Let's Go

Let's Go writers travel on your budget.

"Guides that penetrate the veneer of the holiday brochures and mine the grit of real life."

—*The Economist*

"The writers seem to have experienced every rooster-packed bus and lunar-surfaced mattress about which they write."

—*The New York Times*

"All the dirt, dirt cheap."

—*People*

Great for independent travelers.

"The guides are aimed not only at young budget travelers but at the independent traveler; a sort of streetwise cookbook for traveling alone."

—*The New York Times*

"A guide should tell you what to expect from a destination. Here *Let's Go* shines."

—*The Chicago Tribune*

"An indispensible resource, *Let's Go*'s practical information can be used by every traveler."

—*The Chattanooga Free Press*

Let's Go is completely revised each year.

"A publishing phenomenon...the only major guidebook series updated annually. *Let's Go* is the big kahuna."

—*The Boston Globe*

"Unbeatable: good sight-seeing advice; up-to-date info on restaurants, hotels, and inns; a commitment to money-saving travel; and a wry style that brightens nearly every page."

—*The Washington Post*

All the important information you need.

"*Let's Go* authors provide a comedic element while still providing concise information and thorough coverage of the country. Anything you need to know about budget traveling is detailed in this book."

—*The Chicago Sun-Times*

"*Let's Go* guidebooks take night life seriously."

—*The Chicago Tribune*

Let's Go Publications

Let's Go: Alaska & the Pacific Northwest 2002
Let's Go: Australia 2002
Let's Go: Austria & Switzerland 2002
Let's Go: Amsterdam 2002 **New Title!**
Let's Go: Barcelona 2002 **New Title!**
Let's Go: Boston 2002
Let's Go: Britain & Ireland 2002
Let's Go: California 2002
Let's Go: Central America 2002
Let's Go: China 2002
Let's Go: Eastern Europe 2002
Let's Go: Egypt 2002 **New Title!**
Let's Go: Europe 2002
Let's Go: France 2002
Let's Go: Germany 2002
Let's Go: Greece 2002
Let's Go: India & Nepal 2002
Let's Go: Ireland 2002
Let's Go: Israel 2002
Let's Go: Italy 2002
Let's Go: London 2002
Let's Go: Mexico 2002
Let's Go: Middle East 2002
Let's Go: New York City 2002
Let's Go: New Zealand 2002
Let's Go: Paris 2002
Let's Go: Peru, Ecuador & Bolivia 2002
Let's Go: Rome 2002
Let's Go: San Francisco 2002
Let's Go: South Africa & Southern Africa 2002
Let's Go: Southeast Asia 2002
Let's Go: Spain & Portugal 2002
Let's Go: Southwest USA 2002 **New Title!**
Let's Go: Turkey 2002
Let's Go: USA 2002
Let's Go: Washington, D.C. 2002
Let's Go: Western Europe 2002

Let's Go *Map Guides*

Amsterdam
Berlin
Boston
Chicago
Dublin
Florence
Hong Kong
London
Los Angeles
Madrid
New Orleans
New York City
Paris
Prague
Rome
San Francisco
Seattle
Sydney
Venice
Washington, D.C.

Let's Go

TURKEY 2002

Ben Davis editor
Allison Melia associate editor

researcher-writers
Alexandra D. Cooley
Kyle R. Freeny
Jeremy Greene
Simon Lassman
Cassim Shepard
Noah Carl Waxman

Paul Guilianelli map editor
Naz F. Firoz managing editor

St. Martin's Press New York

HELPING LET'S GO If you want to share your discoveries, suggestions, or corrections, please drop us a line. We read every piece of correspondence, whether a postcard, a 10-page email, or a coconut. Please note that mail received after May 2002 may be too late for the 2003 book, but will be kept for future editions. **Address mail to:**

Let's Go: Turkey
67 Mount Auburn Street
Cambridge, MA 02138
USA

Visit Let's Go at **http://www.letsgo.com,** or send email to:

feedback@letsgo.com
Subject: "Let's Go: Turkey"

In addition to the invaluable travel advice our readers share with us, many are kind enough to offer their services as researchers or editors. Unfortunately, our charter enables us to employ only currently enrolled Harvard students.

Distributed outside the USA and Canada by Macmillan.

ISBN: 0-312-27063-1

First edition
10 9 8 7 6 5 4 3 2 1

Let's Go: Turkey is written by Let's Go Publications, 67 Mount Auburn Street, Cambridge, MA 02138, USA.

Printed in the USA on recycled paper with biodegradable soy ink.

HOW TO USE THIS BOOK

First of all, put the book down, wipe the kebap grease from your fingers, dodge the German tourists careening wildly down the street *en masse*, and take a deep breath. Though we're as proud of *Let's Go: Turkey 2002* as can be, it's not meant to guide you by the hand through this fascinating and endlessly varied country. Instead, it's meant to introduce you to Turkey, until you get a feel for the rhythms of life on the road. After that, your own instincts will serve as the best guide.

ORGANIZATION OF THIS BOOK

INTRODUCTORY MATERIAL. The first chapter if this book, **Discover Turkey,** provides you with an overview of travel in Turkey, including **Suggested Itineraries** that give you an idea of what you shouldn't miss and how long it will take to see it. The **Life & Times** chapter provides you with a general introduction to Turkish art, culture, and history, providing a framework for your own explorations and discoveries. The **Essentials** section outlines the practical information you will need to prepare for and execute your trip.

COVERAGE. The book's chapters are divided regionally, beginning with İstanbul, our choice for the world's greatest city. Our coverage then outlines the country: northwestern Turkey, and the Aegean, Mediterranean, and Black Sea Coasts before winding through the Central Anatolian heartland and ending in the wild, wild east. Our unbeatable coverage of the Turkish Republic of Northern Cyprus will lead you through the quietly crumbling fortresses of one of the world's undiscovered destinations, and our Greek Islands section will allow you to continent-hop with ease. The **black tabs** in the margins will help you to navigate between chapters quickly and easily.

APPENDIX. The appendix contains useful **conversions,** a **phrasebook** of handy Turkish phrases, and a **glossary** of foreign and technical (e.g. architectural) words.

A FEW NOTES ABOUT LET'S GO FORMAT

RANKING ESTABLISHMENTS. In each section (accommodations, food, etc.), we list establishments in order from best to worst. Our absolute favorites are so denoted by the highest honor given out by Let' s Go, the Let's Go thumbs-up (☒).

PHONE CODES AND TELEPHONE NUMBERS. The **phone code** for each region, city, or town appears opposite the name of that region, city, or town, and is denoted by the šicon. **Phone numbers** in text are also preceded by the ☎icon.

GRAYBOXES AND IKONBOXES. Grayboxes at times provide wonderful cultural insight, at times crude humor. In any case, they're usually amusing, so enjoy. **Whiteboxes,** on the other hand, provide important practical information, such as warnings (!), helpful hints and further resources, border crossing information, etc.

NEW FEATURES. Tired of beachside resorts, package tours, and the beaten path? Check out our newly expanded **Eastern Anatolia** section, featuring unbeatable coverage of the Kaçkar Mountains, the Çoruh Valley, and dozens of towns in between. This guide also boasts updated listings for the ever-changing Cappadocian backpacker scene, Turkey's most-touristed.

A NOTE TO OUR READERS The information for this book was gathered by *Let's Go* researchers from May through August of 2001. Each listing is based on one researcher's opinion, formed during his or her visit at a particular time. Those traveling at other times may have different experiences since prices, dates, hours, and conditions are always subject to change. You are urged to check the facts presented in this book beforehand to avoid inconvenience and surprises.

RESEARCHER-WRITERS

Alexandra D. Cooley *Western Mediterranean, Konya*

A whirling dervish of energy and attitude, Alex cruised through one of our longest itineraries with a love of the chill and out-of-the-way to complement her appreciation for the wild and crazy. She shook it all night long at Bodrum, braved package-tourist hell all down the Mediterranean coast, and veered north through Central Anatolia before returning to Antalya as a special guest to a Turkish wedding, all the while cracking wise in her copy and making us thoroughly envious.

Kyle R. Freeny *Aegean Coast and Northwestern Turkey*

This "Turkish-looking American" took the Aegean Coast by storm, sending back fantastic copy and leaving many a broken heart in her wake. Relentlessly pursued by throngs of locals over the course of her entire itinerary, cool-headed and resourceful Kyle drew on her experiences in Gaza to get her through the trip, never failing to regale her editors with stories of how she outwitted even the most cunning of adversaries. This Phi Beta Kappa returns to the states for just two weeks, and then she's off to Cairo for a year to teach kindergarten.

Jeremy Greene *Eastern Anatolia, Eastern Black Sea Coast*

From the *yaylas* of the Kaçkar Mountains to the steaming streets of Diyarbakır, Jeremy conquered one of the toughest routes in entire *Let's Go* series with style and grace. Even a bout with dysentary in Van and a round with *giardia* in şanlıurfa couldn't slow down this med school expert, as he made friends with Turks and Kurds alike throughout Eastern Anatolia, while hiking through waist-deep snow in the Çoruh Valley and discovering ancient Georgian church after ancient Georgian church. From Armenia to Antakya, Jeremy saw it all.

Simon Lassman *Ankara, North Central Anatolia, Black Sea Coast*

Sporting two degrees and speaking six languages—including Turkish, Hebrew, Russian, Arabic, and Japanese—this intrepid Brit ranged across Asia Minor on a wildly ecletic route, exploring Hittite ruins and avoiding *Nataşas* every step of the way. From the *çay* gardens and student hangouts of Ankara to the sunny beaches and sunken ships of Sinop, Simon's Turkish skills and keen eye served him well, resulting in pages and pages of copy fairly crackling with wit and insight.

Cassim Shepard *İstanbul and Northwestern Turkey*

Perceptive Cassim employed his keen powers of observation to penetrate the touristy veneer of İstanbul and discover the city's diamonds in the rough. Equally at home exploring small residential neighborhoods as he was touring some of the world's most famous architectural sites, Cassim sent back reams of thougtful, insightful copy, his prior experience visiting mosques and bazaars ("more than you can shake a stick at") giving him a unique vantage point. This worldly wonder spends next year making films in Fiji. Watch him work his magic (in front of the camera, for a change) on the new television pilot, *Let's Go TV*.

Noah Carl Waxman *Cappadocia, Eastern Mediterranean, Northern Cyprus*

This intrepid backpacker tackled a grueling itinerary with enthusiastic abandon, scoping out some of the best deals in Turkey, and still finding time for plenty of swinging adventures along the way. Tooling around in a 1970 Ford Barracuda convertible, he added a bundle of new establishments to our coverage of Cappadocia, and even a brief sojourn in a Kayseri hospital didn't slow him down. Friendly Noah was right at home wherever he stayed, returning from his trip with many new pals, but, sadly, without a set of cadillac grills.

ACKNOWLEDGMENTS

The Let's Go 2002 series is dedicated to the memory of Haley Surti

WE DRINK RAKI IN HONOR OF: Our crack team of fearless researchers, for braving touts and sketchy meats to send us their fantastic copy. This book is yours. Naz, for endless patience and advice, and the Bump Rule. Erz and Maz, for power hour, happy hour, and many hours in between. Matt, for baseball stats and a second opinion. Jascha for bringing our work to the masses. Paul, for organizational prowess and cartwheels. And, of course, The Boss, for making us Jersey Girls.

BEN GIVES: Intense gratitude to Allison for hard work, general sassiness, and the word "cracktastic." Pink lemonade and mad love to 17A Belmont: P-Funk, Katie B., Saucemaster Jenneral, and Molly. You made the summer. White Russians at Daedalus to Angus, Popper, Matt G., Dehn, Marijeta, George, and the Douglas herself: you're all good like family. 40s of Mickey's to Mazza, JP Flynn, JK, Rishad Mæ, Tiki, and the smilingest rugby team around. Cigarillos and Aquavit to Lizzie, Elliott, and the Swedes, for hospitality and new drinking songs. My first-born to the Ryan & the Harveys, for the greatest place on earth. Love and gratitude to my family, for everything. And, of course, a blink to Katie, for pure news.

ALLISON THANKS: Ben for miles of smiles, Ottoman history lessons, and giving me a job. Thanks to my commuting buddy for fun on the train, lunch dates, and a sixth amazing summer. Lots of love to my family for their guidance and support. *Teşekkür* to the Chalabis for introducing me to this beautiful and fascinating country. Thanks Erz for grrrl power, homerun derby, karaoke (sort of), and Born in the USA; Dad, Annie and Paul for the rides, and the train for (never) being on-time. Highfive to the SFC for another banner year. Hugs and kisses to Deena, Zoe, Sab, Amy, Jules, Liam, Jandro, Sam, Ted, Justin, Aidan and the rest of the gang. *Çök Güzel!*

Editor
Ben Davis
Associate Editor
Allison Melia
Managing Editor
Naz F. Firoz
Map Editor
Paul W. Guilianelli

Publishing Director
Sarah P. Rotman
Editor-in-Chief
Ankur N. Ghosh
Production Manager
Jen Taylor
Cartography Manager
Dan Barnes
Design & Photo Manager
Vanessa Bertozzi
Editorial Managers
Amélie Cherlin, Naz F. Firoz, Matthew Gibson, Sharmi Surianarain, Brian R. Walsh
Financial Manager
Rebecca L. Schoff
Marketing & Publicity Managers
Brady R. Dewar, Katharine Douglas, Marly Ohlsson
New Media Manager
Kevin H. Yip
Online Manager
Alex Lloyd
Personnel Manager
Nathaniel Popper
Production Associates
Steven Aponte, Chris Clayton, Caleb S. Epps, Eduardo Montoya, Melissa Rudolph
Some Design
Melissa Rudolph
Office Coordinators
Efrat Kussell, Peter Richards

Director of Advertising Sales
Adam M. Grant
Senior Advertising Associates
Ariel Shwayder, Kennedy Thorwarth
Advertising Associate
Jennie Timoney
Advertising Artwork Editor
Peter Henderson

President
Cindy L. Rodriguez
General Manager
Robert B. Rombauer
Assistant General Manager
Anne E. Chisholm

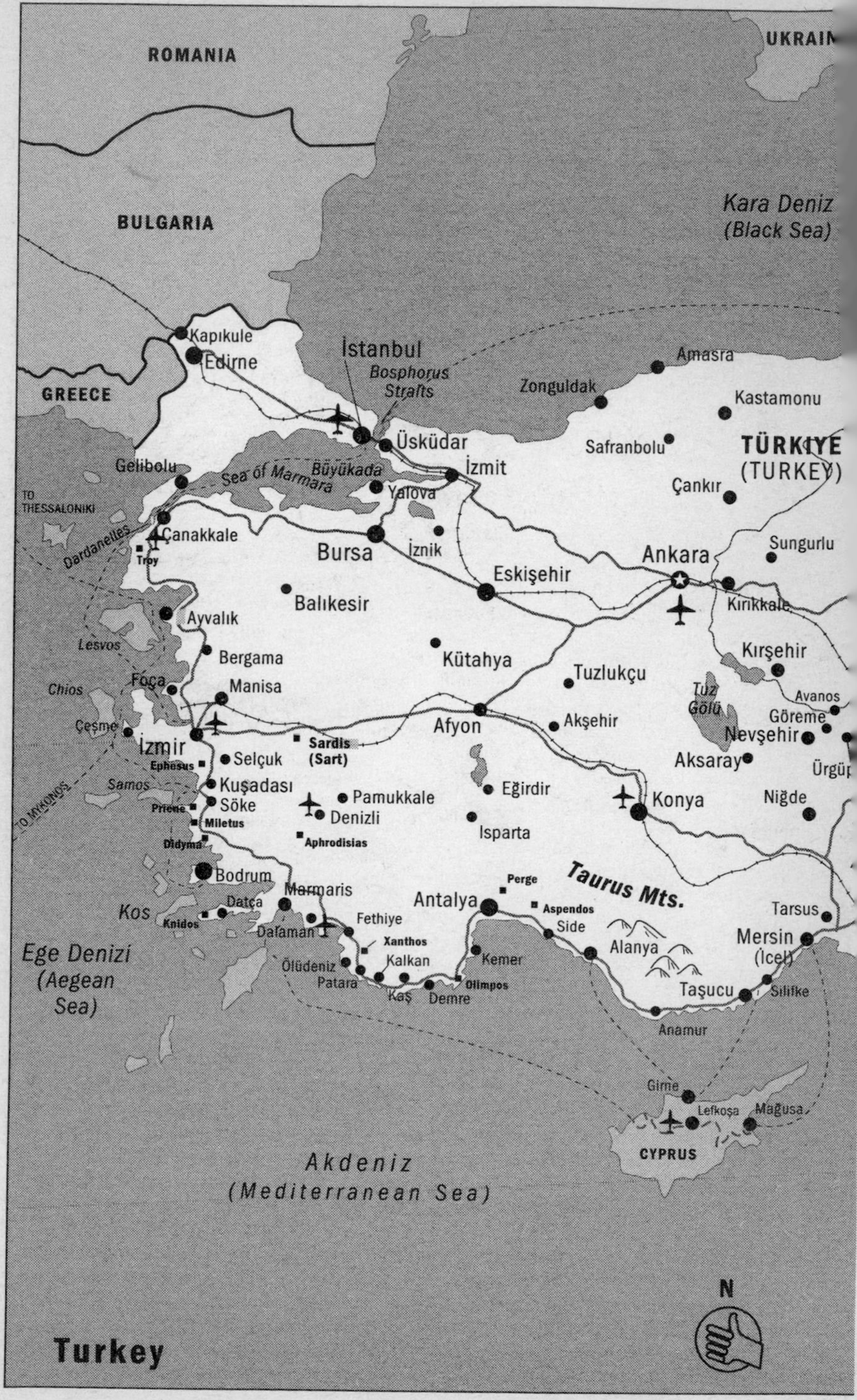
ROMANIA
UKRAIN
BULGARIA
Kara Deniz
(Black Sea)
GREECE
Kapıkule
Edirne
İstanbul
Bosphorus
Straits
Amasra
Zonguldak
Kastamonu
Üsküdar
Safranbolu
TÜRKIYE
(TURKEY)
Gelibolu
Büyükada
Sea of Marmara
İzmit
Çankır
TO
THESSALONIKI
Yalova
Çanakkale
Dardanelles
Troy
Bursa
İznik
Ankara
Sungurlu
Eskişehir
Balıkesir
Kırıkkale
Ayvalık
Lesvos
Bergama
Kütahya
Kırşehir
Tuzlukçu
Chios
Foça
Manisa
Tuz
Gölü
Avanos
Göreme
Çeşme
Afyon
Akşehir
Nevşehir
İzmir
Sardis
(Sart)
Selçuk
Ephesus
Aksaray
Ürgüp
Samos
Kuşadası
Eğirdir
Konya
Niğde
TO MYKONOS
Priene
Söke
Pamukkale
Miletus
Denizli
Isparta
Didyma
Aphrodisias
Bodrum
Perge
Taurus Mts.
Marmaris
Antalya
Aspendos
Tarsus
Kos
Datça
Fethiye
Side
Mersin
(İcel)
Knidos
Dalaman
Xanthos
Alanya
Ege Denizi
(Aegean
Sea)
Ölüdeniz
Kalkan
Kemer
Patara
Kaş
Demre
Olimpos
Taşucu
Silifke
Anamur
Girne
Lefkoşa
Mağusa
CYPRUS
Akdeniz
(Mediterranean Sea)
N
Turkey

RUSSIA
GEORGIA
ARMENIA
IRAN
IRAQ
SYRIA
LEBANON
ISRAEL
JORDAN
Batumi
Sinop
Hopa
Artvin
Rize
Kars
Samsun
Giresun
Yusufeli
Ordu
Trabzon
Kaçkar Mts.
Ayder
Çoruh Valley
Yerevan
Amasya
Gümüşhane
Uzungöl
Bayburt
Igdır
Tokat
Mt. Ararat
Erzurum
Sivas
Erzincan
Doğubeyazıt
Kızılırmak R.
Elazığ
Tatvan
Van Gölü
Van
Kayseri
Malatya
Batman
Nemrut Dağı
Diyarbakır
Şırnak
Kahramanmaraş
Mardin
Şanlıurfa
Gaziantep
Adana
Mosul
Antakya
Harbiye
Aleppo
Euphrates
Tigris
0
200 miles
0
200 kilometers

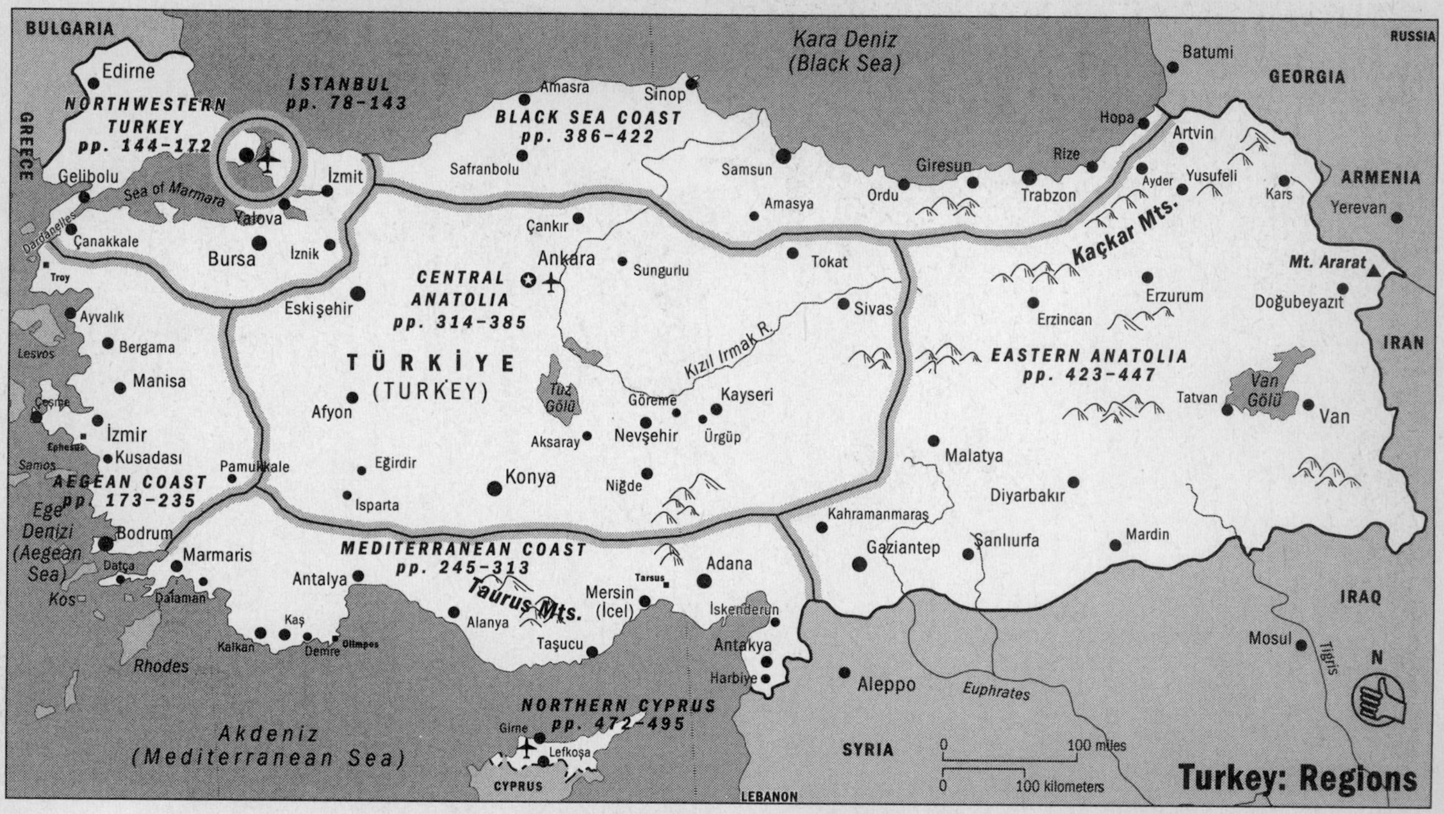
Turkey: Regions
BULGARIA
GREECE
Kara Deniz
(Black Sea)
RUSSIA
GEORGIA
ARMENIA
IRAN
IRAQ
SYRIA
LEBANON
CYPRUS
N
İSTANBUL
pp. 78-143
NORTHWESTERN TURKEY
pp. 144-172
BLACK SEA COAST
pp. 386-422
CENTRAL ANATOLIA
pp. 314-385
EASTERN ANATOLIA
pp. 423-447
AEGEAN COAST
pp. 173-235
MEDITERRANEAN COAST
pp. 245-313
NORTHERN CYPRUS
pp. 472-495
TÜRKİYE
(TURKEY)
Edirne
Gelibolu
Sea of Marmara
Dardanelles
Çanakkale
Troy
Yalova
Bursa
İzmit
İznik
Amasra
Safranbolu
Sinop
Samsun
Amasya
Ordu
Giresun
Trabzon
Rize
Hopa
Batumi
Artvin
Ayder
Yusufeli
Kars
Yerevan
Kaçkar Mts.
Mt. Ararat
Doğubeyazıt
Erzurum
Erzincan
Tokat
Sivas
Çankır
Ankara
Sungurlu
Eskişehir
Kızıl Irmak R.
Tuz Gölü
Göreme
Kayseri
Nevşehir
Ürgüp
Aksaray
Niğde
Konya
Afyon
Eğirdir
Isparta
Pamukkale
Lesvos
Ayvalık
Bergama
Manisa
Çeşme
İzmir
Ephesus
Samos
Kusadası
Ege Denizi
(Aegean Sea)
Bodrum
Datça
Kos
Marmaris
Dalaman
Rhodes
Kalkan
Kaş
Demre
Olimpos
Antalya
Alanya
Taurus Mts.
Mersin
(İcel)
Tarsus
Taşucu
Adana
İskenderun
Antakya
Harbiye
Akdeniz
(Mediterranean Sea)
Girne
Lefkoşa
Kahramanmaraş
Gaziantep
Aleppo
Şanlıurfa
Euphrates
Malatya
Diyarbakır
Mardin
Tatvan
Van Gölü
Van
Mosul
Tigris
0
100 miles
0
100 kilometers

Major Ancient, Hittite, and Byzantine Sites
Black Sea
Mediterranean Sea
Aegean Sea
Sea of Marmara
Dardanelles
Rhodes
Cyprus
BULGARIA
GREECE
GEORGIA
ARMENIA
IRAN
IRAQ
SYRIA
Hadrianople
Byzantium (Constantinople)
(Istanbul)
Nicomedia
Nicaea
Bursa
Ilium (Troy)
Assos
Bergama
Sardis (Sart)
Ephesus
Selçuk
Miletus
Kuşadası
Hieropolis
Halicarnassus
Aphrodisias
Dalyan
Knidos
Fethiye
Xanthos
Patara
Kalkan
Phaselis
Olimpos
Antalya
Parha
Aspendos
Side
Alanya
Taurus Mts.
Konya
Ankara
Tuz Gölü
Amastris
Sinop
Samsun
Kızıl Irmak R.
Hattuşaş
Amasya
Tokat
Sivas
Nevşehir
Tarsus
Adana
Antakya
Gaziantep
Urfa
Harran
Diyarbakır
Trebizond
Erzurum
Mt. Ararat
Lake Van
Van
Tigris
Euphrates
N
0 100 miles
0 100 kilometers

CONTENTS

MAPS

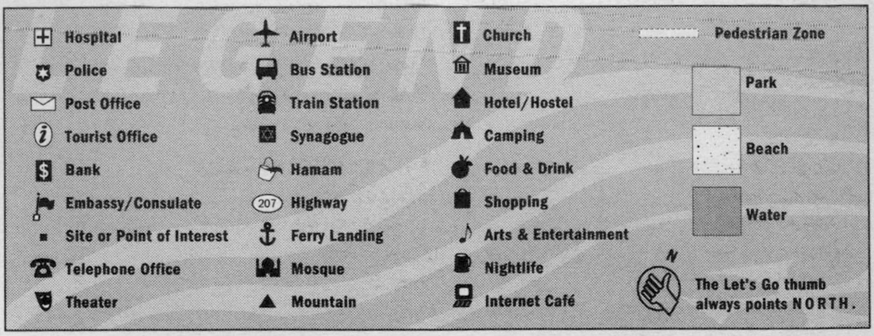

Hospital
Police
Post Office
Tourist Office
Bank
Embassy/Consulate
Site or Point of Interest
Telephone Office
Theater
Airport
Bus Station
Train Station
Synagogue
Hamam
207
Highway
Ferry Landing
Mosque
Mountain
Church
Museum
Hotel/Hostel
Camping
Food & Drink
Shopping
Arts & Entertainment
Nightlife
Internet Café
Pedestrian Zone
Park
Beach
Water
N
The Let's Go thumb always points NORTH.

DISCOVER TURKEY

The modern Republic of Turkey is one of the world's great paradoxes: it is neither Europe, Asia, nor the Middle East, but rather an awe-inspiring amalgam of the three. The empires that carved Asia Minor between them over the past 10,000 years—from the Hittites to the Assyrians, Romans, Byzantines, and Ottomans—each left their distinctive mark, layering history upon history: Urartrian fortresses tower over Armenian churches converted into Selçuk mosques. Though resolutely secular by government decree, every facet of Turkish life is graced by the religious traditions of a 99% Muslim population. The terrain ranges from the ribboned, white sand beaches of the Aegean Coast resort towns, across the great Anatolian plains to the harsh, forbidding peaks of Mt. Ararat in the East. Millionaire playboys pull up to the exclusive clubs of İstanbul in private yachts, while shepherds and farmers scratch out an often desperate living in the boiling lands of the southeast. Millions of tourists every year cram the Sultanahmet district of İstanbul, the glittering western coasts, and the ever-popular moonscapes of Cappadocia, while the rest of Anatolia remains a purist backpacker's paradise: pristine alpine meadows, cliff-side monasteries, medieval churches, tiny fishing villages, and countless cups of *çay* offered by people who take pride in their tradition of hospitality.

FACTS AND FIGURES

CAPITAL Ankara

TYPE OF GOVERNMENT Republican Parliamentary Democracy

POPULATION 66m, and counting

SUFFRAGE 18 yrs. old, universal

ADULT LITERACY 81.6%

LIFE EXPECTANCY women 71.7 yrs; men 66.5 yrs.

PROCLAMATION OF THE REPUBLIC October 29, 1923

LANGUAGE Turkish (official), Kurdish, Arabic

CURRENCY lira (TL)

INFLATION RATE 54%

RELIGIONS 99.8% Muslim (Sunni), .02% Christian and Jewish

TOTAL HIGHWAYS 10,386km

NUMBER OF *RAKI* SHOTS NEEDED TO FEEL INVISIBLE Well, that's up to you.

WHEN TO GO

Turkey's high tourist season is concentrated in the summer months (especially in July and August), when major cities and coastal resorts are infiltrated by hordes of boisterous backpackers. In the late spring and early fall, however, temperatures are milder, many regions of the country are quieter, and prices in the resort areas can drop by up to 10%; unfortunately, a few facilities and sights may also be closed in the off-season. During **Ramazan,** the Islamic holy month, travel may be trickier for non-Muslims, since public eating, drinking and smoking are generally taboo during daylight hours. For details on all the religious holidays and festivals in Turkey, see **Holidays and Festivals,** p. 36.

THINGS TO DO

The sheer diversity of travel options in Turkey makes it attractive to visitors with a wide range of interests. Outdoor enthusiasts, beach bums, gourmets, history buffs, and urban clubhoppers alike will leave Turkey with warm memories of its incomparable local hospitality, deep sense of tradition, and spectacular landscapes. For more specific regional attractions than the ones listed below, see the **Highlights of the Region** section at the beginning of each chapter.

PARADISE CITIES

Spanning thousands of years and dozens of ruling civilizations, Turkey's cities burst at the seams with history, modernity, and humanity. **İstanbul** (p. 78) lays claim to its position as historic head of the mammoth Ottoman Empire, while today it's the country's energetic cosmopolitan champion and ultimate tourist destination. **Ankara** (p. 359), Turkey's sophisticated capital, embraces its leadership in a combination of diplomacy, cultural events and unbeatable museums. To the northwest, **Trabzon** (p. 414), a major Black Sea port city, is an important commerce hub surrounded by lush highland villages. **Antakya** (p. 310), the former ancient city of Antioch, sits on the Syrian border as Turkey's capital of fine cuisine.

DOWN BY THE SEA

Bordered on three sides by sea, Turkey offers up every imaginable flavor of coastline. Rumor has it that Marc Antony imported **Akyaka's powder-white silica** (p. 234) as a gift to Cleopatra on their honeymoon. **Alagadi Beach** (p. 481), on Northern Cyprus, and **Patara** (p. 272) are two of the last preserves of the endangered loggerhead turtles. Munch on fried mussels in **Çengelköy** (p. 133), or try the catch of the day at **Sinop's seaside restaurants** (p. 397). Learn why it's called the "Turkish Riviera:" by day, windsurf at **Altınkum Beach** (p. 199), chew on Turkish taffy-like ice cream in **Antalya** (p. 284), or bronze with the beautiful people at **İçmeler** (p. 252). By night, play it cool in a boater's bar in **Dalyan** (p. 260) or gyrate to bass-heavy beats in **Marmaris's open-air discos** (p. 245). Get set for a transnational nautical booty call in **Bodrum** (p. 224), the "Bedroom of the Mediterranean."

FIRE ON THE MOUNTAIN

Turkey's otherworldly landscapes will make even the most peak-weary rambler's jaw drop. Hikers of all abilities can meet their match among the alien rock clusters of **Cappadocia** (p. 315), the ***yaylas*** (alpine plateaus of northern Turkey; p. 410), or the serene waterfalls of **Butterfly Valley** (p. 272). For a more in-depth experience, join a trek through Turkey's stunning **Kaçkar Mountains** (p. 434). Adrenaline junkies can reach new highs river rafting in the **Çoruh Valley** (p. 432), parasailing over the Mediterranean in **İçmeler** (p. 252), gawking at **Kırkpınar grease wrestlers** (p. 150), skiing on a budget at **Mt. Uludağ** (p. 167), or witnessing bloodless bullfights in **Artvin** (p. 429). From Mediterranean pine groves to Black Sea villages, *Let's Go* gives you the low-down on the best places to commune with the great outdoors.

IT ALL STARTED HERE, BABY

Ancient foreign conquests pay off for history buffs today, as Turkey boasts the world's most outstanding collection of ancient ruins. Some, like **Ephesus** (p. 200) and **Troy** (p. 173), are well placed on the tourist stampede (and for a good reason—don't miss them). At emptier **Miletus** (p. 215) and **Aphrodisias** (p. 221), you'll have some of antiquity's best temples and theaters to yourself. A visit to the **Çatalhöyük** (p. 348), the world's oldest settlement, or the Hittite capital of **Hattuşaş** (p. 375), puts the Greeks' leftovers to shame. Beam ahead a few years to the incomparable Ottoman mosques in **Bursa** (p. 159), **Edirne** (p. 145), and **İstanbul** (p. 78). Heading east will bring you to **Şanlıurfa** (p. 466), "the City of Prophets" and the birthplace of Abraham and Job, and the stunning Armenian ruins of **Ani** (p. 447).

FLYING WITH THE JET SET . . .

Explore the playgrounds of Turkey's rich, famous, and painfully cool at the impossibly posh nightclubs of **İstanbul** (p. 78)—but don't even think of trying to get in unless you can roll up in your own yacht. Next, pop on down to the turquoise waters of the Turkish Riviera and mix with retiring millionaires, pop stars, and famous designers at **Bodrum** (p. 224), **Marmaris** (p. 245), and **Antalya** (p. 284). On your way back up through Anatolia, schmooze with the power brokers of **Ankara** (p. 359) before finally heading to the crystal-blue waters of lush Black Sea retreats, only minutes away from **Sinop** (p. 397), a Neolithic-settlement-turned-resort town.

. . . RUNNING WITH THE PACK . . .

Backpackers have taken over İstanbul's most historic neighborhood, **Sultanahmet** (p. 102). Hip international types trade war stories in the shade of Aya Sofia before moving on down the coast. The (well-)beaten track leads to **Kuşadası** (p. 209), with a detour to the Greek island of **Samos** (p. 240); **Bodrum's discos** (p. 230), with a jaunt to Greek **Kos** (p. 237); **Ölüdeniz's serene shores** (p. 269); **Fethiye's Mediterranean boat trips** (p. 267); and **Olimpos's** treehouses and mysterious mountaintop flame (p. 283). From the coast, backpackers head inland *en masse* to the tripped-out surreal landscapes of **Cappadocia** (p. 315), where they congregate in rock-carved bars and **belly dance** with the pros at **Göreme's "Turkish Nights"** (p. 325).

. . . AND BY YOUR BAD SELF

Badass solo travelers revel in the relatively unexplored delights of Turkey's interior and far-eastern reaches. Trek through waist-deep snow and traverse stunning mountain passes in the **Kaçkar Mountains** (p. 434) before heading to the gorgeous summer villages and ancient churches of the **Çoruh Valley** (p. 432). Keep moving through the wild, wild East to explore the ancient Armenian capital of **Ani** (p. 447) and to roam around a ruined **Kurdish palace** in full view of **Mt. Ararat** (p. 450), before finding a few moments of quiet peace by the shimmering waters of **Lake Van** (p. 451). Ferry yourself to the practically undiscovered beaches and ruins of **Northern Cyprus** (p. 472). And, to make it all go a little smoother, brush up on your Türkçe with the help of our **phrasebook and glossary** (p. 496). Even the most heinously pronounced *teşekkür ederim* is appreciated.

LET'S GO PICKS

BEST WONDERS OF THE ANCIENT WORLD: Turkey boasts a whopping two of the seven: the once-colossal **Temple of Artemis** near Selçuk (p. 208), and the ruins of the **Mausoleum of Halicarnassus** in Bodrum (p. 229).

BEST PLACE TO WATCH NAKED, GRAPPLING MEN (I): Any of İstanbul's dozens of hamams, where you'll see the ancient arts of massage and *kese* practiced like you've never imagined.

BEST WAY TO CLEAR YOUR SINUSES: Indulge in regional specialty **Adana Kebap** (p. 304), a spicy strip of soft meat served with tomatoes, peppers, and bread.

BEST PLACE TO BE EATEN BY FISH: The friendly, flesh-nibbling fish of **Baklıkı Kapıca** (p. 384) provide relief from skin disease and the uncanny sense that you are, well, being eaten by fish.

BEST NIGHT YOU'LL NEVER REMEMBER: Any night spent at Bodrum (p. 224), the notorious "Bedroom of the Mediterranean," where the clothes go flying as quickly as the *rakı* shots go down. Just remember to get a phone number.

BEST FESTIVALS IN ALL TARNATION: Hang with the *VosVoscus* at the **Volkswagen Beetle Festival** in Ordu (p. 399). You'll find bulls, sweat, and testosterone galore at Artvin's annual **Kafkasör Wrestling Festival** (p. 430). Not to be outdone, Selçuk hosts its very own **Camel Wrestling Festival** (p. 217).

BEST WAY TO DRINK FOR FREE: Cappadocia's famous wineries in Göreme (p. 318) and Ürgüp (p. 325) allow you to "sample" new and vintage wines, plus offer wine cellar tours and lectures.

BEST SITE TO COMMUNE WITH YOUR INNER SHEPHERD: On the slopes of **Erciyes Dağı** (p. 341), join scores of shepherds who pitch their tents on the hillsides and graze their sheep during the summer.

BEST PLACE TO WATCH NAKED, GRAPPLING MEN (II): At Edirne's legendary **Kırkpınar Grease Wrestling Festival** (p. 150), where lubed-up men combat each other in black leather pants.

SUGGESTED ITINERARIES

BEST OF TURKEY

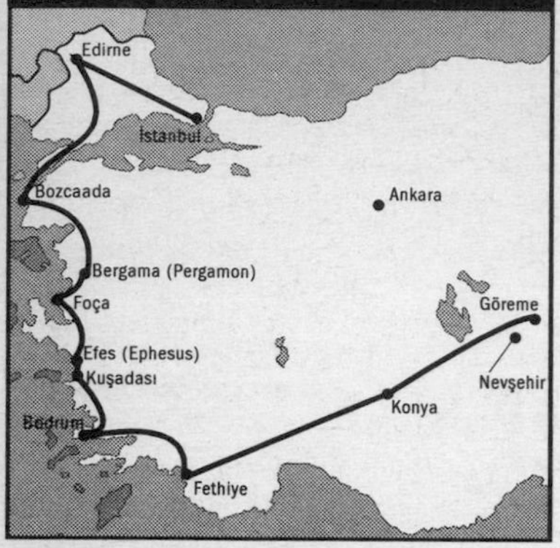

THE BEST OF TURKEY (3 WEEKS) Begin in **İstanbul** (p. 78), the traditional gateway to Turkey. Bargain for baubles, bangles, and beads at Grand Bazaar (p. 115), marvel at luxurious Ottoman palaces, and stand in awe at the magnificent Aya Sofia (p. 105). For evening sweets, tea, and backgammon, head to one of İstanbul's hippest waterfront cafes. Need a break from the city? The Bosphorus ferry lets you kick back and admire the behemoth burg from a distance, stopping for fresh fish sandwiches and fried mussels along the way. Next, head into the heartland to Turkey's bustling capital, **Ankara** (p. 359), where gawk at Atatürk's immense mausoleum and spend hours sipping *çay* in student cafes. A little further south will bring you to the surreal moonscapes and fairy chimneys of Turkey's number-one tourist attraction, **Cappadocia** (p. 315). Bum around Göreme and Nevşehir and get your post-hippy groove on with the thousands of travelers who descend every summer to just like chill, man. Then shake off any lingering relaxation by entering the frenzied world of the Turkish Riviera, where backpackers and jetsetters rub shoulders under the spinning lights of all-night discos. Move up the coast from backpacker-friendly **Fethiye** to **Bodrum**, the legendary "Bedroom of the Mediterranean." Further up the coast awaits the sparkling Aegean Coast, housing the sun-bleached ruins of some of the ancient world's most powerful cities: **Bergama** (p. 184) **Foça** (p. 188), and **Ephesus** (p. 200).

OFF THE BEATEN PATH

OFF THE BEATEN PATH: OUTDOOR ADVENTURES (2 WEEKS) Start with a laid-back trip up Bursa's Mt. Uludağ. Move further inland to take in the surreal landscapes of **Cappadocia** (p. 315) as you hike amid the other-worldly fairy chimneys of the **Rose Valley** (p. 322), the underground cities (p. 324) of **Kaymaklı** and **Derinkuyu,** and the breathtaking beauty of the church-dotted **Ihlara Valley** (p. 332). Marvel at the spectacular frescoes in the Byzantine cave churches of **Göreme** (p. 318). After a hike up **Erciyes Dağı** (p. 341), the tallest mountain in central Turkey, soothe yourself in the hot springs of **Balıklı Kaplıca** (p. 384), where friendly flesh-eating fish bring new meaning to exfoliation. Feeling better? Go for another adrenaline rush of white water rafting along the rivers of the Çoruh Valley, near **Yusufeli** (p. 431) and trek through the pristine **Kaçkar mountains** (p. 434). Then head back west to **Trabzon** (p. 414), a thriving Black Sea port town. Perched on a cliff outside of this city, the awe-inspiring **Sumela Monastery** (p. 420) may cause monk-envy. Give up those dreams of celibacy and follow the Black Sea coast to the pristine **Çambaşı Yayla** (highland plateau) outside of **Ordu** (p. 408), and further to **Ünye** (p. 407), where you can pamper yourself with a divine bath and massage at a hamam (Turkish bath) that was once a Byzantine church. End your adventure with a camp-out on the stunning beaches of **Sinop** (p. 397) before going back to **İstanbul.**

TURKISH RIVIERA

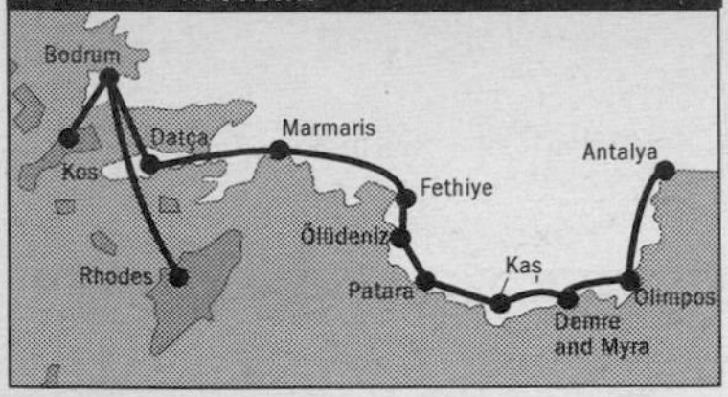

THE TURKISH RIVIERA (12 DAYS) A wonder of the party world, **Bodrum** (p. 224) is the place to pursue hard-core hedonism, whether on a sun-soaked beach or in an open-air dance club. Recover aboard a relaxing Blue Journey boat ride to one of the many nearby Turkish islands and beaches (p. 232). Or hop a continent via a short ferry to the Greek isles of **Kos** and **Rhodes.** Once back on shore, bronze your bod on the secluded beaches of **Datça,** a quiet and charming little town away from it all (p. 255). Get vertical long enough to reach the backpackers' gathering ground of **Fethiye** (p. 263), which works well as a base for daytrips further along the Mediterranean coast to **Ölüdeniz** (p. 269) and the serene **Butterfly Valley** (p. 272). For even more natural wildlife, head to the beaches of **Patara,** where endangered loggerhead turtles lay their eggs (p. 272). Visit **Demre**'s basilica of St. Nicholas (p. 282) and climb among the Lycean rock tombs of **Myra** (p. 282) before being drawn to the eternal flame of **Olimpos** (p. 284). After a night in a treehouse, finish off with a stay in **Antalya,** capital of the Turkish Riviera (p. 284).

BEST OF EASTERN ANATOLIA

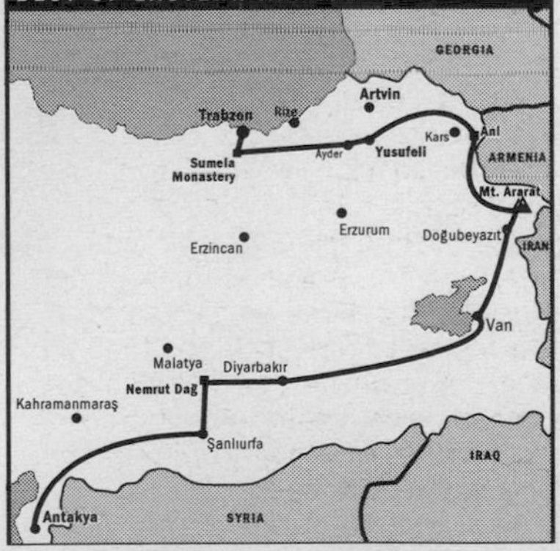

BEST OF EASTERN ANATOLIA (3 WEEKS): Begin in **Trabzon** (p. 414), Turkey's last major outpost along the Black Sea Coast, and visit the spectacularly-situated **Sumela Monastery** (p. 420), clinging to the side of a sheer cliff. Head east through the **Kaçkar Mountains** to the summer plateau village of **Ayder** (p. 425) before trekking across the **Çoruh Valley** to **Yusufeli** (p. 431), stopping along the way only for some white-water rafting and an introduction to Hemşinli culture. From Yusufeli, it's only a hop, skip, and a jump to the majestic Armenian ruins of **Ani** (p. 447), near modern-day **Kars,** and then down to the misty double peaks of **Mt. Ararat** (p. 450), just outside **Doğubeyazıt** (p. 448). After a brief search for Noah's Ark, spend some time relaxing by the deep, crystal waters of **Lake Van** (p. 451) and exploring the region's dozens of eerie, abandoned churches and fortresses. Next, swing by the ancient black basalt walls of **Diyarbakır** (p. 458) before coming face to face with the 2000-year-old statues of Antiochus at **Nemrut Dağ** (p. 464). Finally, wander through the mind-bogglingly old streets of **şanlıurfa** (p. 466), the City of Prophets, on your way to **Antakya** (p. 310), formerly Antioch the current food capital of Turkey.

HISTORY AND CULTURE

HISTORY

Since the first human settlements in Anatolia, Turkey has hosted some of the world's greatest civilizations, each waxing with exuberance and then fading with despair. A journey through Turkey is a chance to retrace the steps of armies, to relive the magnificence of great courts, and to pause for a moment where tragedy has unfolded. Timeless religious, ethnic, and cultural tensions live on here, as they have in every Asia Minor empire before it. The pride and confident nationalism of Turkey today cost the blood and torture of thousands. Despite being the custodian of Hellenic and Roman heritage as well as of the roots of Christianity, it has forever represented foreign intrigue for Europe. Neither a comfortable neighbor nor a suppressible foe, it is the only regional power that walks unhumbled in the Arab world yet demands accord from the west.

ANCIENT ASIA MINOR (7000 BC-36 AD)

7000BC
Beginning of the Neolithic era.

FROM HITTITES TO HELLENES

The beginning of the Neolithic Era in 7000 BC heralded the development of settlements and agriculture. Though the oldest evidence of settlements in Turkey is at **Hacllar,** 25km southeast of Burdur, the most impressive is **Çatalhöyük** (p. 348) on the Konya Plain, where early settlers traded razor sharp obsidian blades in the pre-metalworking era. **Çayönü,** near present-day Elazig, began smelting copper tools, a trade that involved Mesopotamia and the northern Aegean and underwrote the Early Bronze Age (3200-2000 BC) wealth of the Asia Minor cities of **Troy** and **Alacahöyük.**

2000 BC
The Hittites establish an empire in Central Anatolia.

By the Middle Bronze Age (2000 BC), the **Hatti** people of Anatolia were trading with the Assyrians to the south, who delivered clothing and textiles in exchange for much-valued gold, silver, and iron. More importantly, the Assyrian traders introduced the first written records to Anatolia; their cuneiform tablets were left behind in the Hatti capital of **Kanesh,** now Kultepe.

Eventually the Hatti merged with the iron-forging **Hittites,** who migrated south from the Caucuses, adopting Hatti language and religion. The warlike Hittites would dominate central Anatolia for 600 years. From their capital at **Hattuşaş** (modern **Boğazkale,** see p. 374), they waged a series of campaigns against their Mesopotamian and Egyptian neighbors. In 1286 BC, the Hittites defeated Egyptian pharaoh Ramses II at Kadesh and acquired Syria in the history's first recorded treaty.

Despite Hittite dominance in central Anatolia, other ethnic groups began to settle in the area of present-day Turkey. A series of kingdoms rose and fell during the five hundred years following the end of the Hittite Empire, beginning with the **Trojans,** made famous by Homer and Virgil. Scholars believe that the fall of their legendary city at the mouth of the Dardanelles, recounted in the *Iliad* (see p. 173), coincided with the Doric invasions, the mass migration of Sea Peoples across the Aegean, and the end of the Bronze Age, around 1250 BC. The kingdoms of Greek Mycenae, Cyprus, northern Mesopotamia, and Hittite rule of Anatolia ended by 1190 BC, leaving a power vacuum in Anatolia until the unification of the **Urartu** around Lake Van in 875 BC. With their capital at **Tušpa** (modern **Van,** see p. 451), the Urartu demonstrated their engineering skill in the construction of fortresses and canals before being ultimately defeated by the Medes in 580 BC.

The **Phrygians** were related to the Greeks and built their capital at **Gordion** (see p. 373), ruled in the 8th century BC by King Midas, of the legendary golden touch. At the same time, **Ionia,** the central western coast of Anatolia, was a center of trade, science, and culture. Escaping the Doric invasion, Mycenaean Greeks emigrated here in 1100 BC and flourished in cities like **Miletus** until subjugated by Croesus of Lydia in 546 BC. It was in **Smyrna** (modern İzmir, p. 191) that **Homer** wrote the *Iliad* and the *Odyssey* in the Ionian dialect. Miletus, whose original settlers were the Minoans of Crete, became an early center of Greek philosophy and pre-Socratic thought (see p. 215). In the realm of architecture, the enduring Ionic style includes the colossal **Temple of Artemis,** one of the Seven Wonders of the Ancient World (see Ephesus, p. 200). The **Lydians** eventually defeated Miletus and the Ionians, setting up their capital in **Sardis.** They were a Hittite-related people, famous for huge royal tombs and the invention of dice and coined money. The fabulously wealthy King Croesus was routed by Persian Cyrus in Cappadocia in 547 BC, ending the 140-year-old Lydian empire.

In the absence of any political cohesion between the Greek city-states, Cyrus II rapidly extended the Achaemenid Empire of Persia along the coast of Asia Minor and made forays into Greece. Cyrus replaced the city-states with a structure of subordinate *satrapies* (administrative regions) ruled by wealth-hoarding tyrants. Persian culture rarely spread beyond its courts, and apart from the **Mausoleum of Halicarnassus** (see p. 229); little remains from this period today. Greek resistance to Persian rule precipitated the fateful Ionian Revolt of 499 BC, leading to the famous Persian Wars against Athens and Sparta.

ALEXANDER THE GREAT AND THE PAX ROMANA

Persian hegemony over Asia Minor lasted until 333 BC, when their army was routed by Alexander the Great at **İskenderun** It was during this campaign that Alexander chose to slice rather than untie the mythical Gordion knot, thereby making himself the master of Asia (see **Gordion,** p. 373). Alexander's conquests disseminated Greek language and traditions across Asia Minor, from Egypt to the Indian Ocean. Yet with no obvious successor, Alexander's kingdom died with him. On his deathbed in 323 BC, his words, "The kingdom shall go to the strongest," precipitated a carve-up by his generals. To Ptolemy went Egypt and its capital at Alexandria, Lysimachus took Thrace, and Seleucus established control over Syria and much of Asia Minor from **Antioch** (modern **Antakya,** see p. 310). The Attalids of **Pergamon** (modern **Bergama,** see p. 184) won their independence from the Seleucid kingdom 20 years later. Under the Attalids, Pergamon evolved

1286 BC
Hittites defeat Ramses II and acquire Syria.

1250 BC
Troy falls, marking the end of the Bronze Age.

c.1190 BC
Hittite dominance in Central Anatolia comes to an end.

c.875 BC
The Urartu establish a kingdom in the Lake Van region.

c.700 BC
Phrygians invade Anatolia and build their capital at Gordion.

c.600 BC
Lydians establish their capital at Sardis in Western Anatolia.

547 BC
Cyrus II begins expanding the Persian Empire in Asia Minor after uprooting the Lydian Empire.

499 BC
Ionian cities are crushed in the unsuccessful Ionian Revolts.

into a cultural center marked by the impressive Altar of Zeus and its library that rivaled Alexandria's, until the Roman Marc Antony seized its contents as a wedding present for Cleopatra.

Beginning with Rome's defeat of the Greeks at Pydna in 168 BC, it was clear a new era was nigh. Attalus III of Pergamon bequeathed his kingdom to Rome rather than have it conquered, and only King Mithradates of Pontus, now modern **Amasya** (see p. 403), and nearby Tigranes the Great of Armenia, offered significant resistance. Pontus fell in 63 BC to the Roman general Pompey, while Armenia wavered between allegiance to Rome and Parthia to the east. The so-called **Pax Romana** was a time of relative peace, in which local governments enjoyed autonomy so long as they kept the Romans happy, paid their taxes, and let them play soldier. Such tranquility allowed Asia Minor to amass great wealth, finance construction, and revitalize many Aegean trading centers.

CHRISTIANITY AND THE BYZANTINE EMPIRE (36 - 1000)

In 36 AD, St. Paul the Apostle traveled through Asia Minor, spreading Christianity and establishing the seven Churches of Revelation. From Antioch, through Cappadocia, and into Greece, he converted Gentiles while raising the ire of local Jews and pagans. Persecution only lessened in 251, with the third century, following the conversions of the first king, Abgar of Edessa (now **şanlıurfa,** p. 466), and of Gregory the Illuminator in Armenia in 310. In the meantime, the central authority of the Roman Empire was collapsing under the weight of economic tumult and northern invasions, producing a messy civil war. Out of the scramble, **Constantine** emerged in 324 as the sole ruler and became Rome's first Christian Emperor, founding his capital on the old city of Byzantium at the mouth of the Bosphorus. Constantine's successors, however, could not preserve the unity of the empire. In 395 Theodosius partitioned the empire into Hellenistic east and Latin west. Rome was sacked by the Goths in 410, and the Western Empire collapsed in 476.

Things were different in the east, where the Byzantine Empire dominated for the next 600 years. Constantinople remained secure behind its fortifications built by Theodosius II, which can still be seen in modern İstanbul (see **Yedikule,** p. 125). Mass conversion to Christianity created an imperial ideology of universalism and a proliferation of evangelical missions and monasteries. The emperor, the Church, taxation, and the Greek language bound together a cosmopolitan Byzantine culture of Greeks, Syriacs, Egyptian Copts, Armenians, and Slavs.

c.300-600
Seven Ecumenical Councils establish church infrastructure.

Between the 4th and 7th centuries, **Seven Ecumenical Councils** established the structure and clarified Church doctrine. The **Council of Nicaea** in 325 (see **İznik,** p. 169) and the Council of Constantinople in 381 appointed the emperor as the head of both Church and State, exempted the clergy from taxation, and organized the Church into five **patriarchates**—Rome, Constantinople, Alexandria, Antioch, and Jerusalem. Each was headed by a patriarch, who performed religious duties and functioned as a sort of local governor. The early years of the Church were filled with doctrinal debate, heresy, and name-calling. Debates between **Arians,** who believed Christ was subordinate to God, and the **Monophysites,** who emphasized the single divine nature of Christ, challenged official church doctrine and prompted the **Nicene Creed,** a summation of Church doctrine of the Trinity, which ruled that Jesus was simultaneously human and divine.

610-1081
Middle Byzantine period.

This religious dispute caused immense turmoil between the imperial seat in Constantinople and the empire's Monophysite southern and eastern territories. Indeed, it was the persecuted Monophysite provinces of Egypt and Syria that first welcomed Islam during the Middle Byzantine period (610-1081). Disastrous defeats at the hands of the rapidly expanding Arab **Umayyad** dynasty (661-750) led to **Iconoclasm;** a Byzantine belief that their own icons were idolatrous and that defeat was divine punishment. For sixty years starting in 726, all holy images were demolished by imperial order. To the relief of aesthetes, this order was rescinded in 787. Unfortunately, the damage was done; many Byzantine treasures were gone forever, and the empire's three-century decline had begun. Civil wars, as well as those with Slav and Arab neighbors, slowly weakened the empire. At the same time, the isolated patriarchate of Rome began to claim primacy over the other four, leading to doctrinal disputes that culminated in the **Great Schism** between the Orthodox and Roman Catholic churches in 1054.

1054
Schism confirms separation of Roman Catholic and Orthodox churches.

THE GREAT SELÇUK SULTANATE (1055-1335)

THE ARRIVAL OF THE TURKS

c.1000
Arrival of Selçuk Turks in Anatolia.

In the early 11th century, a new group rose to prominence. The **Selçuks'** ancestors are first recorded on 7th-century Mongolian stelae (funerary inscriptions), which testified to a Goturk empire that stretched across the Central Asian steppes. Subsequently, the Turkmen tribes split off into a confederacy loosely based in the western steppes. The Selçuks belonged to one of the Oğuz clans that had migrated westward in the 9th century.

Based near the Aral Sea, several clans of the Oğuz under the leadership of their chief, **Selçuk,** broke away from the confederacy and settled near the lower reaches of the Syr Darya River in Central Asia, where they gradually converted to Sunni Islam. Described by Armenian historians of the day as "long haired Turkmen armed with bow and lance on horses which flew like the wind," they had, by the middle of the 11th century, amassed an empire stretching from Afghanistan to the borders of Fatimid Egypt. Aggressively expanding west, they were poised to deal the crumbling Byzantine empire a crushing blow.

1055
Selçuks are invested with the Sultanate.

Under the leadership of Selçuk's grandson **Tughril-Beg** (1038-1063), the Selçuk Turks crossed into today's Iran, successfully invading Persian lands. At the behest of the embattled caliph of the Sunni **Abbasid Caliphate** in Baghdad, Tughril-Beg defeated the Shi'ite Buyid rulers in 1055. In gratitude, the Abbasid Caliph vested him with the **Sultanate** ("government;" "sultan" literally means "power"). It was the Sultan's duty to defend the *umma* (the Muslim community), eliminate schism and heresy, and to carry on the *jihad* (struggle) against the nations who rejected God and his prophet Muhammed.

1071
The crushing Battle of Manzikert leaves the Byzantine Empire's Anatolian frontier wicked vulnerable.

1075
Süleyman captures Nicaea (˜znik) and organizes the Sultanate of Rum.

While the Great Selçuk Sultans established a state in Persia (today's Iran), the crossing of the Oxus River opened the way for other unruly Turkmen tribes to threaten the borders of the Byzantine Empire. In 1071, Alp Arslan crushed a Byzantine army near Van at the **Battle of Manzikert,** capturing the Christian Emperor and halving Byzantine possessions in Anatolia. The defeat was so disastrous that it was thereafter referred to by Byzantines as "that dreadful day."

Meanwhile, the Anatolian Selçuks became increasingly independent from the Persian Selçuk Sultanate. In 1075, Süleyman, son of Alp Arslan, captured **Nicaea** from the Byzantines and renamed his new capital İznik (see p. 169). Within a decade, his **Sultanate of Rum** had seceded—Anatolia was known to Selçuks as the "land of the Romans."

WE'RE ON A MISSION FROM GOD

1097
The First Crusade nabs ˜znik before heading to the Levant.

1146
The Second Crusade: Turks conquer Balkans.

1190
The Third Crusade: No biggie.

1204
The Fourth Crusade: Latin knights destroy Constantinople.

Urged on by Pope Urban II, the **First Crusade** of Levant-bound French and Norman knights took İznik from the Selçuks in 1097, forcing them to re-establish their capital at **Konya** (see p. 341). Though the Crusaders had taken Antioch and Jerusalem by 1099, the Selçuks recovered it all by 1176. The **Second Crusade** in 1146 provoked the Turks to attack Byzantine Empire; Constantinople lost the Balkan states just as they had lost Armenia a century before. Following the relatively minor **Third Crusade,** the **Fourth Crusade** of 1204 was an unmitigated disaster for the Byzantine Empire. At the behest of a rival for the Byzantine throne, and egged on by Constantinople's trading rival Venice, Latin crusaders ignored Jerusalem and instead sacked the most glorious city in Christendom. The ruin of Constantinople has been described as among the greatest crimes in recorded history. The legacy was short, with Nicaean Greeks recapturing Constantinople from the Latin invaders and reestablishing the empire in 1261. In all, the Crusaders left 100 castles scattered through Anatolia and took home Islamic medicine, philosophy, and science, at the cost of hardened Muslim attitudes and skepticism at home regarding Papal authority.

Taking advantage of a weakened Byzantine empire, Sultan **Kay-Khosrow I** (1192-1205) recaptured Konya in 1205 with the aid of frontier Turkmen tribes. The Sultanate of Rum was reunified and expanded vigorously to the west and to the north, absorbing the remnants of the Byzantine Empire. The conquest of the Mediterranean port of Antalya in 1207 marked a significant political and economic moment in the evolution of the Sultanate—the Selçuks were no longer confined to the interior of the Anatolian plateau, and were ready to set their sights elsewhere.

THE ROARING 13TH CENTURY

By its heyday in the 13th century, the Sultanate of Rum had developed into one of the most important Islamic states of its time. The Sultanate brought stability to its heterogeneous, war-torn population of Greeks, Armenians, Syrians, and Persians through religious and racial tolerance. Unlike prior outside colonizers, this was the first empire to unify and settle in Anatolia.

Under the Selçuks, trade, agriculture, and the arts thrived. The Crusades opened the market for Eastern products in Europe, and the sultans were eager to reap the benefits. Seizing control of the **Silk Route** and Byzantine ports, they built a vast infrastructure to accommodate passing caravans. Hundreds of inns (*kervansaray* or *han*) sprung up along the Anatolian highways, as did fortifications, bridges, and harbors, many of which can still be seen in Turkey today (see **Selçuk Architecture and Decorative Arts,** p. 22). Revenue was channeled into the building of theological seminaries *(medrese)*, mosques, hospitals, asylums, and medical schools. The tremendous Karatay Medrese in Konya (see p. 347), the Çifte Minare Medrese in Erzurum (see p. 440), and the brilliant Gök Medrese in Tokat (see p. 380), stand as architectural testaments to the magnificence of Rum.

c.1200-1300
Flowering of Selçuk culture.

The Rum Selçuks were also prodigious patrons, supporting Islamic philosophers such as **Suhrawardi** and **Ibn al-Arabi,** Turkish and Persian poets like **Yunuş Emre** and **Celeddin-İ-Rumi** (see **I Was Raw,** p. 346). They established insurance for the losses of tradesmen. Attracted by the cultural boom, many Islamic craftsmen, theologians, and Sufi dervishes migrated to the Selçuk realm, where they aided the spread of Islam in Anatolia.

Drawing upon ancient Persian notions of centralized authority, the Sultanate was largely run by Persian-speaking bureaucrats, with Arabic the academic language and Turkish spoken day to day. Led by local chiefs *(beyerli)*, Turkmen tribes made up the military and lived along the Byzantine border. Some served as vassals to their Selçuk lords, and were assembled when needed for expeditions against the Byzantines. By the end of the 13th century, these mercenary tribesmen had become increasingly independent, engaging with the Byzantines on their own initiative.

THE OTTOMAN EMPIRE

THE EARLY YEARS

The **Beylik Period,** which began after Selçuk centralized power collapsed in 1335, featured fragmented politics and competing fiefdoms *(beylik)*. In the free-for-all land-grab that followed the disintegrating Sultanate of Rum, a minor chieftain named **Osman** claimed the northwest corner near Bursa in 1326 and expelled the Byzantines. Though the Selçuk empire was rapidly drawing to a close, it laid the foundations for one of the greatest empires in the history of civilization: the *Osmanlı*, or Ottoman Empire.

1326
Osman's capture of Bursa expels Byzantines. Collapse of centralized power lays the foundation for the Ottoman Empire.

Osman's descendents established their first capital at Bursa (p. 159) and began to expand rapidly through Thrace and the Balkans. The conquest of Greek **Adrianople** (modern **Edirne,** p. 145) in 1361 presaged wholesale conquest of Serbia (1389) and other Balkan states, as Ottoman armies relentlessly encircled the increasingly isolated city of Constantinople. It was after the conquest of Adrianople that **Murad I** (1359-1389) created the **Janissaries** (from *yeni çeri*, "new army'), the first standing army in Europe. Christian boys from the Balkans were conscripted under the *devşirme* system, converted to Islam, and educated. Many advanced to the highest ranks of the military bureaucracy, including the architect Sinan and many Grand Viziers.

1361
Murad I establishes the Ottoman capital at Adrianople.

1362
Murad I creates the Janissaries.

1389
Murad II defeats the Serbs at the Battle of Kosovo Polje, but dies in the attempt.

After the defeat of yet another set of French and Hungarian Crusaders at the Battle of **Nicopolis** in 1396, Ottoman expansion was temporarily halted by the meteoric rise of the Tartar warrior Tamerlane in the east in 1402, who crushed Sultan Beyazıt II at Ankara in 1402, imprisoning the captive sultan in a cage.

1402
Tamerlane crushes Beyaz€t II at Ankara.

1453
Mehmet the Conqueror takes Constantinople, renames it ˜stanbul, and crowns it the jewel of his growing empire.

Filling the vacuum left by Beyazıt's defeat, **Mehmet the Conqueror** completed the empire with his conquest of Constantinople in 1453. First, he murdered all his brothers to eliminate rivals and then built his own castle on the Bosphorus overlooking the defiant city. His army outnumbered the Byzantine defenders by ten to one. When the 54-day siege ended, so did the Byzantine Empire. Mehmet converted the Hagia Sophia basilica into a mosque and renamed the city **İstanbul.**

1512
Sultan Selim I nabs present-day Levant, Egypt, and Arabia, including Islam's top three holy cities.

The early territories of the Ottoman Empire included modern-day Greece, Cyprus, and the Balkans as far as Belgrade. Post-Mehmet, the Ottoman armies of **Selim I** (1512-1520) conquered Syria, Palestine, Egypt, and Arabia. In a single military campaign, the Ottoman Sultan became the guardian of Islam's three holiest cities: Mecca, Medina, and Jerusalem.

Non-Muslims in the empire were generally left to practice their religions freely. Many of the empire's minorities, including Greeks and Jews, were peacefully incorporated into Ottoman society, and most fared better under Muslim authority than they had under the crusading Franks and the Spanish Monarchs. Expansion was characterized by retaining defeated Christian princes as vassals in exchange for loyalty and the absorption of their military. Aside from the occasional ruthless suppression of rebellions, the early days of the Ottoman Empire brought relative peace and prosperity to most.

The sheer size of the Ottoman Empire made central government virtually impossible. Instead, the Porte (as the Ottoman government was known) retained only limited contact with satellite provinces through tax collection and military conscription. Such autonomy among the diverse Ottoman states would ultimately contribute to the decline of the empire.

HOW SÜLEYMAN THE MAGNIFICENT GOT HIS NAME

1520
Accession of Süleyman the Magnificent. Other kings are jealous of his nickname.

1520-1566
Süleyman the Magnificent doubles the empire's size, adds some European flavor, and builds like crazy.

In 1520, **Süleyman** inherited an Ottoman Empire, fresh from conquests in Egypt, Syria and the Arabian peninsula. As Sultan (1520-66), the land-hungry Süleyman doubled the empire's size again, securing borders from the Balkans to Iraq and south to the Arabian Peninsula and Africa. He even gained Hungary for the Ottomans before being halted at the gates of Vienna in 1529. "Magnificent" referred both to his military prowess and to his lavish lifestyle: Süleyman's administrative, artistic, literary, and architectural legacies were equally sensational. As a legislator, he earned the title of **Kanuni** (the Lawgiver), and his patronage of Mimar Sinan, the great Ottoman architect, resulted in some of the most renowned of Ottoman monuments (see **Ottoman Architecture,** p. 23) including 41 mosques in Istanbul alone.

TROUBLES AT HOME, LTROUBLES ABROAD

1566-1574
Süleyman's son Selim the Sot gets wasted, drowns.

Süleyman's most influential wife, **Roxelana,** convinced the Sultan to name her less-than-magnificent offspring as his successor. **Selim the Sot** turned virtually all matters of state over to the Grand Vizier. After Selim's death (he drowned drunk in his tub in 1574), the palace was rife with infighting. This period has been dubbed the **"rule of the women,"** as mothers of potential sultans vied for power by knocking off rival sons. Such tiffs in İstanbul only worsened the government's vulnerable condition.

The sultanates were increasingly transient and inexperienced. Most were crowned without any knowledge of or background in administration, having whiled away years in the harem. With an end to fratricide in 1609, sultans safeguarded their sovereignty by imprisoning rather than killing their male relatives. At times, the women of the harem and the *vezirs* (officials) stepped in to fill the vacuum left by incompetent sultans. Janissaries gained power and made their privileges hereditary, attacking any threats to their status with generalized terror and hooliganism. The word of the sultan was law; he commanded the army, appointed statespersons, and supervised the cabinet ministers *(divan)*. All land was owned by the state, which collected revenue and reclaimed land that was ineffectively farmed for three consecutive years. *Medreses* diversified from religious studies to include language, philosophy, and the sciences. Students lived in cells, studied a fixed set of books rather than for a fixed period of time.

On the economic front, the British and Dutch ditched Middle East trade routes in favor of new Asian ones. Moreover, the discovery of precious metals in the Americas eased European alliance on Ottoman wealth, and caused hideous inflation in the Ottoman provinces. The Porte responded by debasing the currency, causing serious long-term consequences for an exploding population already living in poverty.

The first major blow to the empire's international reputation came with the **Battle of Lepanto** in 1571. Austria's Don Juan led a Holy League that sank 200 of the 245 Turkish ships in an unprecedented naval demolition derby. Afterwards, the pace of Ottoman expansion slowed (Tunis 1574, Azerbaijan 1576, Morocco 1578, and Crete in 1669) and then reversed, with defeat at St. Gotthard (1664) followed by repulsion from Vienna by a Polish-led European coalition in 1683. (According to lore, two mainstays of continental cuisine emerged from the Ottoman siege of Vienna: coffee, which the retreating troops left by the sackful, and croissants, invented by Viennese bakers in the shape of the Turkish standard.) After this series of humiliating Ottoman defeats, the **Treaty of Karlowitz** (1699) surrendered much of their European territories. Russian empress Catherine the Great sought to liberate fellow-Orthodox nation Greece in 1770. Nearly a century of losses to Russia followed, slowing only with western intervention in the 1856 Crimean War.

1571
At the Battle of Lepanto, the Ottomans lose 80% of their fleet and their bad-ass rep.

1699
The Treaty of Karlowitz wrenches half the European territories from Ottoman control.

While the Ottoman borders crumbled, the sultans ran down the empire like the proverbial cash cow. "Let us laugh, let us play, let us enjoy the delights of the world to the full," wrote one court poet, summing up the mentality of the times. Sultan Ahmet III (1703-30) reigned over the Tulip Period, a brief aesthetic revival of the arts. Back in the real world, Ottoman provinces continued to gain increasing autonomy as power away from the crumbling authority of the Porte.

1703-1730
Reign of Amhet III.

THE 19TH CENTURY: REFORM AND REACTION

Well-intentioned **Selim III** tried to stem the tide when he became sultan in 1789. His program, called **Nizam-i-Cedid,** or the "New Order," concentrated on Westernizing the army. The Janissary corps, threatened by these new developments, deposed the sultan in 1807 and murdered him for good mea-

1789
Sultan Selim III implements a "New Order" program to save face and territory; he is rewarded by being deposed and murdered.

sure. By 1812, the picture for the Janissaries was grim. All territory north of the Black Sea was lost, Serbia and Greece had rebelled, and Egypt was becoming increasingly independent. Following their defeats of the Ottomans, Russia and Austria were authorized by treaty to intervene on behalf of non-Muslim Ottoman subjects.

1826
"Auspicious Event" eliminates Janissaries; "euphemisms" become an art form.

Mahmut II succeeded Selim III with great caution. He spent 20 years waging disastrous wars abroad, meanwhile quietly appointing his followers to positions of domestic power. With strong backing assembled by 1826, Mahmut II eliminated the havoc-wreaking Janissaries and their supporters by burning them alive in their barracks (the "Auspicious Event"). Next, he established a secular bureaucracy to effectively replace the ulema, or traditional Islamic leadership

Mahmut II had set the stage for the **Tanzimat** (reorganization). Begun in 1839 by sultans **Abdülmecid I** and **Abdülaziz,** it revamped the army, freed education and media, reduced tax corruption, and changed the administration of the provinces.

THE PLOT THICKENS

During the 19th century, the Ottoman Empire was dubbed "the sick man of Europe." European powers preferred that it remain a buffer state, helping to stabilize the balance of power system established after Napoleon's defeat in 1815. Russia seized as much as it could (Greece, Serbia, Wallacia, Georgia, and Danube ports) before cold stares from the West precipitated a begrudging treaty in 1833. When Egypt seceded in 1838, the Ottomans were too weak to prevent it. Luckily for the Ottomans, England fought the Crimean War (1853-56) on their behalf, restoring some gloss at the price of civil unrest.

1838
Egypt secedes from the Empire.

1839
Tanzimat (reorganization) Period: reform is accelerated to westernize defense and clean up corruption.

1875
Faced with crippling debt from a century of reforms, the empire loses financial control to the European-controlled Ottoman Public Debt Administration.

In addition to military support, European banks and financiers lent the Porte colossal sums of money for war, reforms, and new palaces (see **Dolmabahçe Palace,** p. 128 and **Beylerbeyi Palace,** p. 136). After spiraling further and further into debt the sultanate declared bankruptcy in 1875 and lost financial authority to the European-controlled Ottoman Public Debt Administration. Seizing the moment, virtually every independence-minded province sought to jump the sinking ship, including Greece, Serbia, Bulgaria, Armenia, Bosnia, Lebanon, and Crete.

This crisis inspired a group of bourgeois intellectuals to form a group known as the **Young Ottomans (Yeni Osmanlılar).** One of the most prominent members was **Namık Kemal** (see **Literature,** p. 24), a poet and young functionary convinced that the 19th century "reforms" were both a poor imitation of Europe and an insult to Turkish tradition. The Young Ottomans hoped to save what was left of the empire, and drafted a constitution for Sultan **Abdülhamid II** (1876-1909), only to have him suspend it two years later and assume autocratic rule. Abdülhamid reformed the financial system, shrewdly developed pan-Turkic and Islamic alliances, and courted numerous European powers.

Despite Abdülhamid's advances, dissatisfaction grew and the sultan's forced recall of parliament came too late. Though the Young Turk Revolution of 1908 was put down, **Mustafa Kemal** and Sevket Paşa's 1909 march on İstanbul earned a different reception. Parliamentary deputies met them outside İstanbul and agreed to depose Abdülhamid II in favor of **Mehmet V.**

YOUNG TURKS AND WORLD WAR I

These reforms were unable to stem further military humiliation, however. Albanian uprisings and the Italian invasion of Ottoman North Africa were followed by alliances among the Balkan states of Serbia, Montenegro, Bulgaria, and Greece that lead to the bloody **Balkan Wars** (1912-13). Angered with the government's apparent inability to stem losses in the Balkans, the newfound **Committee for Union and Progress (CUP),** led by powerhouse trio **Talat Paşa, Ahmed Cemal Paşa,** and **Enver Paşa,** rode into İstanbul, shot the minister of war, and declared themselves in effective control of the government.

The Young Turks managed to establish a stable government in 1913. Domestically, their efforts were aimed at amending past failed reforms. This meant a focus upon legal secularization, industrialization, standardization of education, and centralization of power. The Balkan Wars had left the Empire without its European territories, on the eve of the First World War. Seeing Russia as the principal threat, CUP leaders tried to woo Britain and France, who flatly rejected them. Next on the dancecard was Germany, who agreed to an alliance in 1914. Under Mustafa Kemal, the Turks blunted an early Allied assault at **Gallipoli** (see p. 157) by committing all their troops to the high ground and bluffing until reinforcements arrived. Their battle for the Dardanelles restricted the Allies to a kilometer-wide piece of scrub at the price of over 280,000 deaths on both sides. Mustafa Kemal's tactical brilliance and front-line leadership catapulted him to hero status and reignited Turkish nationalism. Apart from this phase, however, the war was a total disaster, a humiliation mitigated only by the nationalistic spur it provided and the new nation it would soon inspire.

More significant in this period was the Armenian genocide of 1915. The decision of Armenian Turks to align with Orthodox Russia during the war ended centuries of peaceful coexistence within Turkey, as many Armenians took up arms against the Ottomans. The government responded brutally, as civilians proved easy prey for the otherwise struggling Turkish army; the result was as many as 1½ million Armenians force-marched, bayonetted off cliffs, incinerated, buried alive, or summarily executed (see **Armenians,** p. 30).

THE CULT OF MUSTAFA KEMAL

In 1918, Turkey surrendered to the allies at Lemnos. The **Treaty of Sèvres** gave the Turkish coast back to Greece and created an independent Armenia and Kurdistan. In March 1920, Britain placed İstanbul under military occupation, breaking up Parliament and exiling its members. The sultan accepted his "empire" of just İstanbul and hinterlands in exchange for keeping his throne. Such a capitulation was anathema to the nationalists, setting the stage for the Turkish War of Independence.

The rebels regrouped in Ankara under Mustafa Kemal, whose successes at Gallipolli and Syria were already legendary. He established a Grand National Assembly and the **National Pact,** which outlined what is modern day Turkey, promised to protect minority populations, and demanded the end of European spheres of influence. At the same time, Turkish nationalists were hard at work, fighting the French in the southeast, the Italians in the southwest, the Armenians in the northeast, and

1876
Young Turks propose new constitution; Sultan Abdülhamid II ditches it.

1908
Young Turk Revolution restores 1876 constitution, replaces Abdülhamid II with Sultan Mehmet V.

1912-1913
Balkan Wars claim the rest of Ottoman-controlled European territories.

1913
The Young Turks seize the government.

1915
Both the defending Turks and especially the invading Allies sustain huge losses at the Battle of Gallipoli.

1915
Armenian genocide in Eastern Anatolia

1918
Turkey surrenders to the Allies. The Treaty of Sèvres proposes carving up Anatolia for European powers.

TURKEY

the Greeks (by far the greatest threat) in western Anatolia. First, the nationalists reclaimed the newly independent Armenia. Next, Mustafa Kemal faced the advancing Greek army, who were marching toward İstanbul with dreams of recapturing the Constantinople for Greece. Greece's enthusiasm outstripped its international support, however, and an army under Mustafa Kemal routed the Greeks in Thrace. An international flotilla was needed to transfer 60,000 trapped refugees from İzmir to safety in Greece. After an armistice was signed on October 11, 1922, Mustafa Kemal and his Grand National Assembly abolished the sultanate, leaving their assembly as the ruling power.

1922
After the two-year Turkish War of Independence, Mustafa Kemal and the Grand National Assembly abolish the sultanate.

THE TREATY OF LAUSANNE

Acknowledging their defeat, the Allies bowed to the Turkish demands in the 1923 **Treaty of Lausanne.** This document recognized newly established Turkish frontiers, demilitarized the Dardanelles and paved the way for an independent Republic of Turkey. The **Population Exchange** of 1923, sought to eliminate anti-minority violence and unrest by removing Greeks from Turkey, and vice-versa. Approximately 500,000 Turkish Muslims left Greece and were replaced by 1.3 million Greeks from Turkey, at the price of property loss, upheaval, and alienation.

1923
Allies recognize Turkish gains in the Treaty of Lausanne. Greece and Turkey agree to a population exchange.

MODERN TURKEY

ATATÜRK'S AGENDA: REDUCE, REUSE, REFORM

Mustafa Kemal became first president of the Turkish Republic in 1923. As part of his campaign to westernize Turkey, he required that all Turks adopt surnames, adding **Atatürk,** or "father of the Turks," to his own name in 1934. He helped implement a Western-style **constitution** and adopted the **Gregorian calendar** and the metric system. Many of his reforms focused on aggressive secularization. This meant abolishing polygamy, doing away with Islamic courts, and instituting secular law codes. In addition, he prohibited the use of the **fez** (traditional Islamic headwear), closed religious schools, and legalized alcohol. By 1928, Islam was no longer the official state religion. Labor codes and agricultural reform were introduced and new banks established to encourage commerce and investment.

Culturally, Atatürk sought to make the country distinctly Turkish. He mandated the Turkification of city names: Angora was changed to Ankara, Smyrna to İzmir, and Adrianople to Edirne. He stepped up his Turkification program by attempting to purge all Arabic and Persian influences. In 1924, Kurdish was banned and the *adhan* (call to prayer) was to be recited in Turkish rather than in classical Arabic.

Though Atatürk's reforms were earth-shaking for all Turkish citizens, they had the greatest impact on **women.** Previously prohibited from holding jobs, women were granted equality with the new **civil code.** He overturned a 1917 bill that had both legalized marriage for girls as young as nine and condoned polygamy. Whereas women were once legally under their husbands' control, the **1923 Suffrage Act** regulated their education and incorporation into society.

It wasn't always smooth sailing for Atatürk. His radical abolishment of the veil fired a debate that still burns today. In 1923 Trabzon's Ali Sukru attacked Atatürk's drinking and legalization of alcohol; his body later turned up in a shallow grave near Atatürk's villa. A plot to assassinate Atatürk ensued, resulting in a mini-purge and 12 public hangings in İzmir. Experimentation with two-party politics allowed the germination of the reform-slowing **People's Republican Party** (PRP) in opposition to Atatürk's Peoples' Party in 1924. Citing Kurdish unrest, Atatürk invoked emergency powers and banned the PRP in 1925.

Atatürk's reforms had delivered Turkey from Ottoman lethargy to the twentieth century. He had replaced the Arabic alphabet with a Latin version by decree in the space of two months. Within a generation, Turks could no longer read the texts, letters, and books of their ancestors. Ties to the old order had been severed forever.

TESTING THE WATERS: A YOUNG NATION-STATE

Shortly before the Second World War, Atatürk died and was replaced by his associate, **İsmet İnönü.** Turkey remained neutral throughout the war until it was compelled to join the Allies in the final weeks of the war.

The Cold War made Turkey a geopolitical gem for both the United States and the Soviet Union. Not only was it within firing range of the Soviet Union, but it also had control over the strategically vital Bosphorus. It was only the financial aid of the Marshall Plan that repelled Russian ambitions in eastern Turkey in 1945. Since then, the United States' military and economic aid to Turkey has remained extensive. Turkey became a full member of NATO in 1952. To its present chagrin, it didn't oppose Greece's membership in 1970—Greece has returned the favor by impeding Turkey's EU membership efforts.

Turkey made a surprisingly peaceful transition from a one-party state to a multi-party democracy. The 1950s were controlled by the Democrats, with Atatürk's former party, the People's Party, in opposition and strongly censored. From 1960, Turkey appeared to herald each new decade with a military coup. Rising domestic output was undone by public debt and inflation, resulting in a People's Party parliamentary walk-out and closure of universities in protest. Though the ensuing coup was bloodless, the trials of nearly 600 Democratic Party members led to fifteen executions.

THE TURBULENT 70S AND 80S

The 1960s represented a leftist and anti-American shift in Turkish politics, with calls for social sector and land reform to address rapid industrialization. Frustrated with the government's inability to deal with protestors, the army intervened in 1971, turning the country over to four years of ineffectual government. The military's handling of political violence in this period attracted international human rights condemnation.

It was during this time that **Abdullah Öcalan** formed the Workers' Party of Kurdistan (PKK is its Kurdish acronym) in order to fight for Kurdish sovereignty. Although the PKK has never represent all Kurds (see p. 29), the PKK would gain prominence among the Kurdish population in the southeast of the country in the following decades.

1923
Mustafa Kemal Atatürk becomes the first president of the Turkish Republic and begins a campaign to westernize the country.

1924
PRP forms in opposition to Atatürk's People's Party.

1925
Atatürk bans the PRP.

1938
Atatürk dies.

1946
Turkey transitions to a multi-party democracy.

1952
Turkey is accepted as a full member of NATO.

1971
The army intervenes in the government, creating a non-party system.

1973
Abdullah Öcalan forms the PKK to fight for Kurdish sovereignty.

1974
Turkey invades Northern Cyprus.

1980
Military coup dissolves political parties.

1982
The army drafts the new constitution.

1983
Three-year martial law ends as Turgut Özal is elected president and enacts initial reforms.

Turkey's foreign relations didn't fare much better. Fearing that independent Cyprus would be annexed by Greece, Turkey invaded the island in 1974, in response to a pro-Greek attempted coup. Economic and arms embargoes were imposed by the West, to which Turkey responded with closure of foreign military installations. By the end of the 70s, however, tensions decreased and normal foreign relations resumed (see **Cyprus in the 20th Century,** p. 476). The decade ended with high unemployment, spiraling inflation, twenty political murders per week and impotent governance.

General Kenan Evren led a bloodless military coup in September 1980, placing both political leaders under house arrest and dissolving political parties. Muslim fundamentalist leader Erbakan was tried for political agitation, and 43,000 others were arrested and, in some cases, tortured. The new 1982 constitution provided for a president who could choose a prime minister, and held that political parties could attain seats in Parliament only if they could claim at least 10% of the vote.

Martial law ended by 1983 with the election of the center-right **Motherland Party (ANAP)** and its leader **Turgut Özal.** Though economic reforms, free-market principles, and emphasis upon trade was promising at first, the decade's worldwide recession sent Turkey into massive inflation, deficit, and unemployment.

Throughout the 1980s, security in eastern Turkey became increasingly precarious. Based in Syria and Iraq, the Kurdistan Workers' Party (PKK) increased its forces and directed a guerilla war against the Turkish state. Civilians were caught in the crossfire: Turkish troops razed villages suspected of helping the PKK, and the PKK razed villages suspected of being pro-government. Meanwhile, the use of the Kurdish language in schools or in the media was banned, as was any expression of sympathy for the Kurds.

TOWARD EUROPE: THE 1990S

The 1990 outbreak of the Gulf War shifted the spotlight, with Özal opening Turkish airbases for the Allied air offensive. This was a robust demonstration of Western alignment, but was undone by further PKK terrorism and the retaliatory bombing of Iraqi Kurd villages by the Turkish airforce in 1992.

1993
Tansu Çiller is elected Turkey's first female Prime Minister.

In May 1993, following Özal's sudden death, the True Path Party elected **Tansu Çiller,** Turkey's first female prime minister. That might have seemed progressive, but later elections showed support for Islamic parties, largely in reaction to a growing income gap between the rich and the poor. Ultimately Çiller was removed for ineffectiveness and corruption.

1998
Islamic Welfare Party dissolved in the name of secularism.

Class tensions mounted in January 1998, when Turkey's highest court dissolved the Islamic Welfare Party and banned its leader, **Necmettin Erbakan,** from politics for five years. Welfare Party members then reorganized themselves into the allegedly secular **Virtue Party,** or **Fazilet,** focused on freedom of expression and democratization. Suspicious opponents of the former Welfare Party, however, believe that the new party's agenda is still Islamically centered. In April 1998, İstanbul mayor and Fazilet supporter **Tayyib Erdogan** was sentenced to ten months in jail for reading a poem describing minarets as "our bayonets."

Turkey's secular **dress code** has also sparked controversy, with the government attempting to curb the wearing of head scarves in universities. Under a new law, a bare head is a requirement for a student ID card photo and, hence, the ability to enter final exams. Religious women students have protested and sidestepped this rule by wearing showy blond wigs over their head scarves and by holding street demonstrations.

As the **European Union** finalized its members list, Turkey's role remained unclear. In 1987, it had applied for full membership, but was rejected in 1989 because its market wasn't developed enough by European standards. Other factors included Turkey's less-than-stellar human rights record, high inflation, and control of Northern Cyprus. European nations also feared that the number of Turkish immigrants working in the rest of Europe would increase if visas were made unnecessary. In early 1995, Turkey was accepted into the European Customs Union, but on the condition that the Turkish Parliament make hundreds of new laws and changes to the constitution by that October. The European Union again denied Turkey candidacy for membership in December 1997. That same year, the EU's selection of Cyprus as a potential candidate angered Turkey, which threatened in late March 1998 to begin a new war with Cyprus (see **Cyprus in the 20th Century,** p. 476).

After several years of unstable coalitions and frequent charges of political corruption, Turkey went to the polls in April 1999 for the first general election since 1995. The results were surprising to most analysts. As expected, the Democratic Left Party (DSP), the party of veteran politician and caretaker **Prime Minister Bülent Ecevit,** triumphed, but he could not form government alone. The surprise coalition partner was DSP's old political foe, the right-wing National Action Party (MHP), led by **Develt Bahçeli.** The Islamic inclined party, **Fazilet,** performed poorly given its successes just a few years before.

RECENT YEARS

Nature has not been kind to Turkey in the past few years. On August 17, 1999, a devastating **earthquake** hit İzmit, near İstanbul. In a space of 45 seconds, it killed approximately 18,000 people, left tens of thousands injured, destroyed 60,000 buildings, and left 200,000 homeless. While neighboring countries and international relief groups raced to the rescue, the Turkish government was seen as slow and disorganized. A **second major quake** struck in mid-November, centered in Duzce, less than 100km from the first epicenter. This one claimed more than 700 lives, injured over 5000, left 80,000 people homeless, and destroyed approximately 750 buildings. Severe winter weather worsened the suffering of homeless refugees from both quakes.

While concentrating on the relief efforts domestically, Turkey received encouraging news from the European Union. The Helsinki European Council meeting in December 1999 nominated Turkey as a full **candidate for membership** to the EU. The Turkish government, however, protested the prerequisite of peace with **Greece** for approval, though relations between the two (especially since the earthquake tragedies) have been improving. Also threatening its membership is Turkey's intransigence on the issue of **Northern Cyprus.**

April 1999
Bülent Ecevit is elected Prime Minister. Abdüllah Öcalan is put on trial.

August to November 1999
Massive earthquakes ravage northwestern Turkey, killing 20,000.

December 1999
Turkey becomes a full candidate for EU membership.

April 2000
Ahmet Necdet Sezer elected 10th president of the Turkish Republic.

Overall, tensions in the southeast decreased since the spring 1999 capture, arrest and death sentence of PKK leader **Abdullah Öcalan.** His capture triggered public demonstrations of joy in many of Turkey's cities, and Kurdish demonstrations of outrage throughout Europe and in Turkey. In light of Öcalan's failing health and his status as an icon for many Kurds, his death sentence is unlikely to ever be carried out. In June 2000, Parliament voted to lift the state of emergency for certain mostly Kurdish southeastern provinces, including Van, which had been in place since fighting with Kurdish guerillas in 1987.

In early May of 2000, the Turkish Grand National Assembly elected **Ahmet Necdet Sezer** the 10th president of the Turkish republic. A judge who had advanced his career up the ranks of the Turkish court system, Sezer stated in his May 16 inaugural speech that he planned to concentrate on higher standards for democracy, secularism, and rule of law.

TURKEY TODAY

The Republic of Turkey is a parliamentary democracy, with a **president** as head of state (**Ahmet Necdet Sezer,** elected in May 2000), and a **prime minister** as the head of the government (**Bülent Ecevit,** elected in April 1999). In 1999, Turkey became a candidate for membership into the European Union (EU), but questions about its economy, human-rights record, and presence in Northern Cyprus have impeded its efforts to join.

Turkey's manufacturing industry is concentrated in the northwest, with textiles as the major export. Turkey's economy has received international attention of late because of soaring inflation rates and overall macroeconomic instability. Notorious for mismanagement and corruption in the past, the Turkish government has been trying to clean up its image by privatizing inefficient state-owned enterprises, particularly in the telecommunications, electricity and natural gas industries.

The waning of the Kurdish guerilla war in the east since the arrest of Abdullah Öcalan has been overshadowed by the economic crisis of 2001. Inflation in Turkey has been at double-digit levels for decades, but it was the decision to float the lira beginning in February 2001 that caused hyperinflation and extreme monetary instability as the lira devalued by almost 40% overnight. **Kermal Dervis,** former vice president of the World Bank, was named minister of the economy in March 2001 and has been charged with healing the crisis in Turkey. In the spring of 2001, the International Monetary Fund (IMF) offered Turkey billions of dollars in aid, stipulating that Turkey reform its corrupt government, end subsidies and privatize state-owned assets. The economic crisis and the high price of aid have left Turkey at a crossroads, reluctant to bend to the whims of the West, but eager to keep pace with the rest of the world.

THE ARTS

A heart in love with beauty never grows old.
—Turkish proverb

VISUAL ARTS

THE GRECO-ROMAN HERITAGE

Turkey boasts two of the **Seven Wonders of the Ancient World,** —the **Temple of Artemis** in Ephesus (see p. 200) and the **Mausoleum of Halicarnassus** in Bodrum (see p. 229). Traces of these and other ruins from the Hellenistic and Roman periods (mid-4th century BC to 3rd century AD) dot Turkey's coast. While the Romans did introduce new architectural innovations—the arch, the vault, the forum, and *thermae* (baths)—they also borrowed heavily from their Greek predecessors, effectively ensuring artistic continuity between these two periods.

Ancient sites such as Ephesus, Miletus, Smyrna, and Pergamon illustrate the organization of Greek political and social life around the *polis* or city-state. **Temples** dedicated to the city-state's patron deity marked the center of religious life, and where geography cooperated, as in Pergamon, these temples occupied the highest point of the city, the acropolis. The **agora** (marketplace) was the center of commercial and political life in the *polis*. A large open space, the *agora* housed countless shops under the **stoas** (colonnades) lining its sides. In oligarchic and democratic city-states, the open space of the *agora* and the nearby **bouleuterion** (council house) functioned as the meeting places for the local government.

The surviving ruins also provide a glimpse into the culture of the period. A society that placed high value on athletics and the athlete, the Greeks built **gymnasia** for physical education and **stadia** for athletic competitions. They also celebrated the human form in the famous naturalistic sculpture scattered throughout the city on pedestals and friezes. For entertainment, the residents of the *polis* attended musical performances in the **odeon** (theater) and theatrical performances in the ubiquitous, semi-circular **amphitheater.** In the Hellenistic period, the auditorium of the amphitheater was built into the hillside, while the Romans used free-standing walls to support the weight of this structure.

THE TIMELESS VISION OF BYZANTIUM

The artistic achievements of Byzantine culture were developed within rigid theological parameters. First codified under the emperor Justinian (527-65 AD), stylized, abstract renderings were more important than naturalistic representation.

ARCHITECTURE. The fourth century, when the early Christians were finally afforded the right to establish their own places of worship, marks the emergence of the Byzantine church. Based on a longitudinal basilica plan, Byzantine churches feature a central nave oriented along an east-west axis. The entrance to the basilica is approached on the western side from a colonnaded outer courtyard. On the eastern side, at the other end of the nave, is the semi-circular apse and the altar. Arched colonnades separate the nave from two parallel side aisles, and the wooden ceiling of the nave is raised above that of the side aisles to incorporate a series of clear windows admitting natural light to the central part of the building.

The most prominent symbol of Byzantine architecture is İstanbul's **Aya Sofia,** built between 532-37 on top of the remains of a church from the era of Constantine (see p. 105). The Aya Sofia features a domed roof centered over a square base, rather than the conventional octagonal kind. By the reign of **Basil I** (867-886), the domed basilicas of Justinian had evolved into a **cross-in-square** plan, featuring four vaulted arms of equal length extending from the domed center. Smaller domes occasionally replaced the vaulted roofs above the four arms of the cross, producing a five-domed church known as the **quincunx.**

DECORATIVE ARTS. Byzantine artistry encompassed a variety of media, from illuminated manuscripts to carved ivory panels, embossed bronze doors and exquisite, jewel-encrusted enamels. The dazzling mosaics and icons decorating Byzantine churches mark the pinnacle of Byzantine craftsmanship, and artists underwent years of spiritual and technical training before portraying sacred subjects. The stylization of Byzantine icons aimed to transmit—not just represent—the spiritual power of the subject.

Byzantine icons employed many different materials, including mosaic, enamel, ivory, gold, and wood. Mosaics were made of **tesserae,** small cubes of stone or ceramic covered in glass or metallic foil. The unique shimmering effect of Byzantine mosaics was achieved by setting gold and silver tesserae at sharp angles to enhance the reflection of light. Excellent examples of Byzantine mosaics can be seen in the Aya Sofia and the **Kariye Camii** (see p. 124).

ISLAMIC ART AND ARCHITECTURE

Because Islam developed in wildly disparate areas, each with its own cultural traditions, Islamic art encompasses a tremendous variety of motifs, materials, and styles. One element common to all Islamic art is the absence of human form, as any attempt to imitate God's divine creation is considered idolatrous and blasphemous. As a result, Islamic artists developed a non-representational artistic language. Calligraphy, floral arabesques, and geometric motifs cover everything from mosques and pottery to metalwork and wood carvings.

THE MOSQUE. The **cami** (Turkish for "mosque") represents the most significant architectural manifestation of Islamic art. As the religious, political, and social center of the Islamic world, mosques often housed schools and libraries in addition to religious facilities. The earliest mosques, based on the layout of the Prophet Muhammed's house in Medina, were simple and functional: large, square prayer halls with open central courtyards. The expansion of the Islamic empire saw the assimilation of Persian, Roman, and Byzantine motifs, which transformed the simple Arabian mosque into a complex affair of tiled domes, vaults, and arches.

The minaret is attached to the outside of the mosque. Originally a small elevated platform, but now a conical tower, it is used by the *müezzin* (crier) to belt out the *adhan* (call to prayer) five times daily. The minarets of most mosques are nowadays equipped with speakers for extra amplification. The mosque courtyard often features a **şadırvan** (fountain) for ritual washing (ablutions) performed before prayer. Inside, the congregation faces the **mihrab,** a niche in the **qibla,** or wall that the congregation faces when praying. To the right of the *mihrab* is the **minber,** a wooden staircase from which the **imam** (spiritual guide) gives the sermon.

All mosques feature spacious, oasis-like interiors—either an airy domed space or an open-air courtyard flanked by cool porticoes. With their roots in Persian and Byzantine models, **domes** are a common feature of mosques. They use a dazzling variety of structural supports to transform the corners of the square base into an octagonal opening for the dome.

Mosques often formed the centerpiece of a larger complex of buildings, and were often flanked by a **medrese** (theological seminary) and **türbe** (tomb). Under the Ottomans, the complex surrounding the mosque developed into a vital social center that served all of a community's needs.

SELÇUK ARCHITECTURE AND DECORATIVE ARTS. During the heyday of the Sultanate of Rum, Selçuk architects undertook extensive public works projects. Using the abundant Anatolian stone and clay, they built mosques, *medrese*, and *türbe*. Rum Selçuk architects modified the designs they inherited from their Iranian counterparts with elements of Syrian and Byzantine architecture, keeping the strict Iranian rectilinear mosque and *medrese* plan, as well as the highly decorated minarets, but roofed over the courtyard.

To safeguard their profitable trade in silks, spices, and slaves, and to provide rest for merchants, the Rum Selçuks built over 100 **kervansaray,** or *hans*, along Anatolian highways, each spaced a day's ride away from the next. These rest stops featured mosques, storage rooms, stables, coffeehouses, hamams, private rooms, and dormitories. The most impressive example of Selçuk *hans* is the **Sultan Han** (see p. 340) outside Kayseri.

Rum Selçuk buildings were characterized by their elaborate stone carvings. Earlier carvings reflect the geometrical asceticism of Syrian and Persian designs, while later carvings, such as those on the facades of Sivas buildings (see p. 382) and on Konya's İnce Minareli (see p. 347), burst into exuberant arabesques and Baroque flourishes. In addition to carvings, the Selçuks enhanced their mosques and *medreses* with glimmering *faïence* (glazed earthenware). The fruit of Iranian craftsmen, Selçuk *faïence* was used to cover walls or minarets, with the best examples at Konya in the Karatay Medrese (see p. 347).

Under Selçuk patronage, decorative arts enjoyed a boom, which was later halted by the 13th-century Mongol invasion. **Glassware** and **textiles** were regular staples of commerce, while new techniques in ceramics and lustre painting created more opportunity for the use of *faïence*. The school of **metalworking** was particularly important, churning out engraved, silver-inlaid candlesticks and bowls.

OTTOMAN ARCHITECTURE. The first Ottoman capital, **Bursa,** is a museum of 14th- and 15th-century Ottoman architecture (see p. 159), combining elements borrowed from Selçuk and European architecture. With the capture of İstanbul in 1453, Ottoman architects were challenged to outdo the vaults and pendentives of the Aya Sofia's spectacular dome (see p. 105). Ottoman architecture reached its pinnacle under the unprecedented patronage of Sultan Süleyman. During Süleyman's rule alone (1520-66), over 80 major mosques and hundreds of other buildings were constructed. **Divan Yolu,** İstanbul's processional avenue, boasts a spectacular collection of these structural wonders. The master architect **Sinan** served Süleyman and his sons as Chief Court Architect from 1538 to 1588, during which time he created a unified style for all of İstanbul and for much of the empire. Trained as a military engineer, Sinan forged an architecture influenced by early Islamic and Byzantine styles. His masterpieces, the **Süleymaniye Camii** in İstanbul (see p. 118) and the **Selimiye Camii** in Edirne (see p. 149), exemplify the harmonious, multi-domed Ottoman trademark style.

Many Ottoman mosques stand at the center of a **külliye** (complex) designed to serve all of a community's needs. *Külliyes* often included a *medrese*, a market, a soup kitchen, a *kervansaray*, and a medical center, all integrated architecturally into a single whole. The most impressive *külliyes* are the Süleymaniye, in İstanbul (see p. 118), and the Beyazıt, in Edirne (see p. 150). Most *külliyes* were established as charitable foundations. Although economic instability has jeopardized these institutions financially, many of them are still functioning.

Sixteenth-century Ottoman architects set a powerful precedent for future structures. Buildings like the Blue Mosque were mere imitations of the Sinan blueprint (see p. 106). In the 18th and 19th centuries, Ottoman architecture, perhaps inspired by the fashions of the Austro-Hungarian Empire, appropriated an ornate, Baroque style, evident in İstanbul's flashiest eyesore, the Dolmabahçe Palace (see p. 128).

OTTOMAN DECORATIVE ARTS. The height of Ottoman decorative arts was tilework. From the 14th to 17th centuries, the Ottomans imported Persian craftsmen in order to develop their ceramic industry in **İznik** (see p. 169), but by 1800 manufacture there had virtually stopped. After a 400-year boom, the ceramics industry in **Kütahya** has experienced a tourist-driven renaissance (see p. 354).

MODERN TURKISH ART. Long before Atatürk's revolution, Ottoman painting had gradually begun to adopt Western forms, thanks to the influence of European artists working at the Ottoman court. In 1883, the **Academy of Fine Arts** was founded by Ottoman artist, museum curator, and archaeologist **Osman Hamdi Bey,** a man thoroughly Westernized in his painting technique as well as in his educational philosophy. Referred to as *the* Academy, the Academy of Fine Arts has had a huge influence on Turkey's major artistic movements: the **Çallı** group of the 20s, the **'D' Group** of the 30s, and the **New Group** of the 40s, 50s, and 60s. Many of the artists who created these movements later became professors at the Academy, and their work is on display at the **Painting and Sculpture Museum** in Ankara (see p. 370).

In 1914, in response to demands of the elite, the Ottoman government opened an Academy of Fine Arts for Women headed by painter **Mihri Müşfil Hanım,** whose work blended İstanbul's conservatism with a Parisian flair for Levantine fashions. In 1926 the Women's Academy merged with the Academy of Fine Arts, and has since produced four generations of recognized women painters.

LITERATURE

Early literature was comprised primarily of oral performance, in which poems were recited, sometimes with musical accompaniment. Traces of this art form are present in the *türkü* (modern Turkish folk song).

Although modern Turkish literature has adopted Western constructs such as the novel and the essay, it often draws from its pre-Ottoman origins. The Sufi poetry of **Celeddin-i-Rumi** and **Yunuş Emre** survived the Ottoman centuries relatively unscathed, as did *The Book of Dede Korkut*, a collection of 12 legends, recounting the travels and trials of the noble Oğuz Turks, the ancestors of modern Turks. This epic provides the modern reader with a good introduction to an important genre in Ottoman literature. Many such epics were rediscovered during the 19th century. With this renewed interest in folk literature came a propagation of the tales of **Nasrettin Hoca,** an amiable, anti-authoritarian, religious man whose parables and fables are known by all Turkish schoolchildren (see **Wise Ass,** p. 351).

Satire has historically been an important element in Turkish literature. A prominent modern Turkish poet, **Namık Kemal,** is famous for his satire of the Ottoman Empire during its final years. The critical poetry of **Nazım Hikmet** brought him both literary fame and exile, a common fate for writers with politically contentious views. A fervent republican and free speech advocate, **Aziz Nesin** is the provocative Alevi writer whose writings sparked the **Sivas Incident** in 1993 (see **Heartbreak Hotel,** p. 383). One of the better known Turkish writers is **Yaşar Kemal,** author of *Memed, My Hawk.* Thrice nominated for the Nobel Prize for Literature, his work has been critical of Turkish society and government, not without recourse: the government recently charged Kemal with anti-Turkish activities. **Orhan Pamuk,** Turkey's best-selling author and one of the few Turkish writers to have received international acclaim, explores the concept of identity through magic realism. His major novels are *The White Castle*, *The New Life*, and *The Black Book.*

MUSIC

During the early Republican period, the only forms of Turkish music that had government approval were classical music and "authentic Turkish" folk music. However, today music in Turkey is varied and exciting, and presents a wide range of forms and styles. The two most common forms, **arabesk** and **taverna,** often have a canned, insipid quality; *arabesk* (called "*minibüs müziği*" for its proliferation on vehicles of all kinds) is an offspring of Arabic pop, while *taverna* combines the influence of Greek music with Turkish cabaret.

In addition to these two types are the urban forms of *sanaat, Türkü,* and *özgün.* **Sanaat,** or "art" music, has preserved 18th-century vocal styles. The late **Zeki Müren** was its most famous performer, although a bit earlier **Bülent Ersoy** had made a name for herself, before her music was banned in 1980, when she had a sex-change operation. Based in folk music, **Türkü** is performed on a diverse mixture of Arab, Western, and Turkish instruments. **Özgun** music is Turkey's protest music, and it often contains politically themed, left-wing lyrics.

On top of the pop music scene is **Tarkan,** the fabulously popular "Turkish Ricky Martin." Also livin' la vida loca is **Kenan Doğlu. Sezan Aksu,** whose concerts draw hordes of screaming devotees, is considered Turkey's most talented musician; in addition to producing her own music, she acts as a mentor for many up-and-coming singers. Also popular is **Sertap Erener,** whose music combines pop and soulful female vocals. **Athena** is a popular Turkish ska band that even performs the occasional Cake cover. In summer, live concerts are performed in outdoor amphitheaters. A Pop Song Festival is held in Çeşme in August (see **Çeşme,** p. 196).

Folk music is celebrated in a variety of local festivals throughout Turkey (see **Music,** p. 24), and it forms the basis for festive rural occasions such as weddings. The troubadour tradition, which has persisted for 1000 years, is still practiced by the **aşıks** in central Anatolia. These traveling minstrels perform poetry set to music on the lute-like *saz*, whose three sets of strings represent the three points of the

Bektaşi/Alevi faith (see p. 28 and p. 31). Along the Black Sea coast, the *tulum* (a two-piped bagpipe) and the *kemençe* (a three-stringed fiddle), are commonly used. **Kurdish folk music** engages its own particular instruments, which include the *blur* (wooden flute), the oboe-like *düdük*, and the *def* (bass drum). The bards of Kurdish music, repositories for Kurdish legend and culture, are the **dengbeys.** Many of them, including the well-known artists **Temo** and **şivan Perwer,** have been exiled because of their politically controversial lyrics.

Ottoman classical music and the ritual music of the Mevlevi dervish order are based on a series of *makams* (500-year-old modal systems) that use a unique tonal system. The compositions of **Abdülkadir Merağî** (15th century), **Prince Dimitiri Cantemir** (17th-18th century), and **Sultan Selim II** and **Tanburi Cemil Bey** (both 19th-20th century) are drawn upon most frequently. Live performances of classical music are given by the Klasik İcra Heyeti of the İstanbul Municipal Conservatory. The annual **Mevlâna Festival,** held in Konya in December, is an excellent opportunity to hear live Mevlevi music (see **Konya,** p. 345).

SOCIETY

ISLAM

About 99% of Turks are Muslim. Jews and Orthodox Christians of Greek, Armenian, and Syrian backgrounds compose the remainder. While Turkey does not have an official state religion, every Turkish citizen's national identification card states his or her creed. Although Atatürk's reforms aimed to secularize the nation, Islam continues to play a key role in the country's political and cultural evolution.

UNDERSTANDING ISLAM

The monotheistic religion of Islam was founded by the Arab prophet **Muhammed** in the 7th century. At the heart of the Islamic faith is the Arabic word *islam* (submission). The believer, or *muslim* (from the active participle of *islam*), accepts complete submission to the will of **Allah** (God) as embodied in the sacred scriptures of Islam, the **Qu'ran** (recitation). The Arabic text is held to be perfect, immutable, and untranslatable—the words of God embodied in the human language.

Informed of his prophetic calling by the Archangel Gabriel, Muhammed became the "seal of the prophets," the end of a long chain of visionaries including such Biblical luminaries as Abraham, Moses, Noah, Elijah, and Jesus. While most Christians view Jesus as both human and divine, Muslims consider Muhammed only as a human messenger of God's word—to Muslims, God is one and unique. Omnipotent and omniscient, the God of the Qu'ran can be a stern judge, particularly when dealing with the ungrateful. Yet for a Muslim, the majesty of God's justice lies in unbounded mercy—all but one of the 114 Qu'ranic *suras*, or chapters, begin, "In the name of God the most Merciful and Compassionate." In Islam, Allah is a God of uncompromising love, guiding all those who sincerely invoke His name.

THE FIVE PILLARS OF ISLAM

All Muslims are charged to adhere to the five pillars of Islam: the profession of faith, prayer fives times daily, alms-giving, fasting during the month of Ramazan, and, if able, the once-in-a-lifetime pilgrimage to Mecca.

The first pillar, upon which membership in the *umma* (community) depends, is the proclamation of faith, the **shahadah:** *La ilaha illa Allah. Ashadu anna Muhammedan rasul Allah.* (There is no god but God. I swear that Muhammed is God's messenger.) Any person who wishes to convert to Islam may do so by reciting the *shahadah* aloud and with heartfelt sincerity.

The second pillar of Islam is **salat** (prayer), performed five times daily, preferably following the call to prayer *(adhan)* by the *müezzins.* Prayers, preceded by

VISITING MOSQUES Many of Turkey's greatest architectural monuments, including tombs and mosques, have religious significance. Visitors are welcome, but they ought to show their respect for the holiness of these places by dressing and acting appropriately. Shorts and skimpy clothing are forbidden inside mosques. Women must cover their arms, heads, and legs, and both sexes should take off their shoes and carry them inside. There are usually shoe racks in the back of the mosques, or caretakers will provide plastic bags for carrying your shoes. Do not take flash photos, never take photos of people in prayer, and avoid visits on Fridays (the holy day) and during prayer times, announced by the call to prayer from the mosque's minarets. Donations are sometimes expected.

ablutions, or ritual cleansing, begin with a declaration of intent and consist of a set cycle of prostrations and recitations in the direction of Mecca. Communal prayer on Fridays, led by the local mosque's *imam* (leader), is particularly encouraged.

The third pillar, **zakat** (purification), is alms-giving, or the religious tax. Every Muslim who can afford to do so is required to give 2.5% of his or her income to the poor. Prior to Atatürk's reforms, the state collected the *zakat*, but it has now largely become a matter of individual responsibility.

Muslims believe that Allah revealed the Qu'ran to Muhammed during the month of **Ramazan** (Ramadan). Fasting during this holy month is the fourth pillar of Islam. Between dawn and sunset, Muslims are forbidden to smoke, have sex, or let any food or water pass their lips. Exceptions exist for travelers, the sick, and women who are pregnant or menstruating. However, travelers should respectfully refrain from eating or drinking outdoors during the day. Ramazan inspires a sense of community among Muslims. They break the fast after the evening *adhan* is heard and begin a night of feasting, visits to friends and relatives, and revelry. Fasting is intended to be an invigorating spiritual exercise, teaching self-control and resistance to desire. The experience of hunger encourages Muslims to be both compassionate toward those less fortunate and grateful for the sustenance that God has provided them. During Ramazan, businesses may close or keep shorter hours.

The last pillar, required once in a lifetime, is the **hajj** (pilgrimage). Only those Muslims who are financially and physically able to fulfill this obligation make the journey to **Mecca** and **Medina** during the last month of the Muslim calendar. The *hajj* is a metaphorical reenactment of the Prophet Muhammed's path, and it serves to unite Muslims. Regardless of gender, wealth, race, or nationality, pilgrims wrap themselves in white and perform the same rituals during the *hajj*.

As with any religion, degrees of interpretation and observance produce a wide range of practices. For more information, try *An Introduction to Islam* by Frederick Denny, *Islam: The Straight Path* by John Esposito, *Vision of Islam* by Sachiko Murata and William Chittick, or *Ideals and Realities of Islam* by Seyyed H. Nasr. Kenneth Cragg and Marston Speight's *Islam from Within* provides a sampling of Islamic texts. If you feel inspired enough to read the Qu'ran, try Muhammed Pickthall's translation, *The Meaning of the Glorious Koran.*

THE HISTORICAL EVOLUTION OF ISLAM

Monotheistic Islam met with staunch opposition in 7th-century polytheist Arabia. In 622, Muhammed fled persecution in his native city of Mecca and escaped to nearby Medina, where he was welcomed as a mediator of a long-standing blood feud. This *hijra* (flight) marks the beginning of the Muslim community and of the Islamic (lunar) calendar. For the next eight years, Muhammed and his community defended themselves against raids, later battling the Meccans and neighboring nomadic tribes. In 630, Mecca surrendered to the Muslims, and numerous Meccans converted to the new faith. This experience established the pattern for *jihad* (struggle). For Muslims, *jihad* has multiple meanings, referring first to the spiritual struggle against one's own desires, second to the struggle to create a righteous Muslim community, and lastly to the struggle against outsiders who wish to harm this community. Sadly, most Westerners have heard only of this last aspect of *jihad*, often removing it from its larger context.

Islam continued to grow after the Muhammed's death. The stories and traditions surrounding the Prophet's life have been passed on as *sunna*, and those who follow the *sunna* (from which the term "Sunni" is derived) in addition to the teachings of the Qu'ran are considered especially devout. The primary source for *sunna* is the **Hadith,** a collection of sayings attributed to Muhammed. A *hadith* was rigorously investigated before it was accepted as true; the tale had to be verified (preferably by those who saw the action), and the greatest weight was given to testimony by Muhammed's followers and relatives.

Of the four Rightly Guided Caliphs *(Rashidun)* who succeeded Muhammed, the fourth, Muhammed's nephew and son-in-law Ali, who lost power and was murdered in 661, was the catalyst for the division between Sunni and Shi'ite Muslims that persists today. The *Shi'at Ali* (Party of Ali), or **Shi'ites,** believed that Ali was the only legitimate successor to Muhammed. Contrary to popular Western perception, Shi'ism is not a creed of fanaticism, but has a sharp focus on **Imams:** mystical guides who are spiritual and sometimes blood descendants of the Prophet through Ali and his wife, Muhammed's daughter Fatima. While most Turkish Muslims today are Sunni, the Shi'ite Alevi comprise a sizeable minority (see **Alevi,** p. 31).

SUFISM

Sufism, the mystical Islamic practice in which Muslims seek divine love and knowledge through a direct personal experience with God, has been vitally important in the development of Islam. Islam spread to Turkey thanks to the efforts of traveling Sufi dervishes, who also established the religion in Central Asia, India, and Sub-Saharan Africa. Sufism began in opposition to the material excess of the **Umayyad caliphate** (661-750), and it sought to refocus the Islamic community on the spiritual goals of Islam. Guided by the Sufi master, the *murid* (disciple) achieves the *tariqa* (path) of Sufism through a strict regimen of ascetic practices. Sufis believe that self-denial, through acts like fasting, permits victory over the ego, the elimination of all thoughts of self in the quest for *fan-fi-Allah* (annihilation in God). Emphasizing universal love between God and humans, Sufi followers are a tolerant and peaceful people, marked by compassion and humility.

Although the Sufis were outside the mainstream of orthodox Islam and some of their more esoteric practices were never far from heresy, the orders enjoyed great privileges in the Ottoman Empire. Under the Ottomans, the Sufi orders lived in lodges (*tekke* in Turkish) that were endowed by the state, rich patrons, and charity. Under Atatürk's 1925 secular reforms, all ceremonies, meetings, and costumes associated with the Sufi orders were officially banned. But the government was unable to suppress such an established religious tradition, and Turkey has witnessed the gradual reemergence of Sufi customs and practice. The English language cannot always adequately translate terms describing Sufism, so consider words like "mystic" and "order" to be approximations.

MEVLEVİ ORDER

> Since in order to speak, one must first listen, learn to speak by listening.
> ——Celeddin-i-Rumi

The Mevlevi order was founded in Konya in the late 13th century by the Persian mystic and poet **Celeddin-i-Rumi** (see p. 346), whose popular title, *Mevlâna* (our master), gave the order its name. Known to the West as the **Whirling Dervishes** because of their ritual dance ceremony, the disciples of the order lived in *tekke*, which included living quarters, prayer room, kitchen, and a galleried *semahane* (dance hall). The Mevlevi's ritual whirl, or *sema*, is a spiritual exercise that allowed disciples to attain a state of union with God. The dancers' tall camel-hair hats represent tombstones, the black cloaks signify tombs, and the white robes a death shroud. In casting off the black cloaks, the dancers set aside all worldly ties and step out of the tomb of the self. Their arms extended—the right palm facing the heavens, the left facing the ground—the dervishes whirl slowly, channeling the mystical energy that makes the world turn.

The Mevlevi impact on poetry, **calligraphy,** and the visual arts from the 14th to 20th century is profound. Perhaps an even more important contribution to Ottoman culture is their development of a **religious music,** as music was frowned upon by Orthodox Islam. In 1954, the Turkish government allowed the Mevlevi ritual dance *(sema)* to be performed for tourists during the week preceding the anniversary of Rumi's death on December 17. Since then, the Mevlevi have gained more freedom to display their dance, and *sema* can be seen almost every other week at the **Galat Mevlihane** in İstanbul (see p. 103). Today the Mevlâna's *türbe* (tomb) in Konya, officially a museum, attracts the faithful (see p. 345).

BEKTAŞI ORDER

> We have recognized the unity of Allah... We have been the intoxicated ones from all eternity—we are butterflies in the divine light.
>
> ——Jevad Paşa

The Bektaşı order of Sufism was founded by **Haci Bektaş Veli,** who was born around 1248 in Iran. Haci Bektaş came to Anatolia in the late 13th century and lived in Kayseri, Kirşehir, and Sivas before founding his monastic complex in Suluca Karahöyük, where he died in 1337. His teachings helped popularize Islam in pre-Ottoman Anatolia, finding a particular resonance among soldiers and peasants. Haci Bektaş espoused a folksy brand of Sufism characterized by maxims like "seek and you shall find." His bestselling self-help book **Makalat** touted the **"Four Doors,"** or steps to enlightenment.

The Bektaşı, originally Sunni, began to assimilate Shi'ite practices in the 16th century. This explains the close ties between the Bektaşı and Shi'ite Alevi communities. The white-capped Bektaşı were famous for their slightly unorthodox behavior, including ritual wine swilling, dancing, and Christian practices such as bread-sharing and the confession of sins. They rose from a rural base to political importance in the 15th century, when their order began to dominate the elite Janissary Ottoman military corps (see p. 11). Bektaşı influence waned after 1826, however, when the "Auspicious Event" (see **The 19th Century: Reform and Reaction,** p. 13) eliminated the Janissary corps. Today, at an annual mid-August gathering, thousands still gather in Hacibektaş to commemorate its namesake with dancing.

WOMEN IN TURKEY

Rapid social change in 20th-century Turkey transformed the social roles of Turkish women, particularly members of the urban upper classes. Rural and poor areas, however, remain largely traditional. In the move to create a progressive republic, **Atatürk's reforms** (see p. 15) gave women nearly the same legal status as men, which included suffrage and the right to hold office. Women began to enter the workforce during World War II, occupying positions as teachers, clerical workers and industrial laborers. By the 1970s, many women held positions in education and health care, and in some regions, women held upper-level positions in fields like law and medicine. In fact, more Turkish women worked in these fields during the early 1980s than did their French and American counterparts. In 1993, **Tansu Çiller** became Turkey's first female prime minister.

The wedding code of the early Republic decreed an end to traditional rituals such as bride fees and arranged marriages, emphasizing marriage as a personal contract between two individuals. The reforms also recognized a woman's right to demand a divorce. While vestiges of the traditional marriage system still exist in rural areas—weddings in these areas often consist of two ceremonies, one civil and the other more religious and family oriented, whereas in urban areas, marriage is a very Western institution.

Because they circumscribed Atatürk's goal of increasing Turkey's population, **abortion** and sterilization were illegal in the early days of the republic. A 1965 law, however, expanded the availability of birth control information and services, and in 1967, abortion was legalized for up to 10 weeks after conception.

While traditional gender roles persist in less modernized areas of the country, women continue to gain power in Turkey. For information on travel for women in Turkey, see **Women Travelers,** p. 71.

MINORITIES

KURDS

The 1999 capture and conviction of Kurdish guerilla leader Abdüllah Öcalan brought increasing international attention to the Kurds, the largest ethnic group in the world without its own nation. An estimated 20 million Kurds live in the regions of eastern Turkey, northern Syria, Iraq, and northern Iran. Between twelve and fifteen million live in Turkey alone, comprising nearly 25% of the population. Divided by international borders and along religious, linguistic, and political lines, the Kurds are far from homogenous. The **Kurdish language,** which is related to Persian, has its roots in northwestern Iran. Of the three distinct dialects spoken by Kurds today, **Kermanji** is the most widely spoken in Turkey. Traditionally, the Kurds pursued a **nomadic lifestyle** of pastoralism, herding sheep and goats and raising horses. After World War I, urbanization and the division of Kurdish lands into disparate nations prevented customary migrations and forced many to settle in towns; however, nomadic lifestyles persist within the more remote regions of Eastern Turkey.

Although they fought alongside Atatürk's forces to establish a Turkish state, the Kurds were repaid not with the foundation of an independent Kurdistan, but with the new Turkish government's policy of **enforced assimilation**—an attempt to create a unified Turkish nation. Kurdish revolts in the 20s and 30s were met with the executions, deportations, and razing of villages that began **armed control** of Eastern Turkey. By 1925 the government had outlawed the Kurdish language, forbidden traditional dress in cities, and encouraged Kurdish migration to the country's urbanized western regions. Kurdish newspapers, television, and radio were also prohibited. Refusing to recognize the Kurds' distinct ethnicity, the Turkish government referred to Kurds as "mountain Turks" until the 1991 Gulf War.

Disaffected by their plight, many Kurds sought to voice their objections and demands through political means. The most famous and extremist Kurdish political group is the **PKK,** or **Worker's Party of Kurdistan.** Founded by political science student **Abdüllah Öcalan** in 1978, the PKK pledged itself to armed struggle in hopes of forming an independent and Marxist Kurdish state.

In the mid-80s, the PKK began to attack Turkish towns in the east and prominent Turkish officials. In response, the government declared **martial law** in the affected areas and armed loyal Kurds to create a defensive force known as the **village guards.** By taking advantage of the lack of Kurdish unity, the government helped to turn Kurds against one another, and the PKK increasingly attacked Kurds who had associated with the Turkish system. In the early 1990s the PKK undertook a series of bombings in heavily touristed coastal cities. These bombs were meant to bring attention to the Kurdish cause by bruising the country's high-revenue tourist industry. The government responded harshly with its own bombings, village evacuations, jailings (often in violation of international human rights legislation), and executions (often under mysterious conditions). By 1999, the continuing conflict had claimed over 30,000 lives.

International perception of the Kurdish issue in recent years has changed from anti-PKK sentiment to criticism of Turkey's human rights policies. The state is torn between its desire to completely quell Kurdish separatism and its interest in placating the international community and the European Union. There has, for instance, been some progress for the Kurds. Though the Kurdish language is still banned in schools and broadcasts, a 1991 decision now permits its use in unofficial settings. The Turkish army, however, has maintained its tough stance against terrorist activities, launching offensives to eradicate the PKK. As a testament to the army's success in weakening the PKK, Öcalan was preparing for a compromise before his capture in February 1999. Though Öcalan offered to broker a ceasefire in exchange for his life and Kurdish minority rights, the court sentenced him to death in June 1999. After the verdict, a renewed outbreak of bombings ensued. Since then, the PKK has announced that it would no longer target civilians, though the potential for violence exists (see **Turkey Today,** p. 20).

ARMENIANS

The ruins of **Ani** (50km east of Kars), a city that rivaled its western brother Constantinople in size, grandeur, and population, still remain to prove the millenial legacy of Armenians in Central Anatolia. Armenians lived under Ottoman rule until the 19th century, when Armenian separatist groups were founded with the hope of establishing an independent Armenian state, often through acts of terrorism.

At the outset of World War I, alliance with the **Russians** offered hope for Armenian independence, and a few thousand Armenians enlisted in the Russian armed forces. On April 20, 1915, Armenians revolted in **Van,** seizing the city's fortress in anticipation of Russian back-up. Fearing the Armenians' alliance with Russia, the Ottoman government (or the military acting independently) initiated a program of **deportation,** relocating Armenians to the Syrian desert. Hundreds of thousands were killed outright during the relocation, and many more died on the march.

Today, both sides dispute the facts, causes, and repercussions of this event. Armenian **casualties** are estimated at about two million, though the Turkish government insists on a much lower figure. The Turkish government denies that the program was officially sanctioned, and claims that it was a spontaneous military response to the threat posed by the Armenians' treasonous alliance with Russia. They assert that the high death count was largely a result of intercommunal warfare between Armenians and Kurds, and that many Turks were killed as well. In any event, the Turkish government claims that all state records of orders and decrees concerning the slaughter, known as *tercih* in Turkish, have been lost or corrupted. Other international sources believe that the incident was the first state-sanctioned genocide of the 20th century.

Armenians and their supporters demand that Turkey officially recognize the genocide and provide some form of apology or compensation. In the 1980s a group known as the **Armenian Secret Army for the Liberation of Armenia (ASALA)** murdered over 30 Turkish diplomats to bring attention to these demands. Many Turks today, however, feel that it is unrealistic and impossible for them to assume responsibility for actions of the Ottomans of almost a century ago.

JEWS

Jews represent a population of about 26,000 in Turkey today, concentrated mainly in İstanbul and with large communities in İzmir and Ankara. 96% of Turkish Jews are of **Sephardic** descent, tracing their lineage back to those who fled Iberia in the 15th century. Some fled the Inquisition, but the majority were expelled after the Christian *reconquista* of Spain and Portugal in 1492. (The term "Sephardic" comes from the Hebrew word for "Spain," though it was originally applied to the area around Sardis to which Jews fled after Nebucchadnezzar's conquest of Jerusalem.) The older generation of Sephardic Jews still speaks **Ladino,** a variant of the 15th-century Judeo-Spanish language, while the Ashkenazis speak Yiddish and the Karaites speak Greek. Dating to the early 15th century, the Ahrida Synagogue in the Balat neighborhood is the oldest of İstanbul's 16 synagogues in use today.

Throughout the **Holocaust,** Turkey extended open refuge to Jews fleeing Nazi persecution, and notable Jewish intellectuals were invited to find safety behind Turkish borders. Upon the establishment of an Israeli state in 1948, 30,000 Jews emigrated from Turkey, and the population has continued to decline steadily.

ALEVİ

The Alevi are Shi'ite Muslims (see **The Historical Evolution of Islam,** p. 26) who adhere to simple moral norms rather than the *Sharia* (Islamic law) and the traditional pillars of Islam. Elements of pre-Islamic Turkish and Persian religions infuse Alevi practice with more mysticism than is present in Sunni Islam. The Alevi believe in direct communion with God without the intermediary of the prayer leader. Thus, the only religious figure is the advice-giving *dede* (wise man). Much like the dervishes, the Alevi celebrate their religion through music and dance in religious ceremonies known as *cem.* That men and women perform these dances together has traditionally been a source of contempt among Sunni Muslims, who emphasize the potential for unholy activities.

The Alevi are estimated to comprise between 15-25% of the population and can be divided into four primary groups based on language: the Azerbaijani Turkish speakers of Eastern Turkey, the Arabic speakers of Southern Turkey, and the more populous Kurdish- and Turkish-speaking groups, concentrated in southeastern and central Anatolia, respectively.

The Alevi have been long-time supporters of the secularization of the state; they embraced Kemalism since it allowed them to fit into mainstream Turkish society, but Sunni-Alevi clashes in the 1970s demonstrated to Turkish officials the difficulty of realizing the unified, homogenous, secular state that Atatürk envisioned. Because of their greater visibility in recent years, the Alevi have become increasingly vulnerable to violence from certain conservative groups, inspiring some radicalized Alevis to draw parallels between their own situation and that of the Kurds; both stand as obstacles to the nationalistic, anti-pluralistic conservative agenda of Turkey's most extreme factions.

THE LAZ, THE HEMŞİN, AND THE CIRCASSIANS

The **Laz,** though present throughout Turkey, are concentrated largely in the eastern regions of the Black Sea coast near the border with Georgia. Numbering approximately 250,000, the Laz have a reputation for being successful businesspeople, as they own and operate many of the Black Sea shipping companies. Their relative affluence often makes them the subject of envy and ethnic jokes among young Turks. It seems likely that they migrated from the war-torn region of **Abkhazia,** the westernmost province of the Republic of Georgia, in the 16th century when they were driven west to Turkey by Arab invaders. Christians until the 16th century, the Laz gradually converted to Islam and became so assimilated that most have completely forgotten their religious heritage. Related to Georgian, the Laz language, *Lazuri,* was purely a spoken one until the 1960s, when its alphabet was codified as a combination of Georgian and Latin letters.

The **Hemşin** people, historically concentrated around Ayder in northeastern Anatolia, are Caucasians like the Laz. Traditional Hemşin villages are suffering from the flight of their youth to urban centers—there are only about 15,000 Hemşin people left in the Ayder region. There is some speculation that the Hemşin might have originated in the area of modern-day Armenia. Like the Laz, the Hemşin people were originally Christian, and even now, their version of Islam is much more relaxed than that of most of their ethnic Turkish neighbors. The Hemşin are traditionally beekeepers and pastry makers (see **Hemşinli,** p. 426).

The **Circassians** (*Çerkes* in Turkish) originated in the northern Caucasus region. With several hundred thousand members, this is the largest Caucasian minority group in Turkey. Most Circassians today are descendants of refugees who were forced to leave their homelands during the 19th-century Russian occupation. The fall of the Soviet Union seemed at first to be a likely catalyst for Circassian repatriation, but the 1992 war in Abkhazia and the subsequent wars in Chechnya served as major deterrents. During the last decade, the Turkish Circassian communities have become more visible and are experiencing a revitalization.

LANGUAGE

Turkish, the official language of Turkey, is spoken by approximately 55 million people domestically, and about one million more abroad. It is the most prominent member of the Turkic language family, which also includes Azerbaijani, Kazakh, Khirgiz, Uyghur, and Uzbek. Turkish is also related to other languages spoken in central Asia such as Mongolian and Manchu. Korean is sometimes included in this group as well. Originally written in Arabic script with strong Arabic and Persian influences, Atatürk reformed the language in 1928 using a romanized alphabet and attempted to purge any foreign borrowings so as to minimize Islam's influence on secular life. This linguistic cleansing was not absolute; common Arabic and Persian words such as *merhaba* (hello) remain.

Visitors with little or no experience with Turkish should not be intimidated. Any attempt at speaking Turkish will be much appreciated by the Turks. (For **pronunciations** and a brief **glossary**, see p. 496). English is widely spoken wherever tourism is big business—mainly in the major coastal resorts. In the rest of Anatolia, only university students tend to know English. A small phrasebook will help greatly during your travels. For more in-depth study, consult *Teach Yourself Turkish* by Pollard and Pollard (New York, 1996. $12.).

CUSTOMS AND ETIQUETTE

Turks value **hospitality** and will frequently go out of their way to welcome travelers, commonly offering to buy visitors a meal or a cup of *çay* (tea). Do not refuse tea unless you have very strong objections; it provides a friendly, easy way to converse with locals. If you are invited to a Turkish house as a guest, it is customary to bring a small gift such as flowers or chocolates and to remove your shoes before entering. A pair of slippers will usually be provided. When chatting with Turks, do not speak with any disrespect or skepticism about Atatürk, founder of modern Turkey, and avoid other sensitive subjects. In particular, do not discuss the Kurdish issue, the PKK, Northern Cyprus, or Turkey's human rights record.

BODY VIBES. In Turkey, **body language** often matters as much as the spoken word. When a Turk raises his chin and clicks his tongue, he means *hayır* (no); this gesture is sometimes accompanied by a shutting of the eyes or the raising of eyebrows. A sideways shake of the head means *anlamadım* (I don't understand), and *evet* (yes) may be signalled by a sharp downward nod. If a Turk waves a hand up and down at you, palm toward the ground, she is signaling you to come, not bidding you farewell. In Turkey the idle habit of snapping the fingers of one hand and then slapping the top of the other fist is considered obscene. It is also considered rude to point your finger or the sole of your shoe toward someone. Though public displays of affection by couples are inappropriate, Turks of both sexes greet each other with a kiss on both cheeks, and often touch or hug one another during conversation. They also tend to stand close to one another when talking.

Turks often stare at one another more than visitors are used to, and women in particular may feel uncomfortable by the stares. Try not to feel threatened by the usually harmless interest. Smiling, regarded in the West as a sign of confidence and outgoing friendliness, is sometimes associated in Turkey with a lack of sincerity or an element of deception. Often, what might appear to be grimness in some Turks may be a mistranslation of an everyday interaction or gesture.

DRESS. Shorts are a sure way to be labeled a tourist, as most Turks, particularly women, do not wear them. Women will probably find a head scarf or a bandana handy, perhaps essential, in more conservative regions. Except in İstanbul and the resort towns of the Aegean and Mediterranean coasts where casual, "beachy" dress is much more widely accepted, scanty clothing sends an audacious or flirtatious signal. Long skirts and lightweight pants are most acceptable, and they are also comfortable and practical, especially in summer. T-shirts are generally acceptable, though you should cover your arms in the more religious parts of the country. Topless bathing is common in some areas along the Aegean and Mediterranean coasts, but unacceptable in other regions. Nude sunbathing is illegal.

LEISURE

Many popular Turkish pastimes still take place in all-male enclaves. A favorite is visiting the local *kıraathane* (coffeehouse), where customers sip coffee or tea over games of *tavla* (backgammon). Another popular game is *OKEY*, which is basically gin rummy played with tiles instead of cards. Men can be found smoking *nargiles* (hookahs) in some corners of Turkey. If you decide to purchase a *nargile* as a souvenir, make sure customs officials do not mistake it for a *water pipe* or *water filtration device* (bong).

THE HAMAM. Because of the Islamic emphasis on cleanliness (pious Muslims perform ablutions before each of the day's five prayers), the baths have been a customary part of daily life since medieval times. They have traditionally functioned as social meeting places, especially for women, who otherwise wouldn't leave the house often. Men and women use separate facilities. Some bathhouses are single-sex, otherwise there will be designated days and times for women *(kadınlar)* and men *(erkekler)*. Consult the sign on the hamam door for a schedule. For more information, check out **Hamam-o-Rama,** below.

SPORTS. The Turkish passion for *spor* transcends religious, cultural, and social barriers. Although Turks do follow other sports, particularly American basketball, they are **futbol** (soccer) fanatics. Of Turkey's numerous soccer teams, only four have risen to national significance: Fenerbahçe, Beşiktas, Galatasaray, and Trabzon Spor. Fans living outside İstanbul or Trabzon generally root for one of these four in addition to their smaller home clubs. All four play very fast, scrappy, world-class soccer. **Fenerbahçe,** hailing from an Asian İstanbul suburb, is immediately recognizable by its blue and yellow team shirts. Nobody, not even die-hard fans of the European Bosphorus counterpart Beşiktaş, really dislikes Fener, the first non-English team ever to beat Manchester United *in* Manchester, in 1997. Commanding the most respect abroad, yellow and red **Galatasaray** is an old, venerated outfit and the reigning Turkish champ. In May of 2000, they made headlines worldwide with their defeat of Britain's Arsenal in the UEFA Cup finals, bringing the trophy and pride to the people of Turkey. **Beşiktas,** the "Black Eagles" in black and white, play very tight soccer, and purple-and-blue **Trabzon Spor** (see p. 419) is the upstart of the bunch, with a zealous fan base consolidated in eastern Turkey.

As in most places where *futbol* reigns supreme, emotions run high at Turkish matches, with fans cheering wildly, chanting and beating on drums. Police confiscate lighters and coins at the entrance to stadiums, but still must use riot shields to protect players coming on and off the field from flying objects thrown by zealous fans. Because of poor maintenance, inadequate facilities and ineffective security, Turkish stadiums were recently deemed unsafe by international soccer officials, although there have been no reported incidents. Disabled travelers should be advised that there is limited handicapped accessibility at stadiums.

HAMAM-O-RAMA Hamams can be intimidating for first-timers, but they're well worth the effort. Pay the entrance fee plus massage and *kese* (abrasive mitt). Bring your own shampoo, soap, and towel, or pay to use the bath's. Some hamams have cubicles *(camekan)* for personal storage. You will be given a large towel *(peştemal)*. Men generally strip and wrap the *peştemal* around their waists, but don't drop that sucker! Turkish women frequently strip naked (in the hamam).

Some hamams have a hot, sauna-like room. After you've worked up a sweat, proceed to the warm main room with its large, heated stone *(göbek taşı)*. Mix hot and cold water and pour it over yourself with the bowl provided.

A wash and **massage** on the large, heated marble stone costs a little more. Usually, the masseur is your gender; female visitors may request a female masseuse. The massage is often very vigorous; try the phrase *"lütfen daha yumuşak"* (gentler please) if need be. The *kese* used can also be purchased at pharmacies. Following the massage and *kese*, you will usually be sponged gently and shampooed. When you're clean as a whistle, rehydrate with water and a have a nap.

Traditional spectator sports such as *cirit oyunu* (tossing javelins at competitors on horseback; see **Wargames,** p. 444) and *deve güresi* (camel wrestling) enjoy a very local following and are generally practiced during festivals. One exception is the **Kırkpınar Grease Wrestling Festival** (see p. 150), held in Edirne in July; it draws a huge crowd and enjoys TV broadcasts throughout Turkey.

FOOD AND DRINK

Contemporary Turkish cuisine reflects its Ottoman heritage. Popular dishes such as *kebap* (kebab) and *pilav* (rice) derive from the traditions of nomadic Central Asian tribes and other civilizations that have swept through Asia Minor. An Assyrian cookbook found during recent excavations shows that similar dishes have been served for thousands of years. Fans of Greek, Armenian, and Middle Eastern food will recognize favorite dishes on Turkish menus, but these neighboring traditions have been reinterpreted and recombined to forge a unique cuisine.

Although Turkish food varies from region to region, some staples will turn up in just about any Turkish kitchen: yogurt, olive oil, bread, rice, lamb, spices, and, above all, fresh produce. Pre-packaged and processed food items are rarely used.

Turks typically start the day with a **breakfast** of freshly baked bread, thick honey, jam, olives, cheese, a soft-boiled egg, sliced tomatoes, and cucumbers, complemented by strong Turkish tea. Many *pansiyons* (small hotels) offer breakfast for a small sum or free of charge.

APPETIZERS AND ACCOMPANIMENTS. Lunch and dinner often begin with *mezes*, hot or cold appetizers which can be a meal in themselves. *Meze* come in many forms, from simple *beyaz peynir* (feta cheese) to complex vegetable dishes. Most menus feature *dolma*, a kind of *meze* whose name comes from the verb meaning to fill or to stuff (not coincidentally the same verb that gives the dolmuş its name). *Dolma* include peppers, grape leaves, and tomatoes stuffed with rice or meat. *İmam bayıldı* (literally, "the priest fainted") is a stuffed eggplant dish. *Börek* is another common *meze* item—a flaky pastry either filled with *kıyma* (meat), *peynir* (cheese), or *ıspınak* (spinach). *Börek* can be *sigara* (long crispy fried rolls which resemble cigarettes), *su* (lasagna-like noodles with cheese filling), or *normal* (flaky pastry dough with filling).

Turkish salads are rarely made with lettuce. More common salad varieties include *çoban salatası* (chopped tomato and cucumber salad), *patlıcan salatası* (pureed eggplant), *yeşil salatası* (green salad, also called *mevsim salatası*—the closest you'll come to an American-style side salad), *cacık* (thin yogurt with cucumbers, often spiced with garlic), and *Amerikan salatası*—an ill-named mixture of peas, carrots, potatoes, and mayonnaise.

Çorba (soup) changes with the seasons. Thicker soups like *mercimek çorbası* (lentil soup) and *domates çorbası* (tomato soup with shredded *kaşar* cheese) are a mainstay in the winter months, while cool, minty yogurt soups dominate summer menus. Inebriated Turks coming back from a wild night on the town often head straight to the nearest *çorba* joint to have a piping-hot bowl of *kırmızı mercimek çorbası* (red lentil soup) or *işkembe çorbası* (tripe soup). Lord knows stomach always tastes better after a good night of drinking.

AAAHH, MEAT. Ubiquity, thy name is **kebap.** Almost every meal in Turkey involves meat, and meat in Turkey is usually lamb. Many restaurants specialize in **köfte** (small, spiced meatballs), **mantı** (tiny meat-filled ravioli), or other meat dishes, and the varieties of this staple are limitless. Coastal Turkey travel merits at least a stop at one of the fish restaurants. Selections vary according to season, region, and the catch of the day; diners choose their *balık* (fish) from the display. Eating fish requires nimble teeth: it's served whole, with bones, head, fins and tail.

VEGETABLES AND FRUIT. The secret ingredient in Turkish cuisine is tasty, fresh-from-the-farm produce, grown (in-season only) along the western and southern coasts. To find the best fruits and veggies available, join the basket-toting women at any of the markets listed in this book. **Carefully wash all produce with bottled or boiled water before taking a bite.** An even better rule of ■ thumb is only to eat peelable fruit. Take the plunge and treat your taste buds to a Turkish favorite: *karpuz* (watermelon) with *beyaz peynir* (feta cheese).

SWEETS. Save room for dessert, which is almost always sticky and sweet. Highlights include *baklava* (a flaky, sweet nut pastry, usually with pistachio), *kadayif* (shredded pastry dough filled with nuts and drenched in syrup), *tavukgöğsu* (a creamy sweet made of pulverized chicken fibers), and *helva* (sesame paste). The *dondurma* (ice cream) manages to be chewy and sticky and frozen all at the same time. Keep an eye out for pudding shops, and sample the *aşure* (fruit pudding), *sütlaç* (rice pudding), *krem karamel* (crème caramel), and *profiterol.*

STREET FOOD. Street food can be a cheap and tasty alternative to restaurant-dining, not to mention a great way to experience authentic Turkish cuisine, particularly if you're on-the-go. The food varies with the season and region, and there is a broad range of quality and freshness. Baked goods like *simit* (a sesame bread ring), *poğaça* (flaky pastry often served with a layer of cheese), and *börek* are safe, as are most dried fruit and nuts. However, buying ice cream on the street may be a bad idea. As always, be cautious, and remember that your stomach may not be used to the benign bacteria found in Turkish food.

Besides the snacks sold on Atatürk Caddesis throughout the nation, Turkey offers the budget traveler a delicious array of inexpensive fast food. Instead of a Big Mac (although they are available), try *gözleme*, a crêpe-tortilla hybrid, filled with cheese, potatoes, spinach, or meat; *kokoreç*, fried, chopped tripe (a cow's stomach lining), usually in sandwiches with tomatoes; *lahmacun*, often called Turkish pizza, a thin rounded bread topped with ground spiced meat; *tost*, a grilled cheese sandwich; or *kumpir*, baked potatoes piled high with toppings.

DRINKS. When in Turkey, do as the Turks do and **always drink only bottled or purified water.** Many establishments use safe water when preparing food, but be sure to do the same yourself. It is also a good idea to keep your mouth closed in the shower.

A half cup full of pure caffeine, *kahve* (Kick-Me-In-The-Face-Turkish coffee) can be ordered *sade* (black), *orta* (medium sweet), or *şekerli* (very sweet). Despite the fame garnered by Turkish coffee, Turkey's national drink remains, without a doubt, *çay* (tea). Served in small, hourglass-shaped glasses, *çay* is strong, black, and everywhere. *Elma çayı* (apple tea), which tastes like warmed apple juice, is an alternative to conventional Turkish tea's strong brew.

PLEASE PASS THE KEBAP Sure, the meaty *kebap* was a treat at first, but after 75 identical meals in a row, you'd rather eat glass. Aside from upscale restaurants, which often offer the same tired menu for Trump-ish prices, your best bet for a wider variety of cheap Turkish cuisine is the *lokanta* (sometimes *lokantası*). These restaurants lie off the tourist path and cater mostly to working men. Their style is usually cafeteria-like: seven or eight dishes will have been prepared for the day, of which two or three are meat-based. The rest are mainly vegetarian (though some may contain unexpected pieces of meat). Everything comes in sized portions and is extremely cheap ($1-2 per serving). For real sampling, request a half-serving. The only drawback to *lokantas* is that women may feel a tad uncomfortable joining the rows of male patrons. Some *lokantas* have an "*aile*" section upstairs, reserved for families and single women, which is usually much cleaner and airier than the men's section. In any case, don't worry about unwanted social contact in the *lokanta*. People usually eat quickly and with no conversation, knowing they soon have to head back to work.

Ayran, a salty yogurt drink, makes appearances with meat dishes and in hot weather. *Meyva suyu* (fruit juice), *maden suyu* (mineral water), and *cola* (Coca-Cola) are also common. *Sahlep*, available only in winter, is a warm, sweet, milky drink made of pulverized orchid root and served with cinnamon.

Alcohol, though widely available, is frowned upon in the more conservative parts of the country. Restaurants that post *içkisiz* in their windows have none, but those with *içkili* are taking special pains to announce alcohol's availability. *Bira* (beer) is ever-popular: *Efes Pilsen* and *Tüborg* are the leading brands—the former is better. The best domestic white wines are *Çankaya*, *Villa Doluca*, and *Kavaklıdere*, made in Cappadocia, while *Yakut* and *Kavaklıdere* produce the finest red. Ice-cold *rakı*, a clear anise-seed liquor that tastes like licorice, is Turkey's national alcohol. Mixed in equal parts with water, which clouds it, *rakı* is similar to Greek *ouzo*, but even stronger. İstanbul's local specialty is *balyoz* (sledge hammer/wrecking ball). Getting wrecked will not be difficult: *balyoz* consists of *rakı*, whiskey, vodka, and gin mixed with orange juice. Bottoms up.

HOLIDAYS AND FESTIVALS

In Turkey, these are of three kinds: national secular, national religious, and local. Since religious holidays are dependent on the lunar calendar, the day they fall on varies from year to year. Local festivals are often dependent upon the harvest, the weather, or the moon, and as such it is difficult to predict exact dates. For specific dates of a given festival, contact the town's tourist office. If you anticipate traveling in a town or region during festival time, check ahead on accommodations, since hotels and pensions in many towns can fill up quickly. For more specific information about the holidays, see the appropriate city section.

Turkey's religious holidays, festivals, and traditions are sometimes overwhelming for travelers. **Ramazan,** which occurs during a different one-month period every year, is a time of fasting for observant Muslims (see **The Five Pillars of Islam,** p. 25). Though tourists are not expected to comply with the holiday, it is important to remember that this is the holiest month of the year for many Turks, and that respect for their customs is imperative. If you're in Turkey during Ramazan, be aware that many restaurants are closed. In those that are open, the clientele will be largely foreign. It is advisable that you not drink, eat, or smoke cigarettes on the street until sunset. *Oruç tutmak* (fasting) is a test of faith, and it is considered disrespectful to tempt the faithful in this way. At sundown, *Ramazan pidesi*, a special, dense flatbread, is used to break the daily fast. The three-day festival of **şeker Bayramı** (Sugar Holiday) occurs at the end of Ramazan, and is celebrated with family gatherings, the giving of sweets to children, and general festivity. **Kurban Bayramı** (Sacrifice Holiday) usually occurs a few months after Ramazan, and involves the large-scale slaughter of sheep, which are purchased on streetcorners by those families who can afford to do so, killed, and then distributed to the poor.

DATE	FESTIVAL	CITY/OBSERVANCE
Nov. 6, 2002 Oct. 27, 2003	Ramazan (Ramadan)	National (religious) Duration is one month; date given is first day. Starting date may vary by one day depending on the sighting of the moon.
Eve of the 28th day of the month of Ramazan	Kadır Gecesi (Eve of Power)	National (religious) Varies with Ramazan.
January 1	Yılbaşı–New Year's Day	National (secular)
Mid-January	Camel Wrestling Festival	Selçuk
December 16, 2001	Sugar Holiday (şeker Bayramı)	National (religious) Date may vary by 1 or 2 days depending on the moon.
March	Film Festival	Ankara
March 18	Sea Victory Celebration	Çanakkale
4 days around the vernal equinox (March 21)	Mesir Macunu ("Power Gum") Festival	Manisa
Feb. 22, 2002 Feb. 11, 2003	Day of the Hajj	National (religious) Varies with Ramazan.
February 12, 2002	Festival of the Sacrifice (Kurban Bayramı)	National (religious) Date varies with the moon.
March/April	Bald Ibis Festival	Gaziantep, şanlıurfa, Birecik
Early April	Film Festival	İstanbul
April 23	Independence Day and Children's Day	National (secular)
April 25	ANZAC DAY	Gelibolu Peninsula
Late April	Power Gum Festival	Manisa
Second week of May	Ephesus Performance Festival	Ephesus
Second week of May	Yacht Festival	Marmaris
May 19	Youth and Sports Day–Atatürk's Birthday	National (secular)
May 20	Black Sea Giresun Aksu Festival	Giresun
May 29	Anniversary of İstanbul's capture in 1453 by Mehmet the Conqueror	İstanbul
Late May/Early June	Song Competition	Pamukkale
June	Strawberry Festival	Bartın
June	International Tea Festival	Rize
June	İzmir Music and Dance Fair	İzmir, Çeşme, Ephesus
June	Wine Competition	Ürgüp
June	Cherry Festival	Tekirdağ
June	Aspendos Opera and Ballet Festival	Serik-Antalya
Third week of June	Bull Wrestling/Caucasus Culture and Arts Festival	Artvin
May 24, 2002	Birth of The Prophet (Peace Be Upon Him)	National (religious) Date varies with the moon.
Last week of June	International Golden Pomegranate Festival	Kemer-Antalya
June/July	Music Festival	İstanbul
July	VW Beetle Festival	Ordu

DATE	FESTIVAL	CITY/OBSERVANCE
July	Golden Hazelnut Festival	Ordu
July	Folk Dance Festival	Samsun
July	Nasreddin Hoca Festival	Akşehir
July	Hittite Festival	Çorum
July 1	Navy Day	National (secular)
Early July	Kırkpınar Grease Wrestling Festival	Edirne
Early July	Bursa Festival	Bursa
Last week of July	Apricot Harvest Festival	Malatya
July/August	Highland Festivals	Trabzon
Mid-August	Hacibektaş Veli Commemoration Ceremony	Hacibektaş
3rd week of August	Pop Song Festival	Çesme
August 26	Armed Forces Day	İstanbul
August 30	Celebration of Turkish Defeat of Greece (1922)	National (secular)
August/September	İzmir International Fair	İzmir
September	Meerschaum (White Gold) Festival	Eskişehir
September	Architectural Treasures and Folklore Week	Safranbolu
First week of September	Golden Apple and Silver Fish Festival	Eğirdir
September 9	Liberation Day (speeches marking the end of the Independence War)	İzmir
September/October	Golden Pistachio Festival	Gaziantep
September/October	Plastic Arts Festival	İstanbul
September/October	Mediterranean Song Contest	Antalya
October	Atatürk Dam Sailing Competition	Alanya
End of October	Yacht Festival/Race Week	Marmaris
October 29	Republic Holiday—Celebration of Atatürk's Declaration of the Republic	National (secular)
November 10, 9:05am	Anniversary of Atatürk's Death (nationwide moment of silence)	National (secular)
December 10-17	Rumi Commemoration—Mevlâna Festival	Konya

ESSENTIALS

DOCUMENTS AND FORMALITIES

TURKISH CONSULAR SERVICES ABROAD

Australia: Embassy: 60 Mugga Way, Red Hill, **Canberra** ACT 2603 (☎(02) 6295 0227; fax 6239 6592; turkembs@ozemail.com.au; http://members.ozemail.com.au/~turkembs.). **Consulates:** 24 Albert Rd. South, 8th fl., **Melbourne** VIC 3205 (☎(03) 9696 6066 or 9696 6046; fax 9696 6104; turkcons@eisa.net.au); 66 Ocean St., P.O. Box 222, Woollahra, **Sydneyolm** NSW 2025 (☎(612) 9328 1155, 9328 1239 or 9363 2587; fax 9362 4533).

Canada: Embassy: 3 Crescent Rd. Rockcliffe, **Ontario** KIM ON1 (☎613-748-3737, 789-3720, or 749-0739; fax 789-3442; turkish@magma.ca).

Ireland: Embassy: 11 Clyde Rd., Ballsbridge, **Dublin** 4 (☎(01) 668 5240 or 660 1623; fax 668 5014; turkemb@iol.ie).

New Zealand: Embassy: 15-17 Murphy St., Level 8, **Wellington** (☎(04) 472 1290 or 472 1292; fax 472 1277; email turkem@xtra.co.nz).

South Africa: Embassy: 1067 Church St., Hatfield, **Pretoria** 0028 (☎(012) 342 6053, 342 6054, or 342 6055; fax 342 6052; pretbe@global.co.za; www.turkishembassy.co.za). **Consulate:** 6 Sandown Valley Crescent 2nd fl., Sandown-Sandton, **Johannesburg** 2001 (☎(011) 884 9060, 884 9061 or 884 9062; fax 884 9064).

UK: Embassy: 43 Belgrave Sq., **London,** SWIX 8PA (☎(020) 7393 0202; fax 7393 0066; info@turkishembassy-london.com; www.turkishembassy-london.com). **Consulate:** Rultand Lodge, Rutland Gardens, Knightsbridge, **London,** SW7 1BW (☎(020) 7589 0949, 7589 0360, or 7584 1078; fax 7584 6235; trcons@globalnet.co.uk).

US: Embassy: 2525 Massachusetts Ave. NW, **Washington, D.C.** 20008 (☎202-612-6700 or 612-6701; fax 612-6744; info@turkey.org; www.turkey.org). **Consulates:** 360 N. Michigan Ave., #1405, **Chicago,** IL 60601 (☎312-263-0644, ext. 28; fax 263-1449; chicago@trconsulate.org); 1990 Post Oak Blvd., #1300, **Houston,** TX 77056 (☎713-622-5849; fax 623-6639; turcon@ix.netcom.com); 4801 Wilshire Blvd., #310, **Los Angeles,** CA 90010 (☎323-937-0118; fax 932-0061; turkcgla@pacbell.net); 821 United Nations Plaza, 5th fl., **New York,** NY 10017 (☎212-949-0160; fax 983-1293; tcbkny@worldnet.att.net).

FOREIGN CONSULAR SERVICES IN TURKEY

Australia: Embassy: 83 Nenehatun Cad., Gazlosmanpaşa, **Ankara** (☎(312) 446 11 80 or 446 11 87; fax 446 11 88). **Consulate:** 58 Tepecik Yolu, Etiler, **İstanbul** (☎(212) 257 70 50 or 257 70 53; fax: 257 70 54).

Canada: Embassy: 75 Nenehatun Cad., Gaziosmanpaşa, **Ankara** (☎(312) 436 12 75, 436 12 76; fax 447 21 73; ankara@dfait-maeci.gc.ca.) **Consulate:** 107/3 Büyükdere Cad., Bengun Han, Gayrettepe, **İstanbul** (☎(212) 272 51 74; fax 272 34 27).

Ireland: Embassy: Ugur Mumcu Cad. MNG Binasi, B Bloc, Kat 3, Gaziomanpaşa, **Ankara** (☎(312) 446 61 72; fax 446 80 61). **Consulate:** 26/A Cumhuriyet Cad., Pegasus Evi, Harbiye, **İstanbul** (☎(212) 246 60 25; fax (212) 248 07 44).

New Zealand: Embassy: 13/4 İran Cad., Kavaklıdere, **Ankara** (☎(312) 467 90 56; fax 467 90 13; newzealand@superonline.com.) **Consulate:** Maya Akar Center, Level 24, 100/102 Buyukdere Cad., Esentepe, **İstanbul** (☎(212) 275 29 89; fax 275 5008).

South Africa: Embassy: 27 Filistin Sok., Gaziosmanpaşa, **Ankara** (☎(312) 446 40 56; fax 446 64 34; saemb@ada.net.tr; www.southafrica.org.tr). **Consulate:** 106 Büyükdere Cad., Esentepe, **İstanbul** (☎(212) 227 52 00; fax 275 76 42).

UK: Embassy: 46/A şehit Ersan Cad., Çankaya, **Ankara** (☎(312) 455 33 44; fax 455 33 56; britembank@ankara.mail.fco.gov.uk; www.britishembassy.org.tr.) **Consulates:** Ucgen Mahallest Dolaplidere Cad., Pirilti Sitesi Kati ilit, Sauna Karisi, **Antalya** (☎(242) 247 70 00/2; fax 243 14 82); Kibris Sehitleri Cad., Konacik Mevkii 401/B, **Bodrum** (☎(252) 317 00 93 or 317 00 94; fax 317 00 95); Ressam Pefik Bursali Cad. No. 40, Zemin Kat 16010, **Bursa** (☎(224) 220 04 36; fax 220 03 31); Meşrutiyet Cad., #34, Tepebaşı, Beyoğlu, PK 33, **İstanbul** (☎(212) 293 75 40; fax 245 49 89); Mahmut Esat Bozkurt Cad., 1442 Sok. No. 49, Alsancak, PK 300, **İzmir** (☎(232) 463 51 51; fax 465 08 58); Yesil Marmaris Tourism and Yacht Management Inc., 118 Barbaros Cad., P.O. Box 8, **Marmaris** (☎(252) 412 64 86; fax 412 45 65); Catoni Maritime Agencies SA, Cakmak Cad. Orta Okulu Sok., No. 3/B, **Mersin** (☎(324) 232 12 48 ; fax 232 29 91).

US: Embassy: 110 Atatürk Bul., Kavaklıdere, **Ankara** (☎(312) 455 55 55; fax 468 61 31). **Consulates:** Atatürk Cad., Vali Yolu, Bossa Apt. Kat 1, **Adana** (☎(322) 459 15 51; fax 457 65 91); 104-108 Meşrutiyet Cad., Tepebaşı, **İstanbul** (☎(212) 251 36 02; fax 251 32 18); Kazim Dirik Cad., Atabay İş Merkezi 13/8, **İzmir** (☎(232) 441 00 72).

PASSPORTS

REQUIREMENTS. Citizens of Australia, Canada, Ireland, New Zealand, South Africa, the UK, and the US need valid passports to enter Turkey and to re-enter their home countries. Turkey does not allow entrance if the holder's passport expires in under six months; returning home with an expired passport is illegal, and may result in a fine.

PHOTOCOPIES. Be sure to photocopy the page of your passport with your photograph, passport number, and other identifying information, as well as any visas, travel insurance policies, plane tickets, or traveler's check serial numbers. Carry one set of copies in a safe place, apart from the originals, and leave another set at home. Consulates also recommend carrying an expired passport or an official copy of a birth certificate separate from other documents.

LOST PASSPORTS. If you lose your passport, immediately notify the local police and the nearest embassy or consulate of your home government. To expedite its replacement, have all available information previously recorded as well as ID and proof of citizenship. Replacements may take weeks to process, and may be valid only for a limited time. Visas stamped in the old passport will be irretrievably lost. In an emergency, ask for immediate, temporary traveling papers that permit entrance to your home country. Your passport is a public document belonging to your nation's government. If you must surrender it to a foreign official, inform the nearest mission of your home country if you don't get it back reasonably quickly.

NEW PASSPORTS. Citizens of Australia, Canada, Ireland, New Zealand, the UK, and the US can apply for a passport at the nearest post office, passport office, or court of law. Citizens of South Africa can apply for a passport at the nearest office of Foreign Affairs. Any new passport or renewal applications must be filed well in advance of the departure date, although most passport offices offer rush services for a very steep fee. Citizens living abroad who need a passport or renewal services should contact the nearest consular service of their home country.

VISAS AND WORK PERMITS

As of August 2001, citizens of Australia, Canada, Ireland, the UK, and the US require a visa—a stamp, sticker, or insert in your passport specifying the purpose of your travel and the permitted duration of your stay—in addition to a valid passport to enter Turkey. A visa costs US$45. Citizens of New Zealand and South Africa do not need visas to enter Turkey. New Zealanders may stay for up to three months with a valid passport, South Africans for up to one month. Though visas can be obtained from a Turkish embassy or consulate in your home country, it is most convenient (and cheapest) to get them at the airport upon arrival in Turkey. US citizens can take advantage of the **Center for International Business and Travel** (**CIBT;** ☎800-925-2428), which secures visas for a variable service charge. They can also be obtained at the border upon entry to Turkey.

Visitors traveling on a tourist visa are not permitted to work, which is authorized only by a **work visa.** Students must obtain a **student visa.** Unlike tourist visas, work visas and student visas must be obtained from the nearest Turkish embassy or consulate prior to arrival in Turkey. Check entrance requirements at the nearest Turkish embassy or consulate (see **Embassies & Consulates Abroad,** on p. 39) for up-to-date information before departure. US citizens may also consult www.pueblo.gsa.gov/cicŤtext/travel/foreign/foreignentryreqs.html.

IDENTIFICATION

When traveling, always carry two or more forms of identification on your person, including at least one form of photo identification; a passport combined with a driver's license or birth certificate is usually adequate. Many establishments, especially banks, may require several forms of identification to cash traveler's checks. Never carry all forms of identification together, in case of theft or loss.

For more information on forms of identification listed below, contact the **International Student Travel Confederation (ISTC),** Herengracht 479, 1017 BS Amsterdam, Netherlands. (☎ +31 (20) 421 28 00; fax 421 28 10; istcinfo@istc.org; www.istc.org)

TEACHER & STUDENT IDENTIFICATION. The **International Student Identity Card (ISIC),** the most widely accepted form of student ID, provides discounts on sights, accommodations, food, and transport. The ISIC is preferable to an institution-specific card (such as a university ID) because it is more likely to be recognized (and honored) abroad. All cardholders have access to a 24hr. emergency helpline for medical, legal, and financial emergencies (in North America call 877-370-ISIC, elsewhere call US collect +1 715-345-0505, UK collect +44 20 8762 8110, or France collect +33 155 633 144), and holders of US-issued cards are also eligible for insurance benefits (see **Insurance,** p. 56). Many student travel agencies issue ISICs, including STA Travel in Australia and New Zealand; Travel CUTS in Canada; usit in the Republic of Ireland and Northern Ireland; SASTS in South Africa; Campus Travel and STA Travel in the UK; and Council Travel (www.counciltravel.com/idcards/default.asp) and STA Travel in the US (see p. 64).

The card is valid from September of one year to December of the following year and costs US$22. Applicants must be degree-seeking students of a secondary or post-secondary school and must be of at least 12 years of age. Because of the proliferation of fake ISICs, some services (particularly airlines) require additional proof of student identity, such as a school ID or a letter attesting to your student status, signed by your registrar and stamped with your school seal. The **International Teacher Identity Card (ITIC)** offers the same insurance coverage as well as similar but limited discounts. The fee is AUS$13, UK£5, or US$22.

YOUTH IDENTIFICATION. The International Student Travel Confederation also issues a discount card to travelers who are 26 or under, but are not students. This one-year **International Youth Travel Card (IYTC)** offers many of the same benefits as the ISIC. Most organizations that sell the ISIC also sell the IYTC (US$22).

CUSTOMS

Upon entering Turkey, you must declare certain valuable items from abroad and pay a duty on the value of those articles that exceed the allowance established by Turkey's customs service. It is wise to make a list, including serial numbers, of any valuables that you carry with you from home; if you register this list with customs before your departure and have an official stamp it, you will avoid import duty charges. Be careful to document items manufactured abroad. Although not all merchants participate, Turkey does have a value-added tax (see **Taxes,** p. 45). For more specific information, **www.turkey.org,** Turkey's official website, has an itemized list of duty-free allowances.

Upon returning home, you must declare all articles acquired abroad and pay a **duty** on the value of articles that exceed the allowance established by your country. Goods and gifts purchased at **duty-free** shops abroad are not exempt from duty or sales tax at your point of return; you must declare these items as well.

MONEY

If you stay in hostels and prepare your own food, expect to spend anywhere from US$15-30 per day. **Accommodations** start at about US$5/$10 per night for a single/double, while a basic sit-down meal costs US$3-5 per person. Carrying cash with you, even in a money belt, is risky but necessary—though most banks will exchange traveler's checks, many establishments (particularly restaurants and shops) in Turkey do not accept them (see **Traveler's Checks,** below).

CURRENCY AND EXCHANGE

A NOTE ON PRICES. *Let's Go* quotes prices effective in the summer of 2001. As the lira has been extremely volatile in recent years, particularly since the macroeconomic crisis of Spring 2001, prices in Turkey may be significantly higher by 2002. Prices are quoted in US dollars to minimize unexpected increases.

The Turkish lira (TL) is the unit of currency in Turkey. Check a large newspaper or the Internet (e.g. www.oanda.com/convert/classic) for the latest exchange rates.

CURRENCY

US$1 = 1,480,000TL	1,000,000 TL = US$0.68
CDN$1 = 969,341TL	1,000,000 TL = CDN$1.04
EUR€1 = 1,351,000TL	1,000,000 TL = EUR€.75
UK£1 = 2,132,295TL	1,000,000 TL = UK£0.47
IR£1 = 1,716,000TL	1,000,000 TL = IR£0.59
AUS$1 = 782,928TL	1,000,000 TL = AUS$1.29
NZ$1 = 642,363TL	1,000,000 TL = NZ$1.57
ZAR1= 179,949TL	1,000,000 TL = ZAR5.60

Notes are in denominations of 10,000,000; 5,000,000; 1,000,000; 500,000; 250,000; and 100,000TL. Coins are in values of 100,000; 50,000; 25,000; 10,000; and 5000 TL. It is cheaper to convert money in Turkey than at home. The post and telephone office (PTT) and banks generally have the best rates. Using an ATM or a credit card (see p. 43) will often get you the best possible rates. Elsewhere, watch out for commission fees. A good rule of thumb is only to go to banks or *döviz (bureaux de change)* that have at most a 5% margin between their buy and sell prices. The most reliable large **banks** in Turkey include Akbank, Koçbank, Garanti Bankası, Yapı ve Kredi, TC Ziraat Bankası, and Türkiye İş Bankası. Because of Turkey's high inflation rate, it is best to convert money on a regular basis despite the one-time commission charges. Keep receipts for departure.

In Turkey, Western currency, particularly US dollars and German marks, is sometimes accepted. It is best to avoid using Western money, however, as throwing it around for preferential treatment may be offensive.

TRAVELER'S CHECKS

Traveler's checks are one of the safest and least troublesome means of carrying funds. Several agencies and banks sell them for a small commission. Each agency provides refunds if checks are lost or stolen, and many provide additional services, such as toll-free refund hotlines abroad, emergency message services, and stolen credit card assistance. Though **American Express** and **Visa** are the most widely recognized, particularly along the Aegean and Mediterranean coasts, traveler's checks are not readily accepted at most establishments. Instead, you will have to cash them at banks or at the post office (PTT).

While traveling, keep check receipts and a record of the checks you've cashed separate from the checks themselves. Also leave a list of check numbers with someone at home. Never countersign checks until you're ready to cash them, and always bring your passport with you to cash them. If your checks are lost or stolen, immediately contact a refund center (of the company that issued your checks) to be reimbursed; they may require a police report verifying the loss or theft. Less-touristed countries may not have refund centers, in which case you may have to wait to be reimbursed. Ask about toll-free refund hotlines and the location of refund centers when purchasing checks, and always carry emergency cash.

American Express: Call ☎(800) 25 19 02 in Australia; ☎(0800) 441 068 in New Zealand; ☎(0800) 521 313 in the UK; ☎800-221-7282 in the US and Canada. Elsewhere call US collect ☎+1 801-964-6665; or visit www.aexp.com. To report lost or stolen checks, call ☎00 (800) 4491 48 20 in Turkey. Checks can be purchased at American Express Travel Service Offices or banks. American Automobile Association (AAA) members may purchase checks commission-free at AAA offices (see p. 70).

Thomas Cook MasterCard: In the US and Canada call ☎800-223-7373; in the UK call ☎(0800) 62 21 01; elsewhere call UK collect ☎+44 (1733) 31 89 50. from Turkey call ☎00 (800) 4491 48 95. Checks available in 13 currencies at 2% commission. Commission-free at Thomas Cook.

Visa: In the US call ☎800-227-6811; in the UK call ☎(0800) 89 50 78; elsewhere call UK collect ☎+44 20 7937 80 91. Call for the location of their nearest office.

CREDIT CARDS

Where accepted, credit cards offer superior exchange rates—up to 5% better than the retail rate used by banks and other currency exchange establishments. Credit cards may also offer services such as insurance or emergency help, and are sometimes required to reserve hotel rooms or rental cars. **MasterCard** and **Visa** are most welcomed; **American Express** cards work at some ATMs and at AmEx offices and major airports. Budget travelers will probably find, however, that few of the establishments they frequent accept credit cards; aside from the occasional splurge, you will probably reserve use of your credit card for financial emergencies.

Credit cards are also useful for **cash advances,** which allow you to withdraw lira instantly from associated banks and ATMs throughout Turkey. However, transaction fees for all credit card advances (up to US$10 per advance, plus 2-3% extra on foreign transactions after conversion) tend to make credit cards a costly way of withdrawing cash. In an emergency, however, the transaction fee may prove worth the cost. To be eligible for an advance, you'll need to get a **Personal Identification Number (PIN)** from your credit card company (see **Cash Cards (ATM Cards),** below). Be sure to check with your credit card company before you leave home; in certain circumstances companies have started to charge foreign transaction fees.

CREDIT CARD COMPANIES. Visa (US ☎800-336-8472) and **MasterCard** (US ☎800-307-7309) are issued in cooperation with banks and other organizations. **American Express** (US ☎800-843-2273) has an annual fee of up to US$55. AmEx cardholders may cash personal checks at AmEx offices abroad, access an emergency medical and legal assistance hotline (24hr.; in North America call ☎800-554-2639, elsewhere call US collect ☎+1 715-343-7977), and enjoy American Express Travel Service benefits (including plane, hotel, and car rental reservation changes; baggage loss and flight insurance; mailgram and international cable services; and held mail). The **Discover Card** (in US call ☎800-347-2683, elsewhere call US ☎+1 801-902-3100) offers cashback bonuses on most purchases, but it may not be accepted in Turkey.

CASH CARDS (ATM CARDS)

Cash cards—popularly called ATM cards—are relatively widespread in most of Turkey. Depending on the system that your home bank uses, you can most likely access your personal bank account from abroad. ATMs get the same wholesale exchange rate as credit cards, but there is often a limit on the amount of money you can withdraw per day (around US$500). There is typically a surcharge of US$1-5 per withdrawal. Be sure to memorize your PIN code in numeric form in case machines elsewhere do not have letters on their keys. Also, if your PIN is longer than four digits, ask your bank whether you need a new number.

The two major international money networks are **Cirrus** (US ☎800-424-7787) and **PLUS** (US ☎800-843-7587). To locate ATMs around the world, call or consult www.visa.com/pd/atm or www.mastercard.com/atm. Banks in Turkey generally don't charge transaction fees, though your bank may charge for withdrawals.

Visa TravelMoney is a system allowing you to access money from any ATM that accepts Visa cards. (For local customer assistance in Turkey, call ☎00-1-800-847-2399.) If you deposit an amount before you travel (plus a small administration fee), then you can withdraw up to that sum. The cards, which give you the same favorable exchange rate for withdrawals as a regular Visa, are especially useful if you plan to travel through many countries. Obtain a card by visiting a nearby Thomas Cook or Citicorp office, calling toll-free in the US 877-394-2247, or checking with your local bank or to see if it issues TravelMoney cards. **Road Cash** issues cards in the US with a minimum US$300 deposit (US ☎877-762-3227; www.roadcash.com).

GETTING MONEY FROM HOME

Turkish law requires that cash advances, money wiring, and the replacement of lost cards or checks are done through a bank. If you need cash immediately, the following organizations may prove helpful.

AMERICAN EXPRESS. Cardholders can withdraw up to US$1000 every 21 days (no service charge, no interest) from their checking accounts at any of AmEx's major offices or representative offices. AmEx "Express Cash" withdrawals from any AmEx ATM in Turkey are automatically debited from the cardholder's checking account or line of credit. Green card holders may withdraw up to US$1000 in any seven-day period (2% transaction fee; minimum US$2.50, maximum US$20). To enroll in Express Cash, cardmembers may call ☎800-227-4669 in the US or ☎212 279 39 80 in Turkey. In Turkey, AmEx's agent is **Akbank.**

WESTERN UNION. Travelers from the US, Canada, and the UK can wire money abroad through Western Union's international money transfer services. In the US, call ☎(800) 325-6000; in Canada ☎(800) 235-0000; in the UK ☎(0800) 833 833. For a complete list of Western Union agents in Turkey visit www.westernunion.com. The rates for sending cash are generally US$10-11 cheaper than with a credit card, and the money is usually available within an hour.

FEDERAL EXPRESS. Some people choose to send cash abroad via FedEx to avoid transmission fees and taxes. While FedEx is reasonably reliable, this method is illegal. FedEx is represented in Turkey by Coneks A.S. and can be reached by calling ☎212 549 04 04. In the US and Canada, FedEx can be reached by calling ☎800-463-3339; in the UK ☎(0800) 12 38 00; in Ireland ☎(800) 535 800; in Australia ☎13 26 10; in New Zealand ☎(0800) 733 339; and in South Africa ☎(011) 923 8000.

STATE DEPARTMENT (US CITIZENS ONLY). In dire emergencies only, the US State Department will forward money within hours to the nearest consular office, which will then disburse it according to instructions for a US$15 fee. If you wish to use this service, you must contact the Overseas Citizens Service division of the US State Department (☎202-647-5225; nights, Sundays, and holidays ☎202-647-4000).

COSTS

The cost of your trip will vary considerably, depending on where you go, how you travel, and where you stay. The single biggest cost of your trip will probably be your round-trip (return) **airfare** to Turkey (see **Getting to Turkey: By Plane,** p. 64). A **railpass** (or **bus pass**) will be another major pre-departure expense Before you go, spend some time calculating a reasonable per-day **budget** that will meet your needs.

STAYING ON A BUDGET. To give you a general idea, a bare-bones day in Turkey (camping or sleeping in hostels/guesthouses, buying food at supermarkets) would cost about US$15; a slightly more comfortable day (sleeping in hostels/guesthouses and the occasional budget hotel, eating one meal a day at a restaurant, going out at night) would run US$25; and for a luxurious day, the sky's the limit. Also, don't forget to factor in emergency reserve funds (at least US$200) when planning how much money you'll need.

Considering that saving just a few dollars a day over the course of your trip might pay for days or weeks of additional travel, the art of penny-pinching is well worth learning. Learn to take advantage of freebies: for example, museums are often free for students with ID, and cities often host free open-air concerts and/or cultural events (especially in the summer). Do your **laundry** in the sink (unless you're explicitly prohibited from doing so). You can split **accommodations** costs (in hotels and some hostels) with trustworthy fellow travelers; multi-bed rooms almost always work out cheaper per person than singles. The same principle will also work for cutting down on the cost of restaurant meals. With that said, don't go overboard with your budget obsession. Though staying within your budget is important, do not do so at the expense of your sanity or health.

TIPPING AND BARGAINING

Even though Turkish salaries often do not take **tipping** into account as a form of income, it is widely expected and accepted. Leaving a bit of small change (around US$1 regardless of the total price) at your table after a meal or with a taxi driver or hotel porter is appreciated as a friendly gesture and a sign of gratitude. Fifteen to twenty-percent tips are only required in very deluxe restaurants. In these establishments, service may be included in the bill *(servis dahil)*, but an additional small tip is usually required.

Bargaining occurs in outdoor food markets, bazaars, some carpet and souvenir shops, and hotels. Walk-in stores that stock conventional goods such as groceries, pharmaceuticals, and clothes have fixed prices. When bargaining, do not be the first to name a price; wait until the salesperson does. Generally, start from a price that is lower than what you intend to pay, but don't offer to pay less than half of the seller's price. Proceed to haggle up from your initial price for something between the two prices. Do not bargain for items that depend upon a guarantee of authenticity or antiquity unless you are an expert in such matters.

TAXES

Not all shops participate, but Turkey does have a 10-20% value-added tax (VAT) known as the *katma değer vergisi* or KDV. It is included in the prices of most goods and services (including meals, lodging, and car rentals). Before you buy, check if the KDV is included in the price to avoid paying it twice. Theoretically, it can be reclaimed at most points of departure, but this requires much persistence. An airport tax of $15 is levied only on international travelers, but it is usually included in the cost of the ticket.

EMERGENCY NUMBERS IN TURKEY. These 24-hour phone numbers can be dialed from any phone in Turkey. At card-operated public phones, you can dial them without inserting a card. At coin-operated phones, you must insert a coin, but it will be returned to you after the call.

Police: ☎155
Ambulance: ☎112
Fire: ☎110
Jandarma (state police in rural areas): ☎156

ESSENTIALS

SAFETY AND SECURITY

Each year, thousands of visitors return home from Turkey with nothing but happy memories. Nonetheless, road safety is an oxymoron, and though tensions in the country have decreased over the past several years since the capture of PKK leader Abdullah Öcalan, they are still present (see **Recent Years,** p. 19). Stay informed of recent developments (see **Staying Informed,** p. 47).

PERSONAL SAFETY

Crime is mainly an issue in large cities in Turkey. Particularly if you are a woman, never admit that you are traveling alone. Extra vigilance is always wise, but there is no need for panic when exploring a new city or region.

EXPLORING. To help avoid unwanted attention, try to **blend in** as much as possible. Respecting local customs (usually, dressing more conservatively) may placate would-be hecklers. Low-profile, conservatively dressed foreigners are less obvious targets for petty theft than gawking camera-toters. Familiarize yourself with your surroundings before setting out, and carry yourself with confidence; if you must check a map on the street, duck into a shop. If you are traveling alone, be sure someone at home knows your itinerary, and never admit that you're traveling alone. You may want to carry a **whistle** to scare off attackers or attract attention if attacked; memorize the emergency numbers above. Whenever possible, *Let's Go* warns of unsafe neighborhoods and areas, but there are some good general tips to follow. When walking at night, stick to busy, well-lit streets and avoid dark alleyways. Buildings in disrepair, vacant lots, and unpopulated areas are all bad signs. The distribution of people can reveal a great deal about the relative safety of the area; look for children playing, women walking in the open, and other signs of an active community. If you feel uncomfortable, leave as quickly and directly as you can, but don't allow fear of the unknown to turn you into a hermit. Careful, persistent exploration will build confidence and make your stay even more rewarding.

SELF DEFENSE. There is no sure-fire way to avoid all the threatening situations you might encounter when you travel, but a good self-defense course will give you concrete ways to react to unwanted advances. **Impact, Prepare, and Model Mugging** can refer you to local self-defense courses in the US (☎800-345-5425). Visit the website at www.impactsafety.org/chapters for a list of nearby chapters. Workshops (2-3hr.) start at US$50; full courses run US$350-500.

TRANSPORTATION. If you are using a **car,** learn local driving signals and wear a seatbelt. Children under 40lbs. should ride only in a specially designed carseat, available for a small fee from most car rental agencies. Study route maps before you hit the road, and if you plan on spending a lot of time on the road, you may want to bring spare parts. If your car breaks down, wait for the police to assist you. For long drives in desolate areas, invest in a cellular phone and a roadside assistance program (see p. 70). Be sure to park your vehicle in a garage or well traveled area, and use a steering wheel locking device in larger cities. **Sleeping in your car** is one of the most dangerous (and often illegal) ways to get your rest. For info on the perils of **hitchhiking,** see p. 67.

TERRORISM

Until recently, the PKK (Kurdistan Workers' Party) and the DHKP/C (formerly Dev Sol) have been responsible for most of the terrorist acts in Turkey. Since the 1999 capture of PKK leader Abdullah Öcalan, however, the group's visibility has declined considerably.

Unfortunately, there was a resurgence of terrorism in Turkey in early 2001, this time at the hands of Chechen exiles and sympathizers. Unlike the PKK, this group has targeted tourists in an attempt to draw attention to their cause—the perceived violence perpetrated against Chechens by the Russian military. Rebels from Chechnya, part of the former Soviet Union, have sought independence from Russia since the mid-1990s. There is a large population of Chechen exiles in Turkey, particularly in İstanbul, which helps to explain Chechen support in Turkey.

After hijacking a Turkish passenger Ferry on the Black Sea in 1996, Muhammed Tokcan, the acknowledged leader of the Chechens in Turkey, spent time in jail, but was released on amnesty in 2000. In March 2001, Chechens hijacked a plane on its way from İstanbul to Moscow, and in April 2001, Chechens and sympathizers stormed the Swissotel in İstanbul, taking 120 hostages. Both acts were attempts to publicize the Chechen cause.

While there is no way to be completely safe, visitors should take certain precautions so as to avoid terrorism. It is wise to stay away from large crowds. Foreign visitors should absolutely steer clear of all political demonstrations. Travelers to Turkey should stay informed of recent political developments. In particular, keep abreast of warnings issued by the U.S. State Department (www.state.gov).

SOUTHEASTERN TURKEY

The dangers of traveling in southeastern Turkey have declined dramatically in the last few years. Once-dangerous cities like Van and Diyarbakır have become prime destinations for independent travelers, and a tourist infrastructure has begun to emerge in the larger cities. Incidents of terrorism, however, are much more frequent in southeastern Turkey than in other parts of the country. As of the summer of 2001, the provinces of Van, Hakkârı, şırnak, Tunceli, Dıyarbakır and Sıırt were still designated as "states of emergency," while the provinces of Muş, Mardin, Batman, Bingöl, and Bıtlış were considered "sensitive areas," one level below state of emergency. In parts of these regions, you can run the remote risk of being kidnapped or even caught in the cross-fire.

Although certain towns in these regions are included in this book (including Muradiye, Van, Diyabakır, Doğubeyazıt, and Mardin), travelers should exercise caution. Above all, be aware of recent developments both before you leave and while on the road (see **Staying Informed,** p. 47). Keep in mind that locals may be inclined to under-emphasize safety precautions and present a more rosy picture of a given town or area than that which actually exists. In most militarized cities, roads close in the afternoon; plan ahead before you travel by bus or car. Do not travel at night. Do not venture away from towns into the hills and mountains or into restricted areas. In order to travel within 5-10km of the borders of Iran, Armenia, and Georgia, you must have a special permit.

STAYING INFORMED. Before you go, read up on Turkey's most recent events and check some of the following websites for the latest travel advisories. Once you're in Turkey, continue to gather information by talking with fellow travelers and reading news stories online. Those considering travel to Eastern Turkey should be in touch with their embassies or consulates in Turkey.

Australian Department of Foreign Affairs and Trade: ☎(02) 6261 1111; www.dfat.gov.au.

Canadian Department of Foreign Affairs and International Trade (DFAIT): In Canada ☎800-267-8376; elsewhere ☎+1 613-944-4000; www.dfait-maeci.gc.ca.

New Zealand Ministry of Foreign Affairs: ☎(04) 494 8500; fax 494 8506; www.mfat.govt.nz/travel.html.

UK Foreign and Commonwealth Office: ☎(020) 7270 1500; www.fco.gov.uk.

US Department of State: ☎202-647-5225; http://travel.state.gov. For *A Safe Trip Abroad*, call ☎202-512-1800.

Expect to be questioned by authorities as to your traveling intentions, and always have your passport on you to present in such situations. Routine police checks become common around some cities: on buses, all men disembark from the bus and stand in a single-file line while officers ask questions and sometimes frisk. Women stay in the bus. Do not adopt a hostile attitude with the authorities—they will do everything in their power to protect you. Do not take photographs of military installations, bridges, power stations, or any other structure which might have military significance. While you should not engage locals in any political discussions, do not be afraid of speaking and interacting with Kurdish civilians.

Travel in eastern Turkey can pose risk, difficulty, and hassle for **women traveling alone.** *Let's Go* does not recommend that women travel alone in this region.

In **Northern Cyprus,** do not use blocked-off roads or cross the Green Line between North and South Cyprus unless you're looking to be deported or imprisoned.

ROAD SAFETY

> **!** Road travel in Turkey is dangerous by European and American standards. Whether taking a bus or driving, travelers in Turkey should educate themselves about road conditions. Only travel on reputable bus companies such as Ulusoy and Varan (see Getting Around: By Bus, p. 68). Avoid road travel at night and in inclement weather. For more information, consult:
>
> **US Embassy Driver Safety Briefing:** www.usis-ankara.org.tr/sec/secdsb.htm.
>
> **Association for Safe International Road Travel:** ☎301-983-5252; fax 983-3663; asirt@erols.com; www.asirt.org. Free information on road safety.

Road conditions in Turkey call for extreme concentration, caution, and defensive driving. About 15 people are killed in Turkey every day in traffic accidents, and Turkey has one of the world's worst traffic safety records. Almost half of all vehicular accidents occur in İstanbul and Ankara; of those, a large percentage happen during evening rush hour. Driving after dark is particularly hazardous, especially given that some drivers do not use their headlights. Drivers are also prone to making sudden traffic moves without warning, including cutting in front of other vehicles from the right and passing on blind curves. Always wear your **seatbelt.** Although many Turks consider it a sign of distrust if passengers fasten their seatbelts, travelers who value their lives will risk the *faux pas* and **buckle up** anyway. Turkish pedestrians often make dastardly attempts at crossing busy streets; be ready to stop suddenly at all times. Accident rates increase in bad weather: roads offer less traction than European roads, becoming oily when wet and icy in winter. Children under 18kg (40lb) should ride only in a specially designed car seat, available for a small fee from most rental agencies.

Sleeping in your car is one of the most dangerous ways to get your rest. If your car breaks down, wait for the police to assist you. Sleeping out in the open can be even more dangerous—camping is recommended only in official, supervised campsites or in wilderness backcountry.

FINANCIAL SECURITY

In large cities and touristed areas, especially İstanbul, pick-pocketing and purse-snatching are quite common. Follow the suggestions below to avoid street crime.

PROTECTING YOUR VALUABLES. There are a few steps you can take to minimize the financial risk associated with traveling. First, **bring as little with you as possible.** Leave expensive watches, jewelry, cameras, and electronic equipment (like your Discman) at home; chances are you'd break them, lose them, or get sick of lugging them around. Second, buy a few combination **padlocks** to secure your belongings either in your pack—which you should never leave unattended—or in a hostel or train station locker. Third, **carry as little cash as possible;** instead carry traveler's checks and ATM/credit cards, keeping them in a **money belt**—not a "fanny pack"—

along with your passport and ID cards. Fourth, **keep a small cash reserve separate from your primary stash.** This should entail about US$50 (US$ or German DM are best) sewn into or stored in the depths of your pack, along with your traveler's check numbers and important photocopies.

CON ARTISTS & PICKPOCKETS. Among the more colorful aspects of large cities are **con artists.** They often work in groups, and children are among the most effective. They possess an innumerable range of ruses. Beware of certain classics: sob stories that require money, rolls of bills "found" on the street, spilled mustard (or spit saliva) on your shoulder that distracts you as your bag disappears. Don't hand over your passport to someone whose authority is questionable (ask to accompany them to a police station if they insist), and **don't ever let your passport out of your sight.** Similarly, don't let your bag out of sight; never trust a "station-porter" who insists on carrying your bag or stowing it in the baggage compartment or a "new friend" who offers to guard your bag while you buy a train ticket or use the restroom. Beware of **pickpockets** in city crowds, especially on public transportation. Also, be alert in public telephone booths. If you must say your calling card number, do so very quietly; if you punch it in, make sure no one can look over your shoulder.

Be careful of in-your-face hustlers, *avcılar* ("hunters") in Turkish, who will try to sell you items, souvenirs, transportation, or lodging. They can make up to 50% commission for each deal. When arriving in a town, have a hotel or pension name in mind. Hawkers and taxi drivers, who will more than likely be working on the same system, will tell you that they know of a better place. They may even say the place you want is full, has burned down, or is experiencing a deadly disease outbreak. Stand firm, carry yourself with confidence, and keep walking. Contact the police if a hustler is particularly insistent.

In large cities such as İstanbul, **street children** may ask for money. Difficult as it is to walk away from a child who appears needy, most Turks believe that giving money will only encourage their parents to keep them in rags on the streets.

ACCOMMODATIONS & TRANSPORTATION. Never leave your belongings unattended; crime occurs in even the most demure-looking hostel or hotel. Bring your own **padlock** for hostel lockers, and don't ever store valuables in any locker.

Be particularly careful on **buses** and **trains;** horror stories abound about determined thieves who wait for travelers to fall asleep. Carry your backpack in front of you where you can see it. When traveling with others, sleep in alternate shifts. When alone, use good judgement in selecting a train compartment: never stay in an empty one, and use a lock to secure your pack to the luggage rack. Try to sleep on top bunks with your luggage stored above you (if not in bed with you), and keep important documents and other valuables on your person.

If traveling by **car,** do not leave valuables (such as radios or luggage) in it while away. If your tape deck or radio is removable, hide it in the trunk or take it with you. If it isn't, try to conceal it. Similarly, hide baggage in the trunk, though savvy thieves can tell if a car is heavily loaded by the way it sits on its tires.

DRUGS AND ALCOHOL

Turkey plays a key role in European drug trafficking, and 75% of drugs seized in Europe have passed through the country. The Turkish government has adopted a stringent policy (including fines and jail sentences) against those caught with drugs. If caught, a meek "I didn't know it was illegal" will not suffice. Remember that you are subject to the laws of the country in which you travel, not to those of your home country, and it is your responsibility to familiarize yourself with these laws before leaving. If you carry **prescription drugs** while you travel, it is vital to have a copy of the prescriptions themselves and a note from a doctor.

Avoid public drunkenness; it is culturally unacceptable in most parts of Turkey and can jeopardize your safety. Since Islam prohibits the consumption of alcohol, it is improper to drink in some of Turkey's more traditional towns and during the holy period of Ramazan (for dates of Ramazan, see **Festivals,** p. 36).

HEALTH

Common sense is the simplest prescription for good health while you travel. Drink lots of fluids to prevent dehydration and constipation, wear sturdy, broken-in shoes and clean socks, and use talcum powder to keep your feet dry.

BEFORE YOU GO

Preparation can help minimize the likelihood of contracting a disease and maximize the chances of receiving effective health care in the event of an emergency. For tips on packing a basic **first-aid kit** and other health essentials, see p. 56.

In your **passport**, write the names of people who may be reached in case of a medical emergency, and also list any allergies or medical conditions. Matching prescriptions to foreign equivalents is not always easy, safe, or possible. Carry up-to-date, legible prescriptions or a statement from your doctor with trade names, manufacturers, chemical names, and dosages. While traveling, be sure to keep all medication in your carry-on luggage.

IMMUNIZATIONS & PRECAUTIONS

Travelers over two years old should be sure that the following vaccines are up to date: MMR (for measles, mumps, and rubella); DTaP or Td (for diptheria, tetanus, and pertussis), OPV (for polio), HbCV (for haemophilus influenza B), and HBV (for hepatitus B). For recommendations on immunizations and prophylaxis, consult the CDC (see below) in the US or the equivalent in your home country, and check with a doctor for guidance. Below is a list of immunizations for travel to Turkey.

If you are concerned about being able to access medical support while traveling, then you may employ special support services. The *MedPass* from **GlobalCare, Inc.,** 2001 Westside Pkwy., #120, Alpharetta, GA 30004, USA (☎800-860-1111; fax 770-475-0058; www.globalems.com), provides 24hr. international medical assistance, support, and medical evacuation resources. The **International Association for Medical Assistance to Travelers (IAMAT;** US ☎716-754-4883, Canada ☎416-652-0137, New Zealand ☎(03) 352 20 53; www.sentex.net/iiamat) has free membership, lists English-speaking doctors worldwide, and offers detailed information on immunization requirements and sanitation. If your regular **insurance** policy does not cover travel abroad, you may wish to purchase additional coverage (see p. 56).

Those with medical conditions (diabetes, allergies to antibiotics, epilepsy, heart conditions) may want to obtain a stainless-steel **Medic Alert** ID tag (first year US$35, annually thereafter US$20), which identifies the condition and gives a 24hr. collect-call number. Contact the Medic Alert Foundation, 2323 Colorado Ave, Turlock, CA 95382, USA (☎888-633-4298; www.medicalert.org).

> **INOCULATION RECOMMENDATIONS.** While there are no required vaccinations for travel to Turkey, Hepatitis A vaccine and/or immune globulin (IG) is recommended. Typhoid is suggested for travelers to less-developed areas away from the Aegean and Mediterranean coasts. Adults traveling to Turkey should consider an additional dose of the Polio vaccine if they have not had one during their adult years. Those traveling for longer periods (more than 6 months) should be inoculated for Hepatitis B, and those intending to hike and camp in Turkey should also be immunized for rabies.

USEFUL ORGANIZATIONS & PUBLICATIONS

The US **Centers for Disease Control and Prevention (CDC;** ☎877-FYI-TRIP; www.cdc.gov/travel), maintains an international fax information service and an international travelers hotline (☎404-332-4559). The CDC's comprehensive booklet *Health Information for International Travel*, an annual rundown of disease, immunization, and general health advice, is free online or US$25 via the Public Health Foundation (☎877-252-1200). Consult the appropriate government agency of your home country for consular information sheets on health and entry requirements (see **Staying Informed,** p. 47). For quick information on health and other travel warnings, call the **Overseas Citizens Services** (☎202-647-5225; after-hours 202-647-4000), or contact a passport agency, embassy or consulate abroad. US citizens can send a self-addressed, stamped envelope to the Overseas Citizens Services, Bureau of Consular Affairs, #4811, US Department of State, Washington, D.C. 20520. For information on medical evacuation services and travel insurance firms, see the US government's website at http://travel.state.gov/medical.html or the **British Foreign and Commonwealth Office** website at www.fco.gov.uk.

For detailed information on travel health, including a country-by-country overview of diseases, try the International Travel Health Guide, Stuart Rose, MD (Travel Medicine, US$24.95; www.travmed.com). For general health information, contact the American Red Cross (☎800-564-1234).

ONCE IN TURKEY

MEDICAL ASSISTANCE ON THE ROAD

If you are in need of medical care in Turkey, an embassy or consulate can provide you with a list of English-speaking doctors. Payment with cash or a credit card is expected at the time of treatment. Serious medical problems should be taken to the *klinik* or hospital *(hastane)*. Private hospitals, located in the more urban areas, tend to provide better care than state-run hospitals *(devlet hastanesi)*, though they are comparably-priced for foreigners, cash payments are expected. For minor troubles, Turkish **pharmacies** *(eczane)* will have remedies. Pharmacies stay open all night on a rotating basis; signs in their windows and in newspapers note which pharmacy is on duty *(nöbetçi)* on a particular night. *Eczane* also sell *esem mat*, small rectangles of mosquito repellent that burn slowly on heat pads that plug into the wall.

ENVIRONMENTAL HAZARDS

Heat exhaustion and dehydration: Heat exhaustion, characterized by dehydration and salt deficiency, can lead to fatigue, headaches, and wooziness. Avoid it by drinking plenty of fluids, eating salty foods (e.g. crackers), and avoiding dehydrating beverages (e.g. alcohol, coffee, tea, and caffeinated soda). Continuous heat stress can eventually lead to heatstroke, characterized by a rising temperature, severe headache, and cessation of sweating. Victims should be cooled off with wet towels and taken to a doctor.

Sunburn: If you're prone to sunburn, bring sunscreen with you (especially in Eastern Turkey, where it's nearly impossible to find) and apply it liberally and often to avoid burns and risk of skin cancer. If you are planning on spending time near water, in the desert, or in the snow, you are at risk of getting burned, even through clouds. If you get sunburned, drink more fluids than usual and apply Calamine or an aloe-based lotion.

Hypothermia and frostbite: A rapid drop in body temperature is the clearest sign of overexposure to cold. Victims may also shiver, feel exhausted, have poor coordination or slurred speech, hallucinate, or suffer amnesia. *Do not let hypothermia victims fall asleep,* or their body temperature will continue to drop and they may die. Keep dry, wear layers, and stay out of the wind to avoid hypothermia. When the temperature is below freezing, watch out for frostbite. If skin turns white, waxy, and cold, do not rub the area. Drink warm beverages, get dry, and slowly warm the area with dry fabric or steady body contact until a doctor can be found.

High altitude: Allow your body a couple of days to adjust to less oxygen before exerting yourself. Alcohol is more potent and UV rays are stronger at high elevations.

INSECT-BORNE DISEASES

Many diseases are transmitted by insects—mainly mosquitoes, fleas, ticks, and lice. Beware of insects in wet or forested areas, especially while hiking and camping. **Mosquitoes** are most active from dusk to dawn. Wear long pants and long sleeves, tuck your pants into your socks, and buy a mosquito net. **Ticks**—responsible for Lyme disease—can be particularly dangerous in rural and forested regions. Pause periodically while walking to brush off ticks using a fine-toothed comb on your neck and scalp. Do not try to remove ticks by burning them or coating them with nail polish remover or petroleum jelly.

Malaria: Malaria is a risk in Southeastern Anatolia, transmitted by *Anopheles* mosquitoes that bite at night. Early symptoms include fever, chills, aches, and fatigue, followed by high fever and sweating, sometimes with vomiting and diarrhea. See a doctor for any flu-like sickness that occurs after travel in a risk area. Left untreated, malaria can cause anemia, kidney failure, coma, and death. It is an especially serious threat to pregnant women. To reduce the risk of contracting malaria, use mosquito repellent, particularly in the evenings and when visiting forested areas, and take prescription oral prophylactics, like **chroloquine** (sold under the name Aralen) or **doxycycline.** Be aware that these drugs can have very serious side effects, including slowed heart rate and nightmares.

Tick-borne encephalitis: A viral infection of the central nervous system transmitted during the summer by tick bites (primarily in wooded areas) or by consumption of unpasteurized dairy products. Symptoms range from nothing to headaches and flu-like symptoms to swelling of the brain (encephalitis). While a vaccine is available in Europe, the immunization schedule is impractical, and the risk of contracting the disease is relatively low, especially if precautions are taken against tick bites.

Lyme disease: A bacterial infection carried by ticks and marked by a circular bull's-eye rash of 2in. or more. Later symptoms include fever, headache, fatigue, and aches and pains. Antibiotics are effective if administered early. Left untreated, Lyme disease can cause problems in joints, the heart, and the nervous system. If you find a tick attached to your skin, grasp the head with tweezers as close to your skin as possible and apply slow, steady traction. Removing a tick within 24hr. greatly reduces the risk of infection.

Leishmaniasis: A parasite transmitted by sand flies. Cutaneous leishmaniasis, characterized by skin lesions including sores, ulcers, and wart-like bumps, occurs in southeastern Turkey and in the Tigris-Euphrates basin. Visceral leishmaniasis *(kala azar),* found along the Aegean, Mediterranean, Sea of Marmara, and Black Sea coasts, affects the internal organs and bone marrow, and common symptoms are fever, weakness, and swelling of the spleen. There are treatments, but no vaccines, for both forms of the disease.

Filariasis: A roundworm infestation transmitted by mosquitoes. Infection causes enlargement of extremities. No vaccine.

FOOD- & WATER-BORNE DISEASES

Prevention is the best cure: be sure that food is properly cooked and the drinking water is clean. In Turkey, where the risk of contracting traveler's diarrhea or other diseases is high, you should never drink unbottled water unless you have treated it. To do so, bring the water to a rolling boil or treat it with **iodine tablets.** Note however, that some parasites such as *giardia* have exteriors that resist iodine treatment, making boiling water more reliable. Bottled water, widely available, is very cheap, and a large bottle typically sells for less than US$.50. In risk areas, don't brush your teeth with tap water or rinse your toothbrush under the faucet, and keep your mouth closed in the shower. Peel fruits and vegetables and avoid ice cubes as well as anything washed in tap water, like salad. Watch out for food from markets or street vendors. Other culprits are raw shellfish, unpasteurized milk, and sauces containing raw eggs. Always wash your hands before eating or bring a quick-drying purifying liquid hand cleaner. Your bowels will thank you.

Traveler's diarrhea: Results from drinking untreated water or eating uncooked foods; a temporary (and fairly common) reaction to bacteria in food. Symptoms include nausea, bloating, urgency, and malaise. Eat quick-energy, non-sugary foods with protein and carbohydrates. Over-the-counter anti-diarrheals (e.g. Immodium) may counteract the problems, but can complicate serious infections. The most dangerous side effect is dehydration; drink 8oz. of water with ½tsp. of sugar or honey and a pinch of salt, try uncaffeinated soft drinks, or munch on salted crackers. If you develop a fever or if symptoms persist for more than 4-5 days, consult a doctor. Also consult a doctor for treatment of diarrhea in children.

Dysentery: Results from a serious intestinal infection caused by certain bacteria. The most common type is bacillary dysentery, also called shigellosis. Symptoms include bloody diarrhea (sometimes mixed with mucus), fever, and abdominal pain and tenderness. Bacillary dysentery generally only lasts one week, but it is highly contagious. Amoebic dysentery, which develops more slowly, is a more serious disease and may cause long-term damage if left untreated. A stool test can determine which kind you have; seek medical help immediately. Dysentery can be treated with the drugs norfloxacin or ciprofloxacin (commonly known as Cipro). If you are traveling in high-risk (especially rural) regions, consider obtaining a prescription before you leave home.

Cholera: An intestinal disease caused by bacteria found in contaminated food. Symptoms include diarrhea, dehydration, vomiting, and muscle cramps. See a doctor immediately; if left untreated, it may be fatal. Antibiotics are available, but the most important treatment is rehydration. Consider getting a vaccine (50% effective) if you have stomach problems (e.g. ulcers) or will be living where the water is not safe.

Hepatitis A: A viral infection of the liver acquired primarily through contaminated water. Symptoms include fatigue, fever, loss of appetite, nausea, dark urine, jaundice, vomiting, aches, and light stools. The risk is highest in rural areas, but is also present in urban districts. Ask your doctor about the vaccine or an injection of immune globulin.

Parasites: Microbes or tapeworms that hide in unsafe water and food. Giardiasis, is acquired by drinking untreated water from streams or lakes. Symptoms include swollen glands or lymph nodes, fever, rashes or itchiness, digestive problems, eye problems, and anemia. Boil water, wear shoes, avoid bugs, and eat only cooked food.

Schistosomiasis: Also known as bilharzia; a parasitic disease caused when larvae of flatworms found in freshwater penetrate unbroken skin. Symptoms include an itchy, localized rash, followed in 4-6 weeks by fever, fatigue, painful urination, diarrhea, loss of appetite, night sweats, and a hive-like rash on the body. If exposed to untreated water, rub the area vigorously with a towel and apply rubbing alcohol. Schistosomiasis can be treated with prescription drugs. In general, avoid swimming in fresh water.

Typhoid fever: Caused by salmonella bacteria; common in villages and rural areas in Turkey. While mostly transmitted through contaminated food and water, Typhoid may also be acquired by direct contact with another person. Early symptoms include fever, headaches, fatigue, loss of appetite, constipation, and a rash on the abdomen or chest. Antibiotics can treat typhoid, but a vaccination (70-90% effective) is recommended.

OTHER INFECTIOUS DISEASES

Rabies: Transmitted through the saliva of infected animals; fatal if untreated. By the time symptoms appear (thirst and muscle spasms), the disease is in its terminal stage. If you are bitten, wash the wound thoroughly, seek immediate medical care, and try to locate the animal. A rabies vaccine, which consists of 3 shots given over a 21-day period, is available but only semi-effective.

Hepatitis B: A viral infection of the liver transmitted via bodily fluids or needle-sharing. Symptoms may not surface until years after infection. Vaccinations are recommended for health-care workers, sexually active travelers, and anyone planning to seek medical treatment abroad. The 3-shot vaccination series must begin 6mos. before traveling.

Hepatitis C: Like Hep B, but the mode of transmission differs. IV drug users, those with occupational exposure to blood, hemodialysis patients, and recipients of blood transfusions are at highest risk, but the disease also be spreads through sexual contact or the sharing of items like razors and toothbrushes that may have traces of blood on them.

AIDS, HIV, & STDS

Though **Acquired Immune Deficiency Syndrome (AIDS)** is a growing problem around the world, it remains relatively uncommon in Turkey. Only about 1000 adults (ages 15-49) in Turkey, 0.01% of the population, were infected with the virus in 2000. HIV is most prevalent in Turkey's large cities—İstanbul, Ankara and İzmir—and along the Black Sea coast, where prostitution is more widespread (see **Nataşas**, p. 409). For detailed information on **AIDS** in Turkey, call the 24hr. hotline of the **US Centers for Disease Control** at ☎800-342-2437, or contact the **Joint United Nations Programme on HIV/AIDS (UNAIDS),** 20, av. Appia, CH-1211 Geneva 27, Switzerland (☎+41 22 791 36 66; fax 22 791 41 87). The Council on International Educational Exchange's pamphlet, *Travel Safe: AIDS and International Travel*, is posted on their website (www.ciee.org/Isp/safety/travelsafe.htm), along with links to other resources.

Sexually transmitted diseases (STDs) such as gonorrhea, chlamydia, genital warts, syphilis, and herpes are easier to catch than HIV and can be equally deadly. Hepatitis B and C are also serious STDs (see above). Though condoms may protect you from some STDs, oral or even tactile contact can lead to transmission. Warning signs include swelling, sores, bumps, or blisters on sex organs, the rectum, or the mouth; burning and pain during urination and bowel movements; itching around sex organs; swelling or redness of the throat; and flu-like symptoms. If these symptoms develop, see a doctor immediately.

WOMEN'S HEALTH

Women traveling in unsanitary conditions are vulnerable to **urinary tract** and **bladder infections,** common and very uncomfortable bacterial conditions that cause a burning sensation and painful (sometimes frequent) urination. To try to avoid these infections, drink plenty of juice rich in vitamin C and clean water, and urinate frequently, especially right after intercourse. Untreated, these infections lead to kidney infections, sterility, and even death. If symptoms persist, see a doctor.

Vaginal yeast infections may flare up in hot and humid climates. Wearing loosely fitting trousers or a skirt and cotton underwear helps, as do over-the-counter remedies like Monistat or Gynelotrimin. Bring supplies from home if you are prone to infection, as they may be difficult to find on the road. In a pinch, some travelers use the natural douche alternative of plain yogurt and lemon juice.

Tampons and **pads** are easy to find in any pharmacy (see **Medical Assistance on the Road,** p. 51). Since your preferred brands might not be available, however, you may want to take supplies along. **Reliable contraceptive devices** will be difficult to find. Women on the pill should bring enough to allow for possible loss or extended stays. Bring a prescription, since forms of the pill vary. Women who use a diaphragm should bring enough contraceptive jelly. Condoms are also hard to come by and are only available in bigger cities.

INSURANCE

Travel insurance generally covers four basic areas: medical/health problems, property loss, trip cancellation/interruption, and emergency evacuation. Although regular insurance policies may well extend to travel-related accidents, it is wise to consider purchasing travel insurance if the cost of potential trip cancellation/interruption or emergency medical evacuation is greater than you can absorb. Prices for separately-purchased travel insurance are about US$50 per week for full coverage, while trip cancellation/interruption separately costs about US$5.50 per US$100 of coverage.

Medical insurance (especially university policies) often covers costs incurred abroad; check with your provider. **US Medicare** does not cover foreign travel. **Canadians** are protected by their home province's health insurance plan for up to 90 days after leaving the country; check with the provincial Ministry of Health or Health Plan Headquarters for details. **Homeowners' insurance** (or your family's coverage) often covers theft during travel and loss of travel documents (like passport, plane ticket or railpass) up to US$500.

ISIC and **ITIC** (see p. 41) provide basic insurance benefits, including US$100 per day of in-hospital sickness for up to 60 days, US$3000 of accident-related medical reimbursement, and US$25,000 for emergency medical transport. Cardholders have access to a toll-free, 24hr. helpline for medical, legal, and financial emergencies overseas (US and Canada ☎877-370-4742, elsewhere call US collect ☎+1 715-345-0505). **American Express** (US ☎800-528-4800) grants most cardholders automatic car rental insurance (collision and theft, but not liability) and ground travel accident coverage of US$100,000 on flight purchases made with the card.

INSURANCE PROVIDERS. Council and **STA** (see p. 64) offer a range of plans that can supplement your basic coverage. Other private insurance providers in the US and Canada include: **Access America** (☎800-284-8300); **Berkely Group/Carefree Travel Insurance** (☎800-323-3149; www.berkely.com); **Globalcare Travel Insurance** (☎800-

821-2488; www.globalcare-cocco.com); and **Travel Assistance International** (☎800-821-2828; www.worldwide-assistance.com). Providers in the **UK** include **Campus Travel** (☎01865 25 80 00) and **Columbus Travel Insurance** (☎020 7375 0011). In **Australia,** try **CIC Insurance** (☎9202 8000).

PACKING

PACK LIGHTLY. lay out only what you absolutely need, then take half the clothes and twice the money. The less you have, the less you have to lose (or store, or carry on your back). Any extra space left will be useful for any souvenirs or items you might pick up along the way. If you plan to hike, see **Wilderness Safety,** p. 57.

LUGGAGE. If you plan to cover most of your itinerary by foot, a sturdy **frame backpack** is unbeatable. (For the basics on buying a pack, see p. 58.) Toting a **suitcase** or **trunk** is fine if you plan to live in one or two cities and explore from there, but inefficient you'll be moving around. In addition to your main piece of luggage, a **daypack** (a small backpack or courier bag) is a must.

CLOTHING. No matter when you're traveling, it's always a good idea to bring a **warm jacket** or wool sweater, a **rain jacket** (Gore-Tex@ is both waterproof and breathable), sturdy shoes or **hiking boots,** and **thick socks. Flip-flops** or waterproof sandals are must-haves for grubby hostel showers. Shorts are acceptable in the more touristed regions along the Aegean and Mediterranean coasts, but completely inappropriate in more conservative parts Turkey. Men should bring light slacks, and women should bring loose-fitting pants or long skirts. For both sexes, short sleeves and baggy T-shirts are fine, but tank tops stand out. Also keep in mind that when visiting religious sites, appropriate attire is required. For more information on women's dress, see **Women Travelers,** p. 71. For advice on hiking attire, see **Camping and the Outdoors,** p. 57.

CONVERTERS & ADAPTERS. In Turkey, electricity is 220 volts AC, enough to fry any 110V North American appliance. 220V electrical appliances don't like 110V current either. Visit a hardware store for an adapter (which changes the shape of the plug) and a converter (which changes the voltage; US$20). Don't make the mistake of using only an adapter (unless appliance instructions explicitly state otherwise). **New Zealanders** and **South Africans** (who both use 220V at home) as well as **Australians** (who use 240/250V) won't need a converter, but will need a set of adapters to use anything electrical.

TOILETRIES. Toothbrushes, towels, cold-water soap, talcum powder (to keep feet dry), deodorant, razors, tampons, and condoms are often available, but may be difficult to find, so bring extras. **Contact lenses,** on the other hand, may be expensive and difficult to find, so bring extra pairs and solution for your trip. Also bring your glasses and a copy of your prescription in case you need an emergency replacement. If you use heat-disinfection, either switch temporarily to a chemical disinfection system (check first to make sure it's safe with your brand of lenses), or buy a 220/240V converter.

FIRST-AID KIT. For a basic first-aid kit, pack: bandages, pain reliever, antibiotic cream, a thermometer, a Swiss Army knife, tweezers, moleskin, decongestant, motion-sickness remedy, diarrhea or upset-stomach medication (Pepto Bismol or Imodium), an antihistamine, sunscreen, insect repellent, burn ointment, and a syringe for emergencies (get an explanatory letter from your doctor).

FILM. Film in Turkey costs about $3-4 for a roll of 36 exposures. It may be more convenient to bring film from home and develop it at home. Also, APS (Advantix) film is expensive and difficult to find. Less serious photographers may want to use a **disposable camera** rather than an expensive, permanent one. Despite disclaimers, airport security X-rays *can* fog film, so buy a lead-lined pouch at a camera store or ask security to hand-inspect it. Always pack film in your carry-on luggage, since higher-intensity X-rays are used on checked luggage.

OTHER USEFUL ITEMS. For safety purposes, you should bring a **money belt** and small **padlock.** Basic **outdoors equipment** (plastic water bottle, compass, waterproof matches, pocketknife, sunglasses, sunscreen, hat) may also prove useful. **Quick repairs** of torn garments can be done on the road with a needle and thread; also consider bringing electrical tape for patching tears. Doing your **laundry** by hand (where allowed) is both cheaper and more convenient than doing it at a laundromat—bring detergent, a small rubber ball to stop up the sink, and string for a makeshift clothes line. Other things you're liable to forget: an umbrella; sealable plastic bags (for damp clothes, soap, food, shampoo, and other spillables); an alarm clock; safety pins; rubber bands; a flashlight; earplugs; garbage bags; and a small calculator.

IMPORTANT DOCUMENTS. Don't forget your passport, traveler's checks, ATM and/or credit cards, and adequate ID (see p. 41).

ACCOMMODATIONS

HOSTELS

Hostels are generally dorm-style accommodations, often in large single-sex rooms with bunk beds. Most in Turkey, however, are known for their welcoming atmosphere and offer private rooms for families and couples. They sometimes have kitchens and utensils, bike or moped rentals, storage areas, and laundry facilities. Hostels in Turkey generally do not have daytime "lock-out" hours or curfew. A bed in a hostel averages around $5-8.

There are very few accredited International Youth Hostels in Turkey, and if you ask for a hostel *(yurt)*, you will most likely be directed to university dormitories. The web page for the umbrella organization **Hostelling International** (www.iyhf.org) may be of some use while researching hosteling in Turkey. Also visit www.hostels.com and www.eurotrip.com/accommodation.

HOTELS AND PENSIONS

Clean, cheap hotels *(otel)* and pensions *(pansiyon)* are available nearly everywhere in Turkey. Basic rooms generally cost $6-8 for singles and $12-16 for doubles. Some establishments may have dorm-style rooms; some may even allow frugal travelers to sleep on their roofs for reduced rates. In most situations, you should have little trouble finding a room; it is still wise, however, to make reservations along the Aegean and Mediterranean coasts during the peak season.

Pensions, the most common form of accommodation, provide a cozy alternative to impersonal hotel rooms. Often they are private homes with rooms available to travelers. Hosts will sometimes go out of their way to be accommodating by giving personalized tours or offering home-cooked meals. On the other hand, many pensions do not provide phones, TVs, or private bathrooms. Pensions that call themselves **aile** (family-style) try to maintain a wholesome atmosphere, and may be the preferred choice for women traveling alone in remote parts of Turkey, particularly the East and the Black Sea coast. In the more touristed areas along the Aegean and Mediterranean coasts, Turks are accustomed to **unmarried male-female couples** staying together. Such relations, however, are often culturally unacceptable in rural and conservative regions, including the Black Sea coast and southeastern Turkey. In these parts of Turkey, unmarried couples may have trouble finding a room together without proof of their marital status, such as wedding rings, a certificate, or the same last name on passports. It is generally a good idea to wear rings to help gain admittance. Men may be turned away from pensions if there are no other men staying in the house.

UNIVERSITY DORMS

Many **colleges and universities** open their residence halls to travelers when school is not in session; some also do so during term-time. These dorms are often close to student areas in large cities such as Ankara and İstanbul. Getting a room usually takes advanced planning, but rates tend to be low. *Let's Go* lists colleges which rent dorms in the **Accommodations** sections of cities and towns where applicable.

CAMPING AND THE OUTDOORS

Camping is more than just a viable means of travel in Turkey, particularly along the Black Sea and Mediterranean coasts and in the East. Most campers consist of Turkish families on vacation, so it is often safe for travelers to camp in designated campgrounds. If you have your own tent, the cost per night per tent is $2.50-$4. Tents can usually be rented for an additional charge. In some places, usually the *yayla* (highland plateaus), camping is free. Generally, camping is not permitted on beaches or in non-designated areas, but you can sometimes secure permission from a member of the *jandarma*. Camping is allowed in all 23 of Turkey's **national parks** and the dozens of nature preserves that dot the countryside. An excellent general resource for travelers planning on camping or spending time in the outdoors is the **Great Outdoor Recreation Pages** (www.gorp.com). **NatureKey** (www.naturekey.com), an online travel resource for Turkey, gives camping tips and features an extensive list of campsites.

For eco-friendly camping, make sure your campsite is at least 150ft. (50m) from water supplies or bodies of water. Similarly, if there are no toilet facilities, do as nature intended far from any water supply or campsite. Always pack your trash in a plastic bag and carry it with you until you reach the next trash can.

WILDERNESS SAFETY

THE GREAT OUTDOORS. Stay warm, stay dry, and stay hydrated. The vast majority of life-threatening wilderness situations can be avoided by following this simple advice. Prepare yourself for an emergency, however, by always packing rain gear, a hat and mittens, a first-aid kit, a reflector, a whistle, high energy food, and extra water for any hike. For what should be included in a first aid kit, see p. 55. Dress in wool or warm layers of synthetic materials designed for the outdoors; never rely on cotton for warmth, as it is useless when wet.

Check **weather forecasts** and pay attention to the skies when hiking, since weather patterns can change suddenly. Whenever possible, let a friend, your hostel, a park ranger, or a local hiking organization know when and where you are hiking. See **Health,** p. 50, for information about outdoor ailments. *Let's Go* does not recommend risking your life by hiking trails beyond your level of skill.

CAMPING AND HIKING EQUIPMENT

WHAT TO BUY...

Good camping equipment is both sturdy and light. Camping equipment is generally more expensive in Australia, New Zealand, and the UK than in North America.

Sleeping Bag: Most sleeping bags are rated by season ("summer" means 30-40°F at night; "four-season" or "winter" often means below 0°F). They are made either of **down** (warmer and lighter, but more expensive, and miserable when wet) or of **synthetic** material (heavier, more durable, and warmer when wet). Prices range US$80-210 for a summer synthetic to US$250-300 for a good down winter bag. **Sleeping bag pads** include foam pads (US$10-20), air mattresses (US$15-50), and Therm-A-Rest self-inflating pads (US$45-80). Bring a **stuff sack** to store your bag and keep it dry.

Tent: The best tents are free-standing (with their own frames and suspension systems), set up quickly, and only require staking in high winds. Low-profile dome tents are the best all-around. Good 2-person tents start at US$90, 4-person at US$300. Seal the seams of your tent with waterproofer, and make sure it has a rain fly. Other tent accessories include a **battery-operated lantern,** a **plastic groundcloth,** and a **nylon tarp.**

Backpack: Internal-frame packs mold better to your back, keep a lower center of gravity, and flex adequately to allow you to hike difficult trails. **External-frame packs** are more comfortable for long hikes over even terrain, as they keep weight higher and distribute it more evenly. Make sure your pack has a strong, padded hip-belt to transfer weight to your legs. Any serious backpacking requires a pack of at least 4000 scubic inches (16,000cc), plus 500 cubic inches for sleeping bags in internal-frame packs. Sturdy backpacks cost anywhere from US$125-420—this is one area in which it doesn't pay to economize. Fill up any pack with something heavy and walk around the store with it to get a sense of how it distributes weight before buying it. Either buy a **waterproof backpack cover,** or store all of your belongings in plastic bags inside your pack.

Boots: Be sure to wear hiking boots with good **ankle support.** They should fit snugly and comfortably over 1-2 pairs of wool socks and thin liner socks. Break in boots over several weeks first in order to spare yourself painful and debilitating blisters.

Other Necessities: Synthetic layers, like those made of polypropylene, and a **pile jacket** will keep you warm even when wet. A **"space blanket"** will help you to retain your body heat and doubles as a groundcloth (US$5-15). Plastic **water bottles** are virtually shatter- and leak-proof. Bring **water-purification tablets** for when you can't boil water. Although most campgrounds provide campfire sites, you may want to bring a small **metal grate** or **grill** of your own. For those places that forbid fires or the gathering of firewood, you'll need a **camp stove** (the classic Coleman starts at US$40) and a propane-filled **fuel bottle** to operate it. Also don't forget a **first-aid kit, pocketknife, insect repellent, calamine lotion,** and **waterproof matches** or a **lighter.**

...AND WHERE TO BUY IT

The mail-order/online companies listed below offer lower prices than many retail stores, but a visit to a local camping or outdoors store will give you a good sense of the look and weight of certain items.

Campmor, 28 Parkway, P.O. Box 700, Upper Saddle River, NJ 07458 (US ☎888-226-7667; elsewhere US ☎+1 201-825-8300; www.campmor.com).

Discount Camping, 880 Main North Rd., Pooraka, South Australia 5095, Australia (☎(08) 8262 3399; www.discountcamping.com.au).

Eastern Mountain Sports (EMS), 327 Jaffrey Rd., Peterborough, NH 03458, USA (☎888-463-6367 or 603-924-7231; www.shopems.com).

L.L. Bean, Freeport, ME 04033 (US and Canada ☎800-441-5713; UK ☎0800 891 297; elsewhere, US ☎+1 207-552-3028; www.llbean.com).

Mountain Designs, P.O. Box 1472, Fortitude Valley, Queensland 4006, Australia (☎(07) 3252 8894; www.mountaindesign.com.au).

Recreational Equipment, Inc. (REI), Sumner, WA 98352, USA (☎800 426-4840 or 253-891-2500; www.rei.com).

YHA Adventure Shop, 14 Southampton St., London, WC2E 7HA, UK (☎020 7836 8541). The main branch of one of Britain's largest outdoor equipment suppliers.

ADVENTURE TRIPS

Organized adventure tours offer another way of exploring the wild. In Turkey, activities include hiking, biking, skiing, kayaking, rafting, climbing, and archaeological digs. Begin by consulting tourism bureaus, which can suggest parks, trails, and outfitters. *Let's Go* lists agencies in Cappadocia, Eastern Anatolia, and the Eastern Black Sea region (see **Cappadocia,** p. 315; **Trekking in the Kaçkars,** p. 434, and **The Çoruh Valley,** p. 429).

KEEPING IN TOUCH

MAIL

SENDING MAIL TO TURKEY. Airmail letters under 1 oz. between North America and Turkey take 4-7 days and cost US$1 or CDN$1.45 (sending a postcard costs about $.50). Allow 6-7 days from Australia (postage AUS$1 for up to 20 grams), 4-8 from Britain (postage £0.36 for up to 20 grams), 6-8 days from Ireland (postage IR£0.32 for 25g), and 6-8 from New Zealand (postage NZ$1.80 for 20g). Mark envelopes "air mail" or "par avion" to avoid having letters sent by sea.

There are several ways to arrange pick-up of letters sent to you by friends and relatives while you are abroad, and most involve the **PTT** (post, telegraph, and telephone office), which are well-marked by their yellow signs. Large PTTs in major urban areas are open M-Sa 8am-midnight, Su 9am-7pm. Major PTTs in İstanbul are open 24 hours. Smaller post offices share the same hours as government offices (M-F 8:30am-12:30pm and 1:30-5:30pm). *Let's Go* lists post offices in the **Practical Information** section for each city and most towns.

General Delivery: Mail can be sent to Turkey through *poste restante* (the International phrase for General Delivery) to almost any city or town with a **PTT** (post, telegraph, and telephone office). To send a letter to someone in Bodrum, address it *poste restante* to: Ryan HARVEY, Poste Restante, Merkez Postanesi, Bodrum 48400, Türkiye. The last name should be capitalized and underlined. The mail will go to a special desk in the central post office *(merkez postanesi)*, unless you specify a post office by street address or postal code. As a rule, it is best to use the largest post office in the area, and mail may be sent there regardless of what is written on the envelope. When possible, it is usually safer and quicker to send mail express or registered. When picking up your mail, bring a form of photo ID, preferably a passport. Some PTTs may charge a small sum for *poste restante,* but it generally does not exceed the cost of domestic postage. If the clerks insist that there is nothing for you, have them check under your first name as well. Some of the smaller PTTs may send you with a slip to a larger PTT in the same city.

American Express: AmEx travel offices throughout the world offer a free **Client Letter Service** (mail held up to 30 days and forwarded upon request) for cardholders who contact them in advance. Address the letter in the same way shown above. Some offices will offer these services to non-cardholders (especially AmEx Travelers Cheque holders), but call ahead to confirm. *Let's Go* lists AmEx office locations for most large cities in **Practical Information** sections; for a complete, free list, call ☎800-528-4800.

SENDING MAIL FROM TURKEY. **Aerogrammes,** printed sheets that fold into envelopes and travel via airmail, are available at post offices. It helps to mark *"uçak ile"* if possible, though "par avion" and "air mail" are universally understood. Tell the vendor the destination: *Avustralya, Kanada, Büyük Bretanya* (Great Britain), *İrlanda, Yeni Zelanda* (New Zealand), *Güney Afrika* (South Africa), or *Amerika.* Most post offices will charge exorbitant fees or simply refuse to send aerogrammes with enclosures. Airmail from Turkey takes about one to two weeks, but longer when sent from smaller towns.

If regular airmail is too slow, there are faster, more expensive, options. The fastest option is *Acele Posta Servisi* (APS), though this may not be available in every PTT. Companies including DHL and Federal Express can also send packages from their offices in larger Turkish cities.

COMPANY	TO OBTAIN A CARD, DIAL:	TO CALL FROM TURKEY, DIAL:
AT&T (US)	888-288-4685	00 (800) 122 77
British Telecom Direct	800 34 51 44	00 (800) 89 0900
Canada Direct	800-668-6878	00 (800) 166 77
Ireland Direct	800 40 00 00	00 (800) 353 1177
MCI (US)	800 444-3333	00 (800) 111 77
Sprint (US)	800 877-4646	00 (800) 144 77
Telkom South Africa	10 219	00 (800) 2711 77
Telestra Australia	13 22 00	00 (800) 6111 77

TELEPHONES

CALLING TURKEY. To call Turkey direct from home, dial:

1. The international access code of your home country. International access codes include: Australia 0011; Ireland 00; New Zealand 00; South Africa 09; UK 00; US and Canada 011. Country codes and city codes are sometimes listed with a zero in front (e.g., 033), but after dialing the international access code, drop successive zeros (with an access code of 011 and a country code of 033, dial 011 33).
2. 90 (Turkey's country code).
3. The city code (found across the header for most cities and towns) and local number.

CALLING FROM TURKEY. A **calling card** is probably the best and cheapest option. Calls are billed either collect or to your account. Many phone companies provide travelers with additional services, such as legal and medical advice, exchange rate information, and translation services. **To obtain a calling card** from your national telecom service before you leave home, contact the appropriate company below. You can usually make direct international calls from public pay phones at the **PTT** (post and telephone office), but if you aren't using a calling card you may need to drop your coins as quickly as your words. Note that a **prepaid card (telekart)** or a token-like **jeton** (both available at the PTT) must be deposited to activate the phone. No credit will be deducted from your card, and your *jeton* will be returned.

If you do dial direct, you must first insert the *telekart* or *jeton.* Since **Turkey's international access code is 00,** you must then dial 0, wait for the tone, and dial 0 again followed by the country code and the number, without pausing. For a helpful list of country codes, see **International Calling Codes,** below. *Telekarts,* which are cheaper and more widely used than the *jeton,* are available in denominations of 30, 60, 100, or 120 *köntur* (credits). Some calls cost more units than others, and during international calls, one credit lasts 2-10 seconds. Regular coins are not accepted. Magnetic-card public phones, abundant in big cities and resort areas, have on-screen instructions in English, French, and German. Calling card calls usually terminate after three minutes if you are calling from a public phone. You can also make use of the **kontörlü telefon** located in the PTT. The officer tells you how much you owe at the end of your call. Since there may be long lines for these phones, especially during the day, try to use one at night at one of the 24-hour PTTs. The same kind of phone is available at some hotels and restaurants, but it may cost you 20-500% more.

The expensive alternative to dialing direct or using a calling card is using an international operator to place a **collect call.** For an international Türk Telekom operator dial ☎115. An English-speaking operator from your home nation can be reached by dialing the access numbers of the appropriate service provider listed above, and they will typically place a collect call even if you don't have one of their phone cards. Although incredibly convenient, in-room hotel calls invariably include an arbitrary and sky-high surcharge (as much as US$10).

INTERNATIONAL CALLING CODES			
Australia	61	N. Cyprus	90 392
Austria	43	Turkey	90
Canada	1	Greece	30
Ireland	353	Italy	39
New Zealand	64	Spain	34
South Africa	13	France	33
United Kingdom	44	Germany	49
United States/Canada	1	Syria	963

CALLING WITHIN TURKEY. With few exceptions, even the smallest village is assessable by phone. Local numbers have seven digits, and area codes have three. (In small towns, numbers start with the same three digits, so you may occasionally be given a four-digit phone number). The number for **directory assistance** in Turkey is ☎118. For operator-assisted calls within Turkey call ☎131. The simplest way to call within the country is to use the prepaid *telekart*, which carry a certain amount of credits depending on the card's denomination (see above). When making a **long-distance** call within Turkey, insert the card into the phone, dial 0, wait for the tone to change to a lower pitch, and dial the area code and the number. A computer indicates how many credits you have left on your card. Phone rates are highest in the morning, lower in the evening, and lowest on Sunday and late at night.

EMAIL AND INTERNET

Internet access is available in most regions of the country, particularly in the more touristed areas of İstanbul, Cappadocia, and the Aegean and Mediterranean coasts. Internet cafes are now common even in more remote areas such as the Black Sea and Eastern Turkey. Prices typically range from US$1-2 per hour. *Let's Go* lists establishments that provide Internet access in the **Practical Information** sections of cities and towns. Web sites, including www.cybercafe.com, can also help you find cybercafes in Turkey.

Though it's sometimes possible to connect to your home server, in most cases this is a slower (and more expensive) option than taking advantage of free **web-based email accounts** (e.g., www.hotmail.com and www.yahoo.com).

TIME ZONES

Turkey and Cyprus are both two hours later than GMT, seven hours later than EST, and 10 hours later than PST. When it is noon in New York, it is 7pm in Turkey and Cyprus. When it is noon in California, it is 10pm in Turkey and Cyprus. When it is noon in London, it is 2pm in Turkey and Cyprus.

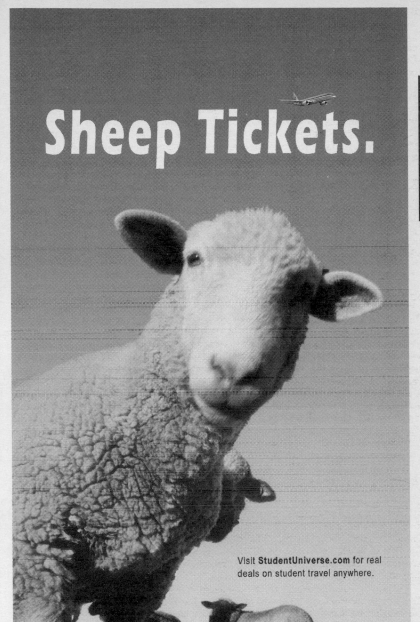

TRANSPORTATION TO TURKEY

BY PLANE

When it comes to airfare, a little effort can save you a bundle. Tickets bought from consolidators are good deals, but last-minute specials, airfare wars, and charter flights often beat these fares. Unfortunately, there are no courier flights to Turkey. The key is to hunt around, to be flexible, and to ask persistently about discounts. Students, seniors, and those under 26 should never pay full price for a ticket.

DETAILS AND TIPS

Timing: Airfares to Turkey peak between June and September. Midweek (M-Th morning) round-trip flights run US$40-50 cheaper than weekend flights, but the latter are generally less crowded and more likely to permit frequent-flier upgrades. Return-date flexibility is usually not an option for budget travelers; traveling with an "open return" ticket can be pricier than fixing a return date when buying the ticket.

Route: Round-trip flights are by far the cheapest. "Open-jaw" (arriving in and departing from different cities) and round-the-world, or RTW, flights are pricier but reasonable alternatives. Patching one-way flights together is the least economical way to travel to Turkey. Flights to İstanbul will offer the most competitive fares, although some airlines will add a connection to İzmir, Antalya, or Ankara for free.

Fares: Round-trip fares to Turkey from the US range from US$750-1000. Fares between November and March (excluding late December) may drop to as low as $500. Round-trip fares from Europe typically cost US$300-600.

BUDGET & STUDENT TRAVEL AGENCIES

While knowledgeable agents specializing in flights to Turkey can make your life easy and help you save money, they may not spend the time to find you the lowest possible fare—they get paid on commission. Travelers holding **ISIC** and **IYTC cards** (see p. 41) qualify for big discounts from student travel agencies. Most flights from budget agencies are on major airlines, but some may sell seats on less reliable chartered aircraft during peak season. For budget travel agencies in Turkey, see individual city listings under **Practical Information.**

A.T.C. Anadolu Tours, 420 Madison Ave., New York, NY, 10017 (☎(888) 262-3658 or (212) 486-4012). Specializes in consolidator tickets to Turkey.

usit world (www.usitworld.com). Over 50 **usit campus** branches in the UK (www.usitcampus.co.uk), including 52 Grosvenor Gardens, **London** SW1W 0AG (☎(0870) 240 10 10); **Manchester** (☎(0161) 273 1880); and **Edinburgh** (☎(0131) 668 3303). Nearly 20 **usit NOW** offices in Ireland, including 19-21 Aston Quay, O'Connell Bridge, **Dublin** 2 (☎(01) 602 16 00; www.usitnow.ie), and **Belfast** (☎(02) 890 327 111; www.usitnow.com). Offices also in Athens, Auckland, Brussels, Frankfurt, Johannesburg, Lisbon, Luxembourg, Madrid, Paris, Sofia, and Warsaw.

Council Travel (www.counciltravel.com). Countless **US offices,** including branches in Atlanta, Boston, Chicago, L.A., New York, San Francisco, Seattle, and Washington, D.C. Check the website or call ☎800-2-COUNCIL (226-8624) for the office nearest you. Another office at 28A Poland St., **London** W1V 3DB (☎(0207) 437 77 67).

CTS Travel, 44 Goodge St., **London** W1T 2AD (☎(0207) 636 00 31; fax 637 53 28; ctsinfo@ctstravel.co.uk).

STA Travel, 7890 S. Hardy Dr., Ste. 110, Tempe AZ 85284 (24hr. reservations and info ☎800-777-0112; fax 480-592-0876; www.sta-travel.com). A student and youth travel organization with over 150 offices worldwide (check website for listing of offices), including **US offices** in Boston, Chicago, L.A., New York, San Francisco, Seattle, and Washington, D.C. Ticket booking, travel insurance, railpasses, and more. In the UK, walk-in office 11 Goodge St., **London** W1T 2PF (☎(0870) 160 60 70. In New Zealand, 10 High St., **Auckland** (☎(09) 309 04 58). In Australia, 366 Lygon St., **Melbourne** Vic 3053 (☎(03) 9349 4344).

Travel CUTS (Canadian Universities Travel Services Limited), 187 College St., **Toronto,** ON M5T 1P7 (☎416-979-2406; fax 979-8167; www.travelcuts.com). 60 offices across Canada. Also in the UK, 295-A Regent St., **London** W1R 7YA (☎(0207) 255 19 44).

COMMERCIAL AIRLINES

The commercial airlines' lowest regular offer is the **APEX** (Advance Purchase Excursion) fare, which provides confirmed reservations and allows "open-jaw" tickets. Generally, reservations must be made seven to 21 days ahead of departure, with seven- to 14-day minimum-stay and up to 90-day maximum-stay restrictions. These fares carry hefty cancellation and change penalties (fees rise in summer). Book peak-season APEX fares early; by May you will have a hard time getting your desired departure date. Use **Microsoft Expedia** (msn.expedia.com) or **Travelocity** (www.travelocity.com) to get an idea of the lowest published fares, then use the resources outlined here to try and beat those fares.

Although APEX fares are probably not the cheapest possible fares, they will give you a sense of the average commercial price, from which to measure other bargains. Specials advertised in newspapers may be cheaper but have more restrictions and fewer available seats. **Turkish Airlines** (THY, *Türk Hava Yolları;* www.thy.com) is the national carrier with offices in: **Chicago** (☎(312) 943-7858), **New York** (☎(212) 339-9602), **Sydney** (☎(02) 9299 8400), **London** (☎(020) 766 93 00), **Capetown** (☎(021) 425 1967), and **Johannesburg** (☎(011) 883 3571). THY offers outstanding discounts during the low season (particularly Nov.-Mar., excluding late Dec.). Most flights are direct to İstanbul, but including a connection to Ankara, İzmir, or Antalya at no additional charge. Other carriers with significant service to Turkey include: Delta Airlines, Northwest Airlines, KLM, United Airlines, Lufthansa, and British Airways.

FLIGHT PLANNING ON THE INTERNET. The Internet is without a doubt one of the best places to look for travel bargains—it's fast and convenient, and you can spend as long as you like exploring options without driving your travel agent insane.

Many airline sites offer special last-minute deals on the Web. You can check out the websites of each airline that flies to Turkey – among them Turkish Airlines (www.thy.com) and many European and North American carriers – or have other sites do the legwork and compile the deals for you—try www.bestfares.com, www.onetravel.com, www.lowestfare.com, and www.travelzoo.com.

STA (www.sta-travel.com), **Council** (www.counciltravel.com), and **StudentUniverse** (www.studentuniverse.com) provide quotes on student tickets, while **Expedia** (msn.expedia.com) and **Travelocity** (www.travelocity.com) offer full travel services. **Priceline** (www.priceline.com) allows you to specify a price, and obligates you to buy any ticket that meets or beats it; be prepared for antisocial hours and odd routes. **Skyauction** (www.skyauction.com) allows you to bid on both last-minute and advance-purchase tickets.

Just one last note—to protect yourself, make sure that the site you use has a secure server before handing over any credit card details. Happy hunting!

OTHER CHEAP ALTERNATIVES

CHARTER FLIGHTS. Tour operators contract charter flights with airlines in order to increase traffic to Turkey during peak season. Charter flights fly less frequently than major airlines, make refunds particularly difficult, and are almost always fully booked. Schedules and itineraries may change or be cancelled at the last moment (as late as 48hr. before the trip, without a full refund), and check-in, boarding, and baggage claim are often much slower. However, they can also be cheaper. **Discount clubs** and **fare brokers** offer members savings on last-minute charter and tour deals. Study contracts closely; you don't want to end up with an unwanted overnight layover.

TICKET CONSOLIDATORS. Ticket consolidators, or **"bucket shops,"** buy unsold tickets in bulk from commercial airlines and sell them at discounted rates. The best place to look is in the Sunday travel section of any major newspaper (such as the *New York Times*), where many bucket shops place tiny ads. Call quickly, as availability is typically extremely limited. Not all bucket shops are reliable, so insist on a receipt that gives full details of restrictions, refunds, and tickets, and pay by credit card (in spite of the 2-5% fee) so you can stop payment if you never receive your tickets. For more information, see www.travel-library.com/air-travel/consolidators.html.

BY TRAIN

Trains run directly to İstanbul from Athens and Bucharest. Some lines may be suspended due to political crises in the Balkans. Eurail passes are not valid in Turkey, but InterRail passes are. The Under 26 InterRail Pass (from US$165) allows either 15 days or one month of unlimited travel within one, two, three, or all of the seven zones into which InterRail divides Europe; the cost is determined by the number of zones the pass covers. The Over 26 InterRail Pass (also zone-based) offers unlimited second-class travel for 22 days for US$220. For information and ticket sales in Europe contact **Student Travel Centre,** 1st fl. 24 Rupert St., London, W1D 6DQ (☎(0207) 437 01 21, 437 63 70, or 434 13 06; fax 734 38 36; http://student-travel-centre.com). If you have a Eurail pass and are traveling from Greece to Turkey, take the train as far as Alexandroupolis, and ride the bus from there. Beware: the 38hr. ride from Athens will wear out even the most seasoned traveler.

BY FERRY

Ferries connect Turkey to Greece, Northern Cyprus, and Italy. Reservations are recommended, especially in high season. Be warned that ferries run on irregular schedules. If you sleep on deck, bring warm clothes and a blanket. Don't forget motion sickness medication, toilet paper, and a hand towel. Bring your own food to avoid high prices on board, and check in at least two hours in advance.

ADDITIONAL INFORMATION: BY PLANE.

The Worldwide Guide to Cheap Airfares, Michael McColl. Insider Publications (US$15).

Discount Airfares: The Insider's Guide, George Hobart. Priceless Publications (US$14).

Air Traveler's Handbook (www.cs.cmu.edu/afs/cs.cmu.edu/user/mkant/Public/Travel/airfare.html).

TravelHUB (www.travelhub.com). A directory of travel agents that includes a searchable database of fares from over 500 consolidators.

Connecting Turkey and **Greece,** ferries run between Ayvalık and Lesvos (see **Ferries,** p. 180), Çeşme and Chios (see p. 197), Kuşadası and Samos (see p. 210), Bodrum and Kos (see p. 225), and Marmaris and Rhodes (with connecting ferries to southern Cyprus and Israel; see p. 247). Between **Italy** and Turkey, ferries connect İzmir and Venice (see p. 193), and Çeşme and Brindisi (see p. 197). Ferries to **Northern Cyprus** leave from Alanya, Taşucu, and Mersin (see p. 473). Individual city listings, referenced above, contain specific information about schedules and fares.

BY THUMB

Let's Go does not recommend hitchhiking. For more information on the dangers associated with hitchhiking, see p. 70. Those who **hitch** between Turkey and Greece usually try to get to İstanbul in one ride from Alexandroupolis or Thessaloniki; there isn't much traffic, and people are not permitted to walk across the border (see **Border Crossing: Greece,** p. 151). Hitchhikers have said that they made sure the license plate number did not get stamped in their passports (but rather on another, disposable piece of paper), so that they wouldn't have to produce the car to leave the country.

ESSENTIALS

LOCAL TRANSPORTATION

BY AIR

Turkish Airlines (*Türk Hava Yolları*, THY) flies to over 30 cities in Turkey, including Adana, Ankara, Antalya, Bodrum, Dalaman, Erzincan, Erzurum, İstanbul, İzmir, Kars, Kayseri, Malatya, Nevşehir, Samsun, Sivas, Trabzon, and Van. **İstanbul** and **Ankara** are the hubs for domestic flights. See individual city listings for schedules and prices. Domestic flights average about US$90 one-way, but passengers ages 12 to 24 may receive a discount. It is often cheaper to purchase tickets for domestic flights in Turkey. In some cities, an airport shuttle bus leaves from the downtown ticket office 30 to 90 minutes before flights (for an extra fee). There are reduced fares for passengers who book international flights with THY.

BY BUS

Frequent, modern, and cheap **buses** run between all sizeable cities. In large cities, the *otogar* (bus station) is often located quite a distance from the city center, but many bus companies have branch offices downtown. Free shuttles called *servis* take ticketed passengers to the otogar. Buy tickets in advance from local offices, or purchase them directly at the station. Tickets are sometimes available on the bus, though you should ask ahead of time—some drivers allow only ticketed passengers aboard. You will need to go from booth to booth to piece together a complete schedule; one company may not divulge competitors' schedules. Many lines provide a 10% discount to ISIC-carrying students. Fares may increase during summer and religious holidays. Passengers are expected to remain in their assigned seats for the duration of the trip.

Because road safety is a serious concern in Turkey (see **Road Safety,** p. 48), *Let's Go* strongly recommends that you **only travel on reputable bus lines,** particularly for long trips. Although these are the most expensive tickets, they are still cheap. The extra money you pay allows the companies to take safety precautions such as giving the drivers rest breaks. Reputable companies include: **Varan, Ulusoy,** and **Kamıl Koç.** Whenever possible, *Let's Go* quotes prices from these companies.

Long routes are often served by **overnight buses.** For greatest comfort, request a window seat in the middle of the bus, away from the driver's radio and behind the overhead window. Every so often, a steward will come around spraying cologne; stretch out your palms to receive a squirt, then rub it over your face and neck. Once or twice during the trip, the bus will stop at a rest area where you can stretch your legs, use the toilets (10¢; paper extra), pray, and purchase overpriced cafeteria grub. The driver will announce the duration of the stop in Turkish, but it might vary by as much as 15 minutes either way, so keep an eye on your bus. If you are stranded, another bus going your way will probably visit the rest complex within a few hours; find the steward to buy a ticket. Nighttime travel is more risky than daytime bus travel. Beware of tourist bureau advice to travel at night in order to maximize touring time. Take care not to travel through poor weather conditions.

In rural parts of Turkey, it is customary to flag buses down from the roadside without reserving a seat in advance. Try to spot the bus's destination sign in the front window. Drivers, who keep an eye out for passengers, stop only if they have an empty seat. A steward hops off to stow your baggage and collect your fare.

Fez Travel, Turkey's flexible "backpacker bus" service, runs around a long loop encompassing İstanbul, Çanakkale, Gallipoli, the Aegean and Mediterranean coasts (including Ephesus, Troy, Kuşadası, Bodrum, Marmaris, Pamukkale, Antalya, and Side), Konya, Cappadocia, Ankara, and Bursa. A season pass (June-Oct. US$175, under 26 US$168) allows you to get on and off along the route at your own whim. There are also various scheduling alternatives, including cheaper passes that cover smaller portions of the route. Buses have English-speaking staff who offer information on accommodations and activities. Contact **Fez Travel,** 15 Akbıyık

Cad., Sultanahmet, İstanbul 5720050. (☎(212) 516 90 24; fax 638 87 64; feztravel@feztravel.com; www.feztravel.com. Tickets can also be purchased through STA in the UK (see **Budget and Student Travel Agencies,** p. 64).

BY DOLMUŞ

Extensive dolmuş (shared taxi) service follows fixed routes within larger cities and between small towns. These are usually vans or minibuses, though occasionally cars are in service as well. They leave as soon as they fill up (*dolmuş* means stuffed), and are almost as cheap as municipal buses (which do not exist in some towns). Best of all, you can get on and off anywhere you like.

BY FERRY

Ferries do not serve the west coast, but a **Turkish Maritime Lines** (TML) cruise ship sails between İstanbul and İzmir (21hr., 1 per week). A weekly boat connects İstanbul with destinations on the Black Sea Coast; for more information, see **The Black Sea Ferry,** p. 388. İstanbul has frequent service to Bandırma and Yalova. Larger ports have ship offices; otherwise, just get on the boat and find the purser.

Most Turkish ferries are comfortable and well-equipped; the cheapest fare class sometimes includes a reclining chair or couchette where you can sleep. Avoid the often astronomically priced cafeteria cuisine by bringing your own food. Fares jump sharply in July and August. Student discounts are often available.

BY TRAIN

Despite low fares, trains within Turkey are no bargain, as they are slow and follow circuitous routes. The Turkish rail system is rivaled only by the Greek system as Europe's most antiquated and least efficient. First-class gets you a slightly more padded seat, but most Turks travel second-class. Since couchettes are available, overnight train trips are preferable to overnight bus trips. Lock your compartment door and keep your valuables on your person. Make reservations at least a few hours in advance at the train station. There is no rail system in Cyprus.

DOLMUŞ DOS AND DON'TS To the uninitiated, mastering this quintessentially Turkish mode of transportation can appear daunting. Travelers can avoid a dolmuş *faux pas* by following these suggestions.

Dolmuş flexibility and price is somewhere between those of taxis and buses. They run along set but unpublished routes, usually beginning from a secret hub somewhere in the city. Dolmuş post their final destinations in their front windows, but if you're headed to an intermediate destination, you'll probably need to ask locals which is the right one for you: *"Bu dolmuş [destination] gidiyor mu?"* (Does this dolmuş go to X?). If you're at a hub, there should be a queue of people waiting to board a queue of dolmuş to your destination. Hop in line and exude savvy.

If you've just jumped on a dolmuş en route, don't stand precariously and fish for your money as the driver pulls away—you'll just make everybody nervous. There's no rush. Take a seat. Keep in mind that you should generally sit next to somebody of the same sex, though as the dolmuş fills up the rule is inevitably broken.

Ask your neighbor or the driver how much it costs to go to your destination: *"X kadar ne kadar?"* (How much is it to X?). Then pass the cash up to someone in the next row, saying the name of your destination and adding "öğrenci" if you're a student. The driver, while racing his stick-shift minibus through tricky traffic, will change your money and pass it back to you. If money is passed to you by somebody else, send it on its way with the same instructions you received.

The driver may remember your stated destination and stop there without any reminder on your part. Otherwise, clearly say *"inecek var"* (getting off) and, as the driver pulls to a stop, calmly squeeze out of your seat and hop off.

BY MOPED AND MOTORCYCLE

Motorized bikes offer an enjoyable, relatively inexpensive way to tour coastal areas and countryside, particularly where there are few cars. They don't use much gas, can be put on trains and ferries, and are a good compromise between the high cost of car travel and the limited range of bicycles. Exercise extreme caution—driving in Turkey can be tricky at best. Your trip to Turkey is not the best time to learn how to ride a moped or motorcycle. They're uncomfortable for long distances, dangerous in the rain, and unpredictable on rough roads and gravel. Always wear a helmet, and never ride with a backpack. Expect to pay about US$20-35 per day; remember to bargain. Motorcycles normally require a license. Ask if the quoted price includes tax and insurance, or you may be hit with an additional fee. Avoid handing your passport over as a deposit; if you have an accident or mechanical failure you may not get it back until you cover all repairs.

BY THUMB

> **!** *Let's Go* strongly urges you to seriously consider the risks before you choose to hitch. We do not recommend hitching as a safe means of transportation.

Those who decide to **hitchhike** in Turkey generally offer to pay half of what the trip would cost by bus. Most Turks, however, refuse payment. Hitchers in Turkey signal with a hand wave or the standard thumb. Travelers in remote parts of Turkey will find that drivers may offer them rides even when they're just waiting for a bus. No one should hitch without careful consideration of the risks involved. After all, any bozo can drive a car.

If you're a woman traveling alone, **do not hitch.** It's too dangerous. Safety issues are always imperative, even for those who are not hitching alone. Safety-minded hitchers avoid getting in the back of a two-door car and never let go of their backpacks. They will not get into a car that they can't get out of again in a hurry. If they ever feel threatened, they insist on being let off, regardless of where they are. Acting as if they are going to open the car door or vomit on the upholstery may get a driver to stop. Hitchhiking at night is particularly dangerous.

BY CAR

Turks drive on the right-hand side of the road, except in Northern Cyprus, where traffic runs on the left side. The speed limit is 50kph (31mph) in cities, 90kph (55mph) on the highways, and 130kph (80mph) on toll roads *(oto yolu)*. Road signs in English make driving somewhat easier. Archaeological and historical sites are indicated by yellow signposts with black writing; village signs have blue writing. Before taking your own car to Turkey, consider the effects of poor roads. If you get into an accident, you must file a report with the police (traffic police ☎118). The **Touring and Automobile Association of Turkey** (TTOK) can provide more information. Their İstanbul office is at I. Oto Sanayi Yanı, Çamlık Cad. 4, Levent 80600 (☎(212) 282 81 40; fax (212) 282 80 42; turing@turing.org.tr; www.turing.org.tr/Turing/emain.html). For safety information, see **Road Safety,** p. 48.

DRIVING PERMITS AND CAR INSURANCE

INTERNATIONAL DRIVING PERMIT (IDP). If you plan to drive a car while in Turkey, you should have an International Driving Permit (IDP). Though Turkey allows travelers to drive with a valid American or Canadian license for a limited time, it may be a good idea to get an IDP anyway in case you're in a situation (e.g., an accident or stranded in a small town) where the police do not know English; information on the IDP is printed in 10 languages.

Your IDP, valid for one year, must be issued in your own country before you depart. An application for an IDP usually needs to include one or two photos, a current local license, an additional form of identification, and a fee.

CAR INSURANCE. Some credit cards cover standard insurance. If you rent, lease, or borrow a car, you will need a **green card,** or **International Insurance Certificate,** to certify that you have liability insurance and that it applies abroad. Green cards can be obtained at car rental agencies, car dealers (for those leasing cars), some travel agencies, and some border crossings. Rental agencies may ask you to purchase theft insurance for countries that they consider to have a high risk of auto theft.

ORIENTATION AND STREET ADDRESSES

Since few Turkish cities follow a grid plan, maps can be difficult to use. To avoid confusion, a three-tiered addressing system is used. *Mahalle* refers to the neighborhood, *cadde* or *bulvar* are avenues or boulevards, and a *sokak* is a street. A slash after the street number, or the word *kat,* introduces the number of the floor, if applicable. *Mahalle(si)* is abbreviated to **Mah.**, *Cadde(si)* to **Cad.**, *Bulvar(ı)* to **Bul.**, and *Sokak* (or *Sokağı*) to **Sok.** Thus, a complete street address in Turkey might look like *Çiğdem Mah. Atatürk Bul. Söğüt Sok. 6/2.* This book, which prints street numbers directly before the streets to which they refer, would list this address as *Atatürk Bul., 6/2 Söğüt Sok, Çiğdem Mah.* It means the second floor of 6 Söğüt St., off Atatürk Ave., in the Çiğdem District. Few addresses will contain all of these parts. In towns and rural areas, the street names may not appear on maps. Rather than searching for street names and building numbers, ask for the place you're seeking: "*Aya Sofia nerede?*" (Where is Aya Sofia?).

ADDITIONAL INFORMATION

WOMEN TRAVELERS

Foreign women, especially those traveling alone, attract significant attention in Turkey. Catcalls and other forms of verbal harassment are common; physical harassment is rare. Regardless of whatever signals a foreign woman intends to send, her foreignness alone may suggest a liberal openness to friendly or amorous advances. Because Western movies and TV often depict women as seductive sex symbols, female travelers are frequently perceived as likely sex partners. However, as long as women expect plenty of attention and take certain common sense precautions, there is no need for paranoia.

More touristed parts of Turkey—İstanbul, Northwestern Turkey, the Aegean and Mediterranean Coasts, Cappadocia, and Ankara—may be more comfortable for women travelers. Female travelers in Anatolia, along the Black Sea, and in Eastern Turkey should be confident and experienced in developing-world travel.

DRESSING FOR SUCCESS. A lot of harassment can be avoided by dressing conservatively. Shorts, short skirts, tight T-shirts, and revealing clothes are unacceptable in all areas of Turkey, including İstanbul, except in the most touristy of Aegean and Mediterranean towns. Women traveling alone might want to avoid such threads even in the latter regions. Generally, the less you look like a tourist, the better off you'll be. Carry a kerchief or scarf to cover your head in mosques and more conservative towns. Wearing a conspicuous **wedding band** may help prevent unwanted overtures. Some travelers report that carrying pictures of a "husband" or "children" is extremely useful to help document marriage status. Even a mention of a husband waiting back at the hotel may be enough to discount your potentially vulnerable, unattached appearance. Many women traveling in Eastern Turkey choose to wear the *chadot*—a traditional, full-length Muslim dress—to discourage unwanted attention.

ACCOMMODATIONS AND FOOD. Sometimes more expensive, slightly more upscale accommodations with single rooms are more secure for a woman traveling alone; however, cheap dorm-style accommodations are often equally good and also can provide invaluable opportunities for meeting other travelers with whom to venture out after dark. Stick to centrally located accommodations to avoid solitary late-night treks or metro rides. For comfortable restaurants, look for establishments with the word "*aile*" ("family") in their names. Although you're free to sit wherever you choose, Turkish women and couples will always sit in the *aile* room, which tends to be furnished better than the men-only "main" room.

STREET SMARTS. On the street, avoid eye contact, and appear confident and directed. Consider approaching older women or couples for directions if you're lost or feel uncomfortable. Customarily, Turkish women seldom walk outside alone, especially after dark. Always carry extra money for a phone call, bus, or taxi. Women and men usually do not sit next to one another on buses and dolmuş. To avoid insinuating interest in her driver, a female traveler should not sit in the front seat of a taxi. **Hitching is never safe** for lone women, or even for women traveling together. Choose train compartments occupied by other women or couples; ask the conductor to put together a women-only compartment if he or she doesn't offer to do so first.

HARASSMENT. The best answer to verbal harassment is no answer at all; feigned deafness, sitting still, and staring straight ahead will do a world of good that reactions usually don't achieve. Alternatively, you can attract attention and show your displeasure by making a scene, perhaps using the expression "*ayıp!*" ("shame!"). A phrase like "*haydi git*" ("go away") may also come in handy. Don't hesitate to seek out a police officer or a passerby if you are being harassed. Rape and other violence against women are still relatively new to Turkish culture, and their incidence is much more rare than in most Western countries. If, at any time, unwanted attention becomes physical and/or threatening, you should yell, scream, and make getting away your first priority. In Turkish, holler "*imdat*" ("eem-DAHT," help) or "*polis*" ("PO-lees," police). Carry a whistle or an airhorn on your keychain, and memorize the emergency number (☎155). An IMPACT Model Mugging self-defense course will not only prepare you for a potential attack, but will also raise your confidence and your awareness of your surroundings (see Personal Safety, p. 46). Women also face some specific health concerns when traveling (see Women's Health, p. 54)

FURTHER READING: WOMEN TRAVELERS.

A Journey of One's Own: Uncommon Advice for the Independent Woman Traveler, Thalia Zepatos. Eighth Mountain Press (US$17).

Adventures in Good Company: The Complete Guide to Women's Tours and Outdoor Trips, Thalia Zepatos. Eighth Mountain Press (US$7).

Active Women Vacation Guide, Evelyn Kaye. Blue Panda Publications (US$18).

Travelers' Tales: Gutsy Women, Travel Tips and Wisdom for the Road, Marybeth Bond. Traveler's Tales (US$8).

TRAVELING ALONE

There are many benefits to traveling alone, including independence and greater interaction with locals. On the other hand, any solo traveler is a more vulnerable target of harassment and street theft. Lone travelers need to be well organized and look confident at all times. Try not to stand out as a tourist, and be especially careful in deserted or very crowded areas. If questioned, never admit that you are traveling alone, and maintain regular contact with someone at home who knows your itinerary. For more tips, pick up *Traveling Solo* by Eleanor Berman (Globe Pequot Press, US$17) or subscribe to Connecting: Solo Travel Network, 689 Park Road, Unit 6, Gibsons, BC V0N 1V7 (☎604-886-9099; www.cstn.org; membership US$28). Alternatively, several services link solo travelers with companions who have similar travel habits and interests; for a newsletter for single travelers seeking travel partners, contact the Travel Companion Exchange, P.O. Box 833, Amityville, NY 11701 (☎631-454-0880 or 800-392-1256; www.whytravelalone.com; subscription US$48).

OLDER TRAVELERS

Older travelers may find traveling in Turkey difficult. Many opt for senior group travel agencies. The following organize trips to Turkey:

ElderTreks, 597 Markham St., Toronto, ON M6G 2L7 (☎800-741-7956; www.eldertreks.com). Adventure travel programs for the 50+ traveler in.

Elderhostel, 11 Ave. de Lafayette, Boston, MA 02111 (☎877-426-8056; www.elderhostel.org). Organizes 1- to 4-week "educational adventures" in Turkey for those 55+.

The Mature Traveler, P.O. Box 15791, Sacramento, CA 95852 (☎800-460-6676). Deals, discounts, and travel packages for the 50+ traveler. Subscription$30.

BISEXUAL, GAY, AND LESBIAN TRAVELERS

Although homosexuality is legal in Turkey and Northern Cyprus, religious and social dictates keep most homosexual activity discreet. Homophobia can be a problem, especially in remote areas; expect authorities to be unsympathetic. Gay and lesbian travelers will benefit from the close contact that Turks maintain with same-sex friends. Public displays of affection should be avoided.

Turkey's urban centers do not lack bars or informal cruising areas (men only), although they may be less obvious. **Lambda İstanbul,** a gay, lesbian, bisexual, and transgendered support group, lists resources and guides to gay-friendly establishments on its webiste (www.qrd.org/www/world/europe/turkey).

For more information on gay and lesbian travel, contact the **International Gay and Lesbian Travel Association,** 52 W. Oakland Park Blvd. #237, Wilton Manors, FL 33311, (☎(954) 776-2626; fax 776-3303; iglta@iglta.com; www.iglta.com), an organization of over 1350 companies serving gay and lesbian travelers worldwide. Call for lists of agents, accommodations, and events. **Out and About** (www.planetout.com) offers a biweekly newsletter addressing gay travel concerns. The **International Lesbian and Gay Association (ILGA),** 81 rue Marché-au-Charbon, B-1000 Brussels, Belgium (☎32 2 502 24 71; www.ilga.org), provides political information, such as homosexuality laws of various countries.

FURTHER READING: BISEXUAL, GAY, AND LESBIAN TRAVELERS.

Spartacus International Gay Guide. Bruno Gmunder Verlag. (US$33).

Damron's Accommodations and *The Women's Traveler.* Damron Travel Guides (US$14-19). For more information, call US ☎(415) 255-0404 or (800) 462-6654 or check their web site (www.damron.com).

Ferrari Guides' Gay Travel A to Z, Ferrari Guides' Men's Travel in Your Pocket, Ferrari Guides' Women's Travel in Your Pocket, and *Ferrari Guides' Inn Places.* Ferrari Guides (US$14-16). For more information, call ☎(602) 863-2408 or ☎(800) 962-2912 or check their website (www.ferrariguides.com).

The Gay Vacation Guide: The Best Trips and How to Plan Them, Mark Chesnut. Citadel Press (US$15).

TRAVELERS WITH DISABILITIES

Turkey and Northern Cyprus are only slowly beginning to respond to the needs of travelers with disabilities. Some hotels, train stations, and airports have installed facilities for the disabled; many of the archaeological sites throughout the region, however, are still not wheelchair accessible. Traveling with disabilities is generally very difficult in Eastern Turkey. It may be difficult for people with disabilities to travel on a budget in Turkey.

Those with disabilities should inform airlines and hotels of their disabilities when making arrangements for travel; some time may be needed to prepare special accommodations. Call ahead to restaurants, hotels, and other facilities about the existence of ramps, the widths of doors, the dimensions of elevators, etc.

Mobility International USA (MIUSA), P.O. Box 10767, Eugene, OR 97440 (☎541-343-1284; www.miusa.org). Sells *A World of Options: A Guide to International Educational Exchange, Community Service, and Travel for Persons with Disabilities* (US$35).

Society for the Advancement of Travel for the Handicapped (SATH), 347 Fifth Ave., #610, New York, NY 10016 (☎212-447-7284; www.sath.org). An advocacy group that publishes free online travel information and the travel magazine *OPEN WORLD* (US$18, free for members). Annual membership US$45, students and seniors US$30.

MINORITY TRAVELERS

In Turkey, Caucasians are a minority. While Turks have a well-deserved reputation for hospitality and openness to strangers, however, travelers of African, Asian, or Latin American descent, especially those traveling alone and/or in non-touristy areas, may have an experience different from that of their Caucasian counterparts. Turks often have no qualms about staring at the unfamiliar, be it beautiful, intriguing, or repulsive. If you're in less-traveled towns and cities, be ready for a few terrified children, puzzled old women, or snickering teenagers. Probably the worst you can expect is a derisive over-the-shoulder remark. You may be faced with a few amusing or even offensive questions, but keep in mind that it's mostly from plain curiosity, without malice or contempt.

A few caveats: dark-skinned travelers should know that, thanks to the power of Hollywood, a distorted cultural representation awaits them, associated with violence and crime. People of East Asian descent are automatically assumed to be Japanese. This may lead to extra deference from people in the tourist industry, as the Japanese have a reputation for lavish spending. Travelers to **Northern Cyprus** may notice quite a few South Asians and Africans on city streets due to the island's ties to the British Empire. Most speak fluent Turkish, so travelers of similar appearance may find themselves expected to do the same.

TRAVELING WITH CHILDREN

Turks and Cypriots adore children. Expect a stream of compliments, advice, candy, and discounts on transportation throughout Turkey and Cyprus. Children under two generally fly for 10% of the adult airfare on international flights (this does not necessarily include a seat). International fares are usually discounted 25% for children between the ages of two and 11. Family vacations will be most enjoyable if you slow your pace and plan ahead. Be sure that children carry some sort of identification in case of an emergency or if they get lost. Consider using a papoose-style device to carry your baby on walking trips. Baby foods are usually only available in pharmacies.

DIETARY CONCERNS

Vegetarians should have no problem finding suitable cuisine in Turkey. **Vegetarian dishes** in Turkey and Cyprus include succulent fruits, colorful salads, tasty breads, *fasülye* (beans), and *börek* (cheese-filled pastry). Vegetarian *meze* (appetizers) are plentiful. In summer, fresh vegetables, fruits, and interesting cheeses abound in the outdoor markets. In well-traveled areas of Turkey, Turks understand the concept of vegetarianism; simply explain, "*Vejetariyanım*" ("I am a vegetarian.") In other areas ask, "*Etsiz yemek var mı?*" ("Do you have food without meat?")

Travelers who keep **kosher** will be hard-pressed to find a kosher restaurant. If you are strict in your observance, consider preparing your own food on the road. A good resource is the *Jewish Travel Guide*, by Michael Zaidner.

ALTERNATIVES TO TOURISM

For an extensive listing of "off-the-beaten-track" and specialty travel opportunities, try the **Specialty Travel Index,** 305 San Anselmo Ave., #313, San Anselmo, CA 94960, USA (☎888-624-4030 or 415-455-1643; www.specialtytravel.com; US$6). **Transitions Abroad** (www.transabroad.com) publishes a bimonthly on-line newsletter for work, study, and specialized travel abroad.

STUDYING ABROAD

Foreign study programs in Turkey vary tremendously in expense, academic focus and quality, living conditions, degree of contact with local students, and exposure to culture and language. If you plan on staying in Turkey for more than three months, you will have to obtain a student visa, available from the Turkish consulates and embassies listed on p. 39.

Most American undergraduates enroll in programs sponsored by US universities. Because English is the language of instruction at many Turkish universities, it is also possible to enroll directly as a special student. Doing so might be less expensive than enrolling in an American university program. Schools that offer study abroad programs to foreigners are listed below.

American Field Service (AFS), 310 SW 4th Ave., #630, Portland, OR 97204, USA (☎800-237-4636; fax 503-241-1653; email afsinfo@afs.org; www.afs.org/usa). Summer, semester, and year-long homestay international exchange programs in Turkey for high school students and graduating high school seniors. Financial aid available.

Beloit College, World Affairs Center, Beloit College, Beloit, WI 53511, USA (☎608-363-2269; www.beloit.edu). A semester program at Marmara University in İstanbul. Also open to non-Beloit students.

Summer Program at Boğaziçi University, İstanbul. Contact Illinois Programs Abroad, 115 International Studies Building, 910 S. 5th St., Champaign, IL 61820, USA (☎217-333-6322; sao@uiuc.edu; www.ips.uiuc.edu/sao/programs/turkey.html). Students choose two or three 7-week classes on the culture, language, and history of Turkey, Central Asia, and the Middle East. Taught at one of Turkey's foremost universities.

Council on International Education Exchange, 205 E. 42nd St., New York, NY 10017, USA (☎888-268-6245; fax 212-822-2699; email info@ciee.org; www.ciee.org). Summer programs at Ankara's Middle East Technical University. For information about study in Turkey, call ☎212-822-2755.

Study Abroad at Middle East Technical University, Ankara. Contact Dr. Shirley Epir, Director, International Relations Office, Rektorluk 501, Middle East Technical University, Ankara 06531 (☎+90 (312) 210 22 98; shirleyj@rorqual.cc.metu.edu.tr; www.metu.edu.tr/MIA/summersc). A 6-week program providing college students with 2 3-credit courses. Offers a wide range of courses on Turkish history, politics, and culture.

State University of New York/Binghamton, Office of International Programs, N.A. Rockefeller Center G-1, P.O. Box 6000, Binghamton University, Binghamton, NY 13902, USA (☎(607) 777-2336; fax 277-2889; oip@binghamton.edu; www.binghamton.edu). Semester, year, and summer programs at İstanbul's Bosphorus University.

TÖMER, 18/1 Ziya Gökalp Cad., Kızılay, Ankara (☎(312) 435 97 81; fax 433 81 90; tanriver@tomer.ankara.edu.tr; www.tomer-ankara.edu.tr). Teaches Turkish in cities across Turkey, including İstanbul, Antalya, Bursa, and İzmir.

FURTHER READING: STUDYING ABROAD.

www.studyabroad.com

Academic Year Abroad 2000/2001. Institute of International Education Books (US$45).

Vacation Study Abroad 2000/2001. Institute of International Education Books (US$43).

Peterson's Study Abroad 2001. Peterson's (US$30).

Peterson's Summer Study Abroad 2001. Peterson's (US$30)

WORKING ABROAD

Finding work in Turkey and Cyprus is difficult, as the government tries to restrict employment to citizens. Foreigners who wish to work in Turkey must obtain a **work visa,** which in turn requires a **permit** issued by the Ministry of the Interior; contact a Turkish diplomatic mission for more information. The brightest prospect for working in Turkey is probably **teaching English.** Students with university credentials might fare quite well, but having your credentials verified can take some time. Various organizations in the US will place you in a (low-paying) teaching job. University foreign language departments may have connections to job openings abroad.

International Schools Services, Educational Staffing Program, P.O. Box 5910, Princeton, NJ 08543, USA (☎609-452-0990; www.iss.edu). Recruits teachers and administrators for American and English schools in Turkey. Program fee US$150.

Office of Overseas Schools, US Department of State, Room H328, SA-1, Washington, D.C. 20522 USA (☎202-261-8200; fax 261-8224; www.state.gov/www/about_state/schools/). Keeps a comprehensive list of schools abroad and agencies that arrange placement for Americans to teach abroad.

VOLUNTEERING

Volunteer jobs are readily available, and many provide room and board in exchange for labor (such as archaeological digs or community projects.)

Archaeological Institute of America, 656 Beacon St., Boston, MA 02215 (☎617-353-9361; www.archaeological.org). The *Archaeological Fieldwork Opportunities Bulletin* (US$16 for non-members) lists field sites throughout Europe (call for info on Turkey). Purchase the bulletin from Kendall/Hunt Publishing, 4050 Westmark Dr., Dubuque, IA 52002, USA (☎800-228-0810).

Gençtur Turizm ve Seyahat Ac. Ltd. (Tourism and Travel Agency), Head Office: Prof. K. İsmail Gürkan Cad., No. 14 Flat 4, Sultanahmet, İstanbul 34100 (☎(212) 520 52 74; fax 519 08 64). Taksim Branch (handles workcamps): İstiklâl Cad., Zambak Sok. 15/5, Taksim, İstanbul 80080 (☎(212) 249 25 15; fax 249 25 54; workcamps@gentur.com.tr; http://genctur.com.) Organizes teenage, group, or international voluntary 2-week summer workcamps and year-round study tours in Turkey.

Volunteers for Peace, 1034 Tiffany Rd., Belmont, VT 05730, USA (☎802-259-2759; www.vfp.org). Arranges placement in workcamps in Turkey. Annual *International Workcamp Directory* US$20. Registration fee US$200. Free newsletter.

FURTHER READING: VOLUNTEERING.

International Jobs: Where They Are, How to Get Them, Eric Koocher. Perseus Books (US$17).

Work Abroad: The Complete Guide to Finding a Job Overseas, Clayton Hubbs. Transitions Abroad (US$16).

International Directory of Voluntary Work, Louise Whetter. Vacation Work Publications (US$16).

Teaching English Abroad, Susan Griffin. Vacation Work (US$17).

Overseas Summer Jobs 2001, Work Your Way Around the World, and *The Directory of Jobs and Careers Abroad.* Peterson's (US$17-18 each).

WEB RESOURCES

Turkey is becoming as wired as a carpet salesman on seven cups of *çay*. The World Wide Web allows travelers to consult official and unofficial sources of information in Turkey and throughout the world and to browse through a vast library of literature and multimedia material about Turkey's past, present, and future. The following is a grab-bag of useful resources.

All About Turkey (www.balsoy.com/Turkiye/index.html). The name says it all.

Center for Middle Eastern Studies (www.fas.harvard.edu/~mideast/inMEres/countries/turkey.html). A spectacular listing of multi-lingual Turkey links.

Learn Practical Turkish (www2.egenet.com.tr/~mastersj/). Covers the language basics and then some. The section on "Off-color Turkish" is not for the faint of heart.

Let's Go (www.letsgo.com/Thumb/mideast/index.htm#). Useful travel-related links.

Republic of Turkey (www.turkey.org). The web site of the Turkish Embassy. Information on travel, history, and current events, from the government's point of view.

Turkish Daily News (www.turkishdailynews.com). Turkey's only English-language daily. Don't believe everything you read.

Turkish Republic of Northern Cyprus (www.trncwashdc.org). Web site of the Northern Cyprus Representative Office, with a variety of semi-helpful information and links.

Türkiye on the Web (www.columbia.edu/cu/libraries/indiv/area/MiddleEast/Turkey.html). Provides a lifetime's worth of Turkey-related web sites.

İSTANBUL

EUROPE ☎212
ASIA ☎216

Straddling two continents and almost three millennia of history, İstanbul exists on an incomprehensible scale. The city occupies a densely historic landscape of Ottoman mosques, Byzantine mosaics, and Roman masonry. The Bosphorus Straits have proven to be the city's lifeline and its curse: the strategic location between two seas and two continents gave birth to the city, but also attracted countless sieges from covetous neighbors. Having withstood innumerable demographic shifts, devastating wars, natural disasters, and foreign occupations, İstanbul is naturally composed of a unique mix of civilizations, a mélange evident not only in architecture and religious practice, but also in everyday life. Conservative women wearing black veils mingle in the swelling crowds with younger women in Western dress, and major religious and historical sights double as the stunningly beautiful backdrops for love scenes in Turkish pop videos.

In its current incarnation, İstanbul is the most crowded and cosmopolitan city in the Turkish Republic. This urban supernova explodes out into the surrounding countryside behind an ever-expanding front of new construction sites, but as no crane or cement truck could possibly hope to keep up with the pace of İstanbulian life, the city remains crowded. New immigrants from the Anatolian hinterland live in shanties on the fringes of the city. These dwellings, called *gecekondus* because they are hastily erected, as if in a single night *(gece)*, were some of the first structures to be leveled in the devastating earthquake of August 1999.

The poverty of İstanbul's *gecekondus* coexists with an ambitious commercialism as audacious and ostentatious as any to be found in New York or London. Yet every level of the city's burgeoning economy remains distinctly İstanbulian: posh, modern nightclubs lend their space to raucous traditional weddings, and modern fast food competes neck-and-neck with boatmen selling fried fish sandwiches.

Even as İstanbul's centuries-long sprawl has engulfed entire towns, each neighborhood of the city retains a distinct character. Some sections of the city are easily accessible to the visitor. The challenge is to see beyond the Ottoman palaces, carpet salesmen, and backpacker bars, and venture out into neighborhood produce markets, back-alley tea shops, and Byzantine fortifications.

İSTANBUL HIGHLIGHTS

TOUR the **Topkapı Palace** (p. 108), one-time residence of Süleyman the Magnificent and his harem, and pore over the visual archives of the Islamic World.

VISIT the **Blue Mosque** (p. 106), the six-minareted wonder whose creation once threatened the singularity of the mosque at Mecca.

WANDER across creaky boards and among ancient columns through the eerie **Underground Cistern** (p. 116) to the partially submerged Gorgon heads.

NAVIGATE the labyrinthine **Grand Bazaar** (p. 115), and bargain for gold, silver, silk, and carpets as you drink bottomless cups of *çay*.

BROWSE Ortaköy's Sunday **silver market** (p. 130) and spend the afternoon playing backgammon with bohemians at a colorful waterfront cafe.

SAMPLE *lokum* at the **Egyptian Spice Bazaar** (p. 122), whose air is thick with the pungent aroma of tea and spices.

HOP on the **Tünel Metro** (p. 126), the oldest subway in the world, to watch a Whirling Dervish show at the Galat Mevlihane on İstiklâl Cad.

BOARD a vintage ferry to the **Prince's Islands** (p. 136) and bike among Greek monasteries before collapsing on the beach to work on that tan.

HISTORY

The traces of the first known settlement in the İstanbul area date to the Paleolithic age. **Mycenaeans** established themselves on the site of modern İstanbul around the 13th century BC. Two hundred years later, settlers founded several fishing villages in the area, one of which occupied the exact site of the Topkapı Palace. It was not until **Megarian** colonists from Greece landed on the Asian shore of the Bosphorus around 700 BC, however, that the city's history was first recorded.

Legend has it that in the 7th century BC, **Byzas,** a Greek speculator looking for prime real estate, consulted the infallible Oracle at Delphi, which told him to settle "opposite the Land of the Blind." As Byzas sailed the Bosphorus, he spotted the Megarian settlement on the Asian shore at Chalcedon (now Kadıköy, one of the centers of Asian İstanbul). Overcome by the glory of the Golden Horn's harbor on the European shore, he decided that the folks at Chalcedon must have been blind to have ignored this site. Byzas and his crew settled here in 667 BC, and Byzas's sister Ramona gave the city its first name in his honor: **Byzantium.**

Roman infighting at the beginning of the 4th century AD determined the city's fate for the next millennium. The abdication of Diocletian in 305 prompted a power struggle between **Constantine,** Emperor of the West, and his rival **Licinius** in the East. The victorious Constantine declared Byzantium "New Rome," renamed it **Constantinople,** and made it the capital of the Eastern Roman Empire, which later became the **Byzantine Empire.** Constantine's enthusiasm for Christianity led to the building of the city's first Christian churches. During the 5th century, Theodosius I supervised the construction of a massive set of fortified walls around the city.

In 532, Emperor **Justinian** was nearly overthrown by the **Nika Revolt,** a dispute among factions of the Hippodrome. He was on the verge of abdicating when his wife, **Theodora,** reproached him for his cowardice. "Purple makes a good shroud," she quipped. Purple being the symbol of imperial honor, Justinian got the message. After five days of bloodshed, he emerged triumphantly to face a ruined city. He eventually restored Constantinople to twice its former glory, undertaking such building projects as the **Aya Sofia** (see p. 105). In the decades following Justinian's reign, besieging Persian, Avar, and Slav armies kept Constantinople continually on her toes. The 7th and 8th centuries saw Arab raiders join the fray, but Theodosius's walls held fast. Finally, the Fourth Crusade broke through Constantinople's seemingly impregnable defenses in 1204. The Latin Crusaders breached the sea walls and plundered the city, occupying it for 60 years. Following Latin rule, the Empire was further weakened by internal crises and skirmishes. The decline of the Byzantine Empire was paralleled by the rise of the **Ottoman Turks,** whose conquests in the 14th century marked the beginning of the **Ottoman Empire.**

By 1451, **Mehmet II,** known as "Fatih," or "the Conqueror," came to lead the Ottomans. The Byzantine emperor controlled little besides the coveted capital city; Anatolia and most of the Balkans were already in Ottoman hands. In 1452, a confident and careful Mehmet commissioned the building of two fortresses on the Bosphorus in anticipation of the conquest. **Rumeli Hisarı** and **Anadolu Hisarı** (the fortresses of Europe and Asia) stood on opposite banks of the Bosphorus and enabled the Ottomans to control the straits. The Byzantine emperor tried to block the Golden Horn but could not foil Mehmet, who had his boats transported by slides to the other end of the straits at night. For his final bombardment of the Theodosian city walls, Mehmet cast the largest cannon in existence.

Constantinople fell to the Ottomans on May 29, 1453. The prophet Muhammed foretold that a commander who bore his name would one day conquer the city, and thus Mehmet (Turkish for Muhammed) secured himself a place in heaven with his victory. The new sultan took to rebuilding and repopulating the city, transforming İstanbul into the exalted administrative, cultural, and commercial center of his empire. Under Ottoman rule, the city developed into an architectural treasure trove, best known for its Imperial mosques. As the Ottoman Empire expanded to Eastern Europe, the Middle East, and North Africa, the capital became one of the

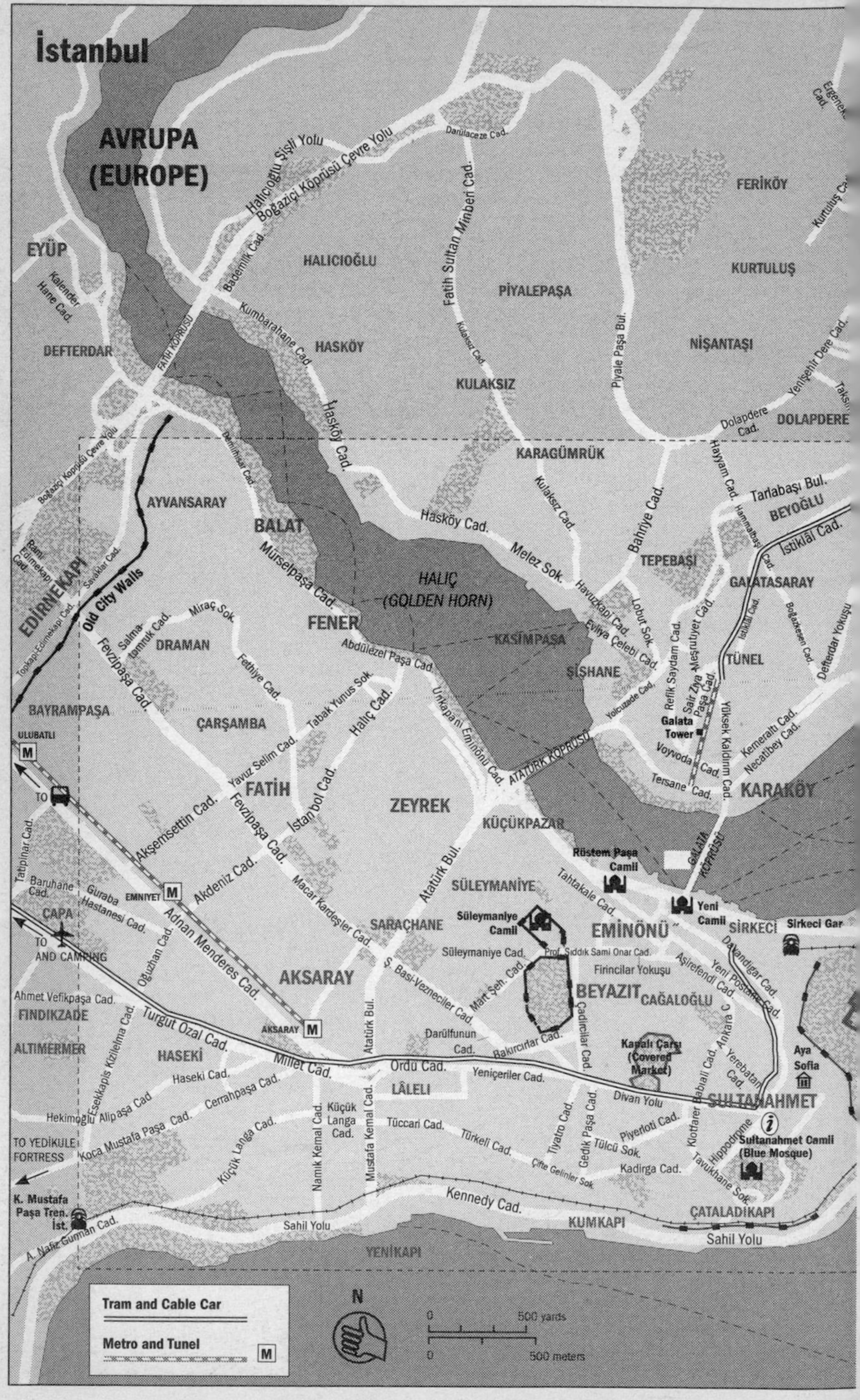
İstanbul
AVRUPA (EUROPE)
EYÜP
Kalender Hane Cad.
DEFTERDAR
Halıcıoğlu Şişli Yolu
Boğaziçi Köprüsü Çevre Yolu
Darülaceze Cad.
Bademlik Cad.
HALICIOĞLU
Fatih Sultan Minberi Cad.
PİYALEPAŞA
FERİKÖY
Kurtuluş Cad.
Ergenekon Cad.
KURTULUŞ
Kumbarahane Cad.
HASKÖY
Kulaksız Cad.
Piyale Paşa Bul.
NİŞANTAŞI
Yenişehir Dere Cad.
FATİH KÖPRÜSÜ
KULAKSIZ
Dolapdere Cad.
DOLAPDERE
Hasköy Cad.
KARAGÜMRÜK
Boğaziçi Köprüsü Çevre Yolu
Demirhisar Cad.
Kulaksız Cad.
Hayyam Cad.
Tarlabaşı Bul.
AYVANSARAY
BALAT
Bahriye Cad.
BEYOĞLU
Hammalbaşı Cad.
İstiklâl Cad.
Hasköy Cad.
Mürselpaşa Cad.
Melez Sok.
TEPEBAŞI
Savaklar Cad.
Rami Edirnekapı Cad.
EDİRNEKAPI
Old City Walls
HALIÇ (GOLDEN HORN)
Havuzkapı Cad.
Lobut Sok.
GALATASARAY
Miraç Sok.
Salma-tomruk Cad.
FENER
KASIMPAŞA
Evliya Çelebi Cad.
Meşrutiyet Cad.
Boğazkesen Cad.
Defterdar Yokuşu
Topkapı-Edirnekapı Cad.
DRAMAN
Fethiye Cad.
Abdülezel Paşa Cad.
ŞİŞHANE
Refik Saydam Cad.
TÜNEL
Fevzipaşa Cad.
Tabak Yunus Sok.
Haliç Cad.
Unkapanı Eminönü Cad.
Yolcuzade Cad.
Şair Ziya Paşa Cad.
BAYRAMPAŞA
ÇARŞAMBA
Galata Tower
Yüksek Kaldırım Cad.
Kemeraltı Cad.
Necatibey Cad.
ULUBATLI
M
Yavuz Selim Cad.
ATATÜRK KÖPRÜSÜ
Voyvoda Cad.
TO
FATİH
İstanbul Cad.
Tersane Cad.
KARAKÖY
Tatipinar Cad.
Akşemsettin Cad.
Fevzipaşa Cad.
ZEYREK
KÜÇÜKPAZAR
Atatürk Bul.
Rüstem Paşa Camii
GALATA KÖPRÜSÜ
Baruhane Cad.
Guraba Hastanesi Cad.
EMNİYET
Akdeniz Cad.
SÜLEYMANİYE
Tahtakale Cad.
Yeni Camii
ÇAPA
Adnan Menderes Cad.
Macar Kardeşler Cad.
SARAÇHANE
Süleymaniye Camii
EMİNÖNÜ
SİRKECİ
Sirkeci Gar
TO AND CAMPING
Oğuzhan Cad.
Süleymaniye Cad.
Prof. Sıddık Sami Onar Cad.
Dayandigar Cad.
Ahmet Vefikpaşa Cad.
AKSARAY
Ş. Basi-Vezneciler Cad.
Mart Şeh. Cad.
Fırıncılar Yokuşu
Aşirefendi Cad.
Yeni Postane Cad.
FINDIKZADE
BEYAZIT
ÇAĞALOĞLU
Ankara C.
Turgut Özal Cad.
AKSARAY
Atatürk Bul.
Darülfunun Cad.
Çadırcılar Cad.
ALTIMERMER
Esekkapis Kızılelma Cad.
HASEKİ
Bakırcılar Cad.
Kapalı Çarşı (Covered Market)
Aya Sofia
Yerebatan Cad.
Millet Cad.
Ordu Cad.
Haseki Cad.
Cerrahpaşa Cad.
Yeniçeriler Cad.
Babıali Cad.
LÂLELİ
Divan Yolu
SULTANAHMET
Hekimoğlu Alipaşa Cad.
Koca Mustafa Paşa Cad.
Küçük Langa Cad.
Tüccari Cad.
Tiyatro Cad.
Gedik Paşa Cad.
Piyerloti Cad.
Klodfarer Cad.
Hippodrome
Sultanahmet Camii (Blue Mosque)
TO YEDİKULE FORTRESS
Küçük Langa Cad.
Namık Kemal Cad.
Mustafa Kemal Cad.
Türkeli Cad.
Tülcü Sok.
Çifte Gelinler Sok.
Kadirga Cad.
Tavukhane Sok.
K. Mustafa Paşa Tren. İst.
Kennedy Cad.
ÇATALADİKAPI
A. Nafiz Gürman Cad.
Sahil Yolu
KUMKAPI
Sahil Yolu
YENİKAPI
Tram and Cable Car
Metro and Tunel
N
0
500 yards
0
500 meters

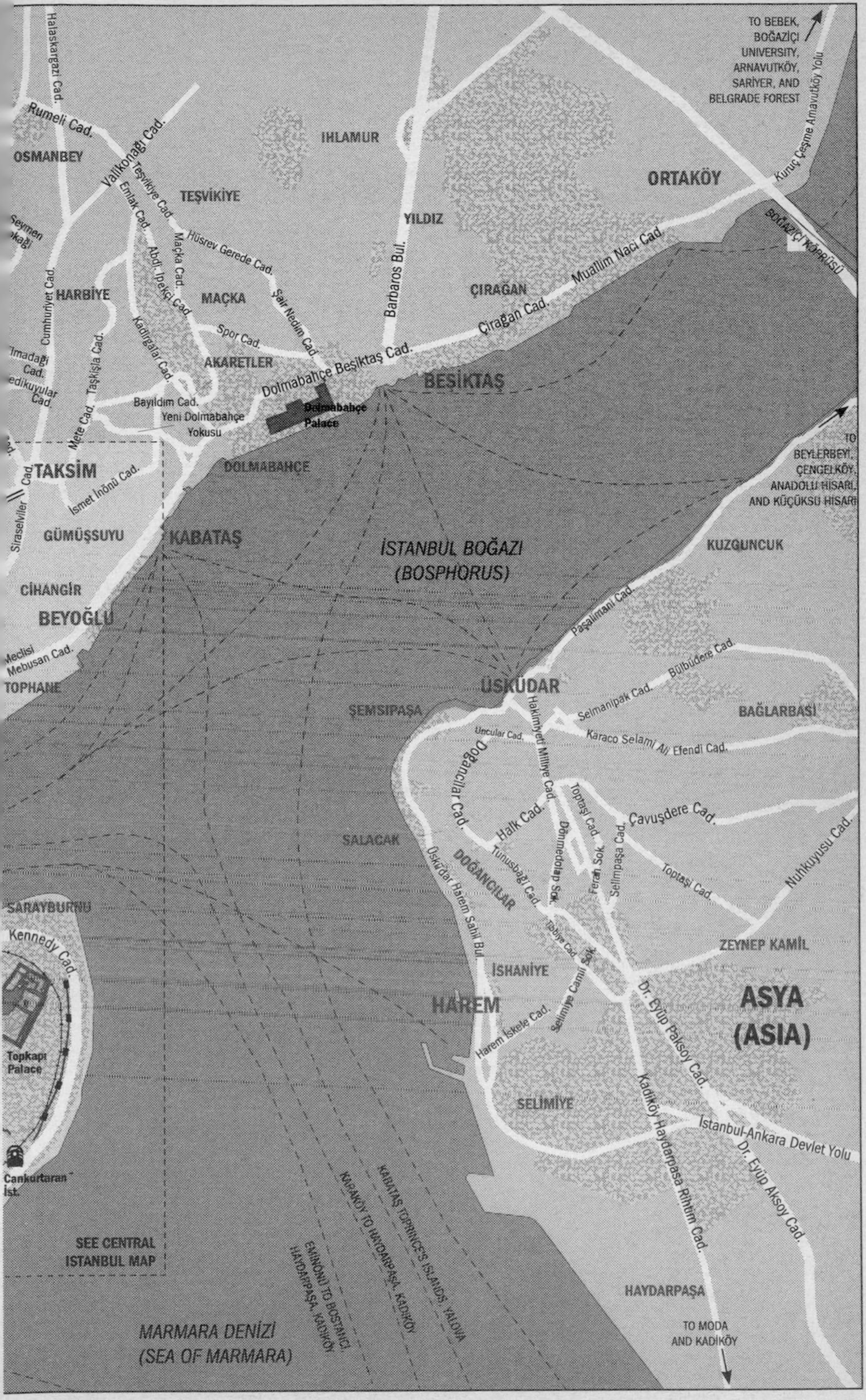
TO BEBEK, BOĞAZİÇİ UNIVERSITY, ARNAVUTKÖY, SARIYER, AND BELGRADE FOREST
Halaskargazi Cad.
Rumeli Cad.
OSMANBEY
Valikonağı Cad.
IHLAMUR
Teşvikiye Cad.
Emlak Cad.
TEŞVİKİYE
ORTAKÖY
Kuruçeşme Arnavutköy Yolu
YILDIZ
Hüsrev Gerede Cad.
Abdi İpekçi Cad.
Maçka Cad.
Boğaziçi Köprüsü
Muallim Naci Cad.
HARBİYE
MAÇKA
Şair Nedim Cad.
Barbaros Bul.
ÇIRAĞAN
Cumhuriyet Cad.
Kadırgalar Cad.
Spor Cad.
Çırağan Cad.
Taşkışla Cad.
AKARETLER
Dolmabahçe Beşiktaş Cad.
BEŞİKTAŞ
Bayıldım Cad.
Yeni Dolmabahçe Yokusu
Dolmabahçe Palace
Mete Cad.
DOLMABAHÇE
TAKSİM
İsmet İnönü Cad.
TO BEYLERBEYİ, ÇENGELKÖY, ANADOLU HİSARI, AND KÜÇÜKSU HİSARI
Sıraselviler Cad.
GÜMÜŞSUYU
KABATAŞ
İSTANBUL BOĞAZI (BOSPHORUS)
KUZGUNCUK
CİHANGİR
BEYOĞLU
Paşalimanı Cad.
Meclisi Mebusan Cad.
Bülbüldere Cad.
TOPHANE
ÜSKÜDAR
Selmanipak Cad.
ŞEMSİPAŞA
BAĞLARBAŞI
Hakimiyeti Milliye Cad.
Karaca Selami Ali Efendi Cad.
Doğancılar Cad.
Toptaşı Cad.
Halk Cad.
Çavuşdere Cad.
Nuhkuyusu Cad.
SALACAK
Dönmedolap Sok.
Tunusbağı Cad.
Selimpaşa Cad.
Feran Sok.
Toptaşı Cad.
DOĞANCILAR
Üsküdar Harem Sahil Bul.
SARAYBURNU
Kennedy Cad.
ZEYNEP KAMİL
İSHANİYE
Selimiye Camii Sok.
HAREM
Dr. Eyüp Paksoy Cad.
ASYA (ASIA)
Harem İskele Cad.
Topkapı Palace
SELİMİYE
Kadıköy Haydarpaşa Rıhtım Cad.
İstanbul-Ankara Devlet Yolu
Dr. Eyüp Aksoy Cad.
Cankurtaran İst.
KABATAŞ TO PRINCE'S ISLANDS, YALOVA
KARAKÖY TO HAYDARPAŞA, KADIKÖY
EMİNÖNÜ TO BOSTANCI, HAYDARPAŞA, KADIKÖY
SEE CENTRAL ISTANBUL MAP
HAYDARPAŞA
MARMARA DENİZİ (SEA OF MARMARA)
TO MODA AND KADIKÖY

Tram and Cable Car
Metro and Tünel
HALİÇ (GOLDEN HORN)
Arda Cad.
Ibadullah Cad.
Hasköy Yolu
BALAT
FENER
St. Stephen of the Bulgars
Orthodox Patriarchate
Fethiye Museum
Kariye Camii (Chora Church)
Old City Walls
Savaklar Cad.
Topkapı Edirnekapı Cad.
Demirhisar Cad.
Mürselpaşa Cad.
Kırkanber Sok.
Malla Şakir Sok.
Mumhanesi Cad.
Çınçınlı Çeşme Sok.
Eğrikapı
Ulubatlı Hasan Sok.
Paşa Hamamı Sok.
Kürküçeşme Sok.
Kamış Sok.
Rifat Ef. Sok.
Çilingir Sok.
Hacı Isa Bostan Sok.
Neşter Sok.
Kaya Cad.
Miraç Sok.
Draman Cad.
Fethiye Cad.
Kalpakçıçeşme Sok.
Kiremit Cad.
Salma Tomruk Cad.
Pr. Naci Şensoy Sok.
Niyazi Mısrı Sok.
KARAGÜMRÜK
Kefevi Sok.
Altışah Sok.
Dilmaç Sok.
Dolapli Bostan Sok.
Manyasa
Ismailağa Cad.
Selimiye Camii
Sultan Selim Sok.
Tabak Yunus Sok.
Sarmaşik Sok.
Prof. Naci Sensoy Cad.
Uzunyol Sok.
Fevzipaşa Cad.
Kefebek S.
Nurettin Tekkesi Sok.
Karakol Sok.
Firin Sok.
Hüseyin Remzi Bey Sok.
Zade Cad.
ÇARŞAMBA
Ispanakci Sok.
Çirakc. Çeş. Sok.
Haliç Cad.
Kara Sarıklı Sok.
Abdülezel Paşa Cad.
Nalıncı Cemal Cad.
Bostan Hamamı Sok.
Boston Sok.
Sofalı Çeşme Sok.
Melekhoca Cad.
Eski Alipaşa Cad.
Hasan Fehmi Paşa Cad.
Beycegiz Fırın Sok.
Saray Ağası Sok.
Altay Sok.
Kabakulak Sok.
Ahşaminare Sok.
Yavuz Selim Cad.
Darüşşafaka Cad.
Kadı Çeşmesi Sok.
Mütfü Hamamı Sok.
Karadeniz Cad.
Cibali Cad.
Salihpaşa Cad.
Keçeciler Cad.
Yusuf Ziyapaşa Sok.
Başhoca Sok.
Başmüezzin Sok.
Tetimmeler Cad.
Sinancamii Sok.
Ali Tekin Sok.
ZEYREK
Unkapanı
Adnan Menderes Bul.
Akbilek Sok.
Zembilci Sok.
Akşemsetin Cad.
Sarıgüzel Cad.
Şemsettin Sami Sok.
Karkut Ata Sok.
Hoca Efendi Sok.
Baş Imam Sok.
Yesarizade Sok.
Fatih Camii
FATİH
Hattat Nazif Sok.
Mıhcılar Cad.
Haydar Cad.
Zeyrek Mehmet P. Sok.
KÜÇÜKPAZAR
Hacıkadın Cad.
SÜLEYMANİYE
Ballıpaşa Cad.
Hüsrevpaşa Sok.
Sarı Nusuh Sok.
Kocasinan Cad.
Zülfi Çeşme Sok.
Fevzipaşa Cad.
Fatih Türbesi Sok.
Zeyrek Sok.
Itfaiye Sok.
Atatürk Bul.
ÇAPA
Guraba Hastanesi Cad.
EMNİYET
Akdeniz Cad.
Mutemet Sok.
Ocaklı Sok.
Okumuşadam Sok.
Macar Kardeşler Cad.
Karaman Sok.
Çamsokağı
Nıyza Sok.
Halıcılar Cad.
Vatanperver Sok.
Açıklar Sok.
Dolap Cad.
Himmet Sok.
Cemal Yener Tosyal Cad.
Kirazcımescit Sok.
Prof. Sıdd
SARAÇHANE
Yeşil Tekke Sok.
Havlucu Sok.
Millet Cad.
Oğuzhan Cad.
Ahmet Vekif Paşa Cad.
FINDIKZADE
Ragıp Bey Sok.
Horhor Cad.
Molla Husrev Toprak Sok.
Belediye (City Hall)
Ş. Baş Yezneciler Cad.
Dedefendi
Süleymaniye Cad.
Besim Ömer Paşa Cad.
Mart Şeh. Cad.
Kimyager Derviş Sok.
Gökalp Ziya Sok.
HASEKİ
YUSUFPAŞA
AKSARAY
Kızılelma Cad.
Tevfik Fikaret Sok.
Özbek Süleyman Efendi Sok.
Yeşiltulumba Sok.
Fevzibey Cad.
Fethibey Cad.
H. Zedeler Sok.
Reşitpaşa Cad.
LALELİ
ÜNİVERSİTE
Ordu Cad.
Yeniçeriler
Haseki Cad.
Cerrahpaşa Cad.
Inkilap Cad.
Tir. Hasan P.Sok.
Aksaray Cad.
Laleli Cad.
Koska Cad.
Mesih Paşa Cad.
Azimkar Sok.
Koca Ragıp Sok.
Sümbül Sinan Sok.
Pehlivan
Tatlıkuyu
Kurban Sok.
Nişancabostanı
Mithatpaşa Cad.
Hekimoğlu Alipaşa Cad.
Küçük Langa Cad.
Hayriye Tüccar Cad.
Esekkapı Sok.
Koca Mustafa Paşa Cad.
Langabostanı Sok.
Mustafa Kemal Cad.
Güvenlik Cad.
Hadımodalar Sok.
Hemşeri Sok.
Türkeli Cad.
Daltaban Yokuşu
Çifte
Mollataşi Cad.
Sepetçi Selim Sok.
Kenanbey Sok.
Telliodalar Cad.
Saraçhane Sok.
Namık Kemal Cad.
Bostani Sok.
YENİKAPI
Kennedy Cad.
Arapzade
A. Nafiz Gürman Cad.
K. Mustafa Paşa Tren. Ist.
Yenikapı Seabus Pier
SEE SOU

TAKSİM
Taksim Buses
BEYOĞLU
GALATASARAY
TEPEBAŞI
Ministry of Tourism
SEE TÜNEL & TAKSİM MAP
KASIMPAŞA
TÜNEL
Tünel Metro Terminal
Galata Tower
CİHANGİR
KABATAŞ
Kabataş Seabus Terminal
DOLMABAHÇE
TOPHANE
KARAKÖY
Karaköy Maritime Terminal
Karaköy Seabus Pier
İSTANBUL BOĞAZI (BOSPHORUS)
THE GOLDEN HORN MAP
SEE SULTANAHMET & SÜLEYMANİYE MAP
Rüstem Paşa Camii
Eminönü Otogar
EMİNÖNÜ
Yeni Camii
Mısır Çarşısı (Egyptian Spice Bazaar)
SİRKECİ
Sirkeci Gar
Süleymaniye Camii & Türbesi
BEYAZIT
Beyazıt Tower
KAPALI ÇARŞI (COVERED MARKET)
Nuruosmaniye Camii
Beyazıt Camii
Gülhane Park
Topkapı Palace
AHIRKAPI
SULTANAHMET
Aya Sofia
Sultanahmet Camii (Blue Mosque)
Cankurtaran İst.
KUMKAPI
ÇATLADIKAPI
Küçük Aya Sofia
İstiklâl Cad.
Tarlabaşı Bul.
Sıraselviler Cad.
Meclisi Mebusan Cad.
Kennedy Cad.
Divan Yolu
Sahil Yolu
Kadırga Limanı Cad.
N
300 yards
300 meters
Central İstanbul

world's major cosmopolitan centers. Neighborhoods such as Galata and Pera were populated almost entirely by foreigners. After more than four centuries, however, the city's fortunes waned along with those of the Empire, and following World War I, Western powers occupied İstanbul. The Westerners were driven out of the city in the 1920s by Mustafa Kemal Atatürk, founder of the modern Turkish Republic.

Upstart Ankara became the capital of the Republic of Turkey in 1923, but İstanbul remains the cultural heart of Turkey. Between 1960 and today, the city's population has increased tenfold, to over 13 million inhabitants.

INTERCITY TRANSPORTATION

Flights: İstanbul's airport, **Atatürk Havaalanı,** is 30km from the city. The domestic and international terminals are 800m apart and are connected by bus (every 20min. 6am-11pm). For information on **visas and entering Turkey,** see **Visas,** p. 40.

To Sultanahmet from the Airport: Take a Havaş shuttle bus from either terminal to Aksaray (every 30min. 6am-9pm, $7). At Aksaray, walk 1 block south to Millet Cad. and take an Eminönü-bound tram to the Sultanahmet stop. The tram is a gray train with orange and blue stripes that runs along the electrical wires overhead. Alternatively, cab it to the Yeşilköy train station and take the commuter rail *(tren)* to Cankarturan, a short walk up the Küçük Ayasafya Cad. hill to hostel land. A taxi to Sultanahmet costs $9.

To Taksim from the Airport: Take a Havaş shuttle to end of the line (every 30min. 6am-9pm, $5).

To the Airport: Have a private service such as **Karasu** (☎638 66 01) or **Zorlu** (☎638 04 35) pick you up from your hostel ($5.50; about every 1½hr.; most hostels can arrange this service). This service can usually only be arranged by a hostel or hotel, sometimes for much cheaper than the posted rate. Alternatively, take the Havaş airport shuttle from the McDonald's in Taksim (45min., every 30min., $6.75).

Cheap fares: Many travel agents offer cheap airfares on charter flights to international destinations out of Atatürk Airport. Sample 1-way airfares include: Amsterdam $145, Berlin $118, London $210, Rome $178, Athens $116, Budapest $110, Tel Aviv $155. See Travel Agencies, p. 92.

Trains: In virtually every case, it's quicker and cheaper to take the bus. All trains to Anatolia leave from **Haydarpaşa Garı** (☎216 336 04 75 or 336 20 63), on the Asian side. To get there, take the ferry from Karaköy pier #7 (every 20min. roughly 6am-midnight, $.65). The pier is halfway between Galata Bridge and the Karaköy tourist office, where rail tickets for Anatolia can be purchased in advance at the TCDD (Turkish Republic State Railway) office upstairs. To reach both, make a right at the end of the bridge if walking from Eminönü, and walk along the waterfront. The office accepts couchette *(kuşet)* reservations for Ankara (2 days in advance, if possible). Haydarpaşa ticket office open daily 7:30am-11:30pm. Tickets also available at the **Sirkeci** station. Europe-bound trains leave from **Sirkeci Garı** (☎212 527 00 50 or 527 00 51), in Eminönü (downhill from Sultanahmet towards the Golden Horn). Connections to most European cities must be made in Athens or Bucharest. Some lines may be temporarily suspended due to Balkan political crises. Call ahead for info and student fares. Many of these destinations offer sleeper cars for about twice the cost, with the price per person decreasing by about $2 for each person with whom you are willing to share a bunk.

Destination	Company	Duration	Times	Price
Ankara	Anadolu Express	9hr.	daily 10pm	$6
Ankara	Ankara Express	9½hr.	daily 10:30pm	$8.80; sleeper $22
Ankara	Başarı Express	7¼hr.	daily 1pm	$12
Ankara	Başkent Express	6½hr.	daily 10am	$9.70
Ankara	Boğaziçi Express	9hr.	daily 1:30pm	$10.60
Ankara	Fatih Express	7½hr.	daily 11:30pm	$9.70
Eskişehir	Eskişehir Express	4½hr.	M, W, F 6:55pm	$9
Gaziantep	Toros Express	27hr.	Tu, Th, Su 8:25am	$10
Kars	Doğu Express	13½hr.	daily 8:35am	$9.60
Konya	Meram Express	12¾hr.	daily 7:20pm	$9.30; sleeper $22
Athens	Ege Express	24hr.	daily 8:20am	$60
Budapest	Balkan Express	40hr.	daily 2:52pm	$90
Bucharest	Bosfor Express	17½hr.	daily 11:55pm	$30

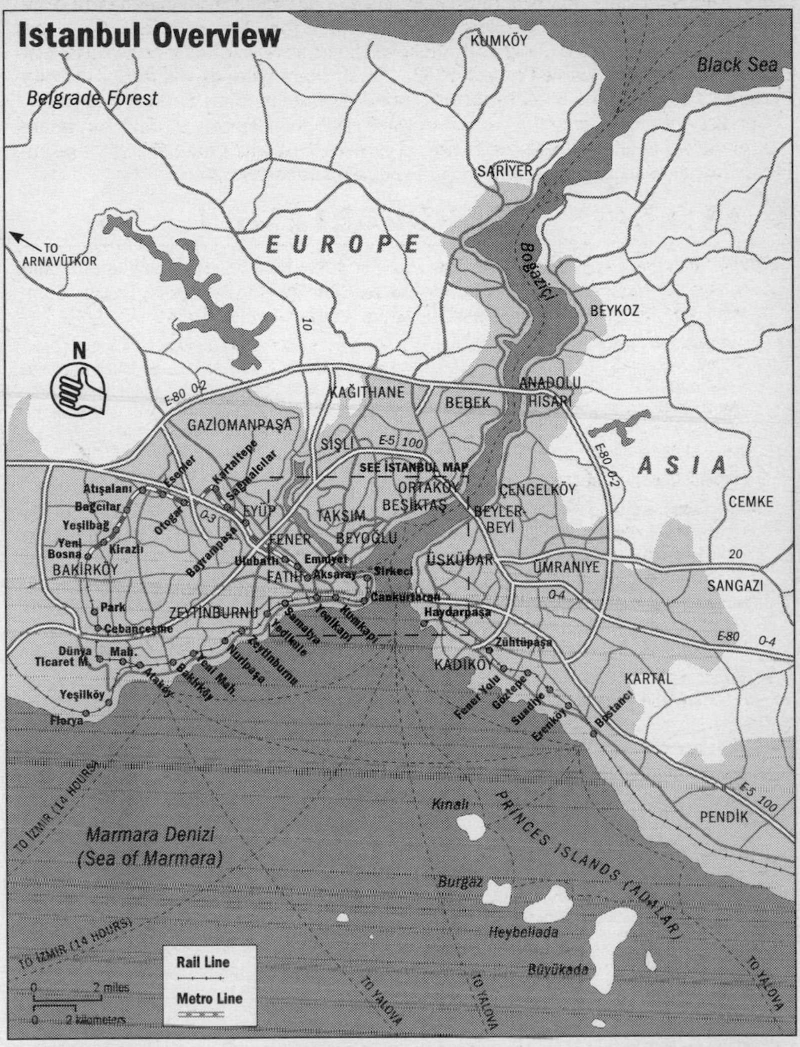

Buses (domestic and international): Inter-city buses leave from the **Esenler Otobüs Terminal** (☎658 00 36) in Esenler, several kilometers from central İstanbul. The otogar is laid out like a giant set of parentheses around the metro stop in the center. Bus companies sell tickets from their offices on the ground floor of the 2 parenthetical buildings, facing inward. Buses depart from the outer side of the building. Each company has a number corresponding to their place along the ticket arcade, from 1 to 167.

To the Bus Terminal from Sultanahmet: Take the tram to Yusufpaşa (1 stop beyond Aksaray; \$.50), cross the overpass from the platform, walk 1min. to the Aksaray metro station on broad Adnan Menderes Bul., and take the metro to the otogar (15min., \$.40). Most companies have courtesy buses, called *servis,* that run to the otogar from Eminönü, Taksim, and other points in the city (free with bus ticket purchase). Certain travel agencies will arrange transportation for free to the bus station if you buy the tickets from them for one of their client bus companies.

Bus companies: Hundreds of buses leave daily for virtually every point in Turkey and for some neighboring countries. Service tends to vary widely in quality and safety, so be careful choosing a company. Travel agencies are perhaps the most convenient way to arrange transportation (calling the companies directly, particularly if you don't speak Turkish, can be difficult and confusing). Otherwise, get to the station with 30min.-1hr. to spare, shop around for the best price to your city, then buy your ticket. For trips within Turkey, **Aydin** (☎658 09 09), **Kamil Koç** (☎658 20 03; No. 147), **Metro** (No. 51), **Nevtur** (☎658 08 65), **Ulusoy** (☎658 30 00; fax 658 30 10; No. 127 in the terminal), **Truva** (☎658 33 86) and **Varan** (☎658 02 74; No. 15-16) are professional and enjoy good reputations. Unfortunately, they don't run to many towns in Eastern Turkey. To get there, you can take a slightly less reputable bus direct from İstanbul (see below) or simply go as far as you can with one of the major companies and then switch over to more reliable regional service. Reservations are recommended, and tickets can be bought in advance at the bus company offices in central İstanbul. Fares increase by about 10-15% during the summer and over religious holidays.

Eastern destinations: Companies with service to more "exotic" locales tend to cluster at the far end of one of the "parentheses," generally in the terminal's highest numbers (look for a big yellow sign for "Van"). **Mar-Soy** (☎658 13 90 or 658 13 91; No. 163) has buses to: **Gaziantep** (12hr.; 1, 4pm; $23); **Mardin** (18hr.; 1, 4pm; $33); and **şanlıurfa** (15hr.; 1, 4pm; $25). **Sivas** has buses to **Erzurum** (18hr.; 2, 4, 7, 10pm; $30) and **Sivas** (13hr.; 5:30, 7:30, 9:30, 11:30pm; $23). **Yeni Van Seyahat** (☎658 33 65 or 658 33 66; No. 163) runs to **Van** (24hr.; 10:30am, 3pm; $32).

International Buses: Unlicensed companies have been known to offer substantial discounts on trips to Western European destinations and then abandon their passengers in Eastern Europe, so choose your company carefully. **Ulusoy** runs to **Athens** (21hr.; Th, Sa 10am; $60, students $51). **Parlak Tur** (☎658 17 55 or 658 17 56; No. 164) runs relatively cheap buses to **Prague** (2 days; Sa 4pm; $100, students $95). For service to **Tehran,** try **İgdir** (No. 165-6), next door to Mar-Soy and Van (36hr., daily 1pm, $30). **Nur** (☎58 05 43 or 658 05 44; No. 47-48) has buses to **Amman** (26hr.; 1:30, 4:30, 7:30pm; $45, students $40); **Damascus** (23hr.; 1:30, 4:30, 7:30pm; $40, students $30); and **Sofia, Bulgaria** (12hr., 6pm, $25).

Destination	Company	Duration	Times (daily)	Price	Students
Adana	Varan	14hr.	6, 7pm	$29	$25.50
Afyon	Pamukkale	7hr.	7 per day 8:30am-11:45pm	$15	$13.50
Ankara	Aydin	6hr.	7 per day 8:15am-1am	$11	
Ankara	Kamil Koç	6hr.	every hr. 6:30am-6:30pm and 8:30pm-2:45am	$22	$20
Antalya	Aydin	12hr.	8:30, 9:15, 10pm	$14	
Antalya	Varan	11hr.	8:30, 9:30pm	$30	$26.50
Bodrum	Aydin	14hr.	8:30, 9:30pm	$15	
Bodrum	Ulusoy	13hr.	8:30, 9:15, 9:30pm	$31	$27
Bursa	Aydin	4½hr.	every 30min.	$6.50	
Bursa	Kamil Koç	4hr.	every 30min.	$9	$8.25
Cappadocia	Aydin	11hr.	every 30min.	$20	
Eskişehir	Pamukkale	6hr.	2:30pm	$12	$11
İzmir	Aydin	9hr.	9am, 1:30, 10:30, 11pm	$12	
Pamukkale	Aydin	10hr.	7 per day 8:30am-11:30pm	$16	
Pamukkale	Pamukkale	10hr.	7 per day 8:30am-11:30pm	$21	$19
Trabzon	Ulusoy	18hr.	1, 5:30, 6:30, 8:30, 10:30pm	$35	$31
Yalova	Kamil Koç	3hr.	every 30min.	$8.50	$6.50

Ferries: Turkish Maritime Lines (☎249 92 22), near pier #7 at Karaköy, to the left of the Haydarpaşa ferry terminal. Look for a building with a blue awning marked *Denizcilik İşletmeleri.* The **Samsun-Trabzon Ferry** traverses the Black Sea, leaving from Saraybumu in İstanbul (M 2pm). (See **The Black Sea Ferry,** p. 388, for details.) Ferries also leave for **Bandırma,** with train connection to İzmir (combination ticket $10-25). Ferries and seabuses cross the Sea of Marmara to **Yalova,** where you can connect to **Bursa** and other points inland (see Yalova: **Practical Information,** p. 167). To **Yalova** from: **Bostancı** (45min.; 6:25am, 5:55pm; $6.50); **Kabataş** (1hr., 6 per day 7:20am-8pm, $7.10); **Kartal** (35min., 8 per day 6:50am-8:15pm, $4.75). The slower ferry, *yolcu vapürü* (☎814 10 20) runs from Kabataş (2½hr.; 9:30am, 2, 6:30pm; $3) and Kartal (4 per day 9am-9:15pm). For local ferry info, see **Getting Around: Ferries,** p. 67.

ORIENTATION

Waterways divide İstanbul into three sections. The **Bosphorus Strait** (Boğaz) separates Asia from Europe. Turks call the western, European side of İstanbul **Avrupa** and the eastern, Asian side **Asya.** The **Golden Horn,** a river originating outside the city, splits Avrupa into northern and southern parts. Directions in İstanbul are usually further specified by city precinct or district (Kadıköy, Taksim, or Fatih).

Most of the famous mosques, historical sites, and tourism facilities are south of the Golden Horn and toward the eastern end of the peninsula, which is framed by the Horn and the Sea of Marmara. The other half of "Europe" is focused on Taksim Square, the commercial and social center of the northern European bank. Two main arteries radiate from the square: **İstiklâl Cad.,** the main downtown shopping street, and **Cumhuriyet Cad.,** which is lined with airline offices and hotels. The Asian side of İstanbul is primarily residential, but offers plenty of rewarding wandering and a more relaxed pace.

Each district is defined much more by its center than by its often unclear borders. Many of these districts were once outlying towns, long since swallowed up by İstanbul's insatiable expansion. European Sultanahmet and Taksim, and Asian Kadıköy, will be the most relevant for most visitors to the city, but memorizing the location of even a few more areas on the map will prove immensely helpful. With help from a map and a keen eye for the many landmarks, you can navigate yourself through the maze of alleys that make up the city.

This chapter is arranged by **discrete neighborhood units.** *Let's Go* recommends that you organize your visit according to those approximate guidelines.

LOCAL TRANSPORTATION

Getting around İstanbul proves fairly easy during the day and evening, with dirt-cheap ferries, buses, shared-taxi dolmuş and trams all making good substitutes for the comparatively expensive private taxis that swell the streets. Even so, the city is gargantuan, and navigating it can be frustrating even for native İstanbullular (plural of Istanbullu, a native of Istanbul). The metropolis must be considered a **series of neighborhoods** rather than a system of coherent streets. Very often streets will change names unannounced as they move from one neighborhood to the next. As the city has grown, the borders between neighborhoods have become nearly imperceptible, and streets appear to change on a whim. Keep the tram and metro in mind as you organize your travel plans—they can usually get you within walking distance of where you want to go, or at least reduce the eventual cab fare. If you know the names of your home and destination neighborhoods, finding a bus or dolmuş should be fairly simple. Heavy traffic can significantly prolong travel time between far-flung neighborhoods, so it's best to focus your day's itinerary on one particular neighborhood or area of the city and explore from morning to evening.

AKBİL AND TICKETS

İstanbul's transportation systems have become somewhat more integrated with the introduction of AKBİL, an electronic ticketing system that works on municipal ferries, buses, trams, seabuses, and the subway (but not dolmuş). Anyone staying longer than three or four days should definitely consider springing for an **AKBİL tab.** After an initial deposit of $5, you can add money to your tab (a little plastic key ring with a magnetic button on the end) in 1,000,000TL increments and save 15-50% on fares when you hold the tab against a reader on the bus or at the station. Deposit credit to your AKBİL from any of the white IETT public bus booths which has the sign *"AKBİL satılır."* Such kiosks are located at most sizeable bus and tram stops, such as Eminönü, Beyazıt, Taksim, Sariyer, Kadıköy, etc. The Kabataş and Eminönü seabus terminals (among other spots) have automated AKBİL 24 machines, which are open 24 hours. These are good to use for seabus trips, since using AKBİL on the boat can save you 15-20% on pricey seabus tickets.

To use the machines, press your tab into the reader and remove it, insert a 1,000,000TL note, and press once more. If you have enough on your tab, the machine beeps once and you may board; otherwise it sounds a lower note and a red light blinks on. Regular tickets are not interchangeable, meaning that you can't use a bus ticket (bought at a kiosk) for the tram or on a bus with a ticket seller on board. Tickets for trams and buses without ticket sellers are available from little white booths, while ferries and seabuses take *jeton* (tokens) available at ferry stops. At the major stations (Eminönü, Beyazıt, Karaköy) it is far less confusing to go to a manned AKBİL booth, indistinguishable from the ticket booths but for the large AKBİL sign. Always be sure to carry plenty of small lira notes so that if you are on a bus with a ticket seller, you won't have to clog up traffic.

BUSES

İstanbul's bus system is a dream, not because of its organization or punctuality, but because there are simply so many buses, with one going wherever you need to go about every 10 minutes. Bus service runs from approximately 5am to midnight, dropping off markedly after about 10:30pm. The real difficulty for newcomers is figuring out where to catch a given bus. The bus system centers on several major stops, from which all buses serving a certain part of the city leave. Hubs include **Eminönü** (in the parking lot on the seaward side of the Egyptian Spice Bazaar), **Aksaray** (Yusufpaşa tram stop), **Beyazıt** (near the tram stop), **Taksim, Beşiktaş,** and **Üsküdar.** It is generally best to go to one of these hubs and then catch the next bus you need from there, although there are a few much-traveled routes along which you can be sure to find the bus you need. Signs on the front of buses indicate the endpoints of the route, and signs on the right-hand side list the major places that the bus passes. Smaller stops aren't always posted. If you do not see your destination listed in the front window, step in and ask the driver: *"Bu otobus [destination] gider mi?"* ("Does this bus go to [destination]?") That should do the trick, or you can simply get on, look a bit lost and say the name of your destination. This will usually get the job done as well.

From **Sultanahmet,** bus #210 leaves from the Aya Sofia Meydanı, crosses the Galata Bridge, and heads up the European Bosphorus shore to Ortaköy and Bebek (every 20min.). From **Aksaray** and **Beyazıt,** multiple buses serve districts to the northwest along the Golden Horn (Yedikule Fortress, Zeyrek, Fatih, Fener, Balat, Edirnekapı, Eyüp). In the big bus lot at the foot of the Galata Bridge in **Eminönü,** six platforms *(peron)* serve different areas to the north and along the Bosphorus: Yeşilköy (#81) and Ataköy (#71) from *peron* #1; Karaköy, Beşiktaş, Bebek (all #22c) from *peron* #3; and Taksim (#46h) from *peron* #5. From Taksim Square, most buses head either north into the suburbs or southwest across the Atatürk Bridge to Aksaray and Beyazıt. Any given route has buses running in the reverse direction as well, and many routes are largely repeated by other buses. When the bus nears your stop, push the button on top of the door to alert the driver.

Even if you are using AKBİL, be sure to have a few spare bus tickets in the event of unexpected bus changes. By the same token, remember to have extra money in case you take a private bus—impossible to differentiate from a public one—which will require that you buy a ticket on board. A final note on buses: when riding the bus, courteous passengers should give their places to elderly riders and women with children if there are no available seats.

DOLMUŞ

Dolmuş, a venerable Turkish tradition, are minibuses that run along a fixed local route. Like buses, they're cheap, and the endpoints of their routes are posted in the front window. Because stops are not announced, it's easiest if you know what your stop looks like or if you want to get off at the end of the line. Dolmuş are generally unnecessary within most of İstanbul since buses are plentiful (with the exception of Kadıköy), but they can be helpful and are much more comfortable than city buses. Dolmuş run only during daylight hours and the early evening, and they are most active at the end of the workday, when people congregate on curbs all over the city, waiting for their ride home. They can be found near most of the major bus hubs, including Aksaray and Eminönü. Dolmuş also congregate around the Hippodrome in the early evening and in front of Aya Sofia throughout the day. The largest and most useful collection of dolmuş is in the side streets north of Taksim Square, where you can catch one to Beşiktaş, Sariyer, Karaköy, Kadıköy, or Aksaray. In neighborhoods far from the bustle of Taksim and Sultanahmet they serve as local group taxis, and it is best to hail them down as they crawl along streets picking up passengers on their way back into the center of İstanbul. For more information on dolmuş travel, see **Dolmuş Do's and Don'ts,** p. 69.

TRAMS, COMMUTER RAIL, AND METRO

The *tramvay* (tram) runs from Eminönü to Zeytinburnu ($.50 per ride). Since it's easy enough to follow the tracks, the tram is very useful for finding your way back to Sultanahmet even if you don't actually take it. A second tram begins behind the large mosque at the Yusufpaşa tram stop in the middle of Adnan Menderes Bul., and it heads to the outer suburbs of İstanbul (Zeytinburnu, Bakırköy, etc.) via the new **otogar** (intercity bus station). Built with consideration for modern İstanbul's sprawling expanse, the tram weaves through many of the city's major neighborhoods. Though there are only a couple of lines, the tram can drop you off within close proximity to many popular destinations.

The city continues to run a beautifully ramshackle **commuter rail** (known locally as *tren*) between Sirkeci Gar and İstanbul's far western suburbs. The upshot of the cars' age is that many of the windows have become stuck halfway down or are missing altogether, making for blessed ventilation and exhilarating views of the sea and ancient city walls along the southern coast of the European side. Watch your step getting on, though, as there are often gaps between the door and the edges of the platform. Despite its defects, the *tren* is a safe option, and many locals use it for their daily commute. For most visitors, the *tren* is good for two things: a more pleasant ride from Sultanahmet to Sirkeci and a cheaper route to the airport. To find the **Cankurtaran** station near Sultanahmet, head downhill and left from the Blue Mosque. The tracks run on an elevated path, parallel to the coastal road. It's a one-stop ride to Sirkeci along the seaside tracks. In the other direction, a 30min. ride goes to Yeşilyürt (near Yeşilköy), from where a cab to the airport is a mere $4. The *tren* runs the same hours as the tram and is just as cheap. Use AKBİL or a *jeton*. The combination of the two-stop **metro** and a trolley along İstiklâl Cad. makes for an easy way to get up to Taksim Square if you want to walk across the bridge from Eminönü and then catch the metro on the other side.

TAXI

Most cabs can be spotted from miles away, since the little yellow street bees have chrome wheels, lots of glittering evil eye protectors, and multiple hood ornaments with names like "saloon" or "sport." Given the chance, taxi drivers are even more reckless and speed-crazed than other İstanbul drivers. This is particularly true after midnight, when all public transportation is closed, roads are more empty, and drivers are eager to give their cars a workout after a day of traffic-jam crawl. Many Turkish taxi drivers are devoid of fear and eager to show off their ability to make their vehicles do maneuvers previously thought possible only on skateboards. If at any point you feel uncomfortable in a taxi, you can and should ask the driver to slow down *(Yavaş lütfen)* or to stop *(Dur!)*. That said, the undaunted say that high-speed cab rides late at night are good fun, and probably the only way you're going to see the blur of neon club signs and headlights of an İstanbul evening at 150mph.

FERRIES

Closer to a respite from the metro grind than a part of it, İstanbul's ferry system transforms mundane public transport into a scenic mini-cruise. They can also shave nearly an hour off transit between İstanbul's European and Asian sections. Ferries run primarily between Europe and Asia, though there is same-side service up the Bosphorus and to more remote points such as Yalova and the Prince's Islands (Adalar). Among the many boats that cluster around this port, the ferries are large white and green ships with yellow smokestacks that often spew a thin black smoke. Timetables are posted at each terminal. Before leaving for a far-off destination, be sure to check that there is a return ferry later in the day.

The following boats depart from the piers clustered around Galata Bridge in Sirkeci (each dock is labeled with the destination): **Üsküdar** (pier 1, every 15-20min. 6:30am-10pm, $.75); **Kadıköy** (pier 2, every 15-20min. 7:30am-8:30pm, $.75); **Prince's Islands** (Adalar) and **Yalova** (from a dock down past pier 1, on the other side of the car ferry; Yalova $3, Adalar $1.50); **Harem** (from a pier labeled "Posta" in large red print among the above piers, every 20min, $.75). To get to **Balat** and the Haydarpaşa train station, take a ferry across the Golden Horn to Karaköy, then catch a boat down to these points. Ferries to Karaköy leave often from the piers on the far side of the Galata Bridge and cost less than $1. From the car ferry near the Adalar dock, other ferries connect the various İstanbul suburbs every 30min. ($1-4). For details, buy a timetable (*feribot tarifesi;* $.60) at any pier.

Points on the Bosphorus are served by less frequent and more expensive day cruises. Some of the ferries to the north shore of the Golden Horn are commuter ferries. Since they leave in the morning and return in the evening, taking an evening ferry could leave you stranded. There is a day cruise that floats up the Golden Horn, docking at places like Fener and Balat and a couple of points further north. But if you're planning for a day in these neighborhoods rather than a day on the boat, it is best to reach these points by land.

Fast Seabus catamarans, each carrying up to 250 passengers, also run along the ferry routes. The seabus generally disembarks in the same area as the ferry, as the two dock in the same place at many destinations. Seabuses (recognizable by their leaping dolphin emblem) are twice as fast as ferries and cost about three to four times as much (average $4-5). Free timetables are available at the booths. You can get the latest updates from Seabus Information (☎216 362 04 44).:

ON THE LOOKOUT: TAXI SCAMS Though İstanbul's cabbies should by no means be considered generally corrupt, scams are widespread. Be especially alert if you don't speak Turkish and are catching a cab in Sultanahmet or Taksim. A common trick is to use the night rate (50% more after midnight) during the day. One light on the meter means day rate; two lights mean night rate. Other common scams are to give foreigners incorrect change, taking advantage of their unfamiliarity with the currency, or to intentionally not reset the cab's meter when you enter. Feel free to fix a price if you don't trust the driver or your ability to recognize an excessively long route. A ride between Sultanahmet and Taksim should be no more than $5 for a group of 3, and few rides in the central İstanbul area should cost more. You can shave $3-4 off a trip from Sultanahmet to Taksim by walking 500m up the tram tracks to Beyazıt and catching a cab there, where it's a straight shot to Taksim. Or if the tram is still running, ride it to the end of the line, get off at Eminönü, and hail one of the many cabs that sits by the waterside around the Galata Bridge. Especially in Sultanahmet, ask your hostel which cab stations are honest, as the cabs who wait in front of Aya Sofia are notoriously unscrupulous.

TRANSPORTATION SUGGESTIONS

FROM THE AIRPORT TO:

SULTANAHMET: From the international terminal, catch a Havaş bus to Aksaray (every 30min. 6am-9pm, $7). From there, catch an Eminönü-bound tram to Sultanahmet (walk uphill along the overpass to the Lâleli tram stop). Alternatively, split a cab ($8), or pick up İstanbul's *tren* in Yeşilyürt to Cankurtaran, which leaves you only a short walk (straight uphill) from Sultanahmet. It's cheaper and more fun than the Havaş, though less direct.

TAKSIM SQUARE: Stay on the Havaş bus. Airport-bound Havaş buses leave from the Havaş office on Cumhuriyet Cad., right off the square.

CAMPGROUNDS (FLORYA/ATAKÖY): They're not far from the airport and you need only take a cab once ($3), as the campgrounds are right next to a stop on the *tren* running frequently to the Sirkeci train station. From here you can either walk or catch buses to most everywhere else.

ASIAN İSTANBUL: Go either to Taksim, from which most of the Asia-bound buses leave, or to Eminönü (see Sultanahmet directions, above), from which both the Üsküdar and Harem Kadıköy ferries leave.

FROM SULTANAHMET TO:

TAKSİM SQUARE: Bus #61B runs infrequently between Beyazıt and Taksim. For faster transport, take the tram (Zeytinburnu-bound) to Yusufpaşa. From the platform, go up onto the overpass, head left, and catch the bus from the stop at the bottom. Taksim-bound buses pass at least every 5min. Alternatively, take a 5min. walk across the Galata Bridge, and catch the metro and then the trolley up to the square—a pleasant way with little hassle or crowds.

EMİNÖNÜ (Spice Bazaar, Ferries, Yeni Cami): Tram it to the end of the line, or walk 10min. along the line. The *tren* runs from Cankurtaran station down the hill from the Blue Mosque to Sirkeci Gar, a stone's throw from Eminönü.

EUROPEAN BOSPHORUS: (Kabataş, Beşiktaş, Arnavutköy, Ortaköy, Bebek; some buses follow inland routes to Rumeli Hisarüstü and Sariyer): Either take bus #210 from Aya Sofia Square *(Meydanı)* or buses #20-25 from Eminönü platform 3. Bus #40KT runs express from Taksim to the ferry port at Kabataş.

YEDİKULE: Take the commuter train from Cankurtaran station in Sultanahmet ($.40). Buses also leave from Eminönü, but from the stop on the waterfront side.

FENER, BALAT, EDİRNEKAPI, EYÜP: Buses run between Beyazıt and Edirnekapı, but it's quickest to tram to Yusufpaşa and then head to the Aksaray bus stop near the Aksaray Metro station on Adnan Menderes Bul. Bus #39E runs to Eyüp. The bus passes through the districts in the order listed above. Eyüp and Eyüp Sultan are essentially the same place.

FATIH: Take a bus marked Fatih or Draman from Beyazit (one stop on the tram from Sultanahmet) and get off at Fatih.

YALOVA: Use the ferry or the less frequent seabus service from Kabataş. Otherwise, take the seabus from Yeni Kapı on the *tren* line (every hr.).

ASIAN BOSPHORUS (Beylerbeyi, Anadolu Kavağı, Kanlica, Paşabahçe): Take a ferry to Üsküdar ($.60). From the main bus stop across from the *iskele* (ferry stop), catch a #15 bus, which will head up the Bosphorus.

PRINCE'S ISLANDS (ADALAR): Take the *"Adalar İskelesi"* ferry from Eminönü, the one closest to Sirkeci train station, next to the car ferry. High-speed catamarans to Adalar depart the Kabataş dock in late afternoon and early evening ($4).

SELİMİYE BARRACKS (Florence Nightingale's chambers): Take a ferry to Üsküdar ($.60). Catch one of the many buses ($.50) or a cab ($2) down to the Harem *iskele*/otogar. For an easier trip, take the ferry to Harem. The barracks can be seen uphill from the water.

KUMKAPI (fish restaurants): Avoid the very short, hot walk along Sahil Yolu during the day by catching the *tren* from Sirkeci or Cankurtaran stations.

PRACTICAL INFORMATION

İSTANBUL STREET SMARTS. Visitors to İstanbul should exercise the same common sense they would use in any large city (see **Personal Safety,** p. 46). "Touts," the men who call out to foreigners (particularly in Sultanahmet), are annoying but ultimately harmless. Feel free to ignore these hawkers; there's no need to even make eye contact (see **Financial Security,** p. 48).

TOURIST AND FINANCIAL SERVICES

Tourist Office: In Sultanahmet, 3 Divan Yolu (☎/fax 518 87 54), in the **white kiosk,** at the north end of the Hippodrome. Open daily 9am-5pm. In Taksim, the main office (☎233 05 92) is in the **Hilton Hotel Arcade** on Cumhuriyet Cad. Open daily 9am-5pm. A less-useful branch is near the **French consulate** (☎245 68 76). Open M-Sa 8:30am-5pm. There is a particularly helpful office in the **Sirkeci train station** (☎511 58 11; open daily 8:30am-5:30pm) and one at **Atatürk Airport** (☎573 41 36; open 24hr.). **Karaköy Maritime Station** (☎249 57 76) has a small booth. Open daily 8:30am-5pm.

Travel Agencies: Tourist agencies line the beginning of Divan Yolu Cad. and Akbıyık Cad., the main backpacker drag in Sultanahmet. Compare prices before sitting down to make a reservation, since there are often special deals at particular agencies, and prices tend to vary in general. That said, *Let's Go* recommends a few: **7-Tur,** 37 Gümüşsuyu Cad., 2nd fl., is İstanbul's STA Travel equivalent, and does all STA ticket changes. From Taksim Sq., walk downhill to the right of Atatürk Cultural Center. ISICs available ($15). **Tur-Ista,** 16 Divan Yolu (☎527 70 85 or 513 71 19), convenient for Sultanahmet, will arrange a free transport to the bus or train station if you buy a ticket through them. **Gençtur,** Prof. K. Ismail Gürkan Cad., Cağaloğlu Hamamı Sok., Kardeşler Iştlanı, 4th fl. (☎520 52 74 or 520 52 75; fax 519 08 64), a 5min. walk from Aya Sofia Meydanı up Yerebatan; the entrance is around the corner from the sign hanging on Yerebatan. Sells ISICs ($10) and GO25 cards ($10). Open M-F 9:30am-5pm, Sa 9:30am-1pm. Taksim branch of Gençtur, 15/5 İstiklâl Cad. (☎249 25 15), organizes volunteer work programs in villages. Open M-Sa 9:30am-6pm. **Indigo Tourism and Travel Agency,** 24 Akbıyık Cad. (☎517 72 66; fax 518 53 33; www.indigo-tour.com), is in the heart of the hotel cluster in Sultanahmet. Sells GO25 cards ($10) and ISIC cards only with valid student ID ($15). Services include bus, ferry, and plane tickets for Europe and the Middle East, airport shuttle service, city and Turkey tours, as well as *poste restante.* Internet upstairs ($1.50 per hr.). Open daily 8:30am-7:30pm; in winter M-Sa 9:30am-6pm.

Consulates: All open M-F. Area code ☎212. **Australia,** 58 Tepecik Yolu, Etiler (☎257 70 50; fax 257 70 54); visas 10am-noon. **Canada,** 107/3 Büyükdere Cad., Bengün Han, Gayrettepe (☎272 51 74; fax 272 34 27). **Ireland** (honorary), 25/A Cumhuriyet Cad., Mobil Altı, Elmadağ (☎246 60 25); visas 9:30-11:30am. **New Zealand,** Level 24, 100-102 Maya Akar Center, Büyükdere Cad., Esentepe (☎275 28 89; fax 275 50 08). **South Africa,** Serbetci Iş Merkezi, 106/15 Büyükdere Cad., Esentepe (☎288 04 28; fax 275 76 42); visas 9am-noon. **UK,** 34 Meşrutiyet Cad., PK33, Beyoğlu/Tepebaşı (☎293 75 40; fax 245 49 89); visas 8:30am-noon. **US,** 104-108 Meşrutiyet Cad., Tepebaşı (☎251 36 02; fax 251 32 18); visas 8:30-11am.

Banks: Currency exchange counters open M-F 8:30am-noon and 1:30-5pm. Most don't charge commission. MC/V **ATM cards** work almost everywhere, and nearly all ATMs have an English-language option. **Pamukbank** machines at the airport, Taksim Sq., and Sirkeci accept practically every kind of card, as do **Garanti Bank** machines. **şekerbank** (1 location on Yenicirler Cad. in Çemberllitaş) and **Akbank** (1 location on Divan Yolu) are also good. Akbank and Vakıf Bank machines also take AmEx. **Yapı ve Kredi, Türkiye İş Bankası, TC Ziraat Bankası,** and **Vakıf Bank** are scattered throughout the city and accept most cards. **Traveler's checks** can be changed at any sizeable branch of the above banks, though the process often takes about 10-15min. and requires more paperwork than seems necessary. Change windows in Sultanahmet offer poor rates and charge 2-4% commission, but are often open late and on the weekends.

American Express: Türk Express, 47/1 Cumhuriyet Cad., 3rd fl. (☎235 95 00), uphill from Taksim Sq., handles lost checks and cards as well as other related AmEx business. Open M-F 9am-6pm. Their office in the Hilton Hotel lobby (☎230 15 15), Cumhuriyet Cad., offers *poste restante* and deals with lost cards when the main office is closed. Open daily 8:30am-8:30pm. Neither branch actually handles the financial side of replacing lost cards or checks, nor do they give cash advances or accept wired money, as Turkish law requires it be done through a bank. AmEx's agent is **Akbank,** with branches across the city. Money is wired without fee if you accept Turkish lira; 1% fee for other currencies. To get a cash advance on your card, you must have a personal check or know the account number and address of your bank. Attempt this service only after visiting an AmEx branch office. Cardholder services until 4pm only.

LOCAL SERVICES

English-Language Bookstores: In Sultanahmet, **kiosks** at the Blue Mosque, on Aya Sofia Meydanı, and on Divan Yolu sell international papers, as does **International Press Büfe** in front of 91 İstiklâl Cad. in Beyoğlu. **Galeri Kayseri,** 58 Divan Yolu (☎512 04 56; galerikayseryi@ihlas.net.tr), caters to thinking tourists. Its helpful owner keeps the shop open daily 9am-9pm. **Balkaya İnşaat Bookstore** at the exit of the Underground Cistern (see p. 116) has a good but sometimes pricey selection of books on the history, poetry, and arts of the region. Convenient for travelers in the backpacker strip, Akbıyık, you can exchange books at the **Traveler's Book exchange** if you're just looking for a trashy novel. For more travel books and contemporary novels, there is the tasteful **Robinson Crusoe,** 389 İstiklâl Cad. (☎293 69 68), where books in English are on the right side of the store. Open M-Sa 9am-9pm, Su 10am-9pm. Off Galatasaray Sq., **Homer Kitabevi,** 28A Yeniçarşı Cad. (☎249 59 02), aims for academic comprehensiveness; you'd be hard-pressed to find an English-language "Gender Theory" section anywhere else in the city. Open M-Sa 9:30am-7:30pm. Walk through a small underwear shop to get upstairs to **Literatür,** 133 İstiklâl Cad. (☎292 41 20). The store has a wide-ranging collection, from art to finance. Open M-Sa 9am-8pm.

Laundromat: Star Laundry, 18 Akbıyık Cad. (☎638 23 02), below Star Pension in Sultanahmet. English spoken. Wash and dry $1.50 per kg; 2kg min. Open daily 8am-8pm.

EMERGENCY AND COMMUNICATIONS

Emergency: ☎155 from any phone.

Tourist Police: In Sultanahmet, at the beginning of Yerebatan Cad. (24hr. hotline ☎527 45 03 or 528 53 69; fax 512 76 76). They speak the best English of all local cops, and their mere presence causes hawkers and postcard-selling kids to scatter.

Pharmacies: The Turkish word for pharmacy (or chemist) is *eczanesi*. All of them offer the basics of personal hygiene (deodorant, toothbrush and paste, hair products, tampons, etc.) and all can fill a prescription. In many cases the pharmacists do not speak English. **Çemberlitaş Eczanesi,** No. 46 Vezirhan Cad. (☎522 69 69), off Divan Yolu by the Çemberlitaş tram stop, is among the most professional and helpful in the neighborhood. The pharmacy also offers optometry services. Open M-Sa 7:30am-8pm. **Ayasofya Eczanesi,** No. 28 Divan Yolu (☎513 72 15; fax 511 80 04), near the main sights, is stocked with all the necessities. Open M-Sa 8:30am-7:30pm. Across the Golden Horn, **Taksim Eczanesi** (☎244 31 95), right off the square on İstiklâl Cad., stocks most everything you could wish for or need. Fills prescriptions. Open M-F 9am-7pm.

Hospitals: American Hospital, Admiral Bristol Hastanesi, 20 Güzelbahçe Sok., Nişantaşı (☎231 40 50), is highly regarded by İstanbul natives and tourists and has many English-speaking doctors. The **German Hospital,** 119 Sıraselviler Cad., Taksim (☎251 71 00, 251 71 01 or 251 71 02), also has a multilingual staff and is more conveniently located for Sultanahmet hostelers. Also available is the **International Hospital,** 82 İstanbul Cad., Yeşilköy (☎663 30 00). All hospitals expect payment with cash or a credit card at the time of treatment. The state-run **Taksim İlkyardım Hastanesi** (Taksim First Aid Hospital), 112 Sıraselviler Cad. (☎252 43 00), offers cheaper services.

Internet Access: Prevalent in low-rent corners and hostels all over Sultanahmet and Taksim. Despite its name, **The Antique Internet Cafe,** 51 Kutlugün Sok., offers a fast connection and big plush chairs in a relaxing spot. Antique also serves tea, cold sodas, and tasty meals (omelettes and salads from $1.50). $1.50 per hr. Open 24hr. **The Sinem Internet Cafe,** 16 Dr. Emin Paşa Sok. (☎513 62 77), in an alley off Divan Yolu by the metro stop, 3 floors up from street level. Waits are rare at this pleasant Sultanahmet cafe with tapestries, cushions, and full drink service. $1.25 per hr. Open daily 9am-midnight. **Cafein Internet Cafe,** 21A Bekar Sok. (☎252 18 66), near the upper end of İstiklâl Cad. $1.20 per hr. Open 10am-11:30pm. The **British Council Library,** 253 İstiklâl Cad., 3rd fl., offers a wider-screen connection. $1.80 per hr. Open Tu 10:30am-8:30pm, W 10:30am-6:30pm, Th-F 10:30am-5:30pm, Sa 9:30am-2:30pm.

PTT: İstanbul has more than 100 post offices. The most convenient for Sultanahmet-dwellers is the yellow booth opposite the entrance to Aya Sofia on Aya Sofia Meydanı, where you can change money and get stamps. The **main branch** is in Sirkeci, 25 Büyük Postane Sok. Stamp and currency exchange services open 8:30am-midnight. 24hr. phones. A branch off the north end of Taksim Sq., at the mouth of Cumhuriyet Cad., is convenient for mailing packages or making calls. 24hr. international phone office, but no collect calls allowed. Open M-F 8am-8pm, Sa 8am-6pm. All PTTs accept packages; if a customs officer is not present, you may be directed to the Kadıköy, Beyazıt, or Tophane (on Rıhtım Cad.) offices. Keep larger packages open so the customs or postal officials can check them if they want. Card phones are a convenient way to make phone calls. You can buy cards with 30, 60, or 100 *kontür* (credits). 1 credit lasts 2-10 seconds during international calls.

Sirkeci postal code: 5270050 and 5270051.

ACCOMMODATIONS & CAMPING

İstanbul's budget accommodations are mainly in touristy **Sultanahmet,** clustered on a few streets just steps away from the city's most awe-inspiring sights. The **Taksim** district, home to many of the city's five-star hotels and a smattering of budget lodgings, is less touristy than Sultanahmet. The side streets around **Sirkeci** railway station and **Aksaray** offer dozens of dirt-cheap hotels, but these neighborhoods are not pleasant places to stay. **Lâleli** is the center of prostitution in İstanbul and should be avoided. Rates can increase by up to 20% in July and August.

SULTANAHMET

This small neighborhood, bounded by the **Blue Mosque, Aya Sofia,** and the walls of the **Topkapı Palace,** is the tourism capital of İstanbul. Hostel accommodations are fairly generic here, and according to some owners, the better hostels tend to fix prices among themselves. The main differences between the hostels usually involve the availability of hot water and other amenities. Most establishments request that you pay one night at a time, and $5-7 is the average going rate for a bed in a dormitory room. Belly dancer performances and *Efes*-sodden happy hours are common evening events in the hostels, whose guests tend to be short-term transients in the city on their way to points east in Turkey, the Greek Islands, or back into Europe. But while the high density of travelers in this four-block area will provide you with a wealth of international acquaintances, getting away from the numerous basement bars and terrace cafes will give you a better chance to experience one of the world's best collections of historic architectural behemoths. In the off-season, usually November through March, prices tend to drop by 10-15%.

CHEAP SLEEPS

İstanbul Hostel, 35 Kutlugün Sok. (☎516 93 80; fax 516 93 84; info@valide.com or istanbulhostel@hotmail.com; www.istanbul-hostel.com). From the path between Aya Sofia and the Blue Mosque, walk south down Tevkifhane Sok., past the Four Seasons Hotel to Kutlugün Sok; the hostel is on your right. This large hostel offers all major amenities, and its breezy, sunny bedrooms and marble-floored bathrooms are the cleanest in town. Has a fireplace, music, nightly movies, satellite TV, and a friendly staff. Breakfast $1. Lunch and dinner $2. **Happy hour** 6:30-9:30pm at downstairs "Buzz Bar" (beer $1.75), which is exceptionally sleaze-free. Superfast **Internet connection** is $.80 per fifteen minutes, $1.70 per 30min., and $2.20 per hr. 24hr. hot water. **Lockers** and **luggage storage** free. Adjacent travel agency. Airport shuttle service with advance booking $2.60 per person. Dorms $6; quads $7; doubles $16; deluxe with TV and bath $30.

Moonlight Pension, 87 Akbıyık Cad. (☎517 54 29 or 518 85 36; fax 516 24 80; moonlight@superonline.com; http://abone.superonline.com/~moonlight). An inexpensive pension a few blocks away from the hustle and bustle of the backpacker scene, Moonlight offers clean, spare rooms and a kind staff. Clear rooftop views, bar, communal kitchen. Cable TV in reception. Fax available. Internet $1.50 per hr. Laundry service $4 per load. Snacks $3. Breakfast $2. 15 rooms; ask for one with a shower (same price). Dorms $5; doubles $16; triples $21. MC/V.

Seagull Pension, Küçük Ayasofya Cad., Aksakal Sok. 22 (☎517 11 42; fax 516 09 72; seagullpension@hotmail.com; www.seagullpension.cjb.net). From Aya Sofya, head down Küçük Ayasofya Cad down the hill toward the Marmara. A block before Kennedy Cad. and the sea, look for the sign on your right. Blissfully removed from the rest of touristy Sultanhamet, this peaceful place provides a great bargain as well as unbeatable access to the sea and the train. Breakfast included on the terrace, where the sea breeze will energize you for a day of trekking around the town. Internet $1.75 per hr. Airport transportation $3.50 per person. 24hr. hot water. Dorms $5, private rooms $8-10.

Nayla Palace Pansion, 22 Kutlugün Sok. (☎516 35 67; fax 516 63 06; nayla@superonline.com). Walk past the Four Seasons, turn right on Kutlugün, head down 2 blocks on the right. A homey atmosphere and quiet garden courtyard make this a good backpacker hideaway. Great view of Marmara from rooftop lounge. Internet $1 per hr. Breakfast included. Dorm beds $5; singles with bath $15; doubles $25, with bath $30; triples with bath $35. Traveler's checks and cash only.

Sultan Hostel, 3 Terbıyık Sok. (☎/fax 516 92 60; sultan@feztravel.com; www.sultanhostel.com), off Akbıyık Cad., around the corner from Orient Hostel. Great views of the sea from the rooftop restaurant and large bar (sandwiches $1.50-3; beer $1.50). The **happy hour** gets very happy (5-8pm). In-house travel office. TV and VCR in common room, with nightly movies. Internet $1.50 per hr. **Belly dancing** Tu and Sa; **water pipe nights** M and Th; **BBQ** F ($2). Breakfast $1.80. Free safe-deposit, luggage storage. 100 beds. 8-bed dorms $6; singles $12; doubles $16; quads $7. MC/V.

Konya Pansiyon, 15/2 Terbıyık Sok. (☎638 36 38). Walk down Adliye Sok., 1 block past Akbıyık Sok., and turn right around the corner. Cheap and cheerful, but expect to get what you pay for: the only furniture you'll find here are the beds. Konya is quiet and tidy, however, and only a block from the action on Akbıyık Sok. Dingy guest kitchen off concrete "garden." Airport transportation $4 per person. Internet $1 per hr. Free safe box. Breakfast $2. Basement dorm $4; regular dorm $5; doubles $14, with shower $30.

THE LUXURY OF A TURKISH PRISON Before its present incarnation as İstanbul's most luxurious (and expensive) accommodation, the ochre-colored Four Seasons Hotel was a less-than-glamorous high-security Turkish prison. Converting it into a four-star hotel a mere four years ago, interior designers maintained the original size of each room and used furniture sparingly in order to harken back to the building's more glorious days. The prison yard used for the inmates' daily exercise now hosts a deluxe restaurant with an Italian chef, and the old watchtower doubles as a site for wedding banquets. Other prison elements have also been restored; one central marble column bears an etched-in prisoner's name with a 1935 date and a pierced heart scribble. While architects left much of the original building intact, one thing that has changed is the price: rooms range from $200-2000 and the 65 available rooms are booked solid. What an escape!

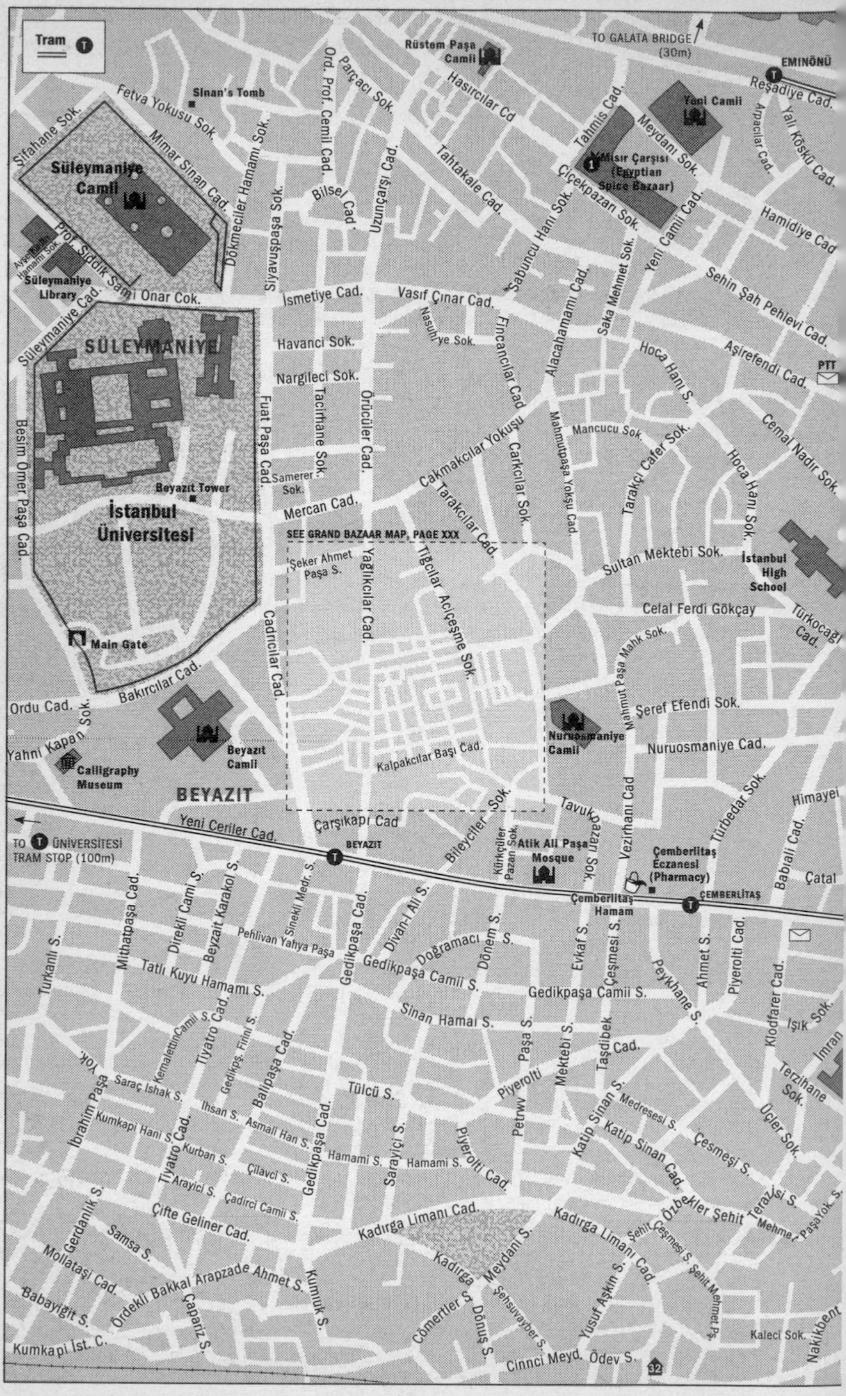
Tram
TO GALATA BRIDGE (30m)
EMINÖNÜ
Rüstem Paşa Camii
Sinan's Tomb
Fetva Yokusu Sok.
Şifahane Sok.
Süleymaniye Camii
Mimar Sinan Cad.
Dökmeciler Hamamı Sok.
Siyavuşpaşa Sok.
Ord. Prof. Cemil Cad.
Parçacı Sok.
Bilsel Cad.
Uzunçarşı Cad.
Hasırcılar Cd
Tahtakale Cad.
Tahmis Cad.
Yeni Camii
Reşadiye Cad.
Arpacılar Cad.
Yalı Köşkü Cad.
Meydanı Sok.
Mısır Çarşısı (Egyptian Spice Bazaar)
Çiçekpazarı Sok.
Yeni Camii Cad.
Hamidiye Cad.
Sabuncu Hanı Sok.
Saka Mehmet Sok.
Alacahamamı Cad.
Şehin Şah Pehlevi Cad.
Aşirefendi Cad.
Hoca Hanı S.
PTT
Prof. Sıddık Sami Onar Cok.
Süleymaniye Library
Süleymaniye Cad.
İsmetiye Cad.
Vasıf Çınar Cad.
Nasuhiye Sok.
Fincancılar Cad.
SÜLEYMANİYE
Havancı Sok.
Nargileci Sok.
Tacirhane Sok.
Örücüler Cad.
Fuat Paşa Cad.
Mahmutpaşa Yokuşu Cad.
Mancucu Sok.
Tarakçı Cafer Sok.
Cemal Nadir Sok.
Hoca Hanı Sok.
Besim Ömer Paşa Cad.
Beyazıt Tower
Samerer Sok.
Çakmakcılar Yokuşu
Çarkçılar Sok.
Mercan Cad.
İstanbul Üniversitesi
Tarakçılar Cad.
SEE GRAND BAZAAR MAP, PAGE XXX
Şeker Ahmet Paşa S.
Yağlıkcılar Cad.
Tığcılar
Acıçeşme Sok.
Sultan Mektebi Sok.
İstanbul High School
Celal Ferdi Gökçay
Türkocağı Cad.
Mahmut Paşa Mahk Sok.
Main Gate
Cadırcılar Cad.
Bakırcılar Cad.
Ordu Cad.
Yahni Kapan Sok.
Şeref Efendi Sok.
Nuruosmaniye Camii
Nuruosmaniye Cad.
Calligraphy Museum
Beyazıt Camii
Kalpakcılar Başı Cad.
BEYAZIT
Vezirhanı Cad.
Tavuk Pazarı Sok.
Türbedar Sok.
Himayei
Yeni Ceriler Cad.
Çarşıkapı Cad
TO ÜNIVERSITESI TRAM STOP (100m)
BEYAZIT
Biteyciler Sok.
Kürkçüler Pazarı Sok.
Atik Ali Paşa Mosque
Çemberlitaş Eczanesi (Pharmacy)
Babıali Cad.
Çatal
Çemberlitaş Hamam
ÇEMBERLİTAŞ
Mithatpaşa Cad.
Direkli Camii S.
Beyzait Karakol S.
Sinekli Medr. S.
Gedikpaşa Cad.
Divan-ı Ali S.
Dönem S.
Evkaf S.
Çeşmesi S.
Ahmet S.
Piyerolti Cad.
Turkanlı S.
Pehlivan Yahya Paşa
Doğramacı S.
Tatlı Kuyu Hamamı S.
Gedikpaşa Camii S.
Peykhane S.
Klodfarer Cad.
Işık Sok.
Sinan Hamai S.
Kemalettin Camii S.
Tiyatro Cad.
Gedikpş. Fırını S.
Ballıpaşa Cad.
Paşa S.
Mektebi S.
Taşdibek Cad.
İmran
Yok.
Saraç Ishak S.
Tülcü S.
Piyerolti
Terzihane Sok.
İbrahim Paşa
Ihsan S.
Kumkapı Hanı S.
Asmalı Han S.
Petrvv
Katip Sinan S.
Medresesi S.
Katip Sinan Cad.
Çeşmeşi S.
Üçler Sok.
Tiyatro Cad.
Kurban S.
Hamami S.
Hamami S.
Sarayiçi S.
Piyerolti Cad
Arayici S.
Çilavcı S.
Çadırcı Camii S.
Gedikpaşa Cad.
Gerdanlık S.
Çifte Geliner Cad.
Kadırga Limanı Cad.
Kadırga Limanı Cad.
Özbekler Şehit
Terazisi S.
Mehmet Paşa Yok. S.
Samsa S.
Mollataşı Cad.
Meydanı S.
Kadırga
Şehit Çeşmesi S.
Şehit Mehmet Ps.
Ördekli Bakkal Arapzade Ahmet S.
Kumluk S.
Yusuf Aşkın S.
Babayiğit S.
Çapariz S.
Cömertler S.
Dönüş S.
Şehsuvarbey S.
Kaleci Sok.
Nakilbent
Kumkapı İst. C.
Cinnci Meyd.
Ödev S.
32

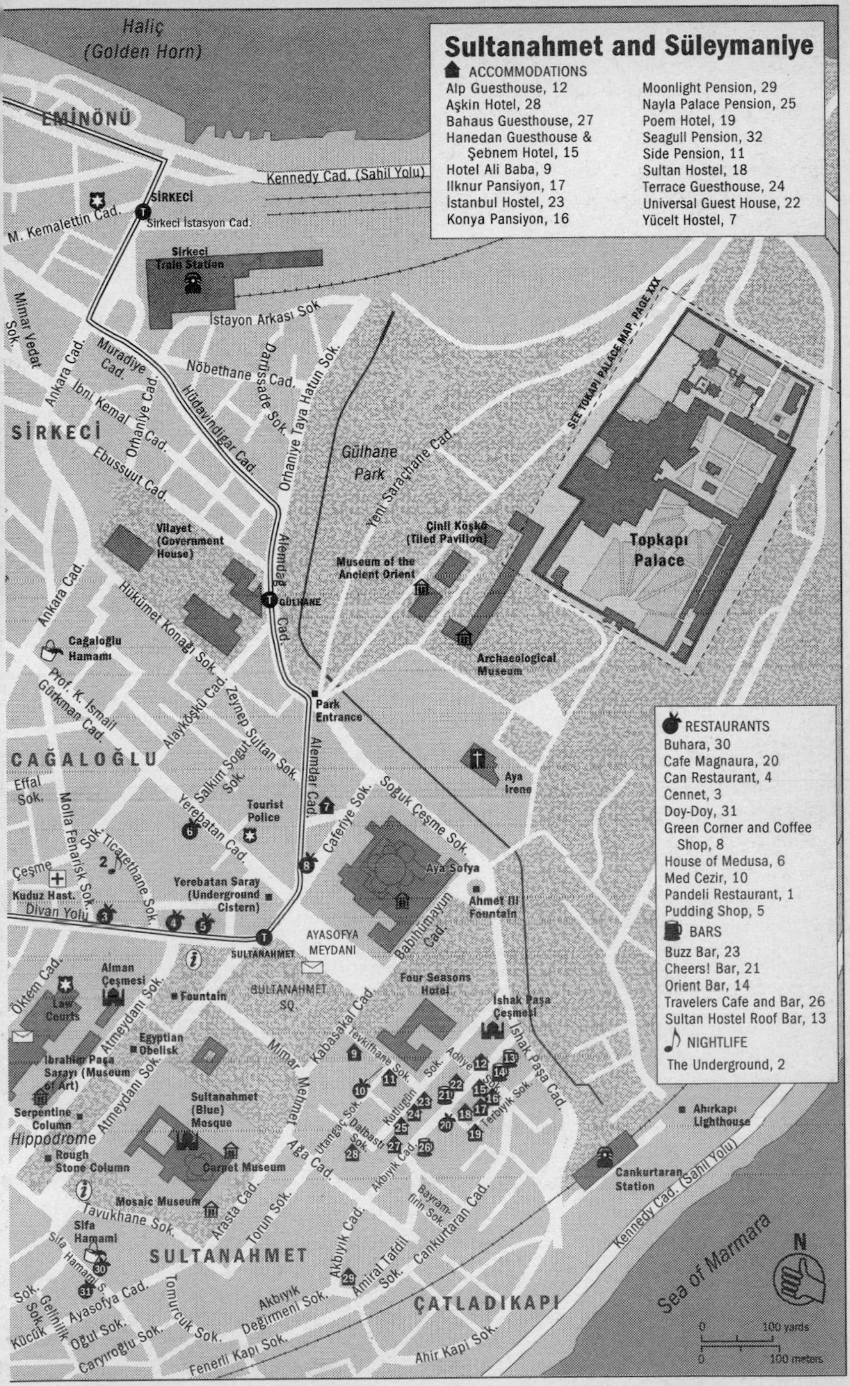
Sultanahmet and Süleymaniye
ACCOMMODATIONS
Alp Guesthouse, 12
Aşkin Hotel, 28
Bahaus Guesthouse, 27
Hanedan Guesthouse & Şebnem Hotel, 15
Hotel Ali Baba, 9
Ilknur Pansiyon, 17
İstanbul Hostel, 23
Konya Pansiyon, 16
Moonlight Pension, 29
Nayla Palace Pension, 25
Poem Hotel, 19
Seagull Pension, 32
Side Pension, 11
Sultan Hostel, 18
Terrace Guesthouse, 24
Universal Guest House, 22
Yücelt Hostel, 7
RESTAURANTS
Buhara, 30
Cafe Magnaura, 20
Can Restaurant, 4
Cennet, 3
Doy-Doy, 31
Green Corner and Coffee Shop, 8
House of Medusa, 6
Med Cezir, 10
Pandeli Restaurant, 1
Pudding Shop, 5
BARS
Buzz Bar, 23
Cheers! Bar, 21
Orient Bar, 14
Travelers Cafe and Bar, 26
Sultan Hostel Roof Bar, 13
NIGHTLIFE
The Underground, 2
Haliç (Golden Horn)
EMİNÖNÜ
SİRKECİ
Kennedy Cad. (Sahil Yolu)
M. Kemalettin Cad.
Sirkeci İstasyon Cad.
Sirkeci Train Station
İstayon Arkası Sok.
SEE TOPKAPI PALACE MAP PAGE XXX
Topkapı Palace
Gülhane Park
Yeni Saraçhane Cad.
Çinli Köşkü (Tiled Pavilion)
Museum of the Ancient Orient
Archaeological Museum
GÜLHANE
Alemdar Cad.
Vilayet (Government House)
Cağaloğlu Hamamı
CAĞALOĞLU
Park Entrance
Aya Irene
Tourist Police
Soğuk Çeşme Sok.
Caferiye Sok.
Aya Sofya
Ahmet III Fountain
Yerebatan Saray (Underground Cistern)
Kuduz Hast.
Divan Yolu
SULTANAHMET
AYASOFYA MEYDANI
SULTANAHMET SQ.
Four Seasons Hotel
İshak Paşa Çeşmesi
Alman Çeşmesi
Law Courts
Fountain
Egyptian Obelisk
İbrahim Paşa Sarayı (Museum of Art)
Serpentine Column
Hippodrome
Rough Stone Column
Sultanahmet (Blue) Mosque
Carpet Museum
Mosaic Museum
Sifa Hamami
Ahırkapı Lighthouse
Cankurtaran Station
Kennedy Cad. (Sahil Yolu)
Sea of Marmara
SULTANAHMET
ÇATLADIKAPI
Ahır Kapı Sok.
Fenerli Kapı Sok.
0 100 yards
0 100 meters
N

Ilknur Pansiyon, Terbıyık Sok., 22 (☎517 68 34 or 517 68 33). One block past Akbıyık on Aldiye, turn right around the corner onto Terbıyık. By far the cheapest place in town, this new pension is run by a delightful Turkish couple and features a pleasantly breezy attic dorm. Claims to have 24hr. hot water. Extensive lending library. Basement terrace offers a guest kitchen, although you'll have to pay for gas. Dorm $3.50; singles with bath $5.80; quads $10.60; prices negotiable for longer stays.

Yücelt Hostel/Interyouth Hostel (HI), 6/1 Caferiye Cad. (☎522 95 01; fax 512 76 28; info@yucelthostel.com; www.yucelthostel.com). From the tram stop at Sultanahmet Sq., walk down Caferiye Cad. on the left side of Aya Sofia. This massive, impersonal, 3-building complex has free billiards, table tennis, computer service, travel library, book exchange, safe boxes, and luggage storage, as well as videos in the rooftop lounge. Clean bathrooms and friendly staff make this a backpacker favorite. Laundry $1.50 per load. Reception claims to speak German and French. Dinner $3. Breakfast $3. 320 beds. Dorms $7-9; singles $18; doubles $18; triples $27. MC/V.

MID-RANGE

Side Pension/Hotel Side, 20 Utangaç Sok. (☎517 65 90; fax 517 65 90; info@sidehotel.com; www.sidehotel.com). Near the entrance of the Four Seasons Hotel. Look for the giant bearded heads. This hotel/pension combination occupies the 2 handsome wooden buildings by the corner of Tevkifhane Sok. and Utangaç Sok. The pension in the newer building offers simple rooms with brightly painted walls, while the hotel provides better furnished rooms with private bathrooms. Breakfast included on rooftop terrace. 24hr. hot water. 40 rooms. Pension singles $20; doubles $25; triples $35. Add $10 for clean, modern bathroom. Hotel singles $40; doubles $50; triples $60. Basement apartment with kitchen, bath, TV also available. Subtract 20% in winter. MC/V.

Bahaus Guesthouse, Akbıyık Cad., 11 Bayram Fırını Sok. (☎517 66 97; fax 517 66 97). From the front of the Blue Mosque, walk down Mimar Mehmet Ağa Cad. 2 blocks, and turn left on Akbıyık Cad. The guesthouse is on your left. This bright yellow, well-decorated hotel has spare, classy rooms and a terrace view of the Sea of Marmara. Free backgammon lessons from the owner. Cable TV in lobby. International phone service. Terrace has various musical instruments for the traveler in need of a tune-up. Breakfast included. 16 rooms. Singles $20; doubles $25, with bath $35; triples $40.

Hotel Ali Baba, Tevkifhane Sok., 12 (☎638 19 67 or 518 00 30; fax 517 17 83; bartamay@hotmail.com; www.istanbulguide.net.tr/hotelalibaba). Turn left at the end of Kabasakal Cad., which runs perpendicular to Ayasofya Meydanı. From here Tevkifhane leads to the Four Seasons, and backpacker-land beyond. Ali Baba is directly across from the Four Seasons, above a carpet shop of the same name; but don't worry, the two operations are completely separate. A great value for backpackers or families. Spacious, comfy rooms with minibar and bathtub/shower. Some with personal balconies. Help-yourself kitchen on a spectacular terrace with views of the Aya Sofia and the Blue Mosque. Singles and doubles $30-35; triples $60. MC/V.

Universal Guest House, Akbıyık Cad., 18 (☎638 22 70; fax 638 22 71; universalguesthouse@yahoo.com). Along the main backpacker strip, Universal has a friendly staff who will trade stories with you in English, French, or Italian at their downstairs Traveler's Cafe, where major renovations are planned for 2002. All 6 rooms have cable, fridge, nice bathroom, and A/C. Breakfast included. Lunch and dinner $5. Singles $20; doubles $25-30.

Alp Guesthouse, Akbıyık Cad., 4 Adliye Sok. (☎517 95 70 or 518 57 28; alpguesthouse@turk.net). Head down Tevkifhane Sok., turn left after the Four Seasons and take the first right. The guesthouse is down 2 blocks on your left. A family-run hotel with Mediterranean ambiance, the Alp boasts spacious, spotless rooms with minibar and international telephone. Some rooms offer views of the Marmara. Frequent BBQs; drinks until 11pm the terrace with superb views of Aya Sofia. Breakfast included. Free airport transport with 3-day stay. Free Internet, safe-deposit, and luggage storage. All 12 rooms with bath. Singles $30; doubles $50; triples $60. Cash and traveler's checks only.

Aşkın Hotel, 16 Dalbastı Sok. (☎638 86 74; fax 638 86 76; hotelaskin@hotmail.com). From Sultanahmet Sq., walk down Mimar Mehmet Ağa Cad., turn left on Utangaç Sok., and take 1st right. 20 rooms decorated in Ottoman style, complete with ornate furniture. Private toilets and clean bathtubs offer the most peace and quiet you'll get outside of a hamam. Reception organizes tours of and cruises on the Bosphorus. Lobby bar with pleasant sitting room. Breakfast included. All 20 rooms with A/C. Singles $40; doubles $60; triples $75; 10% discount if you pay in cash. MC/V.

Hanedan Hotel, Akbıyık Cad., 3 Adliye Sok. (☎516 48 69; fax 517 45 24; www.hanedanhotel.com). Walk down Tevfikhane Sok., turn left after the Four Seasons, and take the 1st right. The hotel is down 2 blocks on the right. Pleasant view from terrace, a beautiful cafeteria, and currency exchange. 24hr. free airport pick-up with minimum 3-day stay. The ultra-friendly staff offers discounted tours (for guests only), travel advice, drinks (beer $2) and free nightly movies. Breakfast included; other meals ($3-5) served on the roof in the summer. Most rooms have bathroom; 2 with view of the water. Singles $25; doubles $35; triples $45.

ISTANBUL

THE BUDGET INDULGENCE

Poem Hotel, Akbıyık Cad., 12 Terbıyık Sok. (☎/fax 517 68 36; hotelpoem@superonline.com). Quiet, luxurious rooms are marked with titles of Turkish poems instead of room numbers; all have Bosphorus views. Turkish breakfast included, served in garden. Female friendly. Free Internet. Lunch, dinner $10. Welcome drink on the house. 12 rooms with safe-deposit, TV, A/C, and superb full bath. Singles $45; doubles $65; triples from $80. Prices 25% lower in winter. MC/V.

Terrace Guesthouse, 39 Kutlugün Sok. (☎638 97 33; fax 638 97 34; terrace@escortnet.com). Charming and peaceful hotel with carpet-lined walls (carpets sold for $125-1000), which hush the noise from outside. Attentive staff. Most rooms offer great views of the sea. Small library/book exchange. Coffee and tea always available. Breakfast included, served on rooftop lounge. Reservations recommended. All 6 rooms have private bath. Singles $45; doubles $60; triples $70. MC/V.

Sebnem Hotel, 1 Akbıyık Cad. (☎517 66 23; fax 638 10 56; sebnemhotel@superonline.com; www.sebnemhotel.com). Walk down Tevflkhane Sok., turn left after the Four Seasons, and take 1st right. Sebnem is down 2 blocks on your right. This pink-walled, converted house has 15 rooms, each with a private, tiled bathroom, canopy bed, and dark wood furniture. Super-deluxe yacht tours can be arranged for a negotiable price, around $80. Safe-deposit provided at desk. Breakfast included, served on terrace. A/C, fridge, and international phone in all rooms. Singles $35; doubles $50; triples $60. MC/V.

TAKSİM

The countless hotels on almost every side street off İstiklâl Cad. are not bad options for cheap sleeps. Most places start around $9; rooms always have private baths and, in many cases, telephones. That tends to be the extent of the amenities and few of the proprietors speak English, but the convenience of location and reasonable cost make these worthwhile.

Hotel As, 26 Bekar Sok. (☎252 65 25; fax 245 00 99). Off upper İstiklâl Cad. Unbeatable price and location make the wear and tear seem charming. Singles and doubles have plenty of room, though their private baths are cramped. Tiny balconies overlook busy cafe alleys. All rooms with bath and phone. 36 rooms, 66 beds. Singles $10; doubles $17; triples $21. Parties of 10 or more: singles $8; doubles $14; triples $18.

Hotel Plaza, 19-21 Aslanyataği Sok. (☎245 32 73; fax 293 70 40). Down Arslanyata Sok., the small side street off Siraselviler. Bear left when Arslanyata turns right. The Plaza is a big, rambling building in a shady courtyard perfectly removed from Taksim's hustle–a good place to write your novel. Quiet, tattered, but classy rooms, some with great Bosphorus views, sitting rooms, fridges, glass tables and large windows. Breakfast included. Singles $20; doubles $40; "student rooms" (rooms showing their age) have negotiable prices depending in the length of your stay, around $7 per night.

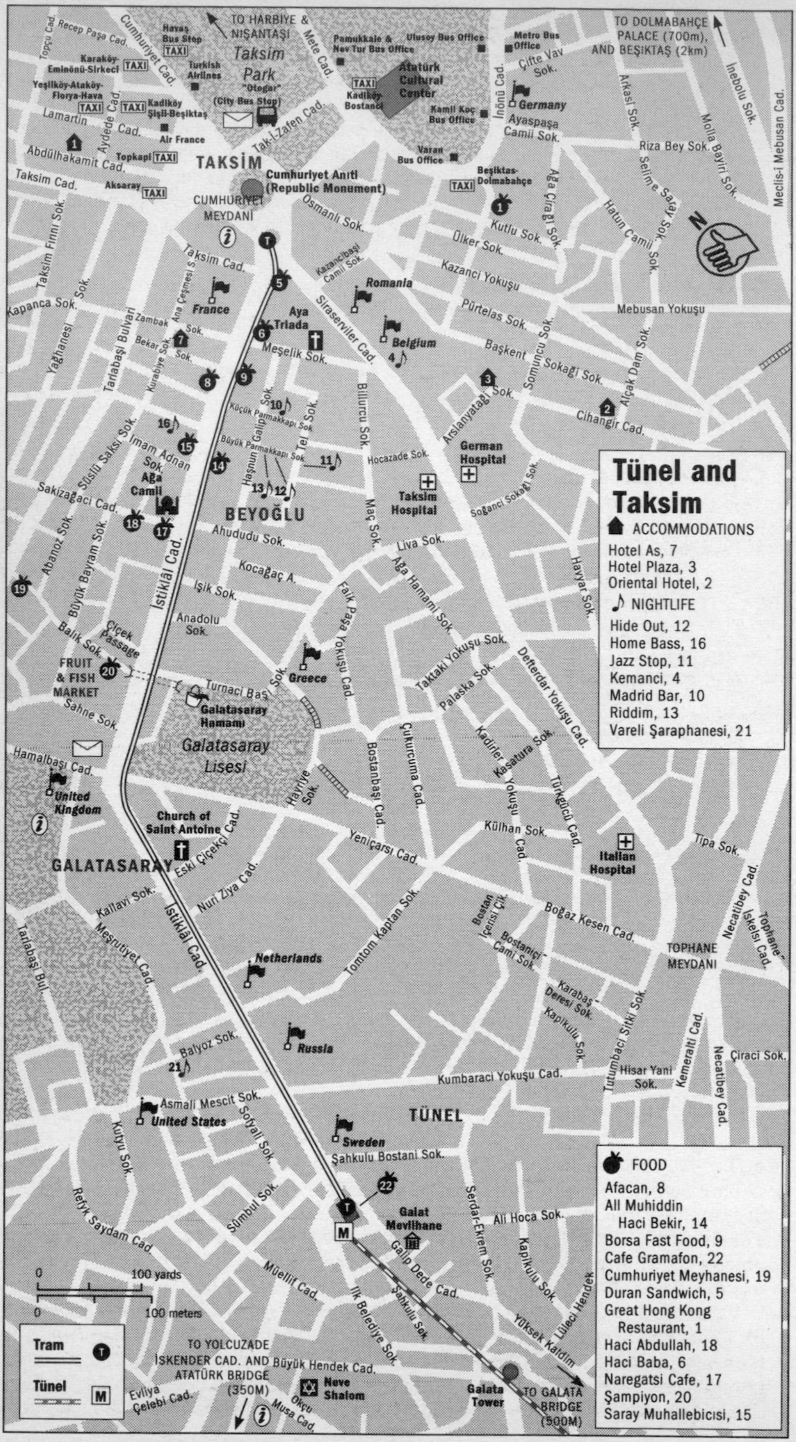

Tünel and Taksim
ACCOMMODATIONS
Hotel As, 7
Hotel Plaza, 3
Oriental Hotel, 2
NIGHTLIFE
Hide Out, 12
Home Bass, 16
Jazz Stop, 11
Kemanci, 4
Madrid Bar, 10
Riddim, 13
Vareli Şaraphanesi, 21
FOOD
Afacan, 8
All Muhiddin Haci Bekir, 14
Borsa Fast Food, 9
Cafe Gramafon, 22
Cumhuriyet Meyhanesi, 19
Duran Sandwich, 5
Great Hong Kong Restaurant, 1
Haci Abdullah, 18
Haci Baba, 6
Naregatsi Cafe, 17
Şampiyon, 20
Saray Muhallebicisi, 15
Tram
Tünel
0
100 yards
0
100 meters
TO HARBİYE & NİŞANTAŞI
TO DOLMABAHÇE PALACE (700m), AND BEŞIKTAŞ (2km)
TO YOLCUZADE İSKENDER CAD. AND ATATÜRK BRIDGE (350M)
TO GALATA BRIDGE (500M)
Taksim Park
TAKSİM
Cumhuriyet Anıtı (Republic Monument)
CUMHURİYET MEYDANI
Atatürk Cultural Center
Havaş Bus Stop
Karaköy-Eminönü-Sirkeci
Yeşilköy-Ataköy-Florya-Hava
Kadiköy Şişli-Beşiktaş
Turkish Airlines
"Otogar" (City Bus Stop)
Air France
Topkapi
Aksaray
Pamukkale & Nev Tur Bus Office
Ulusoy Bus Office
Metro Bus Office
Kadiköy-Bostanci
Kamil Koç Bus Office
Varan Bus Office
Beşiktas-Dolmabahçe
Germany
France
Romania
Belgium
Aya Triada
German Hospital
Taksim Hospital
Ağa Camii
BEYOĞLU
Greece
FRUIT & FISH MARKET
Çiçek Passage
Galatasaray Hamamı
Galatasaray Lisesi
United Kingdom
Church of Saint Antoine
GALATASARAY
Italian Hospital
TOPHANE MEYDANI
Netherlands
Russia
United States
Sweden
TÜNEL
Galata Mevlihane
Galata Tower
Neve Shalom
İstiklâl Cad.
Cumhuriyet Cad.
Mete Cad.
Recep Paşa Cad.
Topçu Cad.
Lamartin Cad.
Aydede Cad.
Abdülhakamit Cad.
Taksim Cad.
Taksim Fırını Sok.
Tak-i-Zafer Cad.
Osmanli Sok.
İnönü Cad.
Çifte Vav Sok.
Ayaspaşa Camii Sok.
Ağa Çiragi Sok.
Kutlu Sok.
Ülker Sok.
Kazanci Yokuşu
Kazancibaşi Camii Sok.
Sıraselviler Cad.
Pürtelas Sok.
Başkent Sokaği Sok.
Somuncu Sok.
Arslanyatağı Sok.
Cihangir Cad.
Alçak Dam Sok.
Mebusan Yokuşu
Arkasi Sok.
Riza Bey Sok.
Selime Saray Sok.
Hatun Camii Sok.
Molla Bayiri Sok.
İnebolu Sok.
Meclis-i Mebusan Cad.
Kapanca Sok.
Yaghanesi Sok.
Tarlabaşı Bulvarı
Zambak Sok.
Ana Çeşmesi S.
Bekar Sok.
Kurabiye Sok.
Meşelik Sok.
Küçük Parmakkapı Sok.
Büyük Parmakkapı Sok.
Hasnun Galip Sok.
Tel Sok.
Billurcu Sok.
Hocazade Sok.
Maç Sok.
Soğanci Sokaği Sok.
Sıslü Saksi Sok.
İmam Adnan Sok.
Sakizağaci Cad.
Abanoz Sok.
Büyük Bayram Sok.
Ahududu Sok.
Kocağaç A.
Işık Sok.
Anadolu Sok.
Liva Sok.
Ağa Hamami Sok.
Faik Paşa Yokuşu Cad.
Hayyat Sok.
Balık Sok.
Turnaci Baş. Sok.
Sahne Sok.
Taktaki Yokuşu Sok.
Palaska Sok.
Defterdar Yokuşu Cad.
Kadirler Yokuşu Cad.
Kasatura Sok.
Türkgücü Cad.
Bostanbaşı Cad.
Çukurcuma Cad.
Hayriye Sok.
Hamalbaşı Cad.
Yeniçarşı Cad.
Külhan Sok.
Tipa Sok.
Eski Çiçekçi Cad.
Nuri Ziya Cad.
Kallavi Sok.
Meşrutiyet Cad.
Tarlabaşı Bul.
Tomtom Kaptan Sok.
Bostan İçerisi Çık.
Bostanici Cami Sok.
Boğaz Kesen Cad.
Necatibey Cad.
Tophane İskelsi Cad.
Karabaş Deresi Sok.
Kapıkulu Sok.
Tutumbaci Sitki Sok.
Kemeralti Cad.
Hisar Yani Sok.
Çiraci Sok.
Balyoz Sok.
Kumbaraci Yokuşu Cad.
Asmali Mescit Sok.
Sofyali Sok.
Kutyu Sok.
Şahkulu Bostani Sok.
Sümbül Sok.
Refik Saydam Cad.
Müellif Cad.
Ali Hoca Sok.
Serdar-Ekrem Sok.
Galip Dede Cad.
Şahkulu Sok.
İlk Belediye Sok.
Kapikulu Sok.
Yüksek Kaldırım
Lüleci Hendek
Büyük Hendek Cad.
Evliya Çelebi Cad.
Okçu Musa Cad.

Oriental Hotel, 60 Cihangir Cad. (☎252 68 70; fax 251 93 21). After leaving Taksim Square, take the 3rd left off Siraserviler onto Soğanci Sok., then a left when the road ends. From Istiklâl Cad., follow Büyük Parmakkapı around its two corners, then take a left and follow that road across Siraserviler onto Soğanci. Follow the road down a short hill, where the hotel is on the left side of a quiet residential street. The short hike from Taksim is worth it if you're in the mood for a more residential atmosphere, along with incredible Bosphorus vistas in 10 of their 20 rooms. Clean rooms with phone. Singles $50; doubles $70; extra bed $20. When staying 10 nights or more, singles $30; doubles $45. Those willing to haggle may be able to get an even better deal.

KADIKÖY AND MODA

Kent Otel, No. 8 Serasker Cad. (☎337 45 18), is an excellent retreat for a few relaxing days in small-town Asia. The small hotel is brand new, and the rooms have balconies, some with views of the old town and Topkapı Palace. Though the rooms do not have their own baths, the shared facilities are modern and exquisitely kept. Haggling may be helpful. Singles $15; doubles $25; triples $35.

CAMPING

The slight savings are hardly worth the hassle and ugliness of city camping. İstanbul's remote campgrounds lie along the commuter rail tracks near the airport. From the airport, take a taxi ($3). From town, take the commuter rail from Sirkeci. None of the campsites rent tents, and be prepared: even the hottest summer days give way to some very cool nights.

Londra Camping (☎560 42 00). On Londra Asfaltı Süt Sanayi Karşısı, 1km from the airport, along the noisy and nerve-grating highway to İstanbul. No bus stop; take a taxi. Far from the center of town, but not from its sounds. Includes cafeteria, bar, and showers. $1.50 without a tent; $2 per tent; $1 to park and sleep in your car; $2 for minivans. 2-person bungalows $10.

Ataköy Tourist Village (☎559 60 08). About 2km from the airport. The "village" has none of the amenities of Londra, but the extra distance from the highway makes it a bit more peaceful. $2 per tent.

FOOD

The dining options in İstanbul run the entire spectrum of quality and value. İstanbul's restaurants, like its clubs and bars, often stick with the golden rule: if it's well-advertised or easy to find, it's not worth doing. Poking around side streets is always worthwhile. Though İstanbul's budget cuisine (under $5) is diverse, a certain amount of creativity is necessary to avoid getting stuck in the *pide*, *kebap*, and *lahmacun* rut. Light dinners of hot or cold *meze* (appetizers), *çorba* (soup), and *salata* (salad) can be inexpensive and satisfying, both for your stomach and your curiosity (see **Food and Drink,** p. 34).

Sultanahmet's heavily advertised "Turkish" restaurants aren't difficult to find, but they often have few Turkish patrons. Much better meals can be found on İstiklâl Cad. and around Taksim. The small Bosphorus towns such as Arnavutköy and Sariyer (on the European side) and Çengelköy (on the Asian side) are the best places for fresh **fish.** In the streets off Cumhuriyet Cad. north of Taksim, the city's high-end restaurants ($20-30 per person) are worked in among the Hilton and other ritzy hotels. Kanlıca, on the Asian side, reputedly has the city's best **yogurt.**

A lamentably overlooked option is food sold by street vendors. Eminönü, like Karaköy across the water, is home to covered boats that fry up **fish sandwiches** on board ($1.50). These are almost always made safe by the vigorous cooking process, despite the questionable composition of the local waters. There are, however, unfortunate exceptions, so watch out. Good **kebap** shops are everywhere, but quality tends to be better in more residential areas. Now and then, *kebap* carts roll by, usually with a small wood fire inside, serving sandwiches with lamb, tomatoes, lettuce, onions and spices—a very tasty, very cheap option. Ortaköy is the place to go for **baked potatoes** stuffed with all kinds of fillings from nacho cheese and salsa to goat cheese and sprinkles of lamb. **Vişne suyu** (sour cherry juice) is sold by vendors in Ottoman dress bearing big steel teapots on their backs. Since the sale of these three foods is supervised by the municipality, prices are fixed at around $.20-.30 for cherry juice and $1 for *kebaps* and potatoes.

Excellent **leblebi** (roasted and salted chickpeas) are often available around the Beyazıt bus stop ($.20-.30 per serving). **Dondurma** (Turkish ice cream) stands are ubiquitous, particularly around Ortaköy. They are hard to miss, as the vendors often clatter their tongs like castanets or play with the scoop of ice cream at the end of their meter-long ice cream scoops. In winter, *vişne suyu* gives away to **sahlep** (a sweet, milky drink made of orchid root and cinnamon) and corn, everywhere during the summer months, is replaced with baked goods, fruits, and nuts.

Travelers who prepare their own food should know that because of space considerations and cultural differences, İstanbul has very few supermarkets. *Migros* is one of the most well known of Turkish supermarket chains, but there are only a couple in the city. Neighborhood markets are a good alternative. Found on corners all over the city, these small shops sell cheese, bread, produce, and drinks, all at rock-bottom prices. Meat is invariably expensive (about $4 for 250g of chicken). A large and fresh selection of produce can be found in the city's **open-air markets;** the best is the daily one in Beşiktaş, near Barbaros Cad. Every Wednesday there is a very good fruit, vegetable, nut, and cheese market along Akbıyık Cad. in Sultanahmet. Two other large open-air markets are centrally located—a general one (including fish) next to Çiçek Pasajı in Beyoğlu, and a **fruit market** next to the Egyptian Spice Bazaar *(Mısır Çarşısı)*, sells mouthwatering sweets.

SULTANAHMET AND DİVAN YOLU

By no means the gastronomical center of İstanbul, Sultanahmet's restaurants are mostly tourist troughs. A simple Turkish meal in this district shouldn't cost much more than $4-5 in any of the cafeteria-style restaurants. There are a number of pricier places scattered throughout the neighborhood and the side streets off Divan Yolu, but for your lira the less expensive eateries can provide just as much flavor as the upscale. Many restaurants have no menu, and hungry customers are encouraged to point and pick from trays of mouth-watering options.

Doy-Doy, 13 şifa Hamamı Sok. (☎517 15 88). From the south end of the Hippodrome, walk down the hill around the edge of the Blue Mosque and look for the blue and yellow sign high in the trees. Easily the best and cheapest of Sultanahmet's crop of cheap eats, 3-story Doy-Doy keeps locals and backpackers coming back for more. The food is simply incomparable. Tasty kebap and refreshing salads ($3.50 and under). The İskender kebap ($2.50) is sublime. From the 4th-story terrace, enjoy an excellent view of the Marmara, the Blue Mosque, and a school yard where local kids play pick-up soccer. Open daily 8:30am-late.

Buhara, just across from Doy-Doy on şifa Hamamı Sok. Almost as good as Doy-Doy, with hefty portions and a better selection of vegetarian options. Munch on fresh bread as you ponder a wide range of mouth-watering choices, the best of which are the Buhara special ($3.50) and the Turkish special kebap ($3). Open daily 9am-late.

Cafe Magnaura, 27 Akbıyık Cad. (☎518 76 22). Down the street from Orient Youth Hostel and Star Pansiyon. Attentive staff serves typical Turkish fare in a romantic, wood-lined interior that opens onto the street. The chicken roll with almonds and pistachios ($6) and the wide array of vegetarian options ($4-7) are delectable. Menu also features international fare (steak and fries $8, delicious pasta $4). Perfect for backpackers looking for a sit-down meal with a clean tablecloth. Open daily 9am-10pm.

Med Cezir, 16 Tevkifhane Sok. (☎517 22 67). Across from the Four Seasons Hotel. One of the better breakfast options in Sultanahmet, this narrow but nicely decorated spot does big Turkish breakfasts for $5. Serves sandwiches ($2-3), scrumptious pizza ($5), and various stuffed potatoes ($4). Come nightfall, the place becomes a pleasant cafe, perfect for watching the high-speed antics of both taxi drivers and the rich and famous at the Four Seasons. 10% service charge. Open daily 8:30am-midnight.

Can Restaurant, 10 Divan Yolu (☎527 70 30). Across the street from the tourist information office at the north end of the Hippodrome. This no-nonsense, dirt-cheap cafeteria offers inexpensive line fare out front and dining tables in the rear. Veggie combination plates start at $1.75, while meat costs a bit more ($2.50-$5). The green beans in tomato sauce ($1) are to die for, and the tomatoes stuffed with rice and lamb ($1.25) are tasty and filling. Open daily 8am-9pm.

Pudding Shop, 6 Divan Yolu (☎522 29 70). A major pit stop for those on the Hippie Trail to the Far and Middle East during the 70s, this family-owned establishment was the setting for the drug deal scene in *Midnight Express.* It is now a self-serve restaurant (meat dishes $2-2.50; veggie dishes $1.50) whose walls are lined with newspaper clippings and notes about its storied past. Finish up with a creme caramel ($1), *keşkül* (vanilla pudding $1), or cappuccino ($1). Continental breakfast served mornings ($2). A/C upstairs. Open daily 7am-11pm.

Pandeli Restaurant, 1 Egyptian Spice Bazaar (☎/fax 522 55 34). The stairs to the 2nd-floor restaurant are right inside the entrance to the bazaar facing the water. The blue tiles give your culinary adventure an underwater feel. Unbelievable fish melts in your mouth to the point you (almost) forget what you're paying ($10-14). Extensive wine list. Tasty yaprak dolması (stuffed vine leaves) and hünkâr beğendi (eggplant with *kebap* $5.75) are specialties. Starters $3-8; main courses $6-14. Open M-Sa noon-4pm.

House of Medusa Restaurant, Yerebatan Cad., 19 Muhteremefendi Sok. (☎511 41 16 or 513 14 28; fax 527 28 22.) A 2min. walk up Yerebatan Cad. from Aya Sofia just across form the tourist police station. This 4-floor, internationally-renowned eatery seats hungry diners on large, comfortable pillows on the floor of the restaurant's upper levels. Delicious *piliç* (chicken stuffed with vegetables; $6) and lamb kebap ($5), savory vegetarian specials ($3-6), and tasty pudding ($2.50) are best capped with their delicious Turkish coffee. Open daily 8am-midnight. AmEx/MC/V. 10% service charge.

The Green Corner (☎522 74 22) on Alemdar Cad., between the tram tracks and Aya Sofia, right next to the Interyouth Hostel. A nice place to unwind after the sensory overload of Aya Sofia, this tree-lined garden cafe features shady outdoor dining, water pipe use any time of day, and good-sized snacks for carnivores; the *kebaps* ($4-5) are fresh but this place specializes in American fare, such as hamburgers ($1) and club sandwiches ($2). Relaxing atmosphere. Open daily noon-12:30am.

Cennet, 90 Divan Yolu (☎ 513 14 16). On the right side of the road as you walk from Sultanahmet toward Aksaray, 3min. from the Sultanahmet tram. Try on traditional Ottoman costumes as you watch women make *gözleme* (Anatolian pancakes) on a griddle in the center of the restaurant. The cheese ($1.75) and the mixed meat pancakes ($2) are divine, but the adventurous palate might enjoy a combination pancake with everything the place has to offer in a single piece of fried dough. *Kebaps* of all sorts are fresh as well ($3). Live Turkish music and dancing every night. Have a tip ready; the musicians are not shy and won't quit. Open daily 10am-midnight.

İSTİKLÂL CAD. AND TAKSİM

The famed **Çiçek Pasajı** (Flower Passage), home of classy but increasingly pricey restaurants, branches off İstiklâl Cad. Look a bit harder in the side streets off İstiklâl Cad. for cheaper bars and cafes where the clientele is mostly Turkish. Hit Taksim Square only if you've got a hankering for the Golden Arches.

Haci Abdullah, 17 Sakizağacı Cad. (☎293 85 61 or 293 08 51), down the street from Ağa Camii is your best bet for insight into what comes out of a real Turkish kitchen (hint: it's not *kebap*). This family-style restaurant has been going strong since 1888, serving it up tasty and friendly, and still finding time to create their specialty pickles, which are available for purchase in large colorful glass vitrines. Entrees run a reasonable $3-6, delicious soups $1. Open daily noon-11pm (kitchen closes at 10:30pm).

Naregatsi Cafe, upstairs at the mouth of Sakizağacı Cad., across from the Ağa Camii. Perhaps the weirdest spot in the Taksim area, Naregatsi serves gourmet cafe fare in the midst of a galactic, high-speed collision of kitsch and concept art. Warhol would feel right at home. Inflatable superheroes, board games, and the occasional live accordion complement the cappuccino (4 flavors, $3.50). The utter singularity of this cafe makes it a must-see—don't miss out on this unique experience. Open noon-11:30pm.

Haci Baba, 49 İstiklâl Cad. (☎ 244 18 86 or 245 43 77), has perfected a wide range of Turkish standards in its nearly 80 years. The unassuming entrance hides a large dining room with a terrace overlooking the courtyard of Aya Triada in back. The menu is extensive, but it's easier to pick something from the deli case in front or help yourself to the immense vegetarian *meze* selection (entrees about $3.50-6.50). 10% service charge. Open daily 10am-10pm. AmEx/MC/V.

Afacan, İstiklâl Cad. 2 locations, one at the top end by the first movie theater and the second at the bottom end, past the Galatasaray Lisesi. Despite the linoleum interior, this is one of the street's better restaurants, specializing in seriously good *kebaps* and *dolma* ($1.50) at the Taksim square location and Turkish Pizza ($1.80) at the other. Top restaurant open daily 10am-midnight; bottom open daily 8am-11pm. MC/V.

şampiyon, Balık Pazarı *(Sahne Sok.),* next to Çiçek Pasajı. Famous across Turkey for the country's best *kokoreç* (grilled tripe cooked with spices and tomatoes). Try the smallest portion, the *çeyrek ekmek kokoreç* ($1.50). For something quick, visit the stand out front for skewers of fried mussels ($1) or fresh mussels stuffed with rice ($.25 each). Open daily 8:30am-midnight.

Cafe Gramafon, 3 Tünel Meydanı (☎293 46 15), on the left as you exit the Tünel station, offers divine Gramafon filet ($8-10) and sandwiches with veggies or meats ($2.50-5) in a mod environment. Delicious salads $4-5; Turkish coffee $1.50; various liquors $6-10. Live jazz W-Sa after 10:30pm. Cover ($5) waived before 11pm. Attracts diverse crowds, though most are moneyed and tragically hip. Open daily 11am-2am.

Cumhuriyet Meyhanesi (☎252 08 86). At the far end of the fish market. In the evenings Turkey's top poets, artists, and journalists migrate between here and the cafes to discuss politics, culture, and other intellectual matters. Serves delectable items such as eggplant salad for $3. Open daily 10am-1am, sometimes later.

Duran Sandwich, 9 İstiklâl Cad. (☎243 52 30). Turkish sandwiches reach a rare level of complexity at this small counter. More than 30 varieties, including caviar and roast beef ($.50 to $4). Open daily 9am-10pm.

Great Hong Kong Restaurant, 12B İnönü Cad., 100m off Taksim Square. A red gateway leads to this lavish Chinese restaurant marooned in Taksim. The full spread of favorites, from hot and sour soup ($2.50) to Huajiao prawns ($8.50), prepared with the Turkish spices you've come to know and love. Open daily noon-3pm and 6-11:30pm.

Borsa Fast Food, 87 İstiklâl Cad. This 3-story fast food restaurant serves quick-fix variations on traditional Turkish cuisine. Try the soup ($1) and artichokes ($2). Vegetarian options. Beer on 3rd fl. Clean, A/C, and raucous. Open daily 8am-midnight.

Saray Muhallebicisi, 102 İstiklâl Cad. A fixture for over 50 years, this pastry shop has expanded to 5 locations all over İstanbul. Marble floors and dark wood tables belie low prices, which keep a constant stream of locals moving through the door. Try the chocolate cake with pistachio ($1.25 per slice). Open daily 6am-midnight.

Ali Muhiddin Haci Bekir, 129 İstiklâl Cad. This place claims to have invented *lokum.* Colossal but pricey Turkish Delight selection ($8-10 per kg). Open 8am-9pm. Another branch at 76 Dolayoba Cad., behind Yeni Camii. MC/V.

FATİH

For those wise enough to leave the fruits and vegetables to the immune locals, try a fresh *sitim,* a round, bagel-like, sesame-seeded bread. They are available everywhere in İstanbul, but hold out for a fresh, hot one in the Fatih's Carşamba district.

Dört Mevsim Restaurant (☎532 01 73), on Haliç Cad. is a delicious local eatery and your best bet for table service and tablecloths in the area. Large speakers play a mix of Turkish and American pop, the TV gives you the update on Turkish sports and news, and you point to your choice of delicious chicken, beef, or lamb *şiş kebaps* ($1.70) plus a large selection of vegetable *mezes*. Cash only.

Cibalikapi Balikçisi Fish Restaurant (☎533 28 46; www.cibalikapbalikcisi.com), right along the Golden Horn, serves good, fresh fish starting at $2.60 and veggies starting at $1.30. Point, and they'll serve it up. MC/V.

Golden Fast Fish, further down the Horn, towards the Atatürk bridge serves various fish specialties ranging from $1.50 to $3.50. More than a roadside stand, this recently renovated self-serve restaurant boasts some of the best fish in town. Cash only.

AKSARAY-LÂLELİ

The Historical Taşhan Restaurant on Fethi Bey Cad. No 55. (☎(212) 526 87 34.), capitalizes on its site's illustrious past: originally built as a guest house for Mustafa III's visitors, it was later used as a military barracks for the janissary. Even if you eat in the breezy garden, the waitstaff will happily show you the Great Hall downstairs, originally a stable for the finest Ottoman steeds, which seats 200 people. Mevlevi whirling dervishes and local folk dances can be organized on request. While the food does little to earn its mark-up (meat dishes $5, salads $2.50, fish $5.50-7), the time warp is well worth it. MC/V. A few paces beyond the restaurant is a beautiful courtyard **cafe**, with delicious *çay* (tea) for $.20 and a large assortment of *nargiles* (hookahs) to rent.

FENER AND BALAT

Tarihi Haliç Işkembecisi. As you walk along the Golden Horn, stop and try the unusual fare at this delightful spot. Their specialty is the *Işkembe Çorbası* (tride soup), a bizarre but curiously appetizing soup of butter, garlic, and shredded fish meat for $1.30. Add lots of garlic. For the adventurous, the menu also features sheep gut for $2.20. MC/V.

SIGHTS

İstanbul's incomparable array of churches, mosques, palaces, and museums can keep a tireless tourist busy for weeks, but five or six days of legwork should be enough to get acquainted with the best of the city's thousands of years of history. Students will find that an ISIC sometimes allows entry to major museums for a reduced fare. Before touring any working religious facilities, see **Visiting Mosques,** p. 26. Perhaps the best way to experience Istanbul is to wander through its residential neighborhoods, away from the sights and the sightseers, up the hills whose streets weave upward from the Golden Horn and the Bosporus, and into the heart of the world's sixth-largest city.

SULTANAHMET

Most budget travelers spend a lot of time in **Sultanahmet,** the area around the Aya Sofia mosque, south of and up the hill from Sirkeci and down to the southwestern tip of the old city. The area is dominated by three of the city's major sights: the Blue Mosque, Aya Sofia, and Topkapı Palace. Within a few hundred yards of each other, the three create a visible testament to the region's varied history, as well as a gigantic tourist trap. Post-sightseeing, reenergize with a pick-up soccer game on the Marmara, or wander up Divan Yolu to get lost in the maze of the Grand Bazaar.

AYA SOFİA (HAGIA SOPHIA)

Museum open Tu-Su 9:30am-4:30pm. Gallery Tu-Su 9:30am-4pm. $6.50, students $2.50.

The Aya Sofia was built by Emperor Justinian after the Nika Riots of 532, in which Hippodrome hooligans had destroyed an earlier structure (see Byzantines, p. 21). To demonstrate his power and restore order, Justinian commissioned the mathematicians Anthemius of Tralles and Isodorus of Miletus to design and build the church. After five years of construction, the exterior of the church was painted blood-red to serve as an unambiguous warning to would-be revolutionaries. The church opened in December 537. Covering an area of 7570 sq. meters and rising to a height of 55.6m, it was the grandest building in the world. Upon entering the church and marvelling at its girth, which was even greater than that of King Solomon's temple in Jerusalem, Justinian reportedly exclaimed, "Solomon, I have outdone you!" Twenty years later, an earthquake revealed a fatal miscalculation by the original architects, bringing the dome crashing to the ground. The task of rebuilding fell to Isador the Younger, nephew of Isadorus. Isador completed his work in 563, having added clumsy exterior buttresses to support the new dome.

From then on, the church began its millennium-long tenure as the most impressive building in the Byzantine world, though it was plundered and desecrated in the 13th century by soldiers of the Fourth Crusade. The Crusaders looted the holy relics, destroyed the exquisite carvings, and seated a prostitute on the patriarch's throne to ridicule the Eastern Church. Despite this humiliation, the Byzantines reclaimed the city and Aya Sofia for another 200 years until the Ottoman conquest.

Mehmet the Conqueror converted Aya Sofia to a mosque, removing all representational art and images and adding a wooden minaret. In the late 16th century, the architect Mimar Sinan undertook a renovation program, adding four minarets. Aya Sofia remained a mosque until 1932, when Atatürk established it as a museum.

THE MUSEUM. Aya Sofia's austere interior amplifies its awesome size. Walking through the main entrance will bring you into the ruins-strewn **exonarthex**, a long, transverse hall common in Byzantine architecture (see **Architecture**, p. 21). The **nave**, reached by crossing the hall, is overshadowed by the massive, gold-leaf mosaic dome. The **mihrab**, the calligraphy-adorned portal pointing towards Mecca, stands awkwardly in the apse, whose two rows of stained glass windows made for a traditional backdrop to the altar during the mosque's Orthodox incarnation. The *minber*, or platform used to address the crowd at Muslim prayer, is the stairway to the right of the *mihrab*. Like the *mihrab*, it was added to the building as part of its reconsecration as a mosque. The elaborate marble square in the floor of the Aya Sofia's main space marks the spot where Byzantine emperors were once crowned.

Move out of the nave toward the south wall of the main floor and peer into the library of Sultan Mahmut I, built in the 1730s. The blue İznik-tiled room features a collection of 18th-century furniture and Koran stands. Crossing back through the nave to the north side of the building, you will reach the **narthex**, a quiet hallway with lace-like column capitals. At the back of the narthex is the famed **sweating pillar**, sheathed in bronze. The pillar has a hole where you can insert your finger to collect the odd drop of water, believed to possess healing powers. Be prepared to wait, though—the perspiration is slow in coming. When you are done here, the climb up to the second floor **gallery** begins at the north end of the exonarthex.

THE GALLERY. The gallery features Byzantine mosaics uncovered from beneath a thick layer of Ottoman plaster, applied to these pieces centuries ago in accordance with regulations on Islamic art. At the end of the climb, turn right, walk down one side of the second floor and turn the corner to the mosaics. Badly damaged from its years under the plaster, the first mosaic depicts Christ listening to the pleas of his mother and John the Baptist. The mosaic on the right depicts Emperor John II Komnenos, his wife Empress Irene, and their son Alexios around Mary and the Christ child. The final mosaic shows Jesus with the Empress Zoë and Constantine Monomachus. The story goes that each time one of Zoë's husbands died, his face would be carved out of the mosaic and the new husband's face would replace it.

BLUE MOSQUE (SULTANAHMET CAMİİ)

Open Tu-Sa 8:30am-12:30pm, 1:45-3:45pm, and 5:30-6:30pm. The Blue Mosque is a working religious facility, so please be courteous—don't attempt to visit during prayer times, which are marked by the call to prayer issued five times daily from all six of the megaphoned minarets. Dress appropriately—head coverings for women and no shorts or tank tops—and speak quietly once inside. On your way out, expect to make a small donation of $1. Tomb open Tu-Su 9:30am-4:30pm. Tomb $1, students free.

Across Sultanahmet Park from Aya Sofia and next to the Hippodrome, the Blue Mosque, or **Sultanahmet Camii,** is a six-minareted, multi-domed structure. Though not blue on the outside, the mosque takes its name from the beautiful blue İznik tiles inside. Completed in 1617, it was Sultan Ahmet's response to Aya Sofia. Though the Blue Mosque is huge, its dimensions don't compete with those of Aya Sofia. Elegantly and intelligently designed, the mosque is buttressed by an internal framework of iron bars across its domes, enabling the entire structure to bend in earthquakes—so far, it has withstood 20. An underground pool moderates the mosque's temperature, keeping it cool in the summer and warm in the winter.

Follow the signs posted along the outside of the mosque to the visitor's entrance on the south side, past the fountains reserved for ceremonial washing. Before entering you should remove your shoes, and women will be provided with necessary head coverings. Once inside, you will find yourself directly under the giant İznik-tiled hemispheres. It's best to visit on a sunny day, when shafts of light enter through the stained-glass windows along the cupola. 16th- and 17th-century Kütahya tiles in characteristically Ottoman floral and geometric patterns grace most of the mosque's surfaces (see **Kütahya,** p. 354).

The barely visible wires hanging from the ceiling support a set of giant light-studded rings. Originally lit with candles, the chandelier structure was intended to create the illusion of tiny starlike lights floating freely in the air. The understated *mihrab*, covered with red and white tile and calligraphic inscriptions, is located along the wall of 17th-century stained-glass windows. A small stone from the Ka'aba at Mecca is almost invisible from the tourists' area.

The entrance to the courtyard is in the wall facing away from Mecca. In typical Ottoman style, the rectangular courtyard has a central fountain and a colonnade with small domes above the arches. The courtyard also holds a sundial that was used to determine prayer times. The mosque's six minarets honor Sultan Ahmet, the sixth sultan to rule after the conquest of Constantinople. Only the mosque at Mecca had six minarets at the time of the Blue Mosque's construction, and the thought of equaling that sacred edifice was considered heretical. Sultan Ahmet bypassed this difficulty by financing the construction of a seventh minaret at Mecca. The mosque has 16 balconies, symbolizing Ahmet's role as the 16th sultan since the beginning of the Ottoman state.

The small, square, single-domed structure in front of the Blue Mosque is **Sultanahmet'in Türbesi,** or Sultan Ahmet's Tomb, which contains the Sultan's remains as well as those of his wife and his sons, Osman II and Murat IV. Contrary to popular belief, the high ratio of small coffins to large ones is not a product of ritual fratricide committed by jealous would-be sultans: though fratricide was a frequent Ottoman practice, it was officially abolished by Sultan Ahmet himself. The small tomb's main attractions are its İznik tiles. The cases of holy relics in the back include strands of the **Prophet Muhammed's beard** and several Koran stands.

On summer evenings, the daily light show romanticizes the history of the mosque's construction. The show is narrated in a different language every night (Turkish, English, French, and German rotate in that order), and even if you don't understand the language of the day, the blue-lit mosque and powerful music make the experience worthwhile.

THE HIPPODROME (AT MEYDANI)

Behind the Blue Mosque, the remains of this ancient Roman circus form a pleasant park whose tranquility contrasts with its turbulent history. Built by the Roman Emperor Septimus Severus in 200 AD, it was the site of chariot races and public executions. Constantine later enlarged the racetrack to 500m on each side.

The Hippodrome played an integral part in the political life of Byzantine Constantinople. The **Hippodrome Factions** arose out of the Hippodrome's seating plan, which was determined by social standing. The "blues" were wealthy citizens seated in the front rows, while "greens" were urban plebians in cheap

İSTANBUL

seats. In one particularly violent demonstration in 532, a protest against the exorbitant taxation policy turned into the bloody Nika Revolt. About 30,000 rioters were eventually subdued (read: massacred), but not before demolishing much of the city.

Two parallel streets, both called **Atmeydanı Sok.,** mark the Hippodrome's long straightaways, while the little semicircular alley behind the Marmara University rectorate is the only surviving bend. The park in the center with the three columns and a gazebo at the north end was a high-walled median divider, against which many unfortunate charioteers were fatally crushed. Along with gladiatorial contests, racing provided an ample supply of corpses from which ancient doctors were able to develop knowledge of human anatomy and medicine.

The northernmost column with hieroglyphics is the **Dikili Taş,** the **Egyptian Obelisk** erected by the Pharoah Thutmosis III in 1500 BC and brought from Egypt to Constantinople in the 4th century by Emperor Theodosius I. At that time, the base was carved with depictions of the life of Theodosius, Byzantine chariot races, and war victories. A few meters away stands all that is left of the **Serpentine Column.** Once an impressive piece of plunder, the column now stands short, its top cut and its bronze gone black. Originally placed at the Oracle of Delphi, the statue consisted of three intertwined snakes whose heads pointed in different directions until Mehmet I conquered the city and decapitated one of them. (one of the original serpent heads is displayed in the "İstanbul Through the Ages" exhibit at the **Archaeological Museum,** p. 113.) The southernmost column is the deteriorating **Column of Constantine,** whose original gold-plated bronze tiling was looted by soldiers of the Fourth Crusade during the sack of Constantinople. The small gazebo with fountains around its base at the other end of the Hippodrome is **Kaiser Wilhem's Fountain.** On the east side of the Hippodrome along Atmeydanı Sok. is **İbrahim Paşa Sarayı,** the **Museum of Turkish and Islamic Art** (see p. 115).

Today, the park's many benches provide a relaxing place to take a break. Vendors sell everything from ice cream to boiled and salted corn.

TOPKAPI PALACE (TOPKAPI SARAYI)

Open W-M 9am-4:30pm. Each day's open galleries are posted next to the ticket window. Harem closes at 4pm. Mandatory tours of the Harem leave every 30min. 9:30am-3:30pm. Palace $6.50, harem $4.

Towering from the high ground at the tip of the old city and hidden behind walls up to 12m high, Topkapı Palace (Topkapı Sarayı) was the nerve center of the Ottoman Empire from the 15th through the 19th century. This sprawling collection of buildings, gardens, and colonnades, whose arrangement clearly disobeys the rules of symmetry and mathematics that traditionally govern Islamic architecture, served as a monument to Ottoman power and glory. The palace is among the greatest structures in Islamic secular architecture, combining a number of different styles within its miles of outer walls. Built by Mehmet the Conqueror between 1458 and 1465 on the strategic Seraglio Point overlooking the Marmara, the palace was originally intended as an administrative center for the Ottoman Empire. When the palace became an imperial residence during the reign of Süleyman the Magnificent, the administrative offices were converted into the Harem (which means "forbidden to enter"), the living quarters for the Sultan, his family, and wives.

The palace is divided into a series of courts, all surrounded by the palace walls. These walls also encompass **Gülhane Park,** whose entrance lies at the Gülhane tram stop, on Alemdar Cad. The palace's main entrance is on Babıhümayun Cad., the cobblestone street off Aya Sofia square. From here, visitors pass machine-gun-toting members of the military and enter into the first of four courtyards, a large walled-in park that also contains the **Archaeological Museum** (see p. 113). The second court makes up the bulk of the palace and was used for carrying out the business of ruling the empire. The third court is the site of the palace school and the sultan's library, and the fourth houses a set of pavilions with views of the Sea of Marmara beyond Gülhane's forest canopy.

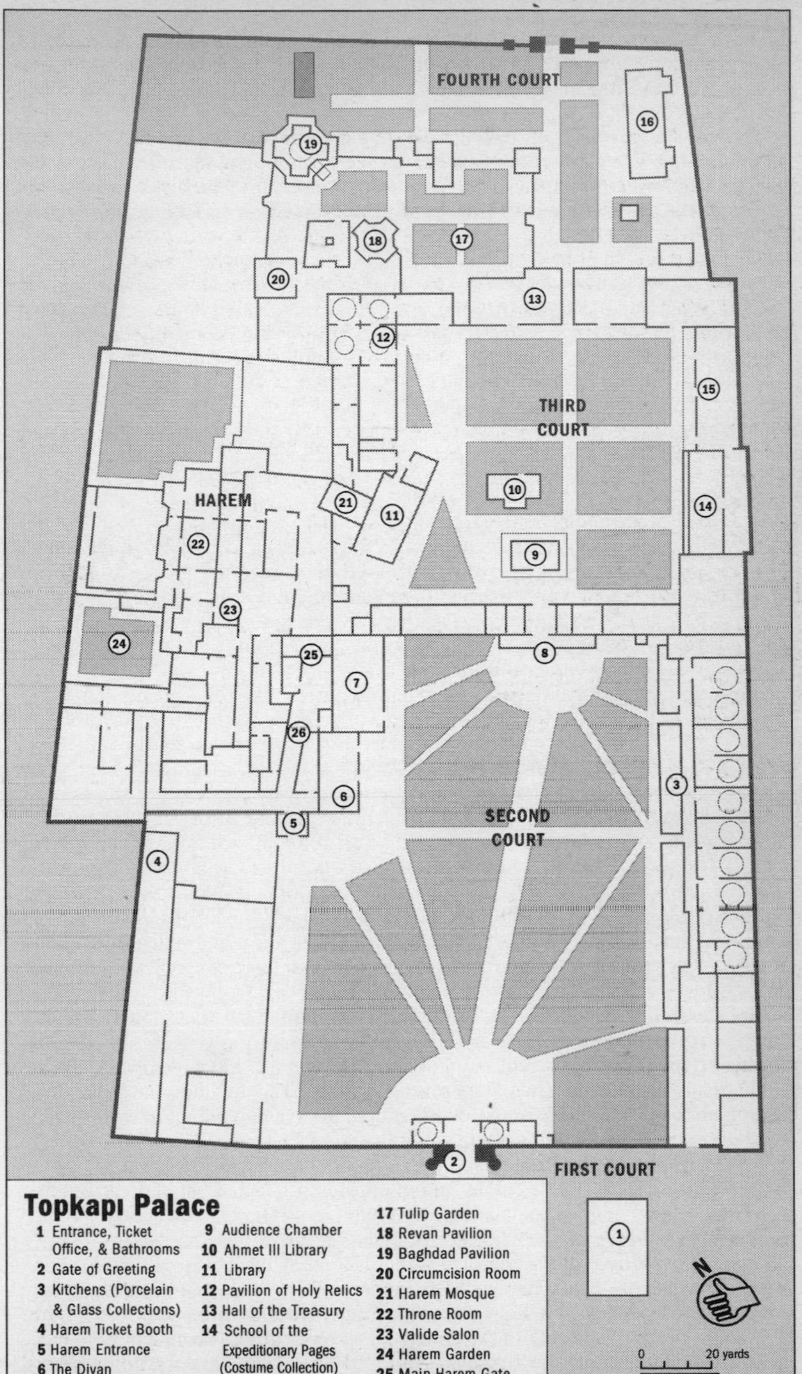

Topkapı Palace

1 Entrance, Ticket Office, & Bathrooms
2 Gate of Greeting
3 Kitchens (Porcelain & Glass Collections)
4 Harem Ticket Booth
5 Harem Entrance
6 The Divan
7 Inner Treasury
8 Gate of Felicity
9 Audience Chamber
10 Ahmet III Library
11 Library
12 Pavilion of Holy Relics
13 Hall of the Treasury
14 School of the Expeditionary Pages (Costume Collection)
15 Palace Treasury
16 Restaurant
17 Tulip Garden
18 Revan Pavilion
19 Baghdad Pavilion
20 Circumcision Room
21 Harem Mosque
22 Throne Room
23 Valide Salon
24 Harem Garden
25 Main Harem Gate
26 Court of the Black Eunuchs

THE FIRST COURT. Follow Babıhümayun Cad. to the Bab-ı-Hümayun, the **Imperial Gate.** At the top are the *tuğra* (seals) of the builder, Mehmet the Conqueror, as well as those of Mahmut II and Abdülaziz, who restored the palace.

The first courtyard, just through the gate, was the center of the Palace, where the general public was permitted entrance to watch executions, trade, and view the nexus of the Empire's glory. The first court consists mostly of a shady park and scattered gardens. On the left stands the **Church of Divine Peace** *(Aya İrini Kilisesi)*, a Byzantine church and a former palace armory. The only way to see the inside of the church is to catch a concert there during either the **İstanbul Festival** or the summer music festivals, which are frequent in June and early July. Next door is the **Imperial Mint,** occasionally open for scholarly symposia and art shows. Its design incorporates an random collection of architectural styles ranging from classical Ottoman to proto-Bauhaus, connected by a narrow-gauge rail line used for transporting bullion. Here coins were minted and the Imperial silverware cast.

THE SECOND COURT. At the end of the first courtyard, the capped conical towers of **Bab-üs-Selam** (Gate of Greeting) mark the entrance to the second court. The design for the two octagonal towers was derived from the battlements of medieval European castles which Süleyman saw during his Eastern European campaigns. The gate itself was built by Sultan Mehmet II in 1542.

The area where guards check tickets and maintain security is the **Kapı Arası.** In Ottoman days, viziers and other emissaries were detained here before receiving permission to enter the palace. The second courtyard formed the business center of the palace. Here, the Janissaries were paid, the Sultan received foreign heads of state, and meetings were held. Inside the gate, six paths lead to different locations within the court. The first path on the left leads to the stables and dungeons. The second path leads to the entrance to the Harem, the Palace's residential center, and the third path leads to the **Privy Chambers** *(Kubbealtı)* and the **Inner Treasury,** both situated along the left wall alongside the Harem entrance. With its window grilles, awnings, walls, and ceilings slathered in gold leaf, the privy chambers were the sight of the Divan council's Tuesday meetings, a gathering of high-ranking Ottoman officials. Of the two grilles here, the one mounted high on the wall contains a peep-hole through which the Sultan could observe his council's deliberations from the Harem. The plush rococo-style room abutting the Council Chamber was where the **Grand Vizier** received foreign dignitaries. Next door, the **Inner Treasury** holds the sultans' swords and various other instruments of cutting, bludgeoning, and hacking. Regrettably, this popular portion of the palace is often closed.

The fifth and sixth paths from the second gate lead to the opposite wall and the **Imperial kitchens,** with their distinctive conical and vaulted chimneys, on the left as you enter the second court. From the narrow alley, the door closest to the entrance to the third court leads into the confectioners' kitchen, displaying glass and porcelain collections. The pastry rolling stone bearing the Imperial seal is the only remaining piece of original kitchen equipment in the building. Back outside on the narrow street, the doors along the opposite, court-side wall lead into the **silver and European porcelain collections,** worth visiting if only to pay homage to the herniated spirits of those who had to schlep the loot in. The last set of doors on the left of the alley open into the palace's deservedly world-famous **Chinese and Japanese porcelain collections.** The Chinese collection is the third largest in the world, featuring pieces from all the major porcelain eras, from the Song through the Ch'ing Dynasties. The Ottomans loved the expert craftsmanship of Chinese porcelain, which was transported along the most difficult of the three major routes of the Silk Road: the water route. The wares traveled along the coasts of India, through the Malacca channel and into the Red Sea. Also worth noting are the kitchen chimneys; one of **Mimar Sinan's** minor commissions, they were built after a fire in 1574 gutted the kitchens.

THE THIRD COURT. Officially known as **Enderun** (literally *inside*), the third court is accessible through the **Gate of Felicity,** also referred to as the **White Eunuchs' Gate** *(Akağalar Kapısı)*. On the second courtyard side of the gate, the white stone in the ground underneath the awning is all that remains of the pedestal which held the sultan's standard whenever he held audience here. The gate shows the beginning of the architectural change from the intricate classical Ottoman order to the showiness of **Dolmabahçe Palace** (see p. 128). It also reveals that even while in use, the Topkapı Palace remained a work in progress.

The building whose awning attaches to the gate is the **Arz Odası,** an **audience chamber** where the sultan met privately with viziers and high-ranking advisers. While it is closed to the public, you can peer inside for a glimpse of the sultan's loveseat-sized throne. The buildings attached to either side of the gate are the quarters and school of the *Enderva Ağas* (Boys of the Inside). Recruited from foreign countries under the *devşirme* system, these boys received preliminary education elsewhere before being brought to the palace to prepare for a life in the service of the sultan (see **The Ottoman Empire,** p. 11). In the center of the courtyard is the **Library of Ahmet III,** also closed to the public. To the right of the library sits the **School of the Expeditionary Pages,** which houses the Palace's **costumes collection.** Follow the evolution of imperial dress from the early days of *kaftans* (long tunics) to the introduction of *şalvar* (baggy trousers) in the late 18th century, right through to the adoption of the fez with Western clothing under Mahmud II.

Moving down along the colonnade brings you to the **Palace Treasury,** subdivided into four rooms of bulletproof display cases covered with the noseprints of eager tourists. The first of these is the **gold objects** room, containing the **chain mail** armor of Murat IV and the sultan's throne. The second hall is reserved for objects embellished with emeralds, including the **legendary Topkapı dagger.** Sultan Mahmut I intended to present it to Nadir Shah of Iran in return for the solid-gold throne displayed elsewhere in the treasury, but Nadir Shah was assassinated before the gift could be received. The next room features various gifts to Ottoman Sultans from European countries. The **Spoonmaker's Diamond,** the world's 7th-largest, earned its nickname because it was traded to a spoonmaker in exchange for three spoons. The highlight of the medals case is the diamond-encrusted anchor, awarded by the German Kaiser to a daring Ottoman sea captain. Also note the silver hand; the small glass compartment reportedly contains some of John the Baptist's bones.

Walking counter-clockwise along the colonnade, you will reach the **Hall of the Treasury,** which now houses 37 portraits, one for each of the 37 sultans. The pride of this collection is the three works commissioned by Murat II: the Shahanshahname (Book of the King of Kings), the Surname (Book of Festivals), and the Hürname (Book of Accomplishments). The **Treasure Dormitory** next door displays a collection of Islamic Art cataloguing the evolution of Selçuk and Mamluk art. Also check out the **shadow theatre display,** with English captions explaining the central role of these figures in Turkish folk culture (see **No Strings Attached,** p. 166).

Just on the other side of the courtyard lies the elegant **Pavilion of Holy Relics,** housing the booty snatched by Selim the Grim after the Ottoman capture of Egypt, as well as gifts sent by the governor of Mecca and Medina upon Selim's victory. The interior is lavishly covered in blue İznik tile, with the names of God and Muhammed on calligraphic seals in the upper corners of the main room. Two further rooms feature extensive Prophet Muhammed memorabilia. In the third room is a soundproof glass cubicle from which the *muezzin* sounds the call to prayer.

HAREM. Cashing in on the associations of debauchery and intrigue conjured up by the word "harem," the Topkapı officials require the purchase of a separate ticket for this, the museum's most popular attraction next to the Spoonmaker's Diamond. "Harem" is actually Arabic; Turks use the word *darüssade*, or house of felicity. The 400-plus rooms housed the sultan, his immediate family, and a small army of servants, eunuchs, and general assistants. Because it was forbidden for men other than the sultan and his sons to live here, the harem became a fount of intrigue and gossip. The rumors included one that claimed the sultans' wives and

SLEEPING YOUR WAY TO THE TOP Though often billed as Hugh Hefner's seventh heaven, the activities of Ottoman **harems** went far beyond his trade. Often, the women inhabitants had been captured in foreign countries or bought as slaves at age five. Concubines were sorted into two groups: the beautiful, who personally served the sultan, and the rest, who started out as rookies *(açemis)*. During their stay at the harem, women were educated in religion, philosophy, and state affairs, and were taught to read and write. At first, they could leave the harem to visit İstanbul, and after nine years they were done with harem service and could ask the sultan for permission to marry. However, if a concubine attracted the sultan's affections or if the sultan spent a night with her, she was promoted to *odalisque*. This position meant she lost her privilege to leave the harem, but her standards of living were improved, and she had chances for further advancement. If she bore the sultan any son, there was a good chance of becoming **Kadın Efendı**, or wife of the sultan (he could have up to 8 of these). If she carried the sultan's first son, she was practically guaranteed to be **Valide Sultan.** Through this system of prestige, the harem women became a powerful, cohesive unit, competently running the affairs of state in the event that the sultan was too mad, weak, or young to rule effectively on his own.

concubines had to crawl on their hands and knees to his bed. Unfortunately, the guided tour of the harem can be anything from highly informative to thoroughly useless, depending on the pace and the distortion of the guide's voice brought on by the building's echoing acoustics. Stand close to the guide or look out for explanatory signs to get the lowdown on the down and dirty.

The harem breaks down into three main sections: the **Eunuchs' Section,** the **Women's Section,** and the **Sultan's Section.** The mandatory guided tour proceeds through the harem in roughly that order, beginning in the **courtyard** with the **Black Eunuchs' Dormitory** on the left, where the lowest ranking eunuchs lived on the top floor, the higher ranking eunuchs on the lower floors, and the chief eunuch on the ground floor. The Black Eunuchs, so named because they were specially recruited from Africa, acted as bodyguards for the sultan and his women, controlled traffic in and out of the harem, and handled other mechanics of harem life.

The women's section of the harem begins with the chambers of the **Valide Sultan,** the sultan's mother. The most powerful of the harem women, the Valide Sultan was greatly influential on her son. Eager to occupy this coveted position, Roxelana, the wife of Süleyman the Magnificent, induced her husband to kill his first son in order to pave the way for the accession of her son, Selim the Sot (see **How Süleyman the Magnificent Got His Name,** p. 12). The first to move her living quarters to Topkapı, she was also the harem's inaugural member. The tour makes its way through the **Queen Mother's chambers** and the smaller apartments of special concubines who served the Queen Mother.

After the Concubines' Courtyard, the tour dives into a maze of unremarkable sitting rooms and bathrooms. You'll pass through the bedroom of Murat III, designed by famed architect Mimar Sinan. Further on, admire the **Fruit Room,** named for the pictures of fruit that adorn every imaginable surface. Before ending, the tour goes through **Hunkon Sofrası,** where the sultan and his esteemed guests delighted in watching belly dancers and tumbling midgets (who lived in the Harem Dwarves' Dormitories). The decor here is eclectic to say the least, with İznik, Ming, and rococo influences all cluttered together. As is typical of Ottoman palace playrooms, the balcony on the far side of the room was for the orchestra.

THE FOURTH COURT. Three passageways lead into the fourth and final palace courtyard. It was among these pavilions, gardens, and fountains that the (in)famous merriments and sordid garden parties of the Tulip Period took place (see **Troubles at Home, Troubles Abroad,** p. 12). Directly in front of the covered entrance to the courtyard, the **Tulip Garden** is now filled with other flowers in well-manicured plots. The courtyard's main attraction is the broad marble terrace with a large central pool and fountain around which the Baghdad, Revan, and Sünnet *köşks* stand. From here you can take in the uninterrupted breathtaking vistas of the Sea of Marmara and the Bosphorus.

The İznik-tiled **Revan Pavilion,** the first room at the top of the stairs to the terrace, was built in 1635 to commemorate Sultan Murat IV's Revan campaign in Iran. The back wall of the Pavilion of the Holy Relics, adjacent to the Revan Pavilion, features a sampler of 15th-century İznik tiles. At the other end of the portico is the **Circumcision Room,** an octagonal chamber that overhangs the edge of the pavilion, built by İbrahim the Mad. Young princes would be clipped into adulthood in this chamber, lined with beautiful (and easy to clean) İznik tiles. The golden canopy overlooking the Sea of Marmara is the **İftariye Köşku,** also built by İbrahim the Mad. It was before these beautiful views that İbrahim and his successors broke the Ramazan fast after sunset. At the far end of the L-shaped terrace stands the **Bağdat Köşku,** Murat I's monument to his capture of Baghdad in 1638. Inside, identical stained-glass windows, matching carpets, and identically paneled doors create astounding radial symmetry. The symmetry is said to be such that if you were to close the door and spin around, you would forget which door you entered through.

İSTANBUL

THE ARCHAEOLOGICAL MUSEUM COMPLEX

The museum complex lies through the gate marked "Archaeological Museums," about 100m downhill from the palace's first courtyard. When the Topkapı Palace is closed, it is possible to enter through Gülhane Park, where a separate road next to the park ticket booths leads to the museum complex. A single ticket theoretically gets you into all 3 museums, although one or another is often closed at any given time. Museum complex open Tu-Su 9:30am-5pm. $5.

TILED PAVILION (ÇİNLİ KÖŞK). The tiled pavilion was built in 1472 by Mehmet the Conqueror to view the athletic competitions below. Originally covered from floor to ceiling in İznik tiles, the sultan's superbox suffered fire and an earthquake which destroyed much of the original *faïence*. The opulent fountain tucked in the corner of the room, off to the right as you enter the *köşk*, is still fringed by its original, delicately patterned İznik tiles. The display covers the full spectrum of Ottoman tilemaking, including some rare early İznik tiles.

THE MUSEUM OF THE ANCIENT ORIENT. This smaller cement building adjacent to the Tiled Pavilion houses treasures so rare that the museum seems reluctant to let anyone see them. Should you have the luck to arrive when it's open, you can expect to find an excellent collection of large stone artifacts from Anatolia, Mesopotamia, and Egypt, dating from the 1st and 2nd millennia BC. The pride of this museum is the **Treaty of Kadesh,** the world's oldest-known written treaty, drafted after a battle between Ramses II of Egypt and the Hittite King Muvatellish ended in a stalemate. A copy of this document graces the entrance to the United Nations.

THE ARCHAEOLOGY MUSEUM (ARKEOLOJİ MUZESİ). Though cursed with an unfortunately generic name, the Archaeology Museum contains one of the world's great collections of Classical and Hellenic art. Built in the middle of the 19th century, the treasures inside were organized into a coherent collection under the curatorship of Ottoman archaeologist Osman Hamdi Bey. To the right of the museum's entrance stands a copy of the famous tear column in the Yerebatan Cistern, though this one lacks the original's green algae. To the left of the entrance are a couple of Roman sarcophagi, noteworthy for their distinct seals showing a letter "p" superimposed on an "x." The two Greek letters, "chi" and "rho," are the first two letters in Jesus' name; the symbol was an early Christian icon.

In the room directly in front of the entrance stands a great statue of **Beş,** the demigod of inexhaustible strength. Heading right leads through the evolution of classical statuary. You can get a good sense of Roman imperial hubris by noticing the heightened similarities between the busts of the Caesars and those of Heracles and Alexander the Great. In the last room of the section are some immense sculptures of Roman gods, including an gigantic **statue of Zeus** from the 2nd century BC and a well-preserved statue of Oceanus, god of the rivers. From the entrance, a left turn leads to the Sidon Sarcophagi section. Excavated by the same Osman Hamdi

Bey, the **Sidon Sarcophagi** are among the most important archaeological finds of all time. Eighteen sarcophagi were found in the royal necropolis of Sidon in Lebanon, and though seven were left in the tomb for various reasons, the remaining 11 were all brought back to İstanbul. The pieces date from the 6th to 4th centuries BC. In the second room of the Sidon Hall rests the **Alexander Sarcophagus.** Modeled on a Greek temple and covered with intricate carvings, the tomb actually holds the Sidonese king Abdalonymous. As a peripheral member of the Sidonese royal family, Abdalonymous was constantly aware that he owed his position to Alexander. His sarcophagus, created long before his death, is an attempt to legitimize his rule through association with Alexander and the kingly sport of lion-hunting.

Follow the stairs to the **"İstanbul Through the Ages"** and the **"Ancient Turkey"** exhibits, the former the winner of a European Museum award. The well-explained İstanbul exhibit describes the city's history from the Bronze Age to the last few centuries. The Ancient Turkey exhibit has artifacts from Troy, made a lot more interesting by the background movie (shown at 10, 11:30am, 1:30, and 3:30pm).

GRAND BAZAAR AND ENVIRONS

To reach the bazaar from Sultanahmet, follow the tram tracks toward Aksaray for five minutes until you see the Nuruosmanıye Camii on the right. Walk one block down Vezirhanı Cad., keeping the mosque on your left. Follow the crowds left into the bazaar (www.grand-bazaar.com). Open M-Sa 9am-7pm, though some stores close an hour or two before the rest of the bazaar.

Consisting of over 4000 shops, several banks, mosques, police stations, fountains, and restaurants, the enormous **Grand Bazaar** (*Kapalı Çarşısı*, "covered bazaar") could be a city in itself. Now the largest of its kind in the world, the Grand Bazaar began in 1461 as a modest affair during the reign of Mehmet the Conqueror. Today, the enormous Kapalı Çarşısı forms the entrance to the mercantile sprawl that

starts at Çemberlitaş and covers the hill down to Eminönü, ending at the **Egyptian Spice Bazaar** *(Mısır Çarşısı)* and the Golden Horn waterfront. This chaotic, labyrinthine world combines all the best and worst of shopping in Turkey. Though the bazaar is loosely organized according to specific themes, much of it is a jumble of shops selling hookah pipes, bright baubles, copper filigree shovels, Byzantine-style icons on red velvet, Turkish daggers, embroidered pillows, carpets, amber jewelry, musical instruments, chess sets, hand puppets, and the ubiquitious evil-eye keychains. Through banter and barter, haggle and hassle, a day spent at the Kapalı Çarşısı is bound to tempt and tantalize even the most experienced traveler.

Navigating the corridors of the Kapalı Çarşısı is no easy task. There are street signs to help you find your way, but unless you're looking for a particular item, you might want to surrender yourself to the pandemonium and simply wander among the merchants' calls. But don't despair—in the event that you have limited time or specific interests, there is some method to the madness. If you enter through the **Nuruosmaniye Kapısı,** the gate near the Çemberlitaş tram stop, you will find yourself on **Kalpakçılarbaşı Cad.,** the goldsellers' avenue that forms the primary east-west spine of the market. The street is lined with jewelers and gold merchants until it opens out onto the **Beyazıt Kapısı,** the gate near the Beyazıt tram stop. The **Kürkçüler Kapısı,** the entrance off Beyazıt Square, feeds into **Kürkçüler Çarşısı,** a giant leather goods bazaar. Takkeciler Cad. and Kuyumcalar Cad. are the main streets running perpendicular to Kalpakcılarbaşı Cad., and also frame the **Old Bazaar,** which holds most of the bazaar's old silver and valuable antiquities. The Old Bazaar begins two blocks below Kalpakçılarbaşı Cad., its entrances marked by painted metal signs. The gold merchants continue on Kuyumcalar, but fine carpets can be found on Takkecelir Cad. as well as the two other streets that wrap around the Old Bazaar.

Around the outside of the bazaar are other interesting opportunities to browse, explore, and empty your pockets. **Fesciler Kapısı,** like both the Beyazıt and Yorguncılar gates, opens onto the open-air clothing market. The market runs along the outside of the bazaar's western wall and is close to the **Sahaflar Çarşısı,** the antique book bazaar. A wide selection of books is available here, along with Koranic inscriptions and university texts. The majority of the books are Turkish, but the few English titles are absolute bargains, starting at about $1 for new paperbacks. When walking out of the Fesciler Kapısı, turn right to find the books. The entrance is just a few meters down on the left. Opposite the book market stands the huge entrance gate of **İstanbul University** (see **Beyazıt,** p. 116). The **Çarşıkapı** entrance, facing Divan Yolu, leads out onto Yağlıkçılar Cad., where ceramics are sold.

OTHER SULTANAHMET SIGHTS

MUSEUM OF TURKISH AND ISLAMIC ART (İBRAHİM PAŞA SARAYI). This superb museum, housed in the palace of Süleyman the Magnificent's Grand Vizier, features a large Islamic art collection organized by period (see **Islamic Art and Architecture,** p. 22). One of the foremost museums of its kind in the world, the museum holds over 40,000 pieces, covering nearly every period of Islamic art. The museum's main wing consists of a long hall with stone artifacts from the early Islamic world, cases of ceramics, carpets, and silver displays. Off the hall lie rooms containing works from specific periods in Islamic and urban development. Among these, the Selçuk exhibits and the Ottoman calligraphy display with *tuğras* (seals) of various Ottoman sultans are particularly impressive. This main corridor leads into the former palace's **Great Hall,** which features a collection of old carpets in decent repair, explained by plaques detailing the origins of certain patterns and motifs. Admire the Qur'an stands and beautiful, handwritten copies of the Qur'an itself. The Great Hall leads outside into a courtyard that also features a tea garden serving *çay* ($.75) and pastries ($2). From here you can see the modern steel and glass renovations that somehow complement the original red brick structure. Off the courtyard is the newly opened ethnographic wing, providing detailed displays of Turkish life and artistic techniques from various time periods. Life-size dioramas include Anatolian village life and 19th-century İstanbul interiors, both clearly explained. *(Museum and cafe open Tu-Su 9:30am-4:30pm. $2, students $1.20.)*

YEREBATAN SARAYI (UNDERGROUND CISTERN). This subterranean "palace" is actually a vast cavern whose shallow water eerily reflects the images of its 336 supporting columns, all illuminated by pulsating colored lighting. The echoing sounds of constantly dripping water and the muted strains of classical tunes will accompany your stroll across the elevated wooden walkways. Watch your step: dripping water makes the floor slippery. Don't miss the pair of columns in the far corner, whose pedestals are a pair of giant **Medusa heads.** Underground walkways originally linked the cistern to Topkapı Palace, but they were blocked to curb rampant trafficking of stolen goods and abducted women. This was also the site of one of the battles between Mahmut II's forces and the Janissaries at the time of the "Auspicious Event" (see **The 19th Century: Reform and Reaction,** p. 13). The cistern is used as the backdrop for various art exhibitions, and the cafe near the exit has a small stage on which local actors perform. At the top of the exit stairs you'll find a small but well-stocked bookstore. Though expensive, the shop has many English-language books on history, poetry, and Islamic art. *(As you stand with your back to Aya Sofia, the entrance is about 175m from the mosque in the small stone kiosk on the left hand side of Yerebatan Cad. Open daily 9:30am-5:30pm. $4, students $3.25.)*

THE MOSAIC MUSEUM. On the site of Emperor Justinian's palace, this museum displays the mosaic from the palace's main hall. Plaques on the wall provide a detailed history of the mosaic, originally laid as a decorative pavement in the palace's main space. The tiles depict nature scenes, hunting, and traditional legends. To get a good look, walk left around the viewing balcony when you enter and pay attention to the explanatory notes along the wall. *(From the exit of the Blue Mosque, walk out into Sultanahmet Sq., turn right, and look for the sign for Arasta Bazaar and the museum. The entrance is on the street side of the carpet bazaar. Open Tu-Su 9:30am-4:30pm. $1.75.)*

THE CARPET MUSEUM. Strictly for hard-core carpet enthusiasts, this small, dimly lit facility displays four centuries' worth of worn-out carpets from all over the Muslim world. With very few display plaques explaining the importance of each carpet fragment, only those with knowledge of the history of Turkish carpets and *kilims* will enjoy this one. Be warned: the carpet shops in the neighborhood are notorious for their high prices. *(At the exit from the Blue Mosque, a ramp about 20m to the right leads up to the museum. Open M-Sa 9am-noon and 1-4pm. $2, students $1.)*

SOUTH OF THE GOLDEN HORN

BEYAZIT

Divan Yolu Cad., the Ottoman processional avenue, leads from Sultanahmet to Beyazıt Meydanı, Beyazıt's main square. A large student district, Beyazıt is home to İstanbul University's main campus and the magnificent **Süleymaniye Camii.** Despite the huge population of students, stores in Beyazıt cater mostly to those weary of haggling in the bazaar. Here, prices are fixed and you won't find any carpet sellers offering you apple *çay* in hopes of brokering a deal. Instead, you will find a young, urban elite going about their business in the shadow of the glorious mosque and Atatürk's imposing statue. Beyazit also has a convenient entrance to the Grand Bazaar, in front of which is a convenient bus stop with a manned AKBİL kiosk; buses from here go everywhere in the old city and Taksim.

ALONG DİVAN YOLU. Walking down the tram line along Divan Yolu from Sultanahmet to Beyazıt, you will pass a number of historical tombs, small graveyards and charming *çay* gardens. The **tomb of Sultan Mahmud II** is housed in a block-long marble structure right before the Çemberlitaş Hamamı (see **Hamams,** p. 138). Although simple compared to earlier burial sanctuaries, the tomb is an example of Ottoman design near the end of the empire. *(Donation required. Dress appropriately.)* The **Press Museum** (Basım Müzesi) displays massive printing presses from Turkey's 100 years of modern publishing history. On the 2nd floor, the Katta Sanat Gallery highlights artwork and handicrafts from contemporary Turkish artists. *(84 Divan Yolu*

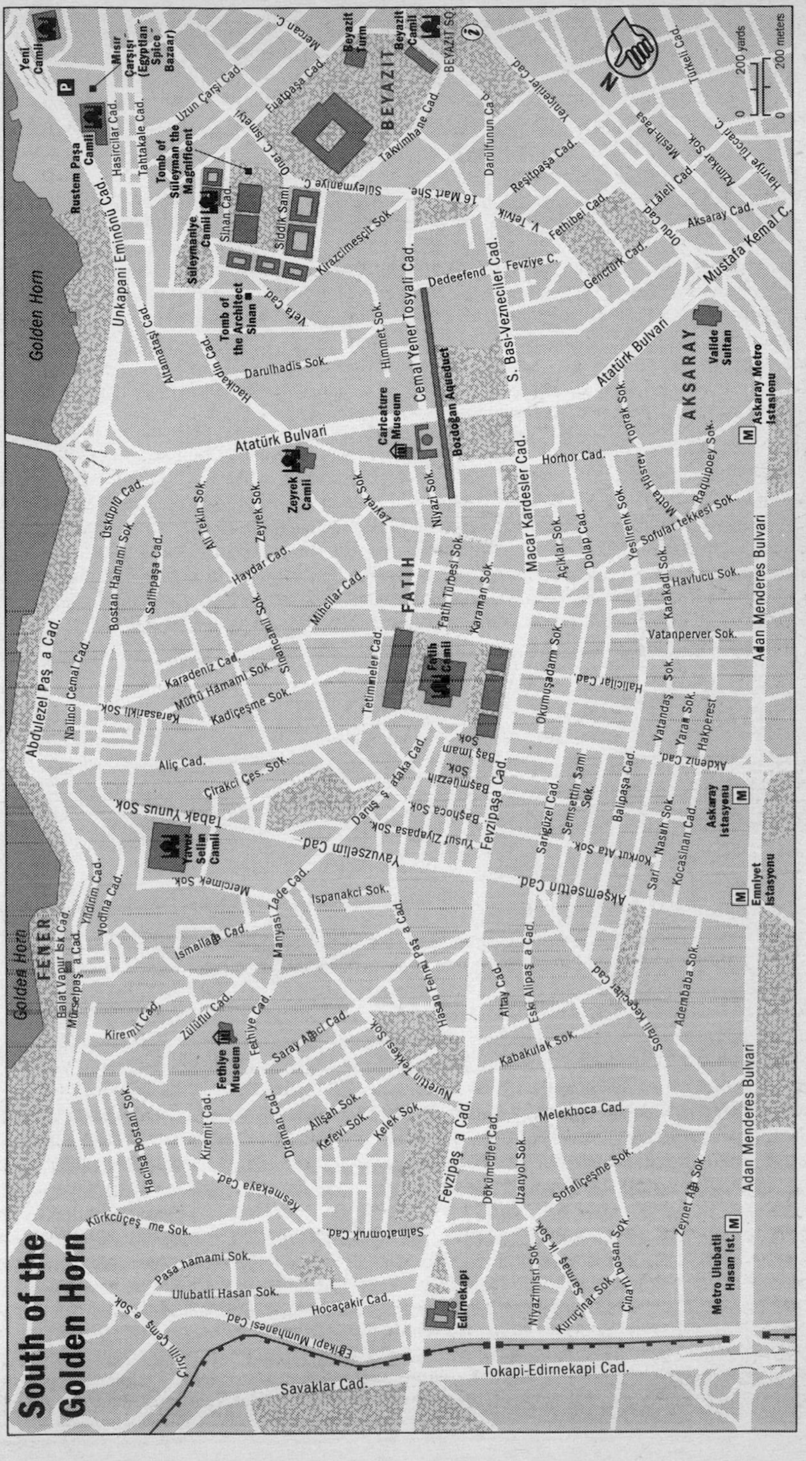
South of the Golden Horn
Golden Horn
FENER
FATIH
BEYAZIT
AKSARAY
Yeni Camii
Mısır Çarşısı (Egyptian Spice Bazaar)
Rustem Paşa Camii
Tomb of Süleyman the Magnificent
Süleymaniye Camii
Tomb of the Architect Sinan
Beyazit Turm
Beyazit Camii
Caricature Museum
Bozdoğan Aqueduct
Zeyrek Camii
Fatih Camii
Yavuz Selim Camii
Fethiye Museum
Edirnekapı
Valide Sultan
Askaray Metro Istasionu
Askaray Istasyonu
Emniyet Istasyonu
Metro Ulubatli Hasan Ist.
Atatürk Bulvari
Adan Menderes Bulvari
Fevzipaşa Cad.
Macar Kardesler Cad.
Cemal Yener Tosyali Cad.
S. Basi-Vezneciler Cad.
Mustafa Kemal C.
Unkapani Eminönü Cad.
Abdulezel Paş a Cad.
Yavuzselim Cad.
Akşemsettin Cad.
Tokapi-Edirnekapi Cad.
Savaklar Cad.
Egrikapi Mumhanesi Cad.
Uzun Çarşi Cad.
Ordu Cad.
Aksaray Cad.
Darulhadis Sok.
Haydar Cad.
Horhor Cad.
Kabakulak Sok.
Melekhoca Cad.
Kesmekaya Cad.
Salmatomruk Cad.
Hocaçakir Cad.
Ulubatli Hasan Sok.
Kürkcüçeş me Sok.
Tabak Yunus Sok.
Aliç Cad.
Karadeniz Cad.
Sofular tekkesi Sok.
Havlucu Sok.
Vatanperver Sok.
Halicilar Cad.
Akdeniz Cad.
0 200 yards
0 200 meters
N

Cad. ☎513 84 58. Open Tu-Su. Free.) Follow Divan Yolu Cad. to the **Tomb of Sinan Paşa,** and pay tribute to the Ottoman Grand Vizier by drinking a cup of *çay* in the adjoining garden. Move from caffeine to nicotine at the Çorlulu Alipaşa Medresesi, a Qur'anic school-turned-shopping complex where *nargile* pipes can be smoked on plush pillows with soul-warming tea.

BEYAZIT SQUARE. Continuing along the tram line brings you to the Beyazıt stop. On the right sidewalk, amid jewelry and soccer clothing stalls, are stone stairs leading up to the large cobblestoned expanse of Beyazıt Meydanı (Beyazıt Square). The square's main stairs are a few meters up the road. Off of the square, there are a number of places to see, beginning with the **Calligraphy Museum** to the left of the main stairs. Located in an old *medrese,* the museum houses a collection of *tuğras* (embellished royal seals) and Qur'ans. Small and dimly lit to preserve the artwork, the museum has a smaller, older collection than the İbrahim Paşa Sarayı (see **Museum of Turkish and Islamic Art,** p. 115). The Calligraphy Museum's permanent collection is primarily from the 13th century, but it also houses temporary exhibits by local artists. *(Open Tu-Sa 9am-4pm. $1.50, students $1.)*

BEYAZIT CAMİİ. Opposite the museum, on the right side of the square, Beyazıt Camii, commissioned by Sultan Beyazıt II (1481-1512), is a good example of the pre-*faïence* period of Ottoman mosque decoration. It also provides a barricade-free opportunity to view one of the oldest standing Imperial mosques in its entirety. Enter the courtyard used for washing up before prayer and take a right, walking around the *şadirvan* to enter the mosque. Though the door is usually covered by a heavy green curtain during the day, the mosque is still open, and the curtain is easily pushed aside. The adjoining courtyard, in the perpetual shade of the mosque, is popular with bead sellers, young men hawking cellular phones, students, and *çay*-drinkers. On the right side as you move toward the used book bazaar is the **Tomb of Sultan Beyazıt II** (1481-1512). The tomb itself is underwhelming, with only a solitary casket and a painted dome. *(Open Tu-Su 9:30am-4:30pm.)*

İSTANBUL UNIVERSITY. The entrance to İstanbul University, to the left of Beyazıt Camii, is a massive arch embellished with gold calligraphy against a deep green background. Nowadays, riot police often stand guard over the small ridge leading up to the entrance, since the university is a hotbed of both Muslim and secular student activism, which occasionally flares up into large, violent demonstrations. Protests and riots, when they do happen, generally occur on Friday afternoons, immediately after prayers. Guards at the gate check IDs, but an ISIC should suffice. The main entrance leads to a long, tree-canopied driveway flanked by a forested park that is frequented by young couples and the occasional stray dog looking for a cool place to sleep. In the center of the main walkway and directly in front of the main campus building, a **statue of Atatürk** in all his glory points out the path of knowledge to a rather muscular male flag bearer and a female torch bearer. To the right of the Atatürk statue is the **Beyazıt Tower,** which serves as a lookout and meteorological station. The building's somber facade reflects its original use as a part of the Ministry of War during the late Ottoman period. Follow the path around to the right to the only public basketball court for miles around. You'll eventually come to a park where students gather to smoke and eat. *(Do not attempt to enter the main campus building without a student escort, since students themselves must pass through metal detectors to enter the building, and the guards are less than friendly.)*

SÜLEYMANİYE KÜLLİYESİ (SÜLEYMANİYE COMPLEX)

From the university, follow the line of stalls to the left of the mosque down the hill of Fuatpaşa Cad. Keep the stone wall on your left; turn left when it does and the mosque will come into view. From Sultanahmet, either walk along the tramvay *(15min.) or take the* tramvay *to the "Üniversite" stop, walk across the square, and take Besim Ömer Paşa Cad. past the walls of the university to Süleymaniye Cad. Open Tu-Su 9:30am-4:30pm, except during prayer.*

To the north of İstanbul University sits the massive, elegant **Süleymaniye Camii,** one of architect Sinan's two great masterpieces. The other is Selimiye Camii in Edirne (see p. 149). Built on one of the seven beautiful hills of Istanbul between 1550-1557 for 700,000 gold dukas, the Süleymaniye Camii is part of a larger **külliye** (complex), which includes **tombs,** an **imaret** (soup kitchen), several **medreses** (Islamic schools), a hospital, a hospice, and a hamam. The mosque's charitable and educational institutions served as an integral part of both the complex and everyday life (see **Ottoman Architecture,** p. 23). Prof. Sıddık Sami Onar Sok. runs between the university and the mosque. The street was formerly known as Tıryakı Çarşısı (The Addicts' Market), after the once-flourishing hashish trade. An entrance on S.S. Onar Sok. leads into the royal cemeteries, where each person has two tombstones—one for the body and one for the soul—with cylindrical-shaped tombstones for men and board-like tombstones edged with flowers for women. Passing through the graveyard brings you to the similarly decorated **royal tombs** of Süleyman I and his wife, Haseki Hürrem. Süleyman's tomb incorporates all three of Sinan's decorative signatures: İznik tiles, stained glass, and painted patterns. The tomb is a superb example of the Ottoman integration of these three elements; fans of İznik tile will appreciate the band of deep blue tile with calligraphy tracing the middle of the room. *(Open Tu-Su 9:30am-4:30pm. $1 donation suggested.)*

Walk along the Süleymaniye Camii's southwest side to the large arch just below the dome. With three columns of honeycomb windows, this arch mirrors those of Aya Sofia. Enter the mosque's central courtyard through the smaller tourist entrance to the left of the main door. Sinan used balconied minarets attached to the main part of the mosque to mark the corners of this courtyard. Columns made from the stones of the royal box at the Hippodrome (see **The Hippodrome** and **The Museum of Turkish and Islamic Art,** p. 115) support the courtyard's 24 domes.

In the spirit of Aya Sofia, the mosque's main attraction is its vast space. The impression of perfect proportions is no accident: the height of the dome (53m) is exactly twice the length of the mosque's walls. The arches' red and white stones highlight their vast size and draw attention to the lines of the dome. The stained-glass windows are the work of the master **Sarhoş İbrahim** (İbrahim the Drunkard), whose great skill, reflected in his exquisite windows, must have surpassed his vice. The wooden lattice curtain in the back left side of the mosque marks off the section where women recite their prayers.

Pick up your shoes on the way out of the mosque, turn right through the gardens along the outside of the courtyard, and, turning left, exit onto şifhane Sok. **Sinan's Tomb** can be reached by following şifhane Sok. to the intersection with Mimar Sinan Cad. The architect's modest tomb is a tribute to the standard Muslim burial rite of roses growing from the earthen open face of a tomb, and the tomb's simple sincerity peacefully gives tribute to the Ottomans' finest artist.

The **Süleyman Library** is behind the busy cafes along the Prof. Sıddık Sami Onal Cad. Originally built by Sinan to store all the old texts scattered throughout the city, the library now stores ancient texts on microfilm.

DOUBLE TROUBLE Various theories of art history abound as to the origin and explanation of the two faces of Medusa that form the base of a pair of Ionic columns in the far left corner of the Yerebatan Sarayı (Underground Cistern). Medusa, the most terrifying of the Gorgon sisters, whose head sprouts vicious snakes instead of hair, frequently guest-stars in ancient Greek and Roman lore. Once a beautiful maiden, Medusa attracted the ire of the goddess Athena, who cursed her with a monstrous form that was capable of turning even the bravest warrior to stone if he but glanced in her direction. Perseus finally slew Medusa by showing her her own reflection in his sword. The mysterious pair of heads in the Cistern conjures up this petrifying ugliness. The third and fourth of the now-separated set lie at the base of the Bosporus Bridge and in Mersin, respectively. Most scholars agree that the heads all came from Didim, but what has confounded art historians for centuries is the fact that all four are arranged at different angles to the ground (the two in the Cistern are upside down and sideways; the other two are reportedly at opposite 45 degree diagonals). The most recent and compelling theory is that the angles represent the angles of reflection in Perseus' sword that ultimately vanquished the monster.

FATİH

Fatih, meaning "the conqueror," is an enclave of strict Muslim conservatism surrounded on all sides by secular, modern İstanbul. As such, it's an insular community, holding fast to such Muslim traditions as the full *chador* of head scarves for women and wool caps and beards for men, earning it the nickname *Küçük Iran* (little Iran). Tourists need only take the usual steps to cover up, particularly no shorts or miniskirts and long sleeves for women (see **Customs and Etiquitte,** p. 32). Fatih is also a stronghold of the **Fazilet Party,** Turkey's most Islamic-leaning Party. *Fazilet*, like the banned Welfare Party before it (see p. 18), has been trying to boost its image through its community's success—there is low crime, good trash collection, and a cleanliness contrasting with that of its northern neighbors, Fener and Balat (see **The Here and Now,** p. 19). Street merchants sell prayer beads, wool caps for men, and copies of the Qur'an. The walk up to Yavuz Selim Camii passes through the district of **Çarşamba** (Wednesday), named after the **market** that fills these streets on that day. It's an experience far more vivid than anything the Grand Bazaar or the Egyptian Spice Bazaar can offer. Fatih is easily reached by a westward walk on şehzadebaşı Cad., which turns into Macar Kardeşler Cad. once over Atatürk Cad., and then changes names again to Fevsı Paşa Cad. when the road reaches the mosque complex. You can also take a Fatih-bound bus from Aksaray. Scope out this part of town on a Wednesday to catch the action along Darruşafaka Cad. A nice walk starts just up the hill from the Draman bus stop, past the defunct Fethiye Museum, at the overlook, with an incredible view of the Golden Horn. Walk down Fethiye Cad., bearing left until you are on Darruşafaka Cad.

FATİH CAMİİ. Unlike İstanbul's other great mosques, which often lie dormant outside of prayer times, Fatih Camii functions as the primary meeting place and social center of the neighborhood. Kids run free on the wide walkways that surround the mosque on all sides, flying kites or kicking soccer balls, while old men, resting with prayer beads, watch from seats along the walls. The stunning mosque was built in 1463, completely destroyed by an earthquake in 1766, and then rebuilt according to the original design, though the interior remains unfinished. While the mosque's outer precincts can be easily explored, visiting the inside requires appropriate clothing and a bit of patience close to prayer times, as the mosque is often full of worshippers. Once inside, however, the mosque is an airy, open, colorful space. Stained glass windows look more like intricately cut mosaics, their small panes winding a wall of design around the *mihrab*. The four corners at the base of the dome have been newly painted, with similar intertwinings of blue, green, vermilion, and deep orange. *(Open Tu-Su 9am-5:30pm. Donations encouraged.)*

YAVUZ SELİM CAMİİ. Named in honor of Sultan Selim the Grim, Yavuz Selim Camii is Fatih's other impressive mosque. When approached from the west, it dominates the view for several hundred meters. Built in a simple square of unadorned, faceted stone, the mosque stands in the center of what was once a complex comprised of *tabhânes* (guesthouses), *imâret* (a meeting place for students and the poor to receive free meals from the sultan), a *sibyan* (pre-school), and tombs. The *tabhâne* rooms adjacent to the mosque reflect the transition from early Ottoman to classical Ottoman architecture. The mosque is far quieter and more inviting than the neighboring Fatih Camii, with groups of children playing soccer and adults congregating on picnic tables in the courtyard. The **tomb of Selim the Grim** is frequented by local visitors coming to pray and leave beads in memory of the sultan. Nicknamed "the Grim" for his fierceness and military success, Selim paved the way for Ottoman guardianship of the three holy cities of Islam. The giant, rectangular hole in the ground in front of the mosque is the last remnant of the **Cistern of Aspar,** one of the city's three Byzantine reservoirs. Formerly a squatter village and shantytown, the reservoir has been converted into an exclusive sports complex, complete with basketball and tennis courts and soccer fields on the far side. You need a membership card to get in. Heading down the staircase by the restrooms will take you to the handsome neighborhood of **Kuçuk Mustafa Paşa**

(not to be confused with the street and bus stop, **Koça Mustafa Paşa,** on the other side of town). *(The mosque, tomb, and cistern lie northwest of Fatih Camii and can be easily reached by retracing your steps back down Darruşafaka and then turning right on Yavuz Selim Cad. Tomb open Tu-Su 9:30am-4:30pm. Donation suggested; $.20 may be required.)*

ZEYREK

Zeyrek and şehzadebaşı, two neighborhoods at either end of the **Aqueduct of Valens** and separated by Atatürk Cad., mark the beginning of greater Fatih, the religiously conservative quarter of İstanbul. Any **bus** from Aksaray to destinations on the Taksim side of the Golden Horn stops at the top of the hill right before the aqueduct at şehzadebaşı, in front of **İstanbul City Hall.** Buses stop again immediately after the aqueduct. From Sultanahmet and the rest of the old city, take the **tram** to the Lâleli stop, walk along the tracks, and turn right before the overpass of Atatürk Cad.

Stretching from Fatih to Beyazıt, the **aqueduct** was built in the 4th century to augment the Roman water system that runs from the Belgrade forest. Diligent maintenance by emperors and sultans kept it in use for 1500 years before it fell into disrepair. When facing the Atatürk bridge and the Golden Horn, the neighborhood on the left side of the street is **Zeyrek,** a conservative Muslim district that is also one of the city's major meat processing areas. Sides of lamb, big buckets of tripe, chickens stripped of head and feathers, and *kebap* are displayed in the windows of butcher shops along İtfaiye Bul. (Fire Station St.), the main street connecting the neighborhood's sights. The area of Zeyrek that's worth seeing weaves in and out of the shade of the aqueduct and the buildings nearby.

Starting from the City Hall, cross Atatürk Bul. and head right toward the aqueduct through the lovely **Saraçhane Park.** The Fatih monument stands on the right side of the park. This bronze **statue of Sultan Mehmet II** (a.k.a. Fatih) astride a leaping horse is flanked on either side by scholars and a group of Janissaries (see p. 11) with their feet firmly planted on the ground. Housed in the Ganzafer Medrese, which presses up against the aqueduct, the **Karikator ve Mizah Müzesi** (Caricature Museum) is a delightful museum. It can be reached by following Atatürk Cad. under the aqueduct and taking the first left onto Kovacılar Sok. The first section exhibits Turkey's more venerated comics from the 50s to the present, such as *Dolmuş*, *Girgir*, *Avni*, and *Nasreddin Hoca* (see **Wise Ass,** p. 351). The collection also contains a number of politically oriented panels from both the Ottoman and Young Turk periods (see **The Young Turks and World War I,** p. 15). Also featured are some rare, less-than-flattering strips of Mustafa Kemal (see p. 15) before his glory days. (☎521 12 64. Open daily, 10am-6pm. Free.)

If you've had your fill of culture, the monolithic **IMÇ Çarşlsithe** on the Zeyrek side of Atatürk Cad. is a 6-block behemoth of a shopping mall. More of an indoor bazaar than a mall, each block is specialized. Block 6 is a crash course in Turkish pop culture. Dozens of CD stores and music production "studios" line its dingy courtyard. Block 2 is devoted entirely to carpets, and the rest cater more to residential interests such as appliances and furniture.

AKSARAY-LÂLELİ

If you come to İstanbul from Europe, or vice versa, you are bound to encounter this bustling section of the old city, since it is a major bus hub and the departure point for the otogar-bound subway. Its streets are lined with display windows, and its sidewalks are full of merchants on the prowl for stragglers looking to buy. The neighborhood is a shopper's paradise for those in the market for leather jackets or *Nataşas* (see p. 409). A large Bulgarian and Russian community has settled in the area, and consequently, many of the signs and advertisements are written in Cyrillic. Stores cater to Russian and Eastern European clothing manufacturers who buy Turkish leather and fabrics to import back home, but you can find anything here among the hodgepodge of happy capitalists. At night, the area is one of İstanbul's centers of prostitution, and its small back streets, lined with windows covered by dark iron shutters, ought to be walked with caution. Despite its seedier side, the Aksaray-Lâleli area, like most of İstanbul, feels safe during the day, bustling with far too many people to be considered at all questionable.

KALENDERHANE CAMII. Formerly the Byzantine Church of Kyriotissa, Kalenderhane Camii is a 9th-century church converted first into a monastery by the Kalender dervishes and subsequently into a mosque. Although it sits unadorned and aging on the outside, the gray and pink marble interior is striking in its simplicity. *(From the "Üniversite" tram stop, walk about 20m downhill along Ordu Cad., take the 1st right after the tram platform onto Büyük Reşit Paşa Cad., walk past the university, and then make a slight right onto Kalender Camii Sok., from which you can see the mosque.)*

LÂLELI CAMII. Rising magically above the din of Ordu Cad., Lâleli Camii is mysteriously quiet inside. This baroque Ottoman mosque has 18 cupolas supported on 14 columns, and has a covered bazaar *(arasta)* below. The tomb of Sultan Mustafa III, who commanded the mosque's baroque design at the hands of court architect Mehmet Tahir, lies at street level near the entrance to the bazaar. This bazaar is much smaller than the Grand Bazaar, and sells mostly clothing for local shoppers. Look for a cafe downstairs. In 1763, Sultan Mustafa III also built an inn just up the hill. Curiously well-preserved, it has since been converted into a restaurant, cafe, and another bazaar. Taşhan Bazaar is one block up from Lâleli Camii; turn right on Gençturk and then right again on Mahvil Sok. *(Downhill along Ordu Cad. from the "Üniversite" tram stop, and immediately next to the "Lâleli" tram stop.)*

EMİNÖNÜ

Alive with the bustle and energy of commerce, Eminönü might be called the home of the real Grand Bazaar. To reach Eminönü from Sultanahmet, head through the northern exits of the Grand Bazaar and downhill through narrow, hawker-lined streets or take the convenient Zeytinburnu-Eminönü tram to the end of the line. From Sultanahmet, it's only a 5-10 minute walk along the tram line downhill. From Taksim, take any bus marked "Eminönü," or take the trolley that runs along İstiklâl Cad. down to the end of the line, hop on the one-stop metro and walk across Galata Bridge into the heart of the neighborhood.

Pigeons, buses, and people swarm the waterfront area. With traffic flying down Kennedy Cad. on one side and the busy port on the other, Eminönü's winding merchant strip can be overwhelming. Watch yourself and your wallet. Food from the seaside stalls can be delicious, but make sure to eat only at the ones that get a lot of business to make sure the food has been replaced since the day before. With your back to the water, Eminönü's three major attractions are, from left to right, Yeni Camii, the Mısır Çarşısı (Egyptian Spice Bazaar), and Rüstem Paşa Camii.

YENİ CAMİİ. Yeni Camii was the last Imperial Classical mosque built by the Ottomans. It is considered to be of lesser quality than some of İstanbul's grander mosques since its tiles are not from İznik and its architect wasn't Sinan. However, for the non-expert, the color and quantity of tiles along the *mihrab* and the *minber* are still impressive. On Fridays at 1pm, the most important Muslim prayers of the week are read. At these times, the Yeni Camii is so crowded that worshippers congregate on the stairs to pray. While tourists are not allowed to enter the mosque during prayer time, this overspill provides a good opportunity to observe unobtrusively the recitation of Muslim prayers.

MISIR ÇARŞISI. The fragrant mixtures of different spices from the Mısır Çarşısı (Egyptian Spice Bazaar) may distract you from the mosque. A stroll through the Mısır Çarşısı's halls is always a sensory overload and one of the most memorable ways to spend an İstanbulian hour or two. The bazaar once handled customs and excise taxes, but today the 80 or so vendors in the L-shaped building sell a mind-boggling array of spices, gold, tea, sweets, honeycombs, nuts, dried fruit, natural Turkish Viagra, a supposedly aphrodisiac perfume, and a bit of unlicensed soccer team paraphernalia. The bazaar's high-vaulted ceilings, saffron- and curry-scented air, and relative lack of tourist-related merchandise lend it an atmosphere more authentic than that of the Grand Bazaar. If you are looking for a bite to eat, **Pandeli Restaurant** (p. 103) sits at the far end of one hallway, above the seaside entrance.

RÜSTEM PAŞA CAMİİ. Leaving the Spice Bazaar by the waterfront gate and turning left leads you back to Eminönü Square and the small but breathtaking Rüstem Paşa Camii. Designed by the illustrious Mimar Sinan, the mosque was constructed in 1561 at the behest of Rüstem, a Grand Vizier. Stunningly beautiful tiles, said to be among İznik's finest, arranged in rare circular patterns, cover practically every surface. The unique main entrance features a nested arch design showcasing all the basic arch forms found in Islamic architecture: first a normal shallow cusp shape, then a tulip shape, and finally a circular shape. Another attractive aspect of the mosque is its small size. Because of the limited space, there is no roped-off section for tourists, so have a close look at the İznik tiles that are more accessible than those in the larger mosques. *(Either cut a path through the densely populated bazaar or walk along Reşadiye Cad. The entrance is on the far side of the mosque, down a small alley. Be on the lookout for a gate marked "Rüstem Paşa Kapısı," through which stairs lead to the mosque. The tourist entrance is to the left of a small courtyard that faces the main entrance.)*

FENER AND BALAT

When advancing his original plan for the attack on the Dardanelles, Winston Churchill asked the war cabinet to imagine the confusion and terror that would fill the "tumbledown wooden houses and narrow cobblestone streets of the Golden Horn" at the sight of British warships. Though most of İstanbul has been paved and concreted in the post-war 20th century, Fener and Balat have retained some of this pre-modern sprawl. İstanbul's Greek and Jewish neighborhoods preserve the look and feel of a town from the 1800s, and despite ramshackle cement houses, the narrow cobblestone streets remain. As the last flickering embers of a once-thriving Greek and Jewish community appear to be dying out, neighborhood conviviality rules the streets, from children playing under the watchful eyes of their mothers to the men playing cards and backgammon in the numerous *spor colubas* in the shade of hanging vines on seemingly every corner.

The easiest way to see Fener and Balat is to take a bus from Eminönü to Unkapanı (a stop on Abdülezel Cad., the wide road that runs along the Golden Horn). Unkapanı-bound buses leave from the Eminönü bus stop. From the Unkapanı bus stop, **Gül Camii** (Church of St. Theodosia) can be reached by continuing along Abdülezel Cad. for 300m in the same direction as the bus, and then turning left onto Kara Sarıklı Cad. Take the second left and then the second right (the streets are unmarked) up the stairs to the mosque. The 12th-century Greek Orthodox church earned its name, Gül (Rose) Camii, in 1453, when the soldiers of Mehmet's army entered the church and found it strewn with roses. The mosque is usually open only for prayers, but the staff can open it for visitors at other times. About 500m farther up Abdülezel Cad. lies the **Greek Orthodox Patriarchate of Phanar.** *Phanar*, as Fener was once known, derives from the Phanariots, a group of wealthy Greek families that lived in the area and served as prominent advisors and administrators in the Ottoman Empire. These rather modest buildings are in fact the Orthodox Christian Church's equivalent to the Vatican; the Church's Patriarchs preside from here. It was also here that the Greek War of Independence began, when the Ottomans hanged Patriarch Gregory V in front of the church's gates. Unfortunately, the church and its dependent buildings are generally closed to casual visitors. About 300m past the patriarchate, **St. Stephen of the Bulgurs** is sandwiched between two roads as the highway splits in two. The church's shiny, magic-castle appearance is a by-product of its completely cast-iron construction.

From the Bulgarian church, **Balat,** the city's Jewish quarter, is only 300m ahead and inland. In marked contrast with Turkey's Greek community, which has had a sometimes difficult relationship with the outside, Jews have always received hospitable treatment. Fleeing persecution during the 1492 Spanish Inquisition, Spanish Jews were encouraged by Beyazıt II to settle in İstanbul (see **Jews,** p. 30). From the Fener bus stop, head one block inland and continue on the road parallel to the shoreline road until you hit Kürçü Çeşme Sok., which leads to the 500-year-old **Ahvida Synagogue,** the city's oldest synagogue. (Open Saturdays only.)

EYÜP

At the far western end of the Golden Horn lies the **necropolis** (city of the dead) of Eyüp, a major Muslim pilgrimage site with added significance for Turkish Muslims. It was here that Eyüp (Job), a companion of the Prophet Muhammed, died in battle during the first Arab siege of Constantinople. When Eyüp's tomb was rediscovered after the Ottoman conquest, Fatih Mehmet had a mausoleum and mosque complex built on the site. Modern Eyüp is synonymous with religious ceremony. Young boys are brought here, accompanied by their celebrating families, for a final prayer before circumcision. The hills overlooking the city are thick with the turban-capped headstones of Ottoman graves, and smaller mausolea line the streets near the two main mosques. It is considered a great privilege to be buried in Eyüp.

EYÜP CAMİİ AND THE TOMB OF EYÜP. Eyüp's primary attraction, Eyüp Camii is the second mosque to grace the site. It dates from 1800, after the one built by Fatih collapsed. With a Baroque exterior and gobs of gold on the inside, its excess is characteristic of later Ottoman art. A long line of the soon-to-be-circumcised boys and their fathers often forms before the *mihrab*, as they wait to pray before the auspicious moment. The boys wear satin capes of blue and white, detailed in gold sequin and a regal plumed hat. After performing the "*Maşallah*" (thanks be to God) prayer, they usually pose for pictures in front of the tomb or in the mosque itself. Directly across from the mosque, in the **Tomb of Eyüp,** lavishly sheathed in İznik tiles and bathed in emerald green light, rests a very large footprint of Muhammed. The mosque is flanked by a beautiful plaza lined with dozens of food, ice cream, cloth stalls, and restaurants. Women should wear head scarves, long sleeves, and long skirts. *(Tomb open daily. Free.)*

CAMİİ KEBIR SOK. AND THE NECROPOLIS. Camii Kebir Sok., the cobblestone street heading from Eyüp to the Golden Horn and the ferry stop, is the main thoroughfare of the old necropolis. Numerous domed mausolea line the street on either side. Regrettably, only the **tombs of Sokollu Mehmet Paşa** and **Siyavus Paşa** are open to the public. The former is more impressive, with deftly crafted stained glass. The excellent İznik panels of Siyavus Paşa's tomb feature an intense, earthen-red hue that modern synthetic dyes have been unable to reproduce. *(Necropolis open Tu-Su 9:30am-4:30pm. Donations encouraged.)*

PIERRE LOTI CAFE. Opened by famous French Turkophile Pierre Loti, this cafe can be reached via a web of cobblestone roads winding through the necropolis. From the well-shaded tables at this graveyard perch, the view extends all the way to the Süleymaniye Camii and Beyazıt tower at İstanbul University. The tea ($.50) and coffee compliment the vista beautifully. An adjacent gift shop is the only place in İstanbul where the prices are listed in French francs. *(From the Eyüp bus or the ferry stop, walk away from the Golden Horn along Camii Kebir Sok. until it turns into another street that runs into Silahtarağa Cad. Head right for 150m, and you'll spot yellow signs showing the way. Alternatively, follow a cobblestone switchback through the graveyard directly to the cafe. The path, a quicker (but steeper) route than the road, begins to the left of the main entrance to Eyüp Camii. A taxi ($2-3) is another option. Open daily 9am-11pm.)*

EDİRNEKAPI

A quiet, residential İstanbuli neighborhood, Edirnekapı lies just outside the old city walls (whose ruins are visible as you peer out the bus windows heading northwest along the Golden Horn). Dense, yet suburban in feel, modern Edirnekapı would hardly merit mention if it were not the site of Kariye Camii, formerly the Church of St. Saviour or Chora Church, now a museum.

KARİYE CAMİİ. Hidden in the back streets of Edirnekapı, Kariye Camii has some of the best-preserved Byzantine mosaics in the world. Although every gilded tile goes against Islamic scriptures concerning representational art, the church managed to escape the fate of Aya Sofia, whose mosaics were either plastered over or torn down. During the 1453 siege, the church's location in Edirnekapı, a defensive nightmare and the weakest spot in the Theodosian

EX-PAT EXTRORDINAIRE During the very end of the Ottoman period, a large community of artists and writers made Eyüp their home. The most famous was the French novelist and travel writer Pierre Loti, a.k.a. Julian Marie Viaud (1850-1923). His Orientalist romance *Aziyade* tells the story of the tragic love affair between a young, daring Loti and a married harem woman during the last days of the Ottoman Empire. He was known for his fez and his loyalty to Turkey during the Balkan conflict and the early part of WWI. He lived in Eyüp from 1876 to 1913. Interestingly, his name has now been appropriated by a chain of pizza restaurants all over İstanbul.

walls, made the odds of Kariye's survival even more improbable. Situated at the base of a small hill outside the walls, Edirnekapı's low location gives the advantage to an attacker's artillery—a position that Mehmet quickly exploited. Enough of St. Saviour Church survived Mehmet's artillery to be repaired and converted into a mosque. Or perhaps Mehmet's army, like many visitors, got lost and couldn't find the place.

The church's mosaics, crafted with gold-leaf tiles, narrate the life of Christ (see **The Timeless Vision of Byzantium,** p. 21). When viewed in the dim light of a candle, the figures appeared much more lifelike, as the candlelight moving over the image gave the illusion of motion. The mosaics are an excellent example of later Byzantine art whose expressive realism influenced Giotto and other Italian painters. If there is no available curator or an English-speaking tour group to listen in on, start your own tour in the narthex (to the left of the entrance behind the ticket window) with the birth of Christ, and continue around the church to behold scenes from the life of Mary, portrayals of Christ's family tree, and portraits of saints, including the manuscript-toting St. Kosmas the Poet, patron saint of writers.

The museum is surrounded by souvenir and food shops, including **Asitâne.** Gourmet olive and cheese plates at this Ottoman restaurant start at $3.50, traditional Turkish entrees from $7-12, and fish from $13.30. A full bar, cocktail menu and list of local wines starting at $10 round out the experience. AmEx/MC/V. *(To reach the Camii, start at the Edirnekapı otogar, heading downhill along Fevzi Paşa Cad., turn left onto Salma Tomruk Cad., then take the second left onto Arat Sok. Open Th-Tu 9am-4:30pm. $1.75 for students, $4.40 general)*

YEDİKULE

At the intersection of Sahil Yolu and Belgrat Kapısı Demirhane Yolu. Yedikule is most conveniently reached by commuter rail from Sirkeci Garı or from the Cankurtaran in Sultanahmet, below the Blue Mosque down by the water. There is very good dolmuş service between Yedikule and Topkapı (the region, not the palace) along Belgrat Kapısı Demirhane Yolu. Museum open Tu-W 9am-4pm. $.80. No student discount.

The Theodosian land walls and the Yedikule (Seven Towers) fortress are the last remnants of the old city's ironclad defenses. This system once included sea walls that ran from Yedikule to the former Byzantine palace of Buceleon and continued around to present-day Eminönü. There, a great iron chain was strung across the Golden Horn whenever invaders threatened. In 1453, the land walls proved to be the weak link in the system when they crumbled under Mehmet's artillery. Ironically, these walls are the only pieces of the city's defenses that survive today.

The current Yedikule fortifications comprise the Byzantine **Golden Gate** and five newer towers which Mehmet added after capturing the city. Theodosius I built the Golden Gate, the two towers with three large brick and stone arches between them, as a triumphal arch through which he and later emperors would enter the city. The arch, sheathed in white marble with gold-plated gates, once served the city as both defense and decoration. To reach the **Marble Tower,** the southernmost section of the Theodosian land walls, turn left outside the Yedikule museum doors and follow the fortress walls to the Yedikule gate. From here, walk along the exterior of the fortress across the train tracks to the sea. More than the Golden Gate, the tower gives a clear sense of the original fortifications.

The two towers directly to the left of the entrance served as a maximum-security **prison** during the early part of the Ottoman Empire until 1839. The first tower, used for prisoners serving long sentences, has their names carved into the wall. The second tower was used for incarceration and beheadings. Though somewhat hard to see from the ground floor, the infamous "well of death," the hole into which heads would roll, still survives. Climb the staircase and walk along the walls to the turret on the entrance side of the fortress to experience the full horror of the "well of death." *(Wear sturdy shoes and watch your head. A flashlight might prove useful.)*

In the far left corner of the fortress' courtyard (which serves as an occasional rock concert venue in the summer), you can enter and climb past some cells to the top. From there, you can see the vast sprawl of İstanbul in all directions, and, just beyond the old city walls, the finely manicured, tiny tracts of farmland. The thin ribbon of land between Belgrat Kapısı Demirhane Yolu and the land walls is home to much of İstanbul's **gypsy community,** which subsists on farming.

NORTH OF THE GOLDEN HORN

TAKSİM SQUARE AND BEYOĞLU

Taksim Square, home of the ritzy Marmaris Hotel and the mammoth Atatürk Cultural Center, draws the rich, the bohemian, and the curious. The square leads into İstiklâl Cad., a cosmopolitan shopping area by day and fast-paced bar and club scene by night. The word "*taksim*" means "distribution," referring to the days when the city's water supply was parceled out from a giant cistern at the top of İstiklâl Cad. Under the approving gaze of the giant Atatürk banner that graces the far end of the main square, Taksim serves as a cement monument to modernization: it's an area of bright lights, big banks, and the industrious insomnia of a great metropolis. Taksim also showcases many of the city's disparate elements: affluent Beyoğlu juxtaposed with poor Galatasaray, and İstanbul's independent artistic community amid multinational banks and consulates.

Present-day Taksim, Beyoğlu, and Galatasaray, through which the İstiklâl Cad. tram runs, stand in what was once known as **Pera** (Greek for "beyond"). Across the Golden Horn from the old city, this area owed its unique demographics to an obscure Byzantine treaty. In the 12th century, when Constantinople began to feel threatened, the emperor allowed the Genoese to set up a colony on the other side of the Golden Horn. Despite the understanding that the Genoese would contribute to the city's defense, they remained neutral when Fatih Mehmet struck in 1453. Over the course of the following three centuries, Pera became the city's foreign quarter, where Greeks, Armenians, Jews, and Russians coexisted. The takeover by the Young Turks introduced a pro-Turkish agenda, largely as a hedge against the European powers who were slowly dividing up the Empire (see **The Young Turks and World War I,** p. 15). Though not overly persecuted, the minority communities of Pera felt ill-at-ease, and some emigrated. By the time of the population exchange in the early 1920s (see **The Treaty of Lausanne,** p. 16), the end of Pera was near, and a Turkification campaign took place, resulting in renaming the area Beyoğlu.

İSTİKLÂL CAD.

Formerly *La Grande Rue de Pera*, İstiklâl Cad. (Freedom Street), unlike any of the other streets radiating off Taksim Sq., retains the appearance and character of its Ottoman and pre-Republican days. Navigating here is easy—almost all the sights, restaurants, and cafes are either on İstiklâl itself or visible from it. The best way to see the street is to start at Taksim Square, work your way down to the end, and catch either the Tünel metro to Karaköy and the Galata Bridge or hop on the streetcar back up İstiklâl Cad. into Taksim.

At the top of İstiklâl Cad., the **tram turnaround** and the **French consulate,** both classic İstanbulian rendezvous spots, are excellent for people-watching. At the center of the square stands one of the finer (among the numerous) monuments to Atatürk and the country's independence. The monument consists of four sculptures each depicting different participants in the country's struggle for freedom. Atatürk himself faces down İstiklâl Cad., surrounded by 15 figures, including politicians, members of the military, and peasants holding children.

Slightly down the hill from the French consulate on the avenue's first side street, the silvery onion domes of **Aya Triada** peek out among the surrounding skyscrapers and hotels. The terrace of Haci Baba restaurant is a good place to contemplate the scene over a cup of *çay*. Visit the 19th-century church's beautiful interior, accessible from Meşelik Sok., on Sunday (service 9-11am), as the sanctuary, like that of many Greek churches in Turkey, is locked the rest of the time. About 100m down İstiklâl Cad. on the left are **Kücük** and **Büyük Parmakkapı Sok.,** two of Taksim's principal **nightlife** streets. Another 200m farther on the right is the **Çiçek Pasajı,** a recently restored cluster of cafes and somewhat pricey restaurants under a high glass roof. Next door, the **Balık Pazar** (fish market) makes for some delicious meals, but restaurants right next door to each other often have drastically different prices, so check a menu before sitting down. On the left, past the **Galatasaray Lisesi,** a leading candidate for the World's Most Beautiful, Best-Located High School, the Roman Catholic **Church of St. Antoine** survives under the care of Franciscan monks. The original St. Antoine was torn down during the construction of the streetcar line, but the present church, built in 1913, is an exact replica containing original paintings and valuables. The sanctuary is especially peaceful in the afternoon, when members of İstanbul's tiny Roman Catholic community drop in for silent prayer in the pale, colored light of the many stained glass windows. (Church open for visitors daily 8am-noon and 3-7pm. Mass in English Su 10am.)

TÜNEL MEYDANI

İstiklâl Cad. rambles downhill for 500m to Tünel Meydanı, the northern terminus of the two-stop Tünel Metro linking İstiklâl Cad. with Yüzbaşı Sabhattin Euren Cad., near Galata Bridge to the west ($.35, with AKBİL $.25). Packed with music stores, Tünel Meydanı is a prime area if you're in the market for traditional Turkish instruments; some shop owners will even point you toward a good instructor. Classy wine and gourmet joints line the picturesque arcade of Tünel Geçidi, across form the Tünel Metro station at the far end of Istiklâl Cad. Walk straight through the Geçidi into the gorgeous Asmanlı Mescid neighborhood, filled with slightly less upscale but no less quality establishments crowding the alleys.

GALATA

Just off Tünel Meydanı, to the left when facing the Tünel station, Galip Dede Cad. plunges into the heart of Galata. **Galat Mevlihane,** the Mevlevi dervish house, is 30m down Galip Dede on the left. The entrance is easy to miss, consisting only of a single gate with a gilded Ottoman *tuğra* (calligraphic seal) above the door. Once a Sufi lodge housing the Mevlevi Order (see **Mevlevi Order,** p. 27), Galat Mevlihane features an octagonal ceremonial hall dating from the 18th century. Two tiers of seats surround the eight-sided floor, with the upper tiers reserved for the *derviş* orchestra, which plays in the box directly above the main entrance during ceremonies. The audience sits in the lower level, surrounded by displays of musical instruments and dervish costumes. The Galat Mevlihane is one of the best places this side of Konya to catch an authentic *sema*, or **whirling dervish show.** Shows are advertised at the ticket booth and usually take place every other Sunday from 3-5pm and on December 17, the anniversary of Mevlâna's death. Much longer and more authentic than the free ones in Gülhane Park, the shows here are well worth the $4 admission. (Museum open W-M 9:30am-4:30pm. $1.75, students $1.)

About 100m down Galip Dede and one street over (look right), the 62m-high **Galata Tower** rises as the area's most prominent landmark, with the best views of the city from the European side. The tower, built by Justinian in 1348, was intended as part of the defensive fortifications around the Genoese colony. When Mehmet II took Constantinople, he allowed the Genoese to keep the tower, but demanded that the walls be torn down. The tower has recently been assaulted by change, with extensive scaffolding and an 8th-floor nightclub ominously promising an "evening that can never be forgotten." The walkway surrounding the nightclub, however, still offers incredible views of Beyoğlu, Taksim and the many mosques of the old city across the water. (Open daily 9am-8pm. $3.25, $2.50 on Mondays.)

MILITARY MUSEUM (ASKERİ MÜZESİ)

Any Mecidiyeköy- or Harbiye-bound vehicle from Taksim Square goes to the museum. Buses and dolmuş leave from the bus stop where Cumhuriyet Cad. hits Taksim Square, in front of the McDonald's. It's only a 10min. walk from the square along the main road just to the right of the bus station. The museum is just after a large high-rise apartment building also (confusingly) named Askeri Müzesi. Open W-Su 9am-5pm. $.65, students $.25; camera $1.50.

With its large collection of artifacts from two military millennia and its unparalleled air-conditioning system, the superb Askeri Müzesi more than makes up for its location 2km from Taksim Sq. Housed in the former Harbiye Military Academy, which was built as a school 1841 and later converted into the Ministry of War by alum Atatürk when the academy moved to Ankara, the first floor of the museum is devoted to weapons, and the second to Turkish military history. It's organized so that visitors must pass through the "Hall of Martyrs," featuring a billboard-size frieze and a list of all the wars in which Turks have fought. The hall also has several display cases containing the martyrs' freshly pressed and cleaned uniforms, with the holes of their fatal wounds left chillingly unmended.

Highlights of the weaponry floor include **Atatürk's classroom,** now a shrine to the leader's memory, complete with the obligatory oversized bronze bust. The exhibits unfold as a chronological lesson in the history of gun mechanics, but some reading into Turkish military history will greatly inform your visit to this large and at times overwhelming display of the glories and tragedies of warfare. Still, the English language plaques are informative (except in the hall of medals, which has no information in English). Mustafa Kemal's report cards show the extent to which he managed to conceal his military genius before Gallipoli. The lower floor also features a display of wartime cloth, with intriguing displays of battlefield tents and flags. Upstairs, the exhibits on Turkish military history, full of medals and uniforms, are very impressive, though a bit inaccessible without knowledge of Turkish. The **Gallipoli exhibit** offers the Turkish version of the battle through a number of exhibits with English explanations. More impressive is the **War of Independence** section, containing a copy of Atatürk's "To the Mediterranean" order and other original documents. The **Mehter Band,** a skilled Janissary band, plays traditional military music in the courtyard (daily 3-4pm).

EUROPEAN BOSPHORUS SHORE

BEŞİKTAŞ

Locals agree that Beşiktaş marks the frontier between westernized İstanbul and the rest of the city. Though the district is less touristy than Sultanahmet and Eminönü, it has a lively and upscale community. Except for the naval museum, housed in a small modern building by the main bus stop, the sights are largely hidden behind giant walls built during the twilight of the Ottoman Empire, when the imperial center was moved from the old city onto the banks of the Bosphorus.

DOLMABAHÇE PALACE

From Taksim Sq., follow İnönü Cad. around the Atatürk Cultural Center to the waterfront, and take a left on Dolmabahçe Cad. The palace is up 400m. Or catch any Sariyer-bound bus for Taksim Sq. Open Tu-W, F-Su 9am-4pm. Mandatory tour of Harem or Selâmlık alone $5, combo ticket $8.50 (2hr.). Tickets may sell out in summer. Reserve ☎ 227 34 41.

Dolmabahçe's extravagant entrance fee is merely a preview of the decadence that awaits. And a penchant for decadence, coupled with hard-core palace and/or late Ottoman enthusiasm, is perhaps the only reason to make the trip. The building borrows its excess indiscriminately from French Baroque, Rococo, and Neoclassical styles, sitting atop the space that **Mehmet the Conqueror** used as a harbor while preparing to conquer Constantinople. Sultan Ahmet I filled in the harbor to make a garden, and hence the palace got the name Dolmabahçe (literally "filled garden").

The obligatory guided tour, which thankfully covers only some of the 285 rooms, begins before the **grand staircase,** where a crystal balustrade and an 1800kg (1 ton) chandelier set the tone for the rest of the tour. The aesthetic merits of the collection are measured in tons of crystal, square meters of handwoven carpet, and pounds of gold leaf. Remarkably, if perhaps uncreatively, every room is symmetrical along two axes, and even the gifts from foreign governments had to come in pairs. The tour arrives next in the **reception hall,** a room complete with bear-hide mats from Tsar Nikolai, clocks from the Napoleons, and other gifts from the likes of Kaiser Wilhelm and George II. From here, the tour is a gilded blur until the **throne room,** where a 36m dome supports the largest chandelier in the palace, a 3500kg (4½ ton) Waterford novelty presented by Queen Victoria. While several parts of the palace have been allowed to fall into disrepair, the throne room is kept splendid for a few official functions, such as the reception of foreign dignitaries, recently including George Bush, Sr.

After the throne room, the focus turns domestic in the **Harem,** the former home of the Imperial family. The Harem's attractions include the **circumcision recovery room,** where young princes would spend about five days in post-operative convalescence (and pain). While there, check out the **giant gold crown** mounted atop the recovery bed and the old black-and-white photo of a prince and his surgeon.

Atatürk's rooms include his death bed, now covered by a silver-filigree Turkish flag, and his clock, which stopped on the day of his death, November 10, 1938. On this day each year, at exactly 9:05am, the entire country ceases activity for a full minute of commemorative silence.

YILDIZ PARKI COMPLEX

Park open daily 9am-10pm; in winter 9am-6pm. Free; $2 if you take a taxi or drive to the köşks or palace. Belediye Müzesi (City Museum) open Tu-Su 9:30am-5pm. $3. Yıldız şale open Tu-W, F-Su 9:30am-5pm. $5. Malta Köşkü open daily 9am-6pm; in winter 9am-5:30pm.

On the far side of central Beşiktaş from Dolmabahçe (about 1km farther down the coastal road) is the main entrance to **Yıldız Parkı,** a heavily wooded park that served as the nerve center of the Ottoman Empire during the 30-year reign of **Abdülhamid II** (see **The Plot Thickens,** p. 14). These days, the park provides some of the best shade possible during the city's hot summers and is one of young İstanbul's favorite make-out spots. Large, sprawling, and uphill in every direction, the park is filled with tall trees that block out the sounds of the nearby city. The **Yıldız Palace Complex,** a collection of *köşk*s (pavilions) and other buildings, is scattered throughout the park. After first serving as the palace of Sultan Abdülhamid II, who retreated to Yıldız from the excesses of Dolmabahçe, the buildings became part of the War Academy during Atatürk's presidency. The main building fell into disrepair until its restoration by the Turkish motoring club and subsequent conversion into two museums, a theater, and offices.

From the park entrance, a steep road leads almost 1km uphill to a T-junction. Immediately at the junction, you can (almost always) find *nargile* (water pipes), *gözleme* (crêpes), and a soda and candy stand. To the left is **Çadır Köşk,** and to the right are **Yıldız şale** and **Malta Köşk.** Built in three chunks in the last two decades of the 19th century, Yıldız şale (Star Chalet) was the palatial guest house of Sultan **Abdülhamid II.** Though the overall decor is relatively understated, the guest house is home to what is unofficially one of the largest carpets in the world; an entire exterior wall was knocked down in order to install it. The luxury lodge also housed Atatürk during the early period of his rule and contains bedrooms that slept various foreign heads of state (including **Kaiser Wilhelm, Charles de Gaulle,** and **Nicolae Ceaucescu**) until the 1970s, when the palace was converted into a museum. The **Belediye Müzesi** contains a medium-sized collection of random household effects from the late Ottoman period, a couple of cabinets worth of *Karagöz* (shadow puppets; see **No Strings Attached,** p. 166), and a rotating exhibit on local handicrafts. About 100m downhill from the palace entrance is the **Malta Köşkü,** a former palace *köşk* turned cafe/bar/*büfe* with an expansive, tree-framed view and an irresistible sweets buffet. **Çadır Köşk** is a pink building with a pond in front. Local nannies bring kids here to feed the ducks.

OTHER SIGHTS IN THE BEŞİKTAŞ AREA

If you leave Dolmabahçe Palace and follow Dolmabahçe Cad. along the walls for about 500m, you will reach the **Deniz Müzesi (Naval Museum)** (☎261 00 40; http://abone.superonline.com/~navalmuseumturk/index.htm), immediately recognizable by its garden full of torpedoes, mines, and the skeletal, scarred hull of an old submarine that sank in the Black Sea. A favorite of both military enthusiasts and the casually curious, the Naval Museum is a quiet yet fascinating inroad into the sheer scope of equipment and ceremony involved in Turkish naval history from 1389 to the present. Amid the larger package tour sights in the vicinity, Deniz Müzesi is that rare museum designed for the expert but equally accessible and intriguing to the layperson. This is in part due to informative and concise English placards explaining the various uses of an exhaustive collection of virtually every piece of equipment used in any number of naval operations. Most of the first building is given over to captured flags and uniforms, though the basement houses stone **lithograph plates** once used for printing Ottoman maps and training manuals. While you can't touch the displays, a huge part of the appeal of the collection of **battleship and submarine equipment** is that the pieces are not behind glass, and that they range from **anti-aircraft artillery** to the **heavy battery range** and **bearing change rate finder.** Other sections include a collection of Ottoman **naval memorabilia** and furnishings taken from Atatürk's official yacht (including a bed he graced for 56 days, as well as items as mundane as butter knives, all labelled with archaeological precision), a mine garden, and a building with imperial **caiques,** the long galleys used by the sultan. The stars of the caique collection are the two very long 17th-century boats with magnificently decorated *köşks*. These were used for ceremonial occasions when the sultan made his entrance on water. (☎261 00 40. Open W-Su 9am-12:30pm and 1:30-5pm. $.85, students $.25.)

On the right, 100m down Dolmabahçe Cad. (which becomes Beşiktaş Cad.), stands the **Barbarossa Memorial,** consisting of a large blackened statue of the Barbary Pirate and admiral of the Ottoman Fleet (a.k.a. "Redbeard") who captured Algiers and Tunis. His tomb lies across from the statue. In summer, the smooth pavement near the memorial attracts hordes of skateboarders and inline skaters.

Back along the shore road further from Dolmabahçe, you will eventually run into **Çirağan Sarayı** (Çirağan Palace), across from Yıldız Parkı. Now an *über*-luxury hotel, the building has been marked by idleness and disuse. Built in 1874, it served as the scene of Sultan Abdul Aziz's murder and then as a prison for Murad IV before being used briefly by the Turkish parliament and finally burning to the ground in 1910. In 1991, the palace was restored as a hotel. While the guards provide a veneer of exclusivity, the palace grounds are open to the public. The interior, however, is neither particularly interesting nor welcoming to sightseers.

ORTAKÖY

Set right on the water, hip Ortaköy positively rages with upper-class partygoers on summer nights (see **Nightlife**, p. 139). The town is essentially one grand cafe, surrounded by old wooden houses and painted in cheerful greens, oranges, and reds. The looming Bosphorus Bridge shades the town by day and provides a dramatic backdrop for the all-night revelry at Paşa Beach. Though pricey, Ortaköy is a perfect place to chill, play backgammon, and drink yet another cup of *çay*.

The relative dearth of sights and the inconvenience of the narrow coastal road insulate Ortaköy from the bustle of more downtown areas like Beşiktaş and Taksim. And despite its proximity to Dolmabahçe Palace and the other big Bosphorus attractions, few tourists go the extra kilometer to get here. The town is a thriving center for young Turks, intellectuals, and socialites. Along the path by the water are a number of small restaurants. Further away from the shore, in the few blocks of winding streets between the water and the center of town, small boutiques sell everything from fine jewelry to pricey foreign magazines. Wedged among the cafes along the main street, the town's Greek Orthodox church and synagogue abut each other about 300m from the ornate stonework of the seaside Ortaköy Camii.

While the food is mouthwatering, it's not cheap. The *kumpir* stands at the mouth of the pedestrian area sell baked potatoes filled with toppings of your choice, including cheese, meat, and assorted vegetables ($2). Stands selling *gözleme* (crêpes, $2.50) operate out of the canopied parking lot off the main road. The waterfront establishments serve meals for about $10 under bright, fluorescently lit canopies, while the inland side of the road is crowded with "traditional" *kebap* and *lahmacun* joints. A good mid-range option is **Bekri şarapevi,** on Yelkovan Sok., which serves a delicious array of appetizers in addition to standard *kebap*-oriented main courses; chicken, lamb and beef *kebaps* go for $3.25, as does their original recipe for *köfte.* Beer seems to be standardized around $1.80 in restaurants, $2.50 in bars. There are no the low-key establishments in Ortaköy—even the dark wood pubs play music loud and all try to book live music when possible.

ARNAVUTKÖY

Tiny Arnavutköy, squished between Ortaköy and Bebek and a pleasant walk from either area, is all about ambience and **fish.** Arnavutköy means "Albanian Village" and after the Albanians, Greeks formed the last minority community to occupy the town. Their *yalıs* (wooden waterfront houses) still stand as an elegant architectural testimony to their fading legacy. Even Arnavutköy's mosque is a modern Mediterranean-style house, with one lonely minaret standing curiously out of place in this European-looking village. Several very good fish restaurants serve the day's catch from the cleaner, upstream end of the Bosphorus. There is also a **Greek Orthodox church** on the continuation of Satiş Meydanı Sok. Follow the street that runs parallel to the coastal road and turn at the "Etiler" signs. (Open daily 9am-4:30pm.) When the church is not open, you can still tour the beautiful adjoining garden during daylight hours. The area has several pleasant cafes, and locals stroll along what has become İstanbul's de facto marina for cruising and touring boats.

BEBEK

Bebek is a university town, home to the south gate of **Bosphorus University** and many of its professors. The Ortaköy end of the town is thick with stores, offices, and *dondurmacılar* (ice cream sellers). Up the Bosphorus, past the small *camii,* are pricey shops and cafes. Many of İstanbul's rich and famous, and numerous American and European expats, call Bebek home. Enormous mansions and posh apartment buildings create a marked distinction between the residents of Bebek and the rest of the city. Bebek Parkı's manicured lawns and polished benches make an ideal spot for observing the rich and famous docking their yachts.

Boğaziçi Üniversitesi (Bosphorus University), originally founded as Robert College by American missionaries in the 19th century, is a short walk along the coastal road toward the Boğaziçi bus stop. From there, you'll see the university entrance gate. Don't worry about the guard—you don't need identification to enter on foot. The long trek to the main campus leads past the school swimming pool and the boys' dormitory. This green oasis in the middle of a chaotic city is the physical embodiment of the campus spirit: an enclave curiously removed from the tensions that plague İstanbul's other major universities. The campus is stunning, and the English-language curriculum is reputedly the finest in Turkey. The *çay* garden near the ATM is a great place to recover from the exertion of the climb.

Follow signs for *"Burc"* as you exit, and you'll be on Kalebaçhe Cad., which weaves through the handsome suburb of upper Hisar and eventually leads to the tower of the **Fortress of Rumeli Kavağı (Rumeli Hisar),** whose main entrance lies about a kilometer upstream from Boğaziçi along the coastal road and is impossible to miss. **Mehmet the Conqueror** built the fortress in 1452 as he prepared to besiege Constantinople, and later, the Ottomans used it to shield the artillery battery that controlled naval traffic at the narrowest point of the Bosphorus. The massive fortifications are impressive even in their state of disrepair. At the entrance, turn right to the theater or left and uphill to the maze of steps and turrets. The views of the Bosphorus from atop the high walls at the back of the fort are stagger-

FLIGHTS OF PASSION In the 17th century, the Galata Tower became the world's **first intercontinental airport,** when an Ottoman daredevil by the name of **Hezarfen Ahmet Çeleb** flew a hang glider from the top of Galata across to the Asian shore, becoming the first man to fly since the mythical Icarus. He was initially rewarded handsomely by Sultan Murat IV, but the *ulema* (official Ottoman Islamic clergy) predictably proclaimed his project satanic, and the sultan banished the aviator to Algeria. In 1997, Turkish director Mustafa Altioklar made the wildly successful film "İstanbul Beneath My Wings" about the legendary flight. The movie's implication that the sultan's change of heart might have been related to a homosexual relationship between the two men enraged conservative Turks, for whom the idea of homosexuality in the Ottoman Porte is an inconceivable sacrilege.

ing. All that remains of the fortress's mosque is the large central space surrounded by the amphitheater. Like many of İstanbul's grand historic sites, Turkish pop and classical concerts are held here in summer. (Fortress open Th-Tu 9am-5pm. $2.)

SARİYER

Sariyer is one of the last bus stops on the European Bosphorus road, and it can take up to 1½hr. to get there by bus (from Eminönü) or dolmuş (from Taksim or Beşiktaş). While architecturally less interesting than Arnavutköy, it does share a laid-back, low-key ambience with the "Albanian Village," as if it still hasn't gotten over its hypnotically beautiful Bosphorus views. Swimmers and picnickers line the shore walls daily, and the most serious citizens seem to be the fishermen staring reflectively at the cliffs across the water. Be sure to try Sariyer's culinary specialty, *börek:* triangles of phyllo dough filled with cheese or meat. Sariyer also hosts an excellent small museum, the **Sadberk Hanım Müzesi,** on Piyasa Cad. 25-29, 400m from the Sariyer dolmuş stop in the direction of Bebek. Built in a cream-colored Armenian house in honor of the wife of a Turkish entrepreneur, the museum has an eclectic collection of the artistic and ethnographic items of the late Sadberk Hanım. The collection includes engrossing embroidery, calligraphy, and illustrated manuscript displays. The highlight, however, is the *faïence* collection, which features fine İznik pieces. *(Museum ☎242 38 13. Open daily 10:30am-6pm; Oct.-Mar. Th-Tu 10am-5pm. $1.50, students $.25.)*

Farther south, toward Bebek, is the port of **Büyükdere,** one stop before Sariyer on the bus. Since Sariyer's port is undergoing massive renovations, watch the ships docking here. In the other direction, toward the Black Sea, is **Rumeli Feneri.** A pleasant, though moderately long, walk from Sariyer will take you to this quaint fisherman's village, a striking contrast to bigger Sariyer. The Genovese, who once occupied the northern shores of the Bosphorus, extended a long metal chain between Rumeli Feneri and Anadolu Feneri at some point in the 18th century to be sure seafarers wouldn't evade their tax on passage under the cover of night. *Feneri* means lighthouse, while *Rumeli* (from Rum, the Turkish word for Rome) refers to the European side of the strait, and *Anadolu* refers to the Asian, Anatolian side. The chain's final incarnation, which included an underwater net to intercept Russian submarines, was removed in 1960.

THE BELGRADE FOREST

! **ON THE LOOKOUT: THE BELGRADE FOREST** The forest has a dangerous reputation. There have been reports of violent crimes perpetrated after sunset. If you are alone, don't go at night.

As İstanbul's last and only old-growth forest, this is where the nature-lovers go to hike, picnic, wash their cars (the water's free), and loll in the cool shade of the tall pines. A former Ottoman hunting ground, Belgrade Forest is also the site of a remarkable network that supplied İstanbul with water for centuries. The forest gets its name from a community of Serbian prisoners, brought here after the capture of Belgrade in 1521 to maintain the water supply system.

Built in stages from the Byzantine period through the reign of Süleyman the Magnificent, the water system remained in use until the beginning of the 1900s, a testimony to the sturdy simplicity of the system's design and the ingenuity of its Serbian caretakers. Scattered around the park are a number of **bends** (large dammed reservoirs) and the remains of the **su terazı** (water towers). These water towers replaced the need for unwieldy aqueducts, and since they worked on the same principle as a gas siphon, they solved the problem of getting water over hills. Water was sent through underground passageways where enough pressure was built up to force it up into a water tower. When the tank filled up, the water was sent back down through the underground channels with enough force to rise up into the next water tower, and so on until the water reached the city.

The best and by far the easiest way to check out the forest and the water works is to catch bus #153, which runs between Sariyer and Bahçeköy every 20 minutes. The end of the line is the town square of Bahçeköy, a village so small that the *müezzin* belts out the call to prayer without amplification. To orient yourself, face uphill with the little tea garden to your right. Behind you and one block downhill is a cheap supermarket, the perfect place to score a bottle of water, *dikmen* wine, or whatever else sustains your wanderlust. Once equipped, there are three ways to get to the forest. To the left and downhill about 45m is the street with signs reading **"Site Bend."** Follow these signs to the edge of the forest, where you can pick up one of the narrow trails up a small, steep hill. At the top, there is a well-worn jeep trail running through the woods. With your back to the forest entrance, head right along the trail for a quarter mile to the bend, a large dam made of massive stone blocks with Arabic inscriptions. The second option is to head right from the main square and backtrack along the bus route. Follow the signs marked **"Bentler,"** 2½km to the entrance of the **Belgrade Forest National Park.** Immediately after the ranger's little hut, the road forks. The right fork leads 1½km past Ottoman springs to the impressive **Valide** and **Yeni Bentler.** The other fork leads to the **Neşet picnic ground** and the **Büyük Bend,** which is larger but farther away (45min. walk each way) than the other bends. Of course, you can also catch a cab from Bahçeköy to the bend for $5 (including $.50 parking fee).

ISTANBUL

ASIAN İSTANBUL

Any #15 bus from Üsküdar heads to Kanlıca, Emirgan, and Anadoluhisan ($.50).

New by İstanbulian standards, the Asian side, like much of the European Bosphorus, is an aggregate of villages that fell outside the old city walls. Because of its residential nature and few sights, Asian İstanbul remains largely undiscovered. As such, *Asya* enjoys a certain reflective distance from the rest of the city—the perfect antidote for the Sultanahmet-weary. An entire day can be spent walking the busy streets and local bazaars without hearing a single "Yes, please!" "Carpet! *Kilim!*" or "Where are you from?" The deal is sweetened by ease of transit—ferries run every 10-15 minutes from Eminönü to Kadıköy for a lovely 15-minute cruise. **Çengelköy's** excellent, inexpensive fish restaurants, **Anadoluhisarı's** small dockside cafes, and **Emirgan's** old-style Turkish houses each merit a visit.

KADIKÖY AND MODA

Kadıköy is the commercial heart of Asian İstanbul and the principal shopping district. There are few tourist sights; instead, Kadıköy offers an honest slice of modern İstanbulian life. The neighborhood's relative lack of pretension makes its crowded markets and narrow stone streets great places to shop for everyday items. And without the tourist tax of more traveled sections of the city, list prices tend to be less ambitious. Kadıköy sits along the Asian Bosphorus shore; south of Üsküdar and Harem, but considerably north of Bostancı. The best way to get there is a ferry from pier 2 in Eminönü (every 15-20min. 7:30am-8:30pm, $.75).

Apart from wandering the back streets off Söğütlüceşme Cad., home to most of the cheap and fairly decent restaurants, Kadıköy's main attraction is **Gen. Azim Gündüz Cad.,** a pedestrian street to the left off Söğütlüçeşme Cad. as you head uphill. The street has slightly cheaper stores than those found along İstiklâl, and has one of the highest concentrations of movie theaters anywhere in İstanbul. These show primarily American films, almost always in English with Turkish subtitles. Turkish movies, unfortunately, are almost never subtitled (tickets $4-6).

A second area for indulgent wandering lies across Söğütlüçeşme Cad. from the dock (on the right as you walk uphill). A small pedestrian square (by the Yapı ve Kredi bank), visible from the dock, leads to a small side street. On the left and 100m up is **Aya Efimia,** an unusual Orthodox church. (Open daily 9:30am-4:30pm.) A right at the church leads onto Mütürder Cad., off of which run the small market streets that comprise Kadıköy's **"old city."** The first street on the left off of Mütürder Cad. is Serasker Cad., home to a luscious fruit market. Continue up Mütürder Cad. and turn left onto Dumlupınar Sok. to tightly packed, ivy-terraced cafes serving up cappuccinos and old jazz, and to the tiny shops displaying obscure books and Turkish comics. In this direction, a right and then a left onto Sakizgülü Sok. leads up to **Kadife Sok.,** a street lined with some of Asia's coolest and most obscure bars and cafes. One of the better places, housed in a basement-level enclave and terrace, is anonymous apart from the **metal crow** out front. Kadife Sok. can also be found by asking for the adjoining Reks Cinema.

The *bat pazarı* **(bazaar)** off Üzelik Sok. (to the right off Söğütlüçeşme Cad., about 100m uphill) is far cheaper than the Grand Bazaar, and sells much more eclectic wares, including icepicks, surfboard leashes, and racks upon racks of black leather shoes. Muvakithane Cad. is another open-air bazaar street, the third right off of Üzelik Sok., where the **Otantik Restaurant,** at No. 62, serves freshly prepared, traditional Anatolian *gözleme* (crêpes) for $2. (☎330 71 44. Open daily 9am-8pm.) Further up is Dellalzade Sok., which branches uphill to the left off Üzelik Sok. The street is occupied solely by antique dealers selling mostly copper and silver goods, and is one of the cheaper places to acquire antiques, real or otherwise.

Moda, right next to Kadıköy (a 15min. walk), used to be one of the city's chief gallery districts, though most of the quality establishments have moved across the strait to Teşvikiye, Beyoğlu, and Nişantaşı, the self-styled "Soho" of İstanbul. These days, the artsy scene has given way to a gentrified, but not artificial, residential community, proud to be the spiritual home of winning futbol team, Fenerbaçhe. To reach Moda, face uphill at the Kadıköy ferry dock, head right to the unmistakable mother of all dolmuş lots, and follow the street that curves uphill from the end of the lot. From here, signs point the way. The surplus of galleries which not so long ago lined Moda Cad., selling entry-level priced modern Turkish art, have mostly turned into furniture stores, but you can still find a few galleries as Moda Cad. snakes its way down to Kadıkoy. The trip to Moda is more than justified by a visit to **Mado,** 256 Moda Cad., which serves ineffably sublime ice cream, easily among the best in the world. As opposed to the ubiquitous Turkish *dondurma,* whose consistency is bizarrely yet appetizingly chewy, the heavenly bliss served by Mado melts in your mouth. While it inevitably has been co-opted by the European side and operates a small location on Istiklâl Cad., a pilgrimage to the original Mado is well worth it. Moda Cad. continues, away from Kadıkoy to a windy point overlooking the Bosphorus. Right by the end of the 200 block, Feritlek Sok. forks to the right off Moda Cad. and heads to a shady spot with park benches perfect for watching local windsurfers flying across the water.

ÜSKÜDAR

Üsküdar is Asian İstanbul's other big suburb. It is accessible from Eminönü by a ferry as quick as it is frequent. Built as Chrysopolis (City of Gold) in 409 BC by the Athenians as a base from which to attack the Byzantines across the Bosphorus, Üsküdar became a major way station at the mouth of the Bosphorus during the Ottoman era. Today, like Fatih on the European side, Üsküdar is relatively devout, though the somewhat more laid-back atmosphere of the Asian peninsula tempers Üsküdar's conservatism just as enjoyably as it does Kadıköy's commercialism. Long, busy streets connect the district's mosques (where visitors are more than welcome) and the atmosphere, while hectic, is pleasant. The streets off İskele Meydanı are perfect for aimless wandering while chewing *dondurma* (there is no "Sultanahmet surcharge" for foreigners).

İskele Meydanı, the square across the street from the ferryboat landing, contains several mosques. Facing inland, the one to the right is the **Yeni Valide Camii,** built by Sultan Ahmet III for his mother. Surrounded by a shady, quiet courtyard with a well-tended garden and exotic flowers, this mosque is a standard example of late Classical Ottoman architecture. The metal cage built into the wall on the Hakimiyet-i Milliye Cad. side, once the tomb of the Valide Sultan, occasionally houses a solitary olive oil dealer, who passes the cans and bottles of oil through the bars. On the other side of İskele Meydanı is the **İskele,** or **Mihrimah Camii,** which was designed by Sinan in 1547. With its waterfront position and large prayer area, the mosque is architecturally reminiscent of the Rüstem Paşa Camii in Eminönü, and is the only Ottoman mosque with an odd number of semidomes (three).

The **Çinli Camii** (Tiled Mosque) contains some of the city's finest İznik tilework, second only to Rüstem Paşa (see p. 123), but it has seen at least one shoddy restoration job. Catch a cab heading inland from Hakimiyet-i Milliye Cad. ($1.50-2). If you decide to make the short, steep walk, follow Hakimiyet-i Milliye Cad., turn left onto Eski Toptaşı Sok., and continue about 1km as the road becomes Dr. Fahri Alabey Cad. The mosque dates from 1640 and the tiles here are generally better than those in Sultanahmet. The unique luster of their terra-cotta and sea-green tints has eluded even the most advanced glaze makers. The mosque is usually kept locked, but either the caretaker or *imam* is always nearby and will show you around. For a small donation, he may even let you climb up the minaret ($1-1.50). About 10m from the mosque, down the hill toward the water, lies the local **Hamam,** one of İstanbul's better small baths (see **Turkish Baths,** p. 138). The prices are reasonable, and while the interior is no architectural masterpiece, the facilities are as elaborate as they come (bath $2; *kese* $1.50; massage $6).

On the outskirts of Üsküdar, near the top of NATO Yolu, is the mysterious and wonderful **Sabri Ertem Otomobil Müzesi,** a trippy excursion into Mr. Ertem's obsessive collection of historic cars, including rare 1930s gangsters' rides from America.

Near Üsküdar rises **Büyük Çamlıca,** the highest point in İstanbul. Take any Ümraniye-bound dolmuş from İskele Meydanı and ask to be dropped off at "Çamlıca." From here, yellow signs point the way to Turistik Çamlıca Cad., the final steep 1½km approach to the hill. The view from the top is fantastic, as the hill lies above the blanket of smog that sometimes clings to the city. On clear days, it's possible to see parts of İstanbul through the haze, and the Uludağ mountain range to the southwest. There's also a great cafe at the summit, serving chocolate-topped *gözleme* and tea by the double-decker pot. (Open daily 9am-midnight.)

NEAR ÜSKÜDAR: SELİMİYE BARRACKS

Looming large over the port and bus station in Harem, the stone and terra-cotta colossus of the **Selimiye Barracks** is also a museum open to the public, containing **Florence Nightingale's chambers** in the same state that they were during her stay here during the Crimean War. It can be reached either by taking the Sirkeci ferry to Harem or any Kadıköy-bound dolmuş from Üsküdar. The barracks are a short walk from the docks. This behemoth was constructed in 1799 by Selim III as part of a failed effort to undermine the power of the Janissaries by creating a separate, parallel corps. The Janissaries voiced objection to this plan by murdering Selim and torching the barracks. Not to be undone, Mahmut II responded by rebuilding the barracks after slaughtering the Janissaries in a puddle of green slime (see **The 19th Century: Reform and Reaction,** p. 13). The British used the barracks as a hospital during the Crimean War, and it was here that Florence Nightingale earned fame as a nurse by reducing the hospital's death rate by 90%. Because the barracks are a working military site, visiting the interior is difficult. According to the tourist office, the barracks are open to visitors on Saturdays from 9am to 4pm; however, this seems to mean nothing to the soldiers on duty if all you can say is "Florence Nightingale." Your best bet is to bring a Turkish speaker along to plead the case, as there's no specific visitors' entrance to the military installment.

ASIAN BOSPHORUS

North up the Asian Bosphorus are a number of small fishing communities, most notably **Çengelköy.** The waterfront fish restaurants here are perfect for enjoying the day's catch and watching the sun sink over **Rumeli Hisarüstü** with the old city in the background. Navigation is pretty straightforward, as all the towns lie along the route of any #15 bus from Üsküdar. The first large village along the shore is **Beylerbeyi,** the former summer residence of Ottoman sultans and the present home of many of İstanbul's super-rich, who live behind big steel gates with portals for machine guns. Downhill and toward the Bosphorus Bridge from the Beylerbeyi bus stop, the massive pink **Beylerbeyi Palace** and its lovely magnolia garden is hard to miss. To get there, jump off the bus at the Çayırbaşı stop, one before the main Beylerneyi stop. Beylerbeyi is a less orgiastic (and less exhausting) version of Dolmabahçe Palace. It was built in little over a year to the melodious strains of an orchestra that Sultan Abdülaziz hired to motivate the workmen. The thoughtful sultan allowed his passion for ships and things nautical to inspire the interior decoration, as paintings of ships adorn many ceilings. Another room takes the naval motif to an absurd climax, with all the furniture and molding decorated with gilded knots and mooring ropes. Many of the ceilings are engraved with poetry in Arabic script. (Open Tu, W, F-Su 9:30am-5pm. $5 mandatory guided tour.)

The next village, **Çengelköy,** is *the* place for **fish** in İstanbul, with a dense pack of well-established *balık* restaurants along the waterfront. The village is also respected for its goat cheese and a special strain of miniature cucumbers. After Çengelköy, **Anadolu Hisarı** is a village built around the Ottoman fortress of the same name. Lying on the Küçüksu Deresi River, this was the Harem ladies' picnic and recreation site, who came only when accompanied by a eunuch bodyguard. From Anadolu Hisarı, head back toward Üsküdar, cross the bridge over the Küçüksu Paresi, and turn left onto Küçüksu Cad. to get to **Küçüksu Kasrı,** another late Ottoman palace used as a hunting lodge by Sultan Abdülaziz. French Baroque on the inside, the house offers an excellent view of the Bosphorus. A visit includes a tour of four or five large salons. (Open Tu, W, F-Su 9am-5pm. $2.75, students $1.)

PRINCE'S ISLANDS (ADALAR)

The craggy Prince's Islands, which locals know simply as the *Adalar* (islands), are a retreat for middle-class İstanbul families looking to escape the metropolis. People do live on the four islands, but the majority run tourist-oriented businesses there or limit their stay to posh summer houses built far up in the hills, away from the shops and hotels around the island's main ports. You can still hear Greek, Spanish, and Hebrew spoken by some of the island's older families, echoing the islands' pre-tourist history. **Büyükada** is by far the busiest island, with the largest selection of markets, hotels, restaurants, and bars. It's also more strictly regulated than the others; while there are more navigable woods and beaches, these areas are often only barely "natural." **Heybeliada** is a giant step downward from Büyükada in terms of facilities, but its giant step up in peace and scenery is somewhat inaccessible. It's best visited as a day trip from Büyükada, via the 5-minute ferry (about 12 throughout the day, free). The other two islands, **Kınalıada** and **Burgazadası,** are even smaller and almost entirely residential, with nothing but restaurants to offer the tourist. The two islands are the first stops along the ferry's island route. **Heybeliada,** the third, is the largest, and the most distant of the islands; Büyükada is last. Prices are high on all the islands if you want a sit-down meal, though the food quality is almost worth it (especially the fruit). It's a good idea to bring lunch with you, or try some of the delicious street food near the port in Büyükada, especially the fried mussels on a stick.

Ferries depart from the north side of Eminönü or Kabataş; look for signs that read "Sirkeci Adalar" (3-4 per day; round-trip $2; from Eminönü). The ferry for the islands is to the right at the bottom of the tramway hill. A faster yet pricier alternative is the **seabus** ($5; from Eminönü, Bostancı and Kabataş in summer).

BÜYÜKADA ☎216

Büyükada is the largest and most enjoyable of the islands. Superb fish restaurants dot the shore, and delicious *kebap* restaurants and *pastane* (pastry shops) line the streets in every direction. A big-time summer retreat, Büyükada offers pine-forested scenery, relatively inaccessible swimming spots, and peaceful walks beyond the busy main drag, making it an excellent daytrip from İstanbul. Thursday is market day along a few streets just off Kadıyoran Cad. in Büyükada, making it an ideal time to visit, before it is overrun by the weekend crowds.

Once off the ferry, you're in the heart of the commercial district. Mercifully, there are no cars or buses on the island—people **walk, bike,** or take **horse-and-buggy rides.** Starting from İsa Çelebi Sok., horse-and-buggy prices start around $8; bike rentals shouldn't cost more than $1 per hr., though prices increase for fancier bikes. As most of the streets are cobblestone, a more comfortable bike is a good investment. For **police,** go to the corner of Lala Hatun Cad. and Kadıyoran Cad., only a block from the main square in a two-story white building (☎382 50 10 or 382 60 36); **emergency:** ☎112. The **hospital** is **Adalar Devlet Hastanesi** (☎382 6228), at 41 Lala Hatun Cad., a five-minute walk up the street from the police station. The **PTT** is at 17 Balık Cad. (Open year-round M-F 9am-6pm, Sa-Su 9am-1pm.)

Most of the hotels here are expensive, luxurious summer retreats. The **Ideal Aile Pansiyon,** 14 Kadıyoran Cad. is the exception: a haunted-house-style masterpiece with huge rooms. (☎382 68 57. $13 per person.) A horde of restaurants occupies the central commercial area by the dock. In the area around the clock tower, small restaurant-cafes spill out onto the street. A rare bargain in this area is **Ferhat Restaurant,** 23 Nisan Cad., #31/A, serving Turkish pizza or *Döner* (chicken or beef) for $2.50, and local spirits for $1. (☎382 60 38. Discounts for large groups of tourists.) On the uphill side are more standard *kebap* and *çay* places, while slightly more expensive (around $7 per meal) eateries line the downhill side. Unbeatable seafood restaurants line the waterfront, offering various kinds *of şiş*, local specialties, and alcohol. Small groceries also sell fresh fruit. Don't miss the great ice cream sold on the main street from the ferry to the clock tower.

Yöruk Ali and **Dil Uzantısı** are good picnic or beach spots. Swimming off the rocks is a tricky but possible alternative. Another option is to take the buggy to **Luna Park** (10-15min., about $7.50), the local amusement park on the far side of the island. **Donkeys** can be rented for $10 per 30min. **St. George's Monastery** claims the highest point on the island. A fully functioning Greek Orthodox monastery complete with a cafe, it can be reached by a 20min. walk up a steep cobblestone path, or by buggy leaving from Yöruk Ali ($1.50 from Yöruk Ali, $7 from the town center). The monks are willing to show the adjoining church to visitors W-Su, but you should call when you get to the island to make sure you don't make the exhausting hike just for the incomparable view. (☎216 382 39 39. Monks speak English, Greek, and all Romance languages.) The adjacent restaurant, **Yücetepe Kır Gazinosu,** is among the cheapest and best places to eat on the island. The family-owned cafe has sprinkled picnic benches all around this high summit, but for those without a bag lunch, try the spicy sausage ($1), and reward yourself for the hike with a cold beer ($1). Luna Park, the donkey rentals, and the path up to St. George's Monastery are all clustered around **Birlik Square,** a spot near the middle of the island where all roads converge before separating out toward the far coast. It's best to park your bikes here before heading up the hill, unless you're feeling particularly masochistic.

HEYBELİADA

TML ferries (but not the seabus) heading outbound from Büyükada to Heybeliada are free, making it a great excursion from Büyükada. Like much of İstanbul, the island was once home to a large Greek population, who left behind a legacy of wooden houses. Heybeliada means "saddle bag," though the island is shaped more like a saddle, with Heybeliada in one of the stirrups.

İSTANBUL

HAIL, TARKAN! Turkey's king of pop can be seen not only on hundreds of billboards (including one in Taksim square that is at least 30m high) but also on every Pepsi can and bottle. His voice booms out of seemingly every storefront and passing car, and graces the dance floors of every nightclub, from the classiest to the seediest. Born in the early 70s in a village in the Kocaeli district, Tarkan got his start singing at weddings around İzmir before skyrocketing to international superstardom. Famous everywhere from Germany to North Africa to India, he is loved nowhere as much as in his native Turkey. Even when a moving company employee attempted to blackmail the rockstar in 2001, forcing him out of the closet after finding incriminating homoerotic photographs in Tarkan's New York residence, the Turkish people rallied around their icon. Clearly, a love this deep goes beyond even the oldest prejudices. Long live the king!

The **Greek Orthodox School of Theology,** atop one of the island's two large hills, is a must-see (roundtrip *fayton* $10). The school also contains the **Aya Triada Monastery,** whose church features some Byzantine relics and a collection of silver inlay and oil paintings as striking as those at St. George's, its sister school on Büyükada.

Bikes can be rented at Trakya Gida, off Ayyıldız Cad. ($1 per hr.; hand-drawn maps $.20). Another option is a **horse-drawn carriage** *(fayton)* ride around the island. Carriages stop near the *iskele:* face inland, head to the right, and look near the basketball courts. Try haggling, particularly if you know the specific stops you want and don't opt for the guided tour. The **Prenset Pension,** 74 Ayyıldız Cad., is one of the cheapest places to stay on the island, but its quality is as good as elsewhere. All of the clean, large rooms have bath and phone. (☎351 81 83. Breakfast included. Haggle or pay $40 per double regardless of occupancy.)

ENTERTAINMENT

HAMAMS (TURKISH BATHS)

İstanbul baths vary immensely in terms of quality. Since this might be your first or only opportunity to experience a Turkish bath, choosing the right hamam is of critical importance. Remember that while most İstanbul baths have either separate women's sections or women's hours, not all have designated female attendants. Women should specifically request female washers. Self-service is always an option, and this desire is best indicated by showing the attendants your bar of soap and wash cloth. Before you go, read **Hamam-o-Rama,** p. 34.

Çemberlitaş Hamamı, 8 Verzirhan Cad. (☎522 79 74). Just a soap-slide away from the Çemberlitaş tram stop. Though a touch touristy, Çemberlitaş is one of the better spots for cleanliness and service. Built by Sinan in 1584, it's also one of the most beautiful. Both the men's and women's sections have marble interiors. Vigorous "towel service" after the bath requires a tip of $1.50-3. Bath with your own towel and soap $9; with a sudsy rubdown, massage and wash $15 (tip included, but after you've changed, the washers wait around, expecting another $1-3). Open daily 6am-midnight.

Çinli Hamamı. In Fatih, near the butcher shops at the end of Itfaiye Cad. Built for the pirate Barbarossa, this bath is excellent, even retaining a few of its original İznik and Kütahya tiles. Large facilities mean ample space on the hot stone. Bath $2.30; *kese* $1.50 massage $3. Both men's and women's sections open daily 8am-8pm.

Mihrimah Hamamı (☎523 04 87). Right next to Mihrimah Mosque on Fevzi Paşa Cad., about 50m from Edirnekapı. Definitely one of the better local baths: it's large, quiet, clean, cheap, and hot. Women's facilities are good, though smaller. Bath $3; massage $2.50. Men's section open 7am-midnight; women's section 8am-7pm.

Galatasaray Hamamı (men ☎244 14 12; women ☎249 43 42). At the end of Turanacıbaşı Sok., off İstiklâl Cad., on a nameless side street across from the Galatasaray high school on Istiklâl; just uphill from Galatasaray. Pricey, a bit touristy, and the place to go if you plan to spill serious lira for an opulent scrubdown. Bath and massage $15.50. Men's section open daily 7am-11pm; women's section 8am-8pm.

CHEAP SETS AND FLOPPED STUNTS Yedikule's dramatic possibilities—high walls to scale, towers to throw people from, and a courtyard for staging pitched battles between armies of extras—have not been lost on Turkish directors. The fortifications are the default "Ottoman castle" set for many low-budget Turkish movies. Footpaths running along the tops of the walls have no handrails and do not run the whole length of the castle's perimeter. This results in several deep, 3m wide chasms whose comic possibilities were more than realized in the Cüneyt Arkın low-budget cinema classic, **Ottoman Eagle.** In the climactic final battle, staged over the sounds of car horns on Sahil Yolu, with the tall buildings of modern İstanbul visible in the background, the hero (played by Arkın) gets thrown down one of these shafts, only to bounce back up on a trampoline barely kept off camera.

Cağaloğlu Hamamı (☎522 24 24). On Yerebatan Cad., 2km up from Yerebatan Cistern in Sultanahmet. This famous hamam, where scenes from *Indiana Jones* were shot, is somewhat disappointing if you like your stone and water ultra-hot—both can tend toward the lukewarm here. $6 for self-service; $20 for the "Sultan treatment" (massage and scrubdown). Men's section open daily 7am-10pm; women's section 8am-8pm.

İSTANBUL

FILMS

Movie theaters showing Hollywood blockbusters and world cinema line İstiklâl Cad. Showings are prominently advertised on billboards outside of the theaters and listed in the nation's large newspapers: *Hürriyet*, *Sabah*, and *Radikal*, among others. Advertisements list theater and showtime information for each film. Most foreign films are shown in the original language with Turkish subtitles, though be sure to ask at the window before you purchase your ticket *(Bu filmı inglizce?)*. Theaters occasionally have films dubbed in the local language, in which case *"Turkce"* will usually be written on the poster. Tickets are $4-6 depending on the showtime, and are usually cheaper for the matinee.

FUTBOL

Futbol (football, soccer), Turkey's national sport, is centered in İstanbul (see **Sports**, p. 33). It's not too expensive to cheer on one of the teams with the rest of the *fanatiks:* ticket prices for İstanbul *futbol* matches rarely exceed $15-20 for very good seats, and can be as low as $3. Tickets are sold at the stadiums. In İstanbul, two easily accessible stadiums are **İnönü Stadium** in Beşiktaş, just off Dolmabahçe Cad., and **Fenerbahçe Stadium,** best reached by taking cab ($2) from Kadıköy. Show up about an hour early to secure a good view, as tickets in the cheap seats are numbered. The season runs September through May.

NIGHTLIFE

But this is a decadent city of loveless lusts,
ready to give up the ghost,
a city of young whores, dead sultans, and the sick
an İstanbul debased.
—İlhan Berk, "İstanbul"

A USER'S GUIDE

Contrary to popular misconceptions, İstanbul has a great nightlife, with the scope and diversity that one would expect in a city of 13 million. Unfortunately, the best clubs and bars are neither well-advertised nor particularly organized, and as a result, bars often have unmarked entrances and clubs are woefully unlisted. Unplanned attempts at club-hopping are ill advised, as they will likely prove fruitless. Women heading out alone at night, aside from taking care to exercise the cautions suggested in the **Safety and Security** section (see p. 46), should consider

ON THE LOOKOUT: NIGHTLIFE SCAMS Foreigners, especially non-Turkish speakers, should exercise caution when meeting new 'friends' out on the town. One of many **tourist scams** involves Turkish men befriending male tourists and leading them to bars where they are soon joined by bands of women. After ordering drinks, the women scram, leaving the tourist with an exorbitant bill. Purchasing drinks for women can also be a front for a prostitution ring. That "drink" might cost you $50, and you may be getting more for your money than you had bargained for. There are also reports of tourists being given drugged drinks and subsequently robbed. While a drink invitation is often simply a gesture of hospitality, use your best judgement when accepting drinks from strangers.

taking cabs. It's also wise to team up with a few other foreigners, Turkish women, or Turkish men you know well. Establishments in Taksim and certainly in Ortaköy tend to be upscale enough to be relatively safe, though there are always exceptions. Cafe-bars and backpacker bars tend to be less threatening than rock bars or clubs. (See **İstanbul Street Smarts,** p. 92.) Men heading out alone or in a pack will have a tough time getting into some of the more upscale clubs and bars. Especially on weekends in the later hours, many places require every man to be accompanied by at least one woman. Although many people, including locals, find this frustrating, clubs insist it is the only way to keep the dance floors "sufficiently" co-ed.

Turkish nightlife generally falls into one of three categories. The first includes male-only *çay* houses, backgammon parlors, and dancing shows. In addition to being boring, they tend to be dingy, poorly lit, and even somewhat unsafe for men as well as women. Though usually not prohibited, women are unwelcome, and should avoid these places. *Let's Go* does not recommend patronage of this sort of establishment. The second category includes **cafe-bars, rock bars,** and **backpacker bars.** Cafe-bars serve light fare, tea, and cappuccino in the afternoon and alcohol in the evening. Generally smaller and more relaxed than the sometimes cavernous rock bars, they play less invasive sounds—often jazz or Latin. Rock bars provide clean fun and include, on one hand, loud, dark halls that tend to blast American and Turkish metal anthems. These can be fun, if you can get over the repetition of watching well-dressed young people banging the gel out of their hair alongside shaggy metalheads. On the other hand are more laid-back establishments that play a mix of classic rock, modern pop, and funk to a young crowd of people looking to relax with a beer. Backpacker bars, probably the best places to meet fellow travelers, are concentrated in the Sultanahmet area and are usually associated with hostels. These bars are convenient and cheap, but they host a markedly familiar, non-Turkish clientele. **Clubs and discos** make up the third nightlife category. The hippest İstanbul clubs often move from unlisted locations in Taksim in the winter to unlisted open-air summer locations throughout the city. Even taxi drivers can't keep up with the itinerant İstanbul night scene. Clubs can be a blast, though often only subtly Turkish and sometimes prohibitively pricey.

SULTANAHMET AREA

Most of the bars listed here are within 100m of each other on Akbıyık Cad., the main backpacker strip, and many standardize their beer prices at $1-1.50 for local brew. Others are a short walk up toward the Sultanahmet tram stop.

Cheers, Akbıyık Cad. The best music on backpacker alley, Cheers attracts locals (except in July and August) as well as the normal tourist crowd to its comfortable, outdoor benches. Delicious fresh fruit soaking in bottled water and a very friendly scene make this one of the best places to grab a beer in the area.

Buzz Bar, 35 Kutlugün Sok., at the Istanbul Hostel. By far the homiest and cleanest of the backpacker bars, Buzz Bar plays nightly movies on their huge satellite TV. Has a very pleasant outdoor seating area for more relaxed conversation. The *Efes* flows just as much upstairs on their sea-view terrace, but it's less of a party than the basement. A brick interior and fireplace make this the place to be in the winter months.

Traveler's Cafe and Bar, Akbıyık. The best place to trade adventures with the super-friendly staff, Traveler's also offers a *nargile* (water pipe) and a delicious, but standard, bar menu. Beer $1.80.

Sultan Hostel Roof Bar, Terbıyık Sok. Around the corner from Orient Hostel, off Akbıyık Sok. A different party every night: belly dancing Tu and Sa; water pipes M and Th; "punch" W. Much less smoky than other places. Beautiful evening view of the Golden Horn and the Sea of Marmara. Sizeable, well-stocked bar. Open daily 8am-2am.

The Underground, 33 Ticarethane Sok. (☎511 62 11). Turn right at the Sultan Pub, by the Sultanahmet tram stop, then take first left; the club is on the left. The only true dance club in Sultanahmet, this basement bar alternates between techno, hip-hop, Turkish pop, and Celine Dion. A student crowd grooves on weekends, some attempting to breakdance to anything and everything the DJ spins. Probably the only place to see the electric slide anywhere in the Western world. Beer $1.80. Domestic liquor $2.20, imported $4.50. Open daily 7pm-2am. No cover.

Orient Bar, 13 Akbıyık Sok. (☎517 94 93). In Orient Youth Hostel. Revelry and dancing abound in this boisterous basement bar. *Nargile* (water pipe) nights (Th, Su 9pm) attract international types; evening belly dancing shows (M, W, F 10pm) inauthentic but entertaining. Decked-out DJ (in retro Volkswagen Bug reincarnated as a DJ booth) plays Turkish and international dance hits. While the DJ is quite skilled in his medleys, you may find that the only clients bopping to the beats are wanton Turkish men waiting for Australian women. Happy hour until 10pm. Open daily 8pm-2am.

TAKSİM SQUARE AND İSTİKLÂL CADDESİ

İstanbul night action is centered around Taksim and İstiklâl Cad., where the bar scene kicks in around 8pm and finishes at about 2 or 3am, while the clubs shut down a few hours later. If you take a bus or a dolmuş to the Taksim area, wandering down İstiklâl Cad. is sure to lead you to a fine club or bar. The density of bars in this area is staggering, with many quality places hiding out in narrow side streets. The list below is certainly not exhaustive, and should serve merely as a starting point for your adventures.

Jazz Stop, around the corner, at the end of Büyük Parmakkapı Sok. A mixed group of music lovers mostly sit while live bands lay the funk, blues, and jazz on thick. The owner, a talented drummer from one of Turkey's oldest and most respected rock groups, occasionally takes part in the jams. Live music nightly 11pm. Beer $3; liquor $6 and up. June-Aug. no cover; Sept.-May F-Sa cover $10. Open daily 11am-4am.

Riddim, 6 Büyük Parmakkapı Sok. If you are looking for Jah, he is here, in the only bar in Taksim dedicated to spinning reggae all night long. Crowd is a mixed group that likes to dance, and the DJs are generally great, spinning the Jamaican export as well as other African and island music. Unattended men will be turned away on weekends. Beer $2.50. Open F-Sa 8pm-4am, Su-Th 9pm-1:30am.

Madrid Bar, İpek Sok. Off Küçük Parmakkapı Sok., which is itself off İstiklâl Cad. An understated bar with a fascination for surrealist Spanish paintings. This small, mellow spot is popular with Turkish students and young foreigners looking for one of the cheapest pints in Taksim ($1.25). Open daily 2pm-2am.

Hide Out, 8/2 Büyük Parmakkapı Sok. (☎244 50 33). The perfect antidote to its deafening next-door neighbor Riddim, Hide Out caters to a slightly older crowd, though it occasionally rocks out to live Latin and Turkish bands W, Sa, Su. Beer $1.30; local spirits $1.80; imported liquors $3.50.

Vareli şaraphanesi, 7/9 Oteller Sok. (☎292 55 16 or 292 55 17) on the corner of Balyoz Sok. Oteller is parallel to İstiklâl down by the Tünel end of the street. Take a right on Balyoz, one of the few well-marked side streets off İstiklâl. This choice wine house is the place to really impress a date. A romantic spot off the beaten path in the scenic neighborhood of Asmanlı Mescit, Vareli offers a large selection of fine wines, running the gamut in price, starting from $4.

Home Bass, 15 Sadri Alısıik Sok. (☎251 00 07), down İstiklâl Cad. on the left. Hip-hoppers will feel right at home at this downstairs club. Though the clientele might not always know the words, the DJ knows the hits and spins until late. Live tunes on weekends include all sorts of "global music." Cover $4 for live performance, but prices vary depending on the act. Beer is cheap ($1.50). Open daily 5pm-4am.

Kemancı (☎251 30 15), consists of 2 clubs 150m down Siraselviler Cad. on the right, up a small flight of stairs in a big archway. The most popular of Taksim's rock bars, this immense downstairs venue draws a large crowd of high-schoolers and college students who come to watch local bands tear through sped-up U2, Judas Priest, and Poison covers. Upstairs, a slightly older crowd cheers as bands pound out loud covers of American tunes. Beer $2.50. Cover F-Sa $12.50, Su-Th $3. Open daily noon-4am.

ORTAKÖY AND THE COASTAL ROAD

The Beşiktaş end of Ortaköy is a maze of upscale hangouts, with hundreds of small cafes and bars offering drinks under the lights of the Bosphorus Bridge. Along the coastal road toward Arnavutköy are a string of open-air clubs, frequented by rich Bosphorus University students, *nouveau riche* swingers, and Turkish celebrities. This scene affords fabulous people-watching, as İstanbul's jet set lets loose beyond the prying eyes of the *hoi polloi.* The cover charges can be astronomical ($18-45), and the bouncers highly selective. Unaccompanied men are unlikely to get past the door. If you're money enough to hit this scene, dress well, be confident, and abuse any out-of-the-ordinary ID you have. Lines outside these places can be long, but if you pick the right one, the rigmarole can be more than worth it. The following bars and clubs are between Ortaköy and Bebek; although the names and decors change often, it's often just a case of an old wine in a new bottle.

China White, 120 Muallim Naci Cad. (☎259 54 80), just under the bridge, is by far the best spot in Ortaköy. No less classy than its sister location in London, a humble entrance leads to an outdoor fun-fest of Asian decor on several tiers of cushy teak terraces. The rich, beautiful and powerful come in all ages and sizes to drink, dance, and, of course, to see and be seen (the multi-tiered seating plan is incredibly conducive to people-watching). While there is no cover, the drinks make it far from a bargain, with *Efes* running you a cool $5, and liquor (all imported) from $9-11. Open daily 7pm-4am.

Paşa Beach Club is a world-famous İstanbul open-air club boasting the longest lines, a latest-model Ferrari lot, the most arrogant bouncers, and the highest cover in the city ($40). Rumor has it that they'll waive the cover if you pull up in your yacht. The club is laughably hard to get into, since you can't even pay the cover without a membership card, for which you must be recommended. Befriending a member or spinning extravagant lies about yourself and your net worth are the best bets here.

Laila, an indoor/outdoor techno club next door to China White, is a notch below the inaccessible decadence of Paşa, but only a few steps down the road. The $30 cover charge is a steal by Ortaköy standards.

Civeli, across the road from Laila, alternates between a relaxed indoor/outdoor bar and restaurant and a scene of bacchanalian mayhem (their logo is a cracked, spilling wineglass). A lot depends on the live (generally Turkish) band and the special events, like wedding receptions. Drinks here are half the price of those at Paşa or Laila (about $5).

SHE Bar is a great, hip spot—particularly in the off-season when wealthy, corpulent businessmen bring their young girlfriends. This bar blasts British punk. Astronomical drink prices ($10) more than compensate for the lack of a cover charge.

Desperado, next door to SHE Bar, is a favorite of Bosphorus University students. It's dim but fun, and the scene is innocent and laid back.

Purple Bar, close to Bebek on the same road, is marked with a weird, black-lit purple sign with almost indecipherable lettering. An exclusive crowd, including, models, actors, and fashionable transvestites, among others, packs the cramped confines. At $12 the cover isn't too bad, and the $5-7 drinks are reasonable.

NORTHWESTERN TURKEY

The only part of the country actually on the European continent, Northwestern Turkey wraps around the Sea of Marmara with a dazzling array of cities and towns. Most of these locales—Mt. Uludağ's ski slopes, Marmara's beach resorts, Termal's hot springs, Bursa's bazaars, and Edirne's mosques—make fantastic quick escapes from İstanbul's urban sprawl. As the dusty streets of the big city filter into winding highways, pavement gives way to terra cotta soil, silvery olive groves, and fields of peach trees. This is, after all, the area that nourished the young Ottoman Empire, and it has two Ottoman capitals, Bursa and Edirne, to show for it. The regions's artistic achievements, including Edirne's masterful architecture, İznik's ceramic tilework, and Bursa's silk, are world-famous. The Gallipoli Battlefields remain a major pilgrimage site for those commemorating the bloody World War I battle for control of the Dardanelles. Whether ferrying the Marmara, bussing through golden sunflower fields in Thrace, or riding a cable car up the heights of Uludağ, traveling in this region allows for a game of rich and eclectic cross-continental hopscotch.

HIGHLIGHTS OF NORTHWESTERN TURKEY

WANDER through Edirne's streets and behold some of the world's finest Ottoman architecture, including **Selimiye Camii** (p. 155), considered Sinan's magnum opus and the most spectacular mosque in Turkey.

GRILL your own meal from the high mountain plateau of **Mt. Uludağ** (p. 173) while the sun sets vermilion over snow-covered fields.

EXPLORE the **Gallipoli Battlefields** and reflect upon the bloodshed at ANZAC Cove (p. 163) as you tour the site of the 1915 conflict.

FOLLOW in the footsteps of emperors and sultans to the **Hot Springs of Termal,** and soak your well-traveled bones in the baths of champions (p. 174).

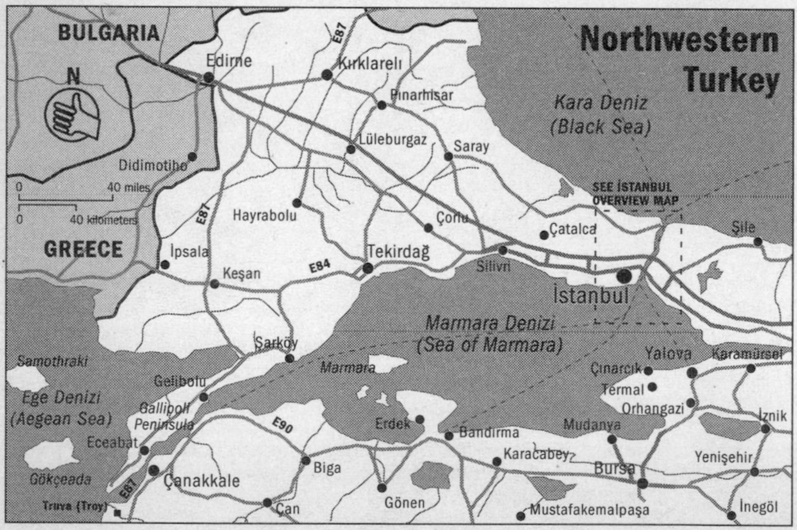

FALL/WINTER 2001 • FREE
student Travels
WORK, STUDY, TRAVEL ABROAD
CZECH IT OUT!
Exploring Prague
and Other Pleasures
in the Czech Republic
BOSTON
Weekend Wandering
in Beantown
INSIDE
Your International
Student Identity Card
(ISIC) Application
PLUS
-Cuba
-Australia
Bedazzled
By BRAZIL
Boundless Attractions From Beautiful Beaches
to Spectacular Festivals to Lush Jungles

THRACE

EDİRNE ☎284

In almost 2000 years of historical prominence, Edirne has enjoyed a mixed and fickle fate, ranging from imperial splendor to hostile occupation. It has been a Roman outpost, an Ottoman capital, and a modern Greek military possession. Nowadays, this sleepy enclave is replete with the friendliness and hospitality that can only be found in cities unused to foreigners. Its status as a border town, however—the source of the city's historically variable fortunes—remains an important part of Edirne's character.

In 125 AD, the Roman Emperor **Hadrian** founded **Adrianople** (Hadrianopolis) and named it, Alexander-style, in his own honor. Under Roman sway, Adrianople was an important garrison town and center of armor production. Latin **Crusaders** dominated the city for a brief period in the 12th century, but it did not fall permanently from Byzantine hands until **Sultan Murat I** conquered it in 1362. Pleased with his latest European possession, Murat made Edirne the capital of his rapidly expanding empire, beautifying it with lavish architecture. Today, Edirne's three remarkable mosques, the **Eski Cami** (Old Mosque), the **Üç şerefeli Camii** (The Three-Balconied Mosque), and the incomparable **Selimiye Camii,** all recall this splendor.

When the capital of the Ottoman Empire shifted to Constantinople in 1453, Edirne retained its prominence as a major stop on the eastern caravan route. In the 19th century, it was still the seventh-largest city in Europe. Now removed from the rest of Turkey, Edirne has a frontier town feel. Although it sits less than 20km from Bulgaria and barely 7km from Greece, crossing into either country from Edirne is inconvenient. Trakya University, the university for European Turkey, keeps the city young. Not coincidentally, the finest brand of *rakı* is made nearby. Modern Edirne clings to its rich history, juxtaposing it with the present day, as 14th-century Ottoman bridges now bear the weight of huge trucks transporting goods from the rest of Europe, an imperial *Kervansaray* is now a beautiful hotel, and a historic bazaar is now the Ali Paşa Çarsisı, Edirne's main shopping mall.

NORTHWEST

TRANSPORTATION

Buses: Numerous bus companies cluster around the parking lot, all selling similarly priced tickets to the region's major cities. Be sure to shop around. *Let's Go* offers the following suggestions, including bus companies: **Ankara** (Edirne Ece Turizm; 9hr., 9:30pm, $20); **Antakya** (Edirne Ece Turizm; 21hr.; 5:30, 7:30pm; $28.25); **Antalya** (Edirne Ece Turizm; 17hr., 7:45pm, $23); **Bursa/Mt. Uludağ** (7hr., 5pm, $16.50); **Çanakkale** (Edirne Ece Turizm; 4hr., 7:45pm, $8.25); **İstanbul** (Edirne Ece Turizm; 3½hr.; 5:30, 7am, then every 30min. until 6:30pm; $5) or (Lüx Edirne Express; 2hr., every 30min. 7am-7pm, $8.25); **İzmir** (Edirne Ece Turizm; 9hr., 7:45pm, $15.50).

Trains: Edirne has 2 train stations. Trains for **İstanbul** (6hr., 7:40am, $4; 4hr. express, M-F 3am, $9) leave from the **Edirne Garı** (☎225 11 55 or 212 09 14), outside Edirne on the İstanbul road. To get to the station, take dolmuş #1 past the otogar toward İstanbul. Ask to be let off at the train station or at **Migros,** a supermarket opposite the station. Trains to **Sofia, Bulgaria** (8hr., 3:30am, $19) leave from the **Kapıkule station** (☎238 23 12). To reach Kapıkule, take a dolmuş from the stand behind Rüstempaşa Kervansaray Otel (every 10min., $.75) or a bus (every hr. until 6pm) from the local station (see listing below).

Local Buses: Although the dolmuş is almost always the cheapest option for local travel, it's sometimes convenient to take the local bus to the border towns **Kapıkule** ($1) or **Karaağaç** ($.75). The local bus station lies 50m up Mimar Sinan Cad., on the left just past the City Hall. Kapıkale and Karaağaç each have their own clearly marked platform.

Dolmuş: Dolmuş leave from the dusty gravel lot behind the Rüstem Paşa Kervansaray Hotel. Each dolmuş travels on one of 4 different circuitous routes, indicated by the colored number in the dolmuş window. Signs posted around the lot indicate the routes denoted by each number. Rides cost $.25-$.45.

Taxis: In the small square off Talat Paşa Cad., past the tourist office (walking from the center of town). Another stand sits between Sera Park and Üç şerefeli Camii. Dial ☎213 56 90 to order a taxi; if you don't speak Turkish it is easier to hail one on the street.

ORIENTATION

Two of Edirne's major roads, **Mimar Sinan Cad.** and **Talat Paşa Cad.,** converge on the fountain at the center of city. From the fountain, with its water-spouting earthenware jugs, you can see the city's three main mosques, and nearly everything of interest is a short walk away. To the south sits **Eski Camii,** the **Bedesten,** and one of the city's central cafe squares. **Talat Paşa Cad.,** the city's main east-west thoroughfare, starts at the fountain and runs through town to the Tunca River. The other half of **Talat Paşa Cad.** begins behind Eski Cami, runs southeast out of the city, and continues on to İstanbul. **Mimar Sinan Cad.** runs up toward the main mosque and Edirne's major **museums.** The city's shops are on **Saraçlar Cad.,** reached by walking on Talat Paşa Cad., away from Selimiye Camii, and making the first left. Further down Talat Paşa Cad., at the intersection with **Maarif Cad.,** you'll find the tourist office and a variety of cheap accommodations. The magnificent **Selimiye Camii,** towers above the city, visible from several kilometers away. Though few of the streets are marked, the large map in the square is a good reference.

PRACTICAL INFORMATION

TOURIST AND FINANCIAL SERVICES

Tourist Office: 17 Talat Paşa Cad. (☎213 92 08), 300m down the road from the center of town. Friendly, helpful staff offers free maps. Open M-F 8:30am-5:30pm; June-Aug. occasionally later and on weekends. The tourism directorate is 750m down the same road on the right.

Bulgarian Consulate: 31 Talat Paşa Cad. (☎225 10 69), about 1km from the center of town down the road to the otogar. 30-day tourist visas: 1-week processing $55, same-day service $70. Multiple-entry visas: 3mos. $66, 6mos. $93, 1yr. $126. Transit visas: single-entry $44, double-entry $63. Open M-F 9am-noon. For info on the Bulgarian border crossing, see p. 157.

Greek Consulate: (☎235 58 04). Take dolmuş #1 to Mega Park (10min., $.25) and find the police station in a gray building. Take the road on the other side of the police station; you will see the Greek flag flying 30m down a side street on the left. Open M-F 10am-noon. For info on the Greek border crossing, see p. 157.

Banks: Türkiye İş Bankası, on Saraçlar Cad., and **Vakıfbank,** further down on Saraçlar Cad., exchange traveler's checks and have a Cirrus/MC/Plus/V ATM. Both open M-F 9am-12:30pm and 1:30-5:30pm. **Akbank,** on Talat Paşa Cad., near the tourist office, has a full-service ATM and can exchange AmEx **traveler's checks.** Open M-F 9am-5:30pm. 50m further down on Talat Paşa Cad., **Garanti** posts its exchange rates in the window (cash only), and has an ATM that accepts all major cards. Open M-F 9am-5pm.

NORTHWEST

EMERGENCY AND COMMUNICATIONS

Emergencies (medical or criminal): ☎155.

Police: (☎213 92 40), far away from the center of town on Mega Park, in a residential area. Take dolmuş #1 to the Mega Park stop (10min., $.25).

Hospitals: Özel Trakya Hastanesi (private, ☎213 92 00 or 213 84 94), just before the Bulgarian consulate on Talat Paşa Cad. **Edirne Devlet Hastanesi** (public, ☎225 46 03), immediately up the hill from the Bulgarian Consulate.

Pharmacy: şifa Eczanesi (☎225 46 36; fax 213 17 77), across the street and down 50m from the tourist office (heading away from town) on Talat Paşa Cad. Open M-F 8:30am-7:30pm. Better-located **Güven Eczanesi** (☎224 65 24) is on Saraçlar Cad., 25m from Talat Paşa Cad. Open M-F 8:30am-7:30pm. MC/V.

Internet Access: Lider Internet Cafe (☎214 67 28). Take an immediate left after the Türkiye İş Bankası on Saraçlar Cad. and walk 250m. The cafe is on the left on the 2nd floor. Modern and well-kept with good, fast connections. ($.65 per hr. Open daily 8am-midnight.) **Eska Iletişim Internet Cafe,** 3 doors down from the Kervansaray Hotel. ($.85 per hr. Open 10am-midnight.) **Kervansaray Hotel** also has an Internet room, which tends to be busier ($.50 per 30min.).

PTT: 17 Saraçlar Cad. Post 8:30am-5pm; phones until 10pm.

Postal code: 22100.

ACCOMMODATIONS

Plenty of places to spend the night are scattered along Maarif Cad., the first left after passing over Saraçlar Cad. on Talat Paşa Cad. Travelers to Edirne during the Kırkpınar Grease Wrestling Festival should call ahead, since the town is filled with spectators for the event during the first week of July. When the flow of travelers through the city falls off, bargaining can be productive.

Efe Hotel, 13 Maarif Cad. (☎213 61 66; fax 213 60 80; www.efehotel.com). Offers luxurious rooms with modern bathrooms, phones, and TV. The friendly staff is the only one in town that speaks English. A/C lobby filled with plants and "English Pub" with live music. Breakfast included. 20 standard rooms, 2 suites (which include seating area and a larger TV). Singles $16.50; doubles $23; triples $27; suites $35.

Hotel Kervansaray, 57 Iki Kapılı Han Cad. (☎225 71 95; fax 212 04 62), a.k.a. Rüstempaşa, runs the length of Eski Cami Altı. It was built in the 1550s as a resting place for camel caravans trudging between Europe and the East. The exquisite gardens, cloistered courtyard, and stone hallways recall early Ottoman days. Modern facilities, including bath, TV, phone, and carpet in each of its 79 rooms. There's also a hamam, parking, 2 bars, and a billiards/Internet parlor. Keep in mind, you are paying for architecture rather than luxury. But you might just find the stupendous architecture worth the trip: it won the prestigious worldwide Aga Khan architecture award in 1980. Singles $30; doubles $60; triples $90. MC/V.

Hotel Aksaray (☎225 39 01), at the intersection of Maarif Cad. and Ali Paşa Ortakapı Cad., a few doors down from the Efe Hotel. Cheap and basic, this well-worn Ottoman house offers small, plain rooms, most with TV, phone, and sink. Singles $5.50, with bath $12.50; doubles $11, with bath $16; triples $13.50, with bath $19.

Park Hotel, 7 Maarif Cad. (☎213 52 76). Nondescript, clean, modern rooms have bath, phone, and TV. Breakfast included. Its business card proudly lists American bar, disco, tavern, and night club all as separate entities, but they are actually one and the same. Singles $12.50; doubles $19.50; triples $21.50. MC/V.

FOOD

TEA GARDENS AND CAFES

şera Park Cafe (☎212 66 30), on Selimiye Meydanı in the park between the Selimiye Camii and Eski Cami, has a breathtaking view of both mosques. The cafe's relaxed atmosphere and elegant central fountain make it a favorite. *Çay* is served either in a traditional small Turkish tea glass ($.25) or in a larger cup ($.40). *Ayran* and *tost* each $.40. Open M-F until midnight, Sa-Su until 2am.

Emirgan Çay Bahçesi, on the far bank of the Meriç, right next to Villa restaurant. Emirgan is the first riverside establishment you come to after crossing the bridge. Though this upbeat outdoor cafe advertises itself as a tea garden, within its canopy are several semi-independent *döner kebap* stands, and Emirgan itself offers delicious Turkish ice cream ($.50), french fries ($.50), and beer ($.85). Open late.

Cafe Antik, 22 Tahmis Cad. (☎212 22 53), farther down from the Selimiye Camii, covers most of the square bordered by the Eski Cami and Kervansaray on 2 sides. Its romantic atmosphere and table umbrellas create an intimate dining space. Selections are nearly identical to those at the other cafes but with slightly better prices and a greater variety of quick snacks (*karışık tost* $.60; hamburgers $1).

Gazlyiz Çay Bahçesi, on the long road up to Beyazıt, 1km off Talat Paşa Cad., just before the high school. In a quiet garden removed from the densely populated residential neighborhood, Gaziyiz feels like a fabled desert oasis. A great place to reward yourself on the way back from a hike before stepping into the center of the city.

RESTAURANTS

Lalezar (☎212 24 89 or 213 06 00). Follow Saraçlar Cad. away from town; the restaurant is to the right of the Meriç River bridge. The walk to the restaurant takes about 20min. (cab ride $2). Outdoor Lalezar is high-class by Edirne standards. No menu, but the language barrier shouldn't be a problem as waiters bring a platter of mouth-watering *mezes* directly to your wooden pavilion, before moving on to the standard *şiş* and *döner* fare, with the added selection of fresh fish. Be warned, there is more being devoured here than the food, as the river's standing water brings tons of mosquitoes. Great views.

Saray Restaurant (☎212 13 92), directly behind the PTT on a short, nameless street. Identifiable by its red awning, the Saray stands out as a local favorite. As you walk in, choose from 8 or 9 dishes prepared for the day ($.50-$1 per serving). Fresh bread and pitchers of cold water come free in endless supply. Open only for lunch.

Yudum Tava Ciğer Salonu (☎212 43 52), faces the square bounded by Talat Paşa Cad., Eski Camii, Hotel Kervansaray, and the row of stores stretching down from the Bedesten. Yudum serves Edirne's specialty, *Tava Ciğer*, lightly breaded, deep fried strips of beef prepared in a large pan ($1). *Ciğer* is an acquired taste, but one worth acquiring, and there's no better place to do so than in this local hangout, indistinguishable from the countless other establishments on the square, but far better than the *Ciğer* stands around the corner. Open daily 4am-10pm.

Villa Restaurant (☎225 20 67), on the far bank of the Meriç River beside a picturesque Ottoman bridge. Like the several other restaurants on the river, the Villa opens only for dinner and is a notch above other small restaurants in town, serving a wide range of delicious dishes (*mezes* $1-2; main courses $3-5). Live music plays regularly.

Edirne Lahmacun (☎225 10 13), across the square from Eski Cami, just down the street from Kervansaray Hotel. A brightly lit eyesore on the otherwise subdued square. Huge servings of top-notch *kebaps* at low prices ($2 per portion). Pastries just as cheap (*baklava* $1.25). Open daily 10:30am-10:30pm.

SWEETS

Final Pastaneleri, 30 Saraçlar Cad. (☎225 42 27). An old standard, with 3 locations in the city. Ice cream at the door, cases full of sweets inside, and cafe seating upstairs. This sweet shop serves puddings, cake, pastries, and an array of cookies that are a cut above the rest on the street ($2.50 per kg). Open daily 9:30am-midnight.

Roma Pastanesi, 99 Saraçlar Cad. This sweet shop has 3 floors, a *dondurma* (ice cream) machine at its entrance, and killer cake ($3 per kg). Open daily 7am-11pm.

SIGHTS

Edirne's three main mosques illustrate the architectural transition from the Selçuk style of Konya and Bursa to the more distinctively Ottoman style of İstanbul. All are packed around the city center, as are Edirne's two museums.

SELİMIYE CAMİİ. Ottoman architect Sinan's self-proclaimed masterpiece, the Selimiye Camii is considered the finest mosque in all of Turkey (see **Ottoman architecture,** p. 25). Because Edirne was near the frontline of the campaign against Hungary, the colossal sultanic mosque was to be a standard-bearer of Islam. Sultan **Selim II** ordered construction to begin in 1567, the year after Sinan died; the mosque was completed in 1575.

In his design, Sinan surpassed the Aya Sofia (Hagia Sophia) in size, structural stability, and aesthetic unity. Eight massive columns support a dome slightly taller and larger in diameter than Aya Sofia's, without relying on semi-domes and side-aisles for support. On the exterior, Sinan augmented the skyward orientation with four slender minarets, each 71m tall. Inside, he illuminated the massive vertical space with 999 windows, giving the interior a weightless, airy feel. The eight potentially awkward columns are seamlessly integrated into the interior design.

The artistic decoration of the mosque—the carving, painting, and tile work—suggest a similarly untouchable mastery. Because Sinan planned closely with his artisans and craftsmen, he knew what he could demand in his designs. The 32m wide interior dome is covered with colorful lace patterns and calligraphic inscriptions. The intricate craftsmanship of the *mimber* and the exquisite tile-work of the *mihrab* are equally breathtaking. Uncharacteristically, Sinan exercised restraint given his penchant for stained glass, and thus the decorative elements evoke a more traditional conception of Islamic visual art. Be sure to approach the mosque from the west, as Sinan intended, passing through the **Kavaflar Arasta** (cobbler's market) and up a stone staircase (marked *Camii Giriş*) to the courtyard.

ESKİ CAMİ. Completed in 1414, the Eski Cami, or Old Mosque, is a prime example of an Ottoman mosque built before the conquest of Constantinople. Built in the style of Bursa's Ulu Camii (see **Bursa Sights,** p. 170), the mosque's rows of arches and pillars capped by nine small domes form a perfect square. Inside, spellbinding calligraphic inscriptions adorn the walls, and the front domes are adorned in intricate floral and botanical scenes. The marble *mihrab* is exquisitely crafted. The interior of the Eski Cami has been under restoration since 1995, but part of it can still be visited. *(On Talat Paşa Cad. at Hürriyet Meydanı.)*

ÜÇ ŞEREFELİ CAMİ. Built of Burgaz limestone on orders from **Murat I,** the Üç şerefeli Cami illustrates an intermediate stage in the development of Ottoman architecture. When completed in 1447, it replaced the Eski Cami as Edirne's primary mosque. The mosque, named for the three balconies *(üç şerefe)* gracing its minarets, features a fine fountain *(şadirvan)*, a tall northwest minaret (overshadowed only by the Selimiye, built two centuries later), and a dome 23m in diameter—the largest in existence at the time of its construction. The domes are painted in different combinations of geometric and floral designs. At the front of the mosque, on either side of the *mihrab*, are two sets of exquisitely handmade wooden doors. *(On Hukumet Cad., the first right off of Talat Paşa Cad., opposite şaraclar Cad.)*

BEYAZIT KÜLLİYESİ (BEYAZIT COMPLEX). Built in the late 1480s by the court architect of **Beyazıt II,** the Beyazıt Külliyesi was a charitably endowed spiritual and physical welfare facility. The centerpiece of the complex is the **Beyazıt Camii.** Multi-domed buildings, once used as schools, hospitals, and asylums, surround the mosque with their handsome courtyards. Only the wing used for medical purposes is open, now housing Trakya University's **Museum of Health.** The cells of the asylum contain displays of medieval and modern medicine, including a room of herbal guidebooks and a graphic display about genital diseases. The teaching hospital that once occupied these buildings was one of the foremost centers of medicine in its time. The long, narrow wing housed the mentally ill, who were soothed by the sounds of running water from courtyard fountains. The polygonal wing, designed to encourage sociability, housed patients with physical ailments. A platform here indicates where musicians stood to play the prescribed music therapy. Today, Trakya University is still renown throughout Turkey for its medical school. *(Follow Horozlu Bayır Cad. from its origin near the Sokullu Hamamı. After it crosses the Tunca River, the road passes through a small thicket and past some fields before it crosses another bend in the river and affords the most picturesque view. Museum open Tu-Su 8:30am-5:30pm. $1.50.)*

OTHER SIGHTS. There are several sights in the center of town that merit a quick look. The **Bedesten,** on Hürriyet Meydanı, is a 500-year-old covered market where leather goods, books, stationery, linens, and postcards can be purchased. On the other side of Hürriyet Meydanı is the **Rüstem Paşa Kervansaray.** This multi-domed structure, designed in the style of the Eski Cami, was built as a resting place for medieval caravan trains. It now serves as a splendid hotel.

Near the Selimiye Camii are two museums of minor interest. In the former *medrese* of the Selimiye Camii, the **Turkish and Islamic Art Museum** contains marble plaques and monumental inscriptions, manuscript Korans, weapons, glass work, weaving, Ottoman furniture, and a special room cataloguing the history of the Kırkpınar Grease Wrestling Festival (see below). *(Open Tu-Su 8am-noon and 1:30-5:30pm. $1.50, students $1.)* The **Ethnography Museum,** across the street, exhibits clothing, carpets, china, coins, and almost every imaginable household item from Ottoman days. *(Open Tu-Su 8:30am-noon and 1:30-5:30pm. $1.50, students $1.)*

If you are tired, relax at one of Edirne's historic hamams. Sinan's 16th-century **Sokollu Hamamı,** beside the Üç şerefeli Camii, is the best and most beautiful. *(☎ 225 21 93. Open daily 7am-11pm for men, 9am-6pm for women. $2.50, with massage $6.25.)*

ENTERTAINMENT

KIRKPINAR GREASE WRESTLING FESTIVAL. Once a year, competitors from all over Turkey travel to Edirne, don giant leather breeches, slather themselves in oil, and hit the mats. The champions of the **Kırkpınar Grease Wrestling Festival** are assured lasting fame and a portrait in the Turkish and Islamic Art Museum (see above). Musical performances, crafts, and folk dancing add to the festive atmosphere. The festival is held during the first week of July. Call the tourist office for info.

NIGHTLIFE

Edirne's modest, non-hotel oriented nightlife centers around the road between the two rivers, off of Alemdar Cad., which is off of Saraçlar Cad. after the stadium. Right next to the huge **Barcelona Disco,** the beautiful outdoor **Garden cafe and bar,** (not to be confused with the garden bar at the Kervansaray hotel) hosts live music in the evenings under an arbor of hanging flowering plants, and serves beer for $1.20. A number of beer gardens line this road between restaurants, making it definitely worth the stroll. A notch above the other hotel bars, **English Pub** at the Efe Hotel, 13 Maarif Cad., is a perfect realization of the Turkish conception of England, with dark wood interiors and plush seats. The **Kervansaray Bar,** at the Kervansaray Hotel, 57 Iki Kapılı Han Cad., is a dark and comfy easy listening lounge, where everyone seems to know the bartender, and you can enjoy a beer for $1.

BORDER CROSSING: BULGARIA

To cross into Bulgaria from Turkey, it is by far most efficient and convenient to take a direct bus from İstanbul. Trying to cross any other way is likely to be a hassle. However, there are a few options for those determined to leave from Edirne.

The border crossing, 18km west of Edirne, is to the left off the road from Edirne to Kapıkule. Either take the local bus into Kapıkule and walk out of town to the crossing zone, or have a dolmuş drop you directly at the entrance (both $1; see **Transportation,** p. 70). Although going on foot is possible (if the guards on duty allow it), the distance of several kilometers between the two border towns makes walking impractical. Turkish taxis will not cross the border or any of the three border checkpoints (passport control, customs, and police), though they run frequently past the Turkish side of the border in search of someone to ferry to Edirne ($20-25 trip). Some travelers hitch a ride on one of the Bulgaria-bound buses from İstanbul or elsewhere. This will make things a lot easier on the Bulgarian side as well, since the first town, Andreevo, has no accommodations. Sofia can be reached via Plovdiv, accessible only by taxi from Andreevo.

BORDER CROSSING: GREECE

Near Pazarkule and just past Karaağaç, the Greek border is less than 7km southwest of Edirne. The border crossing has extremely limited hours of operation (9am-noon). Without private transport, the best way to cross by road into Greece is a direct bus from İstanbul. Nevertheless, the crossing at Pazarkule is possible.

From Edirne, take a taxi to **Pazarkule** (15min., $6.25) or save money by catching the local bus to **Karaağaç** (frequent during the day, $.50; see **Transportation,** p. 70) and walking the remaining 2km to Pazarkule and the border. Between the Turkish and Greek border posts is a 1km no-man's land. Because Greece has declared the border area a military zone, no one may walk this 1km stretch without a military escort. Although Turkish taxis do not drive through to the Greek side, Greek taxis routinely wait at the border to ferry travelers across and on to the next Greek town, Kastanies, where bus and train connections are available.

GALLIPOLI PENINSULA AND THE DARDANELLES

> Pilgrim, be still! The soil you walk upon once engulfed the end of an era. Listen carefully! In this now quiet mound there once beat the heart of a nation.
>
> —Necmettin Halil Olan

The strategic position of the Gallipoli Peninsula on the Dardanelles made it the target of a major Allied offensive in World War I, aimed at keeping Turkey out of the war by bringing British gunboats into İstanbul. The prospect of storming the fields where the fates of Hector and Achilles were decided may have kindled a romantic spark, but the entrenched stalemate that followed the poorly planned assault left 80,000 Turks dead, with over twice as many casualties among the Commonwealth forces. Today, many of the peninsula's memorials and cemeteries are Commonwealth property, owned and maintained jointly by the British, Canadian, Australian, New Zealand, and Indian governments. The battlefields are best visited as a daytrip from the nearby towns of Eceabat, Çanakkale, or Gelibolu.

ÇANAKKALE ☎286

With inexpensive accommodations and frequent bus connections to nearby sights and cities, Çanakkale is an easy base from which to explore Gallipoli and Troy. Though not the most scenic locale, it is improving as the central Cumhuriyet Meydanı is refurbished and local tourist establishments are expanded. If you intend to visit only Gallipoli and not Troy, smaller Eceabat (p. 164) is a more peaceful base.

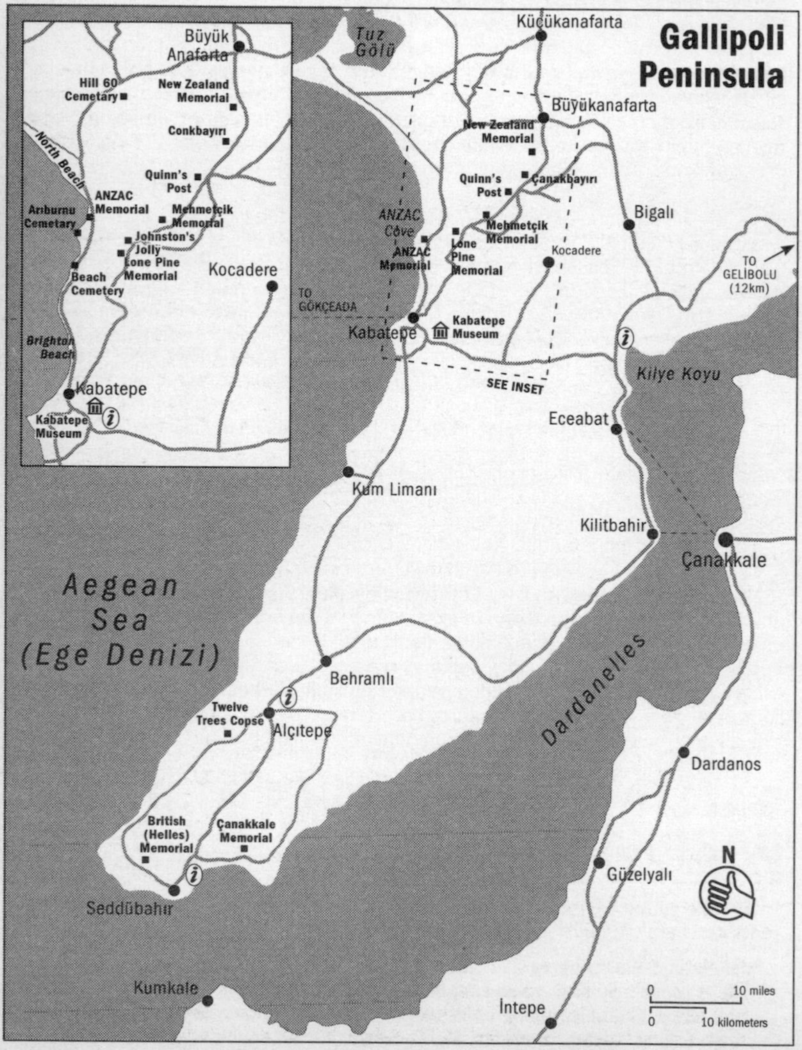

TRANSPORTATION

Ferries from Eceabat arrive at the ferry dock, while those approaching from the Anatolian side arrive at the otogar. To get to the ferry area from the otogar turn left along **Atatürk Cad.,** after 30m make a right onto **Demircioğlu Cad.,** and follow signs marked *"Feribot."*

Buses: The **Kamil Koç** bus company offers the greatest number of trips daily. To: **Ankara** (11hr., 10 per day 7am-1am, $11); **Bursa** (4½hr., 9 per day 7am-1am, $6.50); **İstanbul** (5hr., 7 per day 7am-1am, $9); **İzmir** (5hr., 16 per day 6:45am-2:30am, $8). **Çanakkale Truva** runs buses to Selçuk, including overnight service (6hr.; 8am, 7:30, 11:15pm, 1:45am; $7.50). **Dolmuş** run from under the small bridge over the Sarı Çay inlet to **Troy** (25min., every hr. until early evening, $.75).

Ferries: To **Eceabat** (30min., every hr.). Buy a token ($.50) at the window next to the PTT booth. The smaller ferry to **Kilitbahir** is left of the main docks when facing the sea (about every 15min., $.40). A porter will collect the fare on board.

ORIENTATION AND PRACTICAL INFORMATION

Practically everything relating to budget travel (food, accommodations, and travel agencies) lies within the one-block area around the **ferry dock** and the **clock tower.**

Tourist Office: 67 İskele Meydanı (☎/fax 217 11 87). Helpful, English-speaking staff distributes maps and helps find rooms in the high season.

Tours: Tours of Gallipoli and Troy are available from **TJ's Tours,** through Yellow Rose Pension, and **Hassle Free Travel Agency,** through Anzac House. Afternoon tours include lunch, and all tours include an English-speaking guide, transportation, and admission to the sights. **TJ's Tours** (☎814 31 21; fax 814 31 22; TJs_TOURS@excite.com) provides daily Gallipoli tours (noon, $19) and Troy tours (8:45am, $14) when there is sufficient demand. Call ahead to reserve. **Hassle Free Travel Agency,** 61 Cumhuriyet Meydanı (☎213 59 69; fax 286 29 06; hasslefree@anzachouse.com; www.anzachouse.com), provides daily Gallipoli tours (Apr.-Nov. 11:45am, Dec.-Mar. 10:45am; $19) and almost-daily Troy tours (Apr.-Nov. 8:45am, Dec.-Mar. 7:45am; $14).

ATMs: Several **banks** with Cirrus/MC/Plus/V ATMs stand on a 4-way intersection in a secluded part of the city. To get there, walk up Demircioğlu Cad. away from the ferry docks, and turn right onto Değirmenlik Sok., the 4th right after Anzac House. Follow this street for a few minutes to the intersection. Open M-F 9am-12:30pm and 1:30-5:30pm.

Police: (☎217 52 60), on İnönü Cad., next to the PTT.

Pharmacy: Pelini Eczanesi (☎217 12 60), on Demircioğlou Cad., just down from Anzac House (toward the ferry dock). Many more pharmacies on the right side of Demircioğlu Sok. as you walk away from the ferry docks.

Hospitals: Devlet Hastanesi (public ☎217 10 98), on İnönü Cad. across from the PTT. **Özel Hastanesi** (private ☎217 74 62), on Atatürk Cad., about a 20min. walk from the bridge over the Sarı Çay, away from town.

PTT: Central location on İnönü Cad. Open daily 8am-midnight. There is a small, satellite PTT in front of the ferry docks. Useful for buying stamps and telephone cards.

Postal code: 17100.

ACCOMMODATIONS

Budget accommodations cluster around the clock tower, with many good restaurants and bars only a few steps away.

Efes Hotel, 5 Aralık Sok. (☎217 3256). Walk to the left of the clock tower; hotel is on the left. A completely tiled, spotless hotel with spacious rooms, each with bath. Operated by a lovely, English-speaking Turkish woman. Parking in front. Particularly welcoming to single female travelers. Breakfast $2.50. Singles $7.50; doubles $9; triples $13.50.

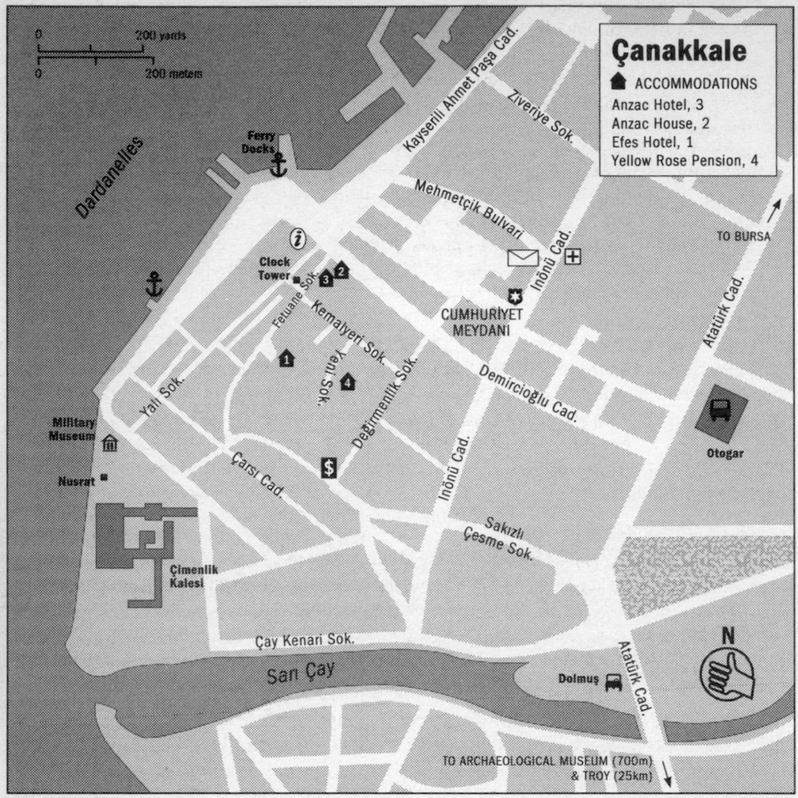

Yellow Rose Pension, 5 Yeni Sok. (☎/fax 217 33 43; yellowrose1@mailexcite.com; www.yellowrose.4mg.com). Turn left onto Kemal Yeri at the clock tower and then right onto Yeni Sok. A popular backpacker hangout, Yellow Rose has clean, moderately cramped single-sex dorm rooms, each with its own bath. Table tennis in garden, window screens, laundry service ($3), and international phone and fax services. *Gallipoli,* starring a young Mel Gibson, is shown each morning before the tour of Gallipoli offered by TJ's tours. Breakfast $1. Internet $1.50 per hr. Dorms $3; singles $6; doubles $9.

Anzac House, 61 Cumhuriyet Meydanı (☎213 59 69; fax 217 29 06; hasslefree@anzachouse.com; www.anzachouse.com), immediately on your right when facing Cumhuriyet Meydanı with your back to the ferry docks. A popular spot with Aussie and Kiwi backpackers, Anzac offers minimalist rooms with spotless sheets and clean, communal bathrooms with hot showers. Laundry service ($3) and Internet access ($1.50 per hr.). Arranges daily Gallipoli and Troy tours through the Hassle Free Tour Agency. *Gallipoli* shown nightly at 9:30pm. Breakfast $.75-1.50; BBQ most evenings in the garden. Reception 24hr. Dorms $3; singles $7; doubles $11. AmEx/MC/V.

Anzac Hotel, 8 Saat Kulesi Meydanı (☎217 77 77; fax 217 20 18). Next to the clock tower. Spotless, unremarkable rooms in this higher-end hotel feature TV and tiled bath. Elevator. Attractive, warmly lit dining area. Singles $11; doubles $20.

FOOD

Many of Çanakkale's restaurants serve the catch of the day along the waterfront, on either side of the ferry docks.

Boğaz 2000, 4 Saat Kulesi Meydanı (☎214 08 88). Step inside, choose small portions, and then sit down and wait for your meal. Tidy with antique photos on the walls and a calming atmosphere. Specialties are *döner kebap* ($1.50) and *Kemal Paşa Tatlısı* (a dessert with cheese inside, $.50). Open daily for lunch and dinner.

Doyum Pide ve Kebap Salonu (☎217 18 66). On the right side of Demircioğlu Cad., a few minutes from the Anzac House (away from the ferry docks). Excellent *iskender kebap* ($1.50) and *lahmacun* ($.25) make Doyum a local favorite. A few English-speaking waiters facilitate ordering off the Turkish menu. Open daily 10am-midnight.

The Yeni Entellektüel, 7 Iskele Meydanı (☎212 37 47), a 1min. walk from Cumhuriyet Meydanı along the waterfront toward the Military Museum. An indoor/outdoor cafe on the waterfront with flowers and an inspiring view of the harbor. Serves an array of *mezes* ($1 each) along with meat and fish entrees ($1.50-3). Open daily 1am-2am. MC/V.

SIGHTS

ÇIMENLIK KALESI (GRASSY CASTLE). About 200m downstream from the harbor lies a combined city park and naval museum. Its shady groves reveal nothing of its significance in the early part of the Gallipoli campaign. The **castle,** originally built in 1462 by Mehmet the Conqueror and reinforced by Abdul Aziz in the 19th century, was a major Turkish battery, containing what little heavy artillery the Turks had. Several Turkish guns from the battle of Gallipoli lie scattered around the park. A replica of the Turkish mine-layer **Nusrat,** with its decks full of racked mines, is also in the park. As a result of Nusrat's daring missions, three large Allied battleships, *Ocean*, *Irresistible*, and *Bouvet*, were destroyed, crippling the Allied attack. In the small, white house by the park entrance, the **Military Museum** exhibits such novelties as a pair of bullets that collided in mid-air. The museum has excellent English translations throughout, and if you have questions, the young Turkish men doing their military service staffing the museum are glad to share their knowledge. *(All three sites open T-W and F-Su 9am-noon and 1:30-5pm. $.50; students $.25.)*

ARCHAEOLOGICAL MUSEUM. This well-displayed collection features items from many local excavations, including those at Troy. Particularly exceptional are several cases of excellent Hellenistic and Roman glassware, including a few colorful Phoenician vessels. Also notable are a large, well-preserved statue of the Roman Emperor Trajan and several cases of Hellenistic funerary objects. The Trojan collection primarily features well-preserved ceramics and household items from each of the various Trojan settlements (see Truva, p. 179). One of the most notable objects recently arrived from the excavation field: an exquisitely crafted sarcophagus. It is the very last piece in the museum (as museum traffic must move essentially in one direction). Though badly damaged, it still shows traces of paint. This museum also displays the wares from which Çanakkale took its name—you can view a number of locally produced earthenware bowls *(çanak)* from the 19th century. *(100 Yuzuncu Yıl Cad. Walk on Atatürk Cad. away from the otogar, about 2km past the bridge. ☎217 67 40. Open daily 6am-5:30pm. $.75, students $.50.)*

ENTERTAINMENT

The city's ever-changing body of short-term visitors and the prevailing quiet during the long off-season make Çanakkale nightlife a lot like the Troy dolmuş: it only really gets going if there are enough people.

The TNT Bar/Garden (☎217 04 70), on Saat Kulesı Meydanı. Probably the best of the bars, drawing in the hostelers to drink and play pool ($2.50 per hr.) to the beat of Turkish and Western rock in a big wooden house. The garden in back serves drinks and quality fare ($3-5) in a romantically lamp-lit, tree-canopied space. Many vegetarian options. Open daily 4pm-3am; in winter 2pm-1am. MC/V.

Baron 7, 19 Fetuahare Sok. (☎214 00 80). Veer to the left of the clock tower when walking from Cumhuriyet Meydanı. Great for getting down with Turkish favorites like Tarkan under a hypnotic strobe light. Open daily 8:30pm-3am; in winter 8:30pm-midnight.

Carıklı, 20 Fetuahane Sok. (☎394 89 50). When you tire of blaring foreign tunes, walk up to the 2nd floor and get groovy with live Turkish music. No food, but plenty of alcohol (foreign and local). Open daily 8pm-2am; in winter 8pm-midnight.

Alesta, 4 Yalı Cad. (☎212 87 32). To the right of the clock tower. This tiny joint serves as the town's low-key but loud bar, blasting REM and other introspective pop in the early evening, before plugging in the woofers for bass-heavy dance music. Happy Hour midnight-2:30am. Open daily 2pm-3am.

ECEABAT

Forty-five kilometers southwest of Gelibolu, Eceabat sits a short ferry ride (every hr., $.50) across the straits from Çanakkale and is the closest major town to the Gallipoli battlefields. The town is particularly hospitable to New Zealanders and Australians, who will find reminders of home at several local establishments. An excellent tour company and cheap accommodations, combined with the location, make Eceabat the best base for exploring the battlefields.

TRANSPORTATION. A minibus to Gelibolu departs every hour until early evening ($.75). In the main square, Eceabat has both a **Çanakkale Truva** office and a **Radar Tur** office for **buses** to: **İstanbul** (5hr., every hr. 7:30am-1:30am, $10); **İzmir** (5hr., every hr. 6am-2am, $7); **Selçuk** (7hr.; 10:30, 11:30pm, 1:15am; $8.50).

ORIENTATION AND PRACTICAL INFORMATION. Eceabat's main square is bordered on one side by the sea and ferry docks. The road running parallel to the sea is **Cumhuriyet Cad.** Facing away from the sea, the road running off to the left one block beyond Cumhuriyet Cad. is **Zübeide Hanım Cad.** İlhami Gezici, nicknamed TJ because of his resemblance to singer Tom Jones, owns and runs **TJ's Tours** (☎814 31 21; fax 814 31 22; TJs_TOURS@excite.com; www.anzacgallipolitours.com). The well-known and well-loved TJ, unparalleled in kindness and helpfulness, gives the tours of the battlefields ($19), tours of Troy when there are sufficient people ($14), and general advice for tourists. Also available through the Boomerang Bar are snorkeling tours of World War I seaside battle sites where adventuresome tourists frequently find unfired bullets, shells, and other war souvenirs. **ATMs** can be found at Is Bankası in the main square and at Ziraat Bankası, located past the Gül Restaurant. **Cyberia Internet Cafe** is located next door to TJ's Hostel (10am-midnight, $1.50 per hr.). The **PTT** is about a 5min. walk along Cumhuriyet Cad. with the sea on your right; there's another branch at the ferry dock.

ACCOMMODATIONS. **TJ's Hostel,** on Cumhuriyet Sok. to the right of the square, serves as the town's main backpacker haven, offering small but clean dorms and private rooms. Friendly, English-speaking staff. Tours of the Gallipoli battlefield leave from the hostel daily at noon. (Dorms $4.50; singles $6; doubles $9.) With more comfort but less atmosphere, **Hotel Eceabat** (☎814 24 58; fax 814 24 61) offers spacious rooms with clean bathrooms, some with balconies, for $6 per person. The bungalows at **Otel Boss,** 10min. down Zübeide Hanim Cad., have a certain rustic kitsch to them (☎814 23 11; $4). Free camping is available on the other end of town at the **Boomerang Bar** (see **Food,** below).

FOOD. The **Vegemite Bar,** to the right of the square, serves Western fare (hamburgers, $.75) and Australian specialties (Vegemite toast, $.75), in addition to alcohol (beer $1, imported drinks $3), and holds a daily BBQ (8-10pm) set to Western pop music. (☎814 14 31. Open noon-2am.) The **Boomerang Bar,** along Cumhuriyet Cad. to the right of the main square, is another little slice of Australia, with a similar menu to Vegemite and plenty of beer ($1). At night, the thump of pop dance music attracts backpackers and locals alike. (☎814 21 44. Open until 2am.) For a more traditional meal, the **Gül,** on the waterfront 20m to the left of the square (facing inland) on Cumhuriyet Cad., serves Turkish pizzas ($1.50) and pick-and-choose appetizers ($.75-1) in both indoor and outdoor dining areas. Vegetarians can find several selections at **Liman** (☎814 10 86), which also serves fish and *kebaps* ($2-3). Follow Cumhuriyet Cad. to the left until it ends.

BATTLEFIELDS OF GALLIPOLI

About 10km northwest of Eceabat lie the battlefields of **Gallipoli.** Shortly after the beginning of World War I, Britain's young First Lord of the Admiralty, **Winston Churchill,** proposed that Britain use its superior naval forces to launch an attack on the Dardanelles, drive Turkey out of the war, and open communications with Russia. After a few unsuccessful attempts on the straits in late 1914 by an Anglo-French fleet, the Allies returned in March 1915, determined to penetrate the waterway. Badly scattered by Turkish mines, the Allied fleet regrouped on the Greek island of **Limnos** and shifted tactics, preparing for an amphibious assault on Turkish forces on the peninsula. The several months spent preparing the Allied expeditionary forces backfired, allowing the Turks time to secure their defenses.

The Allies resolved to land an Anglo-French force at Hellas Point, the mouth of the straits, while **ANZAC** (Australian-New Zealand Army Corps) troops simultaneously invaded the beach north of **Kabatepe.** At daybreak on April 25, 1915, the Anglo-French regiment landed and, at great cost, established a beachhead that they were hard-pressed to expand throughout the rest of the campaign. The ANZACs suffered even more casualties but managed to drive inland slowly, aiming to threaten the Turkish stronghold of **Canakbayırı.** In the face of fierce Turkish resistance, the battle dissolved into a bloody stalemate. The battle of Gallipoli paved the way for its hero, **Atatürk,** to become Turkey's founding father, and temporarily endangered Churchill's career. By the time the unsuccessful Allies withdrew in December 1915, the campaign had claimed the lives of over 80,000 Turkish soldiers and more than 200,000 Allied troops.

The disproportionate sacrifice of the ANZAC troops heightened the sense of sovereignty for Australia and New Zealand within the British Commonwealth. Each year, thousands of Australians and New Zealanders make pilgrimages to Gallipoli's war cemeteries, and April 25, the date of the Allied landing, is an important day of remembrance in both countries. Thousands of Australians and New Zealanders pack every hotel in Çanakkale and Eceabat for the anniversary.

SIGHTS

Gallipoli's battle sights and accompanying memorials are spread out, so your best bet is to take an organized tour, many of which provide lunch, excellent English-speaking guides, and transportation to each of the memorials. Tours are available from Çanakkale (see Çanakkale: Tourist Agencies, p. 158), Eceabat (p. 164), and Gelibolu (p. 164). Bring your swimsuit, since tours often make a short stop for a swim. If you want to visit the area on your own, take a dolmuş to the Kabatepe Müzesi (☎814 12 97) from Eceabat.

MUSEUM. The Museum has a collection of photographs from the battle, as well as old uniforms, weapons, skeletal remains, and two bullets that collided in midair during the fighting. (Open daily 8:30am-noon and 1-5:30pm. $1.20.)

ANZAC COVE. Four kilometers from the museum is ANZAC Cove, where the Australia-New Zealand Army Corps first landed on April 25. The ANZACs had intended to land on the wide shore to the south called Brighton Beach, but their boats were carried north by strong ocean currents and bad leadership. Instead of wide beaches, they found themselves on a narrow strip whose heights were dominated by heavily entrenched Turkish forces. Undeterred, the ANZACs forced their way uphill, dying in droves as they went. The site is marked by a simple stone memorial. A 4min. walk down the road brings you to a larger monument inscribed with a moving tribute by Atatürk to the young men of all nationalities who died fighting.

THE LONE PINE MEMORIAL. Seven kilometers uphill from the museum, this marks the site of an unsuccessful Australian attempt to break the stalemate. The graveyard and monument commemorate the thousands of lives lost in the effort, and visitors can sign a book of remembrance inside.

JOHNSTON'S JOLLY. A short walk north from the Lone Pine brings you to Johnston's Jolly, where the still-visible opposing trenches of the Australians and the Turks are so close together that they actually line both sides of the road. The site is so named because the Australian commander Johnston amused the nearby Turkish soldiers with his jovial antics.

REIS-A-RONI Statues all over Gelibolu celebrate the achievements of the town's local hero Piri Reis, a seaman and cartographer born in Gelibolu in 1470. As an admiral in the Ottoman Navy, he collected new charts and maps from the bazaars of his many ports-of-call. In 1513, he used his extensive library of charts to draw a map of the world. Reis's map resurfaced in 1929, when a group of historians discovered it while poking around in İstanbul's Topkapı Palace. They were astonished to discover that the 1513 map showed the coastal outlines of South and North America and included precise data on Antarctica, supposedly not discovered until 1818. Further studies of Reis's map have suggested that his reference charts may have been drawn from aerial pictures; the rivers, mountain ranges, islands, deserts, and plateaus are drawn with unusual accuracy.

OTHER SIGHTS. More memorials and battle-sites line the road uphill to Conkbayırı, the highest point of the battlefield, controlled throughout by Atatürk's forces. The **New Zealand Memorial** shares this hilltop with a statue of Atatürk.

Tours don't always include the memorials at the southern tip of the peninsula (some 30km from **Kilitbahir,** the town directly across from Çanakkale at the Dardanelles's narrowest point), but these can easily be seen on a separate trip. Take the smaller ferry from Çanakkale to Kilitbahir and then ride one of the regular minibuses to the **Çanakkale Memorial** at **Melles Point,** at the tip of the peninsula.

GELİBOLU ☎286

Though the Battle of Gallipoli (Gelibolu in Turkish) actually occurred many kilometers away at ANZAC Cove and Hellas Point, the peninsula shares its name with its largest town, Gelibolu. Gelibolu is a pleasant destination in its own right, with its quiet atmosphere, fresh fish, and a small but colorful harbor. However, it is the most expensive and least convenient base for touring the battlefields. Eceabat and Çanakkale are both closer to the battle sites and better equipped for budget tourism. Gelibolu is probably best seen as a daytrip from Eceabat.

TRANSPORTATION. From the main square, facing away from the harbor, the otogar is 1km to your left, the museum directly in front, and the Yelkenci and Yılmaz hotels to the right. **Radar Tur** (☎566 64 24) offers non-stop buses to **İstanbul** (4½hr., every hr., $6) and **İzmir** (6½hr., 4 per day, $7). A minibus runs to **Eceabat** (30min., every hr., $.75) from the otogar. Ferries service **Lapseki**, northeast of Çanakkale on the mainland (every hr. 9am-midnight, $.50).

ORIENTATION AND PRACTICAL INFORMATION. Across from the Yılmaz Hotel in the main square, **Atatürk Cad.** leads up to the secondary town square near the top of the hill. **Pharmacies** (all open daily 9am-7pm) and grocery stores line Atatürk Cad.; the **Akbank** with a Cirrus/MC/V **ATM** to the right of the tower museum near the harbor is open daily 9am-12:30pm and 1:30-5pm. The **PTT,** 3 Cumhuriyet Okulu Cad., is open Su-Th 8:30am-5pm for post; daily 7am-11pm for phone cards.

ACCOMMODATIONS. Gelibolu's best accommodations are a short walk from the main square. Down from the square by the water, the **Otel Yelkenci** on Liman Meydanı offers hospitable rooms without bath, but most have a good view of the small harbor ($4). **The Yılmaz Hotel,** 8 Liman Mevkii, offers rooms with shower. It also organizes daily tours (via tape-recorder) of the battlefields ($22). (☎566 12 56 or 566 35 98. Breakfast included. Singles $7; doubles $11; triples $17. 10% *Let's Go* discount.) The **Oya Hotel,** a street over from Atatürk Cad., away from the main square, also offers clean rooms with private baths and TV. (☎566 0392. Handicapped accessible. Breakfast included. Singles $7.50; doubles $11.)

FOOD. The local **seafood** can't be beat. The **Boğaz Restaurant,** 22 Liman Meydanı (☎566 16 06), neighboring **Imren Restaurant** (☎566 23 22), and **Liman Restaurant** (☎566 11 25) have views of the harbor and the fish market from their outdoor tables. Seafood dishes run $2-4; sardines are a local specialty. If fish doesn't float your boat, **Yarımada Lokantası,** 34 Atatürk Cad., is an excellent family restaurant with a large selection of dishes, both meat and vegetarian ($.50-2). Look for the sign outside that reads *"Yarimada Osmanli Mutfaği."* (☎566 12 25. AmEx/MC/V.) For after-dinner *dondurma,* try **Roma,** at the base of Atatürk Cad., across from the Yılmaz Hotel. (☎566 15 14. $1 per scoop. Second location in kiosk along waterfront, halfway to bus station. Open daily 9am-1am.)

SIGHTS. Gelibolu's only legitimate historical sights are the **fortifications** that surround the back side of the harbor. Inside the two-story stone tower, the most distinctive part of the fortification is a dimly lit **museum** displaying Byzantine terracotta lamps, faded reproductions of photographs, and rusted World War I bullets from Gallipoli. *(Open M-W, F 9am-noon and 1-5pm; Sa-Su 8am-noon and 1-5pm. Free.)*

THE EASTERN MARMARA REGION

BURSA ☎224

At the base of the 2km high slopes of Mt. Uludağ, Bursa is one of Turkey's holiest cities, as well as a major industrial center. Surrounded by fertile plains and blessed with vast gardens and parks, the city has earned the moniker "Green Bursa." Since green is also the symbolic color of Islam, the nickname has a double meaning. While the city's 14th-century mosques and tombs still receive visitors, Bursa's robust economy has fueled the development of a wealthy resort area among the towering mountains, including one of Turkey's hottest skiing spots.

Osman, founder of the Ottoman *(Osmanlı)* dynasty, besieged Bursa for nearly a decade before his son Orhan seized the town in 1326 and made it the empire's first capital. The mosques and tombs scattered around the city harken back to the formative stages of Ottoman architecture, when Selçuk influence was still strong.

Despite the relocation of the capital to Edirne and then to İstanbul, Bursa remained an important Ottoman city, bolstered by its role as a center of fine silk production. Today, silk trade remains a major industry in Bursa; the semi-annual silkworm cocoon harvest is held here every June and September. The city is also the original home of Turkish shadow theater, an art that spread all over the Ottoman Empire. Bursa boasts a museum, monument, theater, and annual festival all dedicated to the performance and preservation of the show. The city claims a

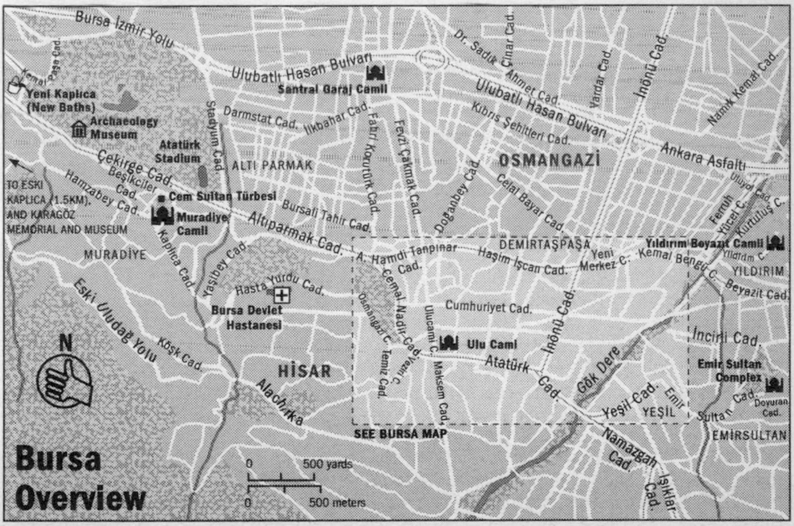

number of culinary triumphs: the *iskender kebap* (lamb meat with tomato sauce served on a bed of bread chunks with yogurt) and *inegöl köfte* (a kind of meatball) were both invented here. Perhaps anticipating the gastric misery resulting from eating too much *kebap*, Sultan Süleyman's Grand Vizier commissioned several mineral baths only a few minutes outside of central Bursa.

These days, travelers must look past Bursa's strip-mall feel to find its rich history, hidden in the infinite maze just off Atatürk Cad. Unconcerned with constant modernization, Bursa hasn't bothered to turn its many historical sites and mosques into museums, instead preferring to let its visitors see them in their current incarnations. The last stop on the fabled Silk Road from China, Bursa's silk markets are still in use, as are its mosques and thermal baths.

TRANSPORTATION

Buses: Bursa's terminal is 20km outside the city center. Local bus #90/A goes directly downtown ($.45). To get back to the bus station, pick up the same bus by the PTT on Atatürk Cad. (30min., every 30min. 6:20am-midnight, $.45). The bus tends to make a number of stops along the way.

Destination	Company	Duration	Times (daily)	Price
Afyon	Kamil Koç	5hr.	6 per day 8:30am-10pm	$6
Amasya	Yeni Amasya Tur	8½hr.	6:30pm	$14.30
Ankara	Kamil Koç	5½hr.	every hr. 6am-3am	$6
Ayvalık	Kamil Koç	5hr.	10 per day 9am-2am	$6
Bodrum	Kamil Koç	9hr.	8:30pm, midnight	$9.60
Çanakkale	Kamil Koç	5hr.	very frequent	$6.50
Çeşme	Kamil Koç	8hr.	2pm, 1:30am	$6.70
Datça	Kamil Koç	12hr.	10:30pm	$10.60
Denizli	Kamil Koç	8½hr.	12:30am	$9
Eskişehir	Kamil Koç	2½hr.	every hr.	$3.30
Fethiye	Kamil Koç	10hr.	8:30, 9:30pm	$11
Giresun	Ulusoy	16hr.	1, 3, 5, 7pm	$20
İstanbul	Kamil Koç	3½hr.	very frequent	$5
İzmir	Kamil Koç	5hr.	every hr.	$5
İznik	Atan Kardeşler	1½hr.	every hr. 7am-7pm	$2
Konya	Kontur	8½hr.	9am, 11pm	$5
Kuşadası	Kamil Koç	7½hr.	noon, 10pm, midnight, 2am	$6.60
Kütahya	Has Tour	2½hr.	1:30, 7pm	$4.50
Marmaris	Kamil Koç	9½hr.	10:30am, 10:30pm, 1am	$9.70
Ordu	Ulusoy	14hr.	1, 3, 5, 7pm	$22.60
Samsun	Ulusoy	12hr.	1, 3, 5, 7pm	$21.50
Trabzon	Ulusoy	18hr.	1, 3, 5, 7pm	$27
Yalova	Yalova Seyahat	50min.	every 30min. 6am-10:30pm	$1.50

Ferries and Seabuses: An excellent way to travel from İstanbul. Ferries and seabuses connect İstanbul and Bursa via Yalova. (For ferry information to Yalova, see **Yalova: Practical Information,** p. 173.) Buses make the hour-long trip from the ferry docks at Yalova to Bursa's terminal every 30-40min. (8am-10pm, $2).

Dolmuş: Bursa has an extensive dolmuş system. Each car takes 4 passengers ($.40-$.60 per person) and leaves from either Atatürk Cad., behind the *Adliye*, or from further down the street, before the Atatürk statue in Heykel. Destinations and stops in between are on a sign on the roof. The city has many garages *(garaj)* from the days before the construction of its terminal. Don't assume that a dolmuş marked "*garaj*" will take you to the one you want. Most garages, however, are a short walk away from Atatürk Cad.

ORIENTATION AND PRACTICAL INFORMATION

Except for the Ulu Cami, which is right on the main road, all of Bursa's sights lie about 1½km east and west of either end of **Atatürk Cad.**, while all of the hotels and restaurants, except those in the Arap şükrü district, are within a block of Atatürk Cad. in the area called **Heykel.**

Tourist Offices: To get to the main tourist office (☎220 18 48), head to the Ulu Cami side of Atatürk Cad., walk past the fountain toward the Atatürk statue, and go down the stairs on the left. Signs point the way. Helpful, English-speaking staff can help with hotel bookings and offers a city guidebook with a detailed map for $1. Open M-Sa 8:30am-6pm; Oct.-Apr. M-Sa 8am-5pm. Another tourist info booth next to the Yeşil Türbesi provides the same. Open July 1-Sept. 15 M-Sa 9am-6pm.

Banks and Currency Exchange: Numerous banks line Atatürk Cad. **Akbank, VakıfBank, Garanti,** and **Pamukbank** all have branches along the main street that can **change foreign currency,** and all have **ATM** machines that accept Cirrus/MC/Plus/V.

English-Language Bookstores: Elt Kitabevi (☎223 41 80), Eski Adliye Karşısı, up Konaaltı Sok. by the old government building, has a selection of periodicals and Penguin and Wordsworth classics. Open daily 9am-8pm. MC/V. **Santana,** 12 R. şefik Bursalı Cad. (☎224 56 42), has a small but carefully selected collection of music. The owner might even dig into his own stacks for something specific. Open daily 10am-9pm.

Emergency: ☎155

Police: (☎221 66 11). There are 2 police stations minutes off Atatürk Cad.; one 2 blocks down İnönü Cad. and the other a 5min. walk on Cemal Nadir Cad., the continuation of Atatürk Cad., toward the tombs of Orhan and Osman Gazi.

Ambulance: ☎111

Hospitals: Hayat Hastanesi (private, ☎225 08 50), just a few blocks from Atatürk Cad. on İnönü Cad. There are signs all the way down the street from the Atatürk statue. **Vatan Hastanesi** (private, ☎220 10 40), further down İnönü Cad. **Devlet Hastanesi** (state, ☎220 00 20). Take a dolmuş from Atatürk Bul.

Internet Access: Elite Internet Cafe, 37 Yeşil Cad. (☎327 03 34), before the overpass leading to the Emir Sultan Cami. $1.30 per hr. Open daily 10am-1am. A couple Internet cafes are 2 blocks uphill from Atatürk Cad., by the large parking garage. The **PTT** has cheap and reasonably fast Internet access ($.30 per hr.), but no disk access.

PTT: Across from Ulu Cami. Open daily 8am-11pm. Airmail services 8am-5:30pm. **Currency exchange** that cashes **traveler's checks.** Open M-F 8:30am-5:30pm.

Postal code: 16300.

ACCOMMODATIONS

A number of Bursa's budget hotels lie off Atatürk Cad., to the south of the PTT. Hotels closer to the main street tend to be noisy.

Otel Güneş, 75 İnebey Cad. (☎222 14 04). 8 basic rooms with linoleum floors and clean, shared baths with Turkish-style toilets. Tidy and quiet. The super-friendly proprietor will talk your ear off about her grandchildren, even if you speak nary a word of Turkish. Plants in the humble lobby give the place a friendly atmosphere. Lockout at 1am. Singles $5; doubles $7.50; triples $14.50; quads $20.

Otel Deniz, 19 Tahtakale Veziri Cad. (☎222 92 38). Keeping the Ulu Cami on the right, walk along Atatürk Cad. and turn left after the Sümerbank. Walk 2 blocks to the end of this street, take a right onto Veziri Cad., and walk 75m. 12 comfortable, quiet rooms around a pleasant courtyard. Shared bath and free laundry. Owner locks up between midnight and 1am. One of the cheapest places in town. Singles $4; doubles $8.

Çeşmeli Otel, 6 Gümüşçeken Cad. (☎/fax 224 15 11), down a street across from the Atatürk statue and a block toward Ulu Cami. This is the place to go if you're willing to spend some extra money. Sparkling, well-furnished rooms with couches, fridges, and TV. Cleaning personnel leaves *lokum* on your pillow. Friendly staff and female owners. Some rooms with A/C. Breakfast included. Singles $20; doubles $35; triples $45.

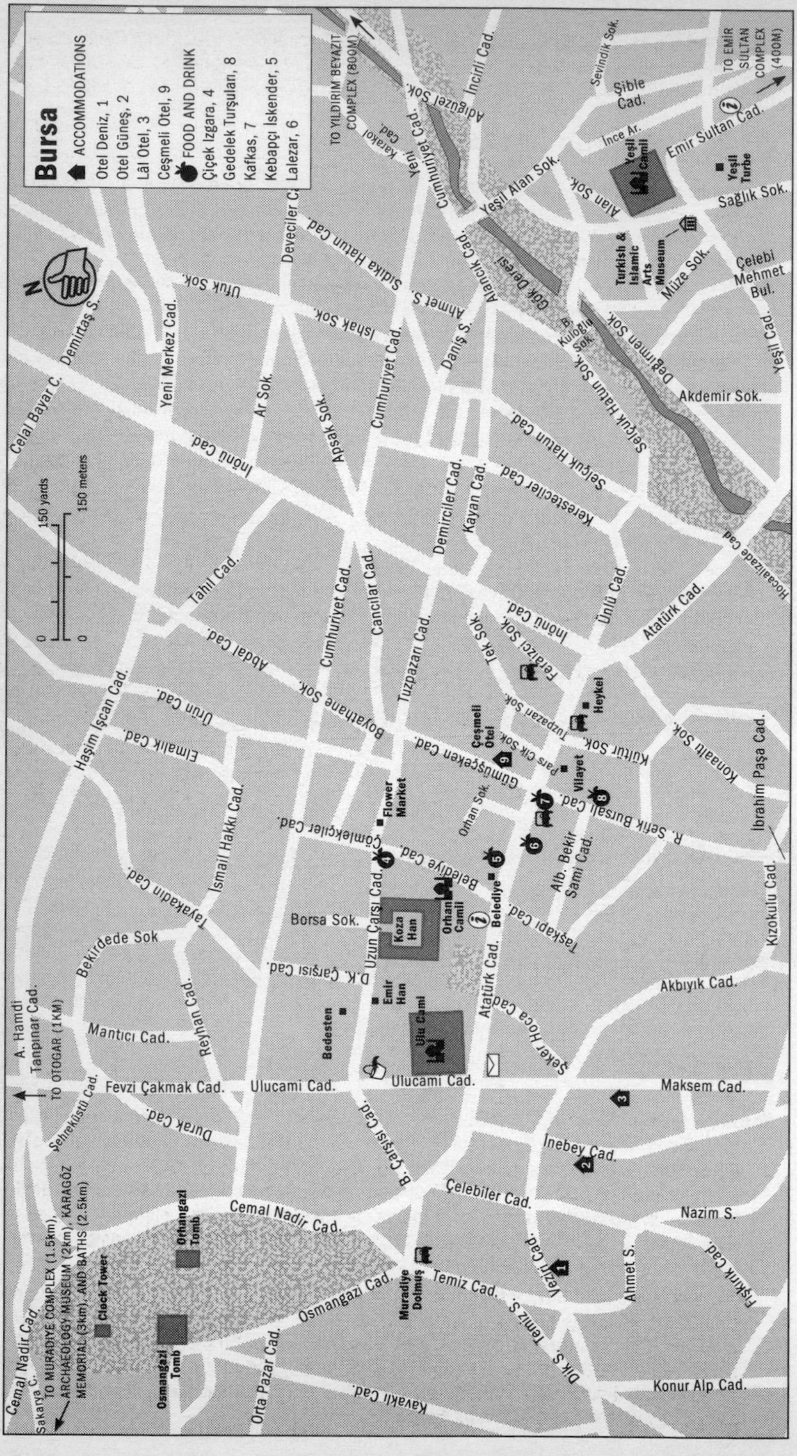
Bursa
ACCOMMODATIONS
Otel Deniz, 1
Otel Güneş, 2
Lâl Otel, 3
Çeşmeli Otel, 9
FOOD AND DRINK
Çiçek Izgara, 4
Gedelek Turşuları, 8
Kafkas, 7
Kebapçı İskender, 5
Lalezar, 6
N
150 yards
150 meters
TO YILDIRIM BEYAZIT COMPLEX (800M)
TO EMİR SULTAN COMPLEX (400M)
TO OTOGAR (1KM)
TO MURADIYE COMPLEX (1.5km), ARCHAEOLOGY MUSEUM (2km), KARAGÖZ MEMORIAL (3km), AND BATHS (2.5km)
Yeşil Camii
Yeşil Turbe
Turkish & Islamic Arts Museum
Koza Han
Orhan Camii
Emir Han
Ulu Camii
Bedesten
Flower Market
Belediye
Vilayet
Heykel
Çeşmeli Otel
Muradiye Dolmuş
Osmangazi Tomb
Orhangazi Tomb
Clock Tower
Gök Deresi
Atatürk Cad.
İnönü Cad.
Cumhuriyet Cad.
Uzun Çarşı Cad.
Ulucami Cad.
Maksem Cad.
Fevzi Çakmak Cad.
Cemal Nadir Cad.
Çelebiler Cad.
İnebey Cad.
Temiz Cad.
Osmangazi Cad.
Kavaklı Cad.
Konur Alp Cad.
Emir Sultan Cad.
Yeşil Alan Sok.
Çelebi Mehmet Bul.
Akdemir Sok.
Hocaalizade Cad.
Ünlü Cad.
Kızokulu Cad.
İbrahim Paşa Cad.
Gümüşçeken Cad.
Tuzpazarı Cad.
Haşim İşcan Cad.
Yeni Merkez Cad.
Celal Bayar C.

Lâl Otel, 79 Maksem Cad. (☎221 17 10). Follow Atatürk Cad. toward Ulu Cami, keeping it on your right, and turn left after the PTT. 21 large, unremarkable rooms with common baths. Hot shower $1.25. Singles $4.70; doubles $7.50; triples $9.60; quads $11.25.

FOOD AND ENTERTAINMENT

You've been eating it all over Turkey, but now you've come to the birthplace of the famous *iskender kebap*. Restaurants specializing in the dish sit between the Atatürk statue and the Green Mosque. Bursa's **Kültür Parkı** district also has decent, though pricier, restaurants and cafes (dolmuş from Heykel, $.30). The Arap şükrü district, next to Tophane Parki and centered around Sakarya Cad., a cobblestone side street off of Cemal Nadir Cad., features fish restaurants, bars, and pubs. To get to Arap şükrü, follow Atatürk Cad. 1½km west, and after passing the park with the Orhan and Osman Gazi tombs, bear left onto Sakarya Cad.

Kebapçı İskender (☎221 46 15) has two locations: a large, posh restaurant at 7 Ünlü Cad. and a smaller one by the Cultural Center on Atatürk Bul. Claims to have invented the *iskender kebap* ($2.50 for a single portion) in 1867. Although this is all they serve, they have perfected it beyond belief. Once served, don't dig in until they bring the pan of browned butter and apply the final fixin'. Open daily 11am-9pm.

Çiçek Izgara, 15 Belediye Cad. (☎221 65 26), in the square behind the large brick and wood building (town hall) on Atatürk Cad. One of Bursa's better restaurants, *Çiçek Izgara* means, literally, "grilled flower." Sit-down service and uniformed waiters. Delicious *köfte* and *kasarlı köfte* (meatballs and cheese; $2). Roasted tomatoes and peppers ($.60) are excellent. Save room for the *Kemalpaşa* dessert, a delectably rich set of cake balls bathed in sugary syrup. Open daily 11am-4pm and 6-9:30pm.

Kalendar Bar/Restaurant, 43 Sakarya Cad. (☎221 00 52). One of the many similar fish restaurants with outdoor seating along the narrow, cobblestone road. Serves fresh fish ($6-8) and *köfte* ($3). Open daily 4pm-1am.

Lalezar, 14/C Ünlü Cad. (☎221 84 24), across from Kebapçı İskender, features a special dish for each day of the week. Try the tasty vegetarian appetizers ($.90) and use great restraint to keep from skipping directly to the desserts, which include *kadayıf* (Turkish delight) in milk and nuts ($.50). Open M-Sa 7am-10pm.

Gedelek Turşuları, on R. şefik Bursalı Cad. Sells nothing but pickled items, including pickled peppers, pickled beans, pickled raspberries, and of course, pickles and pickle juice. Try a glass for $.20 and send your stomach on an adventure.

Kafkas, 31 Atatürk Cad. (☎221 55 49), on the corner of Atatürk Cad. and R. şefik Bursalı Cad., down from Pizza Hut. A Bursa institution, with several city locations. Delectable, reasonably priced chocolates, pastries, and the self-proclaimed best *kestane şekeri* (candied chestnuts) in Bursa ($5 per 800g). Open daily 7:30am-11:30pm. MC/V.

NIGHTLIFE

Indian Cafe and Bar, Oulu Cad., Oylum Çarşi # 21/8 (☎235 02 58). In the Kükürtlu neighborhood. Uniquely hip for this laid-back town, Indian attracts the fashionable of all ages, from alterna-teens to bohemian 20-somethings, with its reasonable prices for beer ($1) and liquor (from $2.50) and its playlist of alternative rock. Surprisingly, Indian is probably the only bar in Turkey that doesn't serve *Efes*, preferring 3 sizes of draft *Tuborg* as well as imported brews (from $3). A good place to rehydrate after the baths in nearby Çekirge. Open daily 11am-1am.

Nihavend Cafe and Bar, #14 Cemal Nadir Cad., which is the same as Atatürk Cad., (☎220 84 96). This tiny bar is easy to miss—head downhill along Atatürk Cad. away from Ulu Camii; the bar is on your right. Favored among 30-40 year-olds. One of the only places to get a cold beer along Atatürk Cad. or anywhere in Heykel. The mercifully air-conditioned pub hosts a nightly *sez* (Turkish 3-stringed instrument) player who sings songs, and all the patrons join in. Beer $1.

Cevriye Bar, 47 Sakarya Cad. (☎224 71 10). In the Arap şükrü district. Hosts live music nightly in its blacklit space with swirling painted walls. Cevriye's overdone decor doesn't promote a particularly party-friendly ambience, but as bars seem to be scarce in Bursa, it's worth a stop if you're in the area. Beer $2; whiskey from $4. Open daily noon-1am.

SIGHTS

Bursa's examples of early Islamic architecture are some of the most stunning in all of Turkey. Largely because the city's Ottoman layout still exists today, most of Bursa's sights lie roughly in a long row along Atatürk Cad. and its continuations.

ULU CAMİ. The immense Ulu Cami stands in the center of town on Atatürk Cad. Though Selçuk in style, with an interior *şadırvan* (fountain), puffy minaret caps, and a sprawling, column-filled interior, the unique layout is the result of a compromise between Sultan Beyazıt I and God. Before the Battle of **Nicopolis** in 1346, Beyazıt promised God that he would build 20 mosques in exchange for victory. After routing his European foes, the Sultan changed his plans, opting instead to build one mosque with 20 domes. The domes are arranged in four rows of five, with the center made of glass, lighting the interior majestically. Beneath the dome is a large fountain, a particularly unique feature. When the land for the mosque was chosen before the start of construction in 1398, one woman refused to move her house from the plot. She was eventually removed, but one cannot pray on a piece of land not given willingly, so the traditional saying goes. To avoid problems, the fountain was built where the woman's house stood. The three main entrances to the mosque feature Persian-style *eyvan*, and the interior columns and walls are adorned in Selçuk calligraphic Qur'an excerpts, instead of tiles or stained glass, setting the mosque apart from others in the region. The *mihrab* contains an astronomical guide with pictures of the planets. *(The mosque is quiet outside of prayer times and is a fine place for contemplation amid the busy town center. Dress appropriately.)*

YEŞİL TÜRBE AND MOSQUE. The gorgeous Yeşil Türbe (Green Tomb) stands atop a hill, its blue-green octagonal base and dome rising high above the surrounding buildings. Inside, everything is covered with beautiful tiles, even the sarcophagus. Sultan Mehmet I, who pulled the Ottoman Empire back together after Tamerlane swept through, is buried here.

Across from the tomb stands the 15th-century Yeşil Camii, whose Selçuk influence is apparent in its brick and stone construction and its onion-shaped minaret caps. The mosque's real beauty is in its interior, where intricately stenciled İznik tiles adorn the walls. The blue and gold *mihrab* demands attention simply for its size (6m wide and almost 11m tall). From the **balcony** that hangs above the entrance, the sultan could enter and pray unobserved, keeping his eyes peeled for potential assassins. The cylinders embedded in the side walls by the entrances to the domed chambers were (and are) used to check the "health" of the building. If they spin freely, all is well; if not, the supports are bearing undue pressure. The dome is one of the first large, central domes used in Ottoman architecture. *(From Heykel, head east along Atatürk Cad., bear right, and continue along Yeşil Cad. following the signs marked "Yeşil." Tomb open daily 8:30am-noon and 1-5:30pm.)*

MURADİYE NECROPOLIS AND MOSQUE. *şehade* (royal sons) are buried in tombs that surround the Muradiye Camii, a testament to the Ottoman practice of fratricide. In order to ensure a smooth succession, the eldest son would execute his younger or weaker brothers. The complex includes 12 tombs, but only 4 are open to the public. Cem Sultan's tomb is spectacular inside, covered in İznik tiles. Adjacent to the tomb is the Muradiye or Murat II Camii, built in the same style as the Yeşil Cami in 1425. *(Catch one of the frequent "Muradiye" dolmuş or buses from the Atatürk Cad./Heykel area. Tombs and mosque open daily 8:30am-noon and 1-5:30pm. $.60.)*

THERMAL BATHS. Bursa's fabled mineral baths are in the *Çekirge* ("Grasshopper") area, to the west of the city. The three-bath complex, **Yeni Kaplıca** (New Baths), is the closest, 300m past the Kültür Parkı. Three adjacent baths, fed by natural thermal springs, feature cavernous bathing pools with tiling, and mosaic work on the walls and floors that is, by itself, worth the admission fee. Bathing options involve varying degrees of service and privacy. The first bath, Yeni Kaplıca, is a men's hamam, built by Süleyman the Magnificent's Grand Vizier, Rüstem Paşa, atop the remains of an even older bath built by Justinian. (Bath $2-4.25; massage $2.50; *kese* $2. Open daily 5am-11pm.) The **Kaynarca** is a women's bath. (Bath $2.50; massage $2.50; *kese* $1. Open daily 7am-10:30pm.) **Karamustafa,** the family bath, has 2- and 4-person cabins available with special water on tap. (2-person cabin $6 per hr.; 4-person $15 per hr. Open daily 7am-11pm.) Karamustafa also has special **mud baths,** where you can soak in a tub of smooth, pasty earth for as long as you like. ($4. Men's mud baths open daily 7am-5pm; women's mud baths open daily 8am-4pm.) *(Take bus #40 or any dolmuş from Heykel with a "Çekirge" sign ($.60). Get off on Çekirge Cad. by the Atatürk Museum, continue walking away from the city center, and bear right at the fork onto Yeni Kaplıca Cad. From here, signs point down the stairs toward the baths.)*

Further west on Çekirge Cad. is the shinier and less crowded ■ **Eski Kaplıca** ("old bath"). This bath was originally built by Murat I, but got its name when ancient Roman baths were discovered around the grounds. Restored by the posh Kervansaray Hotel (among locals, the bath is known simply as "Kervansaray"), this is one of the finest Turkish baths in the country, featuring a hot indoor/outdoor pool where, from the interior side you can swim under a glass partition into the outdoor part. Also offers a hotter pool, and a great massage room. *(On Çekirge Meydanı. Take bus #40 or a Çekirge dolmuş and ask to be let off at the Eski Kaplıca. ☎233 93 00. Men $4, women $3.30;* kese *$3; massage $3. Open daily 7:30am-10:30pm)*

NORTHWEST

BURSA MUSEUMS. Built in 1424 as a *medrese*, the **Turkish and Islamic Arts Museum** *(Turk İslam Eserleri Musezi)* retains its original style, consisting of a rectangular portico with a central garden and classrooms off the sides. The collection is ceramics-oriented, with beautiful İznik pots and vases. The museum also has a costume display in the main lecture hall and a hamam exhibit featuring such items as silver bath clogs and a sultan's towel. Outside are Selçuk and Ottoman stelae and gravestones that illustrate the difference between the angular, raised Selçuk lettering and the flowery, carved Ottoman style. *(On Yeşil Cad., just before the tomb and mosque. Open Tu-Su 8:30am-noon and 1-5pm. $1.50, students $1.)*

On the opposite end of town, the **Bursa Archaeology Museum** *(Arkeoloji Müzesi)* has a decent collection of artifacts pulled from local soil, with a heavy emphasis on Roman items. One of the newer exhibits features an assortment of artifacts and reproductions from the Üçpınar tomb at Balıkesir, but the real highlight is the reconstructed chariot complete with life-size plaster horses. Descriptions and labels are predominantly in Turkish. *(In Bursa's Kültür Parkı on Çekirge Cad. From Heykel, take bus #40 to the Archaeological Museum and Batı Garajı. Open Tu-Su 8:30am-noon and 1-5:30pm. $1.50. Additional $.50 per person to enter Kültür Parkı. Cars $1.50.)*

HANS AND BEDESTEN. On Atatürk Cad., behind the Ulu Cami, stand the **Koza and Emir Hans,** the centers of the city's silk *(ipek)* trade for the past 500 years. Originally built in 1492 by Beyazıt II and later restored by the Aga Khan, the **Koza Han** (cocoon *han*) draws silk cocoon dealers every July and September. The *han* is home to nearly 100 silk shops, which sell the fine local fabric by the bolt, tie, and scarf. In the center of the two-story market's large courtyard is a *masjid* (small mosque). The **Emir Han** concerns itself strictly with the sale of the finished product.

Both *hans* open into the **bedesten** (covered market), architecturally similar to İstanbul's Grand Bazaar. Organized as they were in the 1300s, when Beyazıt commissioned the marketplace, the shops all sell the same merchandise. *(Hans and Bedesten open daily 9am-7am, though some stores close an hour or two earlier than others.)*

KARAGÖZ (SHADOW THEATER). The third week of November each year, the city holds a week-long shadow theater festival, inaugurated at the **Karagöz and Hacivat Memorial** on the road to Çekirge (see **No Strings Attached,** p. 172). The festival includes performances of Turkish shadow theater and of other puppeteering groups from around the world. Across the street from the memorial is the **Karagöz Sanat Evi,** with exhibitions on shadow theater from around the world. The museum also displays traditional clothing and crafts from the villages surrounding Bursa. *(☎232 87 27. Open M-Sa 11am-4pm. $1.50, students $.80.)*

The **Karagöz Antique Shop** is one of the few stores that sells shadow puppets. The master puppeteer R. Sinasi Çelikkol, who owns the shop, gives performances at the Karagöz Sanat Evi every Wednesday and Saturday at 11am. *(12 Eski Aynalı Çarşı, in the Eski Aynalı Çarşı, a marketplace off the bedesten. A former hamam, it's identifiable by its domed ceiling dotted with little lights. ☎221 87 27. Open M-Sa 8:30am-7:30pm.)*

TOMBS OF ORHAN AND OSMAN GAZİ. These tombs were ruined in the earthquake of 1855 and restored in the Baroque style, but perhaps most spectacular is the view over Bursa from the perch by the Bursa clocktower, which was built in 1906. *(Follow Atatürk Cad. to where it fizzles out and becomes Cemal Nadır Cad., and turn left onto Orhangazi Cad., a very steep street marked by "Muradiye" signs. The park will be on you right after leaving Atatürk Cad. Open daily 8:30am-noon and 1-5:30pm. Free.)*

OTHER SIGHTS. The mosque in the **Emir Sultan complex,** popular with devout Muslims, is where fathers take their sons before circumcision. The buildings are bright and well preserved. There's a great view from the park behind the mosque. *(Walk along Yeşil Cad. past the Yeşil Camii to a large underpass on the right. Head to the right of the tunnel, following the sidewalk, and continue uphill to Emir Sultan Cad., which leads to the complex.)*

NORTHWEST

The **Yıldırım Beyazıt Camii** and complex includes an *imaret* (soup kitchen), multiple *medrese*, tombs, and a hospital recognized as the first Ottoman hospital ever built. The complex was built by "the Thunderbolt," Sultan Beyazıt Yıdırım, towards the end of the 14th century. Beyazıt earned his nickname for the *Blitzkrieg*-like tactics he employed in capturing Yugoslavia and Hungary. He died in captivity after succumbing to Tamerlane. Note the so-called "Bursa arch" between the courtyard and the mosque—this architectural device crops up repeatedly in subsequent Ottoman buildings. *(The complex is accessible via the Heykel-Beyazıt Yıldırım dolmuş, the Heykel-Fakulte dolmuş, or any bus with Yıldırım on its route.)*

Back on Atatürk Cad. near the Atatürk statue, is the site of the annual **Bursa Festival,** which kicks off during second or third week of June with a parade down Atatürk Cad. Dancers and musicians from various nations make their way through the city, and afterwards the mayor delivers a speech in front of the Atatürk statue. During the festival, concerts and plays are also held in the Kültür Merkezi.

NO STRINGS ATTACHED Turkish folk shadow puppet theater supposedly began during the reign of the Sultan Orhan Gazi (1324-1359) when two workmen, the stonemason Karagöz and his foreman Hacivat, engaged in conversations so ribald and witty that the entire crew stopped work on the sultan's new mosque in order to listen. An enraged Orhan ordered the execution of the two jokesters, but finding himself bored without their humor, he grew to regret his rash move. An inventive Persian dervish, Mehmet Küscteri, attempted to entertain the melancholy sultan with figures of the late twosome made from transparent camel skin and manipulated from behind a screen lit with oil lamps. Handed down from one puppet-master to the next, Turkish "Karagöz" shows evolved into bewitching spectacles of color, music, bawdy comedy, subtle word-play, and clever political satire. The knavish, amorous, and uneducated character Karagöz ("Black Eye") is recognizable by his black eye and the huge turban that covers his bald head. His polar opposite Hacivat tries to appear erudite, peppering his speech with words of obscure origin that Karagöz perpetually misunderstands. Somehow, Karagöz's street-smart cunning always outdoes everyone, including his pretentious pal. The vignette plots include ludicrous money-making schemes (the two friends once tried to sell the heat of summer and the cold of winter in bottles), or ribaldry (Hacivat in his absence asked the lusty Karagöz to protect the virtue of his none-too-faithful wife). Karagöz enthusiasts are reviving the tradition in Bursa with an annual shadow theater festival, held each year in November (see **Karagöz,** p. 171).

DAYTRIP FROM BURSA: MT. ULUDAĞ

From Bursa, there are two ways of reaching the Uludağ cable car station. The easier method is to take a bus from Peron 1 on Atatürk Cad. Buses 3-C, 3-İ, or any with a "Teleferik" sign in the front window run this route (every 5-10min., $.40). Or catch the dolmuş from behind Adliye and Heykel ($.60). From there, the Teleferik cable car leaves every 40 minutes for the midstation, Kadıyayla, whose only attraction is its gift shop (8min.; runs daily 8am-10pm; round-trip to Kadıyayla $3.50; one way to Sarıalan $3.25, round-trip $7). Another car then continues to Sarıalan about 10min. later.

One of many peaks in the ancient world once called Olympus, this towering, snow-capped mountain is now known as Uludağ, literally "Great Mountain." In winter, the south face (away from Bursa) is a popular ski area (lift tickets $5) surrounded by a cluster of hotels. The ski season runs from December to April, with peak season from January to March. In summer, the Teleferik cable car in Bursa shuttles visitors up the north face to the campgrounds and picnic areas at the Sarıalan plateau. The summit remains snow-covered for most of the year.

Food and fire are both available at the **et mangal restaurants,** which sell meat in grams ($2.80 per 500g) and cook your food on personal, table-side barbecues. While these places don't offer much for vegetarians other than salad, potatoes, and yogurt, food markets in the area sell fresh fruits and vegetables. Camping is only permitted at the campground, **Sarıalan Kamp Yeri,** equipped with toilets, showers, phones, and hot water three days a week. ($2.40 per tent; $3.50 per caravan. Open June 1-Sept.) From Sarıalan, dolmuş make the 8km trip, otherwise it's a two-hour walk to the hotels on the south face (15min.; 8:30am-10:30pm, depart when full; $1). From there it's a challenging 2-3hr. hike to the summit. A second cable car runs from Sarıalan to another picnic and camping area, **Çobankaya.** As there's little of interest in Çobankaya, the primary attraction is the 35min. ride offering views of Bursa. (Open daily 11am-8pm. Round-trip from Sarıalan $3.50.)

NORTHWEST

YALOVA ☎226

Though Yalova is an unattractive warren of forgettable architecture, sub-par restaurants, and hairdressers, its glut of cheap accommodations makes it the best base for visits to the nearby baths at Termal and the beaches of Çınarcık.

TRANSPORTATION. The square is the site of the bus hub and Yalova's only bus company office, **Yalova Seyahat,** housed in a white office near the bus parking lot. The **Seabus** *(deniz otobüsü)*, or **passenger ferry** *(yolcu vapürü)*, leaves from the **car ferry port,** about 400m down the coast in the direction that Atatürk is facing. **Hızlı Feribot İskelesi,** as the port is called, has its own dolmuş and bus hub. Buses for Bursa stop here as well as near Cumhuriyet Meydanı. **Buses** run to: **Ankara** (6hr., 5 per day 8:30am-12:30am, $10); **Antalya** (10hr.; 10:30am, 9:30pm; $15); **Bursa** (1hr., every 30min. 6:30am-9pm, $2.50); **Eskişehir** (4hr.; 8:30, 11am; $6.75); **İstanbul** (3hr., every hr. 8:30am-6:30pm, $5); **İzmir** (6hr.; 10:30, 11:30am, 10:30pm; $8.25). There is also frequent dolmuş service to **Termal** from the square (25min., 7:15am-10:30pm, $.50). **Minibuses** run to **İznik** from the bus parking lot by the ferry port (1½hr., about every hr., $1). **Ferries,** including the *ekspres vapur* and *deniz otobüs*, run between İstanbul and Yalova. The faster **Seabus** (☎812 04 99), identifiable by its dolphin logo, departs for: **Bostancı** (45min., 6:25am, $5); **Kabataş** (1hr., 4 per day 8:30am-6:25pm, $7.50); **Kartal** (35min., 9 per day 7:30am-8:30pm, $4). The **car ferry,** *hızlı feribot* (☎811 13 23), runs from the main dock to **Yenikapı** (2 stops from Sultanahmet's Cankurtaran station, or 3 from Eminönu's Sirkeci) in İstanbul (9 per day 7:15am-9pm; $8 per person per seat, $4 for standing room. $30 per car). On weekends and holidays, ferries leave later and run later into the evening.

ORIENTATION AND PRACTICAL INFORMATION. The stern-faced **statue of Atatürk** in **Cumhuriyet Meydanı** serves as an excellent reference point. The **tourist office** is in front of Atatürk, about 50m down Yalı Cad., the main road along the waterfront. The second-floor office is on the right side of the road when walking away from the square, marked with a small, yellow "Tourist Information" sign. The English-speaking staff can help find lodging. (☎814 21 08; fax 812 30 45. Open daily 8am-noon and 1-5pm; in winter M-F 8am-noon and 1-5pm.) There is a second office right behind the bus station in Cumhuriyet Meydanı. (Open daily 8am-noon and 1-5pm; in winter M-F 8am-noon and 1-5pm.) Though the office staff speaks little English, they can provide maps and guides. The **banks, pharmacies, ATMs,** and **currency exchanges** lie to Atatürk's right, along Cumhuriyet Cad. **Nirvana Internet,** 1 Gazi Paşa Cad., is on the second floor of an office building in the main square (☎811 44 99. $1 per hr. Open daily 10am-midnight.) **Postal code:** 77100.

ACCOMMODATIONS AND FOOD. The new **Hotel 2000,** at the intersection of Yalı Cad. and the Meydanı, is quite a bargain. Its clean singles with double bed, bath, and TV will run you $5 (doubles $10), but many of their rooms have no windows. **Çiftçi Otel 2,** Cumhuriyet Meydanı, 8 Huzur Sok., inland from the main square, offers 30 reasonably priced rooms with bath and TV. (☎814 22 36. Singles $7; doubles $12.50; triples $15.50; quads $18.) For identical prices, **Erdinç Otel,** 8 Yalı Cad. (☎814 40 99), down the street to Atatürk's right, has 13 rooms with bath and TV. In both cases, ask for a room away from the noisy street. Though a bit more expensive, **Fatih Hotel,** 27 Cumhuriyet Cad., is removed from the square to ensure a quiet sleep. Cleaner than the other hotels around the square, each room has TV, phone, and bath. (☎814 95 14. Singles $10; doubles $13; triples $18.)

There are many *kebap* restaurants and pastry shops on Cumhuriyet Cad. Try the **şehir Lokantası** (☎814 28 05), İskele Meydanı, in the main square, for a bowl of soup for $.40 and *kuzu tandır* (oven roasted lamb) for $3. (Open daily 8am-midnight.)

DAYTRIP FROM YALOVA: TERMAL HOT SPRINGS. Having successfully cleansed grime off ancient Greeks, Roman Emperors Constantine and Justinian, Ottoman Sultans, and Atatürk, the **springs** at Termal have entered their third millennium of providing relief from the dusty bustle of İstanbul. Tucked away in the forest 15km south of Yalova, the Termal resort shows no signs of its proximity to either Yalova or İstanbul. The foliage is thick and healthy, and the air is heavy with the scent of ginger. Seizing upon the possibilities offered by this beautiful location, Ottomans built the 16th-century baths, which remain in use today.

Termal's main attractions are its baths and saunas, which serve the precious waters in a variety of ways. **Valide Banyo** is a classic Turkish hamam, with separate sections for males and females. The hot room contains a pool full of the special water. ($1.75, children's discount available. *Kese* $6; massage $6. Open daily 8:30am-5pm; in winter 8:30am-4pm.) The **Sultan Banyo** has private rooms with big tubs and a traditional hamam wash basin, as well as a separate room for changing. (☎675 74 00. 1 person $5 per hr.; 2 people $8.25 per hr.; 3 people $10.75 per hr. Open daily 8am-6pm.) **Kurşunlu Bath,** in the middle of the complex, down by the stream, is the place to enjoy a large open-air pool, sauna, and bath. Arrows point the way to the baths from all parts of the resort. (Pool $4.10; baths and sauna $3.25; private saunas $50 for 1½hr. Open daily 8:30am-10:30pm.) *(Frequent dolmuş leave Yalova from the hub in front of the car ferry terminal and make a stop along the curb in front of Cumhuriyet Meydanı. The Termal resort is the last stop on the route (25min., 7:15am-10:30pm, $.60). Termal can also be visited as a daytrip from İstanbul, if you leave from Kadiköy or Yenikapı, or if you are willing to shell out the $5 for the Bostancı or Kabataş seabus. The ferry ride is only 1hr. long, and Termal is a 20min. dolmuş ride from the ferry port. The bus to Yalova, however, takes at least 3hr., circumnavigating suburban İstanbul before arriving at Kadikoy.)*

TWISTED SISTERS In 304 AD, three virgin sisters, Menodora, Metrodora, and Nymphodora, isolated themselves in the woods near Termal to devote themselves to God. They soon found themselves healing the sick and gleaning the medicinal secrets of the natural hot springs, until rumors of their powers and considerable beauty reached the ears of the Prince of Bithynia. He lavished all manner of gifts upon the sisters, offering them gold and nobles to marry if they would worship the Bithynian idols in exchange. The sisters, however, were resolute in their devotion to the Christian God, even when the Prince threatened torture. Menodora challenged him to collect the finest torture devices from around the world, and still the sisters would not waver, she promised. Unfortunately, she had to keep her promise, as the prince killed each of them by a different elaborate torture scheme. When he had the bodies of the martyred three burned, however, he and the torturers were, as one would expect, consumed by a fire sent from heaven.

İZNİK ☎224

In religious, artistic, and historical significance, the sleepy hamlet of İznik ranks among the most important cities in the world. Archaeologists have found traces of different civilizations on the banks of İznik Lake dating back as far as 2500 BC. Alexander the Great conquered the city, then known as **Nicaea,** before it was incorporated into the Roman Empire in 71 AD. A major religious center, Nicea was the site of ground-breaking councils of the early Christian Church. In 325 AD, Emperor Constantine convened the First Council of Nicaea, condemning the Arian heresy—the belief that Christ was inferior to God. The Council formulated the Nicaean Creed, setting the record straight on Christ's omnipotence (see **Christianity and the Byzantine Empire,** p. 10). The bishops returned in 787, gathering in the local Aya Sofia for the Seventh Ecumenical Council.

In 1081 the Selçuks conquered Nicaea, renamed the city İznik, and made it the capital of the Sultanate of Rum (see **The Great Selçuk Sultanate,** p. 11). Reclaimed by the Byzantines in 1097, the city became part of the nascent Ottoman Empire when Orhan Gazi, son of Osman, drove the Byzantines out for good in 1331. With the fall of Constantinople in 1453 and the relocation of the Ottoman capital, İznik lost its political importance. It gained renown, however, as an artistic center, producing *faïence* on par with Delft porcelain and Ming china.

The discovery of nearby kaolin (glossy clay) and silicon deposits and heightened Persian influence in the city began the golden age of İznik pottery (see **Ottoman Decorative Arts,** p. 25). Sultan Selim the Grim gave the İznik tile industry further impetus when, after conquering parts of Persia in the early 16th century, he sent the skilled potters of Tabriz westwards. At its height, İznik boasted 300 ateliers producing tiles that were used on all the major buildings of the Ottoman Empire. Sadly, by the end of the 1700s, almost all the kilns and workshops had shut down. These days, besides the cheap imitations of the İznik masterpieces available in every gift shop, a new factory near the center of town is working with carefully constructed reproductions of the historic kilns to recreate the magic. They proudly claim that they "almost" have the same colors as the famed ateliers—but not quite. After the close of the original workshops, the town spent the next two centuries sliding into obscurity, with the war of 1922 sealing its fate.

Today, İznik is a passive lakeside town. Speed bumps and laws against honking keep motorists from disturbing the peace of the townsfolk as they drink infinite cups of *çay* in İznik's tea houses and gardens. The scene is even more mellow by the lake, where the natural beauty of a sunset borders on a religious experience.

TRANSPORTATION

Bursa and Yalova are the two main approaches to İznik. Frequent seabus service means arriving from İstanbul via Yalova is no problem (see **Yalova,** p. 173).

Buses: From the otogar to: **Ankara** (5½hr., 9:30am, $7); **Bursa** (1¼hr., every 30min. 6am-7:45pm, $2.40); **İstanbul** (3½hr., 7:45am, $5); **Yalova** (1½hr.; 7:45am, sporadic 9am-7pm; $1.50). Or catch the more frequent Orhangazi bus to Yalova or Bursa.

Ferries: From Yalova (58km away) to **Kabataş, Kartal, Yenikapı** and **Bostancı** in **İstanbul**. See **Transportation,** p. 173.

ORIENTATION AND PRACTICAL INFORMATION

The city's grid-like street plan makes for easy navigation. Two main boulevards, **Kılıçaslan Cad.** and **Atatürk Cad.,** divide İznik into quarters, meeting in the center at Aya Sofia. Most of İznik is enclosed by its ancient walls. The lake *(İznik Gölü)* lies along **Sahil Yolu,** outside the town's western walls.

Tourist Office: (☎757 14 54; fax 757 19 33), near Aya Sofia, inside the large modern building off the park. Friendly staff speaks some English and offers free maps and town guides. Open daily 8:30am-noon and 1-5:30pm; in winter M-F 8am-noon and 1-5pm.

Banks: Türkiye İş Bankası, across the street from Aya Sofia, has a Cirrus/MC/Plus/V **ATM.** Open 9am-12:30pm and 1:30-5:30pm. There is also a **Yapı ve Kredi,** 1 block from the square on Atatürk Cad., with a Cirrus/MC/Plus/V ATM. Open daily 9am-12:30pm and 1:30-5pm. **Akbank,** 1 block off the square on Kılıçaslan Cad., away from the lake, changes AmEx **traveler's checks.** Open daily 9am-12:30pm and 1:30-5:30pm.

Hospital: Devlet Hastanesi (public, ☎757 75 80), a 10min. ride out of town.

Internet Access: Kaynarca Internet at the Kaynarca Hotel and Pansiyon, 1 M. Gündem Sok. (☎757 17 53). One of the only places in town with a flat fee ($.50).

PTT: (☎757 22 22), 150m down Kılıçaslan Cad. towards the lake. Open daily 8am-12:30pm and 1:30-7pm.

Postal Code: 16860.

NORTHWEST

ACCOMMODATIONS & CAMPING

Kaynarca Hotel and Pansiyon (☎757 17 53), at the intersection of Kılıcarslan Cad. and M. Güdem Sok. This is not only the best deal in town, but also the friendliest. Offers a guest kitchen on a beautiful terrace, a clothesline for self-washed clothing, and satellite TV. Brightly colored, homey rooms. Breakfast $2. Dorms (with large, clean, shared bath) $4; singles $7; doubles $11; family rooms (queen-sized bed and single bed) $14.

Burcum Motel, Kemalpaşa Mah., 20 Sahil Yolu (☎757 10 11; fax 757 12 02). A pleasant place to stay, with clean rooms and terraces facing the lake. All 25 rooms have shower, toilet, TV, and phones. 24hr. hot water when full, otherwise available morning and night only. Breakfast included. $11.50 per person.

Cem Pansiyon, 34 Göl Kenarı (☎757 16 87; cempansiyon@mynet.com.tr). After reaching the lake via Kılıçaslan, take a right and walk 300m. Well-kept rooms with superb views. Communal bathroom and shower on every floor. Breakfast $1.80. Singles $8, with a view of the lake $11.50; doubles $12.50, with view $18; triples $23.

Hotel Babacan, 86 Kılıçaslan Cad. (☎757 12 11), at the center of town. Modest rooms vary in quality; rooms with bath are nicer but more expensive. Singles $4.50, with bath $6.10; doubles $7.60, with bath $10; triples $10, with bath 12; quads $13.25.

Camping is possible at a completely facility-less grassy patch, where visitors can pitch a tent for free. Follow Kılıçaslan Cad. toward the lake, turn left at Sahil Yolu, and continue about 275m past Çamlık Restaurant. Anything along the shore there is fair game. Unfortunately, there's nowhere to rent a tent in İznik.

FOOD & NIGHTLIFE

Kirik Çatal, next to the Burcum Motel on Sahil Yolu, has a tasty but standard selection of *mezes* and *kebap,* yet the chicken *şiş* somehow manages to transcend the dish's ubiquity. Be sure to get there in time to watch the sun set over the lake as you dine. *Mezes* $.70-1.50; main courses $2-5; beer $1. Open daily 11am-1pm.

Kar-pi Fast Food (☎757 42 24), across from the Aya Sofia. Cheap, large portions of *kebap* and *lahmacun* ($.50-2). Outstanding *kebap* selection. Choose between open-air seating and the A/C interior. Open daily 11am-midnight.

Çamlık Restaurant, 15 Göl Sahil Yolu (☎757 16 31), at the intersection of Göl Sahili and Kılıçaslan. *Taratör* (spiced garlic yogurt) $.80; grilled *yayın balık* (catfish, a regional specialty) $3. Open daily 9am-1am.

Ceren Pastanesi, 72 Atatürk Cad. (☎757 13 79). This popular pastry shop serves *poğaça* (pastry with cheese) and tea for under $.30. Open daily 6am-midnight.

Tutku Bar, just before the lakeside Sahil Yolu becomes Spandau Bul., across from a playground. If coming from town, take a right when you get to the lake. Indistinguishable in the daytime from the innumerable *çay* gardens along the lake, at night this outdoor, tented space shows soccer and occasionally dubbed action movies on their wide screen TV. Deliciously cold pints of beer just $.70.

SIGHTS

AYA SOFIA. Built by the Byzantines in the 4th century, the Aya Sofia (Church of the Holy Wisdom) was converted to a mosque in 1331 by Osman, the founder of the Ottoman dynasty. After the occupying forces of Tamerlane damaged the building in 1402, it was renovated during the reign of Süleyman the Magnificent (1520-1566) by Sinan, the court architect. Today, it lies in a beautifully evocative state of ruin with only a few pieces of religious art. *(At the town's central intersection. Open daily 9am-noon and 1-4:30pm. $1.65.)*

İZNİK MUSEUM. Sultan Murat I built the **Nilüfer Hatun İmareti** in 1388 in honor of his mother. The building now functions as İznik's museum. A charitable house, the *imaret* once offered food and shelter to traveling students, dervishes, and artisans. Today, it contains İznik porcelain wares and various local stelae, reliefs, and Islamic gravestones. The display case full of ancient coins is a real treat. Look out for the Lysimachean tetradrachm coins bearing the image of Alexander the Great on one side. These coins were used for trade as far away as India and Saudi Arabia. There is also a case of pottery used by the people of Ilıpınar, a part of northwest Anatolia, that dates from 6000-5500 BC. *(Follow Kılıçaslan Cad. away from the center of town. Signs lead the way. Open daily 8:30am-noon and 1-5pm. $1.)*

YEŞİL CAMİ. Across from the museum stands the Yeşil Cami ("Green Mosque"). Designed by Haci Musa in 1371, the well-proportioned building is mostly uninspiring, except for the exquisite, tiled minaret with bands of various geometrical patterns. To catch a glimpse, just look up on your way to the museum.

MURAT HAMAMI. Just south of Aya Sofia, the sagging Murat Hamamı offers cheap baths in a made-to-last facility. The center stone is original and so old that its edges have been rounded from use. The furnace behind the sauna still burns wood rather than propane. *(Standing with your back to the gate of Aya Sofia, turn left, walk 2 blocks, and take another left. The bath is down a block on the left. ☎757 14 59. Open for women 1pm-5pm; for men 8am-1pm and 5pm-midnight. Bath $1.75; massage $1.)*

ÇİNİ KILNS. The large, overgrown clearing across the street from the baths is all that remains of the original, world-famous **İznik kilns.** Excavations in the late 1970s discovered these two kilns and confirmed that they had been in service during İznik's prime tile-making days. Follow İstiklâl Cad. down one block to Kekket Sok., where artisans make modern reproductions of old İznik tile patterns. The tiles are cheap, starting at $2 for simple designs.

ROMAN THEATER. Although the theater was designed to seat 15,000, the remaining ruins offer little hint of the sheer size of the original structure, as most of the theater lies buried under several feet of dirt and crumbled brick. It was supposedly hit by Greek artillery when the city was razed in 1922. Four of the entrance arches

NORTHWEST

still rise out of the rubble. Excavations of the theater site have revealed that the enclosure was used in later years as a sight for kilns, a church, a palace, and ceramic workshops. *(From the center of town, head south along Atatürk Cad. to Tiyatrosu Cad., on the right, where signs point the way to the ruins.)*

CITY GATES. Tiyatrosu Cad. leads through one of the city's seven remaining gates and along the **city walls.** The walls are doubled and even tripled in places with a *fosse* (water-filled ditch) between each section. This degree of fortification, a concrete testament to İznik's former importance, is matched only by the Theodosian Sea Walls in İstanbul. Follow the walls around the city to the four main city gates, of which only three survive. Of these, the **İstanbul Gate** *(İstanbul Kapısı)*, at the north end of Atatürk Cad., is the most impressive. Built at Emperor Vespasian's request, it consists of three concentric gates flanked by high walls.

OTHER SIGHTS. Some of İznik's more ghoulish sights, such as the **Yeraltı Mezar** (an ancient tomb) and the **Byzantine Catacombs,** lie outside the city walls. Visiting these requires a guide from the İznik Museum. Unfortunately, little English is spoken at the museum, so make arrangements through the tourist office a few days in advance. İznik has two other historical sights of interest. The brick-and-mortar **Süleyman Paşa Medrese,** built by the brother of Orhan I on the site of a former Byzantine monastery, is the oldest standing *medrese*, or seminary, in Turkey. Students' cells lined the cramped, porticoed courtyard. The tiny, brick **Haci Özbek Camii,** dingy on the inside and not much better on the outside, is noteworthy for being the oldest Ottoman mosque whose construction date (1333) can be verified. *(Süleyman Paşa Medresse on Kekket Sok., off İstiklâl Cad. Haci Özbek Camii on Kılıçaslan Cad.)*

AEGEAN COAST

Fabulous classical ruins and sublime beaches have helped transform Turkey's once-tranquil Aegean coast into an increasingly popular tourist destination. Framed by 5000 years of history and mythology, the region's rich culture offers an eye-full for photographers, archaeologists, nature-lovers, and hedonists alike. The coast's first foreign visitors were ancient Greeks, who established several ports in the area. As Alexander the Great and subsequent Hellenic rulers pushed their empire east, the ports became centers of commerce for the ancient world. Today, Hellenic ruins—especially extensive at Pergamon, Ephesus, Aphrodisias, and Pamukkale—stand as weathered testaments to the coast's glorious heritage.

Far from just cordoned-off tourist traps, the Aegean's ruins are a natural backdrop to modern life. Broken columns and statuary fill the natural sulfur swimming pools in Pamukkale hotels, standing exactly where they fell when earthquakes toppled them centuries ago. Many restaurants in Aegean coastal towns respectfully reserve their basement floors for mini-exhibits of the ruins on which their foundations were laid. This makes for a spectacular fusion of the booming modern Aegean region with its unparalleled ancient llegacy.

HIGHLIGHTS OF THE AEGEAN COAST

SCAMPER about the ruins of the Temple of Artemis in **Selçuk** (p. 204) and the Mausoleum of Halicarnassus in **Bodrum** (p. 224) to see two of the Seven Wonders of the Ancient World.

FOLLOW in the footsteps of thousands of weary travelers to the calcium-covered travertines of **Pamukkale** (p. 217), one of the world's most beautiful natural baths.

EMBARK on a "Blue Voyage" for a day to explore and swim in the otherwise inaccessible caves, coves, and islands around the **Bodrum Peninsula** (p. 224).

SPEND a day or two amidst the reds and blues of **Ayvalık (p. 180)**, a former Greek fishing village with olive groves, Neo-Classical architecture, and fantastic beaches.

MAKE a pilgrimage to the house in **Selçuk** (p. 208) where the Virgin Mary lived out her last days with St. John.

NORTHERN COAST

TRUVA (TROY)

Site open daily 8am-7pm; in winter, spring, and fall 8am-5pm. $3; students $1.50.

For the casual visitor with no particular attachment to Homer, Troy's jumbled, partially excavated ruins may prove a disappointment. The site is confusing and not immediately striking to the romantic imagination. The hokey wooden horse at the entrance does little to evoke Troy's long-passed grandeur. A tour of the site (provided by the Hassle Free Tour Agency) can help make the stone rubble come alive and shed some light on Troy's complicated history and ongoing excavation. For those with only a passing interest in history who still want to be able to say they visited the famed fortress, an independent visit to Troy should suffice. English-language explanations of the history are scattered throughout.

HISTORY

When Heinrich Schliemann rediscovered Troy in the 1880s, the city had been uninhabited for at least 13 centuries. However, the previous 35 centuries of habitation span a huge continuum of civilization, stretching from the early Bronze age to the later Roman Empire. During 110 years of sporadic excavation, archaeologists have split these periods into comprehensible, clearly numbered units.

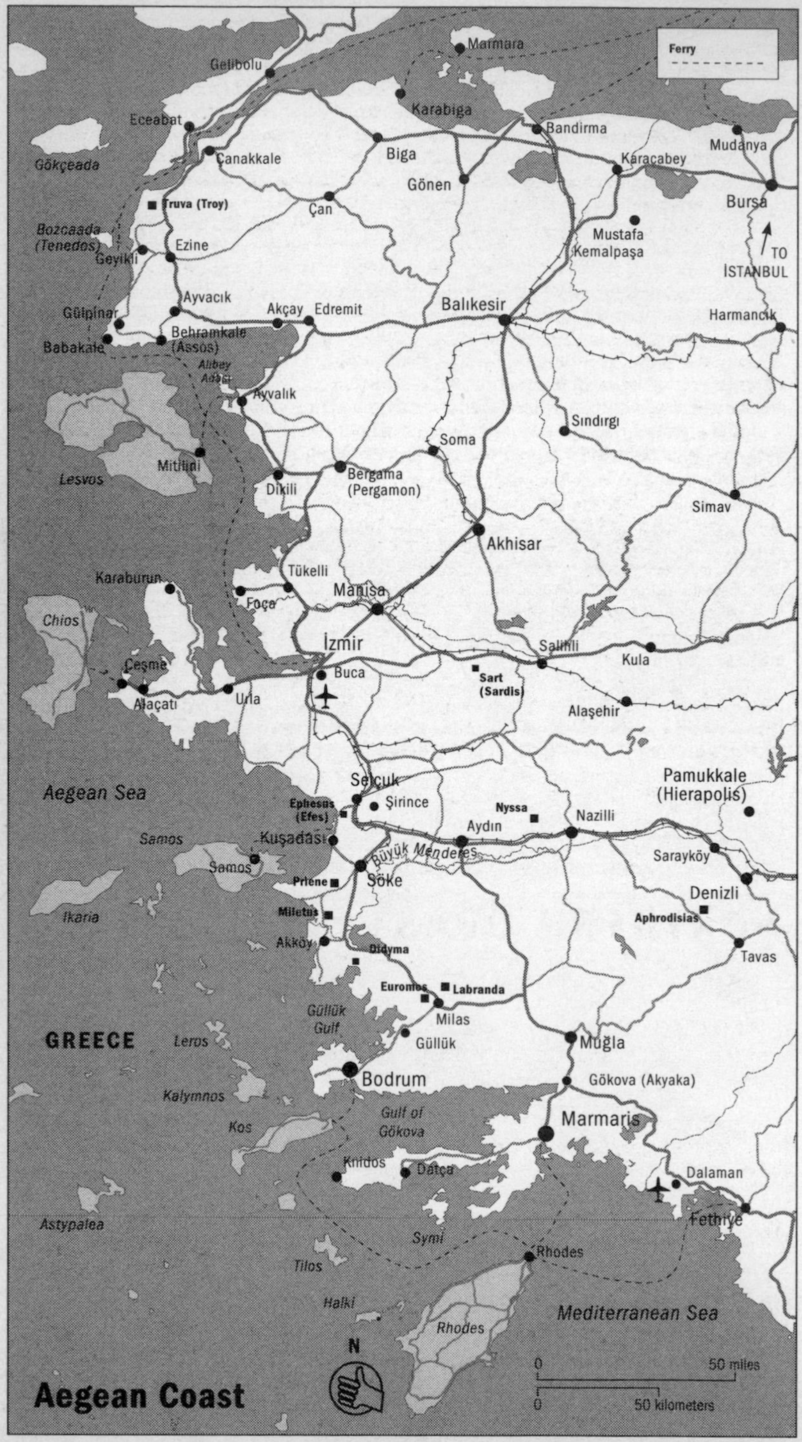

AEGEAN COAST

The first of these smaller units, labeled **Troy I,** dates from about 3000-2500 BC. Once a small fishing settlement, it now consists of walls made of fairly small stones in a huge bone pattern. On top of the first Trojan city lies **Troy II,** an affluent city-state dating from 2500-2200 BC, which Schliemann mistook for the city of the Trojan War. Schliemann believed that the stone ramp, close to which he found the so-called "Treasure of Priam," was used to lead horses up into the city. While there are certainly signs that invaders captured the city, modern scholarship suggests that these conquerors hailed from Asia Minor instead of Greece. After the fall of Troy II, **Troys III-V** (2300-1800 BC) were small, unfortified fishing villages. Newcomers of non-Trojan origin moved into the area around 1800 BC to build the great city of **Troy VI.** The financial successes of this city are visible in the considerably finer workmanship of the smooth walls, often made of sloped, square stones rather than the fitted, uncut stones of the other settlements. Turkish archaeologists hold this city to be the one of epic fame, while American archaeologists believe **Troy VII(a)** (1275-1240 BC) to be the city of Priam. The main evidence supporting this hypothesis is the large number of storage vessels found within Troy VII(a), suggesting that the city prepared for and endured a long siege. No swords, spears, shields, or other signs of war have been unearthed, raising doubts about the famous Trojan War. Nevertheless, the city fell and remained vacant for four centuries until **Troy VIII,** another fishing/farming community, appeared on the site from 700-350 BC.

For the next four centuries, great conquerors passing back and forth across Asia bestowed wealth and attention upon the town, hoping to associate themselves with the Homeric legend. Among the earliest to do this was **Alexander the Great.** After his campaign of conquest crossed into Asia, Alexander traveled to Troy where he sacrificed to **Achilles,** staged games in his honor, and supposedly took the warrior's armor and shield as he headed east to subdue the Persians. **Julius Caesar,** the next superhero to visit Troy, toured the city's remains in 48 BC. He ordered that the ruined temple of Athena be reconstructed and the city rebuilt as **Ilium Novum (Troy IX).** Troy held a special significance for the Julian clan, for—aided by Virgil's poetic imagination—they believed themselves to be the descendants of the Trojan hero **Aeneas.** The senatorial and land-owning classes of Imperial Rome followed suit, claiming lineage from members of the Trojan pantheon.

As Rome collapsed and the Christianized Empire shifted east to Constantinople, Troy fell once again into decline. While there is record that the site was inhabited in the time of Justinian, the city seems to have been largely ignored by royalty and nearly forgotten. Carrying on the tradition of the conqueror/pilgrim, **Sultan Mehmet,** who viewed the ruins in 1444, vowed bloody revenge upon the Greeks for their cruelty toward the people of Asia.

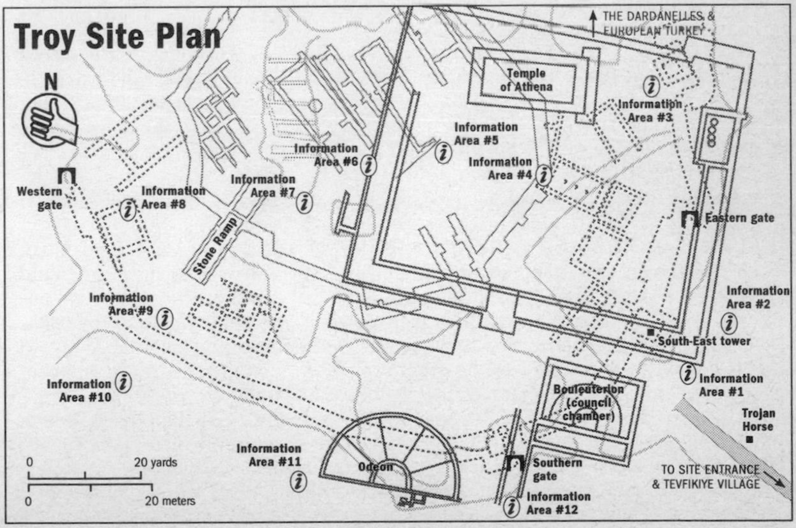

Schliemann's chapter in the story starts in the mid-19th century. Having amassed huge wealth before the age of 40, he left his business to pursue his boyhood dream of finding Troy. Following Frank Calvert's hunch as to the city's location, he broke ground in the 1880s. The ensuing years of excavation produced many treasures and uncovered most of the important features of today's site. In his motives and methods, Schliemann was controversial, straddling the line between amateur archaeologist and crazed looter. Although he did document his work and pay some attention to strata, he still concentrated his efforts on the pursuit of treasure. When his work uncovered the magnificent so-called "Treasure of Priam," he dressed his teenage wife in the gold jewelry and took photos before sending his finds back to Berlin, wholly without permission from the Turkish government. Apart from a few minor pieces in the museum in İstanbul, the treasure disappeared from Berlin at the end of World War II. It resurfaced in Russia a few years ago and is now displayed at the Pushkin Museum of Fine Art in Moscow.

TOURS

Anzac House in Çanakkale offers morning tours through the **Hassle Free Tour Agency** (☎213 59 69; hasslefree@anzachouse.com; $14). **TJ's Tours** (☎814 29 40; fax 814 29 41; TJs_TOURS@excite.com), based in Eceabat, has excellent tours ($14) conducted by İlhami "TJ" Gezici when there are sufficient tourists (see **TJ's Tours**, p. 156). If you decide to visit the site on your own, avoid the cabs ($20-30) and instead take a Troy-bound dolmuş that leaves from the Çanakkale dolmuş lot under the bridge on Atatürk Cad. (every hr. on the half-hour, $.75). It's a good idea to start early to avoid missing the last dolmuş back to Çanakkale.

BOZCAADA (TENEDOS)

Sandy coves, rolling hills, a perpetual cool breeze, and plentiful wine make Bozcaada a natural paradise. The charm of the white-washed, pastel-trimmed houses of the island's only town provides a distinctively Greek feel. Though the island is short on residents (pop. 2500), the summer months see an influx of İstanbulian tourists, recognizable by their number "34" license plates. Even these arrivals aren't enough to crowd the place, though—there's no lack of beach. And there's enough wine to go around: this tiny island supplies more than 10% of Turkey's wine. In antiquity, Tenedos's wine was considered some of the finest in the world. Unfortunately, today's product standard has dropped a little, but it's cheap ($2-4 per bottle) and available everywhere except (maybe) the post office.

TRANSPORTATION. Ferries run from **Geyikli** (Yükyeri dock) to Bozcaada (daily in summer; 10am, 2, 7, 9pm, midnight; $1) and back to Geyikli (daily in summer; 7:30am, noon, 5:30, 8, 11pm). **Minibuses** run from the **Çanakkale** otogar (1hr., every hr., $1) and arrive in Geyikli near the ferry dock. To get to the dock, take a dolmuş from the bus stop to the Yükyeri dock (5min., $.35). Like the several large buses traveling to **İstanbul** and **İzmir, dolmuş** wait for ferries coming back from the island before heading to **Çanakkale** (20min., $.60) and other local destinations.

ORIENTATION AND PRACTICAL INFORMATION. There are two main roads out of town, one running around the south side of the island and one around the north. Of the two, the southern route is longer and better, as its views are closer to the shoreline. Nevertheless, it is possible to combine the two by criss-crossing through the vineyards and forests in the center of the island. Dolmuş to the far side of the island (where the other branch of Ada Cafe lies) leave the main square, though these take a shorter, less scenic route (summer only, 10min., $.50).

While Bozcaada can be navigated by dolmuş at the peak of the tourist season (end of June through August), it is perhaps better explored by **bike.** Rent one at **Ada Cafe,** in the main square (to the left as you face away from the ferry). Ada also provides free maps and an English speaking staffer. (☎697 87 95; www.geocities.com/adaturizm. $1 per hr., $5 per day. Open daily 8:30am-2am, off-season

8:30am-midnight.) Because the afternoon heat, combined with steep hills, is brutal in the summer, cyclists should head out early, wear a hat, and bring **water.** Take special care when sharing the narrow, winding roads with automotive traffic.

Bring extra money with you: Bozcaada is a bad place to go broke. The only **ATM** in town is a **Yapı ve Kredi** that doesn't take foreign cards. The **PTT,** in the main square, is inland from the ferry dock and to the right. (Open daily 7am-11pm; in winter M-F 8:30am-5:30pm, Sa 8:30am-1pm.)

ACCOMMODATIONS, CAMPING, FOOD, AND NIGHTLIFE. Camping, the cheapest way to stay on Bozcaada, is permitted in most places that aren't privately owned, provided that you don't litter, build campfires, or otherwise spoil the land. The official campsite, **Kiraz Camping,** about 3km down the coastal road offers showers, toilets, a public barbecue, and a food stand. Campers stay in the provided tents or bring their own. Free transport is provided between the center of town and the campsite. (☎697 04 60. Open June 20-Aug. $5 per person.)

Many pensions operate out of private homes. The majority of these, which provide a double or the occasional triple, are clean and affordable ($5-9 per room; very negotiable). Owners will often wait at the ferry dock to approach potential guests. It's worthwhile to check out the rooms, which are usually cheaper than comparable hotel options. To avoid bargaining, however, stay at the **Otel Güler Ada.** New, still spiffy, and spacious (except for the 3rd floor), it provides private bath and bug-free surroundings. To get there, take the second road running off the street behind the PTT and make your first right. (☎697 88 99. $9 per person.)

The **Ada Cafe,** to the left as you face the PTT, offers excellent quality breakfast for $1.50, snacks, and red poppy syrup, a juice-like drink diluted with water, $1 per glass. (☎697 87 95. Open daily 8:30am-2am. MC/V.) Another good option is the outdoor **Hafız Çamlık Restaurant,** in the forested area between the soccer field and the square in front of the PTT. In addition to excellent fish ($2-4), it serves traditional dishes at decent prices, including beans for $.75 and *köfte* for $1.25. (☎341 81 67. Open daily 6am-midnight.) Good **fish and meat restaurants** line the small boat harbor, directly across from the ferry landing. The higher prices (salad with meat or fish $4-5) are worth it for the exceptional views of the mainland and the tiny fishing craft that fly postcard-sized Turkish flags. When the rest of the town settles in for the evening, **Salhane,** a local bar at the edge of town, is just getting started. Sit in the modern, dimly lit bar or at a table outside under the canopy of stars and just inches from the sea, accompanied by the sounds of U2 and Eric Clapton. Walk behind the PTT and follow the road along the waterfront.

SIGHTS. The well-preserved **castle** dominates the area around the harbor. The edifice was constructed in the Byzantine period and renovated by the Venetians, Genoese, and Ottomans. Climbing and careful scrambling is permitted on the battlements, which offer bird's-eye views of the town and the harbor. The **museum** exhibits mostly unremarkable 19th-century Turkish household items. It does, however, contain examples of old Turkish money, so you can see pre-inflation 1- and 5-lira coins. (Castle open daily 10am-1pm and 2-7pm. $1; students $.50.)

The island's main attractions, however, are its beaches and cliffs, from which you can gaze out over the cobalt sea. To tour the island by bike, take a left at the first fork on the road out of town and follow the more scenic, southern route. The first 10km of the ride involve huffing and puffing up and racing down the steepest and ugliest of the island's coastal hills, passing the old **lighthouse** at Tuzburun Feneri and the tiny cove with its pebbled beach at **Mermer Burnu.** After this, it's a long, winding descent to Ayana, the first in a 7km stretch of sandy beaches. The beautiful beaches of **Ayana, Ayazma, Solubahçe,** and **Habbele** are the best on the island and the most popular, though they are rarely crowded. Turning right onto the only paved road between Solubahçe and Habbele beaches leads to some of the island's vineyards, where you can get a glimpse of tomorrow's wine today. At Habbele, the paved coastal road peters out, and a left turn takes you down a short dirt road to the other branch of the Ada Cafe. There is no better place on the island to have a

AEGEAN COAST

meal for $1.50-3 (with salad) or a glass of cold water or beer for $1. (Open daily in summer 8:30am-2am.) All of the roads that lead inland in this vicinity pass through a small but pleasant pine forest. About 1km inland, dirt roads off to the left lead to a lighthouse, forested areas, and vineyards at the northwestern tip of the island.

The north side of the island is smaller and less impressive. While it has lots of caves, its beaches are narrower and less sandy. This easier ride leads past the **Horoz Taşları,** where large rocks poke dramatically out of the water.

ASSOS (BEHRAMKALE) ☎286

Despite its stunning ruins and pristine blue water, Assos remains a largely unspoiled tourist destination, catering mostly to wealthy Turkish and German visitors. For the moment, attractive, tasteful hotels far outnumber lurid souvenir shops, but it's difficult to believe that this will last much longer. Apart from the delicate veil of fog that hangs over the narrow stretch of water between the town and the Greek island of **Lesvos,** there's little to complain about in Assos.

Assos's remote location has been one of its major selling points since its founding in the 6th century BC by Methymnian refugees fleeing Lesvos. During the period of its greatest glory in the 4th century BC, the city became a sort of mecca for intellectuals, including **Aristotle,** who taught here before moving on to the Macedonian capital of **Pella** to tutor the young Alexander the Great. After Alexander's untimely death in 323 BC, Assos declined, eventually falling under the rule of Pergamon. The city slipped into oblivion under the Byzantines and Ottomans.

TRANSPORTATION AND PRACTICAL INFORMATION. Modern Assos is a strangely divided community. Half the residents live by the acropolis in the village at the top of the hill, and the remainder stay 2km down and around the hill in the little cluster of buildings by the ancient harbor. The **upper town** contains the local population and the cheaper pensions and restaurants, while the **lower town** caters exclusively to affluent tourists, featuring a number of posh hotels and expensive restaurants. Although the ruins are more accessible from the upper town, the lower town offers amazingly beautiful pebble coves. While dolmuş run between the tombs every hour from mid-June to August, only erratic service connects the towns during the rest of the year. Walking the steep 2km is arduous and inadvisable, and walking it with baggage is out of the question.

To get to Assos, take a **dolmuş** from **Ayvacık** (supposedly every hr. from mid-June to Sept., but sporadic; $.75). Dolmuş stop in the upper town and then continue to the lower half, picking up passengers heading back to Ayvacık. **Postal code:** 17860.

ACCOMMODATIONS AND FOOD. Accommodations and food prices are inversely proportional to altitude; the cheapest way to stay on the beach is to camp. The six campsites are all beyond the glitzy hotels as you walk with the sea on your right. All provide bungalows with toilet and shower ($4-11 per person). Prices vary according to how crowded the grounds are, so if you want to save, come before the middle of June or after August when you can bargain to reduce the fee. Each campground has access to the sea with a swimming dock. Some provide tents as well ($5-6), but you can bring your own. Breakfast is usually included. Tidy but bare rooms with cramped bathrooms and fans can be found at the **Antik Pansiyon,** in the alley in front of the Assos Hotel in the lower town. (☎721 34 52. Breakfast included. Singles $7.50; doubles $15.)

At the top of the mountain, right at the dolmuş stop, the **Dolumay Pension** provides lodging built in the same stone-and-mortar style as the mosque and ruins. (☎721 71 72. Breakfast included. Singles $11; doubles $18.) At the summit, beside the entrance to the Acropolis, is the **Timur Pansiyon,** where you can unload if you want the most stunning views in town. Of the four rooms, two are 200-year-old originals, though their bathrooms have been remodeled. (☎/fax 721 74 49; www.assos.de/timur-pansiyon. Breakfast included. Call for reservations in July and August. Singles $11; doubles $18.)

In the lower town, attached to the Antik Pansiyon, is the relatively cheap **Antik Restaurant,** offering various starters ($1.25 each), fresh fish, and grilled meat for $2.50. (☎ 721 34 52. Open 8am-3:30am.) Other lower town restaurants, all doubling as hotels, include the **Assos, Nazlihan,** and **Behram** (open 24hr.). All dish out tasty meals ($5.50 for several courses) under umbrellas or covered canopies.

The upper town's oldest restaurant, the **Cengiz,** features quality traditional cuisine at excellent prices. The owner has collected 20 volumes of guest books over the 32 years he's been in business. He'll gladly show them over a cup of *çay*. (☎ 721 70 04. Salad, meat, and dessert $3. Open daily 8:30am-midnight.)

SIGHTS. The humpbacked bridge to the left of the modern road into town was once the only way into Assos by land. At the top of the hill, overlooking the village from the edge of a small cliff, is the **Murat Hodavendigar Camii.** Built in 1359 at the behest of Sultan Murat I, it was the first mosque in Assos and stands as a well-preserved example of early Ottoman architecture. The rectangular, elevated stone patio beneath a large awning and the *mihrab* covered with *muqarna* (decorative vault with stalactite decoration) show marked Ottoman influence, but the interior is quite simple, built at a time when the Empire's fortunes could not indulge a more elaborate creation. The Greek inscription over the door acts as a reminder that many of the building materials, including the marble door frame, are *spoglia* (recycled parts; literally "spoils") from a 6th-century church. The mosque is theoretically open 24hr., but if it's locked, ask the ticket-booth attendants to open it.

Next to the mosque lies the entrance to the **acropolis,** the only part of the ruins that charges admission. The pillars on top of the plateau are the remnants of the **Temple of Athena** (c.530 BC), partially rebuilt with funds from *Efes Pilsen*, which has financed all of the excavations in the ancient city. The best part of the visit is the view, since much of the temple, including the reliefs, has been sent to the Archaeological Museum in İstanbul. Locals collect the greenish-tan plants that grow here and dry them for tea, which is sold along the road at $.25 per 50g bag. (Open daily 8am-8pm; in winter 8am-5pm. $2.)

From the village, walk down the hill 300-400m beyond the Cengiz Restaurant. On the left side of the road stands the main gate to the **excavation site** (the "No Admittance to the Excavation Site" signs only apply when people are actually digging). The archaeologists rarely mind visitors as long as they don't interfere with the day's work. The long, stone-paved road that runs through the gate up into the city walls are the remains of the city's Hellenic and Roman **necropolis.** A few stone **sarcophagi,** whose lids were left ajar by medieval grave robbers, lie along the broad street. Assos gained great fame for its sarcophagi after **Pliny the Younger,** as governor of Bithynia, claimed that the local stone could fully dissolve a corpse's flesh within 40 days. The term sarcophagus refers to this very property, deriving from the Greek words for "flesh" (or body) and "to eat."

To the right of the necropolis are the Hellenic **city walls,** fashioned of precisely cut and finished andesite, the igneous rock that provides the building material for almost everything in Assos. A walk on the stone-paved path, through the necropolis and the main gate of the Hellenistic walls, leads into the ancient city. Unlike many other ancient cities, Assos is blessed with never having been built over, and the extent of the site provides insight into its archaeological potential. Marked with *Efes Pilsen* signs, the **gymnasium, Agora Temple, Roman bath, stoa, bouleterion,** and early Christian **churches,** all down the hill through the brush, are far from well-preserved (the partially restored **theater** is an exception). Stick to the clearly trodden path and don't climb on any of the ruins. It is not permitted to approach the theater from above, where the theater is in its weakest state of preservation. Instead, exit the fenced area and walk down the road to approach it from below.

AYVALIK

☎266

Ayvalık's decaying old-world charm and host of exceptional accommodations make it an attractive destination from which to explore the surrounding beaches, olive groves, and small islands. Known for its ornate Neoclassical buildings, Ayvalık was a wealthy Greek settlement until the 1923 population exchange. Hidden away in a maze of narrow cobblestone streets are pastel houses, markets, shops, and people whose traditional lifestyle disappeared in most of Turkey decades ago. Ayvalık's streets are not as clean as those of other Aegean resort towns, and many of its buildings are uninhabited ruins with histories of their own. But when the daily grind of the city becomes too much, the sandy beaches of Sarımsaklı, the serene beauty of Alibey Island, and the stunning views from şeytan Sufrası offer refreshing escapes.

TRANSPORTATION

Buses and Dolmuş: Buses from the otogar go to: **Ankara** (10½hr.; 9, 10:30am, 12:30, 8, 9:30, 10:15, 11:15pm; $12); **İstanbul** (8½hr., 7 per day 8am-11:30pm, $11); **İzmir** (2½hr., 7 per day 6:30am-8:30pm, $3). City buses for **Sarımsaklı beach** ($.40) leave continuously from Cumhuriyet Meydanı near the Tourist Society booth. Minibuses for **Bergama** (11 per day 8:30am-6:30pm, $1.50) leave from the otogar and also stop in front of Cumhuriyet Meydanı.

Ferries: Jale Tur (☎312 27 40), on the docks in Cumhuriyet Meydanı. All year to the Greek island of **Lesbos** (2hr.; W, Th, Sa 6pm; $50). $20 port tax when exiting Greece.

ORIENTATION AND PRACTICAL INFORMATION

The otogar lies on **Atatürk Bul.**, the main road running parallel to the coastline. 1½km from the otogar, with the sea on your right, is **Cumhuriyet Meydanı,** the main square where city buses, taxis, banks, police, and tourist information can be found. Another smaller bus station falls between the otogar and the square, on Atatürk Bul. The other main street, Cumhuriyet Cad., runs parallel to Atatürk Bul. one block away from the sea.

Tourist Office: The main office (☎312 21 22) is just beyond the hospital as you walk away from Cumhuriyet Meydanı with the sea on your right. Open M-F 8:30am-12:30pm and 1:30-5:30pm. A small booth (☎312 31 58) in Cumhuriyet Meydanı on the docks is open June-Sept. M-Sa 10am-2pm and 3-7pm. Both distribute free maps.

Banks: Türkiye İş Bankası (☎312 22 10 or 312 26 08), in Cumhuriyet Meydanı, **exchanges currency** and has a 24hr. Cirrus/MC/Plus/V **ATM.** Open M-F 9am-12:30pm and 1:30-5:30pm.

Police: On Atatürk Bul. in Cumhuriyet Meydanı, next to Türkiye İş Bankası.

Pharmacies: Many line Cumhuriyet Meydanı and Atatürk Bul. **Gültekin Eczanesi** (☎312 12 28) is across from the water in Cumhuriyet Meydanı. Open 8am-7:30pm.

Hospital: Ayvalık Devlet Hastanesi (public, ☎312 63 00), 500m from Cumhuriyet Meydanı with the water on your right. Across from and just beyond a Migros grocery.

Internet Access: Ayvalık Internet Cafe, Atatürk Cad., Nazar Pasaj 14 (☎312 22 75), on the left before the PTT as you walk out of Cumhuriyet Meydanı with the sea on your left. $1.25 per hr. Open daily 9am-11pm; in winter 9am-8pm.

PTT: (☎312 60 41), on Atatürk Bul., about 300m from Cumhuriyet Meydanı as you walk with the sea on your left. Open daily 8:30am-midnight. **Traveler's checks** cashed 8:30am-4:30pm.

Postal Code: 10400.

ACCOMMODATIONS

Ayvalık's accommodations are among the best in Turkey. Its top pensions lie up the hill in the old town's maze of narrow, cobblestoned streets.

Bonjour Pansiyon, 5 Maraşal Çakmak Cad. (☎312 80 85). Follow the road directly across the PTT entrance uphill and into the old city. Originally the home of a priest acting as French ambassador, this pension has been recently restored in turn-of-the-century style. The ceiling paintings are worth looking at even if you are not staying here, and you may not want to leave once you've seen the spacious rooms and met the friendly, welcoming staff. Laundry service $2. Breakfast $3.75. $7.50 per person.

Taksiyarhis Pansiyon, İsmetpaşa Mah., 71 Maraşal Çakmak Cad. (☎312 14 94). Take the 2nd street on the left after the PTT (when walking toward the main square with the sea on your right) and follow it uphill to the signs, which will direct you farther through the old town. Decorated with carpets, sitting pillows, and other bric-a-brac, this eclectic pension has a guest kitchen, a book exchange, and a lovely terrace overlooking the town. Bike rentals ($8 per day) include a map of Alibey Island. Laundry service $6. Enormous breakfast $2.50. $6 per person.

Beliz Pansiyon, 28 Mareşal Çakmak Cad., Fethiye Mah. (☎312 48 97). Follow Talatpaşa Sok. (the 1st street on your right as you exit Cumhuriyet Meydanı with the sea on your left) for 5 blocks away from the sea until you come to the Beliz Pansiyon signs. Run by the vivacious and chic former TV actress Beliz, this pension sports bright yellow walls and colorful pillows. Enjoy the homemade Turkish dinners cooked by Beliz herself ($6), and bring your bathing suit for the daily boat tours she offers of 5 nearby islands ($5). Breakfast included. Bungalow rooms $8 per person; house rooms $9 per person.

Yalı Pansiyon, 25 Balıkhane Sok. (☎312 24 23 or 312 38 19), behind the PTT. The oldest pension in Ayvalık, Yalı abuts the waters of the Aegean so guests can admire the sunset on the horizon from the chairs in the garden, from the balconies of their rooms, or from the water. The setting is tranquil and the location easily accessible. Public kitchen. Breakfast included. Doubles $15; triples $22.

FOOD

Enjoy some *iskender kebap* ($1.50) at the **Osmanlı Mutfagı,** two blocks away from the hubbub of Cumhuriyet Cad. Take a left at the Yapı Kredi bank, about a 1min. walk from Cumhuriyet Meydanı with the sea on your left. (☎312 54 27. Open daily noon-10pm. AmEx/MC/V.) Otherwise, the extremely clean **Kardeşler** restaurant has two branches, one on the docks in front of Cumhuriyet Meydanı (☎313 00 81), which dishes out fresh seafood, an array of salads ($.75), and meat dishes ($1.50-2.50), along with a harbor view. Another branch, called **Kardeşler Kebapci,** on Cumhuriyet Cad., specializes in *kebaps* and other meat selections and features an A/C dining room. (☎312 18 57. Open daily 8am-10pm. AmEx/MC/V.) For *çorba*, *lahmacun*, and *baklava*, visit the **Dayım Ocakbaşı,** across from Kardeşler on Atatürk Cad., with additional seating through the alley by the water. (Open noon-11pm.) **ÖzSüt,** on your left as you exit the square with the sea on your right, is the perfect answer to a sugar craving, with a good selection of attractive desserts like rice pudding and cheesecake. (☎312 23 33. Open daily 11am-midnight. $.70-3.)

SIGHTS

There are few sights to speak of within the town itself. On the walk to the Taksiyarhis Pansiyon is **Saatli Camii** (Clock Tower Mosque), formerly known as the **Church of Agios Yannis** (Church of St. John). The splendor and grace of its former life as a 19th-century Greek church shines through the flaking paint and eroded details. At the time of publication it was closed for a long-overdue renovation. Farther inland and visible on its hillside from Saatli Camii is **Çinanlı Camii** or **Agios Yorgos** (St. George's Church), which boasts Old and New Testament frescoes. Unfortunately, this mosque is also closed for renovation. Next to the Taksiyarhis Pansiyon, off Maraşal Çakmak Cad., the **Taksiyarhis Church** exhibits paintings on fish skins. It is usually closed, but you may be able to peek inside if you find the right moment. Beware the small, ferocious guard dog. Every Thursday there is an **open-air market** on the streets around Cumhuriyet Cad. and Barbaros Cad. In the finest Turkish market tradition, 99% of the stuff for sale is impractical junk, but that in no way takes the fun out of browsing for potential souvenirs.

DAYTRIPS FROM AYVALIK

ŞEYTAN SOFRASI

During July and Aug. dolmuş ($.80) to the site leave daily at 6pm from the Tansaş supermarket, a short walk from Cumhuriyet Meydanı with the sea on your right. The dolmuş wait for visitors to watch the sunset before returning.

To the south of Ayvalık lies the şeytan Sofrası (Devil's Dinner Table), a large rock formation on the summit of a hill that resembles a dinner table only insofar as any flat surface does. Legend has it that hell-raisers met here to feast, citing a giant footprint-shaped dimple in the rock as evidence of the devil's presence. The supremely located **şeytan Cafe** provides the best spot to watch the sunset, serving reasonably priced beverages (beer $.75). The **devil's footprint** lies at the corner of the table farthest from the dolmuş lot, beneath a steel cage, and has been transformed into a demonic wishing well by many a tossed coin. The panoramic view of the coast and the Greek and Turkish islands serves as a heavenly contrast. Even when there aren't enough clouds in the sky for a spectacular sunset, it's worth the trip to watch the islands paint delicate blue silhouettes against a pink sky.

SARIMSAKLI BEACH

Accessible from Ayvalık by dolmuş (every 5-10min. mornings and afternoons; $.40) that depart from the Tansaş supermarket and by buses (every hr., $.40) departing from in front of the harbor in Cumhuriyet Meydanı.

AEGEAN COAST

About 6km south of Ayvalık, Sarımsaklı has some of the best beaches between Bozcaada and Altınkum, with lots of fine, clean sand. The town itself wins slightly less praise, occupying a formidable spot in the great pantheon of tacky beach towns. It's always a quarter past Miller Time here, with an *Efes* chest or a disco bar never more than five meters away. But the beaches, particularly the parts near the shore and away from the central area, have warm water without strong currents or other unexpected surprises. The beach is eerily deserted in the low season.

ALİBEY ISLAND (CUNDA)

*Provided the heat isn't too bad, the best way to explore Alibey Island is by **bike.** The **Taksiyarhis Pension** (see **Ayvalık: Accommodations,** p. 180) rents bikes and provides a map showing a much-recommended scenic route that passes over the bridge connecting the island to the mainland and then continues on through the island's olive groves to the monastery and secluded beaches. (Bikes $8 per day.) **Ferries** run from the dock at Cumhuriyet Meydanı in Aywalik every hr. ($.40). **Buses** also leave from in front of Türkiye İş Bankası in Cumhuriyet Meydanı (every 30min., $.25) and head to the town of Cunda. You can purchase bus tickets at the small ticket window to the right of Türkiye İş Bankası. On Alibey Island, you can buy your bus ticket in the office behind Artur Motel Restaurant, on the cafe-lined seafront.*

Alibey (Sir Ali's) Island is a beautiful escape from the hustle and bustle of Ayvalık. With beaches on the north side, a deserted monastery, and several pleasant fish restaurants along the waterfront in the town of Cunda, there is enough here for an entire day. In the town of Cunda, the old and hauntingly beautiful **Church of Nicolaus** lies about 200m inland. Pigeons fly through its nave, and thick, deeply fissured columns support its domes. Having suffered during the 1922 war with Greece and a 1944 earthquake, the church has more recently been forced to endure graffiti. (Church open daily during daylight hours. Donations welcome.)

Seafood restaurants line the harbor (fish, *mezes*, and salad; $4.50-6), and **Uno Pizza,** behind the harbor, serves up American-style pizza ($1.25-2.25) and the tenderest chicken *şiş* around for $1.50. (☎327 18 28. Open noon-midnight. MC/V.)

CENTRAL COAST

DİKİLI ☎232

Dikili doubles as a fishing town and a beach escape for Turks from İzmir and İstanbul, as well as for foreigners whose luxury liners dock at the local port. While its population increases tenfold in summer, the town still manages to retain a comfortable, homey feel. During the day, vacationers catch rays on the beaches, leaving the streets eerily deserted, only to emerge at night from under their beach umbrellas to stroll along the harbor. It's almost worth an overnight stay just to see the town's main pedestrian boulevard come alive with people of all ages, enjoying the pleasant sea breeze.

ORIENTATION. Most of the activity in Dikili, as in all good beach towns, is centered along the coastline. The *garaj* sits on **S. Sami Akbulut Cad.**, parallel to **Atatürk Cad.**, the pedestrian harbor road. These two north-south streets meet at a traffic circle, as you walk left 20m from the *garaj*. **Uğur Mumcu Cad.** begins across the traffic circle and follows the coastline north. A five-minute walk to the right out of the *garaj*, **Atatürk Meydanı** straddles S. Sami Akbulut Cad. and Atatürk Cad.

TRANSPORTATION AND PRACTICAL INFORMATION. Bus travel to most points outside the immediate vicinity of Dikili requires transfer in **İzmir** (2hr., 21 per day 6am-8pm, $2). Buses also run to **Bursa** (6hr., 9:30am, $7) and **İstanbul** (11hr., 9:30am, $11). Minibuses connect to **Ayvalik** (1hr., 12 per day 8:45am-6:30pm, $1) and **Bergama** (45min., 12 per day 8:30am-7:30pm, $.75).

The **tourist office,** a small kiosk just before Atatürk Meydanı on Atatürk Cad., provides free maps and English-speaking assistance. (☎671 81 63. Open M-F 8:30-12pm and 1-5:30pm.) The **police station** (☎671 26 95) is two blocks up toward the traffic circle. **Türkiye İş Barkişi** sits across from Atatürk Meydanı on S. Sami Akbulut Cad. and has an **ATM** with Cirrus/MC/Plus/V. (Open 9am-12:30pm and 1:30-5:30pm.) **Internet** can be found at Internet Market on S. Sami Akbulut Cad., a few minutes' walk right out of the *garaj*. (☎671 33 77. $.75 per hr.) The **PTT** is up toward the *garaj* from the bank. (Open daily 8am-11pm.) **Postal code:** 35980.

ACCOMMODATIONS. **Günes Pansiyon** offers rooms with private bath and fans, as well as a public kitchen. To get there from the *garaj*, walk right onto S. Sami Akbulut Cad. and turn left at 312 Sok., following the signs. (☎671 48 47. Breakfast included. $5 per person.) **Dikili Pansiyon** is in a quieter location and has fairly clean rooms with private bath; most have balconies. At the traffic circle, follow the second street to the right of Akbulut Cad. until you see signs leading you one block to the right. (☎671 24 54, fax 741 52 07. $5 per person.) Travelers strapped for cash should check out **Özdemir Pansiyon,** on the right of Akbulut Cad. as you walk right out of the *garaj*. It has the cheapest, though perhaps not the most attractive, rooms in town. Shared bath. (☎671 42 95. $2 per person.)

FOOD. Many of Dikili's best restaurants line Çamlaraltı Sok., which runs off S. Sami Akbulut Cad. just opposite Atatürk Meydanı. **Koron 2** is particularly good, with attentive English-speaking service and a greater selection of dishes than most *pide* and *kebap* joints. (☎671 78 79. *Kebaps* $1.50-3.50. Open daily 10am-midnight.) **Sağlam Restaurant,** on the left of Uğur Mumcur Cad. as you walk away from the traffic circle, is owned by the same family that operates two restaurants in Bergama. Spottier service than Koron, but offers an excellent view of the sunset from its waterfront tables. (☎671 33 13. *Mezes* $1; *kebaps* $1.50. Open 10am-midnight.)

C'MON BABY LIGHT MY FIRE In ancient times, only the library in Alexandria surpassed Pergamon's, which contained over 200,000 volumes in repositories all over the city. So great was the Alexandrian's jealousy over the Pergamenes' literary hoard that they made what they thought was a brilliant strategic move: they limited the flow of Egyptian papyrus to Pergamon. The Pergamenes countered by writing all their subsequent volumes on parchment pages made from goat hide, an exponentially more durable, though more expensive, material. The scheming Alexandrians, however, were only temporarily foiled. When the Alexandrian library's fire suppression mechanism experienced a system-wide failure, Marc Antony plundered Pergamon's shelves and presented the whole library to Cleopatra, presumably as a token of his love. In 640, the ill-fated collection was put to the torch by the Caliph Omar and his lieutenant, the aptly named Amr ibn al-Ass. Subscribing to a kind of witch-trial logic, Omar decreed that if the books agreed with the Qur'an, they were unnecessary, and if they disagreed with the Qur'an, they were heretical and fit for combustion. Innumerable works of ancient literature went up in flames and were lost forever, including dozens of plays by Sophocles, Euripides, and Aeschylus.

NIGHTLIFE. As a nightlife alternative to the thumping music and overactive strobe lights of the several disco bars on Uğur Mumcur Cad. (open 10pm-3am), stroll along Cumhuriyet Cad. with the rest of Dikili and grab an ice cream cone ($.10-.50) from a *dondurma* shop or a beer from one of the seaside restaurant-bars ($.75). If you continue down Cumhuriyet Cad., away from the traffic circle, you will eventually hit **Bar Turkuaz,** which features live Turkish music nightly. (☎671 36 08. 10pm-3am. Beer and *rakı* $1.50; whiskey $3.)

SIGHTS. Visitors come to Dikili for one reason—the **beaches.** Filled with coarse, brown sand, beaches run from the traffic circle along Uğur Mumcu Cad. There is a smaller, family beach on Cumhuriyet Cad., past the tourist office.

BERGAMA (PERGAMON) ☎232

The physical layout of Bergama, formerly ancient Pergamon, seems to reflect the ebb and flow of the city's prosperity over time. A dazzling center of cultural activity in antiquity, Pergamon became the capital of the Roman province of Asia and had one of the two largest libraries in the ancient world. The ruins of this great Hellenistic and Roman city dominate the top of the hill. Buildings from later eras, when the city's stature and importance declined, cling lower down at the hill's feet. Greek houses, remnants of more prosperous days during the late-19th century, cluster around the tiny hills of the river banks before giving way to the cement buildings of modern Bergama. Unfortunately, in spite of having some of the most extensive and important ruins in Asia Minor, Bergama is often overlooked. This quiet, attractive town suffers from severe economic depression, mostly due to its location off the main coastal highway and away from the sea, but its calm, unassuming quality, absent in many seaside towns, makes it worth a visit.

Pergamon traces its roots back to the Aeolian Greeks, who built a settlement here in the 9th century. Like many other ancient cities, Pergamon blossomed from the spoils of Alexander the Great's conquest of the Persian empire. Alexander's successor in the region, **Lysimachus,** deposited a hefty booty in the city under the care of **Philetaerus,** who rose from treasurer to ruler when Lysimachus did not return from battle. Philetaerus ruled fairly and generously, maintaining good relations with neighboring cities, and beautified Pergamon with temples and other new buildings. When he chose his nephew **Eumenes I** to succeed him in 263 BC, he established a royal dynasty that would last for five generations. This dynasty expanded Pergamon's empire into Central Anatolia as far as Konya. By the 2nd century BC Pergamon had gotten itself into bed with the increasingly powerful Romans, and in 133 BC **King Attalus II** bequeathed the city to the Roman Empire. Under the Romans, Pergamon became the prosperous capital of the province of Asia. An earthquake in the 2nd century brought the city into a period of irreversible decline, however, and over the next several centuries it passed through the hands of the Byzantines, Crusaders, Lascarids, Arabs, Ottomans, and Greeks.

TRANSPORTATION

Buses: At the *garaj* (☎633 15 45), across from Çamlı Park, about 1½km south of the old town on İzmir Cad. This distance is walkable, but taxi may be preferable ($2). To: **Ankara** (10hr., 9pm, $11); **İstanbul** (10hr.; 10am, 9:15pm; $13); **İzmir** (2hr., every 45min. 6am-7:30pm, $2.25). A *servis* runs to the *garaj* from a smaller bus station near İstiklâl Meydanı. To get there, walk from the square and make the first major left. The bus station is a 2min. walk on your left. When traveling to Bergama, especially from the north, ask for a direct bus since some stop only at the Bergama turnoff on the main highway, 7km from the city. From the main highway, take a dolmuş to the center of town to avoid the heavy cab fare.

ORIENTATION AND PRACTICAL INFORMATION

The Pergamene Acropolis is across the river from the modern city of **Bergama,** while the Asclepion is uphill from **Atatürk Meydanı,** in the modern area. The city's main road runs north-south, winding its way to the acropolis at the northern end. From İzmir to the bus station the road is called **İzmir Cad.,** from the bus station to the northern end of Atatürk Meydanı (the larger of the two squares), it is called **Cumhuriyet Cad.,** and from the northern end of Atatürk Meydanı to **İstiklâl Meydanı,** it is called **Bankalar Cad.** Most pensions and restaurants surround İstiklâl Meydanı.

Tourist Office: (☎631 28 51). From the bus station, take a right onto İzmir Cad. and walk 1km to Cumhuriyet Meydanı. The office is on the left side of the road. Distributes a helpful map with all hotels and pensions labeled. Open M-F 8:30am-noon and 1-5:30pm.

Banks: On the left side of İzmir Cad., about 200m up from the PTT (away from the bus station) are **TC Ziraat Bankası** and **Türkiye İş Bankası.** Both **exchange currency** and have Cirrus/MC/Plus/V **ATMs.** TC Ziraat open M-F 9am-5:30pm. Money exchange closed noon-1pm. Türkiye İş open M-F 9am-12:30pm and 1:30-5:30pm.

Hamams: The historic **Haci Hekim,** 32 Bankalar Cad. (☎632 10 75), is across from the banks. Reasonably clean, it serves Turkish men and tourists of both genders, and is worth a look even if you are not bathing. Bath and massage $7.50. Open daily 7am-midnight. Newly tiled and very clean, the **Sprinter Sauna,** 88 İzmir Cad. (☎632 36 48), south of the *garaj,* serves men and women, and is more comfortable for single female travelers than Haci Hekim, thanks to the availability of female masseurs. Sauna, steam bath, Turkish massage, and full body massage $9. A cafe on the upper level serves hot and cold drinks. Take a dolmuş from the *garaj* and ask for the Serapion or Efsane Hotel, as both are nearby. Alternatively, walk south 500m on İzmir Cad. from the *garaj.* Open daily 1-5pm for women; 8:30am-1pm and 5pm-midnight for men.

Hospital: Bergama Devlet Hastanesi (☎631 28 97 or 631 28 94). Walk from the bus station toward the PTT, turn left where the park ends, go uphill, and turn right.

Police: (☎632 70 01), on İzmir Cad., just past the tourist office.

Internet Access: Köşe Internet (☎631 08 84), on the road to the Asclepion, Galenos Cad., near the center of town. 10 computers at $1 per hr. Open daily 10am-midnight.

PTT: (☎632 39 90), on İzmir Cad. Some English spoken. **Currency exchange** (1% commission) until 5pm. Open daily 8:30am-11pm.

Postal code: 35700.

ACCOMMODATIONS

Pension Athena, 5 İmam Cıkması, Barbaros Mah. (☎633 34 20; aydinathena@hotmail.com; www.athenapension.8m.com). Housed in a restored Ottoman home on the winding road beyond İstiklâl Meydanı to the left. 24hr. hot water, living room with cable TV, public kitchen, enclosed *çay* garden, and rooftop view of the Acropolis. Free map of town, compliments of the friendly management. Laundry $2.25-3. Excellent breakfast $1.50. Internet $.75 per hr. Rooms $4.50, with shower $5.50; a place to throw your sleeping bag out on the roof $1.50. 10% *Let's Go* discount.

Böblingen Pension, 2 Asklepion Cad. (☎633 21 53), on the corner of İzmir Cad. and Asklepion Cad., on the left as you exit the *garaj.* A bit far from the center of town. Clean rooms with private bath. Bar on 4th floor with colorful, Ottoman-style seating. Breakfast included. $5.50 per person.

Berksoy Camping (☎633 25 95). Walk south on İzmir Cad. for 20-30min. No English spoken, so it's probably best to inquire at the tourist office about availability. Amenities include pool and tennis courts. $2.50 per person.

FOOD AND ENTERTAINMENT

Bergama's dining options, mostly family-style *kebap* and *pide* restaurants clustered around İstiklâl Meydanı, are often quite pleasant.

Sağlam 2 Restaurant, 3 İstiklal Meydanı (☎633 20 46). The Sağlam family has all but cornered the dining market, operating 2 restaurants in Bergama and 3 more in other cities. Sağlam 2 offers southeastern Anatolian cuisine, which you can watch being cooked in the traditional brick oven. *Pide* ($1-2.25) and *kebaps* ($1.50-2.50). Live Turkish music on some nights in upstairs bar. Open daily 8am-midnight. AmEx/MC/V.

Sağlam 3, 29 Hükümet Meydanı (☎632 88 97), on the right side of the street before the PTT as you walk north from the otogar. Expansive garden-style seating and 2 Ottoman dining rooms upstairs with rug-covered seats. Similar menu to Sağlam 2, but with more vegetarian options. Open daily 8am-midnight, sometimes later. AmEx/MC/V.

Arzu Pide Salonu, 10 İstiklâl Meydanı (☎631 11 87). 5 kinds of *pide* ($1), *lahmacun* ($.50), and nothing else, with biggest portions in town. Dining area upstairs. Open daily 7:30am-10:30pm.

Pergamon Pension Restaurant, 5 Bankalar Cad. (☎632 34 92). Soft chairs, bright floral tablecloths, a small pool, and natural lighting from skylights add to the charm of this courtyard restaurant housed in an old Ottoman building. Serves meat dishes ($1.50-2.50) and a variety of *mezes* ($1). Open daily 6am-11pm.

SIGHTS

ACROPOLIS

Wear long pants to avoid the relentless thorn bushes and bring plenty of water. Open daily 8:30am-6pm. $2.25, students with ISIC free.

The acropolis of Pergamon looms over the city like a giant, inaccessible, brick-and-marble storm cloud, its treasures protected by steep hills and a high barbed-wire fence. From a lower gate, the ancient, stone-paved road climbs the hill, passing all the ruins and the current excavation sites. The walk up is better than a taxi ride ($5), which follows the modern paved road and misses half the sights. Start at the river (near the Athena Pension), cross the bridge, and proceed through the maze of the old town diagonally to the right and up the hill. Eventually you will meet the paved road that leads to the top. Follow it for a short distance until you reach a gate and a cluster of concrete buildings on the right, where the German excavation team lives and works. To the right of this gate, a little path runs between the road's chain-link fence and the perimeter fence of the archaeological compound, eventually becoming a fairly easy-to-follow trail through the ruins.

Stay on this former **Royal Road** by following the blue dots painted on steps, walls, and other pieces of stone. The first set of rectangular ruins on the left is the **lower agora,** the center of the ancient city's commercial trade. The trail here clings to two of the agora's sides before making a sharp switch back to the right. Farther along is the **gymnasium,** a massive three-tiered complex of exercise halls and baths built on the hillside. In addition to providing a venue for physical exercise, Greek gymnasia also functioned as schools, training young men in philosophy and oratory. Young boys began in the lower gymnasium, today the least impressive and worst preserved of the three, and moved up to the middle level at around age 13. The upper level, built around a large, colonnaded exercise area, included a small theater, a lecture hall, and two bath complexes. In the center of the gymnasium, the largest room, and the most impressive of the ruins, was used for track and field competitions. The remains of the **Temple of Demeter,** marked by a few inscriptions, lie on the path uphill from the upper gymnasium. At the west end, animals were slaughtered as sacrifices to Demeter, the goddess of rebirth, harvest, and fertility.

From here, the road winds around the hill to the left, growing wider and more evenly paved up to the now tree-covered **Altar of Zeus,** built by Eumenes II in commemoration of Attalus's victory over the Gauls. All that remains today are the first four or five tiers of steps on the base; Germans carted off the columns and giant friezes to Berlin, where they have been incorporated into an impressive restoration of the temple. The ticket booth is off to the right, facing the big temples and the city walls. The **Precinct of Athena,** the rectangular ruin closest to the ramp leading from the entrance gate, was the site of Pergamon's famed **library** (see **C'mon Baby Light My Fire,** p. 184).

Carved into the hill for an impressive effect when viewed from the road, the **Hellenistic Theater** once seated 10,000 in nosebleed comfort. Above the theater, the giant **Temple of Trajan** was built for both the cult of Zeus and the imperial cults of Trajan and Hadrian. On the steep bluffs behind the temple were the foundations of the various **royal palaces** of the Attalids, which used to extend into the area now covered by the Temple of Trajan, and a **wishing well.** Wishers throw three coins at the column in the well; supposedly, a wish will come true if one lands on the top.

ASCLEPION AND BERGAMA MUSEUM

Asclepion open 8am-6:30pm. $2.25, students free. The refurbished Bergama museum is toward the bus station about 100m from the Bergama tourist office. Open Tu-Su 8:30am-6:30pm. $1.25, students free.

Pergamon's famed **Asclepion** lies on the west side of town, a relatively easy uphill walk off Atatürk Meydanı, at Galenos Cad. The Asclepion was a shrine to Asclepius, the Greek (and later Roman) demi-god of healing. After the center at Epidauros in Greece, Pergamon's Asclepion was the most famous healing center in the ancient world, and its native son **Galen** was the foremost doctor of his time. An avid promoter of animal dissection and vivisection, Galen served as Asclepion's chief physician. His treatises and theories became the foundation for medical thought in Europe and the Middle East until the mid-17th century.

The site begins with the **Via Tecta,** a broad, colonnaded street connecting the Asclepion with Pergamon proper. Pergamon leads first to the **Propylon,** a small, square building thought to have contained a cult statue of Asclepius. Next door is the **library,** which houses a number of *stelae* covered in Greek inscriptions. Up the stairs to the left is the cylindrical **Temple of Asclepius,** modeled on the Roman Pantheon, and further still is the **healing center,** which consists of six semicircular chambers radiating in a flower-like arrangement from the central domes. Ailing visitors to the Asclepion took part in a kind of dream therapy known as **incubation:** sleeping in the temple, they would be visited in dreams by Asclepius. These dreams, later interpreted by one of the Asclepion's priests, revealed the appropriate treatment, usually a changed diet, hot or cold baths, mud bathing, and exercise. An impressive and perfectly preserved underground tunnel links the healing center to the rest of the complex. The **theater,** which held 3500, staged lectures and other entertainment for the benefit of patients and local citizens.

CLAIRVOYANT CREATURES Strolling along the harbor road of any town along the Aegean, you're bound to come across a fortune-telling rabbit, though it looks like any ordinary bunny. In the gypsy tradition that brought you the dancing bear, these rabbits are trained by street peddlers to pick out a slip of paper from among rows of them, on which is written a detailed fortune. These days, many bunnies have gone multilingual, predicting the future in Turkish, English, and German. Arrange a price in advance, or you may well end up paying a fortune yourself.

The **museum,** arranged like a Roman Villa, surrounds a small, perfectly maintained central courtyard. Grave and dedicatory *stelae* line the surrounding halls. The main room of the museum, at the far end of the courtyard, presents an eclectic collection, including sculptures, glassware, an extensive coin collection, and a large, world-renowned Medusa mosaic. The adjacent **Ethnography Museum,** with its poor lighting and lack of English descriptions seems almost like an afterthought in comparison to the main museum, although it does contain interesting costume displays and one English-language explanation of the carpet-weaving process.

KIZIL AVLU (RED BASILICA)

Open daily 8:30am-6:30pm. $1.50, ISIC holders free.

The remnants of Kızıl Avlu, a pagan temple, stand near the river, İstiklâl Meydanı, and the old part of Bergama. "This is where Satan has his altar," declares Revelations (2:3), citing Kızıl Avlu as one of the Seven Churches of the Apocalypse. This mammoth structure was built in the first half of the 2nd century AD and is dedicated to the Egyptian trio of gods Serapis, Isis, and Harpocrates. At its far end once stood a talking statue of Serapis; priests would climb into the hollow figure to make it "speak." With the advent of Christianity, Kızıl Avlu was converted into the Church of St. John, receiving its twin towers sometime during the Byzantine period. One of these is now a mosque.

FOÇA ☎232

Small, quiet, and attractive, Foça is the North Aegean's other summer resort, rivaling Kuşadası and Ayvalık as the non-Bodrum summer escape. With its large fishing fleet and clear, blue waters, the more-refined Foça offers a welcome variation on Aegean resort towns. Its strategic location near the gulf of İzmir has made the town both a popular resort and a large military center. The navy controls the land south and the *jandarma* training school hugs most of the land on the interior.

In antiquity, Phokaia, as it was called, was a major trading and seafaring center. Herodotus reports that Phokaian shipbuilders built 50-oared galleys capable of ferrying 500 people across the Mediterranean and Black Seas. On trips like these, they founded both the French city of Marseilles and Samsun, on the Black Sea coast. Recent archaeological excavations have revealed segments of the massive walls Herodotus described. Though Foça has declined in importance, it remains true to its ancient character in at least one respect: in ancient Greek, "phokia" means "seal." The town still has a close relationship with its small population of endangered Monk Seals, who have earned Foça's landscape of scree-covered hills and rocky coastline official protection from development. They have become the town's mascot, their black eyes keeping watch from posters, pamphlets, and T-shirts. Some scholars say that the legend of the Sirens, the tantalizing sea nymphs whose songs lured sailors to their deaths, derives from the barking of Foça's seals.

TRANSPORTATION

Buses: From the Foça otogar, buses run to **İzmir** (1½hr., every 30min. 6am-11pm, $1.50), some of which stop along the way in **Yeni Foça** (30min., every hr. 8am-8pm, $.75). **Hanedan**-bound dolmuş service the beach/camping area to the north (every 15min. 8am-midnight, $.25). To reach Foça from the south, catch the direct bus either from İzmir or en route. Approaching from the north, you'll be dropped off at the Foça junction, where either a dolmuş ($.75) or a coach from İzmir can take you the last 20km. The bus/dolmuş stop at this junction is located on the road that runs perpendicular to the north-south highway.

Bike Rental: (☎812 19 69), at the "Motor-rent" sign across from the bus station. Bikes $5 per day; motorcycles $15 per day. Open daily 8am-11pm.

ORIENTATION AND PRACTICAL INFORMATION

Foça lies 20km west of the north-south highway connecting the North Aegean (Çanakkale, Ayvalık, etc.) with İzmir. The town is divided into two main sections: **Eski (old) Foça** and the less attractive **Yeni (new) Foça,** about 10km north, a big resort town, complete with Club Med. Eski Foça consists of a wide strip between the hills and the shore around two harbors—the **Küçük Deniz** (Little Sea) and the **Büyük Deniz** (Big Sea). Most restaurants, accommodations, and other establishments are clustered near the Küçük Deniz, while many sights lie along the Büyük Deniz. Street addresses are largely useless, as Foça numbers its streets rather than naming them. However, the main street, running through town from the otogar down to and along the right side of the Küçük Deniz harbor, does have a name: **Küçük Deniz Sahil Cad.** Leaving the otogar, you'll see the tourist information office almost immediately. Küçük Deniz Sahil Cad. runs to the right of the office.

Tourist Office: (☎812 12 22), near the otogar end of Küçük Deniz Sahil Cad. Organized and well-run. Staff arranges summer boat tours, recommends sights, provides maps and pamphlets, and checks hotel/pension vacancies. Open M-F 8:30am-5:30pm.

Boat Tours: About a dozen summer boat tours leave in the mornings from Küçük Deniz. Tourist office has info. about prices, schedules, and routes.

Banks: Cirrus/MC/Plus/V **ATMs** are at **Türkiye İş Bankası,** on the left side of Küçük Deniz Sahil Caddesi as you walk from the otogar to the harbor, and at **T.C. Ziraat Bankası,** down from Türkiye İş Bankası. They'll also **exchange currency** and cash **traveler's checks** (for an exorbitant fee). Open M-F 9am-12:30pm and 1:30-5:30pm.

Pharmacy: Merkez Eczanesi (☎812 12 31), on the right side of Küçük Deniz Sahil Cad. as you walk toward the harbor, across from Türkiye İş Bankası. Pharmacist Önder Aytuğ speaks French, Italian, and English. Open M-Sa 8:30am-8pm.

Hospital: The main hospital (☎812 14 29) is 30m beyond the Karaçam Hotel on Küçük Deniz Sahil Cad.

Internet Access: Mouse Internet Cafe, just beyond Türkiye İş Bankası. Listen to American Top 40 hits while you email. $.75 per hr. Open daily 9am-1am.

PTT: Across from the tourist office. **Exchanges currency,** cashes **traveler's checks** (when currency is available), and offers *Poste Restante.* Metered phones inside and Türk Telekom phones outside for international calls. Open daily 8am-11pm.

Postal code: 35680.

ACCOMMODATIONS & CAMPING

Depending almost exclusively on summer tourism, Foça's pensions charge according to the volume of business, and, in most cases, prices are somewhat negotiable. Foça's hotels, all located on the waterfront, tend to have a higher opinion of themselves than they ought to, though most are clean.

Siren Pension, İsmet Paşa Mah. 161 Sok. (☎812 26 60; fax 812 62 20). Follow Küçük Deniz Sahil Cad. to the right of the harbor and take a right at the *"Ensar"* sign pointing inland. A large, well-kept family pension with a terrace view of the mountains and the sea. The owners of this mom-and-pop operation speak German and some English. Guest kitchen and most rooms with private bath. Free use of washing machine. Bar, TV, and A/C in living room. Open Mar.-Oct. Breakfast $1. $5 per person.

Ensar Pension, İsmet Paşa Mah. 161 Sok. (☎812 17 77; fax 812 61 59), next to and similar to Siren, but without the stunning view. Caters to families. No alcohol available. Rooms have carpeting and phones. TV room with sewing machine. 24hr. hot water and guest kitchen. Laundry service $3.25 per load. Breakfast $1. $5 per person. MC/V.

Hotel Günes (☎812 19 15; fax 812 21 55). More expensive than the local pensions, but additional amenities include fans, hair dryers, and shower curtains. Includes buffet breakfast. Singles $11; doubles $15.

Ferah Camping (☎812 11 42). No-frills camping on the beach. Travelers come to camp or swim. Electricity, showers (no hot water), and a little restaurant next door. Owners are very generous, especially to weary travelers with slender wallets. Take any "Hanedan" dolmuş from the Foça otogar and ask to be dropped off at Remzi'nin Yeri ($.25). Walk toward the beach; follow the signs. No English spoken. No tents provided. $2 per day.

FOOD

There is no shortage of fresh fish restaurants along the harbor on Küçük Deniz Sahil Cad., nor of *pide*, *kebap*, or even pizza joints. At most harbor front establishments, you can browse the menu first. Be mindful to ask for prices when they are unlisted; once you've been served and given the bill, complaints are futile. The farther inland you go, the more economical the dining becomes.

Rıdvan Usta'nın Yeri (☎812 74 64), Büyük Deniz Cad., on your right as you exit the otogar and head toward the harbor on Küçük Deniz Sahil Cad. Classic Turkish dishes on shiny wooden tables. *Döner kebap* ($1.50), *lahmacun* ($.50), and especially delicious *macar köfte* (meatballs in a cheese sauce; $1.50). Open 24hr. MC/V.

Kordon Restaurant, 8 Küçük Deniz Sahil Cad. (☎812 61 91), in the pedestrian zone on the waterfront. A cut above the rest, Kordon offers foreign specials (chicken schnitzel $3) and fresh fish (priced daily) in an attractive setting. On *futbol* days, a TV is displayed in the front window for outdoor diners. Open daily 9am-1am. MC/V.

Venedik Pizza (☎812 64 14), Aşıklar Yolu Cad., just beyond Deniz Restaurant on the left side of Küçük Deniz. If you're craving a slice of the West (or a close approximation), Venedik bakes pan pizzas to order. Varieties range from vegetable to sausage, tuna, or egg pizzas ($1.50-2). Open daily 8:30am-midnight or 1am. V.

SIGHTS

A number of sights can be seen simply by strolling around Büyük Deniz. Start facing the tourist information office, turn left, and walk on Eski Adliye Sok., which is one block from the sea. You'll pass a sculpture of Atatürk with two children on your left. The **Fatih Camii** appears next on your right. Built sometime between 1455 and 1570, this mosque has undergone extensive repair and thus no longer looks as it originally did. If you walk down to the waterfront and continue with the sea on your left, you'll arrive at the **Beşkapılar (Five Doors)** and city walls, immediately in front of the Temple of Athena. These walls formed the earliest fortifications of Phokaia in the 6th century BC, and have survived intact because of repairs done first by the Byzantines, then later by the Genoese in the late 13th century, and finally by the Ottomans in the 16th century.

Up a small hill and to your right is the excavation site for the **Temple of Athena,** built in the early 6th-century BC. Her temple's location on raised ground, as well as her presence on ancient coins and in ancient inscriptions, demonstrates Athena's importance to the Phokians. To the left on the small hill is the **Kayalar Camii.** This mosque has also undergone numerous renovations since it was first constructed in the 16th or 17th century and also lost much of its original appearance.

A bit farther along on your right is the Phokaia Port, containing the **Kybele Açık Hava Tapınağı** (the Cybele Open Air Temple), a sanctuary carved from stone and dedicated to the goddess **Cybele** in 580 BC. Cybele was the guardian of life and fertility, but, over time, she has come to be associated with having additional powers.

Apart from the Byzantine **mosaics,** a block from the Aydın Motel, which are currently under excavation and not visible, the rest of Foça's sights must be reached by boat since they are in the military zone. The well-restored **Dış Kale** ("Outer Castle") clings to the tip of the point occupied by the navy, and is more impressive than the **fortress.** The **siren rocks** are far off in the ocean near Orak Island. The castle, rocks and island are all visited by boat tours.

İZMİR ☎232

İzmir (pop. 3 million), formerly ancient Smyrna, has risen from a tumultuous past to become Turkey's third-largest city and second-largest port. Reputedly the birthplace of Homer, Smyrna gained prominence in the 9th century BC and thrived before Lydians from Sardis destroyed it about 300 years later. In 334 BC, Alexander the Great conquered the city and refounded it atop Mt. Pagus, now called Kadifekale. During the Roman and Byzantine periods, Smyrna reemerged as a prosperous port. The diversion of the River Hermes protected the harbor from silting up, saving Smyrna from the landlocked fate of its stagnating neighbors. In 1535, Süleyman the Magnificent signed a treaty with France, bringing trade to Smyrna. Beginning with the influx of Christian and Jewish merchants, the city had become a haven for migrants from mainland Greece by the 19th century.

After the Ottoman defeat in World War I, the Greek army occupied İzmir in hopes of uniting the area with mainland Greece. Turkish nationalist leader Mustafa Kemal (Atatürk) defeated the overextended Greek forces who had exhausted themselves in the Anatolian heartland. Greek troops left Smyrna on September 9, 1922, when the city's minority quarters burned. The Asia Minor Disaster, as the events of 1922 came to be called, spelled the end of Greek presence in İzmir.

Along the waterfront, İzmir is a cosmopolitan city with wide boulevards, plazas, and plenty of greenery. Fast cars, luxury hotels, and other signs of conspicuous wealth distinguish the coast. Away from the water, however, much of İzmir is a bleak, factory-laden wasteland; on the outskirts, poverty and uncontrolled industrial expansion combine to produce heartbreaking urban squalor. Still, the city is worth visiting for a few days, especially in June, July, and August, when it hosts the International İzmir Festival, attracting world-renowned musical, dance, and theater performers. In the summer of 2001, the bill included acts ranging from the Vienna Boys choir and the Greek National Theater to Elton John and Sting. Unlike most Aegean towns, summer in İzmir is considered the low season, as many of the city's well-to-do leave town in favor of beach resorts like Foça and Dikili.

TRANSPORTATION

Flights: Airport Adnan Menderes, 20km south of İzmir, connects Turkey to most major European cities. To get to the airport take the Havaş bus from the tourist office (30min., 12 per day 4:15am-8:30pm, $2). Many major airlines serve the airport, but **Turkish Airlines** (airport office ☎274 24 24 or 274 28 00; fax 274 20 33) often has the cheapest flights. The sales office, 1/F Gazi Osman Paşa (info ☎484 12 20, reservations 445 53 63; fax 483 62 81), is just up from the tourist office toward the sea. Open M-Sa 8:30am-8pm, Su 8:30am-5:30pm. To **Ankara** (1hr.; $75, students $60) and **İstanbul** (45min.; $75, students $60).

Buses: For major intercity travel, head to the modern **Yeni Garaj.** Times and prices vary, and buses head just about everywhere. Major destinations on **Kamil Koç** and **Pamukkale** include: **Ankara** (8hr., 12 per day 9am-1am, $9); **Antalya** (8hr., 17 per day 4am-1am, $9); **Bodrum** (via **Selçuk,** 4hr., every hr., $5); **Bursa** (5hr., 10 per day 9am-1am, $6); **İstanbul** (9hr., every hr., $11); **Kuşadası** (1hr., 7 per day 8:30am-7:30pm, $2); **Marmaris** (5hr., every hr. 8am-9pm, $7); **Selçuk** (take a **Bodrum**-bound bus and ask to be let off at Selçuk; 1hr.; $2). For more local destinations including **Manisa** (1hr., every 30min. 6am-9pm, $1.60) and **Sardis** (1½hr., every 30min. 6:25am-10:20pm, $.75), go to the upper level of the terminal to purchase your ticket and board the bus.

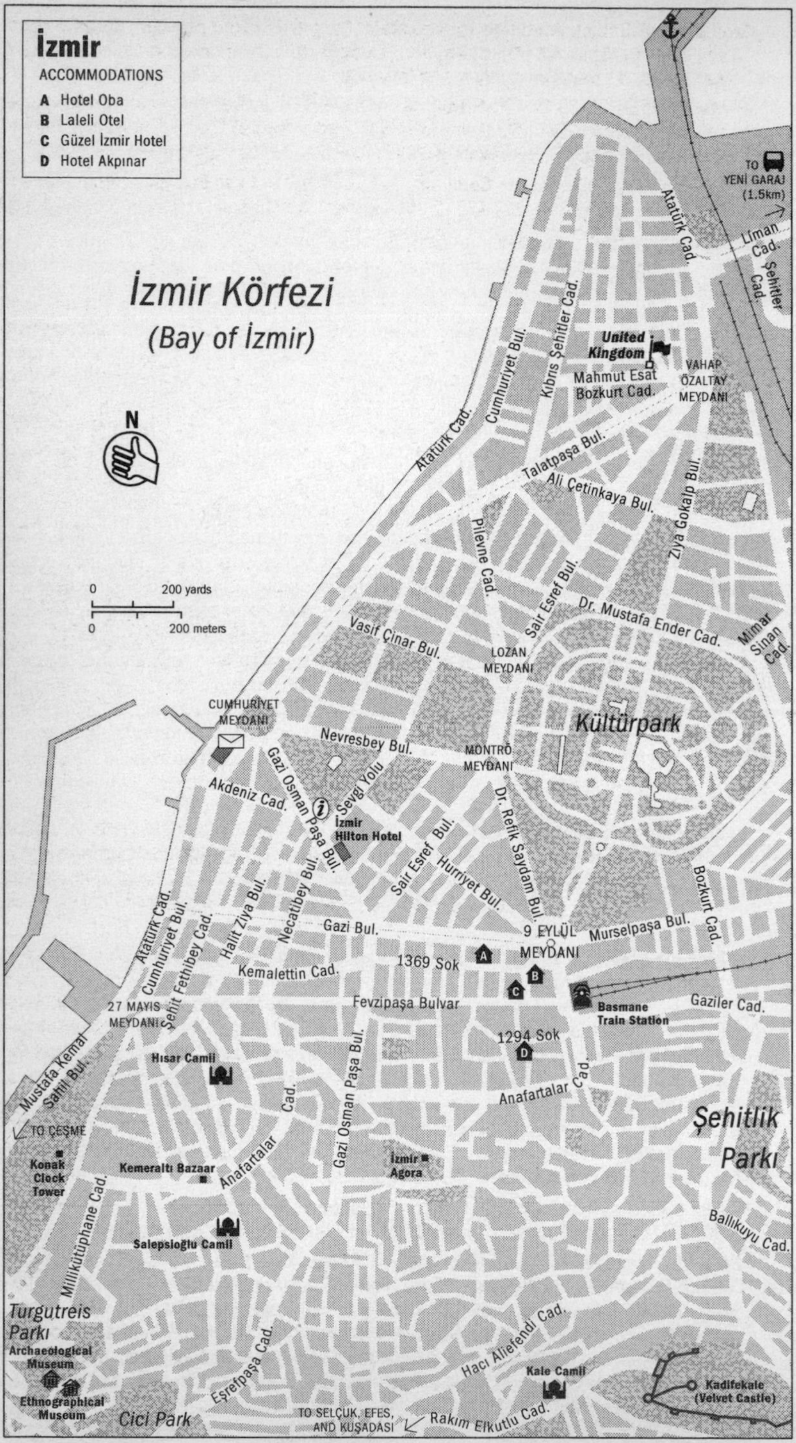
İzmir
ACCOMMODATIONS
A Hotel Oba
B Laleli Otel
C Güzel İzmir Hotel
D Hotel Akpınar
İzmir Körfezi
(Bay of İzmir)
N
0 200 yards
0 200 meters
TO YENİ GARAJ (1.5km)
Atatürk Cad.
Liman Cad.
Şehitler Cad.
Kıbrıs Şehitler Cad.
Cumhuriyet Bul.
United Kingdom
Mahmut Esat Bozkurt Cad.
VAHAP ÖZALTAY MEYDANI
Atatürk Cad.
Talatpaşa Bul.
Ali Çetinkaya Bul.
Ziya Gokalp Bul.
Plevne Cad.
Sair Esref Bul.
Dr. Mustafa Ender Cad.
Mimar Sinan Cad.
Vasif Çinar Bul.
LOZAN MEYDANI
Kültürpark
CUMHURİYET MEYDANI
Nevresbey Bul.
MONTRÖ MEYDANI
Gazi Osman Paşa Bul.
Sevgi Yolu
Akdeniz Cad.
İzmir Hilton Hotel
Dr. Refik Saydam Bul.
Sair Esref Bul.
Hurriyet Bul.
Bozkurt Cad.
Necatibey Bul.
Halit Ziya Bul.
Şehit Fethibey Cad.
Cumhuriyet Bul.
Atatürk Cad.
Gazi Bul.
9 EYLÜL MEYDANI
Murselpaşa Bul.
Kemalettin Cad.
1369 Sok
Fevzipaşa Bulvar
Basmane Train Station
Gaziler Cad.
27 MAYIS MEYDANI
1294 Sok
Mustafa Kemal Sahil Bul.
Hısar Camii
Gazi Osman Paşa Bul.
Anafartalar Cad.
Şehitlik Parkı
TO ÇEŞME
Konak Clock Tower
Kemeraltı Bazaar
Anafartalar Cad.
İzmir Agora
Millikütüphane Cad.
Salepsioğlu Camii
Ballıkuyu Cad.
Turgutreis Parkı
Archaeological Museum
Ethnographical Museum
Cici Park
Eşrefpaşa Cad.
Hacı Aliefendi Cad.
Kale Camii
Kadifekale (Velvet Castle)
TO SELÇUK, EFES, AND KUŞADASI
Rakım Elkutlu Cad.

Trains: From Basmane station to: **Ankara** (13hr.; 6:15, 6:55pm; $8); **Denizli** (6hr.; 7am, 3:15, 6:35pm; $2.50); **Söke** (3hr., 7:08pm, $1.50). Trains stop en route in many other towns. No trains currently run to İstanbul.

Ferries: (☎464 88 89 or 464 88 64; fax 464 78 34), at the Yeni Liman. One ferry per week to **İstanbul** (20hr.; Su 2pm; from $11, students $9). There is a weekly ferry to **Venice, Italy** (3 days; one-way from $172; in winter $145; 15% student discount).

Car Rental: Niyazoğlu Turizm Company, 1/E Gazi Osman Paşa Bul., down from the tourist office (☎483 93 00; fax 483 17 00; info@niyazoglu.com), rents to those 21 and older. From $21 per day. Call or email for reservations.

ORIENTATION

İzmir's principal boulevards radiate from roundabouts, called *meydan.* **Cumhuriyet Meydanı,** on the waterfront, is the city's financial center and the home of travel agencies, fashionable restaurants, consulates, and the PTT. Many budget hotels and inexpensive restaurants, along with several bus company offices and the **Basmane train station,** surround **9 Eylül Meydanı,** the center of the Basmane district. To get there from İzmir's new intercity bus station *(Yeni Garaj),* head to the ground level, where city buses and dolmuş depart. Take city bus #601, 605, 50, 51, 53, 54, or 60. All of these pass near or through 9 Eylül Meydanı, but the best way to make sure you get off in this square is to sit near the bus driver and tell him you want "Basmane Meydanı." Buy bus tickets from the kiosk before boarding ($.25). To return to the *Yeni Garaj,* purchase your bus tickets in one of the bus company offices in 9 Eylül Meydanı and take the company shuttle to the station. If the bus company does not provide service to your destination, they will still allow you to use their shuttle. Locals often give directions based on district. Beyond the Basmane district, more up-scale Alsançak is to the north, near Yeni Liman, and Konak is, predictably, the area near the Konak Clock Tower.

PRACTICAL INFORMATION

TOURIST AND FINANCIAL SERVICES

Tourist Office: Tourism Information Office, 1/1D Gazi Osman Paşa Bul. (☎445 73 90 or 489 92 78; fax 489 92 78). From 9 Eylül Meydanı, walk down Gazi Bul. to the next roundabout, then turn right onto Gazi Osmanpaşa Bul. Look to your right, about 30m up from the İzmir Hilton Hotel. Some English spoken. Great free maps and other info. Open daily 8:30am-5:30pm.

Travel Agencies: The 3 recommended agencies offer a variety of tours, all including an English-speaking guide. **Ramtur,** Gazi Osman Paşa Bul., 3/312 Yeni Asır İşhanı, 3rd fl. (☎425 27 10; fax 483 34 36; info@ramtur.com). Arranges daily tours of İzmir; Ephesus; Pergamon; the Jewish heritage of İzmir, Priene, Miletus, and Didyma; Pamukkale; İstanbul; and Cappadocia. Also assists with airline tickets and İzmir tourist information. Open M-F 9am-7pm, Sa 9am-4pm, Su 9am-1pm. **Opal Travel Agency,** 1 Gazi Osman Paşa Bul. (☎445 67 67; fax 489 88 65), is in the basement of the Büyük Efes Oteli. Daily tours to Bergama, Efes, and Pamukkale. Open M-F 8:30am-7pm, Sa 8:30am-4pm. **Bintur Travel Agency,** 10/1A Gazi Osman Paşa Bul. (☎489 41 00; fax 489 65 64). Deals with hotel reservations. Open M-F 9am-7pm.

Consulates: UK, 49 Mahmut Esat Bozkurt Cad. (☎463 51 51; fax 421 29 14), in Alsancak. **US,** 13 Kazim Dirik Cad., Flat 805 (☎441 00 72 or 441 22 03; fax 441 23 73).

Banks: All national banks and a number of foreign banks have large offices along the waterfront. Smaller banks have offices around Basmane, including a **T.C. Ziraat Bankası,** on the left side of Gazi Bul. when walking east, just before 9 Eylül Meydanı. Includes a Cirrus/MC/V **ATM** and **currency exchange.** Open M-F 9am-12:30pm and 1:30-4:30pm. It's worthwhile to compare rates with the **Efes Döviz** (exchange bureau) on the other side of Gazi Bul. further from 9 Eylül Meydanı, since they are often more favorable. Open daily 7am-6pm.

American Express: 270 Atatürk Cad. (☎463 65 93; fax 422 67 20). In Pamfilya Travel Agency, 15min. from Cumhuriyet Meydanı. Open M-Sa 9am-noon and 1:30-6:30pm.

LOCAL SERVICES

English-Language Bookstore: Net Bookstore, 142/B Cumhuriyet Bul. 142/B (☎421 26 32), at the intersection of Cumhuriyet Bul. and 1375 Sok., north of Cumhuriyet Meydanı. Decent selection of novels and tourist books on Turkey. Open daily 9am-7pm.

Hamam: Hoşgör Hamamı 360 Sok., No. 10 (☎484 03 26), in the Mecidiye district south of Basmane. The hamam is shown on the detailed map distributed by the tourist office. Somewhat far from the Basmane area, but walkable (30min. from 9 Eylül Meydanı). Foreigners are advised to make an appointment. Mixed gender groups welcome. Bath and massage $20. Open daily 7am-11am for both genders, 5pm-midnight for men, 11am-5pm for women.

EMERGENCY AND COMMUNICATIONS

Pharmacies: On almost every corner in the downtown area. **Aşıkoğlu Eczanesi,** 103 Gazi Bul. (☎483 79 63), on the corner of Gazi Bul. and 1362 Sok., 3 blocks west of 9 Eylül Meydanı. Open M-Sa 8am-8pm.

Hospitals: Ege Üniversitesi Tıp Fakültesi (☎343 43 43), in Bornova. 2 state hospitals: **Alsancak Hastanesi** (☎463 64 65), on Talat Paşa Bul., and **Yeşilyurt Devlet Hastanesi,** a.k.a. **Atatürk Hastanesi** (☎243 43 43), Gazeteci Hasan Tahsin Cad., Yeşilyurt.

Internet Access: Seçkin Internet Cafe, 16 Mimarkemalettin Cad. (☎482 14 37), on the left side of the street near the intersection with Cumhuriyet Bul. (walking toward the water). New computers with reliable, if slow, connections. To avoid an inflated fee, make sure to set the price and starting time on arrival. $.75 per hr. Open daily 9am-10pm. The PTT also has 3 computers with Internet access ($.60 per hr.).

PTT: In Cumhuriyet Meydanı. Open M-F 8am-11pm. 24hr. **currency** and **traveler's check exchange** and sale of **phone cards.**

Postal Code: 35000.

AEGEAN COAST

ACCOMMODATIONS

Lâleli Otel, 1368 Sok., No. 5-6 (☎484 09 01 or 484 09 02). Walk 1 block from 9 Eylül Meydanı on 1369 Sok. and turn left. Comfortable, spacious rooms, all with showers and ceiling fans. A clean place to stay for relatively little money. Breakfast $1. $5 per person. AmEx/MC/V.

Hotel Oba, 1369 Sok., No. 27 (☎441 96 05 or 441 96 06; fax 483 81 98), 4 blocks west of 9 Eylül Meydanı, away from the train station. More expensive, but with great amenities, including a lobby bar, and rooms with private bath, TV, and A/C. Worth the extra money if you're planning to spend lots of time in your room. No hot water 10am-8:30pm. Breakfast included. $11 per person.

Hotel Akpınar, 1294 Sok., No. 13 (☎484 16 34; fax 489 46 88). Walk south from 9 Eylül Meydanı on Anafartalar Cad., pass the train station on your left, and make the first right after Fevzıpaşa Bul. Akpınar is quiet, cool, and fairly clean. Every room has a window, but some have views of an airshaft, so it's a good idea to check them out first. TVs in most rooms. Singles $3, with bath $3.50; doubles $4, with bath $5.

Güzel İzmir Hotel, 1368 Sok., No. 8 (☎483 50 69 or 484 66 93). 1 block away from 9 Eylül Meydanı, across the street from Lâleli Hotel. Some chipping paint and cramped quarters, but a good value. TV room. Public phone in lobby. All rooms have showers and fans in summer. $4.50 per person.

FOOD AND ENTERTAINMENT

Güzel İzmir Lokantaları, 1368 Sok., No. 8/B (☎445 05 31), at the Basmane end of the 1369 Sok. Along with 9 Eylül Et Lokantası, Güzel İzmir is the best *lokanta* in the vicinity, offering traditional dishes in a clean setting. Excellent *moussaka* at cheaper-than-average prices. Meat dishes $1, vegetable dishes $.75. Open daily 7am-11pm.

9 Eylül Et Lokantası, 9 Eylül Meydanı, No. 5/B (☎445 05 31). A popular spot offering exceptionally flavorful meat dishes ($1-1.50) and vegetarian options. Try the *taze fasülye* (green beans in tomato sauce; $1). Outdoor tables with a view of the buzzing square. Open daily 5am-11pm.

Basmane Kebap Salonu, 157/A Fevzıpaşa Bul. (☎425 50 19), a few doors down on the right as you walk away from the train station. A display case at the front of this friendly restaurant holds the meats from which you create a *şiş* mix (chicken *şiş* $2; mixed meat $2.50). The specialty is *içli köfte* (meatballs with deep-fried batter; $1.50 each). *Köfte* and *şiş* come in normal or hot "*acılı*" form. Open daily 11am-11:30pm. V.

Sera Cafe-Bar-Restaurant, 190/A Atatürk Cad., Alsancak (☎464 25 95). A bit pricey, this trendy hot spot offers a relaxing sea breeze and a refreshing harbor view. The eclectic decor combines Egyptian and Renaissance motifs. Turkish, Continental, and American breakfasts ($1.50-1.75). Burgers $1.25. Cocktails $2.50. Live Turkish and foreign music every night 9pm until closing. Open daily 7am-3am.

Bolula Hasan Usta, 141/B Cumhuriyet Bul. (☎464 67 26 or 464 67 93), a few minutes north of Cumhuriyet Meydanı. A Parisian-style cafe offering tempting Turkish desserts, including *ekmek kadayıfı* ($.80) and *krem karamel* ($.80). Open daily 7am-midnight.

Kültürpark (☎446 14 56). Entrances at 9 Eylül Meydanı, Montrö Meydanı, Lozan Meydanı, the southern end of Ziya Gökalp Bul., and the western end of Akıncılar Cad. A great center for day- and nightlife, especially during the International Fair (Aug. 15-25). Features various attractions including numerous restaurants, tea gardens, a zoo (open 9am-6pm; $.15), an amusement park (open 11am-midnight), a disco, and a casino (both open 9pm-5am). Crowds are most vigorous on weekends. Open 24hr.

SIGHTS

İzmir's **agora** (marketplace) was built in the 4th century BC, destroyed by an earthquake in 178 AD, and subsequently rebuilt by Emperor Marcus Aurelius. The mediocre remains of ancient columns and more interesting tombstones can be reached by walking south on Gazi Osman Paşa Bul. and turning left on Anafartalar Cad. At the time of publication, the ruins were closed for restoration, but if you're lucky, you might be able to find someone with a key to let you in. Above the city at Mt. Pagus is the **Kadifekale.** Alexander originally built it in the 4th century BC, but various conquerors frequently altered and restored it. The park within the walls of the Kadifekale is intriguing, yet may be unsafe after dark. Dolmuş marked "Mezarlık" leave from in front of the agora entrance on Anafartalar Cad. and ascend the mountain, offering a thrilling panorama of the bay ($.25).

Strolling along Anafartalar Cad. from its origin at the Basmane station, you'll pass evidence of a less-industrialized Turkey—*çay salonu* (tea houses), men smoking *nargile,* children and vendors filling the air with their cries, and colorful streets that eventually turn into İzmir's full-fledged **bazaar** as you cross Gazi Osman Paşa Bul. The bazaar runs at a feverish pace, crowded with shoppers and determined hawkers. Leather, jewelry, and name-brand knockoffs are the most abundant offerings. (Open M-Sa 9am-8pm.)

For a more subdued experience, İzmir's **Archaeological Museum,** near Konak Square, offers what is probably the finest collection of statuary outside of İstanbul. Among finds from Ephesus and other local sites are a elaborate sarcophagi and extraordinary statues. (Open Tu-Su 9am-5pm. $1.50, students $1.) Directly across from the archaeological museum, the **Ethnographical Museum** displays early Ottoman weapons and traditional folk art, mostly from the last century, including *kilims,* costumes, and furniture. (Open Tu-Su 9am-noon and 1-5pm. $.75, students $.35)

In the center of the Konak district lies **Hisar Camii,** İzmir's 400-year-old treasure. Decorated with beguiling floral tiling and fantastic Turkish carpets, this mosque is the most renowned site in İzmir. It is located in the **konak** itself, the late Ottoman clock tower that looms over the intersection of Cumhuriyet Bul. and Atatürk Cad. The annual highlight, the **International İzmir Festival** (www.iksev.org or www.izmirfestival.org.), best reflects the city's cosmopolitan character. Held from mid-June to early August, the festival brings a variety of Turkish and international acts to İzmir, Çeşme, and Ephesus. For tickets and information, call the numbers listed in the back of the İzmir Festival brochure from the tourist office. Considering the quality and reputation of many of the performers, tickets are cheap ($7.50-15).

DAYTRIP FROM İZMIR: SART (SARDIS)

To reach Sardis from İzmir, take a ***bus*** *bound for Salihli from the upper floor of İzmir's Yeni Garaj (1½hr., every 45min. 7am-8:20pm, $.75). Ask to be let off at Sart. You will be dropped near a yellow "Sart Temple of Artemis" sign, amidst the shops and tea houses scattered along the highway. The yellow sign points the way to the Temple of Artemis. The gymnasium, synagogue, and baths are about 50m ahead on your left. Buses back to İzmir run with the same frequency, but cannot be caught along the same road. Turn left instead of right at the yellow Temple of Artemis sign. Follow it to the right as it splits until you reach another highway. Catch the bus on the wide, pull-off area on the other side of the road.*

Sardis (Sart to Turks) was the capital of the **Lydian Empire,** which dominated Aegean Ionia from 680-547 BC. The Lydians embraced and embellished the existing Hellenic culture, giving the world dice and coin minting. Sardis was also an important *satrapy* (administrative center) in the Persian empire and home to one of the seven churches mentioned in the Book of Revelation. Apart from the remains of the Temple of Artemis, most of the ruins at Sardis are Roman or early Byzantine. Though small, Sardis stands out as perhaps the best-restored site in Turkey: it is often difficult to distinguish the replacement marble from the original.

After entering the cluster of ruins on the left side of the highway, proceed to the right along the **West Road** (a.k.a. **Marble Way**), which is lined with a row of **Byzantine shops.** At the end of the Marble Way, turn left to enter the **synagogue,** donated by the Roman authorities to the town's Jewish inhabitants. The patterns of the synagogue's 3rd-century mosaic floors are strangely juxtaposed with the Corinthian and Doric columns above. Beside the synagogue lies the ruined **Palaestra,** where wrestling matches and other sporting events were held. The imposing and magnificently restored two-story structure is the **gymnasium,** the site of a Roman bath house, whose towering columns overshadow a long-deserted **swimming pool.**

AEGEAN COAST

Cross the street and enter Mahmutbey Cad., between the Akçay market and a tea shop, for a wonderful view of Anatolian landscapes. A 1km trek up the paved road brings you to the **Temple of Artemis.** Today, only a few columns remain of the 4th-century BC edifice, but their scrolled capitals are exquisite. Even more impressive are the intricately carved, floral-patterned column bases. On the way to the temple, about 100m up on the left, are the remains of an ancient Roman city wall. 50m farther on the right, catch a glimpse of the ancient **Lydian gold refinery** and a dome from a 12th-century Byzantine **basilica** that was built atop a 5th-century church. On the left, about 800m ahead, you will find a trail to the **pyramid tomb.** Located in the area northwest of the acropolis, the earliest of these tombs dates from the 6th century BC, but it has since been buried by landslides. *(Old city, including the gymnasium, baths, and synagogue, open daily 8am-6pm. $.75, students $.40. Temple open daily 8am-5pm. $.75, students $.40.)*

ÇEŞME ☎232

A breezy seaside village, Çeşme was built around a 14th-century Genoese fortress that was expanded and beautified by 16th-century Ottomans. A little over an hour from İzmir, the town has deservedly gained popularity for its cool climate, crystal clear waters, and proximity to the Greek island of Chios. Daytrippers from Chios keep the myriad restaurants and leather shops in business, and the affluent İzmirites who have weekend houses here ensure an active nightlife in the cafes and bars along the marina. Summer is festival season in Çesme, as the town hosts the Sea Festival/International Pop Song Contest at the end of July and the Çeşme Film Festival at the end of August. For the song contest, bars stay packed, and primary sponsors TEKEL (the state alcohol and tobacco monopoly) and Coca-Cola set up tents along the waterfront for giveaways and contests. Information regarding exact dates for these week-long festivals is available in the tourist office.

TRANSPORTATION

Buses to Çeşme stop either at the new **otogar** or at the top of **İnkılap Cad.** All buses from Çeşme to İzmir pick up passengers at both stops.

Buses: The **otogar** (☎712 64 99) is at the corner of A. Menderes Cad. and Çevre Yolu Cad. From here, Turgutozal Cad. runs down to the sea. To: **Ankara** (10hr.; 9:30pm; $11); **İstanbul** (11hr.; 10am, 9:30pm; $12); **İzmir** (1½hr.; every 20min. 6am-10pm; $2). Most buses to İzmir arrive at the **Üçkuyular** otogar, not the main otogar. However, İzmir-bound buses at 6, 7, 8, 9, 11am, 1, 3, 5, 6, 8, and 9pm continue to the main otogar for a small additional fee. Bus #605 connects Üçkuyular with the main otogar, and any bus running north heads to the center of İzmir (see **İzmir: Transportation,** p. 191).

Ferries: Buy tickets from Ertürk Tourism (see **Travel Agencies**) or any of the tourist offices in town for **Chios** (1hr.; July 1-Aug. 31 Tu-Su; June, Sept. 1-20 T, Th, F, Su; May, Sept. 21-Oct. 31 Tu, Th; Nov. 1.-Apr. 30 Th; $30 one-way, $40 open round-trip; $10 Greek port tax for stays over 1 day). From June-Sept., ferries also depart from the **Turkish Maritime Lines** office (☎712 10 91), on the ferry docks on the south side of the waterfront, for **Brindisi, Italy** (34hr.; Tu 11am, F 11pm; $74, $83 for the deck). To get to the dock from the tourist office, walk along the sea with the water on your right until you reach the large white building marked "TDİ." Open Tu-Th 9am-11pm, Sa-Su 9am-2pm.

Car Rental: Teodan Turizm (☎712 14 81; fax 712 11 55; teodentour@hotmail.com), on the left of İnkilap Cad., rents the cheapest cars and motorbikes in town. For 1-2 days: cars $30; motorbikes $15; bikes $7.50. Open daily 9am-9pm.

ORIENTATION AND PRACTICAL INFORMATION

Shopping and nightlife are centered around **İnkılap Cad.,** a pedestrian street lined with leather shops and ice cream parlors. İnkilap Cad. meets the sea at **Cumhuriyet Meydanı** and runs some 300m to the bus stop up the hill, past Mehmetçik Park on the left. From the otogar, follow **Turgutözal Cad.,** which begins at the corner of the parking lot with the Kamil Koç booth, down to the sea (about 200m), turn right at the sea, and walk 300m to Cumhuriyet Meydanı just past the castle.

Tourist Office: 8 İskele Meydanı (☎/fax 712 66 53), on the waterfront across from the castle and *kervansaray*. Helpful English-speaking staff. Maps and accommodation info available. Open 8:30am-5:30pm, also open in summer Sa-Su 9am-5pm.

Travel Agency: Ertürk Tourism and Travel Agency, Beyazıt Cad., No. 6-7 (☎712 67 68), across from tourist information and next to the *kervansaray*, sells ferry tickets. Open daily 8am-9pm; in winter 9am-6pm.

Banks: TC Ziraat Bankası, in the main square, offers **currency exchange, traveler's check exchange** (M-F 9am-5:30pm), and a Cirrus/MC/Plus/V **ATM.** Just to the left, **Türkiye İş Bankası** has a small currency exchange office. Open daily 9am-11pm.

Police: (☎712 66 27), in the back of the tourist office.

Pharmacy: Çağler Eczanesi (☎712 69 64), on the left side of İnkılap Cad. when walking away from the sea. Open daily 9am-1am.

Hospital: (☎712 07 77), 5km east of town on Çeşme İzmir Yolu, on the right. Take the Ilıca-bound dolmuş from beside the tourist office and ask for "*hastane*" ($.40).

Internet Access: Emre Computer and Internet Cafe, 11 Kutludag Cad. (☎712 67 36). One block from Cumhuriyet Meydanı. Open daily 10am-2am. $.75 per hr. **Melis Cafe** (☎712 12 15) is usually less crowded and has quick connections. Turn left onto Dalyan Cad. from İnkılap Cad. just before Mehmetçik Parkı. Open daily 9am-1am. $.75 per hr.

PTT: (☎712 66 20 or 712 63 48), on the waterfront as you walk away from the tourist office (with the sea on your left). **Currency** and **traveler's check exchange.** Open daily June-Sept. 8am-midnight; Oct.-May M-F 8am-5:30pm.

Postal Code: 35930.

ARCHAEOLOGICAL OBSTACLES One often hears that Turkey has better Roman ruins than Italy and better Greek ruins than Greece. While sites are not so simply ranked, this statement isn't far off the mark. Not only are the better exposed treasures—Ephesus, Aphrodisias, Bergama—dazzling, but much still remains underground, waiting to be unearthed when sufficient funding comes to light. Unfortunately, a number of obstacles stand so firmly in the way that many discoveries will remain buried indefinitely. Money is, of course, the biggest and most long-standing problem. The vast majority of current excavations in Turkey receives funding from international sources: Germans work at Bergama, Americans at Aphrodisias, Austrians at Ephesus, and so forth. The minimal Turkish funding remains largely private; *Efes* beer has generously funded the excavation and restoration work at Assos. The Turkish government, however, has lately created a huge impediment to increased archaeological research. Within the last year it has declared that all substantial ruins excavated must be restored, presumably in the interest of generating tourist sites like those at Ephesus and Bergama. As one can imagine, this requires a serious diversion of funding and energy. Instead of undertaking new excavations and bringing more to scholarly attention, archaeological teams must now spend their limited money on new marble and special architects; therefore, new tourist attractions will come at a considerable cost.

ACCOMMODATIONS & CAMPING

There is no shortage of pensions in Çeşme, but it might be a good idea to make reservations in July and August to get the best rooms.

Filiz Pension, 16 Dellal Sok. (☎712 67 94), just after the shops and restaurants end on İnkılap Cad. (walking away from the square). Turn right onto Mektap Sok. and then immediately right onto Dellal Sok. Refreshingly clean rooms with decorative rugs. Hot water with good pressure. Extra bathrooms and showers on each floor for guests who've already checked out. Guest kitchen. Breakfast $2. Doubles $7.50.

Alim Pension, Tarihi Türk Hamamı Yanı (☎712 83 19; fax 712 83 19), on the corner past the *kervansaray* and hamam as you walk with the sea on your right on Alpaslan Cad. Carpeted rooms with phones and showers, some with balconies overlooking a patch of trees and shrubbery with a fascinating, partially collapsed Ottoman stone house beyond. Primitive guest kitchen in rear garden. Breakfast $1.25. $4 per person.

Avrupalı Pension, 12 Sağ Sok., İnönü Mah. (☎712 70 39). Turn left off İnkılap Cad. (when walking away from the square), and turn left at the sign for Çeşme Pansiyon. Clean rooms with private bath. Lovely, vine-canopied garden and a quiet location. Guest kitchen. Breakfast $1.50. Doubles $7.50; triples $11.

Yalcın Otel, 38 Kale Sok., Musalla Mah. (☎712 69 81; fax 712 06 23). Walk up the hill between the *kervansaray* and the "No Problem" cafe. Follow the alleyway past the Tarhan Pension and take the first left. A bit more upscale than the standard pension. Cozy rooms with bath and phones. Two beautiful terraces looking out over the water. Breakfast included. Doubles $11; triples $19.

Yeni Kervan Pension (☎712 84 96), Kale Sok., Musalla Mah. Walk up the hill between the *kervansaray* and the "No Problem" cafe. Follow the alleyway that goes beyond the Tarhan Pension, turn right at the 1st road, and continue 30m. All rooms have showers and balconies with a garden view. TV lounge and private garden on basement level. Breakfast $1.25. Doubles $7.50; triples $11.

U2 Pension, 2 Muarrem Sok. (☎712 63 81). Centrally located on the left side of İnkılap Cad. as you walk away from the sea, about 150m from the waterfront. Pleasant rooftop terrace overlooking the town. Rooms, some with bath, are small and not quite immaculate. Laundry $7.50 per load. Guest kitchen. Homemade Turkish dinner upon request ($2.25). Breakfast $1.25. Doubles $7.50; triples $9.

Baba Kamp, Altınkum Beach. From the dolmuş stop, face the water, and Baba is the first building on your right. Campground has electricity, water, restaurant, and beach. Open June-Aug. Free if you eat at Baba restaurant, the cheapest around. No tents provided.

FOOD AND ENTERTAINMENT

Mangal Restaurant (☎712 85 21 or 721 10 86), on the corner of Yağcılar Sok. and İnkılap Cad., 200m up from the tourist office, across from the Garden Pub. Enter on Yağcılar Sok., the side street. This 2nd-story open-air restaurant has flawless decor and high ambitions. Excellent food prepared table-side on an enormous barbecue makes Mangal worth the slightly higher prices. Salads $1; pasta dishes $1.50-2; meat dishes from $2.25. Open May-Oct. daily 10am-1am. AmEx/MC/V.

Biz Bize Salonu, 6 İnkılap Cad. (☎712 17 46), on the right side of İnkılap Cad., next to the castle. A favorite among locals, Biz Bize serves some of the best and cheapest *döner,* and not much else. *İskender kebap* $2.25. Open 24hr. MC/V.

Flamingo Cafe and Restaurant, Kervansaray Karşısı (☎712 93 01), right in front of the *Kervansaray.* Outdoor dining under parasols next to a rippling fountain. Spaghetti plates $2-2.25; mushroom and chicken sautés $3.50; *kebaps* $2-2.25. 10% discount for parties of 5 or more. Open May-Sept. daily 8am-1am or later.

Street Bar, Uzun Sok. 4/A (☎712 84 76), on the right corner all the way at the top of İnkılap Cad. when you walk away from the sea. King of the Çeşme club scene, Street Bar has the largest dance floor, A/C, and a retractable roof. Charming decor makes the club resemble a town square. Nightly Turkish and Western hits. Beer $1.50. Cocktails $3.75-5.25. Happy hour before 10pm and after 2am. Open daily 8pm-4am.

Wine Plaza Bar, 27 İnkılap Cad. (☎712 09 58), across from the old basilica. An upscale restaurant by day, by night it serves drinks in an intimate—though hardly stuffy—setting (beer $1.50; wine from $5.25 per bottle). Live music most nights, ranging from traditional Turkish love ballads to Whitney Houston. On livlier evenings, patrons sing along. Open daily 11am-4am.

Garden Bar, 16 İnkılap Cad. (☎610 63 76), close to the square, masked by a donkey statue outside. Another disco bar with an outdoor motif and plenty of plant life. Patrons pack the small dance floor and bust a move to Western and Turkish hits. Beer $1.50; cocktails $4.50-5.50. Open daily 8pm-4am.

SIGHTS

Çeşme's main draw is its superior beaches, easily accessible by dolmuş. With a long ribbon of clean, powder-white sand flanked by clear, warm, blue waters on one side and rolling rush-covered dunes on the other, **Altınkum Beach** is one of Turkey's best. It is also surprisingly free of the crowds that plague other beaches. Dolmuş run to Altınkum from the lot by the tourist office in Çeşme (15min.; June-Sept. every 20min. 8am-8pm, sporadic in winter; $.75).

While Altınkum is the best place to enjoy the sun and sand, **Alaçatı Beach** offers a bit more of a thrill. Situated on a lagoon, it has strong offshore winds, making it one of Turkey's best windsurfing beaches. It hosted the 1998 Quicksilver European Championships, which brought such legendary windsurfers as Robbie Nash to brave the local gales. Several licensed clubs just next to Hotel Süzer rent windsurfing equipment by the hour and the day, and also offer instructional classes. Domuş run to Alaçati from the Çeşme lot (every 20min. in summer during daylight hours, $.40), and stops in town. To catch another dolmuş to the beach, tell the driver you want Hotel Süzer (every hr., $.50). A **public beach** is only a short walk past the PTT (with the sea on your left), although there's not much space to lay out unless you want to fork over $2.25 for a chair and umbrella.

Other major beaches are at **Ilıca, BoYalık, Ildır,** and **Erythrai.** BoYalık is a 25min. walk from Çeşme along Çeşme İzmir Cad., or a short ride on the Ilıca-bound dolmuş. Ask for "BoYalık" ($.40). Ilıca has the additional lure of its famed therapeutic hot springs, water from which can be found at several hotels in town.

The most impressive sight in Çeşme itself is the waterfront **castle** across from the tourist office. Built in 1508 by Sultan Beyazıt II in order to spy on Chios, the castle had 50 cannons and a garrison of 185. Though it was rebuilt in the 18th century, by the 19th century it had lost its military significance. It houses an attractively-displayed but sparse **Archaeological Museum** of common local artifacts, including Roman and 19th-century statues accompanied by little explanation. (Open Tu-Su 8am-noon and 1-6pm. $.75, students $.40.)

The **kervansaray,** built under Süleyman the Magnificent and imaginatively renamed the Hotel Kervansaray, contains a typical Ottoman floor plan with a rectangular frame that opens onto a courtyard. Feel free to poke around. Back up on İnkılap Cad., the shell of the Greek basilica of **Agios Haralambos** is now the town's exhibition center. The finals of the song contest and some of the film festival screenings are held here. It houses ongoing displays of contemporary, local art and handicrafts from June-Oct. (Open daily 9am-midnight.)

EPHESUS REGION

EFES (EPHESUS) ☎232

Stretching from early archaic times to the 6th century AD, Ephesus's glorious prosperity has not gone the way of other notable ancient cities. To this day, Ephesus boasts a concentration of Classical art and architecture surpassed only by Rome and Athens. As both the capital of Roman Asia and the site of a large, wealthy port, Ephesus accumulated almost unparalleled wealth and splendor, the marble specter of which still leaves visitors in awe. The ruins rank first among Turkey's ancient sites in terms of sheer size and state of preservation. No piles of weed-ravaged rubble await imaginative reconstruction work here. Instead, extensive marble roadways and columned avenues create an authentic impression of this ancient, metropolitan gateway to the Eastern world. The best time to visit is right when it opens, before the scorching midday summer sun and throngs of tourists obliterate the last remnants of lingering nighttime cool and silence.

HISTORY

Fiery and intense, Ephesus's history has all the makings of an ancient tragedy. Out of devotion to its patron goddess Artemis, residents maintained the city's location near her colossal temple (now in modern Selçuk), even as they watched their harbor steadily fill with silt from the Cayster River. The recession of the sea had sealed the city's fate by the 6th century, as the harbor deteriorated into a marshy wasteland and eventually became infested with malaria-carrying mosquitoes. A massive epidemic resulted in nearly 200,000 deaths.

Ephesus's origins are equally romantic. The Delphic Oracle prophesied that a fish and a wild boar would determine the site for the founding of the city. After this proclamation, Androclus passed through a seaside village where fish were being roasted along the shore. One fish, covered in burning wood, fell from the fire, igniting a nearby bush and upsetting a wild boar, who tore out from the foliage. Androclus slew the boar, and heeding the oracle, he founded the city on the site.

The ancient traveler Pausanias deemed Ephesus the "most wondrous of the Seven Ancient Wonders" and "the most beautiful work ever created by mankind." The first major structure built entirely of marble and the largest edifice in the ancient Greek world, the **Temple of Artemis** was four times as big as the Parthenon. The 6th-century philosopher Heraclitus was so enamored of this massive monument that he deposited his enigmatic treatise on the nature of the universe in the temple instead of publishing it. He later claimed that no one but the gods could understand his theories anyway. Could be.

Remarkably, the Temple of Artemis was actually built twice. It was set afire during the reign of Mad King Hesostratos in 356 BC on the night of Alexander the Great's birth. According to legend, the pyro-king succeeded only because Artemis—watching over Alexander's birth at the time—was absent. Fittingly, Alexander himself offered to restore the temple when he passed through the city. The Ephesians, however, declined his offer and rebuilt the temple even more splendidly with their own resources and the offerings made by hundreds of thousands of pilgrims. Today, little remains of the magnificent structure. Goths sacked the sanctuary in the 3rd century, and the Byzantines followed suit. Some of the temple's columns can be seen at İstanbul's Aya Sofia and London's British Museum.

Ephesus reached its zenith after 129 BC, when the Romans established the province of Asia with Ephesus as the capital. After Rome, it was second only to Alexandria in population, with more than 250,000 inhabitants. The ruins date primarily from this period. St. Paul, recognizing the significance of the metropolis, arrived in 50 AD and converted a small group of Ephesians to Christianity. Many perceived the development of the new religion as a threat to Artemis and Cybele (mother goddess of Anatolia) and forced St. Paul and his followers to depart. Eventually, Ephesus became a center of Christianity in the Roman Empire, so much so that the Ecumenical Council met here in 431. Pope Paul VI visited the site in 1967 and prayed with a congregation in the ruins of Ephesus's 4th-century church.

TRANSPORTATION AND PRACTICAL INFORMATION

Contrary to the signs and advice given by the tourist offices in Kuşadası, Selçuk, and Samos, the guided tours of Ephesus are not recommended. Ephesus is easily reached by regular dolmuş or by walking from Selçuk, the ruins are in good repair, and there is an abundance of explanatory material. Why spend $30 on what is often a rushed and cursory look at the 2000-acre site? A good guidebook to Ephesus is about $2.50 in Kuşadası's souvenir shops or at the entrance to the site.

Ephesus lies about 2-3km outside of Selçuk along the main Kuşadası-Selçuk road, **Dr. Sabri Yayla Bul.** The easiest way to get to Ephesus from Kuşadası or Selçuk is via the free shuttle service offered by practically every hotel and *pansiyon*. Otherwise, to get to Ephesus from the Kuşadası otogar, take a **dolmuş** to Selçuk and tell the driver to stop at Efes (30min., $.80). From the Selçuk otogar, take a Pamucakkale-bound dolmuş toward Kuşadası (5min.; every 15min., Nov.-Apr. every 30min.; $.60). Taxis also run from Selçuk to Ephesus ($4) and to the House of the Virgin Mary (9km, $15 round-trip including 45min. to visit the house). Ephesus is an easy walk (25min.) from Selçuk along a shady path (beside Dr. Sabri Yayla Bul.) that passes by the spectacular **Ephesus Museum** (see **Selçuk: Sights,** p. 208) and the **Temple of Artemis.** The lower entrance, to which you arrive by dolmuş or on foot, has **toilets** ($.20) and a **PTT** that exchanges money until 4:30pm.

Aside from the stands selling chewy Turkish ice cream, the culinary offerings at the site are unimpressive, though there are some picnic tables just outside the site. Infinitely preferable is the *gözleme* tent just outside the entrance to the Seven Sleepers ($.80; *ayran* $.40). There are currently **no accommodations** in Ephesus.

AEGEAN COAST

EXPLORING EPHESUS

☎892 64 02. Open 8am-7pm. $5.60; students $2.50. Bring water and sunscreen.

VEDIUS GYMNASIUM AND STADIUM. On the left as you walk down the road that goes from Dr. Sabri Yayla Bul. to the lower entrance is the Vedius Gymnasium, built in 150 AD in honor of then-emperor Antonius Pius and Artemis, the city's patron goddess. A marble path connects this structure to the Grand Theater at the head of the Arcadiane. Beyond the vegetation visible from the road lie the horseshoe-shaped remains of the city's stadium, constructed by the Greek architect Lysimachus and then expanded during the reign of Nero. The dual construction highlights the fundamental differences between Hellenic and Roman public entertainment. The original Greek structure would have been a semicircular theater whose shape followed the contours of the land to add a natural emphasis to the staged dramas. The Roman stadium was built atop the old theater for the viewing of such martial spectacles as bloody gladiator games, wild beast hunts, and public executions. You can see the stone supports underneath the seats and the tunnels that served as an ancient world "green room" for wild beasts and gladiators.

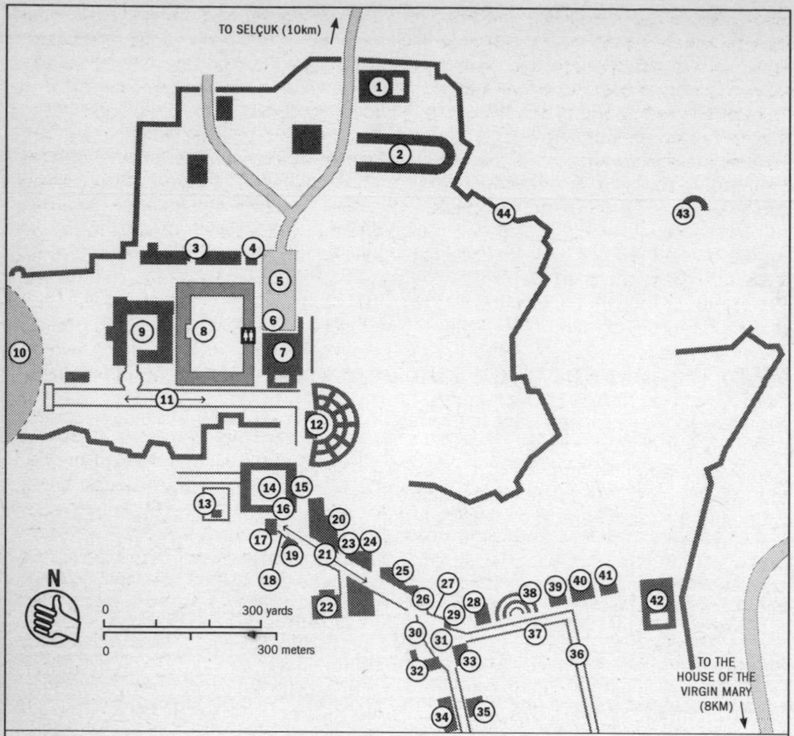

Ephesus

SIGHTS:
Agora, 14
Arcadiane, 11
Archbishop's Palace, 4
Basilica, 39
Baths and Hall of Verulanus, 8
Baths of Scholastica, 24
Baths, brothel, & toilets, 20
Byzantine Walls, 44
Cave of the Seven Sleepers, 43
Church of the Seven Councils, 3
East Gymnasium, 42
Former Harbor, 10
Fountain of Trajan, 25
Gate of Hercules, 26
Gate of Maxeus and Mithridates, 16
Grand Theater, 12
Hadrian's Gate, 18
Harbor Baths, 9
Inscripted Advertisement, 15
Library of Celsus, 17
Lower Gate, 6
Monumental Fountain, 27
Museum of Inscriptions, 34
Octagon, Tomb of Princess Arsinoe, 19
Odeon, 38
Parking Lot and Souvenir Shops, 5
Peristyle House built of Basilica Blocks, 40
Prytaneion, 28
Relief of Nike, 30
Square of Domitian, 31
Stadium, 2
State Agora, 37
Street of Curetes, 21
Temple of Domitian, 32
Temple of Hadrian, 23
Temple of Sarapis, 13
Terrace Houses, 22
Theater Baths and Gymnasium, 7
Tomb of Memmius, 29
Tomb of Pollio, 33
Upper Baths/The Varius' Baths, 41
Upper Gate, 36
Vedius Gymnasium, 1
Water Palace, 35

ON THE WAY TO THE ARCADIANE. Of the three holy Christian sites in the Efes vicinity, only the very long, skinny building of the **Church of the Seven Councils** is in the Ephesus site itself. Just inside the lower entrance, a dirt path leads to the right; follow this path and turn right where it splits to the ruins of the Church. Here, the Ecumenical Council met in 431 AD to iron out the **Nestorian Heresy,** in which the bishop Nestor called into question the humanity of Christ. This was also the site of Pope Paul VI's visit in 1967. Beside the Church of the Seven Councils is the **Archbishop's Palace,** which was destroyed by Arabs in the 6th century AD.

ALONG THE ARCADIANE. Back at the main entrance gate, a tree-lined path leads straight ahead to the Arcadiane, which could loosely be termed Ephesus's main drag. Running from the Grand Theater to what was once the harbor, the magnificent, colonnaded marble avenue would have been thronged with stevedores (men who unload ships' cargoes) and carts bringing wares from ships to sell in the *agora.* The street eventually liquefied into a small marsh, and only a few marble stumps remain of the covered arcade which ran along the sides of the main road. Ephesus was one of only three ancient cities that could afford street lighting. The large expanse of column stones laid out in tidy rows to the left as you face the theater are the remnants of the **Theater Baths and Gymnasium.** This area, used in the Roman Period for training actors, is currently a focus of excavation.

Buried under nothing more than a dense swarm of tourists, the **Grand Theater** is a stunning, 30m by 145m, heavily restored beast. Its *cavea* (seating area), carved into the side of Mt. Pion, had a capacity of 25,000. (Archaeologists have used this number to estimate the population of this and other Hellenistic cities by multiplying the theater capacity by 10.) The hard marble and the sound-catching colonnade across the top gave the theater excellent acoustics. The *skene* (where the scenery and props stand in a modern theater) is a forest of columns, stelae, and statues dating mostly from the reigns of Claudius and Trajan. Denizens of Ephesus placed 89 golden idols of Artemis here to celebrate the goddess's annual festival each April. St. Paul railed against these same false gods. Today, the **International Efes Festival** is held here in September.

THE MARBLE ROAD. From the Grand Theater, you approach the Street of Curetes by walking along the Marble Way. To your right as you walk along the Marble Way is the **agora,** built during the reign of Nero. Currently off-limits, it was once a large commercial area. A square stone in the center marks all that remains of the city's **horologium,** a combination sundial and water clock that kept accurate time. At the southern end of the *agora* is the **Gate of Maxeus and Mithridates,** two wealthy freedmen who had the gate built and dedicated to the first Roman emperor, Augustus. About halfway to the Street of Curetes, on the right-hand edge of the Marble Way, stands a small metal barrier surrounding and protecting a rough-hewn inscription thought to be the world's first advertisement. The inscription consists of a picture of a foot, a cross, a woman, and a heart-shaped blob. The ad-wizards of the day intended this to designate the brothel down the road. The foot indicated the viewer's position as well as the need to walk to the crossroads ahead, represented by the cross. The heart above and to the left of the cross showed the house's position at the intersection, and the woman depicted is just that, a woman. Sailors could follow these clear directions to the **brothel,** which was dedicated to the love goddess Aphrodite.

THE STREET OF CURETES. A slight incline signals the beginning of the Street of Curetes, which connected the city to the Temple of Artemis, now in Selçuk. Ruts in the road are evidence of the enormous concentration of traffic between the temple and the city, and gaps between the slabs reveal glimpses of the city's **sewer system.** At the very bottom of the Street of Curetes is the grand **Library of Celsus,** which was restored by Austrian archaeologists. A memorial to Gaius Julius Celsus and a general fount of knowledge, the library was covered with inscriptions recording important events and once contained 12,000 scrolls. The facade's frontal curvature and the slight thinness of the peripheral columns serve to create an impression of greater width. This tempers the minimizing effect of being sandwiched between the broad *agora* and another building. Scholars suspect that the large building behind the library is the **Temple of Sarapis,** an Egyptian god associated with grain.

Walking up the Street of Curetes from the library, the **brothel** is on your left. Romantic commerce took place by oil light in the windowless side rooms, where archaeologists unearthed the infamous statue of **Priapus,** the god of fertility, now in Selçuk's Efes Müzesi (see p. 208). Near the brothel is a well, still in use, whose waters were thought to make barren women fertile. Adjacent to the brothel are the **Baths of Scholastica,** built in the 5th century at the behest of a wealthy woman. You will find a **public restroom** just beyond the brothel.

Farther up the Street of Curetes you'll see the imposing ruins of the **Temple of Hadrian** on your left. It is marked by its double-layered column construction, several friezes depicting the creation of Ephesus, and a bust of the goddess Cybele that adorns the keystone. The temple was built in 118 AD during Hadrian's rule, atypical for Romans, who usually preferred to deify their emperors only after death. Modest, no? Covering the hillside on the right are the famous stephouses, which the local bourgeoisie called home. Since they are currently under excavation, most are off limits to tourists. A little further up the hill on the left are the ruins of the exquisite **Fountain of Trajan.** A statue of the **Emperor Trajan,** who extended the Roman Empire's borders as far as the Indian Ocean, once stood before the fountain. Today only its base remains.

Two pillars in the middle of the road mark the **Gate of Hercules.** Farther uphill and to the left is the **Prytaneion.** Dedicated to the worship of **Vesta** (Hestia to the Greeks), goddess of the hearth and home, the Prytaneion contained an eternal flame that was tended by the **Vestal Virgins,** a small group of priestesses who served Vesta. Worship of Vesta was of such great significance to Romans that the Vestal Virgins were afforded social standing close to that of men.

Immediately adjacent and in fine repair is the **odeon** (bouleterion), a small, once-covered theater that seated approximately 1500 people. It was used as both a theater and a meeting place. The **state agora** on the right was the heart of political activity from the first century BC until the city's final demise. On the left after the odeon lie the upper **baths.**

TERRACE HOUSES. Just opened to the public in summer 2001, the Terrace Houses, located across from the Temple of Hadrian, are the newest jewel in the Ephesus crown. Believed to date back to the 6th-century Ionian period, the terraces were home to the wealthiest Ephesians in the 2nd century AD. They underwent several restorations in the four centuries that followed. Only two houses are opened to the public, but both have fine examples of **mosaics, frescoes,** and **peristyle architecture** (columned courtyard). Houses had running hot and cold water, a sewage system, and were heated from beneath the floors. Most impressive among the finds are an enormous **domed bath** and remarkably intact frescoes portraying mythological and theatrical scenes. While the site often is bypassed by tourists, it's worth the extra entrance fee just to marvel at how little humankind has really progressed over the past two millennia in terms of domestic architecture and amenities. *(Open daily 8am-6:30pm. $5.60, students $2.50).*

AEGEAN COAST

OTHER SITES. The road that runs by the top entrance of Efes leads to the **House of the Virgin Mary,** where, according to a legend supported by some archaeological and literary evidence, she lived with the Apostle John and later by herself after leaving Jerusalem. *(See **Selçuk: Sights,*** p. 208. *8km. $15 cab ride or a treacherous 1½-2hr. walk).* Much closer to the Ephesus site are the **Caves of the Seven Sleepers,** easily reached by leaving Ephesus through the bottom gate, turning right at the "Seven Sleepers" sign, and walking 10-15min. Legend has it that seven youths fleeing religious persecution under Emperor Decius slept in the cave for what they thought was a night. Upon waking, they discovered that they had slept for 112 years, during which time Christianity had become the official religion of the Empire. Amazed by their story, Emperor Theodosias II built a church atop the caves and decreed that the sleepers' remains be buried there. All that remains of the church is a fence in front of the cave. The youths' tombs are atop the hill by the fence. *(Open 24hr. Free.)*

SELÇUK ☎232

Selçuk is the most convenient base from which to explore nearby Ephesus, and offers several notable archaeological sites of its own, as well as a glut of carpet shops serving—or preying on—the large number of tourists who pass through the town every year. Selçuk's Byzantine Castle dominates the skyline, though it is closed indefinitely for restorations. The İsa Bey Camii, the ruins of the Temple of Artemis, and the Basilica of Saint John, where the apostle is buried, lie just below. The House of the Virgin Mary *(Meryemana)*, where Mary supposedly lived out her last years, can also be reached from Selçuk. The town is home to the famous Camel Wrestling Festival, held annually during the third weekend of January near Pamucak Beach, a short dolmuş ride away (contact the tourist office for info).

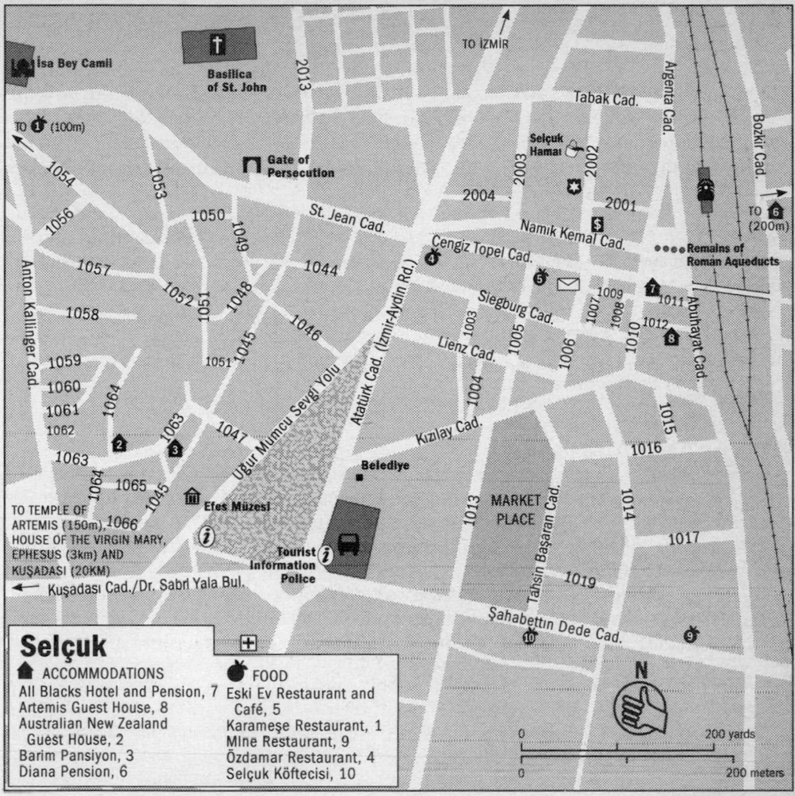

TRANSPORTATION

Buses: The **otogar** is at the intersection of şahabettin Dede Cad. and Atatürk Cad. To: **Ankara** (9hr.; 6:30, 11am, 11pm; $10); **Bodrum** (3hr., every hr. 8:15am-1:15am, $4.50); **Fethiye** (6hr., every 2hr. 8:15am-1am, $7); **İstanbul** (10hr., 5 per day 9:45am-12:30pm, $10); **İzmir** (1hr., every 30min. 6:20am-8:30pm, $1.25); **Marmaris** (4hr.; every hr. 8:45am-7:45pm, midnight, 1:30am; $5). **Minibuses** run to **Kuşadası** (20min.; every 15min. May-Sept. 6:30am-11:30pm, Oct.-Apr. 6:30am-8:30pm; $.80). From May-Sept., you can take a bus directly to **Pamukkale** (3hr.; 8:45, 9:15, 9:45am, 4, 5pm; $5). In the off-season, you must go first to **Denizli** (3hr.; 10:30am, 1, 4, 5:30pm; $3.75) and then catch a dolmuş to **Pamukkale** (20min.).

Trains: To: **Afyon** (10hr., 9:39am, $1.40); **Denizli** (4hr.; 10:37am, 5:04, 8:12pm; $2); **İzmir** (1½hr., 7 per day 6:42am-7:06pm, $.80).

ORIENTATION AND PRACTICAL INFORMATION

The İzmir-Aydın road, **Atatürk Cad,** is one of Selçuk's main drags. **Dr. Sabri Yayla Bul.,** also called **Kuşadası Cad.,** meets Atatürk Cad. from the west, and **şahabettin Dede Cad.** meets Atatürk Cad. from the east to form the town's main crossroads.

Tourist Office: 35 Agora Çarşısı, Atatürk Mah. (☎892 63 28; fax 892 69 45; info@selcukephesus.gen.tr; www.selcuk.gov.tr), at the intersection of Kuşadası Cad. and Atatürk Cad. Free maps. Open M-F 8am-noon and 1-5pm; Apr.-Dec. also open Sa-Su 9am-5pm.

Banks: Türkiye İş Bankası, 17 Namık Kemal Cad., İsabey Mah. (☎892 61 09 or 892 65 14), under the aqueduct. Exit the PTT, turn left, and walk 1 block. **Currency** and **traveler's check exchange** and a Cirrus/MC/Plus/V **ATM.** Open M-F 8:30am-5:30pm.

Hamam: Selçuk Hamamı, 2002 Sok., No. 3 (☎892 61 98). Bath and massage $8; special cream massage $4. Open F noon-5pm for women only; daily 7am-midnight for men and tourists of both sexes.

Police: (☎892 60 16). Office beside Türkiye İş Bankası, and a booth at the corner of the otogar on Atatürk Cad.

Hospital: (☎892 70 36), across Kuşadası Cad. from the tourist office.

Internet Access: Net House Cafe, 7/A Siegburg Cad. (☎892 23 70). To the right, off Atatürk Cad. when walking away from the otogar.

PTT: 1006 Sok., No. 9 (☎892 90 65 or 892 64 25), 1 block west of All Blacks Pension (away from train tracks) on Cengiz Topel Cad. Full service M-F 8:30am-12:30pm and 1:30-5pm. **Currency, traveler's check exchange,** and **phone** open daily 8am-11pm.

Postal Code: 35920.

ACCOMMODATIONS

Selçuk is notorious for having some of the wiliest bus station hawkers in Turkey. Claiming to represent the better pensions, they tell visitors that all pensions in town—except for theirs—are closed. Pension prices are set by the municipality and posted on a board on Atatürk Cad., on the right side in the direction of İzmir. Avoid anyone offering you a spot at their "slightly more expensive" pension. Many of the pensions listed below will pick you up from the bus station if you call, rather than have you face the gauntlet of touts working for their competitors.

AEGEAN COAST

Artemis Guest House ("Jimmy's Place"), Atatürk Mah., 1012 Sok., No. 2 (☎892 61 91; jimmy@egenet.com.tr; www.artemisguesthouse.com). Guests are greeted with a refreshing drink, shown to a carpeted room complete with bath, towels, and fans, and invited to dinner in the garden (nightly, $2.50) or to watch one of owner Jimmy's 100 movies. Staff goes out of its way to please guests and is always working to improve the place. Excellent organized travel information. One of the few gay-friendly establishments in Turkey. Arranges group excursions to the hamam for women. Free transportation to Ephesus, and to Pamucak and Tusan beaches in the morning and from Kuşadası harbor. Internet $.80 per hr. Laundry $2.50. Breakfast $1.60. $5 per person. 2 hotel-style rooms with A/C $30 per night.

All Blacks Hotel and Pension, Atatürk Mah., 1011 Sok., No. 1 (☎892 36 57; abnomads@egenet.com.tr; www.allblacks.8m.com). Named after the famous Kiwi rugby squad. Some of the nicest rooms in the budget circuit, with ultra-clean tile floors and bathrooms. Rooftop terrace with views of the fortress. The ideal place to congregate, relax on cushions, or watch the storks perched on the nearby Roman aqueducts in summer. Wonderful staff. Free transportation to and from Ephesus, Pamucak Beach, and Kuşadası harbor. Ring the bell to enter. Guest kitchen. Laundry $3.75 per load. Internet $1.50 per hr. Breakfast $1.75. Singles $6; doubles $9.

Australian New Zealand Guest House, 7 Prof. Miltner Sok. (☎892 60 50; www.anzturkishguesthouse.com), behind the museum. A backpacker's haven. Terrace on roof with nightly BBQs and Turkish dinners (vegetarian options available). Very sociable. Free service to Ephesus, Kuşadası harbor, and the beach. Trips to şirince for groups of 3 or more. Boat tickets to Samos (Apr.-Nov., $30) and winter trekking packages available. 20% discounts for trekking groups larger than 7. Laundry $3.75 per load. Internet $1.50 per hr. Breakfast and dinner included. Dorms $7; double with bath $15.

Diana Pension, Zafer Mah., 3004 Sok., No. 30 (☎892 12 65; jesseakin@hotmail.com), beyond the railroad tracks. After crossing the bridge, walk 50m with the track on your left, turn right onto 3008 Sok., walk 3 blocks, and turn left onto 3004 Sok., or just follow the signs. Immaculate rooms and bathrooms in a more distant and peaceful location. Cozy garden and terrace with views of the castle. Free transport to Ephesus and şirince. Guest kitchen. 24hr. hot water. Laundry $3.75. Breakfast $1.50. $3.75 per person with bath. Double with A/C $19.

Barım Pansiyon (☎892 69 23), Müze Arkası Sok. Behind the museum. Great decor with bamboo roofing. Hanging plant canopies over the entranceway and garden. Little English spoken. 24hr. hot water. Breakfast $1.75. $4 per person with bath.

FOOD AND ENTERTAINMENT

On Saturdays, locals and tourists flock to huge open-air markets, which feature fresh fruit, cheeses, and spices.

Karameşe Restaurant (☎892 04 66), Tarihi İsabey Camii Önü, beside İsa Bey Camii. The decorating scheme makes this restaurant a sight in itself. A maze of stone paths wind through miniature waterfalls, fountains, and grass-covered gazebos. Bench seating or low tables surrounded by cushions. In the rear, a miniature zoo is home to swans, ostriches, and monkeys. All *ayran* and yogurt made with the milk from on-site cows. *Gözleme* $1.75; *kebap* $1.50; *ayran* $.40. Open daily 9am-3am.

Özdamar Restaurant, 33 Cengiz Topel Cad., Atatürk Mah. (☎892 00 97). Outdoor seating with a view of the castle. Dine on just about any Turkish dish imaginable. Choose from pizza (Italian or Turkish), fish *kebaps* ($2.75), *döner kebap* ($1.50), cold dishes ($.75-1.25), or mixed grill ($2.25). Open daily 8am-midnight.

Eski Ev (Old House) Restaurant and Cafe, Atatürk Mah., 1005 Sok., No. 1/A (☎892 93 57), around the block from the PTT. Quiet dining in the garden of a century-old home. Lamb *şiş kebap* $1.75; *meze* $1.25; bottle of Pamukkale wine $5.25. Open daily 8:30am-1am.

Selçuk Köftecisi, (☎892 66 92), across şahabettin Dede Cad. from the otogar. Patronized by more locals than tourists. Serves *köfte* ($1.25), *şiş* ($1.30), and a deliciously light *keşkül* (pudding, $.60). Open daily 7am-11pm.

Mine Restaurant, 15 şahabettin Dede Cad., Atatürk Mah. (☎892 31 07). Standard look-and-choose restaurant a pleasant distance from the incessant haggling of carpet vendors. *Taş kebap* (meat stew) $1.25; mixed grill $2.25; Turkish breakfast with boiled egg or omelette $1.40. Open daily 8am-midnight. 10% *Let's Go* discount.

SIGHTS

Selçuk's archaeological sights have always been overshadowed by the towering majesty of neighboring Ephesus, but as insights into Muslim, Ancient Greek, and early Christian religious life, they should not be missed.

BASILICA OF ST. JOHN. The colossal and unadvertised Basilica of St. John lies on the site of the apostle's grave. The Byzantine church's entrance is inaccurately called the **Gate of Persecution,** referring to a frieze once believed to depict a Christian being thrown to a lion—it in fact shows Achilles slaying a lion. The 6th-century church, built by Emperor Justinian, would be the seventh-largest cathedral in the world if it were reconstructed today. *(Open daily 8am-7pm. $1.50, students $.75.)*

İSA BEY CAMİİ. This stunning Selçuk mosque lies at the foot of the hill on which the Basilica of St. John and the Ayasoluk Castle stand. Built in 1375 on the order of Aydınoğlu İsa Bey, it features columns taken from Ephesus, which the Ephesians had pilfered from Aswan, Egypt. Restored in 1975, the mosque has regained much of the simple elegance that was eroded by 600 years of wear and tear. Inside the courtyard is an enormous collection of well-preserved Ottoman and Selçuk tombstones and inscriptions. The mosque's facade features Persian-influenced geometric black and white stone inlay. *(Open 10min. before and 10min. after times of prayer.)*

EFES MÜSEZİ. Back in town, directly across from the town's tourist office, Selçuk's **Efes Müzesi (Ephesus Museum)** houses a world-class collection of recent Hellenistic and Roman finds from Ephesus. Most of the earlier finds are in Vienna. The collection includes the infamous statue of **Beş** (Priapus) that graces postcards throughout Turkey, rather tastelessly displayed in a darkened glass box, where you have to push a button for a 10-second peep. While this particular piece was found in the vicinity of the Ephesian brothels, the image of the generously endowed, erect demi-god was not a smutty novelty, but rather a common piece of iconographic currency in the ancient world. The museum also houses an excellent collection of statuary, including a multi-breasted statue of Artemis, exquisite busts of **Eros, Athena, Socrates,** and emperors **Tiberius, Marcus Aurelius,** and **Hadrian.** *(Open daily 8:30am-noon and 1-7pm; in winter 8:30am-noon and 1-5:30pm. $3.)*

TEMPLE OF ARTEMIS. A few hundred meters down Dr. Sabri Yayla Bul. are the sad remains of the **Temple of Artemis.** Once the largest temple in existence and among the Seven Wonders of the Ancient World, it now consists of a lone reconstructed column twisting upward from a bog that approximates the area of the temple's foundation. *(Open daily 8:30am-5:30pm. Free.)*

HOUSE OF THE VIRGIN MARY. Nearer to Selçuk than to any other town, but still a $15 round-trip cab ride away, the tranquil **House of the Virgin Mary** lies 100m off the road from Ephesus to **Bülbüldağı** (Nightingale Mountain). About five years after the death of Christ, St. John is said to have accompanied the Virgin Mary to Ephesus, where they lived in a small house on the slopes of Bülbüldağı. It is a popular pilgrimage destination for both Christians and Muslims, who leave wishes and prayers in the form of tissues tied to chain-link screens. Daily services in the evenings at the house, as well as a 10:30am Sunday mass.

ÇAMLIK STEAM LOCOMOTIVE MUSEUM. Built over the old train station in Çamlik, a short dolmuş ride from Selçuk, this open-air museum exhibits some 30 steam engines once used on the Turkish railways. The oldest, which entered service in 1887, ran on wood rather than coal. Little text is available about the trains, but placards give vital statistics, like manufacturer and maximum speed. *(Catch an Aydin-bound dolmuş and tell the driver you want Çamlik (every 30min., $.60). From the gas station, turn back along the highway toward Selçuk and make the 1st right.)*

DAYTRIP FROM SELÇUK: ŞİRİNCE

*To get to şirince, take the Şirince-bound **dolmuş** that runs from the Selçuk bus station (every 30min. 7:30am-8pm; in winter every hr. 8am-5pm; $.60). From Kuşadası, take the Selçuk-Kuşadası dolmuş ($.90) and switch minibuses at the Selçuk station. To reach St. John the Baptist Church from the dolmuş stop, walk into town with the mosque on your left and take your 1st right. Pass Erdem Pansiyon on your right and turn left at the Ocakbaşı sign. To reach St. Demetrios, turn right at the Ocakbaşı sign and walk to the end of the path.*

Şirince is a rustic enclave cradled in hills of olive and cherry trees—a perfect weekend getaway for those traveling east from Selçuk (7km) or from Kuşadası (25km). Historic churches and a tradition of fine lace handicrafts reflect a local blend of Turkish and Greek influences. şirince, meaning "charming," in Turkish, captivates visitors with cobbled lanes and lush, green hills.

The village also displays the remains of two 19th-century Greek churches. **St. John the Baptist Church** is marked by numerous Byzantine cupolas and a well-preserved Greek inscription dating from 1832. **St. Demetrios Church** was converted from a 19th-century Greek church to a 20th-century mosque after the 1923 Population Exchange (see **The Treaty of Lausanne,** p. 16). Today it is in disrepair, but the frescoes are still visible. The steps that the *muezzin* used are to the right as you stand between the church and the cliff.

Embroidered and crocheted handicrafts are on display in şirince's streets and in the bazaar. Some enterprising locals proffer these fineries in their homes—a sales technique usually initiated by a kindly offer of tea. Unfortunately, as more tourists

THERE'S SOMETHING ABOUT MARY Sixteen kilometers from Selçuk, on the tranquil, leafy slopes of Bülbüldağı (Nightingale Mountain), stands what local tradition, fragmentary archaeological and literary evidence, and now the Vatican say is the House of The Blessed Virgin. It is believed that Mary came here with the Apostle John about five years after the death of Jesus to live out the rest of her life. St. John's connection to Ephesus is well established—his tomb lies in the ruined Basilica of St. John in Selçuk. According to the New Testament, while on the cross, Jesus commended his mother to John's care, telling Mary, "Dear woman, here is your son," and to John, "Here is your mother." From that time on, the disciple took her into his home (John 19:25-27). Given the quantity and strength of evidence, it seems probable that Mary did come to Ephesus and finish her life there. Locating where she lived is a bit harder. Long forgotten to all but local Orthodox Christians who made yearly pilgrimages, the site was discovered toward the end of the 19th century by Lazarist Fathers following the visions of a bed-ridden German nun named Catherine Emmerich (1775-1824). She had never left Germany but could describe the hills surrounding Ephesus with perfect accuracy, leading the Lazarists to the ruins of a 6th- or 7th-century church built over the house. Subsequent archaeological examination has concluded that, in fact, the foundations of the church date from the first century AD. Catherine Emmerich also provided directions and a description of the Virgin's tomb, but as yet archaeologists have found nothing. The enshrined church and nearby spring remain in the care of the Lazarists, and have produced a number of miraculous cures.

come to enjoy this charming respite from the commercialism of coastal towns, the distinction between şirince and the westernized coast becomes less pronounced.

Accommodations in Şirince tend to be comfortable, but since the streets are unnamed, they can be a bit difficult to find. In July and August, call ahead to reserve a room. Signs for **Halil Pansiyon** are up the small hill across from the Artemis Winehouse at the entrance of town. Three cool and relaxing rooms share a bathroom. (☎898 31 28. Laundry $1.60 per load. Breakfast included. $6.50 per person.) The **Huzur Pension** is at the other end of town. After getting off the dolmuş, walk straight up the hill, passing the mosque and the entrance to the covered bazaar on your left. Old wooden cupboards line the bedroom walls of this 150-year-old home. The largest room accommodates up to five people. A triple and a double with bath are also available. (☎898 30 60. Guest kitchen available. Breakfast $2. $4.50 per person.) No English is spoken at either establishment.

Şirince is best known for its strong local wine, available in a variety of fruit flavors at many of the village's restaurants, or at the **Artemis Winehouse,** which also houses the **Şarap Evi Restaurant.** It is by far the largest and most elegant, but also the most commercial, restaurant for many miles around. From the dolmuş stop, Artemis is on your right as you walk away from town. With an unbeatable picturesque setting in a 150-year-old Ottoman schoolhouse, Artemis offers gourmet versions of traditional Turkish fare at standard prices and petite portions. (☎898 32 40. Salads $.80; stuffed mushrooms $1.60; beef $3.25. Wine $3-5 per bottle. Open daily 9am-midnight.) **Ocakbaşı Restaurant,** on a hill overlooking town, cooks delicious traditional Turkish *gözleme* ($.80) on the hearth in the center of the dining area. Stuffed grape leaves ($1.20) are made with leaves grown in their own garden. (☎898 30 94. Open daily 8am-midnight.)

AEGEAN COAST

KUŞADASI ☎256

Named for the pigeons that make their home in the town's 14th-century Genoese castle, Kuşadası ("Bird Island") could hardly have escaped the intense tourism it has received. These days, Kuşadası is an unabashed tourist town, catering to foreign travelers of all stripes. Its picturesque setting on sea-sloping hills, excellent sand beaches, and proximity to the magnificent archeological wonders at Ephesus, Priene, Miletus, and Didyma ensured its transformation a few decades ago from a quiet town to a grand resort. Kuşadası's broad tourist apparatus accommodates every group. Backpackers arrive by ferry from Samos and by bus from the north, and wealthy American and European tourists flood the carpet shops whenever their luxury cruise liners dock in the small harbor, dwarfing other ships and—from a distance—the town itself. Excellent budget hotels and towering, four-star luxury palaces are surrounded by myriad high-end jewelry and carpet shops. As many as 100 pubs dot the city.

TRANSPORTATION

Buses: The *garaj* is on Kahramanlar Sok., about 2km. from the center of town. Most hotels will either provide or pay for transportation from the *garaj*. You can get to the *garaj* from the downtown harbor area by boarding a dolmuş coming from Lady's Beach. Several bus companies serve Kuşadası, including **Pamukkale** (☎612 09 38). To: **Ankara** (9hr., 4 per day 8:30am-10:45pm, $13); **Antalya** (7hr.; 9:30am, 11pm; $10.50); **Bodrum** (2½hr.; 8:30, 9:30am, 6:30pm; $5.60); **Denizli** (3hr., 5 per day 6:30am-9:30pm, $5.60); **Fethiye** (5½hr.; 9:45am, noon; $10.50); **İstanbul** (9hr., 9 per day 9:30am-11:45pm, $13.25); **İzmir** (1½hr., every 30min. 6am-9pm, $2.50); **Marmaris** (4hr.; 10am, 12:30pm; $7.25); **Pamukkale** (3½hr.; 9am, return 5pm; $6.50). Pamukkale can also be reached by dolmuş via **Denizli.** Take the İzmir bus to get to the İzmir **airport.** Call ahead for bus tickets on weekends.

Dolmuş: City dolmuş run between the dolmuş stop on Adnan Menderes Bul. and the lot adjacent to the *garaj*, and also between the harbor area and the *garaj* ($.30). Intercity dolmuş head to **Selçuk** (30min., every 20min. 7:30am-midnight, $.90) via **Ephesus** (ask to be let off), and **Söke** (30min., every 30 min. 7am-11pm, $.90).

Ferries: Ekol Travel beats the official rate. 15% *Let's Go* discount. To **Samos** (1½hr.; daily 8:30am, 4:30pm; in winter 2 per week; $30 including port tax).

AEGEAN COAST

ORIENTATION

The duty-free shop, the **tourist office,** and the **customs office** are all in the port area. Ferry travelers are advised to pay the port tax ($10) in US dollars. The **garaj** is about 2km south of town on **Kahramanlar Sok.** Dolmuş depart from a separate dolmuş stop on **Adnan Menderes Bul.,** a few meters southeast of the intersection of Adnan Menderes Bul. and **İnönü Bul. Liman Cad.** runs inland from the tourist office, passing an ancient **kervansaray** and a covered bazaar. On the other side of the *kervansaray*, the broad, pedestrian-only **Barbaros Hayrettin Paşa Bul.** is home to the PTT, travel agencies, and several banks. Farther east on Atatürk Bul., which runs along the coast, is a medieval watchtower turned modern-day **police station.**

PRACTICAL INFORMATION

Tourist Office: 13 Liman Cad. (☎614 11 03; fax 614 62 95), on the corner of Liman Cad. and Güvercin Ada Sok. Open daily 8am-5:30pm; Oct.-Apr. M-F 8am-noon and 1:30-5:30pm.

Travel Agencies: Ekol Travel with **WorldSpan,** Kıbrıs Cad., 9/1 Buyral Sok. (☎614 55 91; fax 614 26 44). Cheap flights, ferry tickets, luggage storage, room search, message board, car rentals, and emergency help finding English-speaking doctors. 15% *Let's Go* discount on ferry tickets. Open May-Nov. daily 8:30am-10pm; Dec.-Apr. 9am-6pm.

Banks: Several dot the waterfront area. **Türkiye İş Bankası,** on the corner of Atatürk Bul. and Liman Cad., offers 24hr. Cirrus/MC/V **ATM.** Open M-F 9am-12:30pm and 1:30-5pm. **T.C. Ziraat Bankas,** on Barbaros Hayrettin Paşa Bul., changes cash and traveler's checks without a fee. Open 9am-12:30pm and 1:30-5:30pm.

English-Language Bookstores: Kuydaş Kitabevi, 8/B İnönü Bul. (☎614 18 28), sells newspapers, magazines, guidebooks, novels, CDs, and cassettes. Patio in back and modern Turkish art exhibits on the 2nd fl. Staff speaks little English. Open daily 9am-midnight. For cheaper stuff, including a used book collection (half the cover price) and a huge selection of postcards, try **Art Kitabevi,** 57 Sağlık Cad. (☎614 64 54), near the intersection of Sağlık Cad. and Barbaros Cad. Open daily 8:30am-12:30am.

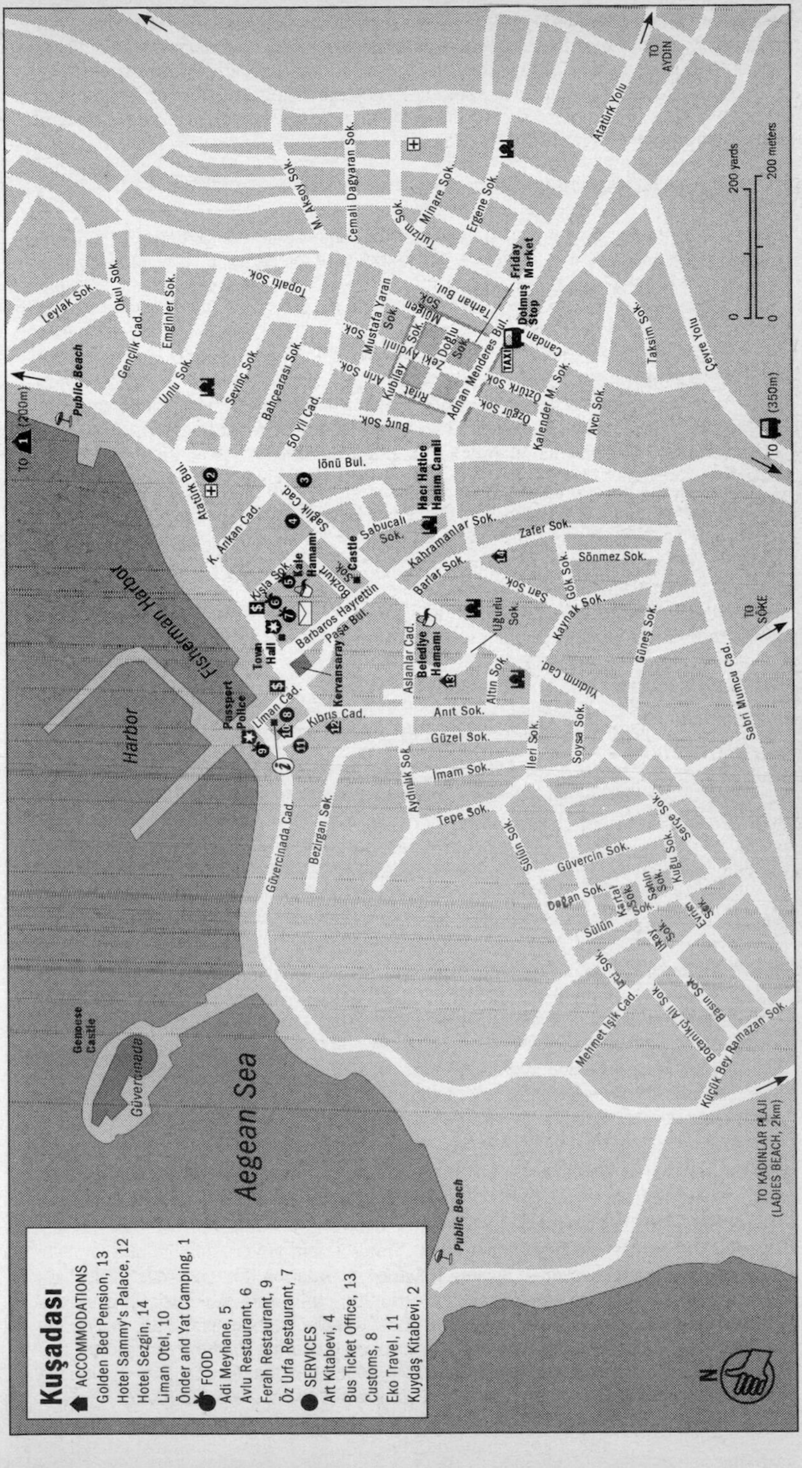

Kuşadası
ACCOMMODATIONS
Golden Bed Pension, 13
Hotel Sammy's Palace, 12
Hotel Sezgin, 14
Liman Otel, 10
Önder and Yat Camping, 1
FOOD
Adi Meyhane, 5
Avlu Restaurant, 6
Ferah Restaurant, 9
Öz Urfa Restaurant, 7
SERVICES
Art Kitabevi, 4
Bus Ticket Office, 13
Customs, 8
Eko Travel, 11
Kuydaş Kitabevi, 2
Aegean Sea
Güvercinada
Genoese Castle
Harbor
Fisherman Harbor
Public Beach
TO 1 (200m)
Passport Police
Town Hall
Kervansaray
Castle
Kale Hamamı
Belediye Hamamı
Hacı Hatice Hanım Camii
Dolmuş Stop
Friday Market
TAXI
TO AYDIN
TO SÖKE
TO (350m)
TO KADINLAR PLAJI (LADIES BEACH, 2km)
200 yards
200 meters
Atatürk Bul.
Atatürk Yolu
Adnan Menderes Bul.
Barbaros Hayrettin Paşa Bul.
Güvercinada Cad.
Liman Cad.
Kıbrıs Cad.
Sağlık Cad.
K. Arıkan Cad.
İönü Bul.
50 Yıl Cad.
Yıldırım Cad.
Sabri Mumcu Cad.
Mehmet Işık Cad.
Aslanlar Cad.
Gençlik Cad.
Çevre Yolu
Küçük Bey Ramazan Sok.
Kahramanlar Sok.
Barlar Sok.
Anıt Sok.
Güzel Sok.
İmam Sok.
Tepe Sok.
Bezirgan Sok.
Aydınlık Sok.
Zafer Sok.
Sönmez Sok.
Kaynak Sok.
Güneş Sok.
Güvercin Sok.
Sülün Sok.
Doğan Sok.
Taksim Sok.
Avcı Sok.
Kalender M. Sok.
Cemali Dagyaran Sok.
M. Aksoy Sok.
Minare Sok.
Ergene Sok.
Turizm Sok.
Tarhan Bul.
Mustafa Yaran Sok.
Topaltı Sok.
Leylak Sok.
Okul Sok.
Emgiller Sok.
Unlu Sok.
Sevinç Sok.
Bahçearası Sok.
Kışla Sok.
Bozkurt Sok.
Sabucalı Sok.
Uğurlu Sok.
Altın Sok.
İleri Sok.
Soysa Sok.
Sarı Sok.
Gök Sok.
Serge Sok.
Kuğu Sok.
Botanikçi Ali Sok.
Basın Sok.

Hamam: Kaleiçi Hamamı (☎614 12 92). Follow signs behind the PTT. Bath and massage $13.60; *çay* or coffee included. Both sexes bathe together. Open daily 8am-9pm.

Police: Headquarters, 6 Atatürk Bul. (☎614 13 82), and **Tourist Police** (☎614 10 22) are in the same building, past the *kervansaray* walking with the sea on your left.

Hospitals: Kuşadası Devlet Hastanesi, 30 Atatürk Bul. (☎614 10 26 or 614 16 14), on the waterfront, past the police station, with the sea on the left. Little English spoken. The Kuşadası **private hospital** *(Kuşadası Özel Hastane),* Türkman Mah. Ant Cad. (☎613 16 16) is a better bet for foreigners.

PTT: (☎614 33 11 or 614 15 79), across from the *kervansaray*, on Barbaros Hayrettin Paşa Bul. Open daily 8am-midnight; in winter 8am-7pm. Phones available 24hr. **Currency** and **traveler's check exchange**.

Postal Code: 09400.

ACCOMMODATIONS & CAMPING

Most budget accommodations are located along Kıbrıs Cad. and near Yıldırım Cad. Reservations are a good idea in July and August.

Liman Otel, Kibris Cad. Buyral Sok., No. 4 (☎614 77 70; fax 614 69 13; hasandegirmenci@usa.net; www.kusadasihotels.com/liman), on the waterfront, past the tourist office, with the sea on your right. Entrance in rear. A slightly more fashionable hotel that still manages to cater to backpackers and budget travelers. Friendly owner Hasan ("Mr. Happy"), a backpacker himself, provides inexpensive interior rooms with no view for those travelers who are willing to sacrifice scenery for savings, and beautiful seaside rooms for vacationers who want it all. Terrific location. Rooftop terrace. All except interior rooms have A/C. 10% discount on any bus ticket. Free transport to and from bus station and Ephesus. Internet $1.50 per hr. Laundry $2 per kg. Breakfast on rooftop $1.50. Dorm $5; interior rooms $7; rear rooms $10; harbor-side rooms $20.

Golden Bed Pension, 4 Aslanlar Cad. (☎614 87 08; fax 612 66 67; goldenbed_anzac@hotmail.com; www.kusadasihotels.com/goldenbed), off Yıldırım Cad. Turn right onto Uğurlu Sok. as you walk up the hill away from the harbor. Owned by a Turkish-Australian couple, this newly renovated pension offers marvelous views of Kuşadası harbor from the balconies and rooftop terrace. Common areas freshly tiled and painted. Free transportation to and from Ephesus; taxi from *garaj* paid. Gay-friendly. Laundry $2.50 per kg. Hamam 25% off. Internet $2 per hr. Nightly chicken and fish BBQs $5. Breakfast $1.60. Dorms $5; $7 per person; doubles with balcony $18.

Hotel Sammy's Palace, 14 Kıbrıs Cad. (☎612 25 88; mobile ☎(532) 274 21 29; fax 612 99 91; sammy@superonline.com; http://abone.superonline.com/~hotelsammyspalace). Ideal for fun-loving, gregarious backpackers always up for a rip-roaring late night complete with drinking games and belly dancing in the hotel common room/bar/dance hall (free nightly in summer). 32 well-furnished, carpeted, peaceful rooms, all with bath and most with balcony, make recuperating from the festivities enjoyable as well. Satellite TV and free movie showings in common room. Cab fares from *garaj* paid by Sammy. Internet access $2 per hr. Laundry $2 per kg. Hamam discount. Dinner and breakfast on rooftop $6. Breakfast alone $2. Roof $2; dorms $5; singles $11; doubles $16. 10% student discount.

Hotel Sezgin, 15 Kahramlar Cad., Zafer Sok. (☎614 42 25; fax 614 64 89; sezgin@ispro.net.tr; www.travelturkey.com). Hotel Sezgin heartily aims to please travelers, especially backpackers, with free transportation to and from the bus station, the Samos ferry, and Ephesus. Organizes a day trip to Priene, Miletus, Didyma, and Altınkum beach. Also 10% off tickets to Samos. Great water pressure. Satellite TV. Internet access $1.60 per hr. Laundry $3 per kg. Lounge and bar. Nightly fish, chicken, and beef BBQ ($3.20), with occasional belly dancing. Breakfast included. $5 per person. *Let's Go* readers stay 3 nights and get the 4th free.

Önder Camping (☎618 15 90 or 618 1518), 15min. walk north of town on Atatürk Bul., with the sea on your left. Swimming pool. Well-kept facilities. Laundry $4. Space for tents $1.60, plus $3.20 per person. Caravans $3.20. Electricity $1.60. 10% *Let's Go* discount. 10% discount at on-site restaurant. No tents provided.

Yat Camping (☎618 15 16). See directions to Önder. Swimming pool. Game room. Laundry $1.20. Space for tents ($1 plus $2 per person). Caravans $1.60. Electricity $.80. 10% discount at on-site restaurant. No tents provided.

FOOD

Avlu Restaurant, 15 Cephane Sok. (☎614 79 95), first left off Barbaros Hayrettin Paşa Bul. as you walk away from the sea. A standard *lokanta* with no menu, just a display of dishes to choose from. Simple decor, fresh food and low prices. Meat dishes $1.25-1.60. Vegetarian dishes $.80. *Tatlı* (dessert) $.40. Open daily 8am-11pm.

Öz Urfa Restaurant, 9 Cephane Sok. (☎614 60 70). A larger, slightly pricier restaurant with an English menu, filled with Turkish favorites. *Döner kebap* $2. Veggie *kebap* plate $2.80. Mixed *meze* plate $2.80. Open daily 8:30am-1am.

Adi Meyhane, 18 Kaleici Bahar Sok. (☎614 34 96), behind the PTT. A romantic nighttime spot, including open-air courtyard with lamp-lighting, fireplaces, and attractive stone walls. Live traditional Turkish music every night (9pm-2am). The most popular dish is Brain Salad ($1.60), but there are plenty of more standard options. Mixed grill $3.20. Beer $1.60. Open daily 9pm-3am.

Ferah Restaurant, 10 Liman Cad. (☎614 12 81). This seafood restaurant is a bit of a splurge, but offers excellent fish and a harbor view of Pidgeon Island. Cold salads $.80-1.20. Shrimp $3.20. Fish *kebaps* $5.60. Open daily 11am-midnight.

SIGHTS

Kuşadası's best-known sights are its shopping areas and its numerous sparkling beaches. While the **Grand Bazaar** and **Barbaros Hayrettin Paşa Bul.** are, contrary to the claims of shop owners, expensive places to shop, it doesn't cost anything to browse the carpet and jewelry stores.

BEACHES. Unfortunately, Kuşadası's clean and sandy beaches are overcrowded. **Kadınlar Plajı** (Ladies' Beach), just 3km from the city, is easily accessible by dolmuş from Adnan Menderes Bul., the otogar, or along the harbor, just in front of Türkiye Iş Bankası. *(10min., in summer every 3min. 7am-midnight, $.40).* Expect to pay to enjoy the sun *(Beach chair $1.60)*, and even more to enjoy the shade *(umbrella $1.60 extra).*

DILEK NATIONAL PARK. A nature reserve just 26km from Kuşadası, this is the best place for swimming, walking, and picnicking. It encompasses four beaches and houses over 30 animal species, including the Anatolian leopard. While overnight camping is not permitted in the park, Dilek offers daytime canyon hiking (6km from entrance gate), **sandy beaches** (İçmeler beach, 1km from the gate, the "first beach"), and **sand-and-pebble shores** (Aydınlık beach, 5km from the gate, the "second beach" and Karvakı beach, 7km from the gate, the "third beach"). Don't leave without seeing **Zeus Mağarası** (Zeus's Cave), opposite the sea, 100m outside the park entrance. Once rumored to be the site of hidden treasure, the cave is full of water bubbling up from the ground. *(Park open daily 8am-7:30pm; extended hours in July-Aug.; off-season 8am-6:30pm. $.80 per person; $1 per motorcycle; $2.80 per car. Dolmuş run from Adnan Menderes and the otogar every 15min. beginning 7:30am, $1.15.)*

PIGEON ISLAND. A trip to Kuşadası would be incomplete without a visit to **Güvercinada** (Pigeon Island), the jutting peninsula that is home to Kuşadası's namesake. Explore the 14th-century Genoese castle, which was converted into a military outpost by the Ottomans in the 19th century, and enjoy a glass of *çay* at any of the various tea houses. *(A 10min. walk from the tourist office with the sea on your right.)*

ENTERTAINMENT AND NIGHTLIFE

The nighttime music and madness of the appropriately named **Barlar Sok.** ("bar street") spills out into streets so brightly lit, it might as well be daytime. The side streets behind the PTT are home to a host of roofless bars featuring live European and Turkish rock. The combination of dozens of discos and no weekday cover charge makes for easy club-hopping.

Heaven, 13 Sakarya Sok. (☎613 24 56), behind the PTT. One of the largest, most popular music clubs. Decorated in mock-Roman style with vines, columns, and a few authentic artifacts, Heaven blasts live Turkish pop in its open-air courtyard every night from 1-4am. Beer $2.80; cocktails $5.60. Cover $6.40 F-Sa, includes 1 domestic drink. Open May-Sept. daily midnight-4am.

Hoppa Club, 15 Tuna Sok. (☎614 98 74), behind the PTT. Another Roman-style bar with columns and statues. Live nightly music (1-4am) in a more intimate setting. Beer $3.20; cocktails $4.80. Cover $8 F-Sa. Open daily 10pm-4am.

Ecstasy, 8 Sakarya Sok. (☎612 81 90), across from Heaven. A disco with sleek decor and plenty of polished steel. "Underground" music along with videos on a large screen. Beer $2.40; *rakı* $3.20; mixed drinks $5.60. Cover $6 F-Sa, includes 1 domestic drink. Open daily 10pm-4am.

Another Bar, 10 Tuna Sok., behind the PTT. A crowded disco with tables amid trees in a roofless courtyard. Live groups perform nightly 11pm-1am, followed by DJ spins until 4am. Beer $2.40; cocktails $4.80. Cover F-Sa $8. Open May-Sept. 10pm-4am.

Jimmy's Irish Bar (☎612 13 18). The first bar on the right on Barlar Sok. The best of several Irish bars in town, Jimmy's fills even in the afternoon when the competition is dead quiet. Wait until 1am for partyers to dance on the tables. "Sheep Brain" (Archers, Grenadine, and Baileys), "Sperm of Barmen" (Archers, Baileys, and Vodka), and other mixed drinks $4; cider $2.80; large *Efes* $2.40. Open daily 8pm-4am.

DAYTRIPS FROM KUŞADASI

Priene, Miletus, and Didyma, arranged in a line along the coast toward Bodrum, make an excellent daytrip from either Selçuk or Kuşadası. Although the 3 sites are grouped as one entity, each has something unique to offer. Priene, set amid beautiful forested slopes, outdoes the other two for its environs, which impart an eerie sense of what the ancient city must have been at its peak. Miletus, in the center of a vast plain, boasts the most ruins of the three, including an impressive 15,000-person theater. Though Didyma's ruins include only one temple, now in the midst of town, it was one of the largest and grandest in the ancient world. While organized guided tours often seem like a canned experience, taking one will ensure that you can visit all three sites in one day, a difficult feat for the independent traveler.

PRIENE (GÜLLÜBAHÇE)

Open daily 8am-8pm; in winter 8am-5pm. $1.20; students $.40. Take the Kamil-Koç bus from Selçuk (9hr., 9:15am, $16). From ***Söke*** *(see p. 233)—easily reached from Kuşadası or Selçuk by dolmuş or on any Bodrum-bound bus—take a* ***dolmuş*** *to* ***Priene*** *(20min., every 15min. 7:30am-7pm, $.40).*

Priene is the most physically demanding of the three sights. Expect a steep uphill climb. Though it was a leading member of the Panionic League, which controlled the Aegean coast after the decline of the Hittite empire, Priene lingered in the shadow of its neighboring economic rival, Miletus. The city's population never exceeded 5000. While its neighbors excelled in commerce, Priene devoted its resources to religion and sports. The city's ruins, on a plateau before the walls of Mt. Mycale, overlook the wanderings of the River Meander. Uphill from the dolmuş stop, ancient walls encircle the ruined city. From the main entrance, the path leads to what was once the main avenue of ancient Priene. Ahead and on the left is the **prytaneum,** the vaulted hearth of the city's sacred flame. Brought from

Athens by the first settlers, the flame was extinguished only when the city was invaded. It was here that diplomats were received, heroes and athletes rewarded, and city administrative matters discussed. Beyond the prytaneum is the unmistakable **bouleterion,** or Senate House, a well-preserved, elegant auditorium. Sacrifices were offered on the inner chamber's huge marble altar to mark the opening and closing of Senate sessions. Only the foundation of the altar remains.

The large building on the right of the path is the **upper gymnasium,** the older of Priene's two educational and physical training facilities. Follow the path to the right in front of the gymnasium and the **Sanctuary of the Egyptian Gods** will be on the right. It was here that Egyptians who arrived in Priene to trade worshipped the gods Isis, Serapis, and Anubis.

Make a left and walk uphill to the 5000-person **theater.** In the front row are five **thrones of honor** with dignified bases carved to look like lions' paws. In front of the theater, beside the upper gymnasium, stands a **Byzantine Church,** built in the 6th century AD with the stones of previous structures. Climb up the hill behind the church to reach the **Temple of Athena,** an edifice that reflects the height of Hellenistic architecture. Alexander the Great financed the project, and Pytheos, the architect whose *chef d'œuvre* was the Mausoleum of Halicarnassus (one of the Seven Wonders of the Ancient World; p. 229), designed it. The temple retains largely intact front steps, interior floors, and five complete columns. The path along the side of the temple takes you to the remains of the **private houses** of Priene, unusually well-preserved examples of pre-Roman domestic architecture.

Exit the Athena Temple from the front, turn right on the stone path, and you'll approach the **Alexandreion,** where Alexander the Great is believed to have resided while liberating Miletus. Later, the house became a sanctuary devoted to him. Beyond is the **Temple of Cybele,** where mostly poor residents worshipped.

Walk back past the Temple of Athena, and the spacious **agora** will be on your right. Women were allowed here only if accompanied by men, either their husbands or slaves. At the center, a public temple once hosted official ceremonies and sacrifices. Beyond the agora is the 3rd-century BC **Temple of Olympic Zeus.** From below the temple, you can gaze down on the **stadium** and lower **gymnasium,** with the names of young athletes inscribed on their walls. On either side of the main hall are small rooms once used for bathing and exercise.

MİLETUS (MİLET)

☎875 50 38 or 875 52 56. Site and museum open daily 8am-8pm; in winter 8am-5:30pm. $1.20, students $.40. Take the Kamil-Koç bus from Selçuk (9hr., 9:15am, $16). From ***Söke*** *(see p. 233)—easily reached from Kuşadası or Selçuk by dolmuş or on any Bodrum-bound bus—take a* ***dolmuş*** *to* ***Miletus*** *(45min., every hr. 7am-2pm, $1.25).*

Now surrounded by arid plains, Miletus once sat upon a thin strip of land surrounded by four separate harbors. Envied for its prosperity and strategic coastal location, the city was destroyed and resettled several times. Eventually, it suffered the same fate as its Ionian neighbors—the silting of its harbors. For centuries, Miletus was a hotbed of commercial and cultural development. In the 5th century BC, the Milesian alphabet was adopted as the standard Greek script. Miletus later became the headquarters of the Ionian school of philosophers, including Thales, Anaximander, and Anaximenes. The city's leadership, however, faltered in 499 BC, when Miletus organized an unsuccessful Ionian revolt against the Persian army. The Persians retaliated by wiping out the entire population of the city, massacring the men and selling the women and children into slavery.

Today, the site's main attraction is the **theater,** which sat 15,000 and was originally at the water's edge. Clearly visible from the Priene-Didyma highway, the strikingly well-preserved structure dates from Hellenistic times, though most of the visible portion was constructed by the Romans. The remaining portions of Miletus are marshy most of the year, sometimes even during the summer. To the right of the theater as you enter the site is a restored 15th-century **kervansaray.** The footpath meandering to the right of the theater leads to the largest Roman baths in

Anatolia, the **Faustina baths,** erected by the wife of Roman Emperor Marcus Aurelius. Visible beyond the baths is the dome of the 15th-century **Ilyas Bey Complex,** which included mosques, *medreses*, and baths, among other unidentified buildings. Further along the road past the baths are the north and south **agoras.** Today, only the pediment on which the gate to the south agora stood is visible, the grand entrance having been moved to Berlin's Pergamon Museum in 1905. Just north of the **south agora** is the **bouleuterion,** where the government assembly met. From the front of the bouleuterion, the **Sacred Way** runs past the **Nymphaeum, Hellenistic Gymnasium, Ionic Stoa,** and **Capitol baths** on the right, and the **north agora** on the left, to the **Delphinium,** the sanctuary of Apollo Delphinus. The temple, whose priests were all sailors, was first constructed to honor Apollo, who supposedly transformed himself into a dolphin and led the Cretans to Miletus.

Beyond the structures that border the Sacred Way lie a few isolated remains. Standing at the north end of this avenue, with the theater to your left, you can see the early 16th-century **Dervish Lodge** to the right, where followers of the Muslim mystic Mevlana studied. The **Inn of Fleas** is to the left. Though the name is not the original one, it is apt for the *kervansaray*-style structure today. Farther to the left is the **synagogue,** built in the Roman Period. North is where the two white marble lion-statues used to sit, nobly surveying the harbor known as the Bay of Lions. There is a small, rather underwhelming **Archaeological Museum** about 500m before the main entrance, featuring sculpture from the site. Even this fragment gives a good impression of the city's former wealth and beauty.

DİDYMA (DİDİM)

Open daily 8am-7pm; in winter 8am-5pm. $1.60. Take the Kamil-Koç bus from Selçuk (9hr., 9:15am, $16). From ***Söke*** *(see p. 233) take a* ***dolmuş*** *to* ***Didyma*** *(1hr., every 15min. 7am-7pm, $1.30).*

Ancient Didyma was the site of a sacred sanctuary to Apollo and an oracle that brought in most of the city's fame and wealth. The first Didyma oracles date from about 600 BC, 100 years before the Persians destroyed the sanctuary. It lay deserted until Alexander the Great's arrival, which supposedly inspired the arid spring miraculously to flow anew. The present sanctuary was begun during the 2nd and 1st centuries BC, but the original plans, like those for Alexander's empire, proved too ambitious and were never completed.

The **temple** at Didyma was the third-largest sacred structure in ancient Asia Minor, after the Temple of Artemis at Ephesus and the Temple of Hera on Samos. As virtually nothing remains of either, the sanctuary at Didyma is the best surviving example of colossal temple architecture. Many of its marble slabs weigh more than 1000kg each. During the Roman period, the unfinished temple attracted pilgrims from all over ancient Greece. A church was constructed on the site in 385 AD after Emperor Theodosius I outlawed pagan oracles, but it suffered extensive damage from an earthquake in 1500. The sacred road from Miletus to Didyma ended at the temple gates. The statues that once lined the final stretch were carried away by the British in 1858 and have been replaced by souvenir shops.

Inside the main gate rests the famous bas-relief of a giant **Medusa head,** once part of an ornate frieze on the temple's exterior. The building's size is only apparent from the stairway to the main facade. All that remains of the more than 100 massive columns are the bases and lower sections. To transport these mammoth chunks of marble, the Greeks constructed long shafts of stone leading to the temple site, lubricated them, and slid the building materials over the slippery surface.

In front of the temple is the spring that the priestesses supposedly tapped when receiving prophecies from Apollo. Begin in the forecourt at the **Hall of Twelve Columns** (also known as the *pronaos*) and continue to the **Hall of Two Columns** (also the *cresmographeion*, or oracle hall), where visitors waited for pronouncements. A sloping corridor leads down to the **sanctuary.** The southeast corner of the **temnos** (the sacred area around the temple) has traces of another **sacred fountain** as well as the foundations of a temple that housed a bronze statue of Apollo.

PAMUKKALE AND APHRODISIAS

PAMUKKALE (HIERAPOLIS) ☎258

Whether as Pamukkale (Cotton Castle) or ancient Hierapolis (Holy City), this village has been drawing the weary to its thermal springs for more than 23 centuries. The Turkish name refers to the surface of the shimmering, snow-white limestone, shaped over millennia by calcium-rich springs. Dripping slowly down the vast mountainside, mineral-rich waters foam and collect in terraces, spilling over cascades of stalactites into milky pools below. Legend has it that the formations are solidified cotton (the area's principal crop) that giants left out to dry.

Overshadowed by natural wonder, Pamukkale's well-preserved Roman ruins and museum have been remarkably underestimated and unadvertised; tourist brochures over the past 20 years have mainly featured photos of people bathing in the calcium pools. Aside from a small footpath running up the mountain face, the terraces are all currently off-limits, having suffered erosion and water pollution at the feet of tourists. While it is not open for bathing, the site is still worth a visit. Although many travelers come to Pamukkale only as a hasty daytrip from Kuşadası or Selçuk, you may want to consider spending the night in the village to best take advantage of its relaxing atmosphere and wealth of sights.

TRANSPORTATION

Buses to Pamukkale stop in Cumhuriyet Meydanı in the center of **Pamukkale Köyü (village).** Most direct buses come from Kuşadası and pass through Selçuk (3½hr.; daily May-Aug. 9am, return 5pm; $6.50), but the more common route is through Denizli (see **Denizli: Transportation,** p. 220). **Dolmuş** run between Denizli and the beginning of the Pamukkale walking path, where Atatürk Cad. meets Mehmet Akif Ersoy Bul. (25min., every 15min. in summer 7am-11pm, $.40). Alternatively, a Pamukkale pension can arrange free pick-up from the Denizli otogar, with the added benefit of bypassing the barrage of pension hawkers at the dolmuş stop.

ORIENTATION AND PRACTICAL INFORMATION

Pamukkale is roughly divided into two areas. **Pamukkale Köyü,** at the foot of the white mountain, is home to many hotels and restaurants. The **Pamukkale site** encompasses the mountain itself, the calcium-rich **pools,** and the ruins of Hierapolis. The path leading to the mountain begins at **Mehmet Akif Bul.,** the road that dolmuş follow to and from Denizli. From the other side of the boulevard, **Atatürk Cad.** leads downhill to **Cumhuriyet Meydanı,** the village's small but central square.

Tourist Office: (☎272 20 77; fax 272 28 82), at the top of the hill, within the site. Open daily 8am-noon and 1:30-6:30pm; in winter M-F 8am-noon and 1-5:30pm.

Tourist Police: (☎272 29 09), at the top of the hill, within the site gates. Open 24hr.

Pharmacy: Denizli Eczanesi (☎272 29 20), Cumhuriyet Meydanı. Open daily 9am-midnight.

Banks: No banks or **ATMs** in Pamukkale.

PTT: Within the site. ☎272 21 21. Open daily 8:30am-6:30pm. Another branch is within the village on Yavuz Selim Cad., 300m from Cumhuriyet Meydanı. ☎272 28 52. Open M-F 8:30am-12:30pm and 1:30-5:30pm.

Site Postal Code: 20285. **Village Postal Code:** 20280.

ACCOMMODATIONS

All of the places listed below have swimming pools filled with Pamukkale thermal water and offer free pickup from the Denizli bus station.

Meltem Guest House, Atatürk Cad., 14 şirin Sok. (☎272 24 13 or 272 31 34; fax 272 24 14; meltemmotel@superonline.com.tr), just outside Cumhuriyet Meydanı. With a warm welcome to backpackers, Meltem offers satellite TV and movies, trips to Aphrodisias ($8), and daily trips to the Red Springs, a "secret waterfall," and a nearby mud bath for a "magic massage" ($12). The tidy rooms all have bath. In winter, guests stay at Meltem Motel, 2 blocks away, with a direct view of Pamukkale Mountain. Internet $1.20 per hr. Laundry $4. Breakfast $1.60. $4 per person; dorms $3.20; rooms with A/C and bath $8 per person; roof $1.60.

Koray Hotel, 27 Fevzi Çakmak Cad. (☎272 23 00 or 272 22 22; fax 272 20 95). Rooms with carpet and bath all face a beautiful inner courtyard, where guests can relax and eat their meals by the pool under grapevines. TV, salon, bar, and glassed-in rooftop restaurant for winter dining. Daily trips to Aphrodisias $8. Internet $1.20 per hr. Breakfast buffet and extensive dinner included. Prices may vary by season but are negotiable. A/C is extra. Singles $16; doubles $24.

Venüs Hotel, 16 Hasan Tahsin Cad. (☎272 21 52). Gleaming white walls and polished bathrooms lend the rooms an air of freshness. All have vine-adorned balconies. Laundry $4. Dinner $4. Breakfast $1.60. Doubles $8; triples $12.

Dört Mevsim Hotel, 19 Hasan Tahsin Cad. (☎272 20 09). Follow the signs for Venüs Hotel and continue 20m. Rooms in this quiet, removed setting overlook a pool and lush flowers. The easygoing owner organizes a daily trip to Aphrodisias for groups of at least 3 people ($6.40). Fantastic *saç kebap* dinners $2.40. All rooms with fans. Breakfast included. Camping $1.60. $4 per person.

FOOD AND ENTERTAINMENT

Most of the pensions serve excellent dinners, making dining elsewhere less of a necessity. The large buffet at the Koray Hotel is particularly impressive. The nightlife in Pamukkale is definitely not as raging as it is on the coast, but you can still find places to get a drink after dinner and dance into the early hours.

Konak Sade (☎272 20 02) on Atatürk Cad., just up the hill from Cumhuriyet Meydanı, on the left. An extensive establishment with a traditional Turkish salon on the upper level. Pool-side terrace seating with a view the Pamukkale mountain. Chicken grill $3.40; *konak sade kebap* $3.80; plenty of ice cream flavors for dessert $1.20. Free swimming for diners. Open daily 9am-2am.

Gürsoy Aile Restaurant, 3 Atatürk Cad. (☎272 22 67), in Cumhuriyet Meydanı. Simple outdoor dining. The house special is *gürsoy kebap* ($2), but salads, omelettes and pasta dishes ($1.20) will satisfy vegetarians. Fish $1.60. Unlimited lunch buffet $4. 10% student discount. Open daily 9am-midnight.

Han Restaurant, 11 Cumhuriyet Meydanı (☎272 25 71), next to Gürsoy Aile. Seating on a porch under thick foliage. Specializes in *kebap* dishes. *Adana kebap* $1.50; eggplant in tomato sauce $.80; mixed potato salad $.80. Open daily 9am-midnight.

Pamukkale Cafe-Bar-Restaurant, 13 Cumhuriyet Meydanı (☎272 21 90 or 272 22 86). Features several fixed menus: 2 are vegetarian ($2.40); others include a glass of wine and either fish ($3.20), chicken ($3.20), or *kebap* ($3.60). A la carte dining also available. Meat, chicken, or cheese sandwiches $1.20. Open daily 9am-midnight.

Paşa Disco and Bar, 1 Mehmet Akif Ersoy Bul. (☎272 21 47), where Atatürk Cad. meets Mehmet Akif Ersoy Bul., across from the entrance to the Pamukkale site. Tunes reverberate with the flashing lights overhead. Beer $1.60. Open daily 9pm-2:30am.

Harem Disco and Bar (☎272 22 52), on Atatürk Cad., uphill from Cumhuriyet Meydanı. A basement disco with modest dance space and carpet-covered sofas. A sign over the door reads *Damsız girilmez,* which means no entrance (for men) if not accompanied by a woman. Don't worry—it doesn't apply to tourists. Beer $1.60. Open daily 8pm-2am.

SIGHTS

MOUNTAINSIDE BATHS. A favorite getaway spot for vacationing Romans almost 2000 years ago, the warm baths at Pamukkale still bubble away. Elegant, shallow pools at the top of the hill (near the road that separates the site from Hierapolis) gradually deepen farther down the slope. The terraces near the center of the formation are the most intricately shaped. All pools are off-limits for bathing due to overuse, and the guards patrolling the site aren't shy with their whistles in cases of transgression. A narrow walkway leading up the face of the slope still allows shoeless visitors to touch the thermal waters, but the occasional gravel patches are hard on the feet and force visitors to concentrate on the ground instead of on the striking scenery. *(Open 24hr. $3.20, students $.80.)*

HIERAPOLIS MUSEUM. Directly across the street from the top of the walking path that leads up the mountain stand the stately archways that once formed the **city bath.** The bath's glossy marble interior has been converted into the spectacular Hierapolis Museum, which houses the finds unearthed by Italian archaeologists. *(☎272 20 34. Open daily 9am-6pm. $1.20, students $.40.)*

RUINS OF HIERAPOLIS. Just past the PTT is a wire fence, with an opening 50m up. From here you can walk to the right to explore the **nymphaeum,** a fountain temple dedicated to the Nymphs, and the remains of the 3rd-century **Temple of Apollo.** Next to the temple is the **Plutonium** (a.k.a. *Cin Deliği*, or Devil's Hole), a pit emitting toxic carbonic acid gas, now marked by a foreboding sign reading "Danger: Poisonous Gas." In ancient times, temple priests used the pit as proof of their power. Carved into the side of the mountain, the enormous **Grand Theater** dominates the vista. The theater is one of the best preserved in Turkey; much of the 25,000 person seating area and many carved stage decorations remain intact.

Farther up the hill and to the left (facing away from the mountain), are the haunting ruins of a 5th-century Christian **basilica,** dedicated to St. Philip, who was martyred in Hieropolis. Farther on the left and back down the hill along the road lie a 3rd-century **bath** that was later converted to a basilica, and a **necropolis,** holding some 1200 tombs and sarcophagi. The tombs vary considerably in size and architectural style, and include house-shaped tombs and rare **tumuli,** recognizable by their circular bases and squat, domed roofs. These plots were prime real estate—it was believed that proximity to the hot springs and vapor-emitting cracks would ease the trip to the underworld. *(The ruins dot the hillside, eventually following the road that leads to Karahayıt. The tourist office provides helpful maps of the sites.)*

SACRED FOUNTAIN. Don't leave Pamukkale without a dip in the sacred fountain at the **Pamukkale Motel Termal.** Warm, fizzy waters bubble at the spring's source, now blocked off to prevent divers from disappearing. On the pool's floor rest the remains of Roman columns, toppled by the earthquake that created the spring. Alongside the pool are cafes (beer $1.60; soft drinks $1.20; sandwiches $1.20) and souvenir shops. *(☎272 20 24. Pool open daily 8am-8pm; in winter 8am-6pm. $4 per 2hr.)*

OTHER SIGHTS. Four kilometers beyond the vehicle entrance to the Pamukkale site is **Karahayıt** (Red Source). Visitors can view the red spring free of charge and swim in the hot spring waters in a pool nearby. *($1.20 per person.)* Karahayıt is accessible by the "Karahayıt-Pamukkale" dolmuş, which leaves from Denizli, and pass by the bottom of the footpath entrance to the Pamukkale site. *(Every 15min. 7am-11pm, $.40.)* 15km beyond Karahayıt are the **mud baths of Gölemezli.** The mud baths are free and always open. They are accessible, however, only with a guided tour. The Meltem Motel offers daily tours that visit the baths.

DENİZLİ ☎258

Fourteenth century North African traveler Ibn Battuta called Denizli "a most important town," and today Denizli is the Aegean region's fastest growing city after İzmir. Garbage-strewn streets and perpetual construction work at the outskirts of town give a bad first impression, but pleasant restaurants and parks line Atatürk Bul. and İstiklâl Cad. An overabundance of chicken statues commemorate Denizli's ties to the poultry industry. Less touristed than nearby Pamukkale but far busier, Denizli offers a nice contrast, if only for a daytrip.

TRANSPORTATION. The otogar and train station (☎268 28 31) sit across from one another on busy İzmir Bul., at the eastern end of town. **Buses** run to: **Ankara** (6hr., 12 per day 7am-1am, $8.80); **Antalya** (5hr., 15 per day 4:30am-2am, $5.60); **Bodrum** (5hr., 5 per day 9:30am-9pm, $5.60); **Bursa** (8hr.; 7:30pm, midnight; $9.60); **Didim (Didyma)** (4hr., 3 per day 6:30am-3pm, $5); **Fethiye** (4hr., 3 per day 9:30am-5:30pm, $4.60); **İstanbul** (10hr.; 6 per day 8:30am-11pm, express after 8:30pm; $14.40); **İzmir** (4hr., 30 per day 4:50am-1am, $4.80); **Konya** (6hr., 5 per day 6am-8pm, $10.50); **Kuşadası** (4hr., take any İzmir bus and get off at Selçuk for a dolmuş, $4); **Marmaris** (4hr., 8 per day 5am-8:30pm, $4.80); **Nazilli** (1hr., take any İzmir bus, $2); **Nevşehir** (10hr., 10pm, $9.60); **Selçuk** (2hr., take any İzmir bus, $4); **Söke** (3hr., take any Didim bus, $4). For **Aphrodisias**, take an İzmir bus to Nazilli, then a minibus to Karacasu, then a dolmuş or taxi to Aphrodisias. **Pamukkale** (30min.; every 15min. 7am-11pm; in winter every 30min. 7am-8pm; $.40). Alternatively, call ahead to a pension in Pamukkale for free pickup. **Trains** run to **İstanbul** (14hr.; 5pm; $8.80); **İzmir** (5hr., 4 per day 5am-3:30pm, $3). There is a 20% student discount with ISIC.

ORIENTATION AND PRACTICAL INFORMATION. The otogar sits on **İzmir Bul.,** one of the city's main arteries. The road running along the side of the otogar opposite the PTT and bus offices, **Turan Güneş Cad.,** eventually ends at **Atatürk Bul.** Follow Atatürk Bul. to the left for 400m to reach Bayramyeri Meydanı, where **İstiklal Cad.,** Atatürk Bul., and **Atatürk Cad.** meet. The train station and otogar are open M-F 8:30am-noon and 1:30-5:30pm; in winter until 5pm. A small 24hr. **police** station (☎241 89 20) is in the otogar, and a larger **24hr. station** (☎241 89 21) is on Atatürk Bul, about 50m from Bayramyeri Meydanı. For medical assistance, go to the **Pamukkale University Hospital,** 42 Doktorler Cad. (☎241 00 34; fax 264 92 57), the best private hospital in the area. A **pharmacy, Atik Eczane,** is just outside of the otogar. (☎262 00 67. Open M-Sa 8am-8pm.) A **PTT** is on Atatürk Bul., 30m beyond the police station. (☎241 01 49. Open daily 7am-11pm.) There is another PTT in the otogar. (Open daily 8:30am-10pm.) **Postal code:** 20100.

ACCOMMODATIONS AND FOOD. **Denizli Pansiyon,** 1993 Sok., No. 14, is about 1km out of town in a pleasant, residential neighborhood. Tidy rooms, all with bath, encircle a shady courtyard with a marble fountain. Free transportation from the otogar and to Pamukkale. Daily trips to Aphrodisias ($8) can be followed by a relaxing swim at **Salda Lake** for an additional $5. (☎261 87 38; mobile ☎(532) 410 39 99; fax 264 49 46. Large breakfast included. Homemade Turkish dinner $4. $5.60 per person.) **Altın Pension,** Topraklık Mah., 633 Sok., No. 4, is a convenient 20m behind the otogar, and offers utilitarian rooms with bath and telephones. Some have TVs. (☎264 54 72; fax 242 76 02. Breakfast $1.60. Singles $4.80, with bath $6.40; doubles with bath $9.60.) For a cushier experience with bath, TV, A/C, and the occasional balcony, head to the 2-star **Yıldırım Hotel,** 632 Sok. No. 13, located conveniently behind the otogar. Ask to see several rooms, since size varies substantially. (☎263 35 90 or 264 50 75; fax 263 35 90. Breakfast included. Singles $12; doubles $16; triples $21; prices slightly negotiable.)

Grab a tasty *kebap, lahmacun* ($.60), or the generous "Special Kervan" mixed plate ($2.80) at the local chain, **Kervan Kebap,** 101 Atatürk Bul. (☎261 62 22), 200m beyond the PTT heading away from Bayrumyeri Meydanı, or 8 Çaybaşı Condağan Parks Karşısı (☎263 07 45), just off Mimar Sinan Cad. before it intersects Atatürk Bul. (Both open daily 8:30am-10pm.) For more sophisticated dining at reasonable prices, the posh **Denizli Evi-Restaurant,** 10 İstiklâl Cad., on the right after the Yeni Ulu Çınar Camii on Deliklıçınar Meydanı, is an excellent choice. (☎263 14 42. Cold dishes from $.80; filet mignon $3.20. Open daily 8pm-midnight.)

GEYRE (APHRODISIAS) ☎256

Aphrodisias's extensive ruins are surrounded by tobacco fields and framed by the majestic Baba Dağ mountain range. Still very much under excavation, the site is expected by some archaeologists to eclipse Ephesus in grandeur after another 50 or 60 years. The site's stadium is remarkably intact and impressive, and the museum is better in many respects than its counterpart in Ephesus.

The city has had nearly as many different names as the goddess Aphrodite, its Classical namesake, had lovers. Before its stint as the center of Greco-Roman worship of the goddess of love and fertility, Aphrodisias was named Ninoe, probably for Aphrodite's antecedent, the Akkadian goddess of love and war. It was later known as Lelegonpolis, Megalopolis, and Plasara until it became the center for the cult of Aphrodite. The rise of the Byzantine Empire saw the city's temples converted to churches, and the name to Stavropolis (City of the Cross), and later, Caria, from which the nearby modern village of Geyre probably takes its name.

Aphrodisias was well known as a center for astronomy, medicine, and mathematics, but above all as a showcase for sculpture. Chiseled from the famed white and bluish-gray marble quarried in the nearby foothills, the finer statues in the Roman Empire were often marked with an imprint from the celebrated Aphrodisian school, which is believed to have operated from the first century BC to the end of the 5th century AD. Under excavation since 1961 by a team from New York University, the modern site contains an enormous theater, an odeon, numerous temples, and the best-preserved Roman stadium in the ancient world.

TRANSPORTATION AND PRACTICAL INFORMATION. The best way to see the ruins is to take a daytrip from Pamukkale. When there is sufficient tourist interest, one bus leaves daily at 9:30am, picking up guests at the various hotels in Pamukkale. The bus departs Aphrodisias at 2:30pm (2hr., round-trip $10). However, many hotels make their own trips if there is enough interest. It is also possible to take a **dolmuş** to **Nazilli** from **Aydın** (45min., every 30min. 6am-midnight, $.90) or **Denizli** (45min., every 30min. 7am-9pm, $1.60), catch a dolmuş from Nazilli to **Karacasu** (30min., every 30min. 7:30am-10:30pm, $1.20), and take another dolmuş from Karacasu onto Aphrodisias (10min., every hr. 9am-6:30pm, $.40), although the service on the last leg of the journey may be unreliable. Karacasu is known for its beautiful red pottery, and artists sell their wares for around $.40 per piece about 500m from the dolmuş stop. The nearest **PTT** is in Geyre. **Postal code:** 09374.

ACCOMMODATIONS AND FOOD. Since Aphrodisias can be visited as a daytrip, there's not much reason to stay in town. The **Aphrodisias Hotel-Restaurant,** operated by Mestan Gökçe Bey (who speaks Turkish, French, and English), is 2km from the Aphrodisias entrance, beyond Chez Mestan. This more elegant hotel offers clean rooms with bath, central heating in the winter, and rugs on the tile floors. All rooms have balconies. (☎448 81 32; fax 448 84 22. Singles $16; doubles $20; triples $24. Camping $4.) The **restaurant** serves up a traditional Turkish plate ($4). Meals are held on the rooftop in winter and in the garden below in summer.

THE RUINS OF APHRODISIAS. At the entrance, the dirt road to the left leads to the large and still acoustically sound **theater,** built in the first century BC. On the theater's *proskenion* (horizontal slab running above the columns) is a dedication, "to the people of Aphrodisias," from Gaius Julius Zoilos, a freed slave who financed the building's construction. Further along the road and on the right, a number of columns mark the remains of the **agora.** The looming structure at the bottom of the hill is **Hadrian's Bath,** equipped with a sauna, frigidarium, and changing rooms. Farther down the road to the right is the **odeon,** once graced by an extraordinary marble mosaic stage, used for concerts and political meetings. The nine columns in front of the odeon form a court which archaeologists christened the **Bishop's Palace** because of the religious artifacts and statues unearthed there.

The highlights of a visit to Aphrodisias are the three magnificent structures at the back of the site. The soaring Ionic columns of the **Temple of Aphrodite** mark the original home of a famous statue of the goddess. Sculpted nearly 2000 years ago, the statue was similar in appearance to the many-breasted Artemis of Ephesus. So far, only copies of the original have been unearthed. The grand structure with elegant, spiral-fluted Corinthian columns and beautiful floral reliefs on its pediment is the **tetrapylon,** the gateway into the ancient city. The name, which means "four gateways" in Greek, refers to the four rows of four columns that comprise the structure. The ancient 30,000 seat **stadium** is one of the best-preserved of its kind. Even the marble blocks that once marked the starting line for foot races are still in the central arena. The first 3 rows of seats were replaced with a tall wall to protect the eager Roman audiences from the violent animal hunts and wrestling matches.

The **museum** near the site entrance displays a breathtaking collection of sculpture. Among the highlights are statues of Aphrodite, her priests, and a satyr carrying the child Dionysus. *(☎448 80 03. Site open daily 8am-8pm; in winter 8am-5pm. $3.20, students $1.20. Museum open daily 9am-6:30pm; in winter 9am-5pm. $3.20, students $1.20.)*

AYDIN ☎256

Aydın was once Tralles, an important Roman scholastic town. Today, despite its palm-lined boulevards and multitude of mosques, Aydın is more worthwhile as a base from which to explore the ruins of Nyssa than as an attraction in itself.

TRANSPORTATION. **Buses** connect Aydın to: **Bodrum** (2½hr.; 10:15am, 2pm, 3:30pm; $3.60); **Fethiye** (5hr., 8 per day 8:30am-11:30pm, $5.20); **İstanbul** (11hr., 5 per day 6am-midnight, $12); **Kuşadası** (1hr., every 10min. 6am-10pm, $1.60); **Marmaris** (2½hr., 14 per day 9:30am-10:30pm, $4). For **Pamukkale,** take a Denizli bus and switch to a dolmuş at the Denizli otogar. From the *gar* at the intersection of Adnan Menderes Bul. and Gençlik Cad., **trains** run to: **Denizli** (3hr., 3 per day 12:15-9:40pm, $1.60); **Söke** (1hr.; 9:30am, 12:30pm; $.60); **İzmir** (Basmane station; 3hr., 6 per day 6am-5:50pm, $1.60). **İstanbul** can be reached via Denizli, and **Selçuk,** via İzmir.

ORIENTATION AND PRACTICAL INFORMATION. The center of Aydın stretches along **Adnan Menderes Bul.,** which runs north-south on a long hill (800m). At a large traffic circle at the bottom of the hill (the southern end), Adnan Menderes Bul. meets **Denizli Bul.** The **otogar** is a short distance from that intersection on Denizli Bul. Restaurants, shops and banks line Adnan Menderes Bul. At the northern end of Adnan Menderes Bul., **Gazi Bul.** runs east-west. From the west, **Gençlik Cad.** meets Adnan Menderes Bul. 100m south of Gazi Bul.

The **tourist office** is on the southeast corner (diagonally from the otogar) of the roundabout where Adnan Menderes Bul. meets Denizli Bul. Staffers speak limited English but distribute helpful Aydin maps. (☎211 27 74; fax 211 28 61. Open May-Oct. 15 8am-noon and 1:30-5:30pm; Oct. 16-April 8am-noon and 1-5pm.) 24hr. MC/V **ATMs** and **TC Ziraat Bankası** are at the intersection of Adnan Menderes Bul. and Gençlik Cad. The **police** (☎225 25 06 or 225 25 07) are on Aydın Denizli Yolu, 500m past the tourist office in the direction opposite the otogar. The local **hospital,** the **SKK Hastenesi** (☎212 92 22), is 400m past the otogar on Denizli Bul., walking away from the tourist office. When heading north on Adnan Menderes Bul., turn left at

Gençlik Cad. and walk about 50m to get to the **PTT.** (Open daily for phones 8am-midnight, postal services 9am-5pm.) **Postal code:** 09000.

ACCOMMODATIONS AND FOOD. Most accommodations are on Adnan Mederes and Gazi Bul. The **Orhan Hotel,** 63 Gazi Bul., is a 20min. walk from the bus station or a short taxi ride. Orhan has clean, large, nicely furnished rooms with A/C, TV and private bath. Some rooms have terraces overlooking the bustling streets below. (☎212 17 13; fax 225 17 81. Breakfast included. Singles $9.60; doubles $12.80; triples $17.60.) The **Baltacı Otel,** 3 Sok., No. 17, is to the right on Gazi Bul. after you walk up Adnan Menderes Bul. Take your first right just after Ramazan Paşa Mosque. Baltacı offers spacious rooms with slightly worn-out furniture and old but tidy bathrooms. (☎225 13 20. Breakfast $1. $5.60 per person.)

Adnan Menderes Bul. is full of ice cream parlors and vendors selling *dondurma*, the gooey wonder that is Turkish ice cream ($.20-.80 per cone). Notable among these is the posh, A/C **Öz Süt,** 91/A Adnan Menderes Bul. (☎212 73 99. Open daily 8:30am-1am.) Plenty of restaurants offering Turkish cuisine also line this street. **Kervan Kebap ve Pide Salonu,** 46/A Adnan Menderes, a few doors up the hill from Kervansaray, is the place to go for Turkish pizza with meat or cheese ($.80) and even egg on top ($.20 extra). *şiş kebap* costs $1.60. (☎213 36 94. Open daily 8am-11pm.) **Kervansaray,** 36 Adnan Menderes Bul., serves *iskender kebap* for $1.60, *çorba* for $.60, and tasty rice pudding for $.80. (☎212 88 79. Open daily 8am-11pm.)

SIGHTS. The **Süleyman Bey Camii** is next to the *gar* (train station) at the intersection of Adnan Menderes Bul. and Gençlik Cad. Notable for the *muqarnas* (stalactite-esque decoration) on its two outer vaults, the mosque also boasts detailed floral brushwork and arabesques that grace the central dome. The **Ramazan Paşa Camii,** 1 block north of the Süleyman Bey Camii, at the intersection of Gazi Bul. and Adnan Menderes Bul., witnessed the meeting held on May 22, 1919, that began the Turkish War of Independence (see **The Cult of Mustafa Kemal,** p. 15). This mosque has simple stained-glass windows and a central dome finished with ornate leaf-like gilding from Turkey's Baroque period.

Tralles, an ancient city known in Roman times for its wealth, lies just north of Aydın. Little remains today; the most prominent features are the **Üc Göz** (Three Arches), which were once part of the gymnasium's vaults. The ruins offer a spectacular view of Aydın and the surrounding mountains. To get to Tralles, catch the dolmuş to **Topyataga** (15min., every 15min. 7am-11pm, $.50) from the corner of Adnan Menderes Bul. and Denizli Yolu. Once there, walk the 1km uphill.

The Aydın Lisesi, 300m past the PTT on Gençlik Cad., hosts the town's annual **traditional dance festival** in late June, drawing international children's dance teams.

DAYTRIP FROM AYDIN: NYSSA. About 30km from Aydın lies ancient Nyssa (in Turkish, *Nysa*, pronounced "Nee-sa"), which was built in the 3rd century BC in two parts, divided by a river. Once home to such thinkers as the Stoic philosopher **Apollonius,** Nyssa now boasts some fairly intact ruins. Just before the site entrance are the poorly preserved **library** and the **gymnasium.** The **stadium,** built to accommodate 30,000 spectators, is situated at the bottom of the ravine, just past the entrance. Seats at the northern end are visible. Most striking is the large **theater,** on the main road 50m past the entrance gate. In Roman days, theater-goers passed through **vomitoria** (archways) on both sides before going to their seats. Across the road from the theater, a circuitous dirt path leads down into a large ravine and through a 115m long **tunnel,** which used to channel the city's water supply. Walking through to the other side brings you back to the main road. Continue and you'll pass the remains of nine **vaulted shops** on your left and the less recognizable remains of the **market basilica** directly across from the shops. Signs point the way to the **bouleterion,** the smaller theater whose entrance gates are still intact. The **agora,** farther up from the bouleterion, contains impressive remains of ancient drainage gullies and three standing Ionic columns. Beneath a thin layer of dirt in the excavated corner of the agora are remnants of the original mosaic floor. The ruins of a Roman bathhouse lie beyond the agora and bouleterion, but as there is

AEGEAN COAST

no path leading to it, the bath is best viewed from across the ravine, just after you pass the ticket office. *(☎351 27 26. Open daily 8am-7pm. $1.20. To reach Nyssa from Aydın, take the dolmuş to Nazilli from the otogar and ask to be dropped at Sultanhisar (30min., $.90). From there you can walk up 3km to Nyssa. In scorching summer months, a taxi is a good option for the journey up, but the walk down is a relatively easy 20min. descent. Catch the dolmuş returning to Aydın on the north side of the highway, across from the arrival spot.)*

BODRUM PENINSULA

BODRUM ☎252

To quote İstanbul designer Cemil İpekçi, met on Cumhuriyet Cad. after an evening of bacchanalian excess: "You can fall in love with anyone in Bodrum, but when you leave, it's gone . . . it's the Bodrum love." With a reputation as the "Bedroom of the Mediterranean," it's easy to see why. Locals and visitors convene in time with the beat of music from countless dance clubs and bars that provides the pulse for a city that comes to life at night.

As light dawns on lazy days, travelers make for the surrounding Acadian Peninsula, home to some of Turkey's best beaches, secluded swimming coves, volcanic islands, and ancient ruins, with the persistence of Bodrum's daily touristic rhythm keeping steady all the while. If music be the food of love, then it is the tourist lira that pays for it. Complete with one of the Seven Wonders of the ancient world, the 4th century BC funerary monument to ancient Halicarnassus' king Mausolus, and as many fake Gucci purses and "I LOVE BODRUM" mugs money can buy, Bodrum is a community in the grand tradition of beach towns. Turkish jet-setters, international yachtsmen, backpackers and package tourists mingle in the day's sight-seeing, shopping, and water sports, searching the evening for "the Bodrum love."

TRANSPORTATION

Flights: The Bodrum Airport is about 45min. out of town. Buses to the airport depart from the otogar ($5). The **Turkish Airlines Office** (☎317 12 03/04), has moved outside of the town's center to the Oasis shopping center in Gümbet, accessible by dolmuş. Open daily 8:30am-7:30pm. To **Ankara** and **İstanbul** (1hr.; 5 per day 6:00am-10:15 pm; İstanbul $106, Ankara $98). Travel needs can also be met by the Turkish Air affiliate **Touralpin Agency,** 6 Çevat şakir Cad. (☎316 87 33 or 316 61 44) opposite the PTT, on your right as you head inland from the castle on Çevat şakir Cad.

Buses: The otogar is on Çevat şakir Cad. Some companies also have offices along Neyzen Teyfik Cad. Companies serving Bodrum include: **Ulusoy** (☎313 04 68 or 313 01 67), **Kamil Koç** (☎313 04 68), and **Pamukkale** (☎316 66 32).

Destination	Company	Duration	Times (daily)	Price	Students
Ankara	Kamil Koç	11hr.	8:30, 10:30pm	$15	$14
Ankara	Pamukkale	11hr.	5, 9pm	$15.50	
Ankara	Ulusoy	11hr.	8:30pm	$21.50	$18.50
Antalya	Kamil Koç	8hr.	9:30am, 10pm	$13	$12
Antalya	Pamukkale	8hr.	9:45am, 10:15pm	$12	
Aydın	Pamukkale	3hr.	9:30am, 4:30pm	$5.50	$5
Bursa	Kamil Koç	9hr.	8:45am, 8, 9:30, 11pm	$14	$13
Bursa	Pamukkale	8hr.	noon, 7:30, 9pm	$12	$11
Bursa	Pamukkale	10hr.	noon, 7:30, 9pm	$13	
Denizli	Pamukkale	5hr.	8:30, 10:30am, 3:30pm	$7.50	$7
Fethiye	Kamil Koç	5hr.	9:30am, 10pm	$9	$8
Fethiye	Pamukkale	5hr.	7:30, 9:45am, 12:30, 10:30pm	$7	
İstanbul	Kamil Koç	13hr.	8:45am, 8, 9:30, 11:30pm	$19	$18
İstanbul	Ulusoy	12hr.	7, 9pm	$26.20	$22.80

Destination	Company	Duration	Times (daily)	Price	Students
İstanbul	Pamukkale	12hr.	noon,7:30, 9pm	$21	
İzmir	Kamil Koç	4hr.	8:45am, noon	$9	$8
İzmir	Pamukkale	4hr.	4am-7pm	$7	
Kadası	Kamil Koç	3hr.	8:45am, noon	$6.50	$6
Kalkan	Pamukkale	7hr.	12:30pm	$9.60	
Kaş	Pamukkale	7½hr.	12:30pm	$10	
Konya	Pamukkale	10hr.	5pm	$16	
Köyceğiz	Kamil Koç	3hr.	9;30am, 10pm	$6	$5
Köyceğiz	Pamukkale	4½hr.	7:30, 9:45am, 12:30, 10:15pm	$5	
Kuşadası	Pamukkale	2½hr.	2am-6pm	$6	
Marmaris	Pamukkale	3hr.	9:30am-4:30pm	$5	
Milas	Kamil Koç	40min.	8:45am-11:30pm	$1.50	
Milas	Pamukkale	1hr.	2am-6pm	$1.80	
Pamukkale	Pamukkale	5hr.	8:30, 10:30am, 3:30pm	$7.50	
Selçuk	Kamil Koç	3.5hr.	8:45, noon	$6.50	$6
Selçuk	Pamukkale	3hr.	2am-6pm	$8	
Side	Pamukkale	10hr.	10:15pm	$15	$14
Yalova	Kamil Koç	11hr.	8:45am, 8,.9:30, 11:30pm	$17	$16
Yalova	Pamukkale	11hr.	noon, 7:30, 9pm	$14.50	

Dolmuş: To **Gümbet** (10min., every 5min, $.60); **Marmaris** (3hr., every hr. 7am-7pm, $6); **Milas** (50 min., every hr. 6am-5pm, $1); **Muğla** (2 hr., every hr. 6am-8pm, $4).

Ferries: Tickets sold through travel agents. **Bodrum Express Lines**, 18 Kale Cad. (☎316 40 67 or 316 10 87; fax 313 00 77), has offices in the otogar and near the castle. Walk past the castle with the marina on your right toward the sea; the office will be on the left. Open 7:30am-11pm. All ferries and hydrofoils leave from the end of the jetty, past the office, and run daily May-Oct. and M, W, F Nov.-Apr. To: **Kos** (1½hr.; daily 9am, return 4:30pm; arrive at the jetty 30 min. early for passport check); **Datça** (M, W, F 9am, return 4:30pm). Children under 11 free. Call for off-season schedule changes.

Hydrofoils: Bodrum Express Lines (☎316 10 87 or 316 40 67; fax 313 00 77). To: **Dalyan** (2½hr., including 1½hr. coach transfer from Gelibolu to Dalyan; Th, Su 8am, return 6pm; $46 including lunch, Dalyan river cruise, and entrance to Kaunos); **Gökova,** a.k.a. the Bodrum-Gellbolu day cruise (1¼hr.; Th, Su 8am, return 6pm; $33 including lunch); **Kos** (20min.; daily 9am, return 4:30pm; $18, round-trip 28); **Marmaris** (2hr., including 20min. coach transfer from Gelibolu to Marmaris; Th, Su 8am, return 6pm; $28, round-trip $37); **Rhodes** (2¼hr.; M-Sa 8:30am, return 5pm; $46, round-trip $57).

Rentals: Botur Agency, 24 Çevat şakir Cad. (☎313 90 52), about 2 blocks on the left from the otogar when facing the sea, rents **cars** ($22-40 per day). **Mopeds** are available at **Team Rent,** 5 1021 Sok (☎313 53 22) off Çevat şakir Cad. before the Botur Agency facing the marina. Open 8am-9pm, $12-24 per day. Or, for three times the price, try **Avis** (☎316 23 33), **Budget** (☎316 3078), or **Hertz** (☎316 1053).

ORIENTATION

Streets in Bodrum are marked by small blue signs, though it is often easier to navigate using landmarks. The main streets in town radiate from the Castle of St. Peter *(Kale)*. **Cumhuriyet Cad.,** the main commercial drag, runs along the water, twisting slightly inland to allow room for a small beach before returning to the sea. Ferries, hydrofoils, and yacht cruises depart from the breakwater and **Kale Cad.,** which runs between the castle and the marina, ending at a mosque. **Belediye Meyd Cad.,** the street that hugs the port's coast between the ships and cafés, turns into **Neyzen Teyfik Cad.,** the western harbor coastal road. Through the canopy of **Carşikale Cad.,** a commercial pedestrian road, **Türkkuyusu Cad.** curves slightly to the left and **Çevat şakir Cad.** branches to the right. **Atatürk Cad.** stems to the right off of Çevat şakir Cad. as it moves away from the harbor.

PRACTICAL INFORMATION

TOURIST AND FINANCIAL SERVICES

Tourist Office: 48 Barış Meydanı (☎316 10 91; fax 316 76 94), at the foot of the castle. Pension information, room listings, and free brochures with maps. Pick up the monthly publication "Aegean Sun," which includes events in and around Bodrum as well as useful information in English and German. Open Apr.-Oct. daily 8:30am-5pm; Nov.-Mar. M-F 8am-noon, 1-5pm.

Travel Agencies: Botur, 24/A Çevat şakir Cad. (☎316 90 52). Open 9am-10:30pm. Organizes bus trips to: **Pamukkale** and **Ephesus** (2 days; W, Th 7:30am; return Su 8pm; $54 includes overnight stay in a 4-star hotel); **Dalyan and Kaunos** (12½ hr.; Th, Su 6:30am, return 8pm; $26). **Village tour** (daily; 11:30am, return flexible; $8).

Consulate: UK, Kıbrıs şehitleri Ca. no. 421 1B (☎317 00 93/4), in Konacik. A 15min. bus ride from Bodrum. Open M-Th 9am-12:30pm, 2:30-4:30pm.

Currency Exchange: At the PTT from 8:30am-midnight. Most exchange booths along the harbor on Kale Cad. and along Cumhuriyet Cad. do not charge commission.

ATMs: Cirrus/Plus/MC/V ATMs located throughout the shopping areas. **Türkiye İş Bankası** (☎316 10 12), on Çevat şakır Cad., is about halfway between the bus station and the castle. Open M-F 9am-12:30pm, 1:30-5:30pm.

LOCAL SERVICES

English Language Bookstores: A 24hr. **book fair** is located across on the corner of Cumhuriyet Cad. and Open from late June-Aug. **D&R Music and Book Store,** 5 Neyzen Teyfik Cad. (☎313 73 62/63/64; fax: 313 74 70), located across from Cizdar Sok, in a small shopping center between Neyzen Teyfik Cad. and the marina, offers an eclectic assortment of English-language "best-sellers." Open daily 8:30am-2am.

Laundromats: Mainly on Türkkuyusu Cad., Çevat şakir Cad., and Atatürk Cad. $4 per load. Most open daily 8am-10pm.

Hamam: The new **Bodrum Hamam** (☎/fax 313 41 29), directly opposite the main exit of the otogar on Çevat şakir Cad., has separate facilities for men and women. Open 6am-midnight. $8-20. The citizens of Bodrum swear by the **Karia Prenses Ottoman Turkish Bath** (☎316 89 71) in the back entrance of the **Karia Prenses Hotel.** To get there, take the Centrum (şe hiriçi) dolmuş from the otogar to the Migros supermarket. With your back to the Migros, take a left and walk down a short block to the hotel. Open Th-Tu 9:30am-8:30pm, W 9:30am-midnight (with a dance club). $10-36.

EMERGENCY AND COMMUNICATIONS

Police: 50 Barış Meydanı (☎316 10 04). At the foot of the castle, next to the tourist office. Open 24hr. **Emergency Police:** (☎316 12 15).

Pharmacies: Especially prevalent on Cumhuriyet Cad., Çevat şakir Cad., and Atatürk Cad. All open daily 8:30am-8pm. All post the nighttime on-duty pharmacy.

Hospital: Bodrum Devlet Hastanesi (☎313 14 20 or 313 21 27), Kıbrıs şehitleri Cad., uphill from the amphitheater. Public and open 24hr; English spoken. **Private Bodrum Hospital** (☎313 65 66). Walk inland on Çevat şakir Cad., take a left onto Artemis Sok., turn left onto Kulcuoğlu Sok., take the 3rd right, and then make the 1st right. English spoken. Open 24hr. Or try the **Universal Hospital** (☎317 15 15) in Konacik.

Internet Access: Reklam Bigisayar Internet, 49 Atatürk Cad. (☎313 38 79), past Uçuluyar Cad. Open April-Sept. 24hr., Oct-Mar 9am-9pm. $1.50 per hr. **Cyber Internet,** 30 Çevat şakir Cad. (☎313 85 47) is a block toward the sea from the otogar in an alleyway to your left. Open 9am-1am. $1 per hr. **Nese-Immuhabbet Internet Café** 85 Türkkusuyu Cad. (☎313 76 08/03) has a lounge and TV as well as internet access. Open 10am-2am, $1 per hour.

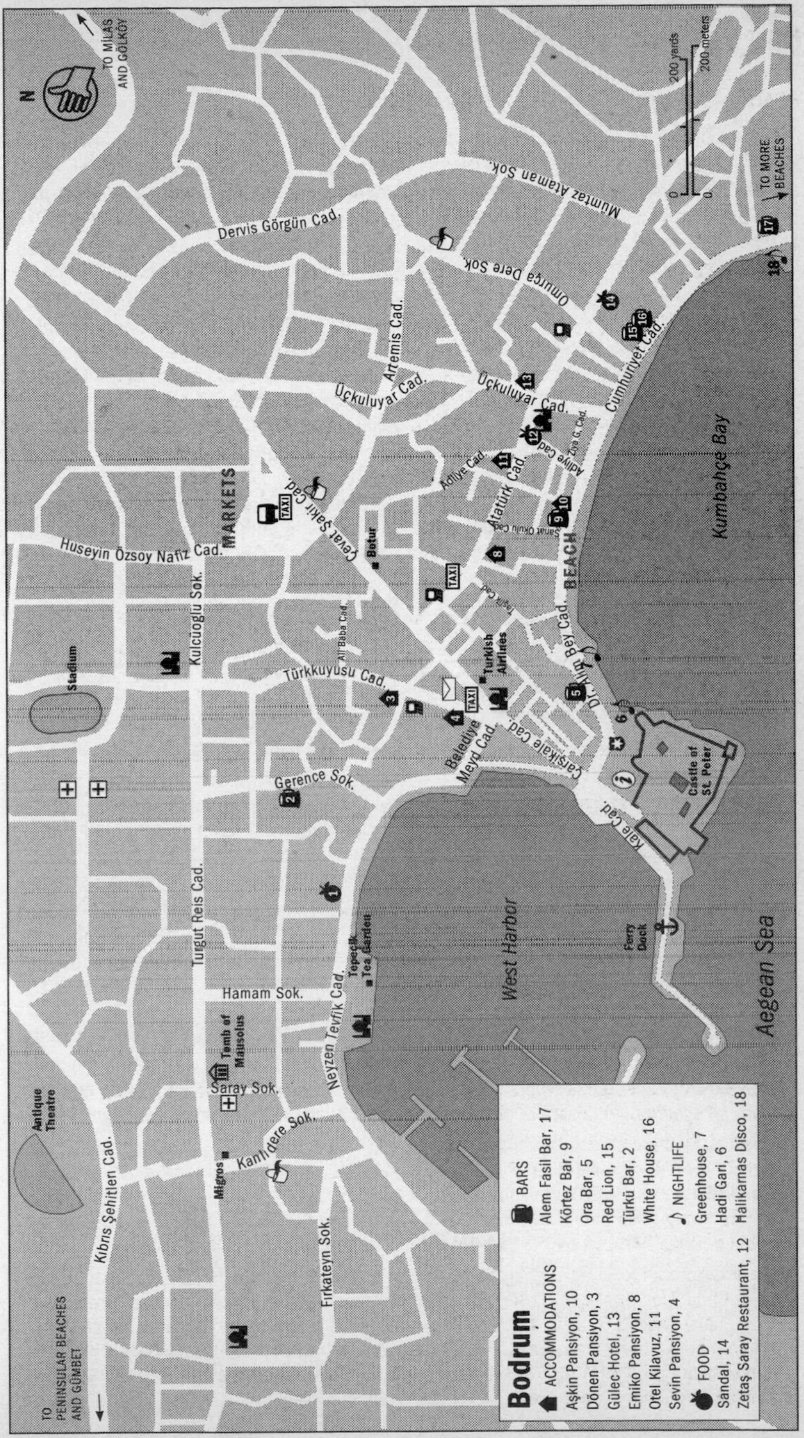
Bodrum
ACCOMMODATIONS
Aşkin Pansiyon, 10
Dönen Pansiyon, 3
Gülec Hotel, 13
Emiko Pansiyon, 8
Otel Kilavuz, 11
Sevin Pansiyon, 4
FOOD
Sandal, 14
Zetaş Saray Restaurant, 12
BARS
Alem Fasil Bar, 17
Körtez Bar, 9
Ora Bar, 5
Red Lion, 15
Türkü Bar, 2
White House, 16
NIGHTLIFE
Greenhouse, 7
Hadi Gari, 6
Halikarnas Disco, 18
TO PENINSULAR BEACHES AND GÜMBET
TO MILAS AND GÜLKÖY
TO MORE BEACHES
N
200 yards
200 meters
Kıbrıs Şehitleri Cad.
Antique Theatre
Migros
Kanlıdere Sok.
Saray Sok.
Tomb of Mausolus
Hamam Sok.
Turgut Reis Cad.
Kulcuoglu Sok.
Stadium
Firkateyn Sok.
Neyzen Tevfik Cad.
Tepecik Tea Garden
West Harbor
Ferry Dock
Aegean Sea
Gerence Sok.
Türkkuyusu Cad.
Ali Baba Cad.
Huseyin Özsoy Nafiz Cad.
MARKETS
Cevat Şakir Cad.
Botur
Turkish Airlines
Belediye Meyd Cad.
Çarşıkale Cad.
Kale Cad.
Castle of St. Peter
Dr. Alim Bey Cad.
BEACH
Sanat Okulu Cad.
Atatürk Cad.
Adliye Cad.
Ziya G. Cad.
Kumbahçe Bay
Üçkuluyar Cad.
Artemis Cad.
Cumhuriyet Cad.
Omurça Dere Sok.
Dervis Görgün Cad.
Mümtaz Ataman Sok.
TAXI

AEGEAN COAST

PTT: (☎316 12 12), on Çevat şakir Cad., 4 blocks from the otogar (when heading toward the castle). *Poste restante,* international phone, stamps and faxes. Open daily 8:30am-midnight. **Postal code:** 48400.

ACCOMMODATIONS

Pensions are plentiful in Bodrum but may require some advance planning. All rates rise in the high season (July and August) when pensions do not have to compete for customers. Single travelers *(tek kişi)* are often given double rooms and may have trouble finding a place in the high season; call ahead in the summer. Cheap pensions cluster behind the PTT and to the left of the castle facing inland.

Emiko Pansiyon, Atatürk Cad., 11 Üslü Sok. (☎/fax 316 55 60). From the otogar, follow Çevat şakir Cad. toward the water, turning left onto Atatürk Cad. After 50m, turn right down the alley marked with a blue sign for the Emiko Pansiyon, not Uslu Sok (which is the next street); it's the 2nd building on your left. Run by Emiko, a gently attentive Japanese woman, this white-washed Mediterranean pension offers 8 simple rooms with baths and hardwood and tile floors. Guests enjoy breakfast under the shade of grape leaves on the stone patio. Guest kitchen. Breakfast $2. Laundry $3. Sept.-Mar. singles $7, doubles $12; Aug. singles $10, doubles $16.

Otel Kilavuz, No. 25 Atatürk Cad. (☎316 38 92; fax 316 2852). From the otogar follow Çevat şakir Cad. toward the castle, turning left onto Atatürk Cad. After 50m, turn left onto Adliye Sok; the hotel is directly before the mosque on your right. This modern hotel has a garden, pool, and bar. Each of the 12 rooms has a large bathroom, phone, and art on the walls. Laundry free with *Let's Go.* Breakfast included. Sept.-Mar. singles $10, doubles $16; June-Aug. singles $13, doubles $20. Discounts with *Let's Go.*

Hotel Güleç, 18 Üçkuyular Cad. (☎316 52 22 or 313 73 91). From the otogar, take Çevat şakir Cad. toward the sea and make a left onto Atatürk Cad. Take a left onto Üçkuyular Cad.; the hotel is on the right. Trimmed by a pleasant garden, this white-washed hotel has fresh, clean rooms replete with oak furnishings and bath. Breakfast and laundry included; discounts for large parties. Apr.-June singles $8, doubles $15; July-Sept. singles $10, doubles $22.

Dönen Pansiyon, Türkkuyusu Cad., 21 1011 Sok (☎316 40 17). Walk inland from the taxi station on Türkkuyusu Cad.; the pension is 3 blocks down on the left, directly after Nese-Immuhabbet Internet Cafe. Run by a friendly family, it has 14 clean if not bright rooms, some with bath. No English spoken. Singles $10, doubles $15, triples $18.

Sevin Pansiyon, 5 Türkkuyusu Cad. (☎316 76 82 or 316 06 00; fax: 313 49 19). About 10m on the left side of Türkkuyusu Cad. when heading inland from the taxi park. 27 ample rooms with bath. Internet access ($1.50 per hr.), car/bike rental ($9 per day) and taxi service to airport available. Breakfast included. Laundry $1.50. Oct.-July: singles $8, doubles $16, triples $20. Aug.-Sept. $25-30.

Aşkin Pansiyon (☎0 543 425 97 50), on a passageway about 20m past Emiko Pansiyon—look for the yellow sign. The rooftop terrace has a splendid view of the sea. 10 very basic rooms, some with bath. Discos nearby make this pansiyon convenient for late-night barhopping, but if you crave quiet, ask for a room in the back. No English spoken. $7.50 per person, $6 with *Let's Go.*

FOOD

Cheap eats in Bodrum consist of the usual kebap stands (kebap and chips $3) and the small cafeteria-style joints on Çevat şakir Cad. (meals $2). Steaming corn on the cob ($.50) is sold from small carts along the main streets, and wherever you turn, fixin's for baked potatoes garnish hot spuds ($1.50).

Sandal, 76 Atatürk Cad. (☎ 316 91 17 or 316 35 59). Turn onto Atatürk Cad. from Çevat şakir Cad. and walk 200m past the mosque on your right. The restaurant is on the block after Omurça Dere Sok on the right. For those craving the taste of the east, Sandal provides an extensive offering of Chinese and Thai food *al fresco.* Munch on *pad thai* under the thatched roof while listening to the rush of the outdoor waterfall. Open daily noon-midnight. Dinner around $10. AmEx/MC/V.

Zetaş Saray Restaurant 12 Atatürk Cad. (☎316 68 48/47). Turn onto Atatürk Cad. from Çevat şakir Cad. and follow it until just before the mosque on your right. Well regarded by Bodrum citizens for the high quality of its Turkish dishes, Zetaş Saray has *kebaps* ($3) and a filling set menu ($7-8) as you listen to the call to prayer from the mosque next door. Vegetarian option available. Reservations for parties of 10+. Handicap accessible. Open 9am-3am. AmEx/MC/V.

Tepeçik Tea Garden, 1 Neyze Teyfik Cad. (☎313 86 66). Follow the road along the coast away from the castle; the tea house will be on your left past a small shopping center. Gaze at the Bodrum coast under the blanket of dried *harıp* leaves or curl up like a sultan on the pillows of an Ottoman corner (*şark*) with apple tea ($.50) and a sandwich ($2-5) in this government-owned tea garden. Prices change annually and remain fixed throughout the year. Open daily 7am-4am.

Karadeniz Patisserie, 13 Cumhuriyet Cad., is the nocturnal sweet tooth's dream. Dazzle your eyes and your gullet with freshly baked sweets, breads, and pastries. Sandwiches and pizza $.60-.90; strawberry tart $1; cakes $6. Open 24hr.

Doyum Büfe 80 Neyzen Teyfik Cad. (☎313 26 75). On Neyzen Teyfik Cad., heading away from the castle. Catch a quick burger and soda, Bodrum-style. Trade your Whopper and Coke for a fried sausage sandwich and *ayran* (a popular yogurt drink, $.40).

SIGHTS

THE RUINS OF HALICARNASSUS. The ruins of ancient Halicarnassus, once one of the largest Mediterranean cities in the ancient world, are Bodrum's best-known attraction. Unfortunately, most of the remains were either destroyed, buried beneath the modern town of Bodrum, or shipped to London. The old **city walls** and what remains of the **theater** are still partly visible. Names, barely visible on the weathered stone steps, pay tribute to those who helped to build the theater. The **Tomb of Mausolus,** one of the Seven Wonders of the Ancient World, marks the resting place of the once-glorious *satrap* (governor) of Halicarnassus. The tomb once rose to a height of 50m, and is the source of the word "mausoleum." A rectangular foundation, stone pedestal, and 36 Ionic columns supported the sepulchral chamber. Covered with a pyramid-shaped roof, the mausoleum was crowned by a statue of Mausolus driving a horse-drawn chariot. Crusaders demolished the structure and used its parts to fortify the Castle of St. Peter. Today the mausoleum site houses a small porch with reconstructions of the mausoleum's friezes and an open-air museum with columnar fragments. The mausoleum itself has been reduced to a pit resembling a Japanese rock garden, populated only by roaming chickens. To see the real goods, head to London's British Museum. *(To reach the Theater, take a dolmuş toward Gümbet on Kıbrıs şehitler Cad. Ask to get off when you see the ruins to your right. To reach the mausoleum, take Kulucüoğlu Sok. from behind the otogar; it will be on your right. Theater and Mausoleum open Tu-Su 8am-noon and 1-5pm. $2.50, students $1.)*

THE CASTLE OF ST. PETER. Sandwiched between Bodrum's two bays, the castle stands watch over the rocky peninsula and the crashing waves below. Crusaders from the Knights of St. John constructed Bodrum's formidable castle during the 15th and 16th centuries. It was built over the ruins of an ancient acropolis and incorporated material from the nearby Mausoleum of Halicarnassus. A transnational effort, the **English, French, German,** and **Italian towers** bear the names of the nations responsible for their construction. Despite their extensive fortifications, the Crusaders's towers were no match for the forces of Süleyman the Magnificent, who overpowered the knights in 1523. Under Ottoman rule, the castle's importance waned, and in 1895 it was converted into a prison. The fortress now houses a museum with maritime and cultural exhibits. The walls of the castle offer an escape from Bodrum's busy streets. Turquoise and amber peacocks parade under flowering trees and bushes. From the towers it is possible to see the entire city as well as some of the neighboring bays. Picnickers will appreciate the peace.

After walking up the stone ramp past a series of gates, enter the castle's lower courtyard on your left at the top of the stairs, where an **amphora exhibit** graces the left wall. Amphoras, two-handled clay jars with rounded bases, were used to carry the wine and olive oil that was traded across the Mediterranean Sea. Opposite the wall is an attractive church which became a mosque under the Ottomans. The **chapel** now houses a model of a sunken vessel and other shipwreck artifacts. Continue uphill to the **Glass Hall,** featuring remnants of the oldest shipwreck ever discovered. The ship sank in the 14th century BC, carrying glass shipments for trade between Egyptian and Anatolian ports.

Once through the gate at the top of the steps, take a left past the public toilets to the **Snake Tower,** home to pottery artifacts, and traverse a stairwell leading to the **Gatineau Tower,** which affords a spectacular view of Bodrum. Once upon a time, this tower acted as a dungeon and torture chamber, as proven by the skeletons found during excavation work. Facing the entrance to the Snake Tower is the **French Tower,** in which rest the remains of a 4th-century BC **Carian Princess.** Scientists have reconstructed the princess's face from her skull structure, and her likeness is on display along with her intact remains and magnificent 4th-century jewelry. Less macabre than it sounds, this exhibit is worth the extra price. Once outside, follow the stairway down to the **English Tower,** whose walls are decorated with Turkish banners, English armor, weapons, and engravings. A new exhibit featuring another ancient shipwreck contains such valuables as **Nefertiti's Seal** and a page from the oldest book in the world. Don't leave the castle without a visit to the **German Tower,** beyond the ostrich cage, by the Snake Tower, replete with banners, stuffed deer heads, and a chandelier reminiscent of the Middle Ages. *(The Castle is the most central landmark in Bodrum. Facing the sea on the harbor, walk left for 300 ft. toward the ferries. ☎316 25 16. Open Tu-Su 8:30am-noon and 12:30-5pm. $5, students with ISIC free. Carian Princess and Glass Wreck open Tu-F 10am-noon and 1-5pm. $2.50.*

AEGEAN COAST

ENTERTAINMENT

Bodrum, a.k.a. the "Bedroom," can be a wild flesh-pot whose excesses seem to bring out everyone's extremes. Loud, exciting discos and calm, sophisticated bars are merely the foreplay to what goes on when the music dies down. Most clubs also open daily as restaurants. Prices rise in July and August. For a wild taste of England in Turkey, hop over the western ridge of Bodrum to Gümbet, where more discos and bars can be found glittering in the night (30min. walk or 10min. dolmuş ride; dolmuş leave the otogar every 5 min.; $.60).

CLUBS

Halikarnas Disco, Z. Müren Cad. On the hill at the end of Cumhuriyet Cad., 1km from the center of town. The second-largest open-air disco in the world, this famed colosseum of rhythm juts out into the ocean, where its strobe lights reflect off the sails of nearby yachts. The club's dressed-to-be-seen clientele makes serious moves on the dance floor, while spectators gaze from above. Daily shows featuring 25 performers, great music, and a celebrity-style entrance tunnel make this club the definitive Bodrum experience. $12 cover charge includes 1 drink. There's a **foam party** on Saturdays in Jul. and Aug. Beer $3.

Temple (☎316 17 21). A popular club where excitable dancing coincides with sly socializing, as the spasmic dance floor lights dart above the flicker of candlelight from the dark wooden bar. Beer $2; *rakı* $2; cocktails $3-6. Open daily 7pm-5am.

Hadi Gari (☎313 80 97). Next to the luminous castle, the oldest disco in Bodrum fuses elegance and funkiness. Stylish customers get down under twinkling white lights on the large outdoor dance floor. Others recline on plush rose and silver cushions in the softly lit interior. An unbeatable view of Bodrum's colorful nightlife. Beer $3; *rakı* $4; cocktails $7-9. Open daily 6pm-4am.

Greenhouse (☎313 09 11). Black lights set off the neon paint at this much-favored dance bar that extends onto the beach. Surreal international newsreels play on a big screen over the indoor bar as enthusiastic international and Turkish DJs spin from the front half of a blue bus. Beer $2; *rakı* $3; cocktails $3.50-6. Open daily midnight-5am.

White House (☎316 40 84). Not to be confused with the one in Washington, D.C., although George W. Bush would still have trouble locating either on a map. An ultra-intense light system illuminates the animated Brits dancing inside and playing on the busy patio. Beer $2; *rakı* $3; cocktails $5. Open 9am-5am.

BARS

Ora Bar, 17 Cumhuriyet Cad. (☎316 39 03). A swanky candle-lit interior with the feel of a castle, where a lively, polished crowd bustles from table to table to the sounds of rock and pop. Popular with a vivacious Turkish crowd. Beer $2.40; *rakı* $3; cocktails $4-6; prices strangely higher on Muslim holidays. Open 7pm-4am.

Türkü Bar, 49 Gerence Sok. (☎316 47 41), in the Maya Hotel lounge. From Nezen Tevifk Cad., walk 90m up Gerence Sok., past the otopark. Far from the hoopla of Cumhuriyet Cad. lies a hotel bar like no other. Decorated like a nomadic tent, Türkü Bar features bands that play 14th-century Turkish and Kurdish standards, aided by a yipping local crowd dancing folkloric dances like they're the macarena. Just clap when everyone else does and you'll be fine. Beer $3.50; *rakı* $3. Music daily from 10:30pm-4am.

Cafe Tömbeki, 10 Carşi Mah. Yusufcanserdi Sok (☎316 13 67), off Cumhuriyet Cad. Slightly removed from the roar of the discos, meet Lewis Carroll's caterpillar at this water-pipe cafe. Try apple, rose, cappuccino, and other tobacco flavors. This reclusive Ottoman *nargile* bar serves no food or alcohol, but provides backgammon boards upon request. Large parties can arrange food in advance. Water pipe $5, tea $1.

Alem Fasıl Bar, 181 Cumhuriyet Cad. (☎313 12 25), near Halikarnas. A wonderfully dark and smoky upstairs den, where acoustic *Fasıl* music will draw out your inner belly-dancer. Beer $5; *rakı* 4; cocktails $7. Open 10pm-4am.

Körfez Bar, 2 Ülsü Sok. (☎316 59 66), on the corner of Cumhuriyet Cad. If Bodrum's repetitive techno-pop has given you a headache, head to this den of classic rock. Down-to-earth customers socialize under the watchful eye of the Jim Morrison posters that line the brick walls. Beer $2; *rakı* $2.40; cocktails $3-5. Open 8am-5am.

Red Lion, 137 Cumhuriyet Cad. (☎316 37 48). For action-packed swigs, touch down at this combination dance and sports bar, where loud crowds watch games on ample TV screens while nodding to house music. Beer $2; *rakı* $3; cocktails $7. Open 4pm-5am.

Lodos Bar, on Cumhuriyet Cad., past the Ora Bar. Playing a fantastic array of English pop music, this joint's svelte layout allows for just enough dancing as befits a bar. A small dark wood patio with underlit water provides a good look at the stars and a romantic setting for . . . well, you know.

Karya Otel (☎313 31 57). Take a much-needed break from Bodrum's discos and unwind at this friendly Cumhuriyet Cad. favorite. Enjoy the refreshing breeze from the sea while sipping coffee or a more exotic concoction with the locals. Great for people watching. Non-alcoholic hot and cold drinks $1; beer $1.20; cocktails $3. Open 24hr.

Sensi (☎316 68 45). For a riotous ride in bar craziness, join the mostly-British crowd at Sensi, where table dancing, karaoke, and wig-wearing 70s nights keep this joint quaking. For those who dare, drown your cares in an alcoholic fishbowl ($18). Beer $1.80; *rakı* $2; cocktails $3.60-5. Open daily 5pm-5am.

DAYTRIPS FROM BODRUM

The Bodrum Peninsula is an extremely popular Turkish vacation spot. Small villages mingle with coastal vistas and offer a more laid-back alternative to the excitement of Bodrum. Explore the peninsula's green northern coast or dry, sandy southern coastline. Several of the peninsula's beaches have recently been awarded the European Blue Flag, an environmental award given to communities that keep their beaches especially clean and safe. In recent years, large resorts have privatized much of the beachfront. All dolmuş to these beaches, which are marked by signs on their front window, depart from Bodrum's otogar.

BLUE JOURNEYS. Çevat şakir Kabaağaç, a writer living in Bodrum between the World Wars, wrote the book *Mavi Yolculuk* ("Blue Journey"), detailing his sailing excursions along Turkey's then-uninhabited southern Aegean coast. These days, tour boats skirt the front of the castle seeking to recreate his journey with trips bound for the beaches on the southern coast of the peninsula. Building on the adventures described in Kabaağaç's book, these so-called "Blue Journeys" are multi-day affairs which take you on more involved tours of the peninsula. These should not be confused with "day tours," which can be a fun alternative to the tourist throngs plaguing the beaches around the city. Itineraries for the tours vary widely; check the tour schedule at the docks at the far end of Cumhuriyet Cad. Popular destinations include the **Akvaryum,** or aquarium, for an early afternoon swim in the turquoise bay; **Kara Ada** (Black Island), where visitors can apply the special orange clay from deep within a cave that is reputed to restore youthful beauty *($.20 entrance fee);* **Meteor** (on the Black Island), whose 20m jump will cure anyone's acrophobia; and **Deveplajı** (Camel Beach), where the trained dromedaries wait to offer rides *($4 for 10min.).* **Lover's Bay** and **Rabbit Bay** offer more swimming and snorkeling. In the high season, tours also include **Orak Island,** which has some of the best swimming spots on the peninsula. There are no cheap hotels in these locales, so stick with daytrips. *(Daily 9am-noon, return 5-6pm; $10-12, lunch included.)*

ORTAKENT. Known by Turks and British connoisseurs as the best beach near Bodrum, Ortakent actually features a certain amount of sand to go with the requisite crystal-blue ocean water. *(Take a dolmuş: 15 min., running 24hr. in high season, $.75.)*

AEGEAN COAST

TURGUT REİS. Named after the famous Turkish pirate and scourge of 16th-century European shipping, Turgut Reis, 18km from Bodrum, is the most accessible point on the west coast of the peninsula. Dolmuş follow a road that was once an ancient trading route. Popular with tourists who prefer relaxing on the beach to dancing in discos, it is usually fairly crowded. To reach the beach, head down Nehemet Hilmi Cad. (the main drag) toward the mosque towers. The beach is to the right of the marina as you face it. If you're up for a walk through fruit-laden groves, follow the small road near the Turgut Reis otogar or take a dolmuş north 4km for the more isolated and enjoyable Kadıkalesi beach. *(Take a dolmuş: 30min., every 10min 6:30am-3:30am; $1.)*

BİTEZ. Recently awarded a Blue Flag in honor of its pristine environment, this narrow beach is popular with British package tourists. Seaside bars have built pontoon docks over the water where you can order drinks while you sunbathe. Windsurfing is popular, with several places offering instruction and rentals. *(Take the dolmuş: 20min., 7:30am-2am (24hr. in high season), $.75. Windsurfing $15 per day.)*

BAĞLA. Famous for its deep clear water, Bağla's lovely beach has been largely overtaken by a British resort company. Windsurfing and dinghies to rent all over the beach, near many great camping areas. *(Best accessible by dolmuş to Bitez and then a short walk. 8am-2am, $1; windsurfing $15 per day.)*

YAHşI. Also awarded a Blue Flag, the rare sand paradise of Yahşı is the longest beach in Bodrum. Flanked by surfers, sunbathers, and olive and tangerine trees, the turquoise waters offer a more serene warmth than other beaches in the area. *(Take a dolmuş: 30min., every 10min. 7:30am-2am, $.80.)*

GÖLKÖY AND TÜRKBÜKÜ. Calmer than the southern coast, the northern end of the peninsula offers swimming docks that stretch into the clear water. The quiet shores of Gölköy and Türkbükü draw sophisticated Turkish tourists and their yachts. *(Dolmuş depart frequently for both beaches: 30min., 8am-midnight; July-Aug. 7am-5am. In Gölköy the dolmuş stops in front of the town's main grocery store, $1.)*

GÜMÜŞLUK (ALSO CALLED MINDOS). The Turkish name means "silvery," referring to ancient silver coins that were discovered in the area. Near the short little sliver of a beach lie the sunken ruins of ancient **Mindos,** a 4th-century BC port impregnable even to Alexander the Great. The site, accessible through daily dives, consists of a 3m-thick city wall and a Roman basilica. Take a boat to **Rabbit Island,** a tiny peninsula 100m from shore that nurtures the furry creatures. *(Take a dolmuş from the Bodrum otogar: 40min., 24hr., $1.40 in high season; $1 all other times. For information on dives, contact the Aegean Prod Dive Center (☎ 316 07 37), on Neyzen Teyfik Cad.)*

LABRANDA (LABRAYNDA)

Because Labraynda is 20km up a steep, winding road in ill-repair, it is not accessible by dolmuş. The site can be reached by private car or taxi ($25-30), but for most travelers, the best way to see it is with a package tour. Some travelers hitch rides on dump trucks heading to a calcium deposit further in the mountains, but this is not advisable. The road to the site starts across the highway from the Milas otogar.

A rough ride over loose stones and thick dust serves as a 45min. rite of passage to this sanctuary of Zeus. One of the least visited sites of ancient Caria, Labraynda was an important religious center devoted to **Zeus Stratios** (aka Zeus Labraundos), a version of the god peculiar only to this sanctuary but attested to in inscriptions from as far away as Athens. The site is exceptional, since its well-preserved ruins, dating to the 7th century BC, precede the Romans. The cult of Zeus Stratios flourished into a cosmic affair complete with oracular signs, banquets, and baths. Today, the flowering terraces of Labraynda provide rich fodder for the honeybees of local villagers and spiritual vistas for lucky travelers.

There are a couple ways to enter. If you encounter a wooden gate, don't be discouraged: just call out and someone will let you in. Directly to the left of the site entrance is **andron A,** where all-male banquets venerating Zeus were held. Behind the *andron* are the **oikoi,** homes for the priests who maintained the site and cult records. Walk through the 4th-century BC **Temple of Zeus,** marked by the remains of Ionic columns, to come face-to-face with a round, chair-like object used during the worship of Zeus. Behind the temple is an oddly shaped *stoa* with raised relief work. About 2m below and 25m ahead, an impressive **stairway** leads to the remnants of the ancient **agora,** where the four open windows on the left once housed shops. On the right stand the **Doric house** and **Byzantine church.** Behind the church is one of the most intriguing finds at Labranda—the domain of the ancient **fish oracle.** Archaeologists think that the columns mark where the priests tempted jewel-bedecked fish with bait. If the fish took the offerings, the oracle was favorable.

For the complete Labranda adventure, climb the hill behind the Temple of Zeus (there's another gate here, but simply pass through) and follow the circuitous path to the exceptionally well-preserved **tomb.** The front chamber of this vaulted structure was once the final resting place of Idrieus' children. In the back lay the man himself and his two wives. On the way out, ask the guide to show you the stone emblazoned with the ax of Zeus Stratios, the focus of the site's cult.

EUROMOS

Euromos is best viewed with a package tour, usually along with Labranda. Open daily 8am-7pm. $1.20, students $.40.

The ancient city of Kyromos became known as Euromos when Caria came under Hellenistic influence in the 4th century BC. A shrine dating from as early as the 6th century BC was dedicated to Zeus and the local god Stratios. Hidden in silvery olive groves, about 50m from the highway, the 2nd-century AD **Temple of Zeus** is a prime example of Roman-era temple architecture, featuring exquisite Corinthian columns. The still-unfluted columns indicate that the temple was never finished. Wealthy residents, whose support is recorded, unusually, on the columns themselves, financed the construction of the elaborate supports.

Notice the intact **architrave,** or stone lintel, running across the top of the columns. A walk around the back of the temple toward the unfinished supports reveals a stone engraved with a double ax, the symbol of Zeus Stratios, and the remains of a decorative lion head on the **sima,** or gutter. Rainwater used to run out of the animal's mouth to the ground. The temple contains the remains of the altar and a curious upright pillar decorated in raised relief, a remnant of the door that led to the sacred inner shrine. Unfortunately, the temple's excellent state of preservation has been marred by shoddy, cement reconstruction work around the foundation. With your back to the length-wise fluted columns, you will see the hilltop remains of the ancient wall enclosing what were the **agora, theater,** and **baths.** Ask the guard to point out the 10,000-seat theater, hidden by grass and olive trees. A keen glance from above reveals a column on the other side of the modern highway; this is part of the ancient *agora* now covered by fields and crops.

AKYAKA (BAY OF GÖKOVA) ☎252

Sitting at the tip of the Bay of Gökova, the serene village of Akyaka is surrounded by a sandy beach and rich pine forests. The undeveloped land around the bay is perfect for camping and exploration. Gökova's river delta, set aside as conservation land, teems with aquatic life, including fish, turtles, and ducks. On the other side of the bay is the island of Sedir, whose white sand is said to have been shipped from Egypt 2000 years ago for Cleopatra and Marc Antony's honeymoon. Although the town is the vacation destination of choice for many locals, its resort amenities are delightfully understated, and its architecture is exquisite.

TRANSPORTATION AND PRACTICAL INFORMATION. Since Gökova lies on the Muğla-Marmaris road, any **bus** heading in either direction can drop you off. **Dolmuş** to **Marmaris** (10am, $1) and **Muğla** (every 30min. 7am-7pm, $.80) leave from the Akyaka dolmuş stop, across from Belediye Park, near the Belediye building on Lütfiye Sakıcı Cad. (the street to the left just before the PTT and *jandarma*).

Navigation can be tough in Akyaka. Though small, the town is not compact, and street names are rarely used. The main road, **Atatürk Cad.,** begins uphill from the town (where minibuses stop) and winds its way down and curves left. After the curve, the pharmacy **Gökova Eczanesi** is on the right side of Atatürk Cad. The owner will open it after hours if medication is urgently needed. (☎243 53 00; after hours ☎243 57 99. Open daily 8am-10pm.) Also on Atatürk Cad., the very helpful **Mepar Tour Office** functions as the tourist office and travel agent, distributing free maps and providing an English-language book exchange. (☎243 55 51; fax 243 55 56. Open daily 8am-10pm.) There are **no banks or ATMs** in the town, but it is possible to change money at the jewelry store next to Mepar Tours (open daily 9am-9pm). The **PTT,** 100m down from Mepar, on the left, offers basic mail and phone services. (☎243 51 42. Open daily 8:30am-12:30pm and 1:30-5:30pm.) **Postal code:** 48650.

Farther down Atatürk Cad., a small road on the left leads to the **National Forest** picnic and camping area. Atatürk Cad. continues for 2km to **Çinar Beach,** which is less crowded than Akyaka's public beach. Lütfiye Sakıcı Cad. runs downhill to Akyaka's **public beach** and waterfront. The beach and the waterfront road has a few restaurants, cafeterias, bars, and souvenir shops.

ACCOMMODATIONS & CAMPING. Because many pensions in Akyaka cater to (mostly Turkish) families, they often have kitchens or apartment-style layouts. Rooms are scarce in summer, so call ahead. Just 5min. from the beach, **Ege Pansiyon** is reachable by turning left off Lütfiye Sakıcı Cad., just before the row of bars and restaurants. Ege offers homey rooms with kitchen, bath, living room, and balcony. (☎243 42 62. $16 per apartment per night.) On Atatürk Cad. across from Mepar Tours, **Server Pansiyon** has apartments (for 3-4 people) with modern bath, fully equipped kitchen, and tile floors. (☎243 54 97; fax 243 55 70. $20 per apartment per night.) To reach Akyaka's campground, **Gökova Orman Kampı,** go down Atatürk Cad. 400m past the PTT to the gates leading to the picnic and camping area. There's overnight camping farther up in the forest. The campground has showers, toilets, electricity, and a restaurant. Bring your own gear. (☎243 50 35. $2.40 per tent or caravan with up to 4 people; bungalow $14.50. Electricity $.80.)

FOOD AND ENTERTAINMENT. Akyaka's culinary offerings include plenty of steak and *kebap* ($3) places in the village center, fresh fish in picturesque settings by the river, and standard variations on Turkish and European cuisine in seaside cafeterias. Nightlife is easygoing. The scenery at **Halil'nin Yeri** is downright gorgeous, especially with the warm lamp light in the evenings; water babbles, ducks quack, and tall green reeds blow right next to your table. To get there from Atatürk Cad., turn left downhill after the pharmacy and walk 300m. (☎243 51 73. Cold dishes $1; grilled meats $2.50-5; fresh fish $5-15; wine $4.50-14 per bottle. Open daily 11am-1am.) For a more casual atmosphere, try one of the restaurants conveniently located at the bottom of Lütfiye Sakıcı Cad., which offer a combination of Turkish standards and Western favorites. On Negiz Sok., to the right off Lütfiye Sakıcı Cad., at the bottom of the hill, the **Caretta Bar** is a rustic, friendly bar playing Turkish and foreign music for a mostly local Turkish crowd. (☎255 63 26. Beer $1.20; *rakı* $1.60; cocktails $3. Open May-Oct. daily 8pm-2am.) The **Tropix Bar,** across from Caretta, is a hip rock 'n' roll joint with comfortable bamboo chairs and outdoor seating. (☎243 50 72. Beer $1.20; Japanese *sake* $4. Open daily 9pm-2am.)

SIGHTS. Enjoying the public beach, with its secluded swimming coves, is Akyaka's main pastime. The beach extends from the right of the pier to the entrance of the pine-laced National Park ($.50). The beach's sandbar stretches nearly 100m into the gulf. Ask at Mepar Tours for information on guided and unguided visits, including daily boat trips to nearby islands, jeep safaris to Gökova Bay and small villages, walking tours, and a river bird-watching trip.

GREEK ISLANDS

KOS

Famous figures in literature and medicine have lounged on the beaches of Kos: **Asclepius,** god of healing; **Hippocrates,** father of modern medicine and the Hippocratic oath; the poet **Theocritus,** and his teacher **Philetas.** In ancient times, Kos was a major trading power with a population of 160,000—eight times that of today. It has passed under control of Italian, German, and British governments. Kos Town draws a young, loud, intoxicated crowd, while relatively unexplored rural Kos attracts more sedate travelers in search of stunning beaches and serene villages.

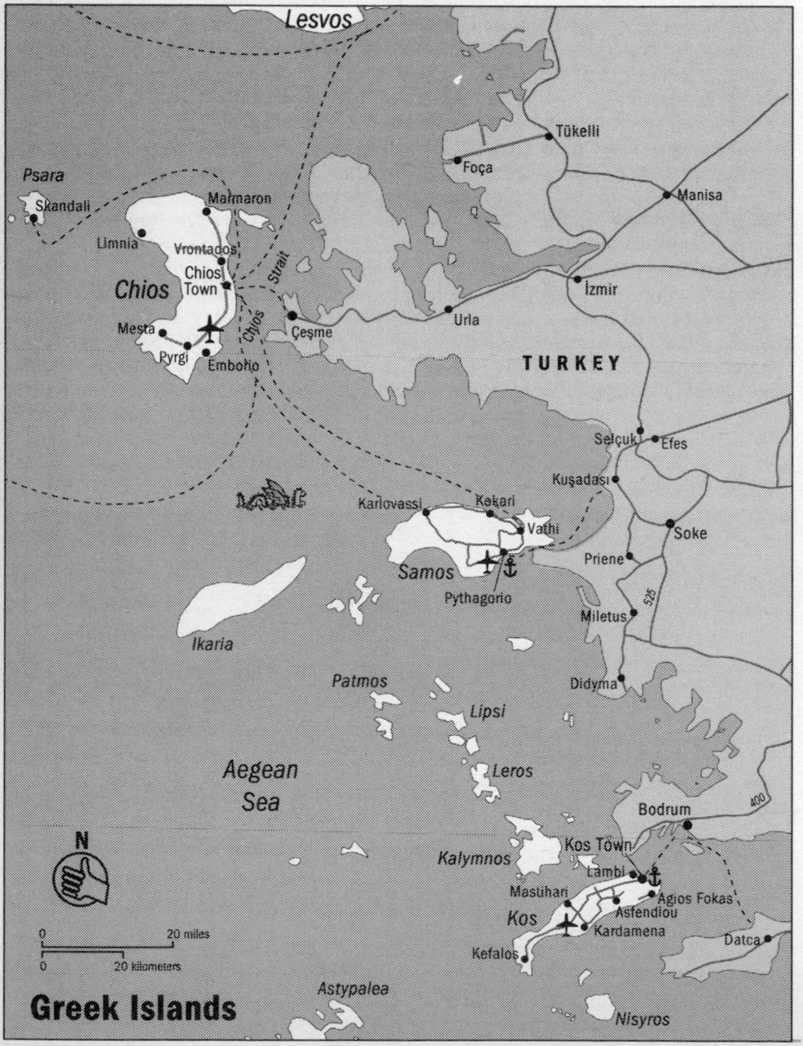

KOS TOWN ☎0242

In Kos Town, the minarets of Ottoman mosques spike above grand Italian mansions, the massive walls of a Crusader fortress, and scattered ruins from the Archaic, Classical, Hellenistic, and Roman eras. The combination of ancient, medieval, and modern makes Kos a historian's paradise by day, while its bars make it a dissipated hotspot by night. It's one of the most expensive towns in the Dodecanese, and package tours leave very few rooms for independent travelers.

ORIENTATION AND PRACTICAL INFORMATION

The dignified walls of the **Castle of the Knights of St. John** overwhelm the vista as ferries pull into the harbor of Kos Town. Walk left (facing inland) from the harbor to reach the **Avenue of Palms,** also known as **Finikon,** framed by the stately trees. Continuing along the waterfront past the Palms leads to **Vassileos Georgios** and the rocky beach alongside it. Turn right onto the Palms, follow it to the next corner of the fortress, and you'll come upon **Akti Koundouriotou,** another waterfront street that wraps around the harbor. The city bus station, boats to Turkey, travel agencies, restaurants, and Kos's thriving nightlife are all here. Branching inland off Akti Koundouriotou are the town's main arteries: **El. Venizelou** leads through a row of travel agencies into the shopping district; **Megalou Alexandrou,** a few blocks down, heads to **Pl. Palaiologou,** the ruins of ancient Kos Town, and the inland villages. The town's other sandy beach begins near the end of Akti Koundouriotou. **Ferries** run to: **Kalymnos** (1¼hr., 1-3 per day, 1800dr/€5.28); **Leros** (2½hr., 1 per day, 2500dr/€7.34); **Patmos** (4hr., 1-2 per day, 3200dr/€9.41); **Piraeus** (11-15hr., 2-3 per day, 5200dr/€15.29); and **Rhodes** (4hr., 2 per day, 4200dr/€12.35). Two per week go to: **Nisyros** (2400dr/€7.06); **Symi** (2800dr/€8.24); **Tilos** (2500dr/€7.35). Boats run to **Bodrum, Turkey** every morning (10,000-13,000dr/€29.41-38.23 round-trip). Turkish boats leave in the afternoon and return the next morning (8000-13,000dr/€23.53-38.23 round-trip). Since travel is international, prices aren't regulated by the Greek government. The **Port Authority** (☎26 594) is at the corner of Megalou Alexandrou and Akti Kountouriotou. Visitors leaving with Turkish boats requiring an overnight stay also need a visa (3000dr). **Buses** (☎22 292, fax 20 263) leave from Kleopatras street near the inland end of Pavlou behind the Olympic Airways office. M-Sa to: **Antimachia** (40min., 6 per day, 500dr/€1.47); **Local buses** leave from Akti Koundouriotou 7 (☎26 276), on the water. To: **Asclepion** (15min., 16 per day); **Agios Fokas** (50 per day); **Messaria** (9 per day); and **Thermae** (20min., 9 per day). Fares cost 150-250dr/€0.44-0.74. **Taxis** (☎22 777 or 22 333) are near the inland end of the Avenue of Palms. Rent a quality bike at **George,** P. Tsaldari 3 (☎28 480), near the port authority. (Mopeds 4000-5000dr/€11.76-14.71 per day, bikes 500-1000dr/€1.47-2.94. Open daily 8am-8pm.) **Greek National Tourist Office,** on Akti Miaouli in the same building as the tourist police, provides maps, brochures, and schedules. (Open M-F 8am-8pm, Sa 8am-3pm.) There's a **National Bank** (☎28 167), behind the Archaeological Museum, one block inland from the water on A.P. Ioannidi. (24hr. **ATM.** Open M-Th 8am-2pm, F 8am-1:30pm.) For **emergencies,** call ☎22 100; **ambulances,** call ☎22 300; for **general information,** call ☎131. The 24hr. **police** (☎22 222), on Akti Miaouli in the big yellow building by the castle, speak some English; the **tourist police** (☎22 444) are in the same place. (Open 7:30am-2pm.)

ACCOMMODATIONS

Hotel vacancies are rare in summer, so start searching for rooms early. Most inexpensive places are on the right side of town if you're facing inland. It's better to seek your own room, since Kos's dock hawks are notorious. The aroma of fresh jasmine is nearly as delightful as Sonia and Alex's hospitality at **Pension Alexis,** Herodotou 9. If rooms are full, the proprietor will set you up with a mattress and sheets on the patio or cut you a deal at his elegant Hotel Afendoulis. Romantic verandas, and common baths. Prices are flexible, especially if you're carrying

Let's Go. Take the first right off Megalou Alexandrou, on the back left corner of the first intersection. (☎28 798 or 25 594. Doubles 5500-95000dr/€16.18-25; triples 9000-10000dr/€26.46-29.41.) Traditional wood-paneled rooms surround a central courtyard at **Hotel Afendoulis,** Evrilpilou 1, down Vas. Georgiou. All have private baths and balcony. Ask about the cheaper cellar rooms. (☎/fax 25 321 or 25 797. Doubles 7500-12000dr/€22.06-35.29.) **Kos Camping** is 3km southeast from the center and accessible by public transport, in a shady, well-maintained setting right across from the beach. (☎23 910 or 23 275. Mini-market, bar, laundry facilities, cooking room, postal services, pool, and security boxes. Your own tent 1100dr/€3.24, rental 13000dr/€3.82. Buses run every 30min. to and from the center.)

FOOD

The fruit and veggie **market** in Pl. Eleftherias, on Vas. Pavlou, inside a large yellow building with a picture of grapes over the doors, is touristy and expensive; mini-markets have cheaper fruit. (Open M-F 7am-9pm, Sa 7am-6pm, Su 10am-2pm.) **Ampavris,** on E. Georgiou, is a true diamond in the rough. Take the road past the Casa Romana; it's about a 15min. walk from town. (Stuffed flower buds 900dr/€2.79, entrees 15000-2000dr/€3-5.50. ☎25 696.) **Hellas,** Psaron 7, at corner of Amerikis, serves huge portions of tasty Greek dishes in a service-friendly atmosphere. (Lamb *kleftiko* 2300dr/€6.76, *moussaka* 1600dr/€4.71. Vegetarian options. Open daily 4-11pm.) **Nick the Fisherman,** Averof 21, at corner of Alikarnasou, brings daily catches straight to your plate at the best *psarotaverna* in town. Ask for Larry's friendly service. (Mussels 2000dr/€5.88, sea-urchins 1800dr/€5.29; entrees from 2000-3000dr/€5.88-8.82 Open 1pm-late.)

NIGHTLIFE

Most bars are in two districts. The first is around **Exarhia** (a.k.a. **Bar Street,** between Akti Koundouriotou and the ancient *agora*, around **Vas. Pavlou**). Beers are 800-1000dr/€2.35-2.94, cocktails 2000dr/€5.88. Most places open at 9pm, fill by 11pm, and rock until dawn. The second district, waterfront **Porfiriou,** hops by day as sun bunnies pregame beachside for the evening's trek to the waterfront dance clubs. **Orfeas** (☎25 713), on the corner of Fenaretis and Vas. Georgiou, shows American movies (2500dr/€7.35). Kitsch (peanut-vending machines) meets de rigeur (elegant candles) at **Fashion Club,** Kanari 2, by the dolphin statue rotary. Kos's most ostentatious club, it's not nearly as pretentious as the bouncers would have you think. (3000dr/€8.82 cover includes a drink. No cover for the cafe in front. ☎22 592.) The former bathhouse of **Hamam Club** (☎28 323) near the *agora*, next to the taxi station in Pl. Diagoras, now soothes you with aural massage: live, outdoor acoustic sets play until midnight over a hopping dance club floor. Enjoy drinks in one of the one-time private bathing rooms. Opposite the beach, **Heaven,** on Zouroudi, has an appropriate cabana theme. A big, loud, popular outdoor disco. (☎23 874. Open Su-Th 10am-4am, Sa-Su 10am-dawn. 2000dr/€5.88 cover.)

SIGHTS

The run-down field of ruins bounded by Nafklirou, Hippocrates, and the waterfront was the **Roman agora;** it's now dominated by a population of sunbathing youth. The remains of a **Temple of Aphrodite** and the more impressive 2nd-century AD **Temple of Hercules** lie beside two Roman roads: the **Cardo** (axis), perpendicular to Grigoriou, and the **Decumana** (broadest), parallel to Grigoriou and intersecting Cardo. Nearby, you'll find an ancient gymnasium, a Roman swimming pool, and an early Christian basilica built over a Roman bath. At the end of the Decumana, the wood-sheltered 3rd-century AD **House of Europa** has a mosaic floor depicting Europa's abduction by Zeus. The **odeum,** a well-preserved Roman theater, lies across the street. The 3rd-century AD **Casa Romana,** uncovered by an Italian archaeologist in 1933, is down Grigoriou. The meager ruins of a **Temple of Dionysus** stand opposite the Casa Romana. *(Open 24hr. Free.)*

Invading Knights of St. John built the massive 15th-century **castle.** The once-movable bridge marks the connecting entrance from the Square of Hippocrates, and linked the island castle to the mainland. Destroyed by an earthquake in 1495, the fortress was rebuilt by Grand Master Pierre d'Aubusson. In the 16th century, elaborate double walls and inner moats resisted Ottoman raids; now, it's a fantastically preserved example of medieval architecture. *(Take the bridge from Pl. Platanou across Finikis. ☎27 927. Ask for the helpful pamphlet available at the door. Open Tu-Su 8:30am-3pm. 1000dr/€2.94, students 500dr/€1.47, EU students free.)* The gigantic **Plane Tree of Hippocrates,** allegedly planted by the great physician 2400 years ago, has grown to an enormous 12m diameter in Pl. Platanou. It's appealing to envision Hippocrates teaching and writing beneath its noble foliage; it's deflating to realize that the tree is only 500 years old. A spring beside it leads toward an ancient sarcophagus used by the Ottomans as a cistern for the **Hadji Hassan Mosque.** Behind the tree, is the monumental **Town Hall,** originally the Italian Governor's Palace. The most impressive Ottoman structure is the **Defterdar Mosque** in Pl. Eleftherias. Nearby, on Diakou, is the abandoned art deco **Synagogue of Kos,** in use until World War II. The city's Byzantine **Greek Orthodox Cathedral** is on the corner of Korai and Ag. Nikolaou. Near the Casa Romana are the ruins of an even older (5th century BC) and more striking Hellenic mansion. *(Open Tu-Su 8:30am-2:30pm. 600dr/€1.76, students and seniors 300dr/€0.88.)*

Hellenistic and late Roman sculptures dominate the **Archaeological Museum.** A celebrated statue, found at the Kos Odeon and presumably of Hippocrates, stands in the northwest room. A 2nd-century AD Roman mosaic in the central courtyard depicts Hippocrates and a colleague entertaining the god Asclepius. Statues of Dionysos, Artemis, and Aphrodite occupy the North room and Atrium. *(In Pl. Eleftherias. ☎28 326. Open Tu-Su 8am-2:30pm. 800dr/€2.35, students 400dr/€1.18.)*

DAYTRIPS FROM KOS TOWN

ASCLEPION. The ancient sanctuary of **Asclepion** devotes itself to the healer god. In the 5th century BC, **Hippocrates** opened the world's first medical school here to encourage the development of a precise medical science. Combining priestly techniques with his own, Hippocrates made Kos the foremost medical center in ancient Greece, and many present-day doctors travel here to take their Hippocratic oaths. Carved into a hill overlooking Kos Town, the Aegean, and Asia Minor, the second- and third-century BC complex contained three levels. A sacred forest of cypress and pine trees still adjoins the site. Inside, you'll find 2nd-century AD Roman baths. The three stacked levels, called *andirons*, remain: the lowest holds a complex of 3rd-century AD Roman baths and a preserved cistern. Climb the 3rd-century BC steps to the remarkable second *andiron* and the elegant columns of the 2nd-century AD **Temple of Apollo** and the 4th-century BC **Minor Temple of Asclepius.** The 60-step climb to the third *andiron* leads to the forested remnants of the **Main Temple of Asclepius** and an overview of the site, Kos Town, and the Turkish coast opposite. *(3.5km west of Kos Town. Take the bus in summer (15min., 16 per day), or a moped. Follow the sign west off the main road, and go as straight as you can. Taxis are 500dr/€1.47. ☎28 763. Open daily Tu-Su 8am-6:30pm. 800dr/€2.35, students 400dr/€1.18.)*

RURAL KOS. Claustrophobes will be pleased at how quickly Kos Town's urban fracas gives way to pastoral landscapes north of town. The island's northern reaches stretch out flat, with bike-laned roads. Pedal along the main road east of town past a sandy, crowded stretch, on the way to the stinky hot springs of **Empros Thermae,** near the road's end and marked by several parked bikes and a Cantina. **Lampi Beach** is at the northernmost tip of the island. A nude beach lies between touristy Tigaki and Marmari. *(Buses run to Empros Thermae (9 per day), Lampi (34 per day), Marmari (10 per day), and Mastihari (4 per day).)* The main road from Kos Town heads 9km southwest to modern **Zipari** and the ruins of the early **Christian Basilica of St. Paul.** From there, a twisting road winds through the green foothills of the Dikeos Mountains to **Asfendiou,** five small settlements that you can hike to in perfect solitude. *(Buses from Kos Town go to Asfendiou (40min., 3 per day, 400dr/€1.18).)* Continue up this road to **Zia,** a delightful little village in the forests of Mt. Dikeos host to spectacular island views. **Ag. Georgios,** in the center of town, also accommodates incredible 13th and 14th-century frescos. South of **Lagoudi,** the prettiest of the five villages, the road becomes a narrow mule path and the hills grow wilder. Uphill 8km, you'll come to the compact **Pyli** ruins, with 14th-century frescoes in a Byzantine church-within-a-castle. *(Buses run from Kos Town (30min., 5 per day, 400dr/€1.18).)* Hills, ravines, and the occasional pasture roll across southern Kos, which is edged by the best **beaches** on the island. Among the beaches stretching to Kardamena, **Camel** is mildly busy and beautiful; **Paradise** is popular; and, farther north, **Magic** is empty and enticingly blue. *(The bus will let you off at any of the beaches.)* A few oceanside ancient columns distinguish **Kefalos,** Kos' ancient capital; head to the surrounding beaches, like picturesque **Limionas.** **Agios Theologos,** a gorgeous, deserted pebbly beach 4km west of Kefalos, is a favorite for nightswimming.

SAMOS

Lush and lovely Samos accommodates a more scholarly crowd than some of its island siblings. Many see Samos as a stepping-stone to Kuşadası and the ruins of Ephesus (p. 200), but this green island has been a destination in its own right for centuries. A procession of architects, sculptors, poets, philosophers, and scientists (among them Pythagoras, Epicurus, Aesop, and Aristarchus, who called the sun the center of the universe 1800 years before Copernicus) have all spent thoughtful hours on Samos's shores.

VATHY (SAMOS TOWN) ☎0273

Palm trees shade quiet inland streets, an engaging archaeological museum stands across from a garden, and red roofs speckle the neighboring hillside of Vathy, also called Samos Town, one of the northeast Aegean's most appealing port cities.

ORIENTATION AND PRACTICAL INFORMATION. Samos Town unfurls around a crescent-shaped waterfront. **Pl. Pythagoras,** identifiable by its four large palm trees, consists of cafes, taxis, and a giant lion statue. Turn onto the side streets between the port and Pl. Pythagoras to hit the most densely packed pension neighborhood on the island. Heading along the waterfront away from the port, past Pl. Pythagoras, will take you to the **Municipal Gardens,** circled by the town's public amenities and the archaeological museum. **Ferries** go to: **Chios** (5hr., 4 per week, 3000dr/€8.80); **Kos** (4hr., 2 per week, 5600dr/€16.43); **Mykonos** (6hr., 6 per week, 5400dr/€15.85); **Naxos** (6hr., 3 per week, 5300dr/€15.55) via **Paros** (4500dr/€13.21); and **Piraeus** (12hr., 1 per day, 7100dr/€20.84); and **Rhodes** (2 per week, 7800dr/€22.89). Catamarans to **Kuşadası, Turkey,** leave from Samos Town 5 times per week (1¼hr.; 10,000dr/€29.35 one-way, 14,000dr/€41.09 open-return; 3000dr/€8.80 Greek port tax). **Buses** follow the waterfront past Pl. Pythagoras, turn left onto Lekati, and continue one block to the **station.** To: **Avlakia** via **Agios Konstantinos** (7 per day), **Chrissi Ammos** (3 per week), **Heraion** (3 per day), **Marathokambs** (1-2 per day), **Pythagorion** (12 per day), **Tsainadon** via **Kokkari** and **Lemonakia** (9 per day), **Vourliotes** (3 per week). **Taxis** (☎28 404), are available 24hr. in Pl. Pythagoras. There's a **tourist office** (☎28 530 or 28 582), one block before Pl. Pythagoras (open July-Aug. M-Sa 8:30am-2pm), and a **National Bank** on the waterfront just beyond Pl. Pythagoras, with a 24hr. **ATM** (open M-Th 8am-2pm, F 8am-1:30pm). The **police** and **tourist police** (☎22 100), are after Pl. Pythagoras on the far right of the waterfront, facing inland; they speak some English. Check email at **Net Cafe** (☎22 535), on the waterfront past Pl. Pythagoras (1000dr/€2.93 per hr.; open 9am-midnight).

GREEK ISLANDS

ACCOMMODATIONS. Call ahead during the high season. If you arrive and all the beds listed below are filled, try the pensions around **Ionia** or ask a travel agent. The cool, traditional rooms of **Pension Trova,** Kalomiris 26, have the occasional bath and balcony. Turn right at the end of the ferry dock and walk 100m along the waterfront to take a left onto E. Stamatiadou before the Hotel Aiolis. Take the second left onto Manoli Kalomiri and head uphill around the bend to hit Kalomiris. (☎27 759. Singles 6000dr/€17.61; doubles 7000dr/€20.53.) Simple, 70s-era rooms surround an elegant courtyard at **Pension Avli,** Areos 2. Areos is the second left off of Manoli Kalomiri. (☎22 939. Doubles 8000dr/€23.48. Open summer only.) The neat rooms of **Pension Dreams,** Areos 9, have fridges, baths, TV and coffee-makers. (☎24 350. Singles 6000dr/€17.61; doubles 7000dr/€20.53; triples 8000dr/€23.48.)

FOOD. Gourmands will find their time well-spent in savoring sweet Samian wine, served at all of the island's nearly indistinguishable restaurants, which otherwise offer a standard spate of traditional meals. **Gregory's,** just past the post office heading inland, is a local favorite. More conveniently located is **Christos,** in Pl. Nicolaos behind Pl. Pythagoras, with outdoor seating for optimal people-watching.

SIGHTS. The phenomenal **Archaeological Museum,** behind the municipal gardens, exhibits Samos' past glory as a commercial and religious center for worshiping Hera. Finds from ancient Heraion, the temple of Hera, and other local digs are enshrined in two recently renovated buildings full of informative notes; you'll find more proof of Heraion's bygone splendor here than in the crumbled remains at the site. The first building houses intricate Laconian ivory carvings of mythological notables, and awesome statues like a colossal 5m **Kouros** from 560 BC. There's also the stunning **Geneleas group.** Named after its sculptor, the nearly life-size votive offering depicts a family; it once graced ancient Heraion's Sacred Way. An exhibit on Hera-worship shows off remarkable offerings made to the goddess. Objects from Ancient Egypt, Cyprus, and the Near East testify to the island's extensive early trade. In the last room, a case of gorgeously nightmarish **protomes** (cauldron handles) is not to be missed. (☎27 469. Open Tu-Su 8:30am-3pm. 800dr/€2.35, seniors and students 400dr/€1.17, EU students free.) In July and August, Samos hosts classical and jazz concerts featuring Greek artists as part of the **Manolis Kalomiris Festival.** Contact the tourist office for a schedule of events.

BEACHES. Most of the northern coast of Samos is easily accessible from the road to **Karlovassi.** Built on a peninsula 10km west of Samos Town is the eminently visitable northern village of **Kokkari. Lemonakia Beach,** 1km west of Kokkari next to Tsamadou, and the wide white beach west of **Avlakia** are both alluring. Kokkari, Lemonakia, and Avlakia are reachable from Samos Town though the irregular KTEL bus service (7-9 buses per day). Infrequent buses (1-2 per day) shouldn't deter you from the splendid beaches of southwest Samos. A couple kilometers west of the peaceful red-roofed hamlet of **Marathokampos** is the spacious beach at **Votsalakia.** A bit farther is an even better beach at **Psili Ammos.**

DAYTRIP FROM VATHY: POLYKRATES' PROJECTS. The ancient city of **Pythagorion** (Πυθαγορειο), once the island's capital, thrived during the 6th century BC under the reign of **Polykrates the Tyrant.** Herodotus reports that Polykrates undertook the three most daring engineering projects in the Hellenic world, among them the **Tunnel of Eupalinos,** 1500m up the hill to the north of town, in fact an underground aqueduct that diverted water from a natural spring to the city below. It may owe its misnomer to its size, which just fits a person. About 200m of damp cavern are open to visitors. To reach the tunnel, walk back inland from the bus stop in town and follow the signs. The 20min. walk to the tunnel entrance passes minor ancient ruins, rolling hills, and grazing goats. *(☎61 400. Open Tu-Su 8:45am-2:45pm, last entrance 2:15pm. 500dr/€1.47, students 300dr/€0.88, EU students free.)* Polykrates' 40m deep **harbor mole** (rock pier) still supports the modern pier. Blocks, columns, walls fragments, and entablatures are strewn throughout Pythagorion like Lincoln Logs after a floorquake—the presentation in the small **Archaeological Museum** is no different. Half the collection fits in the building, and many pieces are haphazardly scattered on the sidewalk in front. *(☎61 400. Open Tu-Su 9am-2:30pm. Free.)* The ruined **Castle of Lycurgus,** on the south side of town, was built in the beginning of the 19th century by Lycurgus, a Samos native and leader in the Greek War for Independence. The **Church of the Transfiguration** is a pale blue variation on classic Orthodox architecture. *(A bus from Samos Town services Pythagorion (20min., 300dr/€0.88). The beach town of Pythagorion, 14km south of Samos Town, sits atop the ancient city of the same name.)* Polykrates' magnum opus is in **Heraion** (Ηπαιον; EAR-ion). Seven centuries of pilgrims worshipped Hera on Samos when Polykrates began enlarging the temple. Eventually, 134 columns supported the 118m-long, 58m-wide 530 BC version of the Temple of Hera; a 525 BC fire wrecked it. A lone standing column remains of the once-majestic colonnade; casts of the Geneleas group, now in the Samos Museum, accompany it. Walk along the beach to return to the temple. If you can't enter through the beachside back gate, a path brings you inland to the main road and main entrance farther along the beach, past two houses. Follow custom: wrap up in your finest toga and carry along a jug of libations on this path, which runs close to the ancient Iera Odos (Sacred Way) from Pythagorion to the temple. *(The bus from Pythagorion (10 min., 300dr/€0.88) stops in Heraion Town. ☎95 277. Open Tu-Su 8:30am-3pm. 800dr/€2.35, students 400dr/€1.17.)*

CHIOS

Chios (KHEE-ohs) is where the wild things *were:* Orion hunted every last beast down, leaving the island's mountainsides to pine and cypress trees, and to native son, Homer. Ever since, human occupants have cultivated and exported the trees' *masticha*—a bittersweet, gummy resin used in a number of things from chewing gum to color TVs. Medieval Genovese and Venetian Crusaders (among them Christopher Columbus) made themselves at home here, and in 1822 Chios hosted a failed Greek nationalist rebellion. A military base and a center of Greek shipping, Chios only recently opened its gates to tourist infiltrators. As its striking volcanic beaches and medieval villages become more accessible, Chios flashes back to the pre-Orion days, as tourists on their way Çeşme do the Wild Thing all night long.

CHIOS TOWN ☎0271

Shipping provides the lion's share of Chios's wealth, and tourists are the exception instead of the rule at the waterfront tavernas and trendy cafes. Inland, a crumbling medieval fortress keeps centuries of island history intact within its decayed bulk—from the days of Byzantine occupation to the Nazi's razing of the town during World War II. Today, tourists and townspeople invade the fallen fortifications daily, partaking of the markets and tavernas that now occupy the fortress.

ORIENTATION AND PRACTICAL INFORMATION. Walking left from the ferry dock along the waterfront, you'll pass a bevy of cafes and restaurants. A right on **Kanari** takes you inland to **Pl. Vounakio,** the social center of town, where most services, buses, and taxis plant themselves on one side or another of the **Municipal Gardens.** Left of Vounakio lies the **market street,** where groceries and bakeries open for business weekday mornings and evenings. Between the ferry dock and the Municipal Gardens, fortress walls hug the Old Town, a residential area with a few small shops and tavernas. **Ferries** go to: **Alexandroupolis** (1 per week, 9000dr/€26.41); **Kos** (1 per week 6am, 6000dr/€17.61); **Lesvos**

(3hr., 1 per week, 3500dr/€10.27); **Limnos** (2 per week, 5500dr/€16.14); **Piraeus** (8 hr., 1-2 per day, 6300dr/€18.49); **Rhodes** (1 per week, 7100dr); **Samos** (4hr., 1 per week, 3300dr/€9.68); and **Çeşme,** Turkey (45min., 1 per day, 17,000dr/€49.89). **Tickets** are available at Hatzelenis Tourist Agency. KTEL **buses** (☎27 507 or 24 257) leave from both sides of Pl. Vounakio, right off the municipal gardens coming from the waterfront. Blue buses (☎23 086), in the plateia on Dimokratias, travel within the vicinity of Chios Town (9km), making 5-6 trips daily to **Daskalopetra, Kontari, Karfas, Karies,** and **Vrondados.** Green buses, on the left side of the municipal gardens, make trips to **Emborios Beach, Pyrgi,** and **Volissos.** To reach the **tourist office,** Kanari 18, turn off the waterfront onto Kanari, walk toward the plateia and look for the "i" sign. They provide maps and help with transportation and accommodations. (☎44 344 or 44 389. Open May-Oct. daily 7am-10pm.) The **Ionian Bank,** Kanari 16, is next to the tourist office and offers a 24hr. **ATM** and **currency exchange.** (☎23 522 or 23 434. Open M-Th 8am-2pm, F 8am-1:30pm.) A 24hr. **hospital** (☎44 303) is 2km north of Chios. **Enter Internet Cafe,** Aigeou 98, on the second floor of a waterfront building, charges 600dr/€1.76 for 30min. (☎41 058. Open 9:30am-late.)

ACCOMMODATIONS. Most of Chios Town's accommodations are on the far end of the waterfront from the ferry dock, in high-ceilinged, turn-of-the-century mansions. In high season, seek help from a tourist agency to get a room. In a yellow building at the far right end of the waterfront, the hospitable owners at **Chios Rooms,** Leofores 114, offer bright and breezy rooms with polished hard-wood floors, most with a sea view and some with bath. (☎20 198. In summer, doubles 8000dr/€23.48; triples 10,000dr/€29.35, 12,000dr/€35.22 with bath. Monthly rental available in winter.) One block behind Aigeou on the waterfront, **Giannis Rooms to Let,** M. Livanou 48, has rooms with baths, a common kitchen, and a lovely backyard garden. (☎27 433. Open May-Oct. Doubles 8000-12,000dr/€23.48-35.22.)

FOOD. Myriad vendors set up shop near Pl. Vounakio. For lunch on the cheap, bite into the fresh *spanakopita* or *tyropita* available in **bakeries.** Love is in the ruins at elegant **Ouzeri Ikobou Plita,** Ag. Giorgios 20, where open-air tables nestle into the tumbledown walls of the Byzantine fortress. To get there, walk past Hatzelenis on Aigeou and make the fourth right. There's no menu; just eyeball the options and pick whatever looks good. Turning off the waterfront on the way to the Archaeology Museum brings you shortly to the **Two Brothers,** on Livanou, who serve good Greek grub in their garden restaurant. (☎21 313.)

SIGHTS. The **Archaeology Museum,** Michalon 10, inland toward the left end of the waterfront, dissects Chios's role in the ancient Aegean world, with an extensive collection of artifacts and detailed explanatory placards. Don't miss the 3rd-century AD statue of Leda and the Swan, with just enough limbs left on both parties to suggest how the dirty deed was done. (☎82 100. Open Tu-Su 8:30am-3pm. 500dr/€1.47, students 300dr/€0.88, EU students free.) Relics of the town's past encircle Pl. Vounakio. To the right of the plateia, the walls of the **Byzantine Castro,** reconstructed by the Genovese, enclose the narrow streets of the **Old Town.** The castle houses a handful of well-restored 14th-century Byzantine wall paintings in the **Justinian Palace** as you enter from Vounakio. (☎26 866. Open Tu-Su 9am-3pm. 500dr/€1.47, students 300dr/€0.88.) The minaret of the nearby **Ottoman Mosque** is visible from far away, though almost every surface has a storefront built in front of it. The main room contains a Byzantine collection, including a short hallway of paintings and a small courtyard of Venetian, Genovese, and Ottoman sculptural pieces. (Open Tu-Sa 10am-1pm, Su 10am-3pm. 500dr/€1.47, students 300dr/€0.88.) The **Folklore Museum,** on the first floor of the **Korais Library,** is next to the **Mitropolis,** Chios Town's cathedral. The collection is extensive, but there are no explanatory placards. (Open M-Th 8am-2pm, F 8am-2pm and 5-7:30pm, Sa 8am-12:30pm.)

DAYTRIPS FROM CHIOS TOWN. On the eastern half of the island, several sites silently recall the invasion of the island by the Ottoman Turks in 1822, among them **Nea Moni** and **Anavatos.** Built in the 11th century, the Nea Moni (New Monastery), 16km west of Chios Town, was inspired by the miraculous appearance of an icon of the Virgin Mary to three hermits. Before entering the main chapel, you'll pass through the inner narthex, featuring stunning 11th-century gold mosaics; their artists are also responsible for the mosaics of Hagia Sophia in Istanbul. An adjoining chapel beside the entrance to the complex houses a memorial to monks and villagers massacred by the Turks in 1822, when the island's population was reduced from 118,000 to 18,000. Elsewhere on the island, 23,000 residents were killed and 47,000 sold into slavery. (Open 9am-1pm and 4-8pm. Free. Dress modestly.) An on-site museum displays church garments and religious items. Open 8:30am-1pm. 500dr/ı1.47. Free Su.)

Anavatos, 15km west of Nea Moni, is a beautiful, abandoned village built into the hillside. The village's women and children flung themselves from these cliffs in resistance to the 1822 invasion. A walk among the ruins of these fortifications provides amazing views of the hills. Stop into the church to the right of the site's entrance to see a spectacular folk-art rendition of the massacre of 1822. (Check with the tourist office or the green bus terminal in Chios for information on excursions to both sites. Taxi drivers may agree to drive you to the site, wait 30min., and bring you back; a taxi-tour of Nea Moni and Anavatos costs around 8000dr/ €23.48.)

The villages in the southern half of the island, called *Mastichochoria*, are home to Chios's famous resin, produced by squat mastic or lentisk trees. **Pyrgi,** high in the hills 25km from Chios, is one of Greece's most beautiful villages, thanks to the black and white geometric designs tattooing its buildings. Pyrgi is also home to the 12th-century **Agioi Apostoloi Church,** a replica of the Nea Moni. Thirteenth-century frescoes and paintings from a Cretan iconography school cover almost every inch of the interior. (Open M-F 9am-3pm. 100dr/ı0.29.) The caretaker can unlock the front gate for you; ask across from the OTE. Access Pyrgi via bus from Chios.

BEACHES. 6km south of Chios Town lies popular, sandy **Karfas,** victim of Chios's latest burst of development. Convenient to both the beach and the amenities of Chios Town, many tourists take up temporary residence here. Blue **buses** run from Pl. Vournakio in Chios. Hatzelenis Tours in Chios Town can set you up with a double with bath and kitchen by the beach at **Villa Anatoli** (š20 002 or 32 235. Doubles 12,000dr/ı35.22). Farther south lies pristine **Emborio,** where beige volcanic cliffs contrast with black stones and deep-blue water below. The green **bus** from Chios Town drops off at the harbor; the first beach is up the only road to the right (facing the water), and a smaller, less crowded shore is up the stairs to your right.

Nine kilometers north of Chios Town, you'll find the pleasant, pebbly shores of **Vrondados** and **Daskalopetra.** Blue **buses** from Pl. Vournakio in Chios Town service both. A 2min. walk from Daskolopetra beach takes you to the **Sanctuary of Cybele.** Here, sitting on the **Stone of Homer,** the bard is rumored to have mentored students. After Daskalopetra, the main roads wind northwest along the coast past Marmaron to **Nagos,** with its gray stone beach—perhaps a popular spot to play hooky from Homer's classes. High in the hills toward the center of the island, the village of **Volissos,** Homer's legendary birthplace, is crowned by a Byzantine fort with a handful of modern-day habitations scattered around it. **Buses** run here from Chios.

MEDITERRANEAN COAST

Alternately chic, garish, and remote, Turkey's Mediterranean coast stretches along lush national parks, sun-soaked beaches, and pine forests. Natural beauty and ancient ruins have made the western Mediterranean one of the most touristed regions in Turkey. While increasingly over-run with pushy touts, Armani sportswear and mega-hotels, the western coast also caters to the backpacker circuit. By day, travelers take tranquil boat trips, hike among waterfalls, and explore submerged ruins; by night, they exchange stories over *Efes*, dance under the stars, and fall asleep in seaside pensions and treehouses.

HIGHLIGHTS OF THE MEDITERRANEAN COAST

HACK your way through an Amazonian forest to find ruins of an ancient city overrun by crabs, turtles, birds, and lizards in **Olimpos** (p. 283).

HIKE up a rocky path through the enchanting **Butterfly Valley** and spend the night in a campsite surrounded by countless nocturnal Jersey Tiger Butterflies (p. 272).

DISCOVER the eternal Promethean flame—the **Chimaera** of Mt. Olimpos (p. 284).

PEER through the clear Mediterranean waters to see the staircases and walls of the sunken city of **Kekova** (p. 281).

VISIT the Mediterranean's only seal colony in the **Blue Caves** near Kaş (p. 280).

WITNESS stunning **Saklıkent Gorge** on a rafting trip along its icy stream (p. 267).

MARMARİS COAST

MARMARİS ☎252

Marmaris's popularity with tourists has engendered a peculiar blend of tradition and transaction. The town bazaar sells both finely crafted traditional wares and forged signature accessories, and local fishermen are increasingly doubling as tour guides ready to ferry tourists to and from uninhabited coastal crannies. What little native charm hasn't been packaged for tourists can be found in this tacky pleasure-haven's namesake, Marmaris Castle. The town owes its name to Süleyman the Magnificent's order to "hang the architect" *(mimarı as)*; exactly what was so distasteful about this understated castle is hard to say, as throngs of appreciative international tourists swarm to the landmark each summer.

One of the ancient Carian kingdom's most important seaports, Marmaris connected Anatolia with Rhodes and Egypt. The natural harbor hosted the naval campaigns of both Süleyman the Magnificent in 1522 and Lord Nelson in 1798. Today, it's a perfect base for whatever touristic designs travelers might have on the pristine coast that stretches away past the town.

TRANSPORTATION

Buses: To reach the otogar (☎412 30 37), walk down Ulusal Egemenlik Bul. from the statue and make a sharp right onto Mustafa Münir Elgin Bul. after the Türk gas station. The bus station is on the left, around the corner from the shopping center. To reach the **Varan** (☎412 09 79) and **Kamil Koç** (☎412 80 76 or 412 06 30) offices, head inland-

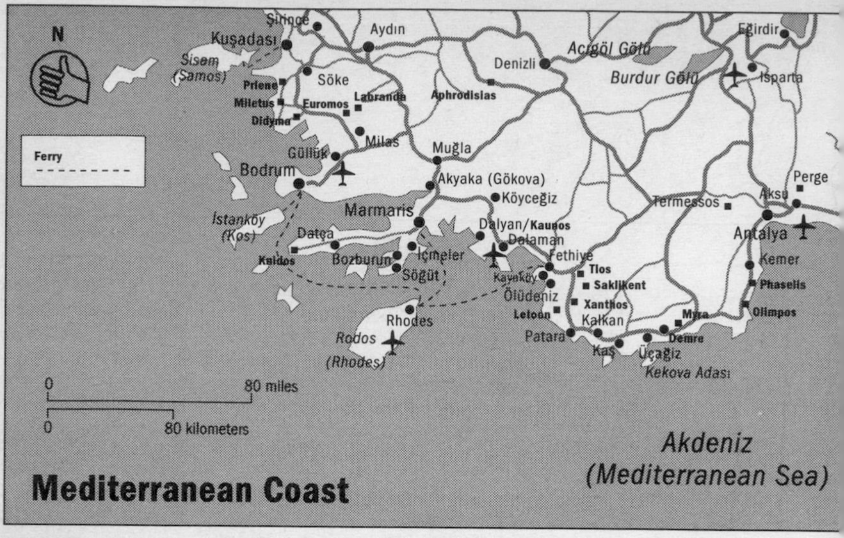

Mediterranean Coast

DESTINATION	COMPANY	DURATION	TIME (DAILY)	PRICE
Ankara	Kamil Koç	10hr.	10am, 9pm	$14
	Pamukkale	11hr.	9:45am, 9, 10, 11pm	$16
Antalya	Pamukkale	7hr.	10am, 11pm	$12
Adana	Kamil Koç	16hr.	6:45pm	$17
Bodrum	Pamukkale	3¾hr.	8:30am-5:30pm; in winter 8:30am-2:30pm	$6
Datça	Pamukkale	2hr.	8 per day 9am-11pm	$3.50
Eskişehir	Kamil Koç	10hr.	7pm	$16
Göreme (Cappadocia)	Aydin Türzim	14hr.	3pm	$18
İstanbul	Kamil Koç	12½hr.	7 per day 9am-1am	$18
	Pamukkale	12½hr.	9:30am, 6:30, 7:30, 9, 10pm	$20
İzmir	Kamil Koç	4½hr.	5:15am-3am	$10
	Pamukkale	4½hr.	9am-3am	$8.50
Kayseri, Sivas	Aydin Türzim	14hr.	3pm	$18
Konya	Kamil Koç	10hr.	4:40, 6:40, 8pm	$14
Kuşadası	Pamukkale	5hr.	10:45am, 6pm	$8
Pamukkale	Pamukkale	4½hr.	8:15am-5:15pm	$7

from the Atatürk statue and take the first left after Tansaş Cad. The **Pamukkale** office (☎412 55 86) is on the first left before Tansaş Cad. For points in eastern Turkey, contact **Aydin Turzim** (☎412 08 52 or 411 03 70) in the otogar.

Intercity dolmuş: From the hub at the Tansaş Shopping Center to: **Dalaman** (2hr., every 30min. 7:30am-10pm, $4); **Fethiye** (3hr., 7:30am-11pm, $5); **İçmeler** (10min., every 5min. 7am-1am, $.50); **Köyceğiz** (1hr., every 30min. 7:30am-10pm, $2); **Milas** (2½hr., 8:30am-9:30pm, $5); **Muğla** (1hr., every 30min. 9am-midnight, $1.50); **Ortaca** (1½hr., 7:30am-10pm, $3.50). Buses to **Bozburun** (1hr.; high season 5 per day 10:30am-7pm, low season noon; $2.50) and **Söğüt** (1½hr.; noon, 3, 5, 8pm; $2) leave from the main otogar. **Kalkan** and **Kaş** can be reached from Fethiye, and **Dalyan** can be reached from Ortaca.

Local Dolmuş: Two main city dolmuş routes both start at Tansaş Shopping Center. One heads straight down Ulusal Egemenlik Bul. to **Beldibi;** the other turns right onto Atatürk Cad. before weaving down backstreets to **Armutalan.**

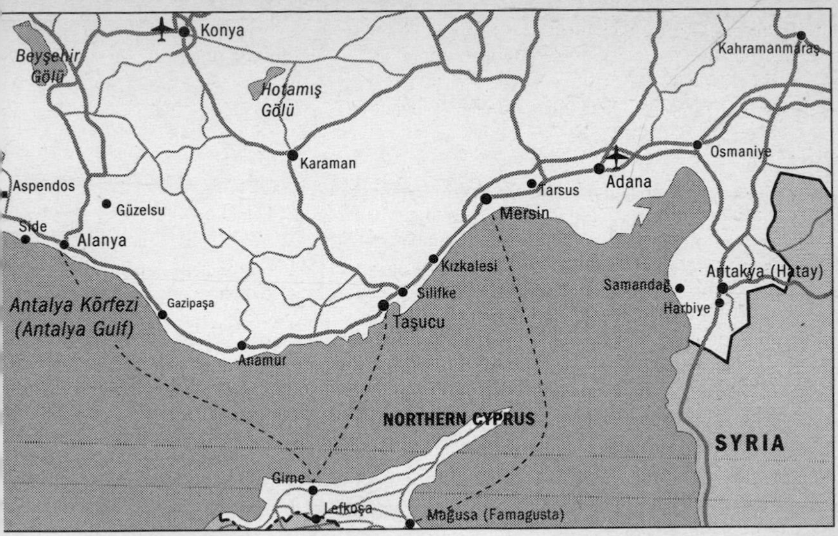

Hydrofoils: To **Rhodes** (1hr.; May-Oct. daily 9:45am and 4:30pm, return 3pm; $40-60). Contact **Engin Tür,** on the waterfront.

Catamarans: To **Rhodes** (1hr.; May-Oct. daily 9:15am, return 4pm; round-trip $40, open return $40). Make reservations one day in advance with any travel agency.

Ferries: Leave for **Rhodes** only when there are enough cars (2hr.; $30, round-trip $40, including port tax). Contact Yeşil Marmaris. Beware, there's more to pay: $10 to get out of Greece, $10 more to get back into Turkey, not to mention the cost of another $45 Turkish visa if required for your country. See **Visas and Work Permits,** p. 40.

ORIENTATION

From the bus station, outside of town on Mustafa Münir Elgin Bul., take a dolmuş ($.40) or taxi ($3) to the town center on **Ulusal Egemenlik Bul.,** where the **Tansaş Shopping Center,** bus offices, and the dolmuş hub can be found. Across from a large school at the intersection of Ulusal Egemenlik Bul. and the sea, the **Atatürk Statue** is a good reference point. Facing the water at the monument, turn left down **Kordon Cad.** to reach the tourist office and harbor. **Barlar Sok.** (Bar Street), the bazaar, and the **castle** are also to the left. **Atatürk Cad.** and **Uzunyalı Cad.** run from the right of the statue. Atatürk Cad. leads to the popular waterfront walkway and public beach before veering right and becoming **Kemal Seyfettin Elgin Bul.** Most smaller streets are numbered Soks. labeled with small blue signs.

PRACTICAL INFORMATION

TOURIST AND FINANCIAL SERVICES

Tourist Office: (☎412 10 35; fax 412 72 77), 250m along Kordon Cad. just outside the bazaar, before the cafes begin on the waterfront. English-speaking and very helpful. Open May-Sept. daily 8:30am-7:30pm; Oct.-Apr. M-F 8am-5pm. **Yeşil Marmaris** (☎412 64 86 or 412 64 88), on the harbor, 30m past the tourist office, can book catamaran and ferry trips to Rhodes (see above). Open daily 7am-11pm. For other travel information, contact the **Turkish Airlines** office, 30 Atatürk Cad. (☎412 37 52).

Budget Travel: Interyouth Hostel, Tepe Mah., 42 Sok No. 45 (☎412 36 87; fax 412 78 25; interyouth@turk.net). They'll help find cheap airline, bus, and boat tickets, arrange jeep and moped rentals, and suggest many scenic trips. There's also an extraordinary Backpacker's Cruise on the hostel's 2 beautiful yachts ($200 for 5 days with English-speaking guide, all-inclusive).

Consulates: UK (☎412 64 86 or 412 64 87; fax 412 50 77), in the Yeşil Marmaris office building on the harbor, around the corner from the tourist office. Open M-F 7:30am-noon and 2:30-5pm.

Banks: Several with **ATMs** on Kemal Seyfettin Elgin Bul., Atatürk Cad., and Kordon Cad. Most open daily; many on Ulusal Egemenik Bul. are open 24hr.

LOCAL SERVICES

English-Language Bookstore: The Marmaris Gymnasium, opposite the Atatürk statue, hosts a **book fair** from mid-June to Nov. offering books in many languages. There's a book exchange in the Interyouth Hostel in the bazaar.

Laundromats: Marina Laundry (☎413 08 45), on Haci Mustafa Sok., near Bar Street. Open daily 9am-11pm. The **Interyouth Hostel** in the bazaar also offers laundry service to non-guests ($5 per load).

Hamams: To reach **Beldibi Hamam,** take a dolmuş (10min., $.40) from Tansaş to Beldibi. $10-15. Open daily 8am-11pm. Closer to the town's center is **Bazaar Hamam** (☎412 44 06), located–you guessed it–in the bazaar. Take the street to the left of the tourist office, and then make the first left. $10-15. Open daily 8am-midnight.

EMERGENCY AND COMMUNICATIONS

Police: (☎412 14 94), on 49 Sok., by Kordon Cad., past the PTT. Little English spoken.

Pharmacies: On every other block throughout the city, generally open 8am-9pm.

Hospital: Public Devlet Hastanesi (☎412 45 49 or 412 10 29), on Datça Yolu Üzeri. From the Atatürk statue, walk 500m up Ulusal Egemenlik Bul., turn left on Datça Cad., and continue 900m uphill. **Private Ahuhetman Hospital** (☎413 14 15), on Kemal Seyfettin Elgin Bul. Follow Atatürk Cad. until it changes to Kemal Seyfettin Elgin Bul., and then make a right on 172 Sok. and a left on 167 Sok. English-speaking doctors and nurses. 24hr. emergency and non-emergency treatment.

Internet Access: Many internet cafes are in the bazaar, especially at the entrance, near the PTT. Most have A/C, charge $1.50 per hr., and are open daily 9am-midnight. **The Blue Internet Cafe** (☎413 63 28) is on Mustafa Muğlalı Cad., past Tansaş Cad. If the need for drunk email is irresistible, try **The Lighthouse** (☎855 64 43), on Yat Limanı Cad. Make a left at the end of Bar St. and follow the canal until you reach a bridge; the Lighthouse is on your left. Open until daily 2am.

PTT: The main PTT (☎412 12 12), on Mustafa Muğlalı Cad., is on the right side heading inland from the Atatürk statue. *Poste restante,* fax, currency exchange, and direct money transfer. Package pickup around the corner. Open daily 8:30am-midnight. A smaller branch is in the bazaar, to the left off Kordon Cad.

Postal Code: 48700.

ACCOMMODATIONS

Interyouth Hostel, Tepe Mah., 42 Sok. No. 45 (☎412 36 87; fax 412 78 23; interyouth@turk.net). Not to be confused with the imposter Interyouth Hostel at Kemeraltı Mah., 14 İyilikataş Mevkii, the real deal is deep within the bazaar. From the Tansaş Shopping Center, enter the bazaar and make your first right. Hospitable managers take care of guests and non-guests alike. The hostel features a book exchange, internet access ($4 per hr.), international phone, free movie rental, and laundry ($5). Can arrange cheap travel. Breakfast in the terrace bar and nightly spaghetti dinners (7:30pm, free for guests). 4-night cruises $200 per person. Dorms $5; July-Aug.: $6; private room $12. $1 discount for ISIC, HI, and IYTC holders.

Sezin Apart-Otel (☎413 61 43; fax 413 14 55). From Mustafa Muğlatı Cad., take a right onto 98 Sok. past the PTT, and then a left onto 91 Sok. The lap of luxury, with a pool, bar, and enormous rooms, each with bath, private kitchen, and balcony. A/C available $15 per room; July-Aug. $25. Discounts with *Let's Go.*

Çubuk Hotel (☎412 67 74; fax 412 67 76). Head down Atatürk Cad. from the statue and turn right on the 1st street after the park; the hotel is on the left corner. 27 carpeted, pastel-hued rooms with bath, phones, balconies, and A/C. Included breakfast served in a room with parakeets. $10 per person; July-Aug. singles $13, doubles $25.

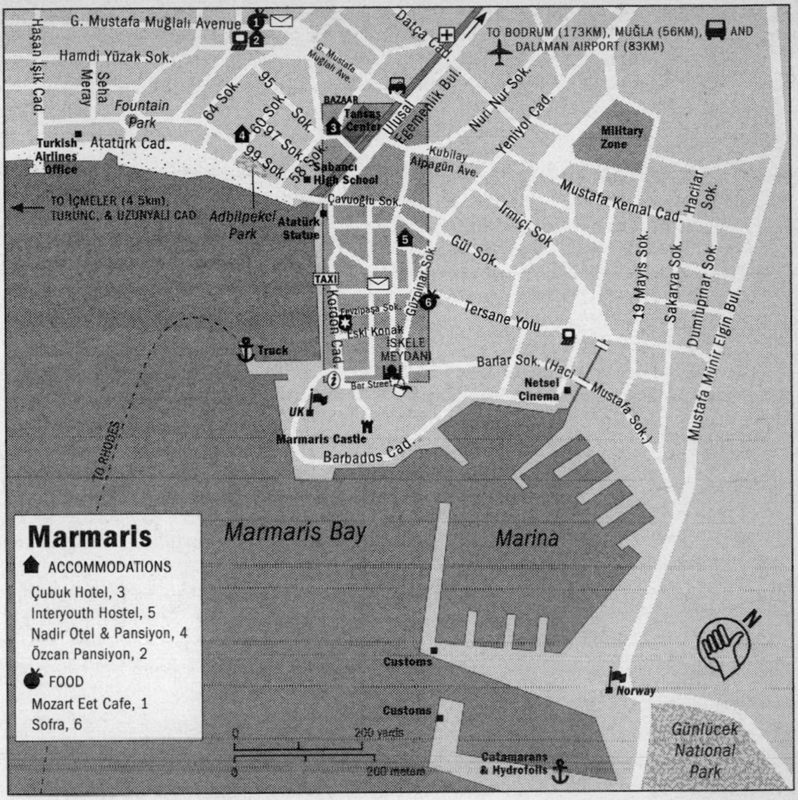

Nadir Otel and Pansiyon, Kemeraltı Mah., 56 Sok. (☎412 11 67 or 412 18 06), the first left off Mustafa Muğlalı Cad. All rooms with TV and balcony. Ask for the side away from the shopping center. The hotel has 24 doubles with bath. Breakfast included. Singles $12; doubles $17; July-Aug. singles $12, doubles $20. The pension offers 20 rooms, some with bath, no breakfast. $5 per person; July-Aug. $8.

Özcan Pansiyon, Kemeraltı Mah., 3 Çam Sok. (☎412 77 61), in a small cul-de-sac off Mustafa Muğlalı Cad. 17 tidy rooms with balconies, most with bath. Communal kitchen. Colorful outside patio/bar. Owner runs 2 boat trips to sites around Marmaris. Laundry and international phone. Breakfast $1.50; July-Aug. $2. $7 per person; off-season $5. Male guests can stay in beds on an outdoor terrace for $3 per person.

FOOD

Marmaris is chock-full of busy, pricey eateries. For cheap fare, try the several small restaurants in the bazaar area or the fast food-style *kebap* places on almost every corner (chicken, meat, and vegetable *kebaps* $3-5). Or carbo-load with a baked potato slathered with toppings ($2-4) at the stands along Atatürk Cad.

Kervansaray Restaurant (☎412 64 84). From the statue, head straight on Ulusal Egemenlik Bul., turn left on Datça Yolu, and take another left on Yunus Nadi Cad.; the restaurant is on the first corner on the right. For $12, feast on a large meal, with Turkish wine or beer and enjoy live Turkish music, wrestling, and traditional folk dances. The finale features the most famous male belly dancer in Marmaris. Ask at the Interyouth Hostel for more information, as groups often go from there. Open daily Apr.-Oct.

Sofra (☎413 26 31), 3 blocks into the bazaar from the PTT, on the right. Well-recommended by the tourist office, Sofra serves *kebaps* ($1-3.50), lamb and mushroom dishes ($4) and European fare ($6) to locals and tourists alike. Enjoy the wine bottle on every table and the music from the record store across the street. Open 24hr.

Eet Cafe Mozart, Mustafa Muğlalı Cad. #1-2-4 (☎413 87 64). Head straight down Ulusal Egemenlik Bul. and turn left on the street after Tansaş Shopping Center; look for the large french-fry man by the PTT. This charming Dutch cafe/patisserie/restaurant serves European fare (fish and chips wrapped in newspaper; $8.50). The chef is open to creating new dishes. Turkish breakfast $2.50; English breakfast $3; apple tart $3; falafel $4.40. Open daily 8:30am-12:30am.

SIGHTS

BEACHES. Only 1500m away from the tourist office, **Günlücek National Park** offers a small, quiet beach and picnic tables set against a lush forest with fragrant frankincense trees. While the lively, crowded beach in Marmaris ($2.50 per person) is great for skin toasting, ice cream licking, and playful frolicking, quieter and prettier beaches in the area are accessible only by boat. Pleasant **İçmeler beach** is, unfortunately, no exception, though the crowds are a bit thinner. *(**Park:** Follow the harbor road past the marina and across the wooden footbridge, or catch a dolmuş from in front of the Tansaş Shopping Center (5min., every 15min., $.40.). **Beach:** dolmuş leave from the front of Tansaş Shopping Center or anywhere along Atatürk Cad. (10min., every 5min. 8am-1am, $.50.). Alternatively, catch the water dolmuş to İçmeler (30min., every 30 min. daily 10am-7pm, $3) from the waterfront next to the Atatürk statue and the tourist office.)*

BOAT TRIPS. Water dolmuş to **Turunç Beach** depart from the waterfront by the Atatürk statue. (45min., daily in summer, every hr. 7am-7pm, $1.) In high season, daily boat trips run to **Dalyan** and **Kaunos** feature **Turtle Beach** and **mud baths** (see **Dalyan and Kaunos,** p. 260). *(Buy tickets from the boats moored on the waterfront across from the bazaar. Summer only; 9:30am, return 7pm; $23 per person; lunch included.)*

Full-day boat tours around both Marmaris and Çiflik Bays stop at **Paradise Island Beach,** the **Akvaryum (aquarium),** several phosphorous caves, and the popular **Turunç Beach.** They continue to the less-crowded **Kumlu Buk Beach,** near the remains of a fortress; the early Byzantine and strangely-named **Pregnant Church;** and the tiny village of Keçi, in the heavily-wooded Nimara Peninsula, which offers spectacular views of the surrounding coastline. *($10-15 per person. Lunch included.)* For a more relaxing tour, contact **Zeus Boat Tours.** Captain Sadık Turgut navigates travelers on lazy, quiet circuits through truly secluded fishing holes he discovered in his fishing days. *(☎247 49 74. $15 per person. Lunch included).* For those in search of a longer voyage, the Interyouth Hostel in the bazaar offers a 4-day boat trip exploring the rugged coast line from Marmaris to Fethiye. *($200 per person.)*

The fine sand beaches of **Kleopatra's Island,** a.k.a. Sedir Adası, are a good daytrip. Legend has it that Marc Antony imported the white sand from the Red Sea some 2100 years ago in an attempt to get Cleopatra into the sack. Those less romantically inclined suspect that fossilized plankton make the sand so white. *(The island can be reached by boat or through an organized tour arranged by any travel agency. A bus will pick up people at 10:30am at a planned meeting place and drive 20min. to Çamlı village, from where a boat will depart for the island. 45min., in summer 17 per day from 10:30am, return 7pm.)*

Travelers can also rent a motorbike ($30 per day) for exploring archaeological sites dotting the Bozburun Peninsula. Inquire at the Interyouth Hostel.

TURGUT WATERFALL. This series of small waterfalls, 35km from Marmaris, is perfect for swimming in the shade or pleasant hikes. Popular but beautiful, with a population of monkeys the summer. *(Take a dolmuş to Turgut from the stop on Datça Yol., one block up from Tansaş. 40min.; 10:30am, 1, 3:30, 6pm; $1.50. Open daily 8am-8pm.)*

OLD TOWN. Meandering through this area of Marmaris rewards the explorer with local color and spectacular views. Small whitewashed buildings cluster on the hill surrounding the castle. Narrow stone passages reveal cats, colorful gardens, and stunning vistas of the sea. The old town is perfect for an afternoon of wandering.

MARMARIS CASTLE. A fertile garden complete with peacocks and turtles fills the inner courtyard of this fairly unremarkable castle, while the paths along the ramparts offer panoramic views of the Marmaris harbor. Built in 1522 by Süleyman the Magnificent, Marmaris's castle was used as a base for the successful campaign against the Crusaders camped out on Rhodes. The castle now exhibits two rooms of stone age, Greek, and Roman pottery from 3000 BC onward and an **ethnography room** of Ottoman material culture. Another room displays changing art collections. *(From the tourist office, take the street to the left, turn left into the bazaar, and then turn right down the narrow alley after the Sultan Restaurant; the castle is at the top of the stone stairs. Open Tu-Su 8:30am-noon and 2-5:30pm. $1.20, students $.60.)*

ENTERTAINMENT

It's hard to tell which is hotter in Marmaris: the burning sun or the blazing nightlife. 11pm is showtime for Barlar Sok., Uzunyalı Cad., and Barbados Cad. (the harbor), when bars and clubs kick into high gear. Loud, bright, and contagious music and neon lights spill onto the street.

To reach **Barlar Sok.** (Bar St.), face the tourist office and take the left road next to the tourist office. Turn left into the bazaar at the next corner and walk straight. Let the music and lights be your guide to a neon sign reading "Bar Street." The somewhat removed **Uzunyalı** is on the opposite side of Marmaris, right on the waterfront past the Atatürk Statue, with larger bars, clubs, and karaoke. **Barbados Cad.** is the pavement along the harbor. Most bars and clubs have no cover, and all clubs feature dancing. Unless otherwise noted, all are open daily year-round. At bars with both indoor and outdoor seating, drinks are usually cheaper outside.

CLUBS

Backstreet (☎412 40 48). On Bar St. An open-air tropical oasis, where ultra-hip dancers groove to international rock and pop while onlookers chill and pool sharks hunt under palm trees along a tiny, fish-filled creek. Beer $2.50; *rakı* $3.50; cocktails $4-8. Open May-Sept. daily 9am-4am.

Greenhouse (☎412 50 71). Halfway down Bar St. Known for its excellent cutting-edge music and comfortable setting, this electric-green, air-conditioned dance club and bar is a Marmaris favorite. Beer $2; *rakı* $3.50; cocktails $5-10. Open daily 9pm-5am.

Beach Club (☎412 11 88). On the beach at the far end of Uzunlyalı. Famous for its cabana-like exterior decorated with fluorescent surfboards and zebra-print bar stools, plus an outdoor bar painted with tropical fish. Inside, the sophisticated surroundings reverberate with the top-notch electronic sounds of hip-hop, house, and Top 40. Beer $1.20-2; *rakı* $2; cocktails (which have a "never say when" philosophy) $5. Open daily 8am-4am in winter Sa-Su 8am-4am. 18+; single men usually not admitted.

Cheers (☎412 67 22). 50m past the Beach Club on Uzunyalı. An outrageously fun disco "theme park" featuring *Grease* and *Saturday Night Fever*. A mega sound system blasts 60s, 70s, and 80s music early in the evening, shifting to techno as the night wears on. Look for flailing limbs and yipping cowboys coming from the direction of the bucking bronco ride. Beer $1.80; *rakı* $3.60; cocktails $4-6 (try the "fishbowls" and you'll be swimming home, $20). Open Apr.-Oct. 8am-4am. 18+ on the dance floor.

BARS

Magic Garden Bar (☎413 12 96), on the right at the beginning of Bar Street. This colorful refuge is a great place to talk and people-watch. Sit at jungle-green terrace tables under a canopy of grapes. Cider $3. Special mixed drinks $7. Open daily 2pm-4am.

B-52 (☎413 45 66), on Bar St. Popcorn at the bar, dancing on the side bar and a young, mobile crowd provide a party so big, it extends into the street and the adjacent establishments. Beer $2.50; *rakı* $3; cocktails $5. Open 24hr.

Ivy Reggae Bar (☎413 65 05), on Barbados Cad., near the Escape Bar. Caribbean bar filled with Bob Marley paraphernalia. Catch the "mixed jammin'" clientele while sipping tropical concoctions under the Hawaiian-style thatched roof. Beer $1.75; *rakı* $2.50; cocktails $5. Open Mar.-Nov. daily 9am-3am.

Marmaris Irish Bar, 87 Bar St. (☎412 66 96), on the left side of Bar St. Flashing lights, contemporary tunes, and a 2-story, dark wood bar allows for much getting jiggy with it. Beer $2; Guiness $5; *rakı* $3. Open daily 8pm-5am.

Escape Bar (☎412 74 17), at the far end of Barbaos St. A cheaper, casual alternative to the flashy nightclubs. Dart boards and surfing posters cover the brick walls; the pool table is ready for action. Friendly backpackers swap travel stories with yacht owners. Beer $1.75; *rakı* $2; cocktails $5. Open daily 8pm-3:30am.

Bedesten Cafe (☎412 72 02), on your left before entering Bar St. If you find the din of Bar St. too oppressive, this secluded water-pipe cafe will soothe your cares with backgammon and snacks ($1-3) in full view of the old mosque's brilliant blue minaret. Water pipe $6; tea $.50; beer $2. Open daily 8am-2am.

İÇMELER ☎252

The next cove down the coast from Marmaris, İçmeler is slowly becoming as crowded as its more famous neighbor. The full-blown concrete conglomerate of tall luxury hotels and neon-signed restaurants now runs all the way down to the beach. It's possible, however, to overlook the package-tour feel of the place and discover İçmeler's superior beach and watersport options. You'll also find some quiet, laid-back pensions a pleasant distance from the beach-front resorts. Frequent dolmuş service to Marmaris, only 10 to 15 minutes away, makes İçmeler a an alternative to lodging in Marmaris while staying within reach of its bars and clubs.

TRANSPORTATION. **Dolmuş** run to **Marmaris** from the beach on Kayabal Cad. or from İnönü Cad. (every 15min. 7am-1am, $.75). **Dolmuş boats** travel to **Marmaris** (30min.; in summer every 30min. 7am-7pm, depart when full; $3) and **Turunç beach** (30min.; in summer 10, 11am, 1, 3pm; return 1:30, 3:30, 4:30pm; $5).

ORIENTATION AND PRACTICAL INFORMATION. Pamukkale (☎455 35 35) and Kamil Koç (☎455 20 69) offices are on Kayabal Cad. Dolmuş and buses enter İçmeler via **Atatürk Cad.** (later **İnönü Cad.**), passing Agua Life water park on the left and turning left down **Kayabal Cad.** and **Cumhuriyet Cad.** Visitors in search of a pension should ask to be let off on İnönü Cad. to reduce walking. Further toward the shore, both run parallel to the beach. Any street to the left off Kayabal Cad. leads first to the residential area with a few pensions then to the huge hotels, and finally to the beach. **Kenan Evren Cad.,** which ends at the beach, links Kayabal Cad. and Cumhuriyet Cad. Streets are very poorly marked, so you'll want to get a map from the Marmaris tourist office.

There is no tourist office in İçmeler, but maps are available in the Marmaris office and from vendors in Marmaris. A more than adequate number of **currency exchanges** and **ATMs** dot Cumhuriyet Cad. and Kenan Evran Cad. There is a **pharmacy** on Kenan Evran Bul., one block from the beach. A small **health clinic, Sağlık Ocağı,** is on the right hand side of 51 Sok., off İnönü Cad., around the corner from the PTT. (☎455 36 98. Open M-Sa 8:30am-noon and 1-5:30pm.) The **police station** (☎455 23 55) is at Kayabal Cad., 72 Sok. No. 3. The **PTT** is on İnönü Cad. (☎455 34 60. Open daily 8am-10pm.) **Postal code:** 48720.

HOW TO DRINK RAKI The art of drinking *rakı*, Turkey's most famous and potent local drink, is a skill deeply ingrained for most Turks and pitifully elusive to most foreigners. Made with aniseed and white grapes, *rakı* contains 40% alcohol and smells strongly of licorice. The best *rakı*, coming from **Tekirdağ,** near İstanbul, is best complemented by white cheese, watermelon, or fish, which bring out the flavor while soothing the stomach from the fiery impact of the liquor. Though most commonly drunk in conjunction with cold water (which turns it a cloudy white), *rakı* is occasionally mixed with orange juice or *salgam,* a spicy turnip juice. However you take it, *rakı* is best drunk slowly—you'll learn to respect its kick—and in the company of good friends. Try drinking spoonful of olive oil beforehand if you want to stay sober.

ACCOMMODATIONS. The pensions located in the residential section between Kayabal Cad. and Cumhuriyet Cad. are the most quiet and cost-effective options in İçmeler. To reach the **Bellevue Hotel,** turn onto Cumhuriyet Cad. off İnönü Cad., making a right at the bar and another right at the first block (68 Sok.). Bellevue will be on your left. A beautiful pool and garden bar are visible from the outside, while modern rooms with carpet, A/C, phone, and bath await within. Breakfast is included. (☎455 26 96; fax 455 40 07. Singles $8; July-Aug. $12.) To find the **Onat Apart,** make a right off Kayabal Cad. just before the Tansaş Center, and a left when the road ends at a schoolhouse. Duplex rooms with kitchens, A/C, balconies, phone, and bath. Look for the owners in the pharmacy next door. (☎455 30 66; fax 455 36 85. $10 per night. AmEx/MC/V.) To get to **Leydi Pansiyon,** turn left off İnönü Cad. (when heading toward Kayabal Cad.) onto 49 Sok. and make a left after two blocks; the pension will be on your right. Surrounded by a garden, the Leydi provides communal bath, kitchen and very rustic rooms. Little English is spoken. (☎455 22 44. 8 rooms. $5 per person.)

FOOD AND ENTERTAINMENT. Along the beach, İçmeler's dining tends toward the pricey, but there are some smaller restaurants that offer good food at a much lower cost. Take a seat at the **Yorkshire Lass Restaurant,** a.k.a. **Captain Bullshit's Place,** 33/A Kayabal Cad., about 300m from the intersection of İnönü Cad. and Kayabal Cad. Join locals Dr. Jimmy and Captain Bullshit for an entertaining and tasty meal. The restaurant serves a smorgasbord of Turkish, English, and Chinese food. (☎455 51 70. Burgers $1.50; 3 course Chinese dinner $7. Open daily 8am-4am.) The **Küçük Ev,** or "Little House," 36 Kayabal Cad., on the right leaving the dolmuş stop, is a popular restaurant dishing out delicious *kebaps* ($3), veggie pizzas, *mezes* ($1.20-$3), and desserts ($2) to outdoor tables. (☎455 21 11 or 455 28 14. Open daily 8am-midnight.) To reach the **Erdem Café and Bar,** head from the bus station down along the shore toward the channel about 75m; the Erden will be on the left. This popular hangout offers great views and simple, cheap food. (☎455 45 59. Sandwiches $1; drinks $1. Open daily 9am-1am.)

İçmeler's nightlife is not as mighty as Marmaris's, but there are a few popular places well worth checking out. Beware that the music has to be turned down at 1am. The buccaneer's dance bar of choice is **Korsan.** Follow the shore with the water to your right over a bridge at the Channel. Make a left after the bridge, walk 150m, and Korsan will be on your right. A tropical fantasy, this wild bar is filled with waterfalls, life-sized pirates, and a stylish crowd nodding to dance music. (☎455 55 97. Beer $2; *rakı* $3.50; cocktails $4. Open daily 5pm-3am.) One block further away from Marmaris, on Ozmangazi Cad., the **Heaven Bar** features European music and a relaxed clientele. There's a summer happy hour from 7:15-10pm. (☎455 20 53. Beer $2; *rakı* $3; cocktails $5. Open daily 8am-2am.) To reach **Deniz Kapısı** (☎455 30 17), walk straight along the beach out of İçmeler. Immediately before the sharp curve in the road, Deniz offers cocktails ($6), karaoke, free use of its beach during the day, and a **Full Monty Show** (Th and Sa) during the summer. It also features **Tom,** the charismatic bartender ranked first in Europe for his mixing skills in 2001. Watch in wonder as he hippy-hippy shakes you up a delicious "Pink Dream" ($5).

SIGHTS. İçmeler's **beach** tends to be cleaner and slightly less crowded than those at Marmaris, although you'll have to pay $1 for your seat. Water sports include the perennial favorites: **parasailing** (15min., $25), **banana boats** (15 min. ride $5), and **paddle boats** ($7.50 per hr.). Equipment is available on the beach or by calling **Mar-Bas Water Sports** (☎455 30 58 or 455 30 59), in the Mar-Bas Hotel in front of Deniz Kapısı bar. Boat lovers can rent a high-powered **speed boat** ($30-$75 per hr.). **Diving centers,** including the **European Diving Centre** (☎455 47 33; fax 455 47 34), near L'Etoile Hotel, one block to the left when headed for the beach on Kenan Evren Bul., offer underwater recreation for all ages and skill levels. ($70 per day; equipment, lunch, and pick-up/drop-off services included.) **Boat trips** run to **Dalyan** and **Kaunos** (daily 9am-7pm, $22.50, lunch included), and, closer to home, the bays around İçmeler (10am-5pm, $12.50). Ask at the harbor for details.

BOZBURUN ☎252

Bozburun lies in a small valley surrounded by the rocky dry hills of the Datça Peninsula. Set against the harbor, Bozburun is a peaceful place for strolling along the waterfront, watching shipwrights assemble the skeletons of embryonic yachts and just enjoying the motion of the ocean. While locals simply jump off the rocks into the sea, timid tourists may prefer the small beach to the right of the harbor.

TRANSPORTATION AND PRACTICAL INFORMATION. To get to Bozburun from Marmaris, catch a dolmuş at the rather distant otogar (to **Bozburun:** 1 hr.; 10:30am, noon, 2:30, 5, 7pm; return 6:30, 8:30, 10am, noon, 4:30pm). Dolmuş depart opposite the mosque, about a block inland from the harbor. In the low season, bargain (hard!) for a taxi from Marmaris to take you to Bozburun and wait to drive you back. There are no taxis in Bozburun.

There are **no banks** or **ATMs,** but most shops will change money with a 20% commission. The **jandarma** (state police; ☎456 20 02), on the harbor to your left, is open 24hr. **Internet** is available at Bazaar Boutique on the left by the harbor. ($1 per 30min. Open daily 9am-11pm.) The **PTT** is next to the mosque. (Open M-F 8:30am-12:30pm and 1:30-5:30pm; Sa-Su 8:30am-noon.) **Postal code:** 48710.

ACCOMMODATIONS AND FOOD. Bozburun's pensions are located on a small dirt road that runs to the left of town as you face the sea. **Pembe Yunus Pansiyon,** 75m farther along the shore from Yılmaz, has a communal kitchen and 20 rooms decorated with dolls. Families or large groups can rent the beautifully modern penthouse, with five beds, kitchen, living room, and bath, for $50 per day. Boat tours are available. (☎456 21 54 or 456 22 11. Breakfast included. $12 per person.) Surrounded by a lush garden, the two-building **Yılmaz Pansiyon** (☎456 21 67) looks out onto the sea. Walk 50m along the harbor, past the *jandarma*. Guests enjoy its ten rooms, most with bath, as well as the communal kitchen. (☎456 21 67. Breakfast $3. $5 per person.) The **Suna Pansiyon,** immediately next door to the Yılmaz, offers seven serviceable rooms, some with blue tile floors and lace curtains. (☎456 21 19. Breakfast $2.50. $5 per person.)

For cheap meals, try the selection of Turkish "home food" and seafood in a pleasant outdoor setting at **Kandil Restaurant.** Head right at the waterfront, walk through the square with a small Atatürk statue; the restaurant is straight ahead. (☎456 22 27. Omelettes $2; steak $4; *şiş* $3.50. Open daily 8am-midnight.) **Gül Cafe Bar,** is about 25m from Kandil Restaurant. Sip cappuccino ($1.25) and nibble fresh crepes ($2) at this classy terrace cafe. (☎456 26 60. Open daily 8am-midnight.)

SÖĞÜT ☎252

The dolmuş ride to Söğüt alone is enticing enough to make the journey out to this village just south of Bozburun. A well-kept travel agent's secret, reserved only for the most astute customer, Söğüt has an untouched wealth of beauty to be found in its tiny pebbled beach, surrounding mountains and breathtaking islands jutting from the miniature bay. The village is spread along the coast and divided by a ridge. Unique in its intimacy, Söğüt also boasts the best fish on the Marmaris coast.

TRANSPORTATION AND PRACTICAL INFORMATION. **Dolmuş** run to **Marmaris** daily from the center of town in front of the mosque (1½hr., 6:30, 9, 11am, 4pm; $2). The town is spread out among three areas. The Aşkin Pansiyon and the Yakomos Pension occupy opposite ends of the town, with the center of the ridge rising between. There are few street names, none of which are marked. There are no **ATMs** or **Banks** in Söğüt, though pensions can **exchange currency.** The **PTT** is in the town center, on Gocupinari Sok., and has an international phone and fax. (Open M-F 8:30am-12:30pm and 1:30-5:30pm; Sa-Su 8am-noon.)

ACCOMMODATIONS AND FOOD. Pensions are on the beach on either side of the center's ridge and are luxurious and cheap. The **Aşkin Pansiyon** is the dolmuş' first stop (of three) in Söğüt, being the only pension on its side of the ridge. Beautiful airy rooms with sliding glass doors opening to a miniature garden.

The pension's beachfront restaurant serves fresh fish ($5-6) and *kebap* ($4). Bus and boat service to town's center or to the other shore free of charge. Boat trips available for $15 per person. Breakfast is included. (☎496 50 93; fax 496 54 51. $15 per room. MC/V.) **Yakanoz Pansiyon,** on the other side of the ridge on the right side of the shore, has clean, friendly rooms, all with bath. Included breakfast is in the blooming garden restaurant. Complimentary car service is available. (Singles $10, doubles $15.) For a rare and unforgettable culinary treat, take your dinner at the quiet, outdoor **Manzara Restaurant** (☎496 51 66), on the road between the center and Yakomo Pansiyon. The restaurant offers an encompassing view of the islands, mountains and valleys surrounding Söğüt. Experience the only fish *kebap* on the Mediterranean coast ($8), savory *şiş* ($5), and free coffee and *çay*.

DATÇA ☎252

With its tranquil small-town atmosphere, Datça offers a more restful experience than the flashing disco balls and wild throngs of Bodrum and Marmaris. The dirt road to Datça twists along the mountainous Datça peninsula, providing occasional glimpses of an emerald string of deserted bays. The road to Datça along the slim, rugged Datça peninsula may be a bit terrifying, with sharp turns and sheer drops, but determined visitors who brave the hair-raising ride will find hospitality, intimate nightlife, and beaches that are both less crowded and more beautiful than those at Bodrum and Marmaris. Small bars line the harbor, where boats lie waiting to depart to the ancient Dorian city of **Knidos** at the tip of the peninsula.

TRANSPORTATION

Buses: Buses leave from the **Pamukkale** office (☎712 33 02 or 712 31 01), on the right-hand side of Atatürk Cad., away from the marina. Open daily 5:30am-noon and 2pm-midnight. All buses traveling inland stop in **Marmaris** (2hr., 10 per day 6am-7pm, $3.50). The **Kamil Koç** office (☎712 34 85) is across the street, also with buses to **Marmaris** (2hr., 11 per day 6am-midnight, $3.50). See **Marmaris: Orientation and Practical Information** (p. 247) for destinations beyond Marmaris.

Ferries and Seabuses: Ferryboat Association (☎712 21 43), at the foot of the hill leading to the marina. To **Bodrum: ferries** (2hr.; May-June M, W, F 9am; July-Sept. daily 9am; $10, round-trip $15; children under 7 free, 7-12 half-price). **Knidos Tour** (☎712 94 64 or 712 94 65), at the marina, for boats to the Greek island **Symi** (9am, return 5pm; $50 including port tax; up to 12 people).

Moped rentals: Çağlayan (☎712 29 15), on the left side of Atatürk Cad., past the police station and PTT. $15 per day including helmets. Open daily 8am-5pm.

Car rentals: Ülken Rent A Car (☎712 90 87 or 712 20 96), to the left of the marina on the road by Atatürk Cad. $40-55 per day, with reductions for multi-day rentals. 18+.

ORIENTATION AND PRACTICAL INFORMATION

Datça's main commercial center is **Atatürk Cad.,** beginning from a **rotary** with a large tree at its center and leading toward Marmaris. An unnamed extension of Atatürk Cad. heads over a hill toward the **marina,** which runs along the bottom.

Tourist office: (☎712 31 63; fax 712 35 46). From the rotary, follow Atatürk Cad. away from the marina, toward Marmaris, and turn left before the police station; the office is on the right, in the same building. English spoken. Open June-Aug. 8:30am-noon and 1-7pm; Sept.-May 8am-noon and 1-5pm.

Bank: Türkiye İş Bankası (☎712 32 72) and others offer **currency exchange.** Open M-F 9am-12:30pm and 1:30-5:30pm. Datça's main road has 3 Cirrus/Plus/MC/V ATMs.

Hamam: Belediye (☎712 94 69). Take Ambarci Cad. from the rotary and turn left after 3 blocks at the "hamam" sign; the hamam is 1 block on the left. Luminous and clean. $8-10. Open daily 7am-10pm.

Police: (☎712 37 92). On the left side of Atatürk Cad., before the PTT. Open 8:30am-3:30pm for official business; 24hr. for emergencies. **Emergencies:** ☎155

Pharmacy: Many line Atatürk Cad. Open daily 8am-9pm.

Hospital: Devlet Hastanesi (☎712 30 82). Follow Atatürk Cad. away from the marina and turn right on Hasan Efendi Cad.

Internet Access: Cici Internet Cafe (☎574 87 60). From the rotary, turn left onto Brüksel Cad.; the cafe is at the end of the street, across from Tunç Pansiyon. Remarkably fast service and kind owner. $1.50 per hr. Open daily 8:30am-midnight.

PTT: (☎712 26 04), on Atatürk Cad., past the police station. *Poste restante,* fax, and currency exchange. Postal window open daily 8:30am-5:30pm. International phone service daily 8am-midnight; in winter 8:30am-5:30pm. Phones open 24hr.

Postal Code: 48900.

ACCOMMODATIONS

Reservations are recommended for the high season (July and August) when room prices usually rise. There are no set reception hours, but you can usually find the owners in nearby stores. While not the norm, Visa and MasterCard can be used.

Tunç Pansiyon (☎712 30 36). From Atatürk Cad., turn left on Brüskel Cad., directly after the rotary; Tunç is on the left. A fancy pension with tiled floor and a stylishly decorated eating area with satellite TV. 22 tidy, modern rooms with large windows and bath. Friendly management. Communal kitchen and laundry (prices vary). Car service to Knidos and Palamutbüken and Mesudiye Beaches. $6 per person; July-Aug. $8 per person.

Aşkin Pansiyon (☎712 34 06 or 712 25 17), on the right hand side of Brüskel Cad., across from Tunç Pansiyon. Look for the bright yellow sign. 22 charming rooms with bath and hot water. During July and Aug., pick fresh grapes from the vines surrounding the terrace and communal kitchen. Boat charting and fishing are available. Little English spoken. Breakfast $2.50. $4 per person; July-Aug $5 per person.

Antalyı Pansiyon (☎712 38 10), on the left side of Atatürk Cad., past Brüskel Cad. Large marble hallways with grand mirrors and colorful rugs. 14 polished rooms with bath, hot water, and balcony. Communal kitchen, TV, and splendid views of the sea from the terrace. Owners can be found in the nearby furniture store. No English spoken. $4 per person; July-Aug. $6 per person.

Mandalina Pansiyon (☎712 49 95). On the right side of Atatürk Cad.'s extension toward the marina. Owners can be found in the neighboring restaurant, named after the pension. 8 large, airy rooms with balcony, great bathrooms, and hot water. Modern communal kitchen. Eat breakfast in their tranquil garden restaurant ($1.50). Little English spoken. $5 per person.

Ilıca Camping (☎/fax 712 34 00), on Taşlık Beach. From the harbor, turn right and walk 150m along the shore. Water sports and grills on the beach. A great alternative to the parade of pensions in town, and a bit like summer camp. The attached restaurant serves beer for $1.25. $2.50 to set up a tent; $3 to tent on the beach. 2-4 person bungalows $6 per person; July-Aug. $8.

FOOD

Travelers can buy fresh food from the small markets on the main road (pine and thyme honey are local specialties) and cook in the communal kitchens of the pensions. Most of the smaller and more traditional restaurants are toward the harbor, before the curve of the main road. The larger and more touristy restaurants, offering views and a wider selection of food options, are at the harbor.

Taraça Restaurant (☎712 30 69), toward the harbor on Atatürk Cad.'s extension. Savor the red snapper (fish prices vary daily) and lamb casserole ($5) while gazing at the bay. Levent, the owner, plays backgammon with customers. Open 8am-late.

Kemal Restaurant (☎712 20 44), toward the harbor on the right side of Atatürk Cad. Once you've chosen your food from the kitchen, enjoy it in a comfortable setting. Vegetarians can enjoy the *çorba* (soup, $1.20). Others can savor the *köfte* (meatballs; $3) or *şiş kebap* ($3). Open M-Sa 8am-10pm.

Karaoğlu Garden House (☎712 30 79). Head toward the harbor and turn left onto a narrow road with a sharp incline just past the foot of the hill; the restaurant is on the right after the road descends. Its spacious terrace offers a superlative 180-degree view of the beach and harbor. Sip wine and savor their specialty: chicken in a clay pot ($4). Vegetarian dishes ($1.50-5).

Nokta Patisserie (☎712 41 89), on the left side of Atatürk Cad. as you walk away from the center square rotary. This cheerful restaurant with a Crayola interior offers home baked cookies and breads ($.20-$1). A colorful array of fruit, crème, and chocolate cakes also available for purchase ($8 per cake).

SIGHTS

Travelers come to Datça for its serene beaches and the impressive remains of the ancient city of **Knidos,** about 30km west of Datça proper (see below). In Datça, boat tours and independent drivers alike should stop at the pebbly, blissful **Palamutbükü** and sandy, raucous **Mesudiye** beaches. Renting a car will allow for stops along the coast where small, isolated beaches lie below the rocky dirt roads. **Kumluk Plajı,** hidden behind the stores along Atatürk Cad., tends to be crowded with tourists staying at the vacation complexes nearby, while the prettier and less-frequented **Taşluk Plajı,** sits to the right of the ships docked at the harbor. Take a dolmuş to Mesudiye (20 min., 4 per day, $1.50) and Palamutbükü (sporadic service; check at the otogar) from the otogar across from the PTT.

As befits a coastal town, Datça hosts a July 1st **Sea Festival.** Young men fearlessly ascend a greasy mast in order to capture the Turkish flag. During the **Culture and Music Festival,** held in the second week of August, pop singers and Turkish folk dancers entertain crowds at the harborside amphitheater. The festivities include an annual **almond festival** in mid-July, when nut growers from all over the peninsula come to Datça to have their produce judged.

ENTERTAINMENT

Lacking the lights and special effects of Bodrum and Marmaris, Datça's animated nightlife consists of small family-run bars perfect for talking and people-watching. For a more mellow evening, join the locals in a leisurely stroll along the harbor or play *tavla* (backgammon) in one of the many *çay* houses.

Eclipse Bar (☎712 43 10), at the foot of the hill by the harbor. Hip, young Turks, backpackers, and surfers socialize with each other and the cool owner. Casual atmosphere featuring the bartender's favorite music: California surf punk/pop. Beer $1.75; *rakı* $2; cocktails $2-5. Open daily noon-4am. Closed in winter.

Marın Bar (☎712 84 38), on the right along the harbor. This glittering open-air disco/bar is surrounded by faux-Classical statuary, blue lights, and American movie posters. Customers bust a move to reggae and Turkish pop. Beer $1.50; *rakı* $2; cocktails $5-9. Open daily 9am-3am; closed in winter.

Sunrise Bar (☎712 95 18). A harbor favorite, catering to a mostly older crowd. Under the twinkling white lights and green foliage, small tables and chairs sprawl all the way to the moored boats. Tourists, sailors, and fishermen discuss sea travels. Beer and *rakı* $1.25; cocktails $2-4. Open daily 8am-3am.

DAYTRIP FROM DATÇA: KNIDOS

Visiting Knidos can easily turn into an all-day affair. ***Taxis*** *happily make the journey (1hr. each way) for a hefty $40. Renting a* ***moped*** *to visit the site is a terrible idea, considering the unpaved, narrow, winding road. A safer (and cheaper) option is to take a* ***boat tour*** *from Datça (daily 9am-6:30pm; $12, with lunch $14). In addition to Knidos, boats often stop for swimming along the southern bays of the peninsula. Call Burak Tour (☎712 37 74; fax 712 30 33) for more information. Site open daily 8am-7pm. $1.50, students $1.*

During the 4th century BC, the port town of **Knidos,** located at the tip of the Datça Peninsula where the Aegean and Mediterranean meet, was a member of the Dorian League. An intellectual center of the ancient world, Knidos was home to **Sostratos,** designer of the Pharos lighthouse at Alexandria (one of the Seven Wonders of the Ancient World) and of the astronomer **Eudoxus.**

Undoubtedly the most impressive feature in Knidos was the now-lost naked **statue of Aphrodite** by Praxiteles. The statue drew tourists such as Cicero and Julius Caesar from afar even in ancient times, and its beauty caused men to weep and attempt to mate with it. Aphrodite's nakedness so offended the inhabitants of Kos, however, that they refused to allow the statue to remain there, banishing it to Knidos before it was lost to history. Despite this crowning monument's absence, Knidos still has enough to make the trek there worthwhile.

Knidos's laissez-faire policy toward visitors makes exploration of the site an open-ended experience. The best way to visit the site is to simply wander around, through, and over the mostly unmarked ruins, pausing every once in a while for a dip in the sea. To the left past the entrance booth is the grass-filled site of the ancient **agora,** and a small **Byzantine church** complete with mosaic floor remains can be found a little farther downhill, as you walk toward the lighthouse on the opposite hilltop. Ascending about 350m higher into the terrace to view the spot of the former ancient **Aphrodite statue,** take a swim from the calmer-than-Knidos shore that separates the two sites. Continuing inland, past the small **odeon** theater, make your way to the **Doric temple.** Nearby are the remains of the world's first **sundial,** used by Eudoxus in the 4th century BC.

Not far down the hill from the sundial are the remains of a large **Byzantine church** at the center of the site, whose Arabic inscriptions and early Christian iconography render it one of the most remarkable sights in Knidos. Back toward the entrance is the **Temple of Dionysus.** The looming remains of the **theater,** which seated 4500 to 8000 spectators, lie by the entrance road. One of Datça's seven castles rests atop the Knidos site's ridge. Built in Knidos's heyday to enable encompassing views of the sea, the castle was used to warn the city in case of an attack. The way to the castle is poorly marked and difficult; ask at the entrance gate.

KÖYCEĞİZ ☎252

Home to various endangered species of birds, turtles, and rare gum-producing liquid amber trees, Köyceğiz is a peaceful town at the northern tip of tranquil Köyceğiz Lake. Though the town itself is a bit of an eyesore, travelers can take comfort in its shores to enjoy a quiet swim or a boat trip to the rejuvenating **Sultaniye hot springs,** the ruins of **Kaunos,** or **Turtle Beach,** or enjoy its surrounding mountains in a hike or a boating trip.

TRANSPORTATION

The otogar is located on Köyceğiz's main street, Atatürk Cad. To reach the town center from the otogar, take a dolmuş (5min., every 10-15min., $.40). **Kamil Koç** (☎262 42 94 or 262 42 08) runs to: **Ankara** (11hr., 7:30pm, $16); **Dalaman** (20min., 7:30am-12:30pm, $.75); **Fethiye** (2hr., 1-7pm, $3); **İstanbul** (13hr., 8pm, $17). **Pamukkale** (☎262 41 64) runs to: **Bodrum** (3½hr.; 1:15, 4pm; $6); **Bursa** (10hr., 7:30pm, $13); **İzmir** (5hr., 9am-5:30pm, $7); **Kaş** (4hr.; 2, 3:45pm; $7); **Marmaris** (45min., 8am-8pm, $2); **Ortaca** (20min., every 20min. 6am-midnight, $1.20). **Dalyan** is accessible via Ortaca. Dolmuş to **Ortaca** (every30 min., 6am-9pm, $.80) leave from the otogar.

ORIENTATION AND PRACTICAL INFORMATION

Köyceğiz, though small, can be a bit confusing since none of its streets are dignified by signs. **Atatürk Cad.,** which runs in front of the **otogar,** heads straight into the town's center, ending in a town square with the mosque and tourist office. Intersecting Atatürk Cad. and running parallel to the lake is **Atatürk Kordon Cad.,** with the PTT and larger hotels. The **tourist office,** opposite the mosque toward the lake on Atatürk Cad., provides maps and accommodations listings. (☎262 47 03. Open

M-F 8:30am-7pm and Sa-Su 9am-6pm; winter M-F 8:30am-noon and 1:30-5pm.) The **Devlet Hastanesi Hospital,** is on a side street opposite the bus station. Look for the blue sign with the large "H." (☎262 47 18. Open 24hr.) To reach the **police station** (☎262 21 74), turn left in front of the central mosque on Atatürk Cad., with your back to the lake. There is a **bank** with an **ATM** on the left side of Atatürk Cad. as you enter town. **Internet access** is available at **Chat Kapi internet Cafe** across from the PTT. ($1.50 per hr. Open 8am-midnight.) For the **PTT,** turn right from Atatürk Cad. as you face the lake, when it runs into the pedestrian square before the mosque. (☎262 46 60. Open 8:30am-noon and 1:30-6pm.) **Postal code:** 48800.

ACCOMMODATIONS

Tango Pension (☎262 32 10; fax 262 43 45; tangopension@superonline.com), on Ali İhsan Kalmaz Cad. Turn right at the water, walk 100m along the waterfront, and follow the signs inland to this bright, peach-colored pension surrounded by a tropical garden. 18 large, modern rooms with bath and balcony, and a dorm room. Friendly and helpful owners. Lively atmosphere. Laundry $4. Windsurfing $6 per hr. Internet $2 per hr. Trekking, sea kayaking, rafting, and biking available. Daily boat trips (10am-7pm) to Turtle Beach, Dalyan, Kaunos, and mud baths ($10 on alternate nights) available June-Aug. Breakfast $2. Dinner $4. Dorms $5; singles $10; doubles $14.

Alila Hotel (☎262 11 50 or 262 11 51). Walk 1 block past the mosque, away from the tourist office; Alila is on the left. A luxurious lakefront hotel with beautiful sculptures and carved wooden ceilings. The spacious rooms have panoramic views of the lake. Garden terrace and swimming pool. Breakfast included. 4 course dinner $5, A/C $2. Singles $8; July and Aug. $10; doubles $16. AmEx/MC/V.

Otel Flora (☎252 4976; fax 262 38 09; alp giray@hotmail.com), on the lake. From the center of town walk 150m; the Flora is on your right. Set in a beautiful garden with frankincense trees, Flora offers 16 clean, modern rooms, some with TV, all with bath and hair dryers. Breakfast included. Free trekking, windsurfing, and bicycles. Delicious 5 course dinner $4. Rooms $8 per person. AmEx/MC/V.

Fulya Pension (☎262 23 01; fulyapansiyon@hotmail.com), next door to the Tango Pension. 17 cheerful doubles and triples, all with bath. Boat trips $10 per person. Breakfast included. Rooms $7.50 per person.

FOOD

Though restaurants abound throughout town, don't be put off by the lakeside joints that offer great views and cheap, scrumptious pancakes ($1-2).

Ali Baba (☎262 31 66). From the tourist office, walk inland 2 blocks; the restaurant is on the right. Delicious homemade Turkish cooking served by charming owners. Full meal $2. Open daily 8am-10pm.

Şamdan Restaurant (☎262 52 82). Down the road on the lake, to the right of the tourist office. Look for the elegant peach and turquoise building. Breezy outdoor restaurant with delicious food and atmospheric hanging lights. Grills $2; *Adana* $2.

Peunguen Pide Salonu (☎262 34 17), on Fevzipaşa Cad., past Ali Baba. Enjoy fresh-baked *pide* ($.40-$1.20) and eclectic decor–bright movie posters and a fish tank.

Eskimo Ice Cream (☎262 36 59). From the tourist office facing inland, walk down the first street going right. Eskimo is on the left. This local secret has been serving delicious homemade ice cream in flavors galore ($1) for 40 years.

SIGHTS

There's a tiny **beach** near the campground, 900m away from town, but swimming stops are included in most boat trips. Boats depart daily from the dock opposite the tourist office for the nearby therapeutic mud baths; **Turtle Beach,** where limited swimming hours (8am-8pm) help ensure the turtles' right to privacy; the ancient

Lycian city of **Kaunos;** and the **Sultaniye thermal springs,** where therapeutic waters reaching 40°C reputedly alleviate stress and rheumatism. (Open 6am-10pm; $.70. Boat trips 10:30am-7pm; $10 with lunch.) Another option is the hour-long moonlight cruise around Lake Köyceğiz (10pm, $2). Catch a boat at the dock or call travel agencies such as **Özay Tourism,** across from the mosque to rent cars ($30-60), scooters ($20), and bikes. (☎262 18 22; fax 262 18 19. Scooters 18+. Cars 21+. Open May-Oct. 8:30am-midnight.) Or try **Şahin Boat** at Tango Pension (☎262 25 01; fax 262 43 45. Open 24hr.) Tango also offers a three-hour **trek,** including a 1hr. jeep ride, lunch, and swimming (9am-7pm, $6).

A small, secluded **waterfall** lies about 10km away from Köyceğiz along the uphill road to Muğla. Known mostly to locals, it's a 10min. walk from the yellow Arboretum sign on the central road, making it the perfect spot for sunbathing and daydreaming. To get to the waterfall, take a dolmuş ($.50) heading to Marmaris or Muğla and ask to be let off near the Arboretum sign. Şahin offers a jeep service to the waterfall (1:30-4:30pm, $1.80).

DALYAN AND KAUNOS (CAUNUS) ☎252

The placid, cobblestoned streets of Dalyan overflow with pleasant restaurants and tacky souvenir shops. The town seems to have grown naturally out of the breezy river beside it—Lycian rock tombs built into the nearby cliffs are visible from the harbor, and thick reed beds teeming with wildlife are just minutes away. A short trip downstream leads to the ancient city of Kaunos and the tranquil Turtle Beach, where endangered sea tortoises are struggling to survive. The Dalyan shore has recently been declared a natural reservation.

Kaunos's origins are unclear. When it became fashionable to live in a city founded by a hero or a god, early residents invented a son of King Miletus, named Caunus, and claimed that he established the city in 3000 BC—the story was probably meant, however, to whitewash the certain attributes of the historical Caunus, including his forbidden love for his sister Bablees. Throughout the ages, Kaunos appears to have fallen under, in order, the Persian, Greek, and Roman Empires. Kaunos had a reputation for being unhealthy; contemporary scholars speculate that the marshy land was infested with malaria-carrying mosquitoes, which eventually drove the Romans away. Still, Kaunos served as a major commercial harbor until the end of Byzantine rule, when silting rendered the harbor unusable.

TRANSPORTATION

Buses: City buses run to **Ortaca** (20min., every 15min., $.40). From Ortaca, **Kamil Koç** (☎284 31 26; in Ortaca ☎282 20 45) and **Pamukkale** (☎284 20 82; in Ortaca ☎282 51 76) send buses to: **Ankara** (12hr.; 8, 8:30pm; $14.50); **Antalya** (5hr., every hr. 8:30am-11:30pm, $8.40); **Bodrum** (4hr., 7 per day 10:30am-7:30pm, $7); **Bursa** (10hr., 5:30pm, $14.50); **Fethiye** (1¼hr., every 30min. 6am-midnight, $2.40); **İstanbul** (14hr.; 5:30, 6:30, 7pm; $22); **İzmir** (5hr., 7am-1:30am, $10); **Kaş** (4hr., 3pm, $7.30); **Kuşadası** (6hr., 11:30pm, $11); **Marmaris** (1½hr., 8:45am-9:45pm, $2.40); **Pamukkale** (4½hr.; 12:15, 1:45, 5:45pm; $7.30).

Dolmuş: The dolmuş from **Ortaca** stops in front of the mosque. Dolmuş run to **Marmaris** and **Fethiye** (every morning 10, 11am, noon; $1.80).

ORIENTATION AND PRACTICAL INFORMATION

The open area with a turtle statue and mosque is a good reference point. Facing the river, walk left along Maraş Sok. to find pensions, restaurants, bars. Maraş Sok. is closed to traffic from 8pm to 7am to allow pedestrians a pleasant evening stroll.

Tourist Office: (☎284 42 35). Tough to find. With your back to the turtle statues, head into the passageway directly across from the statue, by the ice cream parlors. The office will be on your left. Provides maps, accommodations listings, and information in 7 languages. Open 8:30am-noon and 1-6pm; in winter 8:30am-noon and 1-5:30pm.

Boat tours: Offices are behind the turtle statue. The **12 Island Tour** travels to local bays and islands, leaving from Göcek (9am-6pm; $28-32 per person, with lunch). Buses leave for Göcek from the mosque 8am, return 6pm. Cheaper tours travel to Bacardi Bay and other local bays for swimming (10am-6pm, $10 per person). The most popular tours cover the ancient city of Kaunos, mud baths and hot springs, and Turtle Beach (10:30am-6pm; $8 per person, with lunch).

Banks: Several branches with 24-hour **ATMs** in the town center, by the mosque.

Laundromat: (☎284 44 18), on Maraş Sok., across from Dalyan Camping. $5 per load. Open daily 8am-midnight.

Jandarma: (☎284 20 31), on Karakol Sok., off Maraş Sok. Open daily 8am-5:30pm.

Pharmacy: All along Maraş Sok. Open daily 8am-9pm. One is always on 24hr. duty.

Medical Assistance: Sağlık Ocağı (☎284 20 33), on 130 Sok. From Maraş Sok., turn right at the Çelik Hotel sign. Open daily 8:30am-noon and 1:30-5:30pm.

Internet Access: The **inter.net.cafe** is 1 block past the tourist office, on the right of the same small alley. $2 per hr. Open daily 9am-2am. The **Fruit Bar** (see **Food,** below) also offers internet access for $1.50 per hr. Open daily 9am-midnight.

PTT: (☎284 21 21), in front of the mosque. Offers **currency exchange,** *poste restante,* fax, and international phone service. Open daily 8am-midnight.

Postal Code: 48840.

ACCOMMODATIONS

Many small family-run pensions line Dalyan's main street, Maraş Sok. Make sure your room comes with mosquito-netted screens in the summer. Most offer amenities such as pools, air conditioning, gardens, and views of the rock tombs. Bargaining for the rate may be worthwhile.

Gül Motel Pension (☎284 24 67; fax 284 48 03). From the turtle statue, walk down Maraş Sok. and make the 2nd left onto 10 Sok.; Gül will be on the first block to the left. A plant-filled entryway, Ottoman-style tea room, and attractive breakfast terrace accompany large, clean rooms with baths. Some have views of the rock tombs, though they're are a bit louder at night. The owner will make Turkish dinners on request–guests choose the menu. Breakfast included. Singles $7; doubles $12, with A/C $15.

Kristal Pension (☎284 22 63; fax 284 27 43), across from the Gül Pension. Marble floors, garden pool, and a gorgeous terrace. 20 clean rooms with bath and screens, and a great family atmosphere. Breakfast included. Singles $7; doubles $11.

Aktaş Pansiyon (☎284 20 42 or 284 22 73), far down Maraş Sok. on the right. 15 charming rooms with baths, fans and a chalet-like atmosphere, some with great views of the rock tombs. Doubles with A/C $10; triples $20.

Dönmez Hotel (☎284 21 07). From the turtle statue, turn right onto Maraş Sok. Take the 2nd right, and the hotel is on the left. This spacious hotel surrounds a courtyard and fountain. Offers simple rooms with A/C and a swimming pool. Breakfast included, served on a terrace complete with views of the rock tombs. Doubles $15. AmEx/MC/V.

Dalyan Camping, 106 Maraş Sok. (☎/fax 284 41 57). About 350m from the turtle statue. Turn off where the road begins to bend. Don't be discouraged by the entrance; a clean campsite with views of the rock tombs and acropolis lies beyond. The mosquitos are intense–buy repellent for $.50. Modern bathrooms with hot showers. Swimming available. Laundry $4 per 5kg. Large fish dinner $6. Breakfast $2. 2-person tents $5; 2-person bungalows $9; caravans $7.50.

FOOD

Many restaurants along Maraş Sok. offer knockout views of the river. They serve nearly identical Turkish and European menus of *mezes* ($1-4), omelettes ($4), grilled meats ($7-10), and other standard fare. For do-it-yourself eats, visit the open-air market in front of the PTT. (Open Su 8am-8pm.)

The Cool Chili (☎284 48 84). With your back to the turtle statue, take a left, and this chili-pepper-laden restaurant is on the left. Catering to those in search of a decent samosa ($1.75), this vegetarian joint offers such creative delicacies as risotto fritters ($1.75), potato and aubergine curry ($3.75), and sweet *lahssi* ($1.25). Meat is available for carnivores. The Chili also reopens on the latenight to serve out batches of post-clubbing soup to tired, hungry revelers. Open 6pm-midnight; soup available until 4am.

Niobe Restaurant. Take the first left off of Maraş Sok., the restaurant is the 2nd on the left. Offers healthy vegetarian food, including such favorites as vegetable *şis kebaps* ($1.50) and vegetarian pasta ($2.80).

Dalyan Cafe (☎284 50 35), about 60m along Maraş Sok. Enjoy an incredible selection of *gözleme* (pancakes) amid Turkish rugs and traditional low tables. Experiment with fillings like banana, kiwi, cheese, or meat ($1-1.80) and watch your meal created before your eyes. Open daily 7am-2am.

Fruit Bar (☎284 41 64). On Maraş Sok. A cheerful bar where customers can indulge in their wildest fruit fantasies while dreaming of tragically hip Californian smoothie bars. Fruit pizzas ($6); crêpes ($2.50); banana split ($6); melon ice cream ($3); shakes and fresh juices ($1-3). Try the fresh fruit and yogurt drinks ($2). Open daily 9am-midnight.

SIGHTS

Carian **rock tombs,** dating from the 4th century BC, lie opposite the river. Dalyan's other notable sights are best seen on a boat tour. After passing the rock tombs, the boats visit the ruins of ancient **Kaunos.** From the drop-off point at the base of the acropolis, a 600m dirt path leads up to the admission gate and site.

Entering from the gate, an enormous **Roman bath** lies on the right. On the left side of the path, a well-preserved, rounded nave marks a 5th-century **church,** one of the oldest in the area. Walk down the path behind the church toward the remains of a **measuring stone,** used to position the city in relation to wind currents. Between the two, at the bottom of the hill, stand a first-century BC **Doric temple** and a recently discovered **fountain,** where ancient customs information was recorded. Further down the path, the **theater** once held 5000 spectators. *(Open June-Oct. daily 8am-7pm; Nov.-May 9am-5pm. $1.50.)*

The boat tour continues along a circuitous path through reed beds to **İztuzu Beach.** The beach is only open from 8am-8pm in order to allow endangered loggerhead turtles to lay their eggs by night. Bring at least $4 to rent beach chairs with umbrellas, since sunbathing with towels on the turtles' resting area is forbidden (see **Save the Sea Turtle,** p. 482). Alternatively, take a dolmuş (every hr. 8am-7pm) from in front of the mosque. The Kaunos/Turtle Beach tours also stop at local **mud baths** and **thermal springs.** After coating yourself with the restorative mud, relax in the 40°C thermal baths, whose curative powers supposedly extend to arthritis, wrinkles, and stress. *(Open 7am-7:30pm. $.80.)*

ENTERTAINMENT

Dancing Crazy Bar (☎284 47 00), on Maraş Sok., fairly close to the town center. This disco bar has a groovy cave-like interior complete with fake moss, plants, rocks, and flashing colored lights. Lots of room to shake your booty-thang. Plays techno-pop, house, and Turkish pop. Beer $1.50; *rakı* $1.50; cocktails $4. Open daily 7pm-4am.

Blues Bar (☎284 48 15) On Maraş Sok. Join local favorite Murat on guitar for a nightly classic rock jam session and a beer ($1.50). Situated on the Dalyan River with a great view of the rock tombs and a wonderfully chilled-out atmosphere. M night has no music, but cheaper beer ($1). *Rakı* $1.50, cocktails $6-12. Open 2pm-3am.

Albatross Bar (☎284 30 37), on Maraş Sok. Outdoors, with Ottoman-style seating. An excellent spot for people-watching while sipping a beer. A selection of rock, blues, and jazz, with occasional live performances. Beer $1.50. Open daily 5pm-3am.

Nektar Bar (☎284 20 70), on Maraş Sok. An open-air "Secret Garden Bar" complete with lush banana trees, waterfalls, and a twinkling disco bar. Entertain yourself and a newfound friend with a game of backgammon. Plays 60s, 70s, and 80s music. Beer $1.25; *rakı* $1.75; cocktails $5-7. Open 24hr.

FETHİYE COAST

FETHİYE ☎252

A big city with a small-town feel, Fethiye rests peacefully on a harbor surrounded by pine forests and mountains. Its inexpensive pensions and nearby islands make Fethiye a popular stop on the Mediterranean backpacker circuit. Most visitors take daytrips to Ölüdeniz, Butterfly Valley, Kayaköy, or Saklıkent Gorge during the day and later on enjoy Fethiye's winding streets and ancient Lycian rock tombs, whose remains line the surrounding mountains as well as the streets themselves. Integrated into the city's center is a pleasant and orderly bazaar that stretches along the edge of the relatively understated harbor. Though a popular base for exploring the coast, Fethiye has managed to maintain a certain calm, leaving the most of the late-night carousing to Ölüdeniz, its wilder neighbor to the south.

Fethiye rests on ancient Telmessos, founded in the 5th century BC. Telmessos was ruled by the Persians until it joined the Lycian Federation in the 4th century BC. From then, the list of its rulers runs the familiar gamut, including Alexander the Great, the Ptolemies, the Romans, and the Byzantines. The city was called Meğri, "the far city," after its inclusion in the Ottoman Empire in 1424. In 1934, the city was renamed "Fethiye" in honor of a martyred fighter pilot, Fethi Bey.

TRANSPORTATION

Buses: The otogar is on Ölüdeniz Cad. Buses running along the coastal road can drop off passengers anywhere, so there's no need to wait for a bus to a specific destination. **Ulusoy** (☎612 37 37), **Kamil Koç** (☎612 06 36 or 614 19 73), and **Pamukkale** (☎614 14 51 or 614 19 99) have offices on Atatürk Cad. and serve Fethiye. To: **Alanya** (5hr.; 2:15pm, 2:15am; $9); **Ankara** (9hr.; 10, 11pm; $15); **Antalya** (4hr.; 2:15pm, 2:15am; $7); **Bodrum** (4½hr.; 3:30am, 4pm; $8); **Bursa** (10hr.; 5, 10:30pm; $15.50); **Cappadocia** (13hr., 6pm, $14.50); **Eskişehir** (7hr.; 5, 10:30pm; $13.50); **İstanbul** (13hr.; 5, 9, 10:30pm; $18.50); **İzmir** (6½hr., 5:30am-12:30am, $9.50); **Kaş** (2hr.; 3, 7, 9, 10am; $3); **Marmaris** (3hr., 2pm, $5); **Pamukkale** (4½hr, 7 per day 7am-6:30pm, $6.50). To reach **Selçuk,** take the İzmir bus and change in Aydin.

Dolmuş: From the dolmuş stop near the intersection of Hastane and Atatürk Cad. to: **Çalış Beach** (15min., every 3min. 6am-12:30am, $.35); **Ölüdeniz** (20-25min., every 5min. 7am-12:30am, $1.15); **Kayaköy** (40min., every hr. 7am-10pm, $1.50); **Saklıkent** (1hr., every 20min. 7:30am-5pm, $2). **Dolmuş boats** to **Çalış Beach** leave from the waterfront to the right of the main harbor (every 15min. 9:30am-8pm, every 30min. 10pm-midnight; $2).

Taxi: (☎614 44 77), on Atatürk Cad., across from the Atatürk head. 24hr. service.

Mopeds: Levent (☎612 42 16) and **Best Rentals** (☎614 62 03) are side by side on the road past the tourist office toward the *jandarma*. Competition can drive prices down, but they range between $13-15 per day. Both open daily 8am-midnight.

ORIENTATION

The otogar is 2km from the center of town, on the way to Ölüdeniz. If there are no *servis* shuttles to the town center, leave the terminal, cross the street, and wait for a dolmuş heading to Fethiye (about 10min., frequent, $.40). The dolmuş runs on the main street, **Atatürk Cad.**, past a mosque, PTT, and the Atatürk head on a pedestal. As the harbor ends, Atatürk Cad. becomes **Fevzi Çakmak Cad.** Facing the PTT, the harbor, tourist information office, and old town are on the left. The ritzy **Çalış Beach** is to the right along **Sedir Sok.,** which becomes **Akdeniz Cad.** Near the PTT and the edge of the bazaar, **Çarşı Cad.** branches off Atatürk Cad.

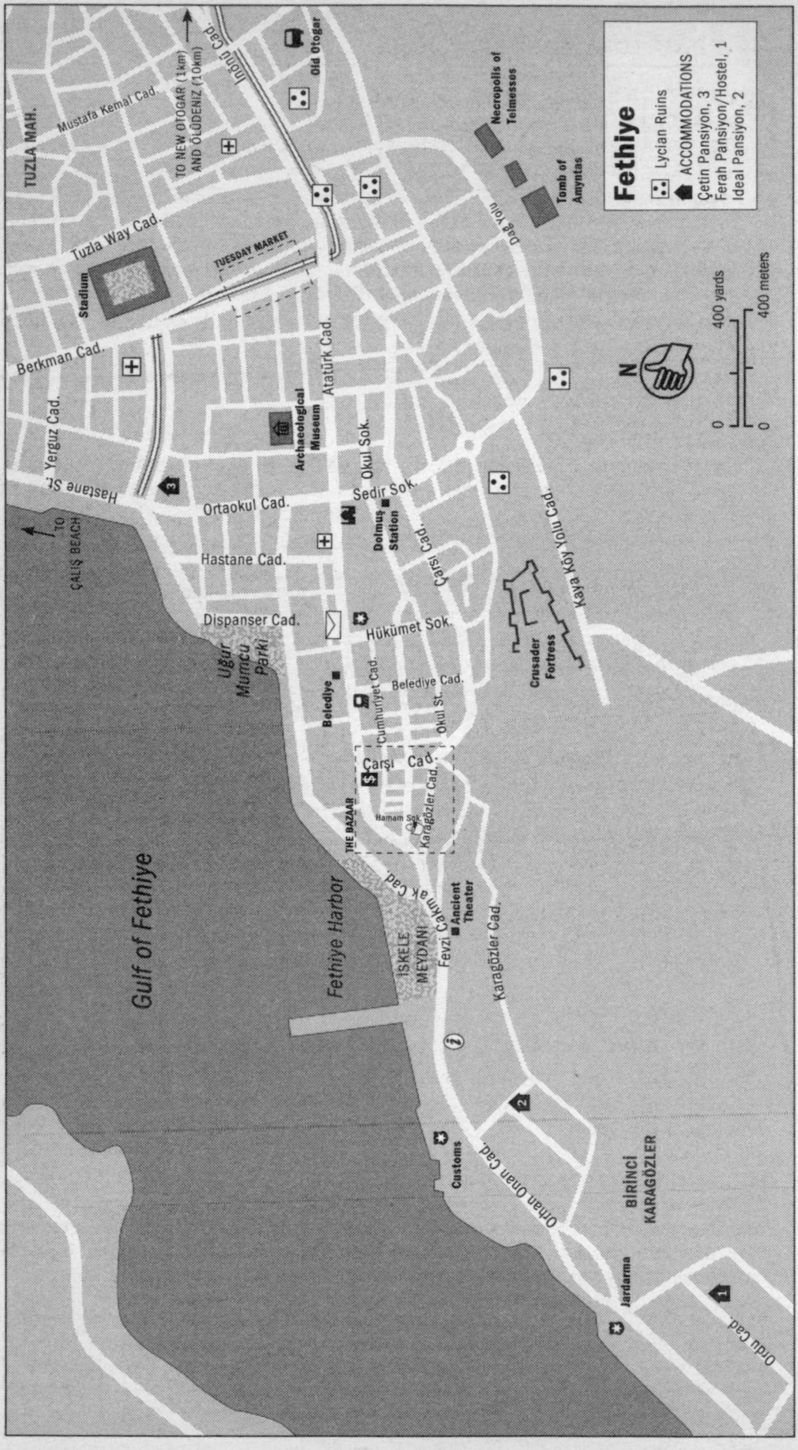
Fethiye
Lycian Ruins
ACCOMMODATIONS
Çetin Pansiyon, 3
Ferah Pansiyon/Hostel, 1
Ideal Pansiyon, 2
400 yards
400 meters
N
TUZLA MAH.
Mustafa Kemal Cad.
TO NEW OTOGAR (1km) AND ÖLÜDENIZ (10km)
İnönü Cad.
Old Otogar
Necropolis of Telmessos
Tomb of Amyntas
Tuzla Way Cad.
TUESDAY MARKET
Stadium
Dağ yolu
Berkman Cad.
Atatürk Cad.
Archaeological Museum
Yerguz Cad.
Okul Sok.
Hastane St.
Ortaokul Cad.
Sedir Sok.
Dolmuş Station
TO ÇALIŞ BEACH
Hastane Cad.
Çarşi Cad.
Kaya Köy Yolu Cad.
Dispanser Cad.
Hükümet Sok.
Crusader Fortress
Uğur Mumcu Parki
Belediye
Cumhuriyet Cad.
Belediye Cad.
Okul St.
Çarşi Cad.
Karagözler Cad.
Hamam Sok.
THE BAZAAR
Gulf of Fethiye
Fethiye Harbor
Fevzi Çakmak Cad.
İSKELE MEYDANI
Ancient Theater
Karagözler Cad.
Customs
Orhan Onan Cad.
BIRINCI KARAGÖZLER
Jardarma
Ordu Cad.

PRACTICAL INFORMATION

TOURIST AND FINANCIAL SERVICES

Tourist Office: 1/A İskele Meydanı (☎/fax 612 19 75), at the end of the harbor, past the Atatürk head and antique theater, toward the *jandarma.* Map and lodging info. Open daily 8:30am-5pm; in winter M-F 8:30am-5pm.

Travel Agencies: Fetur (☎614 20 34; fax 614 38 45; www.fethiye-net.com), 50m past the tourist office on Fevzi Çakmak Cad. Arranges flights and daily tours. Open daily 9am-7pm. **Garfield Tourism and Travel Agency** (☎614 93 12 or 614 93 13; fax 614 25 93), along the harbor on Fevzi Çakmak Cad., offers 3- and 4-day backpacker yacht cruises to Olimpos and the 12 islands ($110-145 July-Sept.; B.Y.O.B.).

Diving: European Diving Center (☎614 97 71; fax 614 97 72) on Atatürk Cad. in the bazaar. Offers beginning and advanced scuba dives ($64).

Banks: On Atatürk Cad., facing the PTT. 24hr. **ATMs. Money exchange,** on the corner of Atatürk and Çarşi Cad., available 8:30am-midnight.

LOCAL SERVICES

English-Language Bookstores: Yay Sat (☎614 11 94), in the bazaar on Cumhurlyet Cad., has the best selection. Open daily 8am-midnight. **Imagine Bookstore** (☎614 84 65), across the street, sells books, maps, and music. Open daily 9:30am-12:30am.

Laundromat: (☎612 56 32). On Çarşı Cad. $3 per load. Open daily 8:30am-8:30pm.

Hamam: (☎614 93 18), in the middle of the bazaar, opposite the Car Cemetery Bar on (you guessed it) Hamam Sok. Soak up history at this 400-year-old bath. $12 per person. Open daily 6am-midnight. For a cheaper and less touristed experience, try the **Kaya Hamam** (☎612 4308), on the right side of the road opposite the otogar. $10 per person. Discounts for large groups. Open daily 6am-11pm.

Market: Along the canal about 500m from the tourist office. Vendors sell clothes, fresh vegetables, and fruit. Open Tu 7am-7pm.

EMERGENCY AND COMMUNICATIONS

Police: (☎614 10 40), around the corner from the tourist office, near the ancient theater. A larger branch (☎614 13 09) is on Atatürk Cad., across from the PTT.

Pharmacies: Many on Atatürk Cad., including **Kestepli Eczanesi Pharmacy** across from the mosque. A very helpful pharmacy can be found right next to the public hospital.

Hospitals: Letoon Hospital (☎612 54 84), on Patlanak Mahaller Cad., has English-speaking doctors. Open 24hr. The public **Devlet Hastanesi** (☎614 40 17 or 614 40 18) is near the PTT at the intersection of Atatürk and Hastane Cad.

Internet Access: Star Ata Internet Cafe (☎612 84 10), on the 3rd fl. of the Star Ata Market on Atatürk Cad. (take the elevator up). $.75 per hr. Open 8am-11pm. **@bakűs Internet Cafe** (☎614 14 22), past the PTT on Atatürk Cad. Scrumptiously fries ($1) to go with internet access at $.75 per hr. Open 9am-midnight.

PTT: On Atatürk Cad., 500m from the tourist office. *Poste restante,* international phone calls, money exchange, and fax. Most services 24hr.

Postal Code: 48300.

ACCOMMODATIONS

Cheap pensions can be found on and around Fevzi Çakmak Cad. Some excellent pensions on Karaözler Ordu Cad. are well worth the brief and scenic walk from the city. Quality varies widely in Fethiye—ask to see a room before checking in.

Ideal Pension (☎614 19 8; idealpension@hotmail.com; www.idealpension.net). Take a left up the large hill as the harbor ends. The peach-colored exterior gives way to helpful, friendly service and 34 clean and orderly rooms. Free pick-up from the otogar. Internet access ($1.50 per hr.), book exchange, laundry ($4), and phenomenal deals with multi-night stays. Breakfast included. $7.50 per person, shared rooms $5.50-6.50.

Ferah Pansiyon, 2. Karagözler Ordu Cad. No. 21 (☎/fax 614 28 16; ferahpension@hotmail.com). Call for free pickup from the otogar. A 10min. walk or a 3min. dolmuş ride ($.35) from Atatürk Cad. (Get off at the *jandarma,* walk up the hill opposite the bay, and take the 1st right; the hostel is on the left.) 9 clean rooms, most with bath, and one terrace dorm room with a view of the bay. Laundry $4. Free use of a nearby pool. Discount at nearby hamam. Home-cooked dinner $4. Breakfast included. Dorms $4; singles $8; doubles $10. 10% discount with *Let's Go.*

Hotel Plaza (☎614 90 30), on Çarşi Cad. An understated hotel with all the amenities. Tidy rooms with telephone, A/C, and TV, right in the center of town. $9 per person.

Pension Çetin, 100 Cad. Dolgu Sahası DSİ Yanı (☎614 61 56; fax 614 77 94). When facing the PTT, head right on Atatürk Cad. and turn left onto Hastane Cad.; a sign for the pension is 100m down on the right side of street. 18 large and comfortable rooms with wood paneling, bath, and balconies. Very friendly and helpful owner. Conveniently close to the Tuesday market. Breakfast $1.50. Singles $6; doubles $12.50.

Artemis Pansiyon (☎612 49 80; fax 612 50 13), down the street from the Ferah Pansiyon, on the right. 14 bright rooms with balconies and bath. Beautiful terrace with harbor view. The multilingual owners used to work as chefs in a 5-star İstanbul hotel and now create gourmet meals for guests. Breakfast included. Singles $8; doubles $14.

FOOD

Çarşı Cad., in the pleasant old town, oozes with great dining possibilities. Options near the harbor have views, but tend to be pricier. On the boardwalk of Çalış Beach (up Hastane Cad. away from the mosque) are restaurants, bars, and cafes.

Meğri Lokantası (☎614 40 47), near the harbor, off Atatürk Cad., before the curve in the road. Huge selection of sumptuous local fare. *Soğuk meze* $1; *şiş* ($3). Open 24hr.

Meğri Restaurant (☎614 40 47), in the main square of the bazaar. A sister establishment of the Lokantası, this large outdoor restaurant specializes in fresh fish and includes an extensive menu with several vegetarian options. Fish $4-7; grilled meat $4-6. Open daily 9am-1am. AmEx/MC/V.

Cumba Restaurant (☎614 60 12), past the tourist office and the amphitheater as Atatürk Cad. turns into Fevzi Çakmak Cad. and the harbor ends. Fresh outdoor dining overlooking the harbor complemented with fresh steak ($4-5) and grilled meats ($3-7). Pick a pomegranate from the white-washed tree when the time is ripe.

Saray Lokantası (☎614 23 67), on Atatürk Cad. opposite the PTT. A humble Turkish kitchen where the weary may rest their feet and their pocketbooks with pizzas ($3-5), *mezes* ($1), and grilled meats ($1-5). Open daily 6:30am-midnight.

Rıhtım Pastanesı, Çarşı Cad. (☎612 38 31). A whole lotta bakin' goin' on. A huge selection of international pastries and classics like baklava (4 for $1). Try a sampling of dozens of mini-tarts ($1.25). Open daily 6am-1am.

SIGHTS

RUINS. The road north into Fethiye climbs steep hillsides thick with pine trees and loud with the shrill chirps of crickets. Isolated from the rest of Asia Minor, this region fostered the development of an insulated Lycian culture in ancient times. Believed to be the descendants of a pre-Hittite Anatolian people, the Lycians remained independent until the Persians gained control in 545 BC. The **necropolis** that remains is the most concrete remnant of Lycian culture. The facades of the cliff-hewn tombs replicate Greek temples down to the pediments, porticoes, and cornices. The tombs themselves are thought to be replicas of Lycian homes. The most notable find at the site is the 4th-century BC **Tomb of Amyntas,** reached by a 200-step climb. You can enter the other tombs as well, though to reach them you must clamber around the rocks. From the necropolis, the remains of the **Fethiye Tower,** built by the Knights of St. John of the Templar, are visible. *(Follow the tiny roads behind Çarşı Cad. to the left and uphill to the rock tombs. Necropolis open 24hr. $1.20.)*

ARCHAEOLOGICAL MUSEUM. Fethiye's museum contains Lycian artifacts from neighboring digs. Upon entering, be sure to check out the display on ancient dress and weaving techniques. Of particular note are the **Stelae of Music** in the back room, a **trilingual stele** from Letoon that helped crack the Lycian dialect, and an unbelievable 19th-century **Greek wooden door** carved with elaborate floral decorations. *(One block from the Devlet Hastanesi on Atatürk Cad., toward the bus station. ☎614 11 50. Open Tu-Su 9am-5pm; in winter 8am-5pm. $1, students $.50.)*

OUTDOOR ACTIVITIES. An evening stroll on the hillside roads above Fethiye offers a fantastic view of the surrounding hillsides, the sea, and yachts in the marina. Eventually, the dirt roads wind into a quiet farming village. For something completely different, one- or three-day boat trips to nearby islands include riotous booze cruises for "backpackers and free-minded travelers." Twelve-island tours usually stop at **Göcek Island** for a quick swim, continue to the resort town Göcek, then on to **Flat Island,** and finally to the **Dock-Yard Island** (where the ruins of an Ottoman dockyard can be seen). Other stops include **Cleopatra's Bath** (where bathing in the spring is said to make you look ten years younger), the Step Cave, and *çay* at Somanlık Bay. The Ölüdeniz-Butterfly Valley tour stops first by Butterfly Valley and continues to the famous beach at Ölüdeniz (see p. 269). There are also trips to Turtle Beach and Dalyan-Kaunos, which include a mud bath ($18; see p. 260). Call a travel agency for details (see Travel Agencies, p. 265). *(Boats depart 10am, return 6:30pm; $11-18; lunch and tea included.)*

Check with a travel agent for **horseback riding** trips to Ölüdeniz and Kayaköy. *(3hr., leaves when there are enough people, $15.)* **River rafting trips** on the Dalaman River are another favorite pastime of Fethiye visitors. *(Daily 8am-6pm. $72. Lunch included.)*

ENTERTAINMENT

Despite its large size, Fethiye's nightlife is relatively quiet: laws require music to turn down at midnight. The bars and clubs are located in the bazaar. For a taste of package tour pizzazz, head down to the string of lively bars along Çarşı Beach.

Ottoman Bar (☎612 11 48). On the right, before Karagözler Sok. runs into Çarşı Cad. Fit for a paşa: fragrant smoke drifts from the large selection of water pipes (try the apple-apricot flavor). The relaxed crowd lounges outdoors in cushion-lined booths when not dancing to tunes. Water pipe $3.50; beer $1.75; *rakı* $2.25. Open daily noon-3am.

Car Cemetery Bar, Hamam Sok. (☎612 78 72). Up the street from the old hamam in the bazaar. Have a cold beer amid deceased car parts. Cocktail names like "orgasm," "sperm of the barman," and "quick fuck" will be sure to spice up your evening. Beer $2; *rakı* $2.25; cocktails $6-7. Open daily 10am-3:30am.

The Music Factory, on Karagözler Sok. A pumping metallic cage with 2 levels of flashing dance floors and stylish, thrashing bodies. House and dance music. Beer $2; *rakı* $2.50; cocktails 2 for $8. Open daily 5pm-5am.

Yes Bar, on Cumhuriyet Cad., above the English bookstore. Enjoy free melon with your drink and watch buff waiters dance with their mirror reflections. Yes–yes–oh–yes! Alternative music. Beer $1.50; *rakı* $2.50; cocktails $5. Open daily 8pm-4am.

DAYTRIPS FROM FETHIYE

SAKLIKENT GORGE

*To get to Saklıkent Gorge from Fethiye, catch the Saklıkent **dolmuş,** opposite the mosque and near the intersection of Hastane Cad. and Atatürk Cad. (45min., every 20min., $2). Otherwise, most travel agents along Fethiye's marina offer a **package tour** ($15). A third choice is to catch a **dolmuş tour** from the main dolmuş station in Fethiye (located opposite the sea on Çarşı Cad., behind the gas station) or from the dolmuş stop next to the mosque. (Every 25min. to Saklıkent, Tlos, and Yaka Park (home to a fish-farm restaurant); May-Sept. 9:30am, return 8pm; $4.) Gorge open summer only 8am-8pm. $.60; students with ID $.30. Let's Go does not recommend going deep into the gorge alone.*

Icy water gushes in from natural springs to flood this 18km deep canyon, leaving incredibly smooth, white stone walls and stone terraces in its wake. Occasional patches of sunshine illuminate striking views of the mountains above the raging rapids. Enter the opening of the gorge and battle rushing water and slippery-smooth surfaces, going as far into the gorge as you feel comfortable. Claustrophobes should run for their lives, but everyone else should relish it. There are ill-fitting plastic shoes for rent in the gorge ($1) and at the River Tree Bar outside the gorge ($.50; $1 if you lose them). Sneakers or other shoes with good traction are a better bet. Enthusiastic young boys are willing to help you through for a price.

A number of local restaurants cater to the hungry adventurer. **Saklıkent,** past the wooden bridge in the mouth of the gorge, serves traditional Turkish food at low Ottoman tables on beautiful patios built over the rushing water. (☎636 85 55. *Köfte* $3.50. Open 7am-8:30pm.) **Kayıp Cennet,** over the bridge in Paradise Park, serves up a huge buffet of cold *mezes*, a main course of fish or chicken ($2), and watermelon for dessert. It also has nifty Ottoman-style seating on small islands in the river. (☎636 84 06 or 636 87 77. Open 24hr.) **River Bar** (☎636 87 67) offers full lunch plates (salad, trout, and fries $6; omelettes $1.20) and popular treehouse **camping** (free for customers; toilets and showers available; breakfast and dinner included; $8 per person; caravan with electricity $4.). The bar also offers **Internet** service, **rafting** expeditions, and **tubing** ($6.50). Sleep for free on cushioned riverside platforms at the neighboring **Kanyon Restaurant** (☎659 00 89); beer is discounted for those who spend the night. Remember, kids: rafting and *rakı* don't mix.

TLOS

Many Fethiye travel agencies offer daily tours to Tlos, which usually include Saklıkent Gorge (see Travel Agencies, p. 265). Alternatively, Saklıkent-Yaka Park-Tlos daytrip dolmuş depart from the station in Fethiye (10:30am, return 4pm; $4; bring your own lunch). A third option is to catch any Saklıkent-bound dolmuş from Fethiye (30min., every 20min., $2); ask to be let off near Tlos and walk 4km uphill from the yellow sign. Open daily 8am-7pm. $1.50.

One of the six major cities of the Lycian Kingdom, Tlos is now home to an eclectic mixture of Lycian, Roman, Byzantine, and Ottoman ruins. Its prominent **castle** is visible from kilometers away. At the entrance to the site, ignore the sign for the castle (20m from the entrance booth). Instead, start at the theater and bath at the back of the ruins and work your way up to the castle. With a seating capacity of 5000 in its heyday, the **theater** still has several intact entrances, including one leading to the stage. Continuing down the road, take a left at the hamam sign and note the desperately overgrown Byzantine church on your left. Beyond the church, is a well-preserved but still unexcavated **Roman bath,** whose high arches once supported a bath and sports center but are now home to a gorgeous view.

Back on the main road and to the left, a large **stadium** stands with arched entryways through which Roman **gladiators** once rushed in anticipation of bloody duels. Continue back toward the castle sign and ascend a small mountain to see 7th-century BC **rock tombs** and well-preserved **Lycian Sarcophagi** with inverted boat-shaped lids. The tombs' corrugated roofs replicate the style used by the Lycians in the roofs of their own homes. A hike up to the **castle-fortress** is rewarded by an incredible view of the valley, the old horse stables, and the rest of the site. Far in the distance, Saklıkent Gorge appears as a massive crack in the mountains.

A favorite place to stop is **Yaka Park Restaurant,** 2km up the road from the Tlos ruins. Fish and chicken meals (both $4) are served at shady tables over falling water. Be sure to tour the fish farm and the twisting waterways that wind through the enormous outdoor eating area, full of the very fish you're about to eat. (☎634 00 36. Open 24hr.) Dolmuş pass the restaurant before arriving in Tlos. Across from the ruins is the **Belleforo Restaurant.** (Meal $3. Room with breakfast $5, with breakfast and dinner $8.) Or try the speckled trout ($3), a local specialty, at the **Tlosaile Restaurant** next door. (☎634 02 20. Open daily 8am-7pm.)

KAYAKÖY

Dolmuş leave for Kayaköy from in front of the mosque in Fethiye (30min., every hr. 7am-8pm, $1.20). Roaming the abandoned town takes about 3hr. (Open daily 9am-6pm. $1.50; free after 6pm.)

Deserted and desolate, the abandoned village of Kayaköy looms eerily over a quiet agricultural valley some 10km from Fethiye. Built in the beginning of the 18th century, Kayaköy was inhabited by 2500 Greeks until the 1923 population exchange (see **The Treaty of Lausanne,** p. 16). Kayaköy was abandoned and the newly arrived Turks refused to move into the village, some say out of respect for those who, like themselves, were forced to leave their homes. Others suggest that the Turks disliked the style of Kayaköy's two-story houses, which had a first floor reserved for animals and the bath outside of the house. Each house was built on the hill, so that its shadow would not fall on another house. The doors, windows, and roofs were taken by the Turks to help build new houses down the road, leaving Kayaköy a haunting shell of what it once was. The Turkish Ministry of Culture made the ghost town a historical monument in the mid-1980s when commercial interests threatened to turn Kayaköy into a holiday village. If sponsors consent, there are plans to build a library and restore some of the houses and the two Orthodox churches.

Three popular hikes can be made from Kayaköy, all beginning from the small white chapel at the top of the Kayaköy ridge. They include a 2hr. hike to Ölüdeniz, winding through cool pine forests, with views of the **Blue Lagoon.** Follow the red trail marks, about every 10m. The lovely and less touristed Cool Water Bay, another popular trek, takes between 45min. and 1½ hr. Gemiler Beach, a 2½hr. hike, passes an exquisite hidden monastery. As signs on the trail do not distinguish between hikes, it may be wise to ask for trekking advice at the popular **Kayaköy Motel and Restaurant,** which has great *mezes* ($1.50), pizza ($2.40), and grilled meats ($4). Crash in one of their 14 rooms or bring a tent and camp for free in the garden by the swimming pool. (☎(258) 618 00 69. Doubles $15.) Next door, the **İstanbul Restaurant** serves tasty *böreks* ($1), french fries ($1.25), soups ($1.25), and various meat dishes. (☎618 01 48. Open daily 8am-midnight.)

ÖLÜDENİZ ☎252

This famous Turkish Riviera retreat caters to both the hippie and glitzy beach town crowds. Although posters of the partially enclosed beach hang on the walls of most Turkish hotels, no picture can convey the sheer beauty of Ölüdeniz's enticing beach and lagoon. Ölüdeniz has been bitten hard by the tourist bug, and it suffers from the usual symptoms of commercial package tours and resorts, including an active nightlife that can at times be distracting for those seeking peace. However, the excellent campsites and the variety of exciting outdoor activities still allow visitors to appreciate the area's glorious natural beauty. Ölüdeniz and Hisarönü, its quieter neighbor to the north, are well placed for daytrips to the Butterfly Valley and nearby bays, and Ölüdeniz has become a popular paragliding spot for amateurs and professionals alike.

UP IN SMOKE Seventy years after the introduction of tobacco to Turkey, a remarkable 80% of men and 50% of women over the age of 18 smoke regularly. Tobacco use seems to be a part of ancient tradition and has been documented in the Qur'an; its popularity has grown to the point where the government has established a monopoly over the production and distribution of the crop. Most black tobacco is relegated to the northern Samsun area, while *Sakrikiz* ("Yellow girl") tobacco is grown in Southeast Anatolia. Few foreign cigarettes have legally made their way into Turkish lungs and are mostly renowned for being a mere touristic accommodation. Any unsanctioned brands are sold under the table along with the cheapest cigarette, *Birinci*, that only comes unfiltered and costs about $.20. Strangely enough, it is not illegal to *smoke* foreign cigarettes, only to sell or buy them. The best and most expensive cigarette in Turkey are *Telkens* (aptly meaning "monopoly"), which sell for about $.80.

TRANSPORTATION AND PRACTICAL INFORMATION

The best way to reach Ölüdeniz is via Fethiye. Dolmuş conveniently stop on the main pebble beach before a curve in the main road. The lagoon and some campgrounds are on the right (when facing the water). To the left along the waterfront is a string of bars, restaurants, other campsites, and paragliding companies.

Dolmuş: In summer, dolmuş run to **Fethiye** (25min., every 10min. 7am-1am, $1.15).

Tourism Cooperative: (☎617 04 38 or 617 01 45; fax 617 01 35), in the small wooden building on the left just up the Fethiye road. Helps with rooms and offers valuable information about boat trips and paragliding. English spoken. Open daily 8:30am-11pm.

Travel Agencies: Living Force (☎/fax 616 67 91; open 8am-11pm), **Traveler's World** (☎617 00 45; fax 617 00 54; belcekiz@superonline.com), and **Adventura** (☎617 03 14; fax 617 03 78), all on the main road along the waterfront, offer tours. Trips to **Camel Beach,** the **Blue Caves,** and **Butterfly Valley** ($8; see p. 272); jeep safaris to **Saklıkent Gorge, Tlos, Patara, Xanthos,** and a local mudbath ($35; see p. 267); and boat service to **Dalyan-Kaunos** ($20; see p. 260). Adventura also offers **paintball** (10am-5pm; $35 includes 50 balls) in a pine forest near Kayaköy; **horseback riding** (8:30am-1:30 and 2-5pm; $20); **diving** ($50); and **river rafting** (9am-6pm; $50, meals included). All agencies book flights.

Hamam: Sultan Hamam Club Belcekiz (☎617 00 77, ext. 774), on the waterfront. Bath and drink $15. Open daily 9am-9pm.

Police: Jandarma (☎617 00 55), 50m toward the lagoon entrance.

Pharmacies: Several line the main road of Hisarönü.

Medical Assistance: Lykia Medical Service (☎616 69 30). Walk 1 block up the road to Fethiye, turn right, and continue 100m. **Esnaf Hospital** (☎616 65 17 or 616 65 13), near Lykia Medical. English spoken. Both open 24hr. Fethiye's **Letöon Hospital** also keeps an ambulance in Ölüdeniz for emergency service.

Internet Access: In the back of **Buzz Bar,** on the waterfront next to Traveler's World. $2.25 per hr. Open daily 10am-10:30pm. **Ölüdeniz Camping, OBA Camping, Crusoe's Bar** (see below) all offer access for $2.50 per hr.

PTT: (☎617 01 29), next to the police station. International phone calls and basic mail services. *Poste restante.* Open daily 10am-7pm; in winter 8:30am-noon and 1:30-5pm.

Postal Code: 48340.

ACCOMMODATIONS

Campsites offer backpackers a laid-back community atmosphere, but **Hisarönü,** the village uphill from the beach, is growing in popularity for its cheap pensions and hi-tech discos. Dolmuş from Fethiye to Ölüdeniz stop there. It is also possible to find a room in one of Ölüdeniz's many hotels for about $8 per person. Ask at the Tourism Cooperative for information on local hotels and bookings.

OBA (☎617 04 70; fax 617 05 22; obamotel@superonline.com). Head uphill from the dolmuş stop and turn right at the OBA sign. This large and friendly campsite is another popular option for backpackers. Laundry $5 per load. Internet $2.50 per hr. International phones available. Excellent bar and restaurant with a special vegetarian menu (meals $6-7; beer $1.50). 30 bungalows. $5 per person; mosquito-netted bed in the large treehouse $2; rooms $7-9. AmEx/MC/V.

Ölüdeniz Camping (☎617 00 48; fax 617 01 81; mmsbar@hotmail.com), 1km along the road to the lagoon entrance (turn right from the dolmuş stop). Call for free pick-up. A loud backpackers' mecca, popular with Aussies and Kiwis. 40 bungalows, a small beach, market, restaurant, and bar. Internet access $2 per hr. 2-for-1 drinks 7-9pm. Breakfast $2-5. Bungalows $5 per person; double bungalows with showers $10; tents $3 per person, with own tent $2; spot in the large treehouse $2; caravans $5.

Ilkiz Hotel (☎617 02 51), across from OBA. Ilkiz has fresh rooms with balconies and bath, a pool, billiards, ping pong, and a playground. Doubles $15, with A/C $20.

FOOD

Food, drink, and revelry cost a pretty penny in Ölüdeniz, especially along the boardwalk, but the quality and service usually match the prices. You can always opt to grab a meal at your campsite.

Hippi Shake (☎617 06 31). From the boardwalk, turn left at the only street that intersects the waterfront strip and walk 10m. *Muesli* $3.40; spicy chicken and tabouli pockets $2.50; burgers and salads $3-4; delicious shakes, smoothies, and desserts $2-3. Open daily 9am-midnight. Closed Nov.-Apr.

Kum-Tur Pide (☎617 00 58; fax 617 03 77), left of the dolmuş stop, at the end of the boardwalk. One of the oldest restaurants in Ölüdeniz. Fantastic traditional food at good prices. Quiet eating area in the shade. Salads $1; *pide* $1-2.25; seafood $2.50-6.

Sugar Shack/Help Bar (☎617 04 98), to the left on the boardwalk. This funky combination bar and snack shack has mouth-watering specials, sizzling fajitas, and "funky and fruity cocktails" ($3). Salads $3-4; pasta dishes $5; a mean chocolate cake $2.40. Beer $1; cocktails $2-6. Open daily 9am-3am; kitchen closes at 11:30pm.

Döner Kebap (☎616 06 09), on the waterfront, past the intersection. Ample portions of chicken and meat served up with a bevy of toppings and Turkish bread. Take away your sandwich and enjoy it right on the beach. Sandwiches $1-3. Open daily 8am-midnight.

Our Place (☎616 69 19), in Hisarönü, on the Fethiye dolmuş route. A delicious selection of vegetarian cuisine. The menu changes every night. Swimming pool, bar (beer $1.20), and a cozy reading area with couches and used books in English. Soup $2; salads $2; main dishes $4-8; outstanding desserts $2-3. Open 11am-3am.

SIGHTS

Its marvelous pebble beach aside, Ölüdeniz's main attraction is the **Blue Lagoon**, an idyllic peninsula of beach cradled in wooded hills and lapped by shining, clear water. Take a blissful, quiet dip in these waters, especially on weekday mornings and evenings when crowds are thinner. Enter from Tabiat Park, on the right of the road from Fethiye, where drinkable water, bathrooms, and showers are available. It's a 20-minute walk to the tip or a $6 taxi ride from the dolmuş station. *(Park and lagoon open 8am-7pm. $.75, cars $3.50.)*

The more daring rival to swimming in the Blue Lagoon is to see it from above by tandem **paragliding.** There are plenty of offices on the boardwalk, including **Sky Sports Paragliding** (☎617 05 11; fax 617 03 24; info@skysports-turkey.com), who will show you their video and set you up for one of several daily flights, with their professional English-speaking staff. Passengers are driven to the top of Baba Dağı ridge (1000 meters) before plunging into the great wide open accompanied by a professional. (Flight time varies with conditions, but the whole experience usually takes about two hours and costs $130. You may have to book a day in advance.) Experienced solo pilots can usually get transportation to the top of the mountain from paragliding companies ($8; another $50 to rent a glider). Paragliding is not without risk; injury due to wind conditions during take-off and landing can occur.

Ölüdeniz is a great base for daily boat excursions. **St. Nicholas Island,** which once housed a thriving Greek community, now offers swimming, a spine-tingling view of the coast, and the remains of a Byzantine basilica. For other tours to places such as **Camel Beach,** the **Blue Caves,** and **Butterfly Valley,** see **Travel Agencies,** p. 270.

ENTERTAINMENT

Ölüdeniz's nightlife focuses on the waterfront, where stores and restaurants burn the midnight oil and a few bars and clubs stay open into the wee hours. Be prepared, though: Ölüdeniz doesn't let loose and dance until the early morning.

Crusoe's Bar (☎617 05 49). Match the twinkle of the moonlit sea with the twinkle in your eye over a drink in the "cabana." Large-screen TVs show major sports events and one English-language movie per night (9pm, free with drink). Pool table available. Beer $2; cocktails $5-6. Open daily noon-5am.

Tonoz Beach Club Bar/Barcelona Night Club/Soho Bar/Chillout Cafe & Restaurant (☎617 05 88), on the street past the Hippi Shake. A massive block-long complex. Sway to top 40 hits as you order another round from your audaciously dressed waiter at Soho Bar. For the late late dance scene, hit up the Barcelona nightclub or plunge into the pool. Happy hour 7:30-8:30pm and 10:30-11:30pm. Open daily 7pm-3am.

Buzz Beach Bar/Buzz Snacks. (☎617 00 45), on the left side of the boardwalk. Chill at this bar or snack at the adjoining cafe. Great view of the water. Internet access ($2 per hr.) and daily specials. Beer $2; cocktails $5. Open daily 9am-3am.

Banana Club/Bar, 175m past the Tonoz Beach Club (when heading away from the beach). This tropical dive offers billiards ($3.50), a sauna (free with drinks), a pool table, darts, a pool, and plenty of strange banana concoctions ($3-6).

DAYTRIP FROM ÖLÜDENİZ: BUTTERFLY VALLEY

Small wooden dolmuş boats heading to Butterfly Valley leave from the beach to the right of Ölüdeniz (45min.; 11am, 2, 4pm; return 1, 5pm; $3 each way). Fancier yacht tours will also take you on a daytrip that includes Butterfly Valley for a much higher price.

Almost indescribably beautiful, this tiny turquoise bay near Ölüdeniz is home to waterfalls and several species of butterflies, including the nocturnal orange and black Jersey Tiger butterfly. After the daytrippers leave, an inviolable silence settles over Butterfly Valley, with only the rolling surf and the occasional strains of a backpacker's guitar to lull visitors to sleep in their huts.

From the entrance to the valley, proceed up the rocky path leading to the two **waterfalls** (follow the blue dots). Though the journey can be made in 25 minutes, most visitors take more time as they relish the butterflies and flowers along the way. Since some stones can be slippery, it's best to wear shoes with good traction. Pay for entry about 30m past the beach ($1). More experienced hikers may opt to take the rocky path (30min-1hr.) up to the quiet, traditional mountain village of **Faralya.** The journey is steep and considered risky. *Let's Go* recommends that those who choose to take this route proceed with caution and not go alone.

Should you decide to spend the night, you can camp on the beach, rent a mattress in a 2-20 person treehouse or hut, or get a bed in one of the three Greek houses for $10 including breakfast and dinner. All accommodations have communal toilets and showers. Food is readily available at discount prices for guests at the Butterfly Valley Shop. Try the spaghetti ($1.25) or sandwiches. (☎642 19 01. Open 24hr.) The **Rock Café,** built into the cliffs, serves juices ($.80) and drinks ($1).

PATARA ☎242

Though this tiny, hard-to-reach village has a few cozy restaurants, its seemingly endless (13mi.) sandy beach is its main attraction. On the way to their daily beach worship, visitors marvel at the imposing ruins that lie peacefully among seaside hills. Remote sand dunes showcase the evening's stars, while streetlights illuminate the mosquito-controlling bats' next meal. The seat of the Roman governor of Lycia, Patara was an important port before its harbor silted up. It was also the birthplace of St. Nicholas, better known as Santa Claus.

TRANSPORTATION AND PRACTICAL INFORMATION

Pamukkale offers **bus** service from Fethiye (1hr., every hr. 7am-7pm, $2). From the bus stop at the Antalya-Patara fork, take a dolmuş into town (2km, $.60). From town, another dolmuş runs to the nearby beach (10min., every 30min. 8am-6pm, $.50). From the dolmuş station (☎843 51 17 or 843 51 18), **dolmuş** run to: **Fethiye** (1hr.; 9:15, 10, 11am, 5pm; $2); **Kalkan** (30min., every hr. 8:45am-6:30pm, $1); **Kaş** (1hr., every hr. 8:45am-6:30pm, $2); and **Saklıkent Gorge** and **Xanthos** (10am, $5). Call **Patara Taksi** (☎843 50 50; from the beach ☎843 52 52) for **taxis.**

Kirca Travel (☎843 52 98; fax 843 50 34; kircatravel@superonline.com), run by the same family as the Flower Pension, offers transport to the airport ($40) and Letöon ($10) as well as treks into the mountains ($10-60). **St. Nikolas Travel,** across from St. Nikolas Pension, offers a variety of boat trips to all the classic Turkish Riviera destinations, including **Kekova, Myra, Ölüdeniz, Butterfly Valley, Kalkan,** and the **Islands.** Tours depart from the office. (☎843 53 08; fax 843 50 24. $18-25 per person; barbecue, lunch, and wine included.) They also offer daily 15km **canoe trips** on the Xanthos River (10am-5pm, $14.50 per person) and trips to **Saklıkent Gorge, Tlos, Letöon,** and **Xanthos.** (Daily 9:30am-6pm, $14.50; see p. 267 and p. 275.) **Han Horse Riding,** next to the PTT in the Vitamin Bar, offers horseback trips along the river and the beach. (☎843 51 55. 2-3hr. tours, depart 7am, 4pm; $32-45 per horse.)

Several places along the road into town and in town offer **Internet access** for $2 per hour. The cheapest access is at Kirca Travel ($1.50 per hr.). A helpful nurse takes the place of a health center. The **PTT,** near the dolmuş station in the town-center, has international **phones** and **currency exchange.** (☎843 52 20. Open daily 10am-10pm, closed Nov.-Apr.) **Postal code:** 07975.

ACCOMMODATIONS

Pensions in the town's center can be a bit loud, but all are subject to the early morning call to prayer from the mosque. Affordable pensions are found on the road into Patara and the road past the dolmuş stop.

Zeybek-2 (☎843 50 86; zeybekpansion@hotmail.com). Patara's ruins and twilight beauty can be seen from the terrace of this pension with clean, beautiful rooms, all with baths, balconies, and fans. Breakfast included. Singles $7; doubles $10.

Flower Pension (☎843 51 64; fax 843 50 34), 200m before the Centrum. Turn right off the main road onto a small dirt road marked by 5 *pansiyon* signs. Call ahead for free pickup from the main road. 11 rooms with colorful woven rugs, bath, screens, balcony, and mosquito nets. Free laundry. Delightful eating area. Delicious homemade Turkish dinner $3.50. Breakfast included. Singles $7.50; doubles $10.

Akay Pension (☎843 50 55; fax 843 51 72), on the right off the main road from Fethiye. A green and pink building next door to the Flower Pension. A wonderful *çay* room and 12 clean rooms with bath and mosquito nets and fan. Homemade Turkish dinners. Breakfast included. $5 per person.

Paradise Pansiyon (☎843 51 90; fax 843 50 78), behind the Akay Pension. This simple pension offers 8 rooms with bath, mosquito netting, terrace, and a fan. Free laundry. Internet access $2. Dinner $3. Breakfast included. Singles $6; doubles $10.

Medusa Camping (☎843 51 93), across from the dolmuş station. Look for the hand-painted green sign. Clean showers and toilets, but a small tent area. Bring your own tent or caravan. $1.50 per person. Electricity $1.

FOOD AND ENTERTAINMENT

Keravansaray (☎843 50 02), past the dolmuş stop, heading out of town. Filling set menus of chicken meat or fish with salad, fruit, pancakes and *mezes* for $4. Requisite Ottoman-style seating under ambiance-evoking lights.

Ayşe's Pancake House (☎843 50 71), in the center of town. A family business specializing in *gözleme* of every variety, including banana-chocolate ($1.50-3.50). They also serve *mantı* (meat ravioli in yogurt sauce). Open daily 8am-midnight.

Bistrot Restaurant (☎843 51 85 or 843 52 31). In the town center under the Otlu Market sign. This cozy eatery serves up southern Turkish cuisine under a lush grape arbor. Try the *içli köfte* (mixed meat, flour, and spices; $3.50), the *Adena aşuresi* (a custard-like dessert with raisins and cinnamon; $1.80), and their special drink, *boğma* ("The Bomb"; $6), to keep you going all night long. Billiard table $3.50 per hr. Internet access $3 per hr. Open daily 8am-4am.

Gipsy Bar (☎843 50 09), across from the dolmuş station. For a late-night game of pool or a little dancing to current hot tunes. Beer $1; *rakı* $1.50. Open daily noon-4am.

Voodoo Bar (☎843 52 73), on the right along the main street as you head to the dolmuş station. A small flower-engulfed refuge. Spend the evening talking over rum ($4) or a beer ($1.50). Open daily 10am-3am; closed Oct.-Mar.

SIGHTS

Patara's calm **beach** is a nesting ground for the shy loggerhead turtle by night (see **Save the Sea Turtle**, p. 482), but by day it's licked by a pleasant surf and is not exceptionally crowded. Strangely enough, there's little swimming to be done due to high sandbars. The nearby Lycian archaeological site is somewhat hidden in the grass, and is largely unimpressive save the **Mettius Modestus Arch**, built in 100 AD, which rests on the right of the road to the beach. A half-covered and well-preserved **amphitheater** lies farther in the field to the right, and is a fine site for an evening picnic after a day of bronzing. A **necropolis** with numerous sarcophagi surrounds the gate. The ruins of Roman baths, a Christian basilica, the **Baths of Vespasian**, and a **theater** lie along the path from the gateway to the sea. May as well take advantage. *(Tickets $4, students $2. Tickets can be purchased on the road to the beach and are good for a week. Both open 8am-8pm. Wear good shoes to the beach or your soles will sizzle.)*

DAYTRIPS FROM PATARA

LETÖON

The best ways to get to Letöon are by taxi from Patara ($20) or daily tours with companies from Ölüdeniz (see p. 270), Patara (see p. 272), Kalkan (see p. 275), or Kaş (see p. 278). Dolmuş from Kaş can drop visitors off about 2km from Letöon in Kinik ($2), where taxis will go the rest of the way ($1.50). Site open daily 8am-7:30pm. $1.50, students $.50.

An impressive archaeological site close to Patara, Letöon was a Lycian religious sanctuary whose ruins date from the Roman and early Byzantine periods. The Lycians founded this site in honor of Leto, who, after giving birth to Zeus's illegitimate children, Artemis and Apollo, came here to escape the wrath of Hera, Zeus's jealous wife. Leto and each of her children have a temple at the site. The central **Leto temple** bears only the marks of the thick Ionic columns that once stood there. **Mosaics** of Apollo's lyre and Artemis's bow and arrow decorate the floor of the **Temple of Apollo.** The **church** behind the temples also bears mosaic floors and a Greek-inscribed tablet that was used to decipher the Lycian language. The large **theater,** opposite the temples, is marked by a remarkably well-preserved entrance pediment, and the outer part of the other entrance is adorned with a row of 16 detailed theater masks representing Dionysus, Silenus, a satyr, a girl, and a comic old woman. The Temple of Leto is slated to be restored in summer 2002.

CIRCUMCISE THIS! There are two Muslim rites essential to a boy's transition into manhood. The first, the circumcision ritual, is meant to emphasize cleanliness and is regarded as a boy's first wedding party; the second being his real marriage and the completion of his masculine development. The ceremony generally occurs during one of the summers during a boy's primary school days (age 6-9) and is done with a pair of closely aged boys, such as brothers or cousins. The day commences with an expansive party and lunch, with the boys' family and neighbors in attendance. After the meal, a caravan parade of decorated cars driven by the men of the party drives through the town streets honking horns, the young boys at the front of the train dressed in sashes reading *Maşalla* ("all the best") and topped off with scepters. The *sünnet meulütü* (circumcision rites) are then administered by a muslim *hoja* after which the circumcision occurs (with anesthetic). The ritual is over after the boys are bedecked in money and gold, given to them as they lay on a bed. The boys must wear special gowns that cannot touch the, er, equipment until after the stitches heal.

XANTHOS

To get to Xanthos, take a Fethiye-bound dolmuş or bus from Patara (15min., $1), Kalkan (1½hr., $1.50), or Kaş, which will actually pass right by the site. Otherwise, take a taxi ($10) or tour from Patara (see p. 272). Site open daily 8am-7:30pm. $2, students $1.

Most notable for their **rock tombs,** the ruins of the ancient Lycian capital of **Xanthos** are perched above the Eşen River, 85km from Fethiye and 22km from Kalkan. In the 6th century BC, the Lycians steeled themselves for a last stand against the Persians. When all hope was lost, they torched the city and fought to the death. The Romans later fortified Xanthos in exchange for military support.

As you climb the road to Xanthos, check out the **Roman city gate,** dedicated to Emperor Vespasian. At the end of the well-preserved **theater,** to the left past the entrance gate, stands the 6th-century BC Lycian **Tomb of the Harpies,** a misnamed structure whose women are presumably Sirens conveying souls to the Isles of the Blessed. The remains of the **acropolis** and a **Byzantine church** are visible from the theater. Make your way past the neighborhood goats to see the 5th-century BC Xanthian **Inscribed Pillar,** the largest and oldest known Lycian inscription, standing across from the theater in the **agora** area. Its 250 lines in the Lycian language, describing Lycian battles in the Peloponnesian Wars, are followed by 12 lines of satire in Greek. Walk 200m through the parking lot to a **Byzantine basilica,** with several large, colored floor mosaics buried beneath a layer of sand. More remote but unique in its highlights is the **necropolis** on the other side of the basilica, with ancient rock tombs and engraved sarcophagi.

KALKAN ☎242

More than just a beach town, tiny Kalkan is a surprisingly sophisticated mini-metropolis that serves as a delightful base for exploring the surrounding coast. Like many Mediterranean towns, this picturesque seaside village has steep cobblestone streets speckled with pensions, varied and inviting restaurants, and small shops teeming with spices, carpets, and jewels. If Kalkan's small, rocky harbor beach disappoints, head 3km toward Kaş for the exquisite sand of Kaputaş Beach.

TRANSPORTATION

Buses, dolmuş, and taxis stop on a hill above the shopping district and harbor.

Buses: Kamil Koç (☎844 24 66) and **Pamukkale** (☎844 33 46) serve Kalkan. To: **Ankara** (10hr., 9pm, $16); **Antalya** (4½hr., 7:35am-6pm, $5.50); **Aydın** (7hr.; 9:30am, 9:30pm; $10); **Bodrum** (6hr., 10am, $10); **Dalaman** (3hr.; 9:30, 10am, 9:30pm; $3.50); **Fethiye** (1½hr., 9am-9:30pm, $2); **İstanbul** (12hr., 7pm, $20); **İzmir** (8hr.; 9:30am, 9:30pm; $11); **Kaş** (30min., 7:30am-6pm, $1); **Kemer** (4¼hr., 7:30am-6pm, $5); **Köyceğiz** (3½hr.; 9:30, 10am, 9:30pm; $5); **Olimpos** (4hr., 7:30am-6pm, $5); **Ortaca** (3hr.; 9:30, 10am; $4); **Selçuk** (7hr.; 9:30, 10am, 9:30, 10:15pm; $12). To reach **Dalyan,** change buses in Ortaca.

Dolmuş: From the stop uphill from the PTT to: **Kaputaş Beach** (15-20min., every 30min., $.60); **Kaş** (every 30min., $1.20); and **Patara** (frequent, $1).

Taxis: (☎844 31 00). Taxis cluster around the bus stop uphill on the main road.

ORIENTATION AND PRACTICAL INFORMATION

Kalkan is on the main road between Fethiye and Kaş. The road downhill passes the PTT and banks before becoming **Hasan Altan Sok.** and entering an area with shops and pensions. The two roads that break off from it, sloping down to the harbor, are possible places to look for pensions and restaurants.

Travel Agencies: ABI Travel (☎844 26 94; fax 844 26 95; www.hitit.co.uk/abi), one of the first offices on the right when entering the main shopping district beyond the dolmuş stop. The English-speaking staff helps with **canoe trip** tickets and plans daytrips to the area's small islands and sites, including **Saklıkent Gorge** and **Tlos, Xanthos** and

Letöon, and the **sunken city of Kekova** ($21-26). They also **rent cars** ($29-50 per day; cheaper for 6 days or more). Open Apr.-Oct. 8:30am-midnight. **Kalamus Specialty Tours** (☎/fax 844 24 56), right before ABI, specializes in tailor-made treks and tours dedicated to showing visitors "the real heart of Turkey." These include daily tours of nomad villages to learn about Lycian archaeology, local architecture, religion, culture and crafts, nature, and photography ($20-30, lunch included). Open daily 9am-11pm.

Bank: TC Ziraat Bankası (☎844 34 26), on the left side of the main road when coming from the bus stop, has a Cirrus/MC/V **ATM.** Open M-F 9am-12:30 and 1:30-6pm. For **currency exchange,** try the one across from Kalamus Trous (open daily 9am-midnight).

Pharmacy: (☎(542) 433 48 12), uphill from the bus stop. Open daily 8am-8pm.

Hospital: Tuana Medical Center (☎844 22 44), up the road and to the right before the dolmuş stop on Kalamar Cad. English-speaking doctors available. Open 24hr.

Internet Access: Osi's Internet Cafe (☎711 53 25), on the harbor, charges $2 per hr. Open daily 9am-midnight. Up the hill from the dolmuş stop and on your first right is **Cimbirik Cafe,** which features an enormous television that plays international sporting events. $2 per hr. Open daily 10am-midnight.

PTT: (☎844 32 30), on the left side of the main road, past the dolmuş station. Has **currency exchange,** fax, and *poste restante.* Open 8am-midnight; in winter 8:30am-7pm.

Postal Code: 07960.

ACCOMMODATIONS

Most of Kalkan's pensions offer A/C at reasonable prices.

Kalamaki Pension (☎844 33 53; fax 844 36 54; cdusakli40@hotmail.com). Follow the road down from the dolmuş station, taking the road as it splits to the left at Moonlight Bar. At the end of the street go downhill and Kalamaki is to the right. 16 beautiful rooms with A/C and bath in a classy hotel. Take your breakfast (included) on the gorgeous rooftop terrace with sea view. Singles $12; doubles $20.

Holiday Pansiyon (☎844 31 54; fax 844 37 77). Uphill from Kalamaki Pension. 8 simple, clean rooms with bath. Some with harbor views. Singles $8; doubles $15.

Öz Pansiyon (☎844 34 44 fax 844 22 22), uphill on the first left after the dolmuş station. Öz is on the right, just over the rainbow. 11 modern rooms with baths, A/C, and balcony. Bright and relaxing terrace with a view to the sea. Breakfast included. Singles $15; doubles $20. MC/V.

Çelik Pension, 9 Yalıboyu Mah. (☎844 21 26), to the left off the main road from the bus stop. 9 clean rooms, most with balcony, bath, and screens. Breakfast served on a modest, flower-shaded rooftop. For quiet, ask for a room away from the noisy bars. Singles $10; doubles $15.

FOOD

Foto'nun Yeri (☎844 34 64). Head uphill from the dolmuş stop and make the first left. A canopied restaurant with great fresh food. Sit up on the wooden platform for an extensive view of Kalkan and, at night, the quiet stars. *Gözleme* $2; *mantı* (ravioli) $3.50; *menemen* (omlette) $3. Open daily 8:30am-midnight.

Ali Baba Lokanta (☎844 36 27). Locals flock to this simple, modest family kitchen for its filling fixed menu ($1.50). Nothing over $4. Open 24hr.

Belgin's Kitchen, 1 Yalıboyu Mah., 2 Nolu Sok. (☎844 36 14), down the main shopping street and off a street to the right past Yalı Cafe. Carpets, low couches, and a relaxed terrace create a pleasant atmosphere. Friendly, family-run business. *Mantı* $4.80; stuffed grape leaves $2.50; *çorba* $1.50. Also serves trout ($7), and yogurt and honey ($2.40). Live traditional Turkish music every night. Open daily 10am-2am.

Özgür Kitchen (☎844 25 69), down the first street toward the harbor from the dolmuş station. A cozy and relaxed spot with a breezy upstairs terrace. Try the delicious *gözleme* ($2-3) and fresh melon juice ($1.50). Omelettes $3-5; *çorba* $1.50; pasta $3.50. 15% discount with ID. Open 9am-1:30am.

SIGHTS

Kalkan has a small but decent beach to the left of the marina (when facing the water). Even better is **Kaputaş Beach,** a wonderful sandy cove with excellent views of the islands, located 15 minutes away by dolmuş. Be prepared for a steep hike between the dolmuş drop-off and parking at the top of the cliff down to the water. Kalkan is also a good place from which to embark on any of the standard boat tours along the Mediterranean coast (see **Travel Agencies,** p. 275).

ENTERTAINMENT

Yacht Point Bar (☎844 20 84). The hottest, hippest, busiest bar in Kalkan. Dim outdoor seating where you can snuggle up to a new friend or bump and grind to Euro-pop. Beer $1.50; *rakı* $2.50; cocktails $7-8. Open daily noon-4am.

Kleo Cafe/Bar (☎844 33 30). Beautiful location with sumptuous lighting and mood music. Behold the bobbing sailboat lights and listen to the lapping ocean while lapping a gin and tonic ($6). Beer $1.50; *rakı* $2.50. Open daily 8:30pm-4am.

Moonlight Bar (☎844 30 43). Head downhill from the bus stop and turn left before the shopping district. A popular nightspot that enjoys good company in daylight, with excellent music and a stylish crowd. Outdoor tables and an indoor dance floor. Beer 1.50; *rakı* $2.50; cocktails $6. Open daily noon-3am.

Yalı Cafe-Bar (☎844 34 90), down from the buses on the main shopping road. Where the elder Brits bop to their own pop. Outside seating. Bright bar and dance floor. Happy hour 6-10pm (buy 2, get 3). Beer $1.25; cocktails $7. Open daily 1pm-3am.

KAŞ COAST

KAŞ ☎242

The serpentine road from Kalkan to Kaş passes glittering inlets dotted with pebble beaches. Sandwiched between sea and mountains, cosmopolitan Kaş is refreshingly hassle-free. Its pleasant streets are lined with inexpensive, hospitable places to stay, excellent restaurants, superior artisan shops, and laid-back bars. A peninsula curves around from one side of the town's harbor, creating a calm, rock-lined lagoon ideal for casting off for a boat trip. Kaş is unique in its character and class, allowing for chances to soak in a little Roman and Lycian history, dance to a hodge-podge of American folk, blues, rock, and Turkish pop, or simply lounge on the waterfront, cocktail in hand. Already renowned as one of the best scuba sites on the Mediterranean, Kaş is building a reputation among paragliding enthusiasts. Launches have recently opened on the same mountains whose hiking trails showcase the area's natural beauty and local culture. Kaş hosts a national arts festival every year at the end of June, when Turks from around the country come to enjoy the professional dance, music, and art displays.

TRANSPORTATION

Buses: The otogar, uphill on Atatürk Cad., is serviced by **Kamil Koç** (☎836 19 49) and **Pamukkale** (☎836 13 10). To: **Ankara** (12hr., 8:30pm, $19); **Antalya** (3hr., every 30min. 7am-7:45pm, $5.40); **Aydın** (6½hr.; 9am, 9pm; $8); **Bodrum** (7hr., 9:30am, $10); **Bursa** (12hr., 8pm, $17); **Dalaman** (3hr.; 9am, 9pm; $7); **Fethiye** (2hr.; 9, 9:30am, 6:30, 8:30, 9pm; $2.50); **İstanbul** (15hr., 6:30pm, $21); **İzmir** (9hr.; 9am, 9pm; $12.50); **Muğla** (5hr.; 9am, 9pm; $6); **Selçuk,** via Aydin. To get to **Olimpos,** take any Antalya-bound bus.

Dolmuş: From the otogar to: **Kalkan** (40min., every 30min. 9:30am-7pm, $1); **Kaputaş Beach** (20min., every 30min. 9:30am-7pm, $1); **Patara** (1hr., every 30min. 9:30am-

7pm, $2); **Saklıkent** and **Xanthos** (10:15am, return 6pm via Kaputaş Beach; $8); **Xanthos** (1¼hr., every 30min. 9:30am-7pm, $2).

Taxis: Yat Taksi (☎836 19 33), on the road toward the harbor on Liman Cad.

Car Rental: Ali Baba Rent-a-Car (☎836 25 01; fax 836 32 25), on Hastane Cad. Motorbikes from $13 per day; cars $30-68 per day. Open daily 8am-midnight.

ORIENTATION AND PRACTICAL INFORMATION

Most of the activity centers around the small harbor along the main street, **Cumhuriyet Cad.** At its west end near the mosque, Cumhuriyet Cad. intersects **Hastane Cad.** before becoming **Atatürk Bul.** and heading out of the city. At its east end, near the Atatürk statue, Cumhuriyet Cad. intersects **Ibrahim Serin Cad.,** which leads to the PTT before turning into **Çukurbağli Sok.** From the Atatürk statue, **Hükümet Cad.** passes above the harbor to the two beaches. The street going uphill behind the tourist office—the one with most of the souvenir shops—is **Uzun Çarşı Cad.**

Tourist Office: 5 Cumhuriyet Meydanı (☎836 12 38; fax 836 16 95), to the left as you face the harbor. A very helpful, English-speaking staff distributes local maps and accommodation info. Open daily 8am-noon and 1-7pm; Nov.-Apr. M-F 8am-5pm.

Travel Agencies: Nearly all agencies offer tours to **Kekova.** Tour prices vary slightly, so shop around before buying a ticket. **BT Adventure and Diving** on Ibrahim Serin Cad. (☎836 37 37; fax 836 16 05; bougainville@superonline.com; www.bougainville-turkey.com), has a friendly staff and offers diving ($30), kayaking trips to Kekova ($30; see p. 281), jeep safaris to Saklıkent Gorge (8:30am-6:30pm, $37 with lunch; see p. 267), and canyoning. Open daily 8:30am-11pm. **Simena Tours,** 1 Elmalı Cad. (☎836 14 16), down the street from the otogar, books airline tickets and arranges popular daytrips to Kekova and Saklıkent Gorge. It also plans canoe tours of Xanthos on Xanthos River (9am-6pm, $24 with lunch; see p. 275) and trips to Gömbe, a traditional village in the mountains near a lake (10am-6pm, $20 with trout lunch). Open 9am-8:30pm. **Dolce Vita Travel Agency** (☎836 16 10; www.dolcevitatravel.org), next to the tourist office, offers friendly and professional service to all the popular sites. **Skysports** (☎836 32 91; fax 836 36 79; arslan@paragliding.org; www.skysports-turkey.com) offers paragliding for $80. Open 8am-11:30pm.

Banks: ATMs are scattered throughout the harbor area and on Atatürk Bul. **Türkiye İş Bankası** (☎836 15 60) is on Atatürk Bul. Open 8:30am-noon and 1:30-5:30pm.

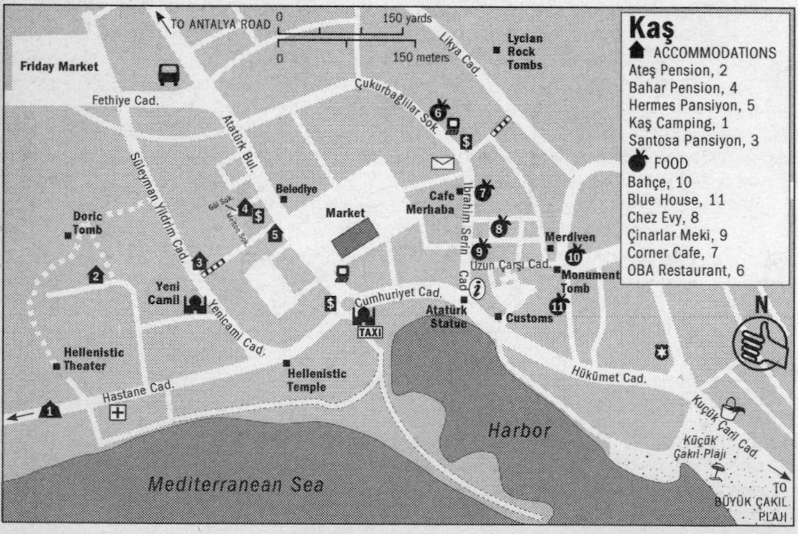

English Language Bookstore: Merdiven (☎836 30 22), directly to the right of the monument tomb, sells used books, maps, and guide books. Open daily 10am-midnight. **Cafe Merhaba** (☎836 18 83), on the corner opposite the PTT, has a selection of international periodicals, and the best cake in Kaş. Open daily 9am-midnight.

Laundromat: Habessos Laundry (☎836 12 63), on Uzun Çarşı Antik Sok., across from Galileo Bookstore. $5 per load, with ironing $7.40. Open daily 8am-midnight.

Hamam: (☎836 30 62), at Hotel Hera on Hükümet Cad. Full service $15.

Police: (☎836 10 24), across from the entrance to the *jandarma* on Hükümet Cad.

Hospital: Private (☎836 11 85), before the campground on Hastane Cad. **Munise Ozan** (☎836 41 42 or 836 41 41), next to Ali Baba Rent-a-Car on Hastane Cad., offers free public health services and is a certified and helpful tourism doctor.

Internet Access: Internet Cafe (☎836 28 45), on Çukurbağlı Cad. $2 per hr. Open daily 9am-midnight. **Turkuaz Internet Cafe** (☎836 20 88), in the market off Atatürk. $2 per hr. Open daily 9am-midnight.

PTT: (☎836 14 50 or 836 14 78), on Çukurbağlı Cad. Walk 50m up from the Atatürk statue on Ibrahim Serin Cad. *Poste restante* available. Open daily 8am-11pm. **Currency exchange** desk open 8:30am-11pm. International phones 24hr.

Postal Code: 07580.

ACCOMMODATIONS

Since pensions tend to jack up their prices in the high season, the search for inexpensive accommodations in July and August will test your haggling abilities. There are many budget pensions on the side streets to the right of Atatürk Bul. (when heading from the otogar to the waterfront), all of which are so close to each other and competing so fiercely that bargaining can significantly ease the strain on your wallet. If you've got some extra cash, the pensions on the hill on the other side of town, with water views and convenient beach access, are worth the money.

Ateş Pension, Yeni Cami Cad. No. 3. (☎836 13 93; atespension@superonline.com). On the right side of Hastane Cad., uphill from the mosque. A popular backpacker hangout with simple rooms, some with bath and balcony, and an adjoining pension with stenciled flowers on the walls and mosquito nets. Ottoman-style breezy rooftop terrace contributes to the laid-back atmosphere. Laundry $3. Free internet. Discounts on local tours and deals with multi-night stays. Breakfast included. Singles $7; doubles $14.

Hermes Pension, 2 İmdi Cad. (☎836 11 73), on the right 1 block in from Atatürk Bul. when walking toward the water from the otogar. Clean, airy, pleasant rooms, all with large bath, tile floors, and balcony. Nice neighborhood. Little English spoken. Breakfast ($2.50) served on terrace with view of the water. Singles $7; doubles $10; triples $14.

Bahar Pension (☎836 13 23). From the otogar, head down Atatürk Bul. toward the sea and take a right onto Gül Sok. Pastel walls illuminate the rooms of this vibrant hostel, topped off by a rooftop terrace. Breakfast included. Singles $9; doubles $13.

Santosa Pansiyon (☎836 17 14). Clean, simple rooms, all with bath and balcony. Barebones but likeable, and right near the mosque (listen for the wake-up call from the *muezzin*). Breakfast included. Singles $6; doubles $12.

Kaş Camping (☎836 10 50), on Hastane Cad., 100m past the theater. Beautiful view, hills, shade, grass, and unreliable hot water. Great oceanside terrace for meals. Breakfast $2.50. Tents $2.50 per person; 2-bed bungalows $10; caravan with electricity $8.

FOOD

Kaş sports dozens of joints complete with beautiful settings and quality food.

Bahçe (☎836 23 70), uphill from the monument tomb. Known for the best *mezes* this side of İstanbul ($1.50-1.75), this enclosed garden restaurant can do it all. Try the fish wrapped in paper ($6.50) or the *saç kavurma* (lamb or beef cooked on the table, $5) for a taste of house specialty. Open daily noon-midnight.

OBA Restaurant (☎836 16 87), uphill from the PTT on Çukurbağlilar Sok., past the internet cafes. A popular green and fresh garden eatery recommended by locals and other Kaş connoisseurs. Interesting dishes include eggplant *kebap* ($3) and *yoğurtlu köfte* (lamb with yogurt, $2.50). *Mezes* $1.25. Open 7am-midnight.

Çinarlar Meki (☎836 28 60), on Ibrahim Serin Cad. A delicious *pide* ($.60) and pizza ($4) restaurant situated in the town's main square. Provides for marvelous people-watching. Beer $1. Open daily 7:30am-12:30am.

Chez Evy, 2 Terzi Sok. (☎836 12 53), up the street and around the corner from the Red Point Bar. If you've got some extra cash, Chez Evy is *the* place to savor exquisite French food in Turkey. Magnificent jasmine-enclosed garden and beautiful Ottoman reclining areas provide an ideal setting for enjoying mushroom-cheese crêpes ($4), a hearty portion of broiled lamb ($8.50), or salad *niçoise* ($5). Open M-Sa 8am-1am.

The Blue House (☎836 21 71), first right uphill from the monument tomb. This extraordinary, antique-filled house has a small, beautiful terrace overlooking the harbor and town. Especially pleasant at night. Soups $1.20; vegetable dishes $1-2; chicken and other grilled meats $4-9. Open 7:30pm-midnight.

Corner Cafe (☎836 14 09), across the street from the PTT. Small but friendly cafe serves yogurt with honey ($2), flavored rice ($1.50), salads ($1.50), pastas, *kebaps*, and fresh fruit juices. Open daily 8am-1am.

Spaghetti House (☎836 40 76). Turn left at the tourist office. Walk straight for 25m and take another left. This gourmet Italian restaurant offers a fantastic selection of pasta and salad at reasonable prices. Savor creamy *tiramisu* ($3) at one of the small outdoor tables. Salads $1.50-3; pasta $1-5; dessert $4-5. Open daily 9am-1am.

Dolphin Cafe and Bar (☎836 35 38). Elegant restaurant next to the Blue House, with a spectacular 2-story terrace and view of the harbor. Outdoor seating. Specializes in seafood $4-7. Delicious *mezes* ($1.25-2) and salads ($1.50-2.50). Open daily 9am-1am.

SIGHTS

The Kaş shoreline is a mixture of white jagged rocks, surrounded by foaming surf and small pebble coves. To the left of the main square, dozens of swimming docks provide the perfect place from which to dive. The entrance to **Küçük Çalık Plajı** (Little Pebble Beach) is atop the hill on Hükümet Cad., 200m uphill to the left as you exit the tourist office. More determined sunbathers and swimmers frequent the less-crowded **Büyük Çakıl Plajı** (Big Pebble Beach), a 15min. walk down the road. Additional bronzing beds such as **Liman Ağzi beach** are in the small alcoves in Kaş's harbor, where the peninsula curves back. These, as well as **Bila beach** with paddle boats and free lounge chairs, can be reached by most boats in the marina. The **Blue Caves,** 15km from Kaş, are home to the Mediterranean's only **seal colony.** The caves are a 20min. swim along the coast—be careful and leave early, before the water becomes too rough. **Doves Cave,** 2km past Kalkan, can be reached only by water. Opposite this grotto, the **Güvercinlik Cave** spouts a cold underwater stream.

The most impressive of the town's historical sites is the **Hellenistic theater,** just past the hospital on Hastane Cad. The only intact ancient structure in Kaş, the solitary theater overlooks the sea and the Greek island of Kastellorizo. During the Lycian Culture and Arts festival (June 28-July 1), the town hosts various concerts and performances here, though the setting sun is a daily event in itself. Follow the path behind the theater 50m to the 4th-century BC **necropolis** with Doric tombs. Up Uzun Çarşı Cad. behind the tourist office, there's a free-standing **Monument Tomb,** also from the same era. A more extensive hike (or dolmuş ride) to the mountain town of **Gömbe** will bring you into contact with the Yoruk people, caretakers of Turkey's traditional nomadic culture. Ask at the local eatery for the trail to the **Yeşil Gölü** (Green Lake) crater lake where cold springs refresh the weary trekker. Kaş also hosts a famous **Friday market** behind the otogar, selling everything from fresh produce to clothing and household items (8am-8pm).

ENTERTAINMENT

Mavi (☎836 18 34), on the harbor to the left of the Atatürk statue. Kaş's first bar has gained more fame from its squatters than from its clientele. Enjoy a lively scene in the bar or perched on the ledge outside, where the frugal can enjoy the music with the help of the "grocer's brew" ($.80). Beer $1.50, *rakı* $2, cocktails $7. Open daily 5pm-3am.

Red Point Bar (☎836 16 05), the 2nd right off Ibrahim Serin Sok. when headed toward the PTT. Look for the small red sign. Situated on a quiet side street, Red Point claims to be the hottest bar in town. Hit this perpetually packed club and dance the night away or talk at the outdoor tables. Beer $1.20, *rakı* ($2). Open daily 6:30pm-3am.

Déjà Vu Bar (☎836 17 47). Facing the harbor, walk left uphill from the Atatürk statue; Déjà Vu is on the right. Throughout the night, laid-back blues and rock flow from the depths of this hip bar. Sit on the star-dappled terrace and sip some of the cheapest beer in Kaş ($1). Vodka $1.75; cappuccino $1.25. Open daily 5:30pm-2:30am.

Hi Jazz Bar (☎836 11 65), across from Chez Evy. Head uphill and turn left after the Red Point Bar. Simple and elegant, this softly-lit bar with photos of jazz artists offers a refreshing break from the usual Mediterranean nightlife scene. Beer $1.50; *rakı* $2; cocktails $5. Open daily 5pm-3am.

Bacchus (☎836 43 78), across from the Blue House. Silvery trees and shimmering, moonlit flowers fill this aromatic garden bar. Turkish and American soft mood music. Beer $1.20; cocktails $5; espresso $1.25; ice cream $1. Open daily 8am-3am.

Han Terrace and Bar (☎836 21 29), across from the PTT. Decorated with hand-made trees, dangling colored lanterns, and light mosaics. Beer $1.50; *rakı* $1.50; cocktails $3.50. Open daily 9am-2:30am.

DAYTRIP FROM KAŞ: THE SUBMERGED CITY OF KEKOVA

Trips from Kaş, often on ***glass-bottom boats,*** *cost around $15. Try a smaller boat ($10) for a more private visit. Kekova can also be visited by* ***sea kayak*** *($30). Kayaking allows for the best views of the ruins, a pleasant lunch in Üçağız (a small coastal village difficult to get to by other means), and some hearty exercise. Inquire at BT Adventure and Diving in Kaş for more details (see p. 278). It's best to visit in the morning when the area is not as crowded. Kekova is also reachable from Kalkan (see p. 275) and Demre (below).*

Off the coast near Üçağız, the Lycian city of Kekova lies submerged under the clear Mediterranean waters. During the eras of Hellenistic and Arab control, the city served as a lookout post and refuge from marauding pirates. From craggy Kekova Island, one can see through calm water to the underwater walls and staircases that collapsed in an earthquake. If the waters are exceptionally smooth, it may be possible to spot an amphora or two, but don't go in expecting to find Atlantis. Above sea level on Kekova Island, a motley assortment of doors and walls still bear evidence of long-gone floors and ceilings. The highlight of the trip is the partially submerged Lycian sarcophagus near the village of Kale, as well as the sight from the village's castle. **Swimming or snorkeling among the ruins is forbidden.**

DEMRE AND MYRA ☎242

The ancient ruins of Myra stretch high into the dry cliffs. The mixture of Lycian rock tombs, sculptures, and a Roman theater is truly awe-inspiring. The offerings of nearby Demre, unfortunately, are not. Its rather drab establishments alternate with unfinished concrete buildings along dusty, hot streets. On the road down from the Beydağları Mountains to Kaş, Demre was once an important member of the Lycian League, and St. Paul is said to have stopped here in 61 AD on his way to Rome. Demre was the diocese of St. Nicholas, better known as **Santa Claus.** The kind-hearted saint, born in Patara (60km west of Demre), became the Bishop of Myra in the early 4th century. The town also has a beach and cold springs.

TRANSPORTATION AND PRACTICAL INFORMATION. Demre's layout is fairly simple. Take a left at the otogar exit and walk 100m to reach the T-junction with the town's main street. To the left 300m is the Church of St. Nicholas. The ruins of Myra are 3km straight from the T-junction. From the otogar, **buses** run to: **Antalya** (3hr., every 30min. 7am-8:45pm, $4); **Fethiye** (3¼hr., every hr. 9am-4:45pm, $4); **Kaş** (1hr., every hr. 8:15am-11:15pm, $1.50). **Myra Otogar Taksi** (☎871 43 43) has **taxis** at the otogar. Other services include: **banks** and an **ATM** on Noel Baba Cad., including a **Türkiye İş Bankaşı** on the way to St. Nicholas Church from the otogar (open 11am-5:30pm); a **police station** (☎871 42 21), near the otogar; and a **PTT**, 200m to the right of the T-junction. (☎871 55 19. Open 8:30am-6pm.) **Postal code:** 07570.

ACCOMMODATIONS AND FOOD. **Kent Pension,** in a bright green building 2½km up the road to Myra, has 10 clean, comfortable rooms with 24hr. hot water and garden-side bungalows with bath. The pension provides tours of Kekova with visits to several bays, the Blue Caves, and a shipyard, as well as shuttles to the beach and cold springs. (☎871 20 42. Dinner $4. Tours $10. Breakfast included. Singles $9; doubles $15; 3-person bungalows $10.) Another option is **Hotel Kiyak,** Merkez Girişi PK 65, a salmon-pink hotel across from the Kekova Pension and near the traffic roundabout. Walk out of town, away from St. Nicholas and Myra. Its 24 large, modern rooms have balconies, bath, phone, and TV. The hotel also organizes Kekova tours ($5-9) and "mountain safaris," with visits to a waterfall, lakes, and a hamam ($23). There's a free shuttle to beach and cold springs. (☎871 45 09. Breakfast included. Singles $7, with A/C $9.50; doubles $15, with A/C $20.)

Demre's dining options are sparse. Inquire about evening meals at pensions, which typically provide reasonable quality and ample portions. Otherwise, you can find a cheap meal along the main road toward St. Nicholas Church. **İpek Restaurant,** near St. Nicholas Church, dishes out Turkish specialties. (☎871 54 48. Hot *meze* $1-1.50; *pide* $1.50. Open daily 8am-midnight.) **İnci Pastanesi,** by the İpek restaurant, sells delicious pastries. (Baklava $3.50 per kg. Open daily 7am-midnight.)

SIGHTS. **Myra** was one of the most important cities in the Lycian League, a federation that included 70 cities, including Xanthos, Patara, Olimpos, and Tlos. Myra was divided into three areas: the **sea necropolis** in the southwest part of the site to the right of the theater, the **acropolis** area and its surrounding walls, and the **river necropolis.** The **rock tombs** built into the sea and the river necropolis are of particularly high quality and are thus off-limits. Some tombs are stylized to imitate wooden beams, and many still have slight traces of color. The river necropolis is less touristed than the sea necropolis, since it requires an arduous climb over thorny, brambled cliffs. The site's other major highlight is a **theater** with 35 consecutive rows of seats and a still-intact stage. Stone tablets engraved with theater mask reliefs lie scattered about the structure. The theater was destroyed by a devastating earthquake in 141 AD, but was later rebuilt and modified to host gladiatorial games. (Open daily 9am-7:30pm; in winter 8am-5:30pm. $1.50, students $.50.)

Demre's other major attraction is the **Church of St. Nicholas,** thought to be built on the site of the famous saint's tomb. An annual Orthodox service takes place in the theater on December 6, the anniversary of St. Nicholas's death. The current structure, which dates from the 8th century, suffered centuries of neglect until the Russian Tsar ordered its repair in the 19th century. Later lost under debris and shifting sand from the Myras River, the church remained hidden until 1956. Excavations since 1989 have uncovered many new rooms but few treasures. Though for the most part barren, the church's stripped walls are illuminated by a few Byzantine frescoes crafted after the Arab invasions of the 11th century, and the church is speckled with tombs from all periods of the church's history.

Scholars have generally agreed that the tomb of St. Nicholas is in the southern nave of the church. In 1087 Italian merchants broke into the tomb and hastily took the remains to Bari, Italy, leaving behind only those that appear in the **Antalya Museum** (see p. 288). The Turkish government's efforts to bring St. Nicholas back to the church have fallen on the deaf ears of Vatican officials for the last 20 years. (Open daily 9am-7:30pm; in winter 8am-5:30pm. $5, students $2.)

OLİMPOS ☎242

Enchanting Olimpos is a true backpacker's town, one of the few budget spots along the Turkish Riviera. Olimpos brings travelers closer to the heavens by giving them the chance to sleep in a treehouse and make a nighttime ascent of the Chimaera, where a naturally occurring flame has burned since ancient times. Roman and Byzantine ruins are close enough to the beach that visitors can partake in nearly simultaneous cerebral and solar stimulation, but the ruins are remote enough to give a sense of forested isolation. But beware: like Homer's Lotus-Eaters, travelers have been known to extend their stays indefinitely.

TRANSPORTATION AND PRACTICAL INFORMATION

To get to Olimpos from Antalya, take a Kaş- or Demre-bound bus and ask to be let off at Olimpos. From Kaş, take an Antalya-bound bus. **Buses** stop at a rest station on the main road. From there, **dolmuş** run down the 10km dirt road that leads to the treehouses (15min., every hr. 8:30am-10pm, $1.25), dropping passengers off at the pensions of their choice. From Olimpos, dolmuş return to the main road (15min., every hr. 8am-6pm, $1.25). Olimpos has **no PTT, pharmacy, bank,** or **police station.** Many pension owners accept US dollars, offer international phone calls, and arrange tours that include trekking or rafting. **Postal code:** 07350.

ACCOMMODATIONS

The Turkish government has classified Olimpos as a "*sit*," or archaeological site, banning the use of concrete. This means no asphalt roads (hence no direct bus service) and no cement building foundations, a potential kiss of death to tourism. Resourceful Olimpians have turned *sit* into gold, building back-to-nature treehouse **pensions,** which line the dirt road to the beach and ruins. Unfortunately, the question is not whether there are bugs, but rather how many and of what kind. Most places also offer pension rooms and sturdy bungalows for an inflated price. Prices are generally standardized, with exceptions noted. (Treehouses $7 per person; bungalows $10 per person; rooms $13 per person.) All prices generally include breakfast and dinner. For less rustic accommodations close to Olimpos and Chimaera, try the pensions in **Çıralı** village, 2km up the beach from Olimpos.

Bayram's Treehouse Pension (☎892 12 43; fax 892 13 99; bayrams1@turk.net; www.bayrams.com). The ultimate Black Hole of Chill, with colorful bungalows and a friendly staff. Internet access $2 per hr. International phone, along with a book exchange and travel arrangements. Close to beach and ruins.

Şaban Pension Bungalows (☎892 12 65; fax 892 13 97; olympossaban_pension@yahoo.com). A relaxed, family-run pension. The dinners alone make a stay here worthwhile. Laundry $3. Internet $2 per hr. Camping $6.

Kadir's Yörük Treehouses (☎892 12 50; fax 892 11 10; treehouse@superonline.com). The first pension at the bottom of the road. More like a sprawling Ewok village than a pension, Kadir's is a post-adolescent summer camp. Guests can watch movies, play volleyball, and chill. At night, Kadir's bar becomes the focus of nightlife. Free shuttle to beach. Laundry $3. Beer $1.25; cocktails $3. Dorm $7; bungalow $12; treehouse $9.

Türkmen Tree Houses (☎892 12 49; fax 892 14 02; turkmen@turkmenpension.com). Treehouses and sparkling showers, a clean kitchen, brand new bungalows, and a beautiful front patio. Free *çay* and coffee throughout your stay. First beer free. Camping $5.

Carreta Carreta, across the road from Şaban. This tiny pension has some of the largest, best-quality, and sturdiest treehouses in Olimpos.

Green Point Camping (☎825 71 82; fax 825 70 94), about 1km up the beach from Olimpos. Great campground with clean toilets and shower. 100m from Çıralı beach. 1-person tent $3.50; 2-person tent $6; 2-person caravan with electricity $12.

"YES, PLEASE" The Turkish language is replete with multipurpose expressions. One particular favorite is *"çok güzel,"* literally "very beautiful," which can be used in reference to pretty much anything one finds agreeable. Another is *"buyurun,"* from the verb *buyurmak* meaning "to order" or "to command." *"Buyurun"* is a prompting word used in a number of different contexts. A waiter bringing food might use it to express "here you are," or a shopkeeper might use it to express "what can I do for you?" The possibilities are endless. Sadly, the linguistic wizard charged with teaching English to generations of Turks decided that there was a direct English translation of *"buyurun:"* specifically, "yes, please." Not only does "yes, please" make no sense in the contexts in which it is so often used by Turkish restaurateurs and hawkers, but the equivalent Turkish *"evet, lütfen"* is equally nonsensical. When you think you'll turn murderous the next time you hear "yes, please," keep in mind that the speaker is trying to find the equivalent of a friendly and welcoming—and untranslatable—expression.

SIGHTS

CHIMAERA. During the 2nd century BC, Olimpos's proximity (7km) to this perpetual flame inspired the residents to worship Hephaestos, god of fire and the forge. They believed the flame to be the breath of the Chimaera, a mythical beast that was part lion, part goat, and part serpent. Geologists have yet to produce a more exciting explanation. They suspect natural methane gas might play some role. In past centuries, the flame was even brighter than it is today; according to ancient reports, ships navigated by it. Chimaera is best seen at night, and bus tours leave Olimpos at 9pm (3hr., $3); ask a pension owner for details. Wear sturdy shoes and bring a flashlight since reaching the flame requires a tricky 20min. uphill hike through unlit mountainous terrain.

RUINS. The ruins at Olimpos are a jumbled pastiche of everything from ancient temples to crumbling walls of medieval castles. Follow the road from the pensions to the beach. The ruins tend to be overgrown with vines and dry bushes, and inhabited by **snakes** and **scorpions,** so be very cautious when exploring the site. About 10m beyond the entrance booth, you can cross the dry river bed to reach a row of tombs and one of the crumbling arches. If you continue on the main path about 40m farther, a small path leads off to the left, climbing uphill past the overgrown **necropolis** to a rather large but unimpressive **archway.** Beyond the archway it is easy to get lost in overgrown orange groves and reeds. The sign at the beginning of the pathway reads simply "temple."

On the other side of the road across the stream are the decrepit **theater** and **medieval walls.** Though it is not unusual to see locals at the stream swimming and drinking, tourists should avoid doing so. Continuing along the main path leads to the **Harbonu memorial tombs** just before the beach, where the best preserved group of ruins looms over the water on a rocky cliff to the right. *(Open 8am-7pm. $5, students $2. Hold on to your ticket stub, as it will be good for multiple entry to the beach and site.)*

ANTALYA GULF COAST

ANTALYA ☎242

Capital of the so-called Turquoise Riviera and linked by air with Munich, Moscow, and Amsterdam, Antalya is a city of many faces. This busy metropolis encircles Kaleiçi ("inside the fortress"), the crescent-shaped old city that brims with cobblestone streets, Ottoman houses, tourist businesses, and carpet dealers. At Kaleiçi's heart, pricey eateries and cutting-edge nightclubs line the ancient walled harbor that once sheltered Roman ships and now welcomes luxury yachts.

Antalya's size might overwhelm the casual visitor, but the city offers something for everyone. Beaches, ruins, waterfalls, an outstanding museum, and restaurants serving Turkish regional specialties and make this place one of the most cosmopolitan in the country. The Antalya Altın Portakal ("Golden Orange") Film Festival held in the fall is a huge affair, screening both international and Turkish titles.

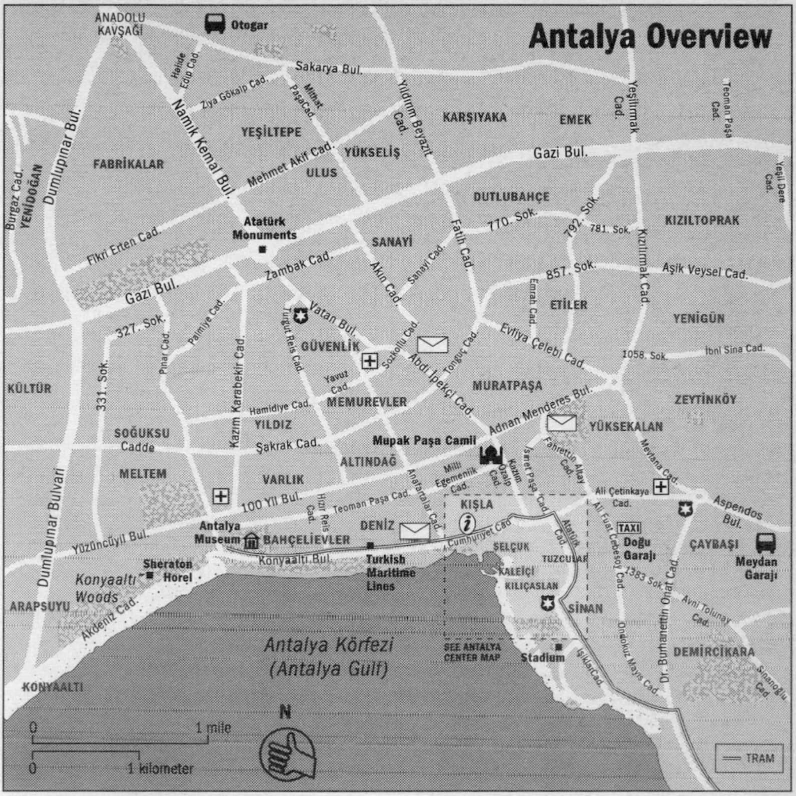

TRANSPORTATION

Flights: Antalya International Airport, 15km from town (domestic flight info ☎330 30 30; international flight info ☎330 36 00). **THY** (reservations ☎444 08 49) has an office on Cumhuriyet Cad., next to the tourist office. Open M-F 10am-7pm, Sa-Su 9am-5:30pm. Buses run between the THY office and Antalya Airport (10 per day 4:45am-2:30am, $3). Flights to **İstanbul** ($61, students $51; round-trip $79, students $61).

Buses: If **Pamukkale** doesn't serve your destination, they'll be able to point you in the right direction. The otogar has 24hr. **luggage storage.** $2 per bag per day.

Dolmuş: Antalya has 2 dolmuş hubs. **Doğu Garaj** sends dolmuş to **Lale** and **Lara Beaches.** To get there from Atatürk Cad., turn right on Ali Çetinkaya Cad., walk 1 block, and turn right at the Start Hotel. The **Meydan Garajı,** at the intersection of Mevlâna Cad., Aspendos Bul., and Ali Çetinkaya Cad., 1½km from the city center, has dolmuş to **Perge** and **Aspendos.** Dolmuş to and from the otogar are white with a blue stripe.

Trams: A new tram system runs from the Antalya Museum along Cumhuriyet Cad., then down Atatürk Cad. to the stadium (every 20 min., $.25). Blue signs mark tram stops.

Vehicle Rental: Available from many agents in Kaleiçi, who require a valid driver's license and minimum age of 21. Daily fees start at $32 per car, $16 per scooter.

DESTINATION	DURATION	TIMES (DAILY)	PRICE
Adana	12hr.	8pm	$16
Alanya	2hr.	9pm-midnight	$3.50
Anamur	4hr.	8pm	$6
Ankara	8hr.	10, 11:30am, 11pm, midnight	$12

DESTINATION	DURATION	TIMES (DAILY)	PRICE
Antakya	15hr.	7:30, 8:30, 9:30pm	$15
Bodrum	8hr.	12:30pm, midnight	$15
Demre	3hr.	every 30min. 5:45am-8pm	$4
Fethiye	5hr.	10:30am, 12:30, 11pm	$6
Göreme (Cappadocia)	9hr.	8:30, 9:30, 10:30pm	$15
İstanbul	12hr.	9:30am, 7:30, 9, 10, 11pm	$16
İzmir	8hr.	6:30am-midnight	$12
Kaş	4hr.	every 30min. 5:45am-8pm	$5
Kayseri	10hr.	8:30, 9:30, 10:30pm	$15
Marmaris	7hr.	10:30am, 11pm	$11
Mersin	10hr.	8pm	$9.50
Olimpos	1¼hr.	every 20min. 5:30am-8:45pm	$1.50
Pamukkale	4hr.	6:30am-midnight	$7
Trabzon	17hr.	5pm	$23

ORIENTATION

In 1997, Antalya gave birth to a gargantuan orange **otogar,** replete with fountains, several **ATMs,** cafes, A/C, a PTT, and labyrinthine bathrooms with seat toilets. Unfortunately, this wonderland is 4km out of town at **Anadolu Kavşağı,** the intersection of Namık Kemal Cad. and Dumlupınar Bul. White buses (every 15min., $.40) run from outside the otogar to the city center, near **Kaleiçi,** the old city. **Işıklar Cad.,** at the intersection of **Kazım Özalp Cad.** and **Cumhuriyet Cad.,** is marked by a brick-red fluted minaret and a stone clock tower. Hostels, restaurants, and historically important ruins and buildings are in this area. The two beaches are on the outskirts of town. **Ali Çentikaya Cad.** leads out of town to the dolmuş garages from the intersection of **Atatürk Cad.** and **Cumhuriyet Cad.** in the old city.

PRACTICAL INFORMATION

TOURIST, FINANCIAL, AND LOCAL SERVICES

Tourist Office: (☎241 17 47), on Atatürk Cad., toward the Antalya Museum. Helpful, English-speaking staff distributes free maps. Open M-F 8am-7pm, Sa 9am-5:30pm.

Travel Agencies: Most pensions will organize tours for you, though they charge a commission unless they run the tours themselves. Try **Akay Tur,** 54 Cumhuriyet Cad. (☎321 88 41; fax 241 98 47). From the clock tower, head 50m west along Cumhuriyet Cad., turn right onto Atatürk Cad., and look for the signs. Tours to: **Perge, Aspendos, Side,** and **Manavgat** (9am-6pm, $40); **Köprülü Kanyon** (9am-6pm; $35, lunch included); **Termessos** and **Upper Düden Waterfall** (Sept.-June 9am-3pm, $25).

Consulates: UK, Dolaplıdere Cad. Pırıltı Sitesi, 1st fl. (☎244 53 13; fax 824 67 03). **The Turkish Republic of Northern Cyprus (TRNC),** Kışla Mah. 35th Sok. Dörteldemir Apt. 11 PK 633 (☎323 43 64).

Banks: For cash transfers, go to **Koç Bank,** opposite Hadrian's Gate on Atatürk Cad. Banks, many with **ATMs,** are clustered about the main streets outside Kaleiçi.

English-Language Bookstores: Owl Bookshop, Barbaros Mah. 21 Akarçeşme Sok. (☎243 57 18), off Hesapçı Sok., 500m into the old city from Hadrian's Gate. Turn left at the Alp Paşa Restaurant. A cat named Pythagoras lurks among back issues of *Harper's,* the *New Yorker,* and an excellent selection of books. Open daily 10am-8pm. **Ardis** (☎247 03 56), in the Setekler Bazaar, past the tourist office on the way out of town. Classic titles and best-sellers. Open daily 7:30am-7:30pm.

Laundromat: Yıkama Laundry, 28 Tabakhane Sok. (☎241 11 74), beside the Anı Pansiyon. Wash and dry $5. Open daily 8am-11pm. Mysteriously, **Öz Ünaller Rent A Car,** 43 Hesapçı Sok. (☎248 93 72), beside the Kesik Minaret, also has a laundry service. $4 per 5kg; ironing $.25 per piece. Open daily 8am-8pm.

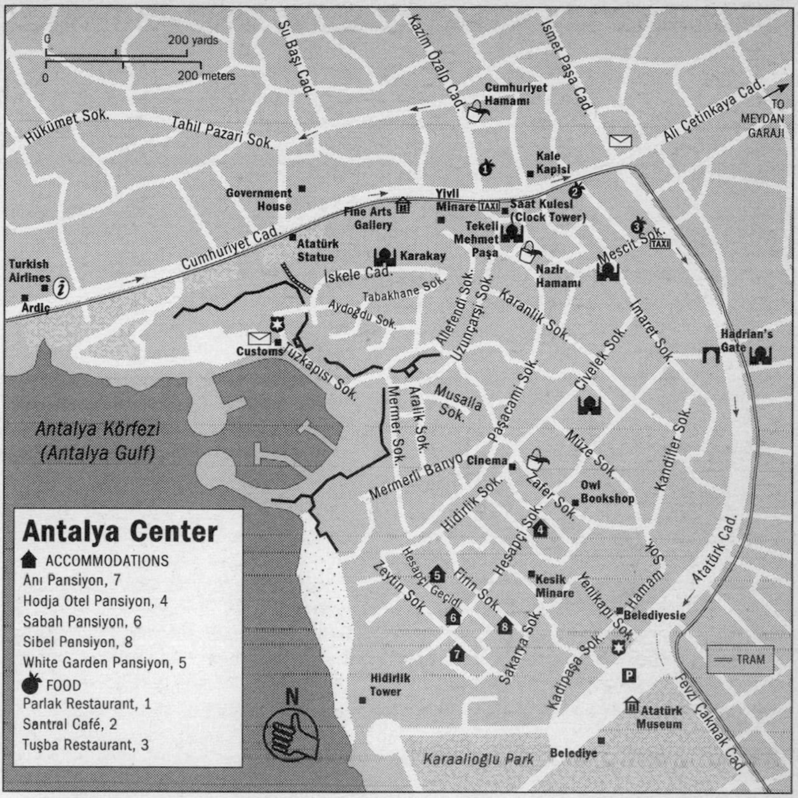

Hamams: Cumhuriyet Hamam (☎244 49 98). From the clock tower, head 1 block north and turn right. $7 per person. Open daily 5am-2am. **Nazır Hamam,** in Kaleiçi, near the Tekeli Mehmet Paşa mosque. Bath, massage, and scrub $7. Open for women M-Th, Sa 10am-5pm; for men Su, F 10am-5pm; for couples daily 5pm-midnight.

EMERGENCY AND COMMUNICATIONS

Tourist Police: (☎/fax 247 03 36). Face the water and turn left on a little street left of the Atatürk bust at the harbor. Little English spoken.

Hospital: The closest hospital to Kaleiçi is the private **Akdeniz Sağlık Vakfı Hastanesi,** 17 Ali Çetinkaya Cad. (☎247 90 01 or 247 90 02; fax 247 90 03), on the left side of Cumhuriyet Cad., 400m past the intersection with Atatürk Cad.

Pharmacies: Many are on Atatürk Cad., opposite the old city walls.

Internet Access: Sörk Cafe, across from Hadrian's Gate, on an alley off Atatürk Cad. $1 per hr. Open daily 8am-midnight. In Kaleiçi, try **Cool Exhibitions** (☎244 56 71), next to Sabah Pansiyon on Hapaçi Sok. $1 per hr. Open daily 8am-midnight.

PTT: To get to the **main branch** (☎243 45 79), head down Cumhuriyet Cad. toward Atatürk Cad. and take the 1st major left onto Anafartalar Cad. Open daily 8:30am-5:30pm for stamps, *poste restante,* and **currency exchange.**

Postal code: 07100 (Kaleiçi). Mail sent *poste restante* should be addressed 07000.

ACCOMMODATIONS

The best place to stay is within the ancient walls of **Kaleiçi,** whose winding streets contain over 200 hotels and pensions. Unless otherwise stated, all include private shower and breakfast. Bargaining may help, especially for students.

White Garden Pansiyon, Hespaçı Gençidi No. 9 (☎241 91 15; fax 241 20 62; garden@mail.koc.net), through Hadrian's Gate in Kaleiçi and down Hespaçı Sok. 15 beautiful rooms that prove that less is more. Nice garden patio and helpful, English-speaking management. Laundry $3. Dinner $1-3. Singles $10; doubles $15.

Sibel Pansiyon, 30 Firin Sok. (☎241 13 16; fax 241 36 56). Take the second right after the Kesik Monument on Hespaçı Sok., past Hadrian's Gate. Large, clean rooms with A/C, and a sunny, overgrown garden. Singles $12; doubles $20.

Sabah Pansiyon, Kaleiçi Kılıçarslan Mah., 60 Hesapçı Sok. (☎247 53 45; fax 247 53 47), toward the harbor. A popular backpackers' hangout with a pleasant courtyard area. Organizes cheap tours. Vegetarian and regular dinners $3.50. Beer $.80. Laundry $4 per load. Bike/scooter rental $15 per day; car rental $24 per day. Singles $7; doubles $8, with bath $13, with A/C $18; roof, couch, or floor $3; camping $2.50-3.

Hodja Otel Pansiyon, Kılıçarslan Mah. 37 Hesapçı Sok. (☎248 94 86; fax 248 94 85). Wonderfully spacious, Hodja has large central hallways, Ottoman paintings, and 12 rooms with bath and fan. Little English spoken. Singles $9.30; doubles $19.

Anı Pansiyon, 26 Tabakhane Sok., Hesapçı Sok. (☎247 00 56). Understated and luxurious, the elegant Anı has large windows, high ceilings, and wooden furniture in a converted Ottoman home setting. Singles $11; doubles $20.

Adalya Tesisleri (☎719 96 35), by the entrance to Lara Beach. Accessible by dolmuş on Atatürk Cad. Tantalizing views of oil tankers. 34 basic bungalow rooms with 2 bunks each go for $2. The "camping" option consists of being given a tent (you can't bring your own) to pitch on concrete platforms. 3-person tents $7; 4-person tents $10.50.

FOOD

Try not to pay the tourist price. The restaurants around the old city arch tend to have a nice atmosphere but overpriced, overrated food. Near the harbor, prices rise in direct proportion to the quality of the view, and the best and cheapest meals are often found in cheap dives a few blocks from the walls of Kaleiçi.

Tuşba Restaurant (☎244 43 81). Facing the street, turn left off of Atatürk Cad. onto Mescit Cad. Tuşba is on the right. The best *kebaps* in Antalya, served sizzling with fresh, warm flatbread ($2.50). Lightning-fast service and free watermelon as a finale.

Parlak Restaurant (☎241 65 53), in the shopping center by the clock tower. Classy, air-conditioned interior and a rotisserie (half chicken $3). Open daily 11am-midnight

Beğirman Börek and Mantı (☎248 53 45), on the first right after the PTT on the way out of town. Delectable *mantı* (Turkish ravioli) in a cheerful, air conditioned, yellow interior. *Börek* $1.20; lemonade $.60. Open daily 7am-10pm.

Santral Cafe and Patisserie. Yum, yum, yum! Superlative tea and pastries ($.30-.50). Also serves cakes, tarts, and ice cream. Outdoor seating.

MEDITERRANEAN COAST

SIGHTS

THE ANTALYA MUSEUM. One of Turkey's finest museums, the Antalya Museum presents exhibits ranging from prehistoric times to the founding of the Turkish Republic. To the left of the entrance is the **Hall of Natural History and Prehistory,** which contains various ancient objects and an example of a **pithas burial:** a skeleton resting in a smashed urn. Past the display, excavations of Phrygian settlements feature amazingly detailed metalwork from the 7th and 8th centuries BC.

The **Salon of Small Objects and Underwater Remains,** down the hall to the right, houses silver and ivory Phrygian statuettes excavated from 8th-century tombs. A blue-lit glass case nearby is littered with "underwater findings," mainly barnacle-encrusted earthenware salvaged from 3rd-century shipwrecks. Down the next hall is the **Hall of Emperors,** home to 2nd- and 3rd-century Roman marble busts from **Perge** (see p. 290). In the next room, the newly refurbished **Salon of the Gods,** are some of the museum's highlights: large 2nd-century statues of Zeus, Aphrodite, Athena, Artemis, Hermes, and Dionysus, as well as their Egyptian sidekicks Serapis, Isis, and Horus. The gem of the collection is a magnificently painted Grecian urn, mysteriously labeled the "Tibet Crater."

The **Icon Hall** across the way displays a small but exceptional collection of Orthodox Christian **icons.** Farther down the hall lies the **Mosaic Salon,** which contains a Seleucid floor mosaic and smaller 6th-century Byzantine works. The **Hall of the Cemetery Culture,** the next room, contains seven beautifully carved sarcophagi, including special ones to escort dogs to the afterlife. The **Hall of Money and Jewelry,** around the corner, contains a few of the **world's first coins,** minted between 640 and 630 BC by the Lydians. These were forged from white gold, or electrium, under the last Lydian king, Croesus. The **Ethnography Salon** displays daily implements of Ottoman and Bedouin life. Check out the elaborate wooden ceiling display near the exit. *(2 Konyaatı Bul., about 2½km from town along Cumhuriyet Bul., which changes its name to Konyaaltı Bul. as it heads out of town. Dolmuş labeled "Konyaaltı/Liman" head along this street, ($.30). Get off when you see the yellow museum signs before the dolmuş heads downhill to the beach.* ☎ *238 56 97. Open Tu-Su 9am-7:30pm; in winter 8am-5pm. $5, students $2.)*

OTHER SIGHTS. Near the entrance to Kaleiçi, at the intersection of Cumhuriyet Cad., stands the symbol of Antalya, the unique red-tinted **Yivli Minare** (fluted minaret). Dating from the 13th century, this minaret was constructed by the Selçuk Sultan Alaeddin Keykubad. Down Atatürk Cad., on the right, stand the three adorned arches of **Hadrian's Gate,** built in 130 AD to commemorate the emperor's visit. Through this gate, about halfway down Hesapçı Sok., is the **Kesik Minare** (Broken Minaret). The mosque traces Antalya's history: it was once a Roman temple, then a domed basilica, and, finally, a Selçuk mosque. At the far end of Hesapçı Sok. is the **Hıdırlık Tower,** believed to have been built as a lighthouse in the 2nd century.

Kaleiçi, a charming district with serpentine streets and old buildings, is a great late afternoon stroll. Founded as Attaleia in the 2nd century BC by King Attalos II of Pergamon, this area is still fortified by Greek, Byzantine, and Selçuk walls.

Antalya's two large and placid beaches, **Lara** and **Konyaaltı,** are both accessible by dolmuş (to Lara from the Doğu Garaj, to Konyaaltı from Konyaaltı Bul.; $.30). Both beaches are free. On the way to Lara, stop off at the **Lower Düden Waterfall,** a cascade that tumbles 20m into the sea. The spectacular **Upper Düden Falls,** about 10km from Antalya, is included in most half-day tours of Termessos (see p. 291).

ENTERTAINMENT

Whether you're looking for an elegant dance club or a more rowdy bar, there's no shortage of nightlife in Antalya. **Cinemas** generally show English-language films with Turkish subtitles. **Oscar,** on Zafer Sok., along Atatürk Cad., shows Hollywood blockbusters and other foreign films ($3.50).

Club Ally, above the harbor on İskele Cad. Easily identified by the intense green laser it shoots across the water at night. The be-all and end-all of nightlife for Antalya's young and wealthy. 10 independently-owned bars encircle a central bar in this spacious outdoor establishment. The evening begins with mellow hip-hop, while bass-heavy dance beats pick up the pace as the night wears on. Beer and *rakı* $3.50; cocktails $10. Cover Su-Th $7.50, F-Sa $10; includes 1 drink. Open daily 10pm-4am.

Club 29 (☎241 62 60 or 247 59 37), uphill along the harbor. Megabass Euro, Turkish, and American pop blasts from all directions on the open dance floor and chic white seats. On weekends, young Turks pack the floor until daybreak. Beer $3.50; *rakı* $5. Cover M-Th $5, F-Sa $7.50. 18+. Open daily 11pm-4am.

Rock Bar (☎248 89 41), downhill from the clock tower. Disgruntled grungesters still upset over Kurt pack this tiny crawl space of a bar, comparing tattoos over beer ($1.50). Loud, angry live music 10:30pm-1:30am. Open daily 2pm-3:30am.

Denizcinin Köşesi (Fisherman's Corner), 1 Yat Limanı (☎247 53 29). Along the harbor. This popular bar spins a range from oldies to contemporary pop music. Beer $1.85; *rakı* $2.25; cocktails $5.85; pizza $5-6. Open daily 9am-5am.

Tequila Mexico Bar, 24 Yat Limanı (☎243 41 15), near the bazaar. This fortress-like bar looms over Antalya's quiet harbor. Low-key and festively decorated, it has nightly music, with live Latin tunes W, F-Sa. Corona $8; tequila $5. Open daily 2pm-6:30am.

DAYTRIPS FROM ANTALYA

PERGE

***Dolmuş** run from Meydan Garajı in Antalya to Aksu (25min., every hr. 7am-10pm, $.75). Ask to be let off at Perge, which is a 2km walk from the highway; beware the hot summer sun. **Daily tours** also visit both Perge and Aspendos ($25-27, admission and lunch included). Talk to your pension owner or contact Akay Travel Service (see Antalya: Travel Agencies, p. 286). Site open May-Oct. daily 7:30am-7pm, Nov.-Apr. 8am-5:30pm. $7.*

The extensive remains of ancient Perge (16km from Antalya) make it easy to imagine what life was like in this prosperous town of over 100,000 inhabitants. The city was supposedly founded by Greek heroes after the Trojan War, but it didn't earn its place in history until it sided with the omnipotent boy-wonder **Alexander the Great** when he stormed through Asia Minor.

Just before the ticket booth is a **theater** featuring fine reliefs of Dionysus, the god of wine and merriment. The entry to the theater leads to an overgrown stairway marked by two bulls' heads—the official entrance for the Emperor and his entourage. The theater is undergoing renovation, and should reopen by 2006. The 12,000-seat **stadium,** past the ticket booth, hosted wild beast fights and athletic events. The wall at the far end protected spectators from the bloodier incidents. For all this danger, however, the victor only took home a measly bottle of olive oil.

The official site entrance is the **Roman gate,** once two stories high and covered with a marble facade, beyond the theater and the stadium. Niches inside the gate mark where statues once stood. Past the gate, on the left, lie the remains of the **athletic complex** and **bath.** Passing through the remains of a large swimming pool and exercise area, enter the bath, a series of three rooms. The first was known as the *frigidarium* (for cold water), the second the *tepidarium* (for warm water), and finally the *caldarium* (for hot water). A stroll through the multi-room complex reveals marble floors and scant bits of marble wall tiling. Under the brick vaults in the last room, fires were built to keep enormous pots of water boiling. The rising steam heated the room and water. The hot water would pass to the warm room and the cold room as heat was lost, finally ending up outside in a water basin known as the *nymphaeum,* which provided drinking water for the whole town.

To the right of the gate is the large **agora.** Here, shops were arranged by trade and inspected by officials known as *agoranomas.* Noteworthy are the intricate black and red mosaic floors of the shop just before the main *agora* complex. The marble columns still standing originally connected to the shops by wooden roofs, forming a covered portico. Directly ahead of the Roman gate are the ruins of the the **Hellenistic Gate.** The city-state of Perge primarily worshipped Artemis, the huntress, but because the townspeople used both the Greek and Latin languages, large stones also bear Artemis's Roman name, Diana. Up ahead, two imposing 3rd-century BC Hellenistic towers mark the beginning of the long, colonnaded **avenue.** Following the avenue to its source will lead you to a beautiful **fountain** and the only remaining statue, the reclining river god **Kestros,** presiding over the once well-stocked water systems. A path to the left affords a stroll past the overgrown **palestra** (gym) and the decayed **northern basilica.** Another walk heads up the steps of the fountain, leading to the **acropolis** and a view over the whole site.

MEDITERRANEAN COAST

ASPENDOS

You may have seen amphitheaters in Italy, France, Dalmatia and Africa; temples in Egypt and Greece; palaces in Crete; you may be sated with antiquity or scornful of it. But you have not seen the theater of Aspendos.

—D.G. Howarth, 1909

*From Antalya, take the bus from Meyden Garajı to Serik (40min., every hr. 8am-6:30pm, $1.75), beyond Perge and Aksu. **Dolmuş** run to Aspendos from the Serik otogar ($.50). Be aware that though the site closes at 7pm, the last Antalya-bound bus from Serik leaves at 6:30pm. ☎(242) 735 74 43. Open daily 7:30am-7pm. $4.50.*

Aspendos's magnificent **theater,** built by the architect Zeno under the reign of Marcus Aurelius (161-180 AD), owes its remarkable state of repair largely to the Selçuks, who restored it as a *kervansaray.* Aspendos arguably has the most magnificent remaining Roman theater in Asia and the single most memorable monument on Turkey's Mediterranean coast. It takes little imagination to envision the ancient tragedies and comedies, the coarse Roman plays, the gladiatorial duels, and mock naval battles for which the theater was filled with water. The acoustics are stunning: send a friend to the back row and she'll hear anything you say.

When Atatürk visited Aspendos, he was so impressed by the remains that he declared it would be used again as a theater, though in recent years many events have been cancelled due to lack of funding. The annual **Aspendos Opera and Ballet Festival** (☎(242) 248 00 08) is still held here during the summer. For details, call the Antalya Kültür Ministry (☎243 43 77). On the right side of the theater is a small **museum** housing sample Roman theater tickets and pictures of Atatürk's visit.

Up the stairs, past the theater, are the **bath** and **gymnasium** complexes, across the highway. The top of the "theater hill" also gives an impressive view over the whole site. Veering to the left up the hill will bring you to the city's **agora** and enormous **nymphaeum** (fountain), on the right. As you circle the fountain, look up for the dolphin and sea turtle engravings on the remaining shelves. Behind both structures is the **odeon,** host to smaller theatrical events and government proceedings. If you're not pooped yet, a trip behind the odeon will bring you to the extensive remains of the marvelous Roman **aqueducts** that dot the landscape.

TERMESSOS

Due to the severe heat, the ruins of Termessos are sometimes closed in July and Aug. Getting to Termessos is easiest with a ***half-day tour*** *from Antalya (10am-3pm, $25). For more info see Antalya:* ***Travel Agencies,*** *p. 286.* ***Buses*** *running to Korkuteli can stop at the entrance of Güllük Dağı National Park, from which it is a grueling 10km (2hr.) climb to the ruins.* ***Taxis*** *run $5 each way. Be aware of the dangers of heatstroke (see p. 51). Wear hiking shoes and pants for the rocky, bramble-covered terrain. Open daily 8am-5pm. $1.50.*

On a mountaintop surrounded by rocky crops and dense undergrowth, **Termessos** wins the grand prize for best location of an ancient city. Termessos was famed for its wildlife and the valor of its Pisidian residents, who withstood Alexander the Great's attack in the 4th century BC. The site is now a collection of well-preserved buildings, including a magnificent theater and a unique water-storage system.

Near the parking lot at the site entrance stand the high stairs and impressive doorway of the **Temple of Artemis.** With the temple on the right, walk up the path past the **city walls,** built in stepwise fashion and now crumbling under the weight of spreading tree growth. About 500m up, past the city gate, is the large **gymnasium-bath complex,** where remains of columnar facades sit opposite arches used for water collection. The path then splits: to the right are the **quarry** and some **rock tombs.** To the left, walk past the unidentified building to the **osbaras portico,** built to make the walk more scenic. Head right at the portico for a stroll through the **agora** to the five enormous **cisterns.** The **heroum** (temple of heroes) stands farther up the walk. Take a left from the heroum to the 600-seat **odeon,** the **gymnasium,** and, best yet, the **theater.** Seating 4200 spectators, the theater's sheer cliffs and surrounding mountains provide a backdrop that once complemented the staged drama.

Back at the unidentified building, continue straight to the imposing **Corinthian temple,** built by Pergamene King Atallus II in the 2nd century BC. Climb up the path to the left to the magnificent, extensive **necropolis** for a view over the while site. For a bit of an adventure, look for the "Agathemeros Mausoleum" sign, in the trees on the left side of the walk, to search for the stunning **Lion's Tomb** and the tomb of King Agathemeros of Termessos. Continue on the path through the necropolis to a small watch tower, 1100m up the mountain, where comfy beds, beverages, binoculars, and a delicious breeze await those who persevere.

Back downhill, a left out of the necropolis and another left at the walk's juncture will bring you to the **tomb of Alcetas,** one of Alexander the Great's best warriors, who befriended the young soldiers of Termessos. Upon learning that he was to be betrayed by the town's elders into the hands of power-hungry rival deputies, Alcetas committed suicide, only to have his body turned over anyway and atrocities inflicted upon it. Upon the recovery of the body by the soldiers of Termessos, this monument was built to house his ravaged remains.

Near the entrance to Güllük Dağı Park is the small **Flora and Fauna Museum,** which contains some stuffed animals and dried plants from the region, as well as photos, Ottoman wares, and treasures excavated from Termessos.

PHASELIS

__Buses__ from either Antalya or Olimpos pass the turnoff for Phaselis (frequent, about $1). Ask to be let off when you see the brown sign. The ruins are about 3km from the highway, and the shady roads make the walk bearable in summer. Pay at a booth 2km up the road from the site. Open daily 8am-6pm; in winter 8am-5:30pm. $4, students $2.

On the road between Antalya and Olimpos, the ancient city of Phaselis is a combination of beaches, Roman ruins, and pine groves. Situated around three natural harbors, the city was founded around 690 BC as a colony of Rhodes. Its location made it a strategic port on the shipping routes between Greece and Syria. Phaselis declined only in the Byzantine period, as Alanya and Antalya grew in prominence.

From the parking lot near the water, pass through the aqueduct to arrive at the military harbor. A second harbor lies to the left, encircled by an uncrowded pebble beach. The town's main road runs to the right, and on the right side of the road, you can amble through the Roman baths. The decomposing theater is 100m down the road and up a short hill on the left. At the end of the 150m Roman road, you'll arrive at the third harbor, now a sandy beach allowing for as fine a swim as Olimpos, without the wayward crowds.

KÖPRÜLÜ KANYON

Akay Tours offers daily trips from Antalya for around $35. Medraft, whose service is a bit more expensive ($52 per person), also offers an optional speedboat exploration of the canyon at the base of the river ($30 for 20min.). *See __Antalya: Travel Agencies,__ p. 286.*

An organized rafting tour to Köprülü Kanyon falls far short of the ideal encounter with nature, what with the crowding and intermittent photo ops; it may, however, be the safest way to see the canyon. After the 2hr. bus ride from Antalya to Köprülü, tourists are dropped near the mouth of the canyon where they can choose to ride the rapids in a two-person kayak or an eight-person boat. By the end of the day, passengers will have taken in breathtaking views of the natural setting at an adrenaline-pounding pace, and paid a pretty penny for it.

SİDE ☎242

Side has all the necessary ingredients for a complete Mediterranean coast vacation: superb Hellenic ruins, parasailing, an illustrious museum, beautiful sandy beaches, and the self-proclaimed "best disco in Europe." You can bargain for leather goods in the crowded pedestrian streets, study up on ancient history in the 7th-century Roman ruins, and make coconut oil libations to the sun god. The town is crammed onto a small peninsula, with the ruins, restaurants, shops, pensions, and banks all within walking distance.

The early history of Side will likely never be fully uncovered. According to residents, the city was colonized by Greeks, who, upon arrival, forgot their mother tongue and instead began speaking a strange, barbarian language. All of the city's inscriptions from before the 3rd century BC are written in a unique and still undeciphered script. Alexander the Great conquered Side in 334 BC and destroyed the Persian Empire in 331. Side later prospered under Roman and Byzantine rule, but, as a result of increasingly ferocious Arab raids and a 10th century conflagration, the population was moved to Antalya.

TRANSPORTATION

Entering Side, you may get dropped at the otogar, but the buses will more likely leave you at a gas station marking the highway turnoff in **Manavgat,** from which dolmuş run to the Side otogar ($.60). From the otogar, a ridiculous-looking, red tractor-drawn **carriage** makes the run to town ($.06). The Manavgat otogar has a better selection of buses departing the region, and it can be reached by dolmuş from Side (every 5 min. 6am-midnight, $.60). Frequent **buses** run from Manavgat to **Alanya** (every 30min. 6am-7pm, $2) and **Antalya** (every 20min. 6am-11pm, $1.50). The Side otogar (☎753 12 86 or 753 42 44), 1km from the tourist center, is a peculiar place: there are bus companies but very few buses. Theoretically, buses leave from Side's otogar to: **Ankara** (10 per day 9am-10:45pm, $13); **Bodrum** (10:45am, 9:45, 10pm; $12); **Bursa** (5 per day 10:45am-11pm, $14); **Eskişehir** (5 per day 10:45am-11pm, $13); **İstanbul** (8 per day 9am-9pm, $18); **İzmir** (7 per day 9am-10:30pm, $14); **Marmaris** (9:30am, $14). You're best off buying your ticket in advance, to ensure that the bus knows to stop in Side en route.

ORIENTATION AND PRACTICAL INFORMATION

The Side **tourist office** is past the otogar and the rusted Luna amusement park, toward the highway. You can snag brochures and a list of Side's 200 pensions and 150 hotels. (☎753 12 65. Open daily 8am-5pm; Sept.-May M-F 8am-5pm.) The **Side Internet Cafe,** marked by a surfboard, is on Small Beach Street, across from the Moonlight restaurant. (☎753 23 99. $1.60 per hr. Open daily 9am-midnight.) **ATMs** and **Exchange Offices** are everywhere on the tourist peninsula. In the event of a **medical emergency,** dial ☎753 12 21. Other services include: the **Side Medical Center** (☎753 1445) and the Manavgat **Government hospital** *(Devlet Hastanesi)* (☎746 4480), across from the tourist office, just off the main street between Side and the highway; the **jandarma** (☎156), which has jurisdiction over Side and may respond faster than the police; and a small **PTT,** in the center of town, with no services beyond post and a **money exchange.** A larger PTT is near the beach west of Side, past the hospital. (Both open 8am-midnight for all services.) **Postal code:** 07330.

ACCOMMODATIONS

A bedroom, a steak, or a leather jacket are never more than 10m away.

Pettino Pansiyon. Walking downhill on Liman Cad., turn left at the Jungle Bar in the middle of town to get to this pleasant, breezy spot. 13 comfortable rooms encircle an arboreal courtyard and bar, where wooden decor adds to the Amazonian ambiance. Breakfast included. $7 per person.

Ani Motel, Buyuk Plaj Yolu (☎753 33 64). With the water on your right, walk past soundwaves. Restaurant has 25 wooden cabins with baths and balconies situated around a well-kept garden. Very close to the entrance to the popular east beach. $6 per person. In 2002, several of the cabins will have A/C for an additional $4.

Beach House Hotel (☎753 10 59 or 753 16 07), on the small eastern beach. Above an ancient Roman villa, this upscale hotel has 20 rooms (with fan and phone) that have been graced by the likes of Simone de Beauvoir. Ocean-view balconies, a terrace bar, and a garden over ancient ruins may inspire you to write your breakthrough novel as well. Breakfast included. Up to 5 guests per room. $13 per person.

Hotel Lale Park Barbaros Sok. Lale Cad., No. 5 (☎753 1131; fax 753 3567; hotellalepark@hotmail.com; www.hotellalepark.com), behind Soundwaves. For the comfort seeker, this hotel offers fully loaded rooms with A/C in a building modeled after an Ottoman mansion. Family owned and operated. Breakfast included in the landscaped garden. Singles $15; doubles $20.

Yaşa Motel (☎753 40 24; fax 753 14 44), on Turgut Reis Cad., next to the parking lot. Near the sea, Yaşa has a charming, if oddly decorated, courtyard and 30 rooms of varying quality, so ask to see a few. Breakfast included. $7-10 per person.

FOOD

No coastal resort would be complete without seafood and a kickin' nightlife. Fine seafood is proferred throughout the city, and slightly pricey restaurants line the waterfront. For savory, affordable Turkish food, try **Uğur Lokantası** (☎753 36 54) on Orkide Sok., where $4 will get you salad and a mean stuffed pepper. For finer dining, hit the **Soundwaves Restaurant** (☎753 10 59), next to the Beach House Hotel. On a picturesque seaside terrace, meat and chicken meals run $5-8, with a slightly pricier seafood menu. Next door, the **Soundwaves Patisserie and Cocktail Bar** is a great lunch spot and serves up a solid cheeseburger ($2.50). The red Christmas-light letters on the sign at **Moonlight Restaurant** are visible all the way down the street. Here seafood, steak, and pasta are served in a romantic courtyard with fabulous views of the moon over the ocean ($4-8). The *döner* joints on Liman Cad. (the main road down to the waterfront) make especially delicious (read: greasy) versions of the Turkish favorite in a frybread wrap for $1.

SIGHTS

Chugging past Side's ancient ruins and arches in a little red tractor gives the illusion of traveling through time. Past the ruins, a Roman footpath along the right-hand side of the paved road enables visitors to retrace the footsteps of ancient Side's residents. In 2001, a laborer came across a terra-cotta pot filled with 1000 Roman gold coins buried just under the topsoil, right next to the modern day road. The **nymphaeum,** a memorial fountain at the entrance to Side, once had a marble facade depicting punishments administered to those who committed sexual sins or who had sinned against the gods. Ironically, modern-day Side is as loose as it gets—get down, get dirty; chances are your neighbors are naughtier than you. The 2nd-century **theater** of Side, which seated 25,000, boasts its role as one of "the largest and most imposing Greco-Roman ruins in Asia Minor." Though 10 years ago the amphitheater was sturdy enough to house the Moscow Circus, today's entrance fee only allows you to walk the 50m fenced-off strip that divides the crumbling upper and lower *cavea,* or seating area. (Open daily 8am-midnight. $4.) The rather unimpressive ruins of two **agora** lie scattered behind the theater. A bit further down the road in the direction of the otogar, ancient **Roman baths** have been converted into an excellent **Archaeological Museum.** A visit to Side is incomplete without seeing this revamped bathhouse, which now houses sarcophagi, marble reliefs, ancient columns, and a breathtaking array of marble statues. (Open Tu-Su 8am-noon and 1-5pm. $4.) At the end of the tiny peninsula, parts of the **Temples of Athena and Apollo** have been rebuilt, making for a spectacular photo spot. Located in a field of razed ruins, the temples' standing columns were repaired and hoisted under the finance and care of an American businesswoman. Beautiful **beaches** extend on either side of the peninsula. To the west, flat stretches make popular sunbathing spots; to the east, some tourists lay sleeping bags on the sand.

NIGHTLIFE

Oxyd Disco, 3km west on the highway outside of Side (taxi $9). The best disco in the area. The bizarre combination of styles—ranging from the Hittite fortress exterior to the industrial piping of the upper dance floor to the space-age rigging over the main dance floor—actually manages to work in this outdoor shrine to postmodernism. A good DJ, fashionable Turks, 2 bars, and an ingenious interior design. Cover $10, includes unlimited domestic drinks. Foreign drinks run about $4. Open daily 11pm-4am.

The Light House, on the water. With a fleet of B-52s cleared for takeoff and plenty of Sex On The Beach, this place is ground zero for mindless carousing. Through the ramped entrance is a giant, open-air, waterfront dance floor with multiple bars. Cover $10, includes domestic drinks. Open daily until 4:30am.

Barracuda Bar and Cafe (☎753 27 24), **Stones Bar** (☎753 36 69), and **Happy Days Bar** (☎753 27 24) all beyond the Athena/Apollo temple (with the water on your right). This side-by-side triumvirate of small dance-bars blasts a mix of Turkish- and Euro-pop with enthusiastic gusto. Dancers bop on small dance floors, though patrons are mostly table-side bar-hoppers. Beer $1.60; *rakı* $2.40; cocktails $6. Open daily 11am-3am.

Jungle Bar (☎753 2235) is a landmark on Liman Cad. at the center of the tourist area. On the second floor of a jewelry store, the name describes the decor. Beer $1.50; mixed drinks range from $2-6.

Blues Bar and Bistro (☎753 11 97), between Jungle Bar and Pettino Pansiyon, this tastefully decorated bar plays a broader selection than its name suggests. Cavernous interior with an outdoorsy ambiance. Houses a winter bar with fireplace. Serves up a tasty Bloody Mary ($4). Beer $1.60. Open daily 11pm-3am. The Bistro, a recent addition, offers standard fare (seafood, pizza, steak) at standard prices ($5-10).

DAYTRIP FROM SIDE: MANAVGAT WATERFALLS

To get to the falls from Side, first take a dolmuş to the Manavgat otogar ($.60) and from there catch another dolmuş to the falls (Manavgat şelalesi; $.60). Day-long tours from Antalya to Perge and Aspendos usually include a visit to the falls ($.40).

Four kilometers north of Manavgat, a set of small falls in a pleasant, shaded area has become a popular escape from the midday heat. Bring a picnic or sip cold drinks purchased from one of the overpriced cafes. Be forewarned: on a hot day, the crowd at the falls can make Side look like a ghost town. If you're just looking for some solitude, try wandering up the road along the river north of the falls.

EASTERN MEDITERRANEAN COAST

ALANYA ☎242

Inching westward along the Mediterranean, Alanya marks the starting line for Turkey's marathon of coastal debauchery. Swarms of Nordic tourists discovered Alanya sometime in the 1980s, rendering the once-idyllic seaside town a maze of apartotels, palm trees, restaurants, shops, and beautiful Scandinavians. Looking beyond the tacky facade, it's easy to see why Alanya is so popular: miles of gorgeous blue-flag beaches, monuments of Selçuk grandeur, and nights of inebrious clubbing combine for some undiluted vacation fun.

TRANSPORTATION

Buses: From the otogar to: **Adana** (9hr., every 1½hr. 7:30am-9pm, $13.50); **Anamur** (3hr., every 1½hr. 7:30am-9pm, $5); **Ankara** (8hr., 6 per day 10am-11pm, $14.50); **Antalya** (2hr., every 1½hr. 7:30am-9pm, $4); **İstanbul** (14hr., 5 per day 8:30am-7:45pm, $20); **İzmir** (10hr.; 10:30am, 6:30, 9pm; $14); **Konya** (4hr., every hr. 7am-11pm, $9); **Mersin** (8hr., every 1½hr. 7:30am-9pm, $11); **Side** (1hr., every 30min. 7:30am-9pm, $2.60); **Taşucu** (6hr., every 1½hr. 7:30am-9pm, $9). The otogar has luggage storage that extorts $1.60 per 20min.

Ferries: Fergün Shipping Co. Ltd. (☎511 55 65; fax 511 53 58), 50m north and uphill from the Kızıl Kule on Atatürk Cad. Sells seabus tickets for **Girne** (W, F 6am; return Tu, Th 4pm; one-way $25, students $20, ages 4-12 $15, under 4 free; round-trip $40, students $30, ages 4-12 $25, under 4 free). Office open 24hr., but erratic.

ORIENTATION AND PRACTICAL INFORMATION

The town's most conspicuous landmark is the **peninsula,** consisting of several hundred vertical meters of cliffs, castles and towers. The two major tourist centers are the famous **Cleopatra's Beach** on the peninsula's western side (to the right facing the water) and the **harbor** on the eastern side. The **otogar** is west of the city center, a few blocks away from the water, along Atatürk Cad., the main road running parallel to the water. The **tourist office** is at the peninsula end of **Güzelyalı Cad.,** the smaller street that runs along Cleopatra's Beach. **İşkele Cad.** is the street that runs downhill to the harbor, the epicenter of Alanya's nightlife. Restaurants, hotels, and counterfeit designer clothing stores are everywhere.

Tourist Office: (☎513 12 40; fax 513 54 36), next to the Damlataş Cave, at the intersection of Damlataş Cad., İsmet İnönü Cad., and Güzelyalı Cad. Consists of an unattended table of free maps and brochures. Open M-F 8:30am-6pm, Sa-Su 9:30am-4pm.

Travel Agency: 2000 Tours, 34/1 Damlataş Cad. (☎512 56 79). Offers Jeep Safari adventure tours through the Taurus Mountains ($25 per person; stops at old Turkish villages and Dim Creek) and historical Perge-Aspendos-Side tours ($25 per person).

Pharmacies: Many line Damlataş Cad., which runs parallel to and south of Atatürk Bul.

Hospital: Besides the numerous, well-advertised international clinics catering to tourists, the **Devlet Hastanesi** (☎513 48 41) provides general medical treatment.

Internet Access: Cafes line Atatürk Cad.; try **My My Donose Chatroom,** closest to the Red Tower. $1.20 per hr. Open daily 10am-1am. Away from the harbor, head to **Eksen Internet Cafe** by taking a left at the Foto Yunus sign on Damlataş Cad. $.80 per hr. Open daily 10am-1am.

PTT: Main office, in the middle of Atatürk Cad. **Postal services, fax,** and **telegraph. Currency** and **traveler's check exchange** daily 9am-11pm.

Postal Code: 07400.

ACCOMMODATIONS

Alanya is awash with hundreds of hotels and pensions. Condominium-like "apartotels" are popular, especially among the European tourists who account for the lion's share of Alanya's visitors. Good deals can be found on Bebek Sok., near the tourist office and Alanya's famed Cleopatra Beach. Night owls might try İskele Cad., whose hotels are a stumble and crawl from the frantic nightlife. Reservations are a good idea in late summer, when hotels in Alanya are often booked full.

Hotel Marina, 80 İskele Cad. (☎513 43 21; fax 513 96 11), by the Red Tower. Cheap, attractive rooms with balconies overlooking the harbor. The lobby has a small bar area and a back room with dart board and pool table. Breakfast included. Singles $10; doubles $15; triples $20.

Mola Otel, 8 Bebek Sok. (☎513 30 21). They call him *"Şişman Amca"* ("Uncle Fatso"). The hotel's congenial proprietor, that is, who relishes the endearing nickname from his days of Ankara ice-cream vending. "Fatso's place" offers 26 comfortable, basic rooms in the heart of Alanya. Breakfast included. Singles $12; doubles $21; triples $28. Add $5 for A/C or $1.50 for fan.

Kalyon Hotel, 123 Atatürk Cad. (☎513 43 92; ☎/fax 513 44 76). Walking away from the water on Bebek Sok., turn left when you hit Atatürk Cad. and walk 50m. Kalyon's exchange services, international newspapers, and pool make it feel like a classy hotel despite the low price. All rooms have balconies, bath, ceiling fans, and funky 70s flavor. Breakfast included. Singles $10; doubles $18.

Baba Hotel, 6 İskele Cad. (☎513 10 32). Apparently this hotel is only for *"yip yips"* (hippies) because of the cheap prices, but hey, that's cool. The 30 rooms are somewhat worn, but bathrooms are surprisingly clean. Fans included. Singles $4, with bath $9; doubles $7, with bath $12.

Sunway Hotel, 2 Bebek Sok. (☎511 18 80; fax 512 75 72). Big with the Nordics and close to the beach, but not the best deal in town. Offers a rooftop terrace, small lobby bar, and rooms with private bath, balcony, and phone. Breakfast included. Room fan $2.40. $14 per person.

FOOD AND ENTERTAINMENT

Tourism has brought many quality dining options to town but has also increased prices. European options, including decent steaks, pizza, and *schnitzel,* mix with the standard Turkish favorites on Alanya's multilingual menus. Recently administered regulations shut down many of Alanya's shabbier eateries, making meat-eating a non-hazardous activity in town. In the nightlife sector, flashy Alanya exudes its share of loud music and disco-light wattage. The most posh and worthy clubs line Rıhtım Cad., along the harbor below İşkele Cad.

Musti's Restaurant and Cafe Bar, 7 Bebek Sok. (☎511 02 76), across from Mola Otel, beneath the apartotels of the same name. Away from the chaos of main streets, this small restaurant, run by friendly staff, presents an eclectic menu of Euro-Turkish and specialty dishes. The Chicken Bombay is to die for ($6). Open daily 8:30pm-midnight.

Cafe Sedir Restaurant, 4 Güzelyalı Cad. (☎512 38 76), down the street from the tourist office. Nightly overflowing crowds make Sedir hard to miss. The fame is well-earned—the polyglot menu fills a 3-ring binder with over 30 house specials, meat and chicken dishes, grills, steaks, salads, and sandwiches ($4-6).

Bistro Bellman, on Rıhtım Cad. This restaurant by "day" (6pm-11pm), club by "night" (11pm-3am) is the place to be seen. Frequent theme parties and a mod crowd animate the dance floor, where hips swivel to techno remixes of otherwise cheesy pop. Nordic tourists vie for majority dominance screaming to chants of "Do we have Sweden/Norway/Denmark in the hoooouuse?!" If you tire of watching the sexy bartenders and sleek patrons, glue yourself to the big screen TVs. Beer $2.50; cocktails $5-6.

James Dean Bar, next door to Bistro Bellman, where everybody aspires to a rebel-without-a-cause slickness. Mellow beginnings have tourists sipping cocktails until the mostly pop selection (expect Madonna) inspires dancers to get their groove on. Beer $2.50; cocktails $4-6. Open daily 9pm-4am.

Zapf Hahn, in the same cluster. An uninspired Top 40 selection and aimless light show attempt to make up in quantity for what they lack in quality. The giant, open-air dance floor sheltered by a corrugated metal canopy, is like a post-apocalyptic pirates' cave gone wild. Beer and *rakı* $2.50. Open daily until 4am.

SIGHTS

Most of Alanya's sights are clustered on the peninsula. Known in ancient times as **Coracesium,** Alanya gained notoriety as a pirate cove until the Roman General Pompey destroyed the town's huge fleet in 67 BC. Marc Antony later conferred the city upon Cleopatra as a gift, resulting in many a souvenir shop named in her honor. Many of the city's great structures date from the 13th century, when the city fell under Selçuk control and was renamed **Alalye** in honor of Sultan Alaeddin Keykubad. Alaiye fell to the Ottomans in 1471.

SELÇUK SIGHTS. The Kızıl Kule (Red Tower), built in 1226 under Sultan Keykubad's reign, is spectacular. The 30m high octagonal structure constructed from red, kiln-baked brick, served as the city's first line of defense against seaborne attack. Soldiers could shoot arrows at ships from five levels while drawing water from the giant cistern built into the tower's spire. The strategic location on the harbor now affords spectacular views of the surrounding area. The Kızıl Kule also houses an Ethnographic Museum, with the usual array of carpets and costumes.

A magnificent 200m walk behind the castle walls from the tower will take you to the only remaining Selçuk-era **tersane** (shipyard) in Turkey. This nursery for Keykubad's navy has five chambers; munitions were stored in the nearby *tophane* (arsenal). *(Tower open Tu-Su 8am-noon and 1:30-5:30pm. $1.65, students $.70.)*

İÇ KALESİ (FORTRESS). At the top of Alanya's headland is a fortress housing a mint, a Byzantine-era monastery, a church, and a cistern. The walls are still mostly intact, and in one corner stands the *adam atacaği* ("place for throwing people"). Now cordoned off, this platform marks the spot from which the condemned were heaved onto the jagged cliffs below. Today, instead of gawking at prisoners, tourists arrive in the early evening to watch the sun set over the ocean. Had the condemned prisoners taken the time to appreciate their plummet, they could have enjoyed one of the most beautiful views on the Mediterranean. The fortress is also worth seeing after dark, when Alanya's lights sparkle like jewels below, and many a car parks at this quintessentially romantic spot. *(You can either trudge the 3km to the top or take a dolmuş (every hr. 7am-8pm, $.30) from the north end of İskele Cad. or opposite the tourist office. Fortress open daily 8am-5:30pm. $2.80, students $1.85.)*

CAVES. Damlataş Cave, accidentally discovered by miners in 1948, is a two-story affair replete with eerie stalactites and stalagmites. The 90-100% humidity inside does wonders for asthma, but the unending flow of tourists that pass through makes it impossible to gaze in solitary awe at the strange workings of Mother Nature. *(Follow the signs along Güzelyalı Cad. in the direction of the peninsula. Open daily in summer 10am-8pm; in winter 10am-5pm. $1.20, students $.60.)*

Far more impressive is the **Dim Cave,** located 9km northeast of town. Dim Cave is an awesome tangle of limestone-dissolved stalactites and stalagmites, measuring 360m long and 10-15m in height. Carbonic acid rainwater continues to drip along the interior, adding to the unearthly formations. Unfortunately, no dolmuş run to Dim Cave, so access is either by tour group, car, or taxi. *(Open daily 9am-8pm. $2.40).* The nearby **Dim Creek** is becoming a popular tourist stop, where visitors swim in the absolutely frigid water. Picnic spots and restaurants are set up along and in the river, with floating raft eateries and waiters wading barefoot to serve. The best pick is **Ada Piknik Motorcu Şevketin Yeri,** where chicken, fish, or meat meals ($3-6) are served on carpeted, pillowed rafts. Further down the creek, a 9m high bridge makes for a heart-stopping plummet to the icy water below.

OTHER SIGHTS. Alanya also has a decent **museum** with exhibits from local Bronze Age excavations to 19th-century Ottoman *kilims*. *(Across from the tourist office. Open Tu-Su 8am-noon and 1:30-5:30pm. $1.15, students $.70.)* Relax during the day at the beautiful **Grand Alanya Büyük Hamam** (☎511 33 44) on Damlataş Cad., where $16 will get you a sauna, jacuzzi, shock pool, *kese*, and 90min. massage. There's also a separate, women-only hamam and a "vitamin bar" for post-scrub indulgence.

MEDITERRANEAN COAST

ANAMUR ☎324

Anamur is a city of many faces. The least attractive of these is the one facing the bus station, so don't be discouraged when you arrive; this is the city center, heavy on dust and concrete. Most visitors stay near the prettier beaches at the İskele (dock), Anamur's tourist district. A laid-back town of 60,000, Anamur is isolated enough that it hasn't been exposed as heavily to the tourist debauchery that has hit the coast further west. For the most part, it's still a popular vacation spot for Turkish families, and pleasant pensions, uncrowded beaches, and a vigorous nightlife make a stay here relaxing and enjoyable. The nearby ruins of ancient Anemurium and the well-preserved Mamure Kale offer more than just a day at the beach.

TRANSPORTATION

Buses: The **otogar** is about 1km downhill from the main square, easily identifiable thanks to an Atatürk statue. Buses travel to: **Adana** (6hr.; 10:30am, 4:30pm; $6); **Alanya** (3hr., 8 per day 9am-midnight, $5); **Ankara** (10hr., 8 per day 7am-11pm, $14); **Antalya** (5hr., 8 per day 9am-midnight, $8); **İstanbul** (16hr.; 2:30, 5pm; $15); **İzmir** (13hr., 3pm, $14); **Konya** (6hr., 8 per day 7am-11pm, $12); **Mersin** (5hr., 6 per day noon-midnight, $6); **Side** (4hr., 8 per day 9am-midnight, $6); **Taşucu** (3hr., 9 per day noon-midnight, $5). Dolmuş run from behind the otogar to the town center (*şehir merkezi*; $.40) and İskele (every 20min. 7am-1am, $.65), contrary to claims of taxi drivers, who charge $7.

Ferries: Two winters ago, **Fergün Maritime** began operating ferries to Northern Cyprus from the Anamur İskele. They stopped running the route in 2001, with plans to have it back up and running in 2002.

ORIENTATION AND PRACTICAL INFORMATION

Tourist Office: (☎814 35 29; www.anamur.gen.tr), on 2nd fl. of the otogar. Provides free maps, directions, and a list of accommodations, but you may be hard-pressed to find an English-speaker. Open M-F 8am-noon and 1-5pm.

Banks: Several near the main square. **Akbank,** on the road to Atatürk's left, has a Cirrus/MC/Plus/V **ATM** and cashes **traveler's checks** without commission. Open M-F 9am-12:30pm and 1:30-5:30pm. On the İskele side of town, a 4-language Cirrus/MC/Plus/V **ATM** is next to the Fergün booth.

Pharmacies: Near the main square.

Hospital: ☎814 10 86.

Internet Access: Idea Internet Cafe, on 2nd fl. of an apartment building, down the road from the main square, walking with Akbank on your right. $1 per hr. Open daily 8am-midnight. **Number 1 Internet Cafe,** behind Eser Pansiyon on the İskele side of town. $1 per hr. Open daily 10am-1am.

PTT: (☎814 10 01), a block downhill and on the right. Offers phone coins, telegraph, and fax, but no money exchange. Open daily 7am-11pm.

Postal Code: 33640.

ACCOMMODATIONS AND FOOD

Anamur's İskele area has more than a dozen pensions with similar facilities (private showers, balconies, breakfast) and fixed prices that are rarely obeyed to the letter (singles $8; doubles $10; triples $12; breakfast $1.60). The best is **Eser Pansiyon.** Run by two retired, English-speaking schoolteachers and their charismatic son, Tayfun, the pension has 11 charming rooms, Internet access for $2.50 per hr., a beautiful garden, and a shaded rooftop terrace. (☎814 23 22. Breakfast included. Singles $6; doubles $10; triples $14.) Another option is **Hotel Bella Roma,** down the street. Its 18 rooms (four with A/C) are equipped with private bath and spacious balconies. (☎816 47 51. $8 per person. Breakfast $2. A/C $2.) For greater indulgence, try **Hotel Dolphine,** 17 İnönü Cad., which offers modern but charmless rooms with A/C, TV, shower, minibar, and phone. (☎814 34 35; fax 814 15 17. Breakfast included. Singles $10; doubles $15; triples $20.) **Pulla Camping** (☎827 11 51), about 1½km from Mamure and accessible by the Mamure dolmuş, sits atop a gorgeous sandy beach. With electricity, toilets, hot showers, and a restaurant, this isn't exactly roughing it. Bring your own tent and stash up to four people for $4.

Restaurants and street food vendors line İskele's main drag, İnönü Cad. It's easy to find good *gözleme* ($.70). Try the cheap, tasty food at **Turtle's Pizza,** including excellent *kumpir* (baked potato stuffed with a Russian salad and peas; $2).

SIGHTS

ANEMURIUM. Nineteenth-century travelers stumbled upon the ruins of Anemurium 1200 years after Arab raids forced out the city's inhabitants. The city reached its height during the early Roman period, 500 to 600 years after its founding in the 4th century BC. It became an episcopal see (an area under the authority of a bishop) during the Byzantine period and existed in relative wealth and peace until a massive 6th-century earthquake. Arab raids pilfered the town just decades later.

The steep Cilician Mountains run behind the city and a climb to the **ridge,** following the **Roman wall** uphill, affords a spectacular view of the ruins of Anemurium on one side and the sea cliffs on the other. A fabulous pebbled **beach** with bamboo umbrellas lies downhill from the city. The ruins include Roman aqueducts, city walls, baths, a gymnasium, an *odeon*, an amphitheater, a *bouleterion*, and several churches. The renowned **necropolis,** Asia Minor's most impressive city of the dead, bursts with 350 tombs carved from gray limestone blocks. Most feature a sarcophagus room and a frescoed antechamber that served as a chapel. Some colored mosaics survive in the nearby **Necropolis Temple.** Most of the city's houses are still being excavated from under the sand dunes, which until recently concealed the remains of a giant **oil lamp factory.** Some 700 terra-cotta oil lamps were unearthed all in one lot, indicating that they were about to be shipped elsewhere.

The drive from Anamur to Anemurium, along the base of the Cilician Mountains, passes through hillsides crammed with hundreds of glass greenhouses, home to the city's famous banana trees. The shores behind the ruins hide some of Anamur's most beauteous beaches. If you're looking for near-isolation and don't mind a 1½km trek to the beach, you can take a taxi directly from the otogar to the ruins ($14). **Alper Pansiyon** offers spacious rooms in a family home. Use of the tidy bathroom, kitchen, and terrace is free. Call ahead. (☎835 11 13. Breakfast $2.50. One double room and two quads. $5 per person.) Continuing down the road to the ruins, you will pass **Dutalti Aile Restaurant** (☎835 10 28) which serves up tasty local favorites in a shady spot with views of the ruins in the distance. *(Most dolmuş stop at the turnoff for a 2km hike to the ruins, but one company goes all the way there at 11am and 4pm. Some İskele hotels and pensions, Eser and Dolphine among them, occasionally organize fishing boat excursions to Anemurium. Taxis run for $17 round-trip, but try bargaining. Site open daily 8am-8pm. $2.50. Wear long pants if you plan to hike to the ridge—the path is lined with thorns.)*

MAMURE KALE. Dramatically jutting out into the sea, this *kale* is one of Anatolia's most impressive castles. A nearby stream feeds the 10m wide moat encircling the structure and leading to the sea. While there are no sea monsters, those who fall in will have to ward off hordes of little turtles. Today, the remains are a veritable playground for all ages—navigate labyrinthine, wildflower-choked rooms, clamber up spiral staircases, and peer through narrow windows at the sea. Come nightfall, Mamure's lights twinkle. *(Dolmuş ($.30) run at least every 30min. from both the city center and the İskele area. You can also walk along the shore to the castle, though that involves swimming across a small creek. Open daily 8am-8pm. $2.50, students $1.50.)*

NIGHTLIFE

When the sun goes down, İnönü Cad. comes to life. Music blasts, lanterns and strings of lights illuminate the streets to near-daylight brightness, car traffic ceases, and the sidewalks overflow with food vendors, souvenir hawkers, and pedestrians looking to enjoy a cool evening. The **Zeyno Bar** has İskele's best live music (folk and pop), drawing a large, lively crowd. (Beer $1.70.) Marking the east end of the İnönü Cad. strip, **Kutlay Bar** gets its crowd dancing every night despite the heat. On the bottom floor of an art-deco-esque apartment building, the **Yakamoz Bar** features dancing, a good selection of Turkish pop, live music, and a young crowd. (Beer $1.80, but beware the nuts—you'll get charged for them.)

The red castle 1km outside of İskele, on the road from Anamur proper, is the **Apollo.** Its walls enclose an open-air dance floor, animated by a first-rate selection of Western and Turkish pop and a dazzling light display. This slick, spacious club has extensive seating areas and an excellent bar. (Beer $2.40; *rakı* $3. Cover $6, includes one drink. Open daily 10pm-4am.)

TAŞUCU ☎324

While storming the rest of Turkish Mediterranean, tourists have overlooked Taşucu, mercifully leaving it free of Benettons, leather dealers, and resort hotels. Though Taşucu is neither a cosmopolitan center nor the seat of glorious ancient civilizations, this small, friendly town is worth visiting for free beaches with pleasant boardwalks and the best transportation to Northern Cyprus.

TRANSPORTATION. From the otogar, **buses** head to: **Adana** (3hr., 9 per day 7:30am-11pm, $5); **Alanya** (6hr., 8 per day 10am-1am, $8); **Anamur** ($3hr., 8 per day 10am-1am, $5); **Ankara** (8hr., 5 per day 9:30am-11:30pm, $12); **Antakya** (6hr.; 8:30am, 1:30, 7:30pm; $8); **Antalya** (8hr., 8 per day 10am-1am, $10); **İstanbul** (15hr.; 4, 9:30pm; $20); **Konya** (4hr., 5 per day 9:30am-11:30pm, $7.20); **Mersin** (2hr., 9 per day 7:30am-11pm, $3); **Side** (7hr., 8 per day 10am-1am, $9.60). **Dolmuş** run to **Silifke** (20min., every 15min., $.40). The **PTT**, across from the dock, and several ferry boat offices sell tickets for the seabus and ferry to **Girne (Kyrenia), Northern Cyprus. Fergün Denizcilik Şti. Ltd.** (☎741 23 23 or 741 37 11) owns the largest, fastest, and most reliable fleet. The **seabus** has daily departures (2½-5hr. depending on weather; 11am; one-way $20, round-trip $38; $1 student discount). Arrive in the morning to make sure your chosen vessel will sail, and then secure a ticket. The **ferry** leaves daily at midnight (6hr.; one-way $15, round-trip $28; $1 student discount).

ORIENTATION AND PRACTICAL INFORMATION. Most of the town occupies a narrow strip between the highway and the sea. Lined with banks and restaurants, the 200m-long strip links the **harbor** and ferry docks at the western end of town to the **otogar** at the opposite end. **Sahil Cad.** runs east of the otogar (perpendicular to the highway), past inviting beaches on the right and affordable accommodations on the left. Further east, the beaches get better and more crowded.

A **Türkiye İş Bankası**, near the harbor, has a Cirrus/MC/Plus/V **ATM.** In a **medical emergency**, call the Sağlık Ocağı (☎741 44 88). The two-story building complex down the road from the PTT houses two **Internet cafes**, both of which charge about $1 per hr. and are open 10am-midnight. The **PTT** is open daily 8am-11pm. No exchange services are available on weekends. **Postal code:** 33900.

ACCOMMODATIONS AND FOOD. Sahil Cad., running east along the sea, has many sunny, similarly priced seaside pensions. **Meltem Pansiyon,** 75 Sahil Cad., all the way down Sahil Cad., is among the best. Its 17 immaculate rooms vary in design. Some have A/C, 12 have private kitchenettes, and all have insect screens for the windows—a much-needed amenity in this part of Turkey. (☎741 43 91. Breakfast $1.60. Singles $8, with A/C $13; doubles $11.30; triples $21.) Closer to the otogar on Sahil Cad., the brand-new, German-run **Dilara Pansiyon** offers seven rooms with bath. (☎741 52 74. Breakfast included. Singles $6.40; doubles $13.) Near the otogar and the sign for Mersin, **Tuğran Pansiyon,** 3 Sahil Cad., offers 16 rooms (six with A/C) with balconies and showers. (☎741 44 93; fax 741 26 92. Breakfast $2. Singles $13; doubles $20.) Taşucu's seafood is both fresh and affordable. Small joints serving decent, cheap seafood are easy to find. For finer dining, try the **Denizkızı Restoran,** overlooking the harbor right across from the dock.

KIZKALESİ ☎324

The majority of visitors to this small resort town are Turks on a short holiday from nearby cities. German tourists and the Americans stationed at İncirlik military base make up much of the rest. Despite the unchecked hotel construction brought on by the recent tourist boom, Kızkalesi still remains fairly small, and it offers hedonistic beaches and a vibrant nightlife. The nearby sites of Kanlıdivane and Adam Kayalar also make fine daytrips, allowing the amateur archaeologist to leave Kızkalesi with something more than memories of sun, sand, and beer.

Legend holds that a king built the castle on the island off the coast to protect his daughter from the untimely death prophesied for her. She lived in splendid near-isolation until a snake, unintentionally hidden in a fruit basket sent by the king's adviser, fulfilled the prediction with a poisonous nibble. A lovely story, but the **Maiden's Castle** (Kızkalesi) and its counterpart on the shore were actually built to protect the Armenian city of Corycus from foreign invaders. Today, these "obstacles" provide the *raison d'être* for the town's tourist industry.

TRANSPORTATION AND PRACTICAL INFORMATION. Nearly all of Kızkalesi's sleeping, eating, and nightlife establishments line the 1km strip of waterfront. **Buses** run through Kızkalesi en route to **Mersin** or **Silifke** (at least every 10min., $.50). There are **no banks** and **no tourist office** in Kızkalesı; the nearest are 25km away in either Erdemli or Mersin. Other services include: the **police** (☎523 22 21); **Kızkalesi Eczane** (☎523 2850); a medical clinic, **Sağlık Ocağı** (☎523 21 39); and the **PTT,** behind the Belediye building, with a string of public phones outside (open M-F 8:30am-12:30pm and 1:30-5:30pm; Sa 8:30am-1pm). **Postal code:** 33790.

ACCOMMODATIONS. Kızkalesi has an astounding number of hotels and pensions, and it is impossible to walk the streets without being hounded by eager cries of "yes, please!" and "*pansiyon?*" The **Best Motel,** 2 Plaj Yolu No. 6, has 12 large but simple rooms with ceiling fans, and the Turkish owners will speak to you in German regardless of your nationality. (☎523 20 74 or 523 25 23. Breakfast $1.60. $5 per room.) For sheer comfort worth far more than its asking price, try the **Yaka Hotel.** Its 16 well-furnished rooms boast phone, A/C, minibar, and even coffee/tea machines. The owner, Yakup Kahveci, is the head honcho of regional tourism and a geyser of information. (☎523 24 44. Breakfast included. Singles $20; doubles $30; triples $40.) Further from the beach, **Sahil Motel,** Mavi Deniz Mah., 2 Plaj Yoluhirişi, is an excellent value. The 21 no-frills rooms are "cooled" by electric fans. (☎523 20 59. Breakfast $2. Singles, doubles, and triples $7, with A/C $10; quads with A/C $13.) Next door to Yaka, the quiet, homey **Hotel Rain** offers 19 rooms with A/C and a killer, included open buffet breakfast. (☎523 27 82. Singles $16; doubles $29.) For 15 nicer, mid-range rooms, try the **Inka Hotel.** All rooms have Mediterranean balcony views. (☎523 21 82; fax 523 26 73. Singles $18, with A/C $24; doubles $29.)

FOOD AND ENTERTAINMENT. Almost all the hotels and pensions in Kizkalesi have full-fledged restaurants that host live singers and lively, table-dancing crowds. Price and quality are consistent with those of their rooms. Other options include **Cafe Rain,** which faces the back of the hotel of the same name. Try the magnificent "rain steak," which comes topped with grilled onions and red peppers ($5). Check out the **Honey Restaurant and Bar** (☎523 24 38), facing the highway, whose owner, Erdoğan, takes credit for introducing *tartuni* (minced meat in a wrap; $1) to Kızkalesi. The mixed Turkish-German menu of this tastefully hip restaurant features a "$3 Ottoman pan" with beef, onions, garlic, and tomatoes.

Nightlife in Kizkalesi consists of drinking and people-watching from the several popular beach bars. Then, after midnight, when outdoor bars are required to stop serving alcohol, the dancing crowd heads to **Oxyd Disco,** where a cavernous interior pulsates with an eclectic mix of music, from Turko-pop to techno. (☎533 260 88 97. Cocktails $3-5. Open daily 10pm-3:30am.)

SIGHTS. The **sea castle,** about 150m from the shore, is Kızkalesi's main attraction. Non-swimmers can catch frequent boats to and from the castle ($3.20). Alternatively, large paddle boats ($4) and smaller "sea bicycles" ($1.60) are rented out on the beach. The walls of the castle reflect the influence of many civilizations, from the Armenians to the Crusaders. Inside, there are ramparts and chambers worth exploring, but its novelty as an island castle is its real attraction. The **land castle,** made partially of pieces salvaged from the ancient city of Corycus, is surrounded by an empty moat. Breaches in the walls afford beautiful views of the water. (Open daily 8am-7pm. $2.40, students $1.60.)

In the rugged "Devil's Glen" valley, 7km north of town, hikers can find the eerily majestic **Adam Kayalar,** a set of 13 Roman reliefs from the first and 2nd centuries AD carved into the face of the valley. The descent is a bit steep, so wear sneakers or boots. The most interesting place near Kızkalesi is the ancient city of **Kanlıdivane** ("Bloody Crazy"), named for its rust-colored soil and rocks. The chasm in the center, over 90m wide and 60m deep, is believed to be the final resting place of criminals and outcasts who were hurled to the bottom. The red rock and shattered buildings evoke the feeling of walking amidst a lost Martian civilization, rendering Kanlıdivane as spooky as it is fascinating. (Open daily 8am-7pm. $1.60.)

Accessing either Adam Kayalar or Kanlıdivane can be difficult; public transportation doesn't service either site. A bus from Kızkalesi can drop you 3km from Kanlıdivane ($.60). The walk is mostly uphill and unpleasant on hot days. While *Let's Go* does not recommend hitchhiking, someone will probably offer you a lift as you trudge up the hill. Hiring a taxi to Kanlıdivane costs $24, to Adam Kayalar $29. With enough tourists, one of the local travel agencies will organize expeditions. On an off day, they may provide a ride that will cost less than a taxi. **Öztop's Rain Travel Agency** (☎532 27 84; oztoprain@superonline.com), next to Cafe Rain, will also organize a 60km tour of local sights (Heaven and Hell Chasms, Adam Kayalar, Kanlıdıvane, Uzuncaburç) for $12 per person.

MERSİN ☎324

A small fishing village 150 years ago, Mersin has blossomed into a mid-sized cosmopolitan city in response to Adana's need for a Mediterranean port. By no means a tourist town, the free stretch of beach and adjoining greenery of Atatürk park, the breezy city center and excellent, cheap hotels still make Mersin a pleasant visit. The city is also useful as a departure point for ferries to Northern Cyprus.

TRANSPORTATION

Flights: The **Turkish Airlines (THY)** office (☎233 02 74) and countless travel agencies with THY banners can book flights from the nearby Adana airport.

Buses: The busy otogar is 1½km from the city center. To: **Adana** (1hr., express, very frequent, $1.60); **Ankara** (7hr.; daily midnight, F-Sa 2:30pm; $15); **Antalya** (6hr.; 11pm, midnight; $10); **İstanbul** (13hr., 6pm, $25); **İzmir** (13hr.; 7am, 6, 7pm; $17); **Konya** (5hr., 7am-6pm, $10); **Nevşehir** (5hr.; 9, 10am, 5pm; $8); **Trabzon** (17hr.; 2, 7pm; $18). To reach the waterfront from the otogar, take a left at the exit, turn right at the T-junction, and take a left at the next main street. From there, head west (walk with the water on your left). Alternatively, dolmuş run from outside the otogar ($.80).

Trains: To reach the *gar* (☎231 12 76), walk 1km from the city center along İsmet İnönü Bul., with the water on your right. Then follow the rotary 200m away from the shore. To: **Adana** (1hr., express trains daily every 30min. 6am-10:30pm, $1); **Ankara** (17½hr., 5:45pm, $9); **İstanbul** (19½hr.; Tu, Th, Sa 7:30pm; $9.30); **Kayseri** (16½hr., 4:20pm, $4.80); **Konya** (7hr.; Tu, Th, Sa 7:30pm en route to İstanbul; $3.60). 20% student discount, 40% handicapped discount. Buses are faster and more reliable, though the train station hosts a pleasant *çay* garden.

Ferries: Turkish Maritime Lines (☎233 98 58), about 1km from the city center along İsmet İnönü Bul. with the water on your right. Ferries depart from the harbor building on the road that forks to the right after Atatürk Park. To **Mağusa, Northern Cyprus** (10hr.; M, W, F 10pm; $24, students with ID $21). Buy tickets on the day of departure.

ORIENTATION AND PRACTICAL INFORMATION

Mersin's center stretches along the waterfront, which marks the city's south side. It consists of pedestrian-dominated streets between **Cumhuriyet Meydanı,** next to the municipality building, and **Gümrük Meydanı,** where the **Ulu Camii** (Great Mosque) stands as a testament to the hideous consequences of the misuse of concrete. **İsmet İnönü Bul.** is the wide road that runs east-west along the waterfront, while the narrower **Atatürk Cad.** runs parallel to it through the city center.

Tourist Office: (☎238 32 71; www.visitmersin.com), near the harbor building, has an English-speaking staff that provides free maps and information. Open daily 8am-noon and 1-5pm; in winter, closed on weekends.

Consulates: Northern Cyprus (☎237 24 82 or 237 24 83). Walk 800m west of the city center along Atatürk Cad. and follow the road 100m as it curves right. The consulate is at the first intersection. Visas can be obtained on arrival in Mağusa, but the consulate will be happy to field any questions. Open M-F 8am-1pm and 2-4pm.

Hospital: Özel Mersin Hastanesi (☎238 00 95) and **Devlet Hastanesi** (☎336 39 50), have reliable facilities and anglophone doctors.

Internet Access: World Internet Cafe, off Atatürk Cad. Head west toward the Northern Cyprus consulate and take a left just before the lights. $2.50 per hr.

PTT: on İsmet İnönü Bul., right next to the "4-star" Mersin Oteli on the eastern end of Gümrük Meydanı. Open daily 8am-7pm. If APS (express mail) just isn't fast enough, try **UPS** or **DHL;** both have offices further down İsmet İnönü Bul., toward the tourist office.

Postal Code: 33100.

ACCOMMODATIONS AND FOOD

The best budget-friendly hotels in Mersin—some of the best in the region—lie on Soğuksu Cad. The best deal is **Hotel Savran,** 46 Soğuksu Cad., whose clean rooms have TV, phone, bath, and A/C. (☎232 44 73. Breakfast included. Singles $6; doubles $10.) Right next door, **Hotel Hitit** offers similar lodgings, with white sheets and towels and a minifridge in each room, but with less impressive baths and no breakfast. (☎231 64 31. $6 per person.) **Gökhan Hotel,** 20 Soğuksu Cad., is the classiest two-star hotel you'll ever see. With all the amenities, a jazzy bar, open buffet breakfast, and sophisticated lounge, Gökhan's rooms are worth far more than their asking price. (☎231 62 56. Singles $12; doubles $20; triples $30.)

There are a variety of good cheap eateries in the town center. Wash down the local specialty *tantuni* (minced meat, onions, lettuce, and tomatoes wrapped up like a tortilla) with *şalgam*, a carrot-juice drink similar to *ayran* (can be sweet or salty). At **Yaprak Tantuni,** on Atatürk Cad., the tasty wraps ($2) make up for what the shabby sitting space lacks. The small outdoor cafes on Atatürk Cad. serve fresh fish ($2.50). **Kukla Kebap,** on Adnan Menderes Bul., about 4km west of the city center, serves some of the best *iskender kebap* in town ($3.50). For a break from seafood and Turkish cuisine, discover **Bella Roma,** located near the Internet cafe about 500m west of the city center on Atatürk Cad. The posters in this Italian restaurant pay homage to Botticelli, Puccini, and Sophia Loren, among others. Choose from a wide variety of pasta dishes ($3-5) or dig into a pizza ($3).

SIGHTS AND ENTERTAINMENT

A relatively young city, Mersin doesn't have much history to draw on. The only "sight" is the rather generically named **Museum,** on Atatürk Cad., just west of Cumhuriyet Meydanı. It displays a pretty standard set of archaeological curios from local excavations. The museum was closed for repairs at the time of publication. (Open T-Su 9am-noon and 1-5pm. $1.25, students $.75.)

If the Mediterranean climate is too much for you, and you boast a Y-chromosome, head to the male-only **5 yol hamam** (Beşyol hamam), about 500m north of the *gar* and 500m east of the Merit Hotel ($2.50; with massage and scrub $6). Take a pleasant stroll amidst *çay* gardens and fishing boats in **Atatürk Park,** which lines the waterfront through the center of town. Sweet-smelling, roasted nuts are $1 per scoop. Chug around the harbor in a pleasure boat ($2.50).

Since the sidewalks in Mersin's center all but roll up after dinner, there is little to enjoy in the way of nightlife. The daytime crowds head west a few kilometers to Adnan Menderes Bul., which runs along the seaside. The area is filled with bars, *çay* gardens, restaurants, and an outdoor movie theater. Catch the blue Poscu dolmuş in front of the PTT and ask to be let off at the Hilton; a short walk along the water leads to some decent restaurants. Otherwise, a cab costs $3-4.

ADANA ☎322

Turkey's sixth-largest city is appropriately named after Adanus, the Greek god of weather. The average June-August temperature is 100°F, with high humidity and a persistent hot wind that seems to issue from a giant invisible hairdryer. If you visit in these months, the weather will probably occupy most of your waking thoughts.

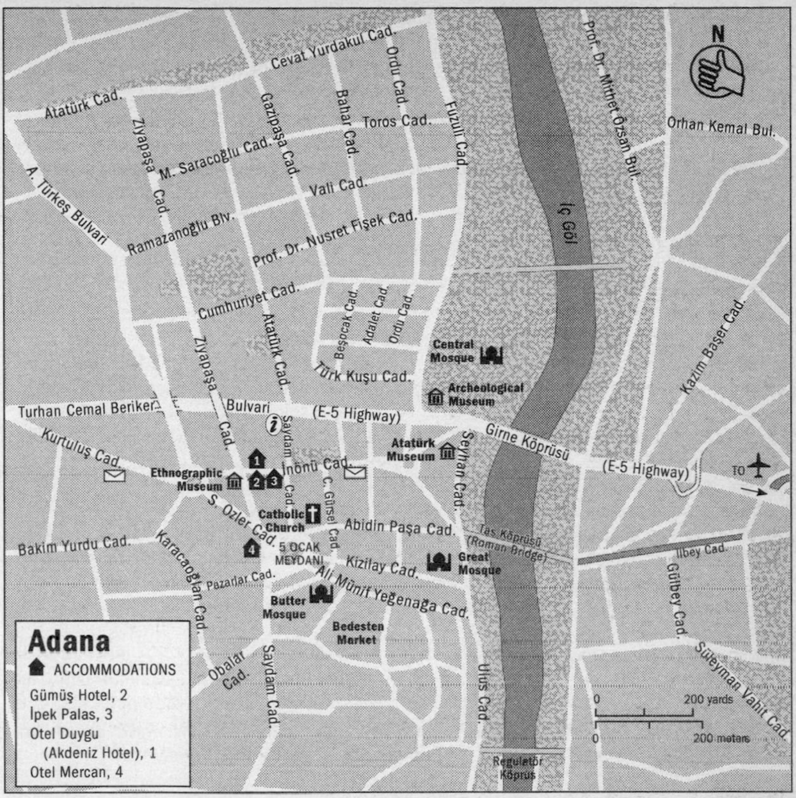

Modern Adana is an agricultural town, wealthy because of its pivotal role in the Turkish textile industry. Its famous *Adana kebap* (spicy minced lamb and herbs, flattened into strips and grilled) tantalizes the eager tastebuds of locals and tourists alike. The nearby US military base at İncirlik does its part for the local economy; Adana has a large otogar and many hotels, and its airport is a stopping point between Northern Cyprus, Antalya, and the Middle East. The city is home to several sights, both historical and modern. The new Sabancı Merkez Camii, the second largest mosque in Turkey, dominates Adana's skyline, looming proudly behind the glittering Roman bridge. In 2000, Adana's proximity to an earthquake zone narrowly saved it from being chosen as the site of a nuclear power reactor.

TRANSPORTATION

Flights: The airport is 4km west of the city center on highway E-5. Frequent buses and dolmuş run to the airport from the stop on Ziya Paşa Cad., across from Hotel Kaza ($.80). The **Turkish Airlines,** 1 Stadyum Cad. (☎454 15 45), on a side street off Atatürk Cad., is across from Atatürk Park. Open M-F 8:30am-5:30pm, Sa 8:30am-noon. To: **Ankara** (2 per day; $50, students $45); **Antalya** (2 per day; $82, students $55); **İstanbul** (3 per day; $140, students $59). **Cyprus Turkish Airlines** (☎363 15 41 or 363 13 75; fax 363 13 75; www.kthy.net), on Çakmak Cad. across from İnönü Park. Flights to **Ercan** (M-F 5:30pm, Sa 6:50am; $65, students $63).

Buses: The larger companies usually offer free *serviş* shuttles between their central offices on highway E-5 (near Akbank) and the otogar (45min.-1hr. before departure), where the squeaking puppets of roaming vendors will drive you insane. To: **Ankara**

(6hr., 4 per day 8am-1pm, $12); **Antakya** (3½hr., 9 per day 8:30am-7pm, $5); **Antalya** (9½hr., every hr. 9am-10pm, $15); **İstanbul** (12½hr., every hr. 9am-11pm, $20); **İzmir** (14hr.; 10:30am, 5pm, midnight; $17); **Kayseri** (6½hr.; 12:30, 4pm, midnight; $7); **Konya** (6½hr., 7 per day 8:30am-midnight, $11); **Mersin** (1½hr., every 30min., $2.50) via **Tarsus** (45min., $1.25). A small dolmuş station on the E-5, by the river and in front of the Sabancı Merkez Cami, services local towns.

Trains: The handsome, old-fashioned *gar* is on İstasyon Cad.; head down Atatürk Cad. past Atatürk Park, and make a left. To: **Ankara** (7½hr., 1:15pm, $7); **Dıyarbakır** (11hr., 4:20pm, $20); **Elazığ** (10hr., 8:40am, $20); **Gaziantep** (6hr., 4:50am, $3.50); **Mersin** (2hr., 29 per day 4:45am-11pm, $1).

ORIENTATION

Adana has few street signs. **Turhan Cemal Beriker Bul.** (a.k.a. the **E-5 highway**) runs from the center of town, past the otogar (5km), and continues along the Mediterranean coast. In town, the landmarks on Turhan Cemal Beriker Bul. are the big Akbank building, the overpass, and the new Sabancı Merkez Camii beside the river. **Atatürk Cad.**, which changes its name to **Saydam Cad.** after passing **İnönü Cad.**, houses the tourist office, hotels, a large Atatürk statue, the PTT, and Atatürk Park. To get to the center of town from the **Merkez Otogar** (bus station), take an E-5 dolmuş from across the road (every 5min., $.40). Be sure to cross the road at the pedestrian overpass, because destination signs are the same in both directions. The dolmuş exits the E-5 about 1km before the Akbank, one block short of the overpass. Disembark here and head for **Kurtuluş Meydanı** (Liberation Square), across from İnönü Cad. If you take a taxi, make sure the meter is turned on ($6-8).

PRACTICAL INFORMATION

Tourist office: (☎363 14 48 or 363 12 87), on Atatürk Cad. This is the garish peach building next to Akbank. English-speaking staff offers those gigantic "yes-I'm-a-tourist-and-can't-fold-a-map" type maps. Open M-F 8am-6pm.

Consulates: US (☎453 91 06), on Atatürk Cad., at the corner of Atatürk Park.

Banks: The landmark **Akbank** is on the corner of T. Cemal Beriker Bul. and Atatürk Cad. Great currency exchange rates and a Cirrus/MC/Plus/V **ATM.**

Currency Exchange: *Döviz* bureaus cluster around Saydam Cad., to the right as you exit the tourist office; try **Yüksek Dövis** (☎563 02 66; fax 563 19 36).

English-Language Bookstore: Yolgeçen Kitabevi, on Atatürk Bul. near the *gar*, sells day-old copies of *USA Today* and the *International Herald Tribune.*

Pharmacies: Throughout town; try Ünlü Eczanesi (☎363 37 75), across the street from the Ethnographic Museum.

Internet Access: Duck into Çakmak Plaza (on Çakmak Cad.), a shopping mall, for a taste of home and some hard-core A/C. On the top floor, the **Electrocom** and **Online Internet Cafes** are scrunched between Pizza Hut and Pizza Han. $1 per hr.

PTT: Main PTT, past the Atatürk statue on Atatürk Cad., open 24hr., with standard stamp, fax, and telegraph services. Smaller 24hr. PTT opposite the *gar* on İstasyon Cad. has **currency exchange** 8am-5pm. Another small PTT on İnönü Cad. open daily 8am-5pm.

Postal Code: 01122.

ACCOMMODATIONS

If you're looking for cleanliness and comfort at a low price, Adana is not the place for you. Apart from the several 5-star hotels ($65-100), most of Adana's two-star facilities cater to businessmen. If sticky nights and the lullaby of a ceiling fan sound unappealing, you're better off forking over extra cash or staying elsewhere.

Otel Mercan, 5 Ocak Meydanı (☎351 26 03), is the best deal in Adana. Clean and plush. All rooms have showers and A/C. Singles $9; doubles $15; triples $22.

Otel Duygu (Akdeniz Hotel), 14 İnönü Cad. (☎363 15 10). Refurbished and reaching for its 3rd star, Duygu offers beautiful rooms with A/C, telephone, TV, and sparkling private baths. Gorgeous room decorations with billowing curtains are fit for a Hollywood set. Breakfast included. Singles $20; doubles $30; triples $40.

Hotel Gümüş, İnönü Cad., No. 87. Small, clean, comfy rooms without A/C capture Adana's burning spirit. Shared but clean *à la turka* toilets. No breakfast service. Singles $5; doubles $8.

İpek Palas, İnönü Cad., No. 89 (☎363 35 12), next door to Hotel Gümüş. Rooms have private showers, A/C, TV, and phones. Breakfast $1.60. $10 per person.

FOOD

Adana's spicy *kebap* specialty will knock your socks off.

Küçük Ev Restaurant (☎363 56 87), off Çakmak Cad., next to the massive Yimpaş shopping center. This food is divine! Beyond the wood-paneled entrance to this former mansion, Ümran Kaçmaz and her team of chefs prepare an unbelievable array of home-cooked foods. A lunchtime selection of 28 meals and dinner palette of 12 includes *sarma* (stuffed grape leaves), *dolma* (stuffed zucchini), and various eggplant specialties. Main courses $1.50-2.50. Ideal for vegetarians, this "little house" is a delightful break from the region's greasy meat dishes. Open M-F 7:30am-8:30pm.

Yeni Onbaşılar (☎363 20 84), on Atatürk Cad., opposite the tourist office and above the Yaza Merhaba clothing store. The most recommended *kebapci* in town, Yeni serves up Adana's spicy specialty ($2), along with a popular *şiş piliç* (chicken *şiş;* $2.80). Open daily 11am-10:30pm.

Bizarre Cafe (☎359 20 67). On the edge of Ocak Meydanı. Far from a misguided claim, the name is quite apt. Pass a mural of muscle-bound waitresses to admire the central fish tank. Burger and fries $2.

Ecem Chicken, 38/B Abidinpaşa Cad. (☎351 12 01). Stands by its specialty. Try the chicken breast ($1.80) or the *kaşarlı* (a chicken and cheese dish; $1.60).

SIGHTS

Walking east along Turhan Cemal Beriker Bul. toward the river, you'll pass the huge **Sabancı Merkez Camii** (Central Mosque), the second largest mosque in both Turkey and the Middle East. (The largest is in Ankara.) Financed by Turkish multi-millionaire businessman Sakıp Sabancı, the mosque is one of his many local projects (check out the Hilton nearby). Though the mosque lacks historical importance, its beauty merits visitors, particularly under the nightly glow of spotlights.

Just before the mosque is Adana's **Archaeological Museum,** one of the few of its kind in this region worth any attention. On display are Hittite sculptures, Roman jewelry, Bronze Age pottery, and coins from various eras. Particularly fascinating are works from the nearby Çukurova excavation and a sunny courtyard of old sarcophagi. (☎454 38 55. Open Tu-Su 8:30am-noon and 1:30-5pm. $1.60.) Leave the museum, turn left, and follow the river to the small **Atatürk Museum,** commemorating a March 15, 1923 visit. The museum features an eerie, life-sized waxwork of the Turkish statesman. At the time of publication, the Atatürk Museum was closed for renovations, but with plans to reopen by summer 2002. (Open Tu-Su 8am-noon and 1-5pm. $1.60, students $.80.) A 5min. walk past the museum lies the famous **Roman bridge,** built by the Roman architect **Auxentus** in the 4th century. Continue past it for 5min. and turn right at the government building to reach the 19th-century **clock tower.** On the right before the clock tower is a park, and just beyond it, the **Ulu Camii** (Great Mosque), built by Halil Bey in 1507 and enlarged in 1541. Halil is buried inside, though current restoration prevents visitors from entering.

Continuing on toward Saydam Cad. leads to **Yağ Camii** (Butter Mosque), an unusual structure that was converted from a church in 1501. Note the roof tiles, more common on Greek mansions than on mosques. The **Catholic church,** serving the city's small Christian community, is down the road to the right, 50m past the Atatürk statue and then down some narrow streets. Press the buzzer to enter. The paintings lining the hall depict St. Paul's vision on the road to Damascus and important events in the life of Christ. Just off İnönü Cad. (follow the sign) is a small **Ethnographic Museum** displaying pistols, coins, and old, handmade *kilims.* (Open Tu-Su 8am-noon and 1:30-5pm. $2.)

On the outskirts of old Adana (toward the residential areas) lies an enormous, man-made **lake** and nearby dam. By day, sun-drenched beaches and *çay* gardens draw carloads of picnickers. Nightfall brings some of Adana's only worthwhile entertainment, as flashy **amusement parks** line the road to innumerable lakeside restaurants and bars. Many of the eateries offer boat-top dining; small boats will ship patrons out to a tiny island and back ($12 per person). From the tourist office, a white dolmuş marked *Cemal Paşa* on top and *Göl* on the destination board will take you all around Adana before stopping at the lake (every 10min., $.50.)

DAYTRIP FROM ADANA: TARSUS

Buses and dolmuş frequently run the Adana-Mersin route, and all stop in Tarsus (45min., every 30min., $1). Catch a dolmuş in Adana by the Merkez Camii or a bus at the otogar.

With over 100,000 inhabitants, Tarsus is not much of a break from the hustle and bustle of Adana. Yet for many, the city's history makes it a must-see. About 30min. west of Adana, the city was both the **birthplace of St. Paul** and the ancient capital of Roman Cilicia in about 63 BC. **Antony and Cleopatra** groupies who have been retracing the couple's rendezvous points along the eastern Mediterranean will also be interested to learn that the couple reportedly "met" here in 41 BC. Across from the massive Atatürk statue in the center of town is **Cleopatra's Gate,** a beautiful arch that once marked the ancient city's entrance. Today, the arch is trapped in a traffic circle, but a vibrant imagination can supply the gold and cavalcade that once greeted Cleopatra's arrival. Her departure made up in gossip what it must have lacked in glory: the ancient town's exit is marked by a less impressive arch near the Eski Cami, called **Kancik Kapısı** ("Bitch Gate"). A few blocks from the major thoroughfare in town is the small courtyard that houses **St. Paul's Well.** Only the round stone slab remains from about 20 AD, when the St. Paul supposedly struck the watering hole. (Courtyard open 8am-5pm. $1.) Following Atatürk Cad. toward the waterfalls, you'll find the **Roman Road Excavations** on your right. You too can play archeologist and explore the emerging artifacts and fascinating ruins. Watch out for unmarked ditches. The **archeological museum,** housed in a *medrese* near the center of town, seems to have had all its artifacts moved elsewhere, except for some fragmentary sarcophagi. The guard will try to extract the admission fee, regardless. (Open Tu-Su 8am-noon and 1-5pm. $1.25, students $.75.)

Overnight options in Tarsus are limited to the four-star hotel by the waterfall ($80) or two in-town options. At **Hotel Zorbaz,** the conspicuous pink building in the center of town, gaudy purple doors mark reasonably clean and spacious rooms with squat toilets. Two lounge rooms each have about 20 leather executive office chairs. (☎622 21 66. Singles $7.30; doubles $11.30; triples $16.) The nearby **Cihan Palas Otel** has bright yellow bedspreads that complement the parakeets in the lobby. Rooms have TVs and tiled baths. (☎624 16 23. Singles $12; doubles $22.)

Tarsus's pleasant but unimpressive **şelale** (waterfall) lies on the edge of town. Tea gardens and restaurants make it a good lunch stop, particularly to try Tarsus's special "cup holder" *lahmacun,* which are shrunken versions of the original. The **Şelale Hasbahçe Restaurant** (☎622 49 23) serves *ızgara* (grilled meats; $3) and a local coffee specialty called *tarsusi.*

THE HATAY

Just east of Adana, the Mediterranean coast hooks southward and the cities take on a decidedly more Arab feel. This is the Hatay, a contested promontory whose identity has long been strained between two larger powers: in the time of Antioch it sat between Rome and Persia; more recently (in the 1930's) the independent Republic of Hatay floated between Turkish and Syrian claims. The Turks won out, and the Hatay joined the Turkish Republic in 1939, but the Hatay's Syrian character is still visible in the omnipresent turbans and unique cuisine found in the streets of the provincial capital Antakya and in İskenderun, its principal port.

İSKENDERUN ☎326

Formerly known as **Alexandretta,** İskenderun was founded by Alexander the Great to commemorate his decisive victory over the Persians at Issus. As the principal port city of Antioch, Alexandretta became a powerful and cosmopolitan burg in its own right. Modern-day İskenderun has retained very little of historical interest, but its waterfront promenades and wide boulevards are pleasant to stroll, and its position on the Mediterranean trade routes has protected the diversity of the towns' Christian, Muslim, and Jewish populations. To the south, some pleasant **beaches** make İskenderun a popular destination for Turkish and Arab tourists.

ORIENTATION AND PRACTICAL INFORMATION. İskenderun is a major waystation for all buses connecting from Antakya to points north and east. Travelers arrive in the **otogar,** 1km north of the town center.

Atatürk Cad. runs along the waterfront park, and intersects the town's two main boulevards, **Sehit Pamir Cad.** and **Ulu Camii Cad.,** at the Atatürk statue. All travelers' needs can be met on these three streets. South on Atatürk Cad., the **tourist office,** 49B Atatürk Cad., has mimeographed maps and brochures. (☎614 16 20. Open M-Sa 8am-noon, 1-5pm.) Next door, the **tourist police** (☎613 61 76) is open daily 24hr. **Banks** and **pharmacies** line Sehit Pamir Cad.; exchange is best at the **Turkiye Iş Bankası,** by the Atatürk statue. The **Devlet Hastahnesi** (☎613 35 70) offers 24hr. medical care. Ambulance ☎122; pharmacy information ☎118. The **PTT** is up Sehit Pamir Cad. on the right. Open 8:30am-5:30pm. **Postal code:** 31200.

ACCOMMODATIONS AND FOOD. Hotel Açikalin, 13 Sehit Pamir Cad. (☎617 37 32) is the best deal in town, with clean air-conditioned rooms and shared bath for $5 per person. Next door, the **Turistik Hotel Imrenay**, 5 Sehit Pamir Cad., is a step up with A/C, bath, fridge, and TV for only a little more. (☎613 21 17. Singles $8.50, doubles $17.) One block over on Ulucamii Cad. No. 16, the **Hotel Cabir** (☎612 33 91) offers well-appointed suites with powerful climate control and spotless bathrooms for $15 per person. For those seeking a more beachside locale, the **Arsuz Otel,** 30min. south on in the resort town of **Uluçinar,** provides 3-star luxury with private beach, restaurant, and waterfront bar. ($20 per person.)

İskenderun has several passable but nondescript *lokantas*; the exception is the atmospheric **Hasan Baba Restaurant,** 35 Ulu Camii Cad. (☎613 27 25), famous for its tasty *iskender kebap* ($3), served in a well-lit garden with fountains and terraces.

SIGHTS. Plenty of Turkish and Syrian tourists come to İskenderun for the nice stretches of **beach** south of the city, which somehow avoid the pollution that fouls the beaches in southern Hatay. The most popular destination is **Uluçinar,** a pretty enough resort town with beachside cafes and sandy beaches over clear water. The coastal highway ends at Uluçinar, but the town has the southernmost outpost of the Kharamanmaraş ice cream chain **46 Edem,** with glorious $.40 cones.

ANTAKYA

☎326

In Antakya, site of the ancient city of **Antioch,** the throngs of tourists diminish, as does the Mediterranean resort atmosphere. Antakya offers sprawling markets in the old sections of town, manicured tea gardens, and the world famous Hatay Museum, housing the world's finest collection of Roman mosaics. It was in Antioch that Christianity received its name; the side of Mt. Stauros is riddled with caves and tunnels where the underground religion was kindled, including the legendary Grotto of Saint Peter—the oldest church in the world.

Seleucus I Nicator, one of Alexander the Great's chief generals, founded Antioch in 300 BC and domineered Asia from here. The population swelled to 500,000, but growth was tumultuous. Internal strife, the neighboring Persian and Roman Empires, a series of plagues and a catastrophic earthquake in 148 BC all threatened the city. Even before Antioch fell to the Romans in 64 BC, this prominent Silk Road stop acquired a reputation for vice and decadence. By 42 BC, equipped with brand new city walls, an acropolis, amphitheater, courthouse, baths, and aqueducts, Antioch was the third-largest city in the Roman Empire and a center of science and commerce. Around 40 AD, the Apostle Peter gathered the first Christian congregation here, converting Antioch and renaming it Theopolis (City of God). Only after losing 200,000 lives in a devastating 6th-century earthquake did the city enter a hopeless decline. Although Justinian rebuilt the city, marauders later trashed his good work, and Antioch's splendor was reduced to ruins.

The crumbling walls along the surrounding mountain ridge are evidence of the city's former glory. Modern-day Antakya thrives in the bustle of its market streets, the buzz of border traffic to Aleppo and Damascus, and the mouth-watering concoctions of Antakya's kitchens, the fusion of Turkish and Syrian palates.

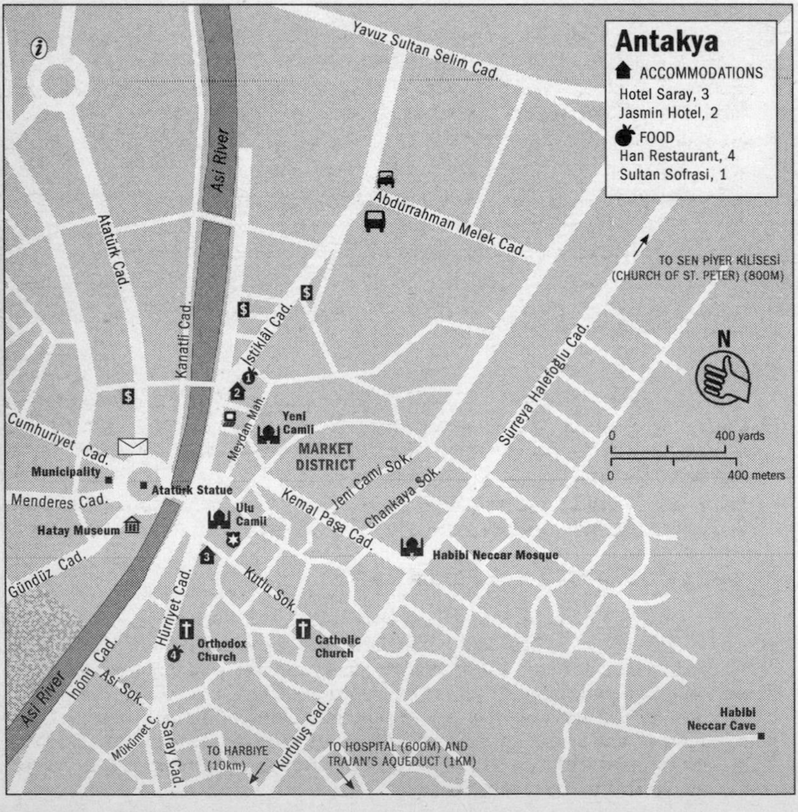

TRANSPORTATION

Buses: To: **Ankara** (10hr., 6 per day 10am-10pm, $13); **Antalya** (14hr., 10 per day 9am-6:15pm, $13); **İstanbul** (16hr., 8 per day 2:30-6pm, $19); **İzmir** (16hr., 4 per day 12:30-7pm, $19); **Kars** (23hr., 3pm, $21); **Kayseri** (8hr.; 9am, 8:30pm; $10); **Mersin** (6hr., 10 per day 9am-8pm, $5); **Trabzon** (20hr., 3:30pm, $18). **International buses: Aleppo** (3-4hr., 4 per day 9am-6pm, $8) and **Damascus** (9hr.; 9:30am, noon; $15). See **Border Crossing: Syria,** p. 313.

Dolmuş: To **Gaziantep** (3hr., every 30min., $4). Across from the otogar, regional and local dolmuş leave for **Samandağ** (30 min, every 15 min, $1), **Harbiye** (20min., every 10min., $.50) and **İskenderun** (30min., every 15min., $1).

ORIENTATION AND PRACTICAL INFORMATION

The **Asi (Orontes) River** divides Antakya, with the otogar, commercial center and hotels on the eastern side. Across the river is the Atatürk statue rotunda, with the **PTT** and **museum** clustered nearby and **Atatürk Cad.** stretching to the north. From the otogar, the center of town is 700m along **İstiklâl Cad.** The museum is visible from here, straight across the river. South of İstiklâl Cad. several hotels, banks, and restaurants cluster along **Hurriyet Cad.**

Tourist Office: (☎216 06 10), in the Valiliki building, at the end of İstiklâl Cad., just past the Antik Beyazıt Hotel. Modest English, some helpful brochures and mimeographed map. Open M-F 8am-noon and 1:30-5:30pm.

Banks: Türkiye İş Bankası, one of the many banks in town, has a branch on İstiklâl Cad., halfway between the center of town and the otogar. Another is just down Hürriyet Cad. from the Saray Hotel. Both offer **currency exchange** and 24hr. Cirrus/MC/Plus/V **ATMs.** The otogar and the exchange office on İstiklâl Cad., across from Vakıf Bank, provide Syrian pounds at more favorable rates (see **Border Crossing: Syria,** p. 313).

Pharmacy: Among the many pharmacies is **Gazipaşa Eczanesi** (☎214 97 04), just down Hürriyet Cad. from the Saray Hotel. Open M-Sa 8:30am-7:30pm.

Hospital: Devlet Hastanesi (☎214 54 30), at Bagri Yanikda, 4km from town, is open 24hr. Dolmuş run from town center ($.30). Taxi $4.

Internet Access: Over 40 outlets, all around $.75 per hr. Some close at 10pm if quiet. **Moda-Net** (☎216 52 90), on Huriyet Cad. 15, is close to Hotel Saray.

PTT: In the center of town. Mail service daily 8:30am-6pm. 24hr. phone service.

Postal Code: 31000.

MEDITERRANEAN COAST

ACCOMMODATIONS

Jasmin Hotel, 14 İstiklâl Cad. (☎212 71 71). Shared bathrooms, rooftop patio, and lawn furniture. Rooms open into a central atrium. Singles $5; doubles $8; triples $10.

Hotel Saray, 3 Hürriyet Cad. (☎/fax 214 90 01), the best of the middle range choices, offers a pleasant breakfast salon and new rooms with bath. Breakfast included. Singles $10; doubles $16; triples $25. Add $5 per room for A/C.

Divan Hotel, 62 İstiklâl Cad. (☎215 15 18), a tidy one-star place with breezy balconies and private bath with excellent showers. $7.50 per person.

FOOD AND ENTERTAINMENT

For the traveler well-inured to the traditional *kebap* and *lokanta* fare, Antakya is an exotic culinary oasis. Among the specialties of the region are hummus and *içli köfte,* often known as *oruk,* a spicy bulgur wheat and red pepper stuffed with seasoned lamb and pine nuts. *Ekşi aşı,* a variation on *oruk,* is served covered in tomato sauce. Vegetarian *mezes* are everywhere and feature lots of thick hummus, eggplants, and garlic. For dessert, *künefe* (or *peynirli kadayıf*) is a baklava-style pastry stuffed with sweet cheese. Much of this Syrian-influenced Turkish cuisine is unavailable in the rest of Turkey.

In the third week of July, Antakya hosts a four-day **music festival,** during which marching bands, DJ carts, and traditional singers fill the streets with howling crowds well past midnight. The beautifully restored **Antik Beyazıt Hotel,** Hukumet Cad. 4, is a must-see example of old Antakyan architecture. Across İstiklâl Cad. from Hotel Divan is the red-light district; avoid anything labeled *"gazino."*

Han Restaurant (☎214 17 16). On Hürriyet Cad. Despite the external appearance, Han has a smashing upper level with a grove of fruit trees. The *mezes* are simply extraordinary. Full meal $4-5. Open 10am-midnight.

Sultan Sofrasi, 18 İstiklâl Cad. (☎213 87 59), is among Antakya's best. Great *Mumbar, aşur* and *sultan sarma* in air-conditioned comfort. Full meal $5-6. Open 7am-10pm.

Anadolu Restaurant, 50/C Hürriyet Cad. (☎215 15 41). 10min. down the street from the Saray Hotel. Popular among locals, Anadolu serves vegetarian *meze* and excellent hummus. Try the *saksuka*: potatoes, eggplants, onions, and tomato sauces topped with yogurt. Outdoor seating. Cheaper than Sultan. Full meal $4-5. Open 10am-midnight.

'46 Edem Dondurma (☎214 53 36). On Atatürk Cad., 100m from the center of town. Serves your favorite fruit flavors as well as 3 varieties of *dövme* ice cream: plain *(sade),* chocolate *(çikolata),* and the heavenly pistachio *(fıstık). Dövme* ("beaten") is pounded, kneaded, and stretched to a thick, gooey consistency.

SIGHTS

HATAY MUSEUM. Except for the ruins of the ancient walls, earthquakes and marauders have destroyed much of Antioch's ancient splendor. Only the breathtaking and world-renowned Hatay Museum hints at the magnificence of the ancient city. The museum houses one of the world's best collections of **Roman mosaics,** assembled by an archaeological team from Princeton University, the British Museum, and the Chicago Oriental Institute. Painstakingly pieced together from thousands of tiny tiles, these huge mosaics depict images with near-photographic precision. Highlights are a 2nd-century wild boar hunt ("A Pig Hunt in Calydonia"), the striking "Personification of Soteria," the small, priapic hunchback mosaic ("The Happy Hunchback"), and a scantily clad man running in horror from an enormous levitating eye radiating farm implements ("Evil Eye"). The most imposing mosaic is the giant 5th-century hunting scene on the floor; climb the spiral staircase for a complete view. An air-conditioned salon houses coins, jewelry and mounted heads. Sarcophagi and additional mosaics fill the garden outside. *(Open Tu-Su 8:30am-noon, 1:30-6pm. $3.50, students $1.50.)*

ST. PETER'S CHURCH (SEN PİYER KİLİSESİ). Founded by the Apostle Peter, who preached here with Paul and Barnabas, this church (a.k.a. St. Peter's Grotto) was built into a cave so that services could be conducted in secret. The original congregation here coined the term "Christianity" to describe their new religion. The hillside above the church, riddled with the remains of tunnels, natural caves, and bits of Antioch's city walls, has been a holy place since pagan times. Inside the cave, an escape tunnel and an ancient baptismal font give a preternatural haunt to the stone altar, still regularly used for services. The external facade was built by 11th century Crusaders; in front a terraced garden offers a pleasant spot to sit with a cup of *çay* and gaze at the city below. A path zigzags 200m to a high relief of a veiled figure, alternately described as a windblown Mary or as the Syrian goddess of Hierapolis flanked by Charon, boatman of Hades. *(To reach the church, walk 2km north on Kurunus Cad. (20min.) and take the erratic city bus #6, or taxi ($2). Open Tu-Su 8am-noon, 1:30-4:30pm. $3, students $1. There is no regular mass; check with the Antakya Catholic Church (☎215 67 03). Relief open Tu-Su 8am-noon, 1:30-5:30pm. Free.)*

DAYTRIP FROM ANTAKYA: MONASTERY OF ST. SIMEON

To reach the site, follow the sign south off the Antakya-Samandağ road just past Karaçay. The road heads uphill 4km before forking right at a white shrine. A track leads a few kilometers farther to the monastery. The Antakya-Samandağ dolmuş (1hr., every 15min., $2) will drop you at the turn-off, if you ask, or at Karaçay, where you can hire a taxi (round-trip $10).

Samandağ, about 30km southwest of Antakya, is a Mediterranean resort popular with Turkish and Syrian tourists. The seaside area, though more appealing than the dreary town, is heavily polluted. Between Samandağ and Antakya lies the **Monastery of St. Simeon Stylites** (the Younger), where Simeon sat on a pillar for 25 years. Driven by the ascetic impulse that characterized Syrian Christianity in the 4th century, Simeon imitated the better-known Simeon the Elder, whose ruined basilica and eroded column are across the border in Syria. He retreated to a deserted mountaintop and chained himself atop a 13m pillar to live the rest of his life in penitent solitude. This isolation did not last long, as he soon attracted crowds of pilgrims, to whom he delivered sermons against the rampant vice of Antioch. A monastery was built around the remains of his pillar. Only the foundations are still intact, but the site continues to draw tourists.

Fifteen minutes southwest of Samandağ on the road to Çevlik are the ancient ruins of **Selucia Pieria (Beşikli Mağara),** an ancient Roman port. Glacial runoff from the nearby mountains threatened the port during heavy rains, so the Romans dug a massive tunnel in the first and second centuries A.D., to divert the water flow. The **Tunnel of Titus** stretches for nearly 2km, from the mountainside down to the beach, at times cutting entirely through the mountain rock. Alongside the tunnel, innumerable Roman tombs were also dug into the rock, including some with magnificent colonnaded facades, holding several-hundred sarcophagi apiece. Hiking trails follow aqueducts through the tunnels and necropoli. At the end of the tunnel, **Club Almina** offers reasonable lodgings, with restaurant, pool, and disco. *(Dolmuş $.35, one way from Samandağ.)*

BORDER CROSSING: SYRIA

The overland crossing at Bab al-Hawa on the Aleppo-Antakya road takes less than 30min. each way. Obtain your Syrian visa in advance from your home country or at the Syrian embassy in Ankara (see p. 363). In theory, only travelers from countries without Syrian embassies can purchase border visas; otherwise they can cost up to $100 at the border. Three-month double-entry visas cost $61. Any passport with evidence of a trip to Israel will be refused a visa or entry.

Several Antakya bus companies, including **Has,** offer service to **Aleppo** (3-4 per day, $8). Avoid Öztur, which uses substandard buses without air conditioning. Allow 4-5 hours for the journey and border formalities. The border has two stops on each side. At one stop on the Turkish side, you will have to leave the bus and go through passport control. Passport control and luggage searches are slower on the Syrian side, sometimes as long as 1½ hours. The Syrian currency is the Syrian pound (S£). Because the official exchange rate (at the time of publication, US$1=S£53.37) is somewhat less than the black market rate, change money in Antakya, where it's legal to exchange at the better rate.

CENTRAL ANATOLIA

While the Aegean and Mediterranean Coasts (a.k.a. the "Turkish Riviera") have become a pastiche of tourist sites and Eurobeaches, and the Black Sea Coast exudes an Eastern European feel, the essence of traditional Turkey is alive and well in the dry, windy mountains of Central Anatolia. The astonishing landscapes and improbable natural formations of Cappadocia are some of the most fascinating in the world, not only for their unearthly aesthetic, but also as testament to the region's tumultuous religious history. The proximity of Cappadocia, an ancient Christian stronghold, to Konya, Turkey's most conservative Islamic city, hints at the area's diversity. Unique for its land and its faiths, Central Anatolia also houses the modern Republic's secular bastion at Ankara and the ruins of a 4000-year-old Hittite capital at Boğazkale. A vibrant culture, welcoming atmosphere, and inspiring landscape characterize these windswept plains of Turkey's heartland.

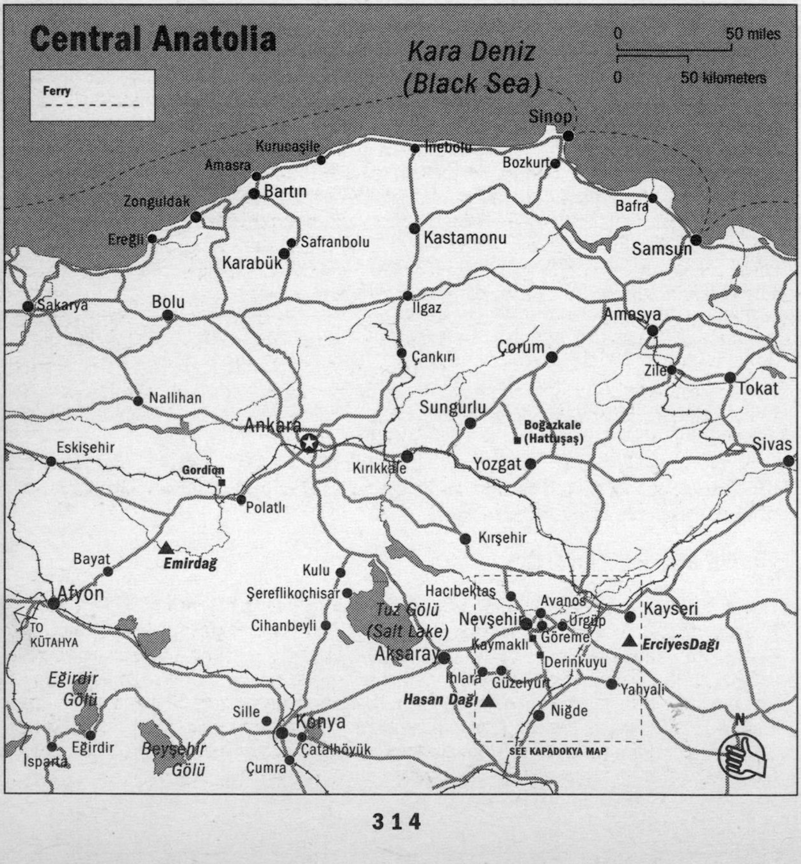

HIGHLIGHTS OF CENTRAL ANATOLIA

GAWK at the mammoth Anıt Kabır, **Atatürk's Mausoleum** in Ankara (p. 384), and discover proof that even clouds mourned the loss of the Father of Turkey.

JOIN pilgrims in **Konya** (p. 341) to pay a visit to the tomb of Celeddin-İ-Rumi, whose disciples founded the famous Sufi order of Whirling Dervishes.

VISIT the **flesh-eating "doctor fish"** at Balıklı Kaplıca (p. 384), where you can treat your psoriasis with the drillers, suckers, and dressers that swim in the hot springs.

MAKE an offering to the Hatti storm god, Teshub, in **Hattuşaş** (p. 375), the 4000-year-old Hittite capital.

GRAB a flashlight and head down into the **Underground Cities of Kaymaklı and Derinkuyu** near Nevşehir (p. 324) to lose yourself in the narrow tunnels of this ancient Christian defensive stronghold.

SLEEP n a cave pension and spend the afternoon at the **Göreme Open-Air Museum** (p. 321), where you can tour six frescoed Byzantine cave churches.

CAPPADOCIA

Cappadocia's enchanting landscape remains unparalleled in history and mystery. Ten million years ago, eruptions from the volcanic Mt. Erciyes (3916m) and Mt. Hasan (3268m) covered the underlying plateaus with **tufa,** a soft stone made of lava, ash, and mud. Rain, wind, and flooding from the Kızılırmak River shaped the tufa into a striking landscape of cone-shaped monoliths called *peribaca* ("fairy chimneys"), grouped in valleys and along gorge ridges. Chunks of hard basalt trapped on the surface of the prehistoric sludge protected the underlying tufa from wind erosion, thus forming bouldered caps on many of the fairy chimneys.

Cappadocia's unique landscape has long been a hotbed of religious activity. From about 525 BC, the fire-worshipping Zoroastrian Persians revered the region's Erciyes Dağ and Hasan Dağ as holy mountains. Early Christians also found inspiration in Cappadocia; by the 4th century, it was a major center for Christian philosophy and civilization. Hiding from Romans, Iconoclasts, Sassanids, and Turks, these hardy Christians carved beautifully frescoed churches and colossal underground cities into the pliant tufa. Throughout Cappadocia's staggering moonscapes, stairs, windows, and sentry holes have been carved into the rock. Many of these "troglodyte dwellings" are still used as houses, storage rooms, or stables, while others have been converted into hotels and bars.

Visitors today are both captivated by the genius of ancient civilizations and inspired by pristine hikes through Cappadocia's bizarre geology, which is sometimes compared to the Grand Canyon on acid. Most travelers reside in the touristy and convenient towns of Göreme and Ürgüp. The more authentic villages of Güzelyurt, Üçhisar, Mustafapaşa, and Ihlara may tempt you to abandon your life plans and become a local shepherd or hiking guide.

If you can only spare a day or two, it is probably easiest to stay in Göreme, visit the spectacular **Open-Air Museum,** and then see the highlights of Cappadocia on one of the local companies' full-day tours.

TRANSPORTATION

From June to September, a dolmuş follows the Ürgüp-Göreme-Çavuşin-Zelve-Avanos circuit (Leaves Ürgüp M-F every 2hr. 10am-6pm; returns from Avanos M-F every 2hr. 9am-5pm). Dolmuş also run frequently between Ürgüp and Mustafapaşa, and Ürgüp and Ortahisar. In winter, most connections within Cappadocia must be made via Nevşehir, from which buses depart every 30min. for all major Cappadocian towns. Transportation within this region costs between $.60 and $2.50. Most visits to southern Cappadocia must be made through Aksaray. Buses from Nevşehir to Ankara stop in Aksaray (every hr., $2.50).

If you have the funds, **car and motorbike rentals** can be a great way to stray from the beaten path and explore the captivating landscape and mysterious caves. Cars start at about $30 per day, though prices skyrocket to about $50 for automatics. **Europcar** (☎341 34 88 or 341 43 15) in Ürgüp rents automatics with A/C for $90 per day. Rental agencies in Göreme and Ürgüp rent **bicycles** ($3 per hr. or $14 per day), **mopeds** ($8 per hr. or $20 per day), and **motorcycles** ($50 per day). **Chimney Tours** next to the Goreme Otogar also boasts a beautiful 5-seater 1970 custom Ford convertible in its rental fleet ($45 per 24hr.).

Guided tours of Cappadocia's major sites are organized by agencies in Göreme and Ürgüp (see Travel Agencies **Tours,** p. 325). Tour packages typically include a day-long tour of the region, as well as bus, lunch, and admission to all sites ($30).

NEVŞEHİR ☎384

Nevşehir serves as Cappadocia's transportation hub, and even "direct" transport to any town in Cappadocia will probably entail a bus switch in Nevşehir. The city is unimpressive to the tourist's eye and a tiresome 2km walk from the otogar. However, Nevşehir's quiet local flavor is visible everywhere: blue-uniformed school children meander the roads as side-street shop owners gossip across clothes racks and backgammon boards.

TRANSPORTATION. Buses leave the otogar for: **Adana** (4hr.; 9am, 1:30, 4:30pm; $7.50); **Alanya** (12hr.; 11am, 7, 9pm; $17.50); **Ankara** (4hr., 11 per day 9am-8pm, $7.50); **Antalya** (10-11hr.; 11am, 7, 8, 9pm; $15); **Bodrum** (14hr., 8:30pm, $18.75); **Bursa** (9hr., 6:30pm, $13.75); **İstanbul** (10hr., 5 per day 7:30-9pm, $15); **İzmir**

(12hr.; 7:30, 9:30pm; $15); **Kayseri** (1½hr., 11 per day 7am-7pm, $2.50); **Konya** (2½hr., 4 per day, $6.25); **Marmaris** (14hr., 8pm); **Mersin** (5hr.; 9am, 1:30, 4:30pm; $7.50). **Dolmuş** leave from the otogar for **Aksaray, Üçhisar, Niğde, Göreme, Ortahisar, Ürgüp, Avanos,** and **Kayseri** (M-Sa every 30min. 7am-7pm, Su every hr. 7am-7pm; Oct-May M-Sa every 30min. 7am-5pm, Su every hr. 7am-5pm; $.75).

ORIENTATION AND PRACTICAL INFORMATION. The two main streets in Nevşehir are the east-west Atatürk Ave., and, perpendicular to it, **Lale Cad.** Lale Cad. runs uphill to the right of the otogar before intersecting Atatürk Ave. (called **Yeni Kayseri Cad.,** east of the Lale Cad. intersection). The Nevşehir Belediye (municipal) buses from Ürgüp and Göreme stop on Lale Cad. before reaching the otogar. The helpful staff at the **Tourist Office,** 14 Yeni Kayseri Cad. (☎213 36 59), one block west of the town's Atatürk statue, offers free maps and brochures, as does **Rock City Travel Agency** (☎212 06 03), on the far east of Atatürk Ave., across from the Nevşehir Museum. The organized staff and anglophone owner handle anything from airplane tickets to $15 guided day tours of Cappadocia. The Nevşehir **hospital** (☎213 12 00), next door to the tourist office, is the town's main facility for medical emergencies. Restaurants, pharmacies, shops, a tea garden, several **ATMs,** and **PTTs** (open M-F 8:30am-12:30pm, 1:30-5:30pm) line Atatürk Ave.

ACCOMMODATIONS, FOOD, AND ENTERTAINMENT. The family-run **Hotel Seven Brothers,** Kayseri Cad., 23 Tusan Sok., has TVs and private baths in each of its 48 rooms. (☎213 49 79 or 212 81 78; fax 213 04 54. Breakfast included. Singles $10; doubles $16. Children under 12 free.) Nearby, **Otel Nisa,** 35 Yeni Kayseri Cad., just off Atatürk Bul., has TVs and private showers in its rooms, some with balcony views. (☎213 58 43 or 212 61 68; fax 213 58 43. Breakfast included. Singles $8; doubles $15; triples $18.) **Şems Otel,** on Atatürk Bul., has well-furnished rooms with private showers. (☎213 35 97; fax 213 08 34. Breakfast included. $10 per person.) Questionable hotels with dirt-cheap rooms ($2-3) dot the western end of Atatürk Ave.

Turkish "fast food" peppers Nevşehir's streets, and you can grab decent kebap, *döner*, and *lahmacun* for under $3. Nightlife in Nevşehir is as non-existent as virgins in a Trabzon "hotel"; instead, spend your time getting massaged, scrubbed, and scraped at the **Damat İbrahim Paşa Hamam,** 43 Camikebir Cad. (☎213 26 58), where $10 buys a divinely complete hamam experience. The hamam is part of the larger Damat İbrahim Paşa mosque-bath-*medrese* complex, completed in 1727.

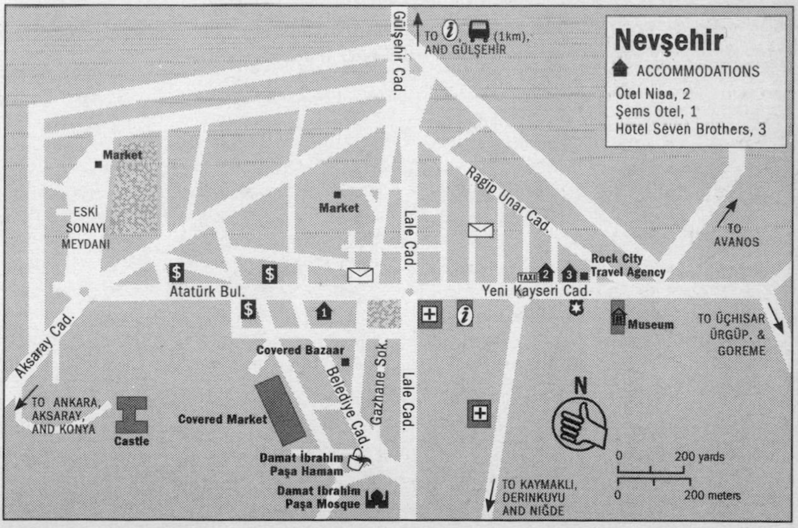

GÖREME ☎384

The village of Göreme is the undisputed capital of Cappadocia's backpacker scene. Scores of tour groups operate out of Göreme, but the city's industry caters largely to the independent traveler. Surrounded by picturesque fairy chimneys, Göreme offers travelers no fewer than 64 pensions, mostly cave dwellings carved into the soft tufa. Its central location makes it the best base for exploring Cappadocia, and the glorious Open-Air Museum is only a short walk away. Despite the tourist traffic, Göreme has retained some of its small-town charm; apple *çay* offerings abound and an extended stay will probably earn you local friends. Be forewarned that visitors have been known to stay permanently in the majestic area; "once you've tasted Göreme's water, you're bound to come back," foretells one local adage. The staggering number of foreign brides (locals say around 200) who've settled here suggests a different allure.

TRANSPORTATION

Buses: Göreme's otogar is in the center of town. Buses travel via **Nevşehir** to: **Alanya** (12hr., 8 per day noon-10:30pm, $16); **Ankara** (4hr., 9 per day 8:15am-midnight, $8); **Antalya** (10hr., 8 per day 6-10:30pm, $15); **Bodrum** (14hr.; 7:30, 9pm, midnight; $20); **Bursa** (10hr.; 5:30, 7:30pm; $16); **Eğirdir** (7hr., 6-10:30pm, $13); **Fethiye** (13hr., 8per day noon-10:30pm, $19.50); **İstanbul** (11hr., 7 per day 8:30am-9pm, $16); **İzmir** (12hr., 6 per day 6:45-10pm, $16); **Kayseri** (1hr., every hour 7am-6:30pm, $3); **Konya** (3hr., 6 per day 8:15am-9pm, $7.30); **Marmaris** (14hr., 5 per day 8pm-midnight, $20); **Mersin** (5hr.; 8am, noon, 12:15, 10pm; $8); **Olimpos** (12hr., 8 per day 6-10:30pm, $19); **Pamukkale** (10hr., 4 per day 7:30pm-midnight, $14); **Selçuk** (13hr., 6 per day 6:45pm-midnight, $19).

ORIENTATION AND PRACTICAL INFORMATION

Finding your way around Göreme is not difficult. The main road heads out west toward Nevşehir and northeast toward Çavuşin. The otogar, just off the main road, is at the eastern end of the town center. A smaller, cobblestone road runs south from the town center. At the eastern end of town, a road up to the Open-Air Museum breaks off from the main road, heading southeast up a hill. Restaurants are mostly near the main road, and pensions are everywhere.

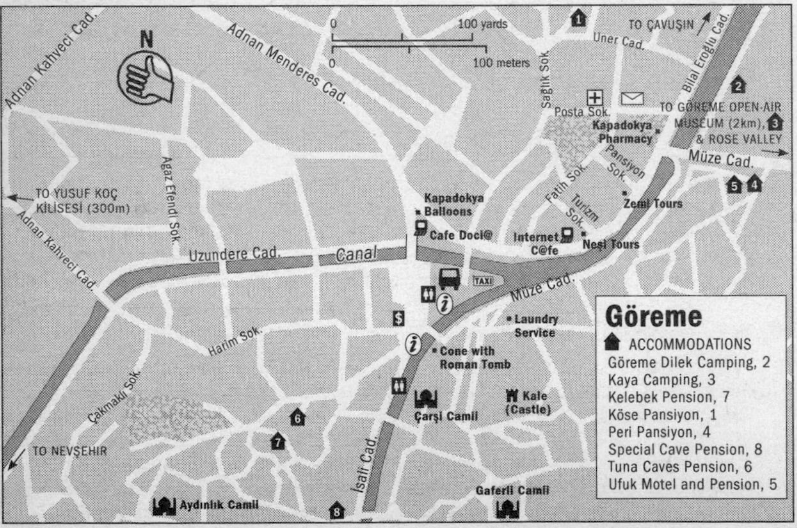

Tourist Office: (☎271 25 58). In the otogar, this cooperative provides info on almost all of Göreme's lodgings. Doing your own research here will acquaint you with Göreme's myriad pensions. Additionally, **Backpacker Information** (on your left as you exit the otogar; ☎271 27 36) can help "the independent traveler" organize an itinerary and offers hostel-based connections through Cappadocia and Turkey's western coast ($10 per day covers lodging and transportation).

Tours: There are many tour companies in Göreme that offer various walking and driving tours (usually $30-$150). In order to find the company best-suited for your needs, as well as to get your money's worth, check that a particular company has insurance, good vehicles and licensed guides (a licensed guide should have an actual license that he can show you). **Alpino Tours** (☎271 27 27; fax 271 27 28; alpino@alpino.com; www.alpino.com.tr) has a very good reputation in town and offers jeep tours (you drive) in addition to its more traditional routes. **Zemi Tours** (☎271 25 76; fax 271 25 77), on the left side of the road leading from the otogar to the Open-Air Museum, offers a unique 2-day Ihlara Gorge Camping Trip ($50 per person) with tents, beds, and meals. **Kapadokya Balloons** (☎271 24 42; fax 271 25 86; www.kapadokyaballoons.com), with an office next door to Cafe Doci@, offers breathtaking 90min. balloon tours, a.k.a. "aerial nature walks," through the Cappadocian landscape. Multilingual, professional pilots Kaili, Mike, and Lars fly as high as 700m and low enough to pick flowers. Balloons fly for 1½hr. with 8 or 12 passengers Apr.-Nov. daily at dawn, weather permitting. They are fully insured and licensed, unlike some other balloon companies in the region. $210 per person, $230 if you pay by credit card; book at least two days in advance.

Banks: Next to the Open-Air Museum. Open daily 9am-5:30pm. There is an **ATM** in the center of Göreme, across from the otogar and to the left.

Laundromat: (☎271 25 79), behind the otogar, across from the Göreme Belediye Handicrafts Market. Wash and dry $7, with ironing $6. Open daily 9am-8pm.

Pharmacy: Kapadokya Pharmacy (☎271 21 37), on the main road near the hospital. Open daily 8am-8pm.

Medical Assistance: The **Göreme Sağlık Ocağı Hospital** (☎271 21 26), near the PTT, is actually a Community Health Clinic, but it also serves medical emergencies.

Internet Access: Cafe Doci@ (see **Food and Entertainment**); **Flintstone's Internet,** next door to Fat Boy's Bar; and **Neşe C@fe.** All open from around 8am until around 11pm and offer cold drinks and a few American-style keyboards to preserve your sanity.

PTT: Though many street-side stores offer PTT services (money exchange, stamps, phone cards), the official post office is on the main road just after the turn-off for the Open-Air Museum. Offers the best exchange rate in town. Open daily 8:30am-12:30pm and 1:30-5:30pm.

Postal code: 50180.

ACCOMMODATIONS & CAMPING

Under Göreme's government, all pensions have fixed minimum prices for non-dormitory rooms: $5 per person, with bath $7, and up to $10 for a single. Establishments designated as starred hotels may charge higher rates. Hit the tourist office (see above) for more complete comparative information on all of Göreme's accommodations, most of which will provide transportation to their establishments if you call ahead. A few pensions accept credit cards, but all of them, like every business in Göreme, strongly prefer that you pay in cash or traveler's checks.

Kelebek Pension (☎271 25 31; fax: 271 27 63; ali@kelebekhotel.com; www.kelebekhotel.com) upholds its reputation as a clean, comfortable, and very well-run pension. Just uphill from Kookabura and Tuna Caves, Kelebek offers cave, fairy chimney, and regular rooms. Each of the several levels of terrace has spectacular views of Göreme and the surrounding valleys. Lounge with satellite TV and English news. Late-arrivals room, complete with shower, open 24hr. for guests wishing to check in the next morning. Dorms $4; fairy chimney rooms $12, with shower $18; super-deluxe $50.

Tuna Caves Pension (☎271 26 81; tunacaves@hotmail.com) Heading from the otogar, take the first right after the ATM and follow the signs. New owners totally refurbished Tuna Caves in 2001 with 17 rooms in an old Greek house. The stone courtyard offers a fireplace and a shady *kilim*-ed lounge area with a stereo. The terrace has a great view. (Cave and non-cave rooms $6, some with shower; dorms $4; deluxe $23).

Special Cave Pension (☎271 23 47; cheilker@yahoo.com) is the coziest cave pension in town and has clean, private showers in every room. The friendly staff, *kilim*-ed terrace, and plush cave bar make this a fun stay. $7 per person.

Köse Pansiyon (☎271 22 94; fax 271 25 77), just behind the PTT. Makeshift Ottoman divans, vine-covered ceilings, swimming pool, ying-yang murals, and helpful Scottish-Turkish owners make Köse quite backpacker friendly. Breakfast $2. Vegetarian and 4-course dinners $4. 2 dorm rooms with mattresses on the floor ($4 per person; bring your own sleeping bag, if possible) and 13 rooms, some with private bath.

Peri Pansiyon (☎271 21 36; fax 271 27 30). On the right, walking east on the road to the Open-Air Museum. Lounge on the sunny, floral courtyard. Tame atmosphere but close to the action at Flintstone's. 4-course dinner ($5) on the wood-panelled *kilim*-ed terrace. 7 cave rooms. Friendly management also offers non-tufa rooms to suit your taste. Singles $7, with bath $10; doubles $20. Cave singles $10, luxury caves $25.

Ufuk Motel and Pension (☎271 21 57; fax 271 25 78; www.ufukpension.com.tr). Next door to Paradise on Göreme Open-Air Museum Way, Ufuk offers 4 cave rooms, 3 with private showers. 11 regular rooms, some with private showers. Garden, wood, and *kilim*-furnished dining terrace with a great view and a dartboard. Laundry $4. Complete dinner $6. Singles $10; doubles $18.

Göreme Dilek Camping (☎271 23 96). Across from Peri Pansiyon. Vast, floral campsite and pool snuggled among phallic rocks. $4.50 per site, $3 per person, $8 per tent, $10 per caravan.

Kaya Camping (☎343 31 00; fax 343 39 84). Walk 5-10 min. uphill from the museum. A superb vista of the opposite valley. Kitchen, pool, and private showers. The environmentally aware will appreciate its solar power. $3 per person, $1.50 per tent.

FOOD AND ENTERTAINMENT

Local Restaurant On the right as you turn onto the road heading to the Open-Air Museum. A recent addition to Göreme's dinning choices, the Turkish crafts and wooden furniture give Local a touch of tradition, and the house specialties are Turkish dishes unique among Göreme's restaurants. Like most tourist establishments in town, Local stays open as long as it has guests.

Fat Boys Bar. The newest bar in town. Its good music, central location in the town's promenade, and cheap happy hour (2 big local beers for $1) have made it an instant success. Backpackers (especially Aussies) often keep Fat Boys fun into the wee hours.

Pacha Bar (☎271 23 40). Well-situated in the middle of Göreme's central promenade and marked by celestial murals, Pacha is often the busiest bar in town. Back to back *Simpsons, Southpark* and *Friends* episodes play every day from 6-8pm and English language films also play in the earlier afternoons. Enjoy beer ($1) or mixed drinks ($3) at the bar or on cushioned benches. Open until business ends.

Sedef Restaurant (☎271 23 56). On the left as you head out of Goreme on Bilal Eroglu Cad. The front porch of the Sedef restaurant is a comfortable place to enjoy some of the best traditional food in town. The bulging stuffed eggplant is sure to please ($1.50), and the local *sez* player and drummer who frequent Sedef during the summer months make meals all the more enjoyable.

Wendy's Wine House (☎271 26 60). Across the canal from Sedef Restaurant, downhill from the otogar. Come in, sit down, and stay a while. Without spending a lot, you can hear some great live folk music, relax with a hookah, and drink some tasty local and import wines. Waterpipe $4; beer $1; a glass of local wine about $3.

Flinstones Bar (☎271 22 48). A revamped cave at the turnoff for the Open-Air Museum. "*Raki* is the answer; I don't remember the question." Fans of Britpop will delight in the DJ's discerning taste. Beer $2. Open until the party ends, around 3am.

Orient Restaurant (☎/fax 271 23 46). A local favorite opposite Yüksel Motel and Cafe Doci@. Charming furniture complements wood floors and cave atmosphere of this restaurant and bar. The sizzling *sac tava* is a must-try house specialty ($4). Entrees and vegetarian dishes $3-4. 5-course daily special $5. Open 7:30am until crowds leave, usually 1am.

Cafe Doci@ (☎271 29 03; www.indigoturizm.com.tr/cafedoci@). To the left as you exit the otogar on the road toward Nevşehir. Mammoth burgers ($3), good beer ($3-5), and good times make this a young backpacker's hotspot. Blaring Ameri/Euro pop draws nightly crowds. A big-screen TV shows American channels and movies during the day. Internet $2 per hr. Opens 8am for breakfast and closes when the partying ends, usually around 2 or 3am.

SIGHTS

GÖREME OPEN-AIR MUSEUM

From Göreme village, follow Open-Air Museum Way about 2km east, walking uphill. Open year-round 8am-5pm. $5.25. Dark Church $10.

With seven Byzantine churches, a convent, and a kitchen/refectory, the Open-Air Museum is a delight to history, art, and religion buffs. In the 4th century, St. Basil founded one of the first Christian monasteries here, setting down religious tenets that influenced the teachings of St. Benedict and, subsequently, the entire Western monastic tradition. Monasticism ended in the 15th century under Turkish rule. From then until the 1923 Population Exchange, the Greeks and Turks used the old churches to store apples, potatoes, and hay. Today, the remains offer tourists an array of Cappadocia's most spectacular frescoes. On weekends, the museum bustles with tourists.

BASIL CHURCH. The empty tufa ditches underfoot were once graves in this early Christian monastery. Though only saints could be buried inside monasteries, the wealthy could buy monastic burials and thus (supposedly) pave their way to paradise. If you use a flashlight and magnifying glass, the artist's fingerprints are just visible on the church's 10th-century frescoes.

ÇARIKLI KİLİSE (SANDAL CHURCH). Çarıklı Kilise earns its name from the footprints below the church's back wall, supposed molds of Jesus' feet. Unfortunately for local mythology, the church only dates from the 11th century.

YILANLI KİLİSE (DRAGON CHURCH). To the right of the entrance, note the area's best-preserved fresco, depicting St. George slaying the dragon. This building is also known as St. Onuphrius Church after its fresco of the hermaphroditic-looking figure of St. Onuphrius. One popular legend claims that the Egyptian girl Onophirios was so beautiful that she could not drive away all the men seeking to ravish her. She prayed for assistance and was granted a long white beard and moustache, which solved all her problems. Another tale tells of St. Onuphrius, who belonged to a 4th-century commune of Egyptian hermits. When a certain St. Paphnutius visited the commune, he was impressed by the moral fervor and self-control of Onuphrius, who is therefore depicted with a beard to represent wisdom. The seemingly full breasts show the artist's technique for depicting strong soldiers; similar "breasts" can be found on many fresco figures, including Jesus.

KARANLIK KILISE (DARK CHURCH). Light filters through a tiny window in the narthex, preserving a set of breathtaking frescoes. By far the most impressive artwork in the museum, its walls depict a number of scenes of Jesus, including His birth, entrance to Bethlehem, Transfiguration, Crucifixion and Resurrection. The dome also houses a rare fresco of a teenage Jesus. Watch your head walking in.

OTHER SIGHTS

NEARBY CHURCHES. A ticket to the Open-Air Museum will also admit you to a number of nearby churches. The first, **Tokalı,** is right outside the museum's entrance and contains three smaller churches and a chapel. Behind the Tokalı Church, about 250m from the entrance, are the **Church of Mother Mary** and the 10th-century **Church of St. Eustathios.** Aynalı is across from Kaya Camping, 600m uphill from the museum entrance. To reach **Saklı** and **El Nazar,** hike 500m uphill to the right from the museum's entrance. Unless you really have a fresco fetish and don't mind asking around for a key, these last churches may not be worth the hike.

KARŞIBUCAK YUSUF KOÇ KİLİSESİ. If you're up for a half-hour's diversion while in Göreme, the Karşıbucak Yusuf Koç Kilisesi is a pleasant visit. Enjoy reasonably well-preserved frescoes as well as a terrific view of Göreme and the surrounding area. *(Keeping the canal on the left from the bus station, take a right on the road just beyond Ottoman House. The second left off this road leads up a hill and left to the church. Free.)*

HIKING

Cappadocia's breathtaking landscape is a hiker's seventh heaven. It's best to start early, as the midday sun can be brutal. Though most of the hikes are moderate, safe, and accessible, *Let's Go* recommends hiking with partners, tour groups, or guides in order to hit all sights, stay safe, and navigate trickier areas. Women traveling alone should especially consider these options, as long, empty trails may cause unease and detract from the hike. Wear hiking boots and long pants to protect your legs from prickly shrubbery.

Some of the best hikes can be found by straying off the road that leads to the Open-Air Museum. About 10 minutes into the walk to the museum, you will see a sign for the **Sword Valley** (see maps from the information center or tour company). This valley is by far the closest, easiest and least-toured valley around Göreme. You will probably have the place to yourself and will be able to explore hundreds of cave ruins scattered around farming plots. Further up the road, **Sunset Point** is about 1km past the museum. Take a left on the dirt road by Kaya Camping, turn left again at the next paved road, and walk for about 3km. The entrance fee ($.60) is a bit criminal, as there are better, free views. But from here, you can descend into the **Kirmizi Vadi (Red Valley),** whose bizarre, multi-colored rock formations make this one of the area's better hikes. The complete Rose Valley hike is 14km long, but there are points of ascent and exit about 3km and 7km into the trek. For the shorter hikes, transportation arrangement (taxi or tour group is your best bet) is necessary, since dolmuş don't pass by. The full hike will bring you to Çavuşin in an hour or two. Take the Avanos-Nevşehir bus or the Avanos-Zelve-Göreme-Ürgüp minibus back to Göreme (every 30min. until 6pm; weekends every hr.). A taxi from Çavuşin to Göreme costs about $5.

PIGEON VALLEY (WHITE VALLEY/BAGLIY). Pigeon Valley can be reached by following the canal west of the otogar. This destination earns its name from the birdhouses carved into its cliffs. According to local folklore, humans and fairies lived together peacefully in the valley until a human and a fairy fell in love. The forbidden romance sparked a war that drove the fairies from the valley forever, transforming them into pigeons. As a gesture of reconciliation, guilt-ridden humans built birdhouses to lure the fairy-pigeons back. The birdhouses also serve a more practical purpose, as the bird droppings are used as fertilizer, particularly for Cappadocia's famous wine and pekmez-making grapes. Pigeon Valley is a confusing hike, as roads become paths, paths become streams, and streams disappear quite frequently. Just be persistent, respect the many gardening patches, and you'll eventually wind up in Üçhisar.

LOVE VALLEY. Located to the north of Göreme, this gorge is affectionately known as "Penis Valley" because of the phallic rock formations that would give even Grade A porn stars a complex. To get there, take a left on the dirt road at the onyx factory on the road to Göreme. Walk about 400m and descend on the right into the valley. You're best off hiking the valley's center, as tufa may crumble underfoot. When in doubt, follow the creek heading northeast and after a couple of hours you'll inevitably end up in Çavuşin. About 1km into the hike, a small ridge divides the valley in two; steer left and the looming penises are hard to miss.

ÜÇHİSAR ☎384

The highest point in Cappadocia, Üçhisar's hidden treasure is its mesmerizing twilight; the "Ancien Village Walking Road" winds in a horseshoe to the town's **kale** (castle), offering visitors a calming panoramic view of the valley and its sunset.

TRANSPORTATION AND PRACTICAL INFORMATION. The Göreme-Nevşehir bus (every 30min., $.70) stops at the road junction less than 1km away from the gigantic fort, which gives the town its name (Üçhisar means "fort on the tip"). No commercial traffic runs through the tiny town center, where you can find the **Üçhisar Eczane** (pharmacy; ☎219 25 00). To get to the town center, simply walk uphill (to your left if you arrive from Göreme) along the main road at the junction where the Dolmuş lets you off.

ACCOMMODATIONS. Üçhisar's accommodations are generally grouped either in the town square (walk down the Ancien Village Walking Road, turn left onto any side street and turn left again into town) or on the road below the kale on the opposite side from the tourist entrance. With the entrance to the kale directly behind you, head down the road in front of you. **Erciyes Pansiyon** is on the right, about 400 yards up. Enjoy warm, family ambiance under the shade of cherry trees. All 12 rooms come with private bath. Try the homemade *pekmez*. (☎219 20 90. Breakfast included. $8 per person.) At the end of the street downhill from La Maison Du Reve, is **Le Jardin de 1001 Nuits,** with numerous shower-equipped fairy chimney rooms and a *kilim*-ed tree house to relax in. (☎219 22 93; fax 219 25 05. Breakfast included. Dorms $6; singles $11; with a nice view $15.) **La Terraces De Üçhisar** is the first of many pensions on the cobblestone road behind and below the *kale* and is a great value with very comfortable, well-furnished, clean rooms. A beautiful old house rebuilt by the French owners into a rather large pension, La Terraces offers live folk music, cave rooms, arched rooms, and regular rooms. (Singles $19; doubles $20.) A little further down the hill is **La Maison Du Reve,** a pension with some of the best views in Cappadocia. There are several terraces, due to the fact that the pension is built into the steep side of the mountain of Üçhisar. ($10 per person. Breakfast included.)

FOOD AND ENTERTAINMENT. At the **Oase Cafe & Bar,** below the *kale*'s valley facade, nightfall is a spectator event. Outdoor tables and a charming mix of Turkish and Texas-style decor makes this the perfect spot to sip a beer under the sinking sun. (☎219 27 60; oase_cafe_bar@email.com. Beer and *rakı* $1.60.) Under a sprawling canopy of trees in the town center, the **Centre Café and Restaurant** (☎219 21 11) is one of the only places in Central Anatolia where you'll find hot dogs on the menu ($1) in addition to your standard Turkish meat meals ($2-4). The **Duyurgan Winery,** on the same road, produces some of Cappadocia's best wines. Enjoy free wine tasting and a tour of the winery. (☎219 29 79. Open 8am-8:30pm.)

SIGHTS. The Üçhisar **kale,** used as a castle until the 14th century, is now Üçhisar's only commercial tourist attraction. Looming high above Cappadocia, it makes for a great climb. (Open 9am-7:30pm, $1.) Üçhisar is also the starting point of a number of good hikes, including Love Valley (see **Hiking,** p. 322). Head toward Göreme and turn left on the dirt road at the onyx factory. Walk about 400m and descend on the right into Love Valley—you'll be in Çavuşin in a couple of hours.

UNDERGROUND CITIES: KAYMAKLI AND DERİNKUYU

By dolmuş, Kaymaklı and Derinkuyu are about 30min. and 45min. from Göreme, respectively, with a connection in Nevşehir. From Göreme, dolmuş run to Nevşehir (every 30min. 6:30am-7pm, $.50) and then go to Kaymaklı ($.60) and Derinkuyu ($.80). Both sites open daily 8am-5pm. Each site $3.75.

Although Cappadocia encompasses almost 30 **underground cities** carved from *tufa*, Kaymaklı and Derinkuyu are the largest. The earliest written mention of Hellenic communities in Derinkuyu and Kaymaklı appears in Xenophon's *Anabasis*, which dates them to at least the 4th century BC. Some think the cities began as cave dwellings that were later used by the Hittites for storage and ambushes. Between the 5th and 10th centuries, the Byzantines expanded them into full-fledged cities that shielded people from Iconoclast and Sassanid raids (see **Christianity and the Byzantine Empire** p. 8).

These underground complexes were designed with mind-boggling ingenuity. Low and narrow passages, easily blocked off by massive millstones, hindered prospective invaders. Wineries consisted of a tub-like area for grape-stomping and a chute that carried the juice into another tub for fermenting. The holes drilled in some pillars suggest that the underground inhabitants enforced strict discipline by chaining and torturing transgressors. It was forbidden for anyone to leave while the cities were occupied, lest their departure give away the hideouts. Strangely enough, no evidence of a permanent settlement has been conclusively found in either Derinkuyu or Kaymaklı.

Derinkuyu, 45m deep with a 55m well, is slightly more impressive than Kaymaklı. With eight levels open to the public, Derinkuyu has sizeable rooms and halls, good lighting, and relatively easy access. Kaymaklı, smaller than Derinkuyu at 35m below ground, boasts a more complex structure. The village has been built around the underground city, so residents could enter storage areas through tunnels in their courtyards. It was common for underground cities to use tunnels for intercity water transport. Rumor has it that a similar Cappadocian tunnel, used for escape rather than carrying water, runs the 9km between Kaymakli and Derinkuyu. In both sites, red arrows lead down, blue arrows up. Although all explorable areas are lit, a flashlight may come in handy, especially because the generator that lights the caves fails every once in a while and can leave the caves pitch-black for minutes at a time. Also, be sure not to miss the **Hard Rock Cafe** on the second story of Kaymakli where a happy old chap will serve you drinks or a water pipe in one of the nicely *kilim*-ed cave alcoves.

ÇAVUŞİN-ZELVE ☎384

The provincial village of Çavuşin may lack Göreme's glory, but it teems with traditional flavor. About 2km down the road from Göreme (heading toward Zelve), this inviting town offers road-weary travelers a glimpse of village life. Tourists in Çavuşin may stumble upon a local wedding, be invited to eat *manti* (Turkish ravioli) in a villager's home, or simply enjoy close proximity to the area's best hikes. Çavuşin's old village originally consisted of Greek dwellings hewn into the surrounding cliffs, made uninhabitable by erosion and earthquakes. These deserted buildings and tufa houses, around which the new village is clustered, make for rewarding exploring. The worn cliffs and caves provide extraordinary valley views. Both the Ürgüp-Avanos minibus and the Göreme-Avanos bus pass through Çavuşin.

While better as a daytrip from Göreme or Ürgüp, Çavuşin does have a number of good pensions. The newly-renovated **Turbel Motel** offers sizeable rooms with nifty log-beam ceilings and one of the most splendid panoramas of the area: a sprawling green valley to one side and the haunting old village to the other. Accommodating francophone owner, Mustafa Kaygisiz, organizes camping trips in the Taurus Mountains. (☎532 70 84; fax 532 70 83. Dinner $5. Breakfast included. Singles $10; doubles $18.) The **Green Motel,** up from the main road and just past the town square, has pricey rooms with bath and a sitting room with Ottoman decor. (☎532 72 28. Singles $20; doubles $30.) A campsite is also available for $5 per tent. For more affordable digs, the nearby **Panorama Pansiyon** (☎532 70 02) offers comfortable rooms with shared bath for $6.50. Dinner at the adjacent restaurant is $4.

The under-visited 5th-century **Church of St. John the Baptist,** the oldest known church in Cappadocia, can be reached by following the town's main road past the old village and climbing either the hill or the tufa and rocks. The sweaty climb is worth the view, even though the frescoes are barely visible. The 10th-century **Çavuşin Church,** on the main road beside the turnoff to the village (look for the steps leading up to the rock face), has some well-preserved frescoes. (Open daily 8am-5pm. $2.)

The **Zelve Open-Air Museum,** consisting of churches and homes carved into three deep valleys, will appeal more to the adventurer than to the art historian. There are very few surviving frescoes, but the complex of tunnels and caves provides hours of gleeful (if tricky) climbing, burrowing, and exploring. The dull way to reach the museum is to take the Ürgüp-Avanos minibus one stop from Çavuşin. With a extra hour or two, you can follow the main road past Çavuşin, take a right up the dirt road behind the pottery shop, and continue to climb for a magnificent ridge walk (beware the heights). (Open daily 8am-5:30pm. $4.) Alternatively, descend into **Paşabağ Valley** (**Monk's Valley,** marked by the street-side shopping 1½km west of Zelve Museum), which is punctuated by mushroom-shaped rock formations and unique three-headed chimneys.

ÜRGÜP ☎384

Ürgüp is characterized by a conglomeration of rock formations, early Christian dwellings, and old Greek mansions. Tourists will appreciate the town's organized information network, central otogar, and proximity to noteworthy villages and points of interest. With fewer pensions and neo-hippies than Göreme, Ürgüp appeals to independent travelers who tirelessly flee the commotion of tourism.

TRANSPORTATION

Buses: English-speaking **Aydın Altan** of **Nevtur** (☎341 43 02) will answer bus-related questions. To: **Adana** (5hr., 3 per day 8am-3pm, $8); **Alanya** (14hr., 4 per day 6-10pm, $18); **Ankara** (5hr., 5 per day 7am-5:30pm, $8); **Antalya** (11hr., 3 per day 6-8pm, $15); **Bodrum** (14hr., 7pm, $19); **Eskişehir** (8hr., 7pm, $11); **Fethiye** (15hr., 3 per day 6-8pm, $19); **İstanbul** (12hr., 4 per day 6-8pm, $16); **İzmir** (12hr., 6:30pm, $16); **Konya** (4hr., 6 per day 8am-7pm, $6); **Kuşadası** (13hr.; 6:30, 7:30pm; $18); **Marmaris** (15hr., 7pm, $19); **Mersin** (5hr., 3 per day 8am-3pm, $8); **Pamukkale** (10hr., 7pm, $15); **Side** (13hr.; 7, 8pm; $15); **Selçuk** (13hr., 6:30pm, $18).

Rental Agencies: Several are near the otogar. Bikes $5-10 per day; mopeds $15-20 per day; cars from $30 per day. Roads are reasonably tame and organized in this area, though only skilled stick-handlers will be able to conquer the hills without stalling. Alternatively, horses ($10 per day) and donkeys ($8 per day), available in the alley behind Europcar, do come with automatic transmission at no extra charge (☎341 38 90).

ORIENTATION AND PRACTICAL INFORMATION

The main square, marked by a hamam and an Atatürk statue, is 20m up **Güllüce Cad.** from the otogar. This road forks uphill into two smaller roads, both near accommodations. Intersecting **Güllüce Cad.** in the main square is **Kayseri Cad.**

Tourist Office: (☎341 40 59). Inside the garden on Kayseri Cad. Follow the signs all over the city. Grab maps and brochures, or drop your bags while you explore. Run by English- and German-speaking Zeki Güzel. Open daily Apr.-Oct. 8am-7pm; Nov.-Mar. 8am-5pm. Alternatively, fork left at the hamam and walk up to the **Turkish Airlines Office,** which doubles as a classier tourist office. Arrange plane tickets, get info, or simply cool off in the stone building that was once Ürgüp's prison. Open daily 8am-5pm.

Tours: The reliable and affordable **Erko Tours** (☎341 32 52; fax 341 37 85; www.erkotours.com.tr), in the otogar, gladly organizes tours of Cappadocia. Upscale and professional **Argeus Tours** (☎341 46 88; www.argeus.com.tr) also operates out of the Turkish Airlines Office. $70 for all-inclusive day tours.

Hamam: Tarihi Şehir Hamamı (☎341 22 41), at the fork in the main square. Co-ed, so bring a friend to this steamy one-room complex. Complete bath with massage (male masseur), *kese* (exfoliating scrub), and sauna. $8 per person. Open daily 7am-11pm.

Pharmacies: There are several near the otogar; walk toward the hamam and **Eczane Ürgüp** (☎341 44 52) is on the left, sandwiched between carpet shops.

Medical Assistance: Call the **hospital** (☎341 40 31), off Kayseri Cad. just behind Tourist Information. The **Cappadocia Health Center,** 28 Dumlupınar Cad. (☎341 54 27 or 341 54 28; fax 341 34 92), offers more private, out-patient clinical care.

Internet Access: Asia Teras (see **Food,** below).

PTT: (☎341 80 12). Turn right out of the tourist office and take the first right uphill. Open daily 8:30am-7pm; in winter 8am-5pm. Offers telephone services, stamps, fax, telegraph, and a **currency exchange** that's closed noon-1:30pm.

Postal Code: 50400.

ACCOMMODATIONS

Ürgüp's hotels and pensions display a range of prices and quality. In general, the standard pensions here cost a little more than in Göreme, where fierce competition has kept prices very budget-friendly.

Hotel Kemer, (☎341 21 68; fax 341 85 16; hotelkemer@hotmail.com), across the street from Hotel Elvan, offers clean, basic rooms with shower and towels. The closest pension to the center of town. $9 per person.

Hotel Surban (☎341 47 61 or 341 46 03; fax 341 32 23). Fork right at the hamam and trudge up the steep hill. Spacious, *kilim*-ed lounge and bar, parking space, cave restaurant, and ping-pong table make Surban ideal for groups, and lots of fun. Rooms with private bath and towels. Singles $15; doubles $25; triples $30.

Hotel Elvan, İstiklâl Cad., 11 Barbaros Hayrettin Sok. (☎341 41 91; fax 341 34 55), downhill from Hotel Akuzun, to the left off the hamam. Maternal Fatma Hanım will boil medicinal teas for her Western guests' weak stomachs. Tidy rooms with private baths. Singles $14; doubles $25; triples $30. MC/V.

Hotel Asia Minor (☎341 46 45; fax 341 27 21; cappadocia50@hotmail.com; http://welcome.to/mevlutshouse.com), 50m up the street from Kemer Hotel. A beautiful 150-year-old Greek mansion with an attractive breakfast garden, and frescoes adorning lobby walls. Breakfast included. All rooms $25-$40.

Elkep Evi (☎341 60 00; elkepevi@superonline.com; www.elkepevi.com). Up the road from Hotel Born, past the Turasan Winery, there are several small and very luxurious cave pensions called ***evis*** (houses). Elkep Evi is the cheapest of these, offering beautifully furnished cave rooms, appropriate for 2 or 3 guests each, with immaculate, white down comforters and comfortable western-style baths. $50 per room.

Türkerler Otel, Camping and Swimming Pool (☎341 33 54). Fork right at the mosque, climb up the hill and steer left at the next fork. Pitch a tent for a couple of bucks on the environs of this tiny pension. Call ahead to check if the swimming pool is in fact filled, and cut a price with the laid-back owners (Turkish business at its best). If camping's lost its novelty, patrons can check into the on-grounds hotel or pension.

Hotel Born. On the way up the hill to Hotel Suburban, Hotel Born is Urgüp's cheapest pension. While the price is certainly right, the old hotel is decidedly lacking in cleanliness and amenities. $3-4 per person.

FOOD

Han Çırağan (☎341 25 66), across the street and to the right of the Atatürk statue. Heavy with Turkish spirit, this restaurant is in a 300-year-old *kervansaray* whose rooms are still used by merchants in horse-drawn carriages. Try the filling Han Çırağan special of *döner* with cheese, mushroom, carrots, and peppers ($4).

Şömine Cafe (☎341 84 42; fax 341 84 43), in the center of the town square, on the second level across the Atatürk statue. With a multilingual menu and professional service, Şömine caters largely to the tourist scene. Try the house specialty, *testi kebap,* a dish of lamb, tomatoes, onions, and garlic roasted in a clay pot. After 6 hours, the pot is broken to reveal a delicious meal for two ($8). Other entrees $2-4.

Asia Teras (☎341 38 39; asiateras@hotmail.com), 20m to the left when exiting the tourist office. Billiards ($2 per hr.) and Internet access ($2.50 per hr.), along with mediocre American food (burgers $1-1.50). Beer $1; *rakı* $2. Open daily 10am-midnight.

Mikro Restaurant (☎341 20 68; fax 341 32 39). A local favorite, serving unbeatable Turkish food, with main courses running about $4. Lucky patrons will catch *mantı* night, when the home-cooked Turkish ravioli leaves everybody smiling.

ENTERTAINMENT

Cappadocia is one of Turkey's largest wine-producing regions, with Ürgüp as its capital. Uphill from Hotel Surban, the renowned **Turasan Winery** supplies 60% of Cappadocia's wines and offers free tours and tastings in its rock-carved wine cellar. Buy cheap wine here (most bottles $2.50-4) or splurge on the more robust '89 vintage for $7.50 or the extra-special '97 Kalecik Karası for $15. (Open 8am-8pm. Tours available until 5pm.) Other shops around the main square offer free tastings. In late September, the Ürgüp **wine festival** brings competitors from France, Italy, Argentina, and the US. If you're still energized after a day of boozing and trooping through Ürgüp's narrow cobblestone streets, put on your dancing shoes.

Kaya Bar (☎235 13 57), Ürgüp's most relaxed bar. Overlooks the town square from the second floor of the large Sukurogullari pastry shop. With either live local music or chill Turkish and American tunes, in addition to an upstairs room with *kilims,* couches, a terrace and a circulating water pipe, folks come to Kaya to hang out and chat. Big with backpackers and some younger locals. Beer $1.50, *rakı* $2.

Prokopi Pub Bar (☎341 64 98), next to Han Çırağan restaurant. Popular with tourists and wealthier locals, this ultra-hip bar plays electronica, dance beats, and American and Brit pop. Dance floor for the inspired or intoxicated. Beer $2.50; *rakı* $3; mixed drinks $4-6. Open until the party dies, usually around 3am.

Bar Barium (☎341 41 98), in the same building as Han Çırağan restaurant. Don't let the strange selection of band posters fool you, this red-lit cave bar plays a solid mix of Turkish and American tunes. Just as happening' as Prokopi but less taxing on your wallet. Beer $1.50; mixed drinks and *rakı* $2.

DAYTRIP FROM ÜRGÜP: SOĞANLI

Getting to the valley on your own isn't easy: a taxi may cost up to $50 and tour companies, which are only marginally cheaper, don't spend much time here. Public transportation only goes to Mustafapaşa. The cheapest way to visit Soğanlı is to rent a scooter ($20, an additional $2.50 for gas) in Ürgüp and brave the Turkish roads armed with nothing but a crash helmet. Valley open daily 8:30am-5:30pm. $1.

About 40km south of Ürgüp, the **Soğanlı Valley** is one of the few places in Cappadocia where beauty remains untarnished by tourism. Thanks to its remote location, you can probably have the place to yourself.

About 150 stone churches sit in the valley, although most have been filled in, destroyed, or converted into birdhouses. The five major churches, all dating from the pre-Ottoman era, are decorated with aged and desecrated frescoes which have not been granted Göreme-style renovations. The **Geyikli Kilise** (Church of the Deer) is at the intersection of the valley's branches. Heading right leads to the **Karabaş Kilise** (Dark Church), notable for the darkened halos that hover over the saints. Down the road is the **Yılanı Kilise** (Snake Church) which has a fresco depicting St. George slaying the dragon. Above the stream, **Kubbeli Kilise** (Domed Church), the largest and most impressive church in the valley, is distinguished by the only rock-carved dome in Cappadocia. The **Tahtalı Kilise** (Wooden Church), at the end of the left valley road, is accessible by a narrow set of stone steps; inside one can just make out a fresco of Christ's descent into hell. Taking either of the two paths through the valley allows you to make a complete circuit in an hour.

Pleasant stops between Ürgüp and Soğanlı include **Damsa Dam,** 5km beyond Mustafapaşa, the only beach environment you're likely to find in Central Anatolia ($.25 per person, $.60 per car). Further down the road, near Cemil, the **Keşlik Monastery** contains a blackened church, a refectory, and a monastery ($.60).

MUSTAFAPAŞA ☎384

With fascinating moonscape valleys, old Greek houses, and Orthodox churches, Mustafapaşa appeals most to hikers and architecture enthusiasts. Formerly known as Sinassos, this friendly village was home to Greeks and Turks alike until the population exchange of 1923. Currently, 96 old Greek houses are under protection by local government and not open to tourists. However, visitors will still be fascinated by the unique mix of Greek and Selçuk architecture; poke around the village and you're likely to get some guidance in seeking out preserved frescoes.

TRANSPORTATION AND PRACTICAL INFORMATION. **Dolmuş** make the 5km run from Ürgüp's otogar to Mustafapaşa (9 per day; M-F 8:15am-6:15pm, return 7:45am-5:45pm; $.65 each way). Dolmuş stop in Mustafapaşa's square, where a shop labeled "Information" sells postcards and trinkets while doubling as the **tourist office.** (Open daily June-Aug. 8:30am-7pm; closed in winter.) On the wall to the left of the door, an imaginatively scaled diagram (be sure to read the labeled distances) indicates the location of the closest sites. Alternatively, walk uphill from the town square and turn left to reach the small, outdoor wooden cabin for **Tourist Information** and keys to the locked churches (see **Sights,** below). In **medical emergencies,** call the Sağlık Ocağı clinic in nearby Ürgüp (☎343 33 64). Around the corner from the tourist office, take the path to the left for the **PTT.** (Open M-F 8am-12:30pm and 1:30-5:30pm; Sa 8am-12:30pm.) **Postal code:** 5042

ACCOMMODATIONS. **Hotel Pacha,** a former Greek mansion, has a beautiful terrace restaurant, with *kilims*, a fireplace, couches, and a bar. The family-run hotel serves a superb home-cooked, five-course dinner for $5.50. (☎358 50 04; fax 353 53 31; pachahotel@hotmail.com; www.hotelpacha.com. 11 rooms. Breakfast included. $10 per person.) **Monastery Pension** downhill and to the left from the dolmuş stop, was once a Greek monastery. The cave bar, complete with disco ball, supplies the only nightlife in Mustafapaşa. (☎353 50 05; fax 353 53 44; monasterypension@yahoo.com. Breakfast included. 13 rooms. $6 per person.) Restful, accommodating **Hotel Cavit** offers 10 clean rooms and a vine-covered terrace for fabulous Turkish breakfasts. (☎353 51 86. Breakfast included. $9.70 per person.) The massive **Hotel Sinassos** provides opulence at an affordable price. A breathtaking restaurant, disco ball, and swanky reception area spell luxury. Large, comfortable rooms with private bath. (☎353 54 34 or 353 51 26. $15 per person.) **Paşa Camping,** next door to Aios Vasilyos church, boasts bathrooms, shower facilities, and a makeshift disco. (☎353 50 18. $1 per person, $1 per tent, $6 per caravan.)

SIGHTS. In addition to the various tours that stop here, Ozgur at **Hotel Pacha** leads hikes around Mustafapaşa's beautiful valleys. The town's most stunning sight is the **Gömede Valley,** whose entrance is a mostly uphill 2km hike from the center of town. Few pains have been taken to make it accessible to hikers; after climbing the cobblestone road from town, turn right onto the dirt path and walk to a paved road. Follow the steep downhill trail (by the water dispenser) to the bottom and up again, then turn right on a dirt path. The valley hike is a moderately difficult 7km trek past pigeon houses and abandoned cave dwellings. On the way, you may see the 1200-year-old **Kara Ala Kilise** (Black and White Church), named for the striking contrast of its frescoes. You can also explore the more spacious **Tavşanlı Kilise** and the recently discovered **Kimistavros Kilise,** whose ceilings are carved with 1100-year-old crosses. (**Gömede Valley** open daily 8am-6:30pm; in winter 8am-5pm. $1.50.) If the valley hike hasn't tired you out, the mountainside cave dwellings of **Golgoli** make another great hiking or driving destination for skilled or 4x4 drivers only. For Golgoli, follow the dirt road that begins at the end of town beyond Monastery Pension; the hike takes approximately 2hr.

Access to Mustafapaşa's two most famous churches requires a key from Tourist Information and a preposterous fee of $7.30. Northwest of the old fountain in the square, a gravel road leads downhill 1km past the Paşa Restaurant to the 7th-century Byzantine **Aios Vasilyos Church.** The visible portion of Aios Vasilyos is an uninspiring stone cubicle the size of a closet, but two flights of stone stairs lead down to a magnificent subterranean church. Because it's carved into the side of the valley, windows let in enough daylight to illuminate some of the frescoes. One such window, the only one accessible from the ground, served as a sentry post: the church could be sealed off by rolling an enormous boulder in front of it. Closer to town, 50m downhill from the town square, the exterior of **Aios Costantinos-Heleni Church** is more impressive than its barren inside.

Much closer to the center of town is **Monastery Valley,** featuring the **Aios Stephanos Kilise, Aios Nikalaos Kilise,** and the **Sinasos Kilise.** The hike itself is just a few kilometers, though without arranged transportation you'll probably have to hike out and back to the entrance. For a taste of regional flavor, try the **Şarap Farbrikası** winery, where you can take a free tour and sample local wines.

AVANOS ☎384

The banks of the nearby wine-colored Kızılırmak, Turkey's longest river, have been providing the potters of Avanos with red, iron-rich clay for centuries. Roughly 100 workshops crowd the area, especially in the cobblestoned Old Town. With workshop signs emblazoned with names like "Chez İsmail," "Chez Barış," "Chez Celebi," and, alarmingly, "Chez Rambo," the town clearly caters to its many foreign visitors. Watch the potters at work or try your own hand at the giant, foot-powered wheels. If clay is your thing, Avanos is close to Cappadocia's major tourist centers as a daytrip, and vibrant and distinct enough for an extended visit.

TRANSPORTATION AND PRACTICAL INFORMATION. To get to Avanos, take the Ürgüp-Göreme-Çavuşin-Zelve-Avanos **dolmuş** (departs Ürgüp M-F every 2hr. 9am-5pm, $.80) or the Göreme-Belediye **buses** (M-F, every 30min. 8am-7pm, $.30). Both stop at the otogar. For more transportation information, see **Cappadocia: Transportation,** p. 315. The **tourist office** is across the river from the otogar. Take a right after crossing the bridge into town and walk 100m. (☎511 43 60. Open M-F 8am-noon and 1:30-5:30pm; closes at 5pm in winter.) Just after the bridge, an uphill stone path on the left leads to the well-marked Old Town, where most of the ceramics studios and a few of the pensions and cafes can be found. The town square, past the tourist office, is marked by several statues (the town's Atatürk monument is on a nearby corner). **Kirkit Voyages** (☎511 32 59, 511 54 40, or 511 45 42; fax 511 21 35; www.kirkirt.com), across from the tourist office, specializes in guided horse tours (2hr. tour $8; half-day tour $24; 10-day camping trips) and rents mountain bikes ($20 per day). The **Alaaddin Hamam** (☎511 50 38), a block to the left after you cross the bridge, is one of Cappadocia's better-equipped bath houses, with a cold, marble "shock pool" for a pre-steam dip. (Open daily 8am-2am; $8.) The **PTT** is just past the square. (Open daily 8am-5:30pm.) **Postal code:** 50500.

ACCOMMODATIONS AND FOOD. On the road from the bridge to the town center, you will see signs on the left for **Vanessa Pansiyon,** where Mukremin, the super-friendly and energetic owner, will give you a tour of the underground city that he is excavating below his pension. Above ground, there are small but comfy rooms, and a *kilim*-ed terrace with two telescopes through which you can see all the way to the Uçhisar castle. Mukremin's record collection and "ethnography collection" of old keys, pots, and other artifacts keep guests busy. ((☎511 38 40. $10 per person.) **Kirkit Pension** offers lodgings in a restored Ottoman stone house behind Kirkit Voyages. The friendly, multilingual owner holds BBQs with live Turkish music when there are enough guests. (☎511 31 48 or 511 32 59; fax 511 21 35. $7 per person; $9 per person with shower and breakfast.) On the bank of the Kızılırmak, behind the Ziraat Bankası and next to the mosque, **Mesut Camping and Restaurant** (☎511 35 45) charges $5 per tent.

Atatürk Cad. is full of fine restaurants in both the Old and New Town. The **Sarıkaya** dining experience includes "Turkish banquets," folklore narrations, music, and dancing, all in a massive restaurant carved into a hillside cave. (Fixed menu; $12 per person.) The **Köşk Mantı Evi,** next to Kirkit Voyages, specializes in *mantı* (Turkish ravioli, $3) and showcases traditional Turkish music in a cozy cave atmosphere. Town favorite **Tuvanna Restaurant** (☎511 44 97; fax 511 26 32) serves Italian-style pizza ($2.50) and spaghetti meals ($3-4), along with an assortment of Turkish cuisine. It's also one of the few places you'll find a non-Turkish toilet while wandering the streets of Avanos, so have a seat. Many small, decent *kafeteriya* line the river. After dark, tourists and locals alike duck into the **Kervanhan,** in the Old Town near the square. The DJ plays Turko-pop and belly-dancing music until 4am. (Beer $3; *rakı* $4.) Just up the street is the predominantly Turkish **Labirent,** offering more of the same. (Beer and *rakı* $3. Open until 4am.)

SIGHTS. In the town square, a clay monument commemorates **pottery** and the other crafts that give Avanos its distinctive character. A trip to Avanos is not complete without a visit to **Chez Galip** and its quirky **hair museum,** one block up from the town square. *Let's Go*-wielding shoppers at the pottery studio can get raging discounts on the beautiful handiwork (consult Galip's assistant). Non-consumers can wander to the hair museum, perhaps the strangest sight in Cappadocia. This cavernous hall in the largest and most renowned of Avanos's pottery shops has been set aside for Galip Körükçü's collection of women's hair. The collection, begun in 1979, now numbers over 100,000 locks and has an entry in the *Guinness Book of World Records.* Each lock of hair is pinned to a wall or ceiling, giving the cavern an unsettling organic feel. Every year, ten locks are chosen, and their former owners are given a 2-week long paid vacation in Avanos, which includes pottery making, carpet weaving, and horseback riding. Good luck, Rapunzel. (☎511 42 40; fax 511 45 43; chzgalip@tr-net.net.tr.; www.chez-galip.com. Open daily 8:30am-9:30pm; in winter 8:30am-6pm.)

NİĞDE ☎388

Niğde's dusty streets swarm with university students, strolling arm in arm. Islamic architecture dominates the town's backdrop of restaurants, bookstores, and pastry shops. Niğde comes alive every Thursday on market day, when fruits and vegetables are sold in the shadows of Selçuk mosques. Architecture aside, this simple lifestyle is none too appealing for tourists, most of whom skip the city entirely and head straight to the nearby Eski Gumeşler Monastery.

TRANSPORTATION. Niğde's otogar, on **Emin Erlşeğil Cad.,** provides connections to: **Adana** (3hr., 7 per day 10am-1am, $7); **Aksaray** (1½hr., every hr. 7:30am-7:30pm, $3); **Ankara** (5hr., every hr. 7:30am-7:30pm, $9); **Antalya** (10hr.; 7:30, 9:30pm; $14); **Erzurum** (12hr.; 6, 9:30pm; $16); **İstanbul** (11hr.; 9:30am, 7, 7:30pm; $16); **İzmir** (12hr.; 7, 9pm; $16); **Kayseri** (1½hr., every hr. 8am-11pm, $3); **Konya** (3hr.; 9:30am, 1:30pm; $8); **Mersin** (3hr., frequent 9am-2:30am, $6); **Nevşehir** (1½hr., every hr. 8am-6pm, $2); **Trabzon** (13hr.; 5:30, 9:30pm; $17).

ORIENTATION AND PRACTICAL INFORMATION. Turning right out of the otogar leads to **Bankalar Cad.,** named for its abundance of **banks** and **ATMs.** Take a left to reach **Atatürk Meydanı,** the town's central square, marked by a statue and a government building. From here, head east on **İstasyon Cad.** past banks and shops to the Thursday market. The **tourist information** office is on the third floor of the large building across the street from the Devlet Hastanesi (government hospital). If you have trouble finding it, one of the locals should be able to direct you. The modern **hospital** (☎232 22 20, 232 22 21, 232 22 22, or 232 22 23), two blocks west of the square, offers the services of several Anglophone doctors. **Internet access** is available at the smoky **Cafe Internet Klas-2,** across from the Ak Medrese. (☎213 35 53 or 233 22 62. $1.60 per 2hr.) The **PTT,** about 100m down the road from Atatürk Meydanı offers stamps, telegraph, and fax services. (Open M-F 8:30am-12:30pm and 1:30-5:30pm.) **Postal code:** 51100.

ACCOMMODATIONS AND FOOD. From ritzy to ramshackle, Niğde's accommodations run the entire comfort gamut. Across the town center from the Atatürk statue is the glitzy, 3-star Hotel Evim—many of Niğde's best deals in accommodations are located in the area behind it. Several two-star hotels offer reasonable rates. Try **Otel Şahin,** where silky blue bedspreads soothe tired backs and clean, spacious rooms come with phone and TV. (☎232 09 51; fax 232 09 53. Breakfast included. Singles $10; doubles $20.) **Otel Nahita,** around the corner, has 30 rooms with phones and balconies, plus a disco bar that fills with local students on weekends. (☎232 53 66; singles $8; doubles $12. Bar cover $1.60, includes one drink.) **Hotel Murat,** across from the Alaeddin Camii clock tower, has clean rooms with shower and TV. (Singles $7; doubles $12; rooms without shower or TV $5.)

Niğde doesn't have a remarkable culinary arsenal. **Bor Cad.,** running south of Atatürk Meydanı, is littered with small *lokantas,* dominated by the Sultan "fast-food" chain. Flashy white decor sparkles inside local favorite **Saruhan** (☎232 21 72), where suspiciously slimming mirrors will whet your appetite for their incredible *döner, kebap,* and *pide* ($2-4). To see the Bohemian side of Anatolia, check out the student-frequented cafes and *okey* salons near the end of Bor Cad.

For a university town of 60,000, Niğde's nightlife is lacking. The tragically hip meet at **Cafe Şamdan,** one block down from the old Bor Garaj on the right, which runs an esoteric category of its own: a "Fast Food, Breakfast, and Chips Salon." Live music (from Turkish folk to Western pop) entertains the cafe's college crowd.

SIGHTS. Niğde's most compelling sight is actually 9km from the city. Dolmuş run between Niğde's otogar and Gümüsler (15min., $.40). The **Eski Gümüşler Monastery** is one of Cappadocia's larger and better-preserved *tufa*-carved structures. Discovered in 1963, the monastery was active in the middle Byzantine era and contains some of the best-preserved frescoes dating back to the 10-12th centuries AD. The three apses depict scenes from the life of Jesus, while the main church features a rare mosaic of a smiling Virgin Mary. Crypts and storage pits dot the courtyard like moon craters, while the upper chambers and the caves outside the monastery make for some fun exploring. Open 8am-noon, 1:30-6:30pm. $2.

Back in town, the **Alaeddin Camii,** built by the Selçuks in 1223, sits atop a hill near the clock tower. One local story about the mosque claims that one of the architects, sick with unrequited love, designed the eastern portal so that the morning summer light creates the outline of a girl's crowned head. Trying to see the head is likely to strain your imagination; recuperate at the *çay* garden next door.

While in Niğde, check out the **Süngür Bey Camii,** south of the Alaeddin Camii. The mosque has been modified by so many different rulers over the centuries that it has come to possess elements of several architectural styles. The **Ak Medrese,** a block away, is worth visiting, if you have time. Built in 1409, this Selçuk-style *medrese* earns its name from the white marble inscriptions above the portal (*ak* means "white"). Niğde's **Archaeological and Ethnographic Museum** was closed for renovations at the time of publication, but is expected to reopen by summer 2002.

IHLARA ☎382

The Ihlara Valley, tucked away between rolling green hills, is one of Central Anatolia's most famous hiking sites. As one approaches Ihlara, a massive gorge (100m deep, 200m wide, and 14km long) suddenly heaves into view, cleaving the surrounding sea of green. Peace-loving Christians found this valley an ideal hideout from nomadic raiders, and now 105 churches and countless dwellings remain carved into the canyon walls. The serene village of Ihlara rests at the southern end of the canyon and makes for the best point of entry into this hidden world.

TRANSPORTATION AND PRACTICAL INFORMATION

Package tours from Göreme and Ürgüp run to the valley, and may be the best option for solo travelers. Dedicated pioneers can catch the Ankara bus to **Aksaray** in **Nevşehir** (1hr., every hr. on the hr., $3), and then take a bus to **Ihlara** (1hr.; 11am, 2, 6pm; $.75). Get off near the turnoff for the valley entrance, by the pensions, to avoid walking to the center of town at the bottom of a steep 1km hill. For emergencies, call the **police** (☎451 20 08). The 24-hour **Eczane pharmacy** (☎453 75 41) is in the town square, on the right side of the road to Derinkuyu. The **hospital** (☎453 70 06) serves standard medical needs. The tiny **PTT** is on the ground floor of the *belediye* building at the turnoff for the valley. It offers standard **phone cards,** stamps, and **telegraph services,** but no money exchange. (☎453 71 00. Open 8:30am-12:30pm and 1:30-5:30pm.) **Postal code:** 68570.

ACCOMMODATIONS AND FOOD

Ihlara's pensions line the road that forks left at the valley entrance. Many pensions will take you to the valley entrance or to Selime in the morning. The only food served outside the pensions is at the excellent **Ihlara Restaurant** (lunch $2-4), near the official entrance to the gorge, and at a cluster of second-rate eateries around the square (*pide* and *kebap* $1.50-3).

Akar Motel (☎453 70 18; fax 453 75 11) offers 10 motel rooms and 8 smaller, homier pension rooms with bath and balcony. Both are clean and comfortable. Breakfast included. Dinner $2-4. $6 per person.

Bişginler Ihlara Pansiyon (☎/fax 453 70 77), has spacious rooms with balconies, hot water, and toilet. Free car or tractor excursions to Hasan Dağ with a *saç tava* picnic and Turkish music (arrange in advance). Cozy restaurant-lounge serves *saç tava* at dinner for $2. 12 rooms. Breakfast included. $8 per person; tents $2.50; campers $6.

Pansiyon Anatolia (☎453 74 40; fax 453 74 39), has a campsite and 15 small rooms, some with showers and balconies. A pleasant, if mysterious, floral smell lingers in the halls. Closed in winter. Breakfast $2.50; dinner $2-4. Tent $3, bed $5. MC/V.

Aslan Camping, Restaurant, and Pension (☎457 30 33), marks Ihlara Valley's 3km point, in the town of Belisirma. Pitching a tent in the valley is illegal, so overnight hikers can party around the Aslan bonfire instead. Restaurant patrons camp for free, otherwise $2 per tent (rentals available). The nearby pension (☎457 30 37) with 22 rooms charges $8 per person, breakfast included.

HIKING THE VALLEY

Most travelers visit the valley on a ***guided tour*** *from Göreme or Ürgüp. These tours usually hike 3km of the valley's 14km, starting at the Ihlara entrance and ending in Belisırma, where a restaurant and campsite mark the official exit point. Continuing north, another official entrance/exit point is halfway into the valley, in Yaprakhisar (the* ***Aksaray bus*** *also passes through here). The full 14km hike ends in the town of Selime, through which the last Aksaray bus passes at 5:30pm. To reach the valley's* ***official entrance*** *from the town square, head 1km uphill toward Aksaray (a sign marks "Ihlara Valley 2km") and take the first main intersection to your right. A paid parking lot and Ihlara Restaurant mark the entrance, where 400 stone stairs bring you down the gorge to the frescoed rock churches. You're best off hiking to Belisırma with the river* *on your right, as most of the stone churches will be on your left. To hike the opposite way (south, from Selime to Ihlara), take the Aksaray bus and get off at Selime. Ask the locals to point you to the valley entrance ("vadı girişi"). Depending on your pace and eagerness to explore, the 14km hike takes about 6hr. The flat and well-worn path involves a few scrambles among the boulders north of Belisırma. (Valley open 8am-7pm. $2, students $1.)*

The Ihlara Valley consists of 14km along the north-south Melendiz River, which runs from Selime to Ihlara village. Sixteen of the valley's 105 churches are open to visitors, and most of these are within 1km of the official valley entrance in Ihlara. The first one you are likely to see is **Ağaçaltı Kilise** (Church Under the Trees), at the base of the stairs leading into the valley. Spectacular blue and white angels encircle the Christ figure on the well-preserved dome. Another 30m south past the Ağaçaltı (to the right after descending the entrance stairs, away from Belisırma) lies the **Pürenliseki Church,** whose faded walls enclose the many martyrs of Sivas. The **Kokar Kilise** (Odorous Church), 70m farther along, celebrates biblical stories with colorful frescoes and ornate geometrical ceiling crosses.

Sümbüllü Kilise, 100m down river from Ağaçaltı Kilise, is noteworthy for its rock facade and five deep, arched bays separated by pillars. Cross the bridge opposite the Sümbüllü Kilise, and walk up the stairs 70m downriver to find the **Yılanlı Kilise** (Snake Church), named for a display of Satan's serpents. Having seen Yılanlı Kilise, you're better off back-tracking, crossing the bridge, and making your way to Belisırma with the river on your right. The walk is on the whole more pleasant, and you're liable to find a few more churches. From Belisırma to Selime, walk downstream, keeping the river on your left for the clearest path.

GÜZELYURT ☎382

About 13km east of Ihlara, pristine hikes, unparalleled hospitality, and fresh sights await travelers in the small town of Güzelyurt, situated on the edge of a rolling, green valley. Its friendly family-run pensions and unspoiled charm welcome visitors to life in a true, traditional Turkish "*köy.*" Don't be fooled by the serene surroundings; mysterious underground cities, horseback riding programs, and nearby hikes are sure to keep you busy.

ORIENTATION AND PRACTICAL INFORMATION. Buses to Güzelyurt leave **Aksaray** (5 per day 11am-6:30pm, return 7:30am-5:30pm; $1.10). Dolmuş don't run between Ihlara and Güzelyurt and taxis cost about $6. In the direction opposite Niğde, follow the gaze of Atatürk's left eyeball, and 50m from the town square, you should see **Sibel Eczane,** the town's **pharmacy** (☎451 26 76). It is run by the outgoing and pleasant Sibel, one of the town's only English-speakers. The **PTT,** a beige building on top of a hill, is situated at the outskirts of town, 10min. from the square. Follow the road toward Niğde and take a right just before the sign for Güzelyurt. (Open M-F 8:30am-12:30pm and 1:30-5:30pm.) **Postal code:** 68500.

ACCOMMODATIONS. There are few places to stay in Güzelyurt. **Otel Karballa,** behind the bust of Atatürk, is housed in a beautiful 19th-century monastery built by the local Greek population, who were evicted in the 1923 population exchange (see **The Cult of Mustafa Kemal,** p. 15). Linked with the French sporting club UCPA, Karballa offers fantastic equestrian programs, hikes to Ihlara and other valleys, mountain biking excursions, and a swimming pool. Meals are served in the refectory once used by the monks. (☎451 21 03 or 451 21 04; fax 451 21 07; karballa@hotmail.com; www.kirkit.com. Activities $16 per person. Dinner $10. Breakfast included. Singles $22; doubles $34.) Cozy **Günalp Pansiyon,** past the road to the monasteries, offers 5 rooms, breakfast, and genuine Turkish hospitality. (☎451 20 76. $8 per person.) **Nalbantoğlu Pansiyon,** which you can find through the town's grocer of the same name, overlooks Güzelyurt's ranch, lake and enchanting sunset. (☎451 21 69. 3 rooms. $8 per person.) **Halil Pension** (☎451 27 07) is a small family pension that offers bed, breakfast, and dinner for $12. To get to Halil, walk 300m down the road to the pharmacy and take a left on Kayabası Sok. The pension is behind a white gate 200m down the road on your left.

SIGHTS. Exploring Güzelyurt's unspoiled sights makes for a regular Tom-and-Huck adventure. Walking down the town square with the Atatürk bust on your left, a sharp right downhill points toward the monasteries. Off this road, signs mark two **underground cities** that don't charge admission and are much smaller than the great cities of Kaymaklı and Derinkuyu. A series of light bulbs lines the narrow tunnels and chambers, where exploration is very do-it-yourself, so bring a flashlight. A third underground city in the center of town is kept locked for safety reasons, ask a blue uniformed police officer for assistance. Monastery Valley and a courtyard with the Camii and Sivişli Churches are down the hill from the underground cities. The paradoxically named **Camii Kilise** (Mosque Church) was originally built in 385 as the Church of St. Gregory of Nationtus. It sported many beautiful frescoes, all of which were whitewashed or stolen when the church was converted into a mosque in 1923. The mosque is seldom used for worship, but villagers are still resistant to the proposal of restoring the frescoes and converting the mosque into a museum. Call out if the door is locked, and someone will arrive to open it. (Open daily 10:15am-8:30pm. $2.) Across from the Camii Kilise and up a very steep set of stone steps is the **Sivişli Kilise** (St. Anargiros Church), formerly a pilgrimage site, with a dome and four columns all carved out of rock. For a fantastic view of the village and valley, climb the stairs to the left of the church.

Monastery Valley itself is a splendid little hike that runs about 4½km and features over 50 churches and monasteries carved out of stone. Follow the steep path to enter the valley; if you hike to the end (about 1hr.), you'll emerge next to the old Greek village of **Siurihisar,** at which point you're best off hiking back in order to avoid a ludicrous cab fare. (Valley open daily 8am-7pm.)

AKSARAY ☎382

Aksaray has seen Assyrians, Hittites, Persians, and Alexander the Great, all of whom wisely moved on once their business was done. In 1470, the Ottomans forcibly transplanted many of the city's residents in order to boost the Muslim population of İstanbul; most travelers will wonder why all Aksarayans didn't jump at the opportunity to leave. A few Selçuk and Karamanoğlu sites aside, noisy and large Aksaray has nothing to offer the traveler but a bus station with connections throughout Cappadocia and the rest of Turkey.

TRANSPORTATION. To get to the main square from the otogar, turn left out of the building, make the first left, and walk 5min. **Buses** run to: **Alanya** (12hr., 8pm, $11); **Ankara** (3hr., frequent 6am-6:30pm, $5); **Antalya** (11hr., 8pm, $10); **Güzelyurt** (1hr., 5 per day 11am-6:30pm, $1); **Ihlara** (1hr., 3 per day 11am-6pm, $.60); **İstanbul** (9hr., frequent 8-10pm, $10); **İzmir** (11hr., 7:30pm, $11); **Kayseri** (2½hr., frequent 5:30am-7pm, $4.25); **Konya** (2hr., frequent 6am-6:15pm, $4.25); **Nevşehir** (1hr., every hr., $2); **Niğde** (1½hr., 6 per day 8am-5pm, $1.50). Nevşehir-Konya and Nevşehir-Ankara buses stop at the Mobil station on the ring road, 2½km from the center of town. Either take a taxi ($5), or walk (ask for the city center: *şehir merkezi*).

ORIENTATION AND PRACTICAL INFORMATION. The **tourist office** (☎212 50 51 or 212 35 63) is on the left a few blocks past the main square. The easiest way to get there is to turn right as you exit the Ulu Camii park. (Supposedly open M-F 8am-5pm. Actual hours are erratic.) A number of **banks** and **ATMs** surround the square, but none offer currency exchange. To change money, head over to any of the *dövis* offices (change bureaus) across from the mosque; try **Aksaray Doviş and Altin,** opposite Aksaray's only Iş Bank, in the city center. The **police** can be reached at ☎215 07 14. Aksaray is home to a large, modern **hospital** (☎212 91 00, 213 10 43, or 213 52 07), at the entrance to town. The two **Internet cafes** charge $1.50 per hr.; one is 100m up the road from the otogar toward the main square, and the other is 50m from the main square toward the tourist office. To find the **PTT,** take a right before the square, walk a few minutes to the park, and turn left—it's across a small side street from the camii. From here, the office, marked by a large roof antenna, is visible. (Open daily 8:30am-12:30pm and 1:30-5:30pm.) **Postal code:** 68100.

ACCOMMODATIONS AND FOOD. Rooms in Aksaray can be very cheap, often for good reason. Women traveling alone and unmarried couples may have difficulty finding accommodations. The ones listed here are among the less questionable. **Tezcancar Hotel,** next door to the central police station *(merkez polis karakotu)*, has a nice restaurant and rooms with TV, phone, and shower. (☎213 84 82. $7 per person.) About 100 meters behind the Kursunlu Mosque, **Ilhara Pension** (☎213 60 83) is a little dingier with basic rooms for $3 per person. If you choose to avoid the city center, you can camp at **Ağaçlı Turistik Tesisleri,** which is accessible only by a $7-8 round-trip taxi ride. (☎215 24 00. $4 per person; $3 per camper.)

The center of town is replete with unremarkable, cheap *lokantas*. The **Golden Apple Pastanesi** (☎213 67 65) is a pastry shop buzzing with the music of teenagers' cell phones and adorned with funky ceiling art. It features Turkish preserves such as *kuru pasta* (stuffed cheese pastries; $4 per kg) and *susamlı peynirli* (salt-covered pastries), along with ice cream and a selection of sweets.

SIGHTS. The **Zinciriye Medresesi,** built in the Karamanoğlu period, is a museum of artifacts from the diverse inhabitants of Aksaray's past. Works of the Hittites, Greeks, Romans, Byzantines, Selçuks, and Ottomans are on display, including a Hittite stone marker, a 3rd-century Roman eagle sculpture, and a cannon from World War I. To get there, head away from the otogar past the city square, turn right, and walk downhill. (Open Tu-Su 8am-noon and 1:30-5:30pm. Free.) Built by the Karamanoğlu in the early 15th century, the **Ulu Camii,** across from the PTT, remains one of the town's religious centers. The Selçuk **Eğri Minare** (Crooked Minaret), five minutes farther up the main road and on the right, was built with red bricks in the 13th century. Its 92 stairs cannot be climbed because the structure is leaning. The street below is partially cordoned off in anticipation of any steel rope failure. Rumors claim that this crooked minaret inspired Pisa's famous tower.

HACIBEKTAŞ ☎384

I have rained with the rain and I have grown as grass.
I have guided aright the country of Rum;
I was Bektaş, who came from Khurasan.
—Hacı Bektaş Veli

Five kilometers from those fabled stones is a village of about 8000 that takes its name from its most romanticized inhabitant. Although the details of Hacı Bektaş Veli's birth and death are unclear, his progressive beliefs inspired a dervish order, the **Bektaşı,** that continued to spread his teachings and to exert religious and political influence in both the Ottoman Empire and in modern Turkey (see **Sufism,** p. 27). Hacıbektaş hosts a **festival** every year from August 16-18 to honor its Sufi namesake. The town has attracted followers for centuries, and today the festival draws thousands of pilgrims from all over Turkey.

TRANSPORTATION AND PRACTICAL INFORMATION. The T-junction where **Atatürk Bul.** (which becomes **Nevşehir Cad.** after the museum) meets **Hacı Bektaş Veli Bul.** marks the center of town. Adorned by a statue of the great Sufi master, this intersection also serves as the local bus stop. A number of bus companies have booths nearby. Buses leave for: **İstanbul** (5:30, 8pm; $13); **İzmir** (6:30, 8:30pm; $13); **Kırşehir** (9, 10am, 2:30, 6:30pm; $1.25); **Mersin** (12:30, 3:30pm; $7.50); **Nevşehir** (8:30, 11:30am, 2:30, 5:30pm; $1.25).

Services include: the **tourist office** (☎441 36 87; open M-F 8am-noon and 1:30-5:30pm); a **pharmacy** (☎441 36 58), opposite the museum; a **hospital** (☎341 30 15 or 341 35 85), down Nevşehir Cad.; and the **PTT,** on Atatürk Bul., between the museum and town square (open daily 8am-12:30pm and 1:30-5:30pm). **Postal code:** 50800.

WHO'S AFRAID OF THE BIG, BAD WOLF?

Over seven centuries ago, a Sufi named Hacı Bektaş Veli warned a shepherd not to lead his sheep onto a certain hill, where the wolves would certainly decimate his flock. The shepherd scoffed at the warning and left his herd grazing unattended for a few moments, when, lo and behold, the sheep were killed by marauding wolves. When the suspicious shepherd found the remains of his flock, he demanded eyewitness testimony to confirm that wolves were to blame. Suddenly, at the behest of Hacı Bektaş Veli, five large rocks on the hill made their way over to the shepherd and affirmed that wolves had indeed killed the sheep.

ACCOMMODATIONS AND FOOD. The **Hotel Hünkar,** in the complex of shops opposite the museum, offers 16 basic rooms and a restaurant/bar. A random photograph of a ski lodge dominates the lobby. (☎441 33 44. Singles with bath $8.) Even more basic is the **Fuat Baba Pensiyon,** down Hacı Bektaş Veli Bul., about 1km from the museum. (☎441 30 70. Singles $5, with bath $7.) Eateries in the town center are decorated with portraits of Hacı Bektaş Veli and serve standard food ($2).

SIGHTS. The **Hacıbektaş Müzesi,** at the end of Atatürk Bul., includes the lodge of the Bektaşı dervishes and the Sufi's tomb. It is centered around three main courtyards, and Anglophone visitors can listen to a recorded walking tour. The mostly unremarkable first courtyard contains the ticket booth and the Three Saints Fountain, built in 1902. Pass through the Door of the Three at the end to enter the second courtyard, dominated by a rectangular pool with a lion-shaped fountain. The **Aş Evi** (dervish kitchen), through the first door on the right, contains a number of cooking utensils, including a massive black cauldron. The second door on the right leads to the small but exquisite **Tekke Mosque.** The series of rooms on the left includes the **Ceremonial Hall,** where Bektaşı ritual ceremonies were held. The nine-vaulted ceiling represents the nine levels of the celestial path. Enter the third courtyard through the Gate of the Six, where you'll pass a corner commemorating Atatürk's visit here in 1919. Filled with the graves of dedicated dervishes, the courtyard has two main buildings which house the dead. To the right, under the shade of the 700-year-old **Wish Tree,** stands the mausoleum of the second greatest Bektaşı, Balım Sultan, who was responsible for spreading the order into Europe. It is said that God will grant the wishes of those who tie ribbons to the tree. To the right as you enter the main building is the tiny room *(çilehane)*, where dervishes meditated to achieve communion with God. Beyond this are several display cases with some of the order's prized artifacts including devices used to help keep dedicated dervishes awake for up to 14 days at a time. Off of the main chamber, called the Forty Saints area, lies Hacı Bektaş Veli's opulent coffin. Doorways in the museum are tiny not because the Bektaşi are unusually petite, but because short entrances make visitors bow humbly before God. Like the Tekke Mosque, this building is holy ground; visitors should dress conservatively and remove their shoes, though it is not necessary for women to wear headscarves. In the Sufi tradition, stepping directly on a doorway's threshold is disrespectful. *(Museum open Tu-Su 8:30am-noon and 1:30-5:30pm. $1.25.)*

KAYSERİ ☎352

Even though Kayseri (pop. 500,000) is easily Cappadocia's largest metropolis, wide streets and large public spaces save the city from claustrophobia and overcrowding. In spite of Kayseri's accumulation of fascinating attractions over the course of its 6000-year history, foreign visitors (though welcome) are unusual here. Despite its Westernized appearance, the city is culturally and religiously conservative; entertainment is scarce, and female tourists should adhere to the dictates of traditional dress. With few tourist traps, this renowned carpet center could be your one-stop shop for cheaper buys than those in İstanbul.

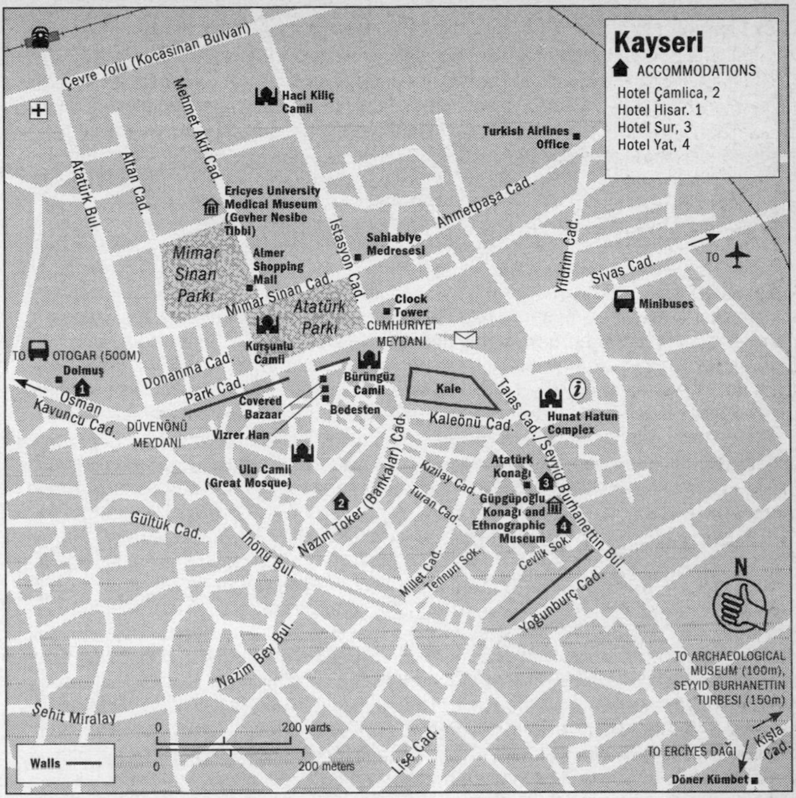

Originally the capital of an independent Cappadocia, the city was renamed Caesaria under the reign of the Roman emperor Tiberius Caesar (14-37 AD). Like most other cities in Anatolia, it then passed from the Romans to the Byzantines, and later to the Selçuks. Kayseri (a derivative of the town's Roman name) blossomed under Selçuk rule. As an important post along trade routes, Kayseri amassed the wealth that financed such 13th-century monuments as the Hunat Hatun Complex and the Gevher Nesibe Tibbiyesi, the world's first medical university.

TRANSPORTATION

Flights: Erkilet Airport (☎338 33 53), 90km northeast of Kayseri down Sivas Cad., is the most organized in Cappadocia. To **İstanbul** (1hr.; daily 9:55am, 9pm; $84, students $67). Buy tickets from the **THY Office,** 1 Yıldırım Cad. (☎222 38 58; fax 222 47 48), which also offers an airport shuttle to the city for $1.60 (call ahead to arrange).

Buses: From the otogar (☎336 43 73), on Osman Kavuncu Cad. to: **Adana** (5hr., frequent 7am-1am, $8); **Aksaray** (2½hr., frequent 9am-5pm, $5); **Ankara** (4½hr., every hr. 7am-2am, $8); **Antalya** (12hr., frequent 5-11:30pm, $11.50); **Bursa** (10hr.; 6:30, 7:30pm; $13); **Erzurum** (9hr., frequent 7-11pm, $13); **İstanbul** (11hr., frequent 9am-10:30pm, $17); **İzmir** (12hr., frequent 6pm-midnight, $17); **Konya** (5hr., frequent 8am-6pm, $8.20); **Kuşadası** (14hr., 6pm, $16); **Mersin** (5hr., frequent 7am-midnight, $8); **Nevşehir** (1½hr., every hr. 7am-2am, $3); **Sivas** (2hr., express, every hr., $5); **Trabzon** (14hr., frequent noon-midnight, $15). Minibuses to **Ürgüp** leave from a stop on Osman Kavuncu Cad., near Düvenönü Meydanı (1½hr., every 2hr. 8am-6pm, $2.50).

Trains: Kayseri's *gar* (☎231 13 13), at the end of Hastane Cad., sends daily trains to: **Adana** (6½hr.; 2:20, 4:40pm; $5); **Ankara** (8½hr.; midnight, 1, 4, 4:30am; $5); **İstanbul** (22½hr.; 4, 4:40am; $7); and **Kars** (17hr., 4:40pm, $7)

ORIENTATION

The otogar is on **Osman Kavuncu Cad.** which meets **Park Cad.** and **İnönü Bul.** at **Düvenönü Meydanı.** From Düvenönü Meydanı, Park Cad. leads to the massive **kale,** a Roman-era stone fortress which dominates the center of town. To the right is **Nazmi Toker Cad.,** known as **Bankalar Cad.** for its many banks, where a massive underpass crosses Park Cad. Kayseri's second main square, marked by the clock tower, is **Cumhuriyet Meydanı,** where Park Cad. meets Sivas Cad. and **Seyyid Burhanettin Bul.** heads away from the fortress, past the Hunat Mosque Complex and the tourist office to the **Döner Kümbet** (Revolving Tomb), the **Archaeological Museum,** and the **Seyyid Burhanettin Türbesi** (tomb).

PRACTICAL INFORMATION

Tourist Office: 61 Kagnı Pazarı (☎222 39 03 or 231 92 95; fax 222 08 79), next door to the Hunat Hatun Complex. English-speaking staff will gladly inundate you with maps and brochures. Open daily 8am-5pm.

ATMs: All over **Bankalar Cad.,** where you'll get lira for your Cirrus/MC/Plus/V.

Hospitals: Erciyes Tıp Fakultesi Hastanesi (☎437 49 01 or 437 4902), **Özel Gülhane Sağlık Merkezi,** 24 Kiçikapu Cad. (☎222 48 54 or 222 48 35), and **Hunat Sağlık Merkezi** (☎221 06 00), next to the Hunat Hatun Complex. All have **ambulance services** and English-speaking doctors. **Emergency:** call ☎336 27 50.

Internet Access: There are a number of Internet cafes in the residential area north of Sivas Cad. and east of the THY office. Slow access costs around $.50 per hr.

PTT: On Sivas Cad. in Cumhuriyet Meydanı. 24hr. phones. Poste Restante. telegraph, fax, and **currency exchange** daily 8:30am-5pm.

Postal Code: 38000.

ACCOMMODATIONS

Since Kayseri is not a backpackers' town, the fancy hotels and even the cheaper, spartan ones tend to be overpriced. Most hotels will negotiate a discount for business groups, but rarely for students. Hotel prices increase by about 25% in the winter, as most visitors (whether businessmen or skiers) come with the snow.

Hotel Yat, 14 Talas Cad. (☎232 73 78 or 232 35 95). has 8 bright, balconied rooms, with orange phones and blue and green walls. Bath $2. Singles $5; doubles $10.

Hotel Hisar, 24 Osman Kavuncu Cad. (☎336 66 44) has several stories of clean but bare rooms, surrounding a skylit central atrium. Free laundry service. $10 per person.

Hotel Sur, 12 Talas Cad. (☎222 43 67; fax 231 3992). Inside the old town walls, by the Ethnographic Museum. Central location and 2-star comfort. Singles $12; doubles $20.

Hotel Çamlıca, Bankalar Cad., 14 Gürcü Sok. (☎232 34 93 or 232 23 54; fax 231 43 44). Bright lounge, tacky palm-tree murals and 70s posters will make you feel like one of Charlie's Angels. Your mission? To conquer the shared *à la turka* toilets at the end of the hall. Breakfast included. Singles $11, with shower $13; doubles $23, with shower $24.

FOOD

Kayseri is the present-day capital of Turkish cold cuts. This is the place for *pastırma* (spicy, salted, sun-dried beef or veal with garlic, pepper, and parsley; $4 per kg), *sucuk* (extremely spicy, well-salted beef sausage resembling a long, thin salami; $3 per kg), and *salam* (salted Turkish salami, similar to *sucuk* but less spicy). Inexpensive picnic fare is also easy to find, as the many bread shops sell loaves of fresh bread for about $.20. Vegetarians might consider the specialty cheese, *tulum peyniri*, or *bal* (honey; $2.50-3.25 per jar), both sold at most food stores. For dessert, try Kayseri's special *kaymaklı ekmek kadayıfı* (fluffy, honey-saturated bread topped with sweetened cream; $1.50), which is not as unbearably sweet as many Turkish desserts. Many inexpensive restaurants line the back streets parallel to Bankalar Cad. Kayseri is not a city that parties until dawn; even most of the restaurants shut down by 10 or 11pm.

İskender Kebap Salonu (☎231 27 69 or 222 69 65), on Millet Cad. behind the fortress. Overwhelmingly recommended by locals, this glossy 3-story restaurant serves an unbeatable meal of *İskender kebap* (thin layers of butter-soaked meat blanketing *pide* bread and served with yogurt) and a tall, foaming *ayran* for just $3.50. Placemats explain the history of *İskender kebap,* for devoted meat historians.

Divan Pastanesi (☎222 39 74). An incredible chain of pastry shops. The best one is just around the corner from İskender Kebap Salonu. Cases of sweets, breads, and pastries hug the sleek glass and metal furniture. Open M-Sa 7:30am-10pm, Su 7:30am-9pm.

Urfa Sofrasi, around the corner from İskender, serves up tasty versions of standard Turkish dishes for about $4. The menu provides pictures of each dish, so consider holding on to it after ordering to study up for future restaurant excursions.

SIGHTS

GEVHER NESİBE TİBBİYESİ. In May 1993, NASA named a newly discovered mountain on Venus after the Selçuk princess **Gevher Nesibe Sultan** in recognition of her contribution to modern science. When she died of tuberculosis in 1204, her elder brother, Giyasettin Keyhüsrev Sultan, commissioned a medical center in her name. The **Gevher Nesibe Tibbiyesi** opened in 1206 as the world's first medical school and most technologically advanced hospital. The hospital treated everyone for free, and patients, doctors, and medical students were admitted regardless of religion. Today its two seminaries house the **Erciyes University Medical Museum,** where you can take a tour of a 13th-century operating room, mental ward, clinic, and hospital. Considering the many difficulties of running a large-scale hospital in the era before electricity, the scope and scale of the facility are impressive. The skylight in the *ameliyat hane* (operating room) concentrates maximum sunlight on the operating table. The equally well-planned *hamam* managed to heat both halves of the building during Kayseri's snowy winters. Perhaps most remarkably, the *akıl hastanesi* (mental hospital) is equipped with one of the earliest known P.A. systems: sound vents in the upper corners of the stone cells enabled a single person upstairs to address all the patients at once. This seminary is not without a tomb of its own—look out for the low-flying sparrows when descending the stairs to the **Gevher Nesibe Sultan Mescidi ve Sandukası** (little mosque), where the princess is interred. Other alcoves are dedicated to relevant quotations from the Qur'an ("Whoever saves one life has in a way resurrected us all") and hospitals founded by Turkish women (from Gevher Nesibe to Valide Sultan in 1845). Atatürk's last brushes with the medical world are also memorialized, including a photo of a syringe, labeled (in Turkish), "The last injection of *extrait hepatique* administered to Atatürk before his death by Dr. M.K. Berk." *(From Park Cad., cut north across Atatürk Parkı and Mimar Sinan Parkı. Open W-Su 8am-5pm. $1.25, students $.75.)*

HUNAT HATUN COMPLEX. Early in the 13th century, Alâadin Keykubad, Sultan of the Anatolian Selçuks (1219-1237), captured the Alanya fortress from its Persian ruler, Kir Vart. One of the conditions of Vart's surrender was that his daughter Hunat ("lady" in Persian) Mahperi Hatun would become the sultan's wife. After her marriage, Lady Hunat (as she is redundantly called in English) converted to Islam and commissioned the **Hunat Hatun Complex** (Külliyesi), made up of the **Hunat Hatun Camii, Türbe** (tomb), **Medrese,** and **Hamam,** which is still functioning and has separate facilities for men and women. *(In the center of town, across from the* kale. *☎231 58 05. Hamam open daily 8:30am-5:30pm. Bath $2.50; massage and scrub $2.50.)*

GÜPGÜPOĞLU KONAĞI AND ETHNOGRAPHIC MUSEUM. Built in the 15th century and later expanded, the **Güpgüpoğlu Konağı** is a beautifully preserved Ottoman mansion, built in 1419. Stroll through the replica kitchen, sitting room, and bride's room, where mannequins in period dress evoke a sense of the life and times of the Ottoman upper crust. Converted into the **Ethnographic Museum,** the rest of the mansion houses a significant collection of coins, guns, costumes, and household objects, mostly from the Ottoman period. *(Staying inside the old city walls, head south from the* kale *about 150m, just beyond Hotel Sur. Güpgüpoğlu Konağı ☎222 95 16. Museum ☎222 21 49. Open Tu-Su 8:30am-5pm. $1.60.)*

ARCHAEOLOGICAL MUSEUM. The first of two halls in this small, fascinating museum displays objects from the Early Bronze Age, along with treasures unearthed from nearby Kültepe, a 6000-year-old settlement that peaked as an Assyrian trading colony (2500-1750 BC). Among the pottery and metalwork are some tablets bearing the earliest writing found in Anatolia, dating to the Neo-Hittite Period. The centerpiece of the second hall is the **Heracles Sarcophagus,** a large marble tomb depicting the 12 labors of Heracles. *(Head down Talas Cad., turn left at Kışla Cad., and follow the signs to the museum. ☎222 21 49. Open daily 8:30am-5pm. $1.)*

CITADEL. First built by the Byzantines in the 6th century, and improved upon by the Selçuks, the massive **kale** is Kayseri's most distinctive landmark and houses its most budget-friendly bazaar. Replete with countless jewelers and cobblers, the *kale* is connected to the even larger, centuries-old covered markets nearby. The oldest, built in 1497, is the **Bedesten bazaar,** near the Ulu Camii. It's connected to the **Vizier Kervansaray** (1723), which still bustles with wool traders and craftsmen.

MOSQUES. West of the fortress, past the bazaar, the **Ulu Camii** (Great Mosque, a.k.a. Camii Kebir or Sultan Cami), constructed in 1134, is Kayseri's oldest mosque. Built on 42 stone pillars by Melik Mehmet Gazi Danişmendoğulları, this mosque's minarets stand 46m high. In the northwest corner of Atatürk Parkı, the **Kurşunlu Camii** (built in 1585) is the only piece of architecture in Kayseri designed by hometown hero Mimar Sinan Eseri (1492-1588), Turkey's most famous architect (see **Ottoman Architecture,** p. 23). Though far smaller than the city's other major mosques, the delicate arches and graceful design are clearly the products of a great master. Next to the *kale,* the immense and beautiful **Bürüngüz Camii** is a 20th-century imitation of the Blue Mosque in İstanbul. As with all mosques, visitors ought to dress conservatively (women preferably with head scarves), remove their shoes before entering, and speak softly while inside.

TOMBS. One of Kayseri's distinguishing features is its wealth of preserved Selçuk tombs. Probably the most interesting is the 13th-century **Döner Kümbet** (Revolving Tomb), on a traffic island down Talas Cad. on the way to Erciyes, south of the *kale.* The 12-sided, cone-roofed tomb does not revolve, but it is said that the pure of heart will see it slowly rotating early in the morning. Though visitors are not allowed inside the tomb, they can peer through a metal grate in the wall.

The sacred **Seyyid Burhanettin Türbesi** was built in the early-13th century for Burhanettin Tirmizi (1165-1244), the first *mevlevi* at Hunat Hatun Medrese. This five-star tomb includes two separate and heavily trafficked prayer rooms for men and women. Inside, you'll find the teacher's enormous sarcophagus under a gargantuan chandelier and a beautiful dome decorated with rows of Selçuk floral designs. *(Turn left at the Döner Türbesi to find the tomb nestled in a little park. Remember to leave your shoes by the door or carry them in a bag. Women may want to wear a head scarf.)*

DAYTRIPS FROM KAYSERİ

SULTAN HAN

Sultan Han is about 45km from Kayseri, and less than 1km from the Kayseri-Sivas highway. To get there, catch one of the Kayseri-Sivas buses and ask to be let off at Sultan Han (every hr., $3). To return to Kayseri, flag down the Sivas-Kayseri minibus at about 20min. past the hour. Open Tu-Su 9am-1pm and 2-6pm. $.60.

The 13th-century Sultan Han, Turkey's second largest *kervansaray*, served as a safe haven for traveling merchants during the Selçuk period (see **Selçuk Architecture and Decorative Arts,** p. 22). Built in 1255 by Vizier Celeddin Karatay, the building now echoes with the incessant calls of bats from the great hall, replacing the murmurs of road-weary travelers and traders. After walking through the old guest quarters and hamam, notice the intricate snake patterns on the *eyvans* (arches) of the mosque in the courtyard. Be sure to climb the stairs to check out the roof and the dome over the great hall.

ERCİYES DAĞI (MT. ERCIYES)

To get to Erciyes, take the Kayseri-Develi dolmuş. The best place to catch it is the small local otogar behind Hotel Yat. The dolmuş leaves as soon as the driver decides it's full, (usually every 30min. 7am-9pm, $.80). Ask to be let off at Kayak Evi. Lifts open daily 8am-5pm. $2 to top. Day pass $15; ski rentals $12.

The snow-capped heights of Erciyes Dağı are clearly visible from Kayseri and serve as a perpetual reminder of the volcanic fury that shaped the Cappadocian landscape. At 3917m, the extinct volcano is the tallest mountain in Central Anatolia. From late October through March, skiers flock to the 2215m high **Tekir Yaylası** (ski track), equipped with two chair lifts, two teleskis, and three beginner's lifts. The accessible part of the mountain runs from the ski base to a point 2770m high and offers skiers altitude of about 550m and heavenly trail conditions. The **Sağlık Ocağı** first-aid clinic (☎342 20 31) caters to winter emergencies. The **Kardelen Restaurant and Disco Bar** (☎342 21 01) at the ski base, is open year-round, though summer meal selections are limited. A true hot spot, Kardelen never loses its party spirit; the disco downstairs pulsates even when sheep are the only passers-by.

In the summer, hiking groups trek the mountain from the ski base up. While experienced mountaineers may climb the west face to the summit (8hr. up; 3hr. down), the melting snow and falling rock render this a dangerous route. Alternatives include a shorter hike to the mountain's bowl and back (8hr.) or a tougher south-side climb to the summit. In any case, be sure to wear sturdy boots and dress in layers. **Kayak Evi,** the year-round hotel at the base of the ski slopes, helps arrange hikes. Groups can call ahead and speak with Veysel, the hotel's Turkish- and German-speaking ski instructor, to arrange a guided hike. (☎342 20 31; fax 342 20 32. Guided hikes $15 per person. $10 per person. Hot-water for groups only; no meals. In winter $35 per person, including bath and meals.) Independent travelers may have problems with logistics, and a trekking tour arranged elsewhere ahead of time may be the best way to attack Erciyes.

KONYA AND ENVIRONS

KONYA ☎332

> Come, come again and again! Come be you unbeliever, idolator or fire worshipper. Whoever you are and whatever your condition come! Our hearth is not the threshold of despair. Even if you have fallen a hundred times, come!
>
> —Celeddin-i-Rumi

Konya (pop. 675,000) brims with the lingering flourishes of the Selçuk dynasty, evoking a world of whirling mystics and hushed prayers in sacred candlelit mosques. The city has long played host to spiritual visionaries. In Roman times, when it was called Iconium, a visit by St. Paul initiated the city's gradual transformation into a Byzantine Orthodox patriarchate. After the Selçuks of Rum invaded and made it their capital in the 11th century, Konya's churches were replaced with the greatest mosques of the era. In 1228, the great Persian poet **Celeddin-i-Rumi,** known to many Turks simply as Mevlâna ("our master"), moved to Konya with his family from their home in Afghanistan. Rumi's poetry and life inspired the now-famous Sufi order known for its Whirling Dervishes. Today, Muslims often stop in Konya to visit Mevlâna's tomb before embarking on the *hajj* to Mecca.

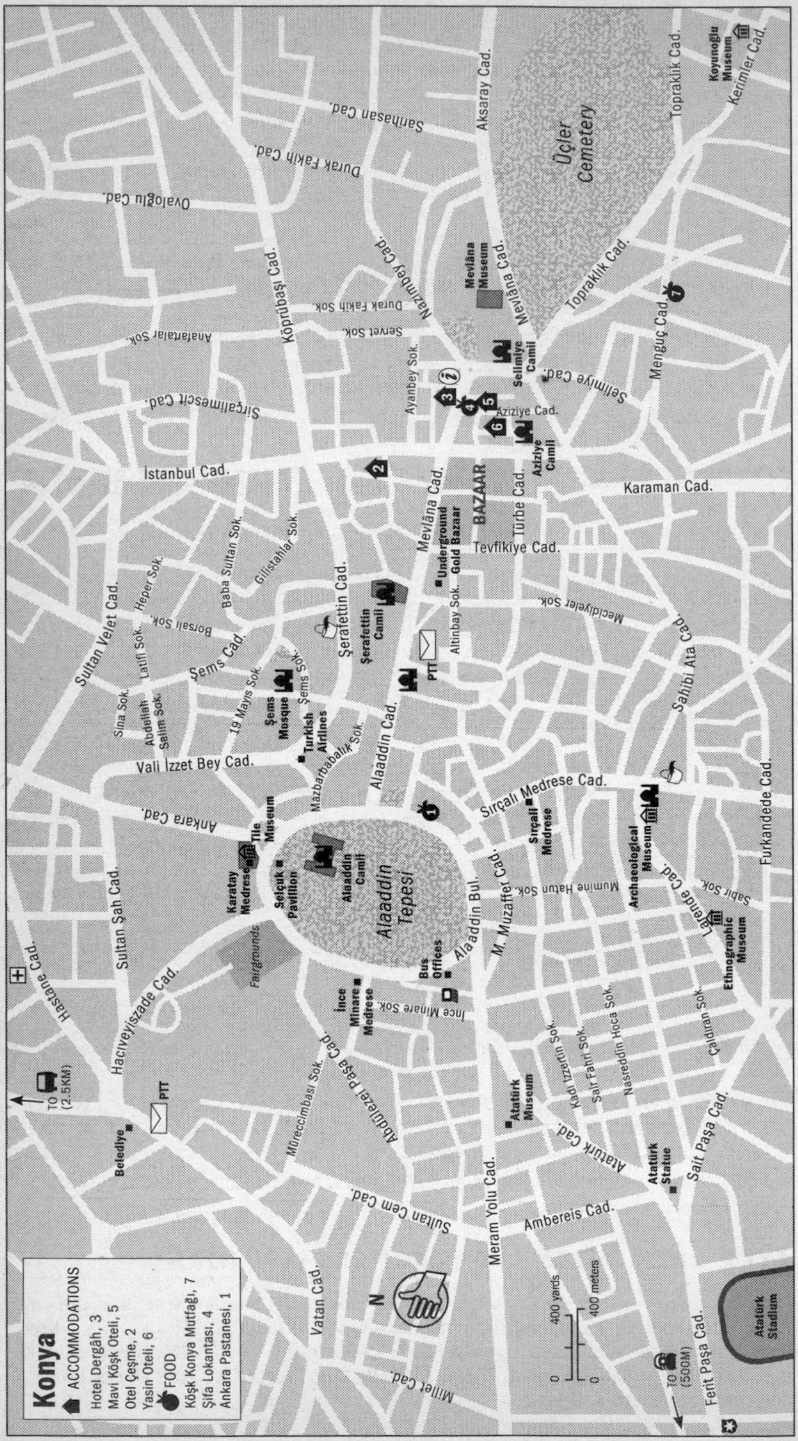
Konya
ACCOMMODATIONS
Hotel Dergâh, 3
Mavi Köşk Oteli, 5
Otel Çeşme, 2
Yasin Oteli, 6
FOOD
Köşk Konya Mutfağı, 7
Şifa Lokantası, 4
Ankara Pastanesi, 1
N
0
400 yards
400 meters
Üçler Cemetery
Mevlâna Museum
Selimiye Camii
Aziziye Camii
BAZAAR
Underground Gold Bazaar
Şerafettin Camii
PTT
Şems Mosque
Turkish Airlines
Tile Museum
Karatay Medrese
Selçuk Pavilion
Alaaddin Camii
Alaaddin Tepesi
Fairgrounds
Bus Offices
İnce Minare Medrese
Sırçalı Medrese
Archaeological Museum
Ethnographic Museum
Koyunoğlu Museum
Atatürk Museum
Atatürk Statue
Atatürk Stadium
Belediye
TO (2.5KM)
TO (500M)
Aksaray Cad.
Sarihasan Cad.
Durak Fakih Cad.
Ovaloğlu Cad.
Nazimbey Cad.
Köprübaşı Cad.
Durak Fakih Sok.
Servet Sok.
Anafartalar Sok.
Sırçalımescit Cad.
İstanbul Cad.
Mevlâna Cad.
Topraklık Cad.
Kerimler Cad.
Menguç Cad.
Selimiye Cad.
Aziziye Cad.
Ayanbey Sok.
Türbe Cad.
Karaman Cad.
Tevfikiye Cad.
Mecidiyeler Sok.
Altınbay Sok.
Şerafettin Cad.
Gilistahlar Sok.
Baba Sultan Sok.
Sultan Velet Cad.
Heper Sok.
Borsalı Sok.
Latifi Sok.
Şems Cad.
Şems Sok.
19 Mayıs Sok.
Sina Sok.
Abdullah Salim Sok.
Vali İzzet Bey Cad.
Mazbarbabatik Sok.
Alaaddin Cad.
Ankara Cad.
Sahibi Ata Cad.
Sırçalı Medrese Cad.
Furkandede Cad.
Sabir Sok.
Larende Cad.
Mümine Hatun Sok.
M. Muzaffer Cad.
Alaaddin Bul.
Sultan Şah Cad.
Hastane Cad.
Hacıveyiszade Cad.
İnce Minare Sok.
Abdülezel Paşa Cad.
Mürecimbaşı Sok.
Kadı İzzettin Sok.
Sair Fahri Sok.
Nasreddin Hoca Sok.
Çaldıran Sok.
Atatürk Cad.
Sait Paşa Cad.
Meram Yolu Cad.
Ambereis Cad.
Sultan Cem Cad.
Vatan Cad.
Millet Cad.
Ferit Paşa Cad.

Despite a large student population, Konya remains one of Turkey's most religiously conservative cities. Konya University, with 45,000 students, has had a huge effect on the city's tolerance, although staunch conservatism remains. Modest, respectful dress may save you uninvited attention; some women travelers choose to wear long skirts and traditional headscarves. Shorts are not recommended for men or women. More information concerning women in public is below.

TRANSPORTATION

Flights: Konya's airport is about 20km out of town. Buses link the PTT and the airport every hr. ($3). The **THY office** (☎351 20 32) is on Alaaddin Bul., off Alaaddin Cad., and offers a service ($3) from the office to the airport. Turkish Airlines flies to İstanbul (1hr.; daily 6:25am; $65, students $50).

Trains: Konya's modest railway station is 2km from the town center on Ferit Paşa Cad. To **İstanbul** (13hr.; daily 5:45, 9pm; $10). To get to town from the *gar*, take a city bus (5min., every 30min., $.60), or catch a dolmuş on Ferit Paşa Cad. (frequent, $.40).

Buses: The otogar is on A. Hilmi Nalcacı Cad. **Özkaymak** (☎265 01 60) and **Aksel** (☎265 01 42) service Konya.

DESTINATION	DURATION	FREQUENCY/TIME	PRICE
Adana	5 hr.	9 per day 6:30am-1:30am	$10
Afyon	3 hr.	6:30, 10am, 3:30, 11pm, midnight	$8
Alanya	5 hr.	6 per day 1am-3:30am	$10
Ankara	4hr.	4am-1am	$8
Antalya	6 hr.	8, 11am, 2, 6pm, midnight	$10
Aydın	8 hr.	9pm	$15
Bodrum	12 hr.	7:30pm	$15.70
Bursa	7 hr.	9am, 2, 9pm, midnight	$15
Denizli	6 hr.	9pm	$13
Erzincan	10 hr.	8pm	$17
Erzurum	12 hr.	5:30pm	$22
Göreme	3 hr.	8, 9, 11am, 2pm	$9
İsparta	4 hr.	4pm	$9
İstanbul	12 hr.	9 per day 10am-midnight	$18
İzmir	8 hr.	7 per day 6:30am-12:30am	$12
Kayseri	5 hr.	9:30am, 6pm	$10
Malatya	10 hr.	10pm, 11:30pm	$18
Marmaris	13 hr.	10:30pm	$18
Mersin	4 hr.	5:30am-1:30am	$10
Milas	9 hr.	7:30pm	$16
Muğla	10 hr.	7:30pm	$16
Sivas	8 hr.	5:30pm, 1:30am	$16

Local Transportation: A **Light Railway** connects Konya University, the otogar on A. Hilmi Nalcacı Cad., and Alaaddin Tepesi. Tickets can be purchased at any of the many stops along the route ($.30, Konya University students $.20).

Taxi: Stations are located throughout the city, mostly near the main tourist sites like Mevlâna Müzesi and Alaaddin Tepesi.

ORIENTATION AND PRACTICAL INFORMATION

Konya's main street runs between the turquoise-domed **Mevlâna tomb** and the circular **Alaaddin Bul.,** which embraces **Alaaddin Tepesi** (Alaaddin Hill), actually a prehistoric burial mound. The section of road closest to the Mevlâna Müzesi and tomb is called **Mevlâna Cad.;** the other half is **Alaaddin Cad.** Most of Konya's sights, hotels, and restaurants are in this area.

Tourist office: 65 Mevlâna Cad. (☎351 10 74; fax 350 64 61). Across from the Mevlâna Müzesi. Look for a green sign. Little English spoken. Take advantage of their free but unhelpful city maps, but take their accommodation and carpet shop advice with a grain of salt. Open M-F 8am-noon and 1:30-5:30pm.

Banks: On either side of Alaaddin Cad. Most have **ATMs.**

Luggage storage: At the otogar. $3 per bag. Open 6am-10pm.

Hamam: (☎353 00 93). For the real deal, head to the hamam across from the PTT, behind Şerafettin Cad. Men's entrance across from the mosque; women's entrance around the corner. Open for men daily 5am-midnight, for women daily 9am-8pm. $5 for the works. The popular **Şifa Sultan Hamam** (☎351 80 34) is down Sırçalı Medrese Cad. Men's entrance across from Şahibi Ata Camii, women's entrance around the corner. Open for women 8am-7pm, for men 9am-midnight. $3 for the works.

Police: (☎322 28 16). On Ferit Paşa Cad., known to locals as Form Cad. Open 24hr.

Hospital: State-run **Nunune Hastanesi** (☎235 45 00), is on Hastane Cad. The receptionists don't speak English, but most doctors do. **TIP Medical Faculty** (☎323 26 00) is on the outskirts of town.

Internet Access: Express Internet City (☎350 78 66), on Alaaddin Bul., near the bus offices. $.80 per hr. Open daily 9am-11pm. **Millennium Internet Cafe,** the first right on Meram Yolu, has 40 quick connections at $.50 per hr. Open daily 9am-midnight.

PTT: (☎352 02 55), on Alaaddin Cad., across from Şerafettin Camii. Postal services open daily 8:30am-5pm. The branch on Vatan Cad. handles most package services.

Postal Code: 42000.

ACCOMMODATIONS

Most of the hotels and pensions are tucked away in alleys off Mevlâna Cad. Room rates are high, but prices tend to be negotiable. Hot water is often only available upon request—be suspicious if it's guaranteed. Women traveling alone should avoid the bazaar and spend extra money to stay in hotels along the main streets.

Mavi Köşk Oteli, Mevlâna Cad., 13 Bostan Çelebi Sok. (☎350 19 04), one block from Mevlâna Müzesi. A standard backpacker haunt, appropriate for groups of 2 or more. 9 rooms with TV, some with bath. Singles $10; doubles $10-12; triples $15.

Yasin Otel (☎351 16 24), in the bazaar, on the second right from Aziziye Cad. Clean, spacious rooms with baths, TVs, and hot water. Breakfast $2. Singles $7; doubles $12.

Otel Çeşme, İstanbul Cad., 35 Akifaşa Sok. (☎351 24 26). Follow Mevlâna Cad. toward Alaaddin Tepesi, turn right on İstanbul Cad., and take the first left. 25 small, spotless rooms with TV and bath. Ask for a room in the back. No English spoken. Singles $12; doubles $15; triples $20; quads $30.

Hotel Bey (☎352 01 73). Take the first right off İstanbul Cad. when headed away from the bazaar. Clean and comfortable rooms, sparkling with less-is-more charm. A good option for women travelers. Breakfast included. Singles $14; doubles $20.

Hotel Dergâh, 19 Mevlâna Cad. (☎351 11 97 or 351 76 61; fax 351 01 16), next to the tourist office. Convenient location. This 2-star hotel features 86 big, somewhat dark rooms with phones and bath. Breakfast included. Rooms $16-30.

FOOD AND ENTERTAINMENT

Konya's specialty is *fırın kebap,* a chunk of oven-roasted mutton served unceremoniously on a *pide,* sometimes under the alias *tandır kebap*—just add yogurt and you could mistake it for *iskender kebap*. Konya is also renowned for its Turkish pizza, here called *etliekmek*. There are plenty of cheap eats on Konya's backstreets, but the atmosphere might be uncomfortable for women traveling alone. Women should choose restaurants that advertise a family *(aile)* section. Unsurprisingly, alcohol is hard to find in this conservative burg.

Köşk Konya Mutfağı (☎352 85 37). With the Mevlâna Müzesi on your left, take a right at the end of Mevlâna Cad., and then take your first right. A bare brick wall and plastic Coke sign conceal a 150-year-old house that serves terrific food. Specialities include *gebzeli çöp kebap* (*kebap* with eggplant; $2.50), *çöp şiş* ($2.50), and *etli yaprak sarması* (meat-stuffed grape leaves with yogurt; $1.50).

Şifa Lokantası, 56 Mevlâna Cad. (☎352 05 19), on the corner of Aziziye Cad. As wholesome as it gets, Şifa will fill you up for $2-3. Vegetarian options. Caters to tourists and families. Open daily 7am-10:30pm.

Dilayla Restaurant, 68 Mevlâna Cad. (☎354 27 40). Past Şifa Lokantası, and smaller and less touristy. Free deliveries, including to Hotel Dergah across the way. Has a comfortable *aile* (family) section. Meals $3-4. Open daily 7am-11pm.

Hotel Şahin, 39 Mevlâna Cad. (☎251 33 50). One of the few bars in Konya. Beer $1.60; vodka $4 per shot; whiskey $6 per shot. This dimly lit establishment is closed to single women. Open until 2am.

Ankara Pastanesi. Turn left from Alaaddin Cad. onto Alaaddin Bul.; the cafe is on the left. Try the delicious milk puddings. Frothy instant coffee provides a quick caffeine fix.

SIGHTS

Konya's museum is dedicated to recalling its Selçuk glory days. The city's architectural riches showcase such classic Selçuk designs as carved loops and swirls, luminous tiles, octagonal or decagonal floor plans, and flowing quotations from the Qur'an. To read more about Selçuk architecture, see **Selçuk Architecture and Decorative Arts,** p. 22. These sights have great religious significance; for tips on visiting Muslim holy places, see **Visiting Mosques,** p. 26.

MEVLÂNA MÜZESİ. Mausoleum, museum, and monument in one, the **Mevlâna Müzesi** (a.k.a. the **Mevlâna Tekke**) is marked by its tower of sea green tiles, erected over a century after Rumi's death. Inside the well-touristed mausoleum lie the turban-domed sarcophagi of Rumi, his father, his oldest son, and his closest disciples. The original site of the museum was a rose garden planted by the sultan for Rumi's father. Later, Sufis who joined the Mevlevi order lodged in the chambers here. In 1954 it was restored as the Mevlâna Museum.

Enter through the "Door of the Dervishes," passing the ticket window. To the immediate right, in front of the kitchen pavilion, is the **Wedding Night Pool,** named for the day of Rumi's death, the night of his union with his Creator. Every year on that date the dervishes would gather around the pool and perform whirling rituals. Today, visitors pray here and drink the sacred water. To the left stands a **fountain** given to the site in 1512 by Sultan Yavuz Selim. The Mevlâna museum and mausoleum is straight ahead, with the entrance to the right. In the first small room, the **reading room,** dervishes recited and copied the Qur'an. Some verses, written in extraordinary Arabic, Persian, and Turkish calligraphy, hang on the walls. In the hushed and colorful main hall, approximately sixty **tombs** hold the bodies of Rumi's family and friends. Male disciples are buried in the tombs capped with turbans; those without turbans hold female disciples. The color of the turban indicates the status of the person buried in the tomb: green means that the person was a family member and white indicates a friend. Bigger turbans represent chiefs of the dervishes. The dervishes used the bowl and chain **Nişan Taş** displayed along the left wall to collect April rainwater, believed to have medicinal properties. To the left of the bowl is a famous line from one of Rumi's poems written in Arabic, Persian, and Turkish: "Either be as you appear, or appear as you are." The two largest and best-lit tombs at the end of the hall hold Rumi and his son, are and often surrounded by chanting pilgrims on the *hajj*. The black silk cloth with gold embroidery that covers the sarcophagi was given by Sultan Abdülhamid II in 1894. Rumi's father is buried in the wooden sarcophagus next to these two tombs.

"I WAS RAW, then I got cooked, and finally got burnt" - Rumi

Mevlâna Celeddin-İ-Rumi, the greatest of all mystical Persian poets, made his home in 13th-century Konya after leaving his native Balkh (now part of Afghanistan) during the Mongol invasion. Following in his father's footsteps, Rumi became a highly respected traditional Islamic scholar and was the head of a *medrese*, a theological school. When Rumi was about 37 years-old, he met **Şems of Tabriz,** a 60-year-old wandering Sufi master from Iran. Şems purposely shattered Rumi's dependence on intellect as the only means for knowing God and, in doing so, revealed Rumi's own source of divinity and the power of love. The two men became inseparable and went into week-long periods of **sohbet,** mystical conversation and merging. Şems mysteriously disappeared in 1248 (he was purportedly murdered by envious members of Mevlâna's entourage). Rumi expressed the wrenching experience and revelations that resulted from this spiritual consummation in spontaneous and ecstatic poetry, music, and dance. Above all, Rumi considered love the greatest guide on the mystical path. His passion-filled poetry of flaming hearts, moonlit gardens, and grievous longing is an account of the meeting, loss, and fervent mystical union of Rumi with Şems, Rumi with God, and Rumi with his true divine self as they all become interchangeable in their spiritual positions of Lover and Beloved.

Rumi's most famous poems were compiled into *Divan-i-Şemseddin-i-Tabriz* (1870 pages, 42,000 lines of poetry) and his later work of lyricism and stories, *Mathrawi* (25,618 couplets). His verses have inspired centuries of readers throughout the Middle East, South Asia, Africa, and the West. After Rumi's death on December 17, 1273 (called his "Wedding Night" with the divine), his disciples founded the Mevlevi Order (see **Mevlevi Order,** p. 27), known abroad as the "Whirling Dervishes" because of their meditative ceremonial dance, or **sema.** For English-speaking readers, Coleman Barks provides an evocative English translation of Rumi's poetry. Anne-Marie Schimmel's *I am Wind, You are Fire* is an excellent introduction to Rumi's life and teachings.

The next room was constructed in the 16th century for the dervishes' **whirling rituals.** Musicians performed on the raised platform, and men watched on the lower platform to the right. Women watched from upstairs. Now the space houses instruments and prayer rugs used by Rumi, crystal chandeliers with ornate marble lattices, Rumi's clothing, and the *serpuş* (hat) of Şems, Rumi's most beloved mentor.

The next room houses manuscripts from the 12th-19th centuries. Among them are old editions of Rumi's work, copies of the Qur'an (one of which fits into a tiny silver pillbox), examples of rich Islamic miniatures, and several specimens of calligraphy. Another box holds part of Muhammed's beard. There are also two strings of prayer beads, used by dervishes for group prayer: assembled on the floor in a circle, the dervishes rotated the large elliptical balls in turn with their prayers.

In the **kitchen pavilion,** across the courtyard from the museum, wax models illustrate the dervishes' daily life. The wax figures show dervishes cooking and eating, all in meditative silence, discussing theological questions, and whirling in a trance. The single figure in the small niche to the left is a *Nevniyaz* (dervish candidate). Candidates sat in a room in the kitchen and prayed for three days. If the dervishes agreed to let him train, he underwent an initiation known as the "1001 days of suffering," in which he had to successfully complete 18 kinds of services, ranging from toilet cleaning to food serving. If he found his shoes in his cell when he woke up in the morning, he continued his service; if they were gone, he had to leave quickly and quietly. Fortunately for the model, his shoes are still there.

Across from the main museum complex are rooms displaying dervish dwellings as well as a 35min. video recounting the museum's history through the evaluation of Rumi and the Mevlevi order. A mesmerizing finale includes the whirling dervishes in action. The film is available in English upon request.

Every year from December 10-17, Konya celebrates Rumi's extraordinary life. The festivities include one of the few opportunities to see whirling dervishes perform. The celebration is popular, so reserve rooms in advance. *(Museum open M 10am-5:30pm, Tu-Su 9am-6pm. $2, students $1. The building is considered a holy place. The staff will lend those wearing shorts a sarong to wrap around their legs. Shoes must be removed and carried. Women should cover their heads. Head scarves are provided at the door.)*

NEAR THE MEVLÂNA MUSEUM. The **Selimiye Camii,** completed in 1587, stands next door to the Mevlâna Müzesi. Konyans gather to pray here under a beautifully decorated tomb and crystal chandeliers that hang almost within arm's reach. The design on the mosque's carpet mimics the one on the dome above.

Aziziye Camii, in the bazaar off İstanbul Cad., was built between 1671 and 1676 at the behest of Sultan Mehmet IV's bookkeeper and renovated in 1891. The mosque's design is a mix of Baroque and Rococo styles. *(Mosques open 8am-6pm.)*

ŞERAFATTİN CAMİİ AND MAUSOLEUM OF ŞEMS. Across from the PTT on Mevlâna Cad. stands the impressive Şerafattin Camii, whose Selçuk mosaic tiles and classic Ottoman minaret suggest the periods of its construction (13th century) and restoration (17th century). If you walk out behind the Şerafettin Camii down the small street past a hamam and into a small park on the left, you will come to the Mausoleum and Mescid of Şems of Tabriz. The Selçuk-style mausoleum, supposedly built on the site where Şems's murdered body was found, contains his wooden catafalque. *(Mausoleum open 9am-6pm.)*

ALAADDİN CAMİİ. The Alaaddin Camii stands atop **Alaaddin Tepesi,** a hill that may well conceal countless as-yet undiscovered layers of human history stretching back to the Bronze Age. Closer to the surface are a park and some quiet tea gardens, crowned by the 13th-century Alaaddin Camii. One of Konya's oldest fixtures, it was built when the region was newly conquered, and its Syrian Selçuk architecture shows the influence of non-Islamic cultures. The mosque now has iron beams that span the *eyvans* (arches) and columns that emerge gracefully from the floor. The visually eloquent *mihrab* (prayer niche), covered in inscriptions and multicolored tiles, compensates for the lack of external decoration. A courtyard within the mosque houses 2 pavilions, containing the bodies of 6 sultans. Tiny stones are stuck in crevices along the outside wall of the mosque, facing the Selçuk Pavilion. Visitors pick up a stone from the area, make a wish or say a prayer, and then throw the stone at the wall. If it sticks, the prayer will be answered or the wish will come true. Downhill from the mosque are the remains of the Alaaddin Palace of Selçuk Sultan Kılıç Arslan II (1156-1192). *(Mosque open daily 9:30am-5:30pm.)*

KARATAY MEDRESE AND TILE MUSEUM. This 13th-century school for teaching the Qur'an and Shar'ia Law to young Selçuks was built by Emir Celâleddin Karatay, a close friend of the Mevlâna and a "voice of reason" to counter Rumi's spiritual and poetic ecstasy. The *medrese* has rather logically become a **tile museum,** since the interior itself is a marvelous example of Selçuk tilework. A tile-covered dome hovers over a square central pool. The now-empty pool, which was open to the sky, reflected the stars at night. Students measured the reflections to learn the distances between stars. The inside of the dome is covered with a pattern of interlinked stars, though age and decay have destroyed the upper tiles. Displays include tiles from Kubadâbâd Palace, near Beyşehir Lake, and ceramic plates from Konya. *(On Alaaddin Bul., across from the Alaaddin Palace. ☎351 19 14. Open daily 9am-noon and 1:30-5:30pm. $1.40.)*

OTHER MUSEUMS. Konya's **Stone and Woodwork Museum** is in the **İnce Minare Medrese** (Medrese of the Slender Minaret). The highlight is a massive stone portal whose arch is engraved with Arabic script and bas-relief plants. The minaret from which the *medrese* took its name was struck by lightning in 1901 but has since been rebuilt. Inside are works from the Selçuk, Karamanoğulları, and Ottoman periods, including winged angels and double-headed eagles carved in stone. The woodwork exhibit features carved doors and shutters and *yazma* stamps. *(On Alaaddin Bul., next to McDonald's. Closed for renovations, the museum should reopen by 2004.)*

Konya's **Archaeological Museum** contains artifacts from prehistoric times to the Byzantine era. One of the 3rd-century Roman sarcophagi on display illustrates the labors of Hercules. The museum also contains extraordinary finds from nearby Çatalhöyük (see below), including the remains of a year-old infant, buried under the floor of her family's house. Ancient toiletries include Roman ivory combs and toothpicks. *(On the small Şuhibi Ata Cad., about 7 blocks south of Alaaddin Tepesi. Open Tu-Su 9am-noon and 1:30-5:30pm. $1.40, children and high school students free.)*

Turn left out of the Archaeological Museum gates to get to the **Ethnographic Museum,** displaying ornate embroidery, clothing, jewelry, metal hats, and hunting equipment that includes a small metal contraption used to make deer noises. *(☎351 89 58. Open Tu-Su 9am-noon and 1:30-5:30pm. $1.40, students $.50, children free.)*

DAYTRIPS FROM KONYA

ÇATALHÖYÜK

The easiest way to get to Çatalhöyük is to take a dolmuş from Konya's otogar to Çümra (45min., 6-7 per day 9am-6pm, $.75), from where a taxi can take you the remaining distance (10min.; $20, try to bargain).

The neolithic town of Çatalhöyük, dating back to the 8th millennium BC, vies with Jericho for the coveted title of "World's First City." Near the town of Çümra, 50km south of Konya, the 9000-year-old town is touted as the most important archaeological site in Turkey. Çatalhöyük was home to between 5000-10,000 people for 1000 years, and was one of the largest and most complex settlements of its time.

Archaeologist James Mellaart discovered the site in 1958. The most sensational objects from Çatalhöyük are the **female figurines,** particularly one of an ample, naked woman, seated on a throne of leopards, who appears to be giving birth. Archaeologists have found carved female breasts that have **vulture beaks** within them. Some conclude that the town was a matriarchal society that worshipped the Mother Goddess, but not enough evidence has been found to support the theory.

Çatalhöyük families lived in compact mud-brick houses which were used for cooking, sleeping, and religious worship. When family members died, they were buried under platforms in the house. About every 100 years, residents would fill in the house and build a new one on top of it, eventually forming a mound 20m high.

The enormous site is slowly being excavated by an international team. Archaeologists eagerly await discoveries about and insight into the ancient culture's art, symbolism, mythology, textiles, use of pottery, metals, and wood, and domesticated plants and animals. Although the most important finds have been whisked to Ankara's **Museum of Anatolian Civilizations** (see p. 369), the site offers a uniquely interactive experience. If you visit the site between July and mid-September, you can watch the excavation in progress and talk with the archaeologists and other workers. Usually, however, a guard will show you around. The site includes museum with finds from the 1993 excavation and a replica of a Çatalhöyük house.

OTHER DAYTRIPS

SİLLE. Sille, 8km from Konya, can be visited in one morning. Visitors come to see the **Aya Elena Kilisesi,** a 4th-century Christian church decorated by more recent frescoes. (Open Tu-Su 9am-4pm. $1.) The two caves facing the church were inhabited at one point. *Sille-bound bus #64 leaves the municipal bus stop (on Alaaddin Cad., across from the PTT) every 30min. ($1), stopping in the middle of Sille's main street, distinguished by the standard-issue Atatürk bust. The PTT is ahead and around the corner (open M-F 8:30am-12:30pm, 1:30-5:30pm), and the church lies 50m past the PTT on the main road.*

MEKE CRATER LAKE. A unique erosion formed the centerpiece for the panoramas and wildlife that surround this aquatic doughnut in an otherwise entirely flat landscape. Nearby **Kilistra,** a purportedly Roman city turned rock-integrated-city à la Cappadocia, is believed to have been a stop on St. Paul's ancient world tour. *(Buses run to nearby Karapınar (2hr., 8am-7pm) from the otogar. A taxi to Kilistra costs $35.)*

WHIRLING DERVISHES Legend holds that Celeddin-I-Rumi's mystical order derived from the great teacher's encounter with the rhythmic banging of a goldsmith's hammer. So sensitive was Rumi to the pounding that he began to spin in ecstasy. A passing *imam* was so engaged that he offered himself to Rumi as a disciple. Since then, the whirling ritual *(sema)* has been fine-tuned and is laden with distinct symbolism, while still retaining its otherworldly effects.

The spiral form is natural to all living things. Through the *sema*, the dervish ("doorway" in Arabic) communes with the divine by imitating one of nature's most innate states. The right palm, upheld to the sky, channels the power of heaven through the dervish's body and out to the earth through the down-turned left palm. The combination of whirling in the manner of the earth's rotation and the transition of energy results in a trance-like state, whose effects on the actor's body have been scientifically documented (they *don't* get dizzy. The dervish's white dress signifies the ego's burial shroud, capped off with the camel hat as the ego's tombstone, indicating the inevitable death of man and his passing importance.

WESTERN ANATOLIA

EĞİRDİR ☎246

No one walks in Eğirdir. It's more of a laid-back amble, cultivated to match the pace of life in this small, conservative fishing town in the Taurus mountains. Under the watchful eye of a nearby military base, Eğirdir is surrounded by Turkey's fourth largest lake, Eğirdir Gölü (540 sq. km), whose color shifts with the strength of the wind, rippling from jade to tones of gray. The lake yields innumerable carp and bass, and in the fall, orchards fill with golden delicious apples.

TRANSPORTATION

Trains: The *istasiyon* (☎311 46 94) is 2km west of downtown, off 2nd Sahil Yolu, and accessible by dolmuş. One slow, unreliable train runs daily to **İstanbul** (15hr.; 5pm; $10, students $8). Station open daily 6am-noon and 5-7pm.

Buses: The otogar (☎311 40 36) is in the town center, between the mosque and the water. To: **Ankara** (7hr.; 10:45am, 12:30pm; $10); **Antalya** (3½hr., 9am-8:30pm, $3.50); **Cappadocia** (8hr.; noon, 9, 11:30pm; $12); **Isparta** (30min., every 15min. 7am-10pm, $.25); **İstanbul** (9hr., 8pm, $14); **İzmir** (7hr., 6 per day 7am-10:30pm, $10); **Konya** (3½hr., every hr. 8:30am-8pm, $8). Frequent **local buses** and dolmuş (every 15 min., 7am-10pm, $.25) leave from behind the mosque, across from the otogar. One runs to **Yeşilada** (1.5km) and the other to the train station and the 3 beaches.

ORIENTATION

The city consists of a peninsula jutting into the lake, **Eğirdir Gölü,** and two islands connected by bridges to the mainland. The city center, marked by a walk-through minaret, a marketplace, several restaurants, and pensions, is on the mainland. The **otogar** sits directly between the minaret and the lake shore. The closer island, little more than a floating *çay* garden, is called **Canada** (JAHN-ah-dah), which means "soul island" or "life island." Most of the town's pensions are on the more bulbous **Yeşilada** (Green Island), which is connected to Canada, eh?

To reach the lake, walk straight from the otogar past the **Atatürk Statue** on the right, and follow the road as it curves left onto **2nd Sahil Yolu.** This street runs past the **PTT** and the **tourist office** to a **soldiers' casino** *(askeri gazinosu)* and several pensions before hitting **Yazla Plajı, Altıkum Plajı,** and **Bedre Plajı. Yenimahalle Cad.** begins to the left of the otogar, and continues past the hospital on to Konya.

PRACTICAL INFORMATION

Tourist Office: 2nd Sahil Yolu No. 13 (☎311 43 88; fax 311 20 98). From the otogar gate, walk straight and follow 2nd Sahil Yolu as it curves up and to the left past the PTT. English spoken. Open M-F 8:30am-5:30pm; in winter M-F 8am-4:30pm.

Banks: Türkiye İş Bankası, on 2nd Sahil Yolu, before the PTT (when walking from the town center) has a V/MC/Cirrus/Plus **ATM.** Several other ATMs dot the town center.

Luggage Storage: At the otogar. $1 per bag. Open roughly 6am-8pm.

Hamam: Erkek Hamam (☎312 36 18), just before the PTT. $6. Open 7:30am-11pm.

Police: (☎311 53 63), on 2nd Sahil Yolu, 20m past the PTT. Open 24hr.

Pharmacy: On Yenimahalle Cad., to the left of the otogar. Open daily 8am-7:30pm.

Hospital: (☎311 64 90), on Yenimahalle Cad. Turn left out of the otogar and walk 300m. Open 24hr. The health center, **Sağlık Ocağı** (☎311 48 55), is next to the hospital. Open daily 8am-5:30pm. Little English spoken.

Internet Access: Gözde Internet (☎311 23 48), the first left after Kervansaray Restaurant, past the otogar. Quick access and cheap rates. $.75 per hr. Open 9am-midnight.

PTT: (☎311 45 90), on 2nd Sahil Yolu on the way to the tourist office. Information and *poste restante* daily 8am-11pm. Express mail M-F 8:30am-12:30pm and 1:30-5:30pm.

Postal Code: 32500.

ACCOMMODATIONS

Since nearly all of Eğirdir's pensions are affordable and comfortable, the added extras can be the deciding factor: the town has no tour agencies, so the services offered by agencies competing for business are paramount. The best are scattered on the mainland and on Yeşilada. Since most don't have singles, they often make single travelers pay for double occupancy during high season (June-Sept.). To save $2-3, let pension representatives at the otogar bid on you with their rivals. Bargaining is acceptable.

Köşk Pension-Restaurant, 37 Yazla Mah. (☎311 43 82; fax 311 61 84), at the top of 2nd Sahil Yolu, 800m from town. Free car service to and from town and the beaches; call for pick-up or meet the driver at the Tuborg/Pepsi sign across from the otogar. Most of the 17 rooms have showers and lake views. Owned by the local Pepsi distributors, Köşk features a free "Pepsi Tur" every Sunday, which shuttles guests in a Pepsi truck 70km south to the scenic Çandır Canyons (9am-9:30pm). Boat tours are also available ($2). Breakfast $3. Singles $6-10; doubles $12-20. Discount with *Let's Go.*

Peace Pension (☎311 24 33; sehsuvar_@hotmail.com; www.peacepension.com). Within Yeşilada, take a left before Choo Choo Pension and a right at the next street. As serene as it gets, with sparkling rooms and a pleasantly shady terrace. Trekking and fishing trips organized. Breakfast $2. $5 per person, with bath $8.

Lale Pension, Kale Mah, 6 Sok. No. 2 (☎312 24 06; fax 311 49 84). Exit the otogar and head right past the castle to the large yellow signs leading to Lale, 2min. from the shore. 9 clean rooms with hardwood floors and bath. The mountaineer owner offers sage advice on trekking, boat trips, and other outdoor activities. Enjoy the astounding terrace view. Laundry $3. Internet $1.50. Breakfast $3.50. $15 per person.

Choo Choo's Pansiyon (☎311 49 26; fax 311 67 64), on Yeşilada Mah. The newest pension on the island, offering clean rooms on the lake, each decorated with the work of a different artist. The hosts, Hüseyin and jovial, St. Nicholas lookalike Choo Choo, arrange boat and fishing trips. Breakfast $2. Singles $8; doubles $15.

Altınkum Plajı Camping (☎311 48 57), on Altınkum Plajı, roughly 2km past the tourist office. Bear right at the "major junction" sign after Köşk. *Plaj*-bound dolmuş leave from across the otogar (every 15min.). Camp with Turkish out-of-towners on Eğirdir's best-loved beach and enjoy electricity, hot showers, and phone. Small tents $1.80; large tents $3; cement shell $6; small double concrete hut with shower and toilet $6.

FOOD AND ENTERTAINMENT

Eğirdir cooks make a mean fish. The local specialities are *sazan* (carp), usually served whole; *levrek* (bass), generally filleted and fried in a light tomato flavored batter; and *karides* (shrimp). All of these are available at the lake-front pension-restaurants of Yeşilada. *Lokantası* and *döner* stands line the town's center.

Kemer Lokantası (☎311 42 47), directly in front of the minaret's entrance on the street. A no-nonsense eatery serving delicious, hearty, meat-and-potatoes standards. Half chicken $.175, *kebaps* $1. Open daily 6am-11pm.

Kervansaray Restaurant (☎311 63 40), next to the otogar. Serves more luxurious meals, with a wine list and an extensive menu including *İzgara çeşitler* (mixed grill; $2.50) and fish ($3-7), all served on a lakefront terrace. *Levrek* comes in a light, crisp tomato batter that must be tasted to be believed ($2.50). Open daily 9am-11pm.

Melodi Restaurant (☎311 48 26), right on the Yeşilada coast. Classy setting with soft lighting and outdoor seating under the trees. The cow brain *meze* in tupperware is a steal at $1. Fish $2.80. Open daily 10am-11pm.

Big Fish Restaurant (☎311 44 13). Veer left as you enter Yeşilada; Big Fish is on the right facing the water. Airy and colorful restaurant with a lovely view, excellent service and scrumptious, fresh fish dishes ($2-9). Open daily 7am-midnight.

Keyasun Disco Bar, past the PTT near the bazaar, is the town's after-hours social center. Off-duty soldiers, and university students pack the small dance floor, drink from the full bar, or sit outside on the terrace in the cool night air. Beer $2. Open daily 9pm-2am.

SIGHTS

BEACHES. The small **Yazla Plajı,** originally a retreat for secondary-school teachers, is now open to the public. Past the Köşk Pension at the top of the hill, signs point to Eğirdir's finest beach, **Altınkum Plajı** (Golden Sand Beach), 1½km farther along 2nd Sahil Yolu. *($.25; parking $.75; dolmuş from town center $.25.)* Some 11km farther is the less-crowded **Bedre Plajı,** accessible by bike or taxi ($8). While there are no real beaches on Yeşilada, you can clamber down the rocky shore and swim wherever you like for free. **Pisidia Tours** (☎311 53 62; fax 311 58 58) runs tours and parties on Lake Eğirdir on a small yacht. The boat's skipper, the enterprising Turko-Australian Aydın Akdüz, lets backpackers sleep on board or camp out on deck under the stars for $4-6.

OUTDOOR ACTIVITIES. Eğirdir will not disappoint nature lovers or adventurers. **Paragliding** ($40), which offers aerial views of the glorious lake, is brand new (check with the tourist office for information). Your best bet for other activities is to find a pension that can organize fishing trips, camping, and other waters ports. Other possibilities include trekking and wind surfing. Prices are negotiable.

WISE ASS Nasrettin Hoca is a fabled 14th-century Ottoman wise man, born in a village near Eğirdir. Spouting wisdom still quoted by Turks today, he traveled the land with his talking blue donkey. One day he arrived at the mosque unprepared for his sermon, and asked the audience if they understood what he was going to tell them. When they all replied "no," he told them that if they didn't understand, there was no point in telling them, and he sat down. The following week when he asked the same question, they all replied "yes." Since they knew what he was going to say, he told them., there was no point in saying it, and so he sat down once again. By the third week, half of the audience said "yes" and the other half said "no," to which Hoca bowed politely and asked those who knew to tell those who did not. Apocryphal Hoca comics often appear on plastic *ayran* cups, most accompanied with English subtitles

Warm hospitality and gorgeous views make the village of **Akpınarköy** a popular trekking destination. The trek begins from behind the hospital and takes about two hours. Twenty-seven kilometers east of Eğirdir lies the 1½km-long **Zindan Cave,** which once served as a Roman temple dedicated to Eurymedon and now serves as the spookiest cave in the region. Explorers should bring a flashlight and a high tolerance for bats. Near the village of Sağrak, 40km southeast of Eğirdir, stands the severely ruined Pisidian city of **Adada,** now consisting of an ancient temple's fallen columns, sarcophagi, and an amphitheater. Coins have been found here dating to the first century BC, although today the site is nearly empty and difficult to reach. Only 25km south of town, **Lake Kovada National Park** teems with wildlife that draws butterfly collectors in the spring. Avid walkers can follow a popular stretch of the **King's Road,** by which Lydian rulers once traveled from Ephesus to Babylon. The trail passes through the **Çandır Canyons** near Lake Kovada. *(Many pensions will run excursions to these sights, especially for groups. Ask your pension owner to help negotiate prices: Zindan $20; Adada $35; National Park $40.)*

OTHER SIGHTS. Poised atop the mosque's archway is one of two **walk-through minarets** in the world. Built by the Selçuks in the 13th century, it is part of the **Hizir Bey Camii.** Walking under the arch is considered good luck. A **castle,** dating from the Lydian kingdom of the 5th century BC, is on the road from the town center to Yeşilada. Atop the castle is a **museum-home,** a reproduction of a 19th-century fishing home. At the foot of the castle in a small green domed hut is the **Tomb of Devran Dede,** a Muslim mystic who was famed for squeezing water from rocks. Eğirdir's **Thursday bazaar** attracts hundreds of neighboring villagers. *(Museum: open during the day; try to find the attendant to let you in. Free.)*

AFYON ☎272

Surrounded by vast fields of innocuous-looking poppies, Afyon ("opium") is a leading producer of the world's opium, grown here legally for pharmaceutical use. Afyon is proud of its role in the War of Independence, when Atatürk made his headquarters here. It also boasts two excellent but rather small museums. If spectacular views are your thing, a climb to the towering Hittite fortress will likely be the highlight of your stay. Modern-day Afyon, however, is a rather nondescript town, so it's best to stop just long enough to see the sights and try some *lokum* (Turkish delight) before getting on your way again.

TRANSPORTATION. Afyon's otogar is on the eastern edge of town along **İsmet İnönü Cad.** To reach the city center, take dolmuş #2 from the stop by the candy store on İsmet İnönü Cad., to **Bankalar Cad.** ($.20). **Buses** to: **Alanya** (6½hr., 10 per day 8am-1am, $10.50); **Ankara** (3hr., 25 per day 5:30am-3:30am, $6.50); **Antalya** (4½hr., 25 per day 7am-1am, $7.50); **Aydın** (via **Denizli:** 5hr., 13 per day 11am-12:30am, $8); **Bodrum** (7hr.; 10:15pm, midnight; $10); **Bursa** (4hr., 13 per day 11:30am-3:30am, $10); **Datça** (8hr., 11, 11:30am, 11:45pm, 12:30am; $13.75); **Denizli** (3hr., 13 per day 11am-12:30am, $6.50); **Eskişehir** (2¼hr., 11 per day 8:45am-1am, $4.25); **İstanbul** (7hr., 15 per day 11am-12:30am, $13); **İzmir** (5hr., 30 per day 8:30am-3am, $7); **Kayseri** (8hr., 2 per day 6pm-midnight, $16); **Kuşadası** (summer only; 7½hr., 5 per day 11am-3am, $10); **Kütahya** (1½hr., 9 per day 7:30am-11:30pm, $3); **Konya** (4hr., 15 per day 12:30pm-3:30am, $8); **Marmaris** (8hr., 5 per day 10:30am-1:30am, $11.25). Students may receive a 10% discount.

The *istasyon,* in the northeast corner of town, sends trains to: **Adana** (11-15hr.; 1:10am, 5:40pm; $2-5); **Denizli** (5-6hr.; 5:55pm, midnight, 2am; $2.50); **Eskişehir** (3-4hr.; 5:10am, 3:50, 11:10pm,; $1.75); **İstanbul** (Haydarpaşa station; 8hr., 8 per day 8:10am-3:30am, $4.50); **Konya** (5hr.; 1:10, 3:50, 9:30pm; $2.50); **Kütahya** (2hr., 5 per day 8:25am-1:20am, $1.50). Prices and travel times vary by train. To get to town from the station, follow Ordu Bulvarı 2km to Hükümet Meydanı.

ORIENTATION AND PRACTICAL INFORMATION. Bankalar Cad. runs from the İmaret Camii in the south to **Hükümet Meydanı** and the tourist office in the north. In between lie most of Afyon's banks, hotels, and restaurants. **Ulu Camii** and the **Mevlevi Camii** sit to the west, where the fortress rises imposingly over the city.

The **tourist office** is on Bankalar Cad., with lots of information, although not much in English. (☎215 65 25; fax 213 26 23. Open daily 8am-noon and 1:30-5:30pm.) As the name suggests, there are numerous **banks** along Bankalar Cad.; the T. C. Ziraat Bankası has an **ATM** and **changes money** and **traveler's checks.** (Open M-F 8:30am-noon and 1:30-5pm.) For bathing, İmaret Camii's 700-year-old **hamam,** 4 Kurtuluş Cad., is the clear choice. (☎215 97 07. Open 6am-midnight. Women $1; men $1.50.) The **hospital,** Afyon Devlet Hastanesi, on Atatürk Cad. can be reached at ☎212 08 02, and the **police emergency number** is ☎155. Reach **Doğuş Internet Cafe,** Dumlupinar 2 Cad., Ersaraç Apt. No. 24/A., by turning off Bankalar Cad. onto Dumlupinar Cad. at the PTT. (☎215 57 20. $1 per hr. Open daily 8:30am-midnight.) The **PTT,** also on Bankalar Cad., has a **currency exchange.** (Postal window open 8am-7pm; exchange open 8:30am-noon and 1:30-5pm.) **Postal code:** 03000.

ACCOMMODATIONS. The cheapest of Afyon's hotels is the **Otel Lale,** 23 Bankalar Cad. Conveniently located across from the İmaret Camii, Lale offers small, simple, hot rooms above the puttering mopeds of Bankalar Cad. (☎215 15 80. Singles $4, doubles with bath $10.50.) **Otel Kafadar,** 2 İmaret Camii Cad., offers very basic rooms, some with gorgeous views of the mosque. There's a Turkish toilet and shower on each floor. (☎215 28 36. Singles $3; doubles $5.50, students $4; triples $8, students $6.50.) Although 2km from town, the **Otel Karaca,** directly opposite the otogar, offers the comforts of a fine hotel at a budget-friendly price. Its bright, carpeted rooms come with TV, bath, phone, and breakfast. (☎215 28 51; fax 213 04 37. Singles $13; doubles $20.)

FOOD & ENTERTAINMENT. Afyon is famous for its Turkish delight (*lokum*) and sausage (*sucuk*), and shops throughout the city display the local wares. For a cheap meal, dine on *pide*, *lahmacun*, or *döner* (all under $2) anywhere along Bankalar Cad. Slightly more upscale, the white tableclothed **İkbal Lokantası,** 21 Uzun Çarsı Cad. (☎215 12 05), serves up tasty three-course meals for under $6. İkbal is about 20m down Üzün Çarsı Cad., a side street off Bankalar Cad. **Kervan Urfa,** 2 Dumlupinar Cad. (☎215 90 43), is simple and functional, with a good selection and fairly cheap prices. Open until 11pm. **Sinema Günleri** in the Afyon Belediyesi Kultur Merkezi, shows English-language movies with subtitles for the homesick. (☎212 09 67. $.75.)

FASHION VICTIM Sultan Mahmut II (r.1809-1839) knew a fashion faux-pas when he saw one.Bound to keep Turkey abreast with European custom, the sultan sought to replace the turban as the official Muslim headgear in 1826. After toying with the possibility of a tri-cornered hat (but rejecting it for its symbolic ties to the Christian Trinity), Mahmut's head was bare no more after a shipment of attractive chapeaux from Tunisia arrived in İstanbul. Though useless for brimming the sun, the fez was close-fitting and thus perfect for the bowing involved in Muslim prayer.

In yet another cultural coup, Atatürk outlawed the once-innovative fez in 1925 as part of his program for modernizing and westernizing his new republic. He implemented the new law by staging what amounted to a fashion show of bowler hats in the extremely conservative Black Sea Coast city of Kastamonu. Atatürk's popularity (not to mention the 3 month prison sentence for anyone caught wearing a fez) ensured his plan's success, and brimmed hats reigned. Today, fez-wearers are still rare: only tourists are allowed to buy them as souvenirs.

SIGHTS. Afyon owes its old name, *Afyonkarahisar* ("The Black Fortress of Opium"), to the mighty rock that dominates the city. A hike up the 500 or so steps to the top of the **fortress** affords a thrilling view of the surrounding area, though some report danger of being mugged in the heights. The panorama is especially striking at sunset, when the call to prayer echoes from all 80 of the city's mosques. The route to the fortress passes Afyon's most striking mosques, the **Mevlevi Camii** and the **Ulu Camii.** Be warned, though: the walk from the center of town to the fortress can take over an hour. To get there, take Üzün Çarsı Cad., which meets Bankalar Cad. across from the Otel Oruçoğlu. After a few blocks, bear right onto Köprübaşı Cad. at the small roundabout. Köprübaşı Cad. becomes Yukarı Pazar Cad. as you walk uphill. Turn left at the POLİS sign and walk up the steps to the Mevlevi Camii, originally the site of Afyon's *mevlevihanesi* (dervish meeting place). The *Mevlevhanesi* was established in the 13th century by Sultan Veled, the son of Celeddin-i-Rumi (see **I Was Raw,** p. 346). Return to Yukarı Pazar Cad. and continue heading uphill to the Ulu Camii (Great Mosque). The Ulu Camii showcases Selçuk mosque construction, with a flat timber roof supported by a forest of more than 40 wooden columns, each capped with a carved *muqarna* (stalactite-shaped) capital. Pray that a guardian caretaker will show up to unlock the doors. Signs at the mosque show the way to the first of the castle's steps.

If your thirst for old mosques hasn't been quenched, back in the center of town stands the **İmaret Camii,** at the southern end of Bankalar Cad. This late Selçuk/early Ottoman mosque provides an oasis of profound silence in this noisy part of town. On the other end of Bankalar Cad., near Hükümet Meydanı and in the otherwise peaceful Anıt Park, the emotionally charged **Victory *(Zafer)* Monument** celebrates Turkish independence. Just across the street, the **Victory Museum** *(Zafer Muzesi)* exhibits weapons, photographs, and other souvenirs of the War of Independence. Most descriptions are in Turkish, but certain museum officials speak limited English. (☎212 09 16. Open daily 8am-noon and 1:30-5:30pm. Free.) Afyon's archaeology museum *(Arkeoloji Müze)* is on Kurtuluş Cad. A small but excellent museum, it clearly explains in English the classical and ancient history of the area. It features a beautifully made sarcophagus of fine white grained marble, full-size statues of Roman senators, and coins, all in excellent condition. (☎215 11 91. Open Tu-Su 8:30am-noon and 1:30-5pm. $1.50, students free.)

KÜTAHYA ☎274

Since the 16th century, Kütahya has been renowned as a center of legendary ceramic artistry. The entire city—mosques, hotels, fountains, and even the bus station—is tiled with intricate patterns of blue and white. Students from Dumlupınar University help keep the city young, and Kütahya's open square, lined with numerous internet cafes and shops, creates a busy street scene. But away from the city center, families still live in aging Ottoman houses and women laboriously wash their rugs in the street. Close to Kütahya rest the dramatic ruins of Aizanoi, an ancient Roman city with a spectacularly well-preserved temple.

TRANSPORTATION

Kütahya is a regional capital sprawled at the base of large hills. The **otogar,** better known as the *çinigar* (tile-station) for its elaborate tile decorations, is about 1km out of town, northeast of the center on **Atatürk Bul.** Much more convenient, however, is the bus **terminal** on Afyon Cad. just off the main square (Belediye Meydanı). All buses leaving the otogar also stop at the centrally located *terminal* about 5min. after their departure.

Buses: To: **Afyon** (1½hr., 6 per day 9:30am-7:30pm, $2.70); **Ankara** (4½hr., 10 per day 8am-2am, $8); **Antalya** (6hr.; 11am, 12:30pm, 1:30am; $10); **Bodrum** (7½hr., 1:30am, $13.75); **Bursa** (2½hr., 7 per day 8:15am-3:30am, $7.50); **Denizli** (4½hr., 2 per day 1:30am-7:30pm, $8.75); **Eskişehir** (1½hr., every hr., $1.50); **İstanbul** (6hr., 9 per day 6am-1:30am, $12.50); **İzmir** (6hr.; 6 per day 10:30am-1:30pm; $9, students $7.50); **Konya** (5hr., 4 per day 11am-1:30am, $10); **Mersin** (10hr., 11am, $16). Buses no longer run to **Kayseri.**

ORIENTATION & PRACTICAL INFORMATION

From the bus station, cross a courtyard onto Atatürk Bul., turn right, and follow the road past many shops, eateries and internet cafés to **Belediye Meydanı,** the main square, with a roundabout, giant clock tower, and beautiful giant ceramic fountain. Starting perpendicular to Atatürk Bul. and running northwest, **Adnan Menderes Bul.** leads to several hotels and ceramics outlets. Across the roundabout from Atatürk Bul. and leading southwest is Kütahya's main drag, **Cumhuriyet Cad.,** featuring numerous banks, hotels, and restaurants, as well as the **PTT** and the **Ulu Camii.** The Dönenler Camii and Kütahya's museums are in the neighborhood of the Ulu Camii; from here scenic winding streets with some fascinating Ottoman houses and really good views lead (fairly steeply) uphill to the fortress.

Tourist Office: A booth is on Belediye Meydanı, providing excellent maps of the city and colorful brochures describing its many attractions. Open M-Sa 9:30am-12:30pm and 1:30-6pm. There's also a less helpful Tourism Director's Office (☎223 19 62), inside the Vilayet Building on Belediye Meydanı.

Hospital: ☎223 60 53. Across from the Vilayet Bina, a 5min. walk up Afyon Cad.

Internet Access: There are dozens of internet cafés in Kütahya. One of the best is **Gence Internet,** No. 11 Asım Gündüz Cad. (☎223 53 63). $.40 per hr. Open 9am-midnight.

PTT: On Cumhuriyet Cad, toward the Ulu Camii and the museums. Telephones and a **currency exchange.** Open 24hr.

Postal Code: 43000.

ACCOMMODATIONS

The best cheap places are scattered around Belediye Meydanı.

Hotel Yüksel, 1 Afyon Cad. (☎212 01 11). Friendly management, and the cheapest rooms in town, with Turkish toilets and showers. Clean doubles with phone $3.

Otel Gönen (☎224 77 99 or 224 78 00; fax 224 78 01), Menderes Buhran, Belediye Meydanı. In the main square. All rooms with private shower, toilet, and TV. Singles $15, students $10.50; doubles $22, students $18.

Otel Köşk, Belediye Meydanı Lise Cad. No.1 (☎216 20 24), in the main square. Well-equipped rooms with hot water, TV, phone, and bath. Singles $6, doubles $9.

Otel Benli, 4 Cumhuriyet Cad. (☎216 13 77). If there's no room anywhere else. Centrally located, with Turkish toilets and somewhat questionable cleanliness. Singles $5, $4 for students; doubles $7, $6 for students; triples $10, $9 for students.

FOOD

Cheap *kebap* restaurants line Cumhuriyet Cad. and Lise Cad., by the roundabout.

Hisar Çaybahçesi, in the *kale* (castle), below the Döner Gazino restaurant. For a unique *çay* experience, order the *semaver,* an elegant teapot-like device which brews tea over hot coals ($1.25 for 2 people). Open 9am-noon.

Antep Sofrası (☎224 39 60), on Atatürk Bul. One of the best restaurants in Kütahya, with a beautiful wooden exterior and delicious food. A hearty meal of *ayran, lahmacun, kebap,* and *baklava* costs about $3. Open 24hr.

Döner Gazino (☎212 10 04), at the top of the *kale.* Take dolmuş #1 to save a half hour's walk uphill from Belediye Meydanı. The best place to spend a late afternoon in Kütahya. Housed in what was once the fortress's central turret, this slowly revolving restaurant provides striking sunset views and refreshing *çay* ($.35). Try the *izgararlar* ($1).

İnci Patisserie has three locations in the city. The best is on Atatürk Bul. (☎223 00 27). From Belediye head toward the otogar; after a short walk you'll see and smell it on your left. A friendly atmosphere to go with an enticing selection of pastries. Doubles as a café with two floors. Open 7am-midnight.

SIGHTS

People come to Kütahya to see **tiles.** Though the industry had withered to one artisan early this century, today it seems like everyone makes tiles. Shops selling local ceramics are concentrated along Atatürk Bul. on the way to the otogar and along Menderes and Abdurahman Kasa Bul. near the roundabout. Every July, Kütahya celebrates its craft for three weeks at the Dumlupınar Fuarı, Turkey's largest **handicrafts fair.** Consult the tourist office for fair dates.

Kütahya's mosques and museums are clustered at the end of Cumhuriyet Cad., a 10min. walk uphill from Belediye Meydanı. Closest to town is the 14th-century **Dönenler Camii** (on Cumhuriyet Cad.), one of the few remaining *mevlevihanesi* (dervish meeting places) in all of Turkey. In dervish services, musicians sat on the platform encircling the central chamber while dervishes revolved on the floor below. Today Dönenler Camii functions only as a mosque. Though covered by thick green carpet, a trap door in the center of the floor leads to a sacred well. For a token donation of about $.25, the mosque's guardian will show you the well and offer you a (dingy) glass of the water—it is said that those who drink from it are headed for heaven. More likely than not, they're headed for stomach problems.

Further along Cumhuriyet Cad. and in the midst of a colorful bazaar lies **Ulu Camii** (Great Mosque), originally built in 1410 but renovated in the 17th century by master architect Sinan. The mosque's *medrese* houses Kütahya's **archaeological museum,** at Börekçiler Mâhallesi, on Ulu Camii Cad. It's worth visiting this small museum for its works ranging from the late Paleolithic era to the Ottoman period, including artifacts from nearby **Aizanoi.** (☎223 69 90. Open Tu-Su 9am-5pm. $1.50, students free.) Kütahya's **Tile Museum** *(Çini Müzesi)* is behind the Ulu Camii on Gediz Cad. Hard-core porcelain enthusiasts will love its displayed works from *çini* masters, some dating from as early as the 14th century. (Open Tu-Su 8:30am-noon and 1:30-5:30pm or so. $.75, students free). The **Kossuth Museum** at Börek Mahallesi, Macar Sokak (Hungarian Street), commemorates **Kossuth Lájos** (1802-1894), the leader of the 1848 Hungarian Revolution, who found refuge in Afyon. Set in a three-story wooden house where he lived, the museum exhibits tell Kossuth's life story and show the house as it was in the 19th century. (☎223 62 14. Open Tu-Su 9am-noon and 1:30-5pm. $1.75; students free.)

No visit to Kütahya is complete without a stop at the sprawling **kale,** where the breathtaking view of the plain and distant mountains compensates for the schlep. Either walk uphill along Ertuğrul Gazi Cad. from the Ulu Camii and then bear left onto Kale Sok., or take dolmuş #1 and ask for the *kale.* The dolmuş will drop you off at a cobblestone path. It's a 15min walk uphill with beautiful views to the top.

Kütahya's most striking **Ottoman houses** line Germiyan Sok., reached by taking a left off Menderes Bul. just after it intersects with Kapan Cad. In order to preserve Kütahya's crumbling architectural heritage, the Turkish Ministry of Culture recently allotted money to purchase and restore five antique houses. Recover from all that walking at one of Kütahya's baths. The 700-year-old **Küçük Hamam,** at 65 Cumhuriyet Cad. near Küçükpark tea garden, houses an elegant marble interior and sauna. (Open 6am-11pm. $1.75, students $1.50.) Built in 1549, **Balıklı Hamam** has twin domed hot-rooms and separate rooms for men and women. (☎223 43 54. $1.75, students $1.50.) To get to Balıklı Hamam, walk along Cumhuriyet Cad. and turn right onto Balıklı Cad., near Küçükpark.

DAYTRIP FROM KÜTAHYA: AIZANOI

The ruins of Aizanoi lie in and around the small town of Çavdarhisar. Buses leave the Kütahya otogar (1½hr., 12 per day 6am-2am, $1.50), stopping at a BP gas station in the center of Çavdarhisar. Ask for the return schedule when you buy your ticket. From the bus stop, walk about 1km west on the road to Emet and Aizanoi, over a small bridge. Site open daily 8am-noon and 1:30-5:30pm. $1, students free.

Among Turkey's Greco-Roman ruins, Aizanoi is special because it is so low-key. The walk to Aizanoi passes through a rural peasant agricultural community, providing a glimpse of Anatolian country life. The incongruity between the old and the new is striking—the 2nd-century temple to Zeus stands opposite a mosque, amid rolling fields and old farmers tending their lands with tractors. Every so often a motorbike whizzes along the road leading to the temple. The temple is about a 15min. walk directly down the road sign-posted for Emet and Aizonoi and over the bridge. You'll pass a couple of coffee shops, lots of ducks, and few passers-by. The friendly guard **Nazim Erras** will let you in and allow you to explore the fallen pillars and stones which litter the site (the effect of a 1970 earthquake). The north and west sides of the temple are in excellent condition and allow you to imagine what the complete structure would have been like. Underneath the temple is a vast barrel-vaulted **chamber.** Research suggests the chamber may have served as an oracle or a storeroom for grain. Such a giant cellar is unusual for Roman temple architecture and is unparalleled in Asia Minor. Exiting the temple, take the road on your right to along a winding farm path to the remains of the **gymnasium, stadium** and **theater complex.** Not much is left of the gymnasium—you may find a shepherd resting with his flock—but continue to the stadium and theatre complex, which remain reasonably well preserved despite the earthquake. Aizanoi is the only known ancient city where the stadium and theater were in one facility. The climb up the stairs to the top of the theater provides a sense of its enormous capacity. On the way back, ask Nazim to show you the **baths,** in a warehouse a short walk away. They feature mosaic floors with mythological figures. The remains of the city's **marketplace** are to the right of the temple on the way back to Çavdarhisar.

If you're hungry, stop for a bite at **Tan-Pa Lokantası** (☎(274) 351 30 07), in front of the BP gas station. While you wait for a bus back to Kütahya, you can fill up here on decent *köfte*, rice, vegetables, and *ayran* for $3.

ESKİŞEHİR ☎222

For tourists, Eskişehir is little more than a busy, somewhat industrial city acting as the transportation gateway into Central Anatolia, with lots of banks and shops, a few clubs, lots of *meerschaum* (a soft, white mineral used for crafting pipes), and some passable museums. For Turks, however, Eskişehir, or "Old City," represents something more: a regional capital with a history stretching back over 3000 years to the Greco-Roman city of Dorylaeum, noted for the curative properties of its thermal baths. As a major industrial transit route, Eskişehir held a vital strategic role in the War of Independence, and today many Turks come from nearby towns for the active nightlife, fueled by a large student community. Though travelers can fill an afternoon or night, most prefer to spend their time and money elsewhere.

TRANSPORTATION. To get to town from the otogar, take any bus and ask for **Köprübaşı,** the central district ($.20, $.15 for students). The bus will stop near a large outdoor TV screen at the intersection of İsmet İnönü Cad. and Cengiz Cad. Alternatively, turn right from the otogar onto Sivrihisar Cad.—the town center is a 20min. walk. **Buses** run from the otogar to **Afyon** (2½hr., every hr., $4); **Alanya** (7hr., 8 per day 11:30am-1:30am, $14); **Ankara** (3hr., every hr. 5am-3pm, $6); **Antalya** (6hr., 8 per day 10:30am-1:30am, $11); **Aydın** (7hr.; 12:30pm, midnight; $15); **Ayvalık** (8hr., 5 per day 11am-11pm, $13); **Bodrum** (11hr., midnight, $16); **Bursa** (2½hr., 10 per day 6am-3:45am, $5); **Çanakkale** (7½hr., 7 per day 10am-1:30am, $12); **Datça** (12hr., 11pm, $19); **Denizli** (5hr., 4 per day 2:30pm-midnight, $9); **Fethiye** (7hr., 10:30pm, $15); **İstanbul** (6hr., every hr. 5am-2am, $10); **İzmir** (6hr., every hr., $13); **Kütahya** (1¼hr., every hr., $1.50); **Marmaris** (11hr., 11pm, $16). Students discounts are roughly 20%, depending on the bus company.

Trains leave Eskişehir's station for **Ankara** (2½hr.; 9-12 per day 5:30am-3:30am; $7, students $6); **İstanbul** (Haydarpaşa station; 4hr.; 10-14 per day 4am-1am; $10, students $8); **İzmir** (11hr.; 7:35am, 10pm, 12:55am; $7, students $5); **Konya** (8hr.; 4:45am, 2:15, 11:56pm; $6, students $5; end of the line is **Karaman**). To reach the city center from the station, turn left and follow İstasyon Cad. until it intersects with İsmet İnönü Cad; turn right here and walk about 1km to the center of town.

ORIENTATION AND PRACTICAL INFORMATION. Eskişehir's center lies between the otogar to the east and the train station to the west. Most hotels are slightly east on **Yunusmene Cad.** and **Sivrihisar Cad.,** which intersect to become **İsmet İnönü Cad.,** the main commercial street. The other main drag is **İki Eylül Cad.** Navigation in Eskişehir is tricky, since streets are rarely labeled and have the habit of changing names at intersections. **İsmet İnönü Cad.** becomes **Sivrihisar Cad.,** which runs parallel to the river and leads to a number of hotels. **İki Eylül Cad.** crosses the river and runs several blocks before turning left. **Hamamyolu Cad.,** parallel to İki Eylül Cad., passes by thermal baths and a park. To get there, take the second left on Köprübaşı Cad., away from the intersection of Sakarya Cad. and Sivrihisar Cad.

The **tourist office,** on the ground floor of the Municipal Building *(Vilayet Binasi)* on İki Eylül Cad., provides colorful brochures about all parts of Turkey except Eskişehir; maps of the city, however, are available. (☎230 17 52; fax 230 13 68. Open daily 8am-5:30pm.) Among the numerous travel agencies is **Sedef Turizm,** 1 İlk Eylül Cad. (☎230 30 71; fax 231 31 67). There are a number of **banks** in the city square and on Sivrihisar Cad., including a Yapı ve Kredi with two **ATMs. Eskişehir Hastanesi (hospital),** Çifteler Cad., ☎237 48 00; staffers speak little English. The **PTT** is on İki Eylül Cad. near the tourist office; there is also one at the otogar.

ACCOMMODATIONS AND FOOD. Otel Divan, 5 Sivrihisar Cad., is the best budget value in town, featuring a central location and clean rooms with Turkish communal toilets and showers on each floor. (☎232 00 31. Singles without TV $7; doubles with TV $15.) Another good budget choice is **Özbek Otel,** 89 Yunusemre Cad., a functional, slightly institutional hotel that's far enough from the main streets to afford a quieter night's sleep. (☎222 231 20 32. Singles $3; doubles $6.) The **Emek Hotel,** on Yunusemre Cad., has pleasant rooms with hot water and friendly management. (☎231 29 40. Singles $8, students $7.50; doubles $14, students $11.) Further down Sivrihisar Cad., the **Çiçek Palas Hotel,** 29 Sivrihisar Cad., has rock-bottom prices and the accommodations to match. Only for the budget fanatic. (☎234 40 56. Singles $2.50; doubles $5.) A pricier option is the **Hotel Arslan,** 107 Yunusemre Cad., with comfortable, clean, well-equipped rooms to go with a spacious lounge area. (☎231 09 09; fax 231 50 18. Singles $10; students $8.)

Finding **cheap eats** is no problem in Eskişehir, as both İki Eylül Cad. and İsmet İnönü Cad. are lined with restaurants and shops selling *döner* with *ayran* for $1 or less. Before you leave, stop by one of the town's sweet shops and try the local *nuga helvası,* a fluffy yet chewy confection peppered with walnuts. Try **Restaurant Ömür,** 20/A Cumhuriyet Mah. Cengiz Topel Cad. (☎234 70 00), an informal diner/restaurant, with a good selection at reasonable prices and a central location. Soup $.50, vegetable dishes $1, *kebap* $1.50. Open 6am-10pm.

SIGHTS. Meerschaum crafts can be found at the otogar or throughout the city; two well-marked shops lie off of İki Eylül Cad. In late September, Eskişehir celebrates its prized craft at the **International White Gold Festival.** If you have some time to kill, check out the finds from nearby Dorylaeuam at the **Archaeology Museum** *(Arkeoloji Müzesi)* on Hasan Polatkan Cad., where you may have the unique experience of having an entire museum to yourself. (Open daily 8:30am-noon, 1:30-5pm. $1.25, students free.) To get there from the tourist office, turn left on Atatürk Cad. and continue until the road ends. Turn right onto Polatkan Bulvar and the museum will be a few hundred meters on your right. Rest your travel-weary bones at Eskişehir's **thermal baths,** said to cure rheumatism, fractures, and kidney stones. A good soaking can be had at the Yeni Kaplua Termal, 5 Hamamyolu Cad. (☎231 15 01. $1; 20% student discount.) For a view into the Eskişehir of an earlier era, check out the restored **Olsmanlı Evi Müzesi** (Museum of the Ottoman House), on

Yeşilefendi Sokak, off Şeyh Sahabetlin Cad, just past the Archaeology Museum on Hasan Polatkan Cad. (Open 9am-noon and 1-4pm. Free.) This area, known as the "Old Town," also contains the historical **Kurşunlu Camii Kulliyesi** (Kurşunlu Mosque Complex), featuring the **Ethnography Museum,** and a 16th-century **mosque.**

NORTH-CENTRAL ANATOLIA

ANKARA ☎312

Ankara's history and character sometimes lead would-be visitors to dismiss the city as a functional, soulless capital city. Such an attitude ignores 3200 years of history and Ankara's place as Turkey's premier college town. Its old houses and twisting streets lie in a confusing tangle beneath imposing Byzantine walls, concealing dozens of cafes with breathtaking views, while nearby Kızılay, the main student area, has bars and an active nightlife to suit all tastes.

Located at the intersection of two Eurasian trade routes, the city was first founded as Ankuwash over 3200 years ago by the Hittites. Legend has it that Ankara was next ruled by the great Phrygian King Midas. Subsequently occupied by Lydians, Galatians, Augustan Romans, Byzantines, and Selçuks, Ankara eventually fell into Ottoman hands. Then known as Angora, the sleepy village was populated mainly by long-haired goats. In 1923, after the Turkish War of Independence, Atatürk built a modern city overnight, more or less from scratch. The curtains of the new nation's Opera House hastily went up, the Painting and Statue Museum was constructed and filled with contemporary Turkish art in just 18 months, and swampland was dredged to make way for the garish Gençlik Park. Modern-day Ankara is an administrative metropolis of parks, tree-lined boulevards, and embassies, providing a microcosmic look at modern Turkey: a multi-layered society with several, sometimes contrasting, identities existing side by side.

INTERCITY TRANSPORTATION

Flights: *Havaş* buses (every ½hr. 4am-11:30pm, $5) to Esenboğa Airport (☎398 00 00) leave from Hipodrom Cad. (next to the train station). Major carriers serving Ankara include: Aeroflot, Air France, Alitalia, Austrian Airlines, British Airways, Canadian Airlines, Delta, Iberia, JAL, KLM, Lufthansa, and Swissair. **Turkish Airlines (THY),** 154 Atatürk Bul., Kavaklıdere (Info and reservations ☎419 28 00; sales ☎468 73 40 or 468 73 41), offers direct flights to: **Adana** (1hr., 3 per day, $68); **Antalya** (1hr., 3 per day, $70); **Bodrum** (1¼hr., 5 per day, $82); **Dalaman** (1¼hr., 4 per day, $82); **Diyarbakır** (1½hr., 2 per day, $68); **Erzurum** (1½hr., 2 per day, $68); **İstanbul** (1hr, 15 per day, $82); **İzmir** (1¼hr., 12 per day, $82); **Sivas** (1hr.; M, Th; $59); **Samsun** (1hr., daily except Sa., $59); **Tokat** (1hr., Tu, $59); and **Trabzon** (1¼hr, 3 per day, $68). Prices and schedules subject to change. Students under 24 and travelers over 65 receive a 25% discount; travelers under 12 receive a 50% discount. It's best to buy tickets 2 days in advance. The private travel agencies between Kızılay and Kavaklıdere are convenient ticket vendors. THY open M-F 8:30am-8pm, Sa-Su 8:30am-5:30pm.

Buses: The **terminal** (a.k.a. AŞTİ or otogar), 5km west of Kızılay in Söğütözü, is the westernmost stop on the Ankaray subway line. Take any train to Kızılay. To get to Ulus from there, transfer to the Metro line and ride 2 stops north to Cumhuriyet Cad., about 400m west of the equestrian statue. Dolmuş ($.60) and city buses ($.50) run from the otogar to Ulus, stopping at Hisarparkı Cad., in the middle of the cheap hotel area. A taxi for the same trip should cost about $6.75; to Kızılay, $8. Scores of bus companies connect Ankara with nearly every point in Turkey. Ask for smaller destinations; chances are that there's a bus going there. For major cities, **Varan,** 34/1 İzmir Cad., Kızılay (☎418 27 06 or 224 00 43), and **Ulusoy,** 18/A İnkılâp Sok., Kızılay (☎419 40 80 or 224 01 72 or 286 53 30), offer safer, faster, and more comfortable transportation. There are no longer direct bus routes to **Afyon, Kemer,** or **Side,** which are instead served by the İzmir bus (for Afyon) and the Antalya bus (for Kemer and Side). Prices and schedules subject to change. Student discounts sometimes available upon request.

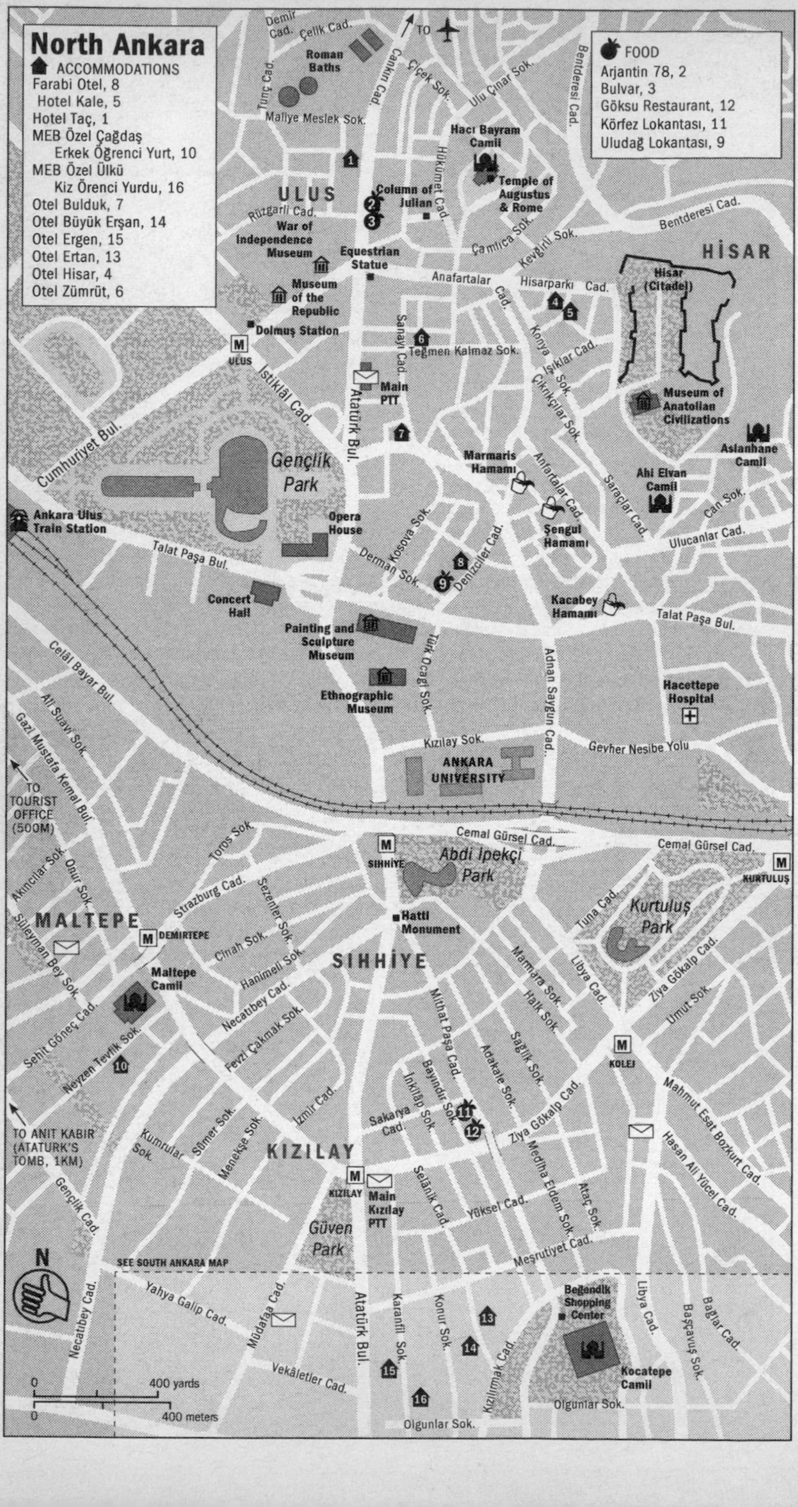
North Ankara
ACCOMMODATIONS
Farabi Otel, 8
Hotel Kale, 5
Hotel Taç, 1
MEB Özel Çağdaş Erkek Öğrenci Yurt, 10
MEB Özel Ülkü Kiz Örenci Yurdu, 16
Otel Bulduk, 7
Otel Büyük Erşan, 14
Otel Ergen, 15
Otel Ertan, 13
Otel Hisar, 4
Otel Zümrüt, 6
FOOD
Arjantin 78, 2
Bulvar, 3
Göksu Restaurant, 12
Körfez Lokantası, 11
Uludağ Lokantası, 9
Roman Baths
Hacı Bayram Camii
Temple of Augustus & Rome
Column of Julian
ULUS
War of Independence Museum
Equestrian Statue
Museum of the Republic
Dolmuş Station
HİSAR
Hisar (Citadel)
Museum of Anatolian Civilizations
Aslanhane Camii
Ahi Elvan Camii
Main PTT
Gençlik Park
Marmaris Hamamı
Şengul Hamamı
Kacabey Hamamı
Ankara Ulus Train Station
Opera House
Concert Hall
Painting and Sculpture Museum
Ethnographic Museum
Hacettepe Hospital
ANKARA UNIVERSITY
TO TOURIST OFFICE (500M)
Abdi Ipekçi Park
Kurtuluş Park
Hatti Monument
MALTEPE
Maltepe Camii
SIHHİYE
KIZILAY
Main Kızılay PTT
Güven Park
TO ANIT KABIR (ATATURK'S TOMB, 1KM)
SEE SOUTH ANKARA MAP
Beğendik Shopping Center
Kocatepe Camii
N
0
400 yards
400 meters

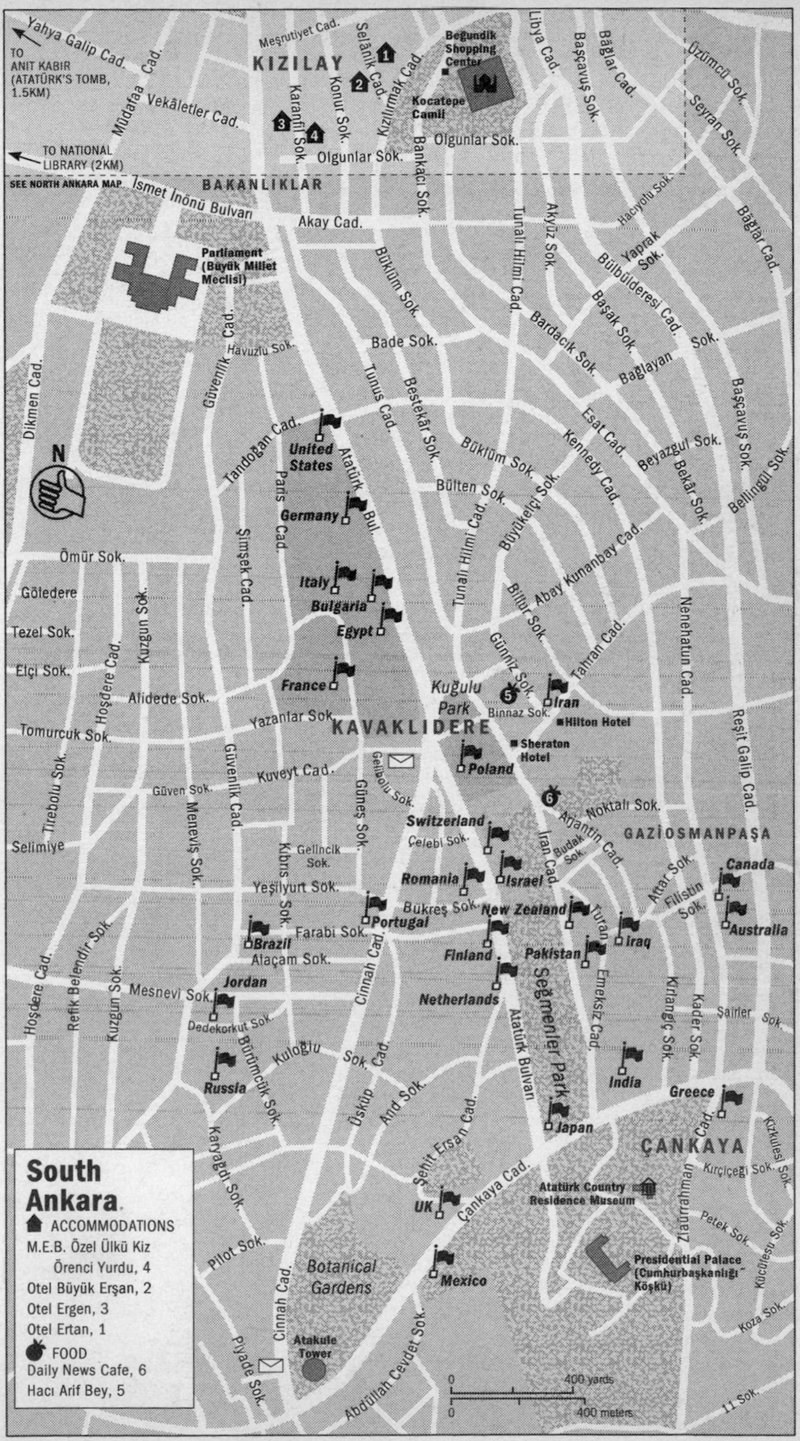

CENTRAL ANATOLIA

DESTINATION	DURATION	FREQUENCY/TIME	PRICE
Adana	7hr.	22 per day 9:30am-midnight	$12
Alanya	7½hr.	21 per day 7am-1am	$20
Antalya	7hr.	34 per day 7am-12:30pm	$13
Bodrum	12hr.	11 per day 7:30-10:30pm	$16.50
Çeşme	9hr.	11:30pm	$16.50
Eskişehır	3hr.	33 per day 7am-10:30pm	$4
Fethiye	8hr.	3 per day; 2 at 9:30pm, 1 at 10pm	$20
İstanbul	5½hr.	150 per day 6:30am-1:30am	$15
İzmir	8hr.	65 per day 7am-12:30am	$13
Kayseri	5hr.	40 per day 7am-1am	$8
Konya	3hr.	75 per day 6am-11pm	$8
Kuşadası	9hr.	10 per day 9am-midnight	$15
Kütahya	4½hr.	11 per day 8am-midnight	$10.50
Marmaris	10hr.	6 per day 9am-11:30pm	$15
Polatlı (for Gordion)	1 hr.	every 30min. 7am-9:30pm	$1.50
Samsun	7 hr.	20 per day 8am-midnight	$10
Sivas	6½ hr.	15 per day 9am-midnight	$12
Sungurlu	3 hr.	12 per day 8:30am-7:30pm	$10
Tokat	6 hr.	10 per day 9am-11pm	$10.50
Trabzon	10 hr.	9 per day 7:30am-8:30pm	$15
Tehran, Iran	36 hr.	M,W, and F 7pm	$35

DESTINATION	DURATION	FREQUENCY/TIME	PRICE
Adana	12 hr.	8:15pm	$9, students $7
Afyon	7 hr.	6:35pm	$7, students $5.50
Diyarbakır	23 hr.	M,W,F,Sa 6:50am; Tu,Th,Su 7:40pm	$10, students $8
Erzurum	22 hr.	2 per day 9am-6:25pm	$9, students $7
Eskişehir	3 hr.	10 per day 8am-11:30pm	$2-31
İstanbul (Haydarpaşa)	6½-9½ hr.	7 per day 8am-11:30pm	$4-35
İzmir (Basmane)	15 hr.	6:10, 6:35, 7:10pm	$9, students $7
Kars	27 hr.	6pm	$9, students $7
Kütahya	7 hr.	2 per day 6:10-7:10pm	$6, students $4.50
Malatya	19 hr.	7:25pm	$6.75
Sivas	12 hr.	6:50am, 6:08, 7:40pm	$5.50, students $4

Trains: The train station *(Ankara Ulus Station)* is connected to Gazi Mustafa Kemal Bul. via a long underground tunnel doubling as a covered market. Follow this tunnel past the last platform to Gazi Mustafa Kemal Bul. The Ankaray stop will be about 300m to the left. Alternatively, walk the 1½km up Cumhuriyet Bul. to Ulus Sq. 20% discount for students and seniors. **Sivas** is served by the Malatya train.

ORIENTATION

The city's main street, **Atatürk Bul.,** runs north-south. At its north end, the **Ulus** precinct consists of dusty cement apartments and crowded markets, all centered around a colossal equestrian monument to Atatürk. To the east of Ulus rises **Hisar** (Citadel), a traditional Anatolian village scattered with upscale restaurants and crowned by the 9th-century **Ankara Fortress** *(Ankara kale)*. Ulus and Hisar comprise **Eskişehir** (Old City) and include most of the sights and the cheapest hotels. A couple of kilometers south of Ulus along Atatürk Bul. is **Sıhhiye,** a commercial neighborhood distinguished mostly by its giant Hittite reindeer. Further south along Atatürk Bul. is **Kızılay,** the center of **Yenişehir** (New City), bustling with bookstores, bars, *kebap* houses, and students from the six nearby universities. West of Kızılay is **Maltepe,** a district full of grim nightclubs and cheap student dorms.

Kavaklıdere, Çankaya, and **Gaziosmanpaşa,** south of Kızılay, represent the stately side of Ankara: lush residential areas of embassies, ministries, five-star hotels, and night clubs. Bus #613 runs the length of Atatürk Bul. from the Atakule tower to the equestrian statue in Ulus. In addition, a new **subway system,** the **Ankaray suburban railway line,** runs east-west from its center in Kızılay. The bus terminal (**AŞTİ** on the signs, otogar to locals) in **Söğütözü** is 5km west of Kızılay, at the westernmost Ankaray subway stop. The railway station *(gar)*, on **Cumhuriyet Bul.**, is 1½km southwest of Ulus Square.

LOCAL TRANSPORTATION

Local Buses: Buses come in 3 flavors: red and green (both government-run), and blue (private). Buy tickets for red and green buses from booths near major bus stops or from street vendors. On the blue buses, pay the conductor after boarding. Tickets on all buses cost $.50, students $.30.

Local Dolmuş: Hubs near Hacı Bayram Camii and at the intersection of Denizciler Cad. and Adnan Saygun Cad. $.35-.60, depending on distance. Student fare available.

Subway: Ankara's new, clean subway system provides possibly the fastest and easiest way to get around the city. The east-west Ankaray line (stations marked by a white "A" on a green background) connects the bus station to Dikimevi, with stops in Tandoğan, Maltepe, Kızılay, and the Colleges (Kolej). The north-south Metro line (white "M" on red background) also stops in Kızılay, running north from there to Sıhhiye, Ulus, and the northwestern suburbs. 5-ride passes $2.50, students $1.50. 6:15am-midnight.

Car Rental: Hertz, 138/B Atatürk Bul., Kavaklıdere (☎468 10 29; fax 468 19 26), and **Avis,** 68/2 Tunus Cad., Kavaklıdere (☎467 23 13; fax 467 57 03), both have airport offices and are more expensive. Both open daily 9am-7pm. **Best Rent A Car,** Büklüm Sok., No. 89/9, Kavaklıdere (☎467 00 08; fax 467 02 05). Rents Fiat Şahin (from $45 per day) and Escorts (from $73 per day). Open M-Sa 8am-7:30pm, Su 8:30am-6pm. **Alara Rent A Car,** 1/A Güniz Sok., Kavaklıdere (☎426 54 75; fax 426 52 63), rents Fiat Şahins (from $30 per day) and air-conditioned Toyotas (from $84 per day). Prices include unlimited mileage and insurance. Open M-Sa 8:30am-7pm.

PRACTICAL INFORMATION

TOURIST AND FINANCIAL SERVICES

Tourist Offices: 121 Gazi Mustafa Kemal Bul. (☎231 55 72). Directly outside the Maltepe stop on Ankaray (from Kızılay, take the train headed toward AŞTİ). The friendly, English-speaking staff provides free city and country maps and can serve as your interpreter to the tourist police (☎303 63 53). Open daily 9am-5pm. The airport tourist office (☎398 03 48) offers similar services. Open 24hr.

Embassies: Bulgaria, 124 Atatürk Bul., Kavaklıdere (☎426 74 55; fax 427 31 78). Visa applications M-F 10am-noon. **Egypt,** 126 Atatürk Bul., Kavaklıdere (☎426 10 26; fax 427 00 99). **Greece,** 9-11 Ziaürrahman Cad., Gaziosmanpaşa (☎436 88 60; fax 446 31 91). Visa applications M-F 9:30am-noon. **Iran,** 10 Tahran Cad., Kavaklıdere (☎427 43 20; fax 468 28 23). Visa applications M-F 3-5pm. **Iraq,** 11 Turan Emeksiz Sok., Gaziosmanpaşa (☎468 74 21; fax 468 48 32). Visa applications M-F 10am-3pm. **Israel,** 85 Mahatma Gandi Cad., Gaziosmanpaşa (☎446 29 20; fax 426 15 33). **Jordan,** 18A Mesnevi Dede Korkut Sok., Aşagı Ayrancı (☎440 20 54; fax 440 43 27). **Lebanon,** 44 Kızkulesi Sok., Gaziosmanpaşa (☎446 74 85; fax 446 10 23). **Northern Cyprus,** 20 Rabat Sok., Gaziosmanpaşa (☎437 60 31; fax 446 52 38). **Russia,** 5 Karyağdı Sok., Çankaya (☎439 21 22; fax 438 39 52). **Syria,** 40 Sedat Simavi Sok., Çankaya (☎440 96 57; visa department ☎440 17 21; fax 438 56 09) Visa applications M-F 8:30-9:30am. For embassies of **Australia, Canada, New Zealand, South Africa,** the **UK,** and the **US,** see **Consular Services in Turkey,** p. 39.

Banks: You can't throw a stone in Kavaklıdere, Kızılay, Maltepe, Ulus, or Sıhhiye without hitting a bank branch. All large banks offer **currency exchange,** but only major banks such as **Akbank** (no commission) and **Garanti** will cash **traveler's checks.** Change offices *(döviz)* along Atatürk Bul. offer slightly better rates (but no traveler's checks). 24hr. **ATMs** can be found on virtually every street corner. **Türkiye İş Bankası, Yapı ve Kredi, Pamukbank,** and **Garanti Bankası** accept V/MC/Cirrus/Plus/Eurocard; Vakıfbank and Akbank also accept AmEx.

Wire Transfers and Moneygrams: Western Union, 27 Meşrutiyet Cad., Kızılay (☎419 88 58). Open M-Sa 9am-5pm. Western Union services also at **MNG Bank,** 84 Uğur Mumcu Cad., Gaziosmanpaşa (☎447 66 50). Open M-F 9am-6pm. AmEx cardholders can send and receive moneygrams at Koçbank by the statue in Ulus Meydanı.

LOCAL SERVICES

Lost Property: Kayip Eşya offices in Esenboğa (☎398 05 50), the **main otogar bus terminal** (☎224 10 10 or 224 01 78), **city municipal buses** (☎384 03 60), and the **Head Security Office** *(Emniyet Müdürlüğü;* ☎303 06 06), on İskitler Cad.

Library: National Library *(Millî Kütüphane),* Bahçelievler (☎212 62 00; fax 223 04 51; www.mkutup.gov.tr). Take the dolmuş ($.35) to Balgat from Kızılay's Güvenpark and ask to be let off at the Millı Kütüphane. Entry to this multi-level, marble, CD-ROM-equipped library will be easier if you have either a form from your embassy (for foreigners living in Turkey) or a research permit, obtained from the Turkish Embassy in your home country. Try using a student ID card or ISIC. Study salons open M-F 9am-8:30pm, Sa-Su 9:30am-6:30pm; stacks open M-F 9am-noon and 1:30-4:30pm.

English Language Bookstores: Most bookstores in Kızılay offer a range of Penguin Classics, Stephen King, and non-fiction. **Dost Kitabevi,** has an extensive and very good selection, with a branch in Kızılay, 11 Karanfil Sok., carrying English language newspapers and magazines. (☎425 24 64. Open M-Sa 9am-10pm, Su noon-7pm.) **Tahran Kitabevi,** 19/A Selânik Cad., Kızılay (☎417 25 50) carries a range of magazines (*The Economist, Newsweek,* etc.) and many books about Turkey. Open M-Sa 9am-12:30pm and 2-7pm. **Turhan Kitabevi,** 8/B Yüksel Cad., Kızılay. From spring to fall, the **open-air book market** on Olgunlar Sok. sells a haphazard range of back-issue US magazines.

Turkish-American Association (Türk-Amerikan Derneği): 20 Cinnah Cad., Kavaklıdere (☎426 26 44; fax 468 25 38; Programs Dept. ☎426 26 48). Cinnah Cad. branches off from Atatürk Bul. south of Bakanlıklar. Take any bus from Atatürk Bul. heading toward Çankaya or Gaziosmanpaşa. Offers Turkish and English classes, art exhibits, ballroom dances, concerts, and a lecture series. Monthly bulletin with events schedule. Small selection of US magazines in the **Graphica Cafe** (tea $.35). Open daily 9am-8:30pm.

The British Council and Cultural Affairs, British Embassy, 41 Esat Cad., Küçükesat 06660 Ankara, (☎424 1644 ext. 118; fax 424 1399; filiz.sanyel@britishcouncil.org.tr). Open to all, the British Council has BBC TV, a nice café, and an excellent library with books on Turkey, English newspapers, and *The Economist.*

Laundromat: Self-service **Ekspres Çamaşır** (☎419 32 32, ext. 272), in Kızılay in the Beğendik shopping mall under the Kocatepe mosque. Go up the first set of motorized ramps and take a right; exit the main shopping area through the corridor and turn left. Wash and dry $3.75. Free locker storage. Open daily 9:30am-9pm. **Bora Çamaşer Yıkamatik,** 16/A Dumlupınar Cad., Cebeci (☎363 42 43), is closer to Ulus. Follow Cemal Gürsel Cad. to the Kurtuluş Ankaray stop, turn left and go underneath the train overpass. From here turn right onto Gerher Nesibe Yolu and then left onto Dumlupınar Cad. Wash and dry $3.75. Open daily 8am-9pm.

Hamams: Şengul Hamamı, 3 Acıçeşme Sok., Ulus (men's section ☎311 03 63; women's section ☎310 22 98), down a small side street off Denizciler Cad., about 200m from the Marmara Otel. Nearly 600 years old, with pool and sauna. $4; massage $1.50. Students 20% off. Open daily 5:30am-11pm. **Karacabey Hamamı,** 101 Talat Paşa Cad., Ulus (☎311 84 47), has a stately wooden antechamber. $3.75; *kese* and massage each $1.25. Open daily 6:30am-11pm. The **Marmara Hamamı** (☎324 25 27), 17 Denizciler Cad., next door to the Marmara Otel in Ulus, has a sauna and a spacious central room. $5; massage $2. Open daily 5am-10pm. Separate women's hamam around the corner (open 8am-6:30pm).

EMERGENCY AND COMMUNICATIONS

24-Hour Pharmacy: Listings of on-duty *(nöbetci)* pharmacies in the *Hürriyet* daily paper (same page as movie listings). On-duty establishments have a sign in their windows.

Hospital: Bayındır Tıp Merkezi, Kızılırmak Mah. #3-3A, 28th Sok., Söğütözü (☎287 90 00), is Ankara's best private hospital. Centrally located, brand-new **Bayındar Kilnik,** 201 Atatürk Bul. (☎428 08 08), Kavaklıdere, is smaller but offers all services. **Hacettepe Üniversitesi Tıp Fakültesi Hastanesi** (☎310 35 45), Hasırcılar Cad., Samonpazarı and **Ankara Üniversitesi Tıp Fakültesi Hastanesi** (☎319 21 60), Tıp Fakültesi Cad., Dikimevi, are the largest university hospitals.

Internet Access: Most of Ankara's internet cafes are in Kızılay, though connection speed and ambiance vary. Many are fairly smoky. Several post connection speeds in their windows. **Internet Center Cafe,** 107 Atatürk Bul. (☎419 27 54; fax 425 79 27), on the 3rd floor of the Engürü İş Hanı, is one of the best. Fast connection, color printing, photocopying, and scanning. $1.25 per hr. Open daily 9am-11pm. Nearby **Intek Internet Cafe,** 47/1 Karanfil Sok. (☎417 17 72), offers speedy connections for $1.25 per hr. *Çay,* coffee, and other snacks. Open daily 8am-midnight. **İrde Internet Cafe,** 31 Selanik Cad., 2nd fl. (☎419 68 56), offers great connections for $1.25 per hr.

PTT: In **Ulus,** on Atatürk Bul., just south of the equestrian statue. Open 24hr., although services are limited at night. *Poste restante.* In **Kızılay,** on Atatürk Bul. just off Kızılay Square, opposite the metro. Open M-Sa 8am-8pm; Su 8:30am-12:30pm, 1:30-7:30pm. In **Kavaklıdere,** on Cinnah Cad. just off the Kavaklıdere roundabout. Open daily 8:30am-12:30pm, 1:30-5pm. In the **train station** on Talat Paşa Cad. Open daily 7am-11pm. All offer full services.

Postal Code: 06443.

ACCOMMODATIONS

KIZILAY

Though more expensive, student-oriented Kızılay is more pleasant than dustier, noisier Ulus. Ulus is nearer to most of the sites; Kızılay is the cultural downtown.

Otel Ertan, 70 Selânik Cad. (☎418 40 84 or 425 15 06). Going south along Atatürk Bul., take the 4th left after McDonald's onto Meşrutiyet Cad., then the 3rd right onto Selanik Cad. Garden in front. Great value on a peaceful street, yet close to the Kızılay nightlife. 20 rooms, all with shower, toilet, and TV. Singles $15.50; doubles $24.50.

Otel Büyük Erşan, 74 Selânik Cad. (☎417 60 45 or 417 60 46; fax 417 49 43), across from Otel Ertan. True to its name, 3-star "Big Erşan" has 85 rooms, each with toilet, shower, TV, and refrigerator, with prices to match. The hotel has a retro feel, like something out of a 60s movie. Singles $26; doubles $38; triples $57.

Hotel Ergen, 48 Karanfil Sok. (☎417 59 06/07/08; fax 425 78 19). Going south along Atatürk Bul., take the 4th left after McDonald's onto Meşrutiyet Cad., then take the next right. Two-star Ergen has 48 rooms, well-furnished with private bath. Most have TV. No hot water 2-8pm. Singles $21, students $15; doubles $30, students $23.

M.E.B. Özel Ülkü Kız Öğrenci Yurdu, 61 Karanfil Sok. (☎419 37 15 or 419 30 67; fax 419 36 49), between Akay Cad. and Meşrutiyet Cad. For female students only. This girls' dormitory provides clean, safe lodgings and a cafeteria. 24hr. hot water. Open July-Sept. Dorms $7 per night, $220 per month; singles $9 per night, $245 per month.

MALTEPE

Just west of Kızılay, Maltepe is the main student residential area, and home to a huge and impressive mosque, some high class hotels and numerous wedding halls. Though somewhat removed from the sights, it is still relatively close to the Kızılay action and escapes the chaotic bustle of Ulus.

M.E.B. Özel Çağdaş Erkek Öğrenci Yurt, 15 Neyzen Tevfik Sok., Maltepe (☎232 29 54 or 232 29 55). From the Demirtepe Ankaray stop, walk 100m along Gazi Mustafa Kemal Bul. with the Maltepe mosque on your right (back toward Kızılay). A set of stairs just past the mosque leads to Neyzen Teufik Sok.; walk uphill until you see the dorm on your left. Most rooms share a bath. TVs and computers are available. Dormitories serve as a co-ed hostel from July-Aug., but only accept male students at other times of the year. Singles $10; doubles $20.

Hitit Öğrenci Yurtları, 96 Gazi Mustafa Kemal Bul. (☎231 02 81 or 231 07 91), on the left as you walk from the Maltepe Ankaray stop back toward Kızılay. This dorm offers dormitory-style lodging to male guests at the unbeatable price of $4 per night, or $11.50 per week. The guard speaks no English, so brush up on your Turkish basics. Shared bathrooms. Prices drop for stays of a month or longer.

ULUS

Ulus is packed with cheap hotels, some more squalid and Dickensian than others. The highest concentration is by the market, east of the equestrian statue.

Otel Hisar, 6 Hisarparkı Cad. (☎311 98 89 or 310 81 28). Walk east from the equestrian statue. Offers simple, comfortable rooms and Hisar views. Among the cheapest in town. Singles $6.50; doubles $11.

Otel Zümrüt, 16 Şehit Teğmen Kalmaz Cad. (☎309 15 54 or 309 01 17). From the statue, follow Atatürk Bul. south; take the 2nd left onto Teğmen Kalmaz Cad. The advantages of a larger hotel at a reasonable price. Comfortable, carpeted rooms with phones. Singles $4.50, with bath $7; doubles $12, with bath $17; triples $17, with bath $21.

Hotel Kale, Anafartalar Cad., 13 Alataş Sok. (☎311 33 93 or 310 35 21). From the statue, follow Anafartalar Cad. toward the Citadel; bear right before it becomes Hisarparkı Cad., and take the 3rd left onto Şan Sok. Hotel Kale is about 150m ahead at the intersection of Şan Sok. and Alataş Sok. Near the center of Ulus, but a quiet distance from any major road. Rooms come with TV, phones, and baths with 24hr. hot water. Singles $13, students $7; doubles $29, students $24; triples $39, students $34.

Farabi Otel, 46 Denizciler Cad. (☎310 07 77; fax 310 09 59). Slightly distant from the other hotels clustered around the Ulus statues, Farabi is a good, quiet alternative near the PTT. Clean singles $5.50, doubles $8.

Hotel Taç, 35 Çankırı Cad. (☎324 31 95 or 324 31 96). North of the statue, Atatürk Bul. becomes Çankırı Cad., a busy, noisy, well-lit street. Lodging here is closer to the Roman ruins and slightly more expensive than elsewhere in Ulus. 35 clean rooms, some with private showers. Singles $8, with shower and toilet $11.50; doubles $16.50, with shower and toilet $19.50.

Otel Bulduk, 26 Sanayi Cad. (☎310 49 15/16/17). Walk south from the equestrian statue along Atatürk Bul., take the first left after the PTT, then turn right onto Sanayi Cad. Bulduk is on the right. A bit more upscale than other hotels in the area, with 68 quiet rooms, all with TV. Singles $13, with bath $16.50; doubles $23, with bath $28.

CAMPING

D.S.İ. Kampı Campground, Bayındır Barajı (☎372 27 31), on the Samsun Yollu Üzeri about 15km from Ankara. By car, take the road to Samsun, past Kayaş; this state-operated campground is on the right. Dolmuş leave the Ulus hubs on Denizciler Cad. and Bentderesi Cad. ($.30). Gas station and cafe nearby. Free use of toilets, showers (24hr. hot water), and laundry. $1.50 per day. Open May 1 until it gets too cold (about Sept.).

FOOD

The main culinary neighborhoods are Kızılay (mid-range), Gençlik Park (cheap), Hisar (upscale, touristy), and Kavaklıdere (upscale, trendy). In addition, just southeast of the Atakule Tower, **Hoşdere Cad.** lays claim to many good restaurants, as does Ahmet Mitat Sok., the side street one block south. For comprehensive supermarkets selling food, rugs, furniture, electronics, watches, shoes, linens, toys, cosmetics, and life insurance, head to **Gima,** with branches on Atatürk Bul. (next to the PTT) in Kızılay and on Anafartalar Cad. in Ulus, or **Beğendik** (open 9am-10:30pm), under the Kocatepe mosque in Kızılay (at the south end of Mithat Paşa Cad.). The **Migros** chain (look for the *MMM* symbol) restricts itself to standard supermarket wares and has branches on Celâl Bayar Bul. in Maltepe and on Uğur Mumcu Cad. in Çankaya. In addition, small, hyper-specialized food stores line the streets of Kavaklıdere, Kızılay, and Ulus. Corn on the cob, rice rolls, and pastries are available from street vendors all over the city.

KIZILAY

Some of Kızılay's streets have been turned into pedestrian zones bustling with a student crowd in restaurants, bars, and cafes. It's hard to go wrong here; just follow the crowds and avoid fast food joints. Numerous shops on **Olgenlar Sok.** sell Kızılay's cheapest meal, the $.75 *döner*. For cheap food outlets and bars, turn onto Karanfil Sok. from Atatürk Bul.; for more upscale (and expensive) food, walk a couple blocks farther from Atatürk Bul., onto Bayındır Sok.

Göksu Restaurant, 22/A Bayındır Sok. (☎431 22 19), is one of the classier places in the neighborhood, with excellent Turkish and European food at mid-range prices (decent filet mignon $4.50). The desserts are particularly delicious. Sit outside on the glass-enclosed patio or inside among the exaggerated but elegant reproductions of Hittite reliefs, while waiters in bowties attend to your needs. Open daily noon-midnight.

Körfez Lokantası, 24 Bayındır Sok. (☎431 14 59). Specializes in seafood ($7-12). *Kiliç* (swordfish), *barbunya* (red mullet), *karides* (prawn), and other dishes available depending on the season. Last food orders 10pm.

Cafe M, 42 Selânik Cad. (☎419 36 65). Join the cell-phone toting collegiate hipsters on the outdoor terrace and look as cool as possible. Try the banana split ($2) or the *tiramisu* ($1.50). Open daily 7am-10:30pm.

Melbo, No. 95 Atatürk Bul. (☎418 03 63), on the top floor of a huge department store. Take the elevator near the PTT entrance. Clearly visible from Atatürk Bul., Melbo offers solid standards with a spectacular view of central Ankara.

Cafe Tenedos, 29/A Kızılırmak Cad. (☎419 34 50), at the intersection of Kızılırmak Cad. and Selânik Sok., west of the Kocatepe mosque. Quality live jazz from Sept.-June. Pleasant patio, wooden interior. Ginger peach soda $2. Open daily 9am-midnight.

ULUS

Since Ulus isn't a particularly compelling neighborhood for restaurants, the quickest and easiest option is to grab a *döner* or *kebap*. Ulus is home to several bakeries; a particularly good one is at the south end of the equestrian statue plaza.

Uludağ Lokantası, 54 Denizciler Cad. (☎309 04 00). A large, reasonably priced restaurant with stellar *kebaps* renowned throughout Ankara. Situated in a large modern building in an otherwise very ordinary area. Try the *özel uludağ kebap* ($1) and the *ekmek kadayıfı* (Turkish sweet pastry with cream, $2).

Tapi Tavuk, 23/A Şehit Teğmen Kalmaz Cad. (☎309 38 16; fax 309 18 15; order in 311 21 11). Decent, inexpensive food in an informal, down-to-earth environment. *Tavuk Şiş* $2.50, *Tavuk köfte* $2, good breakfasts $1. Open 6am-9pm.

Santral Kebap, Orbek Sakağı (☎312 77 57) is a small, friendly, simple restaurant, serving good *kebap* ($1). Open until 11pm.

Arjantin 78, 14/C Çankırı Cad. Kraner İşhanı (☎311 77 12 or 310 16 94 or 310 71 97). One of the best Ulus has to offer, near the Roman ruins, only a few minutes from the hub of Ulus. Serves excellent fish *tavuk* ($.75) and beers in a decidedly smoky atmosphere. Open noon-11pm.

Bulvar, 14/37 Çankırı Cad. (☎311 71 17) is a diner-style joint featuring soups ($.75), *kebap* ($1.50) and desserts ($.75) at very reasonable prices.

HİSAR

To get to the Hisar's several excellent and reasonably priced restaurants, enter the Southern Gate from near the Museum of Anatolian Civilizations. There are several steps leading up on the next road up the hill. You will see several signposts indicating the way to the restaurants perched on the citadel's walls.

Zenger Paşa Konağı, 13 Doyran Sok. (☎311 70 70). Zenger is an impressive and tasteful combination restaurant and museum in a restored 1730 Ottoman house. Clear explanations and displays of pre-Islamic Turkish mythology and customs accompany live Turkish music on an exquisite covered terrace overlooking the city. Excellent food at reasonable prices. Don't leave without trying the delicious *gördeme* crepe specialty ($1). Main courses $2-5. Open daily 10am-11pm; music starts at 7:30pm.

Hisar Kule Lokanta (☎301 78 99). Slightly smaller and with even better prices than its Hisar rivals, this restaurant offers excellent food and stunning views from the roof tower in a relaxing atmosphere. *Patlıcan salatası* $1, *meze* $1.50. Main courses $1.50-3. Open 10am-1am.

Kale Washington, 5-7 Doyran Sok. (☎311 43 44; fax 324 59 59). On the square just to the left, Kale Washington is a classy restaurant with a business-y atmosphere, serving tasty fare on an open-air, canopied terrace. Try the *patlican salatası* (eggplant salad, $2.50). Entrees about $6. Open noon-midnight.

KAVAKLIDERE AND GAZIOSMANPAŞA

Kavaklıdere's glitziness is striking compared to Ulus and the Hisar, as several upscale restaurants compete for well-heeled patrons. It does have its charm, however, and there are plenty of reasonable and enticing restaurants, cafés, and bars. Arjantin Cad. is best avoided unless you're on a serious expense account.

Daily News Cafe, 1 Arjantin Cad. (☎468 45 13). The exception to the pricey restaurants on Arjantin Cad. Newly renovated as an Italian restaurant, but still lined with newspapers, this is a smart, up-market place to while away an afternoon with the upper crust of Ankara society. The perfect spot to spend a relaxing afternoon with a free copy of the English-language *Turkish Daily News*. Sauteed chicken with white wine sauce $6.50. Live music F-M 7:30pm-10:30pm. Open daily 9am-midnight.

Hacı Arif Bey, 48 Güniz Sok. (☎467 00 67; reservations ☎467 57 67). Directly opposite the home of former Turkish President Süleyman Demirel, this large restaurant serves food fit for a king under a huge tent. Often crowded with a decidedly eclectic mix of patrons in a communal atmosphere. *İskender kebap* $3.50; *peynırlı künefe* $1.50.

Dolmax, Tunalıhılmı Cad., Büklüm Sok. (☎467 52 52). This combination restaurant and doll shop has to be seen to be believed. Excellent food served in surreal surroundings with endless shelves of dolls. Chicken fried rice with chef's sauce ($5.50.) Closed for renovations as of Summer 2001, but soon to be re-opened.

Dönen Restaurant (☎440 74 12), atop the Atakule tower in Çankaya. Serves trout ($11) and *ızgara* ($8) as snazzily-dressed guests slowly revolve on a giant mechanized disc. The overpriced food may be justified by the best view in Ankara. Open 10am-1am.

Annem Restaurant, 66 Tunalı Hilmi Cad. (☎426 02 02 or 468 24 10 for reservations). Excellently located at the corner of Tunalı Cad. and Büklüm Sk., this is an upmarket but reasonably priced restaurant in an upscale area. Entrees $2.50. Open noon-midnight.

Deli Dolu Meyhane, 106/6 Tunalı Hilmi Cad. (☎466 06 90). To find the entrance, walk down the alley to the right of the restaurant and into the first apartment building on the left; Deli Dolu is on the third floor. Nightly music creates a lively atmosphere in this traditional wooden restaurant. Try to sit on the balcony for a view of the whole area. Main course $3-5. Open 4pm-3am.

Dolphin Cafe Bar, 99/D Tunalı Hilmi Cad. (☎427 64 68). More of a café-bar with food than a full-scale restaurant, Dolphin Cafe has an intimate, wood-paneled upstairs seating area. Entrees $1-5. Open daily 9:30am-midnight

Hikmet Gökçe Gıda, 108/A Tunalı Hilmi Cad. (☎466 49 49). A solid, popular eatery serving all the basics, Himet is less upscale than many of the others on this road and a convenient alternative to the fast food chains nearby. Seating on the outdoor terrace.

Zeynel, 90/B Tunus Hilmi Cad. (☎466 19 19/20). Turn right on the McDonald's on Tunus Himli Cad. This dessert-and-coffee shop is the first place you'll come across. Try the ice cream *crème caramel*, a Kazandibi specialty. Open 7am -12:30am.

SIGHTS

MUSEUM OF ANATOLIAN CIVILIZATIONS (ANADOLU MEDENIYETLERI MÜZESI). This extraordinary museum, at the foot of the Citadel, is Ankara's most important sight and winner of Europe's Museum of the Year Award in 1997. This restored 15th-century Ottoman building houses a collection of astoundingly old artifacts tracing the history of Anatolia from a 6th millennium BC bone and obsidian razor to Ottoman pottery. The museum's greatest strength is its organization—a U-shaped corridor leads visitors chronologically through the development of human technology, art, and religion. The museum is small enough that a visitor can browse the entire collection without getting "museum feet;" quality, rather than quantity, is the key. Larger artifacts (including sections of the city walls from 950 BC and carved reliefs) are kept in the central room. The museum boasts artifacts from every age of Turkey's ancient history, from Çatalhöyük, the blockbuster of all Neolithic sites; through the early Bronze Age, Assyrian trade colonies, the Phrygian kingdom of Midas, and the Urartrians. Highlights include perfectly preserved Hittite bull vessels; original gate figures from Boğazkale; and a life-size reproduction of King Midas's tomb at Gordion. Equally impressive is the room of 3300-year-old hieroglyphic tablets, ranging from one written by the wife of Ramses II to a tablet of the Hittite Queen Puduhepa. and an underground section featuring ancient coins. The English labeling is reasonably extensive, but if you want more time to absorb Anatolia's rich history, the photo-packed catalogue ($10) explains all. *(2 Gözcü Sok. Walk to the top of Hisarparkı Cad., turn right at the Citadel steps (without climbing them), and follow the Citadel boundaries to a set of steps leading up to the entrance. ☎324 31 60; fax 311 28 39. Museum open Tu-Su 8:30am-5:30pm. $3, students $2.*

ATATÜRK'S MAUSOLEUM (ANIT KABİR). Upon Atatürk's death, Turkey held an international contest to select a plan for his **mausoleum.** The winner, Emin Onat, designed the simple, monumental, Hittite-influenced **Anıt Kabir.** It took nine years to complete and now covers 750,000 sq. meters near Tandoğan Square.

At the mausoleum entrance, six unhappy statues of men and women represent the grief of the Turkish nation upon its father's death. Twenty-four lions, paired Hittite-style and symbolizing power, line the broad stone promenade leading to the mausoleum. Across the vast courtyard is the tomb of **İsmet İnönü,** first prime minister of the Republic and Atatürk's close friend. The mausoleum complex has no fewer than nine towers and two giant victory reliefs, a museum, and a **hall of honors.** Objects on display include Atatürk's 1936 **Lincoln sedan,** his rowing machine, his tie clips, and numerous ceremonial gifts and plaques he received as Turkey's head of state. An excellent series of photographs commemorates Atatürk's career and social life, hobnobbing with Chiang Kai Shek, Hailie Selaissie, and King Abdullah of Jordan, among others. Other photographs taken after his death show **cloud formations** shaped like his profile, suggesting that even the sky mourned his loss. In the Reform Tower, the **Cinevision salon** shows non-stop period documentaries, including some very moving posthumous propaganda films with Chopin soundtracks. "Tell us heavens, tell us flag, clouds, birds, mountains—where is Atatürk now?" Wrap up your tour with a stop at the gift shop for your favorite Atatürk paraphernalia: Atatürk post cards, CD-ROMs, plaques, clocks, and photos. *(Anıt Cad. Take the Ankaray line to Tandoğan and follow the Anıt Kabir signs along Anıt Cad. The unmarked entrance is guarded by two soldiers. It's a 10-minute uphill walk from the gate to the mausoleum entrance. ☎231 79 75. Open M 1:30-5pm, Tu-Su 9am-5pm; winter 9am-4pm. Free.)*

HİSAR. On a high hill overlooking the city, the original, pre-republican hilltown of Ankara remains more or less unchanged, and has managed to preserve a village feel despite being mere meters away from the urban hub. Protected by its imposing Byzantine walls—still in excellent condition—the Hisar provides a vantage point over the new city and the contrasts between the old and the new, and the remarkable range of civilizations to have dominated the city and plains beyond. The network of narrow, twisting streets is full of merchants and craftsmen of every variety, and it's probably the best place in town to go looking for carpets or *kilim*. At the very top of the hill, the eastern tower *(Şark Kulesi)* and the northern tower *(Ak Kale)* offer excellent views. Buy shoes, sheets, and Superman outfits on Çıkrıkçılar Sok., which runs just southwest of the citadel, downhill from the entrance to the Museum of Anatolian Civilizations. From the restaurant area, follow the road uphill and then climb the steps. Descend the Hisar from the other side, toward the **Hacı Bayram Mosque,** for a view of beautiful gardens and a picnic area amid the steps leading down. *(Fortress open 11am-5pm. Free.)*

MOSQUES. The immense **Kocatepe Mosque** looms just east of Kızılay on Mithat Paşa Cad. Completed in 1987, this facility is billed as a 16th-century mosque using 20th-century technology: glowing green digital clocks indicate prayer times. Constructed with dazzling white stone, it shines as one of the world's largest mosques. The stunning stained-glass-and-tiled interior contains a model of the mosque at Medina—a present from King Fahd of Saudi Arabia in 1993. Kocatepe is particularly striking at night, when moths sleep on the white flagstones overlooking the illuminated city and the enormous, round crystal chandeliers inside are lit. After your visit, you can do some upmarket shopping at the Beğendik supermarket and mall—ultra-modern, air-conditioned, and directly underneath the mosque.

Downhill and south of the citadel's towers, in the site of the original village of Ankara, the small, 13th-century **Aslanhane Mosque** (Ahi Şerafettin) bears witness to Ankara's Selçuk legacy. Inside, wooden pillars with Corinthian capitals stretch from the ornate floor to the wooden ceiling, while Selçuk *faïence* tiles adorn the mosque's alcove. One of Ankara's most historically important mosques, the **Hacı Bayram Camii,** among the Roman ruins, is built alongside the tomb of dervish saint Hacı Bayram Veli. To get there, go east from Ulus's equestrian statue on Anafartalar Cad. and take a left at the first major intersection.

ROMAN RUINS. Compared to the Classical ruins of the Aegean and Mediterranean coasts, Ankara's Roman remains are less than impressive. If this is your last and only opportunity to see a piece of Rome, however, you may want to check out the **Roman Baths (Roma Hamamı),** a five-minute walk up Çankırı Cad. from the equestrian statue in Ulus. Turn left as you go up the stairs for the most intact remains and follow the path along until you reach the baths. Built by the **Emperor Caracalla** (212-217), these baths were in continuous use for 500 years. Little is visible today except the well-excavated foundations. The many brick piles supported the floors of the baths and allowed heated air to circulate and warm the tiles. Column capitals, statues, and other fragments are arranged around the grass. *(Open Tu-Su 8:30am-12:30pm, 1:30-5:30pm. $1.50, students free.)*

The inner sanctum of the **Temple of Augustus and Rome *(Ağustos ve Roma Mabedi)*** lies in overgrown ruin directly adjacent to the Hacı Bayram Camii. Romans built the temple in 25 BC on the site of earlier temples to Cybele the Anatolian fertility goddess, and the Phrygian moon god. Later converted to a Byzantine church, the site became holy to Muslims in the 15th century when Hacı Bayram Veli, a dervish saint, was buried here. Guests can ask the guardian of the dervish tomb to unlock the temple gate. To the south toward the vegetable market, the lonely **Column of Julian *(Julianus Sütünü)*,** built in honor of the emperor's 4th-century visit, is now crowned by an immense stork's nest. *(Follow Hükümet Cad. past the fork leading to the Hacı Bayram Camii and take a left.)*

OTHER SIGHTS. At the southernmost end of Atatürk Bul. lie the grounds of the **Presidential Mansion *(Cumhurbaşkanlığı Köşkü)*,** still the home of Turkey's head of state. While you can't tour the current quarters, if you come to the entrance at 5 Ziaürrahman Cad. and leave your passport at the guardhouse, you will be given a tour of **Atatürk's "country residence,"** which dates back to times when Çankaya was still well outside the city. The residence, preserved as Atatürk left it, displays a much more human side of the man than does Anıt Kabir. *(Expect to encounter a heavy security presence. Try proceeding directly to entrance #5.* ☎ *468 63 00. Open Su 1:30-5pm.)*

West of the Presidential Mansion on Çankaya Cad. is the **Atakule Observation Tower.** Enter the mall below and make your way to the central courtyard, where you'll find the tower elevator ($1.25). From the tower's observation deck you can see past Ankara to the farmland and mountains beyond. Just outside the tower is the Botanical Park, one of Ankara's better picnic spots and a favorite of the city's young couples. Housed in a tiny greenhouse within the park are the pleasant, if not particularly exotic, **Botanical Gardens.** *(Bus #613 runs from the equestrian statue in Ulus to the Atakule Tower via Kızılay and Kavaklıdere. Park open daily 24 hr. Free.)*

In Ulus, the first and second Grand National Assembly buildings have been converted into separate, but very similar, historical museums. The First Assembly building, a.k.a. the **War of Independence Museum** (*Kurtuluş Savaşı Müzesi*, 14 Cumhuriyet Bul.), is preserved exactly as it was in the early 1920s. Paintings and photographs tell the story of Turkey's fight for independence, and several rooms are filled with photographs of each member of the original assembly. Next door is the Second Assembly building, or the **Museum of the Republic** *(Cumhuriyet Müzesi)*. Used by the Assembly from 1924 until 1960, this museum is most dramatically distinguished from its partner by an assembly hall full of wax politicians listening attentively as a waxen Atatürk waxes loquacious in his famous Great Speech. Also on display are a few of İsmet İnönü's personal affects, as well as stamps and money used by the republic, including now-inconceivable one-lira notes from the 1930s. None of the museum's descriptions are in English, but an English language brochure is available at the front desk. *(The museums are west of the equestrian statue, toward the Metro stop on Cumhuriyet Bul. War Museum is at #14.* ☎ *310 71 40. $1.50, students $1. Museum of the Republic is at $22.* ☎ *310 53 61. $1.50; 65 and over $.80. Both museums open Tu-Su 8:30am-noon and 1:30-5:30pm.)*

ENTERTAINMENT AND NIGHTLIFE

KIZILAY

Like so many other aspects of the city, Ankara's nightlife is centered in Kızılay, where dozens of bars and multipurpose cafe-bars cover a few city blocks. Manic dancers should be warned, however, that Kızılay's nightlife is of the chat-over-a-beer and listen-to-live-music variety. Pub life is centered on **İnkilâp Sok.** and the even livelier **Bayındır Sok.**, two and three blocks east of Kızılay Sq. Roam the traffic-free streets as you pick the crowd you want to hang with. **S.S.K. Işhane** (Life Insurance Office Building), on the corner of Ziya Gökalp Cad. and Selânik Cad., is the center for bars and clubs. This entire cement block throbs with the bass-kicking sounds from small live music bars. Kızılay's bar prices are fairly uniform: a pint of *Efes*, the local favorite, goes for $1.10-1.50; mixed drinks from $3-4.

Brothers Bar, 61 Selânik Cad. (☎ 419 41 26). At the far end of Selânik Cad., just past the Ertan Hotel. Mellow music and mood. Young musicians play acoustic renditions of Turkish tunes while the large collegiate crowd sings along. Open daily 11am-midnight.

Zx Bar Disco, 14/A Bayındır Sok. (☎ 431 35 35). Packs a 3-floor Turkish pop punch: disco downstairs, live music upstairs, and a bar in the middle of it all. Often crowded, and deservedly so. Beer $1.50. Open daily noon-12:30am.

Nil Bar, 19/C Bayındır Sok. (☎ 431 07 73), and the **Alesta Bar,** 19/B Bayındır Sok. (☎ 431 12 04), open onto the street next door to each other. Pleasant outdoor tables and deafening cover bands playing a mix of Turkish and American rock inside. Beer $1.50. Both bars open daily 9am-midnight.

Gölge Bar, 1-2-3 S.S.K. İşhanı (☎ 434 09 78). Literally "Shadow Bar," Gölge is well-known to the city's youth. Live bands play heavily distorted covers of English rock, from the Rolling Stones to the Cure. The club's dark, smoky space and cheap beer ($1.50) attract an equally nonuniform crowd. Live music nightly, with 2 bands F and Sa. Cover required only after 9pm on F and Sa ($2.50, includes a beer). Open daily 1pm-4am.

Blues Cafe & Bar, 19/16 Bayındır Sok. (☎432 42 46), on the 2nd floor of the building on the corner of Bayındır Sok. and Sakarya Cad. From Nil Bar, turn left, enter the apartment building to the left, and go up the stairs. Makes up for its lack of live music with a well-chosen soundtrack of American blues and rock. Wooden benches arranged around the dark, cozy space are stamped with such names as Bob Marley, Pink Floyd, and Jimi Hendrix. Open daily 11am-12:30am.

May Day Club, Beş Evler Cad., Gençler Birligi Sporklubu Yanı. Quite far out of town, near Anıt Kabir (Atatürk mausoleum). Open only in the summer, when it becomes the place to see and be seen in Ankara for hard-core clubbing.

Zodiac Cafe Pub, 17/B Tunus Cad. (☎419 92 08). A small, intimate music bar, with wooden décor. Much more relaxed and chill than other Kızılay spots. Open 9am-1am.

Türkevi Cafe Restaurant, 36/B Karanfil Sok. (☎312 425 26 16). A lively café/bar with live traditional folk music and dancing every night. Try the house specialty, a delicious *köfte* ($1.50). Beer $1.

İskele Cafe Bar, 14/C Bayındır Sk. (☎433 38 13). A laid-back, chill bar with groovy music and a sedate atmosphere. Live bands play every night. Open until midnight, last entrance 11:30pm.

Metropol Sanat Merkezi Movie House, 76 Selanik Cad., Kızılay (☎425 74 78), across from Brothers Bar. The Movie House offers six screens of artsy and pop films, both Turkish and American. Cool off afterward with a beer at the outdoor bar. Most films $1. Last showing 9:30pm.

Kızılırmak Movie House, 21 Kızılırmak Sok., Kızılay (☎425 53 93), **Derya,** 57 Necatibey Cad., Sıhhiye (☎229 96 18), and **Megapol,** 33 Konur Sok., Kızılay (☎419 44 92) also play British and American films. For listings, check the *Turkish Daily News* or pick up a flyer from any of the theaters.

KAVAKLIDERE

If the mellow/metalhead schizophrenia and pricey lifestyle of Kızılay is getting you down, head to the less crowded, upwardly-mobile bars and clubs scattered around the trendy streets of Kavaklıdere, Gaziosmanpaşa, and Çankaya. Most live music venues have no cover.

Süleyman Nazif Club, 97 Güvenlik Cad. (☎468 57 83). Dance floor with Turkish and Euro techno, where a young, mostly-Turkish crowd lets loose, and a calmer upstairs lounge. Open W-Sa 10pm-2am.

Marilyn Monroe, 54/A Büklüm Sok. (☎428 27 06). Enjoy the Marilyn decor while sipping an *Efes* with the mainly Anglo-American expat crowd. Terrace open in summer. Restaurant attached. Open 10am-midnight.

The North Shield, 111 Güvenlik Cad., Kavaklıdere (☎466 12 66; fax 468 86 91). One of the most popular bars in the area. The mixed crowd at this faux-Scottish pub favors older folks, but includes the weekend student surge. Specializing in Scotch, the North Shield is the only place in Ankara where you can spend $250 on a single glass of 52-year-old malt whisky. Local beers $4, imports $6.50; whiskeys $6.50 and up, up, up. Open daily 11-1:30am.

Likya, SOA/4 Tunus Cad., Kavaklıdere (☎426 27 23), draws a carefully dressed student crowd with its soundtrack of American and European pop tunes. Hair gel recommended. On Thursday the DJ spins all from tango to techno. *Efes* $3. Open daily noon-2am.

Jazz Time Cafe Bar, 4/1 Bilir Sokak (☎488 41 29 or 468 43 48). A good jazz and café bar, parallel to the busy Tunalı Hilmi Cad. Smallish, with less atmosphere than some of the Kızılay hotspots, but with excellent live jazz every night. Open 1pm-1am.

Highland, 53/A Tunus Cad. (☎467 32 35). A more serious and self-conscious place, with steeper prices to boot. Dinner-jacketed bouncers make sure everything goes smoothly. The décor and clientele tend toward the upscale.

Batı Cinema, 151 Atatürk Bul., Kavaklıdere (☎418 83 23; $3.50, students $2), also plays British and American films. For listings, check the *Turkish Daily News* or pick up a flyer from any theater.

Open-air cinema. On the roof of the Kavaklıdere Sheraton (☎468 54 54), with nightly 9:30pm screenings for $7 (summer only). Another place to catch up on American flicks. There's no popcorn, but there is a **bar** (first drink on the house, additional cocktails $3).

ULUS

Most of the clubs, cafes, discos, and movie houses are elsewhere in Ankara, but there are still some diversions in Ulus. **Gençlik Park** is crammed with cheap restaurants and also contains a garish **amusement park** and an artificial lake with rental pleasure boats ($.75 per ½hr.). The park is more than a little tacky, but it's at its best in the early evening, when the lights first come on. Smoke a *nargile* ($2) at the **Kecep Özgen Çay Bahçesi tea house.** (Park open in summer 9am-midnight. Tea house open 7am-midnight.) From November until mid-June, the terra cotta pillared **State Opera and Ballet House** *(Devlet Opera ve Balesi)*, Atatürk Bul. Opera Meydanı holds daily performances. Performance schedules are posted on the bulletin board outside the opera house or available at the tourist office. (☎324 22 10 or 324 20 10. Tickets $5 and $10, students 50% off.) The nearby **Presidential Symphony Orchestra Hall** *(Cumhurbaşkanlığı Senfoni Orkestrası Konser Salonu)*, 38 Talatpaşa Bul., has concerts during the winter only, F 8:30pm and Sa 11am. (☎310 72 90. Tickets $3 or $5; 50% student discount.) **Akün Cinema,** 227 Atatürk Bul., shows American films in the original English (☎427 76 56; $3.50, students $2).

DAYTRIP FROM ANKARA: GORDION

Unfortunately, reaching Gordion can be somewhat difficult. Buses and trains run to Polatlı, the nearest town of any size. ***Non-express trains*** *from Ankara to Eskişehir usually stop here once or twice a day (2hr., $4). From Ulus, catch a bus from Hlik Eski Garajlan (old bus station). The* ***Baysal bus company*** *(☎224 05 42) links Ankara's otogar to Polath (1½hr., every 30min. 7am-9:30pm, $1.50). From Polatlı's bus station, take a service bus into the town center at the train station. A* ***dolmuş*** *leaves from there to Gordion (and adjacent Yassıhöyük) every day but Su (20min., 2 per day 8:30am-3pm, $.75). More likely, you will be forced to hire a* ***taxi*** *($15-25 round-trip). Some find it cheaper to strike a deal with a local who has a car.*

About 100km west of Ankara lie the ruins of the ancient city of Gordion, where the **Phrygians** established their capital in the 8th century BC. The Phrygian King **Midas,** who ruled here, has been immortalized in Greek mythology as the man who greedily wished that everything he touched would turn to gold, with the distastrous result that even his food and drink became golden and inconsumable. Taking pity on the starved, thirsty Midas, Dionysus granted a cure. Centuries later, after the fall of the Phrygian empire, Alexander the Great made Gordion famous once again when he sliced the Gordion knot in half with his sword, thus fulfilling the prophesy that he who successfully untied the knot would rule Asia.

Over 80 burial mounds surround Gordion. About a quarter of them have been excavated over the past 40 years by an archaeological team from the University of Pennsylvania. The most impressive of these towering earth mounds is the **Royal Tomb,** which contained a perfectly preserved "log cabin" made of juniper trunks— one of the oldest standing wooden structures in the world. Inside the cabin lies the intact body of a man in his 60s. Ankara's Museum of Anatolian Civilizations (see p. 369) displays a replica of the tomb. The scale of the tomb can only be understood by traveling the narrow passage to the center of the mound (not recommended for claustrophobes). To get in, ask the attendant at the **museum** across the street. Renovated in 1999, the museum contains fairly well-labeled examples of Bronze Age, Hittite, and Phrygian pottery, as well as photographs documenting the excavations. (Museum open daily 8:30am-5:30pm. $3.50, students free.) The **acropolis,** built and rebuilt during the 8th and 7th centuries BC, stands a good 15-minute walk to the southwest of the museum. To get there, follow the main road through the nearby town until you see signs pointing out the site. Today, the acropolis is likely only exciting to scholars, but a visit does provide an indication of the settlement's considerable size. The complex of mounds is covered with a maze of randomly disintegrating walls, a few still towering to suggest the city's former glory. The Phrygian gate building is the largest monumental fortification in Central Turkey.

BOĞAZKALE ☎364

To locals, Boğazkale is a typical small village where ducks and cows wander oblivious to the passing tractors and children playing in the street. Its unremarkable exterior, however, is misleading: Boğazkale is home to the 4000-year-old remains of the ruined Hittite capital of Hattuşaş. The ancient city, on the outskirts of present-day Boğazkale, just over 200km east of Ankara and 30km off the Samsun highway, is situated 1000m above sea level, in a gorgeous pastoral setting. A designated UNESCO world heritage site, Hattuşaş is easily navigable by car or on foot. Although much has been carted off to various museums around the world, enough of the site remains to suggest the size and glory of the ancient city. The combination of dramatic ruins and landscapes, good places to stay and a peaceful atmosphere makes Boğazkale a unique experience in Turkey.

The 8km loop passing through the Hattuşaş Hittite ruins links the main sites and makes for a beautiful hike through a wild landscape of cliffs and valleys. Three kilometers northeast of the site is Yazılıkaya, an open-air temple that contains bas reliefs of 100 of the 1000 or so Hurrian gods. Back on the main road, Boğazkale's small but impressive museum maintains a collection of the site's artifacts. In the last week of June, Boğazkale and nearby Çorum host a Hittite cultural festival.

TRANSPORTATION AND PRACTICAL INFORMATION

Short of renting a car, the easiest way to get to or from Boğazkale is via **Sungurlu.** Dolmuş leave from Boğazkale's town square (25min.; when full 7am-5:30pm, last return 6pm; $.75). Minibuses also run on weekends. Hattuşaş Pension can arrange transport from Sungurlu or Yozgat. To get to Cappadocia, take a dolmuş to Yozgut, where you can catch a bus to Nevşehir. If you're going from Boğazkale to a smaller destination that may not be served by Sungurlu's small otogar, ask the dolmuş to drop you at the **Mavı Ocak Tesisleri** restaurant and gas station, 6km from Sungurlu and about 25km from Boğazkale on the main Sungurlu-Çorum/Samsun highway. It is a frequent rest stop for buses along the highway.

The two-lane road from Sungurlu is Boğazkale's only real street, which runs past the museum and a few hotels before ending abruptly in the town square. Near the museum, across from the Aşıkoğlu Hotel, a separate road branches off and heads toward Hattuşaş, Yazılıkaya, and two hotels (the Kale and Başkent). The Hattuşaş **ticket office** is one kilometer from the village center. The town square contains **pharmacies,** bakeries, markets, and the **PTT** (open M-F 8:30am-noon and 1-5:30pm). There is also a **T.C. Ziraat Bankası** that exchanges **traveler's checks.** (Open daily 8:30am-noon and 1-5:30pm.) While there are currently **no ATMs** in Boğazkale, there are several in Sungurlu. Next to the Aşıkoğlu Hotel, the **Boğazkale İlce Sağlık Ocağı** (☎452 20 07) is a 24hr. **clinic.** There is a new **internet cafe** next to the Hattuşaş Pension, usually open late ($1 per hr.). **Postal code:** 19310.

ACCOMMODATIONS AND FOOD

The area's only restaurants are in pensions. Outside of that, your only hope for sustenance is the bakery or the grocery store.

Hattuşaş Pension and Restaurant (☎452 20 13; fax 452 29 57; ahattibaykal@hotmail.com). The only hotel in the Cumhuriyet Meydanı. 9 clean, spacious rooms, 2 with private showers and most with a view. The friendly English-speaking owner, Ahmet Baykal, is an excellent source of information. Breakfast $1.50. Singles $7; doubles $12, with shower $14; children under 12 free. MC/V.

Kale Motel and Restaurant (☎/fax 452 31 26). On the road to the Yazılıkaya Hittite temple. Take a right out of the Boğazkale museum and another right at the Petrol Ofisi gas station. This recently renovated motel is 700m up the hill, on the left, and is a 5-10min. walk from Yazılıkaya. All rooms have baths and great balcony views. Nearby hilltop camping with stunning views and outdoor power outlets. Breakfast included. 13 rooms. Singles $7; doubles $10. Camping $2 per tent (bring your own); caravan $3. 25% *Let's Go* discount with student ID.

Başkent Motel Camping (☎452 20 37; fax 452 25 67), on the road toward the Yazılıkaya temple. 18 comfortable, decorated rooms with baths. Başkent's campground has all the advantages of a hilltop location. Singles $11; doubles $20; camping $4.50 per tent, with electricity $6; caravan $4.50, with electricity $6.

Aşıkoğlu Hotel and Restaurant (☎452 20 04; fax 452 21 71), across from the museum, is Boğazkale's upscale, newly renovated, modern hotel. Great, comfortable rooms at very steep prices. All rooms have their own bathroom. Internet access at ridiculous prices ($30 per hr.). Breakfast included. Hotel singles $30, motel $20; hotel doubles $40, motel $30. Camping $2.50 per tent; caravan $2.50.

THE HITTITE SITE

Expect to spend a full day exploring Yazılıkaya and Hattuşaş. For more information on the Hittites, see **From Hittites to Hellenes,** p. 6. Exploring Yazılıkaya and Hattuşaş at a leisurely pace, with a break for a picnic, can easily take an entire day.

Beginning in 1600 BC, the great Hittite kings occupied Hattuşaş for four centuries, competing with Egypt for control of the fertile lands and trade routes of Mesopotamia. They conquered Syria (14th century BC) and battled Pharaoh Ramses II (1285 BC). At the same time, they ruled their civilization with a sophisticated legal code. The Hittite Empire ended around 1200 BC when Hattuşaş was burned, though historians aren't sure exactly who destroyed the city. Possible suspects include vengeful vassals from the Black Sea and invaders from the Greek islands.

The site has two **ticket kiosks,** one at Hattuşaş and one at Yazılıkaya. To get to the Hattuşaş kiosk, follow the road uphill toward the Başkent and Kale motels and then turn right at the Hattuşaş sign. Bring plenty of water and start early before the heat sets in. From the **Hattuşaş** ticket office, signs point to **Yazılıkaya,** about 3km east. *(Both sites open daily 8am-7pm; in winter 8am-6:30pm. $2. The ticket is valid for both Hattuşaş and Yazılıkaya. Since Hattuşaş isn't near any restaurants, you may want to pack a lunch.)*

HATTUŞAŞ. The Hattuşaş road runs from the ticket kiosk in a 7km loop following the city walls. Walking the loop in a counter-clockwise direction, you'll first pass the **Büyük Mabet,** a temple dedicated to the weather god Hatti and the sun goddess Arinna. Today, visitors enter through the *propylon*, or processional entrance, which originally consisted of three (a holy number to Hittites) doors separated by two pools of water. Guards standing in recesses would lay bridges down to admit worshippers. At the Büyük Mabet entrance you'll find salesmen hawking miniature Hittite figures and souvenirs.

Farther in are the quarters of the priests, musicians, scribes, and soothsayers, as well as the temple's warehouses, where thousands of cuneiform tablets documenting commerce were found in 1907. Downhill from the temple were the offices of Assyrian merchants. Here, archaeologists found a parallel text in Akkadian and Hittite hieroglyphics that allowed scholars to translate Hittite. The smooth round holes bored into many of the stones originally held bronze rods that kept the stones together. Also, note the individual shrines to the sun goddess and the weather god, to the right of the entrance. These adjacent rooms, the spiritual heart of the temple, were built of special granite from a quarry over 30km away.

Up the hill, the right fork of the road passes the Hittite kings' ruined summer castle, **Yenicekale,** and then winds steeply up to meet the city walls. On the right is the **Aslanlı Kapı,** or Lion's Gate, consisting of two crumbling doorways framed by lion statues. Only one statue survives. The grooves about a foot above the ground were for the hubs of entering chariot wheels. A photographic computer reproduction posted nearby shows what the gate might have looked like in the 13th century BC. Follow the restored city walls running atop the embankment up the hill to the **Yer Kapı,** or Ground Gate. Popularly known as the **Sfenksli Kapı,** or Sphinx Gate (1250m above sea level), it was guarded by four sphinxes until one was taken to Berlin and another to İstanbul. Only one remains, as the fourth one has been missing since the city's discovery. Climb up the stairs to see the site's most intriguing feature: a 71m-long tunnel leading from inside the city walls to the outside. It was once suggested that the tunnel served a military function, allowing for surprise exits in times of siege. However, scholars now agree that it had a ceremonial function. To get a sense of the wall's overwhelming size, walk though the tunnel, take a left, and walk about 100m along the wall to the corner staircase. Once on top, you can walk back toward the gate, the city's highest point. From here, you can observe several razed *mabet* (temples) and a Byzantine church, now little more than giant blueprints marked out by limestone blocks. The plum tree to your left as you pass through *Sfenksli Kapısı* marks the point where the cuneiform and hieroglyphic-inscribed Boğazkale tablets, now in Ankara, were excavated (see **Museum of Anatolian Civilizations,** p. 369).

Moving eastward and downhill along the wall, the next place of interest is the **Kral Kapı,** or King's Gate. The giant figure is a reproduction; the original is in the Museum of Anatolian Civilizations. Originally believed to be the gate's namesake king, this fellow is actually a war god carrying a battle axe to symbolically defend the gate. Follow the road down a few hundred meters; on your right side are two

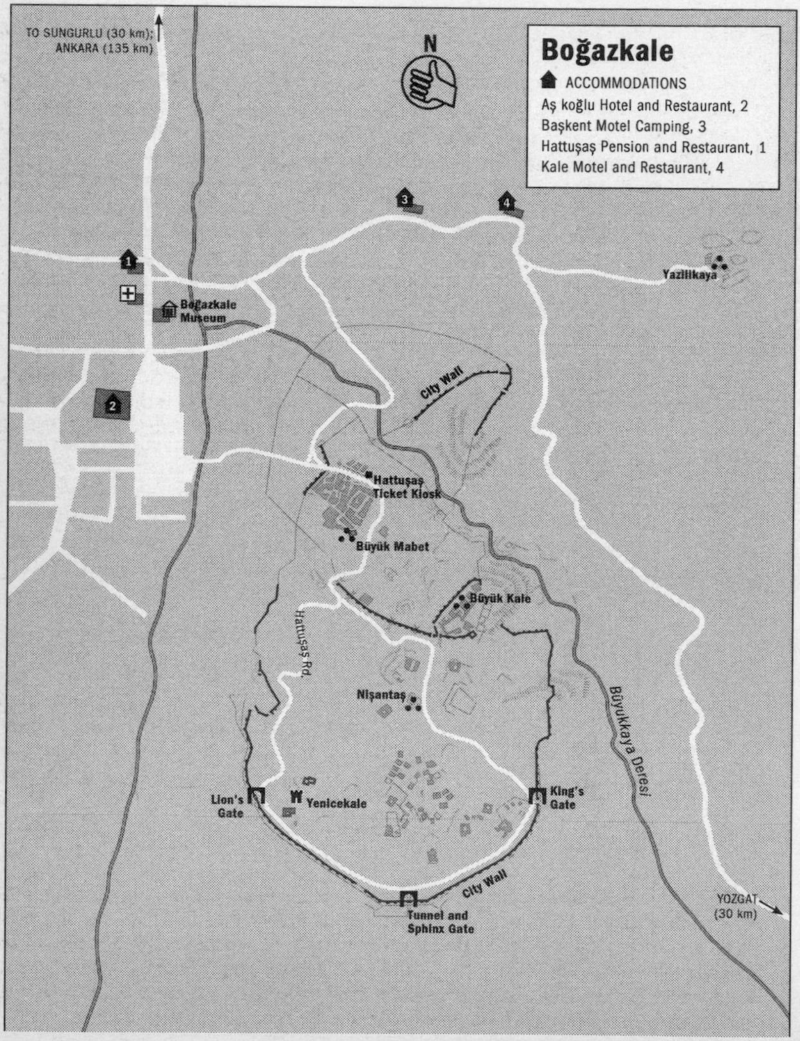

stone chambers, each containing cuneiform characters. Unremarkable **Chamber 1** is less striking than **Chamber 2,** 50m further down. Enter the opening opposite Nişantaş and follow the path up to a large stone, arch-shaped chamber. These were commissioned in 1200 BC by **King Shuppiluliuma II,** the last king of Hattuşaş. The enclosed cult chamber contains a relief of the king holding a symbol with an inscription mentioning a "divine earth road," the symbolic entrance to the underworld. Just across the road is **Nişantaş,** a rocky mound whose eastern side bears a badly weathered 10-line hieroglyphic inscription, believed to be a narration of the deeds of Shuppiluliuma II. Last on the tour, and worth skipping if you're short on time, is the **Büyük Kale,** a ruined complex of archives, offices, and royal apartments linked by courtyards. This was the main fortress of the Hittite kings, and it contained most of their documents. Archaeologists found 8000 cuneiform tablets here, including a treaty between Hattuziliz II and the Egyptian Pharaoh Ramses II. Though the ruins are scattered and difficult to make out, it's easy to appreciate the size and scope of everyday city life. From here it's 1km back to the ticket office.

YAZILIKAYA. The temple of Yazılıkaya is best visited between 11am and 1pm, when the figures carved into the rock are illuminated by the sun directly overhead; shade from the towering grotto easily obscures the bas-relief deities at other times. While in later days the Hittites built large temples at this site, the holy shrine was originally only a series of narrow ravines in the rock (Yazılıkaya is Turkish for "inscribed rock"). These ravines contain reliefs of gods and goddesses on parade. Goddesses appear in profile, wearing long, trailing robes; gods, most wearing kilts, face forward, with their rank indicated by the number of horns on their hats. Their are inscribed over their heads, preceded by an oval ("god" in hieroglyphics).

To the left, **Chamber A** consists of a long, snaking procession of gods and goddesses, increasing in rank toward the head of the procession. Archaeologists suggest that this gallery was used to celebrate the Hittite New Year in the spring. While Hittites had over 1000 deities, most of them were adopted from pre-Hittite peoples native to the area. On the left wall, 42 male gods form a long line, at the back of which are the 12 gods of the underworld; 21 goddesses face them on the right wall. On the far wall, the sculpture culminates in the marriage of the Hittite's two most powerful deities, **Teshub,** the storm god, and **Hepatu,** the sun goddess. Teshub is standing on the backs of two lesser gods, while Hepatu stands on a lion. To the right of Hepatu is a two-headed eagle, a symbol first used by the Hittites. Facing the procession of deities to the right of the entrance stands the famous 2.6m high relief representing **King Tudhaliya IV** (c.1250-1220 BC), astride two mountains and under a winged sun disk. His name appears in hieroglyphics in the bouquet-like object in his right hand. The relief's peculiar white, rubbery surface is the result of a latex reproduction procedure employed by a French archaeologist. Unfortunately, latex is not meant to be used for the reproduction of outdoor reliefs, and the king's now-damaged image will disappear in 20-30 years. **Chamber B,** accessible via a narrow passage to the right of the site's entrance, contains better preserved but less extensive reliefs. On the right wall, a relief of 12 sword-carrying gods is thought to represent the 12 months of the year. Carved into the left wall is the relief of a sword, its hilt formed by 4 lions and its pommel in the shape of **Nergal,** god of the underworld. This chamber may have been used for the death rites of King Tudhaliya IV, who appears to the right of the sword. The niches carved into the rock were most likely used for sacrificial animal offerings.

BOĞAZKALE MUSEUM. The modest Boğazkale Museum features an excellent collection of Hittite bureaucratic paraphernalia, including stone stamps, clay contract envelopes, and cuneiform deeds on stone tablets. Photographs document the progress of the dig, and a large map of the site is very helpful. Labels and explanations are in Turkish. The front desk sells the *Guide to Boğazköy* for $5. *(Dolmuş from Sungurlu pass directly in front. ☎452 20 06. Open daily 8am-5:30pm. $1.25.)*

SUNGURLU ☎364

Sungurlu is a necessary connection on the way to Boğazkale. From the main highway, **Lise Cad.**, between the otogar on the right and a large playing field on the left, runs toward the center of town, passing the large, green **Gençlik Park** before intersecting **Cengiztopel Cad.**, marked by Hotel Fatih. Buses to Sungurlu stop either on the main highway or at the otogar, which sits just off the highway across from a Petrol Ofisi gas station. **Buses** leave the otogar for: **Amasya** (4hr., 9 per day, $7); **Ankara** (3hr.; 13 per day 7:15am-8pm; $4.80, students $3.50); **Antalya** (10hr.; 6, 7, 8pm; $13, students $11.50); **Bodrum** (10hr.; 6:30pm; $13.50, students $12); **Fethiye** (10hr.; 7pm; $13.50, students $13); **İstanbul** (9hr.; 8:30pm; $13, students $12); **İzmir** (10hr.; 8pm; $13, students $12). For other destinations, you may wait at one of the highway rest stops and hop on a bus en route (ask at the otogar for more info). Despite the claims of local taxi drivers, **dolmuş** do head to **Boğazkale,** *leaving* from next to Hotel Fatih and Gençlik Park (30min., leaves when full 8am-6pm, $.65). A private taxi is $8 for a one-way trip to Boğazkale, $24-32 for a full tour of the ruins.

Among the numerous banks, a **Türkiye İş Bankası** that cashes **traveler's checks** and has a Cirrus/MC/Plus/V **ATM** is within sight of the Hotel Fatih. (Open M-F 9am-12:30pm and 1:30-5:30pm.) **Gözde Internet Cafe,** a lengthy walk down Çorum Cad. at 100 yıl hal içi No. 40 (☎365 20 40), charges $1 per hr. The **hospital** (Devlet Hastanesi) can be reached at ☎311 80 07. **Postal code:** 19300.

Crash at **Hotel Fatih,** 24 Cengiztopel Cad., which offers 15 sunny rooms, most with a view and bath; a Turkish toilet is on each floor. (☎311 34 88. Singles $8, with shower $12; doubles $16, with shower $22; triples $24.) In the center of town, across from the Türkiye İş Bankası, is the simple but functional **Otel Ferhat,** 3 Baykal Sok., with 17 basic rooms and one lucky Turkish toilet per floor. (☎311 80 67. Singles $4.50, with bath $5.50; doubles $9.50, with bath $11.) You can find a decent meal at **Birand Restaurant,** inside Özel İdare İşhanı. Follow Lise Cad. past the intersection with Cengiztopel Cad. and take the next right onto Çorum Cad. The comprehensive menu includes *dolma* for $1.50 and cold *mezes* for $1.25. (☎311 99 16. Open daily 6am-11pm.) Crunchy *leblebi* (roasted chickpeas), a regional specialty, are available at dozens of shops throughout town.

TOKAT ☎356

> And the inhabitants live in luxury, and all their property is planted with vines; and there is a multitude of women who make gain from their persons, most of whom are dedicated to the goddess. There, on account of the multitude of prostitutes, outsiders resort in great numbers and keep holiday.
>
> —Strabo, *Geography*

CENTRAL ANATOLIA

Situated in a valley surrounded by rocky hills, the modern city of Tokat is quieter and more conservative than its history would suggest. Step away from the noisy bustle of Gaziosmanpaşa Bul. to find an old city of crumbling Ottoman houses and winding cobblestone streets, where tourists draw crowds of curious children. Tokat's handful of first-rate sights make for a brief but enjoyable stay, especially when combined with the spectacular caves at nearby Ballıca.

Ancient Tokat, or Comana Pontica as Strabo knew it, was the notorious site of a debauched cult dedicated to the Anatolian mother goddess known appropriately as Ma. Annual orgies were held in honor of the goddess, presided over by priests, temple courtesans, a throng of wild flagellants, and frat boys in togas.

Near Tokat in 47 BC, Julius Caesar delivered a crushing defeat to Pharnaces II, the King of Pontus, who had dared attack the Roman provinces of Armenia, Cappadocia, and Galatia. Caesar's and Pharnaces' troops clashed between Tokat and Zile, resulting in the victory that inspired Caesar's famous *"Veni! Vidi! Vici!"* Low-key and unpretentious, modern-day Tokat combines a traditional, unhurried calm with modern streets lined with budget hotels and high-quality museums.

TRANSPORTATION

Flights: The small airport is about 30min. outside town. Tickets to **Ankara** can be purchased at the **THY office,** 206/4 Gaziosmanpaşa Bul., 2nd fl. (☎214 72 54; fax 212 41 69), opposite the Kent Bank. Open M-Sa 8:30am-12:30pm and 1:30-4pm; in summer closes 7pm. Flights Tu at 2:20pm; $58, 25% student discount.) Schedules can be erratic, so phone the THY office in advance.

Buses: Metro, Tokat İtimat and **Topçam** have offices at Cumhuriyet Alanı and at the otogar, near the north end of Gaziosmanpaşa Bul., about 2km from Cumhuriyet Alanı. To: **Adana** (9hr.; 4 per day 1:30-8pm; $16, students $14.50); **Afyon** (10hr.; 9pm; $19, students $17.50); **Alanya** (13hr.; 2pm; $22.50, students $21); **Amasya** (1¾hr., 10 per day 7:30am-9:30pm, $3); **Ankara** (6hr.; 7 per day 7am-12:30am; $13, students $11); **Antalya** (12hr.; 2 per day at 2pm; $21, students $19); **Aydın** (11hr.; 3pm; $19, students $17.50); **Denizli** (12hr.; 3pm; $21, students $19); **Diyarbakır** (10hr.; 4 per day 9-11pm; $19, students $17.50); **Erzincan** (4hr., midnight, $9.50); **Erzurum** (8hr., midnight, $14.50); **İstanbul** (12hr.; 10 per day 9:30am-9:30pm; $19, students $17.50); **İzmir** (14hr.; 4pm; $22.50, students $21); **Kayseri** (5hr.; 4 per day 1:30-8pm; $9.50, students $8); **Malatya** (6hr.; 11pm; $14.50, students $13); **Marmaris** (16hr.; 3pm; $24, students $22.50); **Mersin** (12hr.; 8pm; $16, students $14.50); **Samsun** (4hr.; 10 per day 7:30am-10pm; $8, students $7); **Sivas** (1½hr., 10 per day 7:30am-6pm, $3); **Trabzon** (12hr.; 4 per day 3-10pm; $16, students $14.50). Different companies run on different schedules, so check them all if the times are not convenient.

Local Transportation: Dolmuş ($.30) and buses ($.25) run along Gaziosmanpaşa Bul.

ORIENTATION AND PRACTICAL INFORMATION

Mountains and jagged promontories surround the town on three sides, crowned at one point by a **kale** (fortress). The main street, **Gaziosmanpaşa Bul.,** runs north-south, passing through **Cumhuriyet Alanı,** a large plaza that is the town's center. To get to town from the otogar, take one of the free *servis* shuttles offered by the bus companies. Otherwise, turn left from the bus company offices, walk 400m to a roundabout, and take another left onto Gaziosmanpaşa Bul.

Tourist Office: A tourist information kiosk is on Gaziosmanpaşa Bul., next to the Gök Medrese. Open M-F 9am-12:30pm and 1:30-6pm; Sa-Su 9am-1:30pm and 2-6:30pm.

Banks: A handful of banks with **ATMs** line Gaziosmanpaşa Bul. **Akbank** (☎214 15 95) cashes **traveler's checks** at no commission and accepts Cirrus/MC/Plus/V. Open M-F 9am-12:30pm and 1:30-5:30pm. **TC Ziraat Bank** (☎214 32 50) also cashes traveler's checks. Open M-F 8:30am-noon and 1:30-6pm.

Hamam: Tarihi Ali Paşa Hamamı (see p. 381).

Hospital: Devlet Hastanesi (☎214 54 00). Ardola Sok., south of the main square on the road to Sivas.

Pharmacies: along Gaziosmanpaşa Bul., among them the **Eczane** at No. 79 (☎214 10 73). Open M-Sa 8am-7pm, with rotating service on Su.

Internet Access: 75 Yil Internet Merkezi (☎212 52 98), behind the Meridyen shopping center, in the car park area. Walk south from Cumhuriyet Alanı and take the 2nd left after passing the Latifoğlu Konağı. $1.25 per hr. Open daily 9am-midnight.

PTT: In Cumhuriyet Alanı. *Poste restante* daily 8:30am-6pm. 24hr. phones.

Postal Code: 60000.

ACCOMMODATIONS

Hotel Çağrı, 92 Gaziosmanpaşa Bul. (☎212 10 28), outside Cumhuriyet Alanı, near the bank. Inexpensive, clean, and large but cozy rooms with TV, neatly made beds, and faux-mahogany furniture. 13 rooms, 8 with bath. Singles with bath $9.50; doubles $12, with bath $14.50; triples $17.50, with bath $21. 15% student discount.

Hotel Taç, 1 Vakıf İşhanı (☎214 13 31; fax 212 03 14), across Gaziosmanpaşa Bul. from the Taş Han. 35 spacious pink and white rooms, most with TV. Nice views of the Taş Han and fortress. Breakfast $1.25. Singles $7, with bath $12; doubles $8, with bath $14; triples $22.50, with bath $29.

Otel Plevne, 83 Gaziosmanpaşa Bul. (☎214 22 07), just off Cumhuriyet Alanı. 18 large, clean, comfortable rooms with peeling wallpaper; most have TVs and baths. Laundry service. Breakfast included. Singles $6, with bath $8; doubles $16, with bath $22.50; triples $24, with bath $32. Student discounts available.

Hotel Yeni Çinar, 2 Gaziosmanpaşa Bul. (☎214 00 66 or 213 19 29; fax 213 19 27), near the Türkiye İş Bankası. The highest-quality hotel in the center of Tokat, with brand new, fully equipped rooms with TV, minibar, and bath. Attached is an excellent restaurant (*Tokat kebap* $3). Breakfast $1.25. Singles $18; doubles $30; triples $40. Student discounts available.

FOOD

Though famous for its wines, Tokat is no culinary capital. The two local specialties are *Tokat kebap* (skewered lamb, potatoes, and eggplant; $4), and *çokelekli* (pita bread filled with crumbled cheese and lamb or potatoes; $.80). Inexpensive restaurants line Gaziosmanpaşa Bul. and its neighboring streets. Vegetarians tired of *çokelek* can try *nohut* (stewed chickpeas) at many of the restaurants, but beware the uninvited chunks of lamb that sometimes turn up.

Meridyen Cafe, 49 Gaziosmanpaşa Bul. (☎214 18 00), on the top floor of the Meridyen shopping center. Enjoy an excellent meal and the best view in Tokat from the outdoor terrace tables at this evening student hangout. *İskender kebap* $3; *ayran* $.40. Open daily 10am-10pm; kitchen closes at 9pm.

Bulvar Restaurant, 111 Gaziosmanpaşa Bul., opposite the Otel Taç. Serves the best *Tokat kebap* in town ($3.50), washed down with a bottle of local water ($.25), said to cure kidney, gall, and intestinal miseries. Open daily 6am-midnight.

Gaziantep Sultan Restaurant (☎212 81 81). Just off Cumhuriyet Meydanı, in the Ulaşioğlu İş Merkezi, spread out over two floors. Spacious and friendly. Go for the house specialty, *sultan kebap* ($3). Open daily 6am-11pm.

SIGHTS

GÖK MEDRESE (BLUE SEMINARY). The most visited sight in Tokat, the *medrese* now serves as the town's **museum.** It owes its name to the brilliant tiles that once decorated the entire exterior but are now only visible in the central courtyard. The enamel on these tiles was designed by a formula so distinct that modern-day technology has never been able to reproduce it. The *medrese* was built in the 1270s by the **Mu'in al-Din Süleyman** (a.k.a. "Butterfly"), a Rasputin-like adviser to the Selçuk Sultan Kiliç Arslan IV. Mu'in al-Din fluttered craftily around Kiliç Arslan until, no longer able to bear his lust for power, he had the sultan strangled at a banquet in 1264 and appointed himself regent to the underage successor. Butterfly's remains are reportedly in the Gök Medrese's collection of sarcophagi.

The museum focuses on artifacts unearthed at the Hanözü, Sebastopolis, and Maşat Höyük archaeological digs between Tokat and Zile. In the calligraphy gallery, note the 7½m-long Ottoman diploma required of all tradesmen, listing the owner's every credential from family background to school performance to completed pieces. Other intriguing items on display include local rugs and *kilims*, an exhibit on the making of *yazma* (cloth decorated with woodblock prints), and a wax model of the martyr **Christina,** whose waxy serenity is offset by the faithfully reproduced bloody gash across her throat. This room also has some excellent portraits and Byzantine art. The *medrese* houses the **Kırkkızlar Türbesi** (40 Girls' Mausoleum) which has 20 coffins painted the color of cotton candy. *(Across from the fortress on Gaziosmanpaşa Bul. Open Tu-Su 8:30am-noon and 1-4:30pm. $1.50, students free.)*

OTTOMAN HOUSES. The splendid **Latifoğlu Konaği,** a richly decorated 19th-century Ottoman family mansion, is one of Turkey's finest examples of Ottoman architecture. The sign is easier to see when coming from the north, but the large white house is unmistakable. Enter through the garden. *(On Gaziosmanpaşa Bul., a few blocks south of Cumhuriyet Alanı. ☎214 36 84. Open Tu-Su 8:30am-noon and 1-5pm; in winter 8:30am-noon and 1-4:30pm. $1.50, students free.)* The hilly, stone-paved **Sulu Sokak** to the west of the Ali Paşa Camii brims with less well-maintained Ottoman homes. *(Walk toward Cumhuriyet Alanı from the Taş Han and take a right just before Ali Paşa Camii.)*

TARİHİ ALİ PAŞA HAMAMI. You can't avoid the 425-year-old hamam in Cumhuriyet Alanı. Intentionally or not, its roof sings a glorious architectural ode to the human breast. The roof is made of two giant side-by-side domes, while the smaller domes are studded with nippled glass bulbs. Across the street, Ali Paşa, the hamam's founder, is buried in the garden of the black-domed mosque bearing his name. *(Women 6am-5pm; men 5pm-11pm. Bath $2.25; kese $1.25; massage $1.25.)*

TAŞ HAN. This *kervansaray*, next door to the Gök Medrese, was built in the 17th century for Armenian merchants. Once a major stop on the Silk Route, the Taş Han, at the time of publication, was being converted into a hotel.

OTHER SIGHTS. At the summit of the hill, in his home at 26 Sofyon Mah., **Duran Atılgan** operates a **zurna** shop. These incredibly loud, strident, oboe-like woodwinds are used in Turkish folk music. Altıgan, a self-taught virtuoso, performs on request. Zurnas go for $30-100. *(His house is a bit hard to find; ask passersby for "Duran Amca" or simply the "zurnacı." Walk up Sulu Sok. and after the parade of shops you will see stairs on your left. Take these to the top and ask for "Duran Atılgan." ☎212 04 37.)* North of the shop, the old **fortress** presides over the city. Not much remains, but it has a nice view, and if you climb up during the call to prayer, the town's *muezzins* create a peculiar acoustic effect. *(Head north from Cumhuriyet Alanı; past the museum, you'll see a yellow sign marked "kale." The trip is either a 30min. walk or a $1.50 taxi ride.)*

DAYTRIPS FROM TOKAT

BALLICA MAĞARASI (CAVES)

Buses leave daily for Ballıca from their office at 225 Niksar Yolu Kavşağı, opposite the Yavşaroğlu Dügün Salonu (1hr., Sa-Su 11am, $2.50). Tur 2000 may be willing to arrange group trips on weekdays. Alternatively, hire a taxi to Ballıca and back ($25). Another option is to catch a public bus to Pazar from Tokat's Cumhuriyet Alanı (1hr., $2) and take a taxi to the caves ($5) from in front of the PTT. ☎261 42 36. Open daily 8am-8:30pm. $.75.

A new paved road 25km from Tokat winds up White Mountain *(Akdağ)* 1916m to the entrance of the Ballıca Mağrası. Stalactites and stalagmites of awe-inspiring size have been forming on the marble and limestone walls of these giant caves since the Pleistocene Era, at a rate of 1cm every 400 years. Evidence suggest that some of the caves had human inhabitants in the Hittite period. Ballıca is made up of eight vast chambers that are unseasonably cool in the summer and warm in the winter. Descending hundreds of stairs into a horizonless landscape of jagged and bulbous green rock, punctuated only by the dripping of water and the chattering of bats, visitors have ample opportunity to indulge in *Journey to the Center of the Earth* fantasies. Although there are no English explanations inside the caves, the paths are very well marked, and it is impossible to get lost. A friendly, English-speaking guide (or *Rehber*) can lead you around for $.75 per person. A thorough tour of the caves takes 1-3hr. The caves are a popular stop of elderly asthmatics who believe the air within will help their breathing. A cafe just outside the entrance offers lovely views of the surrounding hills.

Travelers who go through Pazar might want to stop at an old *kervansaray* and the **Belediye İşhanı Sosyal Dayanışma Vakfı,** a blanket and *kilim* school. The school is in the back of the building across from the Belediye Hotel on Pazar's main road; turn toward the PTT and the entrance will be on the left. The weavers don't speak English, but will display their wares, serve you free *çay*, and let you try your hand at *kilim* weaving. *(Kilim school ☎261 20 01. Open M-F 8:30am-12:30pm and 1:30-5pm.)*

KAT

Dolmuş run every hr. from the minibus station, just behind the Gaziosmanpaşa Lisesi (school), off Gaziosmanpaşa Bul. (45min., daily 7am-5:30pm, $.75). Taxi from Tokat $25. Park entry $.50; access to the waters $1.25; to drink and bathe in a private room $7.50.

Budget travelers with ailments of the body, heart, or mind should check out the **healing spring** in Kat. The local tradition is to make a wish in the glade beside the spring, tie a handkerchief to a branch, and drink the spring's water. The area's greatest attractions, however, are the fresh *kiraz* (cherries) sold by farmers at absurdly cheap prices ($.25 per kg). While there's no real reason to sleep here, there is a clean, 8-room hotel. (Singles $8.75; doubles $17.50.)

SİVAS ☎346

A thriving outpost in the dry expanse of Anatolia, Sivas was founded by Hittites in 1500 BC. The city saw the successive rule of Assyrians, Persians, Romans, and Byzantines before flourishing under the control of the Selçuk Sultanate of Rum. Sivas still bears the marked imprint of the Selçuk architectural style. In modern Turkish history, Sivas is renowned as the site of the **Sivas Congress** of September 1919, during which Atatürk sought to fortify Turkish resistance against Allied attempts to partition Anatolia. The traveler arriving at the outskirts of the city would never guess that hidden among the squat, cement-and-glass cityscape are the intricate geometric patterns of one of the best-preserved collections of Selçuk architecture in Anatolia. In addition to being a center for *kilim* production, Sivas is also famous for its massive sheepdogs, bred for power and vigilance and exported to shepherds across Turkey.

TRANSPORTATION

The easiest way to get into town from the otogar is to take one of the many free *servis* buses to the bus company offices in Hükümet Meydanı; ask the driver for the *şehir merkezi* (city center).

Flights: THY office (☎221 11 44) is on İstasyon Cad. Service to **Ankara, Bodrum, Diyarbakır, Erzurum, Gaziantep, İstanbul, İzmir,** and international destinations.

Buses: Sivas Huzur (☎224 06 58), on Atatürk Bul., is reputable and drops their listed price 10% for tourists. To: **Adana** (8hr., 1:30pm, $10); **Afyon** (10hr., 4pm, $15); **Amasya** (3½hr., 2 per day 8am-5pm, $7); **Ankara** (6½hr.; 8, 9am, 1:30pm, midnight, 12:30am; $10); **Bursa** (11hr., 7pm, $15); **Eskişehir** (9hr., 7pm, $13); **İstanbul** (12hr.; 9am, 5:30, 7:30, 9:30pm; $15); **İzmir** (13hr., 4pm, $18); **Kayseri** (2hr., 2 per day 1:30-6:30pm, $5); **Konya** (8hr., 6:30pm, $12); **Mersin** (8½hr., 1:30pm, $10); **Samsun** (5½hr., 8am-5pm, $9); **Tokat** (1½hr., 4 per day 8am-5pm, $3.50). **Minibuses** to nearby destinations such as **Kangal** (1hr., $1) depart from the traffic circle at the downhill end of Atatürk Bul.

ORIENTATION AND PRACTICAL INFORMATION

The city is centered on **Hükümet Meydanı,** the square containing the tourist office and most sights. **Atatürk Bul.,** where most of the banks, hotels, and restaurants are located, runs southeast from here toward the new **otogar,** 3km south of the city. **İnönü Bul. (İstasyon Cad.)** heads southwest from the square toward the train station.

Tourist Office: (☎221 35 35), inside the Valilik building in Hükümet Meydanı; ask the police officer inside for the *"turizm danışma."* Provides a decent city map and brochures. Open M-Sa 8:30am-noon and 1:30-6:30pm.

Banks: Approaching the main square along Atatürk Bul., turn left into Belediye Sok. for **Sekerbank, Ziraat, İş Bankasi, Emlak,** and **Halk.** Additional branches line Atatürk Bul.

Laundromat: Ms. Çiti Laundry, Hikmet Işık Cad., Adliye Arkası (☎223 04 50), directly behind the Valilik building. Wash and dry $2.75. Open M-F 8am-8pm.

HEARTBREAK HOTEL The Otel Madımak is not just another entry in Sivas's pantheon of cheap places to stay. On July 2, 1993, a group of Turkish Alevi intellectuals gathered here for a symposium to honor a 16th-century Ottoman poet, hanged for writing against repression. Among the group was the late Aziz Nesin, Turkish translator of Salman Rushdie's *Satanic Verses*. Nesin's arrival sparked riots in Sivas. Angry mobs chanting religious slogans broke through police gunfire, set fire to the hotel, and surrounded the blaze to prevent rescue squads from entering or controlling the situation. The hotel burned to the ground, killing thirty-seven, though Nesin himself managed to escape by ladder. Though there is no memorial of what happened, the stepped-up police presence every July 2 reveals just how clearly the event lingers in the city's memory (see Alevi, p. 31).

Hamam: Kurşunlu Hamamı, 23 Arap Şeyh Cad. (☎223 24 88), is Sivas's oldest. Follow Atatürk Bul. from the city center and turn right after Otel Ergin; the hamanı is on the right, about 300m ahead. Bath $2; *kese* $1; massage $2. Open daily 4:30am-11pm.

Hospital: (☎221 60 20), north of Hükümet Meydanı. There's also a more convenient Kizilay 24hr. private clinic; $10 per consultation. Turn left off Atatürk Bul. into Belediye Sok.; the hospital is on the first left corner.

Internet Access: Sivas has many cafes in the city center. The **Blue Moon Cafe** (☎221 33 49) is opposite Hotel Fatih on Kursun Cad. $.75 per hr., open until 10:30pm.

PTT: Off Hükümet Meydanı. Open 8:30am-12:30pm and 1:30-5:30pm. Phones 24hr.

Postal Code: 58030.

ACCOMMODATIONS

Most of Sivas's hotels are on Atatürk Bul. There is a cluster close to Hükümet Meydanı, and another 1km further away around Kursun Cad. A local directorate grades hotels and controls prices, but rates are often negotiable.

Otel Akgül, 17 Atatürk Bul. (☎221 12 54), strikes a good balance between quality and price. Rooms away from Atatürk Bul. are quieter. Airy and clean, with 24hr. hot water. Singles $9; doubles $14.

Yavuz Otel (☎225 0204), on Atatürk Cad., is clean and roomy, if a bit dark. The best budget choice, if you can brave hallucinogenic carpets and wallpaper. All rooms with bath. $7.50 per person.

Otel Madımak (☎221 80 27), on Eski Belediye Sok., just off Atatürk Bul. by the PTT, is a 2-star hotel and one of the best in Sivas, desplte Its tragic history (see **Heartbreak Hotel,** below). Recently rebuilt, it has pleasant rooms with bath, upholstered chairs, and elegant two-toned furniture. Singles $15, doubles $25.

Sultan Otel (☎221 29 86), also on Eski Belediye Sok. Similar rooms to Madımak at slightly better prices, with TV and rooftop bar. Singles $12, doubles $24.

FOOD

A number of decent, cheap restaurants are off Atatürk Bul. near the PTT (Aliagacami Sok.). **Liquor** stores are rare. There is one opposite Otel Madımak and another **(Kalkan)** on Hiknet Isin Cad. Both close at midnight. If you're bar-bound, **Akalan,** on Eski Belediye Cad., is a loud, dark, friendly rock-and-roll cave, but only admits couples. (Beer $1. Open until midnight.)

Niyazibey İskender, 4 Eski Belediye Sok. (☎221 34 94), next door to the Madımak Otel, stands above the rest. Interior complete with flowers, wooden columns, and glass chandeliers. Open since 1860, Niyazibey is renowned for its *iskender kebap* ($3) and local specialties such as *papyon kebap* (beef stuffed with cheese and mushrooms, $2).

Büyük Merkez Lokantası, 13 Atatürk Bul. (☎223 64 34). This 3-floor restaurant is popular among locals. Swiftly serves up *kebaps* ($1.70), *börek* ($.90), and a wide variety of local dishes, including light and crust *lahmecuns* ($.50). Open daily 5am-midnight.

SIGHTS AND ENTERTAINMENT

Fortunately for tourists, most Selçuk architecture in Sivas is crammed around the central square. For historical background, see **The Great Selçuk Sultanate,** p. 9.

KALE CAMİİ. This small mosque was built in 1580 during the reign of Sultan Murat III. Its well-preserved frescoes and chandelier of drooping glass teardrops earn it a reputation as the most beautiful Ottoman mosque in Sivas. *(Head along İnönü Bul away from the city center to the first building on the left.)*

SELÇUK SIGHTS. A few steps east across the path from the Kale Camii is the **Büruciye Medrese,** founded in 1271. To the left of the entrance is the tiled *türbe* of the Iranian founder. The tomb's heartfelt inscription reads, "This is the tomb of the humble, homeless servant Muzaffer. May God forgive his sins." Particularly striking is the incredible detail of the interlocking patterns around the doorway.

Follow the cobblestone path farther away from Hükümet Meydanı. On the right is the 13th-century **Çifte Minareli Medrese.** Two red-brick minarets with flecks of remaining blue tile flank the extensive relief of the gateway. Directly opposite is the **Sifaiye Medrese,** built in 1217 under Selçuk Sultan Keykavus I as a hospital, medical school, and asylum. It was converted into a *medrese* in 1768. The courtyard with four *eyvans* (vaulted recesses) now functions as a kind of motley bazaar-cum-tea-garden. Above the large *eyvan* at the end of the courtyard opposite the entrance are two reliefs: on the left, a man surrounded by solar rays, and on the right, a woman with braided hair. Don't miss Sultan Keykavus's enameled *türbe* in the southern wall of the courtyard (to the right when you enter).

Separate from this complex is the **Ulu Cami,** the oldest mosque in Sivas, built in 1196. The interior is a forest of columns (50 in all, arranged in 11 rows). The red-brick minaret was added in the 13th century. *(From the Sifaiye Medrese, return to İnönü Bul., continue walking away from the city center, and after the park ends take the 2nd left onto the wide Cemal Gursel Cad. The Ulu Camii is 500m ahead.)* Follow the yellow signs to the **Gök Medrese,** or Blue Seminary, which was built for the Selçuk vizier Sahip Ata Fahreddin Ali in 1271. You may be permitted to climb the unnerving wooden staircase to the top of one of the minarets. From either the Gök Medrese or the Ulu Cami, it's just a short walk up to the **citadel.** Only the walls remain, but inside are a number of tea gardens with views past the city's boundaries to the mountainous steppe beyond. *(Open daily 7:30am-noon and 1:30-6:30pm. $.90; students $.60.)*

ATATÜRK CONGRESS AND ETHNOGRAPHIC MUSEUM. This museum commemorates the historic council that took place here in 1919. After skipping town in foreign-dominated İstanbul, Atatürk landed in Samsun and proceeded to Amasya and Sivas, organizing meetings with leaders from across Turkey in preparation for the War of Independence and the foundation of the Republic (see **The Cult of Mustafa Kemal,** p. 15). The ethnographic items have English labels, but the extensive descriptions of the Sivas Congress are only in Turkish. *(In the city center, across İnönü Bul. from the Selçuk buildings. Open Tu-Su 8am-noon and 1:30-5:30pm. $1.25, students free.)*

DAYTRIP FROM SIVAS: BALIKLI KAPLICA

Take a bus from Sivas's old bus station to Kangal ($1); from the town center (with a large mosque and an Atatürk statue) take a dolmuş the rest of the way (9am-5pm, less frequent after 3pm; $.60). Dolmuş drivers raise their prices after 5pm. On quieter days, skilled negotiation can yield a $5 round-trip by taxi which includes an hour in the baths. ☎469 11 51. Normal pools $.75; tedavi $10 per day. Pools open daily 7am-noon and 2-7pm.

For a surreal adventure into the realm of bizarre sanatoriums, take a trip out to **Balıklı Kaplıca,** which at first glance is just another Turkish hot spring. Ah, but look closer! The bubbling, selenium-rich waters are the world's only habitat for several species of friendly, **flesh-eating fish.** These fish (designated by the management as drillers, suckers, and dressers), along with the healing properties of the water, have made the spring one of the foremost treatment centers for psoriasis, a non-transmittable skin disease. Patients frustrated with the ineffectiveness of conventional medicine flock here to consume gallons of water and submit to the care of the "doctor fish." It's worth a dip, even for those who don't suffer from psoriasis.

The spring offers two types of pools: "normal" pools for tourists and other casual visitors ($.75 per day paid upon entry to the park), and *tedavi* (treatment) pools for those with skin ailments ($10 per day). An usher wards tourists away from the treatment pools, so only intentional exfoliation or a morbid interest in it will ensure a dip here. While the tickle of tiny bites may feel a bit peculiar at first, you'll soon get used to the fish as they mysteriously hone in on patches of dry, dead skin. (Pools open daily 7am-noon, 2-7pm). The stream passing through the center of the complex is free and fully stocked, providing a less-daunting encounter than the full immersion, although you may encounter the odd "doctor snake," said to combat St. Anthony's fire, another skin ailment. These snakes are small, harmless and, in fact, rarely encountered.

It's not worth staying overnight in Balikli Kaplica, but there are a few options if you're in a pinch: the overpriced **Unsallar Hotel** (☎457 30 36; unsal@alnet.net; singles $30; doubles $50); the **Baraka,** or "Shed" (singles $15; doubles $20); and the nearby campground ($5 per tent). There's food at the site's **market** and decent **restaurant,** also run by Unsallar. (*Tavuk ızgara* $2; *biber dolmasi* $1.50.

BLACK SEA COAST

Along the shores of the Black Sea, the heat of Anatolia gives way to soft sea breezes and tall fir forests descending from high hills to the edge of the sea. Where forests thin out, fields of tobacco and cherries alternate with sloping pastures nibbled by grazing cattle. *Yaylas* and high-altitude villages provide a welcome retreat to escape the summer heat. From Samsun to Trabzon, the Black Sea coast is relatively heavily populated and traveled. West of Samsun, however, lies a different landscape and rhythm. While travel between Samsun and Trabzon is easy, with numerous buses and dolmuş connecting towns along the way, the Black Sea road is in poorer condition and is less often traveled. **The ride is dangerous,** due to both traffic and the road conditions. Despite these drawbacks, those who decide to travel on the coastal road rather than inland will be rewarded with small fishing hamlets, spectacular cliffs jutting straight into the sea, and countless fjords.

HIGHLIGHTS OF THE BLACK SEA REGION

VISIT ancient **Sumela Monastery** (p. 420), beautifully carved into a cave on the side of a sheer cliff and frescoed with the vivid blues and golds of Byzantium.

TURN the clock back centuries as you visit the brilliant restored Ottoman mansions of **Safranbolu** (p. 387), and discover why the town is on the UNESCO World Cultural Heritage List.

LOSE YOURSELF in the tranquil beauty of **Amasya** (p. 403) and explore the mysterious cliff tombs of the Pontic Kings.

BASK in the sun and dine on seafood at the untouristed beaches of Amasra (p. 391).

DIVE into the crystal-clear waters of **Sinop** (p. 397), the northernmost point in Turkey.

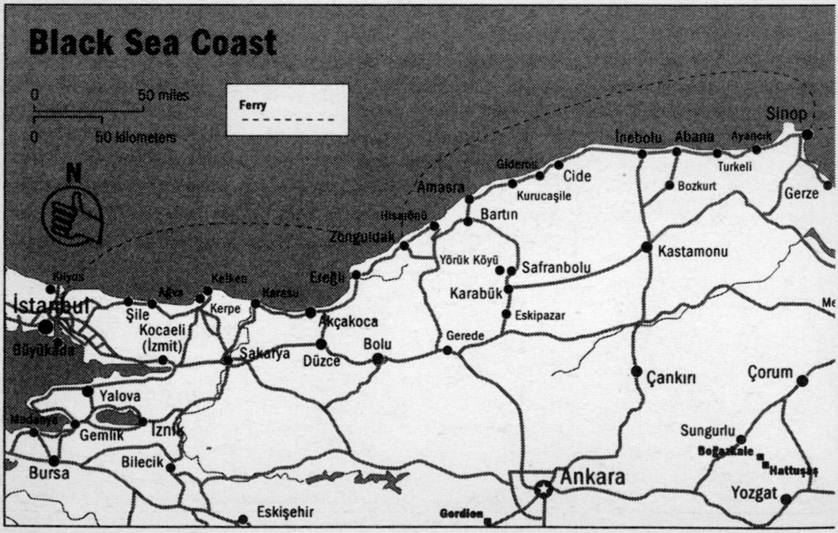

In ancient times, Phoenician and Greek traders esta[illegible] colonies in the few spots where the sheer cliffs break to form natural harbors. The ancient trading posts of Sinop, Trabzon, and Amissos (now Samsun) were all pivotal links on the Byzantine Silk Road. Later, the area was a refuge for the Commenus dynasty as the Ottomans encroached upon Constantinople. After World War I, Mustafa Kemal landed at Samsun to begin the Turkish War of Independence. Until recently, NATO naval bases dotted the coast, staring down Soviet fleets on the horizon. Commerce with Georgia and other former Soviet republics has brought new prosperity, but has also led to a marked increase in prostitution in and around Trabzon.

SAFRANBOLU ☎370

Safranbolu's old city turns back the clock to a 19th-century Ottoman town—nowhere else in Turkey is there such a concentration of old Ottoman houses, making the city somewhat of a living museum. The elegant wooden houses have been well preserved and restored, and new construction is confined to Yeni Safranbolu, the new town, 2km above the old city. The restoration began in 1975, and today, many of the houses are converted to hotels or *gezi evleri* (houses open to visitors). The town was placed on the UNESCO World Cultural Heritage List in 1994 in recognition of its extensive preservation efforts.

TRANSPORTATION

Buses: While direct buses do travel to Safranbolu, you may have to take a dolmuş from the steel manufacturing town of Karabük, 8km away (15min., frequent, leaves when full, $.45). Safranbolu itself is served by **Ulusoy** (☎712 66 44), **Güven** (☎725 21 45), and **Avrupa** (☎712 43 15), which have offices around New Safranbolu's town square. Buses from New Safranbolu to: **Amasra** (2hr., 8:15am, $4); **Ankara** (3hr., 15 per day 5am-8pm, $9); **Antakya** (15hr., 6:30pm, $20); **Bursa** (9hr., 7pm, $15); **Giresun** (9hr., 7pm, $18); **İstanbul** (7hr., 17 per day 7am-11:30pm, $14); **İzmir** (12½hr., 3 per day at 8:30pm, $18); **Kastamonou** (2hr., 6 per day 8am-6pm, $3); **Ordu** (8hr., 6pm, $17); **Rize** (14hr., 6pm, $22); **Samsun** (6hr., 5pm, $14); **Trabzon** (13hr., 6pm, $20).

Taxis: Metered taxis between the old and new town cost about $3. It is only a 30-40min. pleasant, downhill walk from the old town to the new.

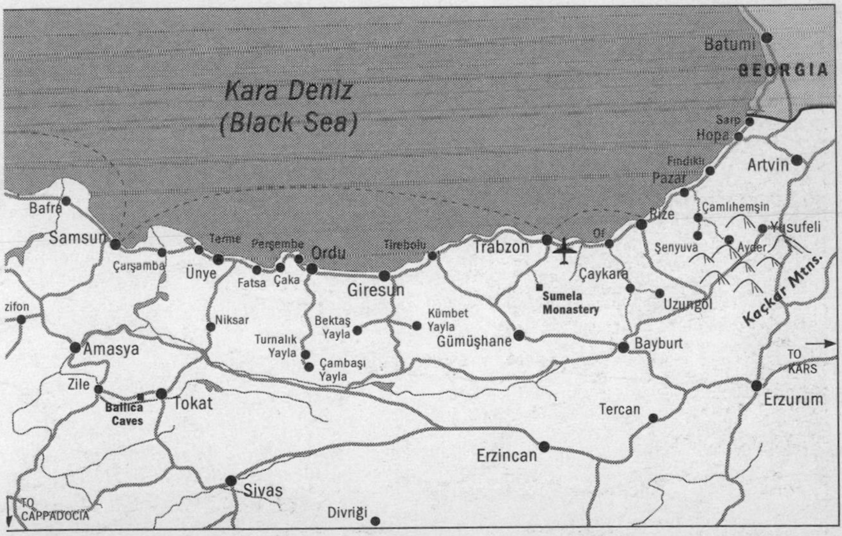

THE BLACK SEA FERRY

For travel in either direction along the Black Sea coast between **İstanbul** (p. 78), **Zonguldak, Sinop** (p. 397), **Trabzon** (p. 414), and **Rize** (p. 420), the Black Sea Ferry provides the most novel, hassle-free, and direct route. Service may also include **Giresun** (p. 410) in the future.

Tickets are sold at Turkish maritime lines offices in each city's harbor area. In İstanbul, make purchases at the Karaköy terminal. The quality of on-board lodging ranges from A/2 (comfortable, with a two-person bunk) to B/4 (crowded, with four people) to airline-style seats ("Pullman seats"), which are the cheapest. Fares from İstanbul:

CLASS	TO SAMSUN	TO TRABZON	TO RIZE
A/2	$34	$59	$60
A/4	$27	$44	$45
B/2	$31	$52	$53
B/4	$24	$39	$40
Seat	$13	$17	$18

The ferries leave İstanbul Mondays at 2pm, from the dock at Sarayburnu, a five-minute walk along the shore from the Sirkeci train station. Boarding starts at 1pm. The boat docks at Samsun around 4pm on Tuesday and at Trabzon about 8am on Wednesday. The return trip leaves Trabzon on Wednesdays at 7pm, hits Samsun at 9am on Thursday, and reaches İstanbul Friday at 1pm.

Though costly, food and drinks are sold on board (the purser on the main deck sells the required restaurant vouchers). A better bet is to bring your own groceries. There are also a few small markets near the pier entrance at Samsun.

If the seas are rough (which is rare in the summer), bring along Dramamine or other over-the-counter motion sickness medications. Even in rough seas, however, the hauntingly beautiful nighttime seascape and the unusual mode of travel make it worthwhile.

ORIENTATION AND PRACTICAL INFORMATION

Safranbolu has two distinct sections: the old town, called **Çarşı,** and the largely uninteresting new one, called **Yeni Safranbolu** or Kıranköy. The heart of Çarşı and its center of transportation is the main square, **Çarşı Meydanı.** If you stand in the square and look toward the old baths, you will see three streets. On the extreme left, **Kastamonu Yollu** leads to the Çarşı Pansiyon. The next street, **Akın Sok.,** runs to the Cinci Han, an old *kervansaray.* To the right, **Yukarı Çarşı Sok.** leads to the Arasna, the site of the tourist office and a number of touristy shops. Behind you, **Hilmi Bayramgil Cad.** runs to the new town.

Tourist Offices: The government-run tourist office, **Turizm Danışma Müdürlüğü,** 5 Arasta Sok. (☎/fax 712 38 63), in the Arasta Bazaar, offers maps. Open daily 8:30am-6pm.

Banks: TC Ziraat Bankası, behind Cinci Han, has an **ATM.** Open M-F 8:30am-noon and 1-5pm. **Currency** and **traveler's check exchange** close at 4:30pm.

Hamam: The 250-year-old **Tarihi Cinci Hamamı,** in the center of Çarşı, is large and clean. Separate sections for men and women. Bath $3; *kese* $.75; massage $1.20. Open for women 10am-8pm, for men 6am-11pm.

Hospital: (☎712 11 87), in the new town, behind the Kız Sağlık Meslek Lisesi.

Internet Access: Only available in New Safranbolu. Try **Cyberland Internet Cafe,** Yavuz İshanı, İnönü Mah., Kaya Erdem Cad. $.80 per hr. Open daily 10am-11pm.

PTT: On Hamamönü Sok., near the Çarşı Pansiyon. Open M-Sa 8:30am-12:30pm and 1:30-5:30pm. A bigger PTT, is on Sadri Artunç Cad., in Bağlar. Open daily 8am-11pm.

Postal Code: 78600.

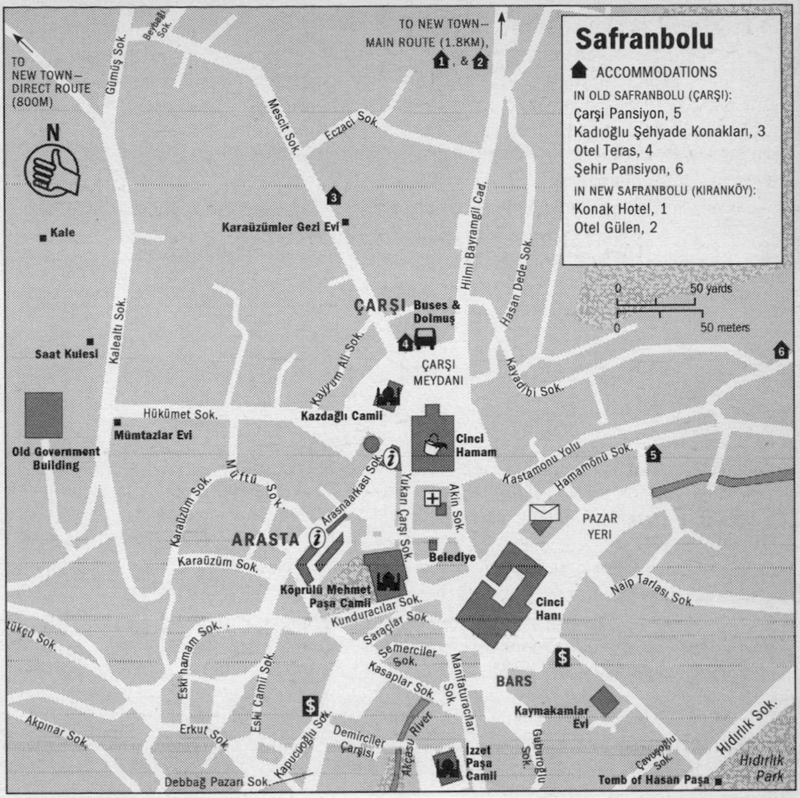

ACCOMMODATIONS

Safranbolu is popular year-round, and accommodations tend to fill up on weekends. If possible, make reservations a few days in advance. New Safranbolu is a hilly 2km road from Çarşı. Frequent dolmuş make the trip, too. Old Safranbolu's accommodations sometimes inflate their prices for tourists.

OLD SAFRANBOLU (ÇARŞI)

Otel Teras, Çarşı Meydanı, 4 Mescit Sok. (☎725 17 48). Conveniently located directly off the main square in a magnificent Ottoman house. 6 decorated, clean, modern rooms with bath and TV at reasonable prices. Breakfast included, served on a pleasant terrace. Singles $16; doubles $24; triples $32.

Çarşı Pansiyon, 1 Bozkurt Sok. (☎725 10 79)., east of the small PTT office. A great budget option, Çarşı has 12 simple rooms, 4 with private bath and 2 with Ottoman-style floor mattresses. Breakfast included. Singles $8; doubles $16; triples $25.

Kadıoğlu Şehzade Konakları, 24 Mescit Sok., Hacıhalıl Mah. (☎725 27 62; fax 712 56). All rooms with bath, phone, and TV. Breakfast included. Singles $19; doubles $32.

Şehir Pansiyon, Akçasu Mah. No. 10 (☎712 19 70), beyond Çarsı, heading 100m uphill on Akçasu Sok., just past the Dağdelen Camii. 8 rooms, 3 with bath, and 4 with hill views. Breakfast included. Singles $14; doubles $24; triples $32.

NEW SAFRANBOLU

Otel Gülen, 2 Utku Sok., Ulu Camii Karşısı (☎725 10 82). From the roundabout in New Safranbolu heading toward Çarşı, take the 2nd right onto Cumhuriyet Cad.; the hotel is about 200m ahead. An incredible bargain. Stay in an authentic Ottoman house with a splendid rustic interior for rock-bottom prices. Charismatic owner offers 9 rooms, 4 with bath. Singles $3; doubles $6.50; triples $9.50.

Konak Hotel, 4 Sağlık Sok. (☎725 24 85), on the left as you walk 150m from the roundabout toward Çarşı. 12 comfortable, clean, renovated rooms, 5 with bath and TV. Breakfast $1.25. Singles $10; doubles $20; triples $32.

FOOD

Safran Ocakbaşı (☎712 10 76), Çarşı Meydanı, Hamamönü Sok. Serves good food in a small, clean restaurant at reasonable prices. *Kanat* (wing) *şiş* $1.30. Free *ayran.*

Karaüzümler Gezi Evi Kafeterya, Hacı Halil Mah., Mescit Sok No. 20 (☎725 14 49), up the road from Otel Teras. This museum-house serves 5 varieties of *gözleme* ($1), with *dolma* ($1.50) and *erik suyu* ($.80), in a lovely garden or inside in the Ottoman salon. Admission to the house is free if you eat in the restaurant.

Kadıoğlu Şehzade Sofrası, 8 Arasta Sok. (☎712 50 91; fax 712 56 57), on the main square. Though a bit touristy, it's one of the places where you can try *kuyu kebap* ($3), made by hanging a whole lamb in a specially prepared underground pit and roasting it for hours, and *Safranbolu bükme* (sweet dessert; $2). Decor includes Ottoman couches, low tables, and a bubbling fountain. Open daily 8am-11pm.

Çevrikköprü Tesisleri (☎737 24 61; fax 737 21 19), about 6km from Safranbolu on the road to Kastamonu. Take one of the hourly dolmuş from Çarşı toward Yörük Köyü and ask to be let off at the restaurant. They specialize in *kuyu kebap.* The meat is particularly tender (250g portion $3). In addition to *gözleme,* baklava, and *pide,* they also have a pool full of live trout ($2). Open daily 9am-midnight.

SIGHTS

OTTOMAN ARCHITECTURE. Safranbolu's highlight is unquestionably its architecture. Traditional wooden mansions are characterized by an overhanging second floor and highly ornate ceiling decorations. Their complex floor plans were designed to maximize comfort and to keep men and women separated. To see the architecture up close, take a peek inside the fancier hotels or visit the *gezi evleri,* restored houses that accept visitors for a small fee.

The best place to start is **Kaymakamlar Evi** (Governor's Residence), the local museum. Enter through the courtyard, where the animals were originally kept. The house has two knockers: each would indicate the gender of the caller to the members of the household, so a resident of the same sex could answer the door. Various tools and utensils are on display in the courtyard, including wooden cone *frustums* used for making *ayran.* Upstairs, the elaborate construction and decoration of the home attest to the complexity and grandeur of Safranbolu's Ottoman houses. One of the most unusual features is the *döner dolabı,* a rotating cabinet set in the wall between the kitchen and the dining room that allowed female residents to serve food to male guests without showing themselves. After your tour, sip tea ($.25) the garden. *(To get to the house from the square, walk along Akın Sok. to the Cinci Han; Kaymakamlar is on the little street past the TC Ziraat Bankası and behind the Cinci Han. ☎712 66 78. $.80, students $.40. Open daily 9am-9pm, in winter 9am-5pm.)*

Kileciler Evi, at the intersection of Akpınar Sok. and Sışayanın Sok., 300m down Manifaturacılar Sok., heading away from the Cinci Han and main square, is worth the walk. This house boasts a gorgeous exterior, trellised balcony, and restored interior. *(☎712 82 00. Open M-F 9am-7pm, Sa-Su 9am-8pm. $.80, students $.40.)*

Other *gezi evleri* include the **Karaüzümler Gezi Evi,** on Mescit Sok. past the Otel Teras. Though more worn than Kaymakamlar, the rough, unfinished, wood-reinforced facade of the this 97-year-old building is an interesting change from the flat white of other mansions. *(Open daily 9am-10pm. $.70, students $.30.)* On Hükümet Sok., high on a hill past the Tahsin Bey Konağı, the Mümtazlar Evi has an interesting octagonal room on the top floor, as well as a tea garden (tea $.25; cappucino $1.25) with a great view. *(☎712 63 59. Open daily 8:30am-midnight. $.80.)*

OTHER SIGHTS. Walk up the narrow broken street past Kaymakamlar Evi to reach **Hıdırlık Tepesi,** a lookout point with fantastic views of Safranbolu in all its antiqued glory. Hıdırlık Tepesi houses the **tomb of Hasan Paşa,** an Ottoman notable exiled to Safranbolu in 1843. Peek through the tiny barred slit to see his elaborately carved wooden tomb and the hundreds of coins thrown in by visitors. Also visit the grave of **Candaroğlu Hıdır Paşa,** who conquered Safranbolu in 1358.

Uphill from the Mümtazlar Evi is the old government building, or **Hükümet Binası,** a 19th-century structure that's prettier from a distance. On Manifaturacılar Sok. past the Cinci Han, the **İzzet Paşa Camii,** built in 1796, has exquisite calligraphy. The more central 17th-century **Köprülü Mehmet Paşa Camii,** across from the Cinci Han, is less exciting, but its courtyard opens onto the very touristed **Yemeniciler Arastası,** the shopping arcade that houses the tourist office. An oval-shaped complex, this was once home to Safranbolu's famous shoe industry. Today, cafes and gift shops crowd the intimate arcade.

ENTERTAINMENT

Most of Safranbolu's nightlife centers around the Cinci Han. There's an excellent range of bars, most offering live music, in the central square.

Beyaz Ev Pub, 18-20 Pazar Yeri (☎712 52 53), behind the Cinci Han. A friendly environment, with great live music and draft beer ($1.50). Be sure to sign their guestbook—a collection of compliments, witticisms, and poems by foreign patrons in various stages of intoxication. Live guitar and *saz* music W and F-Sa. Open daily 11am-2am.

Arasna Bar, Arasta Arkası Sok., No. 4 (☎712 41 70; fax 725 30 82), on the ground floor of the Arasna Hotel. Hosts an enthusiastic crowd on F and Sa, when live music plays from 10pm. Beer $1.75.

Hangar Disco and Bar (☎712 67 27), in Pazar Yeri, behind the Cinci Han. A compact, crowded dance floor in Old Safranbolu's only disco. Beer $2. Cover $3 1-6pm, $4 7pm-3am; first drink and munchies included. Open daily 1pm-2am.

Turku Cafe Bar, 22 Pazar Yeri (☎725 46 66), next to Hangar Disco. Live Turkish folk music W and F-Su 9pm-1am. Beer $1.50. Open 11am-2am.

Safranbolu Photography House and Kültür Café (☎712 65 83). Based in an old stone house just underneath the Hıdırlık Tepesi, this chill cafe-photography gallery is an excellent place to take in Safranbolu from above. The owner, Turqud Ertuğrul, will gladly show you around his pictures of Safranbolu and the house.

AMASRA ☎378

Amasra (pop. 7000) is one of the most spectacularly situated cities on the Black Sea Coast. Straddling two natural harbors with clean, sandy beaches, its natural beauty is striking: craggy cliffs rise above snaking shorelines, rocky islands, and rich blue waters. On top of that, the remains of its considerable medieval fortifications add historic charm and an almost surreal atmosphere. They also provide excellent vantage points from which to survey the town below. Today, however, the town also has several modern, well-equipped pensions and hotels (book ahead in summer), excellent seafood restaurants, and a hassle-free, reasonably priced market for souvenirs (mostly wood work and embroidery).

Over 3000 years of trade and fishing have left Amasra the same quiet beach getaway that Queen Amastris was looking for in the 4th century BC when she founded the town on the site of Sesamos, an ancient Miletian port.

TRANSPORTATION. The main transport hub closest to Amasra is **Bartin,** 16km south, accessible by **dolmuş** (every 30min. 7:30am-9pm; $.80, students $.60). Most major **buses** pass through Bartin. Travelers heading east along the coast to Sinop should be prepared for a long, frustrating journey. The route is serviced only by minibuses and can take a long time. Start very early in the morning; minibuses run rarely in the afternoon and not at all in the evening. Check when buying a ticket whether buses leave from Amasra or Bartin. **Özemniyet** (☎315 10 56) and **AS74** (☎315 17 63) provide direct **bus** service from Amasra to: **Afyon** (9hr., 7pm, $19); **Ankara** (from Bartin: 4½hr., 8 per day 5:30am-1am, $9.50; direct from Amasra: 5:30 and 9:30am, $9); **Antalya** (15hr.; 4:30, 7pm, $20); **Bodrum** (17hr., 7pm, $24); **Bursa** (7hr.; 10am, 5pm; $13); **İstanbul** (8hr., 7 per day 6:30am-11:30pm, $13); **İzmir** (13hr., 5pm, $21). **Minibuses** run to **Bartin** and **Cide** (2½hr.; 7, 11am, 2:30, 7pm; $3).

ORIENTATION AND PRACTICAL INFORMATION. Amasra sits on a peninsula that juts out into the Black Sea, forming two harbors. The western harbor is known as **Küçük Liman** (small harbor), the eastern one is **Büyük Liman** (big harbor). Most of the buses stop in **Atatürk Meydan,** the main square. Opposite is a park that leads to the western harbor. **Küçük Liman Cad.** runs along the western harbor by the hotels before winding left into the fortress. There is a small square on the western harbor, surrounded by the PTT and a number of hotels and restaurants. **Çekiciler Cad.** (the woodworking market) runs east from Küçük Liman Cad. across the peninsula toward the eastern harbor.

In the square, **Türkiye İş Bankası** has an **ATM** and **exchanges currency** and **traveler's checks.** (Open M-F 9am-12:30pm and 1:30-5:30pm.) While there is **no tourist office,** the **Belediye Bina** (municipal building) has a reception desk which can be of assistance. (Open 8am-midnight.) A wonderful English-language resource is the **Aydın Eczanesi,** a **pharmacy** (☎315 23 23) next door to the PTT. Friendly pharmacist Aydın Söğüt, his wife, and his daughter can help with minor currency exchange and, of course, **medical assistance.** (Open daily 8:30am-midnight.) Other services include: the **Devlet Hastanesi** (state **hospital,** ☎315 21 98); **IZO Internet Cafe** on Kum Mah., Barış Sok. No. 3/A (open 9am-midnight; $.90 per hr.); and the **PTT,** on the square by the western harbor. (Open 8am-11pm.) **Postal code**: 74300.

ACCOMMODATIONS. In the summer, make reservations in advance, especially on weekends. Some hotels close down in winter, so phone ahead. Toward the center of town, the **Otel Belvü Palas,** 20 Küçük Liman Cad., has 15 large, clean rooms with whitewashed walls, many with stunning views and all with bath. (☎315 12 37. Singles $13; doubles $25.50; triples $38.50; quads $51.) Across the peninsula, on the eastern harbor, is the small **Amasra Oteli,** 49 General Mithat Ceylan Cad., which offers eight comfortable, carpeted rooms, six with bath and two with sea views. (☎315 17 22; fax 315 30 25. Singles $8; doubles $16; triples $20. Discount for longer stays.) Next door to Amasra Oteli is the larger, more glamorous **Otel Timur,** 57 Çekiciler Cad., sporting marble hallways, hardwood floors, and 18 rooms with immaculate bath, six with sea views and TV. (☎315 25 89; fax 315 32 90. Breakfast included. Singles $10; doubles $20; triples $25.) The **Nur Turistik Pansiyon,** Küçük Liman Mah. Çamlık Sok. No. 3, along the waterfront road, offers 17 rooms, eight with waterfront views. (☎315 10 15. Breakfast included. Singles $8; doubles $20; triples $31.) **Balkaya Pension,** on General Mithal Ceylan Cad., is a new, clean pension. Some rooms have balconies; nine of the rooms have phone, TV, and bathroom. (☎315 14 34; fax 315 14 45. Singles $9; doubles $18; triples $27.)

FOOD. The restaurants along Amasra's western harbor all specialize in fish and offer a range of decor, style, and atmosphere. The large and luxurious **Canlıbalık Restaurant,** 8 Küçük Liman Cad., recognized as the town's best, provides an open-air setting, right next to the sea, with great harbor views. (☎315 26 06. *Barbun* fish $3; *mezgit* fish $2.50; *rakı* $1.25. Open noon-midnight.) **Çinar Restaurant,** 1 Küçük Liman Cad., is an established, central fish restaurant similar to Canlıbalık but will more meat choices. (☎315 10 18.) Near the Timur and Amasra hotels, overlooking the fishing boats in the eastern harbor, **Çeşm-i Cihan Restaurant,** 21 Büyük Liman Cad., serves a wide variety of tasty fish to go with good views. (☎315 10 62. Fish from $3. Open 11am-midnight.) **Liman Restaurant** (☎315 23 48), at the far end of the Büyük Liman Cad., at the end of the harbor, serves *alabalık* (trout; $4), *çupra* fish ($5), and *rakı* ($1.25). Make sure to climb up to the roof terrace for the full experience. For remarkable *gözleme,* head to **Kale Altı Kafeterya,** Çekiciler Cad. No. 37, on the carpenter's road. (☎315 19 21. Open 8am-1am.) **Sormagır Cafe,** Kum Mahallesi K. Liman Cad. No. 24/A, by the citadel, bakes *gözleme* and prepares fillings in front of you. (☎315 34 04. Open until 1am.)

NIGHTLIFE. Take the next left after Canlıbalık, walking toward the ruins, to get to **HAN Bar,** Küçük Liman Cad. No. 17, which has live Turkish music every night and an atmospheric interior. (☎315 27 75. Tuborg beer $1.30, *rakı* $2. Open 10am-3am.) **Su Bar,** Kum Mah., Eyıleoğlu Sok. no 25/B (☎315 13 95), is a new bar with nightly live music and a dance floor. **Teras Cafe and Bar,** Turgut Işık Cad. No. 3, has a chill, informal outdoor atmosphere to go with nightly live music and excellent views of the harbor. (☎315 20 46. Open until 2am.) Amasra's only nightclub, **Beden Altı Disco-Bar,** on Büyük Liman Cad. at the end of the harbor, is an outdoor disco with a huge dance floor, adjacent to Liman Restaurant. ($1.50 cover includes a drink. Beer $1.25. Open in summer 9pm-1am.)

SIGHTS. Amasra is built around its ruins, so it's easy to see them all while strolling around town. Although the town was fortified as far back as the 3rd century BC, the **citadel** that today stands dates from the 9th century AD. Start your tour by following Küçük Liman Cad. from the western harbor left through the fortress gates. Follow the road around until you arrive at an ancient Roman **bridge** connecting the large island of **Boztepe** to the mainland. Turn right onto Kemere Sok. before the bridge and walk uphill to the **Fatih Camii,** Kale İçi Mah., Camii Önü Sok., a ruined 9th-century Byzantine church that was converted into a mosque when Sultan Mehmet II conquered Amasra in 1460. Pass through another gate a little further ahead to reach a **lookout point** atop the fortress walls on the right. Strings of lights affixed to a billboard outline the silhouette of Atatürk on one side and of Sultan Mehmet the Conqueror on the other. A bit further on lies another neglected Byzantine **church.** The frescoes inside have almost completely faded.

The town **museum,** Kum Mah. Çamlık Sok., recently renovated, has miscellaneous items from the Hellenic through Ottoman eras, including a collection of Ottoman pistols. Outside, ancient columns and tablets with Hellenic, Roman, early Christian, and Ottoman inscriptions are being slowly eroded. (☎315 10 06. Open daily 8:30am-5:30pm. $1.50, students $1.25.) Difficult to find but well worth the search is the local **woodworking craft and artisans' market** on Çekiciler Cad.

If you're looking for something a bit wilder than Amasra's semi-urban beaches, head to nearby **Bozköy,** 15km away, a secluded beach with fine sand, clean blue waters, and dramatic green cliffs. The beach houses a cheap campsite. (Open July 1-Sept. 15. $2 per tent.) Bozköy can be reached via minibus (25min., leaves when full 10am-7pm, $.75), or by taxi (about $16.) Make sure you don't miss the last minibus back to Amasra. Two kilometers further east is the small, pleasant town of **Çakraz,** with a more developed but still beautiful beach lined with cafes and a few reasonable hotels. Minibuses from Amasra stop in both Bozköy and nearby Çakraz. Be aware that neither Bozköy nor Çakraz is protected by a bay like Amasra's. Some consider these "open beaches" to carry a greater safety risk.

İNEBOLU ☎366

A low-key fishing town, İnebolu (pop. 1000) serves as a useful coastal connection along the beautiful but poorly served Amasra-Sinop road. The town is popular with Turkish tourists and hotels can fill up in summer, especially on weekends. The trip here from any direction involves spectacular scenery, but the town itself is unexciting; it has little to offer except a rocky beach, some fish restaurants, and a glimpse at a sleepy Turkish resort.

TRANSPORTATION. **Metro** (☎811 49 60) and **Kastamony Özlem** (☎811 39 30) run **buses** from the **otogar** to: **Ankara** (6hr., 8 per day 5am-8pm, $9.50); **Bursa** (8hr.; 6:15, 6:30pm; $14); **İstanbul** (9hr., 5 per day 9am-8pm, $15); **İzmir** (13hr., 6:30pm, $27); **Kastamonu** (1¾hr., 4 per day 8am-9:30pm, $2). **Minibuses** leave the otogar for: **Abana** (every 30min. 9am-7pm; $1.50, students $1.25); **Kastamonu** (1¾hr., 12 per day 6:30am-6pm, $1.50); **Sinop** (3hr.; 2:45, 4:45pm; $6.50, students $5.50). Minibuses also stop at the Petrol Ofisi on the coastal road to drop passengers near the hotels.

ORIENTATION AND PRACTICAL INFORMATION. The coastal road is known as **Zafer Yolu** to the east of the river and as **İsmetpaşa Cad.** to the west. Most hotels are west of the bridge—turn left when facing the coast. **Cumhuriyet Cad.**, the main commercial road, runs inland from the PTT past many shops and a mosque.

There's a basic **tourist office** in a wooden hut on the coastal road, 200m east of the river. (Open June-Sept. daily 11am-7pm.) Banks, including an **Akbank** (open M-F 9am-12:30pm and 1:30-6pm) with an **ATM** and **currency exchange,** line Cumhuriyet Cad. Other services include: **pharmacies** on Cumhuriyet Cad; the **hospital** (☎811 31 94); **internet** at **Internet Cafe,** Boyran Mah., 71/B Şarmin Apt., on the left, past Sahil Pansiyon (☎811 57 50. $1 per hr.); and the **PTT,** on the coastal road. (Open daily 8am-11pm; airmail M-F 8:30am-5:30pm). **Postal code:** 37500.

ACCOMMODATIONS. The **İnebolu Yakamoz Tatil Köyü,** Bayram Mah., İsmet Paşa Cad., 500m west of the town center, has newly renovated motel rooms or small bungalow triples with wooden interiors, bunk beds, and a fridge and kitchen facilities. Call ahead in summer. (☎811 43 05. Motel room $15; triples $13.) Closest to town, **Sahil Pansiyon,** 63 İsmetpaşa Cad., about 400m west of the bridge and up a flight of stairs, offers family-style living in a quiet location. The six clean rooms have common kitchen and Turkish toilet; top floor rooms have a splendid sea view. (☎811 43 98. $4.25 per person.) The rest of the accommodations lie along the beach. The **Huzur Motel,** 8 İsmetpaşa Cad., across from Sahil, has 16 beachside rooms, some with Western toilets. (☎/fax 811 46 52. Doubles $11; triples $13.50.)

FOOD. İnebolu is renowned for its fresh fish. The best establishment in town, the **Gazi Denizcilik Restaurant** (☎822 46 88), on İsmetpaşa Cad., a few hundred meters along the coast toward the hotels, serves a wide variety of fish (*kalkan* $6.50; *barbun* $5) and *pide* ($2.50) on its seaside terrace with excellent views. (☎811 46 88. Open Apr.-Nov. daily 8am-2am.) Also excellent, the **Şehir Restaurant,** on the second floor of the building next to the PTT, has the same owners, menu, and prices, but is open year-round. Try the *Palamut* fish ($3) or *rakı* ($1.25) on the rooftop terrace. (☎811 40 72. Open daily 6am-2am.)

ABANA

☎366

Abana (pop. 3000) is a fast-growing beach resort that has managed to retain an intimate feel. There are plenty of *çay* houses and some pebble beaches, but little other entertainment. Abana is also a major base for campers along the Black Sea Coast—it has one of the only campsites around. Those arriving at the end of July can enjoy the annual **Abana Culture and Art Festival** (☎564 10 08), featuring concerts, art exhibitions, and sports tournaments.

TRANSPORTATION. There is no otogar, so all **buses** stop near the bus company offices in the square. Buy bus tickets either from **Kastamonu Özlem** (☎564 24 24) or **Soner Turizm** (☎564 20 20) for: **Ankara** (7hr., 8:45pm, $11); **İstanbul** (10hr.; 2 buses each at 8:30am and 6:30pm; $16, students $13.50); **Kastamonu** (1½hr.; 6:30pm; $3, students $2.50); **Safranbolu** (6hr.; 5am; $11, students $9.50); **Samsun** (6hr.; 5am; $11, students $9.50); **Zonguldak** (7hr.; Th and Su 9:30am; $11, students $9.50). **Minibuses** service to **İnebolu** (30min.; 8am, 12:30, 2:30pm, then depends on demand; $1.25, students $1) and **Sinop** (2½hr.; 5, 9:15am, 5pm; $5.50, students $4).

ORIENTATION AND PRACTICAL INFORMATION. Hilmi Uran Cad., the town's main street, extends east from the central square, **Cumhuriyet Alanı**, inland, parallel to the sea. The nightlife is concentrated between the square and the coast. Services include: a **tourist office** in a small booth on the square (open June-Sept. daily 8am-midnight); a **TC Ziraat Bankası** with an **ATM** on Hilmi Uran Cad. (open M-F 8am-noon and 1:30-5:30pm); the **hospital** (☎564 11 25); **internet** access at **Beyaz Saray (White House) Internet Cafe,** Merkez Mah., Cumhuriyet Alanı, just off the main square, facing the sea (open 9:30am-1am; $1.25 per hr.); and the **PTT,** next to the Ziraat bank on Hilmi Uran Cad., 130m from the square. (Open M-F 8:30am-12:30pm and 1:30-5:30pm). **Postal Code:** 37970.

ACCOMMODATIONS. Otel Bora, Tahsin Coşkun Cad., directly in Cumhuriyet Alanı. Definitely the best value and the budget choice. Clean rooms, many with balconies overlooking the square, and shared toilets. (☎564 12 60. $6 per person; discount available.) From the square, follow the signs 200m west along the coastal road to **Sahil Pansiyon,** 23 Sahil Cad., a hospitable, family-run place on the seaside with seven quad rooms, four baths, a kitchen, and sea views. (☎564 15 41. More suited to groups or families. $5 per person.) Next door to the Sahil Pansiyon is **Ümit Pansiyon,** 24 Sahil Cad. Six rooms, all with bath, are of better quality than Sahil's, but they cost more. (☎564 11 07. $8 per person.) Along the coastal road east of the square is a cluster of bungalow villages. **Doğan Güneş Camp Cafe,** 600m east of the town center, is a seaside campsite with a cafe, cold water showers, and toilets. (☎564 30 82. Open June-Sept. $4 per tent.)

FOOD AND ENTERTAINMENT. Abana's food is rather unspectacular. The **Köseoğlu Restaurant,** 1 Merkez Mah., in the center of town, has decent fish (*kalkan* $6; *Çiniköp* $4.50) with *rakı* for $1.25 and *revanı* dessert for $.70. (☎564 11 74. Open daily 6am-1am.) A few doors down is **Ümit Ocakbaşı,** 10 Hilmi Uran Cad., which serves *kıymalı pide* for $1.50 and pizza for $3. (☎564 24 29. Open daily 8am-2am; in winter daily 8:30am-9pm.) **Beyaz Saray Restaurant,** Merkez Mah., Kamil Demircioğlu Cad., just off the main square by the sea, has great views, but is perhaps better for an evening drink since the menu is somewhat limited, with *mezgit* fish for $2 and *izgara köfte* for $2. (☎564 28 40. Open daily noon-2am.)

As for entertainment, the town's three main activities are swimming at the beach, sipping tea at the beach, and climbing the nearby hills to look out over the beach. After a day at the beach, head along the coastal road past the campsites to the cluster of **bars** and *çay* gardens, which sometimes offer live Turkish pop. **Bısın Ev,** Cumhuriyet Meydan, just off the square, has a large outside seating area, nice decor, and good *çay*. (Open daily 8:30am-1am.)

KASTAMONU ☎366

An administrative center for Romans, Byzantines, Selçuks, and Ottomans, Kastamonu (pop. 57,000) is still an outpost of activity in the sparse green mountains. As it is the region's transportation hub, travelers headed to Ankara or the nearby coast will most likely pass through here. Kastamonu has many wooden Ottoman houses and old Islamic monuments, and its flowing river and surrounding lush countryside make for a relaxing setting. The town itself is relatively unexciting, but is worth a visit to see its impressive Islamic architecture.

Uphill are many well-preserved, traditional Ottoman houses and the center is dominated by the famous Nasrullah Mosque, built in 1506. Many come on pilgrimages to the tomb of Seyh Saban-İveli, a leader of the Halveti order. The nearby village of Kasbah has what is considered one of Turkey's best wooden mosques.

TRANSPORTATION. Metro (☎214 27 27) and **Kastamony Özlem** (☎214 12 12) provide **bus** service to: **Ankara** (4hr.; 9 per day 5am-midnight; $9.50, students $8); **Bursa** (9hr.; 6:30pm; $17, students $15.50); **Konya** (8hr., 10pm, $16); **İstanbul** (8hr.; 7 per day 10am-11pm; $16, students $14.50); **İzmir** (14hr.; 6:30pm; $27.50, students

$24). **Soner Turizm** (☎212 13 34) runs **minibuses** to **Abana** (1½hr., 10 per day 10:30am-7:30pm, $3). **Doğus** (☎214 17 98) runs buses to **Cide** (2½hr.; 8am, 3, 4:30pm; $1.50). **Demirkaya** (☎214 49 46) runs to **İnebolu** (1hr., 15 per day 10:30am-7:30pm, $2.50) and **Sinop** (3 hr.; 9am, 5:30pm; $6.50).

ORIENTATION AND PRACTICAL INFORMATION. The main road, the north-south **Cumhuriyet Cad.,** runs parallel to the river that bisects the town. It also passes through **Cumhuriyet Meydanı,** the town's central square. **Belediye Cad.,** which runs west from the river, is home to a number of cheaper hotels and restaurants.

The **Tourism Office and Müdürluğu** (Directorate), 15 Nasrullah Meydanı, adjacent to the Nasrullah Camii, is not accustomed to foreign tourists. (☎212 10 62. Open M-F 8am-noon and 1:30-5:30pm). **Internet** is available at **Alem Internet Cafe,** Topçuoğlu Mah., İzbeli Sok. No. 3, on a side street off Cumhuriyet Cad. (☎212 84 02. $1 per hr. Open 9am-1am.) A speedy connection is also available at **Efenet Internet Cafe,** 67-68 Nasrullah İş Merkezi. Walk south along the river and take the second right after Belediye Cad.; it's on the bottom floor of the shop-filled building on the left. ($1 per hr.) Other services include: **banks** in Cumhuriyet Meydanı, including a **Türkiye İş Bankası** with an **ATM** (open 9am-12:30pm and 1:30-5:30pm); the 500-year-old **Araba Pazarı Hamamı,** 80 Belediye Cad., at the end of Belediye Cad. (☎214 57 09; hamam $2.50; *kese* $2; massage $1.75; open for women daily 8am-5pm, for men 5:30am-11pm); the **hospital** (☎214 10 53); and the **PTT** in Cumhuriyet Meydanı (open daily 8:30am-5:30pm). **Postal code:** 37200.

ACCOMMODATIONS. The **Otel Selvi,** 10 Banka Sok., has 54 comfortable rooms, 40 with bath and most with TV. Turn onto Belediye Cad. from Cumhuriyet Cad. and then take the first left. The owner speaks excellent English. (☎214 17 63; fax 212 11 64. Singles $6.50, with bath $10; doubles $11, with bath $17; triples $16, with bath $25.50.) The rest of the hotels are on Cumhuriyet Cad. and can be noisy. The **Otel İdrisoğlu,** 25 Cumhuriyet Cad., has 28 older rooms with private bath and TV. (☎214 17 57; fax 214 79 66. Singles $12, students $8; doubles $19, students $12; triples $25.50, students $22.50.) The cheapest joint in town is the **Otel Ilgaz,** 4 Belediye Cad., off Cumhuriyet Cad., which has 16 very basic rooms, a shared squat toilet, and old shower on each floor. (☎214 11 70. Doubles $8; triples $9.50.)

FOOD. Kastamonu has a number of good, inexpensive *kebap* spots scattered around the square. Many serve the local specialty, *etli ekmek* (minced, spiced meat sandwiched between crispy layers of *pide*). **Fırtına,** Cumhuriyet Cad. No. 5 (☎214 84 40), along the main street, is a brand-new Italian restaurant with excellent food at affordable prices. The **Uludağ Pide ve Kebap Salonu,** 19/D Cumhuriyet Cad., serves great *iskender kebap* for $3 and *ayran* for $.30. (☎214 11 96. Open daily 7am-10:30pm.) Across the river, the comfortable **Kardelen Kebap,** 32 Plevne Cad., provides savory *mercimek çorba* (lentil soup; $.70) and tasty *etli ekmek* ($1.50). (☎212 25 29. Open daily 6:30am-11pm.) After dinner, head to the centrally located **Şengün Pastanesi,** 17/B Cumhuriyet Cad., to sample the local specialty, *sepetçoğlu şekerleme* (a dry, flaky confection; $2.50 per kg), or the delicious *çekme helva,* a white, cube-shaped sweet. (☎214 23 65. Open daily 5am-11pm.)

SIGHTS. Kastamonu's main attractions are its varied examples of Islamic architecture and the view from its ruined castle. In a square near the Otel Selvi is Kastamonu's largest mosque, the **Nasrulla Kadi Camii,** built in 1506. The splendid **Nasrullah Fountain,** in front of the mosque, bears the inscription "The guest who drinks water from the fountain can't keep himself from coming here again." Walk past the Nasrullah Camii and up some stairs to see the historic **Aşır Efendi Han,** a former *kervansaray* for itinerant traders. Nowadays, it is used as a modern shopping center. With your back to the Efendi Han, turn left and take the first left. On the left is the **Yakup Ağa Külliyesi,** a deserted complex that includes a mosque, *medrese,* and kitchen, all built in 1547. Bear right at the fork onto Atabey Sok. toward Kastamonu's oldest mosque, the 13th-century **Atabey Camii,** 500m uphill and well behind the Aşır Efendi Han. A little further uphill, bear right onto Kale Sok., a narrow street that leads to the city's **kale** (castle), a fairly well-preserved complex with a commanding view of the city and surrounding hills. As you enter the *kale*, turn immediately right and try to look inside the main tower. There are stairs leading to the stop. Unfortunately, you have to climb a couple of meters of stone to reach the steps. First constructed by the Byzantines, it achieved its ultimate girth under Tamerlane, when he took the city from the Ottomans in 1402.

The **ethnographic museum,** in the Liva Paşa Konağı on Cumhuriyet Cad., adjacent to the Sağlık Müdürlugu (Health Directorate), contains a variety of craft-related exhibits in a well-restored three-floor Ottoman house. (☎214 01 49. Open Tu-Su 8:30am-noon and 1:30-5pm. $1.50, students $.75.) To get there, start from Cumhuriyet Meydanı, 200m along the river and take the second right.

SİNOP ☎382

One of the most famous ports on the Black Sea Coast, Sinop has provided shelter to sailors since ancient times. Nowadays a resort town popular with young Turks, Sinop's crystal-clear waters and long, sandy beaches are possibly the cleanest in Turkey. Though on the tacky and dusty side, the town itself features the ruins of medieval castles and a lively nightlife around its natural harbor.

Sinop takes its name from Sinope, a mythical nymph who spurned the advances of the thunderbolt-hurling god Zeus. Hoping to lure her into his Olympian sack, he offered to grant her a single wish. Thwarting the horny Olympian's plans, she asked for eternal virginity. Zeus, bound to his promise, isolated her on the tiny mountainous peninsula where modern Sinop now slumbers.

TRANSPORTATION

The larger bus companies don't serve the treacherous road between Sinop west to Amasya; local minibus companies pick up the slack. Sinop has a small otogar, spectacularly and rather bizarrely located in the old city walls. Services can be infrequent so make sure to check the night before. Traveling west can be frustrating and time consuming; start very early.

Buses: Sinop Bırlık (☎261 17 33) and **Sinop Barış** (☎261 51 63) run from the otogar to: **Ankara** (9hr.; 3 per day at 9pm; $16, students $14.50); **Bursa** (10hr.; 2:30pm; $12, students $11); **Giresun** (6hr.; 8pm; $12, students $11); **İstanbul** (11hr.; 9am, 7pm; $28, students $24); **İzmir** (18hr.; 2:30pm; $28, students $24); **Kastamonu** (3hr.; 6 per day 10am-7pm; $8, students $6.50); **Ordu** (6hr., 8pm, $9.50); **Rize** (10hr., 8pm, $14); **Samsun** (3hr.; 10 per day 7am-8pm; $8, students $6.50); **Trabzon** (8hr.; 8pm; $13, students $11); **Ünye** (5hr.; 8pm; $9.50, students $8).

Minibuses: These run westward along the coastal road to **Abana** (2½hr.; 8am, 5:45pm; $5.50, students $4.50) and **Inebolu** (3hr.; 8am, 5:45pm; $6, students $5).

ORIENTATION AND PRACTICAL INFORMATION

The Sinop peninsula juts northeast into the Black Sea. In the center of town, at a large roundabout, **Sakarya Cad.** intersects **Atatürk Cad.,** which runs south toward the harbor and a large square, **Uğur Mumcu Meydanı.** The town's main street, **Sakarya Cad.,** runs from the city center southwest past the **otogar** toward the mainland. The cheap hotels are on Kurtuluş Cad., near the harbor and fish restaurants; follow Sakarya Cad. until it intersects with Atatürk Cad.

Tourist office: (☎261 52 98). Stand in the square with your back to the PTT and turn left; the office is off the road on the right. Open July-Sept. daily 8am-8pm.

Pharmacies: On Sakarya Cad.

Hospital: Atatürk Hastanesi (☎261 45 10). Follow Sakarya Cad. to the town hall and turn right downhill. Open 24hr.

Internet Access: FVT Internet Cafe, Aşıklar Cad. No. 31, on the main coastal road. $.80 per hr. Open daily 9am-midnight.

PTT: In Uğur Mumcu Meydanı. Open daily 8:30am-11pm, mail services until 5pm. 20 phones, available until 11pm.

Postal Code: 57000.

ACCOMMODATIONS

Sinop has plenty of reasonably priced rooms next to the fortifications along the waterfront. Yuvam Belediye Plajı and Karakum Plajı are two of many campsites.

Otel Meral, 19 Kurtuluş Cad. (☎261 31 00). 20 simple, large, sunny rooms, 3 of which have private bath. Rooms on higher floors have stunning harbor views. Solar-powered hot water. Singles $6.50, students $5, with bath $9.50; doubles $12, students $9.50, with bath $19; triples $16, students $14.50; quads with bath $24.

Uğur Aile Pansiyon, 4 İskele Cad. (☎261 59 47), along the waterfront. A budget-friendly place with 9 large rooms, 2 with a great view, common baths, kitchen, and free laundry. Restaurant on the harbor offers good fish. Singles $8, students $6.50; doubles $13, students $9.50; triples $14.50, students $13; quads $19, students $16.

Karakum Tatil Köyü (☎261 26 94; fax 261 26 93). This vacation village on Karakum beach is 2km west of the town center along the coastal road. You can make the trip via the regular dolmuş ($.30) or on foot (30-35min.). Breakfast is included at the hotel, bungalows, and apartment villas. **Hotel:** has 18 simple rooms, all with bath and sea views. Singles $9.50; doubles $19; 2-room suites $32. **Bungalows:** 2-person $22.50; 4-person with kitchen $45. **Apartment villas:** 3-person with kitchen $34. **Campsite:** $4.80 per tent or caravan (open June-Sept.). Good private beach.

Gazi Piknik ve Mesire Yeri (☎260 23 87). Set in a forest by the beach. Turn right from the otogar on Sakarya Cad. and walk 100m; the campsite is on the left. Sinop's largest, cheapest, closest campsite. $4 per tent or caravan. Electricity $.50. Student discount.

FOOD AND ENTERTAINMENT

There are several excellent fish restaurants in the port. Follow the waterfront past the tourist office to the cheap restaurants serving *mantı* and *gözleme.* After a day at the beach, Sinop vacationers play backgammon and *erikriç* (a local version of the game played with tiles) at the waterfront cafes on Kıbrıs Cad.

Saray Restaurant, 18 İskele Cad. (☎261 17 29), on the port waterfront. One of the best fish restaurants in town. Select your own fish from the kitchen. Salmon $4. *Rakı* $1.50. Open daily 9am-4am; in winter daily 9am-midnight.

Balık Restaurant, 1/B İskele Cad. (☎260 33 68), near the port next to the fortress. Possibly the best fish restaurant in town. Serves fresh crab ($.50 per crab). *Rakı* $1.25. Open daily 9am-4am; in winter 9am-midnight.

Burç Cafe (☎260 32 19), atop the citadel's tower. A great place to have *çay* ($.25) and enjoy the view. Live *saz* performances nightly 9pm. Open Apr.-Oct. daily 8am-midnight.

Diogenes Bar, 5 İskele Cad. (☎261 57 21), across from the Uğur Restaurant. Behind the large black door lies Sinop's most vibrant bar. Beer $1.25. Open daily 8pm-4am.

Teleskop Disco, on Karakum Beach, 3km west of the town center and uphill from the coastal road. DJs spin Turkish and foreign dance music. Open daily 9:30pm-very late.

Barbarosa, Tersane Mah. Kurtuluş Cad. 26/2 (☎261 89 16). Caters to a mostly young crowd in a club-like atmosphere. Live bands, playing both Turkish and Western music.

SIGHTS

BEACHES. Beachgoers have a number of options in Sinop's clear, fresh waters. **Akliman Halk Plajı,** 12km from town on the western coast, is long, gorgeous, and uncrowded. *(Dolmuş leave from Uğur Mumcu Meydanı. 20min.; every 30min. M-F 8am-6pm,*

Sa-Su 8am-10pm; $.50.) The **Gazi Piknik ve Mesire Yeri** has a small, quiet beach, usually populated by camping families. *($.50.)* Half a kilometer from central Sinop, **Yuvam Belediye Plajı,** next to the Orman company, is free but quite crowded. It gets better the further you head away from town. The packed and overdeveloped **Karakum Plajı** draws a younger crowd of sun-seekers. *(A 30min. walk or brief dolmuş ride ($.30) northeast from Uğur Mumcu Meydanı along Kıbrıs Cad. Facing the sea from Sinop, turn left. $.35.)* **Boat tours** leave from the port in the center. *($7 per hr.)*

FORTIFICATIONS. Sinop's imposing fortifications date from 770 BC, when the port was settled by Miletian colonists. What stands today is a mish-mash of Pontic and Ottoman renovations. Some remains stand near the otogar, but the walls by the harbor at the end of Atatürk Cad. are much more impressive.

MUSEUM. Most notable for a large Hellenistic sculpture of a deer strangely unconcerned about being devoured by lions, the museum also houses a sizable collection of Greek, Roman, and Ottoman coins, early Bronze Age pottery, and various amphorae. Upstairs is a collection of 19th-century Greek Orthodox icons, including several beautiful Annunciations and a vicious St. George slaying the dragon, and an exhibit on Ottoman calligraphy.

Behind the museum lie the remains of the **Temple of Serapis,** dating to the 4th century BC. Serapis is associated with Asclepius, god of medicine, healing, and dreaming. There is also a memorial to Ottoman soldiers who died after an 1853 surprise Russian attack on the Ottoman navy in Sinop Harbor. *(At the end of Sakarya Cad. Museum closed at time of publication; scheduled to reopen by Summer 2002.)*

SELÇUK SIGHTS. Sinop's two oldest Islamic monuments are the 13th-century rectangular Selçuk **Alaaddin Camii** and **Pervane Medresesi,** next to each other on the north side of Sakarya Cad. The *medresesi* now houses a school, but you can get a peek of the courtyard. Sultan Keykubad built the high-walled mosque—with a single large dome and two small flanking domes—after the Selçuks seized Sinop in 1214. The mosque's *mihrab* is a spectacular example of Selçuk calligraphy in gold and marble. The *medresesi* was built in 1262 after the second sacking of the city.

OTHER SIGHTS. One kilometer from the city center is the **Seyit Bilal Türbesi,** the Selçuk-built tomb of a Muslim martyr. Seyit Bilal was leading an armada to attack Constantinople when a storm forced him into the Byzantine-controlled port of Sinop, where he was decapitated. Legend has it that after his execution, he walked from the city center, at that time located near the Alaaddin Camii, to the site of his tomb—all the while carrying his newly severed head under his arm. While the tomb and its accompanying mosque aren't particularly striking architecturally, the site is exceptionally holy for Sinopean Muslims. *(From the intersection of Sakarya Cad. and Atatürk Cad., continue heading uphill with your back to Sakarya Cad.)*

Abandoned and deteriorating rapidly, the extensive ruins of **Balatlar Kilisesi,** a 7th-century Byzantine church, retains some beautiful frescoes of the evangelists and various saints. *(Near the intersection of Radar Yolu and Kemalettin Sami Paşa Cad., 1km northeast of the museum. To get there, walk uphill from the intersection of Atatürk Cad. and Sakarya Cad. toward the Seyit Bilal Türbesi, but take the right fork after the jandarma road sign.)*

BEETLEMANIA Some things are universal. The Turkish word for Volkswagen driver, *"VosVoscu,"* implies a certain friendly openness. Started five years ago by Beetle fanatic Enis Ayar, the long-haired, energetic owner of Ordu's Ayşığı Cafe, the July festival brings *VosVoscu* together in Ordu's beautiful countryside. Though it varies from year to year, the general plan of each year's festival is the same. After congregating in Ordu, scores of Beetles, which Turks call *Kaplumbağa* (turtles), come from all over the country, and sometimes as far as Greece, and proceed to the highlands, where they camp hike, and drive in a large loop that takes them inland to the 3100m lake, Karagöl, and then back to Giresun. The festival offers fantastic opportunities to relax, hike, eat fresh trout, meet dozens of friendly people, and ogle Mr. Ayar's four converted Beetles; one normal, one jeep one pick-up truck, and one limousine.

SAMSUN

☎362

The largest city on Turkey's Black Sea coast, Samsun is a busy metropolitan center with a long and exotic history. An 1869 fire gutted the city, however, leaving modern-day Samsun few remnants of its past. Famous as the "City of the 19th of May" *(On Dokuz Mayıs)*, the day Atatürk set foot on Anatolian soil and launched the drive for the Turkish Republic, Samsun is now a transportation hub for flight and bus connections. A few quality hotels and museums can make a stay pleasant, but most travelers don't stick around for long.

TRANSPORTATION

The otogar, just off the coastal road on Atatürk Bul., is about 2km east of the city center and main square, Cumhuriyet Meydanı.

Flights: THY office, 8 Kazımpaşa Cad. (☎435 23 30; fax 431 82 60). *Servis* buses run to the airport 1½hr. before each flight ($3), returning to the office after arrivals. The 23km trip costs $20-25 by taxi. To **Ankara** (45min.; F, Su 7:30pm; $52-65) and **İstanbul** (1hr.; daily 6, 10am; also via Ankara; $75-90). 20% student discount.

Trains: On Atatürk Bul., 700m east of Cumhuriyet Meydanı (☎223 50 02 or 223 22 93). To **Sivas** (8hr.; Su-M, W, F 8:20am; $4-5.50) and **Amasya** (2½hr., daily 7pm, $1.25-2).

Buses: If arriving in town, ask to be let off at Cumhuriyet Meydanı, where all the bus companies have offices. 10-20% student discount, depending on the company.

DESTINATION	DURATION	TIMES (DAILY)	PRICE
Adana	12hr.	7, 10:30pm	$15
Alanya	17hr.	5:30pm	$21
Amasya	2½hr.	6 per day 8:30am-5pm	$4
Ankara	6½hr.	15 per day 9am-midnight	$16.50
Antalya	15hr.	5:30, 6:30pm	$24
Bodrum	19hr.	6:30pm	$20
Bursa	13hr.	7pm	$15
Giresun	3½hr.	7:30pm	$5
Hopa	10hr.	8:30am	$14.50
İstanbul	12hr.	9 per day 7:30am-11pm	$24
İzmir	16hr.	5, 6pm	$26
Kayseri	8hr.	9am, 3pm, midnight	$11
Malatya	10½hr.	9:30pm	$11
Marmaris	21hr.	8, 9:30pm	$20
Mersin	12hr.	7, 10:30pm	$13
Ordu	3hr.	7:30, 10pm	$4.50
Rize	8½hr.	5 per day 8:30am-midnight	$13
Sivas	5hr.	5 per day 9am-9:30pm	$9
Tokat	4hr.	5 per day 9am-9:30pm	$8
Ünye	1½hr.	7:30am, 11pm	$2.50

Ferries: East (Tu 8pm) to **Trabzon** (12hr., $3.50-40) and **Rize** (17½hr., $5-42). West (Th 6:30am) to **İstanbul** (30hr., $13.50-50). 20% student discount. The westward boat stops at Sinop and Zonguldak for 30min. each. The ticket office is hard to find: head for the port, 1km west of Cumhuriyet Meydanı. Dolmuş run along Atatürk Bul.; ask for "Liman." Turn right off Atatürk Bul., heading away from the center. Enter the port gates and go to the back of the red building. Climb the stairs and ask for **Alemdarzade office** (☎445 16 05; fax 445 16 04). Open M-Sa 8am-6pm.

ORIENTATION AND PRACTICAL INFORMATION

If there is no free *servis* from the bus company, exit the otogar, cross the main road, and wait under the bridge for the dolmuş ($.30). Ask to be dropped off at **Meydan** (the square). A private taxi costs about $5. The main commercial street, **Kazımpaşa Cad.,** leads west of the main square to **Saat Kulesi Meydanı.** The brick-paved streets to the side contain many of the budget hotels and good restaurants. Farther inland, running parallel to the shore, is **Gazi Cad.,** a pleasant street with many bakeries, bookshops, and banks. The next street along is **Çiflık Cad.** (a.k.a. **İstiklâl Cad.**). Finally, even farther uphill, still parallel to the shore, is **100 Yıl Bul.**

Tourist Office: (☎431 12 28), across Atatürk Bul. from Cumhuriyet Meydanı. Helpful staff speaks English; office has A/C. Be careful: not every tour offered is a good value. Open Apr. 15-Sept. 15 8am-7pm; Sept. 15-Apr. 15 8am-noon and 1:30-5pm.

Travel Agency: Kar Tur, 5/B Kazımpaşa Cad. (☎431 10 26; fax 431 30 60; kartur@ttnet.net.tr). Deals with tour bookings, flight ticket sales, and Ulusoy bus tickets.

Banks: Many with **ATMs** on Gazi Cad., running parallel to Atatürk Bul., 2 blocks inland.

English-Language Bookstore: Dünya Kitabevi, 60 Şevketiye Cad. (☎239 08 49; fax 233 97 53), on a side street off İstiklâl Cad. Periodicals include the *Wall Street Journal, USA Today, Time,* and the *Economist.* Open M-Sa 8:30am-9:30pm; Su 11am-8pm.

Laundromat: Nurpak Kuru Temizleme, 56/B Bahariye Cad. (☎234 53 67), on a side street off İstiklâl Cad. Turn right off İstiklâl Cad. when you reach the Lee Cooper store. Wash and dry $1.25 per kg. Open daily 8am-midnight.

Pharmacies: Many are in and around Cumhuriyet Meydanı.

Hospitals: Devlet Hastanesi (☎230 33 00); **19 Mayıs Üniversitesi Hastanesi** (☎457 60 00); **Büyük Anadolu Hastanesi** (☎435 17 85).

Internet Access: On İstiklâl Cad., including **CEN NET Internet Cafe,** İstiklâl Cad. No. 99 (☎231 26 49). $1 per hr. Open daily 9:30am-midnight. There are slower connections, but a more central location, at **Karteksan Internet Cafe,** 4/1 Orhaniye Geçidi (☎431 83 07), 150m down Mevlevihane Cad., running east from Cumhuriyet Meydanı. $1.50 per hr. Ping-pong $.80 per hr. Open daily 8am-11pm.

PTT: On Kazımpaşa Cad. Mail services 8am-noon and 1-5:30pm. Phones 24hr.

Postal code: 55060.

ACCOMMODATIONS

Most of Samsun's budget hotels are conveniently located just west of the Cumhuriyet Meydanı, along the roads leading to the Saat Kulesi (Clock Tower) Meydanı. For more upscale hotels, head to the establishments in Cumhuriyet Meydanı itself.

Otel Guclu, Pazar Mah., Pazar Cami Sok. No. 4/A (☎431 17 17 or 431 36 50). A good choice right in the center, with modern facilities and friendly staff. New rooms with baths and TVs. Breakfast included. Singles $10; doubles $16.

Otel Necmi, Kale Mah., 6 Bedestan Sok. (☎432 71 64; fax 432 20 29), near the PTT, in the clothes bazaar. A good budget option, with 17 small but clean rooms. Each of the 5 floors has a toilet and shower. Singles $6.50, students $5.50; doubles $12, students $10; triples $19, students $17; quads $25.50, students $22.50.

Divan Otel, Necipbey Cad., 20 Meserret Sok. (☎/fax 431 36 71). Comfortable and friendly. 22 clean rooms with bathroom (and towels). Ask for a room without a TV for a cheaper price. Singles $7; doubles with TV $14; triples with TV $17.

Deniz Otel, Kale Mah., 42 Bankalar Cad. (☎431 58 78), around the corner from Divan. 20 basic rooms. Each of the 4 floors has a shower and toilet. The top floors have a lovely sea view, which only partly justifies the price. Singles $7, students $6; doubles $17.50, students $13; triples $22.50, students $16.

Otel Şirin Bahar, Meşarat Sok., opposite Büyük Camii. A cheap, basic option for those on a very tight budget. Singles $3; doubles $5.

FOOD

Körfez Restaurant, Körfez Mah. No. 15, Kurupelit (☎457 52 91 or 457 53 29), 13km west of the Samsun town center. Take a minibus marked "Atakent-Kurupelit-FAKÜLTE" (15min., $.30), which departs when full from the dolmuş hub on Atatürk Bul., near the Büyük Hotel. Widely renowned for some of the best *pide* dishes in Turkey, Körfez sits on the sea, with a splendid view of Samsun's entire coastline. Try the *karışık yumurtalı pide* ($3) with a *şeftali su* (apricot juice; $1). Live music from 9pm.

Cumhuriyet Lokanta, Saathane Meydanı Şeyhhamza Sok. No.3, 3rd fl. (☎431 21 65). This excellent restaurant, owned by Bülent Kaptan (former president of Samsunspor Football Club), serves a tasty *kara lahana dolma* (vegetable dish; $1.50) and a variety of *kebaps* (from $1.25).

İtimat Balık Lokantası, Cumhuriyet Cad. No. 64-66 (☎420 05 24). 300m east of Cumhuriyet Meydanı, along the coastal road. The fish meals are well worth the long walk from the center. Salmon $5, *Efes* $1.50.

Oskar Restaurant, Belediye Meydanı (☎431 20 40), near the watch tower. With your back to the Büyük Camii and facing the watchtower, take the road in front of you and turn right at a vegetable store. This large establishment with a pleasant wooden interior serves *kuzu tandir* (roasted lamb; $3) and *beğendeli kebap* ($2.50).

Sarnıç Cafe, Bankalar Cd., Anakent İşmerkezi Kat 1 (☎435 78 56 or 435 78 69), at the bottom of the main Anakent Shopping Center. A very pleasant, air-conditioned cafe with *köfte* and *doğum günü*. A great atmosphere, despite the shopping center location.

ENTERTAINMENT AND NIGHTLIFE

Samsunspor Football Club plays from late August until May at the **On Dokuz Mayıs Stadium.** Tickets are available at the stadium the day of the match ($1-3).

Konak Sinemasi (Cinema) (☎431 24 71), İskur Hanı, just above the northeast corner of Cumhuriyet Meydanı. Shows the latest Hollywood films, with Turkish subtitles.

Ata Kum Beach, 6km west of the city center. Since Samsun's beaches are better left unvisited, take a dolmuş here for a relaxing dip.

C Bar (☎233 35 97), on Dr. Damil Cad. 300m down İstıklâl Cad., on a small side street by the Turkmaz Ayakkabı shoe store. A kicking combination bar/club. Tuborg beer $2.25. Open daily 9pm-4am.

Collo Disco, Atatürk Bul. No. 629 (☎432 49 99), adjacent to the Büyük Samsun Oteli. Though pricey, this is one of only a handful of quality clubs along the Black Sea. Beer $4. Cover $4, includes one drink. Open F-Sa 9pm-4am.

SIGHTS

Samsun's **Archaeological Museum** is famous for a well-preserved Roman floor mosaic depicting a battle between the Tritons and the Nereids. It also has some other intriguing exhibits. Quite small, it can be toured in under an hour. One of the most gruesome exhibits is from the excavation of pre-Roman **İkiztepe,** including a dramatic display on the ancient practice of skull surgery. A hole was drilled into the skull to remove evil spirits and avoid dementia. Its practice was widespread in the ancient Middle East. Apparently nearly half the operations were successful. You can see two of the skulls have clear holes, and the hole of the third has been partly healed and covered over. Look out for the excellent coin exhibition, including Hellenistic, Roman, Byzantine, Selçuk, and Ottoman monies. Jewelry, kitchen utensils, and *amphorae*—ancient storage pots also used as containers—dating from 7th century BC are on display. Most exhibits have explanations in English. (☎431 68 28. Open Tu-Su 8:30am-noon and 1-5pm. $1, students $.40.)

Samsun's **Atatürk Museum** is next door to the Archaeological Museum, between the coast and Cumhuriyet Meydanı. Its photo exhibits are extensive, but the museum itself is not particularly gripping. Although nothing to match Anıt Kabir, it does provide a glimpse into Atatürk's personality and the reverence in which he is particularly held in Samsun. (Open Tu-Su 8am-noon and 1-5pm. $1, students $.50.)

DAYTRIP FROM SAMSUN: THE KIZILIRMAK DELTA

Dolmuş run from Samsun to the town of 19 Mayis; from there, the Delta is a 5km walk. Local buses run irregularly throughout the delta. Camping is available, but it's very limited and extremely expensive: $30 for a permit.

Although Samsun itself has a limited number of attractions, it is a good base from which to explore the surrounding countryside. The **Kızılırmak Delta,** 35km from Samsun, is a coastal plain of 50,000 hectares, containing marshes, wetlands, rivers, and swamps. The delta is home to an astonishing array of wildlife: of Turkey's 420 bird species, 316 have been recorded in the delta. In recent years there has been an effort to encourage eco-tourism in this area. At the moment, unfortunately, there are few organized tours, and travelers intent on traveling the delta should treat it as a daytrip from Samsun, setting off very early in the morning. The director of tourism in Samsun offers one at a high price; try to bargain it down.

AMASYA ☎358

Towering cliffs, a quiet river, carved rock tombs, and stately Ottoman houses are all part of Amasya's fortuitous meeting of human and natural architecture. In older areas, the town's pedestrian streets and waterfront houses suggest something like a Turkish Venice, despite the rugged surroundings. Today, Amasya has a relaxed atmosphere. It is most striking when the rock tombs are illuminated at night, towering above the mellow groups drinking *çay* or enjoying Amasya's famous apples.

The birthplace of the geographer Strabo (roughly 63 BC), Amasya was the capital of Pontus, a kingdom of Greek-speaking Persians that arose after the death of Alexander the Great. After a series of costly wars with the Romans, the city was razed by Pompey in 64 BC. Rebuilt as a provincial capital, the town flourished under the Romans and Byzantines before falling in 1071 to the Selçuks, who left a legacy of Islamic monuments. Under the Ottomans, who arrived in 1391, Amasya became a theological and cultural center, with 18 *medresesı* by the 18th century.

TRANSPORTATION

Buses: Arriving buses stop at either the city center or the otogar (☎218 80 12), 3km northeast of town. The larger bus companies provide a free *servis* shuttle to the city center. Otherwise, to get to the center, take any of the city buses ($.30, students $.25) or dolmuş ($.35, students $.30) that stop across the street from the otogar. Some companies will drop you along Atatürk Bul. if they are not terminating in Amasya. Follow this road 600m or so and then turn left to reach the river and center of town. Dolmuş run to the otogar from behind the Atatürk statue in the main square. Otherwise, turn left at the otogar's exit and follow the road straight to the city center. Try to flag down a passing bus heading toward Samsun or Tokat. Buses run from the otogar to: **Ankara** (5½hr.; 7 per day 8:30am-12:30am; $9.50, students $8); **Antalya** (12hr.; 3pm; $22, students $19); **Bursa** (11hr.; 3 per day 6:30-8pm; $19, students $16); **Çorum** (1½hr., frequent, $3); **Denizli** (12hr.; 4pm; $19, students $16); **Diyarbakır** (12hr.; 4 per day 7:30-11:30pm; $19, students $17.50); **Erzurum** (9½hr.; 9:30pm; $19, students $16); **İstanbul** (10hr.; 9 per day 9:30am-11:15pm; $19, students $16); **İzmir** (14hr.; 4 per day at 5pm; $22.50, students $21); **Kayseri** (8hr.; 13 per day; $11); **Marmaris** (15hr.; 4pm; $22.50, students $19); **Samsun** (2hr.; 8am, 11:30pm; $3); **Sivas** (4hr., 12 per day 8am-11:30pm, $3); **Tokat** (1¾hr., 12 per day 8am-11:30pm, $3); **Trabzon** (8hr.; 5 per day 5-10pm; $13, students $11).

Trains: The *gar* (☎218 12 39), on the north bank, is about 2km west of the main square. To get to town, take one of the dolmuş ($.35) or buses ($.30) that stop across the street. Alternatively, turn left out of the station, cross the first bridge, and take another left onto Mustafa Kemal Paşa Cad., which becomes Atatürk Cad. and runs through the center of town. To **Samsun** (3hr.; daily 4:55am; Tu, Th, Sa, Su 2pm; $1.25) and **Sivas** (5½hr.; M, F, Su midnight; $2.25). 60% discount for students and travelers over 60.

ORIENTATION AND PRACTICAL INFORMATION

Amasya is divided by the **Yeşilırmak (Green River),** which runs roughly east-west. The **north bank,** home to Ottoman houses and the cliff tombs of the Pontic Kings, is the older part of town. The tourist office and most restaurants and hotels lie on the **south bank,** either on **Mehmet Paşa Cad.,** the road running immediately along the river, or the more substantial **Atatürk Cad.,** running parallel one block farther south. The city center *(şehir merkezi),* which sits between these two roads, is a large plaza with an Atatürk monument.

Tourist Office: (☎218 74 28; fax 218 33 85), opposite the Yimpaş supermarket in a kiosk along the river's south bank; little English spoken. To get here, turn right from the main square when facing the river. Open Apr. 15 to Sept. 15 M-F 10am-noon and 2-6pm; Sa-Su 1-6pm. Closed in low season.

Banks: Many with **ATMs** line the south bank of the river. **Yapı ve Kredi,** just across the street from the PTT, cashes **traveler's checks** and has a Cirrus/MC/Plus/V **ATM.** Open M-F 9am-12:30pm and 1:30-5pm. **TC Ziraat Bankasi** (☎218 41 53), on Siyat Paşa Bul., will also change traveler's checks. Open M-F 8:30am-6pm.

Hamams: Mustafabey Hamamı (☎218 34 61), just off Mehmet Paşa Cad., 50m east of the tourist office. Divides its single 550-year-old dome between the sexes. Bath $1.50 for women, $2 for men; *kese* $1.25. Open for women 11am-5pm, for men 5-11pm. The 13th-century **Yıldız Hamamı** (☎218 15 94) is across from the Zümrüt Otel on Hazeranlar Sok and a short walk from the entrance to the Pontic tombs. Married couples can enter a private bathing area. Bath $1.50 for women, $2 for men; *kese* $1.25; massage $.70. Open daily 6am-midnight.

Hospital: Devlet Hastanesi (☎218 40 00), on Mustafa Kemal Paşa Cad.

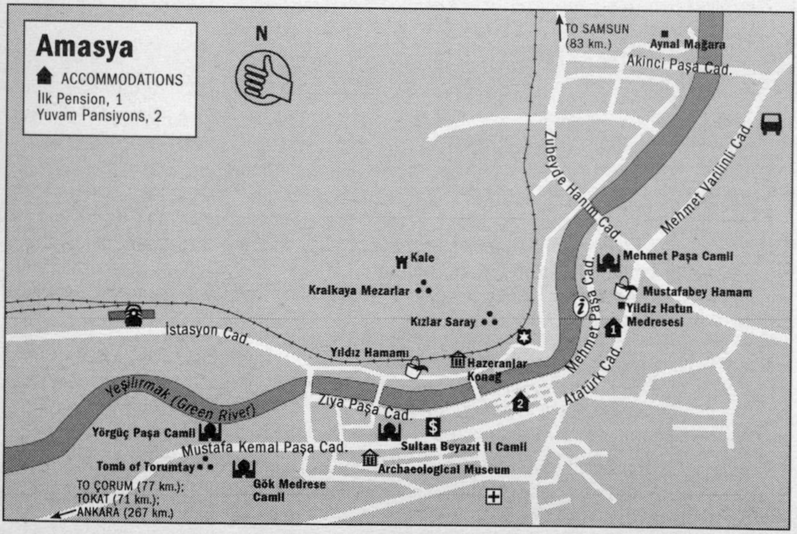

Internet Access: Nokta Internet Cafe, 10 Belediye Dukkanlar (☎218 89 73), next to the Yimpaş grocery on Yavuz Selim Meydanı. $.75 per hr. Open daily 9am-midnight.

PTT: On Mehmet Paşa Cad., 100m west of the main square. Open daily 8:30am-12:30pm and 1:30-5pm. Phone card sales and services 8am-11pm.

Postal Code: 05100.

ACCOMMODATIONS

Amasya's exquisite hotels in restored Ottoman houses sit near more functional, budget accommodations. Expect prices to be slightly steeper here. Though the two Ottoman inns along the river are more expensive than most lodgings in Amasya, their beautiful views and traditional decor make them worth the extra expense. Reservations are recommended during July and August.

İlk Pension, Gümüşlu Ňah., 1 Hitit Sok. (☎218 16 89; fax 218 62 77), down a small side street off Mehmet Paşa Cad., near the Yimpaş supermarket and across the street from the tourist office. Restored by its architect-owner, the 180-year-old pension offers 6 large, decorated rooms. Breakfast $3. Singles $17-34; doubles $25-45. 10% student discount. There's also a 25% discount for architects 45 years and older.

Emin Efendi Pension, Hatoniye Mah., 73 Hazeranlar Sok. (☎212 08 52; fax 212 18 95), on the north bank of the river. Cross over the bridge by the PTT, turn left, and continue 300m. Housed in a 200-year old Ottoman house, the 5 rooms share a bath, and all have a magical view of the river. Singles $22; doubles $33; triples $39.

Yuvam Pansiyons 1 and **2,** 24/1 Atatürk Cad. (☎218 13 42; fax 218 34 09; ariecz@superonline.com), to the left of the main square when facing the river. The **first** is an apartment building with 14 clean but unremarkable rooms, 11 with bath. Breakfast $3. Singles $9.50, with bath $11.50; doubles $16, with bath $19. The **second** pension, farther from the town center but more comfortable, is only open if there are enough guests. Breakfast $3. Singles $13; doubles $26; triples $38. **Camp** in the garden: $4 per tent; $6.50 to use their single tent; $13 for the 2-person tent. Both pensions have kitchens and washing machines ($4 per load), and a 10% student discount.

Yalıboyu Otel, 19/D Ziyapaşa Bul. (☎218 70 29). Each sparkling room in this brand new hotel offers TV and private bath. Excellent rooftop restaurant (*Amasya kebap* $2.50; *Efes* beer $1.50). Breakfast included. Singles $8, with bath $10; doubles $16, $18 with bath; triples $24, $25 with bath.

Zümrüt Otel, 28 Hazeranlar Sok. (☎218 17 69; fax 212 35 54), on the way to the Emin Efendi Pension. Offers 12 cheap rooms with TV and fridges. 4 with river views, 9 with showers. Access to kitchen and stunning rooftop terrace. Very friendly. Breakfast included. $9.50 per person, students $8.

FOOD

Amasya's several *kebap* and *pide* restaurants are filled all day with locals escaping the sun, sipping tea, and taking in the scenery. If you're in more of a do-it-yourself mood, stock up at **Yimpaş,** a supermarket just across the street from the tourist office. (Open daily 8am-10pm.)

Amasya Şehir Derneği Restaurant, 1 Karşıkaya Mah., 1 Tevfik Hafiz Sok., Vilayet Önü (☎218 10 13), in the Öğretmen Evi (teachers' hostel) on the north riverbank, across the bridge from the Atatürk statue. A great terrace just above the river, although the menu is somewhat thin. *Kuzu dolma iç pilav* $3. Open daily 11am-midnight.

Ocakbaşı Restaurant, 5 Ziya Paşa Cad. (☎218 56 92). Face the river from the PTT; turn left on Ziya Paşa Cad. (along the river Mazeranlar Konagi Karşı Geçesi). Serves standard Turkish dishes in an outdoor plaza. *Lahmacun* $.50. Open daily 6am-midnight.

SIGHTS

THE MUMMIES AND THE ARCHAEOLOGICAL MUSEUM. This museum has an impressive collection of artifacts spanning the history of the region. Note the stunning arabesques on the original door of the Selçuk Gök Medrese and the grisly mummified remains of Mongol rulers and their children, on display in the old Selçuk *türbe* (tomb). *(Just past the Sultan Beyazıt Mosque on Atatürk Cad. Open Tu-Su 8:30am-noon and 1:30-5:30pm. $1, students $.50.)*

PONTIC TOMBS. Carved out of the cliffs north of the city are the now-empty **Kralkaya mezarları,** the tombs of the Pontic kings. Though the graffiti-covered tombs are less impressive up close than from below, a climb up offers beautiful panoramic views of the valley and city. At the same site you'll also find the scanty ruins of the palace of the Pontic kings, known as the **Kızlar Sarayı,** or Palace of the Maidens. The site draws its name from the harems that were a part of the palace complex. *(Cross the bridge by the PTT and follow the yellow signs up the hill to the Kralkaya mezarları. Open daily 8:30am-8pm. $1.50, students $.75.)* If you really catch tomb fever, head to the **Aynalı Mağara** (Mirror Cave), a few kilometers northeast of town. As the tomb is not enclosed, you can walk all the way around it to see how it was completely cut away from the rock. *(It's a substantial walk on foot; from the south bank, follow Mehmet Paşa Cad. east past the tourist office, then cross the river at the next bridge, and follow Zübeyde Hanım Cad. to a large roundabout with signs to the tomb. Alternatively, take a $4 round-trip taxi from town.)*

FORTRESS. The ancient 3rd-century BC *kale* looms high above the city. It was renovated first by the Ottomans and again in the 1980s. The extensive ruins and spectacular views of the entire gorge are worth the long and steep hike. Look for the *Cilanbolu* (secret passage), with 150 steps carved into the rock situated at the top. *(From Zubeyde Hanım Cad., on the north bank, follow signs marked "Kale." The walk from the city center takes about 45min.-1 hr.; if you're in a hurry, catch a cab for about $4 one way.)*

OTTOMAN HOUSE MUSEUM (HAZERANLAR KONAĞ). This museum, on the north side of the river opposite Otel Zümrüt, is one of Amasya's best-preserved Ottoman houses, along with the İlk and Emin Efendi Pansiyons. These houses are characterized by wooden or half-timber exteriors and upper floors that extend out over the street. Inside, the complicated floorplans often provide separate stairways and quarters for men and women. Decoration consists of geometrically carved wooden ceilings, and, in the restored houses, *kilims*, carpets, and embroidered cushions. The basement houses a gallery of Turkish modern art. *(Open M-F 8am-noon and 1:30-5:30pm. Museum open Tu-Sa 8am-noon and 1:30-5:30pm. $1.)*

YILDIZ HATUN MEDRESESİ. This **birmarhane,** or insane asylum, 20m on the left as you exit the tourist office, was built in 1308 by the Mongol Sultan Olcaytuas as a hospital, asylum, and medical school. The intricately carved doorway and other features of the building look remarkably Selçuk, revealing the extent to which the Mongols incorporated the architectural styles of the peoples they conquered. Doctors continued to be trained at the Bimarhane up until the 19th century.

MOSQUES. Sultan Beyazıt II Camii, Amasya's largest Islamic monument, was completed in 1486 by Sultan Beyazıt II's eldest son and heir apparent Ahmet. The side areas of the mosque were used as dervish quarters, a feature which disappeared from Ottoman architecture after about 1500. From the mosque, walk through its courtyard and up a flight of stairs to a main road and turn right onto Atatürk Cad. Continue west on Atatürk Cad. past the archaeological museum to the Selçuk **Gök Medrese Camii** (Blue Seminary Mosque). The blue tiles that gave the mosque its name ("gök" means "sky") are now mostly gone, and the spectacular carved door has been moved to the archaeological museum. Still, the intricately carved Selçuk doorway is worth a look. The mosque was built in 1267 by Şerafettin Torumtay, governor of Amasya. He and his family now lie buried on the mosque grounds, in the aptly named **Tomb of Torumtay**. Across the street is the splendid Ottoman ■ **Yörgüç Paşa Camii,** with striking sections of red stone and pristine frescoes. The intimate interior marks a change from the vast vaulted spaces of the larger mosques. Left along the river, with your back to the tourist office, is the early Ottoman **Mehmet Paşa Camii,** a sprawling complex that houses a Qu'ranic school for girls. *(To reach the Beyazıt II Camii, follow the river 1½km west from the PTT.)*

ÜNYE ☎452

Ünye has a rare combination of good beaches, good hotels, campsites, and nearby hiking options. Only 95km east of Samsun, it's easily accessible along the main coastal road from Samsun to Trabzon. Though Ünye's history is thought to extend back to 1270 BC, today it functions mainly as a family-oriented resort town.

TRANSPORTATION. The **otogar,** 1km east of the town center, offers a regular dolmuş connection, but **buses** generally stop at their offices downtown. **Ulusoy** (☎323 61 47), **Metro** (☎323 57 74), and **Eray** (☎324 61 57) run buses to: **Amasya** (4hr.; 5:30, 7, 8pm; $8); **Ankara** (9hr., 5 per day 9am-10:30pm, $12); **Antalya** (16hr.; 3:30, 4, 9:30pm; $24); **Bursa** (13hr., 6 per day 4-9pm, $21); **Çanakkale** (22hr.; 4:30, 6pm; $27); **Eskişehir** (10hr.; 6, 9pm; $16); **İstanbul** (12hr., 9 per day 11am-11pm, $21); **İzmir** (18hr., 8:30pm, $18); **Kayseri** (8hr.; 5, 9pm; $14); **Malatya** (10hr., 7pm, $18); **Mersin** (16hr.; 4, 8pm; $14); **Sinop** (4hr., 3:30pm); **Sivas** (7hr., 7pm, $11); **Trabzon** (5hr., 5:30pm, $6); **Tokat** (6hr., 7pm, $9.50). Student discounts are usually available.

ORIENTATION AND PRACTICAL INFORMATION. The center of town is **Cumhuriyet Meydanı,** a small square along the coast marked by an Atatürk monument. The **tourist office,** 7 Ünye Spor Lokalı Halı Saha Yanı, is about 500m east of the town center, on the coastal road. The director of tourism is helpful and friendly. (☎323 49 52. Open daily M-Sa 8am-6pm; in winter 8am-noon and 1:30-5:30pm.) There's a **Türkiye İş Bankası** with an **ATM** on the coastal road, just east of the main square. (Open M-F 9am-12:30pm and 1:30-5:30pm.) You can reach the **hospital** at ☎323 98 53. **Internet access** is available at **Inter Point Internet Cafe,** Hükümet Cad., Cezmi Sider İshanı. (☎323 22 33. $.80 per hr. Open daily 9am-midnight.) Also try **Millennium Net Cafe,** 21/4 Belediye Cad., Hannadar İşhanı, 3rd fl. (☎ 323 99 53. $1 per hr. Open daily 10am-11pm.) To reach the **PTT,** on Belediye Cad., from the tourist office, cross the street and turn right at the dolmuş stop. (Mail services daily 8am-5:30pm. Telephone services until midnight.) **Postal code:** 52300.

ACCOMMODATIONS. ■ **Otel Güney,** 14 Belediye Cad., in the heart of Cumhuriyet Meydanı, sports a terrace and cafe area with view of the sea at the top to go with 22 clean, comfortable rooms, 14 with bath. (☎323 84 06. Singles with phone $6, with bath, TV, and phone $7; doubles $8, with bath $10; triples $15.) Just outside Cumhuriyet Meydanı, **Otel Burak,** 4 Belediye Cad., offers 14 simple rooms with bath. (☎324 52 16. Singles $6; doubles $10; triples $12. 10% student discount.) The cheapest joint in town is the **Otel Çınar,** 22 Hükümet Cad., down a side street behind the Findikkale bus office in the center of town. The 14 small rooms all come with bath. (☎324 85 48. Singles $4.50, students $4; doubles $8, students $6.)

Even better, take a dolmuş heading west along the coastal road to one of the cheap pensions or beachside campsites that offer Ünye's mellow brand of coastal living. About 1km from the town center, the first place the dolmuş passes is the **Belediye Çamlık Moteli,** which tempts travelers with 13 large, villa-like rooms with bath, a sea view, and a cool, pine tree setting. (☎323 10 85 or 323 13 33. Doubles $12; quads with kitchen $20.) Another 1km farther west are **Gülen Camping** (☎324 73 68), and next door the bigger, better-equipped **Uzunkum Camping,** 62 Atatürk Mah. Uzunkum features showers, toilets, hot water, electricity, a large private beach, and a restaurant. (☎323 20 22. Small tents $5, includes water, electricity, and showers; large tents $6.50; caravan $8. Trout $3; *meze* on request $1.50.)

FOOD. In town, sample the magnificent fish dishes at the **Park Restaurant,** 6 Devlet Sahil Yolu Üzeri, on the waterfront opposite the town square. Try Black Sea fish: *kalkan* ($6) or *levrek* ($6). Reservations are a good idea in summer. (☎323 30 53. Open daily 11am-1am.) Adjacent to the Çamlık Hotel, the **Çamlık Restaurant,** 1km west of town, occupies a lovely tree-lined spot overlooking the sea. (☎323 11 75. Trout $3. Beer $1.25.) **Çakirtepe Restaurant** is about 1km along the coastal road from the center of Ordu toward Uzunkum, and has a good range of fish and meat dishes. (Open daily noon-11pm.)

SIGHTS. Ünye's most important sight is the **Ünye Kalesi,** a Byzantine castle about 5km south of town. From the tourist office, head 300m inland along Niksar Cad. to the dolmuş hub, and ask the drivers about the *kale.* Dolmuş drop you off 2km downhill from the castle (8am-9pm, $.30). Another option is to take a taxi straight to the castle ($6.50). The road leads to the base of the castle, where you'll see a **Pontic tomb** carved into the rock and have an impressive view of the surrounding green hills. A steep and narrow path leads to the top; unfortunately, it is lined with stinging, unfriendly plants and is slippery when wet. Ünye's best **beach** is aptly named *Uzun Kum* ("long sand"), stretching for over a kilometer, about 4km west of the town center (dolmuş $.30).

If cleanliness is next to godliness, you can't go wrong with Ünye's **hamam,** once a 700-year-old **Byzantine church.** The church itself isn't much to look at, but who opens their eyes during an exfoliating massage? (8 Hükümet Cad. Open for men daily 4am-noon; for women noon-5pm. Tourists can bathe in mixed groups; ask at the tourist office. Hamam $2.50; *kese* $1.50.)

Boat tours leave from the dock in the center of town. Tickets are available at **Şahmer Turizm.** (☎634 50 54 or 324 22 09; 30min., in summer every 30min. 8-11pm, $1.50.) The **Asarkaya National Park,** 6km southeast of Ünye, has good picnic facilities and hiking trails in the woods overlooking the sea. Take a dolmuş from the hub opposite the tourist office ($.40, 7am-7pm). On the way from Asarkaya National Park are some **rock tombs.** The director of tourism may offer you a tour; otherwise, walk 4km past the tourist office and ask for *Tozkoparan Kayamezar.*

ORDU ☎452

Built in the shadow of a huge hill called Boztepe, Ordu is a good base from which to visit the glorious *yaylas* (highland plateaus) that rise up farther inland. Its selection of budget hotels is limited, however, and apart from a restored Ottoman house-cum-ethnography museum, there are few sights to speak of: a fire destroyed the old town in 1883. A leading world producer of hazelnuts, Ordu hosts the Golden Hazelnut Festival *(Fındık Şenliği)* in late June and early July, which includes folk music and singing contests.

TRANSPORTATION. **Dolmuş** (line #2) run to and from the **otogar** ($.30), 1km east of the city center. To walk from the otogar to the city center, turn left and follow the highway for 15-20min. Most buses stop in the city center. **Metro** (☎214 12 30) and **Ulusoy** (☎214 16 54) **buses** run to: **Amasya** (6hr.; 5:30pm; $9.50, students $8); **Ankara** (9hr.; 4 per day 9:30am-9pm; $17.50, students $14.50); **Bursa** (15hr.; 5 per day 2:30-7:30pm; $25.50, students $22); **Diyarbakır** (18hr.; 5:30pm; $21, students $19); **Erzincan** (12hr.; 10am; $19, students $17); **Erzurum** (8hr.; 2pm; $16, students $14); **İstanbul** (14hr.; 5 per day 6-8pm; $27, students $22.50); **İzmir** (18hr.; 3 per day 4-8:30pm; $29, students $24); **Konya** (12hr.; 1, 5:30pm; $24, students $21); **Malatya** (12hr.; 5:30pm; $17.50, students $15); **Rize** (6hr.; 11:30am; $7, students $6); **Samsun** (3hr.; every hr. 9am-9pm; $5.50, students $4.50); **Sivas** (11hr.; 5:30pm; $13, students $12); **Trabzon** (4hr.; frequent; $5, students $4); **Tokat** (7hr.; 5:30pm; $13).

ORIENTATION AND PRACTICAL INFORMATION. Ordu lies along the coastal highway **Atatürk Bul.** From Atatürk statue in the city center, on the waterfront, **Hükümet Cad.** runs inland toward the PTT and the museum. **Boztepe,** a majestic hill 8km away, overlooks the entire coast. Forest and sea meet at **Kiraz Limanı,** a harbor 2km west of the city center.

The helpful **tourist office,** 117/A Atatürk Bul., is in the city center and has an English-speaking staff. (☎223 16 08. Open M-Sa 8am-noon and 1-5pm; in winter closed Sa.) Next door, **Çotanak Tur Seyahat Acentası,** 112 Atatürk Bul. (☎225 20 54; fax 214 15 49), sells THY tickets and other travel services. **Banks** with **ATMs** are on Hükümet Cad. Other services include **pharmacies** on Hükümet Cad. and the **hospital** (☎225 01 80; open 24hr.). **Internet access** is at the six-computer **Comuf Internet Cafe,** Süleyman Felek Cad., 58 Kayserilioğlu Sok., along the highway, about 200m west of the city center and opposite the Pikola Cinema. (☎241 63 88; fax 225 29 94. $1 per hr. Open daily 8:30am-midnight.) The **PTT** is 100m up Hükümet Cad. from the coast. (Mail services 8:30am-12:30pm and 1:30-5:30pm.) **Postal code:** 52100.

ACCOMMODATIONS. Ordu's hotels are an uninspiring bunch. The best value, **Otel Kervansaray,** 1 Kazim Karabekir Cad., in the middle of the town square, offers 38 basic rooms, most with bath. With your back to the Atatürk monument, walk left; the hotel's sign is to the right, across the street and behind the municipal building. (☎214 13 30. Singles $5, with bath $6.50; doubles $8, with bath $12; triples $9.50, with bath $14.50.) About 200m farther east along the coast lies the better-quality, 64-room **Turist Hotel,** 134 Atatürk Bul. Sunny rooms overlooking the sea suffer from the noise from the coastal road; a recently renovated section offers quieter choices. All rooms have bath and TV. (☎214 91 15; fax 214 19 50. Breakfast included. Singles $13; doubles $22; triples $30.)

FOOD. Across from the Atatürk Monument, all-purpose cafe-bar-restaurant-art gallery-cinema **Ayışığı** (☎223 28 70), 1 Atatürk Bul., serves delicious local specialties such as *Boztepe kebap* (chicken and *köfte* with peppers, potatoes, garlic, and yogurt; $3) and sauteed mushrooms ($1.40). Run by charismatic Enis Ayar, founder of the Volkswagen Beetle Festival, the restaurant proudly declares "*aile salonumuz yok!*" ("We have no family room!"). On a pier across from the Turist Hotel, **Mıdının Yeri (Midi) Restaurant,** 55 İskele Üstü, offers sea views and a wide selection of Black Sea seafood, including *alabalık* (trout) with salad from $4. (☎214 03 40. Open daily 8am-1am.) **Bulvar Cafe,** Atatürk Bul. No. 98, just west of the main square, offers a wide-ranging English-language menu. (☎223 02 76. Spaghetti $1.50; pizza $2.) Two restaurants dish out the favorites on top of Boztepe. **Boztepe Çamluk Restaurant** (☎229 00 22) is a picnic restaurant—take your food outside and eat in a large garden. The other restaurant, across the road, is a more formal dining option. Both sport unbeatable views of the coast below. Ordu is world famous for its **hazelnuts** and **chocolates,** exported from its Sağra factory to the rest of Europe. At the **Sağra Nuthouse,** 95 Süleyman Felek Cad., you can sample the delicious sweets (hazelnut chocolates $5 per kg).

NATAŞAS The world's oldest profession is legal in Turkey, and trafficking in prostitutes from the former Soviet Union (hence their Turkish name: the *Nataşas*) has increased dramatically since the Union's breakup in 1991. Turkish brothels are supposed to be officially licensed and regulated by health and social service authorities. A 1990 law was passed that set the penalty for abducting or raping a prostitute to be equal to that for crimes against any other woman.

Unofficial estimates suggest there may be as many as 100,000 prostitutes in Turkey. Many women have been abandoned to the brothels after having incurred the scorn of their families. However, a large number have also slipped in unannounced from the former Soviet states. These women may often be the victims of what has grown into a billion-dollar trafficking in women's bodies. Pimps lure desperate former Soviet bloc women under the pretense of offers of employment, marriage, or modeling. These women are frequently abused, threatened, drugged, and raped by pimps who hold their passports and demand that they work to repay the "debt" they have accrued for being taken abroad. As illegal immigrants, they are often left with no political recourse, and their life expectancy averages a grim 35 years.

SIGHTS. The **Ordu Paşaoğlu Konağı,** an impressive 19th-century mansion, is home to the **Ethnography Museum** (☎223 25 96) and stands out clearly from the other, more drab houses along the road. The first floor contains the standard assemblage of carpets, swords, and traditional dress, while the second floor has been decorated in traditional Ottoman fashion. Turn right at the town center, pass the PTT, and turn left into Selimiye Mah., at the intersection of Taşocak Cad. and Erkoçak Sok. (Open daily 9am-noon and 1-5pm. $1.50, students $1.) **Saray Hamam,** Hükümet Cad. No. 49, between the PTT and the Ethnography Museum, offers *kese* for $1.25 and bath for $2. (☎223 30 43. Open daily 5am-11pm, women only Sa 10am-5pm.) The **Belde Hotel,** Kirazlimanı Mevkii, 1km west of the town center, opens its **pool** to non-guests. (☎214 39 87. M-F $5, Sa-Su $6.50.) When night falls, settle into the rhythm of the Black Sea and stroll along the **Kordon** (shoreline), where vendors sell boiled corn, sweets, and nuts. There are **rock tombs** 10km inland from Ordu, in **Bübenköy** and **Dellikkaya.** Dolmuş run from 8am-3pm (1½hr.).

DAYTRIP FROM ORDU: ÇAMBAŞI AND TURNALIK YAYLAS. A visit to Ordu is not complete without a stop in the pristine mountain highlands of Turnalık Yayla and its larger neighbor Çambaşı Yayla (1850m), 2½hr. south of the city. A seemingly endless skyward climb through broken mountain roads leads to this cool, misty paradise with flowering alpine pastures, rocky crags, and icy mountain streams. At 3000m, the weather can be unpredictable: warm, sunny skies can disappear instantly under a blanket of thick fog. When the sun does shine, however, it is hard to be unmoved by the verdant landscapes. *Yaylas* have tiny populations, and services are very limited. Both these *yaylas* are comprised of only one main road with the barest of restaurants and shops.

Çambaşı has a number of cheap, basic hotels along the one main street; try bargaining, since prices are sometimes inflated for Western tourists. **Otal Doğan** has four clean rooms, orthopedic beds, a shared shower, and squat toilet. (☎844 23 03. Singles $3; doubles $6; triples $9.) A much better option for Çambaşı is to follow the signs at the end of the main street for 3km to **Ertaş** (☎214 19 69 or 844 20 10), a restaurant, campground, and trout fishery set in a spectacular valley. Ertaş provides three-person tents for $8 per person (price is the same if you have your own tent) and serves up fresh trout with style ($4 per kg).

If the weather is bad or if you don't fancy camping, try the comfortable **Turnalık Dağ Evi,** in Çelikkıran, just outside Turnalık. This six-room, two-floor lodge is owned by the **Belde Otel** in Ordu and has some of the most stunning views in the area. A *servis* bus makes the 2hr. trip from the hotel in Ordu ($32), but a much cheaper option is to take the minibus heading to Çambaşı and ask to be dropped at Turnalık Dağ Evi. From the drop-off point, a signposted 1km duty road leads to the lodge. The lodge is surrounded by some of the best views in the area, including mini waterfalls. Ask for directions to the nearby fish restaurant. (☎214 39 87. Breakfast $3. Singles $8; doubles $12.)

Twenty-five kilometers beyond Ertaş lies a huge crater, **Karagöl,** at an altitude of 3100m. The trip takes about 2hr. by car, but may require a 4WD vehicle and partial access by foot. There's not much to see at the crater itself, except for a number of small stone settlements. Herders move to Karagöl in the summer; in winter the area is covered in snow. *(Three minibus companies have service from Ordu to Çambaşı (2hr., 6:30am-7pm, $2.50) and Turnalık (1¾hr., 6:30am-7pm, $1.50), of which the best is Çambaşı Seyahat (☎214 47 02), on İsmet Paşa Cad. Çambası and Turnalık are separated by a 20min. drive down steep, winding mountain roads.)*

GİRESUN ☎454

This beautiful coastal city (pop. 75,000) proudly emphasizes its independence and differences from its grittier neighbor, Trabzon. Giresun is large enough to have a good range of hotels, nearby nightlife, and beaches, but small enough to allow visitors to explore on foot and enjoy a relaxed holiday environment. Giresun can also serve as an excellent base for exploring many nearby *yaylas:* mountain communities which offer clean air, a cooler climate, and stunningly lush landscapes.

Giresun has an ancient history. Thought to have been founded in the 8th century BC, its original name was Kerasus, meaning "cherry." It is from here that cherries were introduced to Europe. There is a public circumcision *(sünnet)* festival here in July, but more interesting (depending on your taste) is the **Aksu Festival,** held on May 20. This elaborate pagan fertility ritual, said to have originated in Hittite days, heralds spring and the sowing of new seeds. Participants pass under several iron trivets and circumnavigate the nearby island, throwing 15 stones overboard to symbolically cast away the sorrows of the past.

TRANSPORTATION. Ulusoy, 3 Alparslan Cad. (☎216 44 44), behind the Belediye Binası; **Metro,** Alparslan Cad. No. 5 (☎216 63 63); and **Fındıkkale,** Gazi Cad. No. 5 (☎216 28 28), offer bus service to: **Alanya** (20hr.; 12:30, 1pm; $29, students $27); **Ankara** (11hr.; 5 per day 8am-8:30pm; $15, students $13); **Antalya** (18hr.; 6:30pm; $26, students $24); **Bodrum** (21hr.; 1:30pm; $29, students $24); **Bursa** (15hr.; 4 per day 5pm-2am; $24, students $22.50); **Diyarbakır** (20hr.; 2:30pm; $24, students $22.50); **Erzurum** (10hr.; 2pm; $16, students $14.50); **İstanbul** (15hr.; 9 per day 4-7:30pm; $24, students $21); **İzmir** (18hr.; 5 per day 3pm-3:30am; $25, students $23); **Marmaris** (20hr.; 4:30pm; $24, students $22); **Samsun** (4hr.; every hr. 8am-11:30pm; $5.50, students $5); and **Trabzon** (2hr.; frequent; $2.50, students $2). Dolmuş near the square run east to **Tirebolu** and **Trabzon** and west to **Ordu,** usually departing from east of the Atapark, just under the bridge.

ORIENTATION AND PRACTICAL INFORMATION. Giresun slopes upward from the coast, covering the hills behind it. The **otogar** is on the coast 3km west of the city center on **Atatürk Bul.** It can be reached by free *servis* shuttles provided by the bus companies or by frequent dolmuş, but many bus companies, passing on to further locations, and intercity minibuses will drop you off just outside. The town center is a large pedestrian square, **Atapark,** one block up from the waterfront. Running uphill from here is **Gazi Cad.,** the town's main street, with most of the hotels, restaurants, and banks. The *kale* is sign-posted along Gazi Cad. Cheaper hotels are uphill toward the castle; more expensive ones are near the Atapark.

The **tourist kiosk,** with helpful maps and brochures, is in the Atapark. (☎216 30 07. Open M-Sa 8:30am-6pm.) Also try the **Director of Tourism** *(Türizm Müdürluğu)* at Gazi Cad. No. 72, who speaks English. (☎212 31 90. Open M-F 8am-noon, 1-5pm.) There are several **banks** on Gazi Cad., including a **TC Ziraat Bank** and a **Türkiye İş Bankası** with **ATMs** on the square. (Open daily 8:30am-5:30pm.) **İnanç Internet Cafe,** Suat Akgün Sok., 2nd fl., can be reached by walking 200m up Gazi Cad., on a small side street on the left. (☎214 03 69. Open daily 9:30am-midnight. $.75 per hr.) Others line Gazi Cad., all charging approximately the same price. The **Devlet Hastanesi** (**hospital;** ☎216 10 30) and the **PTT** lie about 1km uphill on Gazi Cad. (Open 8:30am-12:30pm and 1:30-5:30pm. 24hr. telephones.) **Postal code:** 28100.

ACCOMMODATIONS. The **Er-Tur Hotel,** Osmanağa Cad., Çapulacılar Sok. No. 8, is an absolute bargain. With your back to the sea, turn left from the main square and bear right onto a small street. The 25 clean, comfortable rooms all have bath and TV. (☎216 17 57; fax 216 77 62. Singles $9; doubles $17; triples $25.) Many cheaper options lie near the top of the hill, including **Kılıç Otel,** 12 Çınarlar Sok., which has 21 quiet, clean rooms and friendly English-speaking management. Although there's no hot water, a sauna is right next door. Each floor shares a toilet and shower. (☎216 19 52. Singles $3, students $2; doubles $6, students $5; triples $9.50, students $7.) **Otel Bozbağ,** 8 Eski Yağcılar Sok., is a solid budget option. To get there, with your back to the sea, turn left from the main square and then turn right. You should see a large sign at the top of the road. Bozbağ offers 33 adequate rooms, most with phone and TV, half with baths, and terrace, and a quiet location. (☎/fax 216 12 49 or 216 24 68. Breakfast $1.25. Singles $6, with bath $7; doubles $10, with bath $13; triples with bath $19.)

FOOD AND ENTERTAINMENT. The **Tibor Restaurant,** 4/4 İncedayı Sok., is a large tableclothed restaurant offering good views and good food, with a bar to boot. From the Atapark, walk up Gazi Cad., take the first right, and then the first left; Tibor is on the roof of the building on your right. All dishes come with delicious *mısır ekmeği* (cornbread). Go for the *barbun buğlama ve tavası,* or steamed striped mullet with cornflour, for $4. (☎212 28 78. Open 11am-3pm and 6-11pm.) **Deniz Lokanta,** Hacı Miktat Mah., Aplarslan Cad. No. 1, is one block east of the main square, and next to the bus offices. Often very crowded, it offers a good range of dishes in an unpretentious, efficient atmosphere. (☎216 11 58. *Tavuk şiş* $1.50, *ayran* $.30. Open daily 6:30am-11pm.) For dessert, head to the **Balkaya Pastanesi** (☎216 13 15), Gazi Cad., No. 67. Founded in 1932, this landmark serves a tasty *fındıklı* (hazelnut) biscuits ($.30) and the *hindistan cevizli* ($.30).

Aretias Disco-Bar, Teyyaredüzü Mah., Atatürk Bul., No. 1., 5km west of Giresun. Take a dolmuş from the town center to "Aretias." A fun, lively bar with a DJ and dance floor, Aretias is a big draw for many nearby and some not-so-near towns and villages. There is a good range of cocktails and lively, welcoming management. (☎215 56 48. Cover $2, Sa $1. Beer $1.50; *rakı* $2. Open daily 8:30pm-2am.) To reach **Yaman Beach,** to the west of the city, take a dolmuş to *"Yaman plaj."* Enjoy live music nightly in a mellow, low-key atmosphere. (Tuborg beer on tap $1.50.) Up the hill on Gazi Cad., the **Adı-Yok Cafe** ("No-Name Cafe"), 32/B Gazi Cad., functions as a pleasant coffee place during the day and a lively bar at night, featuring student bands. (☎216 69 51. *Çay* $.40; coffee $.90; cappuccino $1.20. No alcohol. Open daily 8am-1am.) A few minutes further up the hill is **Seranad Bar,** 57 Gazi Cad., which has a good young atmosphere with loud Turkish and Western music every night. (☎212 45 44. Beer $1.50; *rakı* $1.80. Open daily noon-3am.) Most of the clubs are about 5km outside town. Take a dolmuş west along the coastal road to **Tayba Turıstık Tesısleri,** Atatürk Bulvarı Teyyere Giresun is bar/disco inside with more seating outside, looking over an excellent view of the coast and sea. Hang out on the small beach. (☎215 12 62. Open daily 8am-2am.)

SIGHTS. The city **museum** is worth a visit. From the Atapark, turn right along the coastal road until you see a lot 1½km down. Turn right up a steep hill and the church should be visible. Housed under the castle in a restored Byzantine Church, it cuts a historical reminder of Giresun's long-departed population in the local architecture. Inside are interesting items of clothing and pottery found in the region as well as some antique photographs. (☎212 13 22. Open M-F 8am-5pm; Sa-Su 8am-noon and 1-3pm. $1.50, students $1.) Another reminder of Giresun's cosmopolitan past is the **Catholic Church,** which at the time of publication was being restored as a children's library. The 19th-century building lacks the charm of the museum, but gives off a peaceful, out-of-place aura. This area is also home to many typical old Giresun houses. (☎216 25 16. Open Tu-Sa 8am-noon and 1-5pm.)

Follow the signs halfway up the Gazi Cad. to the **kale.** The area around the *kale* is one of the liveliest and most attractive parts of Giresun. There are some medieval ruins with good explanations of the history of Giresun in several languages, an impressive **mausoleum** for Osman Ağa, Atatürk's military commander, several food outlets, a large picnic area, *çay* gardens with stunning views, and a "Panorama walkway" with a clear view of the coast and harbor. The steep climb takes about 15 minutes from Gazi Cad.

A couple of kilometers off the coast is a now-deserted **island** with the a ruined castle and monastery. The island still plays a part in local mythology: some believe Jason visited this island during his voyage for the golden fleece. Many visit the island during the AKSU festival (May 20) to make wishes for the future. Boat tours had been suspended as of Summer 2001. Opposite the museum, however, there are many private boats that will take you there for $5-10 (30min. each way).

Dolmuş leave from Giresun's square for **Kümbet Yayla,** a cool highland paradise (2¼hr., 7:30am-4pm, $2). The hotels and restaurants in Kümbet are basic but functional. Staying in a highland village allows for a close-up look at rural life. Travel agencies in Atapark can arrange 4-6 day trekking trips. The best time to visit is the second Sunday in July, when Kümbet hosts its High Plateau Festival.

TİREBOLU ☎454

Tirebolu is one of many small seaside towns along the main coastal highway. The remains of its 14th-century Genoese **Castle of St. John** are now used as an informal *çay* garden. Tirebolu's real attraction, however, lies simply in its relaxed pace: visitors can sit for hours gazing along the coastlines and looking out at the ocean. Tirebolu has enough touristic infrastructure to make it navigable, but is small and undeveloped enough to keep the feel special and intimate.

TRANSPORTATION AND PRACTICAL INFORMATION. Tirebolu has only two main streets: the **coastal highway** and **Gazipaşa Cad.,** the commercial street. Gazipaşa Cad. winds from the castle up the hill and about 1½km around and down to the western bridge and dolmuş lot. The two bridges, one opposite the castle, and the other at the bus drop-off, are excellent navigation marks. Facing the town, with your back to the sea, you'll see set of steep steps 100m from the west bridge. Climb them for the quickest and most scenic route to Gazipaşa Cad.

Buses stop next to the western bridge at the bus and dolmuş lot opposite the two bus offices. **Ulusoy** (☎441 40 62 or 441 29 57) and **Metro** (☎411 49 52) sell tickets to: **Ankara** (11hr.; 4 per day 9am-11pm; $15, students $13.50); **Antalya** (20hr.; noon; $25, students $23); **Erzurum** (8hr.; 3:30pm; $9, students $8.50); **Giresun** (45min., frequent, $1.50) **İstanbul** (16hr.; 10 per day 11:30am-1am; $20, students $18); **Samsun** (5hr.; every hr.; $8, students $6); and **Trabzon** (1½hr.; frequent; $3, students $2). The slightly cheaper **dolmuş** to Giresun and Trabzon departs from the same lot or from various points on Gazipaşa Cad. **Minibuses** to Giresun also stop by the bridge.

Türkiye İş Bankası, halfway up Gazipaşa Cad., can exchange traveler's checks and cash. (☎411 41 04. Open M-F 8:30am-12:30 and 1:30-6pm.) There's also a **TC Ziraat Bank** with an **ATM** on Gazipaşa Cad., near the PTT. (☎411 20 35. Open M-F 8:30am-6pm.) The **police station** (☎411 30 00) is in the dirt lot across from the castle. The **hospital,** Tirebolu Devlet Hastanesi, is near the castle end of Gazipaşa Cad., just after it starts sloping downhill. (☎411 42 78. Open daily 8am-4pm; 24hr. for emergencies.) The hospital houses Tirebolu's best **pharmacy.** (☎411 48 66. Open daily 8am-9pm.) For fast internet access, try **ESO NET Internet Cafe** on Amiral Şükrü Okan Cad. No. 98, on the main coastal highway. ($1.25 per hr. Open daily 9am-midnight.) The **PTT** is on Gazipaşa Cad. Take the stairs up the western bridge and follow the road onto Gazipaşa Cad.

ACCOMMODATIONS, FOOD, AND ENTERTAINMENT. Since Tirebolu has only one functioning hotel, you'd be better off staying in Trabzon or Giresun. **Otel Huzur,** Gazipaşa Cad. No.15 Çintaşı Mah. next to the large mosque, is a 10min. walk uphill from the town center. The hotel is basic and rooms are small, but are clean and comfortable. Most have stunning views. The six rooms share a shower and a Turkish toilet. Request hot water for your shower. (☎411 40 93. Singles $4.50, students $4; doubles $9.50, students $8; triples $14.50, students $12.) Some campers set up tents on the beach east of town.

The standard *kebap* and *pide* joints on Gazipaşa Cad. often have limited menus. There are some mobile fish restaurants just underneath the castle which offer a more scenic setting and better atmosphere. You can also stock your room with fresh fruit, breads, cheese, and other inexpensive goodies from Tirebolu's many markets. Cherries and hazelnuts, both regional specialties, ripen in the summer. Locals love picnics, which go perfectly with the relaxed small town atmosphere. The **beach** just east of the castle is a good place to while away a few hours. It's unremarkable but uncrowded and less dirty than those around the main towns.

Tirebolu's best nighttime attraction the view of the sea, coastline and town from the *çay* house on top of the castle. The Turkish pop music and limited selection of drinks on offer make for a surreal moment. There are also always large groups walking up and down the coastline, especially during university season.

TRABZON ☎462

Trapezus, Trebizond, Trabzon: this city has a rich history and the names to prove it. Contemporary Trabzon is one of Turkey's most cosmopolitan cities. Since the collapse of the Soviet Union and the reopening of Turkey's northeastern borders, Trabzon has resumed its role as an important trade and transport hub for Russia, Georgia, Armenia, Azerbaijan, and Iran. Russian influence is inescapable: Cyrillic lettering competes for prominence with Turkish, and Russian restaurants are almost as easy to find as local ones. While thousands of immigrants helped create an economic boom, the entrepreneurs were also joined by a considerable number of prostitutes, most from the former USSR, who form an inescapable part of the mosaic between the city's Central Square and the Russian bazaar. Trabzon pulses with the dynamic energy of a large border town, and yet is small enough for visitors to appreciate its warmth and explore much of its rich landscape on foot.

Trabzon's history as a commercial port and hilly refuge dates back to the ancient Greek colonists of Miletus, who dubbed their new community Trapezus. During the Greek and Roman periods, Trapezus grew to a commercial center of international scope. Under Alexius Comneni, who sought refuge here from the Crusaders during the sack of Constantinople, the city reached its heyday as the capital of the Trebizond Empire. His dynasty became the longest-lived, and one of the wealthiest, in Greek history—its rulers lived off the profits of trade and local silver mines. The kingdom held out against the Ottomans until 1461 (even longer than Constantinople), when it was seized by Mehmet the Conqueror. Under Ottoman rule, the churches were converted to mosques, and Islam became the dominant religion. Trabzon was invaded by Russian forces in 1916, but reclaimed by the Turks in February 1918. The city has been growing ever since, and with nearly 1.5 million busy residents, it shows no signs of looking back.

TRANSPORTATION

Flights: The airport is a 10min. drive east of the Atatürk Alanı. Dolmuş leave constantly from next to the Hotel Horon, just off the Atatürk Alanı. You can also catch the airport-bound dolmuş along the coastal highway—be sure to ask for "Hava Alanı," because the airport is not the last stop and drivers often speed past. **THY's main office** (☎321 16 80; fax 326 64 34) is at the southwest corner of Atatürk Alanı. To **Ankara** (1½hr.; 10:05am, 7:45pm; $80, students $65); **Antalya** (9:40, 10:05am, 7:20, 7:45pm; $110, students $95); and **İstanbul** (2hr.; 5:40, 9:40am, 7:20pm; $90, students $75). **Azerbaijan Airlines (Hava Yollari),** 35 Maraş Cad., 3rd fl. (☎326 24 97; fax 326 60 29), flies weekly to **Baku** (1¾hr., Su 1:45; $157, students $142).

Buses: The intercity bus terminal (information ☎325 23 43) is 3km east of the main square and easily accessible by dolmuş. **Ulusoy** (☎325 22 01 or 325 21 60) and **Metro** (☎325 72 86) are reliable firms serving: **Ankara** (12hr., 7 per day 7:30am-midnight, $9); **Bursa** (17hr., 4 per day noon-2pm, $33); **Erzurum** (6hr., 6 per day 7am-6pm, $12); **Giresun** (2hr., every hr. 6am-11pm, $4.50); **İstanbul** (18hr., 10 per day 11am-11pm, $25); **İzmir** (23hr., 3 per day 10am-4pm, $40); **Kayseri** (12hr., 2 per day 11:30am-3pm, $21); **Rize** (1¼hr., every 15min. 6am-9pm, $3); **Samsun** (6hr., every hr. 6am-midnight, $8); and **Tirebolu** (2hr., every hr. 6am-11pm, $2). Depending on the company, students may receive a 25% discount.

International buses: Currently, 3 companies provide service to **Georgia. Göktaş** (☎325 04 11 or 325 51 40), **AST/Buse** (☎325 69 82), and **Nuhoğlu** (☎325 48 12) run buses to: **Ardahan** (8hr., 6pm, $15); **Batumi** (5hr., 6pm, $10); **Kutais** (6hr., 6pm, $15); **Posov** (10hr., 6pm, $20); and **Tbilisi** (12hr.; 6pm; $30, students $25). Both **AST/Buse** and **Nuhoğlu** provide service to **Baku, Azerbaijan** (2 days; Tu-Su 6pm; $60, students $50). Ask around in the Russian bazaar: several agents have offices around Camii Yanı, opposite the covered market. Try to bargain. Depending on political conditions, **AST/Buse** also provides service to **Yerevan, Armenia** (24hr.; W, Su 6pm; $40, students $35). Travelers should obtain visas in advance; see **Consulates,** p. 416.

Dolmuş: Trabzon's dolmuş are, in fact, ordinary-looking 4-5 person cars, but, like dolmuş elsewhere, the final destination is listed above the windshield and on a placard on top of the car. Check the price before you board; cars have been known to overcharge foreign tourists. Most dolmuş lines originate in the main Atatürk Alanı, but you can hop on anywhere ($.40, students $.30).

Ferries: The **Turkish Maritime Lines** office (☎321 70 96 or 321 20 18) is just inside the gate at the base of İskele Cad. (which curves down behind Hotel Anıl). Open M-F 8am-5pm. From early June-late Aug., a ferry plugs along between Trabzon, Samsun, and İstanbul. For schedule and rates, see **The Black Sea Ferry**, p. 388. Departs W 7pm. Arrives: **Samsun,** Th 6am; **Sinop,** Th 12:30pm; **Zonguldak,** F 2am; **İstanbul,** F noon.

International Ferries: To **Russia:** All year long, the "COMETA" sea-bus ferry follows the Trabzon-Sochi route to Russia (12hr., 5pm, $50-$100). **Sarı Tur** (☎326 44 84) sells tickets for the two ferries, "Appolonia" and "Karden," which link Trabzon and **Poti, Georgia** (Tu and F; 10hr.; evening departure; $30 one-way, $50 round-trip). Many agents are along İskele Cad., down toward the sea.

ORIENTATION

The heart of Trabzon is the **Meydan** (square). Most of the city's best hotels, restaurants, dolmuş, and services are concentrated within a 500m radius. For some good hotels, take İskele Cad. northeast of the square and then left onto **Güzelhisal Cad. Maraş Cad.** runs west out of the Meydan, leading past banks, exchange outlets, the PTT, and a few historical sites before ending just below the ancient **Aya Sofia.** Running parallel to Maraş Cad. are the pedestrian-only **Kunduracılar Cad.** and charming **Uzun Sok.**, which buzzes with the activity of internet cafes and small food outlets. **Gazipaşa Cad.** is the short main road between Atatürk Alanı's western edge and the coastal highway, **Sahil Yolu,** which leads to the intercity **otogar,** 3km east, and to the airport. To the west, it passes a stretch of *çay* gardens and amusement parks.

PRACTICAL INFORMATION

TOURIST, FINANCIAL, AND LOCAL SERVICES

Tourist Office: Ali Naki Effendi Sok., No. 1. Opposite the southeast corner of Atatürk Alanı, near the Hotel Nur. (☎321 46 59). A well-equipped government tourist office, with some English spoken. Open daily 8am-5:30pm; in winter closed on weekends.

Travel Agencies: Afacan Tour, 40/C İskele Cad. (☎321 58 06; fax 321 70 01), 100m from Usta Hotel. Open in season daily 7:30am-8:30pm. Offers tours of: **Sumela** (daily 10am-3pm, $4.50); **Uzungöl** (Sa-Su 9am-6:30pm, $12); **Ayder** (2hr. travel, Su 9am-7:30pm, $7); and **Karaca Cave and Zigana** (Sa 9am-6:30pm, $8, $12 with lunch). **Usta Tour,** 4 İskele Cad. (☎326 18 70; fax 326 18 71), across from the northeast corner of Atatürk Alanı and adjacent to the Usta Hotel complex. Tours of **Sumela** (Tu and Th 11am-6:30pm; $6.50, students $5.50); **Uzungöl** (W and Sa 9am-6:30pm; $8, students $7); and **Ayder Yayla** (Su 9am-7pm; $11). Open daily 8:30am-5:30pm.

Consulates: Georgian Consulate, 20 Gazipaşa Cad., 2nd fl. (☎326 22 26; fax 326 22 96), quite far down Gazipaşa Cad., approaching the sea. Visas are usually processed the day of demand. Transit visa $15; 2-week visa $40; one-month visa $50. Open M-Sa 9am-12:30pm and 2-6pm. **Iranian Consulate,** Kızıl Toprak Sok. No. 3 (☎326 76 50). Just off Boztepe Cad. Open M, Th, Sa 8am-1pm and 3-5pm; Su 8am-1pm. Allow 2 days. Westerners may be told to seek visas from the Iranian Embassy in Ankara. **Russian Consulate,** Orta Hisar Mahallesi, Refik Cesur Sok. No. 6. (☎326 26 00; fax 326 26 01). US and other Western citizens should generally obtain visas at the Russian Embassy in Ankara. Open M-F 9am-1pm and 3-5pm.

Banks: Trabzon's larger banks are along Maraş Cad., just west of Atatürk Alanı. For traveler's checks try **Akbank** or **TC Ziraat Bank.** (☎326 71 13. Open M-F 8:30am-5pm.) Many **exchange offices** along Maraş Cad. have better rates.

English Language Bookstore: D+R, 17/C Uzun Sok. (☎321 98 55), on the main street southwest of Atatürk Alanı. This branch of the widespread chain has a considerable range of foreign papers and magazines, though the English language books are mainly confined to dictionaries, phrasebooks, and a few classics. Open daily 10am-9pm.

Laundry: Pak Çiti Laundry, Cumhuriyet Mah., Zeytinlik Cad. No. 18/B (☎326 13 51). From Atatürk Alanı, walk down Uzun Sok. until you reach Zeytinlik Cad., then turn left. $4 per load. Student discount available. Open M-Sa 8am-8pm.

EMERGENCY AND COMMUNICATIONS

Police: Trabzon is split into 6 police districts, each with its own telephone number. The best option is to call ☎155. A tourist police office (☎326 30 77) is next to the Kibris Restaurant on the east side of Atatürk Alanı. Open daily 8am-5pm.

Hospitals: Trabzon's best hospital is the **K.T.U. Farabı Hastanesi** (Karadeniz Teknik Üniversitesi Tıp Fakultesi; ☎325 30 11 or 377 50 00). Take any dolmuş marked K.T.U. Another option is the private **Özel Karadeniz Hastanesi** (☎229 70 70). **Nümune Hospital** (☎230 22 97) is 2km west of downtown at the intersection of Maraş Cad. and Faik Dranaz Cad. Take a dolmuş marked "*Hastane*" or "*Nümune*" to the *Nümune Durağı*. There are numerous **pharmacies** on Gazipaşa Cad.

Internet Access: In Atatürk Alanı, try **World Internet Cafe** (☎323 11 34), located on the 2nd fl. of the building adjacent to McDonald's. Open daily 9:30am-1am. Also surf at **Limit Internet Cafe** (☎323 28 94), inside the Corner Hamburger and Pizza joint on the east edge of Atatürk Alanı. $2 per hr. Open daily 7am-11pm. **IPEK Internet Cafe,**

Maraş Cad., İpekyolu İs Merkezi No. 60 (☎323 31 50), on the 2nd fl. of an outside flight of stairs, is pleasant and clean. $1.25 per hr. Open daily 8am-11:30pm.

PTT: 1km west down Maraş Cad. Open daily 8:30am-5:30pm. Telephones open 24 hr.

Postal Code: 61020 (downtown only).

ACCOMMODATIONS

While Trabzon seems to have more hotels per square kilometer than any other city in the world, only a few are off the prostitution circuit. Many, in fact, serve as dormitories for prostitutes and do not admit men. The hotels below have managements dedicated to keeping them safe and free of *Natașas* (see p. 409).

Otel Anıl, Güzelhisar Cad. No. 10 (☎326 72 82 or 326 72 83). Adjacent to Otel Yuvan, 50m off İskele Cad. A good, clean, comfortable, and central hotel. 36 big rooms have carpeting, tiled baths, hot water, and TV. Breakfast included. It's a good idea to reserve during the busy summer months. Singles $10; doubles $18; triples $25.

Hotel Nur, Meydan Camii Sok. No. 10 (☎323 04 45 or 323 04 46; fax 323 04 47). Off Atatürk Alanı, opposite the İskender Paşa Camii, next to the tourist office. Very friendly, helpful management. 15 large, clean rooms, all with shower, toilet, and TV. Fresh watermelon always available at breakfast. Singles $13; doubles $22.50; triples $35.

Hotel Yuvan, Güzelhisar Cad. No. 10 (☎/fax 326 68 23 or 326 68 24). Adjacent to the Otel Anıl, 50m off İskele Cad. This simple, good-value hotel has shower, toilet, and TV in every room. Ask for a room with a view. Singles $6 doubles $10; triples $15.

Hotel Benli (☎321 10 22). Across from İskender Paşa Camii, by the tourist office and Hotel Nur. Provides basic but comfortable rooms in a safe, older hotel. Each floor has a squat toilet and shower. Singles $3, students $2.50; doubles $6, students $5.

FOOD

Trabzon's local cuisine is a mélange of standard Turkish fare, fresh Black Sea fish, and corn, potatoes, and peas from the fertile highlands south of the city. The Meydan supports a dazzling array of restaurants, including dozens of Russian joints, from tasteful dining rooms to late-night upper-story beer halls. Maraş Cad. has a number of more up-market places. A **fruit and vegetable market** lies 1½km west of the square along Maraş Cad. (Open daily 6:30am-9pm.) Cheese, bread, and other basics are cheapest at the **Tan-Şa Supermarket** on the southwest corner of Atatürk Alanı. Lots of fruit and vegetables are available at the **Russian Bazaar,** too.

Şişman Restaurant (☎322 34 45), on the top floor of a building on Maraş Cad., just off Atatürk Alanı. Its outdoor tables provide a good vantage point to observe the ebb and flow of street life below. *Rakı* $1.25, *Efes* $.90. Open daily 9am-1am.

Kebabistan, Maraş Cad. No. 30 (☎321 86 51), opposite the Zorlu Grand Hotel. Among the cleanest and best in Trabzon, with a very good selection of sweets and desserts. *Vali kebap* ($4); *ayran* ($.40). Open daily 11am-11pm.

Güloğlu Restaurant, Atatürk Alanı No. 4/E (☎321 53 32). A recently renovated *kebap* and *lahmacun* salon. Enjoy the A/C while you indulge in the *sarma beyti kebap* ($2) and finish with a 6-piece portion of delicious baklava ($1). Open daily 6am-11pm.

Tad Pizza and Burger (☎321 12 38), on the northeast corner of the main square, opposite the Belediye building. Good for a break from *kebap* and *ayran*, though the hamburgers ($1) might be better called *köfte* burgers. Tad also has a $1 salad bar with specialty called *aşure*, a fruity pudding ($1). Open daily 7am-11pm.

Ev Mamülleri, Gazipaşa Cad. No. 11/A (☎326 24 20), halfway down Gazipaşa Cad., walking toward the sea. Without a doubt the best pastry house in Trabzon. Make sure to taste the delicious *laz börek* ($1.25). Open 7am-midnight.

HALLUCINOGENIC HONEY In the 5th century BC, Cyrus of Persia recruited a ragtag troop of jack-booted Greek thugs to pillage various villages in Asia Minor. Among the 10,000 Greeks was Xenophon, who recorded their misadventures in the *Anabasis*. On the march home, the booty-laden horde happened upon an enormous swarm of bees whose hives brimmed with honey. This particular pillage, however, had payback: some of the soldiers who sampled the nectar ended up unconscious or ill. Those who consumed the ambrosia in moderation reported fantastical visions (who knows what the bees were seeing). The morning after, the entire legion woke up with a wicked hangover and some rich but embarrassing stories. After enduring a few days of rehab and detox from the deleterious effects of too many mind-altering, psychotropic substances, the Hellenes were marching west to Trabzon. It's unknown whether the soldiers suffered flashbacks to their honey-induced trips.

SIGHTS

AYA SOFIA. Now a disused church with excellent, well-preserved frescoes and beautiful interior, Aya Sofia has a history as complex as the city itself. The site originally held a temple of Apollo (117-38) and then a basilica. Comnenian Emperor Manual I (1238-1263) commissioned the construction of the edifice you see today. Orthodox Christians claimed the basilica for the next 200 years, decorating its interior and exterior with frescoes and reliefs. Upon the 1461 Ottoman seizure of Trebizond, the church became a mosque. The Turks briefly used the building as a hospital and munitions depot during part of World War I. A 1960s restoration project uncovered some of Turkey's best frescoes. Though some of the paintings are crumbling, most are visible. Placards subtly positioned around the church explain the frescoes, while preserving the atmosphere of the original building. The main building is surrounded by a garden with views of the Black Sea and is a welcome break from the bustle of Trabzon below. *(Either take a dolmuş from Atatürk Alanı, or, from the old city, take a dolmuş along the coastal highway; ask the driver for Aya Sofia and walk 2 blocks uphill. Museum open Tu-Su 9am-6:30pm. $1, students $.50.)*

TRABZON MUSEUM (TRABZON MÜZESİ). An Italian-style building, the museum was built by a wealthy Greek banker. It was subsequently used as a local headquarters for Atatürk during the War for Independence. Since then, it has had various identities: a courthouse, a trade school for girls, and since April 2001, a museum. The ground floor is now a beautifully restored Baroque museum, offering a glimpse at upper-class Trabzon society of 100 years ago. The living room and dining room constitute one of the best house restorations in the region. In the basement is a display of items found at a dig at **Tabakhane,** near Trabzon. Perhaps the most impressive item is a statue of Hermes. Other items include a collection of ancient coins and icons. *(☎322 38 22; fax 326 18 88. Uzua Sok. Zeytinlik Cad. No. 10.)*

KIZLAR (GIRLS') MONASTERY. This monastery was used by the Greeks until the 1923 **population exchange** (see p. 16). Most interesting is the main chapel, a cave on the south side where scholars claim ceremonies in honor of Mithra (an ancient Persian sun god) were held. Weathered frescoes still decorate the chapel walls. The lookout point 100m below the entrance to the monastery makes a great picnic spot. At daily prayer times, you can hear echoing calls to prayer from dozens of mosques. *(At the time of publication, the monastery was closed indefinitely. To reach it, either walk 2km up Iran Cad., or take a dolmuş to Bötepe. Ask for "Kizlar Monasteri.")*

ATATÜRK KÖŞKÜ (ATATÜRK'S VILLA). Atatürk Köşkü was built at the turn of the century by a wealthy Trabzon Greek. Though the elegant white villa only actually housed "Father Turk" twice, the house is now an Atatürk museum with many photos and memorabilia. Its views and garden are of more interest than the museum itself. *(Take a dolmuş for Çamlık from the meydan or a bus marked "Köşk" for 5km into the hills southwest of the city. Most dolmuş will drop you off at the bottom of a steep hill. They may offer to take you to the top for extra. Open daily 8am-7pm; in winter 8am-5pm. $1.25, students $.75.)*

OTHER RELIGIOUS SITES. St. Anne's Church stands as Trabzon's oldest existing Christian structure, dating from the 7th century, when the Byzantine Emperor Basil I ruled Trebizond. These days it's in a sorry state, boarded up with a coffee house next door. To get there, start from the square and take Maraş Cad. west past the PTT and down an alley on the left (Mısırlıoğlu Aralığı). The church is closed for restoration. Further down Maraş Cad., take a left on Fatih Camii Sok. and walk uphill about 300m. There lies one of the city's treasures, **Fatih Camii,** also known as **Ortahisar Camii.** This mosque was once the cathedral of the *Panagia Chrysokephelos*, the Golden-Headed Virgin. Once a favorite of the Comneni rulers, it was converted to a mosque by Mehmet in 1461, when the floors were carpeted and the exquisite but idolatrous mosaics were covered in plaster. A small portion of the original mosaic remains intact on the east side of the mosque, since it is non-figurative and therefore not offensive to Muslim worshippers.

To reach **Gülbaharhatun Camii,** the Mosque of the Spring Rose, go south from Maraş Cad. to Uzun Cad. Walk west until you reach the south side of **Atapark,** a verdant spot with relaxing *çay* gardens. Gülbaharhatun mosque was built in 1514 by the Ottoman Sultan Selim I in honor of his mother, Ayşe Gülbahar, who is buried in an impressive **tomb** to the left of the ornate mosque. Just up the road on Amasya Sok. is the birthplace of Süleyman the Magnificent.

ENTERTAINMENT

Football. Trabzon is a football town, and adored **Trabzonspor,** the blue-and-burgundy colored local team, plays regularly from late August to late May. The stadium is about 5km east of downtown, on the seaside Spor Cad. Prices vary with the matches, but average about $4 for sheltered seats and $1 for open-air ones.

Saray Sineması, Kasım Oğlu Çıkması No. 15 (☎321 00 06), about 500m west of Atatürk Alanı. Take the 4th left off Uzun Sok. and look up to the left. It shows Hollywood films with Turkish subtitles, and, unlike most places, doesn't show pornography. Most shows start around 8:30pm. $3.50, students $2.50.

Magicworld: Cosmic Bowling and Billiards, Maraş Cad., İpek Yolu İş Merkezi (☎323 33 11), at the basement level, in the mall opposite the Zorlu Grand Hotel. Escape the hectic Turkish rhythm with 5 lanes, 6 pool tables, and a sparkling new cafe and restaurant. Bowling $4.50; billiards $4. Open 10am-midnight.

Russian (Rus) Bazaar, Çömlekçi Mah., begins near the Otel Anıl, at the top of the hill, and continues down to the sea. Shoppers can find anything. Open daily 8am-7pm.

Sekiz Direkli Hamam, Pazarkapı Mah., Hamam Sok. (☎322 10 12). A worthwhile 2km west of the main square. Walk along Maraş Cad. and bear right on İslahane Sok., well before the walls of the old city. Walk down İslahane for 150m, then bear left on Kalkan Oluğ Cad. for 50m. The hamam will be on your right. Rejuvenate yourself with a scrub and massage. Constructed by the Selçuks around 1073 BC and used until 1916, it was renovated 8 years ago with marble and wood paneling. Bath $4.50, *kese* $5.50. Open daily 4:30am-11pm; women only Th 8am-5pm.

Meydan Hamam, Maraş Cad. No. 3 (☎321 38 23), just off Atatürk Alanı. Less beautiful than Sekiz Direkli, but better located. *Kese* $1.25, massage $1.50, bath $3.50. Open daily for men 5am-10:30pm, women 9am-5pm.

NIGHTLIFE

Kibris Restaurant. On the top floor of a building on the east side of the Meydan. The decor is slightly faded, but the outside terrace is a perfect spot to spend an evening watching over the main square. Two-floor restaurant and bar. Open daily 10am-1am.

English Pub, (☎326 88 26) Zorlu Grand Hotel, Maraş Cad. No. 9, 2nd fl. An imitation English pub in Trabzon's ultra-posh, 5-star hotel. The chairs are plush and the pub is tastefully built. Apart from the very expensive *apertifs* and drinks, this is a pleasant and comfortable place to while away the evening. Beer $5. *Rakı* $2. Open daily 5pm-2am.

Efulim Club and Restaurant, Kunduracılar Cad., Ofluoğlu İş Merkezi, 2nd floor (☎326 92 88). Enjoy live music in elegant surroundings. *Efes* $2. Restaurant open daily noon-6pm. Club open 8pm-1am. Bar open until 2am.

High Life Disco, Gazipaşa Cad. Head toward the sea; the disco is on the right 20m before the bridge. A favorite among area students and free of *Nataşas.*

Façuna Night Club (a.k.a. Façino), Grand Hotel Zorlu, Maraş Cad. No. 9, top floor. Drinks may be pricey (*Efes* $4), but the big dance floor of this fashionable hotel club ranks high among Trabzon's slim pickings. Open Sept.-June F-Sa 9pm-2:30am.

DAYTRIP FROM TRABZON: SUMELA MONASTERY

There are three ways to make the trip from Trabzon to the monastery and national park: wallet-bruising taxis (minimum $33 round-trip), dolmuş ($6-10), and organized tours which run from June to September ($5, see Trabzon: ***Travel Agencies,*** *p. 416). Sumela dolmuş leave every day at 10am from the Ulusoy office on the east side of Atatürk Alanı; alternatively, you can negotiate fares with the driver of a Mağka dolmuş loading from 8-11am near Trabzon's* ***Russian Market.****) Tours tend to rush, and the chambers of Sumela are worth exploring on your own, so be sure to give yourself 30min. for the steep climb to and from the monastery. Park $2, students $1.*

Nowhere else in northwestern Anatolia is the region's Byzantine legacy so breathtakingly combined with the jagged, forested landscape than at Sumela Monastery. Approximately 45km southwest of Trabzon, high in the mountains, Sumela was founded in 385 AD by two ambitious Athenian monks who, according to legend, were visited by the Holy Virgin in a dream. Sumela's structures and five-story facade are built into a cliffside cave perched over a lushly-vegetated gorge; the cave provides natural protection from the elements and contributes to its astonishing beauty. The monastery reached the height of its glory in the late Middle Ages, when it had 72 rooms, an immense library, five fully frescoed chapels, and a refectory, much of which are still recognizable. The inner chapel is a spectacular treat even for those wearied by the tourist-track's parade of Byzantine imagery. The three layers of frescoes portray scenes from the Old and New Testaments, as well as enthroned Byzantine emperors. Though tattooed with Turkish, Greek, and English graffiti, the frescoes remain unique and impressive.

A fire 60 years ago destroyed all of the monastery's wooden structures, many of which are currently being renovated. The labyrinthine, honeycombed chambers of the monks' cells, however, remain intact, and photos in the English-language guide ($5) sold at the park gift shop show Sumela in its former glory. At the moment, the restoration team outnumbers visitors. Take advantage of the solitude, stick your head out of a monk's bedroom window, and savor glimpses of the panorama that Sumela's lucky devotees enjoyed for centuries until the 1923 Greco-Turkish population exchange (see **The Treaty of Lausanne,** p. 16).

RİZE ☎462

The lush hills of Rize rise dramatically from its black pebble seacoast in steaming terraces, carpeted with tea plantations and tropical gardens. In a country where the daily rhythm is measured in the clinking of *çay* glasses, Rize is the leading city of tea, a role which commands capital, technology, and respect. With a population over 60,000, Rize is the easternmost major business center on the Black Sea Coast; as an international port town, its streets are packed with an eclectic mix of Azerbaijanis, Russians, and Georgians. Rize has had a long history at the hands of the Black Sea Coast's many rulers; most architectural traces of that history, however, have been lost in the city's concrete modernization. Still, in Rize's hills, travelers can find solace in *çay* gardens perfumed with night blossoms and aromatic tea.

TRANSPORTATION AND PRACTICAL INFORMATION. Dolmuş and minibuses stop on the coastal highway; head one block inland and turn right to find **Belediye Parkı,** the town's center. Two streets bound the park and run parallel to the highway: to the south is **Atatürk Cad.,** while closer to the sea runs **Cumhuriyet Cad.** These two streets contain most travelers' needs, including hotels and banks. By the southwest corner of the park is a traffic circle with an Atatürk statue.

Flights: THY office (☎213 05 91), on Atatürk Cad., just east of the Hotel Efes.

Buses: Ulusoy (☎217 45 45), at the northwest corner of Belediye Parkı, runs from the dolmuş lot on the main highway to: **Ankara** (14hr., 9, 9:30am, 5:30pm; $18); **Bursa** (18hr., 9:30am, 12:30pm; $25); **Erzurum** (6hr., 7:30am, $5); **Giresun** (4hr., frequently 8:30am-10pm, $5); **İstanbul** (18hr.; 11:30am, 3:30, 6pm; $22); **İzmir** (20hr., 10am, $27); **Kastamonu** (20hr., every hr., $23); **Ordu** (5hr., frequent, $8); **Trabzon** (1½hr., frequently 8:30am-10pm, $2.50). The **Artvin Express** (☎212 09 05; 4hr., 4 per day 11am-4pm, $6), which departs from the lane next to Hotel Akarsu, serves **Yusufeli** (8hr., 8am, $10) and **Van** (14hr., 9pm, $12). Dolmuş, the best bet for closer destinations, leave from the big lot on the highway ($1-3).

Tourist Office: (☎213 04 07), in the T. C. Rize Valiliği building, 5 blocks west of town. The director, Atilla Karahasanoglu, can arrange English-speaking advisors. The **tourist information booth** (10am-6pm) is more convenient, in front of the museum and west of the Belediye Parkı.

Tours: Ritur Travel Agency (☎217 88 48; i.h.yildiz@ihlas.net.tr), on the northwest corner of Belediye Parkı. General manager Köksal Bey speaks fluent English. Ritur runs trekking and rafting expeditions. Open daily 8am-5pm. For more info on trekking, see **Trekking in the Kaçkars,** p. 434.

Police: (☎213 03 74), 1km west of the town center, on the main highway.

Pharmacies: Numerous pharmacies line the south side of Belediye Parkı, with rotating 24hr. service. Check the door of any pharmacy for the schedule.

Hospital: The state hospital (☎231 04 91), 1km east of the town center on the coastal highway. Open 24hr.

Internet Access: Rize has 6 internet cafes. The cheapest ($.75 per hr.) are in Belediye Parkı. Most open 8am-11pm.

PTT: On the south side of an open area 25m off the southwest corner of Belediye Parkı. Open daily 8:30am-12:30pm and 1:30-11pm. Phones 24hr.

Postal Code: 53100.

ACCOMMODATIONS. Most of Rize's hotels cater to businessmen's needs: low price, decent cleanliness, a TV lounge, and a touch of prostitution. Most hotels afford a good night's sleep for under $10; below are some of the safer options.

Hotel Akarsu (☎217 17 79). Just west of Belediye Parkı and visible from the PTT. This is a secure family *(aile)* establishment, with shared baths and 24hr. hot water. Clean, standard singles $4; doubles $7.

Hotel Efes (☎214 11 11), on Atatürk Cad., 2 blocks east of Belediye Parkı. Spotless rooms with hot water baths, balconies, and a pleasant roof terrace restaurant. Breakfast included. Singles $15; triples $25.

Kaçkar Hotel, Cumhuriyet Cad. No. 101 (☎213 14 90). Slightly more expensive, the Kaçkar includes a faux-marble entrance, bathtubs, TVs, and rooftop restaurant. Breakfast included. Singles $18; doubles $28.

Hotel Asnur (☎214 17 61), by Luna Park. Strike deals during the off-season with General Manager Ercan Turhan at rizfercan@dedeman.com.tr. Both hotels offer everything conceivable: pool, fitness center, sauna, and vitamin bar. Doubles $60.

FOOD. Rize's highest concentration of *pide* and *kebap* joints is on the north side of Belediye Parkı, stretching east along Cumhuriyet Cad. These Turkish mainstays cost $2-5. The local specialty, *meşhur kuru fasulye* (lamb with cooked beans in sweet tomato sauce), is made especially well at **Huzur Pide & Kebap,** Cumhuriyet Cad. No. 111 (☎217 15 11), for $2. Also try next door, at the **Bekiroğlu Pide Kebap** (☎217 26 62); both places are highly regarded by locals. Stop by **Mis Lahmacun** (☎217 26 06), one block further east along Cumhuriyet Cad., for $.50 Turkish pizzas with beef, chicken, and vegetarian varieties. A slightly more upscale option, the **Müze Kafeterya,** uphill from the PTT, has a veranda and view, and offers fast food and traditional *mulama* (cheese melt dip) and *lahana* (vineleaf parcels). Rize's moneyed young chat in this well-kept, cushioned Ottoman building and its sea-view balcony. (☎214 44 08. Open 9am-10:30pm.)

SIGHTS. Rize is not an exciting town, and tea is the primary focus of most visits. The best place for the *çay* connoisseur and casual enthusiast alike is the **Tea lab,** featuring Ministry of Agriculture greenhouses, laboratories and a rose-scented *çay* garden. At dusk, locals lounge here on patio furniture, gazing over the valley and out to sea. Hike up the road between the PTT and the main mosque, following signs for the "Atatürk Çay Ariştirma Müdürlüğü."

The **Rus Pazarı,** east of town, sells everything from Armenian *kilims* to plastic Stalin pins and three-way flashlights. Take in a view of the city from the **Rize Kalesi,** a small fortress built on a 160m hill above the city. One kilometer east of the center on the water is **Luna Park,** with $1 rides and a promenade. The nightclub of the **Dedeman Hotel** (taxi $4 each way) offers coastline panoramas, live music, and a chance to watch the Rize elite at play. Near the Dedeman, a few black-pebble **beaches** attract bathers during the tropical months of July and August.

HOPA ☎462

Hopa is the last town of note before the border at Sarp, and there's not much to note. Public transport ends in a **dolmuş** lot on the highway. **Otel Huzur,** Cumhuriyet Cad. 25, is the best choice, and will store luggage for those making daytrips into Georgia. (☎(466) 351 40 95. Singles $11.) Numerous diners line the main highway, most east of Otel Huzur. Catch a glimpse of Rize at play nightly after 11pm at **Paparazzi Disco** (☎351 33 65), on Yen Yol Uzeri; beware the $2.50 beer. Hopa's tiny *meydan* holds **ATMs** and the **Internet Cafe** (open until midnight, $.75 per hr.).

GEORGIA ON YOUR MIND? Though years of mutual suspicion simmer, economic liberalization is opening the road between Rize and Georgia frontier city of Batumi. Overlanders to Armenia must also use this route. Minibuses leave for the border from Hopa and other points on the Black Sea highway. Turkish procedures are straightforward and free, while Georgia accounts for any hard currency entering and leaving the country and charges US$3 each way. **They will not accept Turkish currency.** Georgian officials may attempt to extract an additional $5 on the Georgian side. This process is exactly reversed when returning to Turkey from Georgia. Georgian visas cannot be bought at the border, but must be purchased from the consulate in Trabzon ($40, see p. 416). Taxis ($10) and minibuses ($1) run to Batumi. On the way back, Turkish minibuses often refuse to make the short trip to Hopa, hoping for a longer fare to Rize. Some travelers choose to break the cartel by flagging down the first car to pass.

EASTERN ANATOLIA

Welcome to Eastern Turkey, a secret kept even from its own people. Racial and political faultlines traverse this part of the world. Fortunately, tensions have subsided somewhat and once again, one of the world's richest anthropological and historical regions welcomes visitors. Snowy peaks and thundering cascades, the Silk Road and shimmering Van Gölü, hauntingly beautiful Ani and Paşa Palace will, more often than not, be enjoyed without another traveler in sight. After checking passports, once-twitchy police now share apricots and *çay* with travelers. Hotel keepers remember your name, and Eastern Anatolians will consider you their *misafir* (guest) and offer you the utmost hospitality. This is an Eastern Turkey in transition. Internet now allows you to cultivate lifelong friends here. Massive public works programs are returning wealth to the region and Kurdish music and poetry is slowly surfacing after statewide sanctions. Almost no Turks raised in the western part of the country have ever been to Eastern Anatolia, having been taught that the region is war-torn, remote, and impoverished. This negative image of Turkey's frontier lands has also permeated much of the world, leaving the area untouched by all but the most intrepid of travelers. However, the region offers some of Turkey's most astonishing beauty, both natural and man-made.

Situated neatly on a time-worn crossroad, Eastern Anatolia has been the stomping ground of Hittites, Hurrians, Urartians, Assyrians, Persians, Romans, Byzantines, Arabs, Armenians, Mongols, Selçuks, Ottomans, Russians, Kurds, and Turks. In an unending game of musical chairs, push-pull power plays have privileged each civilization separately, leaving behind a heterogeneous legacy of occupation, construction, and war. Eastern Anatolia's pivotal role in contentious and explosive world politics has continued through the 20th century. The Armenian slaughter of 1915 occurred largely within Turkey's eastern border territory, and its ramifications continue to influence world politics from European Union membership negotiations to American congressional lobbies (see **Armenians,** p. 30).

Though tensions have decreased significantly in recent years, travel in Eastern Turkey should be approached with caution. Travelers should be aware of all consular advisories and travel warnings (see **Southeastern Turkey,** p. 47), and should be careful to adhere to local rules and laws. That said, Eastern Turkey has begun to develop a tourist infrastructure, and no traveler should avoid Eastern Turkey solely because of safety concerns.

Let's Go does not recommend that **women** travel alone to Eastern Turkey. Even with a head scarf and long, concealing clothes, women may be considered fair game for wandering eyes and forward flirtations, though the constant accompaniment is almost always benign. To avoid unwanted advances, dress conservatively, memorize some key phrases, particularly about a soon-to-return husband or boyfriend, and stay in more expensive hotels (see **Women Travelers,** p. 71).

The unpredictable nature of travel in Eastern Anatolia requires that travel schedules be flexible. Aside from large luxury buses, arrival and departure times for transportation should be considered tentative.

HIGHLIGHTS OF EASTERN ANATOLIA

EXPLORE the surreal toppled statuary heads upon the man-made summit of **Nemrut Dağı** (p. 464) at dusk and dawn. This grandiose timeless monument of Commagene King Antiochus I stands sentinel over are more recent one, the massive Atatürk Dam.

TRAVERSE the snowy passes of the Kaçkar Mountains, passing crumbling Georgian churches and the sunny *yaylas* (mountain villages) of the Hemşin Valley.

SWIM in the silky waters of **Lake Van,** make pilgrimage by boat to the most beautiful surviving Armenian structure in Anatolia (Akdamar Church; p. 455), then swim in crystal clear Nemrut Golu, within a 3000 meter volcanic crater, all in a day.

JOURNEY to **Şanlıurfa,** the City of Prophets, to see the birth cave of Abraham and the cave that saw Job's body consumed by worms (p. 466).

WANDER Under the shadows of nearby military watchtowers, wander through magnificent **Ani,** the ancient capital of the Armenian Empire (p. 447).

NORTHEAST ANATOLIA

Pitched in battle against industrial modernization, Anatolia's traditions have retreated from its Black Sea shores to the snowy Kaçkar mountain peaks. An elevated waterside freeway is the harbinger of growing commerce, population, and tourism. A recovering economy, political stabilization, and improving relations with neighboring Caucus states are bringing previously unknown comforts to the region. While swimming spots must be shared with an influx of Turkish visitors, stunning Kaçkar treks and windswept highlands can still be enjoyed alone.

Along the sea and in the northwestern Kaçkars, rain falls more days than it doesn't. In the drier northeastern Kaçkars, cascades have carved out tremendous ravines and canyons of orange and yellow bedrock. After hundreds of years, the Hemşin people continue to make their homes here, where they retain autonomous traditions and belief systems. There, *yayla* (highland plateaus) grace the mountainsides, standing as meeting grounds for Hemşin peoples from all over Europe.

HEMŞIN VALLEYS

Moving east and inland from Rize, the Kaçkar mountains become steeper and more lush, and their inhabitants become distinctly Hemşinli (see **The Hemşinli,** p. 426). The physical characteristics of the valleys as are unique as the cultures they contain: a shocking diversity of flora and fauna in the steaming forests of the lower valleys gives way to the misty moors of the upper grasslands. To move up or down the valley is to follow the seasonality of traditional Hemşin life: from the winter villages at the base to the spring *yaylas* of the foothills and the summer *yaylas* in the alpine meadows of the Kaçkars themselves. At every altitude, steeply-pitched stone bridges cross the valleys, and locals and their visiting relatives do their best to make travelers feel at home, pointing them in the right direction for anything from short walks through the hazelnut trees to longer treks over some of the most striking peaks in the Kaçkar Dağları. Plentiful rainfall characterizes this region, so bring waterproof gear and sturdy footwear. Stinging nettle undergrowth necessitates long trousers and sleeves (see **Trekking in the Kaçkars,** p. 434).

Two roads reach the area. From the coastal town of Pazar, it's 17km inland to **Hemşin** itself, a scenic town ill-prepared for tourists. Instead, take the second road 5km east of Pazar and follow a raging river 21km up to **Çamlıhemşin.** Here, the left-hand fork crosses the river and winds up to the rapidly expanding tourist retreat of **Ayder,** while the right leads to the little-touristed **Upper Fırtına Valley** and the handful of scattered buildings comprising **Şenyuva.**

Though the largest town in the Hemşin area and an important waystation for travelers coming to and from the valleys, **Çamlihemşin** is an eyesore on an otherwise beautiful curve in the Fırtına River. There are no hotels in Çamlihemşin, but it is home to the only **pharmacies** and **banks** in Hemşin territory, with a small **hospital** (emergency ☎ 155) on the premises. The large **PTT** is across the bridge. (Open M-F 8:30am-5:30pm.) The **postal code** is 53750.

AYDER ☎ 464

Twenty kilometers up the left-hand fork at Çamlihemşin, the road rises to Ayder, a Hemşin summer village with big ambitions. The ornately-carved blondewood houses of this mist-shrouded village are surrounded by lush forests, open *yayla*, and, increasingly, the concrete totems of the tourist trade. On the far side of the valley, a slender brook fed by melting mountain snow rushes over crags in a series of cascades to join a roaring stream on the valley floor below.

During high season, bus loads of tourists make the trip to breathe fresh mountain air and dip into piping-hot spring water. This influx can mean crowds (especially on weekends), but it also makes Ayder a prime spot for watching Hemşinli festivities unfold as urban exiles return home. The party kicks off the last weekend in May, and reaches fever pitch with the dancing and mingling of the **Ayder Festival.** In late June and early July, bring a good raincoat and selective vision. Unbridled development has overtaxed Ayder's resources, and the town, empty nine months out of the year, can barely cope with the summer influx.

THE HEMŞİNLİ The origins of the Hemşinli people are heavily disputed, but it seems most likely that they are descended from an Armenian tribe that immigrated to the Kaçkar Mountains some 500 years ago, living in virtual isolation for 300 years. Although nominally and linguistically Turkish, the Hemşinli still maintain an independent and unique culture. The best-known markers of Hemşinli culture are the colorful dress of the women and the beauty of their breathtaking *yayla*, the summer villages that rest above the tree-line.

When it's not *yayla* season, traditional Hemşinli live with many people in large homes, relying on cow husbandry and corn cultivation for their livelihoods. During Ottoman rule, the Hemşinli lived in peace, sharing the Kaçkar region with Armenians and Greeks, and absorbing elements of Islam into their lifestyle, albeit a somewhat looser Islam that still allows for some occasional drinking, dancing, and all-out shenanigans. Hemşinli traditionally live on a yearly cycle that follows the seasons. Their winter villages are usually built low in the hills with access to a river, and, as the weather gets warmer, they relocate to higher and higher grass-covered *yaylas*. The traditional house structure *(konak)* is divided into three levels made of stone or wood. The basement level is for animals, the second level for family living, and the top level for drying grass.

Out of economic necessity, Hemşinli families have begun a slow urban migration. Today, many villages are primarily comprised of elderly people, and many of the palatial hillside *konak* are all but empty. The city-dwelling Hemşinli have made a name for themselves all over Turkey as bakers, sweet-shop owners, and master chefs. The diaspora generally returns in full festive force each summer to enjoy the clean air of the *yayla* and to reestablish familial and cultural bonds. Some Hemşinli predict that there will be an increase in the number of people returning permanently to the villages, but that remains to be seen.

TRANSPORTATION AND PRACTICAL INFORMATION

Ayder consists of two sections: **Birinci Ayder** (Lower Ayder) and **İkinci Ayder** (Upper Ayder). Dolmuş stop in the former, home of most of the tourist spots, including hotels, restaurants, hot springs, stores, and the tiny **PTT.** İkinci Ayder, 500m uphill, has some new hotels, many summer villas, and cow pastures. Dolmuş between Ayder and Çamlihemşin ($1) are frequent in summer, but irregular in winter. Ayder charges a $2 **admission fee** for private vehicles, which is collected in a booth 4km from the center of town. Ayder has a famous hot-springy **hamam** but no banks, pharmacies, or hospital services. For any of the latter, visitors must journey down the valley to nearby Çamlihemşin. At the center of town, is a small **PTT** operating out of the back of a van. Open daily 8:30am-6pm. **Postal code:** 53780.

ACCOMMODATIONS

Because of their proximity to the hot springs, few hotels have shower facilities. Most average about $10, but you may get a break early in the season, when prices often haven't been adjusted for inflation. Reservations may be necessary during peak season, especially weekends, and some hotels may not open until the end of June. All offer spectacular views. **Otel Yesilvadi** (☎657 20 50) is the all-around best deal for travelers, with balconies, a fully-equipped kitchen, and an engaging staff. $4 per person; $7 with shower. Down the hill from the Yesilvadi, **trekking guide** Adnan Pirikoğlu runs the **Pirikoğlu Pansiyon** (☎657 20 21) with dorm-style doubles and shared hot water showers. In addition to a shared kitchen, there's laundry for grimy trekkers ($3 for up to 6 kg). $3 per person, $8 with dinner.

A bit farther uphill one can find lodging in more traditional wooden buildings. **Çağlayan Hotel** (☎657 20 73) is a few steps up the hill from lower Ayder and one step up from true asceticism. Its owner (the great-grandson of the founder) combines an English-speaking welcome with Hemşinli authenticity.

Singles $7; doubles $14. A slightly more upscale country-lodge experience can be found at the **Hotel Saray** (☎657 20 01, fax: 657 20 02), toward the lower end of lower Ayder, which occasionally hosts late-night fêtes in its dining room. 15 bathless doubles $15. Between lower and upper Ayder is a popular public campground/picnic site on the river called the **Hoşdere;** treehouses with 4 beds and bath are $20.

The rustic and airy **Kardelen Pansiyon** (☎657 21 07) is secluded 2km up the road from lower Ayder, just above Hoşdere, in the cluster of buildings above the Ayder *yayla*. **Muhammet Önçırak** leaves his İstanbul home every June to run this peaceful 5-room pension that many travelers use as a base for their treks (see **Trekking in the Kaçkars,** p. 434). Before climbing into the Kaçkars, consult the military-issue map hanging on his wall. Open June-Aug. $5 per person. Nature lovers and those strapped for cash can camp for free in the area around his house.

FOOD

Ayder is a good place to try the Hemşinli mountain specialty *muhlama*, a melted mix of cheese, butter, and corn flour that looks like mashed potatoes and behaves like fondue. Fresh bread replaces a spoon. **Dört Mevsim** ("The Four Seasons"), between Birinci Ayder and İkinci Ayder, makes it especially well ($3). Beer, cognac, and *rakı*, among others, are also available. Open 8am-midnight. **Pirikoğlu Lokantası** (☎657 20 21) serves equally wholesome meals. The owner, Adnan Pirikoğlu, is a guide who leads mountain groups (see p. 435) while his brother cooks the local specialty *katneraç* (soup made of corn flour, milk, and butter; $2). Open daily May-Oct, 6am-11pm. Full meals cost about $5.

A late dinner at **Nazlı Çiçek** (☎657 21 30), just before the bridge above lower Ayder, provides the best opportunity to see traditional local dancing (apart from August weekends on the *yayla*). Full meals $3; breakfast $2. Open until 1am. Next door, the **Çise Cafe** (☎657 21 71) stays open until 2 am, and has a cozy fireplace den with full bar and local puddings like *laz boregi*. Next to the picnic sites at the Hoşdere, a few locals sell grilled trout ($2.50) freshly fished from the river.

SIGHTS

Ayder's local **hamam,** below the road by the bridge, is a government-funded natural hot spring housed in the largest and most sophisticated edifice in town. Men (see **The Hamam,** p. 33) might want to wear their own shorts rather than the mildewed pairs provided ($.50). Women can wear bathing suits or a large shirt. Either way, locals will engage you in frank conversation, rarely enjoyed beyond the hamam walls. Water temperatures are close to scalding, but a gradual immersion is rewarding (and safe). The time limit is one hour. Locals swear by the curative properties of the hot water and suggest that swallowing it in large doses resolves all stomach problems—those wary of dysentery and *giardia* would be wise to decline. (Apr.-Oct. 15 daily 7am-7pm. Regular bath $3, private tub $7.50.)

The strongest draw of Ayder, of course, is the serenity of the surrounding *yaylas* and the beckoning slopes of the Kaçkars. Minibuses also run past İkinci Ayder to the Laz *yayla* of **Avusor** (15km, $1), and the Hemşinli **Lower Kavron** (7km, $2), and **Upper Kavron** (12km, $2). Avusor is an important stop along the northern trans-Kaçkar route to Barhal, while the two Kavrons are popular trekking bases on the shoulder of 3932m **Kaçkar Daği.** Only Upper Kavron has facilities, a workers' cottage and diner; otherwise, bring your own. Unless it is a particularly clear day in Ayder, you should expect mists and cool fog, although the warm hospitality and tea unerringly provided by the *yayla* inhabitants helps to take the edge off of the cold and wet. Some travelers prefer to day trek or hitchhike along these routes.

ŞENYUVA VALLEY

Halfway up the Upper Fırtına Valley from Çamlihemşin, sleepy Şenyuva is all but hidden from the casual visitor. The valley itself is empty, and the town's houses and storefronts are shaded by the trees of the high valley walls. Elderly men sit drinking tea and dogs sleep undisturbed on the winding gravel roads; the loudest noise is that of the river cascading through the valleys. Şenyuva's slow, secluded character offers a relaxed and unobtrusive perspective on traditional and contemporary Hemşin life: over a cup of *çay* or an impromptu *tulum* performance, locals are all too happy to discourse on what it means, now and forever, to be Hemşin. Şenyuva offers a first-hand lesson in both contemporary and traditional Hemşin life, and makes an excellent base for trekking excursions.

From Rize or Trabzon, catch a morning dolmuş to Çamlihemşin and continue straight up the valley rather than turning left over the bridge to Ayder. Usually this means taking a private taxi or walking the 5km. Many travelers choose to hitchhike. The valley's only lodge, **Otel Doğa** at Ortankoy (☎651 74 55), was hand-built by İdris Duman, a well-traveled local who speaks English and French. Doğa boasts a spacious living room (the TV gets the BBC), warm beds, hardwood floors, balconies, and meals served on deck overlooking thunderous rapids. Trekking, camping, and luggage storage are available. Two major *yaylas* are accessible from this hotel (see **Trekking in the Kaçkars,** p. 434). Check with Doğa about accommodation options any higher up the valley. $10 per person; $15 with breakfast and dinner.

About 300m up the road from Hotel Doğa stands the high stone arc of the **Ortank Kiprisi Bridge,** built by Hemşin peoples over 200 years ago. Across the road from Hotel Doğa, a gravel track leads to the winter village of **Ortan,** a 15-minute walk up the valley wall and an excellent example of the stone foundations and ornate upper-story woodcarvings that characterize Hemşin architecture. Following the trail from the Ortank bridge, a slightly longer walk leads to the winter village of **Yemişli,** while a side trail off the road to Ortan will take you, after an hour's hike, to the summer *yayla* of **Pokut,** itself a trekking base for the Western Kaçkars. The **Demircioğlu Pensiyon** hosts visitors; ask at the Otel Doğa to help with arrangements.

Zilkale (Bell Castle), a 10 km walk up the valley road, makes a pleasant daytrip. Most likely a minor Armenian or Genoese trading post, this ancient fortress pops into view after about 8 km. Continuing up the Fırtına Valley, after 20 km you will reach the winter village of **Çat,** with modest facilities for travelers. After Çat the crumbling road leads to the *yaylas* of **Elerit, Verçembek,** and **Ciçek.** These remote seasonal villages make excellent bases for exploring the misty Western Kaçkars.

CLEAR WATER, MURKY POLITICS Before the Hemşinli (and *way* before the nation of Turkey), the Fırtına ("Storm") River made its mad rush down the Şenyuva Valley to the Black Sea. But this little river is scheduled for a big change from open air to hydroelectric pipeline, under a government proposal and against local sentiment. Some valley residents and expatriates question the rationale for the project, and say that well-connected contractors will benefit more than citizens living next to a dusty stream-bed. Matters are further complicated by what some local Hemşinli and Laz residents see as a new threat to their cultural independence by a profoundly nationalist government. A functional river supports traditional life, they say, just as hydroelectric power supports an industry blind to all but the most recent past. The struggle continues against what the Turkish government sees as just another necessity of true modernization.

THE ÇORUH VALLEY REGION

The steep gorge of the Çoruh River, which cuts northwest along the southern edge of the Kaçkar Mountains to empty into the Black Sea just across the Georgian border, contains some of Turkey's most stunning historical, cultural, and natural attractions. Unlike the foggy Black Sea slopes, the Çoruh side of the mountain range is bright and arid. The valley walls are ringed by multicolored buttes crowned with thousand year-old churches and Georgian fortresses, and the river valley itself is green with fruit trees and rice paddies. Both Artvin, the valley's biggest city and transport hub, and Yusufeli, the most convenient point of entry into the valley and its sights, make excellent bases for exploration.

ARTVİN ☎466

Artvin is stapled onto a mountainside, overlooking the vast Çoruh River Valley and at the top of a 5km series of switchbacks chiseled into the western slope. The rarefied Artvin air is saturated with smog and waste, sustaining a beleaguered mix of military men, college students, shopkeepers, and prostitutes. For most of the year, Artvin offers little to the visitor except a few tawdry *gazinos* and a dubious nightlife. For one shining weekend in late June/early July, however, it is home to the monumental **Kafkasör Festival,** Turkey's largest and most authentic folk festival. The festival takes place in a grassy *yayla* above town, and its bloodless bullfights, folk dancing, and general hijinks attract a diverse and joyful crowd. Artvin is also the capital of a province stretching from the border with Georgia to the highlands of the Çoruh River, making it a useful travel route inland and a base for supplies for exploring Yusufeli en route to the valley beyond.

TRANSPORTATION

A tiny **otogar** is five steep kilometers from the center of town, near the fortress at the base of the river valley. Local dolmuş ($.80), free shuttle buses, the municipal bus (every 30min., $.50), and taxis ($2) all run from the otogar up to the town center on İnönü Cad. Luckily, most bus and minibus lines will also deposit or pick up passengers from the town center for free.

Flights: The **THY** office (☎212 20 00; fax 212 24 20), in Hotel Karahan. Sells tickets for flights out of Erzurum, Trabzon, and Kars. Open daily 8am-5pm.

Buses: Artvin Express (☎212 13 76 or 212 15 20) has an office across from the enormous municipal building halfway up İnönü Cad. To: **Ankara** (16hr., 2pm, $19); **Erzurum** (4hr.; 6, 11am, 1:30, 5:30pm; $7); **Hopa** (2hr., every hr. 7am-4pm, $2.50); **İstanbul** (22hr., 1pm, $23); **Kars** (5hr., noon, $7); **Rize** (3hr.; 7:30, 10, 11:30am, 12:30pm; $5); **Trabzon** (5hr.; 7:30am, noon, 1, 3, 5pm; $7); **Yusufeli** (1½hr.; 9:30am, noon, 2:30, 5pm; $2.50). Dolmuş from **Hopa** run to **Georgia.**

ORIENTATION AND PRACTICAL INFORMATION

Hotels, restaurants, banks, tea houses, and shops line **İnönü Cad.,** the main street, which runs uphill to a circle at the top of the town. From the top of the circle, **Cumhuriyet Cad.** parallels İnönü on an uphill slope ending at **Cami Meydanı** ("Mosque Square") on the uphill side of Hotel Karahan.

Tourist Office: (☎212 30 71), at the uphill end of İnönü Cad. Amicable English speaker and glossy brochures. Open daily 8am-noon and 1:30-5:30pm.

Banks: Akbank, next to the Artvin Express office. Changes cash and American Express traveler's checks. Open daily 8:30am-5:30pm.

Hamam: (☎212 11 58), appropriately located on Hamam Sok., by the Kaçkar Hotel. Closed for renovations at the time of publication.

Police: (☎212 11 33), next to municipal building on İnönü Cad.

Pharmacy: 6 pharmacies are scattered on İnönü Cad., taking turns staying open 24hr.

Hospital: (☎212 10 40), on the main winding road above the town center.

Internet Access: Multiple options exist and connections are fast. One block uphill from Cumhuriyet Cad., **Casper Internet Cafe** will be on your right on the 2nd floor. $1 per hr. Open daily 10am-midnight. Farther along Inönü Cad. are identical **Sis** and **Arge** cafes.

PTT: Halfway up İnönü Cad. Cash and card phones. Another branch, on İnönü Cad., has *Poste Restante*. Both open daily 8am-12:30pm and 1:30-11pm; phones 24hr.

Postal code: 08000.

ACCOMMODATIONS

Hotels are indifferent to tourists; most are expensive, involved in prostitution, or both. Many are still safe and clean, with *Nataşa* encounters rising as prices fall (See **Nataşas,** p. 409). Reservations are necessary for Kafkasör weekend.

Hotel Ugrak (☎212 65 05). On Hamam Sok, near the Koçkar Hotel. Though a bit worn, bright and clear with valley views and the best bet for value. A bit removed from the late-night scene, with secluded top-floor rooms and laundry facilities. $5 per person.

Kaçkar Oteli (☎212 33 97), on Hamam Sok., just uphill from Çağdaş. From İnönü Cad. follow the steps under the hotel's red sign. Clean, with spacious rooms with showers and seat toilets. $7 per person.

Hotel Çağdaş (☎212 33 33; fax 212 48 51), on İnönü Cad, under a big yellow sign 100m downhill from the PTT. New, wood-paneled rooms have showers and seat toilets. Most rooms are occupied almost entirely by the bed. The nicest rooms in town. Singles $10; doubles $15 with tiled bath.

Hotel Karahan (☎212 18 00), on Cami Meydanı. From İnönü Cad., enter under the sign and walk up 3 flights. Bills itself as the best hotel in town, but its luster has faded and the rates are not justified. All rooms have TV, bath, phone, and balconies with panoramic views. Bar, restaurant, and in-house travel agency. Singles $16; doubles $22.

FOOD

Artvin's ugly *rakı*/gambling/*Nataşa* scene has a reputation for getting rowdy at night. Any establishment termed a *gazino* is probably best avoided.

Hanedan Restaurant (☎212 72 22), on İnönü Cad., near the town center. The watering hole for Artvin's elite, Hanedan has a bar with views of the valley. Meal and beer $3. Open daily 8am-11pm.

Nazar Restoranı (☎212 17 09), at the lower end of İnönü Cad. Decorated with bizarre posters including a rendition of Atatürk in thick felt. A bar and precipitous balcony complement the cheap, excellent food, including delicious *mezes*. Full meal $3. Open daily 10am-midnight.

Bakıroğlu Kebap Salonu (☎212 74 08), 100m uphill from the municipal building on a roof terrace on İnönü Cad. This open-air restaurant has tasty *iskenderun kebap*, a wide selection of *mezes*, and good service in a pleasant atmosphere.

Saklıca Restaurant (☎212 79 82), off İnönü Cad. This real bargain is also the best hidden. Enter the narrow stairway opposite Karahan Hotel and turn left. Be sure to eat upstairs, where the menu is better. Vegetarian options include *fasulye pılaki* (green beans in olive oil; $1). $2 per meal.

Şehir Kukubü (☎212 41 57). This terrace/balcony bar is free of gambling and *Nataşas*, A good place to sip a cold beer and watch the crowds go by.

SIGHTS

The town's calendar is dominated by the annual **Kafkasör Festival,** held at the end of June in Kafkasör *yayla* (10km above Artvin). Thousands of visitors are lured by wrestling and bloodless bullfights, where prime bulls go head to head in a lengthy shoving match, and the owner of the winning animal is publicly honored. Unfortunately, folk-dancing and traditional arts are less visible than they once were. Artvin rooms are nearly impossible to find over the festival weekend—the best and most popular option is to camp in the peaceful forests and open grasslands around the *yayla*. A 15th-century citadel at the base of the valley is now an army base closed to visitors. Dolmuş run to the plateau of **Şavşat,** 30km away, which has breathtaking high glacial lakes and 9th-century **Tibeti** Byzantine church.

YUSUFELİ ☎466

Just 9km off the main Artvin-Erzurum road, Yusufeli offers sweet solace from the urbanization and illicit commerce of its larger neighbors. The town straddles the Barhal River just before its intersection with the Çoruh, leaving hanging pedestrian bridges and terrace cafes jutting out over the rushing rapids. On the drive inland from Artvin, the Çoruh River narrows and the valley walls steepen into dry, crumbling spires and cliffs as the water gets rougher. Yusufeli hosted the world whitewater rafting championships in 1993, and the nearby river includes Grade V and VI rapids. Nearby Georgian churches and close proximity to Tekkale and Barhal make Yusufeli the perfect base from which to explore the Kaçkar region.

TRANSPORTATION AND PRACTICAL INFORMATION

Most transport to Yusufeli will drop you off at the "water junction," a gas station-cum-mosque on the Erzurum-Artvin road. A minibus or taxi will take you the last 9km into town for $2-4; some travelers prefer to hitch a ride, although *Let's Go* does not recommend hitchhiking. **Artvin Express,** in the otogar lot, runs to: **Ankara** (18hr., noon, $18); **Artvin** (2hr., 4 per day 6am-5pm, $3); **Bursa** (22hr., 9am, $23); **Erzurum** (3hr., 2 per day 9-11am, $5); **Hopa** (2½hr., 9am, $8); **İstanbul** (20hr., 10am, $25); **Rize** (4½hr., 9am, $7); **Trabzon** (6hr., 9am, $8). Dolmuş head from the otogar up the Çoruh and Barhal valleys, with prices set according to distance (**Tekkale** $1; **Sarigol** $2; **Barhal** $3; **Yaylalar** and **Olgunlar,** both $3.50). The tourist center of Yusufeli is the rectangular area enclosed by four streets named after Turkish politicians: **İnönü Cad., Enver Paşa Cad., Fevzi Çakmak Cad.,** and **Mustafa Kemal Cad.** İnönü Cad. is the main drag, running along the right bank of the Barhal at the downstream end, and a central otogar near the cluster of hotels at the upstream end. **Ersis Cad.,** on the left bank, passes a few terrace cafes and is home to **Akin Cafe,** Yusufeli's best **internet cafe.** (☎811 38 97. $.75 per hr. Open until 1am.) **Türkiye İs Bankasi,** at the center of town on M. Kemal Cad., is the only place to change **traveler's checks.** A small **hospital** (☎811 20 15) and **police** station are also centrally located. The **PTT** is on İnönü Cad. at the downstream end of town. (Open M-F 8:30am-5:30pm. 24hr. telephones.) **Postal code:** 08800.

FOOD AND ACCOMMODATIONS

Yusufeli's better hotels are all close to each other on İnönü Cad. There's not much variety, but all establishments listed are clean and quiet—the only noise is the rushing of the river. The **Hotel Çiçek Palas** and the jointly managed **Genç Palas** face each other on upper İnönü Cad. and feature bright rooms, hot water, and clean sheets. (☎811 21 02. $3 per person.) The **Hacioğlu Oteli,** on M. Kemal Cad., offers nearly identical accommodations, with terraces and clotheslines. (☎811 35 66. Singles $6; doubles $10.) The **Barhal Hotel,** hanging over the Barhal River about 20m upstream on İnönü Cad, offers sterile rooms with river views and showers. Plans are underway for a rooftop cafe by the summer of 2002. (☎811 31 51. Singles $6; doubles $10; triples $15.) To reach **Greenpeace Camping** and nearby **Akin Camping,** cross the bridge by the Barhal Hotel, turn right, take another right at the T-intersection, and turn left. Both have secluded campsites in a garden, cold shower, and light meals. Those without tents can use sleeping bags or bedding provided in the open-air treehouse *pergulas*. (Open June-Sept. $2-5 per night.)

Dining in Yusufeli, while nothing to write home about, is more varied than you'll find up in the Kaçkars. One of the more popular meeting places is **Çınar Lokantası,** which overlooks the river beneath the Barhal Hotel. Its menu includes fresh trout, *rakı*, vegetarian *mezes*, and *sac tava*, a tasty combination of meat, onions, and peppers, served sizzling in a flat copper wok. (☎811 23 65. Full meal with beer $3.50. Open daily 9am-midnight.) The **Mavi Köşk Restorant,** off İnönü Cad., has delicious food, patio dining, and a well-stocked bar. (☎811 23 29. Full meal about $3.50. Open daily 8am-1am.) Also popular is **Mahsen Restaurant** (☎811 20 08), across the footbridge, with similar fare and the rare advantage of **beer on tap.**

SIGHTS

Yusufeli's most popular sight is the river itself, and several **rafting companies** lead afternoon excursions on the Çoruh or the Barhal. The lucrative rafting/tour industry has provoked a local business war of sorts, with various rafting companies vying for customers. A first-rate German-Dutch rafting company was recently run out of town, taking with it stringent safety standards—few of the remaining tours bother with throwlines or safety kayaks. All outfits use helmets and life jackets, however, and guides are trained in river rescue, so don't be put off the idea completely—rafting past Georgian fortresses in this stunning valley is a singular experience. **Rapid Tür** (☎811 33 93; fax 811 33 93), a new outfit with offices below the Çiçek Palas, is run by Mevrut Bayburtoğlu, who hopes to be internationally accredited by 2002. The **Yusufeli Kayak Raft Dagcilik** is run by Sirali Aydin, owner of the Cinar Restaurant. Excursions with both outfits run $20-30 per day.

Locals **Mehmet Aydin** (mobile ☎(535) 467 93 63) and **Akim Pulat** (mobile ☎(543) 282 08 13) give advice over a cup of *çay* at the Cinar Restaurant and Akin Cafe, respectively. The Cinar has a few hand-drawn maps of the region. A hardscrabble sheep track starts about 100m upstream from Greenpeace camping, leading up the river to an eyrie-like **Georgian castle.** The 5km hike takes about 1½ hours each way. The 14km trip to **Dörtkilise** makes an excellent afternoon hike, with a stop halfway at **Tekkale** for a cold beer or a glass of *çay*. Other daytrips require transportation.

THE ÇORUH VALLEY

Yusufeli is the hub of the upper Çoruh, but local transportation is oriented to the needs of the villager over those of the traveler: ***dolmuş*** *typically leave smaller towns in the morning for Yusufeli and return in the afternoon. This does not present a problem for larger towns with adequate accommodations, such as Barhal and Tekkali, but can make daytripping difficult. Taxis are expensive; many travelers either rent a* ***car*** *in Erzurum ($30-40 per day) or hitchhike, although Let's Go does not recommend hitchhiking. Hand-drawn maps of the region can be found at Cemli's Pension in Tekkale or at the Çinar Restaurant in Yusufeli.*

İŞHAN KİLİSE. Perhaps the most magnificent of the northern Georgian churches, İshan Kilise lies high in the cliffs above the Oltu Çay, a major tributary of the Çoruh some 35km east of Yusufeli. The Oltu Valley is even more stunning than the Çoruh, with painted buttes awash in glorious reds and oranges. Begun in 730 and finished three centuries later, İshan is the oldest church in the valley. The church was enhanced with a Byzantine dome in 1200 before its stewardship passed back into Georgian hands. The immense vault is decorated with deteriorating frescoes depicting the apostles and the visions of Zachariah. *(Take the highway east from Yusufeli to the gas station. Follow the signs first to Erzurum, then bear left toward Olur. Ten to 15km down the road, a sign points left to İşhan Kilise, which is located in a mountain village 5km up the unpaved road. Park at the fountain and take the 5min. path down to the left.)*

ÖŞK VANK KİLİSE. (Fifty kilometers from Yusufeli, Ösk Vank Kilise is one of the world's most beautiful Georgian churches. The well-preserved facade of this airy church features carvings of angels, patrons, and animals. Above the entrance, note a colorful band of frescoed faces next to the image of what may be Öşk Vank itself. Another 25km south toward Erzurum is the Tortum valley, which is home to the church of **Haho** (see p. 441), just outside the town of **Bağbaşı.** *(Back down on the highway south to Erzurum, turn off to Çamlıyamaç for the Öşk Vank Kilise.)*

TEKKALE. About 6km on a paved road up the valley from Yusufeli, Tekkale makes an excellent base for hikes up tributary streams to the area's numerous abandoned **Georgian churches** and *yayla*. Longer hikes lead up past the spring snow line to the peaks and freezing lakes of the southeastern Kaçkars. **Cemil's Pension** (☎811 20 08) offers full room and board for $10 per person, with private rooms downstairs and open-air Black Sea *kilim* platforms upstairs. Even if you don't spend the night, Cemil's garden is an excellent spot for an ice-cold beer or wild trout ($2), grilled on a terrace patio over a rushing brook. Cemil organizes 2- to 3-day hikes from Dörtkilise ti Barhal and other Kaçkar destinations; ask and he may lend you his dog, who will guide you from Tekkale to Dörtkilise and back.

A few kilometers on the paved road past Tekkale is the village of **Peterkale,** with a craggy Georgian fortress. Dolmuş run to Tekkale and Peterkale only in the afternoon ($2). Some travelers choose to hitchhike. Taxis are about $5.

DÖRTKİLİSE AND BAYIRKİLİSE. **Dörtkilise** (literally, "Four Churches") is 7km uphill from Tekkale on the banks of a tributary stream. Only one of the original four churches still stands, and the ruins of the other three have been scattered. The remaining church is a hauntingly beautiful place to spend the evening, and the ground outside makes for a prime campsite. To the right of the church, a small path winds steeply up the valley wall 2km to **Bayırkilise.** At an altitude of 1650m, this minor Georgian church offers spectacular views. From here, it's a fairly level 5km hike north to the small village of **Elecumle.** To complete a loop back down to Tekkale, cut down the switchback path to the road and head the 9km into town. This loop makes for a long day; some may want to catch a ride part way up or down the road. If you have camping equipment (see **Trekking in the Kaçkars,** p. 434) you can continue on from Elecumle up to the high-altitude lakes, **Küçük Göl** (2850m) and **Büyük Göl** (2900m). The climb passes through the *yayla* and villages of **Kusana** and **Salent.** A trail also ascends from Büyük Göl about two hours up to an awesome 3300m pass, and then descends five hours through **Modut** village to the road to Barhal (15km). *(To get to Dörtkilise from Tekkale, follow the signs pointing you up along the dirt road, which climbs up along the left side of the streambed. After 4km, the road crosses to the right of the brook, only to recross 3km later. Just past the second bridge, the church will be visible on the left. If you cross the brook a third time, you've gone too far.)*

BARHAL. From Tekkale, a side road climbs up toward the peaceful mountain village of Barhal (also accessible by a separate road from Yusufeli). The town's center straddles the point where two nameless tributaries join to form the Barhal River; most of the town, however, lies hidden in the ridge above the right-hand (northern) fork. A dirt road follows the fork for 1km before joining the main track. **Karahan Pension** is 50m farther uphill, run by the amiable beekeeper Mehmet Karahan, who provides full board (with fresh honey) and lodging in the treetop open-air top floor of his house. (☎826 20 71. Ask locals for directions. Reservations required. $12 per person.) At the downstream end of town, the **Barhal Pension** has new, wooden rooms occupying the second floor of a house overlooking a bend in the river. Dinner and breakfast included. (☎(466) 826 20 31. $10 per person.) At the foot of Mehmet's driveway, a footbridge crosses the brook, marking the beginning of a steep but short **hike** up the valley wall. The trail begins past the bridge, 20m up to the right at a small hut and threshing stone. The 20min. hike will deposit you at the ruins of a hilltop Georgian chapel with a commanding view of snowy peaks up the two valleys to the north and west. *(2 to 3 dolmuş run daily from Yusufeli to Barhal, one in the afternoon and one in the early evening.)*

YAYLALAR AND OLGUNLAR. Bearing left at the Barhal fork and continuing another 22km into the foothills will bring you to **Yaylalar** and **Olgunlar,** remote summer *yayla* which are the highest spots accessible by car on the southern side of the Kaçkars. Both Yaylalar, below the treeline, and Olgunlar, 3km farther on, are popular bases for exploring the western and southern Kaçkars. There's a **pension** in Yaylalar, and though İsmael, the owner, speaks no English, he can arrange horses and guides. (☎832 20 01. Room and full board $10.) **Ibrahim** and **Osman** run the equivalent pension in Olgunlar (☎832 20 44 or 832 21 00) and also do not speak English. Reservations are required for both pensions; it's best to phone ahead from Yusufeli. **Özkan Şahin** (mobile ☎(532) 505 89 75), a Yusufeli-based mountaineering guide who speaks excellent English, can help translate.

TREKKING IN THE KAÇKARS

The tallest stretch of the Black Sea range, the Kaçkar Dağli—reverently known as the "Pontic Alps"—represent one of the largest glacial formations in Asia Minor and occupy an important spot in the Turkish imagination. The Alpine comparison is apt: treks to the snowy peaks pass through thousand-year-old villages with steeply pitched and ornately carved wooden houses, past glassy lakes and across high meadows carpeted with wild flowers. The terrain ranges from lush, deciduous rainforest in the foothills along the Black Sea coast to arid, eroding steppes southeast in the Artvin and Çoruh Valleys. Trails exist above the tree line in all Kaçkar regions, with spectacular views, lakes, and snow well into the spring.

The Black Sea side of the range is a gently rolling landscape typically shrouded in mist and fog. Immediately across the passes, the Çoruh side of the range is hot, sunny, and dry, and the terrain craggy and steep. The most popular routes pass through the central Kaçkars, crossing from Ayder to Yaylalar and Ogunlar through the **Körahmet** and **Çaymakçur passes** (approx. 3100m), often including a trip to the summit of **Kaçkar Dağ** (3932m), the region's highest peak. Less-crowded but equally stunning routes take trekkers across the northern Kaçkars, from Ayder to Barhal via the **Kırmızı pass** (3200m) and along the northernmost **Altıparmak Ridge.** To the southwest, at the head of the Şenyuva Valley, lie the less well-known misty peaks at the western Kaçkars—also called the "second valley." All in all, there are enough trails, peaks, and lakes to satisfy a dedicated hiker for weeks.

ADVICE AND WARNINGS

Although the Kaçkar meadows and lakes attract trekkers as early as May, the high traverses are impassable without snow equipment until early July, limiting the prime season to July and August. April and May is avalanche season. A more immediate obstacle to trekking here is the lack of any high-quality maps. Matters are complicated by poor trail maintenance, thick afternoon Kaçkar fog, and stinging nettle undergrowth.

Turks are proud of their wilderness, but many litter like bandits, so striking the right balance between responsible trekking and local custom can be tricky. The general rule of thumb is simply to leave the site the way you found it or cleaner. All solid human waste should be buried, and all trash and food scraps packed out. You may also need to remind your guide of the importance of frequent stops for **water.** Below the tree line, regular **fountains** along the trails can be found, above the *yaylas*, the mountain spring water appears to be free of **giardia,** though the cautious hiker should still bring a **filter.** The importance of appropriate **equipment** (good boots, waterproof jacket and pants, hat and gloves, sunglasses and sunblock, for starters) cannot be overstated, as well as food supplies in excess of your planned trip—weather conditions in the peaks are unpredictable and sudden hailstorms can strike well into the summer. At high altitudes, stay warm and hydrated, and ascend less than 1000ft. per day. (See **Environmental Hazards: High altitude,** p. 51.)

DEPARTURE

Most points of departure contain at least one English-speaking local who will be happy to draw out maps and directions for day trips and multi-day treks and guides for hire abound. Prices range according to personal needs, group size, trip duration, and the professionalism of the company. In general, with guides and pensions, it's a good idea to phone ahead. A small advance payment will allow guides to purchase the necessary supplies. As always, **never trek alone.**

YUSUFELİ. Trekkers are drawn to Yusufeli for its dry weather and rafting. Though self-guided trekking takes a little more effort and research, there is an excellent guide service at Barhal Hotel, run by **Sirali Aydin** (☎/fax 811 38 93), head of the local Skiing-Rafting-Mountain Sport club. **Özkan Şahin** (mobile ☎(532) 505 89 75, kackar3932@hotmail.com) is an experienced mountaineer with a full outfit of heavy snow equipment; a two-person 2-day trip runs $150. **Akin Polat** (mobile ☎ (543) 282 08 13) of **Akin Internet** also leads reasonably priced Kaçkar tours from Yusufeli. Stock up on supplies here before heading inland to Barhal or Tekkale.

TEKKALE. The paths leading from Tekkale into the northern and central Kaçkars are steep and difficult; maps can be found at **Cemil's Pension** in Tekkale (☎(466) 811 20 08). Cemil leads a good 3-day trek from Tekkale to Barhal for $50 per day.

BARHAL. The Barhal River splits at the town of Barhal; trails along the right fork lead to the northern Kaçkars, while the left fork heads toward Yaylalar/Olgunlar and the central Kaçkars beyond. The **Karahan Pension** (☎(466) 826 20 71) is an excellent base for exploring the northern Kaçkars—a path from the Barhal Kilise winds up the valley to join a sinuous aqueduct for 7km, which joins the valley road. The road crosses the river twice, cuts a few switchbacks and passes a cemetery before a clear path branches off the road to the left. After 500m, the trail crosses the river again and climbs a ridge to the villages of **Nezana** and **Amanescit.** After Amanescit, a trail to the right leads up to the **Altiparmak** pass, while the aqueduct up the ridge becomes a trail to the glacial lake of Karagöl, which can be reached as a dayhike. Many trekkers find it to be a pleasant campsite at base for dayhikers in the northern Kaçkars; from Karagöl one can turn south to the peak of **Borivan** or west to the *yayla* of **Pişenkaya** and the high pass at **Libler Gölü** beyond.

A quicker route to Libler Gölü from Barhal follows the south fork on the road to Yaylalar for 2km, and then breaks off of the road onto a clear path to the right. The road winds up the valley to Pişenkaya; campsites can be found around Libler Gölü. With a horse and guide ($25-30 per day), supplied by **Mehmet Delioğlu** (☎(466) 826 21 06), the entire trip from Barhal to Ayder can be done in one day.

YAYLALAR/OLGUNLAR. These high and dry *yayla* have good pensions and are the most popular points of departure for the Kaçkar summit and the central trans-Kaçkar route. **İsmail** in Yaylalar (☎(466) 832 20 01) runs the local pension and can arrange horses and guide, although he doesn't speak English. His counterparts in Olgunlar, **İbrahim** and **Osman,** offer room and board (☎(466) 832 20 44 or 832 21 00). Treks include the crater lakes of **Deniz Gölüb** and the so-named **Nameless Lake.**

AYDER. At the lower part of town, **Adnan Pirikoğlu** of **Hotel Pirikoğlu** (☎(464) 657 20 21) leads treks for $50 per day and gives advice about all things mountainous. The town relies on his guidance to help confused English speakers. His favorite, and a very good deal, is a six-day circuit of the Kaçkars, which includes eight crater lakes, **Yukarı Kavron** (3037m, the highest summit in the Kaçkars), lower and upper **Kavron** *yaylas*, **Çaymakçur** *yayla*, and **Denizgölü,** a very deep volcanic lake. Adnan can provide equipment for two people; otherwise, bring your own. He will plan smaller trips for travelers free of charge, and he will store extra gear in his hotel.

Muhammet Önçirak runs the **Kardelen Pension** (☎(464) 657 21 07), a good base for trekking trips. As a member of Turkey's Mountaineering Group, he is a resource for budget travelers hoping to trek cheaply in the Kaçkars. When asked what he charges for guidance, he responds that he will accompany trekkers "in exchange for a bottle of *rakı*." Muhammet has a rare topographic map of the region.

Independent trekkers may want to get a hand-drawn map from Adnan and head up to the pension at **Upper Kavusor** *yayla* (☎(464) 651 73 48), whose proprietor speaks some English. From Kavusor the central and western Kaçkars are easily accessible. In the direction of the northern Kaçkars, the high *yayla* of **Avusor** has no formal pensions, but hospitable locals are likely to offer you some form of lodging or at least let you warm up with some tea by the wood stove.

A well-planned **day hike** from Ayder can get you up to the snowline of Mt. Kaçkar from the **Öküz Yatağı** lake; alternately, the sunny Hemşin *yayla* of **Samistal** can be reached in a day. Talk to Adnan for details and encouragement.

ŞENYUVA. The Doğa Hotel (☎(464) 651 74 55), a riverside lodge in the heart of Hemşin country, is one of the best options for budget travelers seeking help before going their own way. Helpful **İdris Duman** can arrange many daytrips or provide advice about two to four day treks that you can do independently. His treks head into the *yaylas* of the western Kaçkars. He can arrange trips via Çat to the Pokut, Elevit, Polovit, and Apivenek *yaylas* above Şenyuva that include camping or overnight stays in high-elevation lodges—a great deal, despite the wet summer weather. Travelers are welcome to store supplies and equipment at his lodge.

OUTSIDE TREKKING AGENCIES

Trabzon: Usta Tour (☎(462) 326 18 70; fax 326 18 71) has numerous package deals, organized to the last detail by the local mountaineering group. Options include daytrips to Uzungöl or Zigana, Karaca Cave, and 7-day tours of the Pontic Alps regions. They also offer a 3- to 4-day mule trek to *yayla* and crater lakes in the western Kaçkars, roughly $200-$250 per person. Call or fax with questions or reservations. Small groups of 4 to 8 can be accommodated upon arrival.

Rize: RI-TUR Travel Agency (☎(464) 217 14 84; fax 217 14 86; i.h.yildiz@ihlas.net.tr), which operates the town's tourist office and sells international IATA tickets, runs a huge range of regional programs for a hefty price. These can be jointly arranged with international travel agencies so that trips begin and end in İstanbul. The 13-day trans-Kaçkar trips ($770) include the *yaylas* of Yukarı Kavron (the highest peak in the Kaçkars) and a rafting trip on the Çoruh River. Various week-long hiking or trekking packages run about $400-500. Small groups can be accommodated more cheaply with personal transportation and guides ($75 per day). RI-TUR's partner organization in İstanbul is **Interopa Travel** (interopa@escortbet.com).

ERZURUM ☎442

Turkey's highest city, Erzurum sits on an elevated plateau bounded by three mountain ranges. The mountains form the three river valleys that have ensured Erzurum's strategic importance for millennia, with the Aras winding east from the Palandöken mountains to the Caspian Sea, the Tortum Çay coursing north from the Karcapaþara through the Çoruh Valley to the Black Sea, and the Euphrates carving west from the Dumlu Mountains through Central Anatolia. At 1950m elevation, the climate tends toward extremes: winter snowfall is heavy and deep, and summers can be sweltering. Even in the temperate spring and fall, travelers should be prepared for flash hailstorms. When not hailing, however, the sky is clear and bright and the countryside pleasant, making Erzurum an excellent base for daytrips to the southern Georgian churches and the hot springs of Pasinler.

Early 13th-century Arz ar-Rum ("Land of the Romans"), as Erzurum was called by the Arabs and the Turks, prospered under the Selçuk Sultans as a center of trade. After the Mongol invasions, Ottoman Sultan Selim I seized the city in 1515. Russia even had its turn, occupying Erzurum in 1829, 1878, and again during the World War I. In July of 1919, Mustafa Kemal Atatürk chose Erzurum as the site for the Congress of National Delegates in which the principles of the Turkish nationalist movement were established. More recently, Erzurum has become a college town, with a young liberal student population challenging the conservatism of one of Turkey's most old-fashioned and religious cities.

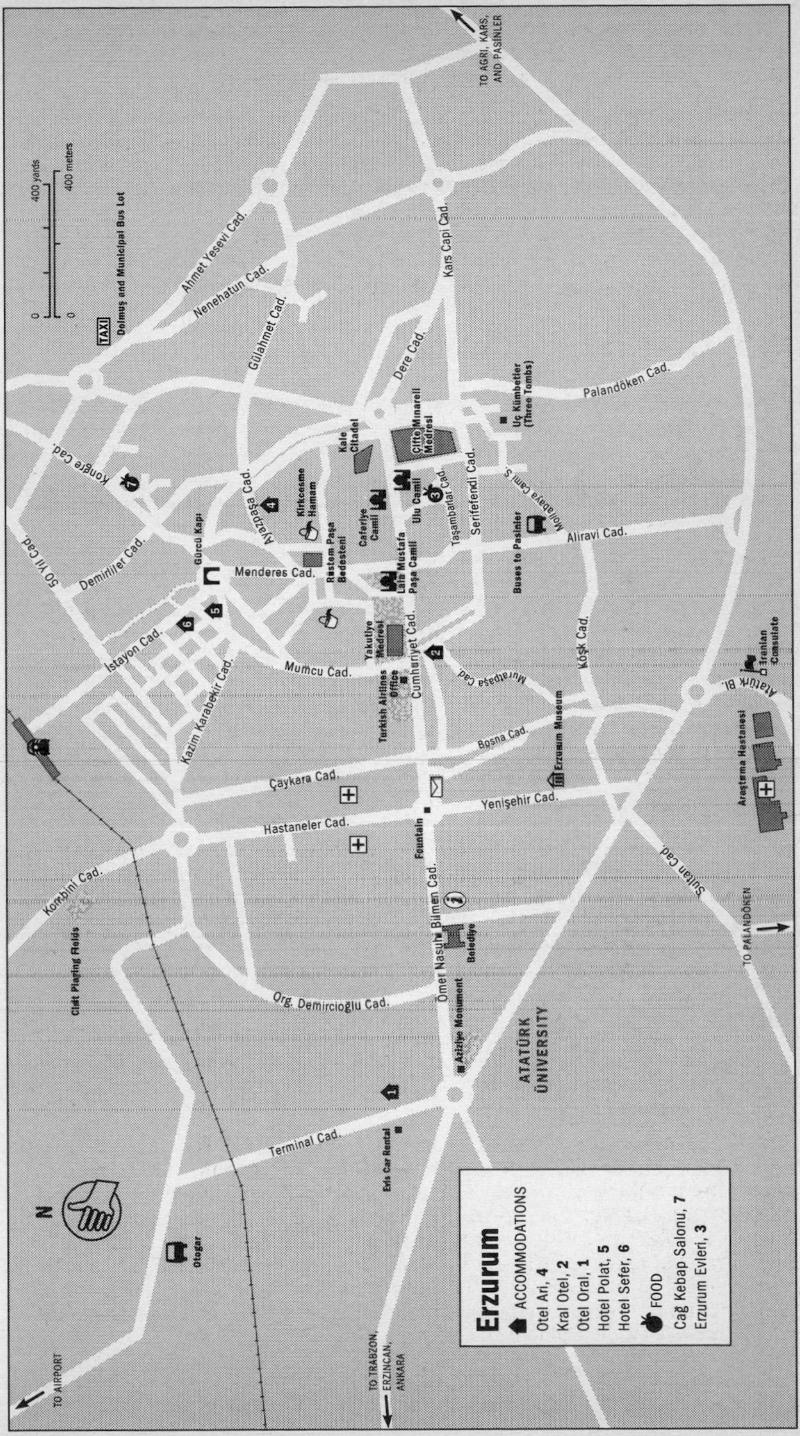
Erzurum
ACCOMMODATIONS
Otel Ari, 4
Kral Otel, 2
Otel Oral, 1
Hotel Polat, 5
Hotel Sefer, 6
FOOD
Cağ Kebap Salonu, 7
Erzurum Evleri, 3
N
400 yards
400 meters
0
TAXI Dolmuş and Municipal Bus Lot
TO AGRI, KARS, AND PASİNLER
TO AIRPORT
TO TRABZON, ERZINCAN, ANKARA
TO PALANDÖKEN
Ahmet Yesevi Cad.
Nenehatun Cad.
Gülahmet Cad.
Kars Capi Cad.
Dere Cad.
Palandöken Cad.
Kongre Cad.
50 Yıl Cad.
Demirtiler Cad.
Ayazpaşa Cad.
Menderes Cad.
Istayon Cad.
Kazim Karabekir Cad.
Mumcu Cad.
Cumhuriyet Cad.
Taşambatar Cad.
Serifefendi Cad.
Mollabeyra Cami S.
Aliravi Cad.
Muratpaşa Cad.
Köşk Cad.
Atatürk Bl.
Bosna Cad.
Çaykara Cad.
Yenişehir Cad.
Hastaneler Cad.
Kombini Cad.
Sultan Cad.
Ömer Nasuhi Bilmen Cad.
Org. Demircioğlu Cad.
Terminal Cad.
Gürcü Kapı
Kirkcesme Hamam
Rüstem Paşa Bedesteni
Caferiye Camii
Kale Citadel
Çifte Minareli Medresi
Ulu Camii
Üç Kümbetler (Three Tombs)
Lala Mustafa Paşa Camii
Yakutiye Medresi
Turkish Airlines Office
Buses to Pasinler
Erzurum Museum
Iranian Consulate
Araştırma Hastanesi
Fountain
Belediye
Cirit Playing Fields
Aziziye Monument
ATATÜRK ÜNIVERSITY
Eris Car Rental
Otogar

TRANSPORTATION

The **otogar** is 3km west of the city center. Most major bus companies provide free shuttles to the town center, and taxis (all have meters) cost approximately $2-3. The main **dolmuş** lot is a short walk northwest of Gürcü Kapı, but directly heading there means navigating a maze of side streets—it's easier but longer to go all the way north on İstasyon Cad. and follow the outer loop around.

Flights: Erzurum's **airport** (☎218 47 98) is a few kilometers out of town on the road to Erzincan, and offers flights to most major cities in Turkey.

Trains: The **train station** (☎218 47 98) is at the northern (downhill) end of the aptly-named İstasyon Cad. Erzurum is the penultimate stop on the line from İstanbul to Kars, with intermediate stops in Erzincan, Eskişehir, Sivas, Kayseri, Ankara.

Buses: Laid out like a miniature international airport, the **otogar** has 4 cardinal wings: 1 for arrivals, 1 for taxis, and 2 for departures. Not many of the major bus companies operate this far east, and the ones that do, including **Ağri** (☎235 20 86), **Dadaş** (☎218 27 88), and **Ulusoy** (☎234 24 06), have scaled-back service. Shop around; look at the bus you'll be taking whenever possible.

Destination	Company	Duration	Daily Times	Price
Adana	Esadaş	8hr.	3:30pm	$13
Ankara	Ağri	13hr.	5 per day 11:30am-7pm	$11
Antalya	Dadaş	18hr.	10:30am, 3:30pm	$17
Doğubeyazıt	Ağri	4hr.	4 per day 11am-4:30pm	$7
Erzincan	Dadaş	3hr.	10am, 2:30, 5pm	$4
İstanbul	Dadaş	19hr.	2, 4, 6, 6:30pm	$14
İzmir	Ağri	20hr.	4:30pm, 10pm	$17
Kars	Doğu Kars	3hr.	5 per day 8:30am-5pm	$5
Sivas	Dadaş	12hr.	5 per day 7:30am-8:30pm	$7
Trabzon	Ulusoy	5hr.	8am, 1, 6pm	$7
Van	Van Seyehat	6hr.	1pm	$9

Dolmuş: Dolmuş and minibuses leave from the **Gölbaş Semt Garajı,** 1km northwest of Gürcü Kapı, to destinations as far as Trabzon, Erzincan, and Kars (generally 9am-6pm). Buses are often faster and more comfortable, and not much more expensive.

ORIENTATION AND PRACTICAL INFORMATION

The heart of modern Erzincan is the park at the intersection of **Cumhuriyet Cad.** and **Mederes Cad.,** which contains the ornate **Ottoman Lala Paşa Camii** and the elaborate **Yakutiye Medrese** as well as a collection of *çay* gardens. Cumhuriyet Cad. runs east to the **Kale** citadel and the double minarets of the **Çifte Minareli Medrese,** and west toward the otogar and the airport. Menderes Cad. runs downhill past the **Rustem Paşa Kervanseray** to reach the **Gürcü Kapı** (Georgian Gate), the center of the old city. From here, **İstasyon Cad.** heads down to the train station.

Tourist Office: (☎218 56 97; fax 218 54 43), on Cemal Gürsel Cad., near the university, has an excellent city map. The director, Muhammet Yoksuç, speaks English. Open daily 8am-7:30pm.

Travel Agency: 11 Tours Travel (☎236 15 15), on Kazim Karabekir Cad., across from the Hotel Polat, organizes local excursions. Little English spoken.

Iranian Consulate: At the southern end of town on Atatürk Bul. (☎316 22 85), on the left about 100m uphill from the traffic circle. Expect a wait and some frustration: western travelers need clearance from Tehran, arranged in advance through a travel agency. M-Th 8:30am-12:30pm and 1:30-4:30pm; Su 8:30am-12:30pm; hours are erratic.

Banks: ATMs line Cumhuriyet Cad. The best place to change money is **TC Ziraat Bankası** on İstasyon Cad. at Gürü Kapı, 50m from Hotel Polat. No commission.

Hamam: Erzurum's finest hamams, the combined male and female establishments at **Kirkcesme** (☎218 23 41), Ayazpaşa Cad. Kirkcesme Sok. 5., just behind the Rustem Paşa Kervanseray, were closed for renovation at the time of publication. Try **Boyahane Hamam,** Cennet Çesme Karşısı Bakırcı M. (☎233 11 76), just south of the Yakutiye Medrese. Men only. $.50. Open daily 10am-7pm.

Pharmacies: On Hastaneler Cad. and Cumhuriyet Cad. Open 24hr.

Hospitals: Numune Hastahanesi is on the well-named Hastaneler Cad. (☎235 07 51). The university-affiliated **Aristirma Hastahanesi,** at the southern end of Atatürk Bul. (☎233 11 22), has several English-speaking physicians. Both are open 24hr.

Internet Access: The student area along Cumhuriyet Cad. is lined with internet cafes. Most charge $.50-.75 per hr. and are open until midnight. The **Cafe'M Lady & Man Internet Center,** at 3 Cumhuriyet Cad., 2nd fl., is open daily 8:30am-1am.

PTT: The main branch lies on Cumhuriyet Cad., 300m west of Menderes Cad. 24hr. international cash phones. No money orders on weekends. Open daily 8am-5:30pm.

Postal Codes: 25000, 25100, and 25200.

ACCOMMODATIONS

In Erzurum, it is worthwhile to avoid the cheapest establishments; for a little extra, you can enjoy the best hotels in town, which have been assigned stars by the Ministry of Tourism. Prices typically include breakfast and bath.

Kral Otel, 18 Erzincan Kapı (☎218 77 84; fax 218 69 73), just south of Cumhuriyet Cad. Possibly the most atmospheric hotel in Eastern Anatolia, the Kral is newly renovated to resemble an archeological excavation of Erzurum: pains have been taken to decorate each floor in the style of a different period: Urartian, Selçuk, Mongol, Ottoman, and modern. The suites are filled with amenities the weary traveler will appreciate, such as tiled bathtubs and writing desks. Singles $15, doubles $21, suites $30. MC/V.

Otel Ari, Ayazpaşa Cad. 22 (☎218 31 41). Central and clean, if a bit frayed at the edges. The best value at $5 per person.

Hotel Polat, 4 Kazim Karabekir Cad. (☎218 16 23), behind the TC Ziraat Bank, just south of Gürgü Kapı. Newly renovated and classy, with TV, phone, hot-water bath, and breakfast on the terrace. Singles $12; doubles $18; triples $24. MC/V.

Otel Oral, 6 Terminal Cad. (☎218 97 40), is the closest hotel to the otogar. Large lobby with huge leather chairs, and excellent but pricey rooms. Singles $25; doubles $38.

Hotel Sefer (☎218 67 14; fax 212 37 75), diagonally across from Polat at the corner on İstasyon Cad. Similar prices, but not quite as nice. Excellent rooms, though noisy at times. Singles $12; doubles $18; triples $24. MC/V.

FOOD

Erzurum has an excellent agricultural base, and the local cuisine reflects its history as a crossroads between Asia and the Mediterranean. Particularly tasty are the *cağ kebap* (prepared on a horizontal spit with lots of butter), *yaprak şarma* (grape leaves stuffed with spicy meat and vegetables), and *manti* (dumplings served with yogurt and tomato sauce). To satisfy your sweet tooth, visit Erzurum's *pastanesis*, overflowing with local pastries such as *kadayıf dolması*, made with angel-hair dough, fresh honey, and nuts.

The **Erzurum Evleri,** one of the most remarkable restaurants in all of eastern Turkey, lies off of Cumhuriyet Cad. in a side alley called Yuzbasi Sok. A carpeted and labyrinthine set of caverns, the Evleri has traditional *kilim* pillow seating on raised or sunken platforms with fountains and caged parakeets, and has served all varieties of Erzurum specialties since 1928. (☎233 20 31. Dinners $3-4. Open 9:30am-11:30pm.) **Güzelyurt,** 54 Cumhuriyet Cad., also serves up some of Erzurum's finest grub, with starched tablecloths and great service. (☎218 15 14. Dinners $3-4. Open 11:30am-midnight.) It is worth the trip out to try the *cağ kebap* at **Dadaş Meşhur Tortum Cağ Kebap Salonu,** 26 Kongre Cad. (☎218 97 26). Sit upstairs by the aquarium but beware: an order of *cağ* is bottomless, and the skewers will keep coming until you burst.

The student population also supports a modest cafe scene on the downhill half of Cumhuriyet Cad. **Salon Asya,** 27 Cumhuriyet Cad., 50m downhill from Menderes Cad., is a popular *kebap* and *lahmacun* spot. (☎212 12 43. Open 5am-1am.) **Donerci Canbaba,** No. 18, offers exemplary *iskender kebap*, with full meals for about $2-3. (☎234 30 13. Open 7:30pm-midnight.) Have dessert and tea at **Kılıçoğlu Sütiş,** 13 Cumhuriyet. (Most desserts under $1. Open until midnight.) Night owls wolf down dessert at **Serender Palisseria,** 32 Cumhuriyet Cad. (☎218 56 45. Open until 1:30am.) A fruit and vegetable market operates daily northeast of Gürcü Kapı.

SIGHTS

Though they span almost 4000 years of history, most of Erzurum's major sights can be explored in about five hours. Starting from the eastern side of the downtown area at the corner of Cumhuriyet Cad. and Tabriz Kapı, you can travel westward (toward the PTT) to the mosque, the castle, museum, and the *kervansaray*.

ÇİFTE MİNARELİ MEDRESE. In 1253, Hüdavend Hatun, the daughter of Sultan Alaeddin Keykubad, commissioned this Qur'anic school, the most lauded of Erzurum's sights. Its twin fluted minarets are tiled in blue and provide the inspiration for the school's name, "The Twin-Minaret Medrese." The rooms that flank the entrance portal on the upper and lower levels were once inhabited by students of the religious school. The Ministry of Tourism recently renovated the courtyard, constructing a high-class *çay* garden where locals and tourists alike find refuge from the summer heat. In back lies the Hatuniye Türbesi, the tomb of Hatun. *(At the eastern end of Cumhuriyet Cad. Çay garden open 8am-11pm.)*

UÇ KÜMBETLER. The more ornate of these three tombs, just south of the Çifte Minareli Medrese, is claimed to house the body of Emir Saluq, founder of the Saltid state. These three structures date from the early-13th to late-14th centuries and bear a distinctive ornamentation.

ULU CAMİİ. Built in 1179 by Melik Mehmet, one of the city's Saltıd rulers, this Selçuk mosque has a dramatically different architectural style from the neighboring Çifte Minareli Medrese. Dim lighting, internal columns, and an unusually low ceiling create a somber, reverent ambiance. An ingenious dome of layered wooden slats lies before an impressive skylight adorned with *muqarnas* (decorative element on mosque walls). A recent restoration has revitalized prayer traffic, so remove your shoes as you enter.

KALE. In the 5th century, Emperor Theodosius II built this citadel at the city's highest point (about 2000m). With each war, the fortress was demolished, and then rebuilt and fortified by the winners. Inside are cannons with Russian and Ottoman inscriptions, a *mescit* (small mosque) from the 12th century that looks like a *kümbet* (tomb), and a clock tower. The clock tower provides splendid views of Erzurum and the vast landscape beyond. Bring a flashlight to explore the dark, steep stairway that climbs to the top. *(From Ulu Camii, head directly north across the street, and walk upward. Open daily 8am-5:30pm. $.50.)*

OTTOMAN MOSQUES. Continue west on Cumhuriyet Cad. to two Ottoman mosques: the **Caferiye Camii** (1645), on the right one block before Menderes Cad., and the **Lala Mustafa Paşa Camii** (1563), at the intersection with Menderes Cad. Lala Mustafa Paşa, the conqueror of Cyprus, commissioned this mosque during his reign over Erzurum. Next door is the **Yakutiye Medrese,** surrounded by fountains, shade trees, and *çay* tables. Lion reliefs and ornate geometric designs decorate the school's west entrance. Today, the *medrese* contains the city's best **museum.** Ethnographic exhibits are displayed in former student rooms. Features include Ottoman arms, ornaments, ceramics, dervish costumes, and manuscripts. *(Museum open M-Sa 9am-noon and 1:30-6:15pm. $1.)*

RÜSTEM PAŞA KERVANSARAY. Because Erzurum was such an important intercontinental trading city, Süleyman the Magnificent's Grand Vizier funded the construction of this *kervansaray*, which served as a travelers' rest stop. Today it houses the **Rüstem Paşa Bedesteni,** a jewelry market with a focus on obsidian, or "black amber," a black volcanic stone mined 150km away in Oltu. Obsidian is often crafted into *tesbih* (prayer beads or worry beads). Prices for the beads start at $5.

ERZURUM MUSEUM. For the intrepid visitor willing to walk uphill along Yenişehir Cad. to reach the museum, a mammoth skeleton and two millennia of coins, pots, and other antiquities await. In the last room, a fractured skull accompanies a starkly one-sided account of the Turkish-Armenian conflicts (see **Armenians**, p. 30). *(Open Tu-Su 8am-5pm. $1.50; students $1.)*

DAYTRIPS FROM ERZURUM

NORTH: HAHO AND THE ÇORUH VALLEY. About 25km north on the road to **Tortum** (60km), the road passes **Dumlu mountain,** the source of the mighty Euphrates. A half-hour dolmuş ride will take you to the village of **Güngömuz;** cross the brook and the trail starts at the base of the hill to your left, climbing the south face before turning east to climb to the **Spring of Euphrates.** The hike is not difficult and takes roughly 2½ hours in each direction, with beautiful views of the valley as a reward at the top. Buy local bread, cheese, and produce from farmers in the village.

Continuing north, the highway passes **Güzel Yayla Pass** at 2010m and descends into the Georgian **Çoruh Valley** (see **The Çoruh Valley,** p. 432), known for its four **Georgian Churches.** The climate and geological strata change rapidly, with fantastic buttes rising out of the Tortum Çay riverbed. About 26km north of Tortum, a humped bridge on the left signals the road to **Bağbaşı,** a village 8km off of the highway which houses **Haho,** one of the best-preserved Georgian churches. Bear right after the bridge and follow the main track to Bağbaşı; Haho is farther up the road.

Haho was built toward the end of the 10th century, and much of the church and monastery owe their good condition to the fact that they have served as the Bağbaşı mosque for several centuries. At the unusual domed gate, a walnut tree presides over a small cemetery; the courtyard is dominated by the 16-sided pointed dome of the spire and the vivid stone carvings of eagles and flying rams that flank the building. Multicolored, glazed enamel tiling is visible on the top of the spire, while the main roof is protected by sheets of aluminum and lower roofs are covered with a thatch of living grass and wildflowers. Behind the main church is the ruined **Chapel of Mary,** which stands over the remains of a tunnel rumored to connect to the other churches in the valley.

Enter the **gallery** from the south, and while taking off your shoes to enter the church, use a flashlight to examine the allegorical stone carvings that flank the church entrance, still the source of much speculation for the local *imam.* To the left, a haloed figure with crossed spears stands atop a **gryphon** and **lion.** On the right, another haloed figure with a small church in his hand rests above **Jonas,** half-eaten in the whale's mouth, being nibbled on the head by two large fish. The carving can also be interpreted to represent the bounty of Christ, rescuing man from the teeth of sin. Inside the church proper, patches of blue fresco in the dome and the apse represent angels and apostles. *(Dolmuş to Bağbaşı leave Erzurum (9am, return 1pm.). The church and mosque are free, but a $1 donation is recommended. A few kilometers down the road, several trout farms have campsites and bungalows, as well as fresh fish lunch.)*

About 5km north of the bridge to Haho, just before the highway crosses the Tortum Çay, a small access road on the right leads to a **Genoese Fortress** that dominates the valley, dating back to when the Genoese controlled the final portion of the Silk Road from Erzurum to the Black Sea. A trail climbs from the access road to a grassy spot near the fortress. farther north on the road to Yusufeli is the Georgian cathedral of **Öşk Vank** in the village of Çamıyamaç and the milky **Tortum Gölü,** from whose 50m waterfall issues the **Çoruh River.**

EAST ALONG THE ARAS RIVER: PASİNLER. A fortress and hot springs tempt travelers to wander about 38km east of Erzurum to **Pasinler,** where 14th-century **Hasan Kale** towers over the town. Originally an Armenian structure, the fortress was rebuilt by the Uzon Hasan (1433-1478), ruler of the White Sheep, a Turkmen tribal federation. On arrival, plan a 40min. round-trip hike from the town. Although the views of the four hot-spring hamams on the other side of the highway below are still impressive, the fortress has been steadily crumbling from neglect and disuse. **Sifali Banyölü Otel** (☎661 32 16) offers private-room baths ($3 per hr.) and doubles with mineral bath ($12). The two-star **Hotel Kale** starts at $3.50 for Roman bath, sauna, and gym. (Private baths $5 per hr. Rooms $7.50 per person.) The pleasant **Büuük Kaplicse Hamam** is a more social option. (Open for women M-Sa 10am-7pm; men M-Sa 7:30-10:30pm, Su all day. Women $.20; men $.50.)

Pasinler has seen better days, and the dusty streets have little to offer the freshly-bathed visitor. The town center is the **Sehitler Parki** at Cumhuriyet Cad., joined to the highway by Belediye Cad. Next to the highway, Belediye Cad. contains the Erzurum **otogar,** the **Aymer Hypermarket, Sanko Bilardo Internet Cafe,** and the best restaurants: **Hajibaba Lok., Saray Lok.** (☎661 47 00), and **Ozlem Lok.** (☎661 34 84), serving standard fare for $1-3. *(Pasinler Beledesi (☎661 35 01) shuttles between Erzurum and Pasinler (every 45min.). It loops through town and can be hailed at the bus stop on İstasyon Cad., opposite Hotel Sefer, or from 500m south of Cumhuriyet Cad.)*

EAST: TERCAN. Tercan is the ideal place to break the 2½hr. journey between Erzurum and Erzincan. Across the road from the gas station, Kervanseray Cad. winds uphill to the splendid **Mama Hatun Türbesi,** built in 1182, which holds the remains of Mama Hatun, a Selçuk princess who helped Saladin conquer this portion of Anatolia. In each of the eight half-circles that form the structure's outer walls, a lesser member of the nobility is buried. At the center is a *mihrab* atop a vaulted tomb. If it is open, head through the door and down the steps to see the sarcophagus, covered in green felt. Above it, the prayer room is still used by pilgrims and pious Muslims, especially women. A winding staircase in the wall across from the *türbesi* leads to the roof and a majestic view of the valley. The ruins of an inn and the kervanseray complete the complex; the kervanseray is scheduled to be renovated by 2002. On the way back down, grab a picnic lunch from the fresh produce bazaar in front of the kervanseray, or stop at the **Kardeşler Lokantasi,** 76 Kervanseray Cad., which is crowded with locals and offers a broad menu, including a delicious *musaka.* (☎441 36 85. Full meal $1-3. Open until 10pm.) If the climb to the *türbesi* has you feeling grimy, the local hamam is right next to the kervanseray. (☎746 4413. Open 4pm-midnight, women only Sat.) There is no reason to stay in Tercan overnight; for those stranded, however, the **Kervanseray Otel,** located diagonally across the highway from the gas station in the white Belediye building, offers clean rooms with bath and hot water. (☎441 25 88. Singles $5; doubles $10.) *(Buses between Erzurum and Erzincan are frequent. Both $2.)*

SOUTH: PALONDÖKEN. Palondöken, 10km of Erzurum, is home to some of Erzurum's best **ski slopes.** The ski season runs from late December to March, but serious skiers can arrange to ski the upper slopes as late as June. In winter, frequent transportation connections are available, but during the summer you'll have to either call a resort to send a car, or pay for a taxi ($19 round-trip). The **Dedeman Hotel** (☎316 24 14), right on the slopes, has a four-star rating and a price to match.

ERZİNCAN ☎446

Erzincan lies in the fertile Euphrates River valley, surrounded by wildflowers and poplar groves and bordered by the Munzur range to the south and the Western extensions of the Kaçkars to the north. An ancient city robbed of its quaintness by a series of natural disasters, Erzincan has quickly rebuilt itself: in 1939, it suffered one of the most devastating earthquakes in Turkish history, which killed more than 30,000 people. A later quake in 1993 (plus a few in between) destroyed most of the buildings of historical interest. The town, however, has recovered rapidly, and commercial and civil industry are booming throughout the downtown area. Students from all over Turkey attend Erzincan's Atatürk University, lending the town a vibrant and somewhat cosmopolitan air. A clean and energetic town, Erzincan is an ideal base for exploring the natural beauty of the upper Euphrates valley.

TRANSPORTATION. The **otogar** is at the far eastern end of town, where Fevsıpaşa Cad. meets the highway. This small, new station boasts a tiny **PTT** and connections to almost everywhere in Turkey. **Buses** travel to: **Adana** (Turay, 12hr., 4pm, $11); **Ankara** (Dadaş; 11hr., 10:30am, 1pm; $17); **Bodrum** (Palandökken, 23hr., 7:30pm, $28); **Diyarbakır** (Turay, 14hr., 12:30pm, $17); **Erzurum** (Esadas, 3hr., 6 per day 10am-4:30pm, $4); **Gaziantep** (Turay, 12hr., 11:30pm, $16); **İstanbul** (Dadaş, 16hr., 4pm, $20); **Kayseri** (Turay, 6hr., 4pm, $19); **Konya** (Palandökken, 11hr., 7:30pm, $18); **Malatya** (Turay; 7hr.; 12:30pm, 11pm, $17); **Şanlıurfa** (Turay, 14hr., 11:30pm, $19); **Sivas** (Yes; 4hr.; 1, 4, 8pm; $4). **Dolmuş** and **minibuses** leave from the dolmuş stop diagonally opposite the otogar. This is the best way to get to **Altintepe** ($.20 each way) and other local destinations. The **train station,** midway between Sivas and Erzurum on the Ankara line, is on the southernmost end of Şubat Cad. One train runs daily in each direction.

ORIENTATION AND PRACTICAL INFORMATION. Erzincan's center is an open pavilion, from which spread **Fevsıpaşa Cad.** to the east, **Ordu Cad.** to the north, **Halitpaşa Cad.** to the west, and **Şubat Cad.** to the south. Traveler services, including 24hr. police, ATMs, and internet cafes can be found near the intersection of these four streets. The **otogar** is on the easternmost end of Fevsıpaşa Cad., and the two blocks between the otogar and the town center contain the best hotels and restaurants. The north end of the central pavilion hosts the **Erzincan Museum** and the **Gemi İs-Merkesi,** an unusual ocean-liner-shaped civic center popular with students. **Atatürk University** is 1km north on Ordu Cad. The **tourist office,** 19 Fevsıpaşa Cad. (☎223 37 92), is in an alley across from Pamuk Bank near the central pavilion on the third floor. **Doğa Sporları Derneği** (☎224 24 42; e-turturizmşemiltd.net) is housed in Elektric Market No. 113 in the Kızılay Işhani building at the corner of Fevsıpaşa Cad. and Şurat Cad. Ask for Rifat Ekinci; he can organize climbing, rafting, skiing, and biking trips. **Grocery stores** line Halitpaşa Cad. The **PTT** is two blocks north of the pavilion on Ordu Cad. (Open M-Sa 7am-11pm.) **Postal code**: 24000.

ACCOMMODATIONS. Many hotels have sprouted up on the two-block stretch of Fevzıpaşa Cad. The following hotels are all close to the otogar, and all offer more or less the same amenities, including TV and hot water showers. **Otel Karakaya,** 40B Fevzipaşa Cad., boasts a lounge with a fish tank and plush furniture. It's clean, comfortable, quiet, and cheap. (☎214 36 73. Singles $6, doubles $10, triples $14.) For a little extra, try the new **Hotel Hanedan,** 34/B Fevzipaşa Cad. (☎224 24 04. Singles $9; doubles $11.) The **Yeni Kiliçar Oteli,** 41 Fevsıpaşa Cad. (☎223 13 80), is dark but clean and well-priced, and **Kervan Otel,** 96 Fevsıpaşa Cad. (☎214 13 64; fax 224 14 13) is closest to the otogar, with the same prices. (Singles $4, with bath $8; doubles $8, with bath $10; triples $9, with bath $12.)

FOOD. Erzincan offers little in the way of *haute cuisine*, but dozens of *kebapçis* and *salonus* line Fevzıpaşa Cad. The clean and well-lit **Evin Kevser,** 14A Fevsıpaşa. Cad. offers decent roasted vegetables in addition to *kebaps* and *lahmecuns*, and features a fountain full of small turtles. (☎212 23 90. Meal $1-3. Open until 10pm.) The **Derya Restoran,** 21/C Fevzıpaşa Cad. (☎223 77 17), offers similar fare until midnight. Popular **Sariyer Işkende Salonu,** 18A Halitpaşa Cad. (☎224 04 36), on the other side of the pavilion, is cheerful and open 24hr. For a step up, **Beyaz Saray,** Vakitler İshani Kat No. 1 (☎224 44 31), on the eastern side of Ordu Cad., offers a more refined atmosphere and particularly flavorful *merkeci* (lentil soup) at bargain prices ($2-4 for a full meal). Of Erzincan's many *çay salonu*, the pillowed and carpeted cave of the **Cafe Çapari,** located on the south mezzanine of the Gemi Is-Merkesiare, is popular with students. What little nightlife Erzincan offers can be found at a few dry discos such as the **Mobidik Cafe,** 29 Hükümet Cad., across from the western side of the Gemi Is-Merkesi, where you can dance to *halay* and Europop under a single disco ball until about 11pm.

WARGAMES The isolated plateaus of Eastern Anatolia have preserved many traditions forgotten by the rest of Turkey; doubtless one of the most striking is the local pastime of *cirit* (pronounced *gee-reet*), still popular in the upper Euphrates valley. Dating back to Selçuk times, when the connections between sport and battle were a bit less abstract, *cirit* is a sort of polo with teeth. Two teams of three to six players on horseback hurl javelins at each other–with intent to hit–as they gallop at full speed across the steppe. The javelins are blunt, but players must be excellent horsemen to compete: to execute one of the key moves, the *eyer boþaltmak* (literally, "to empty the saddle"), a player shifts his entire body onto the side of his galloping horse to evade the incoming missile. Catching an opponent's javelin is the supreme move, but the overall scoring system is more complicated than cricket, as players are docked points for "getting off horse without permission," or simply not attacking correctly. *Cirit* is played regularly on Sundays in the fields outside of Erzurum and Erzincan. For more information contact the Turkish Cirit Federation in Ankara (☎312 331 61 93).

SIGHTS. Altintepe,"the Golden Hill," is an important Urartian site, discovered in 1938 during the construction of the eastern portion of the Turkish railroad (see **From Hittites to Hellenes,** p. 6). Believed to have been constructed between the 7th and 8th centuries BC, Altintepe was once a substantial palace and temple. Resist the taxi temptation and take a $.40 dolmuş from diagonally opposite the otogar. To climb to the ruins from the dolmuş drop-off, you must first cross an irrigation canal intermittently guarded by Sivas-Cangol sheepdogs, then circle around to the back side of the mound to find a climbable aspect. The 5min. ascent offers the intrepid a magnificent view of the Euphrates valley from battlements, platforms, and tumbled columns On the way back, visit the hot springs at **Ekşisu**, where *cirit* is played most Sundays in the spring and summer (See **Wargames,** p. 444).

The **Erzincan Museum,** located in the center of the pavilion, is an elegant high-ceilinged affair bedecked with photographs of the city before the catastrophic 1939 earthquake. Look for the spry octogenarian **Mustafa Nçar**, local musicologist and director of the museum, who has organized a five room suite of his personal effects (including coins, gramophones, musical instruments, textiles, agricultural equipment, woodcarvings, and ox-dung beehouses) as a chronicle of Erzincan's last century. (☎214 80 21. Open M, W 9am-noon; Sa 9am-noon and 2-5pm.)

Erzincan is an excellent base to explore the many **outdoor activities** available in the upper Euphrates valley, including the renowned ski resort at **Akbulut** (☎611 33 88). The tourist office can arrange day trips in the majestic **Munzur mountains,** a 30min. ride from town. Particularly notable is the two-day **paragliding** package: one day of training, and then one day to climb to a suitable spot with a guide and jump off the ridge to the verdant valley below. **Rafting** tours of the upper Euphrates, including grade V rapids, are also available.

KARS ☎474

Formerly an important nexus for rail travel between Turkey and the Soviet Union, Kars has become the last stop on the northeastern railroad thanks to tensions with neighboring Armenia. Isolated on the rugged steppe by the commercial routes that pass the city to the east, Kars combines old-world charm with the dusty realities of modern life. Horse-drawn carts drive alongside automobiles, and a few stately 19th-century buildings founder under the smog and dust of new construction projects. Kars was occupied by the Russians from 1877 to 1920, and their legacy remains in the straight, cobblestone streets and fading Belle Epoque architecture. Tree-lined streets, public parks, and well-lit fountains make central Kars a pleasant place to walk around at night; the main attraction, however, is the Armenian ruins complex at Ani, just 48km to the west.

TRANSPORTATION

Flights: THY, 80 Atatürk Cad. (☎212 38 38), has flights to **Ankara, Diyarbakır, Gaziantep, İstanbul, İzmir,** and **Trabzon.** An airport minibus leaves from the office (daily 8:30am, $1.50).

Buses: Doğu Kars (☎223 33 33), across from the bus station, **Kafkas Kars** (☎223 29 55), and the new **Kars Turgutreis** (☎223 60 38) serve the area. Buses run to: **Ankara** (16hr., 5 per day 9:30am-5pm, $18); **Artvin** (5hr., 8:30am, $9); **Doğubeyazıt** (5hr., 8:30am, $7); **Erzurum** (3hr., 5 per day 9:30am-5:30pm, $5); **İstanbul** (20hr., 5 per day 9:30am-5pm, $27); **Sivas** (10hr., 5 per day 9:30am-5pm, $14); **Trabzon** (8hr.; 8:30, 11:30am; $14); **Van** (7hr., 8:30am, $11); and **Yusufeli** (4hr., 8:30am, $5). All companies have a free bus from their main office to the otogar, 1hr. before departure.

Trains: One per day to **İstanbul,** via **Erzincan, Erzurum, Sivas,** and **Ankara.** Schedules and prices vary; check at the tourist office.

Dolmuş: Eski Otogar, the old bus station 2 blocks east of town center, has become the minibus and dolmuş lot for local destinations. A daily minibus or two leave for **Trabzon** ($12) and **Yusufeli/Artvin** ($6). **Doğubeyazıt** cannot be reached directly. Dolmuş leave for **Iğdır** (every hr. 6am-5pm, $4), where you can connect to other destinations. Dolmuş depart when full to **Sarikamis** (6am-5pm, $1.50), **Selim,** and **Ardahan.**

ORIENTATION AND PRACTICAL INFORMATION

Perhaps the most visible mark of Kars's Russian occupation is its grid-like street plan: main streets run north-south and east-west, forming blocks and long, straight avenues. For the traveler, the intersection of east-west **Fait Bey Cad.** and north-south **Atatürk Cad.** contains most needs and interests. Nearby, the pedestrian mall of **Kasım Bey Cad.** and **Karadağ Cad.** features fountains, shops, and restaurants. To the north the **Kars Kale** towers over the city. To the south of the city are the train tracks. The new **otogar** is 3km east of town and the **airport** 6km to the east.

Tourist Office: (☎212 68 17), 2nd fl. of a gray building on the corner of Karadağ Cad. and Atatürk Cad. in the downtown business district. Open daily 8:30am-5:30pm. Limited English, but helpful photocopied city maps, glossy brochures, and Ani applications (see **Ani,** p. 447).

Banks: Türkiye İş Bankası and **Vaktifbank,** by the corner of Halıt Paşa Cad. and Atatürk Cad., cash traveler's checks. Open 9:30am-12:30pm and 1:30-5:30pm. Many other banks downtown change cash and have 24hr. Cirrus/Plus/MC/V **ATMs.**

Hamams: Kars's two oldest functioning hamams, the **Muradiye** and the **Topçiağlu,** are at the north end of Atatürk Cad., by the old stone bridge at the foot of the citadel. Both are open as early as 5am, and serve men and women alternately; the schedule changes each day, so check the sign over the door (*"erkek"* means men, *"kadın"* means women).

Police and **Tourist Police:** ☎212 47 00.

Hospital: (☎212 56 68 or 212 56 69), on Gazi Ahmet Muhtar Paza Cad. (G.A.M.P Cad.). Large, clean, and open 24hr. **Pharmacies** are on almost every block.

Internet Access: Of Kars's countless internet cafes, **Karizm Internet Cafe** (☎223 61 29), on Fait Bey Cad. at the intersection with Atatürk Cad., has cheap, fast connections. ($.75 per hr.) Open until 1am.

PTT: Main branch on Ordu Cad. between Karadağ Cad. and Fait Bey Cad. There's a side branch on Kazim Bey Cad., on the pedestrian mall. Mail 7am-11pm; 24hr. phones.

ACCOMMODATIONS AND FOOD

Most hotels in Kars are clean, comfortable, and noisy. **Hotel Kervansaray,** 204 Fait Bey Cad. (☎223 19 90), and neighboring **Hotel Nursuray** (☎223 13 64), are super-budget options, centrally located with basic rooms ($4 per person), clean sheets, and shared baths (showers $1). Back rooms are quieter. Another good bet is **Hotel Yıl-**

maz, 146 Küçük Cad., which has well-maintained rooms equipped with showers, TVs, and phones ($7 per person). Its sister hotel **Ahmet Yilmaz,** next door at No. 148, offers similar accommodations. (☎212 17 22. $6 per person.) For a good night's stay in a quieter part of town, try the brand-new **Sim-Er Hotel,** at the new river park, which has luxurious rooms with cable TV, minibars, and tiled baths. (☎212 72 41; fax 212 01 68. Singles $20, doubles $32.)

Kars's cuisine is famous for *çiçek bali*, a kind of thick flower honey, which locals eat by the plateful along with bread, yogurt, and yellow *kaşa* cheese at *kahlvati salonu* (breakfast houses) all over town. The **Bulut Kahlvati Salonu,** next to the Hotel Kervanseray, is a local favorite. As with hotels, restaurants in Kars are cheap and decent, with a couple of splendid exceptions. **Ocakbaşı Restoran,** 176 Atatürk Cad., serves delicious soups, *tavuk dolma* (chicken, walnut, and melted cheese) and *kunëfe* (a birdsnest of hazelnuts, cheese, and honey) for dessert. (☎212 00 56 Full meal $3-4.) **Sema Danla Pastanesi,** 9 Fait Bey Cad., has a broad menu for under $2, with laid-back wicker-chair settings and a trendy college crowd one block east of the Hotel Kervansaray. Vegetarians can ask for *kaşarli pide*, a sort of cheese-*pide*-pizza with some vegetables and egg, at this upbeat salon-style eatery. (☎223 21 18. Open daily 8am-10pm.) A lunchtime crowd always gathers at **Cafe Kristal,** 181 Atatürk Cad., for its cheerful atmosphere, tasty cuisine, and good *döner kebap* (☎223 22 67. Full meal $3.50. Open 8am-10pm.) The **Hukukçular Restaurant** (☎223 29 32), one flight up at the southeast corner of Ordu Cad. and Fait Bey Cad., has a full bar, good *mezes*, and a flair for fish. For nightlife, try **The Planet Cafe Bar,** No. 102 Atatürk Cad. (☎212 69 03), a classy affair with live music on the weekends.

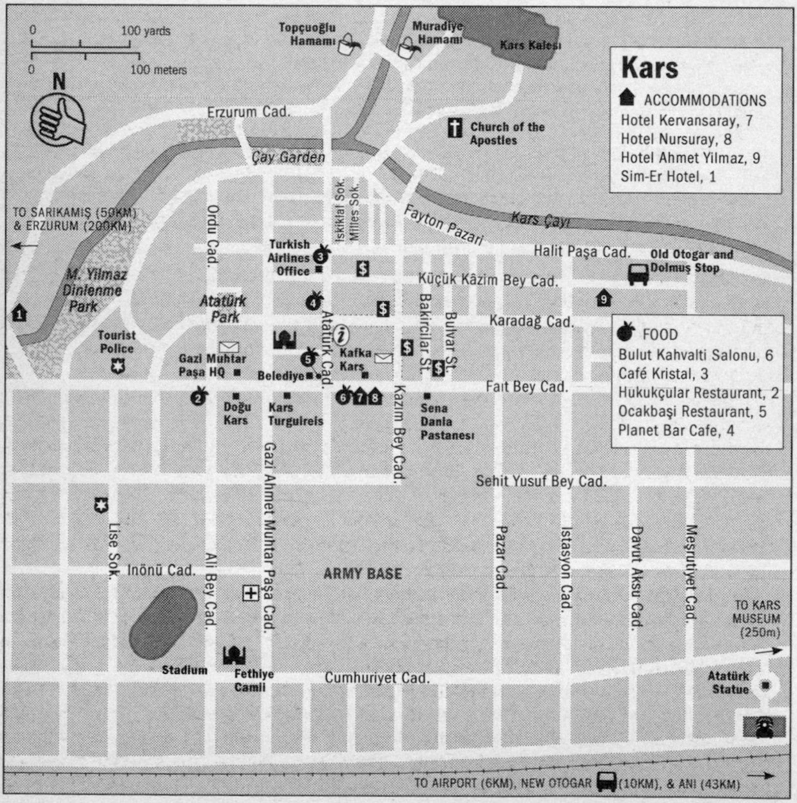

SIGHTS

Most of Kars's sights are clustered at the north end of town, where the **Kars Kale** overlooks the city. It was constructed by either the Armenians or the Selçuks in 1152. After Tamerlane destroyed the building in 1386, Sultan Murat III had it reconstructed in 1579; it remained in service until the 20th century. Inside the citadel, the **Kale Cafe** serves simple meals in a *kilim*-lined room off the old armory. The nearby shrine of **Celal Babab** attracts devotees. (Open daily 9am-6pm. Free.)

On your way up to the Kale, follow the gray path to the **Taş Köprü,** a stone bridge dating from the 15th century and flanked by three **hamams** from the same period (two of which still are still functional; see **Hamams,** above). On the right during the ascent is the **Church of the Apostles,** built by the Bagratid King Abas and repaired by the Ottomans. Today, the church stands abandoned and usually locked. The 12 apostles are still visible, carved in relief on the lower section of the dome. Kars's **museum,** on Cumhuriyet Cad., a 20-minute walk to the south of town, is definitely worth a visit. It features local pottery from 5000 BC to the present as well as Urartian jewelry, photos from local sites, and two tall wooden doors from a church with an interesting eagle relief. Upstairs are *kilims,* old metalworks, weaponry, and ornate embroidered dresses. A visit to the museum is required to obtain a **permit** to visit **Ani,** so you might as well give yourself an extra hour on the way to enjoy the exhibits. (☎212 14 30. Open 8:30am-5:30pm. $3.)

DAYTRIP FROM KARS: THE ANCIENT CITY OF ANİ

Because of its sensitive border location, all visitors to Ani must obtain a ***permit*** *($4, students $1.50). The application process is a complex song-and-dance that begins with a form in the tourist office, which is then stamped by tourist police before a final presentation at the museum where the permits are issued. Passports are required at each point; however, they need not be presented in person. Drivers usually take passengers through the entire permit process (8am-4pm).* ***Çelil Ersözoğlu*** *(☎223 63 23; mobile 0532 226 39 66) is a helpful English-speaking tour guide who will most likely find you before you find him. Staying overnight at Ani is illegal, as is straying, pointing cameras toward Armenia, or climbing Ani's southern fortress (with Turkish flag atop). Jandarma at the gate will check your ticket and hold your passport for the duration of your visit. Heading left from the entrance and walking clockwise makes a 3km circuit that touches all the ruins; allow 3hr. to comfortably visit them all.*

Spread over 5 sq. kilometers on a gorge-bounded peninsula between Turkey and Armenia, Ani's colossal ruins swarm with Turkish military. But don't let that dissuade you: even without the ruins, the 45km ride to Ani is spectacular: wild horses graze over the green landscape dotted with purple and yellow mountain flowers. On a clear day, Mount Ararat (5137m) rises formidably in the distance.

The name Ani comes from the name of the Persian goddess Anahid, who was worshipped by the Urartians at this site. **King Ashot III** (952-977) chose this spot for the capital of Bagratid Armenia. Christian Ani prospered on trade, growing to rival Constantinople. The Byzantines took control in 1045, followed by the Selçuks in 1064. Power traded hands repeatedly between Armenians and Byzantines, until the city was seized two centuries later by the Mongols, who left their mark upon the city's architecture. Harsh weather destroyed many of the great buildings, leaving only the most majestic as a testament to past greatness.

Ani is a triangular plateau wedged southward into the junction of the Alaçay and Arpaçay river canyons, on the west and east, respectively. Armenia lies visibly on the east bank of the Arpaçay. Visitors enter through the **Aslan Kapısı (Lion's Gate),** in the middle of the 10m tall, 2500m long walls. Built in 972, the Lion's Gate is the last remaining of the original seven outer gates along this double wall. After entering through the Lion's Gate, you'll pass through the **Middle Gate,** one of seven gates along the city's inner walls. Heading left along the southeast path will bring you first to the **Church of the Holy Redeemer.** Built in 1034, the church was struck by lightning in 1957, and is now a half-shell with massive piles of rubble. There's a relief of an angel resting over an Armenian cross, with an excavated linseed mill nearby. Inside the half-dome is the **acoustic chimney** used to pipe in music from an unseen choir; traces of a fresco of the Last Supper are visible in an upper archway.

Continue south and pass an 11th-century Selçuk **hamam,** and then head down the slope to find one of the three **Churches of St. Gregory (Tigorn Honents)** that gazes over a ledge onto the Arpaçay River. The conical spire is evocative of Georgian churches, but the many ornate and allegorical friezes carved on all sides—including birds, flowers, tigers, harpies, and other real and imagined creatures—suggest a distinctly Armenian architecture. The entrance preserves **frescoes** of Jesus on the Cross and the Seraphim. Inside, the churches' distinctive frescoes defy scarring graffiti to dazzle the eye in blues, reds, golds, and greens. To the right of the entrance is a depiction of the disquieting saga of **St. Gregory the Illuminator,** who suffered various tortures for his Christian beliefs (the rack, burnings, beatings with thorns, being chained to a volcano with scorpions and snakes), each lovingly rendered on the wall. Other frescoes detail the life of **Hrpsime the Nun** and illustrate traditional Biblical stories such as the Resurrection of Lazarus. Lining all the frescoes are geometrical, floral, and animal motifs still used in local *kilim* production.

Down the valley over a slim path past the **Silk Road** stand the remains of the **Covenant of the Virgins,** from which you can see Armenia and an old bridge across the Arpaçay River. Unfortunately, both sights are currently off-limits to tourists. Walking farther south leads to the largest building in Ani, the domeless **Cathedral of Virgin Mary,** built from 939 to 1001 and designed by Titridates, who previously had collaborated in the restoration of İstanbul's Aya Sofia after earthquake damage. The Selçuks converted the cathedral to a mosque during their reign, but under Christian leaders it reverted to its role as a church. A passage to the left of the altar leads up to a private room; bring a flashlight for safe exploration. Farther southwest lies the **Menüçehir Camii,** built in 1072 and said to be the first mosque in Anatolia. Its climbable minaret bears the uniquely non-Selçuk inscription of Allah's name, and its ceilings bear ornate geometrical motifs. From the mosque's window are views of the river and Armenia. Above the mosque, the 4th-century **citadel** still acts as a strategic location for Turkish soldiers and is often off-limits. Just south of the mosque, a **palace** is currently being excavated.

The rotunda-style **Church of St. Gregory (Abighamrets),** lying northwest of the citadel, has an interesting six-niche design inside. In the center of the plateau is the **Church of the Holy Apostles,** once converted into a *kervansaray* and now mostly rubble. Note the variety of Islamic geometric designs and *muqarnas* (stalactite ornamentations). To the northwest is the massive, circular **Church of St. Gregory,** built by the Armenian King Gegik I, and the **Selçuk Palace.** On your way back to the Middle Gate, try to find the four columns of the old Zoroastrian **fire temple.** Ani's grounds also contain roads, storefronts, and houses; cliffside caves suggest entry points to a vast **underground city** that lay beneath the entire walled compound.

SOUTHEAST ANATOLIA

DOĞUBEYAZIT ☎472

Turkey's portion of the Silk Road ends at Doğubeyazıt, a frontier town that has lured increasing numbers of independent travelers to its ruins and rugged terrain. Flanked to the north by the majestic double peaks of **Ağri Dağ** (Mt. Ararat) and to the south by the hilltop **İşak Paşa Palace,** the valley between teems with traffic from Turkey to Iran. High and dry, with a frontier feel and a dusty, windblown main street, Doğubeyazıt also represents the northeastern border of Turkey's Kurdistan—the "nation" of ethnic Kurds that stretches into Iraq. Visitors in late April may get a chance to take part in the annual Kurdish *nevros* festival, but visitors can enjoy warm Kurdish hospitality and traditional cuisine year-round.

TRANSPORTATION. Most visitors arrive either at the **otogar,** at the east end of Belediye Cad., or the **minibus stop,** at the other end of the same street. No major bus lines operate out of Doğubeyazıt; smaller companies offer limited and indirect service to: **Adana** (13hr., $18); **Ağri** (1hr., $2); **Ankara** (12hr., $20); **Antalya** (22hr., $27); **Erzurum** (4hr., $6); **Gaziantep** (9½hr., $17); **İstanbul** (20hr., $22); **Malatya** (9hr., $15); **Mersin** (16hr., $18); **Sivas** (8hr., $14); **Şanliurfa** (8hr., $15). **Minibuses** leave for **Van** (3hr., $5) via **Çaldiran** ($3) and **Kars** (4hr., $6) via **Iğdir** ($2) from 7am-4pm; be sure to buy your ticket ahead of time as they tend to fill up quickly. **Bus tickets** can be purchased at **Meteor Tourism** (☎312 47 99), at the west end of Belediye Cad. Also at the far west end of Belediye Cad., near the dolmuş stop and above the *çay* house, is the **THY office,** 5 Meyramane Cad. (☎215 95 13), which offers flights out of **Ağri.** Open daily 7am-8pm.

ORIENTATION AND PRACTICAL INFORMATION. Doğubeyazıt's main drag is Belediye Cad., with the **otogar** at the east end and minibuses lining the westernmost intersection with **Büyük Ağri Cad.** Cheap hotels are clustered near the east end of town, and the **PTT** and **banks** are near the middle. **Murat Şahin** (☎312 34 34) and **Ahmet Özgül** (☎(542) 713 25 39; toprak-ararat@hotmail.com) offer free tourist information in English and organize all tours from **Doğanadolu Turzim** at Büyük Ağri Cad., 2nd floor, near the BP sign. **Currency exchange** is available at **T.C. Ziraat Bankası,** on Beleyide Cad. (Open daily 8am-12:30pm and 1:30-5:30pm. No commission.) Cirrus/MC/V **ATMs** are prevalent throughout town. In addition to the **produce bazaar** just east of the minibus stop, a large **supermarket** can be found at the junction of Hastanesi Cad. and Guven Cad. **Pharmacies** are clustered at the intersection of Belediye Cad. and Büyük Cad.; 24hr. service rotates between them. The sparse but clean urgent care facility **Acil Servis** has some English-speaking staff. (☎312 60 42. Open 24hr.) **Internet cafes** line Belediye Cad., the cheapest being **Omega** (☎312 75 48) at the corner of Çarsi Cad., and **Klas** (☎312 49 18), which doubles as a pool hall next door. The **PTT** is on Belediye Cad. (Open daily 8:30am-12:30pm and 1:30-5:30pm. **Phones** available 7am-11pm.) **Postal Code:** 04400.

ACCOMMODATIONS AND FOOD. A cluster of enjoyable, very cheap hotels lies around the far east end of Belediye Cad. Of these, the best value is the **Hotel Kenan,** on Emniyet Cad, which features a *kilim*-lined lobby with an aquarium and rooms with TVs and baths. Breakfast included. (☎312 78 69; fax 312 75 71. Singles $5; doubles $8.) For less money (and less character), try the **Hotel Erzurum,** which has clean but frayed rooms with limited hot water. (☎312 50 80. Singles $2.50; doubles $4.50; triples $7.) **Hotel Tahran,** on Küçük Agri Cad., one block south of Beleyide Cad., near the otogar, also has tidy rooms with bath, at budget prices. (☎312 01 95. Singles $5; doubles $8.) Of Doğubeyazıt's upper-tier hotels, by far the best value is **Hotel Ararat,** a bright and cheery place with balconies and breakfast on a roof terrace looking out toward Mt. Ararat. (☎312 49 88. Singles $5, doubles $8.) Near the Palace (see **Sights,** below), visitors can now stay at **Murat Camping.** Nestled beneath the ruins, guests can camp with access to toilets, hot showers, the restaurant, and traditional evening entertainment. (☎312 34 34. Camping $1 per night; limited doubles with views $5 per person.)

Near the hotels, three restaurants, serving *lokanta*-style food, receive local acclaim. The **Derya Restaurant,** opposite the PTT, is packed with locals. (☎312 34 44. Open 24hr.) Equally good is **Tad Lokantası,** 134 Belediye Cad. (☎312 44 30), serving *kebap* and *asure* (regional Turkish pudding; $.60). The restaurant at **Murat Camping,** at the foot of the İşak Paşa Palace, commands a magnificent view of the valley below. Its specialty is traditional Kurdish fare such *abdigor köfte* (a large, tasty meatball) and the multi-layered *mongol kebap.* After 9pm, the restaurant doubles as a lively nightclub, with singers and dancers imported from İstanbul. (☎312 34 34. Meals $3-4.) For dessert, try **Meşhur Diyarbakır Burma Kadayıfları** (☎312 41 17), on Beleyide Cad., which has several varieties of *kadayıfları,* a filigreed Kurdish delicacy resembling baklava, at $.60 a plate.

SIGHTS. Aside from the spectacular view of Mt. Ararat, the sight most visitors come to Doğubeyazıt to see is the astonishingly well-preserved **Işak Paşa Palace.** The road runs 6km from the Hotel Saruhan to the palace's rock ledge, making for a peaceful 1-1½hr. walk or a $2 taxi ride. In 1685, a local Kurdish chief built the palace using tariffs extracted from Silk Road travelers who passed nearby. The intricacy and beauty of the structure shows taste and nobility, beginning with an ornate entranceway covered in relief work and *muqarnas* (stalactite ornaments). From the southwest corner to the left, walk past the giant holes in the ground that once held a garrison. The large entranceway with lion reliefs leads to the **harem,** the **master's chamber,** and the **kitchen.** A nearby hole in the ground is the archetypal "loo with a view," a squatting toilet that allowed the ruler to gaze at the kingdom. Starting again at the outer courtyard, the northwest corner has an eight-sided **türbet,** a **mosque,** and a **sarcophagus.** (Open daily 6am-5:30pm. $1, students $.50.)

Farther uphill from the palace, next to an Urartian mosque, lies the important **Ahmedi Hami Türbesi,** which holds the remains of **Hani Baba,** considered the first Kurdish author. A 2000-year-old Urartian **fortress,** blending imperceptibly into the mountainside, towers over the entire scene. Ahmet Özgül of Doğanadolu Turzim leads tours of the fortress; those who reach the top early enough can catch the sunrise between the two peaks of Mt. Ararat. Below the palace, shepherds tend their flocks in the ruins of old Doğubeyazıt, destroyed by Russian bombings.

There are several other sites in the Doğubeyazıt area, including the supposed spot where **Noah's Ark** landed **(Uzengili).** One of the world's largest **meteor craters** is 39km from Doğubeyazıt and 5km off the road to Iran. To avoid the hike, most travelers take a taxi ($30) or join a tour. Options include five days in the surrounding areas for $150 per person or tours into Iran. Two-to-three day **horseback riding** expeditions cost $60 per person and include all meals. The route can incorporate **Fish Lake, Uzengili,** nomadic villages, and the Kaplicari **hot springs.** The latter are easily accessible from Diyadin dolmuş (30min., $1) or by contacting any of the local tour companies. **Memet Arik,** Belediye Cad., No. 6 (☎312 67 72; fax 312 77 76), runs regional tours, taking in all the highlights. Pickups can be arranged.

DAYTRIPS FROM DOĞUBEYAZIT: MT. ARARAT

Would-be climbers should contact ***Murat Şahin*** *(☎(543) 635 04 94 or 710 00 67), who has summited the peak 75 times and can help expedite matters such as permits.*

Movement on **Mt. Ararat** is still subject to military restrictions, given the current tensions with Armenia. **Permits** are now being offered to foreign climbers, however, and visitors without a permit can be escorted as high as the snow line (around 3500m) with the invitation of a local and the cooperation of the local jandarma. At present, climbers require a military clearance from Genel Kurmay Baskanligi military headquarters in Ankara. Though a formality, regional approval in Ağri and local military permission cause delay. With the correct papers, climbers pass the two military road blocks and climb to 4200m on day one, then reach the summit early the next morning. Equipment is hard to find in Doğubeyazıt.

On the north face of the mountain lie the ruins of **Korhan** (2000m), a 2500-year-old city. Two **churches** are still intact, and on a clear day climbers can see the modern city of **Jerezan,** the former capital of Armenia. Ararat is still inhabited by nomadic Kurds; at high mountain *yaylas* you are likely to be welcomed by friendly shepherds and their less-than-friendly sheepdogs.

Mt. Ararat borders three countries, but moving between them is not as simple as rolling downhill. Travelers wishing to visit **Armenia** will have no luck here; at the time of publication, the quickest land route to Jerezan was by way of **Georgia.** In both directions, the **Iranian** border (35km east of Doğubeyazıt) is far easier than it has been in previous years. Technically, a letter of invitation must be processed through Tehran, which takes least a week. Well-connected travel agents, such as Murat (see above) can expedite the process by fax in as little as 2 days. The visa itself, however, requires a visit to the Iranian Consulate four hours west, in **Erzurum.** Alcohol, playing cards, pornographic material, and evidence of previous visits to Israel are likely to complicate matters with Iranian officials.

LAKE VAN (VAN GÖLÜ) AND ENVIRONS

The waters of Lake Van are a magical reflecting pool, turquoise by day, fiery red at sunset, and quicksilver after dusk. The silken iridescence of this inland sea comes from its alkaline soda waters, but the mountains and castles along its shores reflect the millennia of volcanic and human activity that have shaped the region. For 3000 years, the area around Lake Van has been Eastern Turkey's most vibrant and fascinating cultural center. In approximately 800 BC, the Urartian Kings established their capital here, building impressive citadels and canals throughout the region. Van's strategic location on the Silk Road *(İpek Yol)* ensured prosperity and power for its rulers. After the Urartians came the Assyrians, Persians, and Armenians, before the Selçuk and then the Ottoman Turks. In the 20th century, Van witnessed the most tragic chapter in the Turkish-Armenian conflict.

To the southeast, the Zob River valley flows toward Hakkâri and Iraq. Present-day Van is the heart of Turkish Kurdistan, and in the early 1990s the area became infamous for PKK tourist abductions. In recent years, however, successful *jandarma* campaigns have all but eliminated the PKK threat, and tourists are once again flocking to Lake Van's shores and the fortresses that surround them.

VAN ☎432

The ruins of **Tuşba** (Old Van) lie on the eastern shore of the great lake in the shadow of a crumbling fortress. Although Van has been the capital of the region for some three millennia, the new city (4km east of the ruins) is barely 80 years old, having been completely rebuilt after the Russian siege of 1915-1918. Van has a long and tragic history of political strife and ethnic upheaval. It was here, in the 1880s, that both the first organized Kurdish rebellion and the first Armenian moves for independence manifested themselves. Armenia's alliance with Russia triggered the forced exile and slaughter of 1.5 million Armenians (see **Armenians,** p. 30). Today, over one million people live in the Van area, and the population (apart from the army and government officials) is almost entirely made up of ethnic Kurds, who are still only provisionally allowed to speak their native language. The modern city is surprisingly secular, with halter tops and jeans for sale in the trendier boutiques along Cumhuriyet Cad. Vibrant, warm, and well-equipped for tourists, Van is a base for exploring the natural and historical marvels of the lake region.

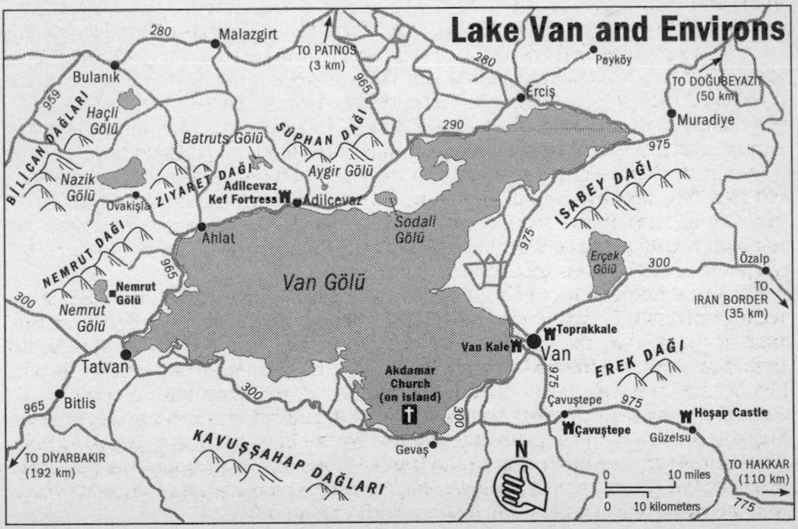

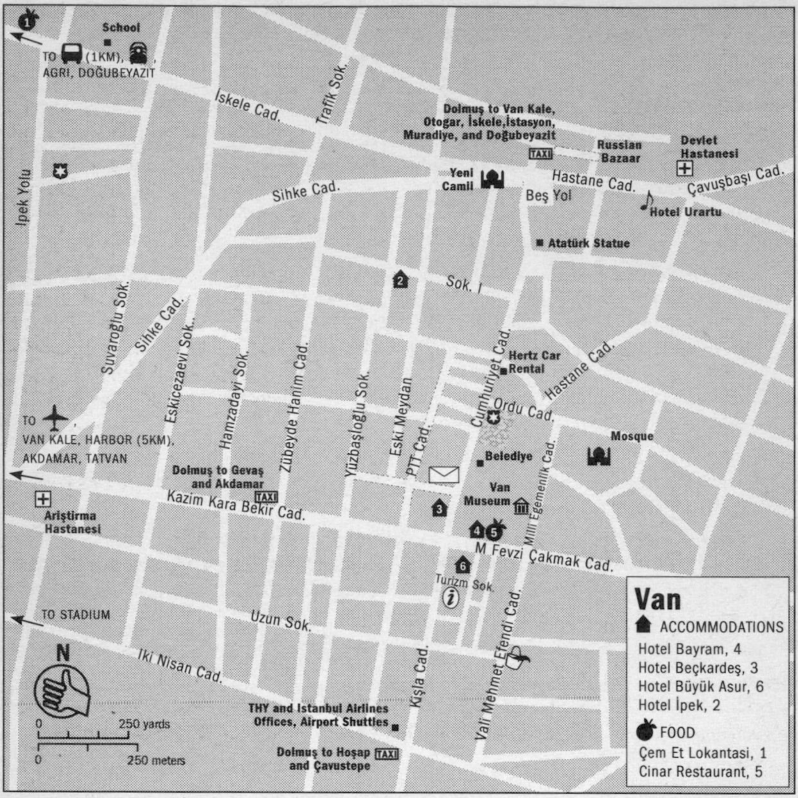

TRANSPORTATION

Minibuses from points north drop off in the center of town at **Beş Yol;** otherwise, most travelers arrive at the **airport** (5km south) or the **otogar** (1½km northwest of the city). Frequent dolmuş marked "İskele-Otogar" go to town ($.30). An airline bus usually meets flights at the airport. Otherwise, walk 300m to the main road for a $.40 dolmuş to avoid the $10 taxi.

Flights: **THY** (☎216 53 54), on the corner of Cumhuriyet Cad. and Ordu Cad., has direct flights to Adana, Ankara, Antalya, İstanbul, and Trabzon, as well as international flights.

Trains: Trains run from the **station** (☎223 13 80) west to **Tatvan, Ankara,** and **İstanbul** by loading onto a **ferry** to cross the lake; schedules are erratic but the trip is worth the wait. International trains run to **Tehran, Iran** (W, Su 6:30pm, $21).

Buses: Van's otogar services most destinations in Turkey. **Best Van** (☎214 28 81), **Star Van** (☎215 06 96), and **Van Gölü** (☎216 33 33) have ticket offices at the corners of K. Karabekir Cad. and Cumhuriyet Cad. Most companies have free transport to the bus station 30min. before departure. To: **Ankara** (18hr., 8 per day, $25); **Antakya** (18hr., 1 per day, $20); **Diyarbakır** (6hr., 6 per day, $11); **Erzurum** (6hr., 4 per day, $11); **İstanbul** (25hr.; 8am, 1pm; $36); **İzmir** (25hr., 3 per day, $37); **Malatya** (11hr., 6 per day, $13); **Şanlıurfa** (10hr., 2 per day, $13); and **Trabzon** (12hr., 1 per day, $20).

Dolmuş: Dolmuş leave 4 times daily in the morning from 200m west of Beş Yol. to: **Çaldıran** ($2); **Doğubeyazıt** ($4); and **Erçis** ($3). Dolmuş to the **Van Kale** leave from 1 block north of Beş Yol; those for points south leave from Cumhuriyet Cad., 1 block south of K. Karabakir Cad.

Car Rental: Several car rental agencies operate out of the airport. **Hertz** is the only one with an office in town, on Cumhuriyet Cad. (☎215 89 90; fax 215 98 91). $45 per day.

ORIENTATION AND PRACTICAL INFORMATION

Cumhuriyet Cad. runs the length of downtown, containing all the traveler's needs between the Atatürk statue at **Iskele Cad. (Beş Yol)** and the tourist information center, just south at **K. Karabakir Cad.** From Cumhuriyet Cad., both of these major streets run west, crossing the **İpek Yol** (Silk Road) before meeting the lake at the **İskele Harbor** and **Van Kale,** respectively.

Tourist Office: (☎216 20 18 or 216 36 75), across from the Asur Otel in a yellow building marked "Turizm Müdürlügü." They offer brochures and a map, but speak little English. Open M-F 8am-noon and 1:30-5:30pm. For more complicated questions, go to the **Buyuk Asur Hotel** (☎216 37 53), across the road, where **Remzi Bozbay** (mobile ☎(542) 784 64 30; rb_asuroteli@hotmail.com) speaks English, offers tourist information, and arranges tours to all sites in the region. His brother runs a *kilim* shop beneath the hotel and also gives tourist advice.

Banks: Vakıf Bank (☎216 11 93) on Cumhuriyet Cad. across the street from the PTT, exchanges **traveler's checks** with no commission. Open daily 8:30am-noon and 1:30-5:30pm. **ATMs** line the main avenue.

Medical and Emergency Services: The state hospital, **Devlet Hastanesi** (☎216 47 06) is 300m south of Beş Yol on İskele Cad. The university-affiliated **Araştirma Hastanesi** (☎216 47 06) is midway between Cumhuriyet Cad. and İpek Yolu on K. Karabekir Cad. Both are large, modern facilities, with ambulance service.

Internet Access: Van Is lIttered with internet cafes. The fastest is **Cafe Net,** upstairs at No. 71/1 on Cumhuriyet Cad.

PTT: (☎214 34 90). On Cumhuriyet Cad. near Sok. 6. Large PTT with *poste restante* service and a row of Türk Telekom phones. **Mail service** open 6am-11pm; **phones** 24hr.

Postal code: 65100.

ACCOMMODATIONS

Most of Van's accommodations are reasonably priced and well-furnished. The very cheapest hotels will entice only the most hard-core of budget travelers; for a little more, it's easy to find clean and comfortable rooms. **Camping** along Van's lakeshore is a beautiful and safe option as long as you stick to designated campgrounds. **Edremit,** 12km southwest of Van, charges $1-2 to set up a tent. Camping on **Akdamar Island** is prohibited, but **Ayanis Kale** and the northeastern shoreline of Lake Van are perfect for camping and swimming along isolated rock beaches. Check with the local *jandarma* or Ramzi Bozbay in Van.

Hotel Büyük Asur, Cumhuriyet Cad. and Turizm Sok. #5 (☎216 87 92). This affordable hotel is a quality traveler's hub with helpful, English-speaking hosts. All rooms have large beds and are well furnished, with 24hr. hot water showers. The lobby boasts a breezy breakfast deck and a traditional *kilim*-pillow lounge. Singles $12; doubles $16.

Hotel Beşkardeş, 16 Cumhuriyet Cad. (☎215 50 30; fax 216 64 66), by the corner of K Karabakir Cad., offers bright, clean rooms with TV. Singles $8; doubles $15.

Hotel Bayram, Cumhuriyet Cad. #1/A (☎216 11 36; fax 214 71 20). Comparable and just 30m from Büyük Asur, Bayram has quiet, newly furnished rooms with tiled bath and shower. Singles $10; doubles $20.

Hotel Ipek, Cumhuriyet Cad., Sok. 1, No. 3 (☎216 30 33). West of Cumhuriyet Cad. Sok. 1, in the heart of the Bit Bazaar. The best of the cheap places. Though basic, some rooms have showers, but share a bath. Singles $4; doubles $8; triples $12.

FOOD

Sadly, Kurdish cuisine has, for the most part, disappeared from restaurant menus, leaving behind standard Turkish fare. Breakfast in Van consists of delightful, fresh honey and *oltu peynir* (Kurdish white cheese with herbs) and is served in many *kahvaltı salonu* (breakfast houses) downtown. Van is a fairly dry city, but alcohol can be found in some small grocery stores; look for the *Efes Pilsen* beer signs. Hotel bars, such as those at the upscale **Hotel Urartu,** across from the Devlet Hastanasi, offer music and drinks until midnight. At dusk, the outdoor *çay-salonus* along the Bit Bazaar fill up with locals.

Merkez Et Lokantasi (☎216 97 01), on the busy corner of İskele Cad. and İpec Yolu. This is Van's best, and worth the 1km trip from town. An artificial waterfall and stunning location complement dishes like *sarma beyti* (spicy garlic mince rolls). The brave of heart can try the delicious *çiğ köfte:* raw meat patties mixed with spices. Meal and soft drink $3-4. Open daily 9am-11pm.

Cinar Restaurant (☎214 66 06), behind the Bayram Hotel. Broad menu, pleasant upstairs location, and the best food on the street. Full meal $3-4. Kitchen closes 9pm.

Çem Et Lokansi (☎215 21 11), on İskele Cad., 100m east of İpek Yolu. This friendly, well-lit restaurant features a wide variety of unidentified bird kebaps grilled in front of you while you dine. Full meal $2-4. Open until 10pm.

SIGHTS

Van's astonishing natural beauty provides a backdrop for a unique blend of Urartian, Armenian, and Kurdish influences. To see them all at the relaxed pace the tranquility of the lake demands, you'll need to plan for a several-day visit. If time is short, give priority to **Akdamar Church, Hoşap Castle, Van Kale,** and **Çavuştepe Fortress** (see **Daytrips from Van,** below).

After the Russians destroyed the old city of Tuşba, the local Kurds and their Turkish rulers built the new city of Van 4km to the east. Consequently, the museum is the only sight of historical importance in the town center, though the fortress and old city are an easy 30min. walk. The elusive **Van cat**—one eye green and one eye blue—is an increasingly rare sight in Van, as is the **cantaloupe melon** fabled to have been invented here. **Carpet** and **kilim** sellers here are the primary distributors for western Turkish dealers. They are in a position to offer the same quality found in tourist areas for up to 70% less. **Sene Kilim,** crafted by Kurdish villagers in Northern Iran and Southeastern Turkey, are easy to find. Do not purchase carpets at high prices unless claims of age and rarity can be authenticated.

VAN MUSEUM. Van's sole historical attraction is one of the better archaeological and ethnographic museums in Eastern Anatolia. The ground floor contains prehistoric finds from **Tilkitepe** as well as Urartian helmets, textile tools, bronze belts, glassware, and cremation bowls. The inner courtyard has large stone carvings of lions and Urartian cuneiform inscriptions. Upstairs is a *kilim* collection and a gallery called the "Genocide section," which displays the remains of eight skeletons and presents a misleading portrayal of the slaughter of Turks by Armenians, conveniently omitting any mention of the Armenian genocide. *(On Seyvit Mehmet Cad., behind the Beyram Hotel. Open daily 8am-noon and 1:30-5:30pm. $1, students $.50.)*

VAN KALE. Van Kale, a nearly 3000-year-old Urartian fortress towering high on rock bluffs, is simply massive: from east to west it stretches nearly 2km, 80m above the surface of the lake. Constructed by King Sarduri I (840-830 BC) and known as Tuşba to the Urartians, it formed the center of their vast kingdom. Though many of the structures were destroyed by the Russian siege, Van Kale's extensive battlements are worth a visit. Start at the lakeside end near the car park and *çay* garden. The large stone slabs near the fishery are ancient **Urartian piers.** Up the hill on the west side lies the locked **burial chamber** of King

Argishti I with inscriptions on the wall. The gate can be unlocked by the caretaker. The king is buried deep in a carved cave with connecting rooms that held the garrison and supplies. Walking up the hill 150m brings you to a flat area that was once the site of the **temple of sacrifice.** The drainage ditch you see was for collecting the animal blood. Pass the **Ottoman palace** to the south end of the fortress, then stumble down a steep rocky hill at the west wall to reach the **burial chambers** of Urartian kings Menua I and Sarduri I. The top of the rock bluff, now bearing the remains of an Ottoman mosque and castle, offers a view of the old city. *(Dolmuş (every 20min., $.30) depart from Beş Yol. Kale $2, students $1. Open 24hr., but escorts at night are recommended. Walking tour requires at least 2hr.; add an extra hour if visiting the old city off the western slopes.)*

OLD VAN (TUŞBA). Today, in **Tuşba** village, burial mounds stand as monuments to the cultural decimation that the area has suffered. The old city is part of a municipal park where locals often gather for late-afternoon picnics and sunset strolls through the ruins. At the base of the fortress, the remains of an **Armenian church** are visible next to the foundation of a *hamam*. The two **Selçuk mosques** have been rebuilt; the southern one is still in use. The one with the peculiar minaret (still climbable with a flashlight and gumption) is what remains of the **Ulu Camii** built by the Persian-influenced Black Sheep Turcomans. *(Open 24hr. Free.)*

DAYTRIPS FROM VAN

A well-planned daytrip can incorporate Hoşap Castle, Lake Van, and a visit to Akdamar Church, arguably the pearls of the Van region.

AKDAMAR CHURCH AND OTHER ARMENIAN CHURCHES

Akdamar Church is 50km west of Van on an island 5km off the coast. ***Dolmuş*** *headed for Gevaş will take you the additional 9km to the boat dock for Akdamar if you clear it with the driver before you board. Dolmuş depart from Van, 400m west of Cumhuriyet Cad. on K. Karabekir Cad. (daily every hr. if full, 6am-5pm; Gevaş $2, Akdamar $2.50). To avoid the hassle, you can also be dropped off at the jetty by any Bitis-bound* ***bus*** *($2). Frequent* ***ferry*** *service from the boat dock allows for convenient transportation to the site (daily every 30min.; if full, 6am-sunset; $3, students $2). When the boat is slow to fill, passengers can split the $30 total and leave promptly.*

Armenians flourished in the Van region for more than two millennia. Here they built villages, churches, and castles, of which little remains; most of their creations have been either razed or converted to mosques. Some scholars argue that Van Armenians are actually descendents of the Urartians, but cultural and linguistic differences make this unlikely. The Armenian kingdom first was united in 95 BC under **Tigranes the Great,** and thrived until it was eclipsed in 1071 by the Selçuks.

Akdamar Island is a popular picnicking destination for Van residents, especially in May, when the almond trees are in blossom. A major architectural and artistic feat, the church is built of sandstone and topped with a characteristic domed ceiling. All evidence of the accompanying palace has disappeared, and the attached monastery remained active until it burned down in the early-20th century.

AKDAMAR The **Church of the Holy Cross,** on Akdamar Island, is a highlight of any visit to Van. The derivation of the name *Akdamar* is traceable through Armenian folklore. The Princess Tamara had fallen in love with a peasant boy on the mainland. Every night she would light a candle on the island, whereupon he would swim out to profess his love. Her father, the king, caught wind of this forbidden love, became very angry, and locked his daughter in the castle. One night the king put the candle on a boat and ordered it moved around the lake. The boy swam in endless circles, and with his last drowning gasp, shouted "Aght Tamara, Aght Tamara!" ("Oh Tamara!").

The surviving reliefs on the outside of the church depict human evolution, as well as Armenian and Christian religious history. These artistic representations once doubled as decorations and as a teaching tool for the community. Beginning in the west, **King Gagik** holds a model of the church, standing next the Bible-clutching **Jesus.** The four Apostles sit in the apse of each outer wall of the church. From the feet of the Apostle on the western wall begins a **vine scroll** depicting bible stories around the entire building, including Adam and Eve, David and Goliath, Samson and Delilah, and Jonah and the Whale. Every figurine's eye sockets originally held jewels that were stolen long ago. The **frescoes** inside are largely dilapidated, though it is clear that the dome's ceiling once depicted the miracle of creation, and the walls displayed the life of Christ. The monastery foundations lie just to the south of the church, while the Turkish flag marks where the castle once stood.

A 13th-century Armenian church called **Çarpanak Kilise** sits on an island 20km east of Akdamar. Akdamar boats will negotiate the trip for large groups. Twenty kilometers over a dirt track lie the ruins of **Yedi Kilise** (Seven Churches). As of Summer 2001, they were not accessible by organized tours.

TO THE SOUTHEAST: URARTIAN FORTRESSES

The road to Hakkâri passes two formidable hilltop fortresses. ***Dolmuş*** *($3) depart from in front of the THY office. The road from Hoşap to Hakkâri is stunning. Unfortunately, as of Summer 2001, Hakkâri province was officially in a* ***state of emergency*** *and not recommended for tourists. Entrance to each castle is $2. Hoşap Castle open 8am-5pm. If the doors are locked, wait for the caretaker in the village below.*

Sixty kilometers south of Van on the road to Hakkâri, the **Hoşap Castle** is one of the greatest Kurdish castles in all of Turkey, and the best-preserved in the region. Built in 1643 by Lord San Süleyman of the Mahmudites (not the magnificent Ottoman lawgiver), the castle was funded by the taxation of travelers en route from Anatolia to northwest Iran. After the erection of his magnificent castle complex, Süleyman reportedly chopped off the hands of the architect to prevent him from building another of equal beauty. The walls are made of a mixture of dirt and pigeon eggs. The entrance gate has two reliefs of chained lions, denoting the gladiatorial matches between animals and men that took place within the castle walls. The upper level contains royal rooms, the harem, and a hamam.

Çavuştepe, formerly known as Sardurihinili, was once a sprawling, three-part castle more than 850m long and 80m high. Built in 764 BC by Sarduri II (764-735 BC), Çavuştepe commanded a strategic position in the Gürpınar Valley until the Scythians destroyed it in the 7th century BC. The temple grounds contain a **sacrifice stone** and a **cuneiform inscription.** The holes near the flag acted as a **water cistern.**

Built in 735 BC by Rusa II, **Toprakkale** (Toprak Castle) is just 4km southeast of Van. At the time of writing, access to Toprakkale was prohibited, as it is in a military zone. Mehir Kapısı's rock niche, a Urartian site between the bluff and the castle, may be open to visitors.

TO THE NORTH: AYANIS AND MURADIYE

Ayanis: There is currently no regular dolmuş to Ayanis from Van. Either organize a private car or hike from the tramway. Head 21km northeast of Van on Ipek Yolu (the Silk Road highway) toward Muradiye, turn left at the sign for Alaköy, and follow the gravel track for 12km. Muradiye: Regular dolmuş ($3) leave from Beş Yol in Van; northbound buses will also drop you off at the falls for the same price.

Forty kilometers northeast of Van, on the edge of the lake, lurks the little-known fortress of **Ayanis.** Built about 2400 years ago by Rusa II and since buried, it is now the focus of archeological excavation, though so far only the temple, the extensive granaries, and the castle spire have been fully uncovered. The drive out to Ayanis is bumpy but strikingly beautiful, passing many a tantalizing empty beach; the view alone is worth the steep scramble to the top of the ruins. Bring a picnic lunch.

The **Muradiye Şelale** (waterfall) lies 100km north of Van and 6km north of Muradiye on the highway. The sign for the waterfall is only visible from the Van direction, and the falls are 300m from the road. Cross the old suspension bridge to walk down to the pools below the falls. Camping is permitted.

TATVAN ☎434

An uninspiring town in a stunning location, Tatvan hugs the eastern end of Lake Van and offers a launch point for a trip to Turkey's second, secretive **Nemrut Dağ.** No, not the place with the big stone heads: this Nemrut is an inactive volcano that holds a breathtaking series of lakes (Nemrut Gölü), and hot springs in a volcanic crater. A dusty, one-horse town, Tatvan is nonetheless a convenient base for exploring the Selçuk tombs and Urartrian fortresses of Lake Van's north coasts.

Set back from the water, Tatvan's services are all along **Cumhuriyet Cad.,** its main thoroughfare, centered around Tatvan Park and the main dolmuş lot opposite. The new **otogar** is on the highway 1km north of town, but most buses will drop you at the town center. The **tourist office** is just above the dolmuş/taxi lot. **Mehet Salici** (☎832 42 28) runs tours of the lake area out of the office. **Pharmacies** and **ATMs** can be found near the park, and the **PTT** (open 7am-11pm) is directly across the street.

Apart from the flagship **Hotel Kardelen,** across from the PTT, most are barebones budget joints. The Kardelen has large, bright, freshly-painted rooms, TVs, minibars, a pleasant terrace restaurant, along with a pool hall. Mehmet, the concierge, speaks English and organizes tours. (☎827 95 00. Rooms $15 per person.) The best option among the mid-range accommodations is **Hotel Altilar,** Cumhuriyet Cad. No. 164, which offers clean, rooms with baths and TVs. (☎827 40 96. Singles $8, doubles $13.) You would be wise to inspect the kitchens of Tatvan's *lokantas* before you eat. **Berivan Restaurant,** Cumhuriyet Cad. No. 12, (☎827 10 51), serves meals from $1-2. Some of the best dining is actually 2½km out of town, along the north shore of the lake. **Supan Adabağ Restaurant** has fresh, tasty *kebaps* ($3) and a breezy view of the lake denied to downtown Tatvan diners.

NEAR TATVAN

NEMRUT GÖLÜ. Nemrut Gölü is a geographic marvel only 15km from Tatvan. Inactive since 1440, this volcano formed Lake Van by closing its outflow. Its vast crater—one of the largest in the world at 49 sq. km—hides a series of crystal-clear lakes at 3050m above sea level. The 90min. taxi ascent costs $20-25 and includes two hours in the crater. The road is just barely navigable by two-wheel drive traffic. Hitching is not only dangerous, but also unrewarding, as the route offers no services and traffic flow is unpredictable. As the road clears the crater lip, the lakes of Nemrut unfold. Half a kilometer into the crater, road signs indicate left to the large lake **(Büyük Gölü)** and should be followed if time is limited. Turning right leads to a series of smaller lakes (less suited to swimming), cozy campsites, hard-to-locate hot springs, and miasmic **thermal chimneys.**

The route to the big (blue) lake is 2km long, after which vehicles must stop 50m from the water's edge. En route, you will pass the small (green) lake, constantly bubbling from its hot thermal springs. Although swimming in the green lake is a bit unappetizing, thanks to thousands of scuttling red water bugs, the blue lake rivals Lake Van in tranquility, with the towering crater walls more than offsetting the appearance of the occasional sea snake. Descending on the northeastern side of the volcano, back toward Lake Van, the road passes **Serinbayır Kilises,** an old Armenian church. From the church, you can catch a view of the lake and mountains.

VAN'S NORTH COAST. Driving the remote northern coast of Lake Van is a highlight of Turkey's southeast, though transport and hitching options are limited. Best Van and Van Gölü offer regular circuits around the lake. The recent detente in regional tensions has eased travel restrictions; the road is now open 24hr.

The Tatvan (western) end of this route contains most of the important sights. First is **Ahlat,** with its famed **Selçuk tombs** *(kümbets)* and **Hasan Padisah's mausoleum.** On the lake side of the highway is the Selçuk rococo **Ulu Kümbet,** flanked with basalt and ringed with several layers of running geometrical and Arabic friezes. On the other side of the road, the hours of the **museum** are erratic and collection meager, but behind it the crooked monuments of the Selçuk **cemetery** stretch on to a dizzying distance. At least nine mausoleums checker Ahlut's landscape, of which the **Boyinler Icümbet** stands out for its unique architecture—incorporating a demi-balustrade of eight columns—and its intact Selçuk mosque.

Next down the road is **Adilcevaz Kef Fortress,** a farther 26km east, whose pretty white and red beachfront promenade stands in the shadows of two Urartian fortresses: **Adilcevaz** and **Ket Kalesi.** Perched on whitestone cliffs, these castles guarded the northwest shores of the lake. Adilcevaz is easy to visit, but Kef Kalesi is in a military zone. **Mehet Salici,** who runs tours out of tourist office in Tatvan (see **Tatvan,** above), organizes tours. A Selçuk mosque sits in Adilcevaz's shadow.

Turn away from the lake here, travel 3km to the village of Aydınlar, and continue farther 6km up to **Sarısu** (taxi $10), with incredible lake views from the shoulder of Mt. Suphan at 2500m. Only extremely fit walkers should consider the 5hr. Suphan ascent, with a small freezing crater lake at the 4053m summit.

DİYARBAKIR (AMED) ☎412

Diyarbakır is one of the world's oldest cities, a fact immediately apparent to any traveler who arrives at this ancient maze of cobbled streets, perched on the shores of the Tigris River in the crook of the Fertile Crescent. The black basalt walls which encircle the city—5km long and reportedly visible from space—are of Roman and Byzantine construction, a relatively recent addition in a place whose archaeological record shows evidence of continuous occupation spanning 7,500 years and 26 distinct civilizations.

Nowadays the crescent isn't so fertile, but the Tigris floodplain still yields bushels of Diyarbakır's famous 50kg watermelons—a welcome treat in a town whose summer heat is regularly above 43°C. Two million citizens, half refugees, live submerged in a timeless cacophony of commerce, and the echo of car horns. In recent years, a massive influx of displaced Kurds has created a second Diyarbakır, this one surrounding the old city walls. To Kurds, Diyarbakır is Amed, their proxy capital. For a people without their own state, the walls offer sanctuary within a sea of perceived repression and injustice. On the surface, Kurds and Turks embrace as brothers. Yet while Kurds cannot carve out a land for themselves, their dreams simmer like the horizon.

TRANSPORTATION

Flights: THY offices (☎228 84 01) are on Inönü Cad.; flights serve: **Ankara, Antalya, Bodrum, İstanbul,** and **Trabzon.** International destinations include **Athens, Berlin, London, Hong Kong, Tripoli,** and **Vienna.**

Bus: The otogar is 4km from town, accessible by dolmuş in front of the hotels on Kilbris Cad. **Mardin** minibuses (1 hr., $3) leave from the intersection of Melek Ahmet and Gazi Cad. Local bus companies include **Öz Diyarbakır** (☎228 93 00), **Diyarbakır Sur** (☎221 08 49), and **Yeni Diyarbakır Seyehat** (☎228 85 30)

DESTINATION	COMPANY	DURATION	TIMES	PRICE
Adana	Öz, Sur, Yeni	8hr.	15 per day 7am-10pm	$11
Afyon	Sur	17hr.	2:30, 5pm	$20
Ankara	Öz, Sur, Yeni	13hr.	9 per day 11:30am-8pm	$18
Antakya	Öz	8hr.	9am, 8, 9:30pm	$12
Bodrum	Öz	24hr.	4pm	$27
Bursa	Öz, Sur, Yeni	19hr.	2:30pm, 3:00pm	$22
Doğubeyazıt	Yeni	8hr.	9pm	$12
Eskişehir	Sur	17hr.	3pm	$22
Gaziantep	Sur, Yeni	5hr.	8 per day 7:30am-5:30pm	$7
İstanbul	Öz, Sur, Yeni	19hr.	11 per day 11:30am-8pm	$22
İzmir	Öz, Yeni	19hr.	4 per day 1-5:30pm	$22

DESTINATION	COMPANY	DURATION	TIMES	PRICE
Konya	Sur, Yeni	12hr.	5 per day 1-5:30pm	$16
Kahta		2hr.	every hr.	$2
Malatya	Sur, Yeni	4hr.	5 per day 1:30-6:30pm	$5
Mardin		1hr.	every hr.	$2
Rize	Öz	20hr.	12:30pm	$22
Şanlıurfa	Sur, Yeni	2½hr.	11 per day 9:30am-11:30pm	$4
Trabzon	Öz	18hr.	12:30pm	$20
Tatvan	Yeni	6hr.	9pm	$6

Taxis: Avoid taxis in Diyarbakır, where the meters spin like a roulette wheel.

ORIENTATION AND PRACTICAL INFORMATION

Diyarbakır's walls are pierced at the cardinal points by four gates. To the north is the **Dağ Kapisi** (Mountain Gate), which houses the tourist office and connects to the southern **Mardin Kapisi** by the north-south **Gazi Cad.** Running from the eastern **Yeni Kapisi** (New Gate) to the western **Urfa Kapisi** is the city's east-west axis. The inner walls are ringed by a single road, named **Kibris Cad.** at the north and **Tursik Cad.** at the south. The only other identifiable street in town is the east-west **İnönü Cad.**, located south of Kibris Cad. The old city is a labyrinth of unmappable alleys.

Tourist Office: In the basement of the **Dağ Kapisi** (☎221 21 73). The director, **Zeki Genes,** speaks some English and can offer you a brochure. Also contact the well-traveled **Ubeydullah Calisir,** nicknamed "Japonali" (☎229 22 71; mobile (535) 259 34 66), who enjoys helping tourists find their way without obligation.

Banks: Every major bank lines Gazi Cad. from the İnönü Cad. intersection toward the center of town. Open 9am-5:30pm. **ATMs** available 24hr.

Hamam: Diyarbakır's oldest hamam is closed indefinitely. Remaining options are Turkish baths attached to the larger hotels. Hotels Dedeman, Turistik, Demir and Kervansaray have pools that charge $8 for a dip. Men can use the city pool just outside the Dağ Kapisi on the way to the Hotel Dedeman for $1.50.

Police: On Gazi Cad., next to Hasan Paşa Hani. Emergency ☎155. Open 24hr.

Pharmacy: Akdeniz Eczane, 11/A Kibris Cad. (☎222 56 68). Open 8am-6:30pm. Part of a rotating pool of pharmacies that remain open 24hr.

Hospital: Devlet Hastanesi (☎228 5430), outside the city walls. Turn left 200m on Yusef Azizoğlu Cad.

Internet Access: The city's 20 cafes are wonderfully concealed, and the joy of discovery almost compensates for slow connections and daily power outages. For **Number 1 Computer Internet House,** cross from the hotels on Kibris Cad, traverse the dolmuş lot, then walk 200m left down Selim Amca Sofra Sal. $.75 per hr.

PTT: The main branch is on the corner of İnönü and Vilayet Cad. Postal services open 8:30am-noon, 1:30-5:30pm.

Postal Code: 21030

ACCOMMODATIONS

Diyarbakır has an excellent range of accommodations, concentrated on İnönü, Kibris and Izzet Paşa Cads. Travelers in summer months may find A/C to be more neccessity than luxury. Room rates are negotiable, however, and giving up breakfast can often be a crucial bargaining point.

Aslan Palas, Kibris Cad. 21 (☎221 12 27). With TV, private bath, and A/C in rooms above the parrot-filled lobby, this is the top choice. Singles $5, doubles $10.

Hotel Kristal (☎224 25 50; fax 224 01 87), in a small alley of Kibris Cad., has large, clean rooms. A bit pricier, but with the added luxuries of a refrigerator, new carpeting, and a tiled bath. Singles $10, doubles $15.

Hotel Kenan, (☎221 66 14), on Izzet Paşa Cad., past İnönü Cad., offers similar accommodations to Aslan Palas, with A/C, private bath, and laundry facilities. $5 per person.

Otel Surkent, Izzet Paşa No. 19 (☎221 66 16), across the street from Kenan, offers the best of the rock-bottom budget options. $2 per person, but you get what you pay for.

Hotel Grand Kervansaray (☎228 96 06), a restored Ottoman *kervanseray,* is at least $50 per night, but its history, architecture, and watermelons in the fountains make it definitely worth a stop.

FOOD

Traditional food reigns in Diyarbakır, where a forlorn Burger King lies exiled beyond the city walls. Speak to locals about the dishes that are heat-labile and best avoided (dairy, pre-cooked, undercooked and reheated). It is considered a crime to leave Diyarbakır without sampling the local watermelon. A cluster of tree-shaded *çay* gardens lie inside the north-west wall of the city and provide picturesque spots to beat the heat; nearby are the old city's best restaurants.

Sarmasik Ocakbasi, 31 Kibris Cad. (☎224 25 97). The best in town for cheap, reliable food. Try *guvec,* delicious crock pot of lamb and vegetable. Full meal $3. Open 24hr.

Tuccarlar, Ticaret Merkezi Kat 1, 5th fl. (☎228 90 21). City views, breezes, great alternatives to kebap (*semiz otu* yogurt, pepper, and juicy *bostane* salad each $1), and live traditional music until 1am.

Guneydoğa Gazeteciler Cemiyeti (☎229 21 17), or "Journalists Club," opposite Tuccarlar and disguised as a *çay* garden, happily serves tourists *içli köfte* (crumbed meat and vegetable ball) and *kie-mumbar* (intestine stuffed with minced meat and vegetable), as well as a full range of drinks. Full meal $5-7.

SIGHTS

A circuit of Diyarbakır's **walls** can be made in a few hours, but the secrets hidden within its labyrinthine center can take days to discover. The walls are among the city's chief draws: 12m high and 5m thick, covered in inscriptions from 12 distinct historical periods. The southern and western walls can be climbed easily, and one can stroll for a good distance atop the fortifications. Within the walls of the old city, several major sites can be seen in just a few hours. Start at the Selçuk **Ulu Camii,** then have a cup of *çay* in the restored **camel market** across the road. The **bazaar,** like the camel market, winds down after 6pm. Finding the **Meryamana Kilisesi,** a 3rd century Aramaic church and convent, requires a plunge into the tangled knot of ancient alleys. Any number of old men or young boys will be happy to guide you; the church is nearly impossible to find without help. This magnificent structure, flanked by carved lions and Aramaic inscriptions, continues to hold services in the original language of Jesus. To the south on Gazi Cad., the restored Ottoman *kervanseray* that has become the **Grand Kervansaray Hotel** is a good place for a drink stop and a dip in the beautiful pool ($8). Next is the restored home of **Cahit Sitki Taranci, Atatürk's house,** south of town, and the **Ducle bridge,** built in 1065.

MARDİN

☎482

Travelers lured by Deyrul Zafarin Monastery to this hilltop city of elegant stone houses perched at the edge of the Syrian desert will discover there is much more to Mardin. Though a perennial hotbed of Kurdish separatist activity, this frontier town lies dormant again, allowing tourists a glimpse of one of Turkey's most intriguing populations. A 10,000 year heritage has woven a patchwork of different cultures together in this upper Mesopotamian city. Even today, Syrian Orthodox goldsmiths and Muslim copperworkers beat out their trades side by side.

TRANSPORTATION. **Mar-Soy** (☎212 95 95), with offices on Birinci Cad., is the only major bus line operating out of Mardin. Buses leave every hr. to **Gaziantep** (5hr., $9), **Diyarbakır** (1hr., $2), and **Şanliurfa** (2½hr., $5). One bus per day leaves for **Adana** (8hr., $12), **Ankara** (13hr., $18), **Antalya** (24hr., $23), **Bursa** (20hr., $25), **Eskişehir** (18hr., $9), **İstanbul** (20hr., $25), **Konya** (12hr., $18), and **Mersin** (9hr., $13).

PRACTICAL INFORMATION. Mardin clings to a rocky hill on the border of the Syrian Desert. The east-west highway runs 500m below **Birinci Cad.**, the main street. From the central Atatürk statue, **dolmuş** stops are located 1km in both directions at either end of Birinci Cad. From these, a *servis* bus will shuttle you to intercity buses around town. Services include: the **tourist office**, set back from the main highway (follow the yellow signs left and up the hill); **banks** on Birinci Cad. with 24-hour **ATMs** (open 9am-5:30pm); the **police** on Yeni Sehir Cad. (open 24hr); **Devlet Hastanesi** (state hospital), next to the PTT on Meydan Cad; the **Yakamos Internet Cafe;** and the **PTT** (open 8:30am-noon, 1:30-5:30pm.) **Postal code:** 47000.

ACCOMMODATIONS, FOOD, AND SIGHTS. The most desirable accommodations in Mardin are not in town at all: the **Deyrul Zafarin Monastery** is happy to host guests—just be sure to get there before the gates lock at sundown. Quality rooms are almost impossible to find in the town's center; the only lodging option is the decrepit **Hotel Bayraktar** (☎212 13 38) on Birinci Cad., by the Atatürk statue. The showers are cold and the beds are old, but the view out back over the Syrian desert is astounding. Singles $5, doubles $7, triples $9. For much, much more, you can enjoy hot water, and air conditioning at the newly renovated **Hotel Bilen** (☎212 55 68), downhill on the east-west highway (singles $20, doubles $40).

Dining options are limited, but the **Turistik Et Lokantasi** (☎212 16 47), on a terrace at the Atatürk Meydanı, goes to great lengths to preserve Mardin's unique cuisine. Try *içli köfte, kiya lamacun, cacik* cucumber yogurt, and the local bitter coffee called *mirra.* Ask to sample the local wine from the Monastery—it's not for sale.

The **Mardin Museum,** on Cumhuriyet Meydanı, is housed in an 1895 building constructed by the patriarch of Antakya, Ignatius Bentham Benni. It boasts a collection spanning 4000 years of Mardin culture, including Roman statuary, Selçuk glasswork, Assyrian urns, and jewelry and pottery dating back to 4000 B.C. from the Girnivaz excavations. (☎21 16 64. Open Tu-Su 8:30am-noon and 1-5pm. $1.) Follow the signs on Birinci Cad. from the museum to find the **Kirklar Kilesesi,** the Syriac cathedral and center of the city's Christian population. Mardin's other churches can be found by their bell-towers—you may even stumble across a service in Aramaic. Just downhill on the west side of town, signs point the way to the exquisite Ottoman **Kasimiye Medresi,** a seminary built in 1457 with high vaulted domes and a central courtyard whose pool is filled by a hillside spring via elaborately carved stone channels. Bring a flashlight to explore the dark and twisting stone stairways, which lead to the upper floors and rooftop.

NEAR MARDİN

DEYRUL ZAFARIN MONASTERY. This monastery is the key reason to visit Mardin. In 451, the Monophysitic congregation of the Syrian Orthodox Church (Jacobites) split from the Byzantine Church after the Council of Chalcedon's debate about the true nature of Christ. It served as the seat of the Syrian Orthodox church from 493 to the 1920s. The hardy Mardin Christian community has dwindled from 2000 to 200 over the past 30 years. The church still uses Aramaic, Jesus' language, as its liturgical tongue. Services are held daily, led by one of the two remaining monks. To the right of the entrance, down a few steps is a prayer room originally used as a temple to Baal in 2000 B.C. Above it is an old mausoleum formerly used as a medical school; the wooden doors are inlaid with lions and serpents. The main chapel still retains patches of its original turquoise coat, and houses a 300-year-old Bible, a 1000-year-old baptismal font, and a 1600-year-old mosaic floor. *(1.5km east of town. Town buses go to within*

1500m (a 20min. walk); buses may detour for an added fee. Taxis $9. Open dawn to dusk. On weekdays, the monks tend to be more hospitable than on weekends, when masses of Turkish tourists descend. Though a few basic cells are available for visitors to stay in, those with a specific religious interest are preferred.)

In **Kiziltepe,** 25km south of Mardin, the 13th-century Ülü mosque with *mihrab* reliefs and a beautiful portal is a fine example of Artukid architecture. The **Öztopraklar Hotel,** on the highway, has spotless new rooms with A/C and private bath (☎312 33 86; singles $10, doubles $20).

MİDYAT AND THE TUR ABDİN PLATEAU. One hour due east of Mardin, the hilltop city of Midyat is perched at the entrance to the Tur Abdin Plateau, the spiritual center of Turkey's tiny Syrian Christian community. Midyat is home to seven Syriac churches, and the surrounding plateau holds several monasteries, including **Mar Gabriel,** the oldest monastery in the world, founded in 397 AD.

Midyat itself is a dusty town divided in two: the newer half, closer to the highway, houses the **hospital** (☎462 11 06), **police station** (☎462 20 56), and the **PTT** (open 7am-11pm), while the older side of town holds the only place to stay, the **Otel Metro,** which offers clean budget options with balconies, bathrooms, and hot water. (☎464 23 17; singles $4, doubles $8); the restaurant downstairs offers decent *mezes* for $1 apiece.

Midyat's skyline is littered with old stone bell towers, and it is easy to explore the Aramaic churches in town. A bit more effort will get you into the heart of the Tur Abdin plateau itself; the most worthwhile sight is the **Mar Gabriel Monastery.** 20km east of Midyat, the mothership of the Turkish Syriac church was founded in A.D. 397 by St. Samuel. Mar Gabriel has withstood centuries of isolation and persecution and continues to thrive as a large monastery/fortress, with many gardens enclosed by its thick stone walls. The gate is flanked by stone lions, while the main chapel contains a breathtaking array of Byzantine mosaic in turquoise and gold. To the rear of the courtyard is a domed hall supported by eight smaller domes, ordered by the Byzantine empress Theodora. Underground, in the mausoleum, the **grave of St. Samuel** is open for display. Visitors may be lucky to receive an audience with the bishop, who speaks excellent English. For other local monasteries, such as the nearby **Meryamana;** ask at Mar Gabriel for advice and directions. A donation is customary for visitors to any monastery.

MALATYA ☎422

Malatya (pop. 800,000) is Turkey's apricot capital and birthplace of Turkey's second president, İnönü. The city lies in a fertile basin, shadowed by a barren range that points the way to the magnificent Nemrut Daği ruins. While most approaches are unremarkable, the journey from the south (Adana or Maraş) is characterized by cascade carved gorges. Malatya's football team, which has only recently joined Turkey's top tier, is the latest jewel in the crown of this glittering modern city. Malatya's open parks and wide, tree-lined boulevards are as pleasant to stroll through as the narrow corridors of its famous apricot bazaar.

TRANSPORTATION

Most travelers arrive in Malatya's palatial **otogar,** 3km west of town. **Dolmuş** connect this station with downtown, passing the train station on the way.

Flights: Cem Tour, 11/1 Galleria İş Merkezi (☎322 66 66; fax 322 84 44), just west of the main square, sells **THY** tickets. Bus service meets each flight and departs from multiple downtown locations 2hr. before departure, sometimes for a fee. THY flies regularly to **Ankara, Bodrum, İstanbul, İzmir,** and international destinations.

Buses: Regular dolmuş link the town center and the **otogar** ($.20). A taxi costs $2-3. To: **Adana** (6hr., 3 per day, $9); **Adiyaman** (3hr., 6 per day, $6); **Ankara** (10hr., 6 per day, $18); **Antakya (Hatay)** (7hr., 3 per day, $10); **Diyarbakır** (4hr., 3 per day, $6);

Doğubeyazıt (15hr., 4 per day, $14); **Erzurum** (8hr., 3 per day, $11); **Gaziantep** (4hr., 6 per day, $6); **İstanbul** (16hr., 6 per day, $20); **Kahramanmaraş** (3½hr., 3 per day, $3); **Kayseri** (5hr., 2 per day, $9); **Konya** (10hr., 2 per day, $16); **Mersin** (7hr., 4 per day, $10); **Sivas** (4hr.,10 per day, $6); **Trabzon** (15hr., 2 per day, $13); and **Van** (9hr., 2 per day, $12). Companies offer shuttles from downtown 30min. before departure.

Trains: The **station** (☎324 77 70) is located 1km west of the statue on Atatürk Cad. The İstanbul-Ankara line and the Adana line run to Malatya. 2 trains run daily to: **Adana, Ankara,** and **İstanbul.**

Car Rental: Meydan Rent A Car (☎325 13 17; fax 323 47 03), 1km west of the town center, rents relatively new Fiats for under $30 per day, with unlimited mileage. A few days is enough to take in Nemrut Dağ, Diyarbakır, Mardin, Midyat, and Şanlıurfa by car.

ORIENTATION AND PRACTICAL INFORMATION

Malatya's main street, **İnönü Cad.**, runs parallel to the Ankara-Van highway and turns into **Atatürk Cad.** on the other side of the İnönü statue at the town center. The statue faces a series of tea gardens that cascade downhill to the market streets, including the famous **coppersmith's** and **apricot bazaars.** Hotels, restaurants, banks, and the PTT are all within a five-minute walk from the İnönü statue.

Tourist Office: Vilayet Binası Kat. 1 (☎323 30 25; fax 324 25 14), on the 1st floor of the Vilayet Hall. English spoken by Bulent, Kemal and Sabrı. If the office is closed, try the *çay* garden in the rear of the building. Open M-F 9m-noon, 1-5pm. Tours to **Nemrut Dağı** depart daily at 11:30am from behind the town hall, in the parking lot next to the tea garden. The $30 fee includes summit lodging at the **Guneş Motel,** dusk then dawn at the site, 2 meals and transport. At the time of writing, however, the Guneş Motel was closed for renovations, and transport-only tours were arranged for $10-15. Hitching or local transport is not advisable due to the remoteness of this location.

Travel Agencies: Cem Tour (see "Flights") offers more expensive tours ($150-$250), including the Atatürk Dam, Huran and Old Ufa. Open daily 8am-8pm.

Banks: Many major banks are in the main square. All are open M-F 8am-noon, 1:30-5:30pm. **Traveler's checks** can be exchanged at **Türkiye İş Bankasi** and **TC Ziraat.**

Hospital: English is spoken at the central, private **Sergi Yip Markezi** (☎325 98 88) on Atatürk Cad. The state-run **Devlet Hastanesi** (☎326 15 70) and the private **Turgut Özal Hastanesi** (☎341 06 60), 17km toward Van, both offer 24hr. care.

Post Office: The main **PTT** (☎322 34 25) is 30m down a small alley off the northwest corner of the main square. Open 8am-noon, 1:30-5:30pm; 24hr. card phones are here and along İnönü Cad.

Postal Code: 44000.

ACCOMMODATIONS AND FOOD

Among Malatya's budget picks, **Park Otel,** 17 Atatürk Cad., 100m east of the square, is a clean, well-lit place with 24hr. hot water. The back rooms are quieter except during the call to prayer. (☎321 16 91. Singles $6; doubles and triples $10.) For similar digs in a darker setting, **Otel Tahran,** along PTT Cad., has simple rooms, private bath, hot water, phones, and a communal kitchenette. (☎324 36 15. Singles $5; doubles $8; triples $12.) Claustrophobes should avoid **Otel Ozen,** across the street at PTT Cad. 18 (☎321 1770), unless $6 doubles suppress symptoms. **Hotel Yeni Sinan,** 6 Atatürk Cad., is the best of the mid-range, with spacious rooms and good bathrooms. (☎321 29 07. Singles $10; doubles $15.)

Mangal Vadisi (☎326 22 00), on Kisla Cad., just off Atatürk Cad., boasts "cook-your-own" Anatolian food in private grill-pits. The menu is familiar, but the *kebaps* are tasty and rich in vegetables ($2-3). Closer to the center, the **Çinar 2001 Kebap Salonu,** 37 Atatürk Cad. (☎322 54 81) offers excellent chicken *sote* and a variety of pizzas to go with their own array of *kebaps* ($1-2). Right in the town center, **Blue**

Bell's Sandwich Cafe, No. 9 Atatürk Cad., delivers faster food ($1-2) and freshly-squeezed orange juice. After dinner, a stroll down the tree-lined and befountained **Fuzuli Cad.** (on the right off Atatürk Cad., 400m from the İnönü statue) will take you past ice cream and dessert spots. **Birinci Pastanesi,** halfway to the museum, has particularly sumptuous offerings. (☎322 19 52. Open daily 7am-1am.)

SIGHTS

Malatya's glass and steel facades offer little in the way of classical architecture, but its shaded trees hold numerous outdoor restaurants and *çay* gardens, the largest of which is **Kernek**, at the end of the promenade on Fuzuli Cad. Here, one can promenade with the locals or dine at the **Kernek Selalesi ve Park Restaurant** (☎323 93 61), which offers cheap food, a view over the entire park, and a water garden.

In the **bazaar** district, sprawling north and east from the Malatya Büyük Otel, vendors peddle everything from head scarves to metal work. Its famous fresh and dried *kaysısı* (apricots) are purveyed in the fantastic **apricot market.** Apricot, raisin, and nut enthusiasts will be stuffed beyond their wildest dreams with handfuls of nuts, candies, and various forms of dried fruit. Couches and tea are provided to help you munch your way through the samples. The nearby **coppersmith's** and **produce markets** are also remarkable. In addition, a roving bazaar sets up tables in different city neighborhoods every day, offering local clothing and perishable goods. The **kilim and carpet bazaar** is on İnönü Cad., opposite the statue, with cheaper carpets than in western Turkey. Near the Malatya Büyük Otel, dusty male travelers can enjoy a Turkish bath in the 125-year-old **Belediye Hamam.** (Bath $2; *kese* $4. Open daily 5am-9pm.) Women can go to the similarly-priced **Saray Palace,** 100m behind the Belediye building. **MalatyaSpor,** the beloved local football team, is a big deal in town, and games are held every Friday, Saturday, and Sunday from August until the end of May. Tickets should be purchased early on the day of the game at the **stadium,** on the opposite end of Fuzui Cad. from the Kerack museum.

Just over 10km away, the town of **Battalgazi** and apricot groves now cover what would have once been **Eski Malatya** (old city of Malatya). Now only the **city walls** and the 13th-century **Ulu Camii** remain. The ancient Hittite site of **Aslantepe** can be reached 4km northeast of the city; contact the tourist information office upon arrival. **Aslantepe** ("Lion Hill"), is best visited in July and August, when the archaeological teams from Rome are actively excavating. Buses to both destinations leave from the dolmuş lot on the highway 500m north of the town center.

NEMRUT DAĞI

Accessible from Malatya (see p. 462), Kahta, Adiyaman, and Şanlıurfa (see p. 466). The site is at the base of a cone-shaped pile of rocks, at the bottom of which are three terraces on the north, west, and east. Open during daylight hours. $3.50, students $2. The Malatya road ends 100m below the eastern terrace, while the road from Kahta ends in a parking lot 1km from the summit. Beside the parking lot is Nemrut Kafeteria, offering 24hr. food, drinks, and a bathroom. Allow at least 2hr. to explore the site, including the walk up. Rough winds can cause chills and dehydration: bring layers and water.

Upon the highest peak in the region (2150m), King **Antiochus I** ordered the construction of a 75m pyramid of rubble, flanked by massive statues, their heads long since decapitated by earthquakes (most recently 1938) and time. At dawn and dusk, solitude and silence prevails on this impressive funerary monument, the calm broken only by the whipping of a constant wind.

The site holds relics dating back to the Commagene kingdom, a border kingdom which managed to fend off the Romans and Persians encroaching from either side between 162 BC and 72 AD. The kingdom was greatest under Antiochus, son of Mithradates, who claimed direct ancestry to **Alexander the Great** on his father's side and to the Persian **Darius the Great** on his mother's, thus embodying the unification of east and west in one royal line. Antiochus is best remembered for installing a brand new pantheon of syncretic gods like "Apollo-Mithras" and "Zeus-Oromas-

A HEAD OF HIS TIME Antiochus's tomb lies buried beneath a man-made mountain of rubble, guarded by towering stone statues. Locked for centuries inside the peak of Mount Nemrut, this burial site, described as the eighth wonder of the ancient world, was discovered in 1881. Since then it has continued to thwart archaeologists and modern investigative technology, with its delicate structure likely to collapse and crush any attempt to burrow toward its possible secrets and treasures. The king has so far clung to his treasures through both might and wile: he put not just heavy bricks in the way, but also Turkish bureaucrats. Denied access to the tomb itself, archaeologists have contented themselves with interpretation of the site's sandstone reliefs, among them, possibly the worlds first horoscope, dating precisely to Antiochus' coronation in 109 BC. Particularly resounding are the texts of Nemrut's many inscriptions, all told in the eerily familiar first-person of Antiochus himself:

Therefore, for this monument a foundations secure from the ravages of time I planned to prepare. In it my body, as it had existed blessedly until old age, after to the heavenly throne of Zeus Oromasdes my divinely loved soul has been sent forth, will sleep for endless eternity.

In the 20th century, archaeologists' dynamite and increased tourist traffic have upped the ante, meaning that the ravages of time may be gaining the upper hand. Exposed again to the elements, reliefs are beginning to erode; propped-up statues have toppled again under the weight of winter snow. In addition, visitors run amok over the barricade-free site. Though there is talk of restoration efforts, locals are sceptical. Only five years ago, a toppled head was restituted for the ludicrous sum of 6 million lira ($10,000). Locals offered to complete the same task with 20 tourists, ten minutes, and a blanket, but to no avail. Perhaps red tape is the one thing that will ensure Nemrut remains as it is for decades to come.

des." He commissioned 10m high statues of these gods in their honor; they are seen bestowing the divine mandate upon a 10m statue of himself. The Herculean labor of constructing this shrine from six-ton stone blocks (not to mention a 75m tall peak (now eroded to 50m) of crushed rock now thought to hide the tomb itself) leads archaeologists to think it may rival Tutankhamen's for wealth and majesty. Meanwhile, the collection of 3m tall stone heads continues to attract visitors to the site. These gargantuan amputata, fallen from the shoulders of crumbled statues, recall Shelley's "Ozymandias."

Careful observation can match fallen heads to the torsos above. The figures on the eastern (sunrise) platform are identical to those on the west (sunrise) side, and there is a rough symmetry from left to right: lion, eagle, Apollo-Mithras, Zeus-Oromasdes, Antiochus, Herades-Aragnes, eagle, and lion. Sunrise and sunset show the site at its most glorious; they also draw massive crowds of Turkish and foreign tourists alike. For a less-crowded snapshot, the site is usually deserted in the middle of the day, and the statues are just as impressive.

If you plan a trip to Nemrut Dağı, you will need to stay in a nearby town. Malatya (p. 462) and Şanlıurfa (p. 466) are probably the better options, as they are pleasant cities in their own right. Kahta and Adiyaman are reasonable bases as well. The bus company Adiyaman Ünal (☎(416) 216 11 12) arranges fast day tours to Nemrut Dağı from Adiyaman. **Kahta** is an oil-town with a dusty main street and a few incongruous 4-star hotels. Nonetheless, it is the closest major town to Nemrut Dağ, and is the best way to see the other surrounding sights within the national park, such as the Roman bridge at **Cendere** and the bas reliefs of **Eski Kaleb** and **Yeni Kale,** all accessible from the Malatya side. Most hotels offer A/C for $7-10 per person, and will offer day tours to Nemrut Dağı (short $28-40 per minivan; long $40-60 per minivan; minivans hold 10-12 people). Nemrut closes from first snowfall (Nov.) until mid-April, though winter walking tours can be arranged. *Jandarma* clear the site after dusk and enforce a non-climbing policy on the unstable rubble pyramid.

ŞANLIURFA ☎414

Though officially known as Şanlıurfa (Glorious Urfa), for its contribution to the struggle for Turkey's independence, this city is known as *Peygamberler Şehri* to Muslims: City of Prophets. Urfa is a place of pilgrimage, being the putative birthplace of Abraham and the home of the prophet Job, as well as ten other Biblical figures including as Jethro, Joseph, and Moses. Şanlıurfa is old, mind-bogglingly old, with newly-excavated temples at Göbeklitepe dating back to 9000 B.C. Urfa has changed hands many times along the millennia: from Hittite to Assyrian to Alexandrine to Commagene, Aramaen, Roman, Persian, Byzantine, Arab, Latin, Selçuk, before finally joining the Ottoman Empire in 1637. These diverse influences have simmered gently in the city to form a distinctive style of architecture, still visible today. Meandering through old narrow streets, you can still catch glimpses of the old stone carvings. Urfa's mansions have open courtyards and cool shaded summer terraces, elegantly carved with crescent moons and vine leaves. Recently, many old mansions have been restored as guest houses and restaurants, and a series of green parks and *çay* gardens have sprung up.

Urfa's economy has boomed with the Southeast Anatolian Project's (GAP's) Atatürk Dam, which, to the chagrin of those downstream, controls the flow of the Euphrates (Fırat) River. Despite oppressive summer heat (up to 50°C by day), the city is a fascinating destination for both travelers and pilgrims, meriting a couple of days for sightseeing and a daytrip the nearby ancient city of **Harran.**

TRANSPORTATION

The otogar is 1½km from the town center. Take a taxi for $4-5, or stop any dolmuş and mention your preferred hotel ($.20), as all listed are on the main route. Some bus companies have free shuttle service to the otogar.

Flights: THY (☎215 33 44), on Atatürk Cad., next door to Şan-Med Hospital, has flights to **Ankara, Antalya, İstanbul, İzmir, Kahramanmaraş,** and **Trabzon.**

Bus: Urfa's otogar is a bustling transport hub. To: **Adana** (5hr., 17 per day, $7); **Ankara** (12hr., 8 per day, $16); **Antakya** (6hr., 3 per day, $8); **Diyarbakır** (3hr., 20 per day, $5); **Doğubeyazıt** (16hr., 4 per day, $22); **Erzurum** (15hr., 2 per day, $16); **Gaziantep** (2hr., 20 per day, $3); **İstanbul** (17hr., 9 per day, $23); **İzmir** (17hr., 2 per day, $23); **Kahramanmaraş** (3hr., 3 per day, $3.50); **Kars** (20hr., 1 per day, $24); **Konya** (12hr., 3 per day, $14); **Malatya** (6hr., 3 per day, $6); **Mardin** (4hr., 5 per day, $6); **Mersin** (3-4hr., 20 per day, $9); **Trabzon** (15hr., 4 per day, $22); **Van** (12hr., 1 per night, $13). **Dolmuş** and **minibuses** leave from the same parking lot.

ORIENTATION AND PRACTICAL INFORMATION

Roads from Diyarbakır (north), Mardin (east), and Gaziantep (west) all meet above the city, at the **Mustafa Kemal Paşa Fountain.** From here **Atatürk Cad.,** changing to **Sarayönü Cad.** and **Dıvan Cad.,** runs south across the Karakoyun River through the center and the old part of town before splintering around the fortress.

Tourist Office: 20m from the doors of the Hotel Edessa (opposite Hasan Pasa Camii), the state tourist office (☎215 24 67) is heralded by marble steps and a small sign. Locals are oblivious to its existence. The office organizes a $17 Harran taxi tour. Open M-F 8am-noon, 1:30-5:30pm. **Tourist police** are one flight down, while the **cultural affairs office** is in an alley around the corner. The unusually helpful **Mahmut Çoban** heads the office and speaks excellent English. (☎(532) 225 12 18.)

Tourist Agencies: Local English teacher Özcan Aslan runs **Harran and Nemrut Tours** (☎215 15 75; mobile ☎(542) 761 30 65; fax 215 11 56). Look for a big yellow canvas sign above the footpath next to the Şan Med Hastenesi, down from İpekpalas Oteli. Open daily 8am-7:30pm. Özcan offers short Harran tours in the morning or evening (3-4hr.; $8 per person, minimum $32 for entire dolmuş). His Nemrut Dağı tour includes

Atatürk Dam, Kahta, Karakus tumulus, the Roman bridge, Arsemia, and Yeni Kale (9am-11pm, dusk at Nemrut; 1am-1pm, dawn at Nemrut; either option $30 per person, 2 person min.). Sunset/sunrise option includes 2 meals and overnight in Kevansaray Hotel for $50 per person. The Mardin tour (6-9pm) visits Deyrul Zafaran Monastery ($25 for 4 people or more). The 2-day option adds Nuysaibin, Jacob's grave, Medyat, Hasankeyf, Batman, food, and lodgings ($60).

Banks: Those with **ATMs** are concentrated around Fuar and Sarayönü Cad.

Hamam: Urfa's oldest hamam is the **Vezir,** just opposite the PTT. Entry $2. Open 8am-12pm for women, 6-11pm for men; hours fluctuate with demand.

Police: (☎313 70 24), across from Golbaşı Park. **Tourist police:** (☎215 60 80).

Hospital: The **Özel Şan-Med Hastanesi** is a good private hospital at the center of town (☎216 27 72, 216 36 16, or 215 43 48). Open 24hr. MC/V. Also downtown, the state-run **Devlet Hastanesi** is on Hastahane Cad., though travelers rarely use it.

Internet: Maviatnet, off Atatürk Cad. by the main circle, is open late. $.50 per hr.

Post Office: The main **PTT** is located between the Şan-Med Hospital and the bazaar. Services include *poste restante* and 24hr. card telephones. Open daily 8am-noon, 1:30-5:30pm. **Internet** services are also available here.

Postal Code: 63100, 63200.

EASTERN ANATOLIA

ACCOMMODATIONS

Urfa's daytime heat persists through the night, so A/C is seriously worth considering in summer. If you elect to go without, make sure to buy bottled water for the night. Because Urfa's visitor flow varies, try negotiating prices from Oct.-May.

Hotel Ugur Palas (☎313 13 40), by the Hotel Harran, off Atatürk Cad. on Koprubasi Cad. Clean and breezy: a budget dream. Tidy rooms with shared baths. $3 per person.

Valiligi Konuk Evi (☎215 93 77), on Vali Fuat Bey Cad. Not as budget-oriented as other Urfa options, but hey, how often do you get the chance to stay in an 800-year old mansion? With only 6 rooms, this exquisitely restored mansion books out in advance. Staff wear traditional dress. Singles $22; doubles $40; suite $50.

Hotel Bakey (☎215 19 79), on Asfalt Cad., off Sarayönü Cad. Popular with tour groups, this fading giant offers A/C and showers for a decent price. Singles $10, doubles $18.

Hotel İpek Palas, 4 Şanmed Hastanesi Arkası (☎215 15 46). Behind the Şan-Med Hospital on Atatürk Cad., in the town center. Clean, quiet rooms with A/C, private hot showers, TV, and phones; cheaper rooms have fans. Singles $12; doubles $18; triples $24.

Otel Doğu, 131 Sarayönü (Atatürk) Cad. (☎215 12 28). With echoing halls and stark, clean rooms, Doğu is a nice choice if you don't need A/C. Back rooms are quieter. Singles $6; double $8; triples $10.

Safak Oteli, on Gol Cad., is the ultimate budget experience. $2 per person.

FOOD

Renowned for its culinary wonders, Urfa's steaming kitchens have a downside: traditional preparation techniques conspire with the weather to leave numerous unwary tourists locked in their latrines. Many foods, especially meats, can quickly become infested with bacteria in the sweltering heat. Local specialties include *patlıcanlı kebap* (eggplant and meatball on a skewer) and *domatesli kebap* (meatball and tomato on a skewer). Another specialty is *içli köfte* (a deep-fried mutton and rice ball), not to be confused with *çiğ köfte*, raw meat with bulgur. Restaurants often give you a complementary dish of *lebeni* (fresh yogurt and bulgur wheat) before your meal, and end with a ritual offering of *mirra* coffee.

Gulizar Konuk Evi (☎215 05 05), by the Ulu Camii. Walk 20m up Irfaniye Sok. from Sarayonu Cad. Housed in a newly-restored Urfan mansion, with *kilim*-carpeted terraces, pigeon houses, and intricate stone latticework. Full meal $3-4. Open until 10pm.

Cardakli Kösk Restaurant (☎217 10 80), next to the Edessa, offers terraces with traffic-free views of the floodlit fortress, and a remarkable menu of Urfa specialties, $3-5.

Güney Lokantası, 17 Köprübaşı (☎313 22 37), across from Hotel İpek Palas., is one of the few welcoming places for vegetarians in the city. They offer about 4 dishes with absolutely no meat, including *fasulye* (beans with red sauce) and *bamya* (okra in tomato-oil sauce). Full meal $2. Open 6am-midnight.

Hotel Edessa has the only Western menu in town, including stroganoff or curry ($4), spaghetti ($2), and crème caramel ($2), in addition to local dishes.

Çay gardens abound in Urfa. Beneath the floodlit fortress, **Gölbaşı** gardens encircle the sacred fish lakes. North of town, **Guresh** and **Millennium Çay Bahesi** flank each other on Atatürk Bul. with **Temigun Bahesi** just before the main stadium.

SIGHTS

A walking tour of Urfa starts on Atatürk Cad., past the post office. Cross the road and visit Urfa's oldest **hamam,** the **Vezir,** then continue around the corner for a cold glass of *biyanbali* from **Serbetci Abdullah** (☎216 77 99), the best source in town. Make sure you visit the **Ulu Camii,** built between 1170 and 1175. It is on the right toward the fortress. The mosque has a beautiful courtyard and a Byzantine bell tower that now serves as a minaret. The engaging *imam* Muhammed Guhadaroğlu enjoys guiding visitors ($1 donation). The first mosque on Göl Cad. is the late Ottoman **Haşon Paşa Camii.** Behind it lies the large **Mevlid Halil Camii,** which houses the supposed **birth cave** of the prophet Abraham. There are separate entrances for men and women; women can go all the way into the sacred cave, while men may only look through a barred fence, praying in the proper direction. (Dress respectably.)

The fantastic **bazaar** begins at the far south end of Atatürk/Sarayönü/Divan Cad, and simply has no peer in Eastern Turkey. Enter any portal for a surreal adventure in the tiny alleys that stretch for kilometers. Each is disorienting, filled with the sounds of machinery and the smell of spices. A few notable space are the dark alleys of the coppersmiths market, the sumptuous displays of silk scarves and *hişvali* embroidery near the Kazzazpazarı bedestan, rows of sheepskins ($3-7), wool, and pigeon-sellers. Most impressive is the local craft of *keçe,* a wool felt pressed and dyed by the sweat of burly, half-naked men in steam rooms. The market's culinary peak is the *tavulc döner* of **Kadiz Usta,** available near the Gümrük Han. If you want to leave, ask for **Gölbaşı,** the park near the pools of sacred carp. On the southwestern side, the **Halil-ür Rahman** mosque stands in a Byzantine church dating to 504 AD. Across the pool is an elegant Ottoman *medrese.*

The entrance to the city's **citadel** is marked by **Corinthian columns,** constructed in 242 BC, from which, according to legend, Nemrut shot firebrands at Abraham. (Open daily 8am-6pm. $2, students $1.) There are two entrances: the stairway on the front wall in the blazing sun and a cave walkway lit by lamps, 50m east. On top, the view is spectacular. Three kilometers south is **Eyyüp Peygamber,** which contains the cave where Job lived for 7 years in physical torture. (Take an "Eyyübe" dolmuş from Atatürk Cad., by the tourist office ($.20). Open daylight hours. $1.)

HOLY CARP! In a cave in Urfa, the prophet Abraham was born in secrecy at a time when King Nemrut had decreed that all children should be put to death. Abraham was fully cognizant of having escaped Nemrut's wrath, and at age 10, seized with monotheistic fervor, he began smashing the city's pagan idols. Nemrut, infuriated with Abraham, ordered a massive bonfire to be lit in the plain below the citadel and had Abraham tossed from the castle turrets into the inferno below. God took pity on Abraham and called on nature to protect him: "O fire, be gentle to Abraham, keep him safe and the fuel cool." A rose garden sprang up around Abraham, the fire became water, and the burning wood turned into fish in the ponds. The pillars, carp, and cave can still be seen today. You can feed the sacred fish with sacred fish food for $.30.

Urfa's **Fine Arts Museum** is on Atatürk Cad. near Kara Meydanı. More of an art school than a gallery, the museum is one of Urfa's old Ottoman houses. One hallmark is the "bearded arch," which ripples upward to a sharp point, like an inverted beard. (Open M-Sa 8am-noon and 1:30-5:30pm; July-Aug. M-F. Free.) The **Archaeological Museum** houses everything from reliefs to jewelry, and on the 2nd floor you'll find Christian icons from the **Ancient Church of the Twelve Apostles,** now the **Fırfırlı Camii.** (Walk on Nusrat Cad. west for 500m; it's on the right. ☎313 15 88. Open daily 8:30am-noon and 1:30-5pm. $2, students $1.) From the carp pools at the southern end of the town, walk 1km north on Vali Fuat Bey Cad. to reach the mosque/church. For Turkish-dubbed western movies, **Emek Aile Sinemas** can be found 50m from Sarayonu Cad. on Fuar Cad. (Showings M-F 2:15, 8:45pm; Sa-Su 3:45pm.)

DAYTRIP FROM ŞANLIURFA: HARRAN

The Akcakale minibus from Şanlıurfa ($1) leaves visitors 10km from the village on the main road. Taxis exploit this fact, and locals in vehicles may charge similarly. $2 is a reasonable round-trip. There are two small lokanstasi near the Harran site, but nothing at Sogmatar.

Harran lies 44km from Şanlıurfa, toward the Syrian border. Harran appears in documents from as far back as 2000 BC, and remarkably was continuously occupied even through the Mongol invasion of 1260 AD. Abraham married here, and his family moved to Harran for a sojourn on their way to Palestine. Harran was home to a religious group known as the **Sabians** in the later centuries of the first millennium. Worshippers of the sun and moon, the Sabians granted equality to men and women, and the **citadel** that stands at the site is supposed to be the remains of a temple to the god of the moon. Further exploration of the site reveals an ancient **castle,** the oldest Islamic **university,** and the supposed site of Abraham's family's house. There is a half-buried underground tunnel and an intact 4km town wall. The **Ulu Camii,** built by the Umayyads in the 8th century, displays an square minaret.

Today the town's inhabitants live in peculiar **beehive-shaped houses,** which are both cool and economical to construct. Youths will often pester and offer to guide visitors; women traveling alone should be wary. Four-hour tours cost $10 per person, while full day tours incorporate **Soğmatar** and the ruins of **Jethro City** ($20 per person; see **Şanlıurfa: Travel Agencies,** p. 466.)

GAZİANTEP ☎342

The largest city in southeast Turkey has a rich heritage dating back to the Stone Age. Yet apart from its fortress, floodlit at night upon a man-made hill, this heritage is giving way to a veneer of modernity. Today, Gaziantep competes with its neighbors for pre-eminence in trade and industry. At night, locals flock to Centenary Park, complete with water gardens, bike tracks, shopping, and a cinema. Beyond the city, a fertile plain of pistachios, olive trees, and vineyards extends in all directions. Gaziantep is a crossroads town for travelers heading west to the Mediterranean coast, south to Antakya and Syria, or east to Van. The Turkish Grand National Assembly granted the town its epithet *Gazi* (war hero/veteran) in 1921 for its resistance to foreign occupation during the War of Independence.

TRANSPORTATION

Flights: THY (☎230 15 65) offers service to over 60 cities worldwide, including **Athens, Cairo, London, Miami, Moscow, New York,** and **Paris.**

Buses: The otogar is a palatial structure 3km north of town. Regular minibuses ($.40) run from İstasyon Cad. at the waterway. **Hidayet Turizm** (☎328 96 96) is one of many companies with offices here. To: **Adana** (3hr., 5 per day, $5); **Ankara** (10hr., 5 per day 7:30am-midnight, $14.50); **Antakya** (3½hr., 9 per day, $5); **Antalya** (14hr.,10 per day, $16); **Diyarbakır** (5½hr., 8 per day, $7); **Erzurum** (6½hr., 4 per day, $15); **İstanbul** (16hr., 6:30am-9pm, $17); **İzmir** (16hr., 2 per day 4-7pm, $17); **Kahramanmaraş** (1hr, plenty, $2.50); **Kars** (19hr., $18); **Kayseri** (8hr., $10); **Sivas** (18hr., 5, 8pm; $11); **Trabzon** (18hr., 6 per day, $18); **Van** (10hr., 9pm, midnight; $14).

Trains: There are 3 rail routes out of Gaziantep. The service to the west runs to tiny Narli to meet the **Adana-Elazig Express** to **Adana, Konya,** and **İstanbul.** One train leaves daily for Narli to meet the **Diyarbakır Express,** via Malatya and Elazig. Another runs east along the Syrian border to a dead end at **Nusaybin,** 50km beyond Mardin. The station (☎323 30 15) lies conveniently enough at the northern end of İstasyon Cad.

ORIENTATION AND PRACTICAL INFORMATION

Gaziantep has a disorderly street plan, centered upon its **Antep Kalesi fortress** and divided by a park-lined waterway, **Allenben Deresi. İstasyon Cad.** crosses the waterway before intersecting with **Atatürk Bul.** to the right and **Eski Saray Cad.** to the left at the town's commercial center.

Tourist Office: A large information office (☎230 99 60) in 100 Year Park. **Uzguy Çinkay** speaks English. Regional info, maps, brochures. Open M-F 8am-noon, 1:30-5:00pm.

Banks: All major banks have **ATMs** and line Atatürk and Eski Saray Cad. Open 9am-noon, 1:30-4pm.

Hamam: 2 of the city's better hamams are in the shadows of the fortress. **Naip** and **Paşa** both admit women by day, before switching to male-only clientele after dusk.

Police: (☎230 18 30). The headquarters are across the Parki on Aksöy Bul. and 4 Cad.

Hospital: Devlet Hastanesi (public, ☎220 93 37). **Sani Konukoğlu Tip Merkezi** (☎220 95 00) provides care at international standards. Most convenient is the private clinic **Özel Hayat Hastenesi** (☎230 60 60) at 17 İstasyon Cad. $10 per patient. 24hr.

Internet Access: The **Eksen Internet Cafe,** 14 Atatürk Bul., 1st fl. (☎231 41 48), 100m from İstasyon Cad. $.75 per hr. Open 8am-midnight.

PTT: On İstasyon Cad., just past Atatürk Cad., on the right. Open 24hr.

Postal Code: 27000

ACCOMMODATIONS

Gaziantep carries the full range of price and quality. Prices are generally negotiable. **Bulvar Palas Oteli,** at 11 İstasyon Cad., has simple rooms and an uneven foyer reminiscent of the Addams Family. (☎231 34 10; singles $7; doubles $10). For slightly nicer accommodations, the **Hotel Büyük Murat,** 15 Suburcu Cad. (☎231 84 49) and the **Hotel Güllüoğlu,** 18 Suburcu Cad. (☎232 43 63) offer nearly equivalent amenities next door to each other just off Eski Savey Cad. Both feature large, clean rooms with full bath; singles $10, doubles $15. The **Hotel Katan** (☎220 69 69), on İstasyon Cad. by the waterway, is a step up, with a terrace restaurant, balcony, and fridge. Singles $15, doubles $20.

FOOD AND ENTERTAINMENT

Wander 500m along Eski Saray Cad. from İstasyon Cad. to **Cavusoğlu** (☎231 30 69) or the less pretty **Cagdas** (☎234 40 00), one block off to the left on Uzun Carsi 14. Both offer quality *kebaps* and *baklava* for $3 per person. (Both open 9am-11pm.) Tucked off İstasyon Cad., on Sayi Ahmet Sok., is quiet **Sadirvan** (☎231 81 88). Visitors to the Anthropological Museum can relax at the nearby **Fuar Restaurant** (☎323 69 69) and sample *alinazik*, a combination of local yogurt dip and *kebap*. Beware the rapidly mounting bill. The uncontested *baklava* master is **Güllüoğlu** on Suburcu Cad. 20. (☎231 22 82. Open 7am-8:30pm.)

Gaziantep's nightlife includes a good deal of prostitution and pornography; check your surroundings carefully before ordering a drink. Close to Güllüoğlu is **Dedikodu,** Gaziantep's favorite **disco,** though ravers would prefer **Taj Mahal,**

3km out of town. Walking from town along the Parki offers outdoor drinking, light dining, and live music, ideal for evenings. After passing the tourist office, look for **Birecikliler Yardimlasma** (☎232 88 81), under the bridge, and **Pegasus.** Just before the mosque is **Incilipmar Sofrasi** (☎234 26 57), with an attached antique shop. Between the mosque and Fevzi Cakmak Bul. is the youthful **Rainbow** (☎338 88 77), run by Eylem Yilmaz. It has nightly music and traditional potato *yufka* cooked on a plate in a nearby tent. The best of the west can be found in the space-age **Begendik** arcade on İstasyon Cad. Its third floor restaurant offers the last profiteroles, lasagna, and donuts before travelers dive into the Anatolian heartland. At the intersection of İstasyon Cad. and Atatürk Cad., a large **cinema/bowling alley** plays first-run, undubbed Hollywood films on six screens (☎220 76 58, $2).

SIGHTS

Day visitors should target Gaziantep's **Archeological Museum** (☎231 11 71), just beyond the stadium on İstasyon Cad., and if possible, the **Ethnographic Museum** (☎230 47 21), on Hamfioğlu Cad. in the Bey district. *(Both are open Tu-Su 8am-noon, 1-5pm.)* **Duluk** village, one of Anatolia's earliest habitations lies 10km north. It contains an archaeological site with Hittite and Roman influences, blended in underground stone churches and mausoleums. Take a minibus from İstasyon Cad. ($1.00) and sit in the village *çay* house until a bus returns. Taxis cost $7 but may not wait for you to explore the site.

Three key sites lie outside Gaziantep. **Belkis** (Zeugma) is just off the Şanlıurfa road, 10km from Nizip village. Hellenistic, Roman and Byzantine influences are combined in a series of villa remnants, many of which will flood with the construction of the Birecik Dam. Check with locals to establish what remains visible after water levels stabilize. **Yesemet** is a field of Hittite statues, progressively excavated over the last 100 years. It is a two-hour detour from the town of Ishlahiye, accesible by taxi. **Rum Kale,** 25km from Yazuveli and 62km from Gaziantep, requires an additional day to visit. This late-Hittite castle is said to have held St. John's biblical manuscripts. Rising water levels from a nearby dam are likely to flood the approaches to Rum Kale, so inquire at tourist information first.

NORTHERN CYPRUS

Along the shores of Northern Cyprus, seductive sunsets and slooooow sailboats reveal the island's easy, breezy attitude. Many civilizations have swept through Cyprus's remote lands, leaving history fans a gold mine of ruins to explore, from medieval castles to mosques-turned-cathedrals. Lazy, hazy days hide a racy secret: come nightfall, harbor-side casinos bubble with crowds of tourists and hard-core gamblers alike. Since the prohibition of casinos in Turkey a few years ago, Northern Cyprus has become a haven for high-rollers. Even if you're not into the extravagant casino thing, Cyprus' quiet Mediterranean beaches, legendary mountains, and magical ruins still merit a few days' visit from mainland Turkey.

Travelers in Northern Cyprus need not feel intimidated by the heavy military presence, which actually grants the island a sense of security. In the cities, policemen lackadaisically direct traffic as blue-beret-wearing UN peacekeepers cruise the streets. Military bases swallow everything from fields to monasteries. Sentries and shepherds walk side by side, and sometimes the sentries *are* the shepherds.

Turkey is the only country that recognizes the "Turkish Republic of Northern Cyprus," which comprises 37% of the entire island. Though officially proclaimed on November 15, 1983, it was more or less established by the 1974 Turkish military action (variously known as the "peace operation" or "invasion," depending on the speaker's point of view). The government of Northern Cyprus, a parliamentary democracy on the British model, is led by President Rauf Denktaş. The official language is Turkish, and the official currency is the Turkish lira. Most of the 175,000 residents are Turkish Cypriots, though about 40,000 are immigrants from the Turkish mainland. A few hundred Brits and Germans also live here, with a number of bonus Brits dropping by their holiday homes in the summer. About half the population speaks English, and many older residents speak Greek.

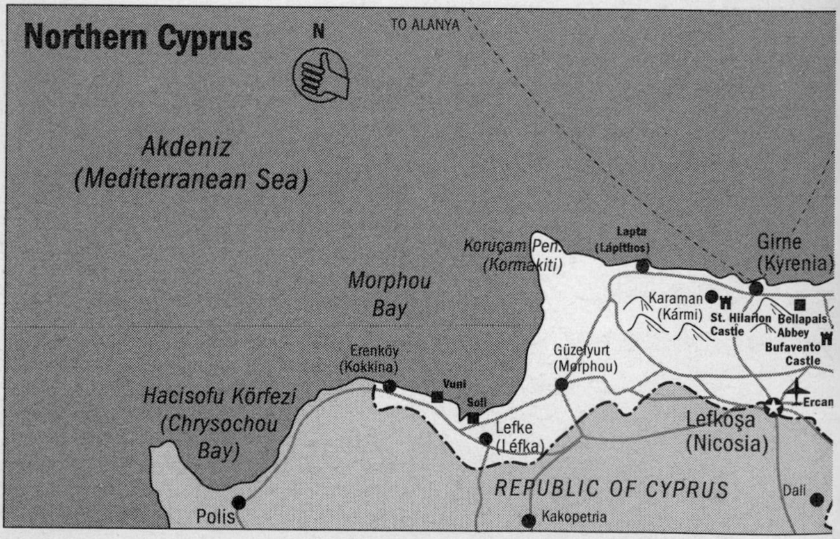

HIGHLIGHTS OF NORTHERN CYPRUS

EXPLORE the fairy-tale beauty of 10th-century **St. Hilarion Castle** (p. 488), a paradisiacal summer house of the ages, coveted as an ancient and modern-day battle prize.

REVISIT Cyprus's royal past in the ghostly halls of **Girne Castle** (p. 486), the dwelling place of the notorious Lusignan ruling family, whose eerie dungeon caged the victims of court politics and intrigues.

JOURNEY among thick cypress groves and silver olive trees to discover the glorious, restored **Bellapais Abbey** (p. 489), whose elegantly crafted cloisters command a majestic view over the sea.

TOUR the extensive ruins that stood preserved in sand in ancient **Salamis** (p. 499) for 1000 years, and gawk at the strange Royal Tombs near **Mağusa** (p. 495).

ESSENTIALS

MONEY

Northern Cyprus uses the same currency as Turkey, the lira. For exchange rates, see p. 44. Due to high inflation, all prices are quoted in US dollars, which are widely accepted for large payments like hotels and car rentals. Many places, particularly along the northern coast, will quote prices and accept payments in British sterling (pounds). Credit cards are generally not accepted on the island, and some ATMs don't take foreign cards, so carrying cash is your best bet.

TRANSPORTATION

TO CYPRUS

The international boundary that divides Cyprus remains nearly impossible to cross. Visitors can enter Northern Cyprus from Southern Cyprus with stringent restrictions and only for a maximum of one day, but they cannot cross the Green Line in the other direction. Borders close at 5pm; see p. 492 for more information

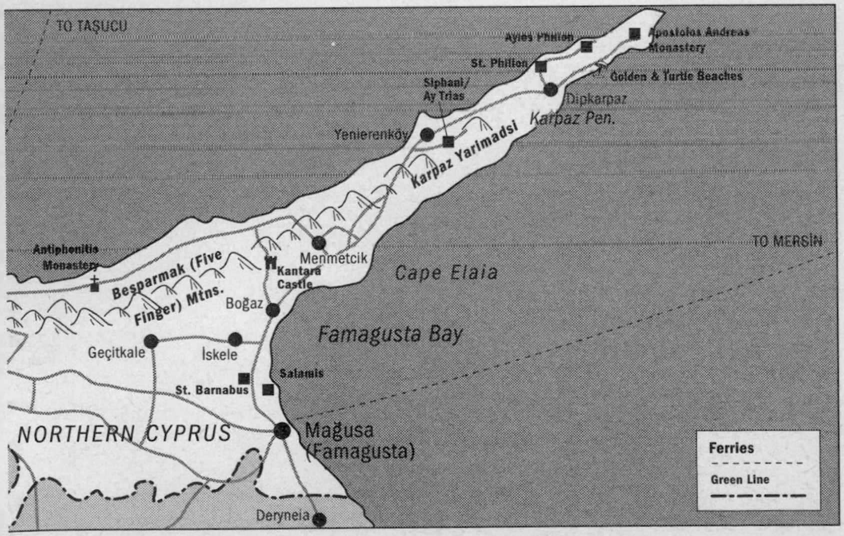

on the Ledra Palace crossing. If you have future plans to visit the south or mainland Greece, ask the immigration official to stamp a separate visa and not your passport upon entering Northern Cyprus. The easiest way to enter Northern Cyprus is via sea or air from Turkey. The best place to catch **ferries** from mainland Turkey is Taşucu, which sends seabuses (2½hr.) and ferries (5hr.) to Girne every day. Less frequent ferries also travel to Girne from Alanya and Anamur, and 3 night ferries per week (10hr.) embark from Mersin to Mağusa. Turkish air carriers are the only ones that fly into Northern Cyprus; flights run between Lefkoşa's **Ercan airport** (☎231 46 39) and most major airports in Turkey. You can get more information from **Cyprus Turkish Airlines'** head office in Lefkoşa. (☎392 228 39 01; info@kthy.net; www.kthy.net.)

WITHIN CYPRUS

If you want to see much of Northern Cyprus, you will have to resign yourself to renting a car. There is efficient dolmuş service between the three major towns of Mağusa, Lefkoşa, and Girne, and it is relatively easy to reach Lapta, Güzelyurt, and Lefke as well. However, many of Northern Cyprus's finest attractions, such as St. Hilarion Castle, Bellapais Abbey, and the Karpaz Peninsula, are miles away from the nearest dolmuş route. Most rental companies will not rent vehicles for fewer than 3 days, and they charge around $35 per day for Suzuki jeeps and Renaults and $50 per day for Nissans with A/C and automatic transmission. In theory, you need to be 25 years old and have a UK or international driver's license to rent a car. In practice, anyone with a driver's license of any kind can rent one. Students should make it clear that they are not at any of the island's English-speaking universities; these students have a well-earned reputation for reckless driving that has caused most rental agencies to refuse them service (see **The Hazards of Being a ZZ-Driver,** p. 494). While Mağusa and Girne are far better bases for island exploration, Lefkoşa also offers a number of affordable rental options. For more information, contact the **Rent-A-Car Association,** based in Girne (☎815 22 72). Gas costs around $.95 per liter, and if you don't take out the maximum possible collision insurance, many agencies require a hefty cash deposit (see **Car Insurance,** p. 73).

> Exercise extreme caution when driving in Northern Cyprus. Winding roads, reckless drivers, and scores of tourists unfamiliar with driving on the left side of the road all provide less-than-optimal road conditions. See **Road Safety,** p. 50.

TOURIST SERVICES

Tourist offices in Northern Cyprus have odd hours, usually scheduled around the noontime heat. An administrative office in Lefkoşa, along with branches in Girne and Mağusa, offers piles of brochures and city maps. Northern Cyprus' touristic press network is actually quite impressive; get your hands on "The Premier Tourist Guide to Northern Cyprus," where you'll find every phone number you could possibly need, plus a number of "pick-me" hotel and restaurant ads.

> **EMERGENCY NUMBERS IN NORTHERN CYPRUS**
> These 24hr. phone numbers can be dialed from any phone in Northern Cyprus. At card-operated public phones you can dial them without inserting a card. At coin-operated phones, you must insert a coin, but it will be returned to you after the call. As with government-sector Turkish hospitals *(Devlet Hastane),* initial emergency medical treatment is free.
> **Police:** ☎155 (in Karpaz dial 381 23 25)
> **Ambulance:** ☎112
> **Forest fire:** ☎177
> **Fire:** ☎199

KEEPING IN TOUCH

Because Northern Cyprus is not recognized by the international community, it is treated as a province of Turkey for postal communication. Mail sent to Northern Cyprus passes first through Mersin and is then shipped to the island. Thus, to send letters to Northern Cyprus, use the postal code "Mersin 10, Turkey." A sample address is: Dan Huntinger, Dome Hotel, Girne, Northern Cyprus, Mersin 10, Turkey. The "TRNC" has its own internationally accepted stamps.

You can call Northern Cyprus the same way you'd call a province in Turkey. From abroad, dial **90** (the **country code**), followed by **392** (the **phone code**). Phonecards from mainland Turkey don't work in Northern Cyprus's pay phones, but post and telecommunication offices sell "TRNC" phonecards. In theory, international operators are accessible via TRNC phone lines, though in practice, American calling cards (e.g AT&T, MCI) do not work.

HANDY TIDBITS

Electricity in Northern Cyprus operates on 240V. Most outlets are English standard plugs, though occasionally you'll find Turkish standard plugs. Appropriate adapters are necessary for electrical appliances.

Cuisine is similar to that of Turkey, though there are number of Cypriot specialties. Particularly, *hellim* cheese (usually made from goat's milk and later boiled) is wildly popular and delicious, with a salty, mozzarella flavor and consistency. Myriad *mezes* and local desserts complement the island's palette and are certainly worth a touch of gluttony.

Like much of mainland Turkey's southern coast, **temperatures** in Northern Cyprus can soar to "way-too-freakin'-hot" (summer's around 34°C). When the mercury's pushing 40, follow the Cypriots and flee the midday heat (11am-4pm).

HISTORY AND CULTURE

ANCIENT CYPRUS

The remains of stone dwellings indicate that Cyprus has been continuously inhabited since 7000 BC. Cyprus's copper deposits made it a key mining and trading center during the Bronze Age, and linguists are unsure whether *kypros*, from which the word "copper" is derived, first referred to the island or to the metal itself.

Regular visits from Mycenaean traders from 1400 to 1150 BC led to the adoption of the Greek language, written notation for commerce, and Hellenistic architectural influences that are still visible today. The **Phoenicians** shared political control with the Greeks until the **Assyrians** washed up in the 7th century BC and dominated the island for 100 years. After the waning of Assyrian power, the Egyptians and then the Persians ruled the island, in the face of much Cypriot resistance. **Alexander the Great** absorbed Cyprus into his growing empire, but after his death in 323 BC, **Ptolemy** claimed the island for Egypt, forcing the last royal family of Salamis to commit suicide. Rome annexed Cyprus in 58 BC, and the Apostle **Paul** introduced Christianity to Cypriots in 45 AD, when Cyprus became the first country in the world to be ruled by a Christian.

BYZANTINE AND OTTOMAN RULE

Roman civic thought, Greek philosophy, and Greek Orthodox tradition melded in Cyprus during the centuries of Byzantine rule. In 1191, **Richard the Lionheart,** en route to Jerusalem, conquered the island. King Richard sold Cyprus to the **Knights Templar,** who returned the gift; the King, in turn, sold it to Guy de Lusignan, a minor French noble. The **Lusignan Dynasty** (1192-1489) brought European feudalism, Gothic architecture, wealth (for the nobles), and a suppression of cultural and religious freedom. In 1489 the **Venetians** annexed the island. In 1570, however, following a two-month siege, Nicosia surrendered to the Ottomans. Famagusta's fall a year later marked the start of the **Ottoman period** in Cyprus.

Under Ottoman rule, feudalism was abolished, peasants were granted land, and the Orthodox Church flourished. As the Ottoman Empire waned in the 19th century, **Britain** defended the Ottoman territories against Russian expansionism. In July of 1878, tired of nursing the "sick man of Europe" without compensation, British forces landed at Larnaka and assumed control of Cyprus. Britain brokered a deal with Turkey whereby the island's excess revenue paid off Ottoman war loans.

CYPRUS IN THE 20TH CENTURY

INDEPENDENCE

After World War II, with the end of the British Empire, **General George Crivas** and **Archbishop Makarios** founded the **EOKA** (National Organization of Cypriot Fighters) an underground Greek movement seeking *enosis*—union with Greece. When the UN vetoed the Greek request to grant Cyprus self-government in 1955, Crivas and the EOKA initiated a round of riots and guerrilla attacks against the British government, attempting to foster popular resistance to colonial rule. In response to increased EOKA activity, the underground **Volkan** (Volcano) group, under the leadership of now-President of Northern Cyprus **Rauf Denktaş,** founded the **TMT** (Turkish Resistance Organization), a paramilitary organization designed to fight the *enosists* and to push for **taksim,** or partition of the island between Greece and Turkey. British, Greek, and Turkish foreign ministers agreed in 1959 to establish an independent Cypriot Republic. On August 16, 1960, Cyprus was granted independence, becoming a member of the UN and the British Commonwealth.

ANNEXATION

The new **constitution** stated that a Greek Cypriot president and a Turkish Cypriot vice-president were to be elected, and that the Greek to Turkish ratio in the House of Representatives would be 70:30. In 1959, Archbishop Makarios became the Republic's first president, and **Fazıl Küçük,** the Turkish Cypriot leader, became vice president. In 1963, Makarios proposed 13 constitutional amendments which implied greater autonomy. When the Turkish government threatened military force in response, renewed violence broke out between the EOKA and TMT, ending in the division of Nicosia along the Green Line. In February 1964, the UN dispatched a "temporary" peacekeeping force that remains today.

In 1968, Makarios and Küçük were both reelected by an overwhelming majority, although in the years following they were subject to several coup plots. Intermittent violence exploded into an international affair in 1974, when the Greek Cypriot National Guard, assisted by the military **junta** in Greece, overthrew Makarios and replaced him with **Nikos Sampson,** a notorious gunman known for shooting up ethnically mixed neighborhoods in Lefkoşa and pushing for immediate *enosis.* Five days later, the Turkish army invaded Cyprus from the north to protect Turkish Cypriots. A half-century after the foundation of the Turkish Republic, the 1923 "population exchange" between Greece and Turkey was repeated in bloody microcosm on Cyprus as families who found themselves on the wrong side of the battle line fled their homes. With the declaration of the Turkish Federal State of Cyprus (TFSC) in early 1975, *taksim* was effectively achieved.

In November 1983, the North declared itself the independent Turkish Republic of Northern Cyprus (TRNC), which only Turkey has recognized. In 1992, the UN reduced their peacekeeping mission significantly. **Glafkos Clerides,** former head of the conservative Democratic Rally (DISY), became head of the Republic of Cyprus in 1993. The reelection of Denktaş in the North helped the negotiation process, and resolution may be possible in the near future. Turkey has threatened to seek unification with Northern Cyprus if the Republic of Cyprus joins the European Union. In early August 1997, Turkey and Northern Cyprus had already agreed to work toward partial defense and economic integration. The agreement, which incensed the Greek government, came just five days before UN-sponsored talks between the two sides were supposed to yield greater cooperation.

WHAT'S TO COME

Periods of tension alternate with periods of relative calm, but there are still threats to future good relations. The announcement in March 1998 that the EU is considering the Republic of Cyprus as a potential member state catalyzed a host of questions as to the future of the island's separate peace. Although Turkey is now a full candidate for membership in the EU, there are concerns about the political future of Northern Cyprus if the Republic of Cyprus's gains admittance into the union.

Though only Turkey has recognized the new state, the self-proclaimed "Turkish Republic of Northern Cyprus" (TRNC) has established trade relations in Europe and with several Arab states. Led by Rauf Denktaş, the TRNC lags far behind the Republic of Cyprus economically, but it is significantly more prosperous than the Turkish mainland. In recent years, the island has seen the arrival of thousands of lower-income settlers from Turkey.

GİRNE AND THE NORTH

GİRNE (KYRENIA)

Girne oozes Britishness, and a small but growing community of British expats lives harmoniously alongside Turkish Cypriots and transient tourists. You can bet on horse and dog races broadcast live from the UK at the Dome Hotel Casino, stay in the Lord Kitchner room at the aptly titled Nostalgia Hotel, shop for Earl Grey tea at any local grocery store, and pay for your fried liver and onions in sterling instead of lira at one of the many British pubs. Girne is ideal if you're looking to spend time sipping cold drinks and doing little else, but don't let the lethargic pace fool you: in and around Girne are treasures for more vivacious spirits to discover.

TRANSPORTATION

Ferries: Tickets for the **Fergün Ferries** can be bought in the main square office (☎815 33 77; open M-F 8am-6pm, Sa 8am-2pm) or at the new harbor, at least 1hr. before departure. Dolmuş run from the new harbor to the main square (supposedly every 30min., $.75). Alternatively, exit the port gates on the right, continue 500m down the road, take

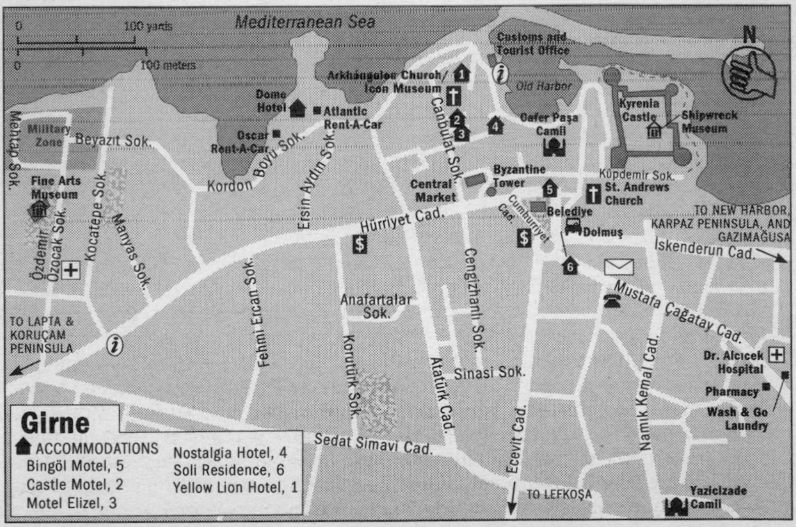

a right at the main intersection onto İskenderun Cad., and walk about 1½km. Fast daily **seabuses** to: **Alanya, Turkey** (3hr.; Tu, Su 4pm; $45, round-trip $60; students $40, round-trip $50), and **Taşucu, Turkey** (2½hr.; daily 9:30am; $29, round-trip $56; students $27, round-trip $53). **Slower ferries** also run to **Taşucu** (5hr.; daily 11:30am; $17, round-trip $33; students $16, round-trip $30). Expect to pay an additional tax of $10 for trips to Alanya and $9 (students $6) for Taşucu. Ferries rarely depart on time.

Dolmuş: From the parking lot off the square, dolmuş run to: **Acapulco Beach and Resort** (5 per day 9:30am-5pm, $.80); **Lapta** (every 15min. 7am-7pm, $1) via **Karaoğlanoğlu** ($.75); **Lefkoşa** (every 15min., $1.35); and **Mağusa** (every 15min., $2.40).

Taxis: Stands are on every street corner. Trips within town, including the new harbor, officially cost $4. There is a list of standard fares. You can also hire your own personal cab for a whole day for $100. Bargaining is worthwhile.

Car Rental: Among many agencies, **Atlantic** (☎815 30 53; fax 815 56 73), in the Dome Hotel, has Renaults (Apr.-June $25 per day; June-Oct. $23; Nov.-Mar. $16), Jeeps (Apr.-June $27 per day; June-Oct. $34; Nov.-Mar. $22), and a range of automatics with A/C (Apr.-June $30 per day; June-Oct. $37; Nov.-Mar. $24). Insurance included. 3-day minimum. Open daily 9am-7pm. Across the street, **Oscar** (☎815 22 72) offers much the same, with a range of Jeeps. Automatic cars and cars with left-side steering are available, but automatic, left-side steering vehicles are a rare commodity.

NORTHERN CYPRUS

ORIENTATION

A wide, grassy mall fills the coast from the harbor to the **Dome Hotel,** a rambling white plaster colonial institution that marks Girne's center of gravity. About 200m along the mall from the Dome, the **old harbor,** now used only by pleasure boats, is near most of the hotels and upscale restaurants. At the far end of the mall rises the massive **Kyrenia Castle.** Turn inland at the castle walls, make a right, and walk uphill to reach a roundabout and modern fountain which mark the **main square,** Girne's overland transportation hub, with dolmuş and taxis galore. From here, **Cumhuriyet Cad.,** which becomes **İskenderun Cad.,** leads toward the **new harbor,** 2km from town, where ferries from Turkey arrive. Behind the main square and to the left runs **Hürriyet Cad.,** the main drag, lined with shops and a few hotels. The streets to the right lead to the seafront; the nearest streets lead to the old harbor.

PRACTICAL INFORMATION

TOURIST, FINANCIAL, AND LOCAL SERVICES

Tourist Office: (☎815 21 45) in the stone ruins across the harbor from the castle. Free city maps of Girne, Lefkoşa, and Mağusa. Open M-F 8am-6pm; Sa-Su 8am-2pm.

Travel Agencies: Possible solution to Northern Cyprus's transportation dilemma. The best is **Kaleidoskop Turizm** (☎815 1818; kaleidos@kktc.net), in the main square behind the bank. The congenial English- and German-speaking manager, Irene Raab, can arrange just about anything. Local sightseeing tours run $30 to Salamis, Mağusa, Güzelyurt, or the like. **Apple Tour** (☎815 54 99; fax 815 18 94), nearby on Ecevit Cad., can arrange half-day tours of the sights near Girne for $30.

Banks: Cirrus/MC/Plus/V **ATMs** are on Hürriyet Cad., near the castle. **Vakıfbank,** in the main square, cashes **traveler's checks.** Open M, Th 8:30am-12:30pm and 2:15-4:15pm; Tu, W, F 8:30am-12:30pm. Banks open M-F 8am-noon. **Exchange offices** are scattered along the street leading from the Atatürk statue left and up to Hürriyet Cad.

Expatriates' Notice Board: In front of PTT, gives info on events and apartment rentals.

English-Language Bookstores: Green Jacket Bookshop, 20 Temmuz Cad. (☎/fax 815 71 30), roughly 1½km from town. From the main square, walk to the end of Hürriyet Cad. and continue for 700m on the coastal road; it's on the left across from the petrol station. A seemingly random selection of novels, non-fiction, and history/guidebooks on Cyprus. Open M-F 9am-1pm and 3:30-6:30pm; Sa 9am-1pm. **BBD,** on Hürriyet Cad., near the square, has a small selection of British newspapers.

Laundromat: Wash and Go Laundry (☎815 18 23). Walking with the hospital on your left, pass the national archives to the 2nd town center. $4.80 per load; $8 per 2 loads. Dry clean $3-5. Open M-Sa 8:30am-1pm and 3-6:30pm.

EMERGENCY AND COMMUNICATIONS

Police: (☎815 20 14 or 815 21 25), on the road immediately beside the castle, just off the harbor and behind the Harbor Club.

Pharmacy: Güven Eczane (☎815 24 09), across from the hospital.

Hospital: Dr. Akçiçek Hospital (☎815 22 66 or 815 22 54), on Cumhuriyet Cad., roughly 100m past the PTT. Clinicians occupy the cottage-like left side, while *"Acil"* marks the emergency entrance to your standard big, white hospital.

Internet Access: The cheapest is **Cafe Net,** well-advertised and across the street from the *jandarma.* $1.60 per hr. Open daily 10am-10pm. **Cafe Online** (☎815 64 28), in the plaza where Hürriyet Cad. and Fehim Ercan Sok. meet. $2.40 per hr. Open M-Sa 10am-6pm. **VIP Net,** where Hürriyet Cad. and Sedat Simavi Cad. converge. $1.80 per hr. Open Su-F 2pm-1am.

Telephones: In the main square, by Cumhuriyet Cad. TRNC phonecards only. The **Telekomunikasyon Dairesi,** opposite the PTT, sells 200-unit cards ($5.25). Open M, Su 8am-1:30pm and 3:30-5pm; Tu-F 8am-1pm; Sa 8am-12:30pm.

PTT: Just off the main square, on Cumhuriyet Cad., offers phones and standard mail services including parcels, stamps, and *poste restante.* Open in summer M 7:30am-noon and 3-5pm; Tu-F 7:30am-noon.

NORTHERN CYPRUS

ACCOMMODATIONS

Accommodations in Girne and the surrounding towns fall into two categories: the luxurious but expensive resort hotels, and the smaller hotels and pensions. The resorts usually cost between $30-100 and are almost always part of a casino, while the smaller hotels and pensions cost $4-20 per night. Rooms with A/C and TV run about $13 per night, but all the less expensive rooms come with a fan. If you have a car, staying outside one of the bigger towns can be quite pleasant. Peaceful rooms close to the sea are easy to find and many are affordable. The quaint alleyways around Girne's harbor also offer several bargain accommodations.

Motel Elizel, 3 Bafra Sok. (☎815 47 74 or 815 82 83; fax 815 82 81). From the town square, walk west (downhill) on Hürriyet Cad. Turn right at the first taxi stand and walk until you see signs for Castle Motel and Motel Elizel in an alley on the right. Friendly, family-run, and the best deal in town. Spacious, clean (if bland) rooms with ceiling fans, some with balconies and mini-fridges. Breakfast $10. $5 per night.

Bingöl Motel, 1 Efeler Cad. (☎815 27 49 or 815 5149), on the main square, across from Set Ristorante. Comfortable but basic rooms with private showers. Ask for the bigger rooms up top. Breakfast $1. $5 per person.

Yellow Lion Motel 23 Eftal Akça Sok. (☎815 93 87; fax 815 3163), behind the tourist office across the harbor from the Castle. Don't let the angry-looking yellow beast out front scare you away. Newly finished rooms have all the goods: TV, A/C, phone, stocked minifridge, and sparkling showers. Breakfast included. Ask to see a few rooms, as they vary greatly in size and some have views of the harbor. $12 per person.

Nostalgia Hotel (☎815 3079 or 815 1375). Each room named after famous personality associated with Cyprus. Giant beds with frilly dust ruffles in deluxe rooms with TV, A/C, phone, balcony and baths. Nice lounge and outdoor restaurant. $16 per person.

Castle Motel, 1 Bafra Sok. (☎815 39 42). Dwarfed by gigantic beds, the clean rooms are equipped with TV, minifridge, high-tech electric fans, and surprisingly beautiful floral baths. Breakfast included. $9 per person.

Soli Residence (☎815 88 70; fax 815 87 80), in the town center, next to the otogar. Run like a huge youth hostel, Soli has 60 2-bedroom suites with sitting space, kitchen, bath, TV, phone, and A/C around a swimming pool. Washing machine and cleaning service. Breakfast included. Singles $18; doubles $28. 20% discount Aug.1-Oct.1.

FOOD

Dine at the harbor, lined with tiny seafood restaurants. The standard $7.50 fish-and-chips combo makes a pleasant enough dinner when accompanied by twilight harborside views. In and around the square, a number of eateries, such as **Dedem** (☎815 33 94), serve typical Turkish food at typical Turkish prices ($2-3). It's best to avoid the fish in these establishments; stick to your *döner* and *çeşit ızgara* (mixed grill). **Supermarkets** offer inexpensive picnic food.

Set Ristorante Italiano (☎815 60 08), adjoining the pension of the same name. Unbeatable ambience and great, affordable food. Set in a Romeo-and-Juliet-esque stone courtyard with draping vines and flowers, this candlelit dining experience is complete with classical music and pasta in all its incarnations. Veggie menu, pizzas and specialty dishes. Starters $3.20; main meals $5-7. Open daily 6-11pm.

Girne Taverna (a.k.a. "Paşa Bahçe Restaurant") (☎815 27 99), on Türkmen Sok., down the street from the Telecommunications office. Serves wildly delicious (though pricey) meals in a garden of grape vines and palm trees. House special *kebap* ($9.80) roasts for 4 hours in the afternoon for an unforgettable meal. Alternatively, a 15-variety Cypriot *meze* special costs $8. Other meals run about $8-12.

Ella's Cafe Bar (☎815 20 16), a "London-style cafe and sandwich bar" across the street from Dome Hotel. A great alternative to standard eateries, Ella's offers home-made cakes and Girne's greatest Nescafe ($2.40). Calling ahead will score you a packed lunch for daytrips and take-outs. Sandwiches $5-7. Kitchen closes 10pm.

The Grapevine, 200m up Ecevit Cad. from the main square. Away from the beauty and bustle of the harbor (but unfortunately next to a gas station), this terraced restaurant serves filling fish and steak dishes ($7-12). Well-stocked bar with $1.20 pints of *Efes.*

NORTHERN CYPRUS

SIGHTS

GİRNE CASTLE. Built by the Byzantines with material plundered from the ruins of a now nonexistent Roman city, the massive castle, Girne's preeminent sight, was later fortified by the Lusignans. In the 15th century, Queen Carlotta, the last true monarch of the Lusignan dynasty, held out here for four years during the siege led by her illegitimate half-brother, the future James II (see **Those Loony Lusignans,** p. 487). After the Venetians rebuilt some of the walls and added several towers, the Ottomans took the fortress in 1570 without firing a single cannon.

A number of the chambers in the well-preserved castle have been set aside for special exhibits and the castle's 6 museums. The **Shipwreck Museum,** across the courtyard, contains the remains of a ship dating back to the time of Alexander the Great (300 BC). The ship and some of the cargo, including 400 wine amphoras from Rhodes and more than 9000 blackened almonds (the crew's dietary staple), are on display. The amusing **Lusignan dungeons,** according to the posted sign, "have been brought back to their former gruesome role as a place to torture or imprison undesirables." Fortunately, these "undesirables" are plaster mannequins and not unmannered tourists. In one room, an anatomically correct Turk is stretched out on the rack. In another, you can peer two stories down through a raised grating at a languid, scantily clad Lady Jeanne, mistress to King James. The queen threw her here after Jeanne gave birth to James's illegitimate son. Other sights in the castle worth a visit are the Byzantine **St. George Church,** exhibits about the excavation of nearby Neolithic and Bronze Age sites, and the Venetian and Lusignan towers. *(Just east of old harbor. Open daily 9am-6pm; in winter 9am-4:45pm. $4, students $.50.)*

BEACHES. The north coast beaches, some of the finest in Cyprus, draw thousands on a good weekend. Most charge a small fee (usually around $2.40) and sit awkwardly below monolithic, multi-storied resorts or "bungalow-style" condo developments. **Kervansaray,** the best of the area's free beaches, lies near the village of **Karaoğlanoğlu,** several kilometers west of Girne. A mostly German and Turkish crowd of sun-bathers and hedonists bake at the popular **Acapulco Beach,** about 4km east of town. The beach

THOSE LOONY LUSIGNANS Girne's castle stands as a giant monument to the Lusignans, the French noble family who took control of Cyprus during a 12th-century crusade. The Lusignans proved that even Crusaders could have dysfunctional families. Raymond de Lusignan's wife, the lovely **Countess Melusine,** was said to turn into a serpent from the waist down every Saturday before eventually becoming the dragon that now haunts her castle in Poitou, France.

Peter I, arguably the greatest of the Lusignan kings (1358-1369), went off to Egypt to recruit soldiers and funding for the Crusades after having seduced his favorite mistress, Lady Jeanne d'Aleman. Peter was later assassinated and dismembered by mutinous barons while in bed with the famed beauty, Lady Echive de Scandelion.

John II ruled Cyprus from 1432 to 1458 under the domineering influence of his unscrupulous and ambitious second wife, Helena Palaeologa. The couple had only one child (Carlotta), but John's mistress, Marietta of Patras, bore him a son, who would later become **King James II.** Never one to leave an offense unreturned, Helena bit off Marietta's nose in a fit of jealousy.

Carlotta fared much worse. Widowed, then orphaned, then remarried to the insipid nonentity Louis of Savoy, she managed in her loneliness to grow quite "close" to her half-brother James. The Lusignan High Court, sensing James was a threat to the purity of the line, poisoned the friendship and drove James to Cairo, where his dynamic ways won the support of the Mamluk Sultan, who lent him a fleet to help him claim the Cypriot crown from his half-sister. In 1460, James took the entire island except for the castle of Girne, in which Carlotta withstood his attacks for four years.

NORTHERN CYPRUS

stretches along the choice Acapulco Resort, where comfortable bungalows surround a tantalizing casino nightlife. **Sunset Beach** is along the road to Lapta. This smaller beach, which also charges $2.40, is an ideal base for Sea Nest Water Sports. *(For Kervansaray, take a taxi ($6) or the Girne-Lapta dolmuş ($.35) from the main square and get off at the "Güler's Fish" sign on the right. For Acapulco, take a minibus from town ($.80) or taxi ($8). $2.40. For Sea Nest Water Sports, ☎851 19 86. Windsurfers $12 per hr.; sailboats $12 per hr.; 1-person canoes $2 per 30min.; 2-person canoes $4 per 30min.; motorboats $2 per 30min.)*

MARINE TURTLE CONSERVATION PROJECT. Not just another pretty stretch of sand, **Alagadi Beach** is the headquarters of the Northern Cyprus Marine Turtle Conservation Project. Initiated in 1992 by Glascow University and the Society for the Protection of Turtles in Northern Cyprus, the project, staffed mostly by university students from the UK, aims to study and protect the **green and loggerhead turtles.**

To avoid alarming the turtles, a maximum of 8-10 visitors can accompany the patrols each night (9pm-dawn) to observe the females nest. When a patrol locates a nesting site, the real treat is watching a turtle patiently lay her eggs, flop awkwardly back to the water, and then glide gracefully out of sight. It's a good idea to arrange your visit in advance to make sure there is space and so the staff will be expecting you. *(15min. drive east of Girne on the coastal road, past Acapulco beach resort and St. Kathleen's restaurant. No public transportation, so drive or hire a taxi ($10 each way; try to bargain). The night on the beach is free, but a $12 donation will get you a T-shirt and $24 will allow you to adopt a turtle. Flash photography not permitted on beach.)*

OTHER SIGHTS. Arkhángelos Church houses a fascinating **Icon Museum** (☎815 53 13). Mostly from the last two centuries, icons line the ground floor and three-tiered balcony. From the upper balcony, you can look across at the magnificent altarpiece depicting Christ in a large golden chalice, surrounded by levitating angel heads. *(Open 9am-1pm and 2-4:45pm. $1.60, students $.40.)*

Girne's **Fine Arts Museum,** a seaside cottage that once belonged to an English governor, lies 1km from the Dome Hotel. Two salons of European paintings give way to several rooms of porcelain Chinese horses, red and gold dragons, and Mt. Fuji fire screens. *(Open daily 9am-1pm and 2-4:45pm. $1.60, students $.40. Because of the intervening military zone, a circuitous route gets you there: walk along Hürriyet Cad., turn right on Özdemir Özocak Sok., and pass the military hospital. Well-marked museum on left.)*

SAVE THE SEA TURTLE The beaches of Northern Cyprus are one of the few remaining nesting sites of the green and loggerhead sea turtles. These remarkable and elusive creatures have been on the earth for nearly 100 million years, but they have been brought to the brink of extinction by human (often tourist-related) pollution and predation of nesting sites by foxes and dogs. The green turtle is classified as "endangered," the loggerhead as "vulnerable." There is still insufficient data on these creatures as most of their 60 to 120 year lifespan is spent at sea, but it is estimated that every year there are 300 to 500 nesting female green turtles and 200 nesting female loggerheads in Cyprus. Sunbathers on Cyprus's beaches should follow a few guidelines. Stay away from the beaches from dusk to dawn. Do not drive on the beaches, since tire ruts can be impassible barriers for hatchlings struggling to reach the sea. Stay close to the water, as nests—normally buried further up the beach—can be disturbed by fires, umbrellas, or anything else that might alter the temperature of the sand in which the offspring are incubating. Finally, do not leave any litter on the beach. For more information about the sea turtles of Northern Cyprus, contact Kutlay Keço, the president of the Society for the Protection of Turtles (SPOT) at the Grapevine Restaurant (☎815 24 96) in Girne or visit the website of the Marine Turtle Conservation Project at www.seaturtle.org/mtrg/.

NIGHTLIFE

Beach-going, moseying, and nap-taking are Girne's most popular entertainment activities for those who aren't into the gambling scene. The peace-loving community has recently passed laws banning loud music late at night, killing the club scene. Nevertheless, the western end of the old harbor has a number of lively bars and casinos that are open all night.

Cafe 34 (☎815 30 56) in the old harbor. The bold loner of loud, pulsating music. Purveyors of Cyprus's best brandy sour and tasteful indoor and outdoor drinking areas, which become jammed with hip Turks and Turk Cypriots on F and Sa nights in high season. *Rakı* and beer $1.80; brandy sour $3. Open daily 10pm-2am.

Shenanigans Irish Pub (☎815 45 21), around the corner from Set, reverberates with laughter and conversation. Patrons lounge on the couches or at the bar, alternately filling and killing their pints. Beer $1.90. Open 6pm-late.

Bar B (☎815 34 22; barbq2000@usa.net), uphill from Yellow Lion Motel at western end of old harbor. Serves up *Efes, rakı* and the rest, all for 25% less than chic waterfront joints. BBQ menu includes steaks ($10), fish ($8), and the standard snack menu, all served in the shade of the cozy courtyard. Open 10am-3pm and 7pm-late.

Sunset Beach (☎821 83 30), on the road to Lapta (technically in Karaoğlanoğlu), features an **outdoor disco** teeming with local youth on summer weekends. Open M-Sa 11pm-3:30am or later, depending on the crowd.

DAYTRIPS FROM GİRNE

ST. HILARION CASTLE

Walking to the castle is prohibited, and dolmuş don't service St. Hilarion, so either rent a ***car*** *or take a* ***taxi*** *($24 round-trip from Girne; 1hr. stop at castle included). From the Girne Town Center, head inland on the main road and follow signs for St. Hilarion from the 2nd rotary. The road to St. Hilarion continues uphill past the castle and makes for some fun dirt road driving with breathtaking and slightly dizzying views. As long as you stay on the coastal side of the mountains, which is hard not to do, the roads all lead down to Lapta. Photos can be taken only after passing military property. Castle open daily 9am-5pm; in winter 9am-1pm and 2-4:45pm. $3.30, students $.40.*

If St. Hilarion Castle looks like something out of a fairy tale, it's because it is: the fortress served as Walt Disney's inspiration when he designed the castle for *Snow White and the Seven Dwarves*. It sprawls across a mountain peak 10km north of Girne. Built in the 10th century over the site of an early monastery, St. Hilarion, together with **Bufavento** and **Kantara** castles, formed part of the Byzantines' early warning system against raiders. After some renovations in the 12th and 13th centuries, the Lusignans transformed it into a glamorous palace of unfettered luxury. Though the castle was abandoned by the Venetians when they conquered the island in 1489, it has endured quite well. Centuries later, in 1964, the Turkish TMT used the castle as a stronghold and garrison from which to push the cause of *taksim* (see **Cyprus in the 20th Century,** p. 482).

While simply gazing upon the castle from a distance is enough to inspire dreams of magic looking-glasses and evil women with self-esteem issues, closer exploration reveals that St. Hilarion kicks the crap out of Disneyan imitations. The castle's walls blend into the mountainside, concealing the tunnels, courtyards, and chambers that make up the steep climb to the top. From the high **Tower of Prince John,** you can gaze out toward Girne far below and look down at where a deluded Prince John of Antioch hurled his Bulgarian bodyguards, suspecting them of treason. Climb 360 steps to the elevated upper ward, where you can walk along the castle's outer walls. The road to the castle has spectacular views, though twisty, cliffside roads are not for the faint of heart.

BEYLERBEYİ (BELLAPAIS ABBEY)

Open daily 8am-7pm. $3.30, students $.40. Ask ticket office about upcoming performances. No public transportation to Beylerbeyi, so hire a taxi ($6.20 one way) or rent a car and follow the signs east out of town.

This tranquil hillside village, 6km east of Girne, contains one of Northern Cyprus's most notable sights, the stunning Gothic **Bellapais Abbey** (a corruption of the French name *Abbaye de la Paix*, or Abbey of Peace). Building began in the late-12th century on a home for Augustinian monks fleeing Jerusalem. Plundered by the Genoese, sacked by the Turks, and snatched by the British (for road-building materials), these days, the abbey basks in restored beauty. Cypress trees tower 30m above the delicately arched cloisters and silvery olive groves. Inside, flying buttresses support the majestic remains of vaulted roofing and romantic stone balconies. Illuminated for artistic performances, Bellapais's nocturnal beauty will take your breath away. The **Kybele Restaurant,** inside the abbey's courtyard, overlooks the sea and serenades guests with baroque and classical music. It serves tasty, if slightly pricey, food and offers a variety of wines to choose from. (☎815 75 31 or 815 75 33. Fish *şiş* $9; local wines $7-8 per bottle. Open daily 11am-11pm.) The village itself is worth a stroll if you have the time. **Erol's Restaurant** (☎815 36 57), in neighboring Ozanköy, 1km from Bellapais on the main road toward Girne, serves stellar Cypriot cuisine, with 24 types of Cypriot *meze* ($4) and vegetarian *şiş kebap* ($4). This popular restaurant often fills up, so reserve in advance.

KARAOĞLANOĞLU

*Karaoğlanoğlu can be reached via the dolmuş to Lapta ($.40) or a taxi ($4). The **PTT** (open daily 8am-1pm and 2-5pm) and a **police station** are in the center of town; head to Girne for other services.*

Four kilometers west of Girne the village of Karaoğlanoğlu offers lovely beaches and excellent accommodations, including some luxurious villas.

The accommodations in Karaoğlanoğlu will leave you wondering why the rest of Northern Cyprus charges so much more. ■ **Silver Waves** offers well-furnished, beachfront apartment rooms with A/C. To get there, follow the signs for the Top Set Hotel, but instead of taking a right into the hotel's parking area, head straight toward the sea. Some rooms come equipped with kitchenettes and A/C. (☎822 24 18 or 822 32 08; fax 223 7691; silverwaves@northcyprus.net. Continental breakfast $2. Singles $12; doubles $20.) The **Şendiniz Hotel** has well-furnished rooms with bath, most with A/C. A number of two-level duplex rooms with balconies and A/C are also available. To get there, follow the signs from the main road. (☎822 24 01; fax 822 22 30. Breakfast included. Singles $10; doubles $20; duplex rooms $24.) For something a bit more posh but worth far more than its price tag, try the **Mountain View Hotel & Bungalows** marked by a series of conspicuous signs to the sea. Plush hotel rooms and multi-room bungalows with A/C, phone, and TV encircle the beautiful pool and bar area. (Breakfast included. Bungalows: singles $14; doubles $21; triples $31. Hotel: singles: $12; doubles $18; triples $27.)

The **Address Restaurant and Brasserie,** 13 Alı Aktaş Sok., makes for some fine seaside dining. Shrimp, *börek*, and cocktails run about $3, while a full fish or meat dinner ranges $7-10. (☎822 35 37. Open daily 12:30-3pm and 7-11pm.) Just within town limits as you head in from Girne, the **Pegasos Restaturant** offers a pretty standard menu backed by a strong bar and excellent conversation. (Open daily 11:30am-midnight.) On the other end of town, **Planter's Bar & Bistro,** 159 Karaoğlanoğlu Cad., serves European and Italian food ($12), with occasional live music. (☎822 22 19. Open daily 6:30pm-when customers leave.)

NORTHERN CYPRUS

LAPTA (LÁPITHOS)

Access Lapta by dolmuş from Girne (frequent 7am-7pm, $.50). The ***police station*** *and* ***PTT*** *(open M-F 8am-1pm and 2-5pm) are on the main road at the base of the mountain.*

The town of Lapta, with its narrow, snake-like roads, covers the base of the mountains, growing in the cracks and sprouting on the jagged bluffs. Once a predominantly Greek village, it is now home to settlers from Paphos. Hotel-owned beaches and casinos provide most of the entertainment. Like many tourist spots, Lapta is separated into two distinct sections, one for locals and the other for visitors. Just north of the municipality borders is the tourist-oriented strip of seaside Lapta, marked by convenience stores, restaurants, discos, and expensive hotels.

Fresh from an afternoon at the beach, hire a taxi ($2.40) to drive up to the **Başpınar** ("headspring"), which has supplied the town's water for over 3,000 years. The view is the real attraction, and the walk downhill (30-45min.) allows you to chase the sun as it dives below the horizon. The brown **mosque** to the left (from the vantage point of the spring) was, like many mosques in Northern Cyprus, formerly an Orthodox church. To the right, the Orthodox **monastery** seems to occupy its own island. On the way, you'll pass three or four wonderfully restored **Greek houses** with fruit gardens, the handiwork of local poet/businessman/politician Doğan Boransel. Rent the houses for $200-$350 per week.

While there are no budget accommodations in Lapta, there are several decent places to eat. **Hilltop Restaurant** (☎821 88 84), by the old monastery, about halfway uphill to the springs, has a pleasant view of the valley below. A relatively tourist-free atmosphere and *kleftigo* (lamb roasted for 3hr. in a pot; $5 with chips and salad) make this place a winner. Hilltop serves a Cypriot specialty: meat and tomatoes seasoned with dried *molehiya* (mint) leaves ($5). **Ali Paşa,** on the water, is a favorite among the Brits. European and Turkish offerings include vegetarian options. (☎821 89 42 or 821 83 29. Lunch $2-3; dinner $5-7.) At **Başpınar** (☎/fax 821 86 61), perched above town by a spring, enjoy the house specialty, a goat dish cooked in a clay pot (Su, W; $6), and views of Lapta. Ask for the *moussaka* (eggplant with rice and yogurt; $7.20) or try some of the 20 *meze* dishes.

At night, Students and young locals frequent the **Golden Bar,** on the beach by the Marmaris Hotel, for its good mix of music (European, American, and Turkish; sometimes live) and a fun clientele. (Beer $2; cocktails $2.50-4.) As for the "nightclubs" on the beach: let their run-down exteriors divert you elsewhere.

LEFKOŞA AND ENVIRONS

LEFKOŞA (NORTH NICOSIA)

Sounds of construction and urban traffic dissolve into the shouts of children at play and the hum of machinery in scattered shops along the **Green Line.** A series of oildrums, barbed wire, steel, and concrete barricades forms a sort of poor man's Berlin Wall, around which the Turkish and Greek Cypriot communities coexist. Tourists wander the streets, among Lefkoşa's older sights, casting a curious eye over the historically and politically salient divide. The mostly residential Lefkoşa lacks Cyprus's coastal appeal, so unless you appreciate the more honest face the town presents, a daytrip from Girne or Mağusa is probably your best bet.

Though it was founded in the 3rd century BC, Lefkoşa did not become the capital of the island until the 10th century AD, when Arab raids forced the Byzantine inhabitants to build a secure inland fortress. In the 12th century, the prosperous city was conquered by Roman Catholic Crusaders, and 200 years later it fell to the Venetians, who built the present city walls. Despite the added defenses, the Ottomans captured the city in 1570, and the arrival of the Turks marked the beginning of the island's modern ethnic conflict. In 1964, the Green Line was established to separate the Greek and Turkish sectors of the city, and ten years later the division was further cemented following the Turkish invasion. **The Green Line is considered a military restricted zone, and photography of the barrier is prohibited.**

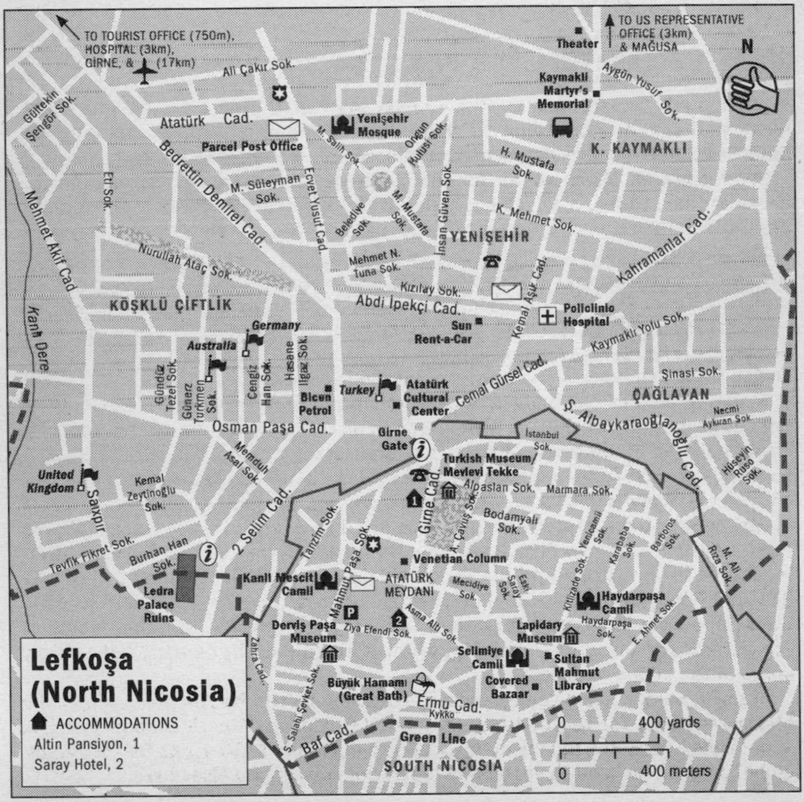

TRANSPORTATION

Flights: Ercan airport, 17km from town, is serviced only by Turkish carriers. Taxis from the airport cost $16; be sure to fix the fare in advance. **Cyprus Turkish Airlines** (☎227 38 20 or 228 39 01) has an office on Atatürk Meydanı. Open M-F 8:30am-1pm, 2:30-5pm; Sa 9am-2pm. All Cyprus Turkish Airlines offices have timetables listing all flight times. Flights to: **Adana** (45min.; M, W, Su 4pm; F 3:30pm, 4pm; round-trip $120); **Ankara** (1hr.; daily at noon; $102, round-trip $135; students $62, round-trip $124); **Antalya** (1hr.; Su-F; $100, round-trip $130; students $60, round-trip $120); **Dalaman** (1¼hr.; W 5pm, Su 8:30am; $100, round-trip $130; students $60, round-trip $120); **İstanbul** (1½hr.; frequent daily flights; $110, round-trip $145; students $66, round-trip $132); **İzmir** (1½hr.; flights M, Th-Sa; $110, round-trip $145; students $66, round-trip $132). 5 flights per week to **Stansted, London**, via Antalya (4hr.; $250, round-trip $300; students $166, round-trip $300), and 2 per week to **Heathrow, London**, via İzmir (4hr., round-trip $316).

Buses and Dolmuş: From the otogar, buses run to: **Lefke** (via **Güzelyurt** every hr. 7am-6:30pm, $1.60); **Girne** (every 15min. 7am-7pm, $1.40); **Mağusa** (every 30min. 7am-7pm, $2). To get to **Ercan Airport,** ride the **Paşaköy** dolmuş and ask to be let off at the airport (1, 2, 4, 4:30pm; $1). Additionally, dolmuş from the town square run the **Lefkoşa-Girne** route (7am-5:30pm, $1.85).

Car Rental: Bicen Petrol, 61 Bedrettin Demirel Cad. (☎223 38 53 or 227 16 80), at the gas station near the roundabout just past the Turkish embassy, rents Renaults and Nissans for a 3 day minimum ($28 per day). **Sun Rent-a-Car,** 10 Abdi İpekci Cad. (☎227 87 87), has jeeps ($50 per day) and automatic Nissans ($55 per day). Open M-Sa 8:30am-6pm, Su 8:30am-3pm.

ORIENTATION AND PRACTICAL INFORMATION

To get to town from the **otogar,** follow **Kemal Aşık Cad.** south for 1km (15min.; walk with the otogar on your right) to **Girne Gate** and the old city walls. From there, **Girne Cad.,** the main street, runs to the main square, **Atatürk Meydanı,** and continues to the **Green Line.** If you arrive from the south at the **Ledra Palace** crossing, walk 500m up the street to a roundabout with a Turkish **victory monolith** in the middle. Follow the city walls to Girne Gate.

Tourist Office: Lefkoşa houses Northern Cyprus's **Ministry of Tourism** (☎228 96 29), inconveniently situated at the extreme northwest of the city on Bedrettin Demirel Cad., 2km from Girne Gate. Deals mostly with administration, though it has an impressive array of brochures and booklets. Welcomes drop-ins. Open M 9am-6pm, Tu-F 9am-5pm; in winter M-F 8am-5pm. A smaller office (☎227 29 94) is more conveniently located just inside Girne Gate, in the stone structure in the middle of the road. English-speaking staff provides free maps. Open M 9am-4pm, Tu-Sa 9am-2pm.

Embassies: Turkey (☎227 23 14), at Bedrettin Demirel Cad., has a full embassy in Northern Cyprus. Open M-F 9am-noon. The following countries have "representative offices," offering some consular services: **Australia,** 20 Güner Türkmen Sok. (☎227 73 32; open Tu, Th 8:30am-12:30pm); **Germany,** 28 Kasım Sok., No.15 (☎227 51 61); **UK,** 29 Mehmet Aleif Cad. (☎228 70 51 or 228 38 61; open M, W, F 9am-1:30pm; Tu, Th 9am-1:30pm and 2:30-5pm); **US,** 6 Saran Sok. (☎225 24 40; open M-F 8am-1pm and 2-3:30pm), 3km out of town. For more info, contact the **Foreign Affairs Office** in Lefkoşa (☎227 23 31 or 228 76 47).

Currency Exchange: Several *döviz* offices along Girne Cad. Open M-F 8am-1pm and 2-4pm. **Banks** close at noon, but the large ones in Atatürk Meydanı reopen from 3:30pm until nighttime. **TC Ziraat Bankası,** on the corner across from the smaller tourist information center, changes traveler's checks. Open M 8am-4pm, Tu-F 8am-1:30pm.

English-Language Bookstore: Rüstem Kitabevi, 26 Girne Cad. (☎228 35 06), just beyond Atatürk Meydanı in the direction of the Green Line. Open since 1937, it has collected a delightful array of Penguin and Oxford paperbacks as well as a wide array of fiction, non-fiction, and books on Cyprus. Open M-F 8am-6pm, Sa 8am-2pm.

Police: (☎228 33 11), on Girne Cad. close to Atatürk Meydanı.

Hospital: (☎228 54 41 or 223 2441). **Burhan Nalbantoğlu Devlet Hastanesı** is 3km from town center on road to Girne, roughly 700m from the Victory Monument.

Telephones: Kontürlü Telefon (metered phone) offices pepper the Old City streets. Your cheapest bet ($.80 per min. to the US) is across the street from tourist office, facing Özner Taxi. **Pembe Telefon,** 30m right of the PTT, has metered booths and sells phone cards. Open M-F 7:30am-2pm and 3:30-5:30pm. The **Government Telecommunications Department** is on Arif Salim Cad., halfway between Girne Gate and the otogar.

Internet Access: On the road into town from Girne (Bedrettin Demirel Cad.), there are a number of well-advertised Internet cafes.

Post Office: (☎228 5448), on Sarayönü Sok., offers standard postal services, plus speedy **APS** delivery. From Girne Gate, take a right off Atatürk Meydanı. Open M 7:30am-2pm and 3:30-6pm; Tu-F 7:30am-2pm and 4-6pm; Sa 8:30am-12:30pm.

ACCOMMODATIONS AND FOOD

Budget travelers may have difficulty finding suitable accommodations in Lefkoşa. The few hotels geared toward tourists ask $20-40 per person and lack charm, while the many pensions generally cater to locals who can't afford apartments. For a roof and a clean bed, one of the best deals is the **Altın Pansiyon,** on the right side of Girne Cad. as you enter the gate, which offers 23 tidy (if cell-like) rooms with shared bath. (☎228 50 49. $11.) Inexpensive **restaurants** crowd the area near the Girne Gate; typical Turkish fare such as *döner kebap* goes for around $1.50. For a shift in routine, try **Cafe Palace,** marked by the massive yellow umbrellas in Atatürk Meydanı, just below the luxurious **Saray Hotel** ($70). Palace serves up burgers (including veggie) in addition to your standard *döner* plate. (☎227 1045. Burgers $1.50, with fries $2.50.) **Havuzbaşı Restaurant** is pressed against a cement wall constituting part of the Green Line. It specializes in non-stop live music and affordable, *kebap*-type meals. (☎228 4004. *Mezes* $.80; meal $3; massive *rakı* bottle $9. Open daily 8am-3am.) Slightly nicer and more expensive joints are near the Selimiye Camii and in the New Town. The classier **Moyra Restaurant,** 32 Osman Paşa Cad., near the Tourism Administrative Office, specializes in a Cypriot menu complete with *şeftale köfte* (meat wrapped with intestines) and the to-die-for *katmer* dessert. (☎228 68 00. Meals $9; cocktails $4.)

SIGHTS

The **Selimiye Camii/St. Sophia Cathedral** is a bizarre sight: an ancient cathedral looming in the shadow of its two soaring minarets. The beautiful flying buttresses, grand vaulted ceilings, and carvings of Christian Saints above the doorways combine with the white-washed interior, prayer rugs, and Islamic calligraphy to make the modern-day mosque a truly unique and awe-inspiring spot.

Refurbished by the Ottomans in 1570, the cathedral was originally built in the Gothic style in 1326 by French architects at the behest of Queen Alix of Champagne. From Atatürk Meydanı, with Girne Gate at your back, continue down Girne Cad., looking left for the twin minarets. Beside it is the **Bedesten,** the 14th-century Orthodox Cathedral of St. Nicholas. Ottomans converted it first into a covered market and then a barn. Next door is the Bedesten's modern successor, where fruit, vegetables, and surprisingly tasteful souvenirs are available at decent prices.

With your back to the Selimiye Camii, head straight for a block and take a left to reach the 700-year-old **Büyük Hamamı,** once part of a 14th-century church. Since the building's construction, Lefkoşa has risen about 2m, leaving the hamam slightly subterranean. (Open daily 8am-10pm. Bath, exfoliation, and massage $15.) Just a dice throw away is the **Kumarcılar Hanı** (Gamblers' Inn). Formerly for 17th-century traveling merchants, it now houses Northern Cyprus's Antiquities Department and a restaurant. (Open M-F 8am-2pm.) A block or two to the east, beyond the Selimiye Camii, is the Gothic-era **Haydarpaşa Camii,** once a Lusignan church and today a gallery. Face the Green Line and follow it to the right to the **Derviş Paşa Museum.**

(Open M 9am-2pm and 3:30-7pm; Tu-Su 9am-7pm. $1.80, students $.40.) The former mansion of a notable 20th-century Cypriot newspaper owner, it has been converted into an unimpressive ethnographic museum displaying clothing and household goods. The **Mevlevi Tekke,** near the tourist office, once a Sufi *tekke*, is now a small Turkish museum housing life-size models of whirling dervishes and Islamic artifacts. (Open M 7:30am-2pm and 3:30-6pm; Tu-F 7:30am-2pm. $3, students $.40.)

DAYTRIPS FROM LEFKOŞA: SOLİ AND VOUNI

On the road stretching from Güzelyurt to Gemikonaği, on the far western rim of Northern Cyprus, lies a patch of Mediterranean coastline short-shrifted by most tourists. The area around **Lefke** has neither Girne's beaches nor Lefkoşa's history, but it is home to the ruins of **Soli** and **Vouni.** Lefke offers a rural reprieve from low-rise, whitewashed cityscapes and from the last stubborn reminders of modernity.

SOLİ

To get to Soli, follow the main road from Güzelyurt (the same road that heads west from Lefkoşa). Without turning off to Lefke (the sign points left to Lefke University), continue straight and follow signs to the ruins. If traveling by ***bus,*** *buy a ticket to Lefke and ask the driver to drop you off at the turn; from there, the hike is about 2-3km. A* ***taxi*** *from Lefke costs $3 (one-way). From Lefkoşa, a taxi runs $40. Renting a vehicle is easier, though more expensive, considering the 3-day minimum. Soli is open daily 8am-7pm. $2.50, students $.50.*

Ancient Soli first attracted Assyrians around 700 BC and was later populated by Greeks. It is said to derive its name from the Athenian law-maker, Solon. The city changed hands, was razed, rebuilt, and abandoned after the Arab raids of the 7th century. Soli's two principal attractions, the **Roman theater** and the **basilica,** were built in the early 3rd and early 5th centuries AD, respectively. The stones that originally made up the 4000-seat theater were shipped off to Port Said in the 19th century to aid in the construction of the Suez Canal. Today's theater is a restored version of the original, located up a set of steep stairs. Christianity has a distinguished history in Soli, since St. Mark was reportedly baptized here. The large 4th-century basilica bears an amazing number of intricate floor mosaics.

VOUNI

The 2nd most popular destination near Lefke (in a popularity contest of two sights), Vouni lies 10km west along the road leading to the Soli ruins. The road to the ruins is a treacherous one with endless blind curves and 1000ft. drops. Jittery travelers should take a taxi and close their eyes (one-way from Lefke $8, from Lefkoşa $40), or skip the trip altogether. Ruins open daily 10am-5pm. $3.25, students $.80.

THE HAZARDS OF BEING A ZZ-DRIVER If you are a young backpacker in Northern Cyprus, you will most likely be confused for a student at the English-language Eastern Mediterranean University in Mağusa. The EMU's international student body of 11,000 consists mostly of affluent mainland Turks and native Turk Cypriots. Large minorities of Pakistani, Sudanese, and West Africans come to EMU as an affordable and relatively close-to-home alternative to the universities in their own countries. A small minority of students from Britain and other English-speaking countries make up the rest. Being identified as an EMU student is generally not a good thing. Purportedly there to get an education, most students are more interested in Northern Cyprus's recreational attractions. Rental agencies are reluctant to rent cars to local students, and the mainland Turks who drive over in their Mercedes-Benz or BMWs are required to bear a special license plate that begins with the letters "ZZ." The notorious "ZZ-driving" refers both to the license plates and to the less-than-straight lines traced by these often inebriated students. Casino- and bar-side streets pulsate with car-stereo music as teenagers cruise by in a motorcade of flashy cars. They're an affable bunch to associate with, but student backpackers might avoid a few cold shoulders from Cypriots by making it clear that they are in fact students from overseas.

Formerly a hilltop palace of 130 rooms, Vouni was built by the Phoenician King of Marion in order to watch over Soli. Abandoned after a fire in 380 BC, Vouni offers little more than a courtyard and a pair of cisterns, though the view of the Mediterranean and Güzelyurt Bay is stunning. According to locals, stolen gold was transported from pirate ships up to the palace via the cistern's tunnels.

MAĞUSA AND THE KARPAZ

MAĞUSA (FAMAGUSTA, GAZİMAGUSA)

The sea around Mağusa is separated from the city by a vast port—one you may have already encountered disguised as the anonymous "seaport in Cyprus" where Shakespeare set his great tragedy *Othello*. In Shakespeare's time, Mağusa was still the world's richest, wildest, most cosmopolitan, and glamorous city, *the* trading post between Christian West and Muslim East—a sort of agglomeration of modern-day New York, Paris, and Hong Kong. Every language could be heard in the streets, from Greek to French, Norse to Persian, Georgian to Amharic. Mağusa itself was, in addition to a point of transit, a supplier of countless luxury exports including filigree cloth, lace, wine, crystals, indigo, saffron, and gum mastic.

Stories hold that two Nestorian Lachas brothers, the city's richest merchant-princes, poured their money into hunting, jousting, and the procuring of women, gradually earning Mağusa, even by the none-too-rigorous standards of the 14th century, a reputation for depravity. St. Bridget of Sweden was especially gloomy in her indictment of "the new Gomorrah." Presumably unnerved, the citizens of Mağusa began church-building with their typical zeal. At one point 365 churches stood within the walls. Only 17 remain.

Crumbling and time-worn monuments to Mağusa's wonder years are scattered about the old city, ringed by the massive city wall. The center of the world no longer, Mağusa seems to have developed a quirky sense of irony at its own fall from grace. A ramble through the old town can take you past a gag shop, a reggae-themed restaurant, or a UN office-cum-barber shop.

Today, in the shadow of former greatness, Mağusa nonchalantly goes about its business. If you're in town around June 27-July 19, you can catch the exceptional **International Famagusta Culture, Art, and Tourism Festival,** which draws musicians, dancers, actors, and artists from all over the world. Performances ranging from reggae concerts to choirs to ballets are held in splendid venues such as the Othello Castle and the Salamis Theater.

TRANSPORTATION

Buses: Run from the poorly organized otogar to: **Dipkarpaz** (2hr.; 1, 4pm, return 5:30am; $1.60); **Girne** (1¼hr., every hr. 7am-8pm, $1.80); **Lefkoşa** (1hr., every hr. 7am-8pm, $1.60). There are also buses out to the villages on the Karpaz Peninsula.

Dolmuş: From the Victory Monument roundabout to **Lefkoşa** (every 30min., $1.60). **Virgo Trans,** on the left as you head toward the otogar, runs to **Girne** (every hr. 7:30-9:30am, 6:30pm; $1.45).

Ferries: Although faster, cheaper, more comfortable sea-buses to Taşucu are available from Girne, **Turkish Maritime Lines** (☎363 59 95, 366 57 86, or 363 67 86; fax 366 78 40) operates ferries to **Mersin** (10hr.; Su, Tu, Th 10pm; $24, students with ID $21). The office hides outside the old city walls, through Canbulat Bastion on Bülent Ecevit Cad. (follow the signs to *Kıbrıs Türk Denizcilik Bilet Satiş Merkezi*). Open in summer 7:30am-2pm, 3:30-6pm; in winter 8am-1pm, 2-5pm. Buy tickets from the port agency.

Car Rental: The petrol station on the left just beyond the otogar rents Renaults ($30 per day). **Deniz Rent-A-Car** (☎378 81 47 or 378 82 98), based at the Mimoza Beach Hotel, 9km north of Mağusa, rents Renaults ($27 per day, with A/C $35) and automatic, A/C Suzukis ($52). Both 3-day minimum.

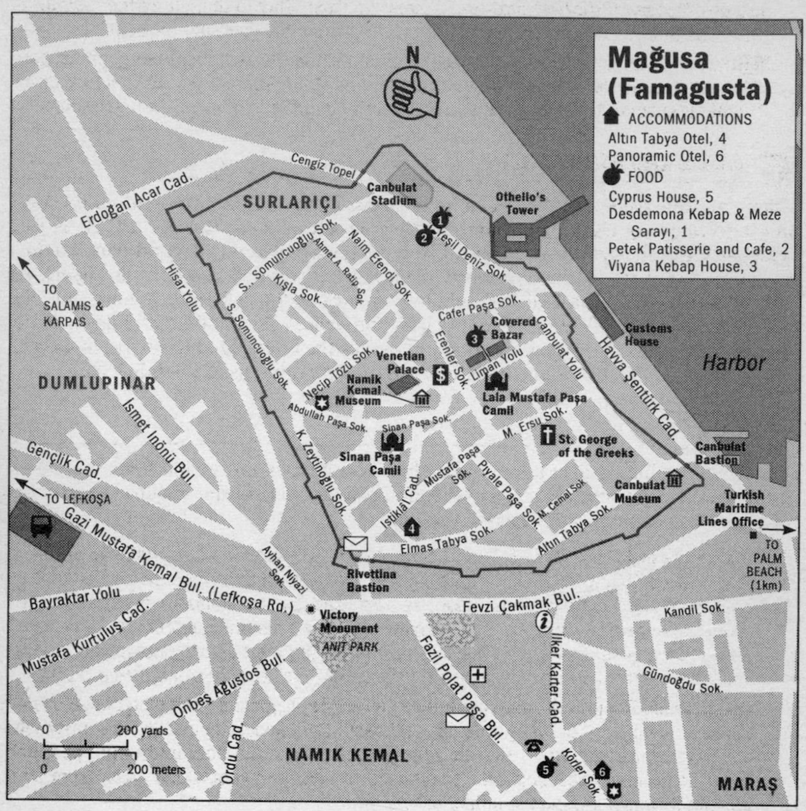

ORIENTATION AND PRACTICAL INFORMATION

Buses stop on the Lefkoşa road (Gazi Mustafa Kemal Bul.). Disembark and turn right; a 250m walk leads to the imposing and vaguely frightening **Victory Monument,** where Atatürk's stern visage emerges from a tower of suffering Turk Cypriots. Behind it are the old city walls. Follow the road outside the walls 500m to the tourist office. The sea is 400m farther away. On the left is the **Canbulat Bastion** and past it, the port where **ferries** arrive. The vacated **Maraş,** now a military zone, lies to the right. The museums, old churches, and Othello Tower are all within the old city.

Tourist Office: On Fevzi Çakmak Bul. Free city maps. English spoken. Open M 7:30am-2pm and 3:30-6pm; Tu-F 7:30am-2pm and 3-6pm; Sa-Su 9am-6pm.

Banks: Türkiye İş Bankası, between the Lala Mustafa Paşa mosque and the Namık Kemal Museum, has one of the city's few Cirrus/MC/Plus/V **ATMs.**

Laundromat: Tözun Temizleme (☎366 48 48). Stay to the right as the road forks 50m south of the Victory Monument rotary, and the cleaners will be on the right, 50m up. Thorough wash and dry $4 per 4kg. Open M-F 8am-1pm and 2-6pm; Sa 8am-2pm.

Police: (☎366 53 10 or 366 53 21), on İlker Karter Cad.

Hospital: The **Mağusa Devlet Hastanesi** (☎366 53 28), on Fazil Polat Paşa Bul., is unmistakably white and yellow.

Telephones: 60 Fazil Polat Paşa Bul. With the tourist office on your left, go left at the first major intersection. 2 card phones; sells phone cards on-site. Open daily 7:30am-8pm.

Internet Access: Cafe Net, next to TC Ziraat Bankası. Stay to the left as the road forks 50m south of the Victory Monument rotary, away from the city wall. $2 per hr.

PTT: Pass the tourist office (on your left) and turn left on the 1st street before the Victory Monument. Open M 7:30am-2pm and 3:30-6pm; Tu-F 7:30am-2pm. No phones at the smaller branch in the bastion, near Land's Gate. Open M 9am-noon, Tu-F 9am-6pm.

ACCOMMODATIONS

There are few decent budget accommodations in Mağusa. If you're intent on staying here anyway, **Panorama Hotel and Restaurant,** next to the main PTT, is the cheapest deal in town. Enjoy breakfast in the terrace garden or wood-paneled dining room for $1.80. 10 clean rooms with shared bath. (☎366 58 80; fax 366 59 90. $6 per person.) **Altın Tabya Otel,** 7 Kızılkule Yolu, just to the right as you enter the old city, has 18 stuffy rooms with ceiling fans and balconies, 14 of which have private baths. Oddly enough, a vast sitting room usurps the majority of hotel space. (☎366 53 63 or 366 25 85. Breakfast included. Singles $20; doubles $25; triples $32.)

NORTHERN CYPRUS

FOOD

Cafes of varying quality pepper the old city. Liman Yolu, which leads between Namık Kemal Museum and Lala Mustafa Paşa mosque all the way to the wall by the port, has a number of fine restaurants.

Petek Patisserie and Cafe 5 Yeşil Deniz Sok. (☎366 4870), about halfway between Canbulat Bastion and Othello's tower, on the opposite side of the street from the city walls. Full snack selection (hamburgers, *tost*, and chips), standard grills menu (i.e. *kebap*), a huge, overcrowded, tropical bird cage, and a central fountain with turtles and leafy plants. Even after you've finished your meal, the trip has only just begun, as the adjoining pastry shop has something for everybody, including homemade ice cream.

Cyprus House Restaurant and Art Gallery (☎366 48 45), across from the phone office. Serves a special steak filet with chips and salad ($7) and octopus ($5) in a tastefully decorated terrace garden. The art gallery features antique pots and pans, pastoral watercolors, and Dalí-esque oils. Live music Tu and Sa nights. Open 11am-3pm and 6pm until stragglers stumble home. MC/V.

Desdemona Kebap & Meze Sarayı, 10m toward the Othello Castle from Canbulat Bastion, across from Petek Patisserie. Serves *meze* meals—20 different hot and cold appetizers, as well as a *kebap* main course. A full *meze* ($9) is enough for two; coffee included. Tack on salad, bottled water, and fresh fruit for $13. Dinner only.

Viyana Kebap House, 19 Liman Yolu (☎366 60 37), across from the Lala Mustafa Paşa Camii. Serves decent *kebap* in a gorgeous grape bower around a fountain, where you can avoid the restaurant's unsightly interior. *Adana kebap* $2.50.

SIGHTS

Though the old town is relatively small, it possesses an impressive number of medieval constructions in varying states of disrepair. The waterfront is consumed by the unattractive seaport; however, beautiful beaches are a short walk away.

OTHELLO'S TOWER. Named in honor of Shakespeare's tragic figure, the castle itself has nothing in common with the story besides its name. Nonetheless, this massive fortification, where Venetians imprisoned the last of the Veronese ruling family for 11 years, makes for some fascinating exploration. Originally built in the 12th century, the tower is Mağusa's oldest standing building. In the 15th century, the Venetians transformed it into an artillery stronghold, reportedly on the advice of a young visitor named Leonardo da Vinci. The large courtyard is still occasionally used for delightful open-air performances, especially during the cultural festival. *(In the northeast corner of the old city. The tower is hard to miss. Head down to the waterfront and follow the city wall north. Open daily 10am-5pm. $2, students $.50.)*

LALA MUSTAFA PAŞA MOSQUE. The Lusignans originally dubbed this Gothic edifice, Mağusa's largest house of God, **St. Nicholas's Cathedral.** When the Ottomans captured Mağusa, they removed all the statuary and representational stained glass, slapped down some carpets, erected the minarets, and—*voilà!*—the gorgeous Lala Mustafa Paşa Mosque. *(In the center of town, on Liman Yolu Cad. As the largest building in town, it is visible from a distance. Small donation expected.)*

BEACHES. The beaches around Mağusa are among the largest and most beautiful on the island. **Palm Beach,** beneath the large hotel of the same name, is the closest. From Canbulat Bastion, follow the sea 1km north. A large stretch of sand extends north of Salamis, where beaches are mostly owned by one hotel or another but are nevertheless hospitable to non-guests. Exemplary and free **Mimoza Beach,** 9km north of Mağusa, is rife with tourists and young people and welcomes non-residents of the commendable three-star **Mimoza Beach Hotel.** (Singles $34; doubles $50.) Some quieter beaches lie up the coast toward the Karpaz Peninsula.

CITY WALLS. The **city walls** and surrounding **moat,** the result of 20 years' labor by 16th-century Venetians, fell somewhat short of their intended purpose: after a vicious year-long siege, Mağusa fell to the Ottomans in 1571. For a spectacular view and an idea of the thickness of the walls, climb the ramps to the **Rivettina Bastion.** The **Canbulat Museum,** inside the **Canbulat Bastion,** houses a small collection of odds and ends including Bronze Age, Venetian, and Ottoman artifacts, a 16th-century hand-printed Koran, and the tomb of the Ottoman commander for whom the museum is named. *(The Rivettina Bastion is immediately left of the entrance to the old city. The Canbulat Bastion is in the southeast corner of the city: from the entrance to the old city, take a right and follow the wall. Museum open daily 8am-7pm. $2, students $.50.)*

OTHER SIGHTS. Facing the entrance of the Lala Mustafa Paşa Mosque, go right for a few blocks to reach the 15th-century **Church of St. George of the Greeks,** which combines Gothic and Byzantine styles. Its original domed roof was destroyed in the Ottoman invasion; cannonball marks are still visible on some walls. On the other side of the Lala Mustafa Paşa Mosque stands the **Church of St. Peter and St. Paul,** complete with flying buttresses. It was built by a 14th-century merchant from the profits of a single business transaction and later converted to the **Sinan Paşa Mosque.** Across the road, a car park infringes on the site of the **Venetian Governor's Palace,** but enough of the walls and ruined staircases still stand to clamber around in. Next to Sinan Paşa Mosque is the **Namık Kemal Museum.** The Ottoman poet Namık Kemal (1840-1888) was exiled to this building from 1873 to 1875 for criticizing the sultan. The upper story contains first editions, photos, letters, and Kemal anecdotes. *(Open M-F 8am-2pm. Free.)* Outside is the **Dungeon.** Head away from Othello's Tower and the sea to pass, on the left, the twin chapels of the **Knights Templar** and the **Knights of St. John of Jerusalem,** which are usually kept locked. Next, go straight to the 14th-century **Nestorian Church,** a.k.a. **Church of St. George the Exiler.**

DAYTRIP FROM MAĞUSA: SALAMIS

Legend has it that Salamis, one of the nine ancient cities of Cyprus, was founded in the 11th century BC by **Teucer,** a hero in the *Iliad* and famed father of the Trojan people. The town was at one time the capital and richest city on the island. The oldest anecdote about Salamis appears in the fifth book of Herodotus, who writes that in 502 BC, the Persian of Amathus decapitated Onesilos of Salamis and hung his head over the city's gates. A swarm of bees moved into the hollowed head and filled it with honeycomb. Interpreting this as a pro-Onesilos gesture by the gods, the Amathusians made yearly sacrifices to their former Salamisian enemy. After Arabs sacked Salamis in the 7th century, it was left covered in sand until its excavation 1000 years later. It was thus spared the looting of the rowdy Middle Ages.

Eight kilometers north of Mağusa, Salamis is divided in two by the road that leads up the Karpaz Peninsula. To the east, between the road and the sea, lie the mostly Roman remains of the ancient city, which include the well-preserved **gymnasium** and the semicircular **theater.** To the west lies the **necropolis of ancient Salamis** and, farther down, the **tomb** of and **museum** in honor of **St. Barnabas.**

The Dipkarpaz bus, leaving from the Mağusa otogar can drop you at the sign-posted turnoff for the ruins (1, 4pm; $.80). Getting back might be more of a challenge, as the return bus only comes by very early in the morning (5:30am). There will probably be no cabs waiting outside the ruins, but you will be sure to find one at the **Mimoza Beach Hotel,** which is a pleasant 30min. walk north of Salamis, along the beach. Cab rides to and from the ruins should cost about $5.

ROMAN SALAMIS. To the right of the entrance stands Salamis's best-preserved building, the **Palaestra** (gymnasium), built by the Emperors Trajan and Hadrian after an earthquake destroyed the city in 76 AD. It was constructed by slaves who transported the columns in small wooden boats from Turkey, Greece, and Italy. The Palaestra's swimming pool is surrounded by beautiful marble statues whose heads were pilfered for use as garden ornaments in the 16th and 17th centuries. Beside the Palaestra lie the elaborate baths, comprised of the **sudatorium** (sweating room), the **caldarium** (hot water baths), and the **frigidarium** (cold rooms). In the central *sudatorium*, a fresco fragment depicts Hylas, Hercules's lover, refusing the water nymphs. The *sudatorium*, in the southeast corner of the structure, contains a couple of surviving mosaic fragments.

To the left, wander through the labyrinth of corridors and ruined walls that were once residences and public buildings. Take the opportunity to marvel at the Roman fascination with temperature control: under many floors, air vaults supported by 2m pillars of terra-cotta tile are exposed. These **hypocausts,** connected by air ducts to outer furnaces, were stoked day and night by slaves. Nearby is the **theater,** built during the reign of Augustus and used for gladiator shows and bawdy plays. The original seating capacity was 15,000. The lower seats are original; the nosebleed seats are 1960s replicas. Today the theater is only occasionally used, usually during the **Mağusa Cultural Festival.** Ask at the entrance of the ruins about upcoming events. From the theater, follow the paved road and bear left at the fork to find other ruins which haven't weathered the centuries quite as well. Just beyond the **late city wall** to the south is the 2000-year-old **agora.** It is surrounded by a wrecked colonnade at the end of a 48km stone aqueduct. The city also contains a **Temple of Zeus** with a podium that affords a view of the *agora*, and three basilicas. Two of them, **St. Epiphanios** and **Kampanopetra,** both have captivating mosaics and views. The third with baptismal basins has no name. *(Site open daily during daylight hours. $3.20, students $.40. Visitors can drive through the ruins, maneuvering around ancient columns like a timorous bull in a china shop. Stop-and-go touring with a car will take a good 90min.; the sights are too spread out to see all of them by foot.)*

CHRISTIAN SALAMIS. The St. Barnabas Monastery, officially the **St. Barnabas Icon and Archaeological Museum,** is 400m up the road from the Necropolis. Some claim that St. Barnabas was a Cypriot Jew from Salamis, educated in Jerusalem, who returned to Cyprus with St. Paul in 45 AD to help spread Christianity. St. Barnabas and St. Paul were initially ill-received in Paphos, where Paul was bound to a pillar and beaten. When he converted the Proconsul to Christianity, however, Cyprus became the first nation with a Christian ruler. In addition to working with Paul, Barnabas was a scribe who used to carry a copy of the Gospel of Matthew with him at all times. Since he had accepted Christianity, the Jews eventually stoned Barnabas to death as a traitor. Some 430 years later, St. Barnabas appeared in a dream to Archbishop Anthemios of Salamis, revealing to the Archbishop the location of his grave. After having the grave opened, the Archbishop took the martyr's remains, identifiable by the Gospel that he carried, to Emperor Zeno in İstanbul. Suitably impressed, Zeno commissioned the building of the Monastery of St. Barnabas and granted autonomy for the Church of Cyprus.

The church, which owes its Greek Orthodox appearance to the renovations of Archbishop Philotheas in 1756, houses a fabulous collection of 19th- and 20th-century icons. Now an archaeological museum, the monastery has a well-arranged and labeled array of artifacts, from 9000-year-old rocks to what might be the only 2600-year-old toys you will ever see—tiny horse-drawn chariots with wheels that actually turn. Finally, 150m from the monastery is the chapel **tomb of St. Barnabas.** If it's locked, get the key from the custodian. The actual body of St. Barnabas has since been moved to Jerusalem. *(Open daily 9am-7pm. $.80, students $.40.)*

THE NECROPOLIS OF SALAMIS. Covering about 7km, the site consists of the small, indoor **Royal Tombs Museum** and a series of excavated tombs dating from the Bronze Age to the Byzantine period. Without a car, getting to the ruins is burdensome, and most visitors won't cover everything. The entombed kings and nobles have long ago disintegrated, and their grave treasures are scattered among faraway museums, but you can peer through the windows at the skeletons of several royal horses unearthed near the surface of the tombs. Accessible from this yard is the stone mausoleum, oddly called **St. Katherine's Prison,** dating from 700 BC. It has yielded countless archaeological curiosities, including an ivory-panelled throne and a bronze cauldron decorated with griffins, now in a southern Cyprus museum. Following the dirt road that passes the ticket booth for another 50m south, you will reach the **Necropolis of Cellarka,** the densest concentration of tombs. *(As you head away from Mağusa, take a left about 500m before the turnoff to Roman Salamis. The ticket office is a short distance up a small dirt road veering off to the left. Driving to the tombs and walking around shouldn't take more than 30min. Open daily 8am-sunset. $3.20, students $.40.)*

KARPAZ PENINSULA

The Karpaz is Northern Cyprus's most remote region, comprised of gently sloping hills covered with shrubs, wildflowers, and the occasional olive and mulberry grove. The peninsula's remote beaches and peaceful accommodations make it a great area to explore and relax . . . if you have elected to rent a car, that is. If not, catch the Karpaz flavor by hopping a **bus** from Mağusa at 1 or 4pm, and stopping briefly in Yenierenköy. The bus from Dipkarpaz leaves for Mağusa every morning at 5:30am. Unfortunately, the sights on the Karpaz are so spread out that a single bus trip will do little good. Most **taxis** charge at least $50 for a trip that includes a stop at the monastery. **Prestige Tours** on Hürriyet Cad. in Girne offers a $40 full-day tour every Thursday, which visits many of the peninsula's major sights.

KANTARA CASTLE. A narrow paved road meanders from Girne along Cyprus' northern coast before turning inland. Traversed by the occasional flock of sheep, this curvy route is popular with tourists: you'll feel like the star of an SUV commercial. A dirt-road turnoff just after Esentepe brings you to the unspoiled Antiphonitis Church, which houses a number of beautiful 12th-century frescoes. Continuing down the coast, you'll reach the gorgeous, 10th-century Kantara Castle. Perched 610m above sea level, Kantara is one of the three Byzantine mountain castles (along with St. Hilarion and Bufavento), and it offers majestic views of the sprawling peninsula. Supposedly a castle of 101 rooms, legend holds that the person to discover the 101st will enter paradise. *(Accessing Kantara can be a pain; 3hr. necessary if coming from Gazimağusa and 1hr. coming from coastal road (the turnoff is well marked). Time permitting, this castle-lover's paradise merits a visit. Open daily 9am-5pm. $1.60, students $.40)*

YENIERENKÖY. Once inland, follow the highway north, and you'll hit the small town of Yenierenköy, a pleasant road stop that offers one of the peninsula's better accommodations. With friendly management and an English-speaking proprietor, **Theresa Hotel** sits 7km past the town, about 50m past the 16th-century Therisos church. It offers 18 comfortable rooms with clean baths, hot water, electricity, and balconies. *(☎374 4266. Breakfast included. Singles $15; doubles $22.)* A seaside restaurant serves fish for about $4 per person and is a great spot to watch the sunset. A few kilometers after the hotel, a marked turnoff to Sipahi will bring you to the 6th-century Basilica of Ay Trias, where breathtaking mosaics sprawl beneath columnar ruins. Before Dipkarpaz, signs will mark a side road to the Eleousa Monastery, 1½km from the main road. While the site is an unimpressive ramble, the neighboring **Elusa Manastırı Pansiyon** is one of the best deals on the peninsula, offering 5 rooms with private bath and shaded restaurant for Karpazian stragglers. *(☎855 85 53. Meals $6. $8 per room: 1 double and 1 single bed.)*

DIPKARPAZ. The highway splits at Dipkarpaz, the largest village on the peninsula, where 400 of the 3000 inhabitants are Greek Cypriots. In the center of town, a road sign marks the right turn that will lead you out to the (Apostolos Andreas) "manastri" and Zafer Burnu (the peninsula's tip). If pressed for time, take the sign's advice and head right to access the area's better sights, arguably the best beaches in the country, and some quiet beachside accommodations and campsites.

Along the 25km stretch of road from Dipkarpaz to the Monastery you'll pass the seaside **Blue Sea Hotel,** which offers 11 well-kept rooms without A/C or fans. *(☎372 23 93. Breakfast included. Singles $15; doubles $20; triples $30.)* Less than 1km further up the peninsula, the **Livana Hotel and Restaurant** caters to the Peter Pan in all of us. Eight treehouse-style bungalows come with double beds, mosquito nets, and *à la turka* outhouses. Not into the Tarzan thing? Try the 14 indoor rooms (9 have private baths), which are genuinely unimpressive, but livable. *(☎372 23 96. Breakfast included. Singles $14.50; doubles $21.)* A few meters walk away, over some dunes, is **Golden Beach,** which earns its name from the flaxen hues of the sand at sunset.

TURTLE BEACH. About 1km down the road from Golden Beach are the white sands of Turtle Beach, one of the most popular beaches on the island for endangered loggerhead and green turtles to nest. In July and August, the turtles dig holes as deep as 1m where they lay eggs. You can crash here at the **Sea Turtle Beach Restaurant & Bar Bungalows,** where bungalows and tents create a summer-camp feel. *(☎372 21 30. Singles $8; doubles $13; tent rental $13; tent owners camp free.)*

APOSTOLOS ANDREAS MONASTERY. The peninsula's claim to fame is the Greek Orthodox **Apostolos Andreas Monastery.** Some Christians believe that St. Andreas traveled to Palestine on a ship navigated by a half-blind captain and struck a rock, bashing open a magical spring that restored the captain's sight. A chandeliered church with a gilded apse marks the spot where the collision occurred. *(Open daylight hours. Free.)* Across the parking lot, municipal-owned rooms (☎372 23 96) with private bath are rented out for $10 per person; get keys and info from the monastery's guards. If you want to see the very tip of Northern Cyprus, a 5km stretch of road leads from the monastery to Zafer Burnu. The view is unbeatable, but its rocky, nightmarish road has left many a visitor desperately pumping a car jack.

AYIOS PHILON AND APHENDIKA. Forking left back in Dipkarpaz will bring you to **Ayios Philon** and **Aphendika.** The former is a 4th-century religious complex touched by a 12th-century Byzantine church. Aphendika contains the ruins of three 6th-century basilicas destroyed by subsequent Arab invasions.

PHRASEBOOK AND GLOSSARY

PRONUNCIATION

Turkish words are spelled with an adapted Roman alphabet. The language is phonetic; each letter has only one sound that is always pronounced distinctly. Nouns are the same in singular and plural. Words are usually accented on the last syllable; special vowels, consonants, and combinations include:

TURKISH	ENGLISH
c	*j* as in jacket
ç	*ch* as in check
ğ	lengthens adjacent vowels
ı / I	(no dot on the "i") *i* as in cousin
i / İ	*ee* as in peace
j	*zh*, like the *s* in pleasure, or *j* as in French *jadis*
ö	*ö* as in German *könig*, or *eu* as in French *deux*
ş	*sh* as in short

TURKISH	ENGLISH
u	*oo* as in boot
â	dipthong of *ea*, or faint *ya*
ü	*ew* as in cue; the French *tu*
ay	*eye* as in pie
ey	*ay* as in play
oy	*oy* as in toy
uy	*oo-ee* as in phooey

APPENDIX

TURKISH PHRASEBOOK

GENERAL

ENGLISH	TURKISH	PRONUNCIATION
Hello.	Merhaba.	mehrhaba
Goodbye (during the day).	Iyi günler.	eee-YEE goon-lehr
Goodbye (in the evening).	İyi akşamlar.	eee-yee ak-SHAM-lahr
Good night.	İyi geceler.	eee-yee geh-jeh-LEHR
What's up/What's new?	Ne haber?	nah-behr?
How are you?	Nasılsın?	nah-sil-sihn?
May it come easy. (greeting to someone who is working)	Kolay gelsin.	koh-lay gehl-seen
Do you speak English?	İngilizce biliyor musun?	een-gul-EEZ-je beel-ee-YOR muh-SUN?
I don't speak Turkish.	Turkçe bilmiyorum.	Toork-che BEEL-mee-YOR-uhm
I am learning Turkish.	Turkçe öğreniyorum.	Toork-che ok-OO-yohr-um
I don't understand.	Anlamadım.	ahn-luh-mah-dim
Where are you from?	Nerelisin?	nehr-eh-LEE-sin?
I am American.	Amerikalıyım.	am-ehr-eh-KALi-yim
I am English.	İngilizim.	EEN-geh-leez-im
I am Irish.	Irlandalıyım.	ihr-lan-DAHLi-yim
I am Australian.	Avustralyalıyım.	ah-vu-STRAHLi-yim
I am from New Zealand.	Yeni Zelandalıyım.	yenih zeh-lan-DAHLi-yim
I am South African.	Güney Afrikalıyım	GUH-ney afri-KALi-yim
I am Canadian.	Kanadalıyım.	kahn-ah-DAHLi-yim
I am Scottish.	İskoçyalıyım.	Ihsk-oCHYAHli-yim.

GENERAL

ENGLISH	TURKISH	PRONUNCIATION
My name is...	İsmim...	Ees-meem...
yes/no/maybe	evet/hayır/belki	eh-veht/hyer/behl-kee
Please	Lütfen.	loot-fahn
Thank you.	Teşekkür ederim.	tesh-ekur edeh-rim
Pardon me.	Pardon.	par-dohn
What time is it?	Saat kaç?	sa-at ka-ch
May I help you?/Go right ahead.	Buyrun.	boy-RUHN
You're welcome/It's nothing.	Bir şey değil.	beer shey dee-eel
What is...	...ne?	neh?
I am a student.	Oğrenciyim.	OH-ren-jee-yeem
How old is...?	...kaç yaşında?	kach yash-in-dah?
who?	kim?	keem?
when?	ne zaman?	neh-zah-mahn?
yesterday/today/tomorrow	dün/bugün/yarın	doon/boogoon/yahr-un
One minute!	Bir dakika!	bee-dak-ka
I'm hungry.	Acıktım.	ach-ik-tim
I'm sorry.	Özür dilerim.	oz-oor deel-er-im
Where is the bathroom?	Tuvalet nerede?	too-walet nehr-e-de?
Help!	İmdat!	EEM-daht!
Police	polis	po-LEES
Can I buy you a drink?	Sana içki ısmarlayabilirmiyim?	SA-na eech-ki us-MAR-lee-ah-BEE-leer-mee-im?

IN A RESTAURANT

ENGLISH	TURKISH	PRONUNCIATION
Do you have food without meat?	Etsiz yemek var mı?	eht seez yemek vahr mi?
I am a vegetarian.	Vejetariyanım.	vej-e-tar-iyan-im
Do you have eggplant salad?	Patlıcan salatası var mı?	paht-lee-jan sahlatasi vahr mi?
Check, please.	Hesap, lütfen.	hesahp, lootfen
I want a glass of water.	Bir bardak su istiyorum.	beer bahr-dak soo eest-eee-yor-uhm
Can I have the salt/pepper?	Tuz/biber alabilirmiyim?	tooz/beeber/ahl-a-bee-leer-meey-um?
What's in...	...neler içinde, acaba?	neh-lehr eech-een-deh, a-jah-bah?
Are you open/closed?	Açık/kapalı mısın?	a-chik/kah-pah-li misin?
I didn't want...	...istemedim.	eestemedim
Compliments to the chef	Ellerine sağlık	ehleh-rih-neh sah-lihk

AILMENTS

ENGLISH	TURKISH	PRONUNCIATION
I need a doctor.	Doktora ihtiyacım var.	dohk-tor-ah eeh-tee-ya-cum vahr
My stomach hurts.	Midem ağrıyor.	mee-dehm ahr-EE-yor
My tooth aches.	Dişim ağrıyor.	dee-sheem ahr-ee-yohr
Where is a pharmacy?	Eczane nerede?	ej-ZAH-ne neh-reh-de?
I am looking for a dentist.	Dişci için arıyorum.	DEESH-jee ahr-ee-yohr-uhm
I have a sore throat.	Boğazım ağrıyor.	bo-AH-zuhm AH-ree-yohr
I have diarrhea.	İshalım var.	EES-hahl-um vahr
I have a cold.	Nezlem var.	nehz-lehm vahr
I have a headache.	Başım ağrıyor.	bash-uhm ahr-ee-yohr
I want medicine.	İlaç istiyorum.	eee-lach-i ee-stee-yohr-uhm

DIRECTIONS

ENGLISH	TURKISH	PRONUNCIATION
Where is...?	...nerede?	nehr-eh-deh?
I am looking for...	...için arıyorum.	eecheen ahr-ee-yohr-uhm
left/right/straight	sol/sağ/doğru	sohl/sa-a/doh-oo
straight (said only to a taxi driver)	düz	dooz
I am going to ...	...ya gidiyorum.	...yah geed-EE-yohr-uhm
Turn left.	Sola dön.	sohl-ah dohn
one-way street	tek yön	teyk yohn
How far is it to...?	...a ne kadar uzakta?	...a neh kahdahr oozakta?
Where is the bus station/airport/ferry?	otogar/hava limanı/feribot nerede?	oh-tow-gahr/hah-vah lumahnu nehr-e-deh?
I'm going to...	...'a gidiyorum	...ah gee-dee-yohr-uhm
I'd like to get off.	Inecek var	EEN-ehjeck vahr
What time does it leave?	Saat kaçta kalkiyor?	sah-at kach-tah kahlk-ee-yohr?
Can I make a ticket reservation?	Rezervasyon yapabilir miyim?	reh-sehrVAH-seeyon yap-a-bee-leer mee-yim?
How long does it take?	Ne kadar sürür?	neh kahdahr SuOOR-oor?
Which bus goes to...?	...a hangi otobüs gider?	...a hahn-gee oto-boos GEE-dehr?
When is the next bus?	Sonraki otobüs kaçta kalkıyor?	sohn-rah-kee oto-boos kach-tah kahlk-EE-yohr?
Can I get out here?	Burada inebilirmiyim?	boor-ah-dah een-eh-bee-leer mee-yum?
Where does it leave from?	Nereden kalkar?	neh-reh-dehn kal-kar?
Slow down, please.	Yavaş lütfen.	yah-vash loot-fahn

IN A HOTEL

ENGLISH	TURKISH	PRONUNCIATION
Is there an available room?	Boş odanız var mı?	bosh odaniz vahr mih?
single room/double room/triple room	tek/çift/üç kişilik	tehk/cheeft/ooch keesheeleek
Can I see it?	Bakabilirmiyim?	buk-ah-beel-EER mee-yeem?
Can we camp here?	Burada kamp yapabilirmiyiz?	boor-ah-dah kamp YA-PA-bee-leer-mee-iz?
Is there hot water?	Sıcak su var mı?	sijak soo vahr mi?
Is there a room with a shower?	Duşlu oda var mı?	DOOSH-lu odah vahr mi?

AT THE MARKET

ENGLISH	TURKISH	PRONUNCIATION
Can I have ____?	Ben ____ alabilirmiyim?	ben ____ ala-beel-EER mee-yeem?
apple/pear/squash	elma/armut/kabak	elmah/armout/kabak
peach/banana/onion	şeftali/muz/soğan	shef-tali/mooz/sohan
How much is...?	...ne kadar?	neh kah-dar?
...is too expensive	...çok pahalı	chok pa-haa-li
No way! Impossible!	Hayır! İmkansiz!	hay-ir! eem-kahn-sizh!
Flattery will get you nowhere.	Yavşayarak bir yere varamazsın.	yahv-sha-YAR-ak beer yereh varah-mahsin

NUMBERS

ENGLISH	TURKISH	PRONUNCIATION
zero	sıfır	si-fihr
one	bir	beer
two	iki	ee-KEE
three	üç	ooch
four	dört	durt

NUMBERS		
ENGLISH	**TURKISH**	**PRONUNCIATION**
five	beş	besh
six	altı	altih
sevn	yedi	ye-DEE
eight	sekiz	SEH-kuz
nine	dokuz	doh-KOOZ
ten	on	ohn
eleven	on bir	ohn beeer
twelve	on iki	ohn eekee
thirteen	on üç	ohn ooch
fifteen	on beş	ohn besh
twenty	yirmi	yeer-mee
twenty-one	yirmi bir	yeer-MEE beer
thirty	otuz	OH-tuhz
thirty-five	otuz beş	OH-tuhz besh
forty	kırk	kuhrk
forty-three	kırk üç	kuhrk ooch
fifty	elli	ahy lee
sixty	altmış	ahlt-mish
seventy	yetmiş	yeht-mish
eighty	seksen	sex-ahn
ninety	doksan	dohk-sahn
one hundred	yüz	yooz
one thousand	bin	been
million	milyon	meel-yohn
billion	milyar	meel-yahr
one and a half	bir büçük	beer booch-ook
one half	yarım	yahr-um
one quarter	çeyrek	chey-rehk

TIME AND HOURS		
ENGLISH	**TURKISH**	**PRONUNCIATION**
open	açık	ach-uk
afternoon	öğleden sonra	oy-leh-dehn sohn-rah
night	gece	ge-je
closed	kapalı	kap-ah-LIH
morning/evening/yesterday	sabah/akşam/dün	sah-bah/aksham/doon

WORDS AND PHRASES		
ENGLISH	**TURKISH**	**PRONUNCIATION**
beautiful/good/delicious	güzel	goo-ZEHL
bad/good	kötü/güzel	koh-too/goo-zehl
sad/happy	üzgün/mutlu	ooz-GOON/moot/LOO
hot/cold	sıcak/soğuk/	sijak/soh-ook
big/little	büyük/küçük	BOO-yook/KOO-chook
Cheers!	Şerefe!	she-reh-FEH
Bon Appetit!	Afiyet olsun.	Ah-FEE-yet ohl-sun
I love you.	Seni seviyorum	sehn-EEE sehv-EE-yohr-uhm
I want to dance.	Dans etmek istiyorum	dahns et-meck ee-STEE-yohr-uhm
Are you a pimp?	Pezvenk misin?	pehs-seh-vehnk mih-sihn?
I accept bribes.	Rüşvet alırım	roosh-veht AL-lih-rihm
I am not interested in you.	Seninle ilgilenmiyorum	sehn-ihn-leh eel-gee-LEHN-mee-yohr-uhm
Shame!	Ayıp!	Ahy-uhp

APPENDIX

GLOSSARY

ada: island
ağa: a minor noble in the Ottoman empire, modern usage refers to a person of local import
agora: marketplace or meeting area of an ancient Roman city
Ağustos: August
aile: family
Akdeniz: Mediterranean Sea
altın: gold
anahtar: key
apse: curved recess at the altar end of a church
Aralık: December
architrave: a wooden or stone lintel (beam) resting on columns.
at: horse
ayran: salty yogurt drink
bakkal: grocery
baklava: try it; you'll like it
balık: fish
bamya: okra
banka: bank
bay: man (as it is written on public bathrooms)
bayan: woman (see above)
bayram: holiday
bedesten: bazaar
belediye: municipal
bema: under Byzantines, flat part of altar; under ancient Greeks a raised platform or podium
bend: dam
bent: dam
benzin: gasoline
bey: a minor Ottoman title, it follows the first name as an honorarium
beyaz peynir: lit. "white cheese," similar to the Greek feta cheese
bilet: ticket
börek: a pastry with fillings, usually cheese
borstal: a British school for delinquent boys providing therapy and vocational training
boş: free, unoccupied
bouleterion: meeting place for local government in ancient Rome.
burada: here
caliph: lit. successor: the civil and religious head of the Muslim faith
camekan: a disrobing room of a *hamam*
cami: (sometimes *"camii,"* depending on modifier) mosque
Cuma: Friday
Cumartesi: Saturday
cumhuriyet: republic
cuneiform: wedge-shaped ancient inscriptions used by the Hitties, Assyrians, Persians, etc.
çarşaf: a bedsheet, or the full-length dress worn by religious Turkish women
Çarşamba: Wednesday
çarşı: market
çay: tea
çeşme: fountain
çiçek: flower
çıkış: exit
çorba: soup
dağ: mountain
deniz: sea
Denizyollari: Turkish Maritime Lines
devlet: state
Dikkat!: Careful!
doktor: doctor
dolma: lit. "stuffed," usually refers to peppers or tomatoes stuffed with rice or meat
dolmuş: shared taxi system, often confused with minibuses, which serve the same function
dolu: full
domates: tomato
döner: thinly shaved meat from a skewer
durak: stop
dürüm: sandwich of döner wrapped in a thin flour tortilla
eczane: pharmacy
Ege Deniz: Aegean Sea
Ekim: October
eski: old
et: meat
Eylül: September
exedra: semicircular niche
exonarthex: a transverse vestibule preceding the facade in a Byzantine church
eyvan: domed side chamber of an Ottoman religious building
ezan: Muslim call to prayer
faïence: A general term used to refer to various kinds of glazed earthenware and porcelain
gar: train station
garaj: small bus station
gazete: newspaper
gazeteci: journalist
ghazi: warrior for the Islamic faith
giriş: entrance
göbek taşı: lit. navel stone; the platform in the middle of the hot room of a *hamam*
göl: lake
gözleme: crêpe-like pancake with fillings
gümüş: silver
gün: day
hamam: Turkish bath
han: inn, usually in towns; also a title of a prince or a ruler
hanım: polite form of address for women, it attaches to the 1st name; analogous to "Bey"
hastane: hospital
hava alanı: airport
Hazıran: June
hicri (hijra): the Muslim dating system, wherein time is measured from 622, the date of Mohammed's flight from Mecca to Medina
hisar: fortress
hoca: teacher in charge of religious instruction.
hürriyet: freedom, liberty
ızgara: grill; grilled food
içecekler: beverages
içki: alcoholic beverages
imam: prayer leader at a mosque
imaret: charitable house for travelers, often attached to a medrese
indirim: sale/discount
isim: name
iskele: ferry/dock or jetty
istasiyon: train station
istiklal: independence
iwan: also eyvan, a vaulted or domed recess open on one side
jihad: purification, struggle with one's self
kaaba: shrine at Mecca containing a sacred black stone
kaftan: long robe or tunic
kahve: coffee
kale: castle, citadel
kapı: gate
kaplıca: developed hot springs
Karadeniz: Black Sea
Kasım: November
kervansaray: hotel located along a trade route
kese: exfoliatory scrub in a *hamam*
khan: respectful title, refers to lords or members of nobility (Mongol derivation)
kilim: tapestry weave mat
kilise: church
kitap: book
köfte: spiced meatballs
köşk: pavilion, kiosk
köpek: dog

kufic: thick, angular Arabic script attributed to the scholars of Kufa
kümbet: tomb or mausoleum
lahmacun: often called Turkish pizza, it is bread topped with ground meat and spices
liman: harbor
lokanta: restaurant
lokum: Turkish Delight
makarna: pasta
mahalle: district or neighborhood or a larger municipality or postal area
mantı: stuffed pasta, similâr to ravioli
Mart: March
Mayıs: May
medrese: Islamic theological school teaching Islamic law (Shar'ia)
mescit: a prayer hall without a mimber; not used for the Friday prayer
Mevlana: lit. "master," Sufi spiritual leader; often used to refer to Rumi
meydan: town square
meze: appetizers—little salads and spreads that precede a full meal
mihrab: a niche elaborated into an ornate portal, it indicates the direction of Mecca and therefore of prayer
mimar: architect
mimber: The hooded dais reached by long stairs from which the Friday prayer is conducted
minare: Turkish for minaret; tall spires flanking mosques from which the call to prayer is issued
muezzin: mosque officer responsible for the call to prayer
muqarna: decorated transitional element between walls and vault, often with a stalactite appearance
müze: museum
namaz: pen-air mescit or camii, especially for the army
naos: a temple or the cella of a temple
nargile: hookah
narthex: narrow vestibule along the west side of a church
nave: the principle, lengthwise aisle of a church
necropolis: cemetery
nehir: river
nöbetçi: on duty
Nısan: April
nymphaeum: temple of the Nymphs, an ornamental fountain with statues
Ocak: January
oda: room
orada: there
otel: hotel
otobüs: bus
otogar: bus station
öğrenci: student
pancration: an athletic contest involving wrestling and boxing
pansiyon: typical accommodation.
patlıcan: eggplant
park yeri: car park
Pazar: Sunday
Pazartesi: Monday
Perşembe: Thursday
pide: not to be confused with pita bread, pide is bread filled with cheese or meat
polis: police
proscenium: a raised platform in front of the stage-building used by Roman actors
PTT: post office (Posta Telefon Teleğraf)
Ramazan: The Muslim month-long fast
saat: hour or time
sağ: right
salata: salad
Salı: Tuesday
saray: palace
sarhoş: drunk
satrap: lit. "protector of the country," a governor under the ancient Persian Empire
saz: long-necked, fretted, stringed instrument used in Turkish folk music
sebze: vegetable
Selçuk: the first Turkish state in Anatolia (11th-13th centuries)
sema: a dervish ceremony
sima: the gutter of a classical building
sol: left
squinch: support, usually in the shape of an arch.
su: water
Sufi: an adherent to one of the mystical branches of Islam; sects include Mevlevi, Bektaşı and Naqshbandi
sultan: lit. "power," the ruler of the Ottoman Empire
süt: milk
stelae: narrow stone slab set upright bearing writing or decoration; used as a grave marker
stoa: a colonnade or unattached portico
şadirvan: fountain
şarap: wine
şehir merkezi: city center
şerefe: balcony of a minaret, also used in drinking as a toast ("To your health")
Şubat: February
tatlı: lit. "sweet," usually refers to dessert
tavla: backgammon
tekke: Sufi lodge
Temmuz: July
THY: Turkish Airways (Türk Hava Yolları)
TML: Turkish Maritime Lines
transept: the "wings" of a church, perpendicular to the nave
tufa: soft rock
tuğra: the seal of a sultan
türbe: freestanding tomb
tuvalet: toilet
ulema: Ottoman religious intelligentsia
umma: Muslim community
Valide Sultan: The mother of the sultan
vezir: Vizier, the chief advisor to the Sultan, responsible for managing state affairs
yabancı: foreigner
yalı: ornate wooden house along the Bosphorous
yasak: forbidden, prohibited
yayla: flat grassy highland area
yeni: new
yer: room/place
yiyecekler: food
yok: indicates a lack of something
yol: road

INDEX

INDEX

M

N

O

P

INDEX

ABOUT LET'S GO

FORTY-TWO YEARS OF WISDOM

For over four decades, travelers crisscrossing the continents have relied on *Let's Go* for inside information on the hippest backstreet cafes, the most pristine secluded beaches, and the best routes from border to border. *Let's Go: Europe*, now in its 42nd edition and translated into seven languages, reigns as the world's bestselling international travel guide. In the last 20 years, our rugged researchers have stretched the frontiers of backpacking and expanded our coverage into the Americas, Australia, Asia, and Africa (including the new *Let's Go: Egypt* and the more comprehensive, multi-country jaunt through *Let's Go: South Africa & Southern Africa*). Our new-and-improved City Guide series continues to grow with new guides to perennial European favorites Amsterdam and Barcelona. This year we are also unveiling *Let's Go: Southwest USA*, the flagship of our new outdoor Adventure Guide series, which is complete with special roadtripping tips and itineraries, more coverage of adventure activities like hiking and mountain biking, and first-person accounts of life on the road.

It all started in 1960 when a handful of well-traveled students at Harvard University handed out a 20-page mimeographed pamphlet offering a collection of their tips on budget travel to passengers on student charter flights to Europe. The following year, in response to the instant popularity of the first volume, students traveling to Europe researched the first full-fledged edition of *Let's Go: Europe*. Throughout the 60s and 70s, our guides reflected the times—in 1969, for example, we taught you how to get from Paris to Prague on "no dollars a day" by singing in the street. In the 90s we focused in on the world's most exciting urban areas to produce in-depth, fold-out map guides, now with 20 titles (from Hong Kong to Chicago) and counting. Our new guides bring the total number of titles to 57, each infused with the spirit of adventure and voice of opinion that travelers around the world have come to count on. But some things never change: our guides are still researched, written, and produced entirely by students who know first-hand how to see the world on the cheap.

HOW WE DO IT

Each guide is completely revised and thoroughly updated every year by a well-traveled set of nearly 300 students. Every spring, we recruit over 200 researchers and 90 editors to overhaul every book. After several months of training, researcher-writers hit the road for seven weeks of exploration, from Anchorage to Adelaide, Estonia to El Salvador, Iceland to Indonesia. Hired for their rare combination of budget travel sense, writing ability, stamina, and courage, these adventurous travelers know that train strikes, stolen luggage, food poisoning, and marriage proposals are all part of a day's work. Back at our offices, editors work from spring to fall, massaging copy written on Himalayan bus rides into witty, informative prose. A student staff of typesetters, cartographers, publicists, and managers keeps our lively team together. In September, the collected efforts of the summer are delivered to our printer, who turns them into books in record time, so that you have the most up-to-date information available for your vacation. Even as you read this, work on next year's editions is well underway.

WHY WE DO IT

We don't think of budget travel as the last recourse of the destitute; we believe that it's the only way to travel. Our books will ease your anxieties and answer your questions about the basics—so you can get off the beaten track and explore. Once you learn the ropes, we encourage you to put *Let's Go* down and strike out on your own. You know as well as we that the best discoveries are often those you make yourself. When you find something worth sharing, please drop us a line. We're Let's Go Publications, 67 Mount Auburn St., Cambridge, MA 02138, USA (feedback@letsgo.com). For more info, visit our website, www.letsgo.com.

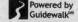

Will you have enough stories to tell your grandchildren?
Yahoo! Travel
Do You Yahoo!?